KU-406-826

Second Edition

CORPORATE FINANCIAL MANAGEMENT

ARNIN(

Gle[illegible], PhD
[illegible]niversity of [illegible]

FINANCIAL TIMES
Prentice Hall

An imprint of Pearson Education

Harlow, England · London · New York · Reading, Massachusetts · San Francisco · Toronto · Don Mills, Ontario · Sydney
Tokyo · Singapore · Hong Kong · Seoul · Taipei · Cape Town · Madrid · Mexico City · Amsterdam · Munich · Paris · Milan

TO LESLEY, MY WIFE, FOR HER LOVING SUPPORT AND ENCOURAGEMENT

Pearson Education Limited

Edinburgh Gate
Harlow
Essex CM20 2JE
England

and Associated Companies throughout the world

Visit us on the World Wide Web at:
http://www.pearsoneduc.com

First published in Great Britain under the
Financial Times Pitman Publishing imprint in 1998
Second edition published in 2002

© Financial Times Professional Limited 1998
© Pearson Education Limited 2002

The right of Glen Arnold to be identified as Author of this Work has been asserted by him in accordance with the Copyright, Designs and Patents Act 1988.

ISBN 0 273 65148 X

British Library Cataloguing-in-Publication Data
A CIP catalogue record for this book can be obtained from the British Library

Library of Congress Cataloging-in-Publication Data
Arnold, Glen.
Corporate financial management / Glen Arnold.-- 2nd ed.
p. cm.
Includes bibliographical references and index.
ISBN 0-273-65148-X (alk. paper)
1. Corporations--Finance--Management. 2. Corporations--Finance. I. Title.

HG4026 .A755 2001
658.15--dc21

2001056924

All rights reserved; no part of this publication may be reproduced, stored in a retrieval system, or transmitted in any form or by any means, elecronic, mechanical, photocopying, recording, or otherwise without either the prior written permission of the Publishers or a licence permitting restricted copying in the United Kingdom issued by the Copyright Licensing Agency Ltd, 90 Tottenham Court Road, London W1P 0LP.

10 9 8 7 6 5 4 3 2 1
08 07 06 05 04 03 02

Typeset in 10/12 pt Sabon by 30
Printed and bound by Rotolito Lombarda, Italy

Neither the author nor the publisher can accept responsibility for any loss occasioned to any person who either acts or refrains from acting as a result of any statement in this book.

BRIEF CONTENTS

Topics covered in the book *xi*
Introduction to the book *xii*
Acknowledgements *xix*

Part I INTRODUCTION

1 The financial world *3*

Part II THE INVESTMENT DECISION

2 Project appraisal: Net present value and internal rate of return *51*
Appendix 2.1 Mathematical tools for finance *83*
3 Project appraisal: Cash flow and applications *95*
4 The decision-making process for investment appraisal *135*
5 Project appraisal: Capital rationing, taxation and inflation *164*

Part III RISK AND RETURN

6 Risk and project appraisal *189*
7 Portfolio theory *235*
8 The capital asset pricing model and multi-factor models *285*
Appendix 8.1 Note on arithmetic and geometric means *322*

Part IV SOURCES OF FINANCE

9 Stock markets *335*
10 Raising equity capital *385*
11 Long-term debt finance *457*
12 Short-term and medium-term finance *510*
13 Treasury and working capital management *551*
14 Stock market efficiency *603*

Part V CORPORATE VALUE

15 Value-based management *655*
16 Managing a value-based company and the cost of capital *695*
17 Valuing shares *755*
18 Capital structure *801*
Appendix 18.1 Asset beta *834*
Appendix 18.2 Adjusted present value (APV) *835*
19 Dividend policy *845*
20 Mergers *868*

Part VI MANAGING RISK

21 Derivatives *923*
Appendix 21.1 Option pricing *955*
22 Managing exchange-rate risk *966*

APPENDICES

I Future value of £1 at compound interest *1009*
II Present value of £1 at compound interest *1010*
III Present value of an annuity of £1 at compound interest *1011*
IV Future value of an annuity of £1 at compound interest *1012*
V Areas under the standardised normal distribution *1013*
VI Answers to the mathematical tools exercises in Appendix 2.1 *1014*
VII Solutions to selected questions and problems *1015*

Glossary *1037*
Bibliography *1061*
Index *1077*

CONTENTS

TOPICS COVERED IN THE BOOK *xi*

INTRODUCTION TO THE BOOK *xii*
Aims of the book – Themes in the book – Student learning features – Support for lecturers

ACKNOWLEDGEMENTS *xix*

Part I INTRODUCTION

1 THE FINANCIAL WORLD *3*

Introduction 3
Learning objectives 4
The objective of the firm *4*
Case study 1.1 Cadbury Schweppes *4*
Ownership and control *16*
Primitive and modern economies *19*
The role of the financial manager *22*
The flow of funds and financial intermediation *25*
Growth in the financial services sector *31*
The financial system *34*
Concluding comments 41
Key points and concepts 42
References and further reading 44
Websites 46
Self-review questions 46
Questions and problems 47
Assignments 47
Chapter notes 48

Part II THE INVESTMENT DECISION

2 PROJECT APPRAISAL: NET PRESENT VALUE AND INTERNAL RATE OF RETURN *51*

Introduction 51
Case study 2.1 Kingfisher *52*
Learning objectives 52
Value creation and corporate investment *53*
Net present value and internal rate of return *57*
Modified internal rate of return *77*
Concluding comments 81
Key points and concepts 81
Appendix 2.1 Mathematical tools for finance 83
Case study 2.2 Jacques Chirac's attempt to help Eurotunnel *85*
Exercise 2.1 Mathematical tools exercises 90
References and further reading 91
Self-review questions 92
Questions and problems 92
Assignments 93
Chapter note 93

3 PROJECT APPRAISAL: CASH FLOW AND APPLICATIONS *95*

Introduction 95
Case study 3.1 Airbus's Superjumbo *96*
Learning objectives 97
Quality of information *97*
Are profit calculations useful for estimating project viability? *98*
The replacement decision *110*
Replacement cycles *113*
When to introduce a new machine *118*
Drawbacks of the annual equivalent annuity method *119*
Timing of projects *120*
The make or buy decision *121*
Fluctuating output *122*
Concluding comments 123
Key points and concepts 123
References and further reading 124
Self-review questions 125
Questions and problems 126
Assignments 134
Chapter note 134

4 THE DECISION-MAKING PROCESS FOR INVESTMENT APPRAISAL *135*

Introduction 135
Case study 4.1 The Noddy and Big Ears project *136*
Case study 4.2 Bentley output to rise on £600m investment *136*
Learning objectives 137
Evidence on the employment of appraisal techniques *137*

Payback *137*
Accounting rate of return *141*
Internal rate of return: reasons for continued popularity *144*
The 'science' and the 'art' of investment appraisal *145*
The investment process *148*
Concluding comments 154
Key points and concepts 155
References and further reading 156
Self-review questions 160
Questions and problems 161
Assignment 163

5 PROJECT APPRAISAL: CAPITAL RATIONING, TAXATION AND INFLATION *164*

Introduction 164
Case study 5.1 The £200 billion gamble *164*
Learning objectives 165
Capital rationing *165*
Taxation and investment appraisal *170*
Inflation *172*
Case study 5.2 Eurotunnel's inflation allowance *173*
Concluding comments 179
Key points and concepts 179
References and further reading 180
Self-review questions 181
Questions and problems 181
Assignments 186
Chapter notes 186

Part III RISK AND RETURN

6 RISK AND PROJECT APPRAISAL *189*

Case study 6.1 Eurotunnel and Camelot *189*
Introduction 190
Learning objectives 190
What is risk? *190*
Adjusting for risk through the discount rate *193*
Sensitivity analysis *194*
Scenario analysis *199*
Probability analysis *200*
The risk of insolvency *212*
Problems of using probability analysis *217*
Evidence of risk analysis in practice *218*
Case study 6.2 RJB Mining: Risky coalfields *219*
Concluding comments 224
Key points and concepts 225
References and further reading 226
Self-review questions 227
Questions and problems 228
Assignments 234
Chapter note 234

7 PORTFOLIO THEORY *235*

Introduction 235
Learning objectives 236
Holding period returns *236*
Expected returns and standard deviation for shares *238*
Combinations of investments *241*
Portfolio expected returns and standard deviation *249*
Dominance and the efficient frontier *254*
Indifference curves *257*
Choosing the optimal portfolio *259*
The boundaries of diversification *261*
Extension to a large number of securities *264*
Evidence on the benefits of diversification *266*
The capital market line *269*
A practical application of portfolio theory *272*
Problems with portfolio theory *273*
Concluding comments 274
Key points and concepts 275
References and further reading 276
Website 278
Self-review questions 278
Questions and problems 279
Assignments 284
Chapter notes 284

8 THE CAPITAL ASSET PRICING MODEL AND MULTI-FACTOR MODELS *285*

Introduction 285
Learning objectives 286
Case study 8.1 Pigs might fly *287*
A short history of shares, bonds and bills *287*
The capital asset pricing model *295*
Factor models *311*
The arbitrage pricing theory *314*
The three-factor model *315*
An alternative approach to the risk–return relationship *316*
Project appraisal and systematic risk *317*

Sceptics's views – Alternative perspectives of risk *319*
Concluding comments 321
Appendix 8.1 Note on arithmetic and geometric means 322
Key points and concepts 324
References and further reading 325
Self-review questions 328
Questions and problems 328
Assignments 330
Chapter notes 331

Part IV SOURCES OF FINANCE

9 STOCK MARKETS *335*
Case study 9.1 Oxford BioMedica *335*
Introduction 335
Learning objectives 336
Stock exchanges around the world *336*
Globalisation of financial flows *346*
The importance of a well-run stock exchange *350*
The London Stock Exchange *353*
The UK equity markets available to companies *358*
Tasks for stock exchanges *364*
Trading systems *364*
The ownership of UK quoted shares *372*
Regulation *370*
Understanding the figures in the financial pages *375*
Taxation and corporate finance *379*
Concluding comments 379
Key points and concepts 380
References and further reading 382
Websites 383
Self-review questions 383
Questions and problems 384
Assignments 384
Chapter notes 384

10 RAISING EQUITY CAPITAL *385*
Case study 10.1 To float or not to float? *385*
Introduction 386
Learning objectives 387
What is equity capital? *387*
Preference shares *390*
Some unusual types of shares *392*
Floating on the Official List *393*
Methods of issue *399*
Timetable for a new offer *404*
How does an AIM flotation differ from one on the Official List? *408*
The costs of new issues *410*
Rights issues *413*
Other equity issues *419*
Scrip issues *422*
Warrants *423*
Equity finance for unquoted firms *423*
Case study 10.2 Confidence reaps a rich reward *426*
Disillusionment and dissatisfaction with quotation *435*
Concluding comments 436
Key points and concepts 436
References and further reading 439
Websites 440
Appendix 10.1 Reasons for and against floating 441
Self-review questions 453
Questions and problems 454
Assignment 456
Chapter notes 456

11 LONG-TERM DEBT FINANCE *457*
Introduction 457
Learning objectives 457
Some fundamental features of debt finance *458*
Bonds *459*
Bank borrowing *463*
Syndicated loans *466*
Credit rating *467*
Mezzanine debt and high-yield (junk) bonds *471*
Case study 11.1 The junk bond wizard: Michael Milken *471*
Convertible bonds *475*
Case study 11.2 Greenhills *476*
Case study 11.3 BPB Industries plc *477*
Valuing bonds *478*
International sources of debt finance *482*
Project finance *490*
Sale and leaseback *492*
Securitisation *494*
The term structure of interest rates *495*
Eurotunnel *500*
Concluding comments 501
Key points and concepts 502
References and further reading 504
Websites 505
Self-review questions 505
Questions and problems 506
Assignments 509
Chapter notes 509

12 SHORT-TERM AND MEDIUM-TERM FINANCE *510*

Introduction *510*
Learning objectives *511*
Bank sources *511*
Trade credit *514*
Trade debtor management *520*
Factoring *524*
Hire purchase *529*
Leasing *532*
Bills of exchange *539*
Acceptance credits (or bank bills or banker's acceptance) *540*
Concluding comments *541*
Key points and concepts *544*
References and further reading *545*
Websites *546*
Self-review questions *546*
Questions and problems *547*
Assignments *550*
Chapter note *550*

13 TREASURY AND WORKING CAPITAL MANAGEMENT *551*

Introduction *551*
Learning objectives *552*
Case study 13.1 Treasury policy at Kingfisher *555*
Financing *556*
Case study 13.2 Philips goes for relationship banking *564*
Risk management *564*
Working capital management *568*
Investment of temporary surplus funds *589*
Concluding comments *592*
Key points and concepts *593*
References and further reading *595*
Websites *596*
Self-review questions *596*
Questions and problems *597*
Assignments *602*
Chapter notes *602*

14 STOCK MARKET EFFICIENCY *603*

Introduction *603*
Learning objectives *604*
What is meant by efficiency? *604*
Random walks *608*
The three levels of efficiency *610*
Weak-form tests *610*
Semi-strong form tests *615*
Strong-form tests *631*
Behavioural finance *633*
Misconceptions about the efficient market hypothesis *638*
Implications of the EMH for investors *639*
Implications of the EMH for companies *640*
Concluding comments *641*
Key points and concepts *642*
References and further reading *643*
Self-review questions *649*
Questions and problems *650*
Assignment *652*
Chapter notes *652*

Part V CORPORATE VALUE

15 VALUE-BASED MANAGEMENT *655*

Introduction *655*
Learning objectives *658*
Value creation and value destruction *658*
Earnings-based management *663*
How a business creates value *669*
Measuring value creation: External metrics *677*
Concluding comments *685*
Key points and concepts *685*
References and further reading *688*
Self-review questions *690*
Questions and problems *690*
Assignments *693*
Chapter notes *693*

16 MANAGING A VALUE-BASED COMPANY AND THE COST OF CAPITAL *695*

Introduction *695*
Learning objectives *695*
An overview of the application of the value principles *696*
Case study 16.1 Strategy, planning and budgeting at Lloyds TSB *710*
Measuring value creation: internal metrics *710*
Case study 16.2 The use of economic profit is becoming more widespread *721*
The cost of capital *725*
Empirical evidence of corporate practice *735*
Implementation issues *738*
Fundamental beta *741*
Some thoughts on the costs of capital *741*

Concluding comments 742
Key points and concepts 743
References and further reading 746
Self-review questions 749
Questions and problems 749
Assignments 753
Chapter notes 753

17 VALUING SHARES *755*

Introduction 755
Learning objectives 755
Case study 17.1 Amazon.com and Orange *756*
Valuation using net asset value (NAV) *757*
Valuation using income-flow methods *760*
The dividend valuation models *760*
Price–earnings ratio (PER) model *771*
Valuation using cash flow *776*
Valuation using owner earnings *780*
Valuing unquoted shares *781*
Unusual companies *782*
Managerial control and valuation *784*
Concluding comments 789
Key points and concepts 789
References and further reading 792
Self-review questions 792
Questions and problems 793
Assignments 800
Chapter notes 800

18 CAPITAL STRUCTURE *801*

Introduction 801
Learning objectives 802
Case study 18.1 The balance between debt and ordinary share capital *803*
What do we mean by 'gearing'? *804*
The effect of gearing *809*
The value of the firm and the cost of capital *814*
Does the cost of capital (WACC) decrease with higher debt levels? *815*
Modigliani and Miller's argument in a world with no taxes *816*
The capital structure decision in a world with tax *820*
Additional considerations *822*
Some further thoughts on debt finance *829*
Concluding comments 832
Appendix 18.1 Asset beta 834
Appendix 18.2 Adjusted present value (APV) 835
Key points and concepts 837
References and further reading 839
Self-review questions 840
Questions and problems 841
Assignments 844
Chapter notes 844

19 DIVIDEND POLICY *845*

Introduction 845
Learning objectives 846
Defining the problem *846*
Modigliani and Miller's dividend irrelevancy proposition *847*
Dividends as a residual *849*
Clientele effects *851*
Taxation *852*
Dividends as conveyors of information *852*
Resolution of uncertainty *854*
Owner control (agency theory) *855*
Scrip dividends *856*
Share buy-backs and special dividends *856*
A round-up of the arguments *858*
Concluding comments 860
Key points and concepts 861
References and further reading 862
Self-review questions 863
Questions and problems 863
Assignments 866
Chapter notes 867

20 MERGERS *868*

Introduction 868
Learning objectives 868
The merger decision *869*
Definitions and semantics *869*
Merger statistics *870*
Merger motives *872*
Case study 20.1 Economies of scale in oil *876*
Financing mergers *884*
The merger process *889*
The impact of mergers *896*
Managing mergers *900*
Concluding comments 910
Key points and concepts 910
References and further reading 913
Websites 915
Self-review questions 915
Questions and problems 916
Assignment 918
Chapter notes 919

Part VI MANAGING RISK

21 DERIVATIVES *923*

Introduction 923
Learning objectives 924
A long history *924*
Options *924*
Forwards *936*
Futures *937*
Forward rate agreements (FRAs) *947*
Caps *949*
Swaps *950*
Derivatives users *952*
Concluding comments 955
Appendix 21.1 Option pricing 955
Key points and concepts 957
References and further reading 959
Websites 960
Self-review questions 960
Questions and problems 961
Assignments 965
Chapter notes 965

22 MANAGING EXCHANGE-RATE RISK *966*

Introduction 966
Case study 22.1 What a difference a few percentage point moves on the exchange rate make *966*
Learning objectives 967
The effects of exchange-rate changes *967*
Volatility in foreign exchange *968*
The foreign exchange markets *970*
Exchange rates *973*
Types of foreign-exchange risk *979*
Transaction risk hedging strategies *981*
Managing translation risk *989*
Managing economic risk *992*
Exchange-rate determination *994*
Concluding comments 999
Key points and concepts 999
References and further reading 1001
Websites 1001
Self-review questions 1002
Questions and problems 1002
Assignments 1005
Chapter notes 1005

APPENDICES

I Future value of £1 at compound interest *1009*

II Present value of £1 at compound interest *1010*

III Present value of an annuity of £1 at compound interest *1011*

IV The future value of an annuity of £1 at compound interest *1012*

V Areas under the standardised normal distribution *1013*

VI Answers to the mathematical tools exercises in Appendix 2.1 *1014*

VII Solutions to selected questions and problems *1015*

GLOSSARY *1037*
BIBLIOGRAPHY *1061*
INDEX *1077*

TOPICS COVERED IN THE BOOK

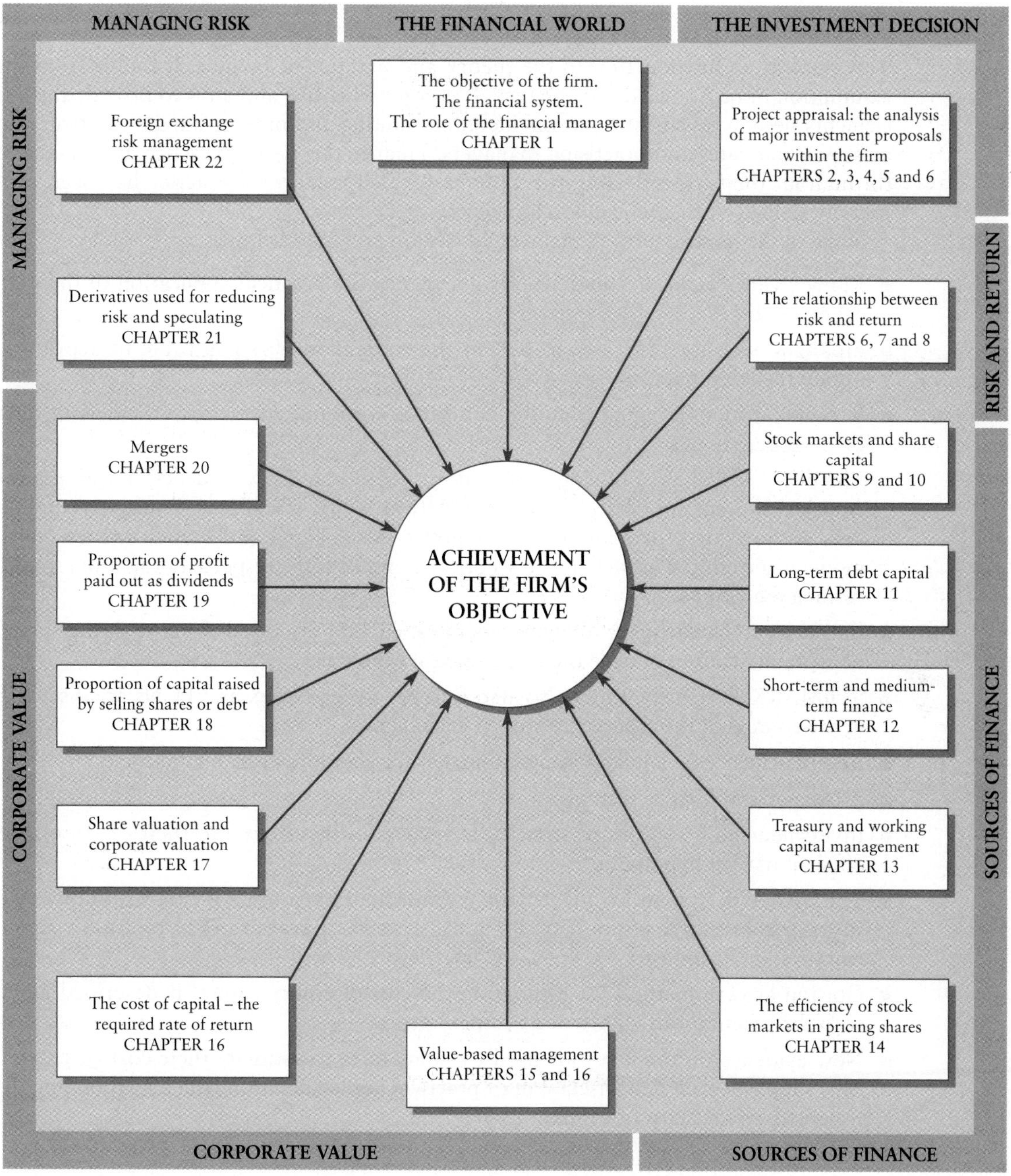
MANAGING RISK
THE FINANCIAL WORLD
THE INVESTMENT DECISION
The objective of the firm. The financial system. The role of the financial manager CHAPTER 1
Foreign exchange risk management CHAPTER 22
Project appraisal: the analysis of major investment proposals within the firm CHAPTERS 2, 3, 4, 5 and 6
Derivatives used for reducing risk and speculating CHAPTER 21
RISK AND RETURN
The relationship between risk and return CHAPTERS 6, 7 and 8
Mergers CHAPTER 20
Stock markets and share capital CHAPTERS 9 and 10
ACHIEVEMENT OF THE FIRM'S OBJECTIVE
Proportion of profit paid out as dividends CHAPTER 19
Long-term debt capital CHAPTER 11
Proportion of capital raised by selling shares or debt CHAPTER 18
Short-term and medium-term finance CHAPTER 12
Share valuation and corporate valuation CHAPTER 17
Treasury and working capital management CHAPTER 13
The cost of capital – the required rate of return CHAPTER 16
Value-based management CHAPTERS 15 and 16
The efficiency of stock markets in pricing shares CHAPTER 14
CORPORATE VALUE
SOURCES OF FINANCE

INTRODUCTION TO THE BOOK

Aims of the book

This book is an introduction to the theory and practice of finance. It builds from the assumption of no knowledge of finance. It is comprehensive and aims to provide the key elements needed by business management, accounting and other groups of undergraduates, postgraduates and practising managers. Finance theory and practice are integrated throughout the text, reflecting the extent to which real world practice has been profoundly shaped by theoretical developments.

Some of the new features in this second edition are listed below.

- Many recent *Financial Times* articles illustrating the practical application of theoretical material.
- Financial website addresses to permit the student to pursue a topic in depth and obtain the latest data.
- Recent statistics – ranging from the number of corporate mergers, to the default rates on corporate bonds.
- The discussion of asset pricing models now incorporates new evidence concerning the equity risk premium (sharply revised downwards) for UK shares. Equity risk premiums are provided for many other countries. Also, Fama and French's three-factor model is introduced as well as the sceptical views of some respected practitioners concerning the CAPM.
- European stock exchange alliances, mergers, etc. are discussed along with the spread of an equity culture outside the Anglo-Saxon economies.
- techMARK, Euronext, Virt-x, Nasdaq Europe, Jiway, Norex and ECNs are discussed in the context of the theoretical role of exchanges.
- Recent evidence on equity pricing anomalies (or should that be inefficiencies?)
- A behavioural finance section.
- Investment philosophies of some very successful investors and their views on the efficient market hypothesis.
- The TRRACK system for identifying extraordinary resources giving the company a superior competitive position so that it can beat the average rates of return on capital employed in its industry.
- Gordon growth method for estimating the cost of equity capital is described along with the practical difficulties of its employment.
- New evidence on the methods used by companies to estimate their cost of capital. This supplements a new discussion of practical implementation issues surrounding the weighted average cost of capital.
- Share valuation using owner earnings.
- Asset beta – described with assumptions highlighted to discourage improper use.
- Adjusted present value – emphasis on caution required for real-world use.

- Mergers as a way of destroying shareholder wealth – the views of practitioners.
- The influence of a current-account deficit and capital flow on exchange rates.

Themes in the book

Practical orientation

Every chapter describes and illustrates how financial techniques are used in the practical world of business. Throughout the text insight is offered into how and why practice may sometimes differ from sound theory. For example, in making major investment decisions, managers still use techniques with little theoretical backing (e.g. payback) alongside the more theoretically acceptable approaches. The extent of the use of traditional appraisal methods was revealed in a survey to which 96 finance directors from the largest UK-based firms responded. Their choice of analytical technique is not dismissed or regarded as 'bad practice', but there is an exploration of the reasons for the retention of these simple rule-of-thumb methods. This book uses theory, algebra and economic models where these are considered essential to assist learning about better decision making. Where these are introduced, however, they must always have passed the practicality test: 'Is this knowledge sufficiently useful out there, in the real world, to make it worth while for the reader to study it?' If it is not, then it is not included.

Clear, accessible style

Great care has been taken to explain sometimes difficult topics in an interesting and comprehensible way. An informal language style, and an incremental approach, which builds knowledge in a series of easily achieved steps, leads the reader to a high level of knowledge with as little pain as possible. The large panel of reviewers of the book assisted in the process of developing a text that is, we hope, comprehensive and easy to read.

Integration with other disciplines

Finance should never be regarded as a subject in isolation, separated from the workings of the rest of the organisation. This text, when considering the link between theoretical methods and practical financial decision making, recognises a wide range of other influences, from strategy to psychology. For example, important new developments in business thinking in the 1980s and 1990s has led to the adoption of shareholder value management, which integrates finance, strategy and organisational resource. Value-based management principles are sweeping across boardrooms the world over. This is the first major corporate finance textbook to recognise fully the importance of value-based approaches to managing companies today. The origins of the principles in the finance literature are described, and the significance and pervasiveness of the managerial challenge are explored.

Real-world relevance

Experience of teaching finance to undergraduates, postgraduates and managers on short courses has led to the conclusion that, in order to generate enthusiasm and commitment to the subject, it is vital to continually show the relevance of the material to what is going on in the world beyond the textbook. Therefore, this book incorporates vignettes/short case studies as well as a very large number of examples of real companies making decisions which draw on the models, concepts and ideas of finance management.

A UK / international perspective

There is a primary focus on the UK, but also regular reference to international financial markets and institutions. Care has been taken to avoid giving a parochial perspective and the international character of the book has been enhanced by the detailed evaluation of each chapter by a number of respected academics teaching at universities in Europe, Asia and Africa. The richly integrated world of modern finance requires that a text of this nature reflects the globalised character of much financial activity. The financial world has moved on in the last few years with the development of new financial markets and methods of trading, and this is fully reflected in the text.

A re-evaluation of classical finance theory

There is considerable debate about the validity of the theories of the 1950s and 1960s which underpin much of modern finance, stimulated by fresh evidence generated in the 1990s. For example, the theories concerning the relationship between the risk of a financial security and its expected return is under dispute, with some saying the old measure of risk, beta, is dead or dying. This issue and other financial economics theories are presented along with their assumptions and a consideration of recent revisions.

Real-world case examples

The publishers are part of the Pearson Group, which also includes the *Financial Times* and the *Investors Chronicle* (and part ownership of *The Economist*). It has been possible to include much more than the usual quantity of real-world case examples in this book by drawing on material from the *Financial Times*, *Investors Chronicle* and *The Economist*. The aim of these extracts is to bring the subject of finance to life for readers. A typical example is shown in Exhibit 1, which is used to illustrate some of the financial issues explored in the book.

Exhibit 1

3i spins to Ministry of Sound

FT

Cash injection to fund global expansion

By Ashling O'Connor, Media Correspondent

Nearly a decade after the Ministry of Sound nightclub first opened its doors to clubbers in Elephant & Castle, the dance music operator has secured the financial backing needed to expand beyond its south London base.

James Palumbo, Ministry's ex-Etonian founder, has sold nearly 20 per cent of the business to 3i, the private equity group, to fund growth in its media and music operations.

Under the deal, expected to be announced today, 3i is investing £24m cash for new shares, valuing the company in excess of £120m.

The move marks the next stage of development for Ministry, which has ambitions to be a global brand and will seek acquisitions in music and media. . . .

The deal with 3i also heralds a flotation of Ministry in two to three years.

Ministry had sales of about £80m in 2000 and pre-tax profits of £6m–£7m. This year turnover is expected to be £100m and operating profits about £10m.

The company's advisers believe Ministry can at least treble its turnover in three to four years.

Dan Adler, investment manager for media and leisure at 3i, said: 'Ministry is a media company. We hope it can be developed into a globally-recognised brand.' . . .

Ministry's music division, which accounts for 80–85 per cent of group revenues, has sold 15m albums, such as the *Chill Out* session compilation CDs, which recently reached number one. It has seven record labels.

Just 3 per cent of Ministry's turnover now comes from the club. The rest is from CDs, a magazine, a website and a digital radio station. It syndicates a Ministry show to 150 stations. It also organises live events.

Source: *Financial Times*, 9 August 2001, p. 22. Reprinted with permission.

This article touches on many of the financial decisions which are explored in greater detail later in the book. Money is being raised to invest in the next stage of development of the Ministry of Sound. There are two main pillars of finance:

1 *Raising finance and knowledge of financial markets* In the case of the Ministry of Sound the £24m is being injected from a venture capital fund, 3i, immediately. There are also plans to float on a stock exchange 'in two or three years'. This will allow the company to tap a wider array of investors (sources of finance are considered in the book in Chapters 9–14).
2 *Investment in real assets, tangible or intangible* There are techniques which help the process of deciding whether to make a major investment – these are discussed early in the book (Chapters 2–6). The Ministry of Sound will be investing in a number of areas (including its brand, magazine and CDs). It will need rigorous techniques to assist with the selection of projects. Amongst other things it will have to consider the risk relative to the reward on investments (risk and return are considered in Chapters 6, 7 and 8).

Another area of decision making for investors and management alike is the question of the most appropriate mixture of sources of finance: should the company borrow most of the money it needs, or should it obtain a larger proportion from shareholders? This is the 'gearing' question (*see* Chapter 18). Other financial decisions likely to affect the Ministry of Sound which are not mentioned in the article, but which may well be of importance for the company in the future, include:

- What proportion of profits should be distributed as dividends each year? (See Chapter 19.)
- What factors are to be considered when contemplating a merger with another company? (*See* Chapter 20.)
- What type of debt finance to use? Is bank borrowing better than selling a corporate bond? Should the Eurobond or the syndicated loan market be tapped? What are the advantages and disadvantages of financing equipment with a lease or hire purchase? (*See* Chapters 11 and 12.)
- How will the company's shares be valued on the stock market once the company has been floated? (See Chapter 17.) Does the market do a good job of pricing shares, taking into account the future potential of the company, or does it act in perverse and unpredictable ways? (*See* Chapter 14.)
- Should the company use derivative financial instruments, such as futures, options and swaps, to reduce its risk exposure to changes in interest rates or exchange rates? (*See* Chapters 21 and 22.)

These are just a few of the financial issues that have to be tackled by the modern corporation and trying to answer these questions forms the basis for this book.

Student learning features

Each of the chapters has the following elements to help the learning process:

- ***Learning objectives*** This section sets out the expected competencies to be gained by reading the chapter.
- ***Introduction*** The intention here is to engage the attention of the reader by discussing the importance and relevance of the topic to real business decisions.

- ***Worked examples*** New techniques are illustrated in the text, with sections which present problems, followed by detailed answers.
- ***Mathematical explanations*** Students with a limited mathematical ability should not be put off by this text. The basics are covered early and in a simple style. New skills are fully explained and illustrated, as and when required.
- ***Case studies and articles*** Extracts from recent articles from the *Financial Times*, *Investors Chronicle* and other sources are used to demonstrate the arguments in the chapter, to add a different dimension to an issue, or merely to show that it is worth taking time to understand the material because this sort of decision is being made in day-to-day business.
- ***Key points and concepts*** At the end of each chapter an outline is given of the essentials of what has been covered. New concepts, jargon and equations are summarised for easy referral.
- ***References and further reading*** One of the features of this text is the short commentaries which follow the list of articles and books referred to in the body of the chapter, or which are suggested for the interested student to pursue a topic in greater depth. This allows students to be selective in their follow-up reading. So, for example, if on the one hand a particular article takes a high-level, algebraic and theoretical approach or, on the other hand, is an easy-to-read introduction to the subject, this is highlighted, permitting the student to decide whether to obtain the article. A list of useful websites is also included
- ***Self-review questions*** These short questions are designed to prompt the reader to recall the main elements of the topic. They can act as a revision aid and highlight areas requiring more attention.
- ***Questions and problems*** These vary in the amount of time required, from 5 minutes to 45 minutes or more. Many are taken from university second year and final year undergraduate examinations, and MBA module examinations. They allow the student to demonstrate a thorough understanding of the material presented in the chapter. Some of these questions necessitate the integration of knowledge from previous chapters with the present chapter. The answers to many of the questions can be found in Appendix VII at the end of the book.
- ***Assignments*** These are projects which require the reader to investigate real-world practice in a firm and relate this to the concepts and techniques learned in the chapter. These assignments can be used both as learning aids and as a way of helping firms to examine the relationship between current practice and finance theory and frameworks.
- ***Glossary and Appendices*** At the end of the book is an extensive Glossary of terms, allowing the student quickly to find the meaning of new technical terms or jargon. There is also a Bibliography of references for further reading. Appendices give a future value table (Appendix I), present value table (Appendix II), present value of annuity table (Appendix III), future value of an annuity (Appendix IV), area under the standardised normal distribution (Appendix V), answers to questions in the Chapter 2 Appendix reviewing mathematical tools for finance (Appendix VI), and answers to the numerical questions and problems (Appendix VII) – with the exception of those question numbers followed by an asterisk (*), which are answered in the *Lecturer's Guide*. Answers to discussion questions, essay and reports questions can be found by reading

the text. Some questions, marked †, are left for the tutor or lecturer to discuss, with no answer which the student may access.

Support for lecturers

The website dedicated to this book contains a section designed to add value to the student learning process (for example by providing updated newspaper articles illustrating the concepts discussed in the chapters) and also includes a section for lecturers who adopt the book. The site has:

- Over 500 PowerPoint slides, which can also be downloaded as OHP masters.
- Extra questions and answers.
- Multiple-choice questions bank.
- Additional *Financial Times/Investors Chronicle* case material with a short commentary; this will be added to every few months to ensure it is up to date, and may be useful for illustrating lectures.
- Links to other websites, for example major stock exchanges around the world, banks, LIFFE and other derivatives markets, international financial press, and professional bodies.

Lecturer's Guide

This contains:

- Supplementary material for chapters, including learning objectives and key points and concepts listings.
- A multiple-choice question bank (also available on the website).
- Answers to the questions and problems marked with an asterisk * in the book.

Target readership

The book is aimed at second/final year undergraduates of accounting and finance, business/management studies, banking and economics, as well as postgraduate students on MBA/MSc courses in the UK, Europe and the rest of the world. It would be helpful if the student has an elementary knowledge of statistics, algebra, accounting and microeconomics, but this is not essential.

The practising manager, whether or not a specialist in financial decision making, should find the book useful – not least to understand the language and concepts of business and financial markets.

Students studying for examinations for the professional bodies will benefit from this text. The material is valuable for those working towards a qualification of one of the following organisations:

- Institute of Chartered Accountants in England and Wales
- Institute of Chartered Accountants of Scotland
- Chartered Institute of Public Finance and Accountancy
- Association of Chartered Certified Accountants
- Chartered Institute of Management Accountants

- Institute of Chartered Secretaries and Administrators
- Chartered Institute of Bankers

The applicability of finance knowledge for all organisations

Most of the theories and practical examples in the book are directed at the business operating in a competitive market environment. However, the fundamental principles and truths revealed by the logic and frameworks of finance are applicable to organisations other than commercial firms. Sound financial decision making is necessary in non-profit organisations and public sector bodies, ranging from schools and hospitals to charities and churches, and so the principles contained within the book have validity and applicability to any organisation needing to make decisions involving money.

A Companion Website accompanies
CORPORATE FINANCIAL MANAGEMENT, 2nd edition

Visit the *Corporate Financial Management* Companion Website at www.booksites.net/arnold to find valuable teaching and learning material including:

For Students:
- Study material designed to help you improve your results
- Comprehensive learning objectives detailing what you need to know
- Multiple-choice questions to test your learning
- Links to relevant sites on the World Wide Web
- Extra case studies

For Lecturers:
- A secure, password-protected site with teaching material
- A downloadable version of the full *Lecturer's Guide* with solutions to questions not answered in the book
- Over 500 downloadable PowerPoint slides
- A syllabus manager that will build and host your very own course web page

ACKNOWLEDGEMENTS

My thanks to the following for their help in the preparation of this book:

The international panel of reviewers for the major contribution they made to providing realism, balance and accuracy:

Drs A.W.M. Berndsen, Erasmus University of Rotterdam, The Netherlands
Dr Johan De Villiers, Stellenbosch University, South Africa
David K. Ding, Nanyang University, Singapore
Helen Keady, Nottingham Business School, Nottingham Trent University
Steve Toms, School of Management, University of Nottingham
Peijie Wang, Manchester School of Management, UMIST
Ian Jackson, Staffordshire University
Ruth Bender, Cranfield University
Vijay Lee, Southbank University
Jean Bellemans, Boston University, Brussels, and United Business Institutes, Brussels, Belgium
Lars Vangaard, University of Southern Denmark
Dr Jan Jakobsen, Copenhagen Business School, Denmark
Ann Rinsler, Kingston University

The 96 finance directors who responded to a financial survey in 1997, for contributing to our understanding of modern financial practice.

The publishing team at Pearson Education, particularly Pat Bond, Paula Harris, Anna Herbert, Jacqueline Senior, Colin Reed and Liz Tarrant, and editor Susan Faircloth for their patience, professionalism and faith.

The *Financial Times*, *Investors Chronicle*, the London Stock Exchange and all those organisations and individuals acknowledged in the text, for allowing the use of their material.

Christopher Purser, former treasurer of Glynwed (now Aga Foodservice Group plc) and Council member of the Association of Corporate Treasurers, for his helpful insights into corporate treasury management.

We are grateful to the following for permission to reproduce copyright material:

Case study 1.1 reprinted by permission of Cadbury Schweppes plc (*Annual Report and Form 20-F, 1999*); Case studies 2.1 and 13.1 reprinted by permission of Kingfisher plc; Cases 5.2 and 11.2, and Exhibits 1.17, 7.46, 7.58, 8.13, 10.7, 11.31, 14.7, 14.12, 16.20, 17.5 and 20.18 reproduced with permission of the *Investors Chronicle*; Case Study 13.2 reprinted with kind permission of *Corporate Finance*, Euromoney Institutional Investor PLC (if you would like to subscribe to *Corporate Finance* please contact Esther Rodd at + 44 20 7779 8062); Case Study 16.1 from 'Lessons from practice: VMP at Lloyds TSB' in G. Arnold and M. Davies (editors) *Value-based*

Management, copyright 2000, © John Wiley & Sons Limited, reproduced with permission (Davies, M., 2000); the artist Robert Thompson for the cartoon in Exhibit 1.6; Exhibit 4.1 data reproduced with permission of the author (Pike, R.H., 1988), Exhibit 4.1 data from *Journal of Business Finance and Accounting*, 23(1) January, reprinted with permission of Blackwell Publishers and with permission of the author (Pike, R.H., 1996); Exhibits 4.1, 4.9, 4.10, 5.14, 6.30, 16.24, 16.25, 16.26 from *Journal of Business Finance and Accounting*, 27(5/6) June/July, 603-26 (Arnold, G.C. and Hatzopoulos, P.D., 2000) and Exhibit 4.8 from *Journal of Accounting Research* 27, 1989 supplement, 10 (Bernard, V. and Thomas, J.K., 1989), reprinted with permission of Blackwell Publishers; Exhibits 14.9, 14.10, 19.1, 20.9 and 20.15 copyrighted material, reproduced with permission of the author Warren E. Buffett; Exhibits 7.49, 7.50 and 7.51 copyright 1974 and 1988, Association for Investment Management and Research,* reproduced and republished from *Financial Analysts Journal* with permission from the Association for Investment Management and Research, all rights reserved; Exhibit 7.52 from Solnik, Bruno, *International Investment*, 1st edn, Exhibit 4.3 (p. 112), © Pearson Education Limited 2000, reprinted with permission (Solnik, B., 2000); Exhibits 8.2, 8.3, 8.10 and 8.11 reprinted by permission of the authors (Dimson, E., Marsh, P. and Staunton, M., 2001); Exhibits 8.25 and 8.26 reprinted with permission of Institutional Investors Inc.; Exhibits 9.6, 9.18, 9.19, 9.22 and 10.6 reprinted with permission of the London Stock Exchange Inc.; Exhibit 10.30 from *BVCA Performance Measurement Survey* 2000, conducted by PricewaterhouseCoopers, reprinted with permission (BVCA, 2000); Exhibit 11.9 reprinted with permission from Standard & Poor's; Exhibits 11.16 and 11.17 reproduced with permission from BIS *Quarterly Review*, www.BIS.org; Exhibits 12.9 and 18.4 reprinted with permission of Lloyds UDT Ltd, formerly Lloyds Bowmaker Ltd; Exhibit 13.2 from ACT's 'Five pillars of wisdom', reprinted with kind permission of The Association of Corporate Treasurers (unpublished), and the extract on p. 555 from *The Role of Corporate Treasurer*, 13 February, reprinted by permission of Aga Foodservices Group plc (formerly Glynwed International plc) and the author (Purser, C.R., 1997); Exhibit 13.3 reprinted with permission of Thames Water; Exhibit 15.7 adapted with the permission of The Free Press, A Division of Simon & Schuster, Inc., from *The Value Imperative: Managing for Superior Shareholder Returns* by James M. McTaggart, Peter W. Kontes and Michael C. Mankins. Copyright © 1994 The Free Press; Case study 11.3 reprinted by permission of BPB plc; the extract on p. 879 reprinted by permission of John Kay, copyright © John Kay, economist; the extract on pp. 319-20 reprinted with the permission of Simon & Schuster from *Contrarian Investment Strategies* by David Dreman, copyright © 1998 by Dreman Contrarian Group, Inc. (Dreman, D. 1998); Warren E. Buffett for the extracts on pp. 320-1, 627, 698, 845 and 878, copyrighted material, reproduced with permission of the author. Exhibit 9.31 is reproduced by permission of Virt-x Investment Exchange; Exhibits 7.56, 7.57, 8.4, 8.5, 8.6, 8.7, 8.8 and 8.9 reprinted with permission from Barclays Capital; Exhibit 9.14 from 'Rebuilt by Wall Street', *Financial Times*, 25 January 2000, © David Hale; Exhibit 13.15 from 'Amazon spreads its risks', *Financial Times*, 12 June 2001, © Tim Jackson. Crown copyright material is reproduced under class licence number CO1 W0000039 with permission of the Controller of HMSO and the Queen's Printer for Scotland in Exhibits 9.33 and 20.1. Exhibit 15.22 is reproduced with permission of the *Sunday Times*. © Times Newspapers Limited. Exhibits 1.8, 8.17, 9.31, 15.3, 15.4, 15.5, 16.27, 17.9, 17.10, 17.13, 20.12, 20.8, 22.1, 22.2, 22.3 and 22.4 are reproduced with permission from Thomson Financial. © Thomson Financial.

We are grateful to the Financial Times Limited for permission to reprint the following material:

Exhibits 1, 1.2, 1.3, 1.4, 1.5, 1.6, 1.8, 1.9, 1.10, 1.11, 1.12, 1.21, 1.24, 1.25, 4.7, 8.12, 8.21, 9.2, 9.3, 9.4, 9.5, 9.9, 9.11, 9.12, 9.13, 9.16, 9.20, 9.21, 9.22, 9.23, 9.24, 9.25, 9.28, 9.32, 9.35, 9.36, 10.3, 10.4, 10.8, 10.9, 10.11, 10.12, 10.13, 10.15, 10.17, 10.18, 10.19, 10.21, 10.22, 10.23, 10.24, 10.27, 10.28, 10.29, 10.31, 10.32, 10.33, 10.34, 10.36, 10.37, 10.38, 10.39, 10.40, 10.41, 10.42, 10.43, 10.44, 10.45, 10.46, 10.47, 10.48, 10.49, 10.50, 10.51, 10.52, 10.53, 10.54, 10.55, 10.56, 11.2, 11.4, 11.6, 11.7, 11.8, 11.10, 11.11, 11.14, 11.19, 11.20, 11.21, 11.24, 11.25, 11.26, 11.27, 11.30, 12.2, 12.3, 12.7, 12.13, 12.18, 12.20, 12.21, 12.24, 13.4, 13.9, 13.35, 13.37, 14.11, 15.2, 15.6, 15.13, 15.19, 15.20, 17.2, 17.4, 17.6, 17.7, 17.8, 17.11, 17.13, 17.15, 17.19, 17.20, 18.5, 18.11, 18.17, 18.19, 18.22, 18.23, 18.24, 19.2, 19.3, 19.5, 19.6, 19.7, 20.2, 20.3, 20.5, 20.6, 20.8, 20.14, 20.16, 20.19, 20.23, 20.24, 20.26, 20.29, 21.1, 21.6, 21.11, 21.13, 21.14, 21.15, 21.17, 21.18, 21.19, 21.21, 21.24, 21.26, 22.5, 22.6, 22.7, 22.8, 22.9, 22.11, 22.12, 22.15, 22.16, 22.17, 22.18 and 22.19; Case Studies 2.1, 2.2, 3.1, 4.2 and 6.2.

In some instances we have been unable to trace the owners of copyright material, and we would appreciate any information that would enable us to do so.

*CFA® and Chartered Financial Analyst™ are trademarks owned by the Association for Investment Management and Research (AIMR®). The Association for Investment Management and Research does not endorse, promote, review, or warrant the accuracy of the products or services offered by Pearson Education. EVA® is a registered trademark of Stern Stewart and Co. Many of the designations used by manufacturers and sellers to distinguish their products are claimed as trademarks. Pearson Education has made every attempt to supply trademark information about manufacturers and their products mentioned in this book.

Part I

INTRODUCTION

1 The financial world

Chapter 1

THE FINANCIAL WORLD

INTRODUCTION

Before getting carried away with specific financial issues and technical detail, it is important to gain a broad perspective by looking at the fundamental questions and the place of finance in the overall scheme of things. The finance function is a vital one, both within an individual organisation and for society as a whole. In the UK, for example, the financial services industry accounts for about as large a proportion of national output as the whole of manufacturing industry. This shift in demand and resource has accelerated rapidly since 1970 and, if the trend continues, it will not be long before finance employs more people and attracts more purchasing power than all the manufacturing industries put together. To some this is a cause of great alarm and regret but, given that this trend has occurred at a time when free choice in the market-place largely dictates what is produced, presumably there must be something useful that financial firms are providing. We will examine the key role played by financial intermediaries and markets in a modern economy, and how an efficient and innovative financial sector contributes greatly to the ability of other sectors to produce efficiently. One of the vital roles of the financial sector is to encourage the mobilisation of savings to put them to productive use through investment. Without a vibrant and adaptable finance sector all parts of the economy would be starved of investment and society would be poorer.

This chapter also considers the most fundamental question facing anyone trying to make decisions within an organisation – what is the objective of the business? Without clarity on this point it is very difficult to run a business in a purposeful and effective manner. The resolution of this question is somewhat clouded in the large, modern corporation by the tendency for the owners to be distant from the running of the enterprise. Professional managers are usually left in control and they have objectives which may or may not match those of the owners.

Finally, to help the reader become orientated, a brief rundown is given of the roles, size and activities of the major types of financial institutions and markets. A little bit of jargon-busting early on will no doubt be welcomed.

Learning objectives

It is no good learning mathematical techniques and theory if you lack an overview of what finance is about. At the end of this chapter the reader will have a balanced perspective on the purpose and value of the finance function, at both the corporate and the national level. More specifically, the reader should be able to:

- describe alternative views on the purpose of the business and show the importance to any organisation of clarity on this point;
- describe the impact of the divorce of corporate ownership from day-to-day managerial control;
- explain the role of the financial manager;
- detail the value of financial intermediaries;
- show an appreciation of the function of the major financial institutions and markets.

THE OBJECTIVE OF THE FIRM

Cadbury Schweppes has a clear statement of its objective in the 1999 Annual Report – see Case study 1.1.

CASE STUDY 1.1

Cadbury Schweppes

Cadbury Schweppes' objective is growth in shareowner value. The strategy by which it will achieve this objective is:

- Focusing on its core growth markets of beverages and confectionery
- Developing robust, sustainable market positions which are built on a platform of strong brands with supported franchises
- Expanding its market share through innovation in products, packaging and route to market where economically profitable
- Enhancing its market positions by acquisitions or disposals where they are on strategy, value-creating and available

Managing for Value is the process which supports the achievement of this strategy.

The Chairman in 1999, Sir Dominic Cadbury, expands on the theme of the purpose of the Company in his letter in the Business Review 1999:

> 'In the latter half of the 1990s we focused more closely on the creation of shareowner value through the adoption of Managing for Value ("MFV") in 1997. During 1999 our MFV programme was extended throughout the Group, establishing a new discipline to, and understanding of, our management of the business. Growth and scale are important; but in global markets, where competition is intense, a complete understanding of value-creation is essential.
>
> With a clear vision of what value-creation means, we are confident of achieving sustainable earnings growth in 2000 and beyond.
>
> Our value analysis has already had far-reaching consequences. The sale of our beverages brands recognised the comparative disadvantage they suffered in smaller markets. It was in shareowners' best interest to obtain optimum value for them by finding the most appropriate owner.'

Source: Cadbury Schweppes Annual Report and Form 20-F 1999. Reprinted with permission.

This book is all about practical decision making in the real world. When people have to make choices in the harsh environment in which modern businesses have to operate, it is necessary to be clear about the purpose of the organisation; to be clear about what objective is set for management to achieve. A multitude of small decisions are made every day; more importantly, every now and then major strategic commitments of resources are made. It is imperative that the management teams are aware of, respect and contribute to the fundamental objective of the firm in all these large and small decisions. Imagine the chaos and confusion that could result from the opposite situation where there is no clear, accepted objective. The outcome of each decision, and the direction of the firm, will become random and rudderless. One manager on one occasion will decide to grant long holidays and a shorter working week, believing that the purpose of the institution's existence is to benefit employees; while on another occasion a different manager sacks 'surplus' staff and imposes lower wages, seeing the need to look after the owner's interests as a first priority. So, before we can make decisions in the field of finance we need to establish what it is we are trying to achieve.

You have probably encountered elsewhere the question, 'In whose interests is the firm run?' This is largely a political and philosophical question and many books have been written on the subject. Here we will provide a brief overview of the debate because of its central importance to making choices in finance. The list of interested parties in Exhibit 1.1 could be extended, but no doubt you can accept the point from this shortened version that there are a number of claimants on a firm.

Sound financial management is necessary for the survival of the firm and for its growth. Therefore all of these stakeholders, to some extent, have an interest in seeing sensible financial decisions being taken. Many business decisions do not involve a conflict between the objectives of each of the stakeholders. However, there are occasions when someone has to decide which claimants are to have their objectives maximised, and which are merely to be satisficed – that is, given just enough of a return to make their contributions.

There are some strong views held on this subject. The pro-capitalist economists, such as Friedrich Hayek and Milton Friedman, believe that making shareholders' interests the paramount objective will benefit both the firm and society at large. This approach is not quite as extreme as it sounds because these thinkers generally accept that unbridled

Exhibit 1.1 A company has responsibilities to a number of interested parties

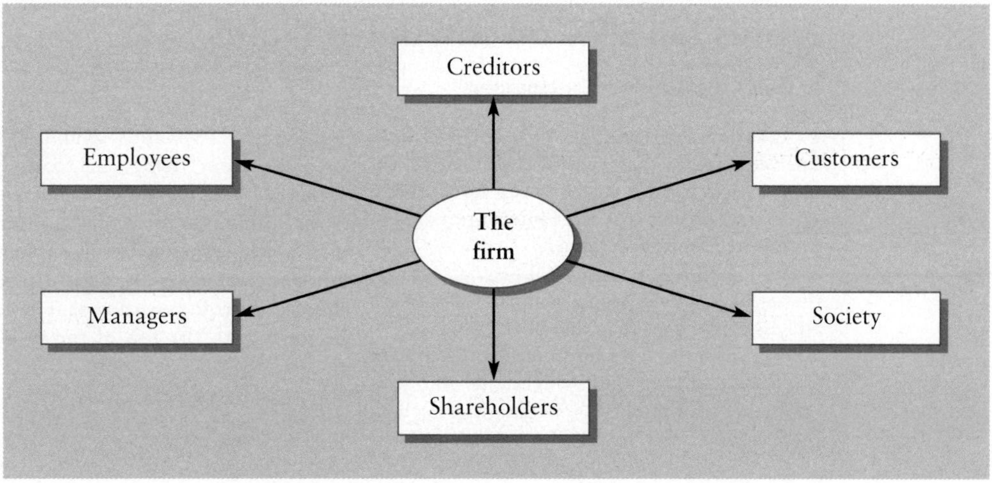

pursuit of shareholder returns, to the point of widespread pollution, murder and extortion, will not be in society's best interest and so add the proviso that maximising shareholder wealth is the desired objective provided that firms remain within 'the rules of the game'.

At the opposite end of the political or philosophical spectrum are the left-wing advocates of the primacy of workers' rights and rewards. The belief here is that labour should have its rewards maximised. The employees should have all that is left over, after the other parties have been satisfied. Shareholders are given just enough of a return to provide capital, suppliers are given just enough to supply raw materials and so on.

Standing somewhere in the middle are those keen on a balanced stakeholder approach. Here the (often conflicting) interests of each of the claimants is somehow maximised but within the constraints set by the necessity to compromise in order to provide a fair return to the other stakeholders.

Some possible objectives

A firm can choose from an infinitely long list of possible objectives. Some of these will appear noble and easily justified, others remain hidden, implicit, embarrassing, even subconscious. The following represent some of the most frequently encountered.

- ***Achieving a target market share*** In some industrial sectors to achieve a high share of the market gives high rewards. These may be in the form of improved profitability, survival chances or status. Quite often the winning of a particular market share is set as an objective because it acts as a proxy for other, more profound objectives, such as generating the maximum returns to shareholders. On other occasions matters can get out of hand and there is an obsessive pursuit of market share with only a thin veneer of shareholder wealth espousement – *see* Exhibit 1.2.
- ***Keeping employee agitation to a minimum*** Here, return to the organisation's owners is kept to a minimum necessary level. All surplus resources are directed to mollifying employees. Managers would be very reluctant to admit publicly that they place a high priority on reducing workplace tension, encouraging peace by appeasement and thereby, it is hoped, reducing their own stress levels, but actions tend to speak louder

Exhibit 1.2

Profits fall 39% on scheduled flights

FT

By Kevin Done, Aerospace Correspondent

International airlines last year suffered a 39 per cent fall in the net profits of their scheduled services to $1.9bn, the lowest level for five years, according to the International Air Transport Association (Iata).

Pierre Jeanniot, Iata director-general, warned that airlines should 'stop chasing the chimera of endless traffic growth at any price'.

'If governments are no longer going to subsidise such folly,' he said, 'why should we?'

The net profitability of international scheduled services fell to $1.9bn last year from $3.1bn in 1998 and $5bn in 1997, under pressure from rising fuel costs and falling yields resulting from widespread overcapacity.

Mr Jeanniot warned that most airline strategies continued to be based on market growth and on increasing market share instead of being driven by profits. Airline shareholders should be moved 'to the top of the priority list for rewards'.

Source: Financial Times, 5 April 2000, p. 13. Reprinted with permission.

than words. An example of this kind of prioritisation was evident in a number of state-owned UK industries in the 1960s and 1970s. Unemployment levels were low, workers were in a strong bargaining position and there were, generally, state funds available to bail out a loss-making firm. In these circumstances it was easier to buy peace by acquiescing to union demands than to fight on the picket lines.

- *Survival* There are circumstances where the overriding objective becomes the survival of the firm. Severe economic or market shock may force managers to focus purely on short-term issues to ensure the continuance of the business. They end up paying little attention to long-term growth and return to owners. However this focus is clearly inadequate in the long run – there must be other goals. If survival were the only objective then putting all the firm's cash reserves into a bank savings account might be the best option. When managers say that their objective is survival what they generally mean is the avoidance of large risks which endanger the firm's future. This may lead to a greater aversion to risk, and a rejection of activities that shareholders might wish the firm to undertake. Shareholders are in a position to diversify their investments: if one firm goes bankrupt they may be disappointed but they have other companies' shares to fall back on. However the managers of that one firm may have the majority of their income, prestige and security linked to the continuing existence of that firm. These managers may deliberately avoid high-risk/high-return investments and therefore deprive the owners of the possibility of large gains.
- *Creating an ever-expanding empire* This is an objective which is rarely openly discussed, but it seems reasonable to propose that some managers drive a firm forward, via organic growth or mergers, because of a desire to run an ever-larger enterprise. Often these motives become clearer with hindsight; when, for instance, a firm meets a calamitous end the *post mortem* often reveals that profit and efficiency were given second place to growth. The volume of sales, number of employees or overall stock market value of the firm have a much closer correlation with senior executive salaries, perks and status than do returns to shareholder funds. This may motivate some individuals to promote growth.
- *Maximisation of profit* This is a much more acceptable objective, although not everyone would agree that maximation of profit should be the firm's purpose.
- *Maximisation of long-term shareholder wealth* While many commentators concentrate on profit maximisation, finance experts are aware of a number of drawbacks of profit. The maximisation of the returns to shareholders in the long term is considered to be a superior goal. We look at the differences between profit maximisation and wealth maximisation later.

This list of possible objectives can easily be extended but it is not possible within the scope of this book to examine each of them. Suffice it to say, there can be an enormous variety of objectives and a large potential for conflict and confusion. We have to introduce some sort of order.

The assumed objective for finance

The company should make investment and financing decisions with the aim of maximising long-term shareholder wealth. Throughout the remainder of this book we will assume that the firm gives primacy of purpose to the wealth of shareholders. This assumption is made mainly on practical grounds, but there are respectable theoretical justifications too.

The practical reason

If one may assume that the decision-making agents of the firm (managers) are acting in the best interests of shareholders then decisions on such matters as which investment projects to undertake, or which method of financing to use, can be made much more simply. If the firm has a multiplicity of objectives, imagine the difficulty in deciding whether to introduce a new, more efficient machine to produce the firm's widgets, where the new machine both will be more labour efficient (thereby creating redundancies), and will eliminate the need to buy from one half of the firm's suppliers. If one focuses solely on the benefits to shareholders a clear decision can be made. This entire book is about decision-making tools to aid those choices. These range from whether to produce a component in-house, to whether to buy another company. If for each decision scenario we have to contemplate a number of different objectives or some vague balance of stakeholder interests, the task is going to be much more complex. Once the basic decision-making frameworks are understood within the tight confines of shareholder wealth maximisation, we can allow for complications caused by the modification of this assumption. For instance, shareholder wealth maximisation is clearly not the only consideration motivating actions of organisations such as Body Shop or the Co-operative Bank, each with publicly stated ethical principles. GlaxoSmithKline is coming under pressure from some of its shareholders to balance its shareholder wealth objective with generosity to AIDS victims – *see* Exhibit 1.3. It may be that the positive image created by providing cheap drugs to Africans is good for shareholders. On the other hand, it could be that the directors have to make a trade-off decision – greater generosity means less for shareholders. Real-world decision making can be agonisingly hard.

The theoretical reasons

The 'contractual theory' views the firm as a network of contracts, actual and implicit, which specify the roles to be played by various participants in the organisation. For instance, the workers make both an explicit (employment contract) and an implicit (show initiative, reliability, etc.) deal with the firm to provide their services in return for salary and other benefits, and suppliers deliver necessary inputs in return for a known payment. Each party has well-defined rights and pay-offs. Most of the participants bargain for a limited risk and a fixed pay-off. Banks, for example, when they lend to a firm, often strenuously try to reduce risk by making sure that the firm is generating sufficient cash flow to repay, that there are assets that can be seized if the loan is not repaid and so on. The bankers' bargain, like that of many of the parties, is a low-risk one and so, the argument goes, they should be rewarded with just the bare minimum for them to provide their service to the firm. Shareholders, on the other hand, are asked to put money into the business at high risk. The deal here is, 'You give us your £10,000 nest egg that you need for your retirement and we, the directors of the firm, do not promise that you will receive a dividend or even see your capital again. We will try our hardest to produce a return on your money but we cannot give any guarantees. Sorry.' Thus the firm's owners are exposed to the possibilities that the firm may go bankrupt and all will be lost. Because of this unfair balance of risk between the different potential claimants on a firm's resources it seems only fair that the owners should be entitled to any surplus returns which result after all the other parties have been satisfied. Another theoretical reason hinges on the practicalities of operating in a free market system. In such a capitalist system, it is argued, if a firm chooses to reduce returns to shareholders because, say, it wishes to direct more of the firm's surplus to the workers, then this firm will find it difficult to survive. Some shareholders will sell their

Exhibit 1.3

GSK under pressure over drugs for poor

FT

Investors support Oxfam campaign to secure cheaper medicines for developing countries

By David Pilling in London

Large institutional investors in GlaxoSmithKline will this week throw their weight behind a campaign to force the newly merged Anglo-American drugs group to do more to make vital medicines available in developing countries.

Among those backing the campaign, to be launched today by Oxfam, is Friends Ivory Simes, which has £30bn under management and about £1bn invested in GSK. Oxfam is singling out GSK, the £120bn pharmaceutical giant, as part of a campaign focused on what it sees as the abuse of drug patents in denying poor countries access to cheaper medicines.

The issue of access to drugs has been highlighted by the HIV epidemic, which threatens to kill at least 30m people. It has been championed by Médecins sans Frontières, as well as by the author John Le Carré, whose novel *The Constant Gardener* portrays an industry devoid of morality.

Campaigners have accused drug companies of putting profits before lives in the developing world.

Craig Mackenzie, director of governance of Friends Ivory Simes, which manages Friends Provident's pension money, said 'If millions of Africans are dying of preventable diseases and one reason is that drug companies are charging too much, you have a serious reputational risk.'

Mr Mackenzie said institutional investors were taking ethical issues more seriously following last year's Pensions Act, which requires funds to detail their stance on such matters.

Mr Mackenzie said several large investors would meet on Wednesday to discuss how GSK could do more.

Oxfam, part of whose pension fund is also invested in GSK, accused the company of systematically using patent rules to 'squeeze low-cost copies of branded medicines off the market'. It urged GSK to forego patents in Ghana, Uganda and South Africa where it said the company was using legal manoeuvres to block imports of cheap medicines.

GSK said it was disappointed that its 'extensive' drug donation programmes – dismissed by Oxfam as 'islands of philanthropy' – had not been acknowledged. It said it had offered to slash the cost of Aids medicine in Africa, but that governments had been slow to respond.

The company said patents were essential to stimulate investment in research. To argue that breaking or selectively applying patents would solve health disparities was naive, it said.

'If you start having patents in one country but not in another, it undermines the whole patent system. Where do you draw the line?'

Source: *Financial Times*, 12 February 2001, p. 23. Reprinted with permission.

shares and invest in other firms more orientated towards their benefit. In the long run those individuals who do retain their shares may be amenable to a takeover bid from a firm which does concentrate on shareholder wealth creation. The acquirer will anticipate being able to cut costs, not least by lowering the returns to labour. In the absence of a takeover the company would be unable to raise more finance from shareholders and this might result in slow growth and liquidity problems and possibly corporate death, throwing all employees out of work. For over 200 years it has been argued that society is best served by businesses focusing on returns to the owner. Adam Smith (1776) expressed the argument very effectively:

> The businessman by directing ... industry in such a manner as its produce may be of the greatest value, intends only his own gain, and he is in this, as in many other cases, led by an invisible hand to promote an end which was no part of his intention. Nor is it always the worse for society that it was no part of it. By pursuing his own interest he frequently promotes that of the society more effectually than when he really intends to promote it. I have never known much good done by those who affected to trade for the public good. It is an affectation, indeed, not very common among merchants.
>
> *Source*: Adam Smith, *The Wealth of Nations*, 1776, p. 400.

One final, and powerful reason for advancing shareholders' interests above all others (subject to the rules of the game) is very simple: they own the firm and therefore deserve any surplus it produces.

This is not the place to advocate one philosophical approach or another which is applicable to all organisations at all times. Many organisations are clearly not shareholder wealth maximisers and are quite comfortable with that. Charities, government departments and other non-profit organisations are fully justified in emphasising a different set of values to those espoused by the commercial firm. The reader is asked to be prepared for two levels of thought when using this book. While it focuses on corporate shareholder wealth decision making, it may be necessary to make small or large modifications to be able to apply the same frameworks and theories to organisations with different goals.

Football clubs are organisations that often have different objectives from commercial organisations. As Exhibit 1.4 shows, many fans of Newcastle United believe that the objectives of their club changed for the worse when it became a company quoted on the London Stock Exchange. A confusion of objectives can make decision making complex and suspect.

Exhibit 1.4

It's not all black and white for Newcastle

FT

Disgruntled fans are blaming the 'plc' for the club's lack of success

By Patrick Harverson

At professional football clubs, when things start to go badly wrong on the pitch it is traditional to blame the manager, the chairman, or the board of directors.

Not any more. As more and more clubs have begun to list their shares on the stock market, the 'plc' has slowly emerged as the favoured scapegoat of the disgruntled fans.

Take Newcastle United, a team lying six points above the Premiership's relegation zone after losing five of its last six league games. Despite its precarious position, the club has continued to sell some of its best players, and seems in no hurry to buy any replacements.

Although Kenny Dalglish, the team manager, has been criticised for the club's predicament, most of the blame has been heaped on the publicly quoted company that owns the club, and the institutional shareholders which hold shares in that company.

The fans believe Dalglish has been forced to sell players by the board of the plc, which is under pressure from City institutions to tighten its financial belt ahead of the planned £42m redevelopment of its St James' Park ground. Consequently, even though a net £12.5m has been raised from player sales in the past 12 months, there is still not enough money available to improve the playing squad.

The fans also think that if the club had remained private and in the hands of its former chairman, Sir John Hall – the local millionaire whose wealth provided the foundation for the club's rebirth in the 1990s – the team would still be buying new players and challenging for the Premiership title.

It is a persuasive argument, but is it true? And is it inevitable that quoted clubs will always remain vulnerable to the suspicion that they are running the business primarily for the benefit of the shareholders, and not the supporters?

With £31m of cash in the bank at the end of its last financial year, Newcastle is certainly not short of money. The situation, explains Ms Dixon, is that Mr Dalglish has the funds to spend on players, but has been unable to get the ones he wanted.

Of course, the manager does not have a blank cheque. 'Like any business we have a strategy and we operate within a budget,' says Ms Dixon. 'We would have that whether we were private or public.'

Mark Edwards of the financial public relations firm Buchanan Communications advises several top clubs. He says: 'When a club announces plans to float, the first thing that comes up in the local press is the question of what happens if there's a choice between paying a dividend to shareholders or buying a player. These sorts of questions are being raised, but they are probably not being answered fully enough by the clubs.'

Source: *Financial Times*, 24/25 January 1998, p. 18. Reprinted with permission.

Exhibit 1.5 illustrates that a major debate is taking place in Germany about the objective of the firm.

Exhibit 1.5

Whirlwinds of change

FT

Vodafone AirTouch's takeover of Mannesmann will be a landmark in Germany's momentous journey towards a different model of capitalism, says John Plender

Vodafone AirTouch's victory in its bid to control Germany's Mannesmann is of profound historical importance.

At one level it suggests that, in the global competition between national political systems and economic institutions, the adversarial Anglo-American style of capitalism has won ground at the expense of the consensual German stakeholder model. The rules of the post-war German settlement between capital and labour are being radically rewritten from the outside, to the advantage of shareholders.

At another level Germany's 'insider' financial system, in which the banks have played a dominant role, has been opened up to a genuine market in corporate control. For good measure Vodafone, the British telecommunications group, deployed the hostile bid techniques deplored earlier by Chancellor Gerhard Schröder.

The question now is how far convergence between the different systems will go. In one specific sense the Germans have already overtaken the US. Klaus Esser, Mannesmann's chairman, has shown himself far more sensitive to shareholder interests in the course of the bid battle than is usually the case with hostile bids in the US.

There are also limits to the speed of Germany's retreat from stakeholding. Gerhard Fels, Jürgen Matthes and Claus Schnabel argue in a recent paper for the think-tank that deeply embedded values are likely to prevent full convergence on the US model.

Companies, they say, 'are regarded as social institutions, not just as the property of their shareholders. Employees, trade unions and various other stakeholders have a strong say in corporate governance and in labour relations through legal requirements for power-sharing and through the traditional principle of consensus-seeking.'

A . . . worrying outcome might be that, with business, politicians and public differing so markedly in their respective appetites for reform, Germany could end up with the worst of both worlds: Anglo-American governance increasing the pressure for efficiency, while German labour market practice ensures that globally acceptable returns, and thus new jobs, could still only be generated abroad.

Source: *Financial Times*, 4 February 2000, p. 18. Reprinted with permission.

What is shareholder wealth?

Maximising wealth can be defined as maximising purchasing power. The way in which an enterprise enables its owners to indulge in the pleasures of purchasing and consumption is by paying them a dividend. The promise of a flow of cash in the form of dividends is what prompts investors to sacrifice immediate consumption and hand over their savings to a management team through the purchase of shares. Shareholders are interested in a flow of dividends over a long time horizon and not necessarily in a quick payback. Take the electronics giant Philips: it could raise vast sums for short-term dividend payouts by ceasing all research and development (R&D) and selling off surplus sites. But this would not maximise shareholder wealth because, by retaining funds within the business, it is believed that new products and ideas, springing from the R&D programme, will produce much higher dividends in the future. Maximising shareholder wealth means maximising the flow of dividends to shareholders *through time* – there is a long-term perspective.

If a company's shares are quoted on a stock exchange, and that stock exchange, through the actions of numerous buyers and sellers, prices shares appropriately given the firm's potential, then the prospective future dividend flow should be reflected in the share price. Thus, on this assumption of efficient share pricing we may take the current share price as our measure of shareholder wealth. (This assumption is examined in Chapter 14 when we look at the efficient markets hypothesis.) Thus, if the actions of directors, in their investment decisions, are beneficial to shareholders the share price will rise. If they make poor investments in real assets then future dividends will be reduced, and the share price will fall. The comments in Exhibit 1.6 from the *Financial Times* introduce the concept of shareholder value which is discussed in Chapters 15 and 16 – note for now that it involves more than good performance in product markets.

Exhibit 1.6

Never mind the price, feel the value

FT

When you say 'shareholder value', do you sound convincing?

If you do, you're on your way to the top, or there already. It's one of those tests for modern business people: you just *have* to take shareholder value seriously.

But saying it with appropriate reverence, even writing mission statements about it, is easy. The hard work only starts when you try to put it into practice.

How *can* companies create shareholder value? And how they can make sure the world realises what they're doing?

The two questions are closely linked. The concept of shareholder value straddles two different markets: the product market in which a company's goods and services trade; and the stock market, in which its equity changes hands.

MY SHAREHOLDERS DON'T UNDERSTAND ME MS PEMBERTON
ROBERT THOMPSON

The snag is that a company can do well in its product market but still fail to realise its potential shareholder value.

There's no substitute for good product-market performance, of course; and any multi-line business also has to allocate capital properly between its subsidiaries.

But that may not be enough. If the share price is to reflect that success, investors must believe in the company's current management and future prospects. And if they don't you can kiss shareholder value goodbye.

How do you get investors to believe in you and your future? Talking to them helps. So does a convincing annual report.

Source: *Financial Times*, 17 January 1996. Reprinted with permission.

Illustration © Robert Thompson. Reprinted with permission.

Profit maximisation is not the same as shareholder wealth maximisation

Profit is a concept developed by accountants to aid decision-making, one decision being to judge the quality of stewardship shown over the owner's funds. The accountant has to take what is a continuous process, a business activity stretching over many years, and split this into accounting periods of say, a year, or six months. To some extent this exercise is bound to be artificial and fraught with problems. There are many reasons why accounting profit may not be a good proxy for shareholder wealth. Here are five of them:

- ***Prospects*** Imagine that there are two firms that have reported identical profits but one firm is more highly valued by its shareholders than the other. One possible reason for this is that recent profit figures fail to reflect the relative potential of the two firms. The stock market will give a higher share value to the company which shows the greater future growth outlook. Perhaps one set of managers have chosen a short-term approach and raised their profits in the near term but have sacrificed long-term prospects. One way of achieving this is to raise prices and slash marketing spend – over the subsequent year profits might be boosted as customers are unable to switch suppliers immediately. Over the long term, however, competitors will respond and profits will fall.

- *Risk* Again two firms could report identical historic profit figures and have future prospects which indicate that they will produce the same average annual returns. However one firm's returns are subject to much greater variability and so there will be years of losses and, in a particularly bad year, the possibility of bankruptcy. Exhibit 1.7 shows two firms which have identical average profit but Volatile Joe's profit is subject to much greater risk than that of Steady Eddie. Shareholders are likely to value the firm with stable income flows more highly than one with high risk.

Exhibit 1.7 Two firms with identical average profits but different risk levels

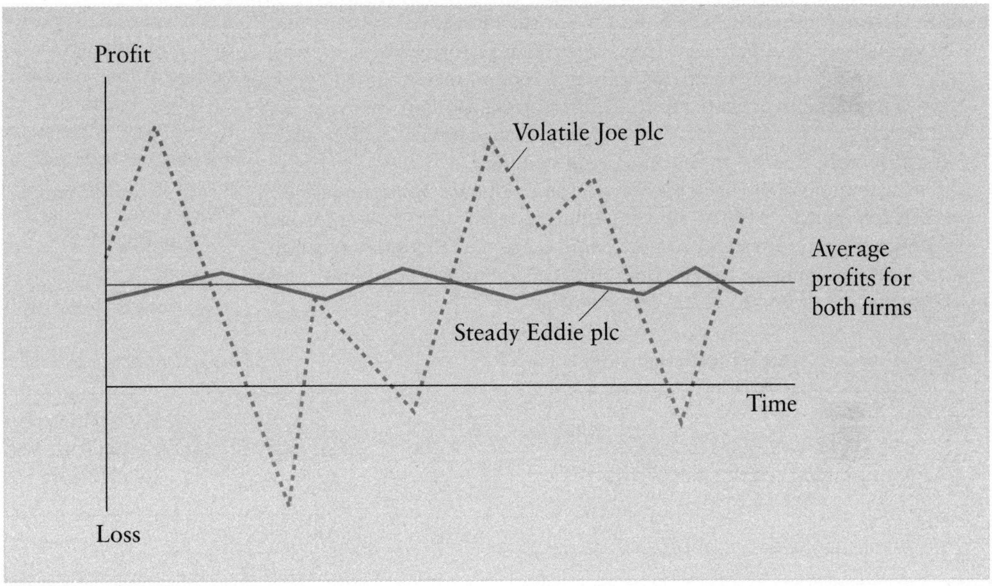

- *Accounting problems* Drawing up a set of accounts is not as scientific and objective as some people try to make out. There is plenty of scope for judgement, guesswork or even cynical manipulation. Imagine the difficulty facing the company accountant and auditors of a clothes retailer when trying to value a dress which has been on sale for six months. Let us suppose the dress cost the firm £50. Perhaps this should go into the balance sheet and then the profit and loss account will not be affected. But what if the store manager says that he can only sell that dress if it is reduced to £30, and contradicting him the managing director says that if a little more effort was made £40 could be achieved? Which figure is the person who drafts the financial accounts going to take? Profits can vary significantly depending on a multitude of small judgements like this. Another difficult accounting issue is demonstrated in Exhibit 1.8 – just when does a sale add to profits?

Exhibit 1.8

Opening a blind eye to tech stocks' figure-flattering

FT

Investors and analysts are concerned some companies are exploiting holes in accounting rules, say Caroline Daniel and Michael Peel

Investors and analysts are growing increasingly concerned that some companies are exploiting holes in accounting rules to give their turnover a more flattering look.

Institutions complain that their search for potential winners in volatile markets is hindered by companies that confuse the issue by booking tomorrow's sales today.

'In a strongly growing period, markets tend to be blind to some of these accounting issues,' says one UK technology fund manager. 'But when top line growth decelerates there is more emphasis on the financial details.'

Last month, shares in Lucent, the telecommunications equipment maker, fell sharply after it said it had overstated turnover because of a suspected accounting irregularity. The company refused to reveal further details of what it called a 'revenue recognition issue' until an investigation had been completed.

The question of revenue recognition is at the heart of the British debate, which revolves around the question of when a sale becomes a sale. For many companies, such as traditional retailers, the answer is easy – the sale is a sale once the goods have been passed to the customer.

But the boundaries become more blurred in sectors such as software, where companies might have ongoing obligations to provide customers with services such as advice and upgrades.

Some software businesses, such as Logica, take a prudent approach and recognise the sales in increments as they complete their contract.

But others take the more adventurous option of booking the full value of the sale as soon as product is handed over, even though their obligations may continue for many months.

Changes in revenue recognition policies can have a big impact, as ITNet, the computer services company, illustrated last month.

The group announced it would take a profits write-off of between £10m and £11m this year as a result of changing its accounting policy for long-term contracts.

A key point is that companies taking an aggressive line on accounting are not contravening any regulations, because Britain lacks clear standards on revenue recognition.

Source: *Financial Times*, 1 December 2000, p. 26. Reprinted with permission.

ITNet

Share price relative to the FTSE TechMark 100

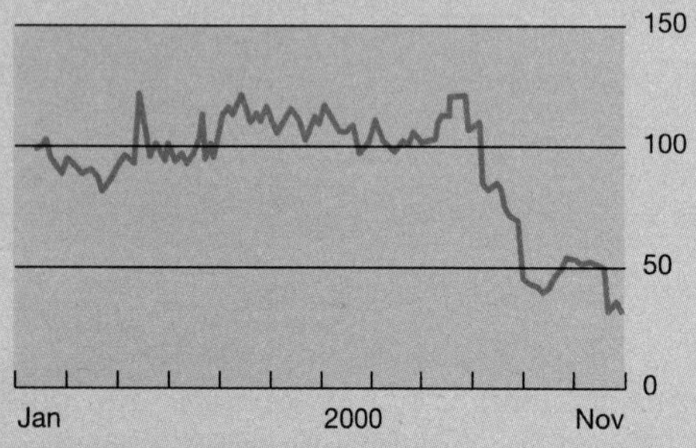

Source: Thomson Financial Datastream

Cedar Group

Share price relative to the FTSE TechMark 100

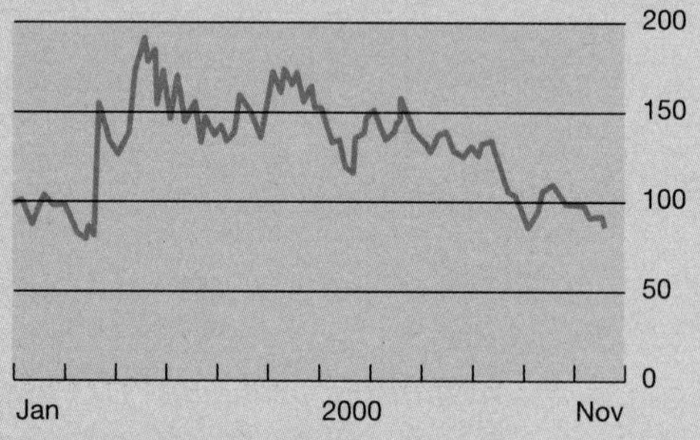

Source: Thomson Financial Datastream

- *Communication* Investors realise and accept that buying a share is risky. However they like to reduce their uncertainty and nervousness by finding out as much as they can about the firm. If the firm is reluctant to tell shareholders about such matters as the origin of reported profits, then investors generally will tend to avoid those shares. Fears are likely to arise in the minds of poorly informed investors: did the profits come from the most risky activities and might they therefore disappear next year? Is the company being used to run guns to unsavoury regimes abroad? The senior executives of large quoted firms spend a great deal of time explaining their strategies, sources of income and future investment plans to the large institutional shareholders to make sure that these investors are aware of the quality of the firm and its prospects. Firms that ignore the importance of communication and image in the investment community may be doing their shareholders a disservice as the share price might fall. Barclays seems to be aware of its responsibilities in this respect – see Exhibit 1.9.

Exhibit 1.9 More information leads to higher shareholder value . . .

Barclays to separate its revenue sources

FT

Barclays plans to disclose significantly more information about earnings from different operations this year in an effort to improve its stock market valuation.

Mr Martin Taylor, chief executive, intends to publish revenues and costs from operations within investment banking and UK retail banking.

Until now, the bank has only given the overall figures for these divisions.

In its interim results announcement later this summer, the bank is likely to list separately revenues from investment banking, asset management, UK personal retail banking, and small and medium-sized business banking in the UK.

Mr Taylor hopes investors will be able to value the bank's earnings more accurately from these figures. Asset management earnings are relatively high quality because they tend to be more consistent than those in investment banking.

Barclays also hopes that by showing the exact extent of its small business lending it will be able to reassure investors. Three-quarters of its earnings volatility in the past 15 years have come from bad debts on this lending.

A split between personal and small business banking would put Barclays among the leading banks in terms of disclosure. National Westminster only splits earnings between NatWest Markets, its investment bank, and its UK retail bank.

Source: John Gapper, Banking Editor, *Financial Times*, 14 May 1996, p. 22. Reprinted with permission.

The London Stock Exchange encourages companies to improve their communication with shareholders – *see* Exhibit 1.10.

Exhibit 1.10

Stock exchange in shareholder relations advice

FT

By David Blackwell

The stock exchange is today sending every listed small company a guide to improving relations with shareholders.

Its main recommendation is for a Statement of Prospects to be published in the annual report. It also urges companies to explore the internet and other ways of making available information that will enable potential investors to make value judgements more easily.

The move follows the increasing pressure on small companies as they fall off investors' radar screens. They are becoming less important to institutions that are increasing in size as the financial services industry consolidates.

Source: *Financial Times*, 8 February 1999, p. 21. Reprinted with permission.

- *Additional capital* Profits can be increased simply by making use of more shareholders' money. If shareholders inject more money into the company or the firm merely retains profits (which belong to shareholders) their future profits can rise, but the return on shareholders' money may fall to less than what is available elsewhere for the same level of risk. This is shareholder wealth destructive.

OWNERSHIP AND CONTROL

The problem

In theory the shareholders, being the owners of the firm, control its activities. In practice, the large modern corporation has a very diffuse and fragmented set of shareholders and control often lies in the hands of directors. It is extremely difficult to marshall thousands of shareholders, each with a small stake in the business, to push for change. Thus in many firms we have what is called a separation, or a divorce, of ownership and control. In times past the directors would usually be the same individuals as the owners. Today, however, less than 1 per cent of the shares of most of the UK's 100 largest quoted firms are owned by the directors and only four out of 10 directors of listed companies own any shares in their business.

The separation of ownership and control raises worries that the management team may pursue objectives attractive to them, but which are not necessarily beneficial to the shareholders – this is termed 'managerialism'. This conflict is an example of the principal–agent problem. The principals (the shareholders) have to find ways of ensuring that their agents (the managers) act in their interests. This means incurring costs, 'agency costs', to (a) monitor managers' behaviour, and (b) create incentive schemes and controls for managers to encourage the pursuit of shareholders' wealth maximisation. These costs arise in addition to the agency cost of the loss of wealth caused by the extent to which prevention measures do not work and managers continue to pursue non-shareholder wealth goals.

Some solutions?

Various methods have been used to try to align the actions of senior management with the interests of shareholders, that is, to achieve 'goal congruence'.

- ***Linking rewards to shareholder wealth improvements*** A technique widely employed in UK industry is to grant directors and other senior managers share options. These permit managers to purchase shares at some date in the future at a price which is fixed now. If the share price rises significantly between the date when the option was granted and the date when the shares can be bought the manager can make a fortune by buying at the pre-arranged price and then selling in the market-place. For example in 2002 managers might be granted the right to buy shares in 2007 at a price of £1.50. If the market price moves to say £2.30 in 2007 the managers can buy and then sell the shares, making a gain of 80p. The managers under such a scheme have a clear interest in achieving a rise in share price and thus congruence comes about to some extent. An alternative method is to allot shares to managers if they achieve certain performance targets, for example, growth in earnings per share or return on assets.
- ***Sackings*** The threat of being sacked with the accompanying humiliation and financial loss may encourage managers not to diverge too far from the shareholders' wealth path. However this method is employed in extreme circumstances only. It is sometimes difficult to implement because of difficulties of making a co-ordinated shareholder effort.
- ***Selling shares and the takeover threat*** Over 60 per cent of the shares of the typical companies quoted on the London stock market are owned by financial institutions such as pension and insurance funds. These organisations generally are not prepared

to put large resources into monitoring and controlling all the hundreds of firms of which they own a part. Quite often their first response, if they observe that management is not acting in what they regard as their best interest, is to sell the share rather than intervene. This will result in a lower share price, making the raising of funds more difficult. If this process continues the firm may become vulnerable to a merger bid by another group of managers, resulting in a loss of top management posts. Fear of being taken over can establish some sort of backstop position to prevent shareholder wealth considerations being totally ignored.

- *Corporate governance regulations* There is a considerable range of legislation and other regulatory pressures designed to encourage directors to act in shareholders' interests. The Companies Acts require certain minimum standards of behaviour, as does the Stock Exchange. There is the back-up of the Serious Fraud Office (SFO) and the financial industry regulators – *see* Chapter 9. Following a number of financial scandals, such as the Maxwell affair, the Cadbury, Greenbury and Hampel reports on corporate governance attempted to improve the accountability of powerful directors. Under these non-statutory proposals, the board of directors should no longer be dominated by a single individual acting as both the chairman and chief executive. Also the non-executive directors should have more power to represent shareholder interests; in particular, at least three independently minded non-executives should be on the board of a large company and they should predominate in decisions connected with directors' remuneration and auditing of the firm's accounts.
- *Information flow* The accounting profession, the stock exchange and the investing institutions have conducted a continuous battle to encourage or force firms to release more accurate, timely and detailed information concerning their operations. The quality of corporate accounts and annual reports has generally improved, as has the availability of other forms of information flowing to investors and analysts, such as company briefings and press announcements. This all helps to monitor firms, and identify any wealth-destroying actions by wayward managers early, but as a number of recent scandals have shown, matters are still far from perfect.

Corporate governance in other countries

The UK and other so-called Anglo-Saxon economies – the USA, Australia, etc. – are much more stock-market orientated than many other countries and a very strong distinction is made between investors and managers. In many continental European countries the stock exchange plays a less pivotal role in providing finance and influencing the actions of directors. Much heavier emphasis is placed on debt finance and this entails a slightly different set of principal–agent restraints, in that there tend to be more rules and legal restrictions. It is said that the Anglo-Saxon reliance on an active stock market and the takeover mechanism is an inefficient way of encouraging management to modify their actions. German companies have two boards to supervise the firm's strategy and operations. The supervisory board has a wide range of outside directors representing the numerous interest groups, not least of which are the bankers. Below this is the executive board, which implements the strategy. The information, power and influence that the banks have in Germany is often significantly greater than it is for their counterparts in the more financial-market-orientated economies.

In some countries the interests of shareholders are often placed far below those of the controlling managers. However progress is being made, as the article in Exhibit 1.11 demonstrates.

Exhibit 1.11

A big voice for the small man

FT

John Plender meets a campaigner for the rights of shareholders in Korea's chaebol

In global corporate governance, South Korea is frontier territory in spite of its status as a member of the Organisation for Economic Co-operation and Development. So Professor Jang Hasung of Korea University, an outspoken campaigner for shareholder rights, has taken on one of the world's more stressful law and order jobs.

Working under the banner of the People's Solidarity for Participatory Democracy (PSPD), a Korean civic group campaigning against the abuse of power by government, the judiciary and big business, he has targeted the country's big five *chaebol*. These sprawling, opaque conglomerates are notorious for the abuse of conflicts of interest between their controlling families and minority shareholders.

'What we want is a fair outcome of the market process,' says the professor. 'We did a great job in Korea on development, but for 30 years fairness has been lacking because of cronyism and the rest. So the rich are not respected and the average person is very negative about the *chaebol*.' . . .

One of his earliest targets was Korea First Bank. Large sums had been lent illegally to the failed Hanbo Steel Group, which was involved in a loans-for-bribes scandal. In 1998, the PSPD's legal action forced the bank's former management to reimburse Won 40bn (£23m) for losses arising from mismanagement and abuse of power.

But Professor Jang's biggest victory has been at SK Telekom, Korea's leading mobile phone group, where he wanted to prevent this very profitable part of the SK *chaebol* from bailing out weaker sister companies.

Here he succeeded in securing the appointment of outside directors and amending the company articles to increase transparency and impose a Won 10bn ceiling on deals with SK sister companies. The chief officer and president of the company even apologised to minority shareholders for excessive profit-taking and insider trading.

Since then, the professor's chief priority has been to secure change at Samsung Electronics, the jewel in the crown of Korea's second-ranked *chaebol*.

It is a tougher target. Prof Jang negotiated improvements in corporate governance with management before the last annual shareholders' meeting. There was give and take, he says. 'But to my despair, one day before the meeting, I was told the chairman did not like the negotiated deal.' The directors then proposed a Won 1,000bn threshold for deals with sister companies.

'This was outrageous,' he says. 'I have never seen anything like it – a mere pretence.' While outside directors were appointed to the board, PSPD's nominee was rejected.

But the professor did not give up, even though many of the foreign investors, with 52 per cent of the equity, failed to back him. A shareholders' meeting that was expected to last 20 minutes ran for 13 hours, as he drilled the executives over hidden subsidies made to the group's failed car company.

He also began legal action calling for the Samsung chairman and other executives to reimburse Won 300bn to the group for other incestuous and illegal transactions.

The activist professor acknowledges that traditional corporate governance remedies are imperfect in a Korean context. Non-executive directors may well be golf partners of the executives. The web of obligations that bind Koreans is a hindrance in persuading non-executive directors to play a proper monitoring role. 'When shareholder value issues arise,' he says, 'the problem is they never raise a voice on the board.'

The professor has concentrated on shareholder value because an immediate priority in dealing with the *chaebol* has been to prevent shareholders being robbed. 'If shareholders' rights are not protected,' he asserts, 'no other stakeholders will be protected. With shareholder rights, others get a safety net.'

But the overriding aim is to legitimise the workings of capitalism in Korea. So far, the impact of the professor and his small group of supporters has been out of all proportion to their numbers and resources.

Source: *Financial Times*, 4 May 2000, p. 15. Reprinted with permission.

In the absence of good corporate governance it is difficult for a firm to obtain funds for expansion – *see* the trouble Russian companies are having in Exhibit 1.12.

Exhibit 1.12

S&P plans new type of rating for Russian groups

FT

By Arkady Ostrovsky in Moscow

Standard & Poor's, the international credit rating agency, will next month launch a product allowing the rating of Russian companies according to corporate governance standards.

Poor standards of corporate governance are among the most pressing issues in the Russian economy, which analysts say slow down foreign and domestic investment and undermine Russian growth.

The new product, whose launch will coincide with the OECD's round table on corporate governance, will rank companies according to their compliance with standards of governance rather than their financial position.

Investors say any instrument allowing measurement of corporate governance risk could be of great value.

The lack of transparency, poor business practices and disrespect for minority shareholders are among the biggest risks for investors in Russia. Last month Norilsk Nickel, one of Russia's largest commodity companies, came under fire from minority shareholders for failing to inform them about the company's restructuring plan and diluting their stakes.

Nick Bradley, director of corporate governance services at S&P, said companies would be evaluated according to four main criteria, including the transparency of the ownership structure, relationship with investors, financial transparency and level of disclosure, and the structure of the board of directors.

Mr Bradley said the service could be paid for by a company itself, or by a foreign investor who is interested in taking a stake in a Russian company.

Source: *Financial Times*, 11 October 2000, p. 37. Reprinted with permission.

PRIMITIVE AND MODERN ECONOMIES

A simple economy

Before we proceed to discuss the role of the financial manager and the part played by various financial institutions it is useful to gain an overview of the economy and the place of the financial system within society. To see the role of the financial sector in perspective it is, perhaps, of value to try to imagine a society without any financial services. Imagine how people would go about their daily business in the absence of either money or financial institutions. This sort of economy is represented in Exhibit 1.13. Here there are only two sectors in society. The business sector produces goods and services, making use of the resources of labour, land and commodities which are owned by the household sector. The household sector is paid with the goods and services produced by the business sector. (In such a simple economy we do not have to concern ourselves with a government sector or a foreign trade sector.)

In this economy there is no money and therefore there are two choices open to the household sector upon receipt of the goods and services:

1 *Consumption* Commodities can be consumed now either by taking those specific items provided from the place of work and enjoying their consumption directly, or, under a barter system, by exchanging them with other households to widen the variety of consumption.

2 *Investment* Some immediate consumption could be foregone so that resources can be put into building assets which will produce a higher level of consumption in the

Exhibit 1.13 Flows within a simple economy – production level

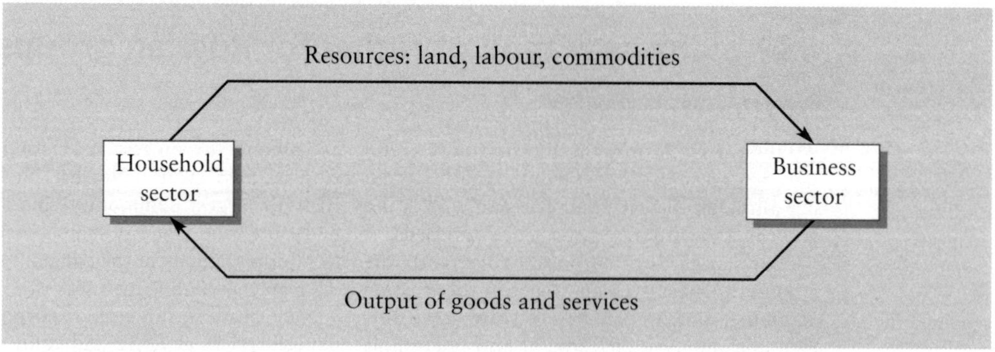

future. For instance, a worker takes payment in the form of a plough so that in future years when he enters the productive (business) sector he can produce more food per acre.

The introduction of money

Under a barter system much time and effort is expended in searching out other households interested in trade. It quickly becomes apparent that a tool is needed to help make transactions more efficient. People will need something into which all goods and services received can be converted. That something would have to be small and portable, it would have to hold its value over a long period of time and have general acceptability. This will enable people to take the commodities given in exchange for, say, labour and then avoid the necessity of, say, carrying the bushels of wheat to market to exchange them for bricks. Instead money could be paid in exchange for labour, and money taken to the market to buy bricks. Various things have been used as a means of exchange ranging from cowry shells to cigarettes (in prisons particularly) but the most popular has been a metal, usually gold or silver. The introduction of money into the system creates monetary as well as real flows of goods and services – *see* Exhibit 1.14.

Exhibit 1.14 Flows within a simple economy – production level plus money

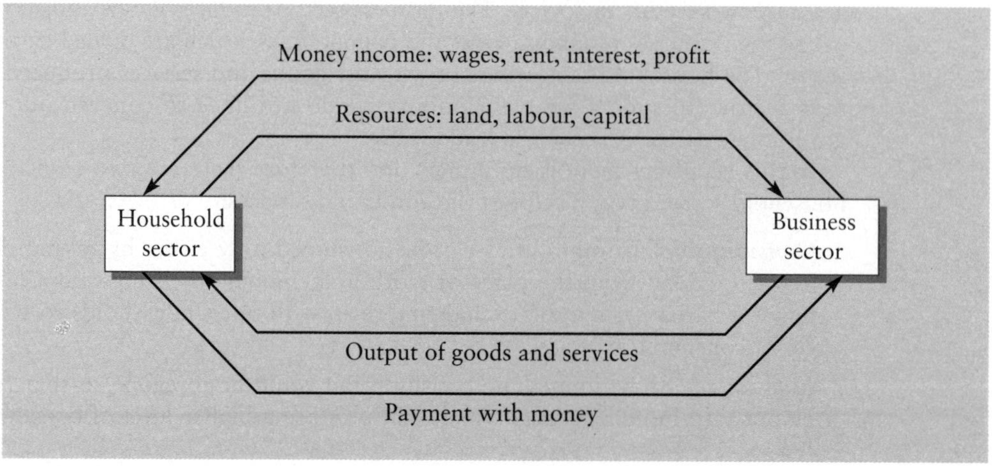

Investment in a money economy

Investment involves resources being laid aside now to produce a return in the future, for instance, today's consumption is reduced in order to put resources into building a factory and the creation of machine tools to produce goods in later years. Most investment takes place in the business sector but it is not the business sector consumption which is reduced if investment is to take place, as all resources are ultimately owned by households. Society needs individuals who are prepared to sacrifice consumption now and to wait for investments to come to fruition. These capitalists are willing to defer consumption and put their funds at risk within the business sector but only if they anticipate a suitable return. In a modern, sophisticated economy there are large-scale flows of investment resources from the ultimate owners (individuals who make up households) to the business sector. Even the profits of previous years' endeavours retained within the business belong to households – they have merely permitted firms to hold on to those resources for further investments on their behalf.

Investment in the twenty-first century is on a grand scale and the time gap between sacrifice and return has in many cases grown very large. This has increased the risks to any one individual investor and so investments tend to be made via pooled funds drawing on the savings of many thousands of households. A capital market has developed to assist the flow of funds between the business and household sectors. Amongst their other functions the financial markets reduce risk through their regulatory regimes and insistence on a high level of disclosure of information. In these more advanced financial structures businesses issue securities which give the holder the right to receive income in specified circumstances. Those that hold debt securities have a relatively high certainty of receiving a flow of interest. Those that buy a security called a share have less surety about what they will receive but, because the return is based on a share of profit, they expect to gain a higher return than if they had merely lent money to the firm.

In Exhibit 1.15 we can see household savings going into business investment. In exchange for this investment the business sector issues securities which show the claims that households have over firms. This exhibit shows three interconnected systems. The

Exhibit 1.15 Flows within a modern economy

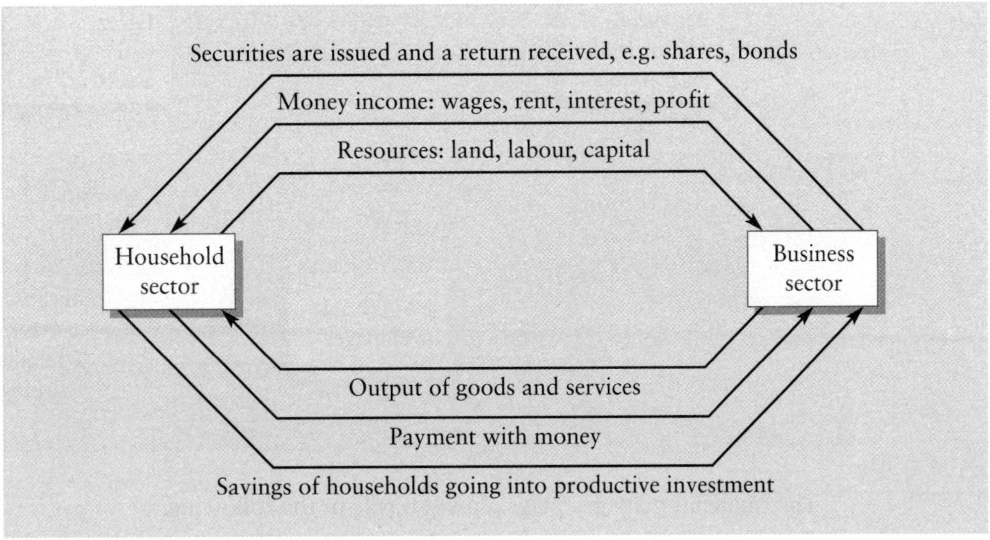

first is the flow of real goods and services. The second is a flow of money. The third is the investment system which enables production and consumption to be increased in the future. It is mainly in facilitating the flow of investment finance that the financial sector has a role in our society. The financial system increases the efficiency of the real economy by encouraging the flow of funds to productive uses.

THE ROLE OF THE FINANCIAL MANAGER

To be able to carry on a business a company needs real assets. These real assets may be tangible, such as buildings, plant, machinery, vehicles and so on. Alternatively a firm may invest in intangible real assets, for example patents, expertise, licensing rights, etc. To obtain these real assets corporations sell financial claims to raise money; to lenders a bundle of rights are sold within a loan contract, to shareholders rights over the ownership of a company are sold as well as the right to receive a proportion of profits produced. The financial manager has the task of both raising finance by selling financial claims and advising on the use of those funds within the business. This is illustrated in Exhibit 1.16.

Exhibit 1.16 The flow of cash between capital markets and the firm's operations

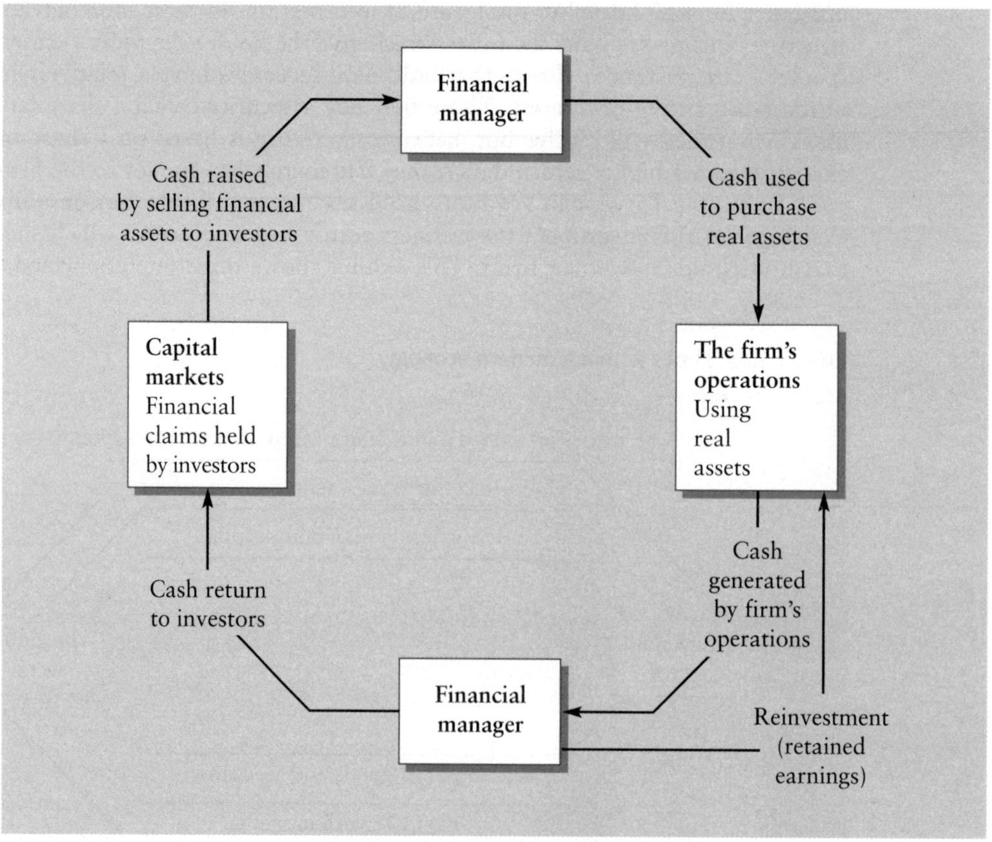

The financial manager plays a pivotal role in the following:

Interaction with the financial markets

In order to raise finance a knowledge is needed of the financial markets and the way in which they operate. To raise share (equity) capital awareness of the rigours and processes involved in 'taking a new company to market' might be useful. For instance, what is the role of an issuing house? What services do brokers, accountants, solicitors, etc. provide to a company wishing to float? Once a company is quoted on a stock market it is going to be useful to know about ways of raising additional equity capital – what about rights issues and open offers?

Knowledge of exchanges such as the Alternative Investment Market (UK) or the European market Euronext might be valuable. If the firm does not wish to have its shares quoted on an exchange perhaps an investigation needs to be made into the possibility of raising money through the venture capital industry.

Understanding how shares are priced and what it is that shareholders are looking for when sacrificing present consumption to make an investment could help the firm to tailor its strategy, operations and financing decisions to suit their owners. These, and dozens of other equity finance questions, are part of the remit of the finance expert within the firm.

Another major source of finance comes from banks. Understanding the operation of banks and what concerns them when lending to a firm may enable you to present your case better, to negotiate improved terms and obtain finance which fits the cash-flow patterns of the firm. Then there are ways of borrowing which by-pass banks. Bonds could be issued either domestically or internationally. Medium-term notes, commercial paper, leasing, hire purchase and factoring are other possibilities.

Once a knowledge has been gained of each of these alternative financial instruments and of the operation of their respective financial markets, then the financial manager has to consider the issue of the correct balance between the different types. What proportion of debt to equity? What proportion of short-term finance to long-term finance and so on?

Perhaps you can already appreciate that the finance function is far from a boring 'bean-counting' role. It is a dynamic function with a constant need for up-to-date and relevant knowledge. The success or failure of the entire business may rest on the quality of the interaction between the firm and the financial markets. The financial manager stands at the interface between the two.

Investment

Decisions have to be made concerning how much to invest in real assets and which specific projects to undertake. In addition to providing analytical techniques to aid these sorts of decisions the financial expert has to be aware of a wide variety of factors which might have some influence on the wisdom of proceeding with a particular investment. These range from corporate strategy and budgeting restrictions to culture and the commitment of individuals likely to be called upon to support an activity.

Treasury management

The management of cash may fall under the aegis of the financial manager. Many firms have large sums of cash which need to be managed properly to obtain a high return for shareholders. Other areas of responsibility might include inventory control, creditor and debtor management and issues of solvency and liquidity.

Risk management

Companies that enter into transactions abroad, for example exporters, are often subject to risk: they may be uncertain about the sum of money (in their own currency) that they will actually receive on the deal. Three or four months after sending the goods they may receive a quantity of yen or dollars but at the time the deal was struck they did not know the quantity of the home currency that could be bought with the foreign currency. Managing and reducing exchange rate risk is yet another area calling on the skills of the finance director.

Likewise, exposure to interest rate changes and commodity price fluctuations can be reduced by using hedging techniques. These often employ instruments such as futures, options, swaps and forward agreements. Misunderstanding these derivatives and their appropriate employment can lead to disaster – for example, the Barings Bank fiasco, in which a major bank was brought to bankruptcy through the misuse and misunderstanding of derivatives.

Strategy

Managers need to formulate and implement long-term plans to maximise shareholder wealth. This means selecting markets and activities in which the firm, given its resources, has a competitive edge. Managers need to distinguish between those products or markets that generate value for the firm and those that destroy value. The financial manager has a pivotal role in this strategic analysis.

Exhibit 1.17 demonstrates the centrality of the finance function.

Exhibit 1.17

More than just a number cruncher

Ask a well-informed private investor for views on chief executives and you'll get enough material to fill four filing cabinets. But pose the same question about finance directors and you'll be lucky if the answers fit on an envelope.

Finance directors have been comparatively low profile (mostly) men and (occasionally) women, ignored by the press unless, like hapless Stuart Straddling, finance director of Wickes, they're thrust into the limelight by a messy accounting scandal.

But dig a little deeper and you discover that while finance directors may not have public images, they're often the quiet voice of authority in a company.

Richard Lapthorne, finance director of British Aerospace, commands huge respect in the City and is viewed by some analysts as being the power behind the throne. Richard Brooke, finance director of BSkyB, may not be as colourful as that company's boss, Sam Chisholm, but he is regarded as a heavyweight who knows as much about the satellite broadcasting business as his chief executive.

There are two types of finance director: the chief finance officer who has been bred by the company, man and boy, and the 'career finance director' who is parachuted in at board level.

A good example of the first category is Rob Rowley at Reuters, who joined as an assistant financial manager in 1978, moved up via various financial positions and was named finance director in 1990.

A more flamboyant career path was taken by Roy Gardner, who joined British Gas as group finance director in 1994 and has recently been named chief executive designate of British Gas Energy.

Money, skills and politics too

Before reaching those Olympian heights, the finance director has to master accounting, treasury functions, City and investor relations and tax. International exposure, takeover experience and ability to handle pan-European acquisitions can be handy for a job with a multinational or a conglomerate. Political savvy is a useful attribute, too.

In theory, these skills are portable and finance directors can move between industries – Simon Moffat, finance director of drug developer Celltech, has a food-manufacturing background. Gerald Corbett, Grand Metropolitan's finance director, did the same job at Redland, the buildings-material supplier, and cut his managerial teeth at retailer Dixons.

But most finance directors stay in the same industry. Rebecca Winnington Ingram, of investment bank Morgan Stanley, says: 'A finance director may be great at performing treasury swaps but, if he knows nothing about the underlying industry, he's not much use.'

Given the weight of the role – closeness to the chief executive, input into corporate strategy and detailed knowledge of the company – the finance director might seem an obvious successor to the chief executive. That is borne out by some recent senior appointments in industry. Derek Bonham, chief executive of Hanson, was Hanson's former finance director, and Nigel Stapleton, finance director of Reed Elsevier, has recently been named chief executive.

'The FD will speak for the company in the chief executive's absence, might even be likened to a deputy chief executive,' he says, pointing to Tomkins's Greg Hutchins (chief executive) and Ian Duncan (finance director) as one such pairing, Sir Richard Greenbury and Keith Oates at Marks and Spencer as another.

Source: Tracy Hofman, *Investors Chronicle*, 16 August 1996. Reprinted with kind permission of *Investors Chronicle*.

THE FLOW OF FUNDS AND FINANCIAL INTERMEDIATION

Exhibit 1.16 looked at the simple relationship between a firm and investors. Unfortunately the real world is somewhat more complicated and the flow of funds within the financial system involves a number of other institutions and agencies. Exhibit 1.18 is a more realistic representation of the financial interactions between different groups in society.

Households generally place the largest proportion of their savings with financial institutions. These organisations then put that money to work. Some of it is lent back to members of the household sector in the form of, say, a mortgage to purchase a house, or as a personal loan. Some of the money is used to buy securities issued by the business sector. The institutions will expect a return on these loans and shares which flows back in the form of interest and dividends. However they are often prepared for businesses to retain profit within the firm for further investment in the hope of greater returns in the future. The government sector enters into the financial system in a number of ways, two of which are shown in Exhibit 1.18. Taxes are taken from businesses and this adds a further dimension to the financial manager's job – for example, taking taxation into account when selecting sources of finance and when approving investment proposals. Second, governments usually fail to match their revenues with their expenditure and therefore borrow significant sums from the financial institutions. The diagram in Exhibit 1.18 remains a gross simplification, it has not allowed for overseas financial transactions, for example, but it does demonstrate a crucial role for financial institutions in an advanced market economy.

Primary investors

Typically the household sector is in financial surplus. This sector contains the savers of society. It is these individuals who become the main providers of funds used for investment in the business sector. Primary investors tend to prefer to exchange their cash for financial assets which (a) allow them to get their money back quickly should they need to (with low transaction cost of doing so) and (b) have a high degree of certainty over the amount they will receive back. That is, primary investors like high liquidity and low risk. Lending directly to a firm with a project proposal to build a North Sea oil platform which will not be sold until five years have passed is not a high-liquidity and low-risk investment. However, putting money into a sock under the bed is (if we exclude the possibility of the risk of sock theft).

Exhibit 1.18 The flow of funds and financial intermediation

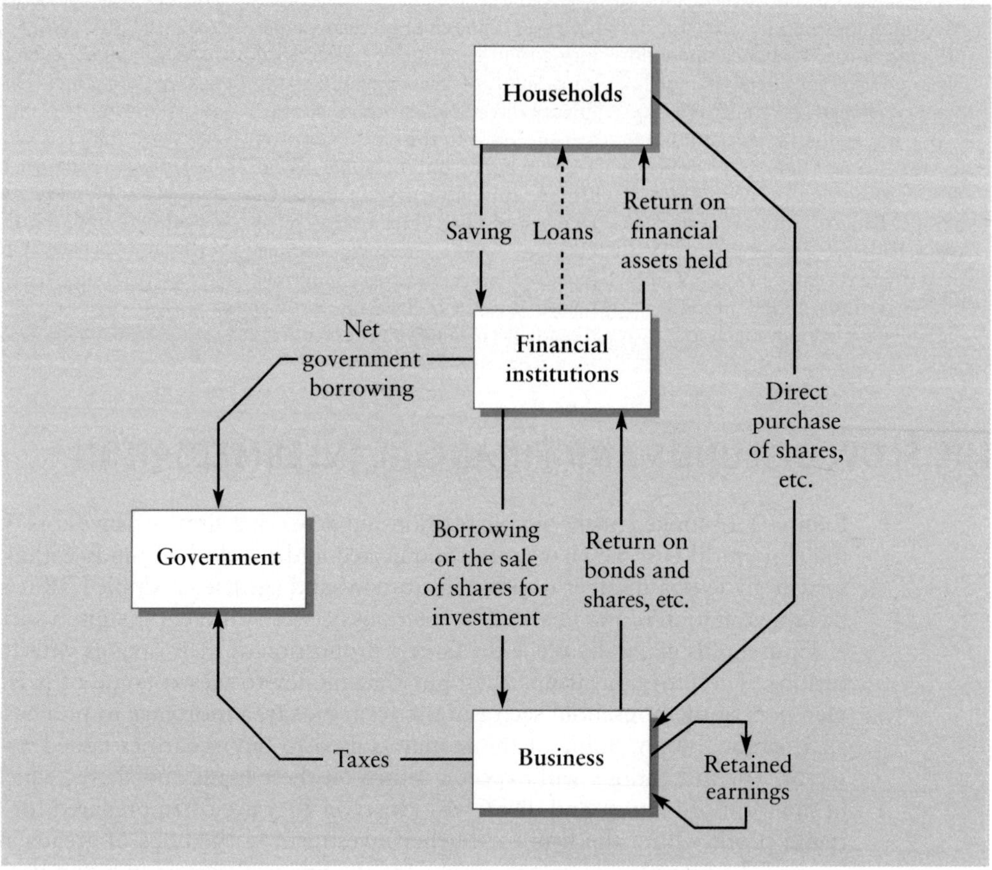

Ultimate borrowers

In our simplified model the ultimate borrowers are in the business sector. These firms are trying to maximise the wealth generated by their activities. To do this companies need to invest in real plant, equipment and other assets, often for long periods of time. The firms, in order to serve their social function, need to attract funds for use over many years. Also these funds are to be put at risk, sometimes very high risk. (Here we are using the term 'borrower' broadly to include all forms of finance, even 'borrowing' by selling shares.)

Conflict of preferences

We have a conflict of preference between the primary investors wanting low-cost liquidity and certainty, and the ultimate borrowers wanting long-term risk-bearing capital. A further complicating factor is that savers usually save on a small scale, £100 here or £200 there, whereas businesses are likely to need large sums of money. Imagine some of the problems that would occur in a society which did not have any financial intermediaries. Here lending and share buying will occur only as a result of direct contact and negotiation between two parties. If there were no organised market where financial securities could be sold on to other investors the fund provider, once committed, would be trapped in an illiquid investment. Also the costs that the two parties might incur in

Exhibit 1.19 Savings into investment in an economy without financial intermediaries

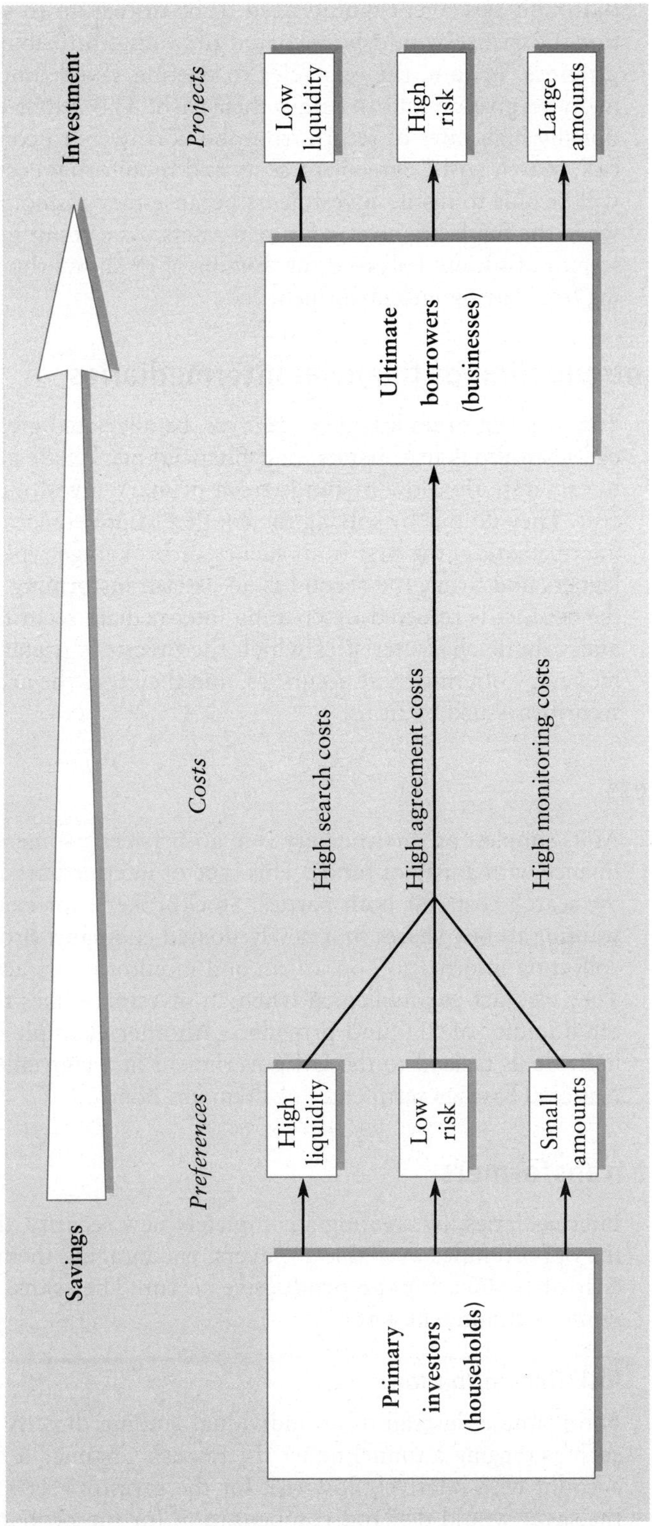

searching to find each other in the first place might be considerable. Following contact a thorough agreement would need to be drawn up to safeguard the investor, and additional expense would be incurred obtaining information to monitor the firm and its progress. In sum, the obstacles to putting saved funds to productive use would lead many to give up and to retain their cash. Those that do persevere will demand exceptionally high rates of return from the borrowers to compensate them for poor liquidity, risk, search costs, agreement costs and monitoring costs. This will mean that few firms will be able to justify investments because they cannot obtain those high levels of return when the funds are invested in real assets. As a result few investments take place and the wealth of society fails to grow. Exhibit 1.19 shows (by the top arrow) little money flowing from saving into investment.

The introduction of financial intermediaries

The problem of under-investment can be alleviated greatly by the introduction of financial institutions (e.g. banks) and financial markets (e.g. a stock exchange). Their role is to facilitate the flow of funds from primary investors to ultimate borrowers at a low cost. They do this by solving the conflict of preferences. There are two types of financial intermediation; the first is an agency or brokerage type operation which brings together lenders and firms, the second is an asset-transforming type of intermediation, in which the conflict is resolved by creating intermediate securities which have the risk, liquidity and volume characteristics which the investors prefer. The financial institution raises money by offering these securities, and then uses the acquired funds to purchase primary securities issued by firms.

Brokers

At its simplest an intermediary is a 'go-between', someone who matches up a provider of finance with a user of funds. This type of intermediary is particularly useful for reducing the search costs for both parties. Stockbrokers, for example, make it easy for investors wanting to buy shares in a newly floated company. Brokers may also have some skill at collecting information on a firm and monitoring its activities, saving the investor time. They also act as middlemen when an investor wishes to sell to another, thus enhancing the liquidity of the fund providers. Another example is the Post Office which enables individuals to lend to the UK government in a convenient and cheap manner by buying National Savings certificates or Premium Bonds.

Asset transformers

Intermediaries, by creating a completely new security, the intermediate security, increase the opportunities available to savers, encouraging them to invest and thus reducing the cost of finance for the productive sector. The transformation function can act in a number of different ways.

Risk transformation

For example, instead of an individual lending directly to a business with a great idea, such as digging a tunnel under the English Channel, a bank creates a deposit or current account with relatively low risk for the investor's savings. Lending directly to the firm the saver would demand compensation for the probability of default on the loan and therefore the business would have to pay a very high rate of interest which would inhibit investment. The bank acting as an intermediary creates a special kind of security called a bank account agreement. The intermediary then uses the funds attracted by the new financial asset to buy a security issued by the tunnel owner (the primary security) when it obtains long-term debt capital. Because of the extra security that a lender has by holding a bank account as a financial asset rather than by making a loan direct to a firm, the lender is prepared to accept a lower rate of interest and the ultimate borrower obtains funds at a relatively low cost. The bank is able to reduce its risk exposure to any one project by diversifying its loan portfolio amongst a number of firms. It can also reduce risk by building up expertise in assessing and monitoring firms and their associated risk. Another example of risk transformation is when unit or investment trusts take savers' funds and spread these over a wide range of company shares.

Maturity (liquidity) transformation

The fact that a bank lends long term for a risky venture does not mean that the primary lender is subjected to illiquidity. Liquidity is not a problem because banks maintain sufficient liquid funds to meet their liabilities when they arise. You can walk into a bank and take the money from your account at short notice because the bank, given its size, exploits economies of scale and anticipates that only a small fraction of its customers will withdraw their money on any one day. Banks and building societies play an important role in borrowing 'short' and lending 'long'.

Volume transformation

Many institutions gather small amounts of money from numerous savers and re-package these sums into larger bundles for investment in the business sector. Apart from the banks and building societies, unit trusts are important here. It is uneconomic for an investor with, say, £50 per month, who wants to invest in shares, to buy small quantities periodically. Unit trusts gather together hundreds of individuals' monthly savings and invest them in a broad range of shares, thereby exploiting economies in transaction costs.

Intermediaries' economies of scale

The intermediary is able to accept lending to (and investing in shares of) companies at a lower rate of return because of the economies of scale enjoyed compared with the primary investor. These economies of scale include:

(a) *Efficiencies in gathering information* on the riskiness of lending to a particular firm. Individuals do not have access to the same data sources or expert analysis.
(b) *Risk spreading* Intermediaries are able to spread funds across a large number of borrowers and thereby reduce overall risk. Individual investors may be unable to do this.
(c) *Transaction costs* They are able to reduce the search, agreement and monitoring costs that would be incurred by savers and borrowers in a direct transaction. Banks, for example, are convenient, safe locations with standardised types of securities. Savers do not have to spend time examining the contract they are entering upon when, say, they open a bank account. How many of us read the small print when we opened a bank account?

The reduced information costs, convenience and passed-on benefits from the economies of operating on a large scale mean that primary investors are motivated to place their savings with intermediaries.

Exhibit 1.20 Savings into investment in an economy with financial intermediaries and financial markets

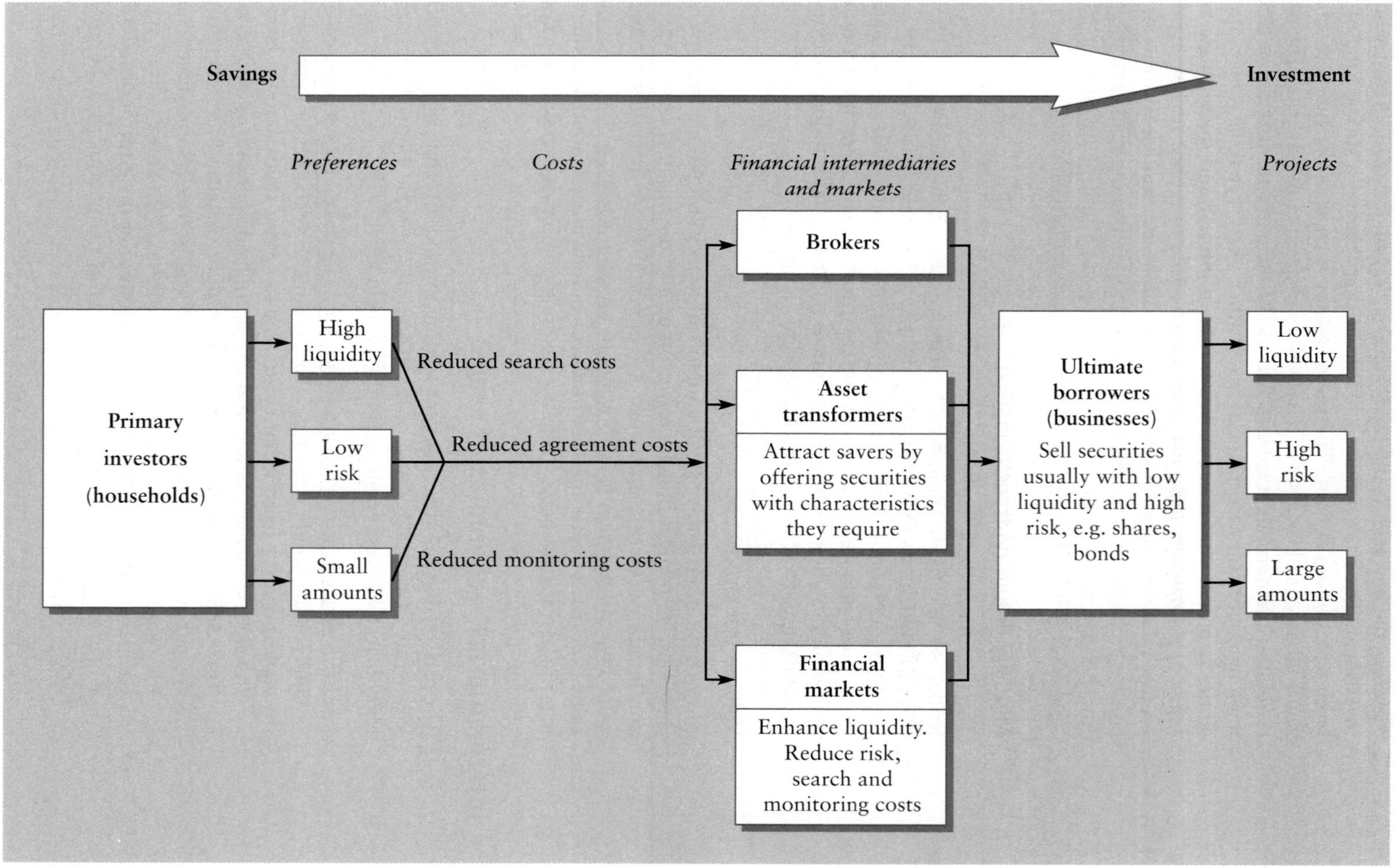

Financial markets

A financial market, such as a stock exchange, has two aspects; there is the *primary market* where funds are raised from investors by the firm, and there is the *secondary market* in which investors buy and sell shares, bonds, etc. between each other. These securities are generally long term and so it is beneficial for the original buyer to be able to sell on to other investors. In this way the firm achieves its objective of raising finance that will stay in the firm for a lengthy period and the investor has retained the ability to liquidate (turn into cash) a holding by selling to another investor. In addition a well-regulated exchange encourages investment by reducing search, agreement and monitoring costs – *see* Exhibit 1.20.

GROWTH IN THE FINANCIAL SERVICES SECTOR

The financial services sector has grown rapidly in the post-war period. It now represents a significant proportion of total economic activity, not just in the UK, but across the world. We define the core of the financial sector as banking (including building societies), insurance and various investment services. There are one or two other activities, such as accounting, which may or may not be included depending on your perspective. Firms operating in the financial services sector have, arguably, been the most dynamic, innovative and adaptable companies in the world over the past 20 years.

Some reasons for the growth of financial services in the UK

There are a number of reasons for the growth of the financial services sector. These include:

1 *High income elasticity*. This means that as consumers have become increasingly wealthy the demand for financial services has grown by a disproportionate amount. Thus a larger share of national income is devoted to paying this sector fees, etc. to provide services because people desire the benefits offered. Firms have also bought an ever-widening range of financial services from the institutions which have been able to respond quickly to the needs of corporations.

2 *International comparative advantage*. London is the world's leading financial centre in a number of markets, for instance international share trading and Eurobond dealing. It is the place where the most currency transactions take place – over £400bn per day. It is also a major player in the fund management, insurance and derivative markets. It is certainly Europe's leading financial centre. One of the reasons for London's maintaining this dominance is that it possesses a comparative advantage in providing global financial services. This advantage stems, not least, from the critical mass of collective expertise which it is difficult for rivals to emulate – *see* Exhibit 1.21.

Dynamism, innovation and adaptation – three decades of change

Since the 1970s there has been a remarkably proactive response by the financial sector to changes in the market environment. New financial instruments, techniques of intermediation and markets have been developed with impressive speed. Instruments which even in the early 1980s did not exist have sprung to prominence to create multi-billion pound markets, with thousands of employees serving that market.

Exhibit 1.21

London is 'gateway to euro-zone'

FT

Clementi says City outpacing Frankfurt and Paris

By Alan Beattie, Economics Correspondent

London will continue to act as the gateway for investment into the euro-zone, David Clementi, deputy governor of the Bank of England, said yesterday.

Speaking in Tokyo, Mr Clementi said London had tightened its grip on euro-denominated markets since the launch of the euro two years ago, despite not having joined the single currency.

'The City of London does not depend on the currency used by the UK,' Mr Clementi said.

'Financial activity will be carried on where it can be carried on most conveniently, profitably and efficiently.'

Mr Clementi said that London's dominance in foreign exchange, derivatives, cross-border bank lending and euro-denominated international bond markets meant that it was outpacing Frankfurt and Paris as an international financial centre.

'Deep and liquid euro markets have become well established in London,' he said. 'They have replaced the previous, more segmented markets in the old national currencies like the Deutschemark and the French franc.'

Mr Clementi, the deputy governor with responsibility for promoting the UK as a financial centre, said that London's success rested on its flexible labour laws, low tax levels and 'non-bureaucratic but rigorous', approach to financial regulation.

His verdict on the first two years of trading in the euro throws weight behind the argument that the UK's position as a global financial centre has survived unscathed its decision not to participate in the first wave of monetary union. The effect on the competitive position of the UK's financial services industry is one of the Treasury's five tests for entry into the euro.

More than half of underwritten euro-denominated international bonds were issued in London, which also has a 70 per cent share of secondary trading in the market, the deputy governor said.

He added that the capitalisation of the London Stock Exchange was nearly double that of either Frankfurt or Paris.

Source: *Financial Times*, 14 February 2000, p. 6. Reprinted with permission.

Until the mid-1970s there were clearly delineated roles for different types of financial institutions. Banks did banking, insurance firms provided insurance, building societies granted mortgages and so on. There was little competition between the different sectors, and cartel-like arrangements meant that there was only limited competition within each sector. Some effort was made in the 1970s to increase the competitive pressures, particularly for banks. The arrival of large numbers of foreign banks in London helped the process of reform in the UK but the system remained firmly bound by restrictions, particularly in defining the activities firms could undertake.

The real breakthrough came in the 1980s. The guiding philosophy of achieving efficiency through competition led to large-scale deregulation of activities and pricing. There was widespread competitive invasion of market segments. Banks became much more active in the mortgage market and set up insurance operations, stockbroking arms, unit trusts and many other services. Building societies, on the other hand, started to invade the territory of the banks and offered personal loans, credit cards, cheque accounts. They even went into estate agency, stockbroking and insurance underwriting. The ultimate invasion happened when Abbey National decided to convert from a building society to a bank in 1989. The Stock Exchange was deregulated in 1986 (in what is known as 'Big bang') and this move enabled it to compete more effectively on a global scale and reduce the costs of dealing in shares, particularly for the large institutional investors.

The 1970s and early 1980s were periods of volatile interest rates and exchange rates. This resulted in greater uncertainty for businesses. New financial instruments were developed to help manage risk. The volume of trading in LIFFE (the London International Financial Futures and Options Exchange) has rocketed since it was opened in 1982 – it now handles over £358bn worth of business every day.[1] Likewise the volume of swaps, options, futures, etc. traded in the informal 'over-the-counter' market (i.e. not on a regulated exchange) has grown exponentially.

Through the 1980s the trend towards globalisation in financial product trading and services continued apace. Increasingly a world-wide market was established. It became possible for a company to have its shares quoted in New York, London, Frankfurt and Tokyo as well as its home exchange in Africa. Bond selling and trading became global and currencies were traded 24 hours a day. International banking took on an increasingly high profile, not least because the multinational corporations demanded that their banks provide multi-faceted services ranging from borrowing in a foreign currency to helping manage cash. The globalisation trend was assisted greatly by the abolition of exchange controls in 1979 in the UK, followed by other leading economies during the 1980s. (Before 1979 UK residents were restricted in the amount of foreign assets they could buy because of limits placed on the purchase of foreign currency.)

Vast investments have been made in computing and telecommunications systems to cut costs and provide improved services. Automated teller machines (ATMs), banking by telephone, and payment by EFTPOS (electronic funds transfer at point of sale) are now commonplace and taken for granted by consumers. A more advanced use of technological innovation is in the global trading of the ever-expanding range of financial instruments. It became possible to sit on a beach in the Caribbean and trade pork belly futures in Chicago, interest rate options in London and shares in Singapore. In the 1990s there was a continuation of the blurring of the boundaries between different types of financial institutions to the point where organisations such as J.P. Morgan Chase, and Barclays are referred to as 'financial supermarkets' (or 'universal banks') offering a wide range of services. The irony is that just as this title was being bandied about, the food supermarket giants such as Sainsbury's and Tesco set up comprehensive banking services, following a path trodden by a number of other non-banking corporations. Marks and Spencer provide credit cards, personal loans and even pensions. Virgin Direct sells life insurance, pensions and Individual Savings Accounts (ISAs) over the telephone. Also, a number of large building societies (e.g. Halifax, Alliance and Leicester and the Woolwich) decided to follow Abbey National and become banks. This has enabled them to undertake an even wider range of activities and to tap further the wholesale financial markets for funds. The internet has provided a new means of supplying financial services and lowered the barrier to entry into the industry. New banking, stockbroking and insurance services have sprung up. The internet allows people to trade millions of shares at the touch of a button from the comfort of their home, to transfer the proceeds between bank accounts and to search websites for data, company reports, newspaper reports, insurance quotations and so on – all much more cheaply than ever before.

The globalisation of business and investment decisions has continued making national economies increasingly interdependent. Borrowers use the international financial markets to seek the cheapest funds, and investors look in all parts of the globe for the highest returns. Some idea of the extent of global financial flows can be gained by contrasting the *daily* turnover of foreign exchange (approximately £1,500bn)[2] with the *annual* output of all the goods and services produced by the people in the UK (£950bn).[3]

Exhibit 1.22 Main features of change in financial services

1970s	• Roles strictly demarcated
1980s	• Deregulation • Competitive invasions of market segments • Globalisation
1990s and 2000s	• Continuation of boundary blurring • Increasing international focus • Disintermediation • New products (e.g. ever more exotic derivatives) • Internet services/trading

Another feature of recent years has been the development of disintermediation. This means borrowing firms by-passing the banks and obtaining debt finance by selling debt securities, such as bonds, in the market. The purchasers can be individuals but are more usually the large savings institutions such as pension funds and insurance funds. Banks, having lost some interest income from lending to these large firms, have concentrated instead on fee income gained by arranging the sale and distribution of these securities as well as underwriting their issue.

A summary of the history of the financial services sector is provided in Exhibit 1.22.

THE FINANCIAL SYSTEM

To assist with orientating the reader within the financial system and to carry out more jargon-busting, a brief outline of the main financial services sectors and markets is given here.

The institutions

The banking sector

Retail banks

Put at its simplest, the retail banks take (small) deposits from the public which are re-packaged and lent to businesses and households. This is generally high-volume and low-value business which contrasts with wholesale banking which is low volume but each transaction is for high value. The distinction between retail and wholesale banks has become blurred over recent years as the large institutions have diversified their operations. The retail banks operate nationwide branch networks and a subset of banks provide a cheque clearance system (transferring money from one account to another) – these are the *clearing* banks. The five largest UK clearing banks are Barclays, Lloyds TSB, Royal Bank of Scotland (including NatWest), HSBC and Abbey National. Loans, overdrafts and mortgages are the main forms of retail bank lending and total lending amounted to £1,284bn in mid-2000.[4] The trend has been for retail banks to reduce their reliance on retail deposits and raise more wholesale funds from the money markets. They also get together with other banks if a large loan is required by a borrower (say £150m) rather than provide the full amount themselves as this would create an excessive exposure to one customer – this is called syndicate lending, discussed in Chapter 11.

Wholesale banks

The terms wholesale bank, merchant bank and investment bank are often used interchangeably. There are subtle differences but for most practical purposes they can be regarded as the same. These institutions tend to deal in large sums of money – at least £250,000 – although some have set up retail arms. They concentrate on dealing with other large organisations, corporations, institutional investors and governments. While they undertake some lending their main focus is on generating commission income by providing advice and facilitating deals. There are five main areas of activity:

- ***Raising external finance for companies*** These banks provide advice and arrange finance for corporate clients. Sometimes they provide loans themselves, but often they assist the setting up of a bank syndicate or make arrangements with other institutions. They will advise and assist a firm issuing a bond, they have expertise in helping firms float on the Stock Exchange and make rights issues. They may 'underwrite' a bond or share issue. (This means that they will buy any part of the issue not taken up by other investors – *see* Chapter 10). This assures the corporation that it will receive the funds it needs for its investment programme.
- ***Broking and dealing*** They act as agents for the buying and selling of securities on the financial markets, including shares, bonds and Eurobonds. Some also have market-making arms which assist the operation of secondary markets (*see* Chapter 9). They also trade in the markets on their own account and assist companies with export finance.
- ***Fund management (asset management)*** The investment banks offer services to rich individuals who lack the time or expertise to deal with their own investment strategies. They also manage unit and investment trusts as well as the portfolios of some pension funds and insurance companies. In addition corporations often have short-term cash flows which need managing efficiently (treasury management).
- ***Assistance in industrial restructuring*** Merchant banks earn large fees from advising acquirers on mergers and assisting with the merger process. They also gain by helping target firms avoid being taken over too cheaply. Advising governments on privatisations has become an important source of fee income. Indeed, the expertise built up in the UK in the 1980s led to a major export industry as governments around the world needed to draw on the bankers' body of knowledge to help privatise large chunks of state-controlled industries. Corporate disposal programmes, such as selling off a division in a management buyout (MBO), may also need the services of a wholesale bank.
- ***Assisting risk management using derivatives*** Risk can be reduced through hedging strategies using futures, options, swaps and the like. However this is a complex area with large room for error and terrible penalties if a mistake is made (*see* Chapter 21). The banks may have specialist knowledge to offer in this area.

International banks

There are two types of international banking:

- *Foreign banking* transactions in sterling with non-UK residents (lending/borrowing, etc.) by UK banks.
- *Eurocurrency banking* for transactions in a currency other than that of the host country. Thus for UK banks this involves transactions in currencies other than sterling with both residents and non-residents (Chapter 11 considers this further).

The major part of international banking these days is borrowing and lending in foreign currencies. There are over 550 non-UK banks operating in London, the most prominent of which are American, German and Japanese. Their initial function was mainly to provide services for their own nationals, for example for export and import transactions, but nowadays their main emphasis is in the Eurocurrency market. Often funds are held in the UK for the purpose of trading and speculation on the foreign exchange market.

Building societies

Building societies collect funds from millions of savers by enticing them to put their money in interest-bearing accounts. The vast majority of that deposited money is then lent to people wishing to buy a home – in the form of a mortgage. Thus, they take in short-term deposits and they lend money for long periods, usually for 25 years. More recently building societies have diversified their sources of finance (e.g. using the wholesale financial markets) and increased the range of services they offer. In 2000 they had loans outstanding to house buyers and other borrowers of about £134bn.[5] The moves by the biggest societies to convert to banks has diminished building societies' significance in the mortgage market.

Finance houses

Finance houses are responsible for the financing of hire purchase agreements and other instalment credit, for example, leasing. If you buy a large durable good such as a car or a washing machine you often find that the sales assistant also tries to get you interested in taking the item on credit, so you pay for it over a period of, say, three years. It is usually not the retailer that provides the finance for the credit. The retailer usually works in conjunction with a finance house which pays the retailer the full purchase price of the good and therefore becomes the owner. You, the customer, get to use the good, but in return you have to make regular payments to the finance house, including interest. Under a hire purchase agreement, when you have made enough payments you will become the owner. Under leasing the finance house retains ownership (for more detail *see* Chapter 12). Finance houses also provide factoring services – providing cash to firms in return for receiving income from the firms' debtors when they pay up. Most of the large finance houses are subsidiaries of the major conglomerate banks. The size of the market is in the region of £10bn–£12bn (new finance provided by Finance and Leasing Association members each year).[6]

Long-term savings institutions

Pension funds

Pension funds are set up to provide pensions for members. For example, the University Superannuation Scheme (USS), to which university lecturers belong, takes about

6.35 per cent of working members' salaries each month and puts it into the fund. In addition the employing organisation pays money into the scheme. When a member retires the USS will pay a pension. Between the time of making a contribution and retirement, which may be decades, the pension trustees oversee the management of the fund. They may place some or all of the fund with specialist investment managers. This is a particularly attractive form of saving because of the generous tax relief provided. The long time horizon of the pension business means that large sums are built up and available for investment. In 2001 this sum had reached over £800bn. A typical allocation of a fund is:

- 50–70 per cent in UK shares;
- 10 per cent lending to UK government by buying bonds and bills;
- 5 per cent property;
- 10–20 per cent overseas securities;
- 5–10 per cent other.

Insurance funds

Insurance companies engage in two types of activities:

- *General insurance* This is insurance against specific contingencies such as fire, theft, accident, generally for a one-year period. The money collected in premiums is mostly held in financial assets which are relatively short term and liquid so that short-term commitments can be met.
- *Life assurance* With *term assurance*, your life is assured for a specified period. If you die your beneficiaries get a pay-out. If you live you get nothing at the end of the period. With *whole-of-life* policies, the insurance company pays a capital sum upon death whenever this occurs. *Endowment* policies are more interesting from a financial systems perspective because they act as a savings vehicle as well as cover against death. The premium will be larger but after a number of years have passed the insurance company pays a substantial sum of money even if you are still alive. The life company has to take the premiums paid over, say, 10 or 25 years, and invest them wisely to satisfy its commitment to the policy holder. Millions of UK house buyers purchase with an endowment mortgage. They simply pay interest to the lender (e.g. a building society) while also placing premiums into an endowment fund. The hope is that after 25 years or so the value of the accumulated fund will equal or be greater than the capital value of the loan.

Life assurance companies also provide *annuities*. Here a policy holder pays an initial lump sum and in return receives regular payments in subsequent years. They have also moved into personal pensions.

Life assurance companies had over £900bn under management in 2001.[7] A typical fund allocation is:

- 40–50 per cent UK shares;
- 20 per cent lending to UK government;
- 10 per cent property;
- 10 –15 per cent overseas securities;
- 5–10 per cent other.

The risk spreaders

These institutions allow small savers a stake in a large diversified portfolio.

Unit trusts

Unit trusts are 'open-ended' funds, so the size of the fund and the number of units depends on the amount of money investors wish to put into the fund. If a fund of one million units suddenly doubled in size because of an inflow of investor funds it would become a fund of two million units through the creation and selling of more units. The buying and selling prices of the units are determined by the value of the fund. So if a two-million unit fund is invested in £2m worth of shares in the UK stock market the value of each unit will be £1. If over a period the value of the shares rises to £3m, the units will be worth £1.50 each. Unit holders sell units back to the managers of the unit trust if they want to liquidate their holding. The manager would then either sell the units to another investor or sell some of the underlying investments to raise cash to pay the unit holder. The units are usually quoted at two prices depending on whether you are buying (higher) or selling. There is also usually an initial charge and an on-going management charge for running the fund. Trustees supervise the funds to safeguard the interests of unit holders but employ managers to make the investment decisions – *see* Exhibit 1.23.

Exhibit 1.23 Unit trust investors, trustees and managers

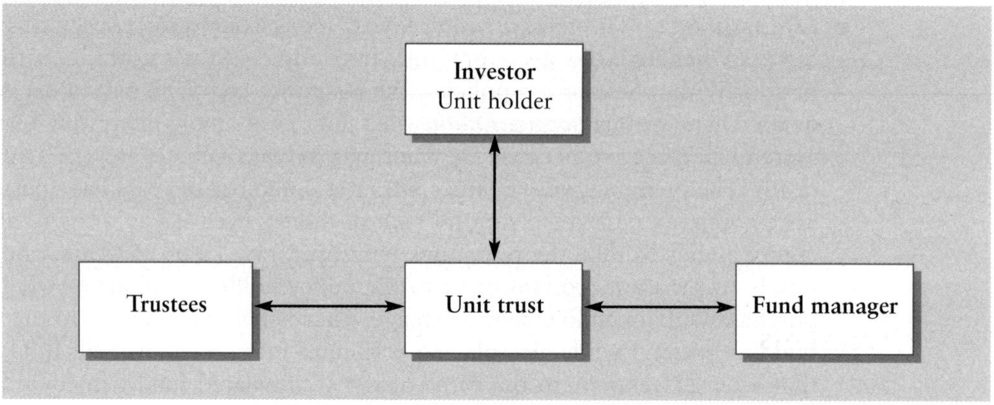

There is a wide choice of unit trust (over 1,000) specialising in different types of investments ranging from Japanese equities to privatised European companies. Of the £260bn (2001) invested, 50–60 per cent is devoted to UK company securities with the remainder mostly devoted to overseas company securities. Instruments similar to unit trusts are called mutual funds in other countries. For an example of a unit trust *see* Exhibit 1.24.

Investment trusts

Investment trusts differ from unit trusts by virtue of the fact that they are companies (rather than trusts!) able to issue shares and other securities. Investors can purchase these securities when the investment trust is first launched or purchase shares in the secondary market from other investors. These are known as closed-end funds because the company itself is closed to new investors – if you wished to invest your money you would go to an existing investor and not buy from the company. Investment trusts usu-

Exhibit 1.24 Unit trust offered by one of the 150+ managers

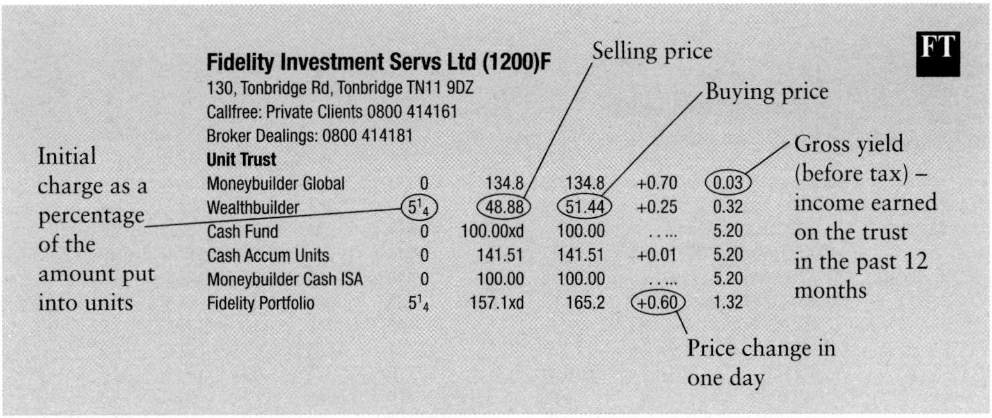

Fidelity Investment Servs Ltd (1200)F
130, Tonbridge Rd, Tonbridge TN11 9DZ
Callfree: Private Clients 0800 414161
Broker Dealings: 0800 414181

Unit Trust					
Moneybuilder Global	0	134.8	134.8	+0.70	0.03
Wealthbuilder	5¼	48.88	51.44	+0.25	0.32
Cash Fund	0	100.00xd	100.00	.....	5.20
Cash Accum Units	0	141.51	141.51	+0.01	5.20
Moneybuilder Cash ISA	0	100.00	100.00	.....	5.20
Fidelity Portfolio	5¼	157.1xd	165.2	+0.60	1.32

Source: *Financial Times*, 9 March 2001. Reprinted with permission.

ally spread the investors' funds across a range of other companies' shares. They are also more inclined to invest in a broader range of assets than unit trusts – even property and unlisted shares. Approximately one-half of the money devoted to UK investment trusts (£65bn) is put into UK securities, with the remainder placed in overseas securities. The managers of these funds are able to borrow in order to invest. This has the effect of increasing returns to shareholders when things go well. Correspondingly if the value of the underlying investments falls the return to shareholders falls even more, because of the obligation to meet interest charges.

Open-ended investment companies (OEICs)

Open-ended investment companies are hybrid risk-spreading instruments which allow an investment in an open-ended fund. Designed to be more flexible and transparent than either investment or unit trusts, OEICs have just one price. However, as with unit trusts, OEICs can issue more shares, in line with demand from investors, and they can borrow.

The markets

The money markets

The money markets are wholesale markets (usually involving transactions of £500,000 or more) which enable borrowing on a short-term basis (less than one year). The banks are particularly active in this market – both as lenders and as borrowers. Large corporations, local government bodies and non-banking financial institutions also lend when they have surplus cash and borrow when short of money.

The bond markets

A bond is merely a document which sets out the borrower's promise to pay sums of money in the future – usually regular interest plus a capital amount upon the maturity of the bond. These are long-dated securities (in excess of one year) issued by a variety of organisations including governments and corporations. The UK bond markets are over three centuries old and during that time they have developed very large and sophisticated primary and secondary sub-markets encompassing gilts (UK government bonds),

Exhibit 1.25 Some of the investment trusts (companies) listed in the *Financial Times*

FT

Investment companies

Notes	Price	+ or –	52 week high	52 week low	Yield	NAV	Dis or Pm(–)
3i ♣†	1333	–11	1797	1001	0.9	1017.1	–31.1
3i Bioscience ♣	543	–7	757½	357½	–	593.7	8.5
3i European Technology	57½	–¼	136½	53	–	56.2	–2.3
3i Smllr Quoted Cos †	243	+1	318	215	1.7	282.4	13.9
3i UK Select	110xd	+½	119	103	2.5	128.3	14.3
ACM Euro Enhanced	89	+½	106	86	10.1	84.0	–6.0
AIM Distribution ‡s	115	......	163	110	2.0	135.5	15.2
AIM Trust ♣	363	......	491	285	–	352.5	–3.0
AIM VCT s	176½xd	......	270	170	0.8	183.3	3.7
AIM VCT 2	92½	......	120	85	–	96.1	3.8
Aberdeen Asian Smlr ♣	93½	......	119	88	1.3	113.4	17.5
Warrants	35¾	......	53	32½	–	–	–
Aberdeen Convertible ♣	97	+½	111	96	8.4	86.3	–12.4
Aberdeen Devlpt Capital ♣†	72½	......	77½	58½	4.8	70.4	–3.0
Zero Div Pref	71	......	73	61½	–	64.4	–10.3
Aberdeen Emrg Ecos ♣	67¾	+¾	78	60	–	83.6	18.9
Warrants	17	+1	22½	12¾	–	–	–
Aberdeen High Inc ♣†	86½	......	118	85½	11.6	70.5	–22.7
Aberseen Latin Amer ♣	66½	......	77¼	58½	–	83.2	20.1
Warrants	15¾	......	26	15½	–	–	–
Aberdeen New Dawn ♣	185	......	195½	152½	0.9	220.1	16.0
Aberdeen New Thai ♣	40½	–¾	48½	33½	0.6	45.6	11.2
Aberdeen Pfd ♣	116	......	153	115½	15.2	88.5	–31.1
5⅜pc RPI Deb 2007	£114$\frac{3}{16}$	–$\frac{3}{32}$	£116$\frac{5}{16}$	£113	4.8	–	–
Units 8¼pc Ln' 23	£102$\frac{29}{32}$	–$\frac{15}{32}$	£105⅜	£98$\frac{23}{32}$	8.0	–	–
Aberdeen Pfd Zero Dv Pf	272½	......	277½	245¾	–	269.9	–1.0
Aberdeen Pf Scs ZDv Pf 08	110	......	111¾	101	–	102.7	–7.2
Aberforth Smllr	337½	......	338	233¾	2.6	378.4	10.8

Change in price in one day

Net asset value. The value of the investment owned by the investment trust per share

The discount on the trust's share price compared with it NAV per share as a percentage

Closing price

Gross yield: dividend income before tax as a percentage of the share price

Source: *Financial Times*, 9 March 2001. Reprinted with permission.

corporate bonds, local authority bonds and Eurobonds, amongst others. The annual turnover of gilt-edged stocks alone is over £1,692bn and the government has over £380bn (2001) of bond debt outstanding. Bonds as a source of finance for firms will be examined in Chapter 11.

The foreign exchange markets (Forex or FX)

The foreign exchange markets are the markets in which one currency is exchanged for another. They include the *spot* market where currencies are bought and sold for 'immediate' delivery (in reality, two days later) and the *forward* markets, where the deal is agreed now to exchange currencies at some fixed point in the future. Also currency *futures* and *options* and other forex derivatives are employed to hedge risk and to speculate. The forex markets are dominated by the major banks, with dealing taking place 24 hours a day around the globe. Chapter 22 looks at how a company could use the forex market to facilitate international trade and reduce the risk attached to business transactions abroad.

The share markets

The London Stock Exchange is an important potential source of long-term equity (ownership) capital. Firms can raise finance in the primary market by a new issue, a rights issue, open offer, etc., either in the main listed London Market (the Official List), the techMARK, or on the Alternative Investment Market. Subsequently investors are able to buy and sell to each other on the very active secondary market. Chapters 9 and 10 examine stock markets and the raising of equity capital.

The derivative markets

A derivative is a financial instrument derived from other financial securities or some other underlying asset. For example, a future is the right to buy something (e.g. currency, shares, bond) at some date in the future at an agreed price. This *right* becomes a saleable derived financial instrument. The performance of the derivative depends on the behaviour of the underlying asset. These markets are concerned with the management and transfer of risk. They can be used to reduce risk (hedging) or to speculate. The London International Financial Futures and Options Exchange (LIFFE) trades options and futures in shares, bonds and interest rates. This used to be the only one of the markets listed here to have a trading floor where face-to-face dealing took place on an open outcry system (traders shouting and signalling to each other, face-to-face in a trading pit, the price at which they are willing to buy and sell). Now all the financial markets (money, bond, forex, derivative and share markets) are conducted using computers (and telephones) from isolated trading rooms located in the major financial institutions. In the derivative markets a high proportion of trade takes place on what is called the over-the-counter (OTC) market rather than on a regulated exchange. The OTC market flexibility allows the creation of tailor-made derivatives to suit a client's risk situation. The practical use of derivatives is examined in Chapter 21.

CONCLUDING COMMENTS

We now have a clear guiding principle set as our objective for the myriad financial decisions discussed later in this book: maximise shareholder wealth. Whether we are considering a major investment programme, or trying to decide on the best kind of finance to use, the criterion of creating value for shareholders over the long run will be paramount. A single objective is set primarily for practical reasons to aid exposition in this text, and anyone wishing to set another goal should not be discouraged from doing so. Many of the techniques described in later chapters will be applicable to organisations with other purposes as they stand, others will need slight modification.

There is an old joke about financial service firms: they just shovel money from one place to another making sure that some of it sticks to the shovel. The implication is that they contribute little to the well-being of society. Extremists even go so far as to regard these firms as parasites on the 'really productive' parts of the economies. And yet very few people avoid extensive use of financial services. Most have bank and building society accounts, pay insurance premiums and contribute to pension schemes. People do not put their money into a bank account unless they get something in return. Likewise building societies, insurance companies, pension funds, unit trusts, merchant banks and so on can only survive if they offer a service people find beneficial and are willing to pay for. Describing the mobilisation and employment of money in the service of productive investment as pointless or merely 'shovelling it around the system' is as logical as saying that the transport firms which bring goods to the high street do not provide a valuable service because there is an absence of a tangible 'thing' created by their activities.

Final thought

If 200 years ago, when the economy was mainly agrarian, you had told people that one day less than 2 per cent of the working population would produce all the food required for a population of 59 million you would have been laughed out of town. Given the lessons of the history of the last 200 years, where will the balance of economic power go over the next few decades in terms of employment and output?

KEY POINTS AND CONCEPTS

- Firms should clearly define the **objective** of the enterprise to provide a focus for decision making.
- **Sound financial management** is necessary for the achievement of all **stakeholder** goals.
- Some stakeholders will have their returns **satisficed** – given just enough to make their contribution. One (or more) group(s) will have their returns **maximised** – given any surplus after all others have been satisfied.
- The assumed objective of the firm for finance is to **maximise shareholder wealth.** Reasons:
  - **practical**, a single objective leads to clearer decisions;
  - the **contractual theory**;
  - **survival** in a competitive world;
  - it is better for **society**;
  - they **own** the firm.
- **Maximising shareholder wealth** is **maximising purchasing power** or **maximising the flow of discounted cash flow** to shareholders over a long time horizon. In an efficient stock market this equates to **maximising the current share price.**
- **Profit maximisation** is not the same as shareholder wealth maximisation. Some factors a profit comparison does not allow for:
  - future prospects;
  - risk;
  - accounting problems;
  - communication;
  - additional capital.
- Large corporations usually have a **separation of ownership and control.** This may lead to **managerialism** where the agent (the managers) take decisions primarily with their interests in mind rather than those of the principals (the shareholders). This is a **principal–agent problem.** Some solutions:
  - link managerial rewards to shareholder wealth improvement;
  - sackings;
  - selling shares and the takeover threat;
  - corporate governance regulation;
  - improve information flow.

- The efficiency of production and the well-being of consumers can be improved with the introduction of **money** to a **barter economy**.
- **Financial institutions and markets** encourage growth and progress by **mobilising savings** and encouraging investment.
- Financial managers contribute to firms' success primarily through **investment and finance decisions**. Their knowledge of financial markets, investment appraisal methods, treasury and risk management techniques are vital for company growth and stability.
- Financial institutions encourage the flow of saving into investment by acting as **brokers** and **asset transformers**, thus alleviating the **conflict of preferences** between the **primary investors** (households) and the **ultimate borrowers** (firms).
- **Asset transformation** is the creation of an intermediate security with characteristics appealing to the primary investor to attract funds, which are then made available to the ultimate borrower in a form appropriate to them. Types of asset transformation:
  - risk transformation;
  - maturity transformation;
  - volume transformation.
- Intermediaries are able to transform assets and encourage the flow of funds because of their **economies of scale** *vis-à-vis* the individual investor:
  - efficiencies in gathering information;
  - risk spreading;
  - transaction costs.
- The **secondary markets** in financial securities encourage investment by enabling investor liquidity (being able to sell quickly and cheaply to another investor) while providing the firm with long-term funds.
- The **financial services sector** has grown to be of great economic significance in the UK. Reasons:
  - high income elasticity;
  - international comparative advantage.
- The financial sector has shown remarkable **dynamism, innovation and adaptability** over the last three decades. Deregulation, new technology, globalisation and the rapid development of new financial products have characterised this sector.
- **Banking sector:**
  - **Retail banks** – high-volume and low-value business.
  - **Wholesale banks** – low-volume and high-value business. Mostly fee based.
  - **International banks** – mostly Eurocurrency transactions.
  - **Building societies** – still primarily small deposits aggregated for mortgage lending.
  - **Finance houses** – hire purchase, leasing, factoring.
- **Long-term savings institutions:**
  - **Pension funds** – major investors in financial assets.
  - **Insurance funds** – life assurance and endowment policies provide large investment funds.

- The risk spreaders:
  - **Unit trusts** – genuine trusts which are open-ended investment vehicles.
  - **Investment trusts** – companies which invest in other companies' financial securities, particularly shares.
  - **Open-ended investment companies** (OEICs) – a hybrid between unit and investment trusts.
- The markets:
  - **The money markets** are short-term wholesale lending and/or borrowing markets.
  - **The bond markets** deal in long-term bond debt issued by corporations, governments, local authorities and so on, and usually have a secondary market.
  - **The foreign exchange market** – one currency is exchanged for another.
  - **The share market** – primary and secondary trading in companies' shares takes place on the official list of the London Stock Exchange, techMARK and the Alternative Investment Market.
  - **The derivatives market** – LIFFE dominates the 'exchange-traded' derivatives market in options and futures. However there is a flourishing over-the-counter market.

REFERENCES AND FURTHER READING

Anthony, R.N. (1960) 'The trouble with profit maximisation', *Harvard Business Review*, Nov.–Dec., pp. 126–34. Challenges the conventional economic view of profit maximisation on grounds of realism and morality.

Arnold, G.C. (2000) 'Tracing the development of value-based management'. In Glen Arnold and Matt Davies (eds), *Value-based Management: Context and Application*. London: Wiley. A more detailed discussion of the objective of the firm is presented.

Blake, D. (2000) *Financial Market Analysis*. 2nd edn. London: Wiley. A more detailed introduction to the financial markets.

Brett, M. (2000) *How to Read the Financial Pages*, 5th edn. London: Random House. A well-written simple guide to the financial markets.

Buckle, M. and Thompson, J. (1995) *The UK Financial System*. 2nd edn. Manchester: Manchester University Press. Clear, elegant and concise description.

'The Cadbury Report' (1992) *Report of the Committee on the Financial aspects of Corporate Governance*. London: Gee. The first and most thorough of the three reports on corporate governance – easy to read.

Cannon, T. (1994) *Social Responsibility*. London: Pitman Publishing. A clear discussion of the corporate objective and governance.

Copeland, T., Koller, T. and Murrin, J. (1996) *Valuation*. 2nd edn. New York: McKinsey and Co. Inc. Contends that shareholder wealth should be the focus of managerial actions.

Donaldson, G. (1963) 'Financial goals: management vs. stockholders', *Harvard Business Review*, May–June, pp. 116–29. Clear and concise discussion of the conflict of interest between managers and shareholders.

Doyle, P. (1994) 'Setting business objectives and measuring performance', *Journal of General Management*, Winter, pp. 1–19. Western firms are over-focused on short-term financial goals (profit, ROI). Reconciling the interests of stakeholders should not be difficult as they are 'satisficers' rather than maximisers.

Fama, E.F. (1980) 'Agency problems and the theory of the firm', *Journal of Political Economy*, Spring, pp. 288–307. Explains how the separation of ownership and control can lead to an efficient form of economic organisation.

Friedman, M. (1970) 'The social responsibility of business is to increase its profits', *New York Times Magazine*, 30 Sept. A viewpoint on the objective of the firm.

Galbraith, J. (1967) 'The goals of an industrial system' (excerpt from *The new industrial state*). Reproduced in H.I. Ansoff, *Business Strategy*, London: Penguin, 1969. Survival, sales and expansion of the 'technostructure' are emphasised as the goals in real-world corporations.

Gardiner, E. and Molyneux, P. (eds) (1996) *Investment banking: theory and practice*. London: Euromoney Books. An overview of merchant banking.

'The Greenbury Report' (1995) *Directors' remuneration: report of a Study Group chaired by Sir Richard Greenbury*. London: Gee. One of the three reports designed to improve corporate governance.

Grinyer, J.R. (1986) 'An alternative to maximisation of shareholder wealth in capital budgeting decisions', *Accounting and Business Research*, Autumn, pp. 319–26. Discusses the maximisation of monetary surplus as an alternative to shareholder wealth.

'The Hampel Report' (1998) *The Committee on Corporate Governance, Final report*. London: Gee. The final report attempting to improve corporate behaviour.

Hart, O.D. (1995a) *Firms, Contracts and Financial Structure*. Oxford: Clarendon Press. A clear articulation of the principal–agent problem.

Hart, O.D. (1995b) 'Corporate governance: some theory and implications'. *Economic Journal*, 105, pp. 678–9. Principal–agent problem discussed.

Hayek, F.A. (1969) 'The corporation in a democratic society: in whose interests ought it and will it be run?' Reprinted in H.I. Ansoff, *Business Strategy*, London: Penguin, 1969. Objective should be long-run return on owners' capital subject to restraint by general legal and moral rules.

Jensen, M.C. (1986) 'Agency costs of free cash flow, corporate finance and takeovers', *American Economic Review*, 76, pp. 323–9. Agency cost theory applied to the issue of the use to which managers put business cash inflows.

Jensen, M.C. and Meckling, W.H. (1976) 'Theory of the firm: managerial behavior, agency costs and ownership structure', *Journal of Financial Economics*, Oct., Vol. 3, pp. 305–60. Seminal work on agency theory.

Keasey, K., Thompson, S. and Wright, M. (1997) *Corporate Governance: Economic, Management and Financial Issues*. Oxford: Oxford University Press. An edited collection of monographs, some of which deal with the question of the objective of the firm.

Levinson, M. (1999) *Guide to Financial Markets*. London: The Economist Books. A clear, brief account of modern financial markets.

Sheridan, T. and Kendall, N. (1992) *Corporate Governance*. London: Pitman Publishing. Discussion of the way in which modern corporations are directed and governed.

Simon, H.A. (1959) 'Theories of decision making in economics and behavioural science', *American Economic Review*, June. Traditional economic theories are challenged, drawing on psychology. Discusses the goals of the firm: satisficing vs. maximising.

Simon, H.A. (1964) 'On the concept of organisational goals', *Administrative Science Quarterly*, 9(1), June, pp. 1–22. Discusses the complexity of goal setting.

Smith, A. (1776) *The Wealth of Nations*. Reproduced in 1910 in two volumes by J.M. Dent, London. An early viewpoint on the objective of the firm.

Vaitilingam, R. (2001) *The Financial Times Guide to using the Financial Pages*. 4th edn. London: Financial Times Prentice Hall. Good introductory source of information. Clear and concise.

Williamson, O. (1963) 'Managerial discretion and business behaviour', *American Economic Review*, 53, pp. 1033–57. Managerial security, power, prestige, etc. are powerful motivating forces. These goals may lead to less than profit maximising behaviour.

WEBSITES

Association of British Insurers www.abi.org.uk
Association of Investment Trust Companies www.aitc.co.uk
Association of Unit Trusts and Investment Funds www.autif.org.uk
Bank of England www.bankofengland.co.uk
British Bankers Association www.bankfacts.org.uk
British Venture Capital Association www.bvca.co.uk
Building Societies Association www.bsa.org.uk
Chartered Institute of Bankers www.cib.org.uk
Companies House www.companieshouse.gov.uk
Finance and Leasing association www.fla.org.uk
Financial Times www.FT.com
National Association of Pension Funds www.napf.co.uk
London International Financial Futures and Options Exchange www.liffe.com or www.liffe.co.uk
London Stock Exchange www.londonstockexchange.com

SELF-REVIEW QUESTIONS

1 Why is it important to specify a goal for the corporation?

2 How can 'goal congruence' for managers and shareholders be achieved?

3 How does money assist the well-being of society?

4 What are the economies of scale of intermediaries?

5 Distinguish between a primary market and a secondary market. How does the secondary market aid the effectiveness of the primary market?

6 Illustrate the flow of funds between primary investors and ultimate borrowers in a modern economy. Give examples of intermediary activity.

7 List as many financial intermediaries as you can. Describe the nature of their intermediation and explain the intermediate securities they create.

8 What is the principal–agent problem?

9 What is the 'contractual theory'? Do you regard it as a strong argument?

10 What difficulties might arise in state-owned industries in making financial decisions?

11 Briefly describe the following types of decisions (give examples):
a Financing
b Investment
c Treasury
d Risk management
e Strategic.

12 Briefly explain the role of the following:
   a The money markets
   b The bond markets
   c The foreign exchange markets
   d The share markets
   e The derivatives market.

QUESTIONS AND PROBLEMS

1 Explain the rationale for selecting shareholder wealth maximisation as the objective of the firm. Include a consideration of profit maximisation as an alternative goal.

2 What benefits are derived from the financial services sector which have led to its growth over recent years in terms of employment and share of GDP?

3 What is managerialism and how might it be incompatible with shareholder interests?

4 Why has an increasing share of household savings been channelled through financial intermediaries?

5 Discuss the relationship between economic growth and the development of a financial services sector.

6 Firm A has a stock market value of £20m (number of shares in issue x share price), while firm B is valued at £15m. The firms have similar profit histories:

	Firm A	*Firm B*
1997	1.5	1.8
1998	1.6	1.0
1999	1.7	2.3
2000	1.8	1.5
2001	2.0	2.0

Provide reasons why, despite the same total profit over the last five years, shareholders regard firm A as being worth £5m more (extend your thoughts beyond the numbers in the table).

7 The chief executive of Geight plc receives a salary of £80,000 plus 4 per cent of sales. Will this encourage the adoption of decisions which are shareholder wealth enhancing? How might you change matters to persuade the chief executive to focus on shareholder wealth in all decision-making?

ASSIGNMENTS

1 Consider the organisations where you have worked in the past and the people you have come into contact with. List as many objectives as you can, explicit or implicit, that have been revealed to, or suspected, by you. To what extent was goal congruence between different stakeholders achieved? How might the efforts of all individuals be channelled more effectively?

2 Review all the financial services you or your firm purchase. Try to establish a rough estimate of the cost of using each financial intermediary and write a balanced report considering whether you or your firm should continue to pay for that service.

CHAPTER NOTES

1 LIFFE: www.liffe.co.uk
2 BIS.
3 Office for National Statistics, *UK National Accounts* (*The Blue Book*).
4 Office for National Statistics, *Financial Statistics*.
5 Office for National Statistics, *Financial Statistics*.
6 Finance and Leasing Association.
7 Office for National Statistics, *Financial Statistics*.
8 Bank of England.

Part II

THE INVESTMENT DECISION

2 Project appraisal: Net present value and internal rate of return

3 Project appraisal: Cash flow and applications

4 The decision-making process for investment appraisal

5 Project appraisal: Capital rationing, taxation and inflation

Chapter 2

PROJECT APPRAISAL: NET PRESENT VALUE AND INTERNAL RATE OF RETURN

INTRODUCTION

Shareholders supply funds to a firm for a reason. That reason, generally, is to receive a return on their precious resources. The return is generated by management using the finance provided to invest in real assets. It is vital for the health of the firm and the economic welfare of the finance providers that management employ the best techniques available when analysing which of all the possible investment opportunities will give the best return.

Someone (or a group) within the organisation may have to take the bold decision on whether it is better to build a new factory or extend the old; whether it is wiser to use an empty piece of land for a multi-storey car park or to invest a larger sum and build a shopping centre; whether shareholders would be better off if the firm returned their money in the form of dividends because shareholders can obtain a better return elsewhere, or whether the firm should pursue its expansion plan and invest in that new chain of hotels, or that large car showroom, or the new football stand.

These sorts of decisions require not only brave people, but informed people; individuals of the required calibre need to be informed about a range of issues: for example, the market environment and level of demand for the proposed activity, the internal environment, culture and capabilities of the firm, the types and levels of cost elements in the proposed area of activity, and, of course, an understanding of the risk and uncertainty appertaining to the project.

Kingfisher presumably considered all these factors before making their multi-million pound investments – *see* Case study 2.1.

CASE STUDY 2.1

Kingfisher

The 2000 annual report for Kingfisher shows that the company spent £817m investing in the business. The chairman, Sir John Banham, comments:

> This year was characterized by record organic growth and a wide range of innovations and investments . . . including the £23.3 million costs of e-commerce and other new channel development . . . We also grew our business in new markets, for example expanding rapidly in Poland, a fast growing DIY market, and we opened our first store, a B&Q, in China. Overall the group opened 120 new stores . . . we have also gained massively from our investment in LibertySurf, the French Internet Service Provider.

Kingfisher not only invested in stores around the world. It had investment projects in: building strong retail brands; improving sourcing and supply chain management systems; e-commerce channels to customers and suppliers; fulfilment and delivery; property; and in a whole host of other assets and activities designed to create value for shareholders.

Bravery, information, knowledge and a sense of proportion are all essential ingredients when undertaking the onerous task of investing other people's money, but there is another element which is also of crucial importance, that is, the employment of an investment appraisal technique which leads to the 'correct' decision; a technique which takes into account the fundamental considerations.

In this chapter we examine two approaches to evaluating investments within the firm. Both emphasise the central importance of the concept of the time value of money and are thus described as Discounted Cash Flow (DCF) techniques. Net present value (NPV) and internal rate of return (IRR) are in common usage in most large commercial organisations and are regarded as more complete than the traditional techniques of payback and accounting rate of return (e.g. Return on Capital Employed – ROCE). The relative merits and demerits of these alternative methods are discussed in Chapter 4 in conjunction with a consideration of some of the practical issues of project implementation. In this chapter we concentrate on gaining an understanding of how net present value and internal rate of return are calculated, as well as their theoretical under-pinnings.

Learning objectives

By the end of the chapter the student should be able to demonstrate an understanding of the fundamental theoretical justifications for using discounted cash flow techniques in analysing major investment decisions, based on the concepts of the time value of money and the opportunity cost of capital. More specifically the student should be able to:

- calculate net present value and internal rate of return;
- show an appreciation of the relationship between net present value and internal rate of return;
- describe and explain at least two potential problems that can arise with internal rate of return in specific circumstances;
- demonstrate awareness of the propensity for management to favour a percentage measure of investment performance and be able to use the modified internal rate of return.

VALUE CREATION AND CORPORATE INVESTMENT

The objective of investment within the firm is to create value for its owners, the shareholders. The purpose of allocating money to a particular division or project is to generate a cash inflow in the future, significantly greater than the amount invested. Thus, put most simply, the project appraisal decision is one involving the comparison of the amount of cash put into an investment with the amount of cash returned. The key phrase and the tricky issue is 'significantly greater than'. For instance, would you, as part-owner of a firm, be content if that firm asked you to swap £10,000 of your hard-earned money for some new shares so that the management team could invest it in order to hand back to you, in five years, the £10,000 plus £1,000? Is this a significant return? Would you feel that your wealth had been enhanced if you were aware that by investing the £10,000 yourself, by, for instance, lending to the government, you could have received a 5 per cent return per year? Or that you could obtain a return of 15 per cent per annum by investing in other shares on the stock market? Naturally, you would feel let down by a management team that offered a return of less than 2 per cent per year when you had alternative courses of action which would have produced much more.

This line of thought is leading us to a central concept in finance and, indeed, in business generally – the time value of money. Investors have alternative uses for their funds and they therefore have an opportunity cost if money is invested in a corporate project. The *investor's opportunity cost* is the sacrifice of the return available on the forgone alternative.

Investments must generate at least enough cash for all investors to obtain their required returns. If they produce less than the investor's opportunity cost then the wealth of shareholders will decline.

Exhibit 2.1 summarises the process of good investment appraisal. The acheivement of value or wealth creation is determined not only by the future cash flows to be derived from a project but also by the timing of those cash flows and by making an allowance for the fact that time has value.

Exhibit 2.1 Investment appraisal: objective, inputs and process

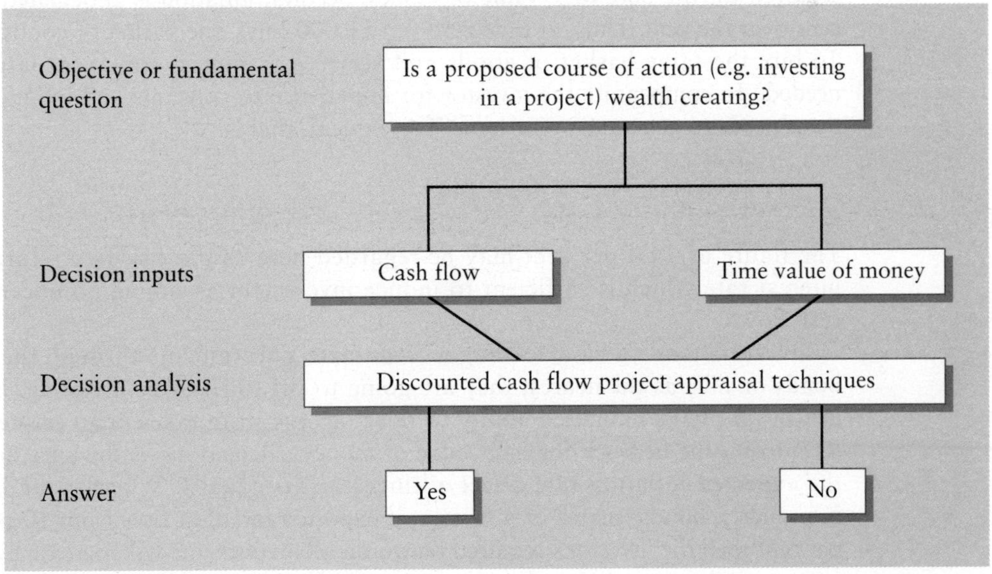

The time value of money

When people undertake to set aside money for investment something has to be given up now. For instance, if someone buys shares in a firm or lends to a business there is a sacrifice of consumption. One of the incentives to save is the possibility of gaining a higher level of future consumption by sacrificing some present consumption. Therefore, it is apparent that compensation is required to induce people to make a consumption sacrifice. Compensation will be required for at least three things:

- ***Time*** That is, individuals generally prefer to have £1.00 today than £1.00 in five years' time. To put this formally: the utility of £1.00 now is greater than £1.00 received five years hence. Individuals are predisposed towards *impatience to consume*, thus they need an appropriate reward to begin the saving process. The rate of exchange between certain future consumption and certain current consumption is the *pure rate of interest* – this occurs even in a world of no inflation and no risk. If you lived in such a world you might be willing to sacrifice £100 of consumption now if you were compensated with £104 to be received in one year. This would mean that your pure rate of interest is 4 per cent.
- ***Inflation*** The price of time (or the interest rate needed to compensate for time preference) exists even when there is no inflation, simply because people generally prefer consumption now to consumption later. If there is inflation then the providers of finance will have to be compensated for that loss in purchasing power as well as for time.
- ***Risk*** The promise of the receipt of a sum of money some years hence generally carries with it an element of risk; the payout may not take place or the amount may be less than expected. Risk simply means that the future return has a variety of possible values. Thus, the issuer of a security, whether it be a share, a bond or a bank account, must be prepared to compensate the investor for time, inflation and risk involved, otherwise no one will be willing to buy the security.

Take the case of Mrs Ann Investor who is considering a £1,000 one-year investment and requires compensation for three elements of time value. First, a return of 4 per cent is required for the pure time value of money. Second, inflation is anticipated to be 10 per cent over the year. Thus, at time zero (t_0) £1,000 buys one basket of goods and services. To buy the same basket of goods and services at time t_1 (one year later) £1,100 is needed. To compensate the investor for impatience to consume and inflation the investment needs to generate a return of 14.4 per cent, that is:

$$(1 + 0.04)(1 + 0.1) - 1 = 0.144$$

The figure of 14.4 per cent may be regarded here as the risk-free return (RFR), the interest rate which is sufficient to induce investment assuming no uncertainty about cash flows.

Investors tend to view lending to reputable governments through the purchase of bonds or bills as the nearest they are going to get to risk-free investing, because these institutions have unlimited ability to raise income from taxes or to create money. The RFR forms the bedrock for time value of money calculations as the pure time value and the expected inflation rate affect all investments equally. Whether the investment is in property, bonds, shares or a factory, if expected inflation rises from 10 per cent to 12 per cent then the investor's required return on all investments will increase by 2 per cent.

However, different investment categories carry different degrees of uncertainty about the outcome of the investment. For instance, an investment on the Russian stock market, with its high volatility, may be regarded as more risky than the purchase of a share in BP with its steady growth prospects. Investors require different risk premiums on top of the RFR to reflect the perceived level of extra risk. Thus:

Required return = **RFR + Risk premium**
(Time value of money)

In the case of Mrs Ann Investor, the risk premium pushes up the total return required to, say, 19 per cent, thus giving full compensation for all three elements of the time value of money.

Discounted cash flow

The net present value and internal rate of return techniques, both being discounted cash flow methods, take into account the time value of money. Exhibit 2.2, which presents Project Alpha, suggests that on a straightforward analysis, Project Alpha generates more cash inflows than outflows. An outlay of £2,000 produces £2,400.

Exhibit 2.2 Project Alpha, simple cash flow

Points in time (yearly intervals)	*Cash flows (£)*
0 Now	–2,000
1 (1 year from now)	+600
2	+600
3	+600
4	+600

However, we may be foolish to accept Project Alpha on the basis of this crude methodology. The £600 cash flows occur at different times and are therefore worth different amounts to a person standing at time zero. Quite naturally, such an individual would value the £600 received in one year more highly than the £600 received after four years. In other words, the present value of the pounds (at time zero) depends on when they are received.

It would be useful to convert all these different 'qualities' of pounds to a common currency, to some sort of common denominator. The conversion process is achieved by discounting all future cash flows by the time value of money, thereby expressing them as an equivalent amount received at time zero. The process of discounting relies on a variant of the compounding formula:

$$F = P\,(1 + i)^n$$

where F = future value
P = present value
i = interest rate
n = number of years over which compounding takes place

Note

It will be most important for many readers to turn to Appendix 2.1 at this point to get to grips with the key mathematical tools which will be used in this chapter and throughout the rest of the book. Readers are also strongly advised to attempt the Appendix 2.1 exercises (answers for which are provided in Appendix VI at the end of the book).

Thus, if a saver deposited £100 in a bank account paying interest at 8 per cent per annum, after three years the account will contain £125.97:

$$F = 100\ (1 + 0.08)^3 = £125.97$$

This formula can be changed so that we can answer the following question: 'How much must I deposit in the bank now to receive £125.97 in three years?'

$$P = \frac{F}{(1+i)^n} \text{ or } F \times \frac{1}{(1+i)^n}$$

$$P = \frac{125.97}{(1+0.08)^3} = 100$$

In this second case we have discounted the £125.97 back to a present value of £100. If this technique is now applied to Project Alpha to convert all the money cash flows of future years into their present value equivalents the result is as follows (assuming that the time value of money is 19 per cent).

Exhibit 2.3 Project Alpha, discounted cash flow

Points in time (yearly intervals)	*Cash flows (£)*	*Discounted cash flows (£)*
0	–2,000	–2,000.00
1	+600	$\frac{600}{1+0.19}$ = +504.20
2	+600	$\frac{600}{(1+0.19)^2}$ = +423.70
3	+600	$\frac{600}{(1+0.19)^3}$ = +356.05
4	+600	$\frac{600}{(1+0.19)^4}$ = +299.20

We can see that, when these future pounds are converted to a common denominator, this investment involves a larger outflow (£2,000) than inflow (£1,583.15). In other words the return on the £2,000 is less than 19 per cent.

Technical aside

If your calculator has a 'powers' function (usually represented by x^y or y^x) then compounding and discounting can be accomplished relatively quickly. Alternatively, you may obtain discount factors from the table in Appendix II at the end of the book. If we take the discounting of the fourth year's cash flow for Alpha as an illustration:

Calculator: $\frac{1}{(1 + 0.19)^4} \times 600$

Input 1.19
Press y^x (or x^y)
Input 4
Press =
Display 2.0053
Press $^1/_x$
Display 0.4987
Multiply by 600
Answer 299.20.

Using Appendix II, look down the column 19% and along the row 4 years to find discount factor of 0.4987:

$$0.4987 \times 600 = 299.20$$

NET PRESENT VALUE AND INTERNAL RATE OF RETURN

Net present value: examples and definitions

The conceptual justification for, and the mathematics of, the net present value and internal rate of return methods of project appraisal will be illustrated through an imaginary but realistic decision-making process at the firm of Hard Decisions plc. This example, in addition to describing techniques, demonstrates the centrality of some key concepts such as opportunity cost and time value of money and shows the wealth-destroying effect of ignoring these issues.

Imagine you are the finance director of a large publicly quoted company called Hard Decisions plc. The board of directors have agreed that the objective of the firm should be shareholder wealth maximisation. Recently, the board appointed a new director, Mr Brightspark, as an 'ideas' man. He has a reputation as someone who can see opportunities where others see only problems. He has been hired especially to seek out new avenues for expansion and make better use of existing assets. In the past few weeks Mr Brightspark has been looking at some land that the company owns near the centre of Birmingham. This is a ten-acre site on which the flagship factory of the firm once stood; but that was 30 years ago and the site is now derelict. Mr Brightspark announces to a board meeting that he has three alternative proposals concerning the ten-acre site.

Mr Brightspark stands up to speak: Proposal 1 is to spend £5m clearing the site, cleaning it up, and decontaminating it. [The factory that stood on the site was used for chemical production.] It would then be possible to sell the ten acres to property developers for a sum of £12m in one year's time. Thus, we will make a profit of £7m over a one-year period.

Proposal 1: Clean up and sell – Mr Brightspark's figures

Clearing the site plus decontamination payable, t_0	–£5m
Sell the site in one year, t_1	£12m
Profit	£7m

The chairman of the board stops Mr Brightspark at that point and turns to you, in your capacity as the financial expert on the board, to ask what you think of the first proposal. Because you have studied assiduously on your Financial Management course you are able to make the following observations:

Point 1 This company is valued by the stock market at £100m because our investors are content that the rate of return they receive from us is consistent with the going rate for our risk class of shares; that is, 15 per cent per annum. In other words, the opportunity cost for our shareholders of buying shares in this firm is 15 per cent. (Hard Decisions is an all-equity firm, no debt capital has been raised.) The alternative to investing their money with us is to invest it in another firm with similar risk characteristics yielding 15 per cent per annum. Thus, we may take this *opportunity cost of capital* as our minimum required return from any project we undertake. This idea of opportunity cost can perhaps be better explained by the use of a diagram (*see* Exhibit 2.4).

If we give a return of less than 15 per cent then shareholders will lose out because they can obtain 15 per cent elsewhere and will, thus, suffer an opportunity cost.

We, as managers of shareholders' money, need to use a discount rate of 15 per cent for any project of the same risk class that we analyse. The discount rate is the opportunity cost of investing in the project rather than the capital markets, for example, buying shares in other firms giving a 15 per cent return. Instead of accepting this project the firm can always give the cash to the shareholders and let them invest it in financial assets.

Exhibit 2.4 The investment decision: alternative uses of firm's funds

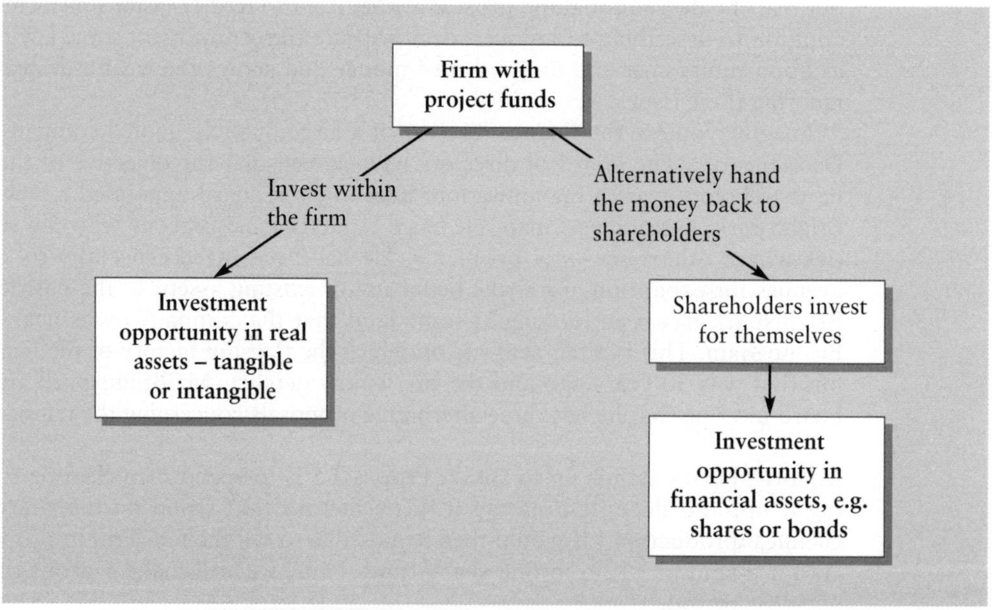

Point 2 I believe I am right in saying that we have received numerous offers for the ten-acre site over the past year. A reasonable estimate of its immediate sale value would be £6m. That is, I could call up one of the firms keen to get its hands on the site and squeeze out a price of about £6m. This £6m is an opportunity cost of the project, in that it is the value of the best alternative course of action. Thus, we should add to Mr Brightspark's £5m of clean-up costs the £6m of opportunity cost because we are truly sacrificing £11m to put this proposal into operation. If we did not go ahead with Mr Brightspartks' proposal, but sold the site as it is, we could raise our bank balance by £6m, plus the £5m saved by not paying clean-up costs.

Proposal 1: Clean up and sell – Year t_0 cash flows

Immediate sale value (opportunity cost)	£6m
Clean up, etc.	£5m
Total sacrifice at t_0	£11m

Point 3 I can accept Mr Brightspark's final sale price of £12m as being valid in the sense that he has, I know, employed some high quality experts to do the sum, but I do have a problem with comparing the initial outlay *directly* with the final cash flow on a simple *nominal* sum basis. The £12m is to be received in one year's time, whereas the £5m is to be handed over to the clean-up firm immediately, and the £6m opportunity cost sacrifice, by not selling the site, is being made immediately.

If we were to take the £11m initial cost of the project and invest it in financial assets of the same risk class as this firm, giving a return of 15 per cent, then the value of that investment at the end of one year would be £12.65m. Investing this sum in alternative investments:

$$F = P(1 + k)$$

where k = the opportunity cost of capital:

$$11(1 + 0.15) = £12.65\text{m}$$

This is more than the return promised by Mr Brightspark.

Another way of looking at this problem is to calculate the net present value of the project. We start with the classic formula for net present value:

$$\text{NPV} = F_0 + \frac{F_1}{(1 + k)^n}$$

where F_0 = cash flow at time zero (t_0), and
F_1 = cash flow at time one (t_1), one year after time zero:

$$\text{NPV} = -11 + \frac{12}{1 + 0.15} = -11 + 10.43 = -0.56\text{m}$$

All cash flows are expressed in the common currency of pounds at time zero. Thus, everything is in present value terms. When the positives and negatives are netted out we have the *net* present value. The decision rules for net present value are:

NPV ≥ 0 Accept
NPV < 0 Reject

An investment proposal's net present value is derived by discounting the future net cash receipts at a rate which reflects the value of the alternative use of the funds, summing them over the life of the proposal and deducting the initial outlay.

In conclusion, Ladies and Gentlemen, given the choice between:

(a) selling the site immediately raising £6m and saving £5m of expenditure – a total of £11m, or
(b) developing the site along the lines of Mr Brightspark's proposal,

I would choose to sell it immediately because £11m would get a better return elsewhere.

The chairman thanks you and asks Mr Brightspark to explain Project Proposal 2.

Mr Brightspark: Proposal 2 consists of paying £5m immediately for a clean-up. Then, over the next two years, spending another £14m building an office complex. Tenants would not be found immediately on completion of the building. The office units would be let gradually over the following three years. Finally, when the office complex is fully let, in six years' time, it would be sold to an institution, such as a pension fund, for the sum of £40m (*see* Exhibit 2.5).

Proposal 2: Office complex – Mr Brightspark's figures

Exhibit 2.5

Points in time (yearly intervals)	*Cash flows (£m)*	*Event*
0 (now)	–5	Clean-up costs
0 (now)	–6	Opportunity cost
1	–4	Building cost
2	–10	Building cost
3	+1	Net rental income $\frac{1}{4}$ of offices let
4	+2	Net rental income $\frac{1}{2}$ of offices let
5	+4	Net rental income All offices let
6	+40	Office complex sold
TOTAL	+22	Inflow £47m Outflow £25m
PROFIT	22	

(*Note*: Mr Brightspark has accepted the validity of your argument about the opportunity cost of the alternative 'project' of selling the land immediately and has quickly added this –£6m to the figures.)

Mr Brightspark claims an almost doubling of the money invested (£25m invested over the first two years leads to an inflow of £47m).

The chairman turns to you and asks: Is this project really so beneficial to our shareholders?

You reply: The message rammed home to me by my finance textbook was that the best method of assessing whether a project is shareholder wealth enhancing is to discount all its cash flows at the opportunity cost of capital. This will enable a calculation of the net present value of those cash flows.

$$\text{NPV} = F_0 + \frac{F_1}{1+k} + \frac{F_2}{(1+k)^2} + \frac{F_3}{(1+k)^3} \cdots + \frac{F_n}{(1+k)^n}$$

So, given that Mr Brightspark's figures are true cash flows, I can calculate the NPV of Proposal 2 – *see* Exhibit 2.6.

Proposal 2: Net present values

Exhibit 2.6

Points in time (yearly intervals)	*Cash flows (£m)*		*Discounted cash flows (£m)*
0	-5		-5
0	-6		-6
1	-4	$\frac{-4}{(1+0.15)}$	-3.48
2	-10	$\frac{-10}{(1+0.15)^2}$	-7.56
3	1	$\frac{1}{(1+0.15)^3}$	0.66
4	2	$\frac{2}{(1+0.15)^4}$	1.14
5	4	$\frac{4}{(1+0.15)^5}$	1.99
6	40	$\frac{40}{(1+0.15)^6}$	17.29
Net present value			-0.96

Because the NPV is less than 0, we would serve our shareholders better by selling the site and saving the money spent on clearing and building and putting that money into financial assets yielding 15 per cent per annum. Shareholders would end up with more in Year 6.

The chairman thanks you and asks Mr Brightspark for his third proposal.

Mr Brightspark: Proposal 3 involves the use of the site for a factory to manufacture the product 'Worldbeater'. We have been producing 'Worldbeater' from our Liverpool factory for the past ten years. Despite its name, we have confined the selling of it to the UK market. I propose the setting up of a second 'Worldbeater' factory which will serve the European market. The figures are as follows (*see* Exhibit 2.7).

Proposal 3: Manufacture of 'Worldbeater' – Mr Brightspark's figures

Exhibit 2.7

Points in time (yearly intervals)	*Cash flows (£m)*	*Event*
0	–5	Clean-up
0	–6	Opportunity cost
1	–10	Factory building
2	0	
3 to infinity	+5	Net income from additional sales of 'Worldbeater'

Note: Revenue is gained in Year 2 from sales but this is exactly offset by the cash flows created by the costs of production and distribution. The figures for Year 3 and all subsequent years are net cash flows, that is, cash outflows are subtracted from cash inflows generated by sales.

The chairman turns to you and asks your advice.

You reply: Worldbeater is a well-established product and has been very successful. I am happy to take the cash flow figures given by Mr Brightspark as the basis for my calculations, which are as follows (*see* Exhibit 2.8).

Proposal 3: Worldbeater manufacturing plant

This project gives an NPV which is positive, and therefore is shareholder wealth enhancing. The third project gives a rate of return which is greater than 15 per cent per annum. It provides a return of 15 per cent plus a present value of £5.5m. Based on these figures I would recommend that the board looks into proposal 3 in more detail.

The chairman thanks you and suggests that this proposal be put to the vote.

Mr Brightspark (interrupts): Just a minute, are we not taking a lot on trust here? Our finance expert has stated that the way to evaluate these proposals is by using the NPV method, but in the firms where I have worked in the past, the internal rate of return (IRR) method of investment appraisal was used. I would like to see how these three proposals shape up when the IRR calculations are done.

The chairman turns to you and asks you to explain the IRR method, and to apply it to the figures provided by Mr Brightspark.

Exhibit 2.8

Points in time (yearly intervals)	*Cash flows (£m)*		*Discounted cash flows (£m)*
0	−11		−11
1	−10	$\frac{-10}{(1+0.15)}$	−8.7
2	0		
3 to infinity	5	Value of perpetuity at time t_2: $P = \frac{F}{k} = \frac{5}{0.15} = 33.33.$	
		This has to be discounted back two years: $\frac{33.33}{(1+0.15)^2}$	= 25.20
Net present value			+5.5

Note: If these calculations are confusing you are advised to read the mathematical Appendix 2.1 at the end of this chapter.

Before continuing this boardroom drama it might be useful at this point to broaden the understanding of NPV by considering two worked examples.

Worked example 2.1 Camrat plc

Camrat plc requires a return on investment of at least 10 per cent per annum over the life of a project in order to meet the opportunity cost of its shareholders (Camrat is financed entirely by equity). The dynamic and thrusting strategic development team have been examining the possibility of entering the new market area of mosaic floor tiles. This will require an immediate outlay of £1m for factory purchase and tooling-up which will be followed by *net* (i.e. after all cash outflows, e.g. wages, variable costs, etc.) cash inflows of £0.2m in one year, and £0.3m in two years' time. Thereafter, annual net cash inflows will be £180,000.

Required

Given these cash flows, will this investment provide a 10 per cent return (per annum) over the life of the project? Assume for simplicity that all cash flows arise on anniversary dates.

Answer

First, lay out the cash flows with precise timing. (Note: the assumption that all cash flows arise on anniversary dates allows us to do this very simply.)

Points in time (yearly intervals)	0	1	2	3 to infinity
Cash flows (£)	−1m	0.2m	0.3m	0.18m

Second, discount these cash flows to their present value equivalents.

Points in time	0	1	2	3 to infinity
	F_0	$\frac{F_1}{1+k}$	$\frac{F_2}{(1+k)^n}$	$\frac{F_3}{k} \times \frac{1}{(1+k)^2}$
	−1m	$\frac{0.2}{1+0.1}$	$\frac{0.3}{(1+0.1)^2}$	$\frac{0.18}{0.1}$ This discounts back two years: $\frac{0.18/0.1}{(1+0.1)^2}$
	−1m	0.1818	0.2479	$\frac{1.8}{(1.1)^2} = 1.4876$

Note

The perpetuity formula can be used on the assumption that the first payment arises one year from the time at which we are valuing. So, if the first inflow arises at time 3 we are valuing the perpetuity as though we are standing at time 2. The objective of this exercise is not to convert all cash flows to time 2 values, but rather to time 0 value. Therefore, it is necessary to discount the perpetuity value by two years.

Third, net out the discounted cash flows to give the net present value.

	−1.0000
	+0.1818
	+0.2479
	+1.4876
Net present value	+0.9173

Conclusion

The positive NPV result demonstrates that this project gives not only a return of 10 per cent per annum but a large surplus above and beyond a 10 per cent per annum return. This is an extremely attractive project: on a £1m investment the surplus generated beyond the opportunity cost of the shareholders (their time value of money) is £917,300; thus by accepting this project we would increase shareholder wealth by this amount.

Worked example 2.2 Actarm plc

Actarm plc is examining two projects, A and B. The cash flows are as follows:

	A £	B £
Initial outflow, t_0	240,000	240,000
Cash inflows:		
Time 1 (one year after t_0)	200,000	20,000
Time 2	100,000	120,000
Time 3	20,000	220,000

Using discount rates of 8 per cent, and then 16 per cent, calculate the NPVs and state which project is superior. Why do you get a different preference depending on the discount rate used?

Answer

Using 8 per cent as the discount rate:

$$NPV = F_0 + \frac{F_1}{1+k} + \frac{F_2}{(1+k)^2} + \frac{F_3}{(1+k)^3}$$

Project A

$$-240{,}000 + \frac{200{,}000}{1+0.08} + \frac{100{,}000}{(1+0.08)^2} + \frac{20{,}000}{(1+0.08)^3}$$

$$-240{,}000 + 185{,}185 + 85{,}734 + 15{,}877 = +£46{,}796$$

Project B

$$-240{,}000 + \frac{20{,}000}{1+0.08} + \frac{120{,}000}{(1+0.08)^2} + \frac{220{,}000}{(1+0.08)^3}$$

$$-240{,}000 + 18{,}519 + 102{,}881 + 174{,}643 = +£56{,}043$$

Using an 8 per cent discount rate both projects produce positive NPVs and therefore would enhance shareholder wealth. However, Project B is superior because it creates more value than Project A. Thus, if the accepting of one project excludes the possibility of accepting the other then B is preferred.

Using 16 per cent as the discount rate:

Project A

$$-240{,}000 + \frac{200{,}000}{1.16} + \frac{100{,}000}{(1.16)^2} + \frac{20{,}000}{(1.16)^3}$$

$$-240{,}000 + 172{,}414 + 74{,}316 + 12{,}813 = +£19{,}543$$

Project B

$$-240{,}000 + \frac{20{,}000}{1.16} + \frac{120{,}000}{(1.16)^2} + \frac{220{,}000}{(1.16)^3}$$

$$-240{,}000 + 17{,}241 + 89{,}180 + 140{,}945 = +£7{,}366$$

With a 16 per cent discount rate Project A generates more shareholder value and so would be preferred to Project B. This is despite the fact that Project B, in pure undiscounted cash flow terms, produces an additional £40,000.

The different ranking (order of superiority) occurs because Project B has the bulk of its cash flows occurring towards the end of the project's life. These large distant cash flows, when discounted at a high discount rate, become relatively small compared with those of Project A, which has its high cash flows discounted by only one year.

We now return to Hard Decisions plc. The chairman has asked you to explain internal rate of return (IRR).

You respond: The internal rate of return is a very popular method of project appraisal and it has much to commend it. In particular it takes into account the time value of money. I am not surprised to find that Mr Brightspark has encountered this appraisal technique in his previous employment. Basically, what the IRR tells you is the rate of interest you will receive by putting your money into a project. It describes by how much the cash inflows exceed the cash outflows on an annualised percentage basis, taking account of the timing of those cash flows.

The internal rate of return is the rate of return which equates the present value of future cash flows with the outlay (or, for some projects, it equates discounted future cash outflows with initial inflow):

Outlay = Future cash flows discounted at rate *r*

Thus:

$$F_0 = \frac{F_1}{1+r} + \frac{F_2}{(1+r)^2} + \frac{F_3}{(1+r)^3} \cdots \frac{F_n}{(1+r)^n}$$

IRR is also referred to as the 'yield' of a project.

Alternatively, the internal rate of return, r, is the discount rate at which the net present value is zero. It is the value for r which makes the following equation hold:

$$F_0 + \frac{F_1}{1+r} + \frac{F_2}{(1+r)^2} + \frac{F_3}{(1+r)^3} \cdots \frac{F_n}{(1+r)^n} = 0$$

(*Note*: in the first formula F_0 is expressed as a positive number, whereas in the second it is usually a negative.)

These two equations amount to the same thing. They both require knowledge of the cash flows and their precise timing. The element which is unknown is the rate of interest which will make the time-adjusted outflows and inflows equal to each other.

I apologise, Ladies and Gentlemen, if this all sounds like too much jargon. Perhaps it would be helpful if you could see the IRR calculation in action. Let's apply the formula to Mr Brightspark's Proposal 1.

Proposal 1: Internal rate of return

Using the second version of the formula, our objective is to find an r which makes the discounted inflow at time 1 of £12m plus the initial £11m outflow equal to zero:

$$F_0 + \frac{F_1}{1+r} = 0$$

$$-11 + \frac{12}{1 + r} = 0$$

The method I would recommend for establishing r is trial and error (assuming we do not have the relevant computer program available). So, to start with, simply pick an interest rate and plug it into the formula.

Let us try 5 per cent:

$$-11 + \frac{12}{1 + 0.05} = £0.42857\text{m} \text{ or } £428,571$$

A 5 per cent rate is not correct because the discounted cash flows do not total to zero. The surplus of approximately £0.43m suggests that a higher interest rate will be more suitable. This will reduce the present value of the future cash inflow.

Try 10 per cent:

$$-11 + \frac{12}{1 + 0.1} = -0.0909 \text{ or } -£90,909$$

Again, we have not hit on the correct discount rate.

Try 9 per cent:

$$-11 + \frac{12}{1 + 0.09} = +0.009174 \text{ or } +£9,174$$

The last two calculations tell us that the interest rate which equates to the present value of the cash flows lies somewhere between 9 per cent and 10 per cent. The precise rate can be found through interpolation.

Interpolation for Proposal 1

First, display all the facts so far established (*see* Exhibit 2.9).

Exhibit 2.9 Interpolation

r	9%	?	10%
Net present value	+£9,174	0	–£90,909
Point	A	B	C

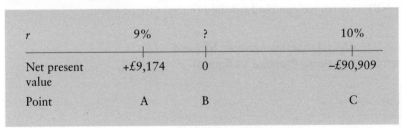

Exhibit 2.9 illustrates that there is a yield rate (r) which lies between 9 per cent and 10 per cent which will produce an NPV of zero. The way to find that interest rate is to first find the distance between points A and B, as a proportion of the entire distance between points A and C.

$$\frac{A \rightarrow B}{A \rightarrow C} = \frac{9,174 - 0}{9,174 + 90,909} = 0.0917$$

Thus the ? lies at a distance of 0.0917 away from the 9 per cent point.

Thus, IRR:

$$= 9 + \left(\frac{9,174}{100,083}\right) \times (10 - 9) = 9.0917 \text{ per cent}$$

To double-check our result:

$$-11 + \frac{12}{1 + 0.090917}$$

$$-11 + 11 = 0$$

Internal rate of return: examples and definitions

The rule for internal rate of return decisions is:

If $k > r$ reject

If the opportunity cost of capital (k) is greater than the internal rate of return (r) on a project then the investor is better served by not going ahead with the project and applying the money to the best alternative use.

If $k \leq r$ accept

Here, the project under consideration produces the same or a higher yield than investment elsewhere for a similar risk level.

The IRR of Proposal 1 is 9.091 per cent, which is significantly below the 15 per cent opportunity cost of capital used by Hard Decisions plc. Therefore, using the IRR method as well as the NPV method, this project should be rejected.

It might be enlightening to consider the relationship between NPV and IRR. Exhibits 2.10 and 2.11 show what happens to NPV as the discount rate is varied between zero and 10 per cent for Proposal 1. At a zero discount rate the £12m received in one year is not discounted at all, so the NPV of £1m is simply the difference between the two cash flows. When the discount rate is raised to 10 per cent the present value of the year 1 cash flow becomes less than the current outlay. Where the line crosses the x axis, i.e. when NPV is zero, we can read off the internal rate of return.

Exhibit 2.10 The relationship between NPV and the discount rate (using Proposal 1's figures)

Discount rate (%)	*NPV*
10	−90,909
9.0917	0
9	9,174
8	111,111
7	214,953
6	320,755
5	428,571
4	538,461
3	650,485
2	764,706
1	881,188
0	1,000,000

Exhibit 2.11 The relationship between NPV and the discount rate for Project Proposal 1

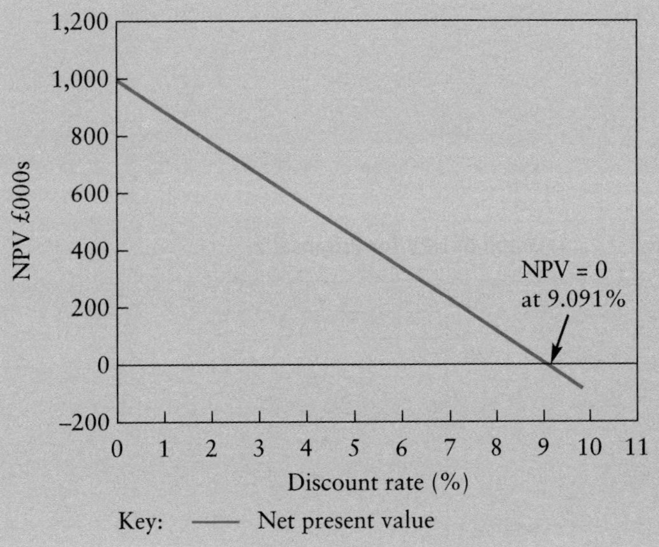

It should be noted that, in the case of Project Proposal 1 the NPV/discount rate relationship is nearly a straight line. This is an unusual case. When cash flows occur over a number of years the line is likely to be more curved and concave to the origin (at least for 'conventional cash flows' – conventional and non-conventional cash flows are discussed later in the chapter).

If the board will bear with me I can quickly run through the IRR calculations for Project Proposals 2 and 3.

Proposal 2: IRR

To calculate the IRR for Proposal 2 we first lay out the cash flows in the discount formula:

$$-11 + \frac{-4}{(1+r)} + \frac{-10}{(1+r)^2} + \frac{1}{(1+r)^3}$$

$$+ \frac{2}{(1+r)^4} + \frac{4}{(1+r)^5} + \frac{40}{(1+r)^6} = 0$$

Then we try alternative discount rates to find a rate, *r*, that gives a zero NPV:

Try 14 per cent:

NPV (approx.) = −£0.043 or −£43,000

At 13 per cent:

NPV = £932,000

Interpolation[1] is required to find an internal rate of return accurate to at least one decimal place (*see* Exhibit 2.12).

$$13 + \frac{932,000}{975,000} \times (14 - 13) = 13.96\%$$

Exhibit 2.12 Interpolation

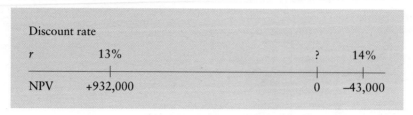

Exhibit 2.13 Graph of NPV for Proposal 2

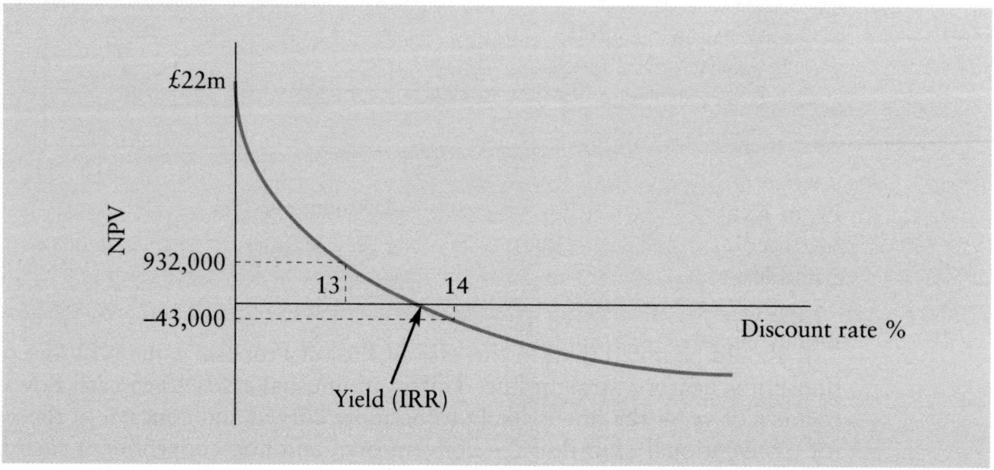

From Exhibit 2.13, we see that this project produces an IRR less than the opportunity cost of shareholders' funds; therefore it should be rejected under the IRR method. The curvature of the line is exaggerated to demonstrate the absence of linearity and emphasise the importance of having a fairly small gap in trial and error interest rates prior to interpolation. The interpolation formula assumes a straight line between the two discount rates chosen and this may lead to a false result. The effect of taking a wide range of interest rates can be illustrated if we calculate on the basis of 5 per cent and 30 per cent.

At 5 per cent, NPV of Project 2 = £11.6121m.

At 30 per cent, NPV of Project 2 = –£9.4743m.

$$5 + \left(\frac{11.6121}{11.6121 + 9.4743}\right)(30 - 5) = 18.77\%$$

Exhibit 2.14 Linear interpolation

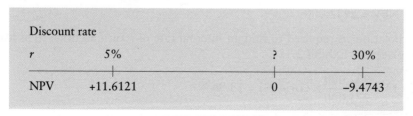

Exhibit 2.15 Graph of NPV for Proposal 2 – using exaggerated linear interpolation

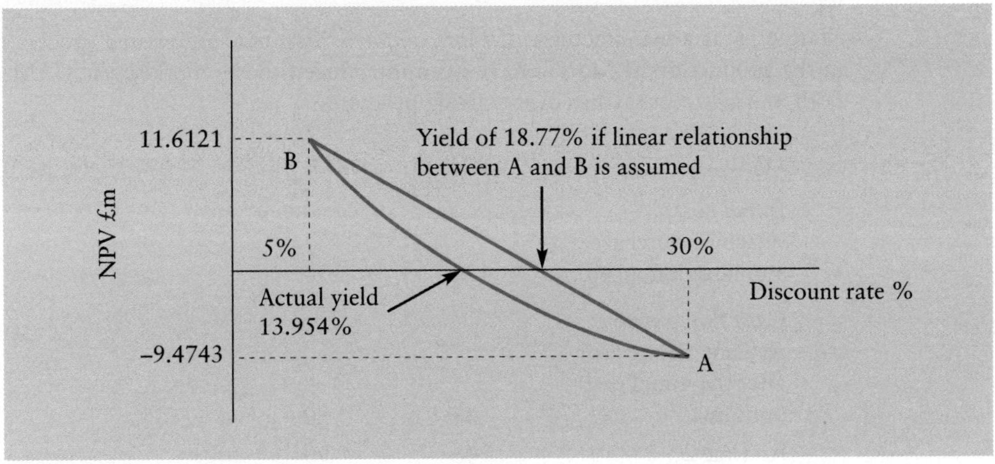

From Exhibit 2.15 we see that the non-linearity of the relationship between NPV and the discount rate has created an IRR almost 5 per cent removed from the true IRR. This could lead to an erroneous acceptance of this project given the company's hurdle rate of 15 per cent. In reality this project yields less than the company could earn by placing its money elsewhere for the same risk level.

Proposal 3: IRR

$$F_0 + \frac{F_1}{1+r} + \frac{F_3/r}{(1+r)^2} = 0$$

Try 19 per cent:

$$-11 + \frac{-10}{1+0.19} + \frac{5/0.19}{(1+0.19)^2} = -£0.82\text{m}$$

Try 18 per cent:

$$-11 + \frac{-10}{1+0.18} + \frac{5/0.18}{(1+0.18)^2} = £0.475\text{m}$$

Exhibit 2.16 Linear interpolation

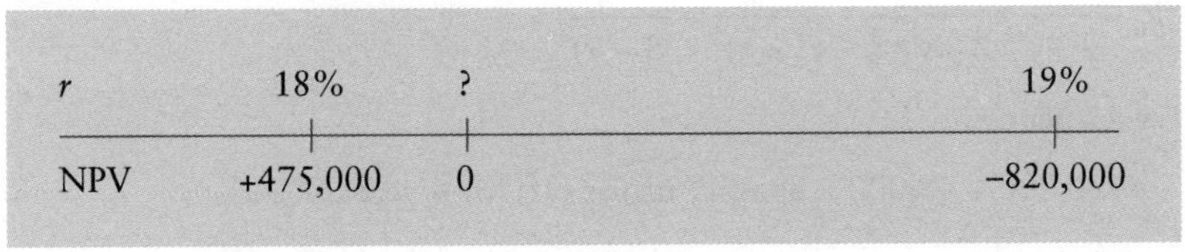

$$18 + \frac{475{,}000}{1{,}295{,}000} \times (19 - 18) = 18.37\%$$

Project 3 produces an internal rate of return of 18.37 per cent which is higher than the opportunity cost of capital and therefore is to be commended.

We temporarily leave the saga of Mr Brightspark and his proposals to reinforce understanding of NPV and IRR through the worked example of Martac plc.

Worked example 2.3 Martac plc

Martac plc is a manufacturer of *Martac-aphro*. Two new automated process machines used in the production of Martac have been introduced to the market, the CAM and the ATR. Both will give cost savings over existing processes:

£000s	*CAM*	*ATR*
Initial cost (machine purchase and installation, etc.)	120	250
Cash flow savings:		
At Time 1 (one year after the initial cash outflow)	48	90
At Time 2	48	90
At Time 3	48	90
At Time 4	48	90

All other factors remain constant and the firm has access to large amounts of capital. The required return on projects is 8 per cent.

Required

(a) Calculate the IRR for CAM.
(b) Calculate the IRR for ATR.
(c) Based on IRR which machine would you purchase?
(d) Calculate the NPV for each machine.
(e) Based on NPV which machine would you buy?
(f) Is IRR or NPV the better decision tool?

Answers

In this problem the total cash flows associated with the alternative projects are not given. Instead the incremental cash flows are provided, for example, the additional savings available over the existing costs of production. This, however, is sufficient for a decision to be made about which machine to purchase.

(a) IRR for CAM

$$F_0 + \frac{F_1}{1+r} + \frac{F_2}{(1+r)^2} + \frac{F_3}{(1+r)^3} + \frac{F_4}{(1+r)^4} = 0$$

Try 22 per cent:

$-120{,}000 + 48{,}000 \times$ annuity factor (af) for 4 years @ 22%

(*See* Appendix 2.1 for annuity calculations and Appendix III at the end of the book for an annuity table.)

The annuity factor tells us the present value of four lots of £1 received at four annual intervals. This is 2.4936, meaning that the £4 in present value terms is worth just over £2.49.

$-120{,}000 + 48{,}000 \times 2.4936 = -£307.20$

Try 21 per cent:

$$-120{,}000 + 48{,}000 \times \text{annuity factor (af) for 4 years @ } 21\%$$

$$-120{,}000 + 48{,}000 \times 2.5404 = +£1{,}939.20$$

Exhibit 2.17 Interpolation

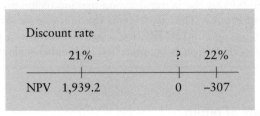

Discount rate	21%	?	22%
NPV	1,939.2	0	−307

$$21 + \left(\frac{1939.2}{1939.2 + 307}\right) \times (22 - 21) = 21.86\%$$

(b) IRR for ATR

Try 16 per cent:

$$-250{,}000 + 90{,}000 \times 2.7982 = +£1{,}838$$

Try 17 per cent:

$$-250{,}000 + 90{,}000 \times 2.7432 = -£3{,}112$$

Exhibit 2.18 Interpolation

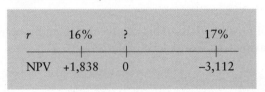

r	16%	?	17%
NPV	+1,838	0	−3,112

$$16 + \left(\frac{1{,}838}{1{,}838 + 3{,}112}\right) \times (17 - 16) = 16.37\%$$

(c) Choice of machine on basis of IRR

If IRR is the only decision tool available then as long as the IRRs exceed the discount rate (or cost of capital) the project with the higher IRR might appear to be the preferred choice. In this case CAM ranks higher than ATR.

(d) NPV for machines: CAM

$$-120{,}000 + 48{,}000 \times 3.3121 = +£38{,}981$$

NPV for ATR

$$-250{,}000 + 90{,}000 \times 3.3121 = +£48{,}089$$

(e) Choice of machine on basis of NPV

ATR generates a return which has a present value of £48,089 in addition to the minimum return on capital required. This is larger than for CAM and therefore ATR ranks higher than CAM if NPV is used as the decision tool.

(f) Choice of decision tool

This problem has produced conflicting decision outcomes, which depend on the project appraisal method employed. NPV is the better decision-making technique because it measures in absolute amounts of money. That is, it gives the increase in shareholder wealth available by accepting a project. In contrast IRR expresses its return as a percentage which may result in an inferior low-scale project being preferred to a higher-scale project.

Problems with internal rate of return

We now return to Hard Decisions plc.

Mr Brightspark: I have noticed your tendency to prefer NPV to any other method. Yet, in the three projects we have been discussing, NPV and IRR give the same decision recommendation. So, why not use IRR more often?

You reply: It is true that the NPV and IRR methods of capital investment appraisal are closely related. Both are 'time-adjusted' measures of profitability. The NPV and IRR methods gave the same result in the cases we have considered today because the problems associated with the IRR method are not present in the figures we have been working with. In the appraisal of other projects we may encounter the severe limitations of the IRR method and therefore I prefer to stick to the theoretically superior NPV technique.

I will illustrate two of the most important problems, multiple solutions and ranking.

Multiple solutions

There may be a number of possible IRRs. This can be explained by examining the problems Mr Flummoxed is having (*see* Worked example 2.4).

Worked example 2.4 Mr Flummoxed

Mr Flummoxed of Deadhead plc has always used the IRR method of project appraisal. He has started to have doubts about its usefulness after examining the proposal, 'Project Oscillation'.

Project Oscillation

Points in time (yearly intervals)	0	1	2
Cash flow	–3,000	+15,000	–13,000

Internal rates of return are found at 11.56 per cent *and* 288.4 per cent.

Given that Deadhead plc has a required rate of return of 20 per cent, it is impossible to decide whether to implement Project Oscillation using an unadjusted IRR methodology.

The cause of multiple solutions is unconventional cash flows. Conventional cash flows occur when an outflow is followed by a series of inflows or a cash inflow is followed by a series of cash outflows. Unconventional cash flows are a series of cash flows with more than one change in sign. In the case of Project Oscillation the sign changes from negative to positive once, and from positive to negative once. These two sign changes provide a clue to the number of possible solutions or IRRs. Multiple yields can be adjusted for whilst still using the IRR method, but the simplest approach is to use the NPV method.

Ranking

The IRR decision rule does not always rank projects in the same way as the NPV method. Sometimes it is important to find out, not only which project gives a positive return, but which one gives the greater positive return. For instance, projects may be mutually exclusive, that is, only one may be undertaken and a choice has to be made. The use of IRR alone sometimes leads to a poor choice (*see* Exhibit 2.19).

Exhibit 2.19 Ranking

Project	*Cash flows £m*		*IRR%*	*NPV (at 15%)*
	Time 0	*One year later*		
A	–20	+40	100%	+14.78m
B	–40	+70	75%	+20.87m

NPV at different discount rates

Discount rate (%)	*Project A*	*Project B*
0	20	30
20	13.33	18.33
50	6.67	6.67
75	2.86	0
100	0	–5
125	–2.22	–8.89

From Exhibit 2.20 (p. 76), it is clear that the ranking of the projects by their IRRs is constant at 75 per cent and 100 per cent, regardless of the opportunity cost of capital (discount rate). Project A is always the better. On the other hand, ranking the projects by the NPV method is not fixed. The NPV ranking depends on the discount rate assumed. Thus, if the discount rate used in the NPV calculation is higher than 50 per cent, the ranking under both IRR and NPV would be the same, i.e. Project A is superior. If the discount rate falls below 50 per cent, Project B is the better choice. One of the major elements leading to the theoretical dominance of NPV is that it takes into account the scale of investment; thus the shareholders are made better off by undertaking Project B by £20.87m because the initial size of the project was larger. NPVs are measured in absolute amounts.

The board of directors of Hard Decisions are now ready for a coffee break and time to digest these concepts and techniques. The chairman thanks you for your clarity and rigorous analysis. He also thanks Mr Brightspark for originating three imaginative and thought-provoking proposals to take the business forward towards its goal of shareholder wealth enhancement.

Exhibit 2.20 NPV at different discount rates

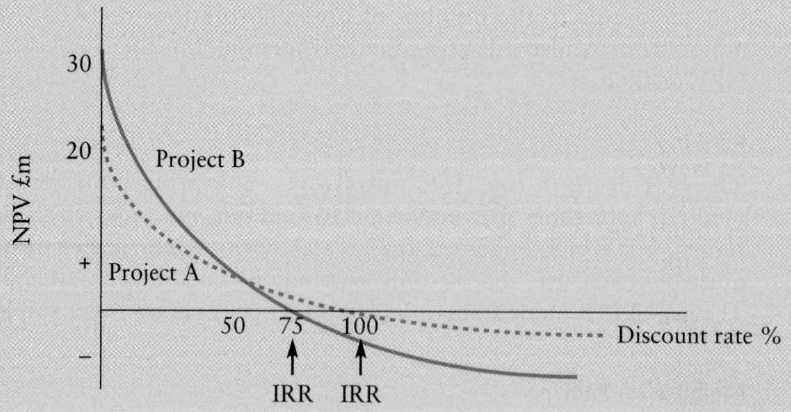

Summary of the characteristics of NPV and IRR

Exhibit 2.21 summarises the characteristics of NPV and IRR.

Exhibit 2.21 Characteristics of NPV and IRR

NPV	*IRR*
■ It recognises that £1 today is worth more than £1 tomorrow.	■ Also takes into account the time value of money.
■ In conditions where all worthwhile projects can be accepted (i.e. no mutual exclusivity) it maximises shareholder utility. Projects with a positive NPV should be accepted since they increase shareholder wealth, while those with negative NPVs decrease shareholder wealth.	■ In situations of non-mutual exclusivity, shareholder wealth is maximised if all projects with a yield higher than the opportunity cost of capital are accepted, while those with a return less than the time value of money are rejected.
■ It takes into account investment size – absolute amounts of wealth change.	■ Fails to measure in terms of absolute amounts of wealth changes. It measures percentage returns and this may cause ranking problems in conditions of mutual exclusivity, i.e. the wrong project may be rejected.
■ This is not as intuitively understandable as a percentage measure.	■ It is easier to communicate a percentage return than NPV to other managers and employees, who may not be familiar with the details of project appraisal techniques. The appeal of quick recognition and conveyance of understanding should not be belittled or underestimated.
■ It can handle non-conventional cash flows.	■ Non-conventional cash flows cause problems, e.g. multiple solutions.
■ Additivity is possible: because present values are all measured in today's £s they can be added together. Thus the returns (NPVs) of a group of projects can be calculated.	■ Additivity is not possible.

MODIFIED INTERNAL RATE OF RETURN

The fourth characteristic listed for IRR in Exhibit 2.21 is a powerful force driving its adoption in the practical world of business where few individuals have exposed themselves to the rigours of financial decision-making models, and therefore may not comprehend NPV. These issues are examined in more detail in Chapter 4, but it is perhaps worth explaining now the consequences of sticking rigidly to IRR.

One problem centres on the reinvestment assumption. With NPV it is assumed that cash inflows arising during the life of the project are reinvested at the opportunity cost of capital. In contrast the IRR implicitly assumes that the cash inflows that are received, say, half-way through a project, can be reinvested elsewhere at a rate equal to the IRR until the end of the project's life. This is intuitively unacceptable. In the real world, if a firm invested in a very high-yielding project and some cash was returned after a short period, this firm would be unlikely to be able to deposit this cash elsewhere until the end of the project and reach the same extraordinary high yield, and yet this is what the IRR implicitly assumes. The more likely eventuality is that the intra-project cash inflows will be invested at the 'going rate' or the opportunity cost of capital. In other words, the firm's normal discount rate is the better estimate of the reinvestment rate. The effect of this erroneous reinvestment assumption is to inflate the IRR of the project under examination.

For example, Project K below has a very high IRR, at 61.8 per cent; thus the £1,000 received after one year is assumed to be taken back into the firm and then placed in another investment, again yielding 61.8 per cent until time 2. This is obviously absurd: if such an investment existed why has the firm not already invested in it – given its cost of capital of only 15 per cent?

Project K (required rate of return 15 per cent)

Points in time (yearly intervals)	0	1	2
Cash flows (£)	–1,000	+1,000	+1,000

IRR

Try 60 per cent: NPV = 15.63.
Try 62 per cent: NPV = –1.68.

Interpolation

Exhibit 2.22 Interpolation, Project K

$$60 + \left(\frac{15.63}{15.63 + 1.68}\right) \times (62 - 60) = 61.8\%$$

The reinvestment assumption of 61.8 per cent, for the £1,000 receivable at time 1, is clearly unrealistic, especially in light of the fact that most investors can only obtain a return of 15 per cent for taking this level of risk.

The IRR of Project K assumes the following:

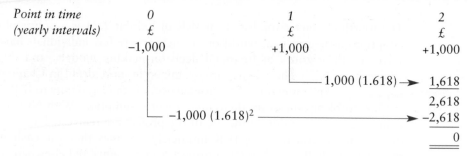

Point in time	*0*		*1*	*2*
(yearly intervals)	£		£	£
	–1,000		+1,000	+1,000
			1,000 (1.618) →	1,618
				2,618
		–1,000 $(1.618)^2$ →		–2,618
				0

The £2,618 compounded cash flows at the terminal date of the project are equivalent to taking the original investment of £1,000 and compounding it for two years at 61.8 per cent. However, an NPV calculation assumes that the intra-project cash inflow is invested at 15 per cent:

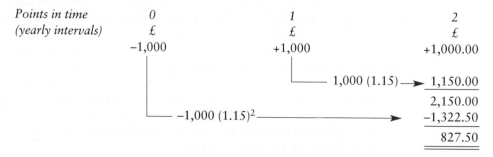

Points in time	*0*		*1*	*2*
(yearly intervals)	£		£	£
	–1,000		+1,000	+1,000.00
			1,000 (1.15) →	1,150.00
				2,150.00
		–1,000 $(1.15)^2$ →		–1,322.50
				827.50

Discounting £827.50 back two years gives the NPV of £625.71.

If, for reasons of pragmatism or communication within the firm, it is necessary to describe a project appraisal in terms of a percentage, then it is recommended that the modified internal rate of return (MIRR) is used. This takes as its starting point the notion that, for the sake of consistency with NPV, any cash inflows arising during the project are reinvested at the opportunity cost of funds. That is, at the rate of return available on the next best alternative use of the funds in either financial or real assets. The MIRR is the rate of return, m, which, if used to compound the initial investment amount (the original cash outlay) produces the same terminal value as the project cash inflows. The value of the project's cash inflows at the end of the project's life after they have been expressed in the terminal date's £s is achieved through compounding. In other words, the common currency this time is not time 0 £s, but time 4, or time 6, or time 'n' £s.

What we are attempting to do is find that rate of compounding which will equate the terminal value of the intra-project cash flows with the terminal value of the initial investment.

Modified internal rate of return for Project K

First, calculate the terminal value of the cash flows excluding the t_0 investment using the opportunity cost of capital.

			Terminal value (£)
t_1	1,000 (1.15)		1,150.00
t_2	1,000	already expressed as a terminal value because it occurs on the date of termination	1,000.00
		Total terminal value	2,150.00

The modified internal rate of return is the rate of compounding applied to the original investment necessary to produce a future (terminal) value of £2,150.00 two years later.

$$1{,}000\,(1 + m)^2 = 2{,}150.00$$

Solve for m. (The mathematical tools – *see* Appendix 2.1 – may be useful here.) Divide both sides of the equation by 1,000:

$$(1 + m)^2 = \frac{2{,}150}{1{,}000}$$

Then, take roots to the power of 2 of both sides of the equation:

$$\sqrt[2]{(1 + m)^2} = \sqrt[2]{\frac{2{,}150}{1{,}000}}$$

$$m = \sqrt[2]{\frac{2{,}150}{1{,}000}} - 1 = 0.466 \text{ or } 46.6\%$$

or more generally:

$$m = \sqrt[n]{\frac{F}{P}} - 1$$

Thus, the MIRR is 46.6 per cent compared with the IRR of 61.8 per cent. In the case of Project K this reduced rate is still very high and the project is accepted under either rule. However, in a number of situations, the calculation of the MIRR may alter the decision given under the IRR method. This is true in the worked example of Switcharound plc for projects Tic and Cit, which are mutually exclusive projects and thus ranking is important.

Worked example 2.5 **Switcharound plc**

The business development team of Switcharound plc has been working to find uses for a vacated factory. The two projects it has selected for further consideration by senior management both have a life of only three years, because the site will be flattened in three years when a new motorway is constructed. On the basis of IRR the business development team is leaning towards acceptance of Cit but it knows that the key Senior Manager is aware of MIRR and therefore feels it is necessary to present the data calculated through both techniques. The opportunity cost of capital is 10 per cent.

Cash flows

Points in time (yearly intervals)	*0*	*1*	*2*	*3*	*IRR*
Tic (£m)	–1	0.5	0.5	0.5	23.4%
Cit (£m)	–1	1.1	0.1	0.16	27.7%

However, on the basis of MIRR, a different preference emerges.

Tic: MIRR

		Terminal value £m
t_1	$0.5 \times (1.1)^2$	0.605
t_2	0.5×1.1	0.550
t_3	0.5	0.500
Total terminal value		1.655

$$1{,}000{,}000\ (1 + m)^3 = 1{,}655{,}000$$

$$m = \sqrt[n]{\frac{F}{P}} - 1$$

$$m = \sqrt[3]{\frac{1{,}655{,}000}{1{,}000{,}000}} - 1 = 0.183 \text{ or } 18.3\%$$

Cit: MIRR

		Terminal value £m
t_1	$1.1 \times (1.1)^2$	1.331
t_2	0.1×1.1	0.110
t_3	0.16	0.16
Total terminal value		1.601

$$1{,}000{,}000\ (1 + m)^3 = 1{,}601{,}000$$

$$m = \sqrt[n]{\frac{F}{P}} - 1$$

$$m = \sqrt[3]{\frac{1{,}601{,}000}{1{,}000{,}000}} - 1 = 0.17 \text{ or } 17\%$$

Of course, a more satisfactory answer can be obtained by calculating NPVs, but the result may not be persuasive if the senior management team do not understand NPVs.

NPVs for Tic and Cit

Tic $-1 + 0.5 \times$ annuity factor, 3 years @10%

$-1 + 0.5 \times 2.4868 = 0.243400$ or £243,400

Cit

$$-1 + \frac{1.1}{1 + 0.1} + \frac{0.1}{(1 + 0.1)^2} + \frac{0.16}{(1 + 0.1)^3} = 0.202855 \text{ or } £202{,}855$$

Therefore, Tic contributes more towards shareholder wealth.

Summary table

Ranking

	NPV	*IRR*	*MIRR*
Tic	£243,400 (1)	23.4% (2)	18.3% (1)
Cit	£202,855 (2)	27.7% (1)	17.0% (2)

CONCLUDING COMMENTS

This chapter has provided insight into the key factors for consideration when an organisation is contemplating using financial (or other) resources for investment. The analysis has been based on the assumption that the objective of any such investment is to maximise economic benefits to the owners of the enterprise. To achieve such an objective requires allowance for the opportunity cost of capital or time value of money as well as robust analysis of relevant cash flows. Given that time has a value, the precise timing of cash flows is important for project analysis. The net present value (NPV) and internal rate of return (IRR) methods of project appraisal are both discounted cash flow techniques and therefore allow for the time value of money. However, the IRR method does present problems in a few special circumstances and so the theoretically preferred method is NPV. On the other hand, NPV requires diligent studying and thought in order to be fully understood, and therefore it is not surprising to find in the workplace a bias in favour of communicating a project's viability in terms of percentages. Most large organisations, in fact, use three or four methods of project appraisal, rather than rely on only one for both rigorous analysis and communication – *see* Chapter 4 for more detail. If a percentage approach is regarded as essential in a particular organisational setting then the MIRR is to be preferred to the IRR, or the distinctly poor accounting rate of return (e.g. return on capital employed). Not only does the MIRR rank projects more appropriately and so is useful in mutual exclusivity situations; it also avoids biasing upward expectations of returns from an investment. The fundamental conclusion of this chapter is that the best method for maximising shareholder wealth in assessing investment projects is net present value.

KEY POINTS AND CONCEPTS

- ***Time value of money*** has three component parts each requiring compensation for a delay in the receipt of cash:
  - the pure time value, or impatience to consume,
  - inflation,
  - risk.
- ***Opportunity cost of capital*** is the yield forgone on the best available investment alternative – the risk level of the alternative being the same as the project under consideration.
- Taking account of the time value of money and opportunity cost of capital in project appraisal leads to **discounted cash flow analysis** (DCF).

- **Net present value** (NPV) is the present value of the future cash flows after netting out the initial cash flow. Present values are achieved by discounting at the opportunity cost of capital.

$$NPV = F_0 + \frac{F_1}{1+k} + \frac{F_2}{(1+k)^2} + \dots \frac{F_n}{(1+k)^n}$$

- **The net present value decision rules** are:

  NPV $\geqslant$ 0 accept
  NPV $<$ 0 reject

- **Internal rate of return** (IRR) is the discount rate which, when applied to the cash flows of a project, results in a zero net present value. It is an 'r' which results in the following formula being true:

$$F_0 + \frac{F_1}{1+r} + \frac{F_2}{(1+r)^2} + \dots \frac{F_n}{(1+r)^n} = 0$$

- **The internal rate of return decision rule** is:

  IRR $\geqslant$ opportunity cost of capital – accept
  IRR $<$ opportunity cost of capital – reject

- IRR is poor at handling situations of unconventional cash flows. **Multiple solutions** can be the result.
- There are circumstances when IRR ranks one project higher than another, whereas NPV ranks the projects in the opposite order. This **ranking problem** becomes an important issue in situations of mutual exclusivity.
- NPV measures in **absolute amounts of money**. IRR is a percentage measure.
- IRR assumes that intra-project cash flows can be invested at a rate of return equal to the IRR. This biases the IRR calculation.
- If a percentage measure is required, perhaps for communication within an organisation, then the **modified internal rate of return** (MIRR) is to be preferred to the IRR.

APPENDIX 2.1 MATHEMATICAL TOOLS FOR FINANCE

The purpose of this appendix is to explain essential mathematical skills that will be needed for the remainder of this book. The author has no love of mathematics for its own sake and so only those techniques of direct relevance to the subject matter of this textbook will be covered in this section.

Simple and compound interest

When there are time delays between receipts and payments of financial sums we need to make use of the concepts of simple and compound interest.

Simple interest

Interest is paid only on the original principal. No interest is paid on the accumulated interest payments.

Example 1

Suppose that a sum of £10 is deposited in a bank account that pays 12 per cent per annum. At the end of year 1 the investor has £11.20 in the account. That is:

$$F = P(1 + i)$$
$$11.20 = 10(1 + 0.12)$$

where F = Future value, P = Present value, i = Interest rate.

At the end of five years:

$$F = P(1 + in)$$

where n = number of years. Thus,

$$16 = 10(1 + 0.12 \times 5)$$

The initial sum, called the principal, is multiplied by the interest rate to give the annual return. Note from the example that the 12 per cent return is a constant amount each year. Interest is not earned on the interest already accumulated from previous years.

Compound interest

The more usual situation in the real world is for interest to be paid on the sum which accumulates – whether or not that sum comes from the principal or from the interest received in previous periods. Interest is paid on the accumulated interest and principal.

Example 2

An investment of £10 is made at an interest rate of 12 per cent with the interest being compounded. In one year the capital will grow by 12 per cent to £11.20. In the second year the capital will grow by 12 per cent, but this time the growth will be on the accumulated value of £11.20 and thus will amount to an extra £1.34. At the end of two years:

$$F = P(1 + i)\,(1 + i)$$
$$F = 11.20(1 + i)$$
$$F = 12.54$$

Alternatively,

$$F = P(1 + i)^2$$

Exhibit 2.23 displays the future value of £1 invested at a number of different interest rates and for alternative numbers of years. This is extracted from Appendix I at the end of the book.

Exhibit 2.23 The future value of £1

	Interest rate (per cent per annum)				
Year	*1*	*2*	*5*	*12*	*15*
1	1.0100	1.0200	1.0500	1.1200	1.1500
2	1.0201	1.0404	1.1025	1.2544	1.3225
3	1.0303	1.0612	1.1576	1.4049	1.5209
4	1.0406	1.0824	1.2155	1.5735	1.7490
5	1.0510	1.1041	1.2763	1.7623	2.0113

From the second row of the table in Exhibit 2.23 we can read that £1 invested for two years at 12 per cent amounts to £1.2544. Thus, the investment of £10 provides a future capital sum 1.2544 times the original amount:

$$£10 \times 1.2544 = £12.544$$

Over five years the result is:

$$F = P\,(1 + i)^n$$
$$17.62 = 10(1 + 0.12)^5$$

The interest on the accumulated interest is therefore the difference between the total arising from simple interest and that from compound interest:

$$17.62 - 16.00 = 1.62$$

Almost all investments pay compound interest and so we will be using compounding throughout the book.

Present values

There are many occasions in financial management when you are given the future sums and need to find out what those future sums are worth in present-value terms today. For example, you wish to know how much you would have to put aside today which will accumulate, with compounded interest, to a defined sum in the future; or you are given the choice between receiving £200 in five years or £100 now and wish to know which is the better option, given anticipated interest rates; or a project gives a return of £1m in three years for an outlay of £800,000 now and you need to establish if this is the best use of the £800,000. By the process of discounting a sum of money to be received in the future is given a monetary value today.

Example 3

If we anticipate the receipt of £17.62 in five years' time we can determine its present value. Rearrangement of the compound formula, and assuming a discount rate of 12 per cent, gives:

$$P = \frac{F}{(1+i)^n} \text{ or } P = F \times \frac{1}{(1+i)^n}$$

$$10 = \frac{17.62}{(1+0.12)^5}$$

Alternatively, discount factors may be used, as shown in Exhibit 2.24 (this is an extract from Appendix II at the end of the book). The factor needed to discount £1 receivable in five years when the discount rate is 12 per cent is 0.5674.

Therefore the present value of £17.62 is:

$$0.5674 \times £17.62 = £10$$

Exhibit 2.24 The present value of £1

	Interest rate (per cent per annum)				
Year	*1*	*5*	*10*	*12*	*15*
1	0.9901	0.9524	0.9091	0.8929	0.8696
2	0.9803	0.9070	0.8264	0.7972	0.7561
3	0.9706	0.8638	0.7513	0.7118	0.6575
4	0.9610	0.8227	0.6830	0.6355	0.5718
5	0.9515	0.7835	0.6209	0.5674	0.4972

Examining the present value table in Exhibit 2.24 you can see that as the discount rate increases the present value goes down. Also the further into the future the money is to be received, the less valuable it is in today's terms. Distant cash flows discounted at a high rate have a small present value; for instance, £1,000 receivable in 20 years when the discount rate is 17 per cent has a present value of £43.30. Viewed from another angle, if you invested £43.30 for 20 years it would accumulate to £1,000 if interest compounds at 17 per cent.

CASE STUDY 2.2 The effect of compounding over long periods

Jacques Chirac's attempt to help Eurotunnel

FT

In May 1996, when Eurotunnel seemed to be headed for bankruptcy, Jacques Chirac, the French president, urged that Eurotunnel's franchise to operate the Channel tunnel be extended by between 20 and 30 years. He was concerned at the impact of the financial problems on hundreds of thousands of small shareholders in the UK and France. In the spring of 1996 the concession was due to end in 2052. In the City the move was regarded as 'brilliant public relations' and it was thought that it might encourage other parties, especially the bankers, to make concessions in the negotiation of a reprieve package. However, the impact on the company would be limited as one banker said, 'The value in current money of revenues in 60 or 70 years' time is actually quite low.' The *Financial Times* commented that 'Analysts estimated that a 30-year extension could increase the value of the company by £100m –£500m. This compares with the group's debts of £8.4bn.'

Source: *Financial Times*, 16 May 1996. Reprinted with permission.

Determining the rate of interest

Sometimes you wish to calculate the rate of return that a project is earning. For instance, a savings company may offer to pay you £10,000 in five years if you deposit £8,000 now, when interest rates on accounts elsewhere are offering 6 per cent per annum. In order to make a comparison you need to know the annual rate being offered by the savings company. Thus, we need to find i in the discounting equation.

To be able to calculate i it is necessary to rearrange the compounding formula. Since:

$$F = P(1 + i)^n$$

first, divide both sides by P:

$$F/P = (1 + i)^n$$

(The Ps on the right side cancel out.)

Second, take the root to the power n of both sides and subtract 1 from each side:

$$i = \sqrt[n]{[F/P]} - 1 \text{ or } i = [F/P]^{1/n} - 1$$

Example 4

In the case of a five-year investment requiring an outlay of £10 and having a future value of £17.62 the rate of return is:

$$i = \sqrt[5]{\frac{17.62}{10}} - 1 \quad i = 12\%$$

$$i = [17.62/10]^{1/5} - 1 \quad i = 12\%$$

Technical aside

You can use the $\sqrt[x]{y}$ or the $\sqrt[y]{x}$ button, depending on the calculator.

Alternatively, use the future value table, an extract of which is shown in Exhibit 2.23. In our example, the return on £1 worth of investment over five years is:

$$\frac{17.62}{10} = 1.762$$

In the body of the Future Value table look at the year 5 row for a future value of 1.762. Read off the interest rate of 12 per cent.

An interesting application of this technique outside finance is to use it to put into perspective the pronouncements of politicians. For example, in 1994 John Major made a speech to the Conservative Party conference promising to double national income (the total quantity of goods and services produced) within 25 years. This sounds impressive, but let us see how ambitious this is in terms of an annual percentage increase.

$$i = \sqrt[25]{\frac{F}{P}} - 1$$

F, future income, is double P, the present income.

$$i = \sqrt[25]{\frac{2}{1}} - 1 = 0.0281 \text{ or } 2.81\%$$

The result is not too bad compared with the previous 20 years. However, performance in the 1950s and 1960s was better and countries in the Far East have annual rates of growth of between 5 per cent and 10 per cent.

The investment period

Rearranging the standard equation so that we can find n (the number of years of the investment), we create the following equation:

$$F = P(1 + i)^n$$
$$F/P = (1 + i)^n$$
$$\log(F/P) = \log(1 + i)^n$$
$$n = \frac{\log(F/P)}{\log(1 + i)}$$

Example 5

How many years does it take for £10 to grow to £17.62 when the interest rate is 12 per cent?

$$n = \frac{\log(17.62/10)}{\log(1 + 0.12)} \quad \text{Therefore } n = 5 \text{ years}$$

An application outside finance

How many years will it take for China to double its real national income if growth rates continue at 10 per cent per annum?
Answer:

$$n = \frac{\log(2/1)}{\log(1 + 0.1)} = 7.3 \text{ years (quadrupling in less than 15 years)}$$

Annuities

Quite often there is not just one payment at the end of a certain number of years. There can be a series of identical payments made over a period of years. For instance:

- bonds usually pay a regular rate of interest;
- individuals can buy, from saving plan companies, the right to receive a number of identical payments over a number of years;
- a business might invest in a project which, it is estimated, will give regular cash inflows over a period of years;
- a typical house mortgage is an annuity.

An annuity is a series of payments or receipts of equal amounts. We are able to calculate the present value of this set of payments.

Example 6

For a regular payment of £10 per year for five years, when the interest rate is 12 per cent, we can calculate the present value of the annuity by three methods.

Method 1

$$P_{an} = \frac{A}{(1+i)} + \frac{A}{(1+i)^2} + \frac{A}{(1+i)^3} + \frac{A}{(1+i)^4} + \frac{A}{(1+i)^5}$$

where A = the periodic receipt.

$$P_{10,5} = \frac{10}{(1.12)} + \frac{10}{(1.12)^2} + \frac{10}{(1.12)^3} + \frac{10}{(1.12)^4} + \frac{10}{(1.12)^5} = £36.05$$

Method 2

Using the derived formula:

$$P_{an} = \frac{1 - 1/(1+i)^n}{i} \times A$$

$$P_{10,5} = \frac{1 - 1/(1+0.12)^5}{0.12} \times 10 = £36.05$$

Method 3

Use the 'Present Value of an Annuity' table. (*See* Exhibit 2.25, an extract from the more complete annuity table at the end of the book in Appendix III.) Here we simply look along the year 5 row and 12 per cent column to find the figure of 3.605. This refers to the present value of five annual receipts of £1. Therefore we multiply by £10:

3.605 × £10 = £36.05

Exhibit 2.25 The present value of an annuity of £1 per annum

	Interest rate (per cent per annum)				
Year	*1*	*5*	*10*	*12*	*15*
1	0.9901	0.9524	0.9091	0.8929	0.8696
2	1.9704	1.8594	1.7355	1.6901	1.6257
3	2.9410	2.7232	2.4868	2.4018	2.2832
4	3.9020	3.5459	3.1699	3.0373	2.8550
5	4.8535	4.3295	3.7908	3.6048	3.3522

The student is strongly advised against using Method 1. This was presented for conceptual understanding only. For any but the simplest cases, this method can be very time consuming.

Perpetuities

Some contracts run indefinitely and there is no end to the payments. Perpetuities are rare in the private sector, but certain government securities do not have an end date; that is, the amount paid when the bond was purchased by the lender will never be repaid, only interest payments are made. For example, the UK government has issued Consolidated Stocks or War Loans which will never be redeemed. Also, in a number of project appraisals or share valuations it is useful to assume that regular annual payments go on forever. Perpetuities are annuities which continue indefinitely. The value of a perpetuity is simply the annual amount received divided by the interest rate when the latter is expressed as a decimal.

$$P = \frac{A}{i}$$

If £10 is to be received as an indefinite annual payment then the present value, at a discount rate of 12 per cent, is:

$$P = \frac{10}{0.12} = £83.33$$

It is very important to note that in order to use this formula we are assuming that the first payment arises 365 days after the time at which we are standing (the present time or time zero).

Discounting semi-annually, monthly and daily

Sometimes financial transactions take place on the basis that interest will be calculated more frequently than once a year. For instance, if a bank account paid 12 per cent nominal return per year, but credited 6 per cent after half a year, in the second half of the year interest could be earned on the interest credited after the first six months. This will mean that the true annual rate of interest will be greater than 12 per cent.

The greater the frequency with which interest is earned, the higher the future value of the deposit.

Example 7

If you put £10 in a bank account earning 12 per cent per annum then your return after one year is:

$$10(1 + 0.12) = £11.20$$

If the interest is compounded semi-annually (at a nominal annual rate of 12 per cent):

$$10(1 + [0.12/2])(1 + [0.12/2]) = 10(1 + [0.12/2])^2 = £11.236$$

In Example 7 the difference between annual compounding and semi-annual compounding is an extra 3.6p. After six months the bank credits the account with 60p in interest so that in the following six months the investor earns 6 per cent on the £10.60.

If the interest is compounded quarterly:

$$10(1 + [0.12/4])^4 = £11.255$$

Daily compounding:

$$10(1 + [0.12/365])^{365} = £11.2747$$

Example 8

If £10 is deposited in a bank account that compounds interest quarterly and the nominal return per year is 12 per cent, how much will be in the account after eight years?

$$10(1 + [0.12/4])^{4 \times 8} = £25.75$$

Continuous compounding

If the compounding frequency is taken to the limit we say that there is continuous compounding. When the number of compounding periods approaches infinity the future value is found by $F = Pe^{in}$ where e is the value of the exponential function. This is set as 2.71828 (to five decimal places, as shown on a scientific calculator).

So, the future value of £10 deposited in a bank paying 12 per cent nominal compounded continuously after eight years is:

$$10 \times 2.71828^{0.12\times 8} = £26.12$$

Converting monthly and daily rates to annual rates

Sometimes you are presented with a monthly or daily rate of interest and wish to know what that is equivalent to in terms of Annual Percentage Rates (APR).

If m is the monthly interest or discount rate, then over 12 months:

$$(1 + m)^{12} = 1 + i$$

where i is the annual compound rate.

$$i = (1 + m)^{12} - 1$$

Thus, if a credit card company charges 1.5 per cent per month, the annual percentage rate (APR) is:

$$i = (1 + 0.015)^{12} - 1 = 19.56\%$$

If you want to find the monthly rate when you are given the APR:

$$m = (1 + i)^{1/12} - 1 \quad \text{or} \quad m = \sqrt[12]{(1 + i)} - 1$$

$$m = (1 + 0.1956)^{1/12} - 1 = 0.015 = 1.5\%$$

Daily rate:

$$(1 + d)^{365} = 1 + i$$

where d is the daily discount rate.

The following exercises will consolidate the knowledge gained by reading through this appendix (answers are provided at the end of the book in Appendix VI).

MATHEMATICAL TOOLS EXERCISES

1 The rate of interest is 8 per cent. What will a £100 investment be worth in three years' time if the rate of interest is 8 per cent, using: (a) simple interest? (b) annual compound interest?

2 You plan to invest £10,000 in the shares of a company.
(a) If the value of the shares increases by 5 per cent a year, what will be the value of the shares in 20 years?
(b) If the value of the shares increases by 15 per cent a year, what will be the value of the shares in 20 years?

3 How long will it take you to double your money if you invest it at: (a) 5 per cent? (b) 15 per cent?

4 As a winner of a lottery you can choose one of the following prizes:
(a) £1,000,000 now.
(b) £1,700,000 at the end of five years.
(c) £135,000 a year for ever, starting in one year.
(d) £200,000 for each of the next 10 years, starting in one year.
If the interest rate is 9 per cent, which is the most valuable prize?

5 A bank lends a customer £5,000. At the end of 10 years he repays this amount plus interest. The amount he repays is £8,950. What is the rate of interest charged by the bank?

6 The Morbid Memorial Garden company will maintain a garden plot around your grave for a payment of £50 now, followed by annual payments, in perpetuity, of £50. How much would you have to put into an account which was to make these payments if the account guaranteed an interest rate of 8 per cent?

7 If the flat (nominal annual) rate of interest is 14 per cent and compounding takes place monthly, what is the effective annual rate of interest (the Annual Percentage Rate)?

8 What is the present value of £100 to be received in 10 years' time when the interest rate (nominal annual) is 12 per cent and (a) annual discounting is used? (b) semi-annual discounting is used?

9 What sum must be invested now to provide an amount of £18,000 at the end of 15 years if interest is to accumulate at 8 per cent for the first 10 years and 12 per cent thereafter?

10 How much must be invested now to provide an amount of £10,000 in six years' time assuming interest is compounded quarterly at a nominal annual rate of 8 per cent? What is the effective annual rate?

11 Supersalesman offers you an annuity of £800 per annum for 10 years. The price he asks is £4,800. Assuming you could earn 11 per cent on alternative investments would you buy the annuity?

12 Punter buys a car on hire purchase paying five annual instalments of £1,500, the first being an immediate cash deposit. Assuming an interest rate of 8 per cent is being charged by the hire purchase company, how much is the current *cash* price of the car?

REFERENCES AND FURTHER READING

Bierman, H. and Smidt, S. (1992) *The Capital Budgeting Decision*, 8th edn. New York: Macmillan. A clear introductory exposition of the concepts discussed in this chapter.

Dean, J. (1951) *Capital Budgeting*. New York: Columbia University Press. Dean introduced an analytical framework for a systemised approach to investment within the firm based on discounted cash flow. Easy to read.

Fama, E.F. and Miller, M.H. (1972) *The Theory of Finance*. New York: Holt, Rinehart & Winston. A more detailed consideration of IRR and NPV.

Fisher, I. (1930) *The Theory of Interest*. Reprinted in 1977 by Porcupine Press. Originator of the present value rule.

Hirshleifer, J. (1958) 'On the theory of optimal investment decision', *Journal of Political Economy*, 66 (August), pp. 329–52. Early theory.

Hirshleifer, J. (1961) 'Risk, the discount rate and investment decisions'. *American Economic Review*, May, pp. 112–20. Theoretical justification for the use of net present value.

McDaniel, W.R., McCarty, D.E. and Jessell, K.A. (1988) 'Discounted cash flow with explicit reinvestment rates: Tutorial and extension', *The Financial Review*, August. Modified internal rate of return discussed in more detail as well as other theoretical developments.

Solomon, E. (1963) *The Theory of Financial Management*. New York: Columbia University Press. An early advocate of net present value.

Wilkes, F.M. (1980) 'On multiple rates of return', *Journal of Business, Finance and Accounting*, 7(4). Theoretical treatment of a specific issue.

SELF-REVIEW QUESTIONS

1 What are the theoretical justifications for the NPV decision rules?

2 Explain what is meant by conventional and unconventional cash flows and what problems they might cause in investment appraisal.

3 Define the time value of money.

4 What is the reinvestment assumption for project cash flows under IRR? Why is this problematical? How can it be corrected?

5 Rearrange the compounding equation to solve for: (a) the annual interest rate, and (b) the number of years over which compounding takes place.

6 What is the 'yield' of a project?

7 Discuss the statement: 'The IRR method is better than the NPV method for choosing which projects to invest in because the cost of capital is not needed at the outset.'

8 Explain why it is possible to obtain an inaccurate result using the trial and error method of IRR when a wide difference of two discount rates is used for interpolation.

QUESTIONS AND PROBLEMS

1 Proast plc is considering two investment projects whose cash flows are:

Points in time (yearly intervals)	*Project A*	*Project B*
0	–120,000	–120,000
1	60,000	15,000
2	45,000	45,000
3	42,000	55,000
4	18,000	60,000

The company's required rate of return is 15 per cent.

a Advise the company whether to undertake the two projects.

b Indicate the maximum outlay in year 0 for each project before it ceases to be viable.

2 Highflyer plc has two possible projects to consider. It cannot do both – they are mutually exclusive. The cash flows are:

Points in time (yearly intervals)	*Project A*	*Project B*
0	–420,000	–100,000
1	150,000	75,000
2	150,000	75,000
3	150,000	0
4	150,000	0

Highflyer's cost of capital is 12 per cent. Assume unlimited funds. These are the only cash flows associated with the projects.

a Calculate the internal rate of return (IRR) for each project.

b Calculate the net present value (NPV) for each project.

c Compare and explain the results in (a) and (b) and indicate which project the company should undertake and why.

3* Mr Baffled, the managing director of Confused plc, has heard that the internal rate of return (IRR) method of investment appraisal is the best modern approach. He is trying to apply the IRR method to two new projects.

	Cash flows		
Year	*0*	*1*	*2*
Project C	−3,000	+14,950	−12,990
Project D	−3,000	+7,500	−5,000

a Calculate the IRRs of the two projects.

b Explain why Mr Baffled is having difficulties with the IRR method.

c Advise Confused whether to accept either or both projects. (Assume a discount rate of 25 per cent.)

4 Using a 13 per cent discount rate find the NPV of a project with the following cash flows:

Points in time (yearly intervals)	t_0	t_1	t_2	t_3
Cash flow (£)	−300	+260	−200	+600

How many IRRs would you expect to find for this project?

5† a Find the total terminal value of the following cash flows when compounded at 15 per cent. Cash flows occur at annual intervals and the fourth year's cash flow is the last.

Points in time (yearly intervals)	t_1	t_2	t_3	t_4
Cash flow (£)	+200	+300	+250	+400

b If £900 is the initial cash outflow at time 0 calculate the compounding rate that will equate the initial cash outflow with the terminal value as calculated in (a) above.

c You have calculated the modified internal rate of return (MIRR), now calculate the IRR for comparison.

6† a If the cost of capital is 14 per cent find the modified internal rate of return for the following investment and state if you would implement it.

Points in time (yearly intervals)	t_0	t_1	t_2	t_3	t_4
Cash flow	−9,300	5,400	3,100	2,800	600

b Is this project to be accepted under the internal rate of return method?

7* Seddet International is considering four major projects which have either two- or three-year lives. The firm has raised all of its capital in the form of equity and has never borrowed money. This is partly due to the success of the business in generating income and partly due to an insistence by the dominant managing director that borrowing is to be avoided if at all possible. Shareholders in Seddet International regard the firm as relatively risky, given its existing portfolio of projects. Other firms' shares in this risk class have generally given a return of 16 per cent per annum and this is taken as the opportunity cost of capital for the investment projects. The risk level for the proposed projects is the same as that of the existing range of activities.

Project

	Net cash flows			
Points in time (yearly intervals)	t_0	t_1	t_2	t_3
A	–5,266	2,500	2,500	2,500
B	–8,000	0	0	10,000
C	–2,100	200	2,900	0
D	–1,975	1,600	800	0

Ignore taxation and inflation.

a The managing director has been on a one-day intensive course to learn about project appraisal techniques. Unfortunately, during the one slot given over to NPV he had to leave the room to deal with a business crisis, and therefore does not understand it. He vaguely understands IRR and insists that you use this to calculate which of the four projects should be proceeded with, if there are no limitations on the number which can be undertaken.

b State which is the best project if they are mutually exclusive (i.e. accepting one excludes the possibility of accepting another), using IRR.

c Use the NPV decision rule to rank the projects and explain why, under conditions of mutual exclusivity, the selected project differs from that under (b).

d Write a report for the managing director, detailing the value of the net present value method for shareholder wealth enhancement and explaining why it may be considered of greater use than IRR.

ASSIGNMENTS

1 Try to discover the extent to which NPV, IRR and MIRR are used in your organisation. Also try to gauge the degree of appreciation of the problems of using IRR.

2 If possible, obtain data on a real project, historical or proposed, and analyse it using the techniques learned in this chapter.

CHAPTER NOTE

1 Interpolation (with a conventional cash flow project) always overstates the actual IRR.

Chapter 3

PROJECT APPRAISAL: CASH FLOW AND APPLICATIONS

INTRODUCTION

The last chapter outlined the process of project evaluation. This required consideration of the fundamental elements; first, recognition of the fact that time has a value and that money received in the future has to be discounted at the opportunity cost of capital; second, the identification of relevant cash flows that are to be subject to the discounting procedure. It is to this second issue that we now turn.

This chapter examines the estimation of the cash flows appropriate for good decision-making. The relevant cash flows are not always obvious and easy to obtain and therefore diligent data collection and rigorous analysis are required. Defining and measuring future receipts and outlays accurately is central to successful project appraisal.

In the following Case study Airbus would have had to consider carefully which projected cash flows are, and are not, relevant to the decision whether to go ahead with producing an aircraft capable of carrying 555 passengers.

Having completed the essential groundwork the chapter moves on to demonstrate the practical application of the net present value (NPV) method. This deals with important business decisions, such as whether to replace a machine with a new more efficient (but expensive) version or whether it is better to persevere with the old machine for a few more years despite its rising maintenance costs and higher raw material inputs. Another area examined is replacement cycles, that is, if you have machinery which costs more to run as it gets older and you know that you will continue to need this type of machine and therefore have to replace it at some stage should you regularly replace after one year or two, three or four years? An example is a car hire company that replaces its fleet of cars on a regular cycle. Other topics include the make or buy decision and optimal timing for the implementation of a project.

CASE STUDY 3.1 Will it fly?

Airbus's superjumbo

Surely one of the biggest investment appraisal decisions ever made was when Airbus decided to go ahead and produce the A380 superjumbo. This is one of those 'bet the company' type investments. A massive $10,700 million will be needed to create this monster aircraft.

It was touch and go all through 2000 as to whether Airbus would dare to invest so much money. Before they said 'yes let's do it' they had to have firm orders for at least 50 aircraft. Finally, just before Christmas the sixth major buyer signed up, to take the order book to 50 'definites' and 42 on option (the airlines have the right to buy, but not the obligation).

The A380 will be significantly larger than Boeing's highly successful 747. It will carry 555 passengers (compared with 416). It will also cut direct operating costs for the airlines by 15–20 per cent compared with Boeing's 747-400 and will be able to fly 10% further (8,150 nautical miles).

So, where is all the money on development and build going? This is a project at the cutting edge of technology. The remarkable innovations cost a tremendous amount in terms of up-front cost but the benefit will be spread out over many decades.

Here are some of the innovations:

- New, weight-saving materials.
- Better aerodynamics.
- Lower airframe weight.
- Carbon-fibre central wingbox.
- 40 per cent of the structure and components will be made from new carbon components and metal alloys.
- Upper fuselage shell is not to be aluminium but 'Glare', a laminate with alternative layers of aluminium and glass-fibre reinforced adhesive.
- Innovative hydraulic systems.
- Improved air conditioning.

Airbus reckon that they need to sell at least 250 aircraft to break even in cash-flow terms (presumably meaning that nominal cumulative cash inflows equal nominal cumulative cash

Rivalry in the skies: contrasting views

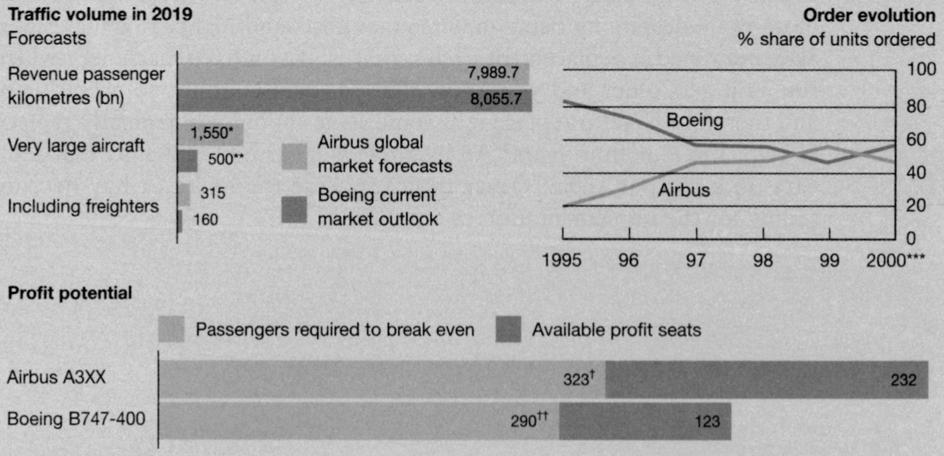

* 500 seats and above ** Larger than 747 *** Includes announcements from Farnborough Air Show 2000
† Assuming same revenue per passenger as B747-400 †† Break-even load factor assumed for B747-400; 70%

Source: *Financial Times*, 2 November 2000, p. 28 Reprinted with permission. Data from Airbus.

outflows). To achieve a positive net present value would require the sale of hundreds more aircraft. Each aircraft has a list price of around $216m – $230m – but don't pay too much attention to that, as airlines receive substantial discounts. At full tilt something like 96,000 people will be working on this aircraft.

And yet it could so easily have been abandoned. Boeing had decided not to develop a superjumbo because it estimated the maximum market at 500 aircraft – they believe that airlines are generally content to continue using the 747. Airbus estimated the market for jumbos and superjumbos at 1,550. It expects to take two-thirds of that business, worth $400bn in today's prices.

This is a high impact project appraisal if ever there was one. Many of the techniques you have learned in Chapter 2 and will learn in this chapter will have been employed by the management of Airbus to help them decide whether or not to press the button to 'go' or the button to 'stop'.

Learning objectives

By the end of this chapter the reader will be able to identify and apply relevant and incremental cash flows in net present value calculations. The reader will also be able to recognise and deal with sunk costs, incidental costs and allocated overheads and be able to employ this knowledge to the following:

- the replacement decision/the replacement cycle;
- the calculation of annual equivalent annuities;
- the make or buy decision;
- optimal timing of investment;
- fluctuating output situations.

QUALITY OF INFORMATION

Good decisions are born of good information. This principle applies to all types of business decisions but is especially appropriate in the case of capital investment decisions in which a substantial proportion of the firm's assets can be put at risk. Obtaining relevant and high-quality information reduces the extent of the risk for the enterprise. Information varies greatly in its reliability, which often depends upon its source. The financial manager or analyst is often dependent on the knowledge and experience of other specialists within the organisation to supply data. For example the marketing team may be able to provide an estimate of likely demand while the production team could help establish the costs per unit. Allowance will have to be made for any bias that may creep into the information passed on; for instance, a manager who is particularly keen on encouraging the firm to expand in a particular geographical area might tend to be over-optimistic concerning the market demand. Some aspects of project appraisal might be able to use high-quality information whereas other aspects have a lower quality. Take the case of the investment in a new lorry for a courier firm; the cost of purchase can be estimated with high precision, whereas the reaction of competitor firms is subject to much more uncertainty.

The sources of information which are useful as inputs for decision making vary widely; from accounting systems and special investigations, to those of the informal, 'just-between-you-and-me-and-the-gatepost' type. Whatever its source all information should, as far as possible, have the following characteristics:

- relevance;
- completeness;
- consistency;
- accuracy;
- reliability;
- timeliness;
- low cost of collection compared with benefit.

ARE PROFIT CALCULATIONS USEFUL FOR ESTIMATING PROJECT VIABILITY?

Accountants often produce a wealth of numerical information about an organisation and its individual operations. It is tempting to simply take the profit figures for a project and put these into the NPV formula as a substitute for cash flow. A further reason advanced for favouring profit-based evaluations is that managers are often familiar with the notion of 'the bottom line' and frequently their performance is judged using profit. However, as was noted in Chapter 1, determining whether a project is 'profitable' is not the same as achieving shareholder wealth maximisation.

Profit is a concept developed by accountants in order to assist them with auditing and reporting. Profit figures are derived by taking what is a continuous process, a change in a company's worth over time, and allocating these changes to discrete periods of time, say a year (*see* Exhibit 3.1). This is a difficult task. It is a complex task with rules, principles and conventions in abundance.

Exhibit 3.1 Business activity is a continuous process; this is difficult to capture in periodic accounts

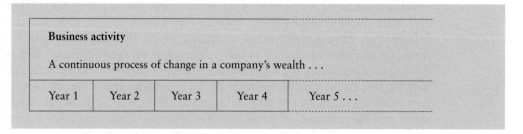

Business activity A continuous process of change in a company's wealth . . .				
Year 1	Year 2	Year 3	Year 4	Year 5 . . .

Profit uses two carefully defined concepts: income and expenses. Income is not cash inflow, it is the amount earned from business activity whether or not the cash has actually been handed over. So, if a £1,000 sofa has been sold on two years' credit the accountant's income arises in the year of sale despite the fact that cash actually flows in two years later. Expense relates the use of an asset to a particular time period whether or not any cash outflow relating to that item occurs in that period. If a firm pays immediately for a machine which will have a ten-year useful life it does not write off the full cost of the machine against the first year's profit, but allocates a proportion of the cost to each of the next ten years. The cash outflow occurs in the first year but the expense (use) of the asset occurs over ten years.

Shareholders make current consumption sacrifices, or they give up the return available elsewhere when they choose to invest their money in a firm. They do this in anticipation of receiving more £s in the future than they laid out. Hence what is of interest to them are the future cash flows and the precise timing of these cash flows. The accountant does a difficult and important job but the profit figures produced are not suitable for project appraisal. Profit is a poor approach for two main reasons, first, depreciation and second, working capital.

Depreciation

Accounting profit is calculated after deducting depreciation, whereas what we are interested in is net cash inflows for a year. Depreciation should not be deducted to calculate net cash inflows. For example, if a firm buys a machine for £20,000 which is expected to be productive for four years and have a zero scrap value, the firm's accountant may allocate the depreciation on the machine over the four years to give the profit figures of say, a stable £7,000 per year. The reason for doing this may be so that the full impact of the £20,000 payout in the first year is not allocated solely to that year's profit and loss account, but is spread over the economic life of the asset. This makes good sense for calculating accounting profit. However, this is not appropriate for project appraisal based on NPV because these figures are not true cash flows. We need to focus on the cash flows at the precise time they occur and should not discount back to time zero the figure of £7,000, but cash flows at the time they occur. The contrast between profit figures and cash flow figures is shown in the example of Quarpro plc (*see* Exhibit 3.2).

Exhibit 3.2 Quarpro plc: An example of adjustment to profit and loss account

Machine cost £20,000, at time 0. Productive life of four years.

Accountant's figures

Year	1 £	2 £	3 £	4 £
Profit before depreciation	12,000	12,000	12,000	12,000
Depreciation	5,000	5,000	5,000	5,000
Profit after depreciation	7,000	7,000	7,000	7,000

Cash flow

Point in time (yearly intervals)	0 £	1 £	2 £	3 £	4 £
Cash outflow	–20,000				
Cash inflow		12,000	12,000	12,000	12,000

Working capital

When a project is accepted and implemented the firm may have to invest in more than the large and obvious depreciable assets such as machines, buildings, vehicles and so forth. Investment in a new project often requires an additional investment in working capital, that is, the difference between short-term assets and liabilities. The main short-term assets are cash, inventories and debtors. The principal short-term liabilities are creditors.

So, a firm might take on a project which involves an increase in the requirements for one of these types of working capital. Each of these will be taken in turn.

Cash floats

It may be that the proposed project requires the firm to have a much higher amount of cash float. For instance, a firm setting up a betting shop may have to consider not only the cash outflow for building or refurbishment, but also the amount of extra cash float needed to meet unexpectedly large betting payouts. Thus, we have to take into account this additional aspect of cash inputs when evaluating the size of the initial investment. This is despite the fact that the cash float will be recoverable at some date in the future (for instance, when the shop is closed in, e.g., three years' time). The fact that this cash is being used and is therefore not available to shareholders means that a sacrifice has been made at a particular point. The owners of that money rightfully expect to receive a suitable return while that money is tied up and unavailable for them to use as they wish.

Stock (inventories)

Examples of stock are raw materials and finished goods. If a project is undertaken which raises the level of inventories then this additional cash outflow has to be allowed for. So, for a retail business opening a number of new shops the additional expenditure on stock is a form of investment. This extra cash being tied up will not be recognised by the profit and loss accounts because all that has happened is that one asset, cash, has been swapped for another, inventory. However the cash use has to be recognised in any NPV calculation. With some projects there may be a reduction in inventory levels. This may happen in the case of the replacement of an inefficient machine with a new piece of equipment. In this case the stock reduction releases cash and so results in a positive cash flow.

Debtors

Accounting convention dictates that if a sale is made during a year it is brought into the profit and loss account for that year. But in many cases a sale might be made on credit and all the firm has is a promise that cash will be paid in the future, the cash inflow has not materialised in the year the sale was recorded. Also, at the start of the financial year this firm may have had some outstanding debtors, that is, other firms or individuals owing this firm money, and in the early months of the year cash inflow is boosted by those other firms paying off their debt.

If we want to calculate the cash flow for the year then the annual profit figure has to be adjusted to exclude the closing balance of debtors (cash owed by customers at the end of the year but not yet paid over), and include the opening balance of debtors (cash owed by the customers at the beginning of the year which is actually received in this year for sales that took place the previous year).

Creditors

Creditors are suppliers to the firm to whom cash payment is due. If creditors rise as a result of a course of action then this is effectively an increase in lending by those firms to this firm, and the cash flow has improved. If the creditor level falls then this firm is effectively experiencing a reduction in cash flow.

Thus we may have four working capital adjustments to make to the profit and loss account figures to arrive at cash flow figures. The value of the firm's investment in net working capital, associated with a project, is found by the:

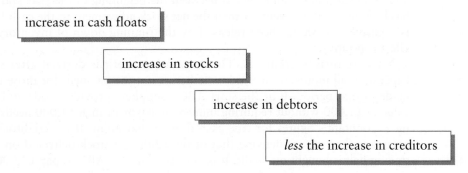

increase in cash floats

increase in stocks

increase in debtors

less the increase in creditors

Net operating cash flow

The net operating cash flow associated with a new investment is equal to the profit, with depreciation added back plus or minus any change in working capital. If the project results in an increase in working capital then:

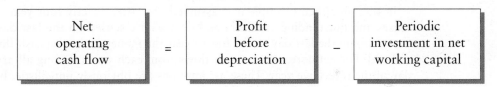

Net operating cash flow	=	Profit before depreciation	–	Periodic investment in net working capital

An example of the differences between profit and cash flow

We now turn to an example of a firm, ABC plc, carrying out a project appraisal. The finance manager has been provided with forecast profit and loss accounts and has to adjust these figures to arrive at cash flow. This project will require investment in machinery of £20,000 at the outset. The machinery will have a useful life of four years and a zero scrap value when production ceases at the end of the fourth year.

ABC's business involves dealing with numerous customers and the cash flows within any particular week are unpredictable. It therefore needs to maintain a cash float of £5,000 to be able to pay for day-to-day expenses. (Note: this cash float is not used up, and cannot therefore be regarded as a cost – in some weeks cash outflows are simply greater than cash inflows and to provide adequate liquidity £5,000 is needed for the firm to operate efficiently. The £5,000 will not be needed when output ceases.)

To produce the product it will be necessary to have a stock of raw materials close to hand. The investment in this form of inventory together with the cash committed to work in progress and finished goods amounts to £2,000 at the beginning of production. However, more cash (an extra £1,000) is expected to be required for this purpose at the end of the second year. When the new business is begun a large proportion of raw materials will come from suppliers who will grant additional credit. Therefore the level of creditors will rise by £1,000 over the period of the project.

To illustrate some of the differences between profit and cash flow there follows a conversion from projected accounting figures to cash flow. First it is necessary to add back the depreciation and instead account for the cost of the machine at time 0, the start date for the project when the cash actually left the firm. This is shown in Exhibit 3.3. To capture the cash flow effect of the investment in inventories (stock) we need to see if any additional cash has been required between the beginning of the year and its end. If cash has been invested in inventory then the net stock adjustment to the cash flow calculation is negative. If cash has been released by the running down of inventory the cash flow effect is positive.

Now we turn to creditors. The accounting profit is derived after subtracting the expense of all inputs in a period, whether or not the payment for those inputs has been made in that period. If at the start ABC's suppliers provide goods and services to the value of £1,000 without requiring immediate payment then £1,000 needs to be added to the accountant's figures for true cash flow at that point. If the creditor's adjustment is not made then we are denying that of the £2,000 of stock delivered on the first day of trading half is bought on credit. It is not necessary for ABC to pay £2,000 at the start to suppliers; they pay only £1,000 and thus the creditor adjustment shows a positive cash flow at time 0, offsetting the outflow on stock. (In other examples, later in the book, it may be assumed that all stock is bought on trade credit and therefore there would not be a cash outflow for stock payments at time 0. In these examples all creditor and debtor adjustments are made at the year ends and not at time 0.) In subsequent years the prior year's creditor debts actually paid match the amount outstanding at the year end, thus no net cash flow effect adjustment is necessary.

In this simplified example it is assumed that after exactly four years all production ceases and outstanding creditors and debtors are settled on the last day of the fourth year. Also on the last day of the fourth year the money tied up in cash float and stock is released. Furthermore, the net cash flows from each year's trading all arrive on the last day of the respective year. These assumptions are obviously unrealistic, but to make the example more realistic would add to its complexity.

Incremental cash flows

A fundamental principle in project appraisal is to include only incremental cash flows. These are defined as the cash flows dependent on the project's implementation. If a project is accepted only those cash flows that are induced by the investment at time 0 and in subsequent years are regarded as incremental. Some of these cash flows are easy to establish but others are much more difficult to pin down.

Incremental cash flow	=	Cash flow for firm with the project	–	Cash flow for firm without project

There follow some guide posts for finding relevant/incremental cash flows.

Exhibit 3.3 ABC plc: an example of profit to cash flow conversion

- Machinery cost £20,000 at time 0, life of four years, zero scrap value.
- Extra cash floats required: £5,000, at time 0.
- Additional work in progress: £2,000 at time 0, £3,000 at time 2.
- Increase in creditors: £1,000.

ABC plc			*Accounting year*		
Point in time (yearly intervals)	*0* £	*1* £	*2* £	*3* £	*4* £
Accounting profit		7,000	7,000	7,000	7,000
Add back depreciation		5,000	5,000	5,000	5,000
		12,000	**12,000**	**12,000**	**12,000**
Initial machine cost	**–20,000**				
Cash float	**–5,000**				**5,000**
Stock					
Closing stock	2,000	2,000	3,000	3,000	0
Opening stock		2,000	2,000	3,000	3,000
Net stock adjustment (Outflow –tive, Inflow +tive)	**–2,000**	**0**	**–1,000**	**0**	**+3,000**
Creditors					
End of year	1,000	1,000	1,000	1,000	0
Start of year		1,000	1,000	1,000	–1,000
Cash flow effect of creditors (Outflow –tive, Inflow +tive)	**+1,000**	**0**	**0**	**0**	**–1,000**
Net operating cash flow	**–26,000**	**12,000**	**11,000**	**12,000**	**19,000**

Point in time (yearly intervals)	*0*	*1*	*2*	*3*	*4*
Cash flow	–26,000	12,000	11,000	12,000	19,000

Cost of capital 12%

$$\text{NPV} = -26{,}000 + \frac{12{,}000}{(1+0.12)} + \frac{11{,}000}{(1+0.12)^2} + \frac{12{,}000}{(1+0.12)^3}$$

$$+ \frac{19{,}000}{(1+0.12)^4} = +£14{,}099$$

This project produces a positive NPV, i.e. it generates a return which is more than the required rate of 12%, and therefore should be accepted.

Include all opportunity costs

The direct inputs into a project are generally easy to understand and measure. However, quite often a project uses resources which already exist within the firm but which are in short supply and which cannot be replaced in the immediate future. That is, the project under consideration may be taking resources away from other projects. The loss of net cash flows from these other projects is termed an opportunity cost. For example, a firm may be considering a project that makes use of a factory which at present is empty. Because it is empty we should not automatically assume that the opportunity cost is zero. Perhaps the firm could engage in the alternative project of renting out the factory to another firm. The forgone rental income is a cost of the project under consideration.

Likewise if a project uses the services of specialist personnel this may be regarded as having an opportunity cost. The loss of these people to other parts of the organisation may reduce cash flows on other projects. If they cannot be replaced with equally able individuals then the opportunity cost will be the lost net cash flows. If equally able hired replacements are found then the extra cost imposed, by the additional salaries etc., on other projects should be regarded as an opportunity cost of the new project under consideration.

For a third example of opportunity cost, imagine your firm bought, when the price was low, a stock of platinum to use as a raw material. The total cost was £1m. It would be illogical to sell the final manufactured product at a price based on the old platinum value if the same quantity would now cost £3m. An alternative course of action would be to sell the platinum in its existing state, rather than to produce the manufactured product. The current market value of the raw platinum (£3m) would then be the opportunity cost.

Include all incidental effects

It is possible for a new project to either increase or reduce sales of other products of the company. Take the case of an airline company trying to decide whether to go ahead with a project to fly between the USA and Japan. The direct cash flows of selling tickets, etc. on these flights may not give a positive NPV. However, if the additional net revenue is included, from extra passengers choosing this airline firm for flights between, say, Europe and the USA, because it now offers a more complete world-wide service, the project may be viable.

On the other hand if a clothes retailer opens a second or a third outlet in the same town, it is likely to find custom is reduced at the original store. This loss elsewhere in the organisation becomes a relevant cash flow in the appraisal of the *new* project, that is, the new shop.

In the soft drink business the introduction of a new brand can reduce the sales of the older brands. This is not to say that a company should never risk any cannibalisation, only that if a new product is to be launched it should not be viewed in isolation. All incremental effects have to be allowed for, including those effects not directly associated with the new product or service.

Royal Dutch/Shell are to include the incidental effect of carbon emissions in all future projects – *see* Exhibit 3.4.

Exhibit 3.4

Environmental cost included in project appraisals

Royal Dutch/Shell, the Anglo-Dutch energy company, decided, in 2000, to include a cost for carbon emissions in all big projects. Each project is now required to achieve a satisfactory internal rate of return after the deduction of $5 per tonne of carbon dioxide in the years 2005–2009, rising to $20 per tonne in 2010.

Ignore sunk costs

Do not include sunk costs. For example, the project to build Concorde involved an enormous expenditure in design and manufacture. At the point where it had to be decided whether to put the aeroplane into service, the costs of development became irrelevant to the decision. Only incremental costs and inflows should be considered. The development costs are in the past and are bygones; they should be ignored. The money spent on development is irrecoverable, whatever the decision on whether to fly the plane. Similarly with Eurotunnel, the fact that the overspend runs into billions of pounds and the tunnel service is unlikely to make a profit does not mean that the incremental cost of using some electricity to power the trains and the cost of employing some train drivers should not be incurred. The £9bn+ already spent is irrelevant to the decision on whether to transport passengers and freight between France and the UK. So long as incremental costs are less than incremental benefits (cash flows when discounted) then the service should operate.

A common mistake in this area is to regard pre-project survey work already carried out or committed to (market demand screening, scientific study, geological survey, etc.) as a relevant cost. After all, the cost would not have been incurred but for the possibility of going ahead with the project. However, at the point of decision on whether to proceed, the survey cost is sunk – it will be incurred whether or not implementation takes place, and it therefore is not incremental. Sunk costs can be either costs for intangibles (such as research and development expenses), or costs for tangibles that may not be used for other purposes (such as the cost of the Eurotunnel). When dealing with sunk costs it is sometimes necessary to be resolute in the face of comments such as, 'good money is being thrown after bad' but always remember the 'bad' money outflow happened in the past and is no longer an input factor into a rigorous decision-making process.

Be careful with overheads

Overheads consist of such items as managerial salaries, rent, light, heat, etc. These are costs that are not directly associated with any one part of the firm or one project. An accountant often allocates these overhead costs amongst the various projects a firm is involved in. When trying to assess the viability of a project we should only include the incremental or extra expenses that would be incurred by going ahead with a project. Many of the general overhead expenses may be incurred regardless of whether the project takes place.

There are two types of overhead. The first type is truly incremental costs resulting from a project. For example, extra electricity, rental and administrative staff costs may be incurred by going ahead rather than abstaining. The second type of overhead consists of such items as head office managerial salaries, legal expertise, public relations, research and development and even the corporate jet. These costs are not directly associated with any one part of the firm or one project and will be incurred regardless of whether the project under consideration is embarked upon. The accountant generally charges a proportion of this overhead to particular divisions and projects. When trying to assess the viability of a project only the incremental costs incurred by going ahead are relevant. Those costs which are unaffected are irrelevant.

Dealing with interest

Interest on funds borrowed to invest does represent a cash outflow. However, it is wrong to include this element in the cash flow calculations. **To repeat, interest should not be deducted from the net cash flows.** This is because if it were subtracted this would amount to double counting because the opportunity cost of capital used to discount the cash flows already incorporates a cost of these funds. The net cash flows are reduced to a present value by allowing for the weighted average cost of finance to give a return to shareholders and lenders. If the un-discounted cash flows also had interest deducted there would be a serious understatement of NPV. For more details see Chapter 16 on the calculation of the firm's discount rate (cost of capital).

Worked example 3.1 Tamcar plc

The accountants at Tamcar plc, manufacturers of hairpieces, are trying to analyse the viability of a proposed new division, 'Baldies heaven'. They estimate that this project will have a life of four years before the market is swamped by the lifting of the present EU import ban on hairpieces. The estimated sales, made on three months' credit, are as follows:

Year	*Sales (£)*
20X1	1.5m
20X2	2.0m
20X3	2.5m
20X4	3.0m

Cash flows from sales may be regarded as occurring on the last day of the year and there are no bad debts.

Costs of production likewise can be assumed to be paid for on the last day of the year. There are no creditors.

Year	*Cost of production (£)*
20X1	0.75m
20X2	1.00m
20X3	1.25m
20X4	1.50m

At the start of the project an investment of £1m will be required in buildings, plant and machinery. These items will have a net worth of zero at the end of this project. The accountants depreciate the plant and machinery at 25 per cent per annum on a straight line basis.

A cash float of £0.5m will be required at the start. Also stocks will increase by £0.3m. These are both recoverable at the end of the project's life.

A £1m invoice for last year's scientific study of 'Baldies heaven' hairpiece technology (e.g. wind resistance and comb-ability) has yet to be paid.

The head office always allocates a proportion of central expenses to all divisions and projects. The share to be borne by 'Baldies heaven' is £500,000 per annum. The head office costs are unaffected by the new project.

The accountants have produced the following profit and loss accounts:

Year	*20X1* £m	*20X2* £m	*20X3* £m	*20X4* £m
Sales	1.50	2.00	2.50	3.00
Costs of production	0.75	1.00	1.25	1.50
Depreciation	0.25	0.25	0.25	0.25
Scientific survey	0.25	0.25	0.25	0.25
Head office	0.50	0.50	0.50	0.50
Profit/loss	–0.25	0	0.25	0.50

Accountants' summary

Investment: £2m Return: £0.5m over 4 years

$$\text{Average Return on Investment (ROI)} = \frac{\text{Average profit}}{\text{Investment}} = \frac{0.5 \div 4}{2} = 0.0625 \text{ or } 6.25\%$$

Recommendation: do not proceed with this project as 6.25% is a poor return.

Required

Calculate the Net Present Value and recommend whether to accept this project or invest elsewhere.

Assume

- No inflation or tax.
- The return required on projects of this risk class is 11%.
- Start date of the project is 1.1.20X1.

Answer

- Depreciation is not a cash flow and should be excluded.
- The scientific survey is a sunk cost. This will not alter whether Tamcar chooses to go ahead or refuses to invest – it is irrelevant to the NPV calculation.
- Head office costs will be constant regardless of the decision to accept or reject the project, they are not incremental.

The sales figures shown in the first line of the table below are not the true cash receipts for each of those years because three months' credit is granted. Thus, in year one only three-quarters of £1.5m is actually received. An adjustment for debtors shows that one-quarter of the first year's sales are deducted. Thus £375,000 is received in the second year and therefore this is added to time 2's cash flow. However, one-quarter of the £2m of time 2's sales is subtracted because this is not received until the following year.

An assumption has been made concerning the receipt of debtor payments after production and distribution has ceased. In 20X4 sales are on the last day and given the three months' credit, cash is received after three months at time 4.25.

Tamcar cash flows

Time (annual intervals)	0	1	2	3	4	4.25
Year	*20X1*	*20X1*	*20X2*	*20X3*	*20X4*	*20X5*
Sales		+1.5	+2.0	+2.5	+3.0	
Buildings, plant, machinery	−1.0					
Cash float	−0.5				+0.5	
Stocks	−0.3				+0.3	
Costs of production		−0.75	−1.0	−1.25	−1.50	
Adjustment for debtors						
Opening debtors	*0*	*0*	*0.375*	*0.500*	*0.625*	*0.75*
Closing debtors	*0*	*0.375*	*0.500*	*0.625*	*0.750*	*0*
Cash flow adjustment for debtors		−0.375	−0.125	−0.125	−0.125	
Cash flow	−1.8	+0.375	+0.875	+1.125	+2.175	+0.75

Net present value

$$-1.8 + \frac{0.375}{(1.11)} + \frac{0.875}{(1.11)^2} + \frac{1.125}{(1.11)^3} + \frac{2.175}{(1.11)^4} + \frac{0.75}{(1.11)^{4.25}}$$

−1.8	+0.338	0.710	0.823	+1.433	+0.481

NPV = + £1.985m

This is a project that adds significantly to shareholder wealth, producing £1.985m more than the minimum rate of return of 11 per cent required by the firm's finance providers.

Worked example 3.2 The International Seed Company (TISC)

As the newly appointed financial manager of TISC you are about to analyse a proposal for the marketing and distribution of a range of genetically engineered vegetable seeds which have been developed by a bio-technology firm. This firm will supply the seeds and permit TISC to market and distribute them under a licence.

Market research, costing £100,000, has already been carried out to establish the likely demand. After three years TISC will withdraw from the market because it anticipates that these products will be superseded by further bio-technological developments.

The annual payment to the bio-technology firm will be £1m for the licence; this will be payable at the end of each accounting year.

Also £500,000 will be needed initially to buy a fleet of vehicles for distribution. These vehicles will be sold at the end of the third year for £200,000.

There will be a need for a packaging and administrative facility. TISC is large and has a suitable factory with offices, which at present are empty. Head office has stated that they will let this space to your project at a reduced rent of £200,000 per annum payable at the end of the accounting year (the open market rental value is £1m p.a.).

The project would start on 1.1.20X1 and would not be subject to any taxation because of its special status as a growth industry. A relatively junior and inexperienced accountant has prepared forecast profit and loss accounts for the project as shown in the following table.

Year	*20X1*	*20X2*	*20X3*
Sales	5 *(£m)*	6 *(£m)*	6 *(£m)*
Costs			
Market research	0.1		
Raw material (seeds)	2.0	2.4	2.4
Licence	1.0	1.0	1.0
Vehicle fleet depreciation	0.1	0.1	0.1
Direct wages	0.5	0.5	0.5
Rent	0.2	0.2	0.2
Overhead	0.5	0.5	0.5
Variable transport costs	0.5	0.5	0.5
Profit	0.1	0.8	0.8

By expanding its product range with these new seeds the firm expects to attract a great deal of publicity which will improve the market position, and thus the profitability, of its other products. The benefit is estimated at £100,000 for each of the three years.

Head office normally allocates a proportion of its costs to any new project as part of its budgeting/costing process. This will be £100,000 for this project and has been included in the figures calculated for overhead by the accountant. The remainder of the overhead is directly related to the project.

The direct wages, seed purchases, overhead and variable transport costs can be assumed to be paid at the end of each year. Likewise, sales revenue may be assumed to be received at the end of each year. The firm will grant two months' credit to its customers. An initial cash float of £1m will be needed. This will be returned at the end of the third year.

Assume no inflation. An appropriate discount rate is 15 per cent.

Required

Assess the viability of the proposed project using the discounted cash flow technique you feel to be most appropriate.

Suggestion

Try to answer this question before reading the model answer.

Answer

Notes

- Market research cost is non-incremental.
- Opportunity cost of factory is £1m per annum.
- Vehicle depreciation does not belong in a cash flow calculation.
- The effect on TISC's other products is an incidental benefit.
- Head office cost apportionment should be excluded.

Cash flows						
£m	*20X1 start*	*20X1 end*	*20X2 end*	*20X3 end*	*20X3 end*	*20X4 2 months*
Inflows						
Sales		5.0	6.0	6.0		
Benefit to divisions		0.1	0.1	0.1		
Cash at end					1.0	
Vehicles					0.2	
Total inflows	0	5.1	6.1	6.1	1.2	0
Outflows						
Licence		1.0	1.0	1.0		
Vehicles	0.5					
Property rent (opportunity cost)		1.0	1.0	1.0		
Raw materials		2.0	2.4	2.4		
Direct wages		0.5	0.5	0.5		
Overheads		0.4	0.4	0.4		
Variable transport		0.5	0.5	0.5		
Initial cash	1.0					
Cash flows after outflows	−1.5	−0.3	0.3	0.3	1.2	0
Adjustment for debtors						
Debtor: start		0	0.833	1.00		1.0
end		0.833	1.000	1.00		0
Cash flow effect of debtors		−0.833	−0.167	0	0	+1.0
Cash flows	**−1.5**	**−1.133**	**+0.133**	**+0.3**	**+1.2**	**+1.0**

Net present value

$$NPV = -1.5 \quad \frac{-1.133}{(1.15)} + \frac{0.133}{(1.15)^2} + \frac{0.3}{(1.15)^3}$$

$$+ \frac{1.2}{(1.15)^3} + \frac{1.00}{(1.15)^{3.167}}$$

NPV = −1.5 − 0.985 + 0.101 + 0.197 + 0.789 + 0.642 = −£0.756

Conclusion

Do not proceed with the project as it returns less than 15 per cent.

The Severn river crossing consortium had to pay a great deal of attention to the estimated relevant cash flows associated with building and operating the new bridge linking Wales and England. Many thought that they had overestimated the likely revenue and therefore would destroy shareholder wealth. Only time will tell. *See* Exhibit 3.5.

Exhibit 3.5

The New Severn River Crossing

One of the biggest UK projects in the mid-1990s was the construction of a second bridge linking South Wales and England. The £330m 3-mile bridge was constructed under the government's Private Finance Initiative (PFI). The deal is as follows: a franchise is awarded to the Severn River Crossing, plc (SRC) to operate and receive toll income on the two Severn bridges for a period of 30 years. In return SRC had to build and finance the second bridge and maintain both for the period of the franchise. SRC has four shareholders, Laing and GTM Entrepose with 35% each, Bank of America International Finance Corporation with 15%, and BZW, the investment bank, with 15%.

The first Severn bridge carried 19m vehicles in 1995/96, at a toll rate of £3.80 for a car, £7.70 for a small goods vehicle and £11.50 for a heavy goods vehicle to enter Wales (the eastward journey is toll free). The government has imposed caps on the rate of increase of these tolls to the retail price index. Also there is to be no subsidy from government. The construction consortium were criticised for making a cut-price bid to win the franchise. However, they are confident volumes will rise significantly over the next three decades to justify their investment.

Source: Based on *Financial Times*, 15 May 1996.

THE REPLACEMENT DECISION

In the dynamic and competitive world of business it is important to review operations continually to ensure efficient production. Technological change brings with it the danger that a competitor has reduced costs and has leaped ahead. Thus, it is often wise to examine, say, the machinery used in the production process to see if it should be replaced with a new improved version. This is a continual process in many industries, and the frustrating aspect is that the existing machine may have years of useful life left in it. Despite this the right decision is sometimes to dispose of the old and bring in the new. If your firm does not produce at lowest cost, another one will.

In making a replacement decision the increased costs associated with the purchase and installation of the new machine have to be weighed against the savings from switching to the new method of production. In other words the incremental cash flows are the focus of attention. The worked example of Amtarc plc demonstrates the incremental approach.

Worked example 3.3 Amtarc plc

Amtarc plc produces Tarcs with a machine which is now four years old. The management team estimates that this machine has a useful life of four more years before it will be sold for scrap, raising £10,000.

Q-leap, a manufacturer of machines suitable for Tarc production, has offered its new computer-controlled Q-2000 to Amtarc for a cost of £800,000 payable immediately.

If Amtarc sold its existing machine now, on the secondhand market, it would receive £70,000. (Its book value, after depreciation, is £150,000.) The Q-2000 will have a life of four years before being sold for scrap for £20,000.

The attractive features of the Q-2000 are its lower raw material wastage and its reduced labour requirements. Selling price and variable overhead will be the same as for the old machine.

The accountants have prepared the figures shown below on the assumption that output will remain constant at last year's level of 100,000 Tarcs per annum.

	Profit per unit of Tarc	
	Old machine	*Q-2000*
	£	£
Sale price	45	45
Costs		
Labour	10	9
Materials	15	14
Variable overhead	7	7
Fixed overhead		
factory admin., etc.	5	5
depreciation	0.35	1.95
Profit per Tarc	7.65	8.05

The depreciation per unit has been calculated as follows:

$$\frac{\text{Total depreciation for a year}}{\text{Output for a year}}$$

Old machine: $\frac{(150{,}000 - 10{,}000)/4}{100{,}000} = £0.35$

Q-2000: $\frac{(800{,}000 - 20{,}000)/4}{100{,}000} = £1.95$

An additional benefit of the Q-2000 will be the reduction in required raw material buffer stocks – releasing £120,000 at the outset. However, because of the lower labour needs, redundancy payments of £50,000 will be necessary after one year.

Assume

- No inflation or tax.
- The required rate of return is 10 per cent.
- To simplify the analysis sales, labour costs, raw material costs and variable overhead costs all occur on the last day of each year.

Required

Using the NPV method decide whether to continue using the old machine or to purchase the Q-2000.

Hints

Remember to undertake incremental analysis. That is, analyse only the difference in cash flow which will result from the decision to go ahead with the purchase. Remember to include the £10,000 opportunity cost of scrapping the old machine in four years if the Q-2000 is purchased.

Answers

Stage 1
Note the irrelevant information:

1 Depreciation is not a cash flow and should not be included.
2 The book value of the machine is merely an accounting entry and has little relationship with the market value. Theoretically book value has no influence on the decision. (In practice, however, senior management may be reluctant to write off the surplus book value through the profit and loss account as this may prejudice an observer's view of their performance – despite there being no change in the underlying economic position.)

Stage 2
Work out the annual incremental cost savings.

	Savings per Tarc		
	Old machine £	*Q-2000* £	*Saving* £
Labour	10	9	1
Materials	15	14	1
Total saving			2

Total annual saving £2 × 100,000 = £200,000.

Stage 3 Incremental cash flow table

Time £000s	*0*	*1*	*2*	*3*	*4*
Purchase of Q-2000	–800				
Scrap of old machine	+70				
Raw material stocks	+120				
Opportunity cost (old machine)					–10
Redundancy payments		–50			
Sale of Q-2000					+20
Annual cost savings		+200	+200	+200	+200
	–610	+150	+200	+200	+210

Stage 4 Calculate NPV

Discounted cash flows

$$-610 + \frac{150}{1.1} + \frac{200}{(1.1)^2} + \frac{200}{(1.1)^3} + \frac{210}{(1.1)^4}$$

NPV = –£14,660.

The negative NPV indicates that shareholder wealth will be higher if the existing machine is retained.

REPLACEMENT CYCLES

Many business assets, machinery and vehicles especially, become increasingly expensive to operate and maintain as they become older. This rising cost burden prompts the thought that there must be a point when it is better to buy a replacement than to face rising repair bills. Assets such as vehicles are often replaced on a regular cycle, say every two or three years, depending on the comparison between the benefit to be derived by delaying the replacement decision (that is, the postponed cash outflow associated with the purchase of new assets) and the cost in terms of higher maintenance costs (and lower secondhand value achieved with the sale of the used asset).

Consider the case of a car rental firm which is considering a switch to a new type of car. The cars cost £10,000 and a choice has to be made between four alternative (mutually exclusive) projects (four alternative regular replacement cycles). Project 1 is to sell the cars on the secondhand market after one year for £7,000. Project 2 is to sell after two years for £5,000. Projects 3 and 4 are three-year and four-year cycles and will produce £3,000 and £1,000 respectively on the secondhand market. The cost of maintenance rises from £500 in the first year to £900 in the second, £1,200 in the third and £2,500 in the fourth. The cars are not worth keeping for more than four years because of the bad publicity associated with breakdowns. The revenue streams and other costs are unaffected by which cycle is selected. We will focus on achieving the lowest present value of the costs.

If we make the simplifying assumption that all the cash flows occur at annual intervals then the relevant cash flows are as set out in Exhibit 3.6.

Exhibit 3.6 Relevant cash flows

	Point in time (yearly intervals)	*0*	*1*	*2*	*3*	*4*
Project 1		£				
Replace after one year	Purchase cost	−10,000				
	Maintenance		−500			
	Sale proceeds		+7,000			
	Net cash flow	−10,000	+6,500			
Project 2						
Replace after two years	Purchase cost	−10,000				
	Maintenance		−500	−900		
	Sale proceeds			+5,000		
	Net cash flow	−10,000	−500	+4,100		
Project 3						
Replace after three years	Purchase cost	−10,000				
	Maintenance		−500	−900	−1,200	
	Sale proceeds				+3,000	
	Net cash flow	−10,000	−500	−900	+1,800	

Exhibit 3.6 Relevant cash flows *continued*

	Point in time (yearly intervals)	*0*	*1*	*2*	*3*	*4*
Project 4						
Replace after four years	Purchase cost	−10,000				
	Maintenance		−500	−900	−1,200	−2,500
	Sale proceeds					+1,000
	Net cash flow	−10,000	−500	−900	−1,200	−1,500

Assuming a discount rate of 10 per cent the Present Values (PVs) of costs of one cycle of the projects are:

$$PV_1 \quad -10{,}000 + \frac{6{,}500}{1.1} = -4{,}090.90$$

$$PV_2 \quad -10{,}000 - \frac{500}{1.1} + \frac{4{,}100}{(1.1)^2} = -7{,}066.12$$

$$PV_3 \quad -10{,}000 - \frac{500}{1.1} + \frac{900}{(1.1)^2} + \frac{1{,}800}{(1.1)^3} = -9{,}845.98$$

$$PV_4 \quad -10{,}000 - \frac{500}{1.1} - \frac{900}{(1.1)^2} - \frac{1{,}200}{(1.1)^3} - \frac{1{,}500}{(1.1)^4} = -13{,}124.44$$

At first sight the figures in Exhibit 3.6 might suggest that the first project is the best. Such a conclusion would be based on the normal rule with mutually exclusive projects of selecting the one with the lowest present value of costs. However, this is not a standard situation because purchases and sales of vehicles have to be allowed for far beyond the first round in the replacement cycle. If we can make the assumption that there are no increases in costs and the cars can be replaced with identical models on regular cycles in the future[1] then the pattern of cash flows for the third project, for example, are as shown in Exhibit 3.7.

Exhibit 3.7 Cash flows for Project 3

Time (years)	*0*	*1*	*2*	*3*	*4*	*5*	*6*	*7 ...*
Cash flows (£)								
1st generation	−10,000	−500	−900	+1,800				
2nd generation				−10,000	−500	−900	+1,800	
3rd generation							−10,000	−500 ...

One way of dealing with a long-lived project of this kind is to calculate the present values of numerous cycles stretching into the future. This can then be compared with other projects' present values calculated in a similarly time-consuming fashion.

Fortunately there is a much quicker technique available called the annual equivalent annuity method (AEA). This third project involves three cash outflows followed by a cash inflow within one cycle as shown in Exhibit 3.8.

Exhibit 3.8 Cash outflows and cash inflow in one cycle

Time (years)	*0*	*1*	*2*	*3*
Cash flows (£)	–10,000	–500	–900	+1,800

This produces a one-cycle present value of –£9,845.98. The annual equivalent annuity (AEA) method finds the amount that would be paid in each of the next three years if each annual payment were identical and the three payments gave the same (equivalent) present value of –£9,845.98, that is, the constant amount which would replace the ? in Exhibit 3.9.

Exhibit 3.9 Using the AEA

Time (years)	*0*	*1*	*2*	*3*	*Present value*
Actual cash flows (£)	–10,000	–500	–900	+1,800	–9,845.98
Annual equivalent annuity (£)		?	?	?	–9,845.98

(Recall that the first cash flow under an 'immediate' annuity arises after one year.)

To find the AEA we need to employ the annuity table in Appendix III. This table gives the value of a series of £1 cash flows occurring at annual intervals in terms of present money. Normally these 'annuity factors' (af) are multiplied by the amount of the cash flow that is received regularly, the annuity (A), to obtain the present value, PV. In this case we already know the PV and we can obtain the af by looking at the three-year row and the 10 per cent column. The missing element is the annual annuity.

$$\text{PV} = \text{A} \times \text{af}$$

$$\text{or A} = \frac{\text{PV}}{\text{af}}$$

In the case of the three-year replacement:

$$\text{A} = \frac{-£9,845.98}{2.4869} = -£3,959.14$$

Thus, two alternative sets of cash flows give the same present value (*see* Exhibit 3.10).

Exhibit 3.10 Present value, calculated by Cash flow 1 and cash flow 2

Time (years)	*0* £	*1*	*2*	*3*
Cash flow 1	–10,000	–500	–900	+1,800
Cash flow 2		–3,959.14	–3,959.14	–3,959.14

The second generation of cars bought at the end of the third year will have a cost of –£9,845.98 when discounted to the end of the third year (assuming both zero inflation and that the discount rate remains at 10 per cent). The present value of the costs of this second generation of vehicle is equivalent to the present value of an annuity of –£3,959.14. Thus replacing the car every three years is equivalent to a cash flow of –£3,959.14 every year to infinity (see Exhibit 3.11).

Exhibit 3.11 Replacing the car every three years

Time (years)	*0*	*1*	*2*	*3*	*4*	*5*	*6*	*7 ...*
Cash flows (£)								
First generation	–10,000	–500	–900	+1,800				
Second generation				–10,000	–500	–900	+1,800	
Third generation							–10,000	–500 ...
Annual equivalent annuity	0	–3,959.14	–3,959.14	–3,959.14	–3,959.14	–3,959.14	–3,959.14	–3,959.14

If all the other projects are converted to their annual equivalent annuities a comparison can be made.

Exhibit 3.12 Using AEAs for all projects

Cycle	*Present value of one cycle (PV)*	*Annuity factor (af)*	*Annual equivalent annuity (PV/af)*
1 year	–4,090.90	0.9091	–4,500.00
2 years	–7,066.12	1.7355	–4,071.52
3 years	–9,845.98	2.4869	–3,959.14
4 years	–13,124.44	3.1699	–4,140.33

Thus Project 3 requires the lowest equivalent annual cash flow and is the optimal replacement cycle. This is over £540 per year cheaper than replacing the car every year.

A valid alternative to the annual equivalent annuity is the lowest common multiple (LCM) method. Here the alternatives are compared using the present value of the costs over a time-span equal to the lowest common multiple of the cycle lengths. So the cash flow for 12 cycles of Project 1 would be discounted and compared with six cycles of Project 2, four cycles of Project 3 and three cycles of Project 4. The AEA method is the simplest and quickest method in cases where the lowest common multiple is high. For instance the LCM of five-, six- and seven-year cycles is 35 years, and involves a great many calculations.

Worked example 3.4 Brrum plc

Suppose the firm Brrum has to decide between two machines, A and B, to replace an old worn-out one. Whichever new machine is chosen it will be replaced on a regular cycle. Both machines produce the same level of output. Because they produce exactly the same output we do not need to examine the cash inflows at all to choose between the machines; we can concentrate solely on establishing the lower-cost machine.

Brrum plc

- Machine A costs £30m, lasts three years and costs £8m a year to run.
- Machine B costs £20m, lasts two years and costs £12m a year to run.

Cash flows

Point in time (yearly intervals)	*0*	*1*	*2*	*3*	*PV (6%)*
Machine A (£m)	–30	–8	–8	–8	–51.38
Machine B (£m)	–20	–12	–12	–	–42.00

Because Machine B has a lower PV of cost, should we jump to the conclusion that this is the better option? Well, Machine B will have to be replaced one year before Machine A and therefore, there are further cash flows to consider and discount.

If we were to assume a constant discount rate of 6 per cent and no change in costs over a number of future years, then we can make a comparison between the two machines. To do this we need to convert the total PV of the costs to a cost per year. We convert the PV of the costs associated with each machine to the equivalent annuity.

Machine A

Machine A has a PV of –£51.38m. We need to find an annuity with a PV of –£51.38 which has regular equal costs occurring at years 1, 2 and 3.

Look in the annuity table along the row of three years and down the column of 6% to get the three-year annuity factor.

Machine A

PV = Annual annuity payment (A) × 3-year annuity factor (af)

$-51.38 = A \times 2.673$

$A = -51.38/2.673 = -£19.22$m per year

Point in time (yearly intervals)	*0*	*1*	*2*	*3*	*PV (6%)*
Cash flows (£m)	–30	–8	–8	–8	–51.38
Equivalent 3-year annuity (£m)		–19.22	–19.22	–19.22	–51.38

When Machine A needs to be replaced at the end of the third year, if we can assume it is replaced by a machine of equal cost we again have a PV of costs for the Year 3 of £51.38m dated at Year 3. This too has an equivalent annuity of –£19.22m. Thus, the –£19.22m annual costs is an annual cost for many years beyond Year 3.

Machine B

PV = A × af

$-42 = A \times 1.8334$

$A = -42/1.8334 = -£22.908$m

Point in time (yearly intervals)	*0*	*1*	*2*	*PV (6%)*
Cash flows (£m)	–20	–12	–12	–42
Equivalent 2-year annuity (£m)		–22.91	–22.91	–42

Again, if we assume that at the end of two years the machine is replaced with an identical one, with identical costs, then the annuity of –£22.91m can be assumed to be continuing into the future.

Comparing the annual annuities
Machine A: (£m) –19.22.
Machine B: (£m) –22.91.

When we compare the annual annuities we see that Machine A, in fact, has the lower annual cost and is therefore the better buy.

WHEN TO INTRODUCE A NEW MACHINE

Businesses, when switching from one kind of a machine to another, have to decide on the timing of that switch. The best option may not be to dispose of the old machine immediately. It may be better to wait for a year or two because the costs of running the old machine may amount to less than the equivalent annual cost of starting a regular cycle with replacements. However, eventually the old machine is going to become more costly due to its lower efficiency, increased repair bills or declining secondhand value. Let us return to the case of the car rental firm. It has been established that when a replacement cycle is begun for the new type of car, it should be a three-year cycle. The existing type of car used by the firm has a potential further life of two years. The firm is considering three alternative courses of action. The first is to sell the old vehicles immediately, raising £7,000 per car, and then begin a three-year replacement cycle with the new type of car. The second possibility is to spend £500 now to service the vehicles ready for another year's use. At the end of the year the cars could be sold for £5,200 each. The third option is to pay £500 for servicing now, followed by a further £2,000 in one year to maintain the vehicles on the road for a second year, after which they would be sold for £1,800. The easiest approach for dealing with a problem of this nature is to calculate NPVs for all the possible alternatives. We will assume that the revenue aspect of this car rental business can be ignored as this will not change regardless of which option is selected. The relevant cash flows are shown in Exhibit 3.13. Note that the annual equivalent annuity cash flow, rather than the actual cash flows for the three-year cycle of new cars, is incorporated and is assumed to continue to infinity. It is therefore a perpetuity.

(Note that the sums of £3,959.14 are perpetuities starting at Times 1, 2 and 3, and so are valued at Times 0, 1 and 2. The latter two therefore have to be discounted back one and two years respectively). The switch to the new cars should take place after one year. Thereafter the new cars should be replaced every three years. This policy is over £800 cheaper than selling off the old cars immediately.

The net present value calculations are as set out in Exhibit 3.14.

Exhibit 3.13 Cash flow per car (excluding operating revenues, etc.)

Point in time (yearly intervals)		*0*	*1*	*2*	*3 → ∞*
Option 1 – sell old car at time 0	Secondhand value	+7,000			
	New car		−3,959.14	−3,959.14	−3,959.14
	Net cash flow	+7,000	−3,959.14	−3,959.14	−3,959.14
Option 2 – sell old car after one year	Secondhand value		+5,200		
	Maintenance	−500			
	New car			−3,959.14	−3,959.14
	Net cash flow	−500	+5,200	−3,959.14	−3,959.14
Option 3 – sell old car after two years	Secondhand value			+1,800	
	Maintenance	−500	−2,000		
	New car				−3,959.14
	Net cash flow	−500	−2,000	+1,800	−3,959.14

Exhibit 3.14 NPV calculations

Option 1: $$+7{,}000 - \frac{3{,}959.14}{0.1} = -£32{,}591.4$$

Option 2: $$-500 + \frac{5{,}200}{1.1} - \frac{3{,}959.14}{0.1} \times \frac{1}{1.1} = -£31{,}764.91$$

Option 3: $$-500 - \frac{2{,}000}{1.1} + \frac{1{,}800}{(1.1)^2} - \frac{3{,}959.14}{0.1} \times \frac{1}{(1.1)^2} = -£33{,}550.74$$

DRAWBACKS OF THE ANNUAL EQUIVALENT ANNUITY METHOD

It is important to note that annual equivalent annuity analysis relies on there being a high degree of predictability of cash flows stretching into the future. While the technique can be modified reasonably satisfactorily for the problems caused by inflation we may encounter severe problems if the assets in question are susceptible to a high degree of technical change and associated cash flows. An example here would be computer hardware where simultaneously, over short time periods both technical capability increases and cost of purchase decreases. The absence of predictability means that the AEA approach is not suitable in a number of situations. The requirement that identical replacement takes place can be a severe limitation but the AEA approach can be used for approximate analysis, which is sufficient for practical decisions in many situations – provided the analyst does not become too preoccupied with mathematical preciseness and remembers that good judgement is also required.

TIMING OF PROJECTS

In some industries the mutually exclusive projects facing the firm may simply be whether to take a particular course of action now or to make shareholders better off by considering another possibility, for instance, to implement the action in a future year. It may be that taking action now would produce a positive NPV and is therefore attractive. However, by delaying action an even higher NPV can be obtained. Take the case of Lochglen distillery. Ten years ago it laid down a number of vats of whisky. These have a higher market value the older the whisky becomes. The issue facing the management team is to decide in which of the next seven years to bottle and sell it. The table in Exhibit 3.15 gives the net cash flows available for each of the seven alternative projects.

Exhibit 3.15 Lochglen distillery's choices

	Year of bottling						
Point in time (yearly intervals)	*0*	*1*	*2*	*3*	*4*	*5*	*6*
Net cash flow £000s per vat	60	75	90	103	116	129	139
Percentage change on previous year		25%	20%	14.4%	12.6%	11.2%	7.8%

The longer the firm refrains from harvesting, the greater the size of the money inflow. However, this does not necessarily imply that shareholders will be best served by delaying as long as possible. They have an opportunity cost for their funds and therefore the firm must produce an adequate return over a period of time. In the case of Lochglen the assumption is that the firm requires a 9 per cent return on projects. The calculation of the NPVs for each project is easy (*see* Exhibit 3.16).

As shown in Exhibit 3.16, the optimal point is at Year 5 when the whisky has reached the ripe old age of 15. Note also that prior to the fifth year the value increased at an annual rate greater than 9 per cent. After Year 5 (or 15 years old) the rate of increase is less than the cost of capital. Another way of viewing this is to say that, if the whisky was sold when at 15 years old the cash received could be invested elsewhere (for the same level of risk) and receive a return of 9 per cent, which is more than the 7.8 per cent available by holding the whisky one more year.

Exhibit 3.16 NPVs for Lochglen distillery's choices

	Year of bottling						
Point in time (yearly intervals)	*0*	*1*	*2*	*3*	*4*	*5*	*6*
£000s per vat		$\frac{75}{1.09}$	$\frac{90}{(1.09)^2}$	$\frac{103}{(1.09)^3}$	$\frac{116}{(1.09)^4}$	$\frac{129}{(1.09)^5}$	$\frac{139}{(1.09)^6}$
Net present value	60	68.8	75.8	79.5	82.2	83.8	82.9

THE MAKE OR BUY DECISION

A perennial issue which many organisations have to address is whether it is better to buy a particular item, such as a component, from a supplier or to produce the item in-house. If the firm produces for itself it will incur the costs of set-up as well as the on-going annual costs. These costs can be avoided by buying in but this has the potential drawback that the firm may be forced to pay a high market price. This is essentially an incremented cash flow problem. We need to establish the difference between the costs of set-up and production in-house and the costs of purchase. Take the case of Davis and Davies plc who manufacture fishing rods. At the moment they buy in the 'eyes' for the rods from I'spies plc at £1 per set. They expect to make use of 100,000 sets per annum for the next few years. If Davis and Davies were to produce their own 'eyes' they would have to spend £40,000 immediately on machinery, setting up and training. The machinery will have a life of four years and the annual cost of production of 100,000 sets will be £80,000, £85,000, £92,000 and £100,000 respectively. The cost of bought-in components is not expected to remain at £1 per set. The more realistic estimates are £105,000 for Year 1, followed by £120,000, £128,000 and £132,000 for Years 2 to 4 respectively, for 100,000 sets per year. The new machinery will be installed in an empty factory the open market rental value of which is £20,000 per annum and the firm's cost of capital is 11 per cent. The extra cash flows associated with in-house production compared with buying in are as set out in Exhibit 3.17.

As the incremental NPV is negative Davis and Davies should continue to purchase 'eyes'. The present values of the future annual savings are worth less than the initial investment for self-production.

Exhibit 3.17 Cash flows for producing 'eyes' in-house

Points in time (yearly intervals) *£000s*	*0*	*1*	*2*	*3*	*4*
1 Cash flows of self-production	40	80	85	92	100
2 Plus opportunity costs		20	20	20	20
3 Relevant cash flows of making	40	100	105	112	120
4 Costs of purchasing component		105	120	128	132
Incremented cash flow due to making (line 4 – line 3)	–40	5	15	16	12

Net present value of incremental cash flows

$$-40 + \frac{5}{1.11} + \frac{15}{(1.11)^2} + \frac{16}{(1.11)^3} + \frac{12}{(1.11)^4}$$

NPV = –£3,717

FLUCTUATING OUTPUT

Many businesses and individual machines operate at less than full capacity for long periods of time. Sometimes this is due to the nature of the firm's business. For instance, electricity demand fluctuates through the day and over the year. Fluctuating output can produce some interesting problems for project appraisal analysis. Take the case of the Potato Sorting Company, which grades and bags potatoes in terms of size and quality. During the summer and autumn its two machines work at full capacity, which is the equivalent of 20,000 bags per machine per year. However, in the six months of the winter and spring the machines work at half capacity because fewer home grown potatoes need to be sorted. The operating cost of the machine per bag is 20 pence. The machines were installed over 50 years ago and can be regarded as still having a very long productive life. Despite this they have no secondhand value because modern machines called Fastsort now dominate the market. Fastsort has an identical capacity to the old machine but its running cost is only 10 pence per bag. These machines are also expected to be productive indefinitely, but they cost £12,000 each to purchase and install. The new production manager is keen on getting rid of the two old machines and replacing them with two Fastsort machines. She has presented the figures given in Exhibit 3.18 to a board meeting on the assumption of a cost of capital of 10 per cent.

The production manager has identified a way to save the firm £6,000 and is duly proud of her presentation. The newly appointed finance director thanks her for bringing this issue to the attention of the board but thinks that they should consider a third possibility. This is to replace only one of the machines. The virtue of this approach is that

Exhibit 3.18 Comparison of old machines with Fastsort

Cost of two old machines

Output per machine per year =	rate of 20,000 p.a. for six months 20,000 × 0.5	=	10,000
+	rate of 10,000 p.a. for six months 10,000 × 0.5	=	5,000
			15,000

15,000 bags @ 20p × 2 = £6,000.

Present value of a perpetuity of £6,000: $\frac{6,000}{0.1} = £60,000$

Cost of the Fastsorts

Annual output – same as under old machines, 30,000 bags p.a.

Annual operating cost 30,000 × 10p = £3,000

Present value of operating costs $\frac{3,000}{0.1} = £30,000$

Plus initial investment	£24,000
Overall cost in present value terms	£54,000

during the slack six months only the Fastsort will be used and can be supplemented with the old machine during the busy period, thus avoiding £12,000 of initial investment. The figures work out as set out in Exhibit 3.19.

Exhibit 3.19 Replacing only one old machine

	Fastsort	*Old machine*
Output	20,000 bags	10,000 bags
Initial investment	£12,000	
Operating costs	10p × 20,000 = £2,000	20p × 10,000 = £2,000
Present value of operating costs	$\frac{2,000}{0.1}$ = £20,000	$\frac{2,000}{0.1}$ = £20,000
Total present value	£12,000 + £20,000	+ £20,000 = £52,000

The board decides to replace only one of the machines as this saves £8,000 compared with £6,000 under the production manager's proposal.

CONCLUDING COMMENTS

Finding appropriate cash flows to include in a project appraisal often involves some difficulty in data collection and requires some thoughtfulness in applying the concepts of incremental cash flow. The reader who has diligently worked through this chapter and has overcome the barriers to understanding may be more than a little annoyed at being told that the understanding of these issues is merely one of the stages leading to successful application of net present value to practical business problems. The logical, mathematical and conceptual knowledge presented above has to be married to an appreciation of real-world limitations imposed by the awkward fact that it is people who have to be persuaded to act to implement a plan. This is an issue examined in the next chapter. Further real-world complications such as the existence of risk, of inflation and taxation and of limits placed on availability of capital are covered in subsequent chapters.

KEY POINTS AND CONCEPTS

- **Raw data** have to be checked for accuracy, reliability, timeliness, expense of collection, etc.
- **Depreciation** is not a cash flow and should be excluded.
- **Profit** is a poor substitute for cash flow. For example, working capital adjustments may be needed to modify the profit figures for NPV analysis.
- Analyse on the basis of **incremental cash flows**. That is the difference between the cash flows arising if the project is implemented and the cash flows if the project is not implemented:

  - **opportunity costs** associated with, say, using an asset which has an alternative employment are relevant;
  - **incidental effects**, that is, cash flow effects throughout the organisation, should be considered along with the obvious direct effects;
  - **sunk costs** – costs which will not change regardless of the decision to proceed are clearly irrelevant;
  - **allocated overhead** is a non-incremental cost and is irrelevant;
  - **interest** should not be double counted by both including interest as a cash flow and including it as an element in the discount rate.

- **The replacement decision** is an example of the application of incremental cash flow analysis.

- **Annual equivalent annuities** (**AEA**) can be employed to estimate the **optimal replacement cycle** for an asset under certain restrictive assumptions. The **lowest common multiple** (**LCM**) method is sometimes employed for short-lived assets.

- Whether to **repair** the old machine or sell it and **buy** a **new machine** is a very common business dilemma. Incremental cash flow analysis helps us to solve these types of problems. Other applications include **the timing of projects**, the issue of **fluctuating output** and the **make** or **buy** decision.

REFERENCES AND FURTHER READING

Bierman, H. and Smidt, S. (1992) *The Capital Budgeting Decision*, 8th edn. New York: Macmillan. Chapters 5 and 7 are particularly useful for a student at introductory level.

Carsberg, B.V. (1975) *Economics of Business Decisions*. Harmondsworth: Penguin. An economist's perspective on relevant cash flows.

Coulthurst, N.J. (1986) 'The application of the incremental principle in capital investment project evaluation', *Accounting and Business Research*, Autumn. A discussion of the theoretical and practical application of the incremental cash flow principle.

Damodaran, A. (1999) *Applied Corporate Finance*. New York: Wiley. A clear account of some of the issues discussed in this chapter.

Gordon, L.A. and Stark, A.W. (1989) 'Accounting and economic rates of return: a note on depreciation and other accruals', *Journal of Business Finance and Accounting*, 16(3), pp. 425–32. Considers the problem of depreciation – an algebraic approach.

Pohlman, R.A., Santiago, E.S. and Markel, F.L. (1988) 'Cash flow estimation practices of larger firms', *Financial Management*, Summer. Evidence on large US corporation cash flow estimation practices.

Reinhardt, U.E. (1973) 'Break-even analysis for Lockheed's Tristar: an application of financial theory', *Journal of Finance*, 28, pp. 821–38, September. An interesting application of the principle of the opportunity cost of funds.

Wilkes, F.M. (1983) *Capital Budgeting Techniques*, 2nd edn. Chichester: Wiley. Useful if your maths is up to scratch.

Wright, M.G. (1973) *Discounted Cash Flow*, 2nd edn. Maidenhead: McGraw-Hill. Chapter 4 deals with cash flows at an introductory level.

SELF-REVIEW QUESTIONS

1 Imagine the Ministry of Defence have spent £50m researching and developing a new guided weapon system. Explain why this fact may be irrelevant to the decision on whether to go ahead with production.

2 'Those business school graduates don't know what they are talking about. We have to allocate overheads to every department and activity. If we simply excluded this cost there would be a big lump of costs not written off. All projects must bear some central overhead.' Discuss this statement.

3 What is an annual equivalent annuity?

4 What are the two main techniques available for evaluating mutually exclusive projects with different lengths of life? Why is it not valid simply to use NPVs?

5 Arcmat plc owns a factory which at present is empty. Mrs Hambicious, a business strategist, has been working on a proposal for using the factory for doll manufacture. This will require complete modernisation. Mrs Hambicious is a little confused about project appraisal and has asked your advice about which of the following are relevant and incremental cash flows.

a The future cost of modernising the factory.

b The £100,000 spent two months ago on a market survey investigating the demand for these plastic dolls.

c Machines to produce the dolls – cost £10m payable on delivery.

d Depreciation on the machines.

e Arcmat's other product lines are expected to be more popular due to the complementary nature of the new doll range with these existing products – the net cash flow effect is anticipated at £1m.

f Three senior managers will be drafted in from other divisions for a period of a year.

g A proportion of the US head office costs.

h The tax saving due to the plant investment being offset against taxable income.

i The £1m of additional raw material stock required at the start of production.

j The interest that will be charged on the £20m bank loan needed to initiate this project.

k The cost of the utility services installed last year.

6 In a 'make or buy' type of decision should we also consider factors not easily quantified such as security of supply, convenience and the morale of the workforce? (This question is meant to start you thinking about the issues discussed in Chapter 4. You are not expected to give a detailed answer yet.)

7 'Depreciation is a cost recognised by tax authorities so why don't you use it in project appraisal?' Help the person who made this statement.

8 A firm is considering the implementation of a new project to produce slippers. The equipment to be used has sufficient spare capacity to allow this new production without affecting existing product ranges. The production manager suggests that because the equipment has been paid for it is a sunk cost and should not be included in the project appraisal calculations. Do you accept his argument?

QUESTIONS AND PROBLEMS

1 The Tenby-Sandersfoot Dock company is considering the reopening of one of its mothballed loading docks. Repairs and new equipment will cost £250,000. To operate the new dock will require additional dockside employees costing £70,000 p.a. There will also be a need for additional administrative staff and other overheads such as extra stationery, insurance and telephone costs amounting to £85,000 p.a. Electricity and other energy used on the dock is anticipated to cost £40,000 p.a. The London head office will allocate £50,000 of its (unchanged) costs to this project. Other docks will experience a reduction in receipts of about £20,000 due to some degree of cannibalisation. Annual fees expected from the new dock are £255,000 p.a.

Assume

- all cash flows arise at the year end except the initial repair and equipment costs which are incurred at the outset;
- no tax or inflation;
- no sales are made on credit.

a Lay out the net annual cash flow calculations. Explain your reasoning.

b Assume an infinite life for the project and a cost of capital of 17 per cent. What is the net present value?

2 A senior management team at Railcam, a supplier to the railway industry, is trying to prepare a cash flow forecast for the years 20X1–20X5. The estimated sales are:

Year	*20X1*	*20X2*	*20X3*	*20X4*	*20X5*
Sales (£)	20m	22m	24m	21m	25m

These sales will be made on three months' credit and there will be no bad debts.

There are only three cost elements. First, wages amounting to £6m p.a. Second, raw materials costing one-half of sales for the year. Raw material suppliers grant three months of credit. Third, direct overhead at £5m per year.

Calculate the net operating cash flow for the years 20X2–20X4. Start date: 1.1.20X1.

3 (*Examination level*) Pine Ltd have spent £20,000 researching the prospects for a new range of products. If it were decided that production is to go ahead an investment of £240,000 in capital equipment on 1 January 20X1 would be required.

The accounts department has produced budgeted profit and loss statements for each of the next five years for the project. At the end of the fifth year the capital equipment will be sold and production will cease.

The capital equipment is expected to be sold for scrap on 31.12.20X5 for £40,000.

	Year end 31.12.20X1	*Year end 31.12.20X2*	*Year end 31.12.20X3*	*Year end 31.12.20X4*	*Year end 31.12.20X5*
Sales	400	400	400	320	200
Materials	240	240	240	192	120
Other variable costs	40	40	40	32	20
Fixed overheads	20	20	24	24	24
Depreciation	40	40	40	40	40
Net profit/(loss)	60	60	56	32	(4)

(All figures in £000s)

When production is started it will be necessary to raise material stock levels by £30,000 and other working capital by £20,000.

It may be assumed that payment for materials, other variable costs and fixed overheads are made at the end of each year.

Both the additional stock and other working capital increases will be released at the end of the project.

Customers receive one year's credit from the firm.

The fixed overhead figures in the budgeted accounts have two elements – 60 per cent is due to a reallocation of existing overheads, 40 per cent is directly incurred because of the take-up of the project.

For the purposes of this appraisal you may regard all receipts and payments as occurring at the year end to which they relate, unless otherwise stated. The company's cost of capital is 12 per cent.

Assume no inflation or tax.

Required

a Use the net present value method of project appraisal to advise the company on whether to go ahead with the proposed project.

b Explain to a management team unfamiliar with discounted cash flow appraisal techniques the significance and value of the NPV method.

4* (*Examination level*) Mercia plc owns two acres of derelict land near to the centre of a major UK city. The firm has received an invoice for £50,000 from consultants who were given the task of analysis, investigation and design of some project proposals for using the land. The consultants outline the two best proposals to a meeting of the board of Mercia.

Proposal 1 is to spend £150,000 levelling the site and then constructing a six-level car park at an additional cost of £1,600,000. The earthmoving firm will be paid £150,000 on the start date and the construction firm will be paid £1.4m on the start date, with the balance payable 24 months' later.

It is expected that the car park will be fully operational as from the completion date (365 days after the earthmovers first begin).

The annual income from ticket sales will be £600,000 to an infinite horizon. Operational costs (attendants, security, power, etc.) will be £100,000 per annum. The consultants have also apportioned £60,000 of Mercia's central overhead costs (created by the London-based head office and the executive jet) to this project.

The consultants present their analysis in terms of a commonly used measure of project viability, that of payback.

This investment idea is not original; Mercia investigated a similar project two years ago and discovered that there are some costs which have been ignored by the consultants. First, the local council will require a payment of £100,000 one year after the completion of the construction for its inspection services and a trading and environmental impact licence. Second, senior management will have to leave aside work on other projects, resulting in delays and reduced income from these projects amounting to £50,000 per year once the car park is operational. Also, the proposal is subject to depreciation of one- fiftieth (1/50) of the earthmoving and construction costs each year.

Proposal 2 is for a health club. An experienced company will, for a total cost of £9m payable at the start of the project, design and construct the buildings and supply all the equipment. It will be ready for Mercia's use one year after construction begins. Revenue from customers will be £5m per annum and operating costs will be £4m per annum. The consultants allocate £70,000 of central general head office overhead costs for each year from the start. After two years of operating the health club Mercia will sell it for a total of £11m.

Information not considered by the consultants for Proposal 2

The £9m investment includes £5m in buildings not subject to depreciation. It also includes £4m in equipment, 10 per cent of which has to be replaced each year. This has not been included in the operating costs.

A new executive will be needed to oversee the project from the start of the project – costing £100,000 per annum.

The consultants recommend that the board of Mercia accept the second proposal and reject the first.

Assume:

- If the site was sold with no further work carried out it would fetch £100,000.
- No inflation or tax.
- The cost of capital for Mercia is 10 per cent.
- It can be assumed, for simplicity of analysis, that all cash flows occur at year ends except those occurring at the start of the project.

Required

a Calculate the net present value of each proposal.
State whether you would recommend Proposal 1 or 2.

b Calculate the internal rate of return for each proposed project.

5* (*Examination level*) Mines International plc
The Albanian government is auctioning the rights to mine copper in the east of the country. Mines International plc (MI) is considering the amount they would be prepared to pay as a lump sum for the five-year licence. The auction is to take place very soon and the cash will have to be paid immediately following the auction.

In addition to the lump sum the Albanian government will expect annual payments of £500,000 to cover 'administration'. If MI wins the licence, production would not start until one year later because it will take a year to prepare the site and buy in equipment. To begin production MI would have to commission the manufacture of specialist engineering equipment costing £9.5m, half of which is payable immediately, with the remainder due in one year.

MI has already conducted a survey of the site which showed a potential productive life of four years with its new machine. The survey cost £300,000 and is payable immediately.

The accounts department have produced the following projected profit and loss accounts.

	Year				
Projected profit and loss (£m)	*1*	*2*	*3*	*4*	*5*
Sales	0	8	9	9	7
Less expenses					
Materials and consumables	0.6	0.4	0.5	0.5	0.4
Wages	0.3	0.7	0.7	0.7	0.7
Overheads	0.4	0.5	0.6	0.6	0.5
Depreciation of equipment	0	2.0	2.0	2.0	2.0
Albanian govt. payments	0.5	0.5	0.5	0.5	0.5
Survey costs written off	0.3				
Profit (loss) excluding licence fee	(2.1)	3.9	4.7	4.7	2.9

The following additional information is available:

(a) Payments and receipts arise at the year ends unless otherwise stated.

(b) The initial lump sum payment has been excluded from the projected accounts as this is unknown at the outset.

(c) The customers of MI demand and receive a credit period of three months.

(d) The suppliers of materials and consumables grant a credit period of three months.

(e) The overheads contain an annual charge of £200,000 which represents an apportionment of head office costs. This is an expense which would be incurred whether or not the project proceeds. The remainder of the overheads relate directly to the project.

(f) The new equipment will have a resale value at the end of the fifth year of £1.5m.

(g) During the whole of Year 3 a specialised item of machinery will be needed, which is currently being used by another division of MI. This division will therefore incur hire costs of £100,000 for the period the machinery is on loan.

(h) The project will require additional cash reserves of £1m to be held in Albania throughout the project for operational purposes. These are recoverable at the end of the project.

(i) The Albanian government will make a one-off refund of 'administration' charges three months after the end of the fifth year of £200,000.

The company's cost of capital is 12 per cent.

Ignore taxation, inflation and exchange rate movements and controls.

Required

a Calculate the maximum amount MI should bid in the auction.

b What would be the Internal Rate of Return on the project if MI did not have to pay for the licence?

c The board of directors have never been on a finance course and do not understand any of the finance jargon. However, they have asked you to persuade them that the appraisal method you have used in (a) above can be relied on. Prepare a presentation for the board of directors explaining the reasoning and justification for using your chosen project appraisal technique and your treatment of specific items in the accounts. You will need to explain concepts such as the time value of money, opportunity cost and sunk cost in plain English.

6 Find the annual equivalent annuity at 13 per cent for the following cash flow:

Point in time (yearly intervals)	*0*	*1*	*2*	*3*
Cash flow (£)	−5,000	+2,000	+2,200	+3,500

7* (*Examination question if combined with question 8*) Reds plc is attempting to decide a replacement cycle for new machinery. This machinery costs £10,000 to purchase. Operating and maintenance costs for the future years are:

Point in time (yearly intervals)	*0*	*1*	*2*	*3*
Operating and maintenance costs (£)	0	12,000	13,000	14,000

The values available from the sale of the machinery on the secondhand market are:

Point in time (yearly intervals)	*0*	*1*	*2*	*3*
Second hand value (£)	0	8,000	6,500	3,500

Assume

- replacement by an identical machine to an infinite horizon;
- no inflation, tax or risk;
- the cost of capital is 11 per cent.

Should Reds replace this new machine on a one-, two- or three-year cycle?

8* The firm Reds plc in Question 7 has not yet purchased the new machinery and is considering postponing such a cash outflow for a year or two. If it were to replace the existing machine it could be sold immediately for £4,000. If the firm persevered with the old machine for a further year then £2,000 would have to be spent immediately to recondition it. The machine could then be sold for £3,000 in 12 months' time. The third possibility is to spend £2,000 now, on reconditioning, and £1,000 on maintenance in one year, and finally sell the machine for £1,500, 24 months from now. Assuming all other factors remain constant regardless of which option is chosen, which date would you recommend for the commencement of the replacement cycle?

9 Quite plc has an ageing piece of equipment which is less efficient than more modern equivalents. This equipment will continue to operate for another 15 years but operating and maintenance costs will be £3,500 per year. Alternatively it could be sold, raising £2,000 now, and replaced with its modern equivalent which costs £7,000 but has reduced operating and maintenance costs at £3,000 per year. This machine could be sold at the end of its 15-year life for scrap for £500. The third possibility is to spend £2,500 for an immediate overhaul of the old machine which will improve its efficiency for the rest of its life, so that operating and maintenance costs become £3,200 per annum. The old machine will have a zero scrap value in 15 years, whether or not it is overhauled. Quite plc requires a return of 9 per cent on projects in this risk class. Select the best course of action. (Assume that cash flows arise at the year ends.)

10* The managing director of Curt plc is irritated that the supplier for the component widgets has recently increased prices by another 10 per cent following similar rises for each of the last five years. Based on the assumption that this pattern will continue, the cost of these widgets will be:

Points in time (yearly intervals)	*1*	*2*	*3*	*4*	*5*
Payments for widgets (£)	100,000	110,000	121,000	133,100	146,410

The managing director is convinced that the expertise for the manufacture of widgets exists within Curt. He therefore proposes the purchase of the necessary machine tools and other items of equipment to produce widgets in-house, at a cost of £70,000. The net cash outflows associated with this course of action are:

Points in time (yearly intervals)	*0*	*1*	*2*	*3*	*4*	*5*
Cash outflows	70,000	80,000	82,000	84,000	86,000	88,000

Note: The figures include the £70,000 for equipment and operating costs, etc.

The machinery has a life of five years and can be sold for scrap at the end of its life for £10,000. This is not included in the £88,000 for year 5. The installation of the new machine will require the attention of the technical services manager during the first year. She will have to abandon other projects as a result, causing a loss of net income of £48,000 from those projects. This cost has not been included in the above figures.

The discount rate is 16 per cent, and all cash flows occur at year ends except the initial investment.

Help Curt plc to decide whether to produce widgets for itself. What other factors might influence this decision?

11† The Borough Company is to replace its existing machinery. It has a choice between two new types of machine having different lives. The machines have the following costs:

Points in time (yearly intervals)		*Machine X*	*Machine Y*
0	Initial investment	£20,000	£25,000
1	Operating costs	£5,000	£4,000
2	Operating costs	£5,000	£4,000
3	Operating costs	£5,000	£4,000
4	Operating costs		£4,000

Each machine will be replaced at the end of its life by identical machines with identical costs. This cycle will continue indefinitely. The cost of capital is 13 per cent.

Which machine should Borough buy?

12* Netq plc manufactures Qtrans, for which demand fluctuates seasonally. Netq has two machines, each with a productive capacity of 1,000 Qtrans per year. For four months of the year each machine operates at full capacity. For a further four months the machines operate at three-quarters of their full capacity and for the remaining months they produce at half capacity. The operating costs of producing a Qtran is £4 and the machines are expected to be productive to an indefinite horizon. Netq is considering scrapping the old machines (for which the firm will receive nothing) and replacing them with new improved versions. These machines are also expected to last forever if properly maintained but they cost £7,000 each. Operating costs (including maintenance) will, however, fall to £1.80 per Qtran. The firm's cost of capital is 13 per cent. Should Netq replace both of its machines, one of them, or neither? Assume output is the same under each option and that the new machines have the same productive capacity as the old.

13 Clipper owns 100 acres of mature woodland and is trying to decide when to harvest the trees. If it harvests immediately the net cash flow, after paying the professional loggers, will be £10,000. If it waits a year the trees will grow, so that the net cash flow will be £12,000. In two years, £14,000 can be obtained. After three years have elapsed, the cash flow will be £15,500, and thereafter will increase in value by £1,000 per annum.

Calculate the best time to cut the trees given a cost of capital of 10 per cent.

14* (*Examination level*) Opti plc operates a single machine to produce its output. The senior management are trying to choose between four possibilities. First, sell the machine on the secondhand market and buy a new one at the end of one year. Second, sell in the secondhand market and replace at the end of two years. The third is to replace after three years. Finally, the machine could be scrapped at the end of its useful life after four years. These replacement cycles are expected to continue indefinitely. The management team believe that all such replacements will be for financially identical equipment, i.e., the cash inflows produced by the new and old equipment are the same. However, the cost of maintenance and operations increases with the age of the machine. These costs are shown in the table, along with the secondhand and scrap values.

Points in time (yearly intervals)	*0*	*1*	*2*	*3*	*4*
Initial outlay (£)	20,000				
Operating and maintenance costs (£)		6,000	8,000	10,000	12,000
Secondhand/scrap value (£)		12,000	9,000	6,000	2,000

Assume

- The cost of capital is 10 per cent.
- No inflation.
- No technological advances.
- No tax.
- All cash flows occur on anniversary dates.

Required

Choose the length of the replacement cycle which minimises the present values of the costs.

15 (*Examination level*) Hazel plc produces one of the components used in the manufacture of car bumpers. The production manager is keen on obtaining modern equipment and he has come to you, the finance director, with details concerning two alternative machines, A and B.

The cash flows and other assumptions are as follows.

		£000s	£000s	£000s
Points in time (yearly intervals)	*0*	*1*	*2*	*3*
Machine A	–200	+220	+242	0
Machine B	–240	+220	+242	+266

Machine A would have to be replaced by an identical machine on a two-year cycle.
Machine B would be replaced by an identical machine every three years.
It is considered reasonable to assume that the cash flows for the future replacements of A and B are the same as in the above table.
The opportunity cost of capital for Hazel is 15 per cent.
Ignore taxation.
The acceptance of either project would leave the company's risk unchanged.
The cash flows occur on anniversary dates.

Required

a Calculate the net present value of Machine A for its two-year life.

b Calculate the net present value of Machine B for its three-year life.

c Calculate the annual equivalent annuities for Machines A and B and recommend which machine should be selected.

d You are aware that the production manager gets very enthusiastic about new machinery and this may cloud his judgement. You suggest the third possibility, which is to continue production with Machine C which was purchased five years ago for £400,000. This is expected to produce +£160,000 per year. It has a scrap value now of £87,000 and is expected to last another five years. At the end of its useful life it will have a scrap value of £20,000.

Should C be kept for another five years?

e The production manager asks why you are discounting the cash flows. Briefly explain the time value of money and its components.

ASSIGNMENTS

1 Try to obtain budgeted profit and loss accounts for a proposed project and by combining these with other data produce cash flow estimates for the project. Calculate the NPV and contrast your conclusions on the viability of the project with that suggested by the profit and loss projections.

2 Examine some items of machinery (e.g. shop-floor machine tools, vehicles, computers). Consider whether to replace these items with the modern equivalent, taking into account increased maintenance costs, loss or gain of customer sales, secondhand values, higher productivity, etc.

3 Apply the technique of annual equivalent annuities to an asset which is replaced on a regular cycle. Consider alternative cycle lengths.

CHAPTER NOTE

1 This is a bold assumption. More realistic assumptions could be made, e.g. allowing for inflation, but the complexity that this produces is beyond the scope of this book.

Chapter 4

THE DECISION-MAKING PROCESS FOR INVESTMENT APPRAISAL

INTRODUCTION

An organisation may be viewed simply as a collection of projects, some of which were started a long time ago, some only recently begun, many are major 'strategic' projects and others minor operating-unit-level schemes. It is in the nature of business for change to occur, and through change old activities, profit centres and methods die, to be replaced by the new. Without a continuous process of regeneration firms will cease to progress and be unable to compete in a dynamic environment. It is vital that the processes and systems that lead to the development of new production methods, new markets and products, and so on are efficient. That is, both the project appraisal techniques and the entire process of proposal creation and selection lead to the achievement of the objective of the organisation. Poor appraisal technique, set within the framework of an investment process that does not ask the right questions and which provides erroneous conclusions, will destroy the wealth of shareholders.

The payback and accounting rate of return (ARR) methods of evaluating capital investment proposals have historically been, and continue to be, very popular approaches. This is despite the best efforts of a number of writers to denigrate them. It is important to understand the disadvantages of these methods, but it is also useful to be aware of why practical business people still see a great deal of merit in observing the outcome of these calculations.

The employment of project appraisal techniques must be seen as merely one of the stages in the process of the allocation of resources within a firm. The appraisal stage can be reached only after ideas for the use of capital resources have been generated and those ideas have been filtered through a consideration of the strategic, budgetary and business resource capabilities of the firm. Following the appraisal stage are the approval, implementation and post-completion auditing stages.

Any capital allocation system has to be viewed in the light of the complexity of organisational life. This aspect has been ignored in Chapters 2 and 3, where mechanical analysis is applied. The balance is corrected in this chapter. Investment, whether in intangible assets, as in the case of Noddy (*see* Case study 4.1), or tangible, as in the case of Bentley cars (*see* Case study 4.2), need to be thoroughly evaluated. This chapter considers the process of project development, appraisal and post-investment monitoring.

CASE STUDY 4.1

The Noddy and Big Ears project

In March 1996 Trocadero paid £13m for the copyright and trade marks of all the works of Enid Blyton. These include 700 books, 10,000 stories and a range of characters. The company believes that the Blyton stories have been under-exploited compared with Thomas the Tank Engine. The merchandising of Thomas brings in hundreds of millions whereas Noddy earned only £150,000 in merchandising in 1995/96. The Famous Five earned a mere £5,000.

The characters' popularity will be built upon in Japan and the USA. The BBC will continue to distribute the television series of Noddy as well as videos, audio tapes and associated books and magazines. Efforts to merchandise Noddy and other Enid Blyton characters will be stepped up including Blyton parades every day in the Trocadero in London, a travelling Noddy show and a deal with a big retail group to bring Noddy to every High Street.

Source: Based on *Financial Times*, May 1996.

CASE STUDY 4.2

Bentley output to rise on £600m investment

FT

By John Griffiths

Production of Bentley cars, already due to leap from 2,000 to 9,000 annually over the next three years under a £600m investment programme, may be expanded further under plans being developed within Volkswagen group, Bentley's owner for the past three years.

'We have a huge vision for the brand in the long run – we certainly don't see 9,000 a year as the limiting factor,' said Tony Gott, the chief executive of Bentley Motor Cars.

Further expansion can be undertaken 'without taking Bentley downmarket', said Mr Gott.

Executives at the luxury carmaker, which currently manufactures Rolls-Royce as well as Bentley models at Crewe in Cheshire, are understood to be studying a number of other niches of the world car market in which the brand could compete.

These range from very high performance 'super-cars' to luxurious four-wheel-drive recreational vehicles.

Bentley could produce such vehicles without necessarily dropping prices below the £85,000-plus at which a 'cheaper' Bentley is expected to be priced when it is launched in 2003.

Some £500m is already being invested in new models, plus approaching £100m on doubling the size of assembly buildings and installing new research, development and engineering facilities.

Employment at the Crewe facility is to rise by about 1,000 people to 3,500 over the next three years.

Source: *Financial Times*, 23 January 2001, p. 6. Reprinted with permission.

Learning objectives

The main outcome expected from this chapter is that the reader is aware of both traditional and discounted cash flow investment appraisal techniques and the extent of their use. The reader should also be aware that these techniques are a small part of the overall capital-allocation planning process. This includes knowledge of:

- empirical evidence on techniques used;
- the calculation of payback, discounted payback and accounting rate of return (ARR);
- the drawbacks and attractions of payback and ARR;
- the balance to be struck between mathematical precision and imprecise reality;
- the capital-allocation planning process.

EVIDENCE ON THE EMPLOYMENT OF APPRAISAL TECHNIQUES

A number of surveys enquiring into the appraisal methods used in practice have been conducted over the past 20 years. The results from surveys conducted by Pike and by the author jointly with Panos Hatzopoulos are displayed in Exhibit 4.1. Some striking features emerge from these and other studies. Payback remains in wide use, despite the increasing application of discounted cash flow techniques. Internal rate of return is at least as popular as net present value. However, NPV is gaining rapid acceptance. Accounting rate of return continues to be the laggard, but is still used in over 50 per cent of large firms. One observation that is emphasised in many studies is the tendency for decision makers to use more than one method. In the 1997 study 67 per cent of firms use three or four of these techniques. These methods are regarded as being complementary rather than competitors.

There is an indication in the literature that while some methods have superior theoretical justification, other, simpler methods are used for purposes such as communicating project viability and gaining commitment throughout an organisation. It is also suggested that those who sponsor and advance projects within organisations like to have the option of presenting their case in an alternative form which shows the proposal in the best light.

Another clear observation from the literature is that small and medium-sized firms use the sophisticated formal procedures less than their larger brethren.

PAYBACK

The payback period for a capital investment is the length of time before the cumulated stream of forecasted cash flows equals the initial investment.

The decision rule is that if a project's payback period is less than or equal to a predetermined threshold figure it is acceptable.

Exhibit 4.1 Appraisal techniques used

	Proportion of companies using technique							
	Pike surveys[a]				*Arnold and Hatzopoulos survey*[b]			
	1975 %	*1980 %*	*1986 %*	*1992 %*	*1997 Small %*	*Medium %*	*Large %*	*Total %*
Payback	73	81	92	94	71	75	66	70
Accounting rate of return	51	49	56	50	62	50	55	56
Internal rate of return	44	57	75	81	76	83	84	81
Net present value	32	39	68	74	62	79	97	80

Capital budget (per year) for companies in Arnold and Hatzopoulos study approx.
Small: £1–50m. Medium: £1–100m. Large: £100m+

Notes

(a) Pike's studies focus on 100 large UK firms.

(b) In the Arnold and Hatzopoulos study (2000), 300 finance directors of UK companies taken from *The Times 1000* (London: Times Books), ranked according to capital employed (excluding investment trusts), were asked dozens of questions about project appraisal techniques, sources of finance and performance measurement. The first 100 (Large size) of the sample are the top 100; another 100 are in the rankings at 250–400 (Medium size); the final 100 are ranked 820–1,000 (Small size). The capital employed ranges between £1.3bn and £24bn for the large firms, £207m and £400m for the medium-sized firms, and £40m and £60m for the small companies. Ninety-six usable replies were received: 38 large, 24 medium and 34 small.

Sources: Pike (1988 and 1996) and Arnold and Hatzopoulos (2000).

Consider the case of Tradfirm's three mutually exclusive proposed investments (see Exhibit 4.2):

Exhibit 4.2 Tradfirm

	Cash flows (£m)						
Points in time (yearly intervals)	*0*	*1*	*2*	*3*	*4*	*5*	*6*
Project A	−10	6	2	1	1	2	2
Project B	−10	1	1	2	6	2	2
Project C	−10	3	2	2	2	15	10

Note: Production ceases after six years, and all cash flows occur on anniversary dates.

There is a board room battle in Tradfirm, with older members preferring the payback rule. They set four years as the decision benchmark. For both A and B the £10m initial outflow is recouped after four years. In the case of C it takes five years for the cash inflows to cumulate to £10m. Thus payback for the three projects is as follows:

Project A:	4 years
Project B:	4 years
Project C:	5 years

If the payback rule is rigidly applied, the older members of the board will reject the third project, and they are left with a degree of indecisiveness over whether to accept A or B. The younger members prefer the NPV rule and are thus able to offer a clear decision.

In order to calculate the net present value, first calculate the annual writing-down allowances (WDA). Note that each year the WDA is equal to 25 per cent of the asset value at the start of the year. (*See* Exhibit 5.5).

The next step is to derive, the project's incremental taxable income and to calculate the tax payments (Exhibit 5.6).

Finally, the total cash flows and NPV are calculated (*see* Exhibit 5.7).

Exhibit 5.5 Calculation of written-down value

Point in time (yearly intervals)	*Annual writing-down allowance* £	*Written-down value* £
0	0	1,000,000
1	1,000,000 × 0.25 = 250,000	750,000
2	750,000 × 0.25 = 187,500	562,500
3	562,500 × 0.25 = 140,625	421,875
4	421,875 × 0.25 = 105,469	316,406

Exhibit 5.6 Calculation of corporation tax

Year	*1* £	*2* £	*3* £	*4* £
Net income before writing-down allowance and tax	400,000	400,000	220,000	240,000
Less writing-down allowance	250,000	187,500	140,625	105,469
Incremental taxable income	150,000	212,500	79,375	134,531
Tax at 30% of incremental taxable income	45,000	63,750	23,813	40,359

Exhibit 5.7 Calculation of cash flows

Year	*0* £	*1* £	*2* £	*3* £	*4* £
Incremental cash flow before tax	−1,000,000	400,000	400,000	220,000	240,000
Sale of machine					316,406
Tax	0	45,000	−63,750	−23,813	−40,359
Net cash flow	−1,000,000	355,000	336,250	196,187	516,047
Discounted cash flow	−1,000,000 +	$\frac{355,000}{1.12}$ +	$\frac{336,250}{(1.12)^2}$ +	$\frac{196,187}{(1.12)^3}$ +	$\frac{516,047}{(1.12)^4}$
	−1,000,000	+316,964	+268,056	+139,642	+327,957

Net present value = + £52,619

The assumption that the machine can be sold at the end of the fourth year, for an amount equal to the written-down value, may be unrealistic. It may turn out that the machine is sold for the larger sum of £440,000. If this is the case, a *balancing charge* will need to be made, because by the end of the third year the Inland Revenue have already permitted write-offs against taxable profit such that the machine is shown as having a written-down value of £421,875.

A year later its market value is found to be £440,000. The balancing charge is equal to the sale value at Time 4 minus the written-down book value at Time 3, viz:

£440,000 – £421,875 = £18,125

Taxable profits for Year 4 are now:

	£
Pre-tax cash flows	240,000
Plus balancing charge	18,125
	258,125

This results in a tax payment of £258,125 × 0.30 = £77,438 rather than £40,359.

Of course, the analyst does not have to wait until the actual sale of the asset to make these modifications to a proposed project's projected cash flows. It may be possible to estimate a realistic scrap value at the outset.

An alternative scenario, where the scrap value is less than the Year 4 written-down value, will require a balancing allowance. If the disposal value is £300,000 then the machine cost the firm £700,000 (£1,000,000 – £300,000) but the tax writing-down allowances amount to only £683,594 (£1,000,000 – £316,406). The firm will effectively be overcharged by the Inland Revenue. In this case a balancing adjustment, amounting to £16,406 (£700,000 – £683,594) is made to reduce the tax payable – see Exhibit 5.8.

Exhibit 5.8 Year 4 taxable profits

	£
Pre-tax cash flows	240,000
Less annual writing-down allowance	105,469
Less balancing allowance	16,406
Taxable profits	118,125
Tax payable @ 30%	35,438

INFLATION

Annual inflation in the UK has varied from 1 per cent to 26 per cent since 1945. It is important to adapt investment appraisal methods to cope with the phenomenon of price movements. Future rates of inflation are unlikely to be precisely forecasted, nevertheless, we will assume in the analysis that follows that we can anticipate inflation with reasonable accuracy. Unanticipated inflation is an additional source of risk and methods of dealing with this are described in the next chapter. Case study 5.2 shows the importance of allowing for inflation.

CASE STUDY 5.2

Eurotunnel's inflation allowance

Peter Puplett, writing in the *Investors Chronicle*, pointed out some of the forecasting errors made in Eurotunnel's pathfinder prospectus issued in November 1987, one of which was to do with inflation:

> The total cost of the project was stated as £4,874m in the prospectus, as shown in the table. The uplift directors made for inflation was less than 14%, even though they knew the project would take at least six years to complete.

General inflation in the UK was far higher than 14 per cent over this period. The projected costs, therefore, were too low.

1987 Eurotunnel costs

	£m
Construction @ 1987 prices	2,788
Corporate costs @ 1987 prices	642
	3,430
Plus:	
Provision for inflation	469
Building cost	3,899
Net financing costs	975
Total project cost	4,874

Source: Based on *Investors Chronicle*, 19 April 1996, p. 20.

Two types of inflation can be distinguished. *Specific inflation* refers to the price changes of an individual good or service. *General inflation* is the reduced purchasing power of money and is measured by an overall price index which follows the price changes of a 'basket' of goods and services through time. Even if there was no general inflation, specific items and sectors might experience price rises.

Inflation creates two problems for project appraisal. First, the estimation of future cash flows is made more troublesome. The project appraiser will have to estimate the degree to which future cash flows will be inflated. Second, the rate of return required by the firm's security holders, such as shareholders, will rise if inflation rises. Thus, inflation has an impact on the discount rate used in investment evaluation. We will look at the second problem in more detail first.

'Real' and 'money' rates of return

A point was made in Chapter 2 of demonstrating that the rate of return represented by the discount rate usually takes account of three types of compensation:

- the pure time value of money, or impatience to consume;
- risk;
- inflation.

Thus, the interest rates quoted in the financial markets are sufficiently high to compensate for all three elements. A 10-year loan to a reputable government (such as the purchase of a bond) may pay an interest rate of 9 per cent per annum. Some of this is compensation for time preference and a little for risk, but the majority of that interest is likely to be compensation for future inflation. It is the same for the cost of capital for a business. When it issues financial securities, the returns offered include a large element of inflation compensation.

To illustrate: even in a situation of no inflation, given the choice between receiving goods and services now or receiving them some time in the future, shareholders would rather receive them now. If these pure time and risk preferences were valued, the value might turn out to be 8 per cent per annum. That is, in a world without inflation, investors are indifferent as to whether they receive a given basket of commodities today or receive a basket of commodities which is 8 per cent larger in one year's time.

The *real rate of return* is defined as the rate of return that would be required in the absence of inflation. In the example in Exhibit 5.9, the real rate of return is 8 per cent.

If we change the assumption so that prices do rise then investors will demand compensation for general inflation. They will require a larger monetary amount at Time 1 to buy 1.08 baskets. If inflation is 4 per cent then the money value of the commodities at Time 1, which would leave the investor indifferent when comparing it with one basket at Time 0, is:

$$1.08 \times 1.04 = 1.1232$$

That is, investors will be indifferent as to whether they hold £1,000 now or receive £1,123.20 one year hence. Since the money cash flow of £1,123.20 at Time 1 is financially equivalent to £1,000 now, the *money rate of return* is 12.32 per cent. The *money rate of return* includes a return to compensate for inflation.

Exhibit 5.9 Rate of return without inflation

Time 0		Time 1		
1 basket of goods and services	← indifferent → from	1 basket of goods and services	+	0.08 of a basket of goods and services

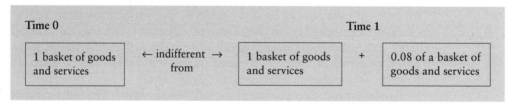

The generalised relationship between real rates of return and money (or market, or nominal) rates of return and inflation is expressed in Fisher's (1930) equation:

$$(1 + \text{money rate of return}) = (1 + \text{real rate of return}) \times (1 + \text{anticipated rate of inflation})$$

$$(1 + m) = (1 + h) \times (1 + i)$$

$$(1 + 0.1232) = (1 + 0.08) \times (1 + 0.04)$$

'Money' cash flows and 'real' cash flows

We have now established two possible discount rates, the money discount rate and the real discount rate. There are two alternative ways of adjusting for the effect of future inflation on cash flows. The first is to estimate the likely specific inflation rates for each of the inflows and outflows of cash and calculate the actual monetary amount paid or received in the year that the flow occurs. This is the money cash flow or the nominal cash flow.

With a *money cash flow*, all future cash flows are expressed in the prices expected to rule when the cash flow occurs.

The other possibility is to measure the cash flows in terms of real prices. That is, all future cash flows are expressed in terms of, say, Time 0's prices.

With *real cash flows*, future cash flows are expressed in terms of constant purchasing power.

Adjusting for inflation

There are two correct methods of adjusting for inflation when calculating net present value. They will lead to the same answer.

- *Approach 1* Estimate the cash flows in money terms and use a money discount rate.
- *Approach 2* Estimate the cash flows in real terms and use a real discount rate.

For now we will leave discussion of conversion to real prices and focus on the calculations using money cash flow. This will be done through the examination of an appraisal for Amplify plc.

Worked example 5.3 Amplify plc

Cash flow in money terms and money discount rate

Amplify plc is considering a project which would require an outlay of £2.4m at the outset. The money cash flows receivable from sales will depend on the specific inflation rate for Amplify's product. This is anticipated to be 6 per cent per annum. Cash outflows consist of three elements: labour, materials and overheads. Labour costs are expected to increase at 9 per cent per year, materials by 12 per cent and overheads by 8 per cent. The discount rate of 12.32 per cent that Amplify uses is a money discount rate, including an allowance for inflation. One of the key rules of project appraisal is now followed: if the discount rate is stated in money terms, then consistency requires that the cash flows be estimated in money terms. (It is surprising how often this rule is broken.)

$$\text{NPV} = M_0 + \frac{M_1}{1 + \text{m}} + \frac{M_2}{(1 + m)^2} \cdots \frac{M_n}{(1 + m)^n}$$

where M = actual or money cash flow
m = actual or money rate of return.

Annual cash flows in present (Time 0) prices are as follows:

	£m	*Inflation*
Sales	2	6%
Labour costs	0.3	9%
Material costs	0.6	12%
Overhead	0.06	8%

All cash flows occur at year ends except for the initial outflow.

The first stage is to calculate the money cash flows. We need to restate the inflows and outflows for each of the years at the amount actually changing hands in nominal terms. (*See* Exhibit 5.10.)

Exhibit 5.10 Amplify plc: Money cash flow

Point in time (yearly intervals)	*Cash flow before allowing for price rises £m*	*Inflation adjustment*	*Money cash flow £m*
0 Initial outflow	–2.4	1	–2.4
1 Sales	2	1.06	2.12
Labour	–0.3	1.09	–0.327
Materials	–0.6	1.12	–0.672
Overheads	–0.06	1.08	–0.065
Net money cash flow for Year 1			+1.056
2 Sales	2	$(1.06)^2$	2.247
Labour	–0.3	$(1.09)^2$	–0.356
Materials	–0.6	$(1.12)^2$	–0.753
Overheads	–0.06	$(1.08)^2$	–0.070
Net money cash flow for Year 2			+1.068
3 Sales	2	$(1.06)^3$	2.382
Labour	–0.3	$(1.09)^3$	–0.389
Materials	–0.6	$(1.12)^3$	–0.843
Overheads	–0.06	$(1.08)^3$	–0.076
Net money cash flow for Year 3			+1.074

Then we discount at the money rate of return (*see* Exhibit 5.11).

Exhibit 5.11 Amplify plc: Money cash flows discounted at the money discount rate

Point in time (yearly intervals)	*0*	*1*	*2*	*3*
			£m	
Undiscounted cash flows	–2.4	1.056	1.068	1.074
Discounting calculation	–2.4	$\frac{1.056}{1 + 0.1232}$	$\frac{1.068}{(1 + 0.1232)^2}$	$\frac{1.074}{(1 + 0.1232)^3}$
Discounted cash flows	–2.4	0.9402	0.8466	0.7579

Net present value = +£0.1447 million.

This project produces a positive NPV and is therefore to be recommended.

Cash flow in real terms and real discount rate

The second approach is to calculate the net present value by discounting real cash flow by the real discount rate. A real cash flow is obtainable by discounting the money cash flow by the general rate of inflation, thereby converting it to its current purchasing power equivalent.

The general inflation rate is derived from Fisher's equation given above:

$$(1 + m) = (1 + h) \times (1 + i),$$

where m = money rate of return;
h = real rate of return;
i = inflation rate.

m is given as 0.1232, h as 0.08, i as 0.04.

$$i = \frac{(1 + m)}{(1 + h)} - 1 = \frac{1 + 0.1232}{1 + 0.08} - 1 = 0.04$$

Under this method net present value, becomes:

$$\text{NPV} = \text{R}_0 + \frac{\text{R}_1}{1 + h} + \frac{\text{R}_2}{(1 + h)^2} + \frac{\text{R}_3}{(1 + h)^3} + \ldots$$

The net present value is equal to the sum of the real cash flows R_t discounted at a real rate of interest, h.

The first stage is to discount money cash flows by the general inflation rate to establish real cash flows (Exhibit 5.12).

Exhibit 5.12 Amplify plc: Discounting money cash flow by the general inflation rate

Points in time (yearly intervals)	*Cash flow £m*	*Calculation*	*Real cash flow £m*
0	–2.4	–	–2.4
1	1.056	$\frac{1.056}{1 + 0.04}$	1.0154
2	1.068	$\frac{1.068}{(1 + 0.04)^2}$	0.9874
3	1.074	$\frac{1.074}{(1 + 0.04)^3}$	0.9548

The second task is to discount real cash flows at the real discount rate (Exhibit 5.13).

Note that the net present value is the same as before. To discount at the general inflation rate, i, followed by discounting at the real rate of return, h, is arithmetically the same as discounting money cash flows at the money rate,[3] m.

Also note that the money cash flows are deflated by the general rate of inflation, not by the specific rates. This is because the ultimate beneficiaries of this project are interested in their ability to purchase a basket of goods generally and not their ability to buy any one good, and therefore the link between the real cost of capital and the money cost of capital is the general inflation rate.

Exhibit 5.13 Amplify plc: Real cash flows discounted at the real discount rate

Point in time (yearly intervals)	*0 £m*	*1 £m*	*2 £m*	*3 £m*
Real cash flow	−2.4	1.0154	0.9874	0.9548
Discounting calculation	−2.4	$\frac{1.0154}{1 + 0.08}$	$\frac{0.9874}{(1 + 0.08)^2}$	$\frac{0.9548}{(1 + 0.08)^3}$
Discounted cash flow	−2.4	0.9402	0.8465	0.7580

Net present value = +£0.1447m.

The two methods for adjusting for inflation produce the same result and therefore it does not matter which method is used. The first method, using money discount rates, has the virtue of requiring only one stage of discounting.

Internal rate of return and inflation

The logic applied to the NPV analysis can be transferred to an internal rate of return approach. That is, two acceptable methods are possible, either:

(a) compare the IRR of the money cash flows with the opportunity cost of capital expressed in money terms; or

(b) compare the IRR of the real cash flows with the opportunity cost of capital expressed in real terms.

A warning

Never do either of the following:

1 Discount money cash flows with the real discount rate. This gives an apparent NPV much larger than the true NPV and so will result in erroneous decisions to accept projects which are not shareholder wealth enhancing.

2 Discount real cash flows with the money discount rate. This will reduce the NPV from its true value which causes the rejection of projects which will be shareholder wealth enhancing.

The treatment of inflation practice

Exhibit 5.14 shows that UK companies generally either specify cash flow in constant prices and apply a real rate of return or express cash flows in inflated price terms and discount at the market rate of return.

Exhibit 5.14 Inflation adjustment methods used for investment appraisal by UK firms

	Small %	*Medium-sized* %	*Large* %	*Composite* %
Specify cash flow in constant prices and apply a real rate of return	47	29	45	42
All cash flows expressed in inflated price terms and discounted at the market rate of return	18	42	55	39
Considered at risk analysis or sensitivity stage	21	13	16	17
No adjustment	18	21	3	13
Other	0	0	3	1

Source: Arnold and Hatzopoulos (2000).

CONCLUDING COMMENTS

This chapter deals with some of the more technical aspects of project appraisal. These are issues that are of great concern to managers and should never be neglected in an investment evaluation. Serious misunderstanding and poor decision making can result from a failure to consider all relevant information.

KEY POINTS AND CONCEPTS

- **Soft capital rationing** – internal management-imposed limits on investment expenditure despite the availability of positive NPV projects.
- **Hard capital rationing** – externally imposed limits on investment expenditure in the presence of positive NPV projects.
- For **divisible one-period capital rationing problems**, focus on the returns per £ of outlay:

$$\text{Profitability index} = \frac{\text{Gross present value}}{\text{Initial outlay}}$$

$$\text{Benefit-cost ratio} = \frac{\text{Net present value}}{\text{Initial outlay}}$$

- For **indivisible one-period capital rationing problems**, examine all the feasible alternative combinations.
- Two rules for **allowing for taxation** in project appraisal:
  - include incremental tax effects of a project as a cash outflow;
  - get the timing right.

- **Taxable profits are not the same as accounting profits.** For example, depreciation is not allowed for in the taxable profit calculation, but writing-down allowances are permitted.
- **Specific inflation** – price changes of an individual good or service over a period of time.
- **General inflation** – the reduced purchasing power of money.
- General inflation affects the rate of return required on projects:
  - **real rate of return** – the return required in the absence of inflation;
  - **money rate of return** – includes a return to compensate for inflation.
- **Fisher's equation**

  (1 + money rate of return) = (1 + real rate of return) × (1 + anticipated rate of inflation)

  $(1 + m) = (1 + h) \times (1 + i)$

- Inflation affects future cash flows:
  - **money cash flows** – all future cash flows are expressed in the prices expected to rule when the cash flow occurs;
  - **real cash flows** – future cash flows are expressed in constant purchasing power.
- **Adjusting for inflation in project appraisal:**
  - Approach 1 – Estimate the cash flows in money terms and use a money discount rate.
  - Approach 2 – Estimate the cash flows in real terms and use a real discount rate.

REFERENCES AND FURTHER READING

Arnold, G.C. and Hatzopoulos, P.D. (2000) 'The theory-practice gap in capital budgeting: evidence from the United Kingdom', *Journal of Business Finance and Accounting*, 27(5) and (6), June/July, pp. 603–26. Empirical evidence on the treatment of inflation.

Bierman, H. and Smidt, S. (1992) *The Capital Budgeting Decision*, 8th edn. New York: Macmillan.

Carsberg, B.V. and Hope, A. (1976) *Business Investment Decisions Under Inflation: Theory and Practice*. London: Institute of Chartered Accountants in England and Wales. A study of investment appraisal practices adopted by large British firms with particular reference to the treatment of inflation. Clear description of NPV theory, suitable for the beginner.

Coulthurst, N.J. (1986) 'Accounting for inflation in capital investment: state of the art and science', *Accounting and Business Research*, Winter, pp. 33–42. A clear account of the impact of inflation on project appraisal. Also considers empirical evidence on the adjustments made in practice. Good for the beginner.

Fama, E.F. (1981) 'Stock returns, real activity, inflation and money', *American Economic Review*, 71 (Sept.), pp. 545–64. On the complex relationship between returns on shares and inflation – high level economics.

Fisher, I. (1930) *The Theory of Interest*. New York: Macmillan. Early theory – interest rates and inflation.

Pike, R.H. (1983) 'The capital budgeting behaviour and corporate characteristics of capital-constrained firms', *Journal of Business Finance and Accounting*, 10(4), Winter, pp. 663–71. Examines real-world evidence on capital rationing and its effects – easy to read.

Samuels, J.M., Wilkes, F.M. and Brayshaw, R.E. (1996) *Management of Company Finance*, 6th edn. London: Chapman and Hall. More detailed consideration of linear and integer programming.

SELF-REVIEW QUESTIONS

1 Explain why hard and soft rationing occur.

2 If the general rate of inflation is 5 per cent and the market rate of interest is 9 per cent, what is the real interest rate?

3 Explain the alternative methods of dealing with inflation in project appraisal.

4 Why not simply rank projects on the basis of the highest NPV in conditions of capital rationing?

5 Distinguish between a money cash flow and a real cash flow.

6 How should tax be allowed for in project appraisal?

7 Why is capital rationing impossible in perfect capital markets?

8 What are a balancing charge and a balance allowance for capital items subject to a writing-down allowance?

9 Describe the two major effects inflation has on the evaluation of investments.

10 Name two great 'don'ts' in inflation adjustment for projects and explain the consequences of ignoring these.

11 What will be the effect of under-allowance for future inflation when using a money discount rate?

QUESTIONS AND PROBLEMS

1 The washer division of Plumber plc is permitted to spend £5m on investment projects at time zero. The cash flows for five proposed projects are:

	Points in time (yearly intervals)				
	0	*1*	*2*	*3*	*4*
Project	*£m*	*£m*	*£m*	*£m*	*£m*
A	−1.5	0.5	0.5	1.0	1.0
B	−2.0	0	0	0	4.0
C	−1.8	0	0	1.2	1.2
D	−3.0	1.2	1.2	1.2	1.2
E	−0.5	0.3	0.3	0.3	0.3

The cost of capital is 12 per cent, all projects are divisible and none may be repeated. The projects are not mutually exclusive.

a Which projects should be undertaken to maximise NPV in the presence of the capital constraint?

b If the division was able to undertake all positive NPV projects, what level of NPV could be achieved?

c If you now assume that these projects are indivisible, how would you allocate the available £5m?

2 The Telescope Company plc is considering five projects:

Project	*Initial outlay*	*Profitability index*
A	6,000	1.2
B	4,000	1.05
C	10,000	1.6
D	8,000	1.4
E	7,000	1.3

Projects C and D are mutually exclusive and the firm has £20,000 available for investment. All projects can only be undertaken once and are divisible. What is the maximum possible NPV?

3 The business insurance premiums of £20,000 for the next year have just been paid. What will these premiums be in three years' time, if the specific rate of inflation for insurance premiums is 8 per cent per annum?

If the money rate of return is 17 per cent and the general inflation rate is anticipated to average 9 per cent over three years, what is the present value of the insurance premiums payable at Time 3?

4* (*Examination level*) Wishbone plc is considering two mutually exclusive projects. Project X requires an immediate cash outflow of £2.5m and Project Y requires £2m. If there was no inflation then the cash flows for the three-year life of each of the projects would be:

Annual cash flows	*Project X*		*Project Y*	
	£	£	£	£
Inflow from sales		2,100,000		1,900,000
Cash outflows:				
Materials	800,000		200,000	
Labour	300,000		700,000	
Overheads	100,000		50,000	
		(1,200,000)		(950,000)
Net cash flow		900,000		950,000

These cash flows can be assumed to arise at the year ends of each of the three years.

Specific annual inflation rates have been estimated for each of the cash flow elements.

Sales	5%
Materials	4%
Labour	10%
Overheads	7%

The money cost of capital is 17 per cent per annum.

a Use the money cash flows and money cost of capital to calculate the NPV of the two projects and recommend the most appropriate course of action.

b Now assume that the general inflation rate is anticipated to be 8 per cent per annum. Calculate the real cash flows and the real cost of capital and use these to calculate the NPVs.

5 Hose plc is trying to make a decision on whether to make a commitment of £800,000 now to a project with a life of seven years. At present prices the project will return net cash flows of £150,000 per annum at the year ends. Prices are not expected to remain constant and general inflation is anticipated at 6 per cent per annum. The annual net cash inflows of this project are expected to rise in accordance with general inflation. The money rate of return is 13 per cent. Advise Hose on the viability of this project.

6 A machine costs £10,000 and has a five-year life. By how much can taxable profit be reduced through the writing-down allowance (WDA) in the third year, if the annual WDA is 25 per cent on a declining balance? If the tax rate is 30 per cent, what is the present value of the WDA in Year 4 to the machine's owners?

If the machine has a scrap value of £1,000 after five years, what will be the fifth year's adjustment to the WDA?

The required rate of return is 10 per cent.

7* Bedford Onions plc is examining the possibility of purchasing a machine for a new venture. The machine will cost £50,000, have a four-year life and a scrap value of £10,000. An additional investment of £15,000 in working capital will be needed at the outset. This is recoverable at the end of the project. The accountant's figures for the annual trading accounts are as follows:

	£
Sales	100,000
Labour	(20,000)
Materials	(10,000)
Direct overhead	(20,000)
Allocated overhead	(15,000)
Depreciation	(10,000)
Annual profit	25,000

Allocated overhead consists of central administrative costs which are incurred with or without this project. The machine will be eligible for a 25 per cent writing-down allowance (on a declining balance). Tax is payable at 30 per cent.

For a project of this risk class a minimum return of 14 per cent is considered acceptable. Assume no inflation or risk

Required

Calculate the net present value of this investment.

8* (*Examination level*) Clipper plc is considering five project proposals. They are summarised below:

Project	*Initial investment (£000)*	*Annual revenue (£000)*	*Annual fixed costs (£000)*	*Life of project (years)*
A	10	20	5	3
B	30	30	10	5
C	15	18	6	4
D	12	17	8	10
E	18	8	2	15

Variable costs are 40 per cent of annual revenue. Projects D and E are mutually exclusive. Each project can only be undertaken once and each is divisible.

Assume

- The cash flows are confined to within the lifetime of each project.
- The cost of capital is 10 per cent.
- No inflation.
- No risk.
- No tax.
- All cash flows occur on anniversary dates.

If the firm has a limit of £40,000 for investment in projects at Time 0, what is the optimal allocation of this sum among these projects, and what is the maximum net present value obtainable?

9[†] (*Examination level*)

a Oppton plc's managers are ambitious and wish to expand their range of activities. They have produced a report for the parent company's board of directors detailing five projects requiring large initial investments. After reading the report the main board directors said that they have a policy of permitting subsidiary managers to select investment projects without head office interference. However, they do set a limit on the amount spent in any one period. In the case of Oppton this limit is to be £110,000 at Time 0 for these projects, which if accepted will commence immediately. The five projects are not mutually exclusive (that is, taking on one does not exclude the possibility of taking on another), each one can only be undertaken once and they are all divisible.

The cash flow details are as follows:

	Point in time (yearly intervals)				
	0 (£000)	*1 (£000)*	*2 (£000)*	*3 (£000)*	*4 (£000)*
Project 1	–35	0	60	0	0
Project 2	–50	30	30	30	0
Project 3	–20	10	10	10	10
Project 4	–30	15	15	15	15
Project 5	–60	70	0	0	0

None of the projects lasts more than four years and cash flows are confined to within the four-year horizon.

Assume

- The cost of capital is 10 per cent.
- No inflation.
- No tax.
- All cash flows occur on anniversary dates.

What is the optimal allocation of the £110,000 and the resulting net present value?

b Distinguish between 'soft' and 'hard' capital rationing and explain why these forms of rationing occur.

10† Cartma plc's superb strategic planning group have identified five projects they judge to be shareholder wealth enhancing, and therefore feel that the firm should make these investment commitments.

The figures are:

Point in time (yearly intervals)	*0 £m*	*1 £m*	*2 £m*	*3 £m*	*4 £m*	*5 £m*	*NPV*
Project A							
Cash flow	−10	0	0	+20	0	0	
Discounted cash flows	−10	0	0	$20/(1.1)^3$	0	0	+5
Project B							
Cash flow	−15	5	5	5	5	5	
Discounted cash flow	−15	5 × Annuity factor for 5 years @ 10%					
	−15	+ 5 × 3.7908					+3.95
Project C							
Cash flow	−8	1	12	0	0	0	
Discounted cash flows	−8	1/1.1	$12/(1.1)^2$	0	0	0	+2.83
Project D							
Cash flow	−5	2	2	2	2	2	
Discounted cash flow	−5	2 × Annuity factor for 5 years @ 10%					
	−5	+ 2 × 3.7908					+2.58
Project E							
Cash flow	−4	0	0	3	3	3	
Discounted cash flow	−4	$((3 \times \text{Annuity factor for 3 years @ } 10\%)/(1.1))^2$					
	−4	0	0	$\dfrac{3 \times 2.4868}{(1.1)^2}$			+2.17

The strategic planning group are keen on getting approval for the release of £42m to invest in all these projects. However, Cartma is a subsidiary of PQT and the holding company board have placed limits on the amount of funds available in any one year for major capital projects for each of its subsidiaries. They were prompted to do this by the poor response of debt holders to a recent capital raising exercise due to the already high borrowing levels. Also they feel a need to counteract the excessive enthusiasm in subsidiary strategic planning groups which could lead to over-rapid expansion if all positive NPV projects are accepted, placing a strain on management talent. The limit that has been imposed on Cartma for the forthcoming year is £38m.

Assume

- No inflation or tax.
- The rate of return required on projects of this risk class is 10 per cent.
- All project cash flows are confined within the five-year period.
- All projects are divisible (a fraction of the project can be undertaken), and none can be undertaken more than once.

What is the maximum NPV available if projects are selected on the basis of NPV alone and the limit of £38m is adhered to?

Now calculate profitability indices (or benefit-cost ratios) for each project and calculate the maximum potential NPV.

ASSIGNMENTS

1 Investigate the capital rationing constraints placed on a firm you are familiar with. Are these primarily soft or hard forms of rationing? Are they justified? What are the economic costs of this rationing? What actions do you suggest to circumvent irrational constraints?

2 Write a report on how inflation and tax are allowed for in project appraisal within a firm you know well. To what extent are the rules advocated in this chapter obeyed?

CHAPTER NOTES

1 The use of these terms is often muddled and they may be used interchangeably in the literature and in practice, so you should ensure that it is clearly understood how the ratio used in a particular situation is calculated.

2 If we are dealing with after-tax cash flows the discount rate will be the after-tax discount rate.

3 Often, in practice, to calculate future cash flows the analyst, instead of allowing for specific inflation rates, will make the simplifying assumption that all prices will stay the same, at Time 0's prices.

Part III

RISK AND RETURN

6 Risk and project appraisal

7 Portfolio theory

8 The capital asset pricing model and multi-factor models

Chapter 6

RISK AND PROJECT APPRAISAL

CASE STUDY 6.1 Two risky ventures . . .

one that did not pay off . . .

Eurotunnel

In 1996 Eurotunnel, with £8.56bn of debts and interest of £2m per day, was forced into negotiations with its 225 banks to try to ensure its financial survival. Eurotunnel is unlikely to pay a dividend in the near future and shareholders have lost hundreds of millions of pounds. The risky plan, using £1bn of funds provided by equity shareholders and £5bn by lenders, to build the tunnel has turned out much worse than expected. The total cost has doubled, there was a delay in starting commercial operations and competing ferry companies have responded aggressively.

and one that did . . .

Camelot

Camelot bid for, and won, the right to create the UK's national lottery. They invested in a vast computer network linking 30,000 retail outlets and paid for three hundred man years to develop specialised software. Camelot also had to train 91,000 staff to operate the system, which can handle over 30,000 transactions a minute, and spend large amounts on marketing. The gamble seems to have paid off. In the first year of operation total sales of £5.2bn produced a pre-tax profit of £77.5m – they hit the £1m+ jackpot every week. The owners of Camelot – Cadbury Schweppes, De La Rue, GTech, ICL and Racal Electronics – have a political battle on their hands trying to persuade the public and authorities that they took a risk and things happened to turn out well. It could have been so different; they could have made a multimillion pound investment followed by public indifference and enormous losses.

Sources: Eurotunnel – based on *Investors Chronicle*, 19 April 1996; Camelot – based on *Financial Times*, 5 June 1996.

Exhibit 6.2 Frequency distribution of probability of supermarkets

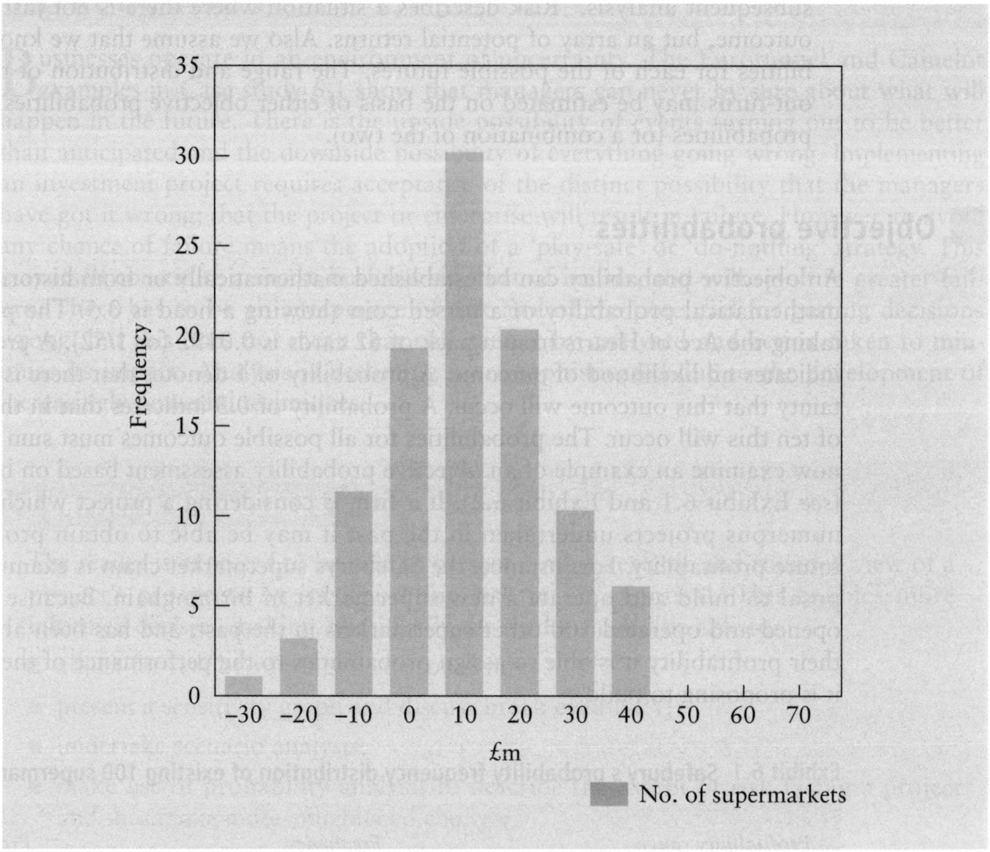

Subjective probabilities

In many project assessments there is a complete absence of any past record to help in the creation of the distribution of probabilities profile. For instance, the product may be completely new, or a foreign market is to be entered. In situations like these, subjective probabilities are likely to dominate, that is, personal judgement of the range of outcomes along with the likelihood of their occurrence. Managers, individually or collectively, must assign probability numbers to a range of outcomes.

It must be acknowledged that the probabilities assigned to particular eventualities are unlikely to be entirely accurate and thus the decision making that follows may be subject to some margin of error. But consider the alternative of merely stating the most likely outcomes. This can lead to less well-informed decisions and greater errors. For example, a firm might be considering two mutually exclusive projects, A and B. Both projects are expected to be shareholder wealth enhancing, based on the estimate of the most likely outcome. The most likely outcome for A is for it to be shareholder wealth enhancing, with a 95 per cent chance of occurrence. Similarly the most likely outcome for B is a shareholder wealth enhancing return, with a 55 per cent chance of occurrence (*see* Exhibit 6.3).

Exhibit 6.3 Probability outcome for two projects

Outcome	*Project A probability*	*Project B probability*
Shareholder wealth enhancing	0.95	0.55
Not shareholder wealth enhancing	0.05	0.45

By using probabilities, a more informed decision is made. The project appraiser has been forced to consider the degree of confidence in the estimate of expected viability. It is clear that Project A is unlikely to fail, whereas Project B has a fairly high likelihood of failure. We will examine in detail the use of probability distribution for considering risk later in the chapter. We now turn to more pragmatic, rule-of-thumb and intuitively easier methods for dealing with project risk.

ADJUSTING FOR RISK THROUGH THE DISCOUNT RATE

A traditional and still popular method of allowing for risk in project appraisal is the risk premium approach. The logic behind this is simple: investors require a greater reward for accepting a higher risk, thus the more risky the project the higher is the minimum acceptable rate of return. In this approach a number of percentage points (the premium)

Exhibit 6.4 Adjusting for risk – Sunflower plc

Level of risk	*Risk-free rate (%)*	*Risk premium (%)*	*Risk-adjusted rate (%)*
Low	9	+3	12
Medium	9	+6	15
High	9	+10	19

The project currently being considered has the following cash flows:

Point in time (yearly intervals)	0	1	2
Cash flow (£)	–100	55	70

If the project is judged to be low risk:

$$\text{NPV} = -100 + \frac{55}{1+0.12} + \frac{70}{(1+0.12)^2} = +£4.91$$

Accept.

If the project is judged to be medium risk:

$$\text{NPV} = -100 + \frac{55}{1+0.15} + \frac{70}{(1+0.15)^2} = +£0.76$$

Accept.

If the project is judged to be high risk:

$$\text{NPV} = -100 + \frac{55}{1+0.19} + \frac{70}{(1+0.19)^2} = -£4.35$$

Reject.

are added to the risk-free discount rate. (The risk-free rate of return is usually taken from the rate available on government bonds.) The risk-adjusted discount rate is then used to calculate net present value in the normal manner.

An example is provided by Sunflower plc, which adjusts for risk through the discount rate by adding various risk premiums to the risk-free rate depending on whether the proposed project is judged to be low, medium or high risk (*see* Exhibit 6.4).

This is an easy approach to understand and adopt, which explains its continued popularity.

Drawbacks of the risk-adjusted discount rate method

The risk-adjusted discount rate method relies on an accurate assessment of the riskiness of a project. Risk perception and judgement are bound to be, to some extent, subjective and susceptible to personal bias. There may also be a high degree of arbitrariness in the selection of risk premiums. In reality it is extremely difficult to allocate projects to risk classes and identify appropriate risk premiums as personal analysis and casual observation can easily dominate.

SENSITIVITY ANALYSIS

The net present values calculated in previous chapters gave a static picture of the likely future out-turn of an investment project. In many business situations it is desirable to generate a more complete and realistic impression of what may happen to NPV in conditions of uncertainty. Net present value calculations rely on the appraiser making assumptions about some crucial variables: for example the sale price of the product, the cost of labour and the amount of initial investment are all set at single values for input into the formula. It might be enlightening to examine the degree to which the viability of the project changes, as measured by NPV, as the assumed values of these key variables are altered. An interesting question to ask might be: if the sale price was raised by 10 per cent, by what percentage would NPV increase? In other words, it would be useful to know how sensitive NPV is to changes in component values. Sensitivity analysis is essentially a 'what-if' analysis, for example what if labour costs are 5 per cent lower? or what if the raw materials double in price? By carrying out a series of calculations it is possible to build up a picture of the nature of the risks facing the project and their impact on project profitability. Sensitivity analysis can identify the extent to which variables may change before a negative NPV is produced. A series of 'what-if' questions are examined in the example of Acmart plc.

Worked example 6.1 Acmart plc

Acmart plc has developed a new product line called Marts. The marketing department in conjunction with senior managers from other disciplines have estimated the likely demand for Marts at 1,000,000 per year, at a price of £1, for the four-year life of the project. (Marts are used in mobile telecommunications relay stations and the market is expected to cease to exist or be technologically superseded after four years.)

If we can assume perfect certainty about the future then the cash flows associated with Marts are as set out in Exhibit 6.5.

The finance department have estimated that the appropriate required rate of return on a project of this risk class is 15 per cent. They have also calculated the expected net present value.

Exhibit 6.5 Cash flows of Marts

Initial investment	£800,000	
Cash flow per unit		£
Sale price		1.00
Costs		
Labour	0.20	
Materials	0.40	
Relevant overhead	0.10	
		0.70
Cash flow per unit		0.30

Annual cash flow = 30p × 1,000,000 = £300,000.
Present value of annual cash flows = 300,000 × annuity factor for 4 years @ 15%

		£
	= 300,000 × 2.855	= 856,500
Less initial investment		–800,000
Net present value		+56,500

The finance department are aware that when the proposal is placed before the capital investment committee they will want to know how the project NPV changes if certain key assumptions are altered. As part of the report the finance team ask some 'what-if' questions and draw a sensitivity graph.

- What if the price achieved is only 95p for sales of 1m units (all other factors remaining constant)?

  Annual cash flow = 25p × 1m = £250,000.

	£
250,000 × 2.855	713,750
Less initial investment	800,000
Net present value	–86,250

- What if the price rose by 1 per cent?

  Annual cash flow = 31p × 1m = £310,000.

	£
310,000 × 2.855	885,050
Less initial investment	800,000
Net present value	+85,050

- What if the quantity demanded is 5 per cent more than anticipated?

  Annual cash flow = 30p × 1.05m = £315,000.

	£
315,000 × 2.855	899,325
Less initial investment	800,000
Net present value	+99,325

- What if the quantity demanded is 10 per cent less than expected?

  Annual cash flow = 30p × 900,000 = £270,000.

	£
270,000 × 2.855	770,850
Less initial investment	800,000
Net present value	–29,150

- What if the appropriate discount rate is 20 per cent higher than originally assumed (that is, it is 18 per cent rather than 15 per cent)?

  300,000 × annuity factor for 4 years @ 18%.

	£
300,000 × 2.6901	807,030
Less initial investment	800,000
	+7,030

- What if the discount rate is 10 per cent lower than assumed (that is, it becomes 13.5 per cent)?

  300,000 × annuity factor for 4 years @ 13.5%.

	£
300,000 × 2.9441	883,230
Less initial investment	800,000
	+83,230

These findings can be summarised more clearly in a sensitivity graph (*see* Exhibit 6.6).

An examination of the sensitivity graph in Exhibit 6.6 gives a clear indication of those variables to which NPV is most responsive. This sort of technique can then be extended to consider the key factors that might cause a project to become unviable. This allows the management team to concentrate their analysis, by examining in detail the probability of actual events occurring which would alter the most critical variables. They may also look for ways

Exhibit 6.6 Sensitivity graph for Marts

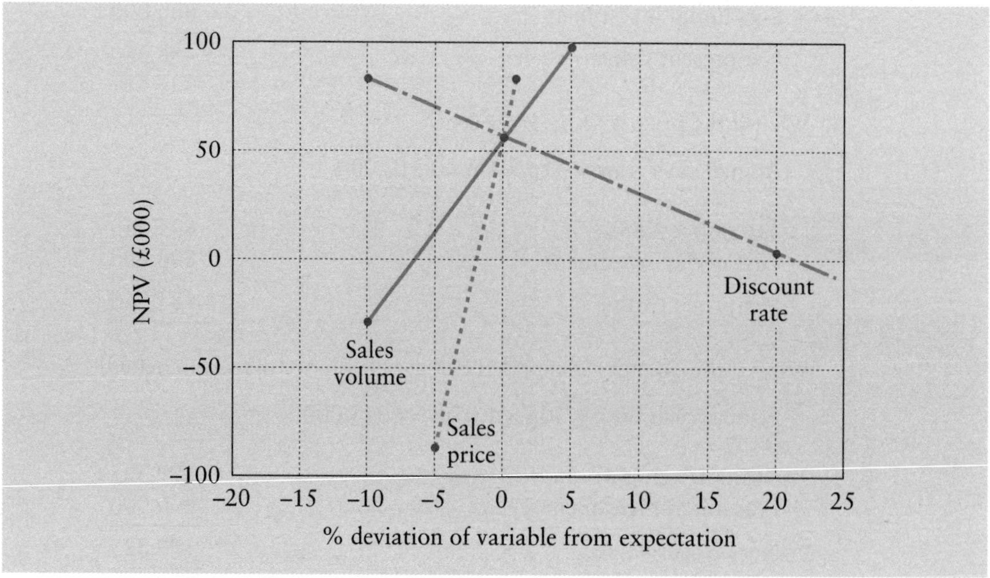

of controlling the factors to which NPV is most sensitive in any future project implementation. For example, if a small change in material costs has a large impact, the managers may investigate ways of fixing the price of material inputs.

The break-even NPV

The break-even point, where NPV is zero, is a key concern of management. If the NPV is below zero the project is rejected; if it is above zero it is accepted.

The finance team at Acmart now calculate the extent to which some of the variables can change before the decision to accept changes to a decision to reject. (We will not go through all the possible variables.)

Initial investment

A rise of £56,500 will leave NPV at zero. A percentage increase of:

$$\frac{£56,500}{£800,000} \times 100 = 7.06\%$$

Sales price

The cash flow per unit (after costs), c, can fall to 28 pence before break-even is reached:

$$800,000 = c \times 1,000,000 \times 2.855$$

$$c = \frac{800,000}{2.855 \times 1,000,000} = 0.2802$$

Thus the price can decline by only 2 per cent from the original price of £1. An alternative approach is to look up the point at which the sales price line crosses the NPV axis in the sensitivity graph.

Material cost

If the cash flow per unit can fall to 28 pence before break-even is reached 2 pence can be added to the price of materials before the project produces a negative net present value (assuming all other factors remain constant). In percentage terms the material cost can rise by 5 per cent $((2 \div 40) \times 100)$ before break-even is reached.

Discount rate

We need to calculate the annuity factor that will lead to the four annual inflows of £300,000 equalling the initial outflow of £800,000 after discounting.

$$300,000 \times \text{annuity factor} = 800,000$$

$$\text{Annuity factor (four-year annuity)} = \frac{800,000}{300,000} = 2.667$$

The interest rate corresponding to a four-year annuity factor of 2.667 is approximately 18.5 per cent. This is a percentage rise of 23.33 per cent.

$$\frac{18.5 - 15}{15} \times 100 = 23.33$$

This project is relatively insensitive to a change in the discount rate but highly responsive to a change in the sales price. This observation may lead the managers to request further work to improve the level of confidence in the sales projections.

Advantages of using sensitivity analysis

Sensitivity analysis has the following advantages:

- ***Information for decision making*** At the very least it allows the decision makers to be more informed about project sensitivities, to know the room they have for judgemental error and to decide whether they are prepared to accept the risks.
- ***To direct search*** It may lead to an indication of where further investigation might be worth while. The collection of data can be time consuming and expensive. If sensitivity analysis points to some variables being more crucial than others, then search time and money can be concentrated.
- ***To make contingency plans*** During the implementation phase of the investment process the original sensitivity analysis can be used to highlight those factors which have the greatest impact on NPV. Then these parameters can be monitored for deviation from projected values. The management team can draw on contingency plans if the key parameters differ significantly from the estimates. For example, a project may be highly sensitive to the price of a bought-in component. The management team after recognising this from the sensitivity analysis prepare contingency plans to: (a) buy the component from an alternative supplier, should the present one increase prices excessively, (b) produce the component in-house, or (c) modify the product so that a substitute component can be used. Which of the three is implemented, if any, will be decided as events unfold.

Drawbacks of sensitivity analysis

The absence of any formal assignment of probabilities to the variations of the parameters is a potential limitation of sensitivity analysis. For Marts the discount rate can change by 23.33 per cent before break-even NPV is reached, whereas the price can only change by 2 per cent. Thus, at first glance, you would conclude that NPV is more vulnerable to the price changes than to variability in the discount rate. However, if you are now told that the market price for Marts is controlled by government regulations and therefore there is a very low probability of the price changing, whereas the probability of the discount rate rising by more than 23.33 per cent is high, you might change your assessment of the nature of the relative risks. This is another example where following the strict mathematical formula is a poor substitute for judgement. At the decision-making stage the formal sensitivity analysis must be read in the light of subjective or objective probabilities of the parameter changing.

The second major criticism of sensitivity analysis is that each variable is changed in isolation while all other factors remain constant. In the real world it is perfectly conceivable that a number of factors will change simultaneously. For example, if inflation is higher then both anticipated selling prices and input prices are likely to be raised. The next section presents a partial solution to this problem.

SCENARIO ANALYSIS

With sensitivity analysis we change one variable at a time and look at the result. Managers may be especially concerned about situations where a number of factors change. They are often interested in establishing a worst-case and a best-case scenario. That is, what NPV

Exhibit 6.7 Acmart plc: Project proposal for the production of Marts – worst-case and best-case scenarios

Worst-case scenario

Sales	900,000 units
Price	90p
Initial investment	£850,000
Project life	3 years
Discount rate	17%
Labour costs	22p
Material costs	45p
Overhead	11p

Cash flow per unit		£
Sale price		0.90
Costs		
Labour	0.22	
Material	0.45	
Overhead	0.11	
		0.78
Cash flow per unit		0.12

Annual cash flow = 0.12 × 900,000 = £108,000

	£
Present value of cash flows 108,000 × 2.2096 =	238,637
Less initial investment	–850,000
Net present value	–611,363

Best-case scenario

Sales	1,200,000 units
Price	120p
Initial investment	£770,000
Project life	4 years
Discount rate	14%
Labour costs	19p
Material costs	38p
Overhead	9p

Cash flow per unit		£
Sale price		1.20
Costs		
Labour	0.19	
Material	0.38	
Overhead	0.09	
		0.66
Cash flow per unit		0.54

Annual cash flow = 0.54 × 1,200,000 = £648,000

	£
Present value of cash flows 648,000 × 2.9137 =	1,888,078
Less initial investment	–770,000
Net present value	1,118,078

will result if all the assumptions made initially turned out to be too optimistic? And what would be the result if, in the event, matters went extremely well on all fronts?

Exhibit 6.7 describes a worst-case and a best-case scenario for Marts.

Having carried out sensitivity, break-even NPV and scenario analysis the management team have a more complete picture of the project. They then need to apply the vital element of judgement to make a sound decision.

PROBABILITY ANALYSIS

A further technique to assist the evaluation of the risk associated with a project is to use probability analysis. If management have obtained, through a mixture of objective and subjective methods, the probabilities of various outcomes this will help them to decide whether to go ahead with a project or to abandon the idea. We will look at this sort of decision making for the firm Pentagon plc.

Pentagon plc is trying to decide between five mutually exclusive one-year projects (see Exhibit 6.8).

Exhibit 6.8 Pentagon plc: Use of probability analysis

	Return	*Probability of return occurring*
Project 1	16	1.0
Project 2	20	1.0
Project 3	–16	0.25
	36	0.50
	48	0.25
Project 4	–8	0.25
	16	0.50
	24	0.25
Project 5	–40	0.10
	0	0.60
	100	0.30

Proposals 1 and 2 represent perfectly certain outcomes. These might be investments in, say, government bonds for Project 1 and a bond issued by a highly respectable firm such as Unilever or ICI in the case of Project 2. For both projects the chance of the issues defaulting is so small as to be regarded as zero. These securities carry no risk. However, Project 2 has a higher return and is therefore the obvious preferred choice. (These bonds, with different returns for zero risk, only exist in an inefficient market environment; market efficiency is discussed in Chapter 14.)

In comparing Project 2 with Projects 3, 4 and 5 we have a problem: which of the possible outcomes should we compare with Project 2's outcome of 20? Take Project 3 as an example. If the outcome is –16 then clearly Project 2 is preferred. However, if the outcome is 36, or even better, 48, then Project 3 is preferred to Project 2.

Expected return

A tool that will be useful for helping Pentagon choose between these projects is the expected return.

The *expected return* is the mean or average outcome calculated by weighting each of the possible outcomes by the probability of occurrence and then summing the result (*see* Exhibit 6.9).

Algebraically:

$$\bar{x} = x_1 p_1 + x_2 p_2 + \dots x_n p_n$$

or

$$\bar{x} = \sum_{i=1}^{i=n} (x_i p_i)$$

where $\bar{x}$ = the expected return;
i = each of the possible outcomes (outcome 1 to outcome n)
p = probability of outcome i occurring
n = the number of possible outcomes

Exhibit 6.9 Pentagon plc: Expected returns

Pentagon plc	*Expected returns*	
	16 × 1	16
Project 2	20 × 1	20
Project 3	−16 × 0.25 = −4	
	36 × 0.50 = 18	
	48 × 0.25 = 12	
		26
Project 4	−8 × 0.25 = −2	
	16 × 0.50 = 8	
	24 × 0.25 = 6	
		12
Project 5	−40 × 0.1 = −4	
	0 × 0.6 = 0	
	100 × 0.3 = 30	
		26

The preparation of probability distributions gives the management team some impression of likely out-turns. The additional calculation of expected returns adds a further dimension to the informed vision of the decision maker. Looking at expected returns is more enlightening than simply examining the single most likely outcome which is significantly different from the expected return of 26. For Project 5 the most likely outcome of 0 is not very informative and does not take into account the range of potential outcomes.

It is important to appreciate what these statistics are telling you. The expected return represents the outcome expected if the project is undertaken many times. If Project 4 was undertaken 1,000 times then on average the return would be 12. If the project was undertaken only once, as is the case in most business situations, there would be no guarantee that the actual outcome would equal the expected outcome.

The projects with the highest expected returns turn out to be Projects 3 and 5, each with an expected return of 26. However, we cannot get any further in our decision making by using just the expected return formula. This is because the formula fails to take account of risk. Risk is concerned with the likelihood that the actual performance might diverge from what is expected. Note that risk in this context has both positive and negative possibilities of diverging from the mean, whereas in everyday speech 'risk' usually has only negative connotations. If we plot the possible outcomes for Projects 3 and 5 against their probabilities of occurrence we get an impression that the outcome of Project 5 is more uncertain than the outcome of Project 3 (*see* Exhibit 6.10).

Exhibit 6.10 Pentagon plc: Probability distribution for Projects 3 and 5

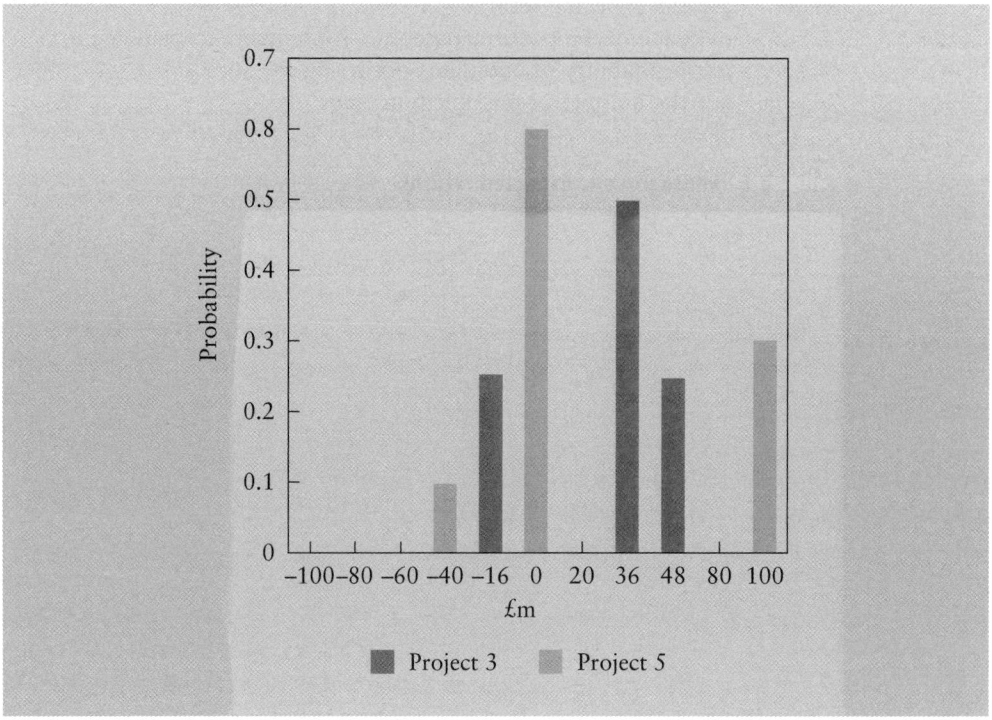

The range of possible outcomes is relatively narrow for Project 3 and therefore presents an impression of lower risk. This is only a general indication. We need a more precise measurement of the dispersion of possible outcomes. This is provided by the standard deviation.

Standard deviation

The standard deviation, σ, is a statistical measure of the dispersion around the expected value. The standard deviation is the square root of the variance, σ^2.

$$\text{Variance of } x = \sigma_x^2 = (x_1 - \bar{x})^2 p_1 + (x_2 - \bar{x})^2 p_2 + \dots (x_n - \bar{x})^2 p_n$$

$$\text{or} \quad \sigma_x^2 = \sum_{i=1}^{i=n} \{(x_i - \bar{x})^2 p_i\}$$

Standard deviation

$$\sigma_x = \sqrt{\sigma_x^2} \text{ or } \sqrt{\sum_{i=1}^{i=n} \{(x_i - \bar{x})^2 p_i\}}$$

To calculate the variance, first obtain the deviation of each potential outcome from the expected outcome $(x_i - \bar{x})$. Second, square the result $(x_i - \bar{x})^2$. Third, multiply by the probability of the outcome occurring $(x_i - \bar{x})^2 p_i$. Finally, add together the results of all these calculations. Note that the variances are very large numbers compared with the original potential outcome. This is because the variance measures in pounds squared or returns squared, etc. Thus, the next stage is to obtain the standard deviation σ, by taking the square root of the variance. This measures variability around the expected value in straightforward pound or return terms. The standard deviation provides a common yardstick to use when comparing the dispersions of possible outcomes for a number of projects. The variance and standard deviation calculations for Pentagon are shown in Exhibit 6.11.

If we now put together the two sets of measurements about the five projects we might be able to make a decision on which one should be selected, as shown in Exhibit 6.12.

Project 1 would not, presumably, be chosen by anyone. Also, Project 4 is obviously inferior to Project 2 because it has both a lower expected return and a higher standard deviation. That leaves us with Projects 2, 3 and 5. To choose between these we need to introduce a little utility theory in order to appreciate the significance of the standard deviation figures.

Risk and utility

Utility theory recognises that money in itself is unimportant to human beings. What is important is the well-being, satisfaction or utility to be derived from money. For most people a doubling of annual income will not double annual well-being. Money is used to buy goods and services. The first £8,000 of income will buy the most essential items – food, clothing, shelter, etc. Thus an individual going from an income of zero to one of £8,000 will experience a large increase in utility. If income is increased by a further £8,000 then utility will increase again, but the size of the increase will be less than for this first £8,000, because the goods and services bought with the second £8,000 provide less additional satisfaction. If the process of adding incremental amounts to annual income is continued then, when the individual has an income of, say, £150,000, the additional utility derived from a further £8,000 becomes very small. For most people the additional utility from consumption diminishes as consumption increases. This is the concept of *diminishing marginal utility*. Now consider the case of an individual who must choose between two alternative investments, A and B (*see* Exhibit 6.13).

Exhibit 6.11 Pentagon plc: Calculating the standard deviations for the five projects

	Outcome (return)	*Probability*	*Expected return*	*Deviation*	*Deviation squared*	*Deviation squared times probability*
Project	x_i	p_i	$\bar{x}$	$x_i - \bar{x}$	$(x_i - \bar{x})^2$	$(x_i - \bar{x})^2 p_i$
1	16	1.0	16	0	0	0
2	20	1.0	20	0	0	0
3	–16	0.25	26	–42	1,764	441
	36	0.5	26	10	100	50
	48	0.25	26	22	484	121
					Variance =	612
					Standard deviation =	24.7
4	–8	0.25	12	–20	400	100
	16	0.5	12	4	16	8
	24	0.25	12	12	144	36
					Variance =	144
					Standard deviation =	12
5	–40	0.1	26	–66	4,356	436
	0	0.6	26	–26	676	406
	100	0.3	26	74	5,476	1,643
					Variance =	2,485
					Standard deviation =	49.8

Exhibit 6.12 Pentagon plc: Expected return and standard deviation

	Expected return $\bar{x}$	*Standard deviation* σ_x
Project 1	16	0
Project 2	20	0
Project 3	26	24.7
Project 4	12	12
Project 5	26	49.8

Exhibit 6.13 Returns and utility

	Investment A		*Investment B*	
	Return	*Probability*	*Return*	*Probability*
Poor economic conditions	2,000	0.5	0	0.5
Good economic conditions	6,000	0.5	8,000	0.5
Expected return	4,000		4,000	

Both investments give an expected return of £4,000, but the outcomes of B are more widely dispersed. In other words, Investment B is more risky than Investment A. Suppose the individual has invested in A but is considering shifting all her money to B. As a result, in a poor year she will receive £2,000 less on Investment B than she would have received if she had stayed with A. In a good year Investment B will provide £2,000 more than if she had left her money in A. So the question is: is it worthwhile to shift from Investment A to Investment B? The answer hinges on the concept of diminishing marginal utility. While Investments A and B have the same expected returns they have different utilities. The extra utility associated with B in a good year is small compared with the loss of utility in a bad year when returns fall by an extra £2,000. Investment A is preferred because utility is higher for the first £2,000 of return than for the last £2,000 of return (increasing return from £6,000 to £8,000 by switching from A to B). Investors whose preferences are characterised by diminishing marginal utility are called risk averters.

A *risk averter* prefers a more certain return to an alternative with an equal but more risky expected outcome. The alternative to being a risk averter is to be a risk lover (risk seeker). These investors are highly optimistic and have a preference rather than an aversion for risk. For these people the marginal utility of each £ increases.

A *risk lover* prefers a more uncertain alternative to an alternative with an equal but less risky expected outcome. These are rare individuals and it is usually assumed that shareholders are risk averters. When faced with two investments, each with the same expected return, they will select the one with the lower standard deviation or variance. This brings us to the mean-variance rule.

Mean-variance rule

Project X will be preferred to Project Y if at least one of the following conditions apply:

1 The expected return of X is at least equal to the expected return of Y, and the variance is less than that of Y.

2 The expected return of X exceeds that of Y and the variance is equal to or less than that of Y.

So, returning to Pentagon plc, we can see from Exhibit 6.14 that Project 5 can be eliminated from any further consideration using the mean-variance rule because it has the same expected return as Project 3 but a wider dispersion of possible outcomes.

Projects 1, 4 and 5 are recognisably inferior, leaving a choice between Projects 2 and 3. From this point on there is no simple answer. The solution depends on the risk-return utility attitude of the decision maker. This is fundamentally a matter for subjective judgement and different investors will make different choices. To know which project will be chosen, one needs knowledge of the specific utility characteristics of the decision maker – the extent to which the disutility of greater risk is offset (in the mind of the individual) by the increased utility of greater reward. Some adventurous owners or managers will be willing to accept some risk if the expected return is high and so will opt for Project 3, whilst others will be more risk averse and will choose Project 2. (Chapter 7 introduces indifference curves which may be used to help decide between Projects 2 and 3). One of the factors in the equation is that variability (standard deviation) may not be a worry if the project forms a small part of a person's wealth or a small part of the firm's assets. Also variability may be diversified away to some extent and therefore may be of less concern – *see* Chapter 7.

Exhibit 6.14 Pentagon plc: Expected returns and standard deviations

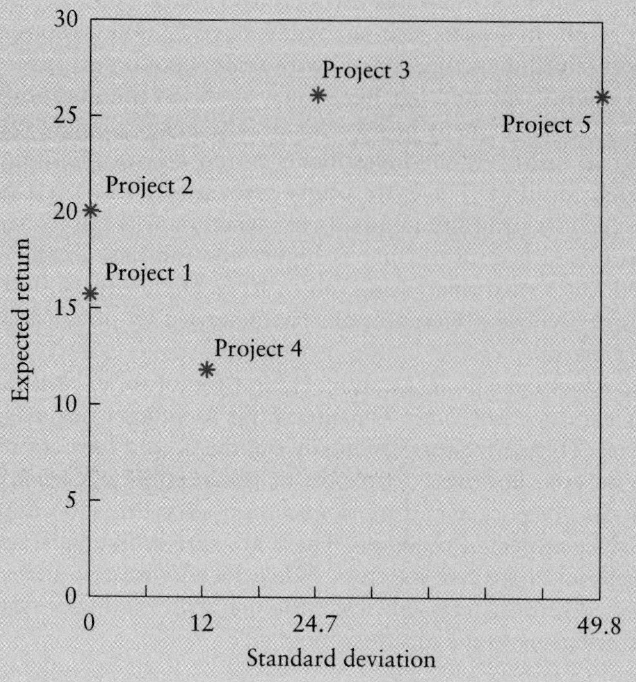

Expected net present values and standard deviation

In the example of Pentagon plc we have simply taken the potential returns of the projects as given. Now we will look at a project under circumstances of risk when you are not handed the *returns*, but have to calculate the NPV and the standard deviation of NPV using the cash flows associated with the investment. In addition, these cash flows will occur over a number of years and so the analysis becomes both more sophisticated and more challenging. First, the notation of the statistical formulae needs to be changed.

The expected net present value is:

$$\overline{NPV} = \sum_{i=1}^{i=n} (NPV_i p_i)$$

where $\overline{NPV}$ = expected net present value;
NPV_i = the NPV if outcome i occurs;
p_i = probability of outcome i occurring;
n = number of possible outcomes.

The standard deviation of the net present value is:

$$\sigma_{NPV} = \sqrt{\sum_{i=1}^{i=n} \{(NPV_i - \overline{NPV})^2 \, p_i\}}$$

This more realistic application of probability analysis will be illustrated through the example of Horizon plc.

Horizon plc buys old pubs and invests a great deal of money on refurbishment and marketing. It then sells the pubs at the end of two years in what the firm hopes is a transformed and thriving state. The management are considering buying one of the pubs close to a university campus. To purchase the freehold will cost, at Time 0, £500,000. The cost of refurbishment will be paid at the outset to the shop-fitting firm which Horizon always uses (in order to obtain a discount). Thus an additional £200,000 will be spent at Time 0.

Purchase price, t_0	£500,000
Refurbishment, t_0	£200,000
	£700,000

Experience has taught the management team of Horizon that pub retailing is a very unpredictable game. Customers are fickle and the slightest change in fashion or trend and the level of customers drops dramatically. Through a mixture of objective historical data analysis and subjective 'expert' judgement the managers have concluded that there is a 60 per cent probability that the pub will become a trendy place to be seen in and meet people. There is a 40 per cent chance that potential customers will not switch to this revamped hostelry within the first year.

The Year 1 cash flows are as follows:

	Probability	*Cash flow at end of Year 1*
Good customer response	0.6	100,000
Poor customer response	0.4	10,000

Note: For simplicity it is assumed that all cash flows arise at the year ends.

If the response of customers is good in the first year there are three possibilities for the second year.

1 The customer flow will increase further and the pub can be sold at the end of the second year for a large sum. The total of the net operating cash flows for the second year and the sale proceeds will be £2m. This eventuality has a probability of 0.1 or 10 per cent.

2 Customer levels will be the same as in the first year and at the end of the second year the total cash flows will be £1.6m. The probability of this is 0.7 or 70 per cent.

3 Many customers will abandon the pub. This may happen because of competitor action, for example other pubs in the area are relaunched, or perhaps the fashion changes. The result will be that the pub will have a net cash outflow on trading, and will have a much lower selling price. The result will be a cash inflow for the year of only £800,000. This has a 20 per cent chance of occurring.

If, however, the response in the first year is poor then one of two eventualities may occur in the second year:

1 Matters continue to deteriorate and sales fall further. At the end of the second year the cash flows from trading and the sale of the pub total only £700,000. This has a probability of 0.5, or a 50–50 chance.

2 In the second year sales rise, resulting in a total t_2 cash flow of £1.2m. Probability: 0.5.

The conditional probabilities for the second year are as follows:

If the first year elicits a *good response* then:

	Probability	*Cash flow at end of Year 2*
1 Sales increase in second year	0.1	£2m
or		
2 Sales are constant	0.7	£1.6m
or		
3 Sales decrease	0.2	£0.8m

If the first year elicits a *poor response* then:

	Probability	*Cash flow at end of Year 2*
1 Sales fall further	0.5	£0.7m
or		
2 Sales rise slightly	0.5	£1.2m

Note: All figures include net trading income plus sale of pub.

To be able to calculate the expected return and standard deviation for a project of this nature, we first need to establish the probability of each of the possible outcomes. This is shown in Exhibit 6.15. This shows that there are five possible outcomes. The probability that the initial expenditure is followed by a cash inflow of £100,000 after one year, and £2m after two years (that is, outcome *a*) is very low. This is as we might expect given that this is an extreme, positive outcome. The overall probability of this path being followed is the first year's probability (0.6) multiplied by the second year's probability (0.1) to give 0.06 or a 6 per cent chance of occurrence. The most likely outcome is for the first year to be successful (£100,000) followed by a continuation of the same sales level resulting in Year 2 cash flow of £1.6m (outcome *b*) with a probability of 0.42.

The second stage is to calculate the expected return making use of the probabilities calculated in Exhibit 6.15 – *see* Exhibit 6.16.

Now the standard deviation for this pub project can be calculated – *see* Exhibit 6.17.

Now that the management team have a calculated expected NPV of £407,000 and a standard deviation of £367,000 they are in a position to make a more informed decision. The probability analysis can be taken on to further stages; for example, an additional dimension that may affect their judgement of the worth of the project is the probability of certain extreme eventualities occurring, such as the project out-turn being so bad as to lead to the insolvency of the company. This technique is described later. First we broaden the application of probability analysis.

Exhibit 6.15 An event tree showing the probabilities of the possible returns for Horizon plc

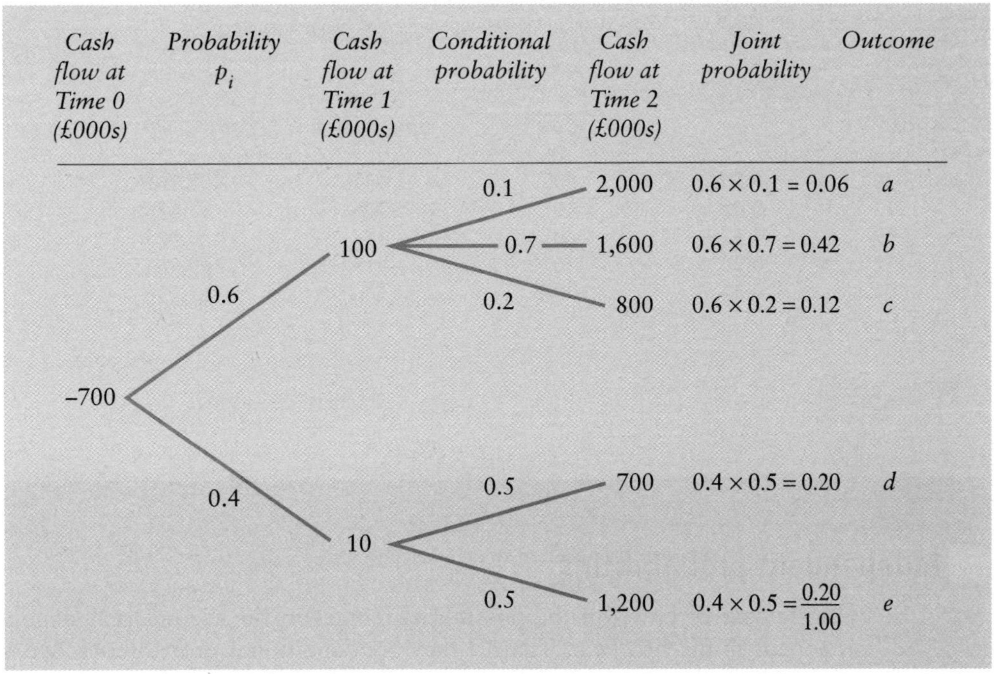

Exhibit 6.16 Expected net present value, Horizon plc

Outcome		*Net present values (£000s)*	*NPV × Probability*
a	$-700 + \frac{100}{1.1} + \frac{2,000}{(1.1)^2}$	= 1,044	1,044 × 0.06 = 63
b	$-700 + \frac{100}{1.1} + \frac{1,600}{(1.1)^2}$	= 713	713 × 0.42 = 300
c	$-700 + \frac{100}{1.1} + \frac{800}{(1.1)^2}$	= 52	52 × 0.12 = 6
d	$-700 + \frac{10}{1.1} + \frac{700}{(1.1)^2}$	= –112	–112 × 0.20 = –22
e	$-700 + \frac{10}{1.1} + \frac{1,200}{(1.1)^2}$	= 301	301 × 0.20 = 60
Expected net present value			407 or £407,000

Note: Assuming a 10% opportunity cost of capital

Exhibit 6.17 Standard deviation for Horizon plc

	Outcome £000s NPV_i	Probability p_i	Expected NPV $\overline{NPV}$	Deviation $NPV_i - \overline{NPV}$	Deviation squared $(NPV_i - \overline{NPV})^2$	Deviation squared times probability $(NPV_i - \overline{NPV})^2 p_i$
a	1,044	0.06	407	637	405,769	24,346
b	713	0.42	407	306	93,636	39,327
c	52	0.12	407	–355	126,025	15,123
d	–112	0.20	407	–519	269,361	53,872
e	301	0.20	407	–106	11,236	2,247
					Variance =	134,915
					Standard deviation = $\sqrt{134,915}$ =	367
					or	£367,000

Independent probabilities

In the case of Horizon the possible outcomes in the second year depend upon what happens in the first year. That is, they are conditional probabilities. We now turn to a case where the second year's outcomes are independent of what happens in the first year, and therefore there can be any combination of first and second year outcomes (*see* Exhibit 6.18).

Exhibit 6.18 Independent probabilities

Year 1		*Year 2*	
Cash flow (£000s)	*Probability*	*Cash flow (£000s)*	*Probability*
100	0.2	50	0.6
150	0.7	160	0.4
180	0.1		

The six possible overall outcomes are (£000s):

- 100 + 50
- 100 + 160
- 150 + 50
- 150 + 160
- 180 + 50
- 180 + 160

The initial cash outflow is £150,000. One method of calculating the expected NPV is to first calculate the expected return in each year (*see* Exhibit 6.19).

Exhibit 6.19 Expected return per year

Year 1

Cash flow (£000s)	*Probability*	*Cash flow × probability (£000s)*
100	0.2	20
150	0.7	105
180	0.1	18
		143

Year 2

Cash flow (£000s)	*Probability*	*Cash flow × probability (£000s)*
50	0.6	30
160	0.4	64
		94

Note: The discount rate is 10%.

The expected NPV is given by:

$$-150 + \frac{143}{1.1} + \frac{94}{(1.1)^2} = +57.69 \text{ or } £57{,}690$$

Expected NPV and standard deviation can be computed in one table as shown in Exhibit 6.20.

This project has an expected out-turn of £57,690 but a fairly high standard deviation of £49,300. This means that there is a distinct possibility of the out-turn being significantly under £57,690, at say £27,690, or £17,690, or even –£1,090. On the other hand, there are similar chances of obtaining £87,690, or £97,690, or even £116,470. To put more precise probability estimates on particular outcomes occurring we need to understand the Z statistic. It is to this that we now turn. The Z statistic will be explained by using it to tackle the problem of the probability of a project leading to insolvency.

Exhibit 6.20 Expected NPV and standard deviation

Cash flow Year 1	*(£000s) Year 2*	*Probability* p_i	*NPV*	*NPV* × p_i	*Expected* NPV	$(NPV_i - \overline{NPV})^2 p_i$
100	50	0.2 × 0.6 = 0.12	–17.77	–2.13	57.69	683.31
100	160	0.2 × 0.4 = 0.08	73.14	5.85	57.69	19.10
150	50	0.7 × 0.6 = 0.42	27.69	11.63	57.69	378.00
150	160	0.7 × 0.4 = 0.28	118.59	33.21	57.69	1,038.47
180	50	0.1 × 0.6 = 0.06	54.96	3.30	57.69	0.45
180	160	0.1 × 0.4 = 0.04	145.87	5.83	57.69	311.03
		1.00	Expected NPV	57.69		

Variance σ^2 = 2,430.36
Standard deviation σ = 49.3

THE RISK OF INSOLVENCY

On occasions a project may be so large relative to the size of the firm that if the worst-case scenario occurred the firm would be made bankrupt. It is sometimes of interest to managers to know the probability that a project will have a sufficiently poor outcome as to threaten the survival of the company. We can estimate this probability if we know the shape of the probability distribution. We usually assume that the probability distribution of a project's potential return is 'normal' and 'bell-shaped' (*see* Exhibit 6.21).

Exhibit 6.21 The normal curve

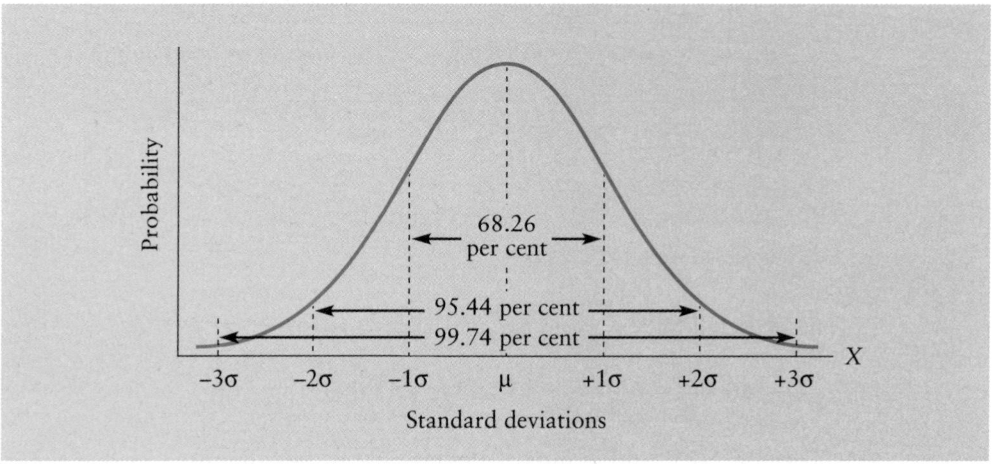

The distribution of possible outcomes is symmetrical about the expected return, μ. This means that the probability of an outcome, x, occurring between the expected return and one standard deviation away from the expected return is 34.13 per cent (one half of 68.26 per cent). That is, the chances of the outcome landing in the shaded area of Exhibit 6.22 is 34.13 per cent.

Exhibit 6.22 Probability of outcome being between expected return and one standard deviation from expected return

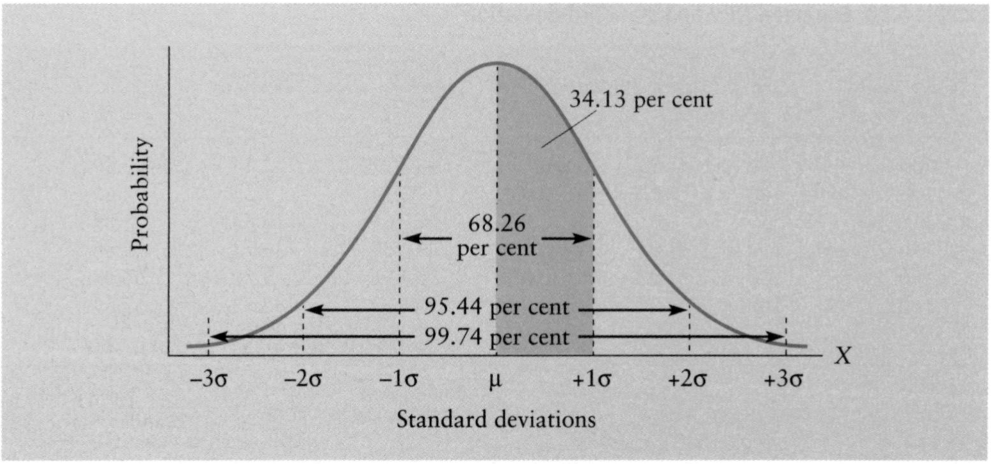

The probability of the outcome being between the expected value and two standard deviations from the expected value is 47.72 per cent (one-half of 95.44 per cent). To find the probability that the outcome will be between two particular values we first need to obtain the Z statistic. This simply shows the number of standard deviations from the mean to the value that interests you.

$$Z = \frac{X - \mu}{\sigma}$$

where Z is the number of standard deviations from the mean;
X is the outcome that you are concerned about;
μ is the mean of the possible outcomes;
σ is the standard deviation of the outcome distribution.

We also need to use the standard normal distribution table. This is in Appendix V at the end of the book but an extract is presented in Exhibit 6.23.

There is a very small probability of the outcome being more than three standard deviations from the mean or expected value. The probability of being more than three standard deviations greater than the mean is 0.13 per cent (50 per cent – 49.87 per cent).

The use of the standard normal distribution table will be illustrated by the example of Roulette plc.

Exhibit 6.23 The standard normal distribution

Value of the Z statistic	*Probability that X lies within Z standard deviations above (or below) the expected value (%)*
0.0	0.00
0.2	7.93
0.4	15.54
0.6	22.57
0.8	28.81
1.0	34.13
1.2	38.49
1.4	41.92
1.6	44.52
1.8	46.41
2.0	47.72
2.2	48.61
2.4	49.18
2.6	49.53
2.8	49.74
3.0	49.87

Worked example 6.2 Roulette plc

Roulette plc is considering undertaking a very large project and if the economy fails to grow there is a risk that the losses on this project will cause the liquidation of the firm. It can take a maximum loss of £5m and still keep the rest of the business afloat. But if the loss is more than £5m the firm will become bankrupt. The managers are keen to know the percentage probability that more than £5m will be lost.

The expected return has already been calculated at £8m but there is a wide variety of possible outcomes. If the economy booms the firm will make a fortune. If it is reasonably strong they will make a respectable return and if there is zero or negative growth large sums will be lost. These returns are judged to be normally distributed, that is, a bell-shaped distribution. The standard deviation is £6.5m.

To calculate the probability of insolvency we first calculate the Z statistic, when the X in which we are interested is at a value of –5.

$$Z = \frac{X - \mu}{\sigma}$$

$$Z = \frac{-5 - 8}{6.5} = -2$$

The value of –2 means that the distance between the expected outcome and the point of bankruptcy is two standard deviations. From the standard normal distribution table (Appendix V) we can see that the probability that the return will lie between the mean and two standard deviations below the mean is 47.72 per cent (*see* Exhibit 6.24).

Exhibit 6.24 Probability of outcome between μ and 2σ from μ

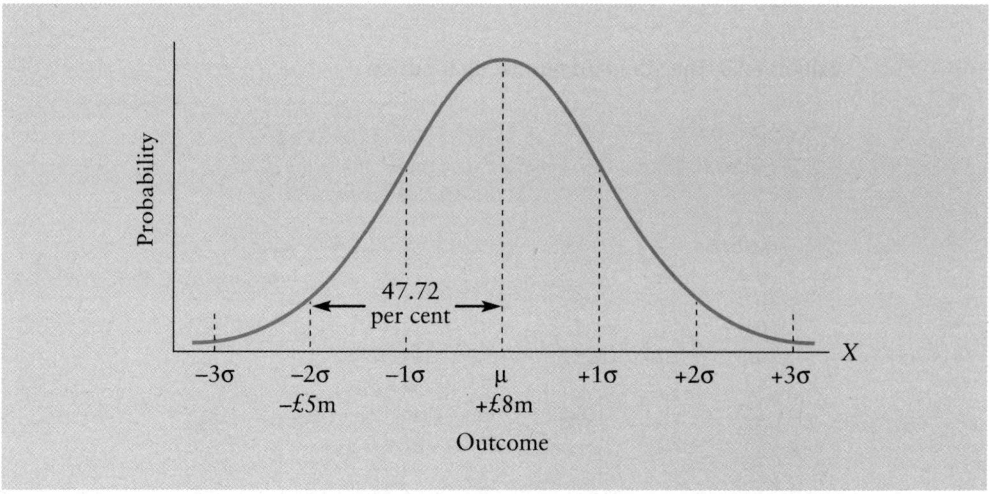

The probability distribution is symmetrical about the mean; therefore, the probability that the return will be above the mean is 50 per cent. Thus, the probability of the firm achieving a return greater than a loss of £5m is 97.72 per cent (47.72 per cent plus 50 per cent). To make the final decision on whether to proceed with this project we need to consider the owners' and the managers' attitude to this particular level of risk of insolvency. This is likely to vary from one company to another. In some situations shareholders and managers will have well-diversified interests and so are reasonably sanguine about this risk. Other decision makers will not even take a 2.28 per cent (100 per cent – 97.72 per cent) chance of insolvency.

Interpreting probability distributions using different discount rates

In calculating NPVs and their standard deviations, two alternative discount rates may be used:

- the risk-free discount rate;
- a risk-adjusted discount rate (that is, with a risk premium added).

Regardless of which of these is used to calculate the probability of certain eventualities through the standard normal distribution, careful interpretation of the results is needed. This is illustrated through the example of Brightlight plc.

Brightlight plc is considering a project with the cash flows shown in Exhibit 6.25.

Exhibit 6.25 Brightlight plc: cash flows

Initial outlay 100

Economic conditions	*Time (year)* 1	2	*Probability of economic event* p_i
Economic boom	130	130	0.15
Good growth	110	110	0.20
Growth	90	90	0.30
Poor growth	70	70	0.20
Recession	50	50	0.15

The risk-free discount rate is 6 per cent. Applying this the project produces an expected NPV of 65 and a standard deviation of 46.4 *see* Exhibit 6.26.

Exhibit 6.26 Applying the risk-free discount rate

Economic conditions	*NPV*	*NPV* $\times p_i$	$(NPV - \overline{NPV})^2 p_i$
Economic boom	138.342	20.7513	806.725
Good growth	101.674	20.3348	268.908
Growth	65.006	19.5018	0.000
Poor growth	28.338	5.6676	268.908
Recession	–8.330	–1.2495	806.725
		Expected NPV = 65.0060	Variance = 2,151.266

Standard deviation = $\sqrt{2,151.27}$ = 46.4

The management team are interested in discovering the probability of the project producing a negative NPV if the risk-free discount rate is used. Thus, in the Z statistic formula, X is set at a value of 0:

$$Z = \frac{X - \mu}{\sigma}$$

$$Z = \frac{0 - 65}{46.4} = -1.4$$

The probability of the outcome giving an NPV of between 0 and +65 is 41.92 per cent (1.4 standard deviations) according to Appendix V. Therefore, the probability of a negative NPV (the shaded area in Exhibit 6.27) is 8.08 per cent (50 per cent – 41.92 per cent). The interpretation of this result is that there is an 8.08 per cent probability of this project producing a return of *less than the risk-free rate*. The decision now has to be made as to whether this probability is acceptable, given that the rate set is merely the risk-free rate. If a number of mutually exclusive projects were being compared then to be consistent the risk-free rate must be used for all of them.

Exhibit 6.27 Probability distribution for Brightlight (risk-free discount rate)

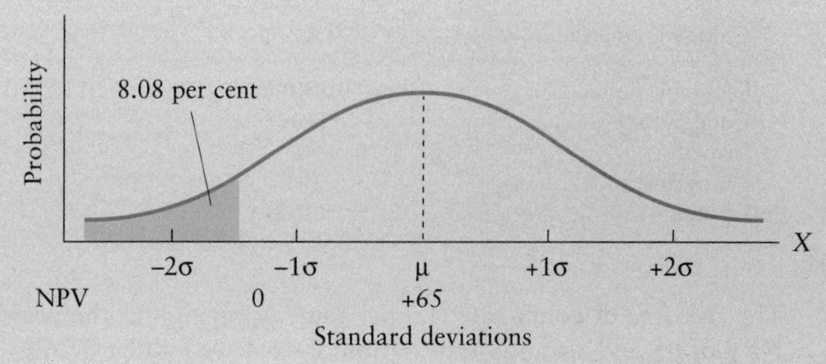

Brightlight also considers this project using a discount rate with a risk premium of 5 per cent added to the risk-free rate, that is, 6 + 5 = 11 per cent (*see* Exhibit 6.28).

Exhibit 6.28 Applying a discount rate including a risk premium of 5 per cent

Economic conditions	*NPV*	*NPV × p_i*	*$(NPV - \overline{NPV})^2 p_i$*
Boom	122.625	18.394	703.8375
Good growth	88.375	17.675	234.6125
Growth	54.125	16.237	0
Poor growth	19.875	3.975	234.6125
Recession	−14.375	−2.156	703.8375
		Expected NPV = 54.125	Variance = 1,876.90
			Standard deviation = 43.3

The probability of a negative NPV is:

$$Z = \frac{X - \mu}{\sigma}$$

$$Z = \frac{0 - 54.125}{43.30} = -1.25$$

A standard deviation of 1.25 gives a probability of 39.44 per cent of the outcome being between X and μ. Thus the probability of the project producing less than the required return of 11 per cent is 10.56 per cent (50 per cent – 39.44 per cent). Using the risk-adjusted discount rate tells the appraiser that this project is expected to produce a positive NPV of 54.125 when using a discount rate which takes account of risk. Also, if it is decided to implement this project, there is a 10.56 per cent probability of the decision being incorrect, in the sense that the NPV will turn out to be negative and therefore will not be shareholder wealth enhancing (*see* Exhibit 6.29).

Exhibit 6.29 Probability distribution for Brightlight risk-adjusted discount rate

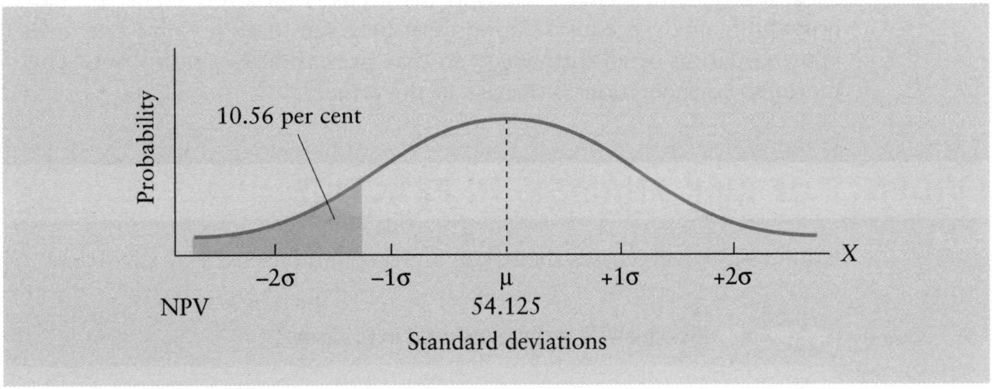

PROBLEMS OF USING PROBABILITY ANALYSIS

Too much faith can be placed in quantified subjective probabilities

When dealing with events occurring in the future, managers can usually only make informed guesses as to likely outcomes and their probabilities of occurrence. A danger lies in placing too much emphasis on analysis of these subjective estimates once they are converted to numerical form. It is all too easy to carry out detailed computations with accuracy to the nth degree, forgetting that the fundamental data usually have a small objective base. Again, mathematical purity is no substitute for thoughtful judgement.

The alternative to the assignment of probabilities, that of using only the most likely outcome estimate in the decision-making process, is both more restricted in vision and equally subjective. At least probability analysis forces the decision maker to explicitly recognise a range of outcomes and the basis on which they are estimated, and to express the degree of confidence in the estimates.

Too complicated for all managers to understand

Investment decision making and subsequent implementation often require the understanding and commitment of large numbers of individuals. Probability analysis can be a poor communicating tool if important employees do not understand what the numbers mean. Perhaps here there is a need for education combined with good presentation.

Projects may be viewed in isolation

The context of the firm may be an important variable, determining whether a single project is too risky to accept and therefore a project should never be viewed in isolation. Take a firm with a large base of stable low-risk activities. It may be willing to accept a high-risk project because the overall profits might be very large and even if the worst happened the firm will survive. On the other hand a firm that has a large number of risky projects may only accept further proposals if they are low risk.

The other aspect to bear in mind here is the extent to which a project increases or reduces the overall risk of the firm. This is based on the degree of negative covariance of project returns. (This is an aspect of portfolio theory which is discussed in the next chapter.)

Despite these drawbacks, probability analysis has an important advantage over scenario analysis. In scenario analysis the focus is on a few highly probable scenarios. In probability analysis consideration must be given to all possible outcomes (or at least an approximation of all outcomes) so that probabilities sum to one. This forces a more thorough consideration of the risk of the project.

EVIDENCE OF RISK ANALYSIS IN PRACTICE

Exhibit 6.30 summarises the risk analysis techniques used by UK firms.

Exhibit 6.30 Risk analysis techniques used in UK firms

	Small %	*Medium* %	*Large* %	*Total* %
Sensitivity/Scenario analysis	82	83	89	85
Reduced payback period	15	42	11	20
Risk-adjusted discount rate	42	71	50	52
Probability analysis	27	21	42	31
Beta analysis	3	0	5	3
Subjective assessment	44	33	55	46

Source: Arnold and Hatzopoulos (2000) sample of 96 firms: 34 small, 24 medium, 38 large. Survey date July 1997.

UK firms have increased the extent of risk analysis in project appraisal over the past twenty years (evident from surveys conducted by Pike (1988, 1996) and Ho and Pike (1991)). This trend has been encouraged by a greater awareness of the techniques and aided by the availability of computing software. Sensitivity and scenario analysis remain the most widely adopted approaches. Probability analysis is now used more widely than in the past but few smaller firms use it on a regular basis. Beta analysis, based on the capital-asset pricing model (discussed in Chapter 8) is rarely used. Simple, rule-of-thumb approaches have not been replaced by the more complex methods. Firms tend to be pragmatic and to use a multiplicity of techniques in a complementary fashion.

CASE STUDY 6.2

RJB Mining: risky coalfields

Background

RJB Mining, led by Richard Budge, was a small company only recently quoted on the London Stock Exchange, when in November 1994 it tried to raise over £1bn of funds to buy the English mining regions of British Coal. In the accounts to 1994, RJB Mining made pre-tax profits of £12m on a turnover of £75m and was capitalised on the stock exchange at less than £160m.

The sale of the 17 deep mines and 16 open cast sites was part of the UK government's privatisation programme and RJB was negotiating around a price of £914m, at least 50 per cent more than the nearest rival. If RJB's projections were correct and it could produce profits of over £200m per year, then £914m could be regarded as cheap. But it is a large 'if'. Richard Budge had a hard time trying to persuade City institutions that the project was viable. Together with advisers Barclays de Zoete Wedd, the company set about the task of trying to raise £425m in equity and £628m in debt to both finance the bid and provide working capital. In some parts of the financial world there was great scepticism concerning the projections put forward by RJB. The key features are these:

Financial projections

Year end Dec 31

(£m)	*95*	*96*	*97*	*98*	*99*	*Total*
Turnover	1,244	1,276	1,258	1,218	1,238	6,234
Costs	1,073	1,052	1,029	1,033	1,031	
Profit before interest and taxation	171	224	229	185	207	1,016
Pro-forma net interest	(55)	(36)	(18)	1	13	
Profit before taxation	116	188	211	186	220	
Operating cash flow*	255	278	292	269	261	1,355
Cumulative cash flow*	255	533	825	1,094	1,355	

*Before interest, dividents and taxation. NB. Projections exclude results for the existing RJB Group.

Key assumptions

	95	*96*	*97*	*98*	*99*
Volume sold (million tonnes)	35.3	35.7	34.7	34.1	33.8
Volume produced (million tonnes)	33.4	34.4	33.6	33.6	35.2
Ave selling price/GJ (1994 prices) (£)	1.43	1.40	1.38	1.32	1.32
Ave cost/tonne (£) (incl. overheads and inflation)	30.4	29.5	29.7	30.3	30.5

Inflation 3 per cent a year.

►

Market requirements for coal*

	Conservative case Mar 31 2000	*Favourable case Mar 31 2000*	*RJB projection Dec 31 1999*
ESI	27.1	43.0	
Industrial	6.4	8.5	
Domestic	2.0	3.0	
Total	**35.5**	**54.5**	**33.8**

* Million tonnes.

RJB was thought, by some analysts, to have overestimated the size of the post-1998 market by a large percentage and that even the 'conservative' estimates were at the high end of the likely outcome. Mr Charles Kernot, an analyst at Credit Lyonnais Laing, commented, 'He may be able to make £220m in 1998, but it looks tight.'

The bank lenders were being asked to provide £528m (the remaining £100m was to be derived from a corporate bond issue) on the expectation that RJB would have paid them back all their capital before 1998. The year 1998 is so important, because prior to that date the company would have firm contracts, inherited from British Coal, to sell 29m tonnes a year to the electricity generators at agreed prices. Thus, a total annual volume of around 35m tonnes for the first three years seemed credible. Raising the debt capital was likely to be less troublesome than the equity. Potential shareholders were concerned about the less predictable years after 1998. RJB were confident that volumes and prices would not fall dramatically, whereas others suggested that RJB would struggle to sell 25m tonnes a year and the price would fall to £1.15 a gigajoule or less, given the potential for intense competition.

Source for data: *Financial Times*, 18 November 1994. Reprinted with permission.

Note: RJB Mining changed its name to UK Coal in 2001.

Some risk analysis

For the purposes of analysing this case study we will make a number of bold simplifying assumptions in order to make the analysis manageable in the context of this textbook. The estimates that follow are based on one of many potential adjustments to the basic data. You may like to make your own assumptions and forecasts based on alternative perspectives. (The author is not privy to non-public data held only by RJB and therefore is unable to provide a true representation of the prospects for this project.)

The financial projections for turnover and operating cash flow are as set out in Exhibit 6.31.

Exhibit 6.31 Turnover and cash flow projections

Year £m	*1995*	*1996*	*1997*	*1998*	*1999*
Turnover	1,244	1,276	1,258	1,218	1,238
Operating cash flow	255	278	292	269	261

We will assume that the annual cash flows for the year 2000 and beyond are the same as for 1999.

Imagine you are an analyst advising a pension fund on whether to provide equity and debt finance for this enterprise and you believe the following outcomes are possible:

1 Turnover is the same as RJB's projections – probability 0.25.
2 Turnover is 10 per cent greater than RJB's projections – probability 0.10.
3 Turnover is 25 per cent less than the projections – probability 0.65.

To simplify the calculations, assume costs, interest and tax are unaffected by turnover changes, thus any lost or gained turnover feeds directly into cash flows. (This is an unforgivable over-simplification of the real world, but the calculation would be too complicated for the reader to focus on the risk analysis if more realistic assumptions were made.) Also, the 'operating cash flows' as calculated by RJB are truly reflective of the theoretically correct cash flows we would arrive at using our textbook knowledge.

The risk-free cost of capital is 9 per cent, time 0 is 1.1.95 and the cash flows occur at year ends.

Expected net present value assuming £914m is the initial outflow

If turnover is as expected:

$$\text{NPV} = -914 + \frac{255}{1.09} + \frac{278}{(1.09)^2} + \frac{292}{(1.09)^3} + \frac{269}{(1.09)^4} + \frac{261}{(1.09)^5} + \frac{261}{0.09} \div (1.09)^5 = £2{,}024\text{m}$$

If turnover is 10 per cent greater than projections

Time (years)	*0*	*1*	*2*	*3*	*4*	*5*	*6→∞*
RJB's projected cash flows (£m)	–914	255	278	292	269	261	261
plus 10% of projected turnover		124.4	127.6	125.8	121.8	123.8	123.8
	–914	379.4	405.6	417.8	390.8	384.8	384.8

Discounted cash flows:

$$\text{NPV} = -914 + \frac{379.4}{1.09} + \frac{405.6}{(1.09)^2} + \frac{417.8}{(1.09)^3} + \frac{390.8}{(1.09)^4} + \frac{384.8}{(1.09)^5} + \frac{384.8}{0.09} \div (1.09)^5 = £3{,}403.84\text{m}$$

If turnover is 25 per cent less than projections

Time (years)	*0*	*1*	*2*	*3*	*4*	*5*	*6→∞*
RJB's projected cash flows (£m)	–914	255	278	292	269	261	261
less 25% of projected turnover		311	319	314.5	304.5	309.5	309.5
	–914	–56	–41	–22.5	–35.5	–48.5	–48.5

Discounted cash flows:

$$NPV = -914 - \frac{56}{1.09} - \frac{41}{(1.09)^2} - \frac{22.5}{(1.09)^3} - \frac{35.5}{(1.09)^4} - \frac{48.5}{(1.09)^5} - \frac{48.5}{0.09} \div (1.09)^5 = -£1{,}424.17\text{m}$$

Expected NPV

$$(2{,}024.42 \times 0.25) + (3{,}403.84 \times 0.1) + (-1{,}424.17 \times 0.65) = -£79.22\text{m}$$

Standard deviation of NPV

NPV	*Probability, p_i*	*Expected NPV ($\overline{NPV}$)*	*$(NPV - \overline{NPV})^2 p_i$*
2024.42	0.25	–79.22	1,106,304
3403.84	0.1	–79.22	1,213,157
–1424.17	0.65	–79.22	1,175,814
		Variance =	3,495,275
		Standard deviation =	1,869.56

If we assume that the distribution of returns is normal and bell-shaped, we can answer some further questions.

What is the probability of the rate of return being less than the required rate of return (9 per cent)?

This question relates to the probability of a negative NPV (*see* Exhibit 6.32).

Exhibit 6.32 Probability of negative NPV

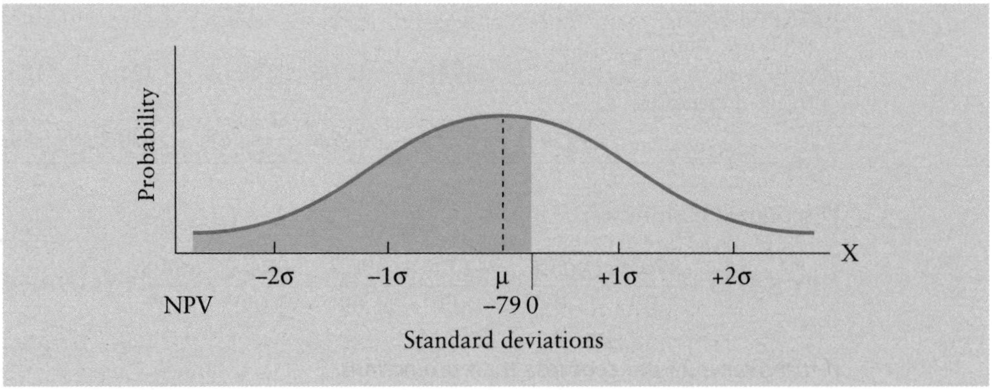

$$Z = \frac{X - \mu}{\sigma}$$

$$Z = \frac{0 - (-79.22)}{1{,}869.56} = 0.0424$$

The probability of an outcome between –79.22 and 0 = 1.6%.
Therefore the probability of an outcome less than 0 = 51.6%.

If insolvency occurs at an NPV of negative £200m, what is the probability of insolvency?

$$Z = \frac{X - \mu}{\sigma}$$

$$Z = \frac{-200 - (-79.22)}{1,869.56} = -0.065$$

The probability of an outcome between –200 and –79.22 = 2.6%.
The probability of insolvency = 50% – 2.6% = 47.4%.

If the champagne corks can start to fly at an NPV of £1,000m, what is the probability of this being achieved?

$$Z = \frac{X - \mu}{\sigma}$$

$$Z = \frac{1,000 - (-79.22)}{1,869.56} = 0.577$$

The probability of an outcome between –79.22 and 1,000 = 21.8%.
The probability of an outcome greater than £1,000m = 50% – 21.8% = 28.8%.

The data can be used to practise risk profiling by employing the other techniques shown in this chapter. Perhaps the reader would like to make a few assumptions and practise using the risk-adjusted discount rate method, sensitivity and scenario analysis.

Comment

In this analysis we have taken a much more pessimistic view of the prospects than did RJB. Perhaps it is far too pessimistic to assume that there is a 65 per cent chance that turnover will be only 75 per cent of the level forecast by the professionals at RJB and BZW. Having completed the statistical analysis we have a better picture of the nature of this project and can make far more informed choices. However, we cannot second-guess the risk appetite of the pension fund managers, given their particular context.

At the end of the negotiating period, RJB Mining paid £99m less than was first mooted, at £815m, and it raised a total of £894m mainly from the major institutions, although a few small shareholders did contribute. By mid-1995 the company had performed so well that it reduced its bank debt to around £150m. By mid-1996 RJB was regarded as having such a strong balance sheet, with gearing at 49 per cent, that the group felt confident enough to announce a £100m share buy-back programme. In addition, the company started an overseas expansion, spending £71.5m to acquire 43 per cent of CIM Resources of Australia. The share price almost doubled during the 18 months following the English coalfields purchase. However it collapsed in late 1997 as reports on the negotiations over the electricity generator contracts starting in 1998 were pessimistic.

Events after 1998

Life got a lot tougher for RJB. As can be seen from Exhibit 6.33 turnover was much less than projected at the time of the fund raising: for example, for 1999 it was expected to be £1,238m; it was actually £688m. With the deregulation of the electricity generating industry there was a rush to produce electricity using gas and the demand for coal slumped. The electricity producers were in a strong bargaining position when negotiating

Exhibit 6.33 RJB

		1997	*1998*	*1999*	*2000*
Turnover	£m	1,125	823	688	705
Profit before interest and tax (and exceptional items)	£m	190	60	28	(31)
Costs	£m	942	764	675	736
Net interest	£m	19	20	17	8
Operating cash flow	£m	281	96	85	82
Volume sold (million tonnes)		31.2	25.9	22.5	22.2
Average selling price £/GJ (current price)	£	1.60	1.40	1.25	1.26
Average income/tonne	£	35	31	29.3	n/a
Average cost/tonne	£	30	29	28.8	n/a
Market requirements for coal		54	54	45	n/a

Sources: Financial Times (numerous articles), RJB annual reports and accounts, www.rjb.co.uk

future coal prices, especially as the price on the international market for coal was depressed. RJB sells 85 per cent of its coal to the electricity producers and so was unable to resist the pressure to lower prices.

In the 1998 report Chief executive, Richard Budge wrote: 'Although we have been successful in agreeing additional sales contracts, they are for significantly reduced volumes and at lower prices than we previously received . . . RJB Mining's industrial and domestic sales declined by 24% with an overall market decline of 15% and increased penetration of imported coal due to a combination of low world coal prices and the strength of sterling.'

Matters worsened in the following year. In the 1999 report John Robinson, Chairman, wrote: 'Current generator contracts are for volumes and prices significantly below those of the previous year . . . coal prices [were at] . . . a 25-year low'. Richard Budge wrote: 'total thermal coal use in the UK fell by 17% compared with 1998, to 45 million tonnes . . . a result of new gas-fired generation facilities'.

Low volume and low prices resulted in operating cash flow being much lower than forecast. One saving grace was the lower operating costs than originally estimated allowing positive operating cash flows.

The share price, which had peaked at 625p in 1996, slumped to 25p in 2000. The original £400m or more of shareholders' money had been reduced to about £30m. An American company attempted to buy RJB – mainly because it held property assets worth more than the value of its shares. In March 2001 Richard Budge left the company, just as coal prices started to lift and the firm benefited from an injection of grant money from the UK government totalling £75m (designed to keep coal mines open).

CONCLUDING COMMENTS

This chapter, and the previous one, have dealt with some of the more sophisticated aspects of project analysis. They have, hopefully, encouraged the reader to consider a wider range of factors when embarking on investment appraisal. Taking into account more real-world influences such as inflation, rationing, tax and risk will enable the appraiser and the decision maker to obtain a clearer picture of the nature of the proposal being discussed. Greater realism and more information clears away some of the fog which envelops many capital investment decision-making processes.

However, this chapter has focused primarily on the technical/mathematical aspects of the appraisal stage of the investment process sequence. While these aspects should not be belittled, as we ought to improve the analysis wherever we can, it should be noted that a successful programme of investment usually rests far more on quality management of other stages in the process. Issues of human communication, enthusiasm and commitment are as vital to investment returns as, for example, assessing risk correctly. Also note that the level of mathematical complexity and precision could be taken up a few notches from this point. Readers interested in greater depth are advised to read specialised books and periodicals in this area. But beware of the danger of precision at the expense of perspective – always try to see the wood rather than the trees.

KEY POINTS AND CONCEPTS

- **Risk** – more than one possible outcome.
- **Objective probability** – likelihood of outcomes established mathematically or from historic data.
- **Subjective probability** – personal judgement of the likely range of outcomes along with the likelihood of their occurrence.
- **Risk can be allowed for by raising or lowering the discount rate:**

  Advantages: easy to adopt and understand;
  some theoretical support.

  Drawbacks: susceptible to subjectivity in risk premium and risk class allocation.

- **Sensitivity analysis** views a project's NPV under alternative assumed values of variables, changed one at a time. It permits a broader picture to be presented, enables search resources to be more efficiently directed and allows contingency plans to be made.

  Drawbacks of sensitivity analysis:
  – does not assign probabilities and these may need to be added for a fuller picture;
  – each variable is changed in isolation.

- **Scenario analysis** permits a number of factors to be changed simultaneously. Allows best- and worst-case scenarios.
- **Probability analysis** allows for more precision in judging project viability.
- **Expected return** – the mean or average outcome is calculated by weighting each of the possible outcomes by the probability of occurrence and then summing the result:

$$\bar{x} = \sum_{i=1}^{i=n} (x_i \, p_i)$$

- **Standard deviation** – a measure of dispersion around the expected value:

$$\sigma_x = \sqrt{\sigma_x^2} \text{ or } \sqrt{\sum_{i=1}^{i=n} \{(x_i - \bar{x})^2 \, p_i\}}$$

- It is assumed that most people are **risk averters** who demonstrate **diminishing marginal utility**, preferring less risk to more risk.

- **Mean-variance rule:**

  Project X will be preferred to Project Y if at least one of the following conditions apply:

  1 The expected return of X is at least equal to the expected return of Y, and the variance is less than that of Y.

  2 The expected return of X exceeds that of Y and the variance is equal to or less than that of Y.

- If a normal, bell-shaped distribution of possible outcomes can be assumed, the probabilities of various events, for example insolvency, can be calculated using the **Z statistic.**

$$Z = \frac{X - \mu}{\sigma}$$

- **Careful interpretation** is needed when using a risk-free discount rather than a risk-adjusted discount rate for probability analysis.

- **Problems with probability analysis:**
  - undue faith can be placed in quantified results;
  - can be too complicated for general understanding and communication;
  - projects may be viewed in isolation rather than as part of the firm's mixture of projects.

- Sensitivity analysis and scenario analysis are the most popular methods of allowing for project risk.

REFERENCES AND FURTHER READING

Arnold, G.C. and Hartzopoulos, P.D. (2000) 'The theory-practice gap in capital budgeting: evidence from the United Kingdom', *Journal of Business Finance and Accounting*, 27(5) and (6), June/July, pp. 603–26. Discussion on the use of alternative risk adjustment methods is provided.

Hertz, D.B. (1964) 'Risk analysis in capital investment', *Harvard Business Review*, January/February, pp. 95–106. Excellent discussion of risk and the use of probability analysis.

Hertz, D.B and Thomas, H. (1984) *Practical Risk Analysis: An Approach through Case Histories*. Chichester: Wiley. Contains some interesting case studies of companies applying the principles and techniques discussed in this chapter.

Hillier, F.S. (1963) 'The derivation of probabilistic information for the evaluation of risky investments', *Management Science*, April, pp. 443–57. The use of standard deviation in project appraisal.

Ho, S. and Pike, R.H. (1991) 'Risk analysis in capital budgeting contexts: simple or sophisticated', *Accounting and Business Research*, Summer, pp. 227–38. Excellent survey of risk-handling techniques adopted in 146 large companies.

Magee, J.F. (1964a) 'Decision trees for decision making', *Harvard Business Review*, July/August, pp. 126–38. The use of decision trees is explained in clear terms.

Magee, J.F. (1964b) 'How to use decision trees in capital investment', *Harvard Business Review*, September/October, pp. 79–96. Decision trees applied to project appraisal.

Markowitz, H. (1959) *Portfolio Selection*. New York: Wiley. Utility foundations of mean-variance analysis.

Pike, R.H. (1988) 'An empirical study of the adoption of sophisticated capital budgeting practices and decision-making effectiveness', *Accounting and Business Research*, 18(72), pp. 341–51. Interesting evidence on the practical use of risk analysis techniques.

Pike, R.H. (1996) 'A longitudinal survey of capital budgeting practices', *Journal of Business Finance and Accounting*, 23(1), January. Clearly described evidence on the capital investment appraisal practices of major UK companies.

Swalm, R.O. (1966) 'Utility theory – insights into risk taking', *Harvard Business Review*, November/December, pp. 123–36. An accessible account of utility theory.

SELF-REVIEW QUESTIONS

1 Explain, with reference to probability and sensitivity analysis, why the examination of the most likely outcome of an investment in isolation can both be limiting and give a false impression.

2 What do you understand by the following?

a Risk-lover;

b Diminishing marginal utility;

c Standard deviation.

3 Discuss the consequences of the quantification of personal judgements about future eventualities. Are we right to undertake precise analysis on this sort of basis?

4 Explain the attraction of using more than one method to examine risk in project appraisal.

5 Why has the development of powerful computers helped the more widespread adoption of scenario analysis?

6 Suggest reasons why probability analysis is used so infrequently by major international corporations.

7 'The flatter the line on the sensitivity graph, the less attention we have to pay to that variable.' Is the executive who made this statement correct in all cases?

8 If one project has a higher standard deviation and a higher expected return than another, can we use the mean-variance rule?

9 What does it mean if a project has a probability of a negative NPV of 20 per cent when (a) the risk-free discount rate is used, (b) the risk-adjusted discount rate is used?

10 What is the probability of an outcome being within 0.5 of a standard deviation from the expected outcome?

QUESTIONS AND PROBLEMS

1 Calculate the NPV of the following project with a discount rate of 9 per cent.

Point in time (yearly intervals)	*0*	*1*	*2*	*3*	*4*
Cash flow (£000s)	–800	300	250	400	500

Now examine the impact on NPV of raising the discount rate by the following risk premiums:

a 3 percentage points;

b 6 percentage points.

2* (*Examination level*) Cashion International are considering a project that is susceptible to risk. An initial investment of £90,000 will be followed by three years with the following 'most likely' cash flows (there is no inflation or tax):

	£	£
Annual sales (volume of 100,000 units multiplied by estimated sales price of £2)		200,000
Annual costs		
Labour	100,000	
Materials	40,000	
Other	10,000	
	150,000	(150,000)
		50,000

The initial investment consists of £70,000 in machines, which have a zero scrap value at the end of the three-year life of the project and £20,000 in additional working capital which is recoverable at the end. The discount rate is 10 per cent.

Required

a Draw a sensitivity graph showing the sensitivity of NPV to changes in the following:
- sales price;
- labour costs;
- material costs;
- discount rate.

b For the four variables considered in (a) state the break-even point and the percentage deviation from 'most likely' levels before break-even NPV is reached (assuming all other variables remain constant).

3* Use the data in question 2 to calculate the NPV in two alternative scenarios:

Worst-case scenario

Sales volume	90,000
Sales price	£1.90
Labour costs	£110,000
Material costs	£44,000
Other costs	£13,000
Project life	3 years
Discount rate	13%
Initial investment	£90,000

Best-case scenario

Sales volume	110,000
Sales price	£2.15
Labour costs	£95,000
Material costs	£39,000
Other costs	£9,000
Project life	3 years
Discount rate	10%
Initial investment	£90,000

4 (*Examination level*) A company is trying to decide whether to make a £400,000 investment in a new product area. The project will last 10 years and the £400,000 of machinery will have a zero scrap value. Other best estimate forecasts are:

- sales volume of 22,000 units per year;
- sales price £21 per unit;
- variable direct costs £16 per unit.

There are no other costs and inflation and tax are not relevant.

a The senior management team have asked you to calculate the internal rate of return (IRR) of this project based on these estimates.

b To gain a broader picture they also want you to recalculate IRR on the assumption that each of the following variables changes adversely by 5 per cent in turn:

- sales volume;
- sales price;
- variable direct costs.

c Explain to the management team how this analysis can help to direct attention and further work to improve the likelihood of a successful project implementation.

5 Project W may yield a return of £2m with a probability of 0.3, or a return of £4m with a probability of 0.7. Project X may earn a negative return of £2m with a probability of 0.3 or a positive return of £8m with a probability of 0.7. Project Y yields a return of £2m which is certain. Compare the mean return and risk of each project.

6 The returns from a project are normally distributed with a mean of £220,000 and a standard deviation of £160,000. If the project loses more than £80,000 the company will be made insolvent. What is the probability of insolvency?

7† (*Examination level*) Toughnut plc is considering a two-year project that has the following probability distribution of returns:

Year 1		*Year 2*	
Return	*Probability*	*Return*	*Probability*
8,000	0.1	4,000	0.3
10,000	0.6	8,000	0.7
12,000	0.3		

The events in each year are independent of other years (that is, there are no conditional probabilities). An outlay of £15,000 is payable at Time 0 and the other cash flows are receivable at the year ends. The risk-adjusted discount rate is 11 per cent.

Calculate:

a The expected NPV.

b The standard deviation of NPV.

c The probability of the NPV being less than zero assuming a normal distribution of return – (bell-shaped and symmetrical about the mean).

d Interpret the figure calculated in (c).

8 A project with an initial outlay of £1m has a 0.2 probability of producing a return of £800,000 in Year 1 and a 0.8 probability of delivering a return of £500,000 in Year 1. If the £800,000 result occurs then the second year could return either £700,000 (probability of 0.5) or £300,000 (probability of 0.5). If the £500,000 result for Year 1 occurs then either £600,000 (probability 0.7) or £400,000 (probability 0.3) could be received in the second year. All cash flows occur on anniversary dates. The discount rate is 12 per cent.
Calculate the expected return and standard deviation.

9† A project requires an immediate outflow of cash of £400,000 in return for the following probable cash flows:

State of economy	*Probability*	*End of Year 1(£)*	*End of Year 2(£)*
Recession	0.3	100,000	150,000
Growth	0.5	300,000	350,000
Boom	0.2	500,000	550,000

Assume that the state of the economy will be the same in the second year as in the first. The risk-free rate of return is 8 per cent. There is no tax or inflation.

a Write down the project's most likely NPV.

b Calculate the expected return.

c Calculate the standard deviation.

d Assuming the distribution of returns to be normal and bell-shaped what is the probability of a positive NPV based on the risk-free rate?

10 (*Examination level*) RJW plc is a quoted firm which operates ten lignite mines in Wales. It has total assets of £50m and the value of its shares is £90m. RJW plc's directors perceive a great opportunity in the UK government's privatisation drive. They have held preliminary discussions with the government about the purchase of the 25 lignite mines in England. The purchase price suggested by the Treasury is £900m.

For two months the directors have been engaged in a fund-raising campaign to persuade City financial institutions to provide £500m of new equity capital for RJW and £400m of fixed interest rate debt capital in the form of bank loans.

You are a senior analyst with the fund management arm of Klein-Ben Wensons and last week you listened attentively to RJW's presentation. You were impressed by their determination, acumen and track record but have some concerns about their figures for the new project.

RJW's projections are as follows, excluding the cost of purchasing the mines:

Table 1: Cash flows for the English lignite mines: RJW's estimate

Time t	*0*	*1*	*2*	*3*	*4*	*5 and all subsequent years*
Sales (£m) (cash inflows)		1,200	1,250	1,300	1,320	1,350
Less operating costs (£m) (cash flows)		1,070	1,105	1,150	1,190	1,200
Net cash flows (£m)		130	145	150	130	150

You believe the probability of RJW's projections being correct to be 50 per cent (or 0.5). You also estimate that there is a chance that RJW's estimates are over-cautious. There is a 30 per cent probability of the cash flows being as shown in Table 2 (excluding the cost of purchasing the mines).

Table 2: A more optimistic forecast

Time t	*0*	*1*	*2*	*3*	*4*	*5 and all subsequent years*
Sales (£m) (cash inflows)		1,360	1,416.7	1,473.33	1,496	1,530
Less operating costs (£m) (cash outflows)		1,100	1,140	1,190	1,225	1,250
Net cash flows(£m)		260	276.7	283.33	271	280

On the other hand, events may not turn out as well as RJW's estimates. There is a 20 per cent probability that the cash flows will be as shown in Table 3.

Table 3: A more pessimistic scenario (excluding purchase cost of mines)

Time t	*0*	*1*	*2*	*3*	*4*	*5 and all subsequent years*
Sales (£m) (cash inflows)		1,166.67	1,216.7	1,266.67	1,144	1,170
Less operating costs (£m)(cash outflows)		1,070	1,105	1,150	1,165	1,150
Net cash flows(£m)		96.67	111.7	116.67	–21	20

Assume:

1 The cost of capital can be taken to be 14 per cent.

2 Cash flows will arise at year ends except the initial payment to the government which occurs at Time 0.

Required

a Calculate the expected net present value (NPV) and the standard deviation of the NPV for the project to buy the English lignite mines if £900m is taken to be the initial cash outflow.

b There is a chance that events will turn out to be much worse than RJW would like. If the net present value of the English operation turns out to be worse than negative £550m, RJW will be liquidated. What is the probability of avoiding liquidation?

c If the NPV is greater than positive £100m then the share price of RJW will start to rise rapidly in two or three years after the purchase. What is the probability of this occurring?

11† (*Examination level*) Alder plc is considering four projects, for which the cash flows have been calculated as follows:

	Points in time (yearly intervals)					
Project	*0*	*1*	*2*	*3*	*4*	*5*
A	–£500,000	+£600,000				Project ends after 1 year.
B	–£200,000	+£200,000	£150,000			Project ends after 2 years.
C	–£700,000	0	£1million			Project ends after 2 years.
D	–£150,000	+£60,000	+£60,000	+£60,000	+£60,000	Project ends after 4 years.

The appropriate rate of discount is judged to be 10 per cent.

Accepting one of the projects does not exclude the possibility of accepting another one, and each can only be undertaken once.

Assume that the annual cash flows arise on the anniversary dates of the initial outlay and that there is no inflation or tax.

Required

a Calculate the net present value for each of the projects on the assumption that the cash flows are not subject to any risk. Rank the projects on the basis of these calculations, assuming there is no capital rationing.

b Briefly explain two reasons why you might regard net present value as being superior to internal rate of return for project appraisal.

c Now assume that at Time 0 only £700,000 of capital is available for project investment. Calculate the wisest allocation of these funds to achieve the optimum return on the assumption that each of the projects is divisible (fractions may be undertaken). What is the highest net present value achievable?

d A change in the law now makes the outcome of Project D subject to risk because the cash flows depend upon the actions of central government. The project will still require an initial cash outflow of £150,000. If the government licensing agency decides at Time 0 to permit Alder a licence for a trial production and sale of the product, then the net cash flow for the first year will be +£50,000. If the agency decides to allow the product to go on sale under a four-year licence without a trial run the cash inflow in Year 1 will be +£70,000. The probability of a trial run is 50 per cent and the probability of full licensing is 50 per cent.

If the trial run takes place then there are two possibilities for future cash flows. The first, with a probability of 30 per cent, is that the product is subsequently given a full licence for the remaining three years, resulting in a cash flow of +£60,000 per year. The second possibility, with a probability of 70 per cent, is that the government does not grant a licence and production and sales cease after the first year.

If a full licence is granted in the first year then there are two possible sets of cash flows for the subsequent three years. First, the product sells very well, producing an annual net cash flow of +£80,000 – this has a probability of 60 per cent. Secondly, the product sells less well, producing annual cash flows of +£60,000 – this has a probability of 40 per cent.

The management wish you to calculate the probability of this product producing a negative net present value (assume a normal distribution).

12* (*Examination level*) The UK manufacturer of footwear, Willow plc, is considering a major investment in a new product area, novelty umbrellas. It hopes that these products will become fashion icons.

The following information has been collected:

- The project will have a limited life of 11 years.
- The initial investment in plant and machinery will be £1m and a marketing budget of £200,000 will be allocated to the first year.
- The net cash flows before depreciation of plant and machinery and before marketing expenditure for each umbrella will be £1.
- The products will be introduced both in the UK and in France.
- The marketing costs in Years 2 to 11 will be £50,000 per annum.
- If the product catches the imagination of the consumer in both countries then sales in the first year are anticipated at 1m umbrellas.
- If the fashion press ignore the new products in one country but become enthusiastic in the other the sales will be 700,000 umbrellas in Year 1.
- If the marketing launch is unsuccessful in both countries, first year sales will be 200,000 umbrellas.

The probability of each of these events occurring is:

- 1m sales: 0.3
- 0.7m sales: 0.4
- 0.2m sales: 0.3

If the first year is a success in both countries then two possibilities are envisaged:

a Sales levels are maintained at 1m units per annum for the next 10 years – probability 0.3.

b The product is seen as a temporary fad and sales fall to 100,000 units for the remain ing 10 years – probability 0.7.

If success is achieved in only one country in the first year then for the remaining 10 years there is:

a a 0.4 probability of maintaining the annual sales at 700,000 units; and

b a 0.6 probability of sales immediately falling to 50,000 units per year.

If the marketing launch is unsuccessful in both countries then production will cease after the first year.

The plant and machinery will have no alternative use once installed and will have no scrap value.

The annual cash flows and marketing costs will be payable at each year end.

Assume:

- Cost of capital: 10 per cent.
- No inflation or taxation.
- No exchange rate changes.

Required

a Calculate the expected net present value for the project.

b Calculate the standard deviation for the project.

c If the project produces a net present value less than minus £1m the directors fear that the company will be vulnerable to bankruptcy. Calculate the probability of the firm avoiding bankruptcy. Assume a normal distribution.

ASSIGNMENTS

1 Gather together sufficient data on a recent or forthcoming investment in a firm you know well to be able to carry out the following forms of risk analysis:

a Sensitivity analysis.

b Scenario analysis.

c Risk-adjusted return analysis.

d Probability analysis (expected return, standard deviation, probabilities of various eventualities).

Write a report giving as full a picture of the project as possible.

2 Comment on the quality of risk assessment for major investments within your firm. Provide implications and recommendations sections in your report.

CHAPTER NOTE

1 Strictly speaking, risk occurs when specific probabilities can be assigned to the possible outcomes. Uncertainty applies in cases when it is not possible to assign probabilities.

Chapter 7

PORTFOLIO THEORY

INTRODUCTION

The principles discussed in this chapter are as old as the hills. If you are facing a future which is uncertain, as most of us do, you will be vulnerable to negative shocks if you rely on a single source of income. It is less risky to have diverse sources of income or, to put it another way, to hold a portfolio of assets or investments. You do not need to study high-level portfolio theory to be aware of the common sense behind the adage 'don't put all your eggs in one basket'.

Here we examine the extent of risk reduction when an investor switches from complete commitment to one asset, for example shares in one company or one project, to the position where resources are split between two or more assets. By doing so it is possible to maintain returns while reducing risk. In this chapter we will focus on the use of portfolio theory particularly in the context of investment in financial securities, for instance shares in companies. The reader needs to be aware, however, that the fundamental techniques have much wider application – for example, observing the risk-reducing effect of having a diversity of projects within the firm.

The basis of portfolio theory was first developed in 1952 by Harry Markowitz. The thinking behind the explanation of the risk-reducing effect of spreading investment across a range of assets is that in a portfolio unexpected bad news concerning one company will be compensated for to some extent by unexpected good news about another. Markowitz gave us the tools for identifying portfolios which give the highest return for a particular level of risk. Investors can then select the optimum risk-return trade-off for themselves, depending on the extent of personal risk aversion. For example, a retired person dependent on investments for income may prefer a low-risk and low-return portfolio, whereas a young person with alternative sources of income may prefer to choose a portfolio with a higher return and concomitant higher risk. The fundamental point is this: despite the different preferences, each investor will be able to invest in an efficient portfolio; that is, one that gives the highest return for a given level of risk.

Learning objectives

This chapter should enable the student to understand, describe and explain in a formal way the interactions between investments and the risk-reducing properties of portfolios. This includes:

- calculating two-asset portfolio expected returns and standard deviations;
- estimating measures of the extent of interaction – covariance and correlation coefficients;
- being able to describe dominance, identify efficient portfolios and then apply utility theory to obtain optimum portfolios;
- recognise the properties of the multi-asset portfolio set and demonstrate the theory behind the capital market line.

HOLDING PERIOD RETURNS

To invest in a share is to become part owner of a business. If the business performs well then high returns will be earned. If the business does less well the holders of other types of securities, for instance the lenders, have the right to demand their contractual return before the ordinary shareholders receive anything. This can result in the share investor receiving little or nothing. The return earned on a share is defined by the holding period returns: R. For one year this is:

$$\text{Return} = \frac{\text{Dividends received} + (\text{Share price at end of period} - \text{Purchase price})}{\text{Purchase price}}$$

$$R = \frac{D_1 + P_1 - P_0}{P_0}$$

The return is the money received less the cost, where P_0 is the purchase price, P_1 the securities value at the end of the holding period and D_1 the dividend paid during the period (usually assumed to occur at the end, for ease of calculations). Thus the return on a share consists of two parts: first, a dividend; and second, a capital gain (or loss), $P_1 - P_0$. For example if a share was bought for £2, and paid a dividend after one year of 10p and the share was sold for £2.20 after one year the return was:

$$\frac{0.10 + 2.20 - 2.00}{2} = 0.15 \text{ or } 15\%$$

If another share produced a holding period return of, say, 10 per cent over a six-month period we cannot make a direct comparison between the two investments. However, a one-year return and a six-month return are related through the formula:

$$(1 + s)^2 = 1 + R$$

where: s = semi-annual rate,
R = annual rate[1]

Thus if the semi-annual return is converted to an annual rate we have a true comparison (*see* Exhibit 7.1).

Exhibit 7.1 Comparison of returns

First investment	*Second investment*
	$(1 + 0.1)^2 = 1 + R$
	$R = (1 + 0.1)^2 - 1$
Return = 0.15 or 15%	Return = 0.21 or 21%

For a three-year holding period, with dividends received at Time 1, 2 and 3 (yearly intervals) the annual rate of return is obtained by solving for R in the following formula:

$$P_0 = \frac{D_1}{1 + R} + \frac{D_2}{(1 + R)^2} + \frac{D_3}{(1 + R)^3} + \frac{P_3}{(1 + R)^3}$$

So, for example if the initial share price was £1 and the share price three years later (P_3) was £1.20 and a dividend of 6p was paid at the end of Year 1 (D_1), 7p was paid at the end of Year 2 (D_2) and 8p was paid at the end of Year 3 (D_3), the annual rate of return can be found by trial and error:

Try 13%

	Pence	*Discounted*
D_1	6	5.31
D_2	7	5.48
D_3	8	5.54
P_3	120	83.17
		99.50

Try 12%

	Pence	*Discounted*
D_1	6	5.36
D_2	7	5.58
D_3	8	5.69
P_3	120	85.41
		102.04

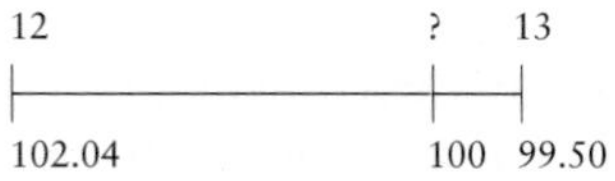

$$12 + [2.04/(102.04 - 99.50)](13 - 12) = 12.8\%$$

If the annual rate of return was 12.8 per cent then the three-year holding period return was (assuming dividend income was reinvested at the internal rate of return):

$$(1 + 0.128)^3 - 1 = 43.5\%$$

or,

$$P(1 + i)^n = F$$

$$£100(1 + 0.128)^3 = £143.52$$

The analysis so far has been backward looking, as it focused on the certain returns that have already been received. Given perfect hindsight it is easy to make a choice between investments. When making investment decisions we are concerned with the future. The only certain fact the investor has is the price P_0 to be paid. The uncertainty over the future dividend has to be taken into account and, in addition, the even more difficult task of estimating the market value of the share at the end of the period has to be undertaken. Pearson, the owner of the *Financial Times,* has steadily raised its dividend year on year and therefore the estimation of the dividend one year hence can be predicted with a reasonable amount of confidence. However forecasting the future share price is more formidable. This is subject to a number of influences ranging from the talent of the editorial team to the general sentiment in the stock market about macroeconomic matters.

So when dealing with the future we have to talk about expected returns. An expected return is derived by considering a variety of possibilities and weighting the possible outcomes by the probability of occurrence. The list of possible outcomes along with their probability of occurrence is called the frequency function.

EXPECTED RETURNS AND STANDARD DEVIATION FOR SHARES

A frequency function or probability distribution for shares in Ace plc is described in Exhibit 7.2. If the economy booms over the next year then the return will be 20 per cent. If normal growth occurs the return will be 5 per cent. A recession will produce a negative return, losing an investor 10 per cent of the original investment.

Exhibit 7.2 Ace plc

A share costs 100p to purchase now and the estimates of returns for the next year are as follows.

Event	*Estimated selling price, P_1*	*Estimated dividend, D_1*	*Return R_i*	*Probability*
Economic boom	114p	6p	+20%	0.2
Normal growth	100p	5p	+5%	0.6
Recession	86p	4p	–10%	0.2
				1.0

The example shown in Exhibit 7.2 lists only three possibilities. This small number was chosen in order to simplify the analysis, but it is possible to imagine that in reality there would be a number of intermediate out-turns, such as a return of 6 per cent or –2 per cent. Each potential outcome would have a defined probability of occurrence but the probability of all the outcomes would sum to 1.0. This more sophisticated approach to probability distribution is illustrated in Exhibit 7.3 where the distribution is assumed to be normal, symmetrical and bell shaped.

We could add to the three possible events shown in Exhibit 7.2, for example slow growth, bad recession, moderate recession and so on, and thereby draw up a more complete representation of the distribution of the probabilities of eventualities.

Exhibit 7.3 A normal distribution

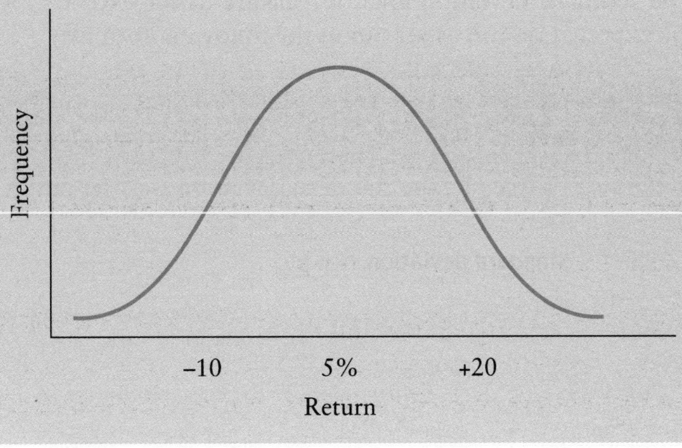

However to represent all the possibilities would be an enormous task and the table would become unwieldy. Furthermore, the data we are dealing with, namely, future events, do not form a suitable base for such precision. We are better off representing the possible outcomes in terms of two summary statistics, the expected return and standard deviation.

The expected return

The expected return is represented by the following formula:

$$\bar{R} = \sum_{i=1}^{n} R_i p_i$$

where

$\bar{R}$ = expected return
R_i = return if event i occurs
p_i = probability of event i occurring
n = number of events

In the case of Ace plc the expected return is as set out in Exhibit 7.4.

Exhibit 7.4 Expected return, Ace plc

Event	*Probability of event* p_i	*Return* R_i	$R_i \times p_i$	
Boom	0.2	+20	4	
Growth	0.6	+5	3	
Recession	0.2	–10	–2	
		Expected returns	5	or 5%

Standard deviation

The standard deviation gives a measure of the extent to which outcomes vary around the expected return, as set out in the following formula:

$$\sigma = \sqrt{\sum_{i=1}^{n}(R_i - \bar{R}_i)^2 p_i}$$

In the case of Ace plc, the standard deviation is as set out in Exhibit 7.5.

Exhibit 7.5 Standard deviation, Ace plc

Probability p_i	*Return* R_i	*Expected return* $\bar{R}_i$	*Deviation* $R_i - \bar{R}_i$	*Deviation squared × probability* $(R_i - \bar{R}_i)^2 p_i$
0.2	20%	5%	15	45
0.6	5%	5%	0	0
0.2	–10%	5%	–15	45
			Variance σ^2	90
			Standard deviation σ	9.49%

Comparing shares

If we contrast the expected return and standard deviation of Ace with that for a share in a second company, Bravo, then using the mean-variance rule described in the last chapter we would establish a preference for Ace (*see* Exhibits 7.6 and 7.7).

Exhibit 7.6 Returns for a share in Bravo plc

Event	*Return* R_i	*Probability* p_i
Boom	–15%	0.2
Growth	+5%	0.6
Recession	+25%	0.2
		1.0

Thus, Exhibit 7.6 indicates that the expected return on Bravo is:

$$(-15 \times 0.2) + (5 \times 0.6) + (25 \times 0.2) = 5 \text{ per cent.}$$

The standard deviation for Bravo is as set out in Exhibit 7.7.

If we had to choose between these two shares then we would say that Ace is preferable to Bravo for a risk-averse investor because both shares have an expected return of 5 per cent but the standard deviation for Ace is lower at 9.49.

Exhibit 7.7 Standard deviation, Bravo plc

Probability p_i	*Return* R_i	*Expected return* $\bar{R}_i$	*Deviation* $R_i - \bar{R}_i$	*Deviation squared × probability* $(R_i - \bar{R}_i)^2 p_i$
0.2	–15%	5%	–20	80
0.6	+5%	5%	0	0
0.2	+25%	5%	+20	80
1.0			Variance σ^2	160
			Standard deviation σ	12.65%

COMBINATIONS OF INVESTMENTS

In the last section we confined our choice to two options – either invest all the money in Ace, or, alternatively, invest everything in Bravo. If the option were taken to invest in Ace then over a few years the returns might turn out to be as shown in Exhibit 7.8.

Exhibit 7.8 Hypothetical pattern of returns for Ace plc

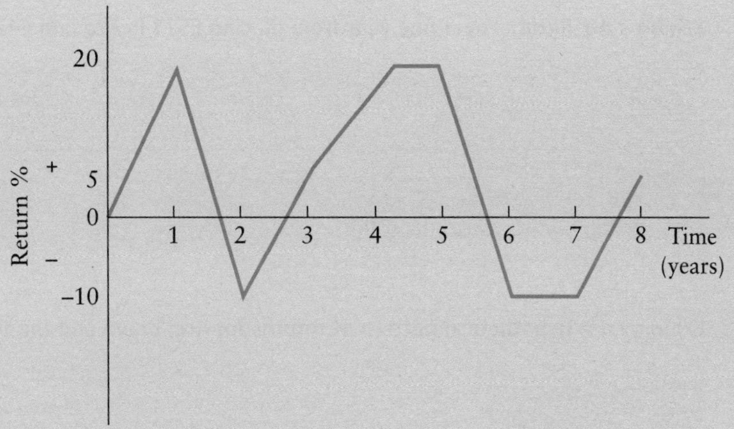

Note, in Exhibit 7.8, the large variability from one year to the next. The returns on Ace are high when the economy is doing well but fall dramatically when recession strikes. There are numerous industries which seem to follow this sort of pattern. For example, the luxury car market is vulnerable to the ups and downs of the economy, as are the hotel and consumer goods sectors.

If all funds were invested in Bravo in isolation then the patterns of future returns might turn out as shown in Exhibit 7.9.

Bravo is in the sort of industry that performs best in recession years; for example, it could be an insolvency practice. Again, note the wild swings in returns from year to year.

Exhibit 7.9 Hypothetical pattern of returns for Bravo plc

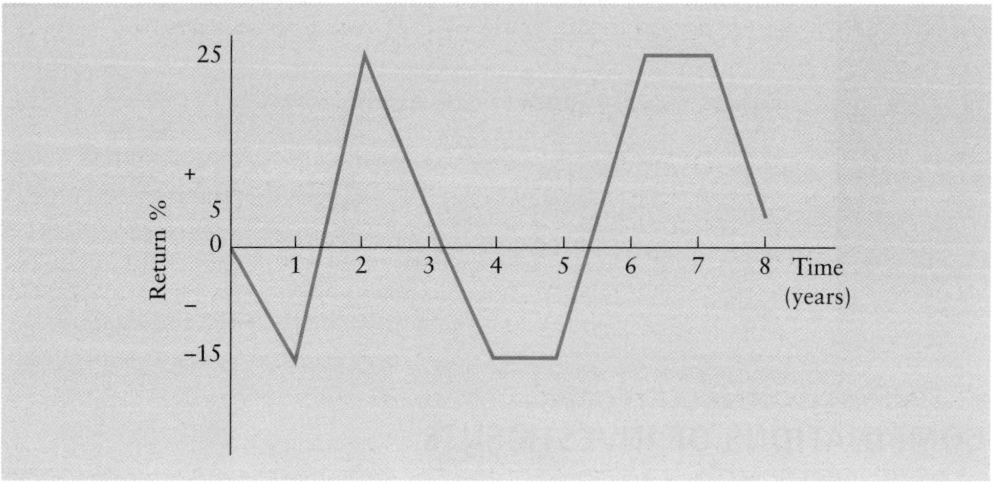

Now assume that the investor is not confined to a pure investment in either Ace's shares or Bravo's shares. Another possibility is to buy a portfolio, in other words, to split the fund between the two companies. We will examine the effect on return and risk of placing £571 of a fund totalling £1,000 into Ace, and £429 into Bravo (see Exhibits 7.10 and 7.11).

Exhibit 7.10 Returns over one year from placing £571 in Ace and £429 in Bravo

Event	*Returns Ace* £	*Returns Bravo* £	*Overall returns on £1,000*	*Percentage returns*
Boom	571(1.2) = 685	429 – 429(0.15) = 365	1,050	5%
Growth	571(1.05) = 600	429(1.05) = 450	1,050	5%
Recession	571 – 571(0.1) = 514	429(1.25) = 536	1,050	5%

Exhibit 7.11 Hypothetical pattern of returns for Ace, Bravo and the two-asset portfolio

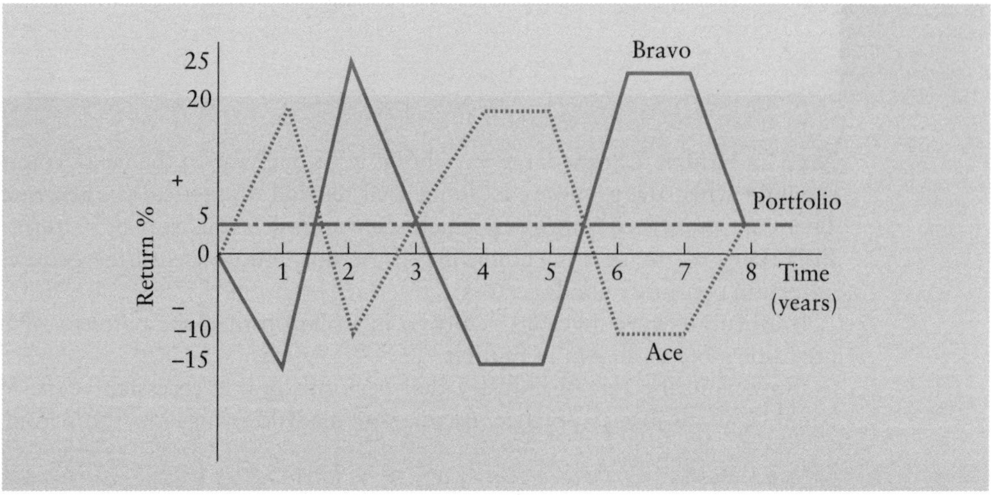

By spreading the investment between these two companies we have achieved complete certainty. Year after year a constant return of 5 per cent is assured rather than the fluctuations experienced if only one share is chosen. Risk has been reduced to zero.

Perfect negative correlation

Under conditions of perfect negative correlation we have a dramatic demonstration of how the risk (degree of deviation from the expected value) on a portfolio can be less than the risk of the individual constituents. The risk becomes zero because the returns on Bravo are highest in circumstances when the returns on Ace are at their lowest, and vice versa. The co-movement of the returns on Ace and Bravo is such that they exactly offset one another. That is, they exhibit *perfect negative correlation*.

Perfect positive correlation

By contrast to the relationship of perfect negative correlation between Ace and Bravo Exhibit 7.12 shows that the returns on Ace and Clara move exactly in step. This is called *perfect positive correlation*.

Exhibit 7.12 Annual returns on Ace and Clara

Event i	*Probability* p_i	*Returns on Ace* %	*Returns on Clara* %
Boom	0.2	+20	+50
Growth	0.6	+5	+15
Recession	0.2	–10	–20

If a portfolio were constructed from equal investments of Ace and Clara the result would be as shown in Exhibit 7.13.

Exhibit 7.13 Returns over a one-year period from placing £500 in Ace and £500 in Clara

Event i	*Returns Ace* £	*Returns Clara* £	*Overall return on* £1,000	*Percentage return*
Boom	600	750	1,350	35%
Growth	525	575	1,100	10%
Recession	450	400	850	–15%

The situation portrayed in Exhibit 7.13 indicates that, compared with investing all the funds in Ace, the portfolio has a wider dispersion of possible percentage return outcomes. A higher percentage return is earned in a good year and a lower return in a recession year. However the portfolio returns are less volatile than an investment in Clara alone. There is a general rule for a portfolio consisting of perfectly positively correlated returns: both the expected returns and the standard deviation of the portfolio are weighted averages of returns and standard deviations of the constituents respectively. Thus because half of the portfolio is from Ace and half from Clara the expected return is half-way between the two individual shares. Also the degree of oscillation is half-way between the small variability of Ace and the large variability of Clara. Perfectly positively correlated investments are at the opposite extreme to perfectly negatively correlated investments. In the former case risk is not reduced through diversification, it is merely averaged. In the latter case risk can be completely eliminated by selecting the appropriate proportions of each investment.

A typical pattern of returns over an eight-year period might be as shown in Exhibit 7.14 for Ace and Clara and a 50:50 portfolio.

Exhibit 7.14 Hypothetical pattern of returns for Ace and Clara

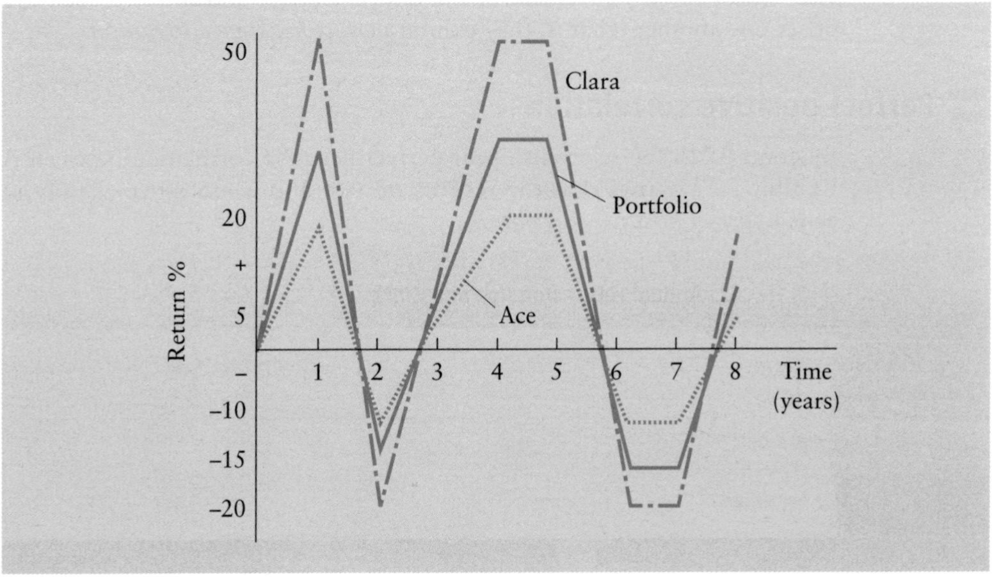

Independent investments

A third possibility is that the returns on shares in two firms are completely unrelated. It is possible within a portfolio of two statistically independent shares to find that when one firm gives a high return the other one may give a high return *or* it may give a low return: that is, we are unable to state any correlation between the returns. The example of X and Y in Exhibits 7.15–7.18 shows the effect on risk of this kind of zero correlation situation when two shares are brought together in a portfolio. Shares in X have a 0.5 probability of producing a return of 35 per cent and a 0.5 probability of producing a return of negative 25 per cent. Shares in Y have exactly the same returns and probabilities but which of the two outcomes will occur is totally independent of the outcome for X.

Exhibit 7.15 Expected returns for shares in X and shares in Y

Expected return for shares in X	*Expected return for shares in Y*
Return × Probability	Return × Probability
– 25 × 0.5 = –12.5	–25 × 0.5 = –12.5
35 × 0.5 = 17.5	35 × 0.5 = 17.5
5.0%	5.0%

Exhibit 7.16 Standard deviations for X or Y as single investments

Return R_i	*Probability* p_i	*Expected return* $\bar{R}_i$	*Deviation* $R_i - \bar{R}$	*Deviation squared × probability* $(R_i - \bar{R})^2 p_i$
–25%	0.5	5%	–30	450
35%	0.5	5%	30	450
			Variance σ^2	900
			Standard deviation σ	30%

If a 50:50 portfolio is created we see that the expected returns remain at 5 per cent, but the standard deviation is reduced (*see* Exhibits 7.17 and 7.18).

Exhibit 7.17 A mixed portfolio: 50 per cent of the fund invested in X and 50 per cent in Y, expected return

Possible outcome combinations	*Joint returns*	*Joint probability*	*Return × probability*
Both firms do badly	–25	0.5 × 0.5 = 0.25	–25 × 0.25 = –6.25
X does badly Y does well	5	0.5 × 0.5 = 0.25	5 × 0.25 = 1.25
X does well Y does badly	5	0.5 × 0.5 = 0.25	5 × 0.25 = 1.25
Both firms do well	35	0.5 × 0.5 = 0.25	35 × 0.25 = 8.75
		1.00	Expected return 5.00%

Exhibit 7.18 Standard deviation, mixed portfolio

Return R_i	*Probability* p_i	*Expected return* $\bar{R}$	*Deviation* $R_i - \bar{R}$	*Deviation squared × probability* $(R_i - \bar{R})^2 p_i$
–25	0.25	5	–30	225
5	0.50	5	0	0
35	0.25	5	30	225
			Variance σ^2	450
			Standard deviation σ	21.21%

The reason for the reduction in risk from a standard deviation of 30 (as shown in Exhibit 7.16) to one of 21.21 (as shown in Exhibit 7.18), is that there is now a third possible outcome. Previously the only outcomes were –25 and +35. Now it is possible that one investment will give a positive result and one will give a negative result. The overall effect is that there is a 50 per cent chance of an outcome being +5. The diversified portfolio reduces the dispersion of the outcomes and the chance of suffering a major loss of 25 per cent is lowered from a probability of 0.5 to only 0.25 for the mixed portfolio.

A correlation scale

We have examined three extreme positions which will provide the foundation for more detailed consideration of portfolios. The case of Ace and Bravo demonstrated that when investments produce good or bad outcomes which vary in exact opposition to each other, risk can be eliminated. This relationship, described as perfect negative correlation, can be assigned the number –1 on a correlation scale which ranges from –1 to +1. The second example, of Ace and Clara, showed a situation where returns on both shares were affected by the same events and these returns moved in lock-step with one another. This sort of perfect positive correlation can be assigned a value of +1 on a correlation scale. The third case, of X and Y where returns are independent, showed that risk is not entirely eliminated but it can be reduced. (Extreme outcomes are still possible, but they are less likely.) Independent investments are assigned a value of zero on the correlation scale (*see* Exhibit 7.19).

Exhibit 7.19 Correlation scale

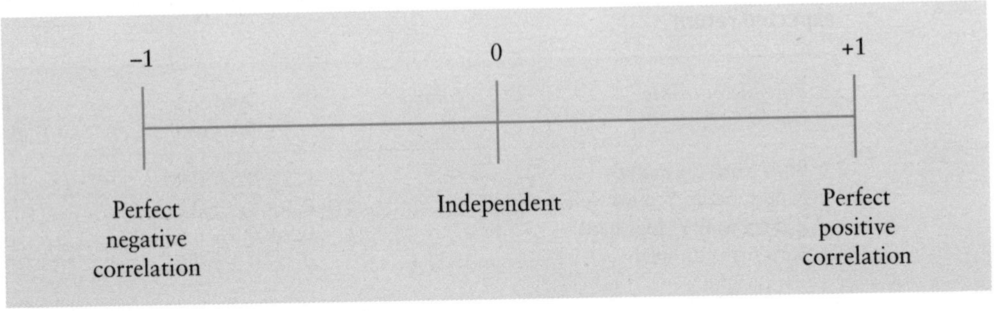

This leads to an important conclusion from portfolio theory:

So long as the returns of constituent assets of a portfolio are not perfectly positively correlated, diversification can reduce risk. The degree of risk reduction depends on:

(a) the extent of statistical interdependence between the returns of the different investments: the more negative the better; and
(b) the number of securities over which to spread the risk: the greater the number, the lower the risk.

This is an amazing conclusion because it is only in the very extreme and rare situation of perfect positive correlation that risk is not reduced.

It is all very well focusing on these three unusual types of relationships but what about the majority of investments in shares, projects or whatever? Real-world assets tend to have returns which have some degree of correlation with other assets but this is neither perfect nor zero. It is to this slightly more complex situation we now turn.

Initially the mathematics of portfolio theory may seem daunting but they do break down into manageable components. The algebra and theory are necessary to gain a true appreciation of the uses of portfolio theory, but the technical aspects are kept to a minimum.

The effects of diversification when security returns are not perfectly correlated

We will now look at the risk-reducing effects of diversification when two financial securities, two shares, have only a small degree of interrelatedness between their returns. Suppose that an investor has a chance of either investing all funds in one company, A or B, or investing a fraction in one with the remainder purchasing shares in the other. The returns on these companies respond differently to the general activity within the economy. Company A does particularly well when the economy is booming. Company B does best when there is normal growth in the economy. Both do badly in a recession. There is some degree of 'togetherness' or correlation of the movement of the returns, but not much (*see* Exhibit 7.20).

Exhibit 7.20 Returns on shares A and B for alternative economic states

Event i *State of the economy*	*Probability* p_i	*Return on A* R_A	*Return on B* R_B
Boom	0.3	20%	3%
Growth	0.4	10%	35%
Recession	0.3	0%	–5%

Before examining portfolio risk and returns we first calculate the expected return and standard deviation for each of the companies' shares as single investments (*see* Exhibits 7.21–7.25).

Exhibit 7.21 Company A: Expected return

Probability p_i	*Return* R_A	$R_A \times p_i$
0.3	20	6
0.4	10	4
0.3	0	0
		10%

Exhibit 7.22 Company A: Standard deviation

Probability p_i	*Return* R_i	*Expected return* $\bar{R}_A$	*Deviation* $(R_A - \bar{R}_A)$	*Deviation squared × probability* $(R_A - \bar{R}_A)^2 p_i$
0.3	20	10	10	30
0.4	10	10	0	0
0.3	0	10	–10	30
			Variance σ^2	60
			Standard deviation σ	7.75%

Exhibit 7.23 Company B: Expected return

Probability p_i	*Return* R_B	$R_B \times p_i$
0.3	3	0.9
0.4	35	14.0
0.3	–5	–1.5
		13.4%

Exhibit 7.24 Company B: Standard deviation

Probability p_i	*Return* R_B	*Expected return* $\bar{R}_B$	*Deviation* $(R_B - \bar{R}_B)$	*Deviation squared × probability* $(R_B - \bar{R}_B)^2 \, p_i$
0.3	3	13.4	10.4	32.45
0.4	35	13.4	21.6	186.62
0.3	–5	13.4	–18.4	101.57
			Variance σ^2	320.64
			Standard deviation σ	17.91%

Exhibit 7.25 Summary table: Expected returns and standard deviations for Companies A and B

	Expected return	*Standard deviation*
Company A	10%	7.75%
Company B	13.4%	17.91%

Compared with A, Company B is expected to give a higher return but also has a higher level of risk. If the results are plotted on a diagram we can give an impression of the relative risk-return profiles (*see* Exhibit 7.26).

Exhibit 7.26 Return and standard deviation for shares in firms A and B

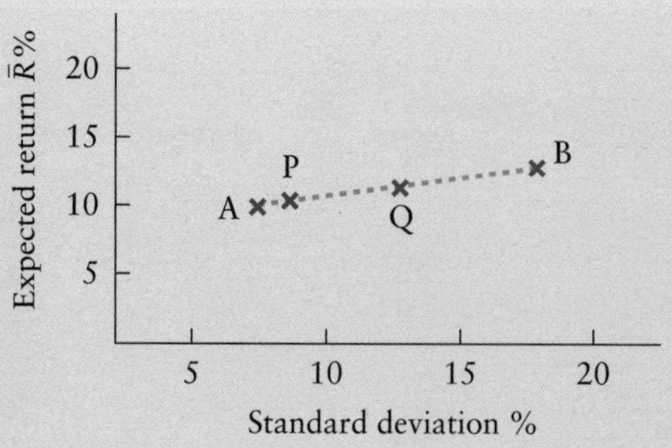

From a first glance at Exhibit 7.26 it might be thought that it is possible to invest in different proportions of A and B and obtain a risk-return combination somewhere along the dotted line. That is, a two-asset portfolio of A and B has an expected return which is a weighted average of the expected returns on the individual investments *and* the standard deviation is a weighted average of the risk of A and B depending on the proportions of the portfolio devoted to A and B. So if point Q represented a 50:50 split of capital between A and B the expected return, following this logic, would be:

$$(10 \times 0.5) + (13.4 \times 0.5) = 11.7\%$$

and the standard deviation would be:

$$(7.75 \times 0.5) + (17.91 \times 0.5) = 12.83\%$$

Point P represents 90 per cent of the fund in A and 10 per cent in B. If this portfolio was on the dotted line the expected return would be:

$$(10 \times 0.9) + (13.4 \times 0.1) = 10.34\%$$

and the standard deviation would be:

$$(7.75 \times 0.9) + (17.91 \times 0.1) = 8.766\%$$

However, this would be **wrong** because the risk of any portfolio of A and B is less than the weighted average of the two individual standard deviations. You can, in fact, reduce risk at each level of return by investing in a portfolio of A and B. This brings us to a general rule in portfolio theory:

Portfolio returns are a weighted average of the expected returns on the individual investment . . .
BUT . . .
Portfolio standard deviation is less than the weighted average risk of the individual investments, except for perfectly positively correlated investments.

PORTFOLIO EXPECTED RETURNS AND STANDARD DEVIATION

The rule stated above will now be illustrated by calculating the expected return and standard deviation when 90 per cent of the portfolio funds are placed in A and 10 per cent are placed in B.

Expected returns, two-asset portfolio

The expected returns from a two-asset portfolio are as follows.

Proportion of funds in A = a = 0.90
Proportion of funds in B = $1 - a$ = 0.10

The expected return of a portfolio R_p is solely related to the proportion of wealth invested in each constituent. Thus we simply multiply the expected return of each individual investment by their weights in the portfolio, 90 per cent for A and 10 per cent for B.

$$\bar{R}_p = a\bar{R}_A + (1 - a)\bar{R}_B$$

$$\bar{R}_p = 0.90 \times 10 + 0.10 \times 13.4 = 10.34\%$$

Standard deviation, two-asset portfolio

Now comes the formula that for decades has made the hearts of students sink when first seen – the formula for the standard deviation of a two-asset portfolio. This is:

$$\sigma_p = \sqrt{a^2\,\sigma^2_A + (1-a)^2\,\sigma^2_B + 2a(1-a)\,\text{cov}\,(R_A, R_B)}$$

where

σ_p = portfolio standard deviation

σ^2_A = variance of investment A

σ^2_B = variance of investment B

cov (R_A, R_B) = covariance of A and B

The formula for the standard deviation of a two-asset portfolio may seem daunting at first. However, the component parts are fairly straightforward. To make the formula easier to understand it is useful to break it down to three terms:

1 The first term, $a^2\sigma^2_A$, is the variance for A multiplied by the square of its weight – in the example $a^2 = 0.90^2$.
2 The second term $(1-a)^2\sigma^2_B$, is the variance for the second investment B multiplied by the square of its weight in the portfolio, 0.10^2.
3 The third term, $2a(1-a)$ cov (R_A, R_B), focuses on the covariance of the returns of A and B, which is examined below.

When the results of all three calculations are added together the square root is taken to give the standard deviation of the portfolio. The only piece of information not yet available is the covariance. This is considered next.

Covariance

The covariance measures the extent to which the returns on two investments 'co-vary' or 'co-move'. If the returns tend to go up together and go down together then the covariance will be a positive number. If, however, the returns on one investment move in the opposite direction to the returns on another when a particular event occurs then these securities will exhibit negative covariance. If there is no co-movement at all, that is, the returns are independent of each other, the covariance will be zero. This positive–zero–negative scale should sound familiar, as covariance and the correlation coefficient are closely related. However the correlation coefficient scale has a strictly limited range from –1 to +1 whereas the covariance can be any positive or negative value. The covariance formula is:

$$\text{cov}\,(R_A, R_B) = \sum_{i=1}^{n} \{(R_A - \bar{R}_A)(R_B - \bar{R}_B)p_i\}$$

To calculate covariance take each of the possible events that could occur in turn and calculate the extent to which the returns on investment A differ from expected return $(R_A - \bar{R}_A)$ – and note whether this is a positive or negative deviation. Follow this with a similar deviation calculation for an investment in B if those particular circumstances (that is, boom, recession, etc.) prevail $(R_B - \bar{R}_B)$. Then multiply the deviation of A by the deviation of B and the probability of that event occurring, p_i. (Note that if the deviations are both in a positive direction away from the mean, that is, a higher return than average, or both negative, then the overall calculation will be positive. If one of the deviations is negative while the other is positive the overall result is negative.) Finally the results from all the potential events are added together to give the covariance.

Applying the formula to A and B will help to clarify matters (*see* Exhibit 7.27).

Exhibit 7.27 Covariance

Event and probability of event p_i		*Returns* R_A	R_B	*Expected returns* $\bar{R}_A$	$\bar{R}_B$	*Deviations* $R_A - \bar{R}_A$	$R_B - \bar{R}_B$	*Deviation of A × deviation of B × probability* $(R_A - \bar{R}_A)(R_B - \bar{R}_B)p_i$
Boom	0.3	20	3	10	13.4	10	−10.4	10 × −10.4 × 0.3 = −31.2
Growth	0.4	10	35	10	13.4	0	21.6	0 × 21.6 × 0.4 = 0
Recession	0.3	0	−5	10	13.4	−10	−18.4	−10 × −18.4 × 0.3 = 55.2
								Covariance of A and B, cov (R_A, R_B) = +24

It is worth spending a little time dwelling on the covariance and seeing how a positive or negative covariance comes about. In the calculation for A and B the 'Boom' eventuality contributed a negative 31.2 to the overall covariance. This is because A does particularly well in boom conditions and the returns are well above expected returns, but B does badly compared with its expected return of 13.4 and therefore the co-movement of returns is a negative one. In a recession both firms experience poor returns compared with their expected values, thus the contribution to the overall covariance is positive because they move together. This second element of co-movement outweighs that of the boom possibility and so the total covariance is positive 24.

Now that we have the final piece of information to plug into the standard deviation formula we can work out the risk resulting from splitting the fund, with 90 per cent invested in A and 10 per cent in B.

$$\sigma_p = \sqrt{a^2\sigma^2_A + (1-a)^2\,\sigma^2_B + 2a\,(1-a)\,\text{cov}\,(R_A, R_B)}$$

$$\sigma_p = \sqrt{0.90^2 \times 60 + 0.10^2 \times 320.64 + 2 \times 0.90 \times 0.10 \times 24}$$

$$\sigma_p = \sqrt{48.6 + 3.206 + 4.32}$$

$$\sigma_p = 7.49\%$$

A 90:10 portfolio gives both a higher return and a lower standard deviation than a simple investment in A alone (*see* Exhibit 7.28).

Exhibit 7.28 Summary table: expected return and standard deviation

	Expected return (%)	*Standard deviation (%)*
All invested in Company A	10	7.75
All invested in Company B	13.4	17.91
Invested in a portfolio (90% in A, 10% in B)	10.34	7.49

In the example shown in Exhibit 7.29 the degree of risk reduction is so slight because the returns on A and B are positively correlated. Later we will consider the example of Augustus and Brown, two shares which exhibit negative correlation. Before that, it will be useful to examine the relationship between covariance and the correlation coefficient.

Exhibit 7.29 Expected returns and standard deviation for A and B and a 90:10 portfolio of A and B

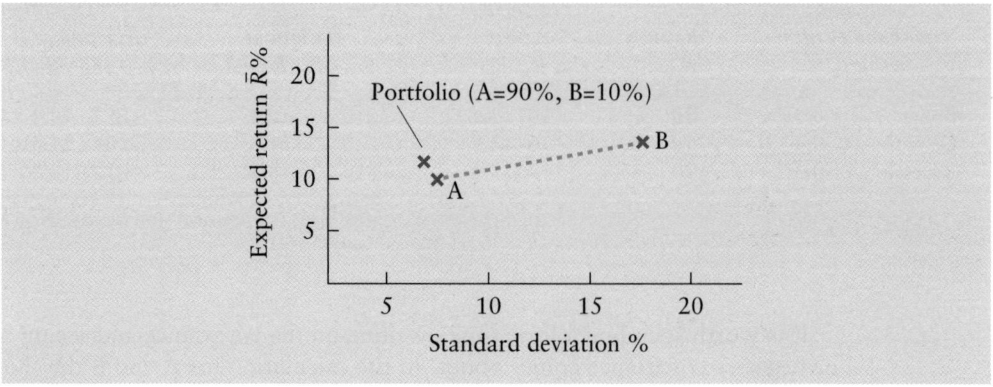

Correlation coefficient

Both the covariance and the correlation coefficient measure the degree to which returns move together. The covariance can take on any value and so it is difficult to use the covariance to compare relationships between pairs of investments. A 'standardised covariance' with a scale of interrelatedness is often more useful. This is what the correlation coefficient gives us. To calculate the correlation coefficient, R_{AB}, divide the covariance by the product (multiplied together) of the individual investment standard deviations.

So for investments A and B:

$$R_{AB} = \frac{\text{cov}\,(R_A, R_B)}{\sigma_A\,\sigma_B}$$

$$R_{AB} = \frac{24}{7.75 \times 17.91} = +0.1729$$

The correlation coefficient has the same properties as the covariance but it measures co-movement on a scale of –1 to +1 which makes comparisons easier. It also can be used as an alternative method of calculating portfolio standard deviation:

$$\text{If } R_{AB} = \frac{\text{cov}\,(R_A, R_B)}{\sigma_A\,\sigma_B} \text{ then cov } (R_A, R_B) = R_{AB}\sigma_A\sigma_B$$

This can then be used in the portfolio standard deviation formula:

$$\sigma_p = \sqrt{a^2\,\sigma^2{}_A + (1-a)^2\sigma^2{}_B + 2a\,(1-a)\,R_{AB}\sigma_A\sigma_B}$$

Exhibit 7.30 illustrates the case of perfect positively correlated returns (R_{FG} = +1) for the shares F and G. All the plot points lie on a straight upward sloping line.

Exhibit 7.30 Perfect positive correlation

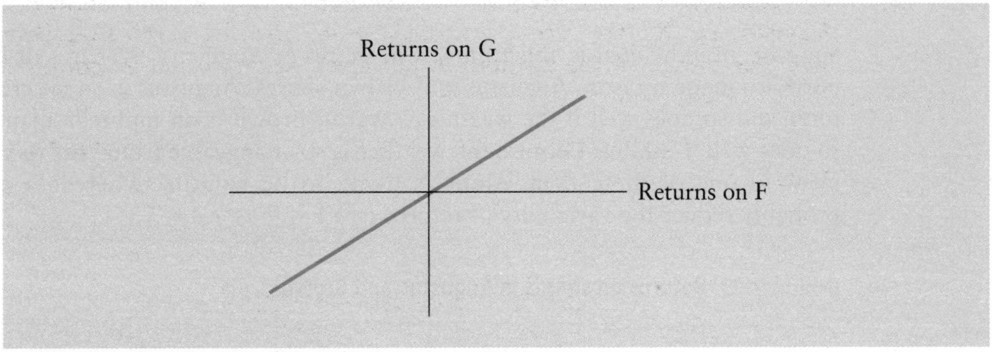

If the returns on G vary in an exactly opposite way to the returns on F we have perfect negative correlation, $R_{FG} = -1$ (*see* Exhibit 7.31).

Exhibit 7.31 Perfect negative correlation

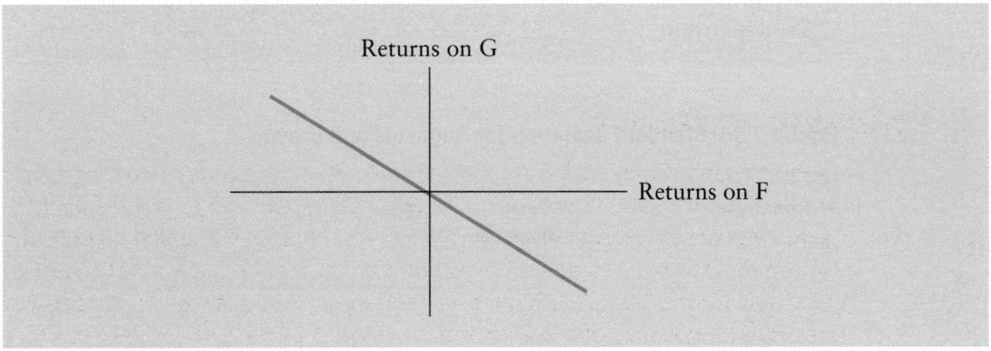

If the securities have a zero correlation coefficient ($R = 0$) we are unable to show a line representing the degree of co-movement (*see* Exhibit 7.32).

Exhibit 7.32 Zero correlation coefficient

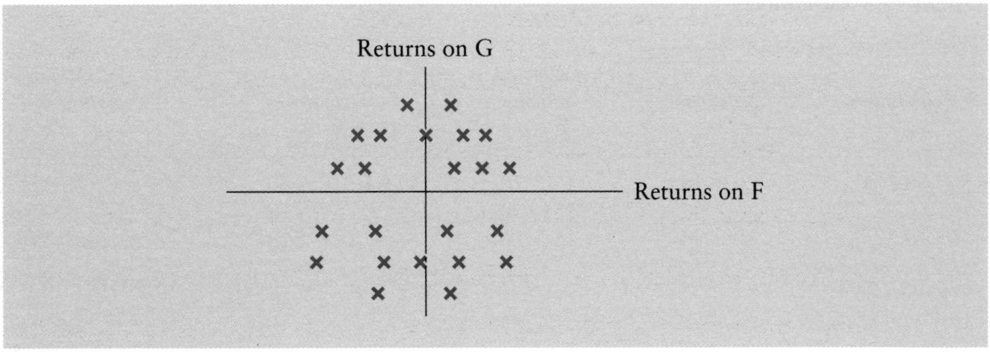

DOMINANCE AND THE EFFICIENT FRONTIER

Suppose an individual is able to invest in shares of Augustus, in shares of Brown or in a portfolio made up from Augustus and Brown shares. Augustus is an ice cream manufacturer and so does well if the weather is warm. Brown is an umbrella manufacturer and so does well if it rains. Because the weather is so changeable from year to year an investment in one of these firms alone is likely to be volatile, whereas a portfolio will probably reduce the variability of returns (*see* Exhibits 7.33–7.35).

Exhibit 7.33 Returns on shares in Augustus and Brown

Event (weather for season)	*Probability of event*	*Returns on Augustus*	*Returns on Brown*
	p_i	R_A	R_B
Warm	0.2	20%	–10%
Average	0.6	15%	22%
Wet	0.2	10%	44%
Expected return		15%	20%

Exhibit 7.34 Standard deviation for Augustus and Brown

Probability p_i	*Returns on Augustus* R_A	$(R_A - \bar{R}_A)^2 p_i$	*Returns on Brown* R_B	$(R_B - \bar{R}_B)^2 p_i$
0.2	20	5	–10	180.0
0.6	15	0	22	2.4
0.2	10	5	44	115.2
	Variance, σ^2_A	10	Variance, σ^2_B	297.6
	Standard deviation, σ_A	3.162	Standard deviation, σ_B	17.25

Exhibit 7.35 Covariance

Probability p_i	*Returns* R_A	R_B	*Expected returns* $\bar{R}_A$	$\bar{R}_B$	*Deviations* $R_A - \bar{R}_A$	$R_B - \bar{R}_B$	*Deviation of A × deviation of B × probability* $(R_A - \bar{R}_A)(R_B - \bar{R}_B)p_i$	
0.2	20	–10	15	20	5	–30	5 × –30 × 0.2 =	–30
0.6	15	22	15	20	0	2	0 × 2 × 0.6 =	0
0.2	10	44	15	20	–5	24	–5 × 24 × 0.2 =	–24
							Covariance (R_A, R_B) =	–54

The correlation coefficient is:

$$R_{AB} = \frac{\text{cov}\,(R_A, R_B)}{\sigma_A\,\sigma_B}$$

$$R_{AB} = \frac{-54}{3.162 \times 17.25} = -0.99$$

There are an infinite number of different potential combinations of Augustus and Brown shares giving different levels of risk and return. To make the analysis easier we will examine only five portfolios. These are shown in Exhibit 7.36.

Exhibit 7.36 Risk-return correlations: two-asset portfolios for Augustus and Brown

Portfolio	*Augustus weighting (%)*	*Brown weighting (%)*	*Expected return (%)*	*Standard deviation*	
A	100	0	15		= 3.16
J	90	10	15.5	$\sqrt{0.9^2 \times 10 + 0.1^2 \times 297.6 + 2 \times 0.9 \times 0.1 \times -54}$	= 1.16
K	85	15	15.75	$\sqrt{0.85^2 \times 10 + 0.15^2 \times 297.6 + 2 \times 0.85 \times 0.15 \times -54}$	= 0.39
L	80	20	16.0	$\sqrt{0.8^2 \times 10 + 0.2^2 \times 297.6 + 2 \times 0.8 \times 0.2 \times -54}$	= 1.01
M	50	50	17.5	$\sqrt{0.5^2 \times 10 + 0.5^2 \times 297.6 + 2 \times 0.5 \times 0.5 \times -54}$	= 7.06
N	25	75	18.75	$\sqrt{0.25^2 \times 10 + 0.75^2 \times 297.6 + 2 \times 0.25 \times 0.75 \times -54}$	=12.2
B	0	100	20		=17.25

Exhibit 7.37 shows the risk-return profile for alternative portfolios. Portfolio K is very close to the minimum risk combination that actually occurs at a portfolio consisting of 84.6 per cent in Augustus and 15.4 per cent in Brown. The formula for calculating this minimum standard deviation point is shown in Worked example 7.1.

The risk-return line drawn, sometimes called the opportunity set, or feasible set, has two sections. The first, with a solid line, from point K to point B, represents all the *efficient* portfolios. This is called the *efficiency frontier*. Portfolios between K and A are *dominated* by the efficient portfolios. Take L and J as examples: they have the same risk levels but portfolio L dominates portfolio J because it has a better return. All the portfolios between K and A are *inefficient* because for each possibility there is an alternative combination of Augustus and Brown on the solid line K to B which provides a higher return for the same risk.

An efficient portfolio is a combination of investments which maximises the expected return for a given standard deviation.

Exhibit 7.37 Risk-return profile for alternative portfolios of Augustus and Brown

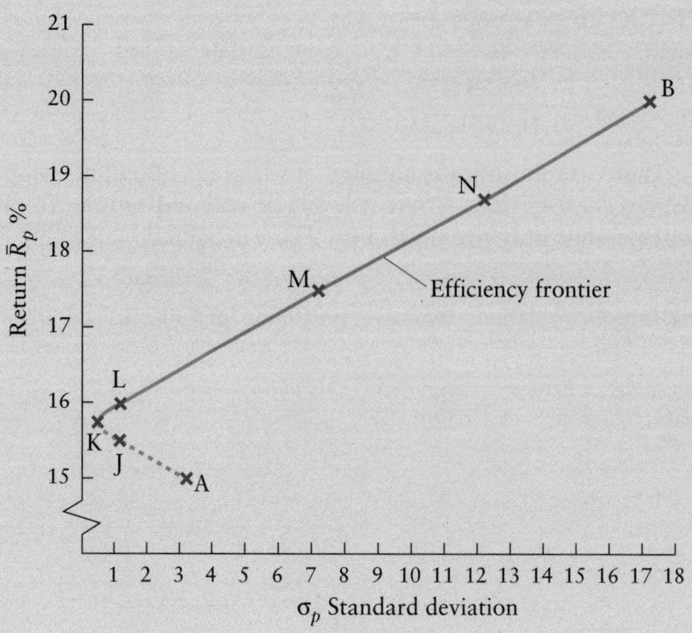

Worked example 7.1 Finding the minimum standard deviation for combinations of two securities

If a fund is to be split between two securities, A and B, and a is the fraction to be allocated to A, then the value for a which results in the lowest standard deviation is given by:

$$a = \frac{\sigma_B^2 - \text{cov}\,(R_A, R_B)}{\sigma_A^2 + \sigma_B^2 - 2\,\text{cov}\,(R_A, R_B)}$$

In the case of Augustus and Brown:

$$a = \frac{297.6 - (-54)}{10 + 297.6 - 2 \times -54} = 0.846 \text{ or } 84.6\%$$

To obtain the minimum standard deviation (or variance) place 84.6 per cent of the fund in Augustus and 15.4 per cent in Brown.

We can now calculate the minimum standard deviation:

$$\sigma_p = \sqrt{a^2\,\sigma^2{}_A + (1-a)^2\,\sigma^2{}_B + 2a\,(1-a)\,\text{cov}\,(R_A, R_B)}$$

$$\sigma_p = \sqrt{0.846^2 \times 10 + 0.154^2 \times 297.6 + 2 \times 0.846 \times 0.154 \times -54}$$

$$\sigma_p = 0.38\%$$

Thus, an extremely risk-averse individual who was choosing a combination of shares in Augustus and Brown can achieve a very low variation of income of a tiny standard deviation of 0.38 per cent by allocating 84.6 per cent of the investment fund to Augustus.

Identifying the efficient portfolios helps in the quest to find the optimal portfolio for an investor as it eliminates a number of inferior possibilities from further consideration. However, there remains a large range of risk-return combinations available in the efficient zone and we need a tool to enable us to find the best portfolio for an individual given that person's degree of risk aversion. For instance a highly risk-averse person will probably select a portfolio with a high proportion of Augustus (but not greater than 84.6 per cent) perhaps settling for the low-return and low-risk combination represented by portfolio L. A less risk-averse investor may be prepared to accept the high standard deviation of portfolio N if compensated by the expectation of greater reward. To be more accurate in choosing between efficient portfolios we need to be able to represent the decision makers' attitude towards risk. Indifference curves help us to do this.

INDIFFERENCE CURVES

Indifference curve analysis draws on the concept of utility to present alternative trade-offs between risk and return each equally acceptable to the investor. Every individual will exhibit unique preferences for risk and return and so everyone has a unique set of indifference curves. Consider Mr Chisholm who is hypothetically allocated portfolio W represented in Exhibit 7.38. This portfolio has a return of 10 per cent and a standard deviation of 16 per cent. Now imagine you asked Mr Chisholm, 'If we were to change the constituents of the portfolio so that the risk increased to a standard deviation of 20 per cent how much extra return would you require to compensate for the increased risk to leave your overall utility unchanged?' According to this simple model an extra return of 4 per cent is required. That is, Mr Chisholm is indifferent between W and the portfolio Z with a standard deviation of 20 per cent and return of 14 per cent. His utility (or well-being) is identical for each portfolio.

Exhibit 7.38 Indifference curve for Mr Chisholm

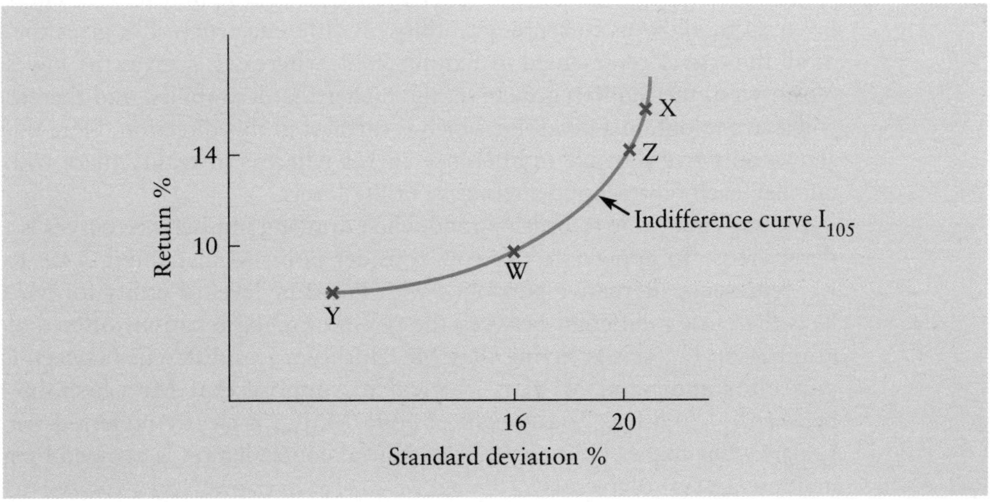

In fact all the risk-return combinations along the indifference curve I_{105} in Exhibit 7.38 have the same level of desirability to Mr Chisholm. Portfolio X has a higher risk than portfolio Y and is therefore less desirable on this factor. However, exactly offsetting this is the attraction of the increased return.

Now consider Exhibit 7.39 where there are a number of indifference curves drawn for Mr Chisholm. Even though Mr Chisholm is indifferent between W and Z, he will not be indifferent between W and S. Portfolio S has the same level of risk as W but provides a higher level of return and is therefore preferable.

Likewise portfolio T is preferred to portfolio Z because for the same level of return a lower risk is obtainable. All portfolios along I_{110} provide a higher utility than any of the portfolios along I_{105}.

Exhibit 7.39 A map of indifference curves

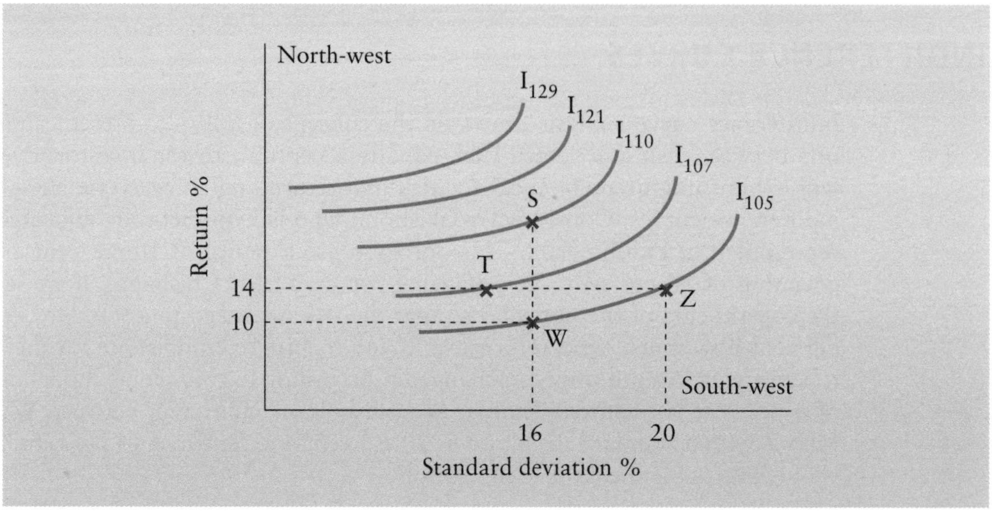

Similarly I_{121} portfolios are better than I_{110}. (These indifference curve numbers are invented to allow us to represent utility.) Indifference curve I_{129} gives the highest utility of all the curves represented in Exhibit 7.39, whereas I_{105} gives the lowest. The further 'north-west' the indifference curve, the higher the desirability, and therefore an investor will strive to obtain a portfolio which is furthest in this direction. Note that Exhibit 7.39 shows only five possible indifference curves whereas in reality there will be an infinite number, each representing alternative utility levels.

An important rule to bear in mind when drawing indifference curves is that they must never cross. To appreciate this rule consider point M in Exhibit 7.40. Remember that I_{105} represents alternative portfolios with the same level of utility for Mr Chisholm and he is therefore indifferent between the risk-return combinations offered along I_{105}. If M also lies on I_{101} this is saying that Mr Chisholm is indifferent between any of the I_{101} portfolios and point M. It is illogical to suppose that Mr Chisholm is indifferent between I_{105} and I_{101}. To the right of point M, I_{105} is clearly preferred. To the left of M, I_{101} gives the higher utility level. This logical contradiction is avoided by never allowing indifference curves to cross.

Mr Chisholm's personality and circumstances led to the drawing of his unique indifference curves with their particular slope. Other investors may be less risk averse than Mr Chisholm, in which case the increase in return required to compensate for each unit of increased risk will be less. That is, the indifference curves will have a lower slope.

Exhibit 7.40 Intersecting indifference curves

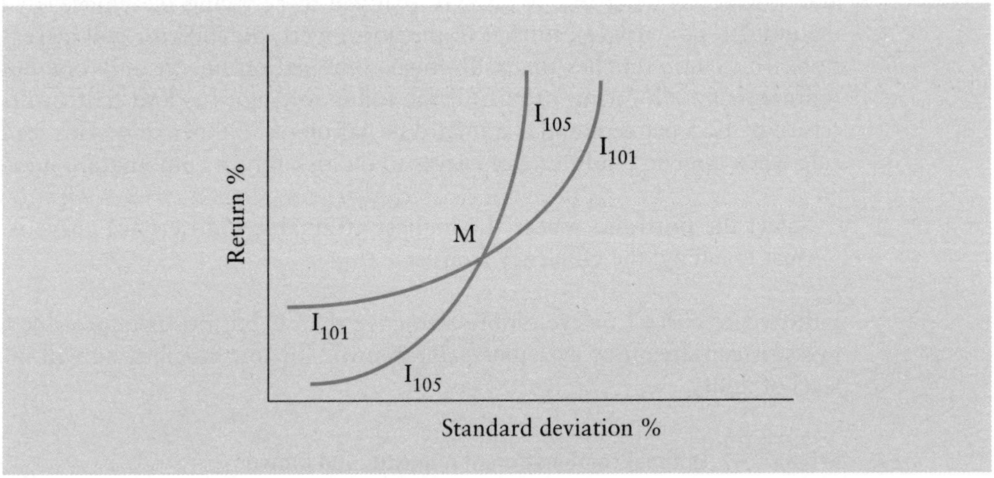

This is represented in Exhibit 7.41(b). Alternatively, individuals may be less tolerant of risk and exhibit steeply sloped indifference curves, as demonstrated in Exhibit 7.41(c). Here large increases in return are required for small increases in risk.

Exhibit 7.41 Varying degrees of risk aversion as represented by indifference curves

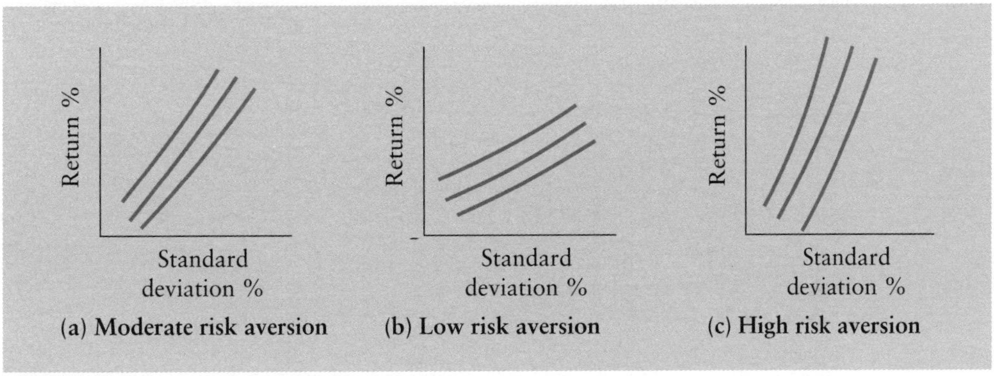

CHOOSING THE OPTIMAL PORTFOLIO

We can now return to the investor considering investment in Augustus and Brown and apply indifference curve analysis to find the optimal portfolio. By assuming that this investor is moderately risk averse we can draw three of his indifference curves on to the risk-return profile diagram for two-asset portfolios of Augustus and Brown. This is shown in Exhibit 7.42. One option available is to select portfolio N, putting 25 per cent of the fund into Augustus and the remainder in Brown. This will give a respectable expected return of 18.75 per cent for a risk level of 12.2 per cent for the standard deviation. It is interesting to note that this investor would be just as content with the return of 15.5 per cent on portfolio J if risk were reduced to a standard deviation of 1.16 per cent. I_1 represents quite a high level of utility and the investor would achieve a high level of well-being selecting either N or J. However this is not the highest level of utility available – which is what the investor is assumed to be trying to achieve. By moving on to the indifference curve I_2, further to the north-west, the investor will increase his satisfaction. This curve touches the risk-return combination line at only one point, M, which represents an allocation of half of the funds to Augustus and half to Brown, giving a return of 17.5 per cent and a standard deviation of 7.06 per cent. This leads to a general rule when applying indifference curves to the risk-return combination line:

> **Select the portfolio where the highest attainable indifference curve is tangential to (just touching) the efficiency frontier.**

Indifference curve I_3 is even more attractive than I_2 but this is impossible to obtain. The investor can dream of ever-increasing returns for low risk but he will not achieve this level of utility.

Exhibit 7.42 Optimal combination of Augustus and Brown

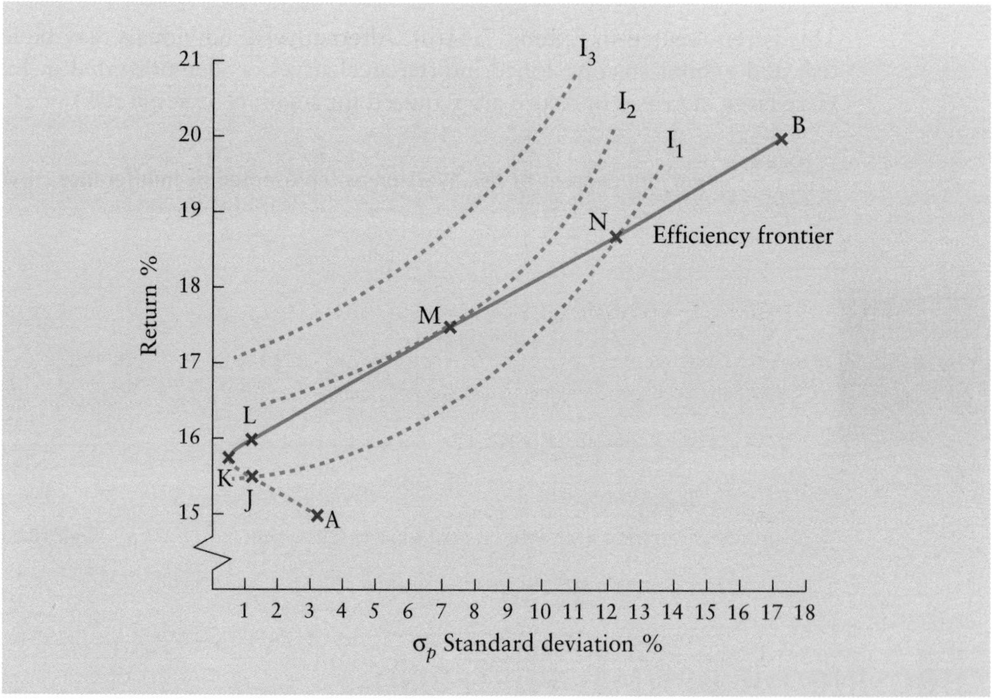

Problems with indifference curve analysis

Obtaining indifference curves for individuals is time consuming and difficult. It is also subject to error. Try estimating your own risk-return preferences and your own degree of risk-aversion to gain an impression involved in drawing up curves from subjective material such as thoughts and feelings. Even if you did arrive at firm conclusions at one specific time, are you confident that these will not change as your circumstances alter? It is plain that there are serious drawbacks to excessive reliance on mathematically precise curves when they are based on imprecise opinion. However it would be wrong to 'throw the baby out with bathwater' and reject utility analysis completely. The model used does give us a representation of the different risk tolerances of individuals and permits us to come to approximate conclusions concerning likely optimal portfolios for particular individuals based on their risk-reward preferences. For instance a highly risk-averse person is unlikely to elect to place all funds in Brown but will tend to select portfolios close to L or K. The exact allocation is less important than the general principles of (a) identifying efficient portfolios and (b) selecting an efficient portfolio which roughly matches the degree of risk aversion of the decision maker.

THE BOUNDARIES OF DIVERSIFICATION

We can now consider the extreme circumstances of perfect negative and zero correlation to demonstrate the outer boundaries of the risk-return relationships.

Consider the two securities C and D, the expected returns and standard deviations for which are presented in Exhibit 7.43.

Exhibit 7.43 Expected return and standard deviation, Companies C and D

	Company C	*Company D*
Expected return	$\bar{R}_C = 15\%$	$\bar{R}_D = 22\%$
Standard deviation	$\sigma_C = 3\%$	$\sigma_D = 9\%$

Perfect negative correlation

If we first assume that C and D are perfectly negatively correlated, $R_{CD} = -1$, then the point of minimum standard deviation is found as follows:

a = proportion of funds invested in C

$$a = \frac{\sigma_D^2 - \text{cov}\,(R_C, R_D)}{\sigma_C^2 + \sigma_D^2 - 2\,\text{cov}\,(R_C, R_D)}$$

or

$$a = \frac{\sigma_D^2 - R_{CD}\,\sigma_C\sigma_D}{\sigma_C^2 + \sigma_D^2 - 2R_{CD}\,\sigma_C\sigma_D}$$

$$a = \frac{9^2 - (-1 \times 3 \times 9)}{3^2 + 9^2 - (2 \times -1 \times 3 \times 9)} = 0.75$$

The portfolio which will reduce risk to zero is one which consists of 75 per cent of C and 25 per cent of D.

The return available on this portfolio is:

$$R_P = aR_C + (1 - a)\,R_D$$

$$= 0.75 \times 15 + 0.25 \times 22 = 16.75\%$$

To confirm that this allocation will give the minimum risk the portfolio standard deviation could be calculated.

$$\sigma_P = \sqrt{a^2\sigma_C^2 + (1-a)^2\sigma_D^2 + 2a(1-a)\,R_{CD}\,\sigma_C\,\sigma_D}$$

$$\sigma_P = \sqrt{0.75^2 \times 3^2 + 0.25^2 \times 9^2 + 2 \times 0.75 \times 0.25 \times -1 \times 3 \times 9} = 0$$

This minimum variance portfolio has been labelled E in Exhibit 7.44. In the circumstances of a correlation coefficient of –1 all the other risk-return combinations are described by the dog-legged line CED. This describes the left boundary of the feasible set of portfolio risk-return lines.

Exhibit 7.44 The boundaries of diversification

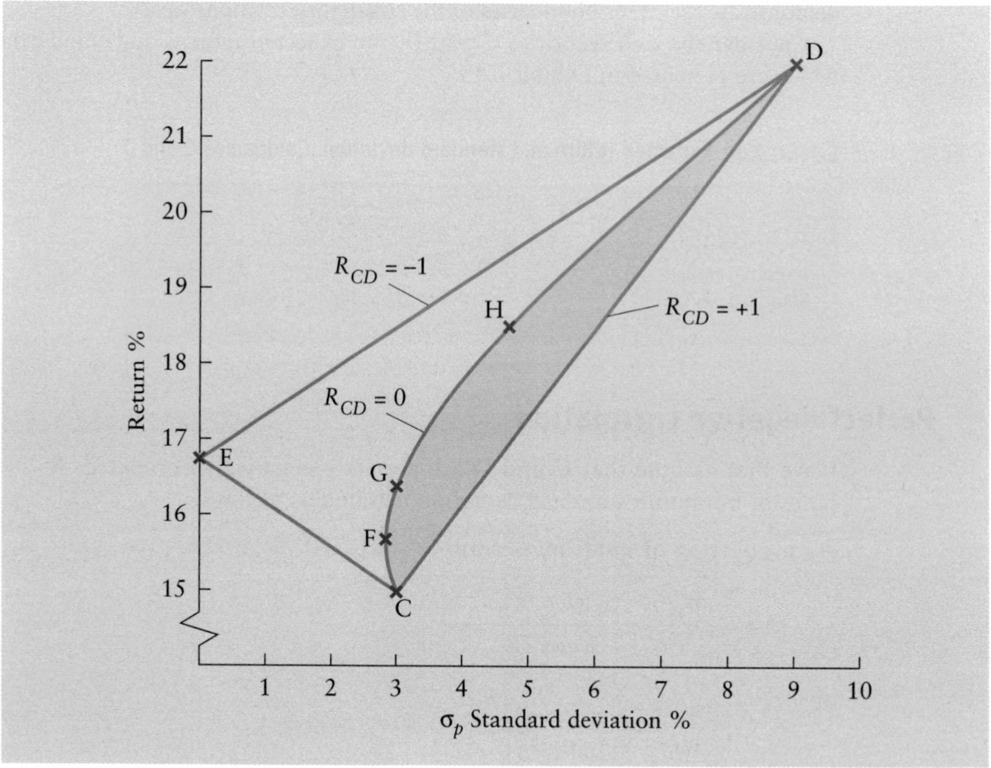

Perfect positive correlation

The risk-return line for portfolios of C and D under the assumption of a correlation coefficient of +1 is a straight line joining C and D. Risk is at a maximum for each level of return for a portfolio consisting of perfectly positively correlated securities. This line forms the right boundary of possible portfolios. If the investment fund is evenly split between C and D both the expected return and the standard deviation will be weighted averages of those for single shares:

Expected return: (15 × 0.5) + (22 × 0.5) = 18.5%
Standard deviation: (3 × 0.5) + (9 × 0.5) = 6%

Zero correlation

The risk-return portfolio combinations for all correlation coefficients of less than +1 lie to the left of the line CD and exhibit non-linearity (that is, they are curved). The non-linearity becomes increasingly pronounced as the correlation coefficient approaches –1. The line CFGHD represents an intermediate level of the risk-reducing effect of diversification. For this line the correlation coefficient between C and D is set at 0. The plot points for the various portfolios are shown in Exhibit 7.45.

Exhibit 7.45 Risk-return combinations for C and D with a correlation coefficient of 0

Portfolio	*C weighting (%)*	*D weighting (%)*	*Expected return (%)*	*Standard deviation*
C	100	0	15	3.00
F	90	10	15.7	$\sqrt{0.9^2 \times 3^2 + 0.1^2 \times 9^2 + 0} = 2.85$
G	80	20	16.4	$\sqrt{0.8^2 \times 3^2 + 0.2^2 \times 9^2 + 0} = 3.00$
H	50	50	18.5	$\sqrt{0.5^2 \times 3^2 + 0.5^2 \times 9^2 + 0} = 4.74$
D	0	100	22	9.00

For most investments in the real world, correlation coefficients tend to lie between 0 and +1. This is because general economic changes influence the returns on securities in similar ways, to a greater or lesser extent. This is particularly true for the returns on shares. This implies that risk reduction is possible through diversification but the total elimination of risk is unlikely. The shaded area in Exhibit 7.44 represents the risk-return region for two-asset portfolios for most ordinary shares.

Portfolio theory has been adopted even by private investors. The article in Exhibit 7.46 is one of many discussing the qualities of shares in terms of covariances and standard deviations.

Exhibit 7.46

The dangers of risk

In this week's instalment of our monthly series on how to build more efficient portfolios of investments, we explain why even low-risk portfolios may not be as safe as they seem

How do you build a low-risk equity portfolio? If you think the answer is simply to stuff it with low-risk shares, go to the back of the class. If you want to reduce the riskiness of your portfolio, simply looking at the riskiness of individual shares isn't enough. You must also consider the covariances between shares – the degree to which they rise and fall together . . . two risky shares can make a safer portfolio, if one rises when the other falls.

A simple example shows how important covariances are. Imagine that since the start of 1998 your shareholdings had comprised equal weightings of just two stocks – Bass and Granada. Since 1988, this portfolio would have had a standard deviation of quarterly returns of 11.06 per cent. That's riskier than Bass alone. But had your portfolio comprised Bass and HSBC, its standard deviation would have been 9.35 per cent. Replacing Granada

▶

Exhibit 7.46 continued

with HSBC would have cut your risk by 15 per cent, even though HSBC is a riskier stock than Granada.

This is possible because the covariance between Bass and HSBC is much lower than that between Bass and Granada. So falls in Bass have often been offset by rises in HSBC, and vice versa. Even high-risk stocks can have a place in a low-risk portfolio, if they have low covariances with other stocks. Not only is this a simple lesson, it's also a profitable one. Higher-risk stocks often have higher returns. So if you can get some of these in your portfolio, you may be able to achieve little risk without giving up decent returns.

In building a low-risk portfolio, your task, therefore, is to find stocks with low covariances. Sadly, this is harder than it sounds. Covariances, like share returns themselves, can vary over time. Just as past returns are no guide to future returns, so past covariances may be no guide to future covariances.

Take, for example, BP and J Sainsbury. Since the start of 1988, the covariance between the two – again using quarterly returns – has been minus five. That's very low indeed, suggesting the two stocks will often move in different directions. Often, but not always. Between December 1993 and March 1994, Sainsbury's price fell by over 15 per cent. But BP's price also fell, by 3 per cent. On that occasion, BP would have offered no protection against a fall in Sainsbury's price.

Source: *Investors Chronicle*, 7 August 1998, p. 11. Reprinted with permission.

EXTENSION TO A LARGE NUMBER OF SECURITIES

To ensure that the analysis is manageable we have so far confined ourselves to two-asset portfolios. Investors rarely construct portfolios from shares in just two firms. Most realise that if risk can be reduced by moving from a single investment to a portfolio of two shares it can be further reduced by adding a third and fourth security, and so on. Consider the three securities represented in Exhibit 7.47. If the investor were to limit the extent of diversification by dividing the fund between two shares, three possible portfolio risk-return combination lines are possible. Curve 1 represents portfolios made by varying allocations of a fund between A and B. Curve 2 shows the alternative risk and return profiles available by investing in B and C; and Curve 3 represents A and C portfolios. With three securities the additional option arises of creating three-asset portfolios. Curve 4 shows the further reduction in return fluctuations resulting from adding the third share.

For two-asset portfolios the alternative risk-return combinations are shown by a line or curve. For a three- (or more) asset portfolio the possible combinations are represented by an area. Thus any risk-return combination within the shaded area of Exhibit 7.47 is potentially available to the investor. However most of them will be unattractive because they are dominated by other efficient alternatives. In fact the rational investor will only be interested in portfolios lying on the upper part of Curve 4. This is the efficiency frontier or efficient boundary. If the number of securities is raised the area representing the whole population of potential risk-return combinations comes to resemble an umbrella battling against a strong wind.

From Exhibit 7.47 it is not possible to establish which portfolio a rational investor would choose. This would depend on the individual's attitude to risk. Two types of investor attitudes are shown in Exhibit 7.48 by drawing two sets of indifference curves. Indifference curves I_H are for a highly risk-averse person who would select the multi-asset portfolio U, which gives a relatively low return combined with a low risk. The less risk-averse person's attitude to risk is displayed in the indifference curves I_L. This person will buy portfolio V, accepting high risk but also anticipating high return. In this manner both investors achieve their optimum portfolios and the highest possible levels of utility.

Exhibit 7.47 A three-asset portfolio

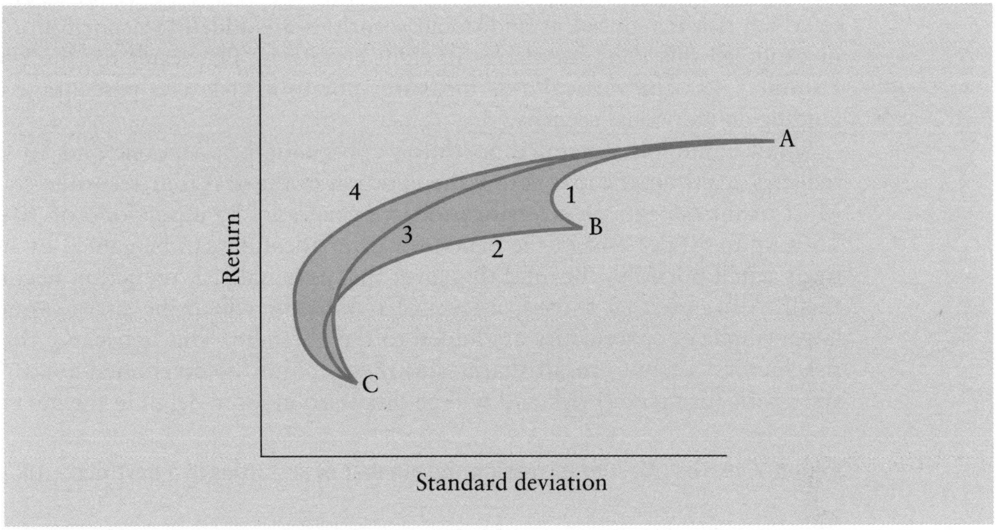

Exhibit 7.48 The opportunity set for multi-security portfolios and portfolio selection for a highly risk-averse person and for a slightly risk-averse person.

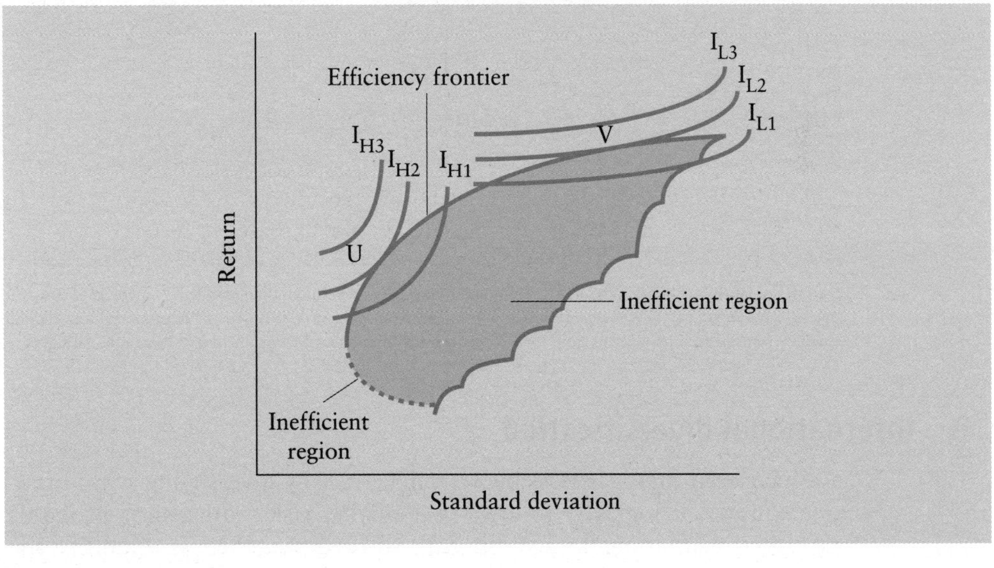

EVIDENCE ON THE BENEFITS OF DIVERSIFICATION

A crucial question for a risk-averse investor is: 'How many securities should be included in a portfolio to achieve a reasonable degree of risk reduction?' Obviously the greater the number of securities the lower the risk. But many investors, particularly small ones, are not keen on dividing their resources into ever smaller amounts, particularly given the transaction cost of buying financial securities. So it would be useful to know the extent to which risk is reduced as additional securities are added to a portfolio. Solnik (1974) investigated this issue for shares in eight countries. The result for the UK is shown in Exhibit 7.49. The vertical axis measures portfolio risk as a percentage of the risk of holding an individual security.

Solnik randomly generated portfolios containing between one and 50 shares. Risk is reduced in a dramatic manner by the addition of the first four securities to the portfolio. Most of the benefits of diversification are generated by a portfolio of 10–15 securities. Thus up to 90 per cent of the benefit of diversification can be gained by holding a relatively small portfolio. Beyond this level the marginal risk reduction becomes relatively small. Also note that there is a level of risk below which the curve cannot fall even if larger numbers of securities are added to the portfolio. This is because there are certain risk factors common to all shares and these cannot be diversified away. This is called systematic (or market) risk and will be discussed in more detail in the next chapter.

Exhibit 7.49 The effect of increasing the number of securities in a portfolio – UK shares

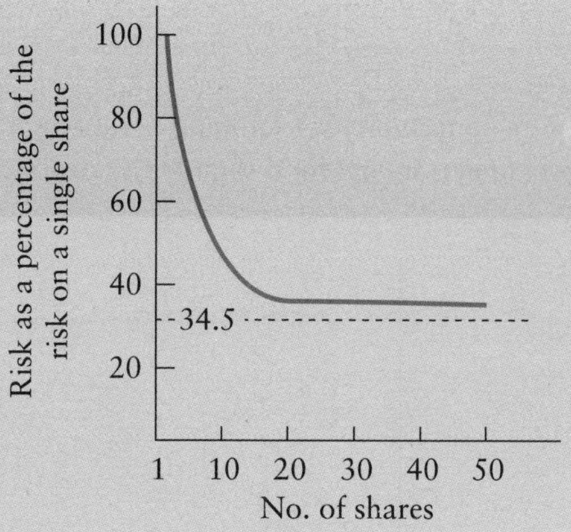

Source: Solnik, B.H. (1974) 'Why not diversify internationally rather than domestically?', *Financial Analysts Journal*, July–August, pp. 48–54. Copyright 1974, Association for Investment Management and Research. Reproduced and republished from *Financial Analysts Journal* with permission from the Association for Investment Management and Research. All rights reserved.

International diversification

We have seen that it is possible to reduce risk by diversifying within the boundaries of one country. It logically follows that further risk reduction is probably available by investing internationally. Exhibit 7.49 showed that there is a limit to the gains experienced by spreading investment across a range of shares in one country. This is because of the economy-wide risk factors such as interest rates and the level of economic activity, which influence all share returns simultaneously. Researchers have demonstrated that this limit can be side-stepped to some extent and that substantial further benefits can be attained through portfolio diversification into foreign shares. Solnik (1974) described a study for Germany in which 43.8 per cent of risk remains even after complete diversification through buying shares within the domestic stock market. While the figures for France and the USA were better, at 32.67 per cent and 27 per cent respectively, there was still a large amount of risk remaining, which could be reduced further by purchasing shares in other countries (*see* Exhibit 7.50).

Exhibit 7.50 The effect of increasing portfolio size with domestic shares

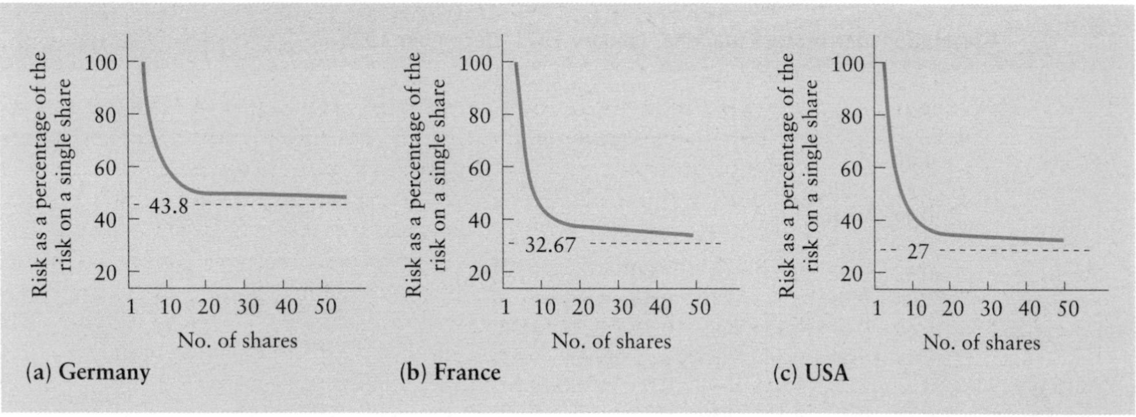

Source: Solnik, B.H. (1974) 'Why not diversify internationally rather than domestically?', *Financial Analysts Journal*, July–August, pp. 48–54. Copyright 1974, Association for Investment Management and Research. Reproduced and republished from *Financial Analysts Journal* with permission from the Association for Investment Management and Research. All rights reserved.

The benefits of international diversification shown in Exhibit 7.51 are very significant. An internationally diversified portfolio reduced risk to less than half the level of a domestically focused portfolio. The international portfolio was almost one-tenth as risky as holding a single company's shares.

Exhibit 7.51 Benefits of international diversification

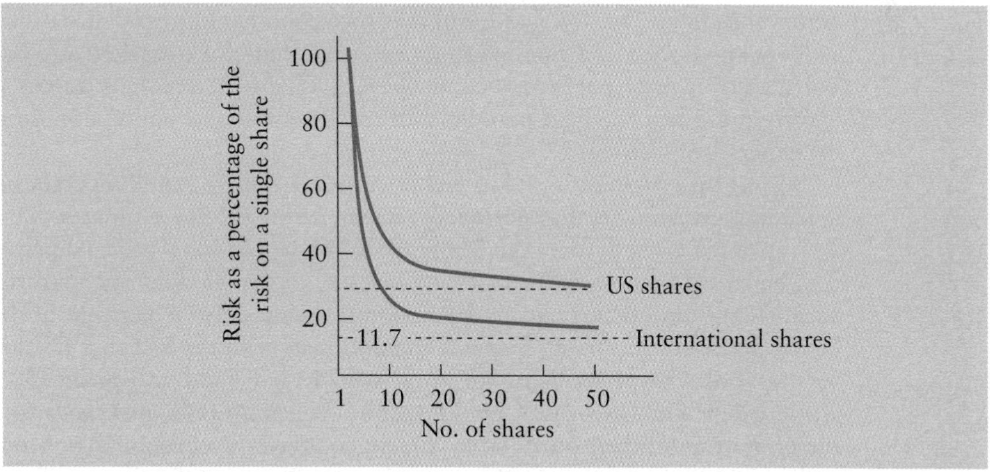

Source: Solnik, B.H. (1974) 'Why not diversify internationally rather than domestically?', *Financial Analysts Journal*, July–August, pp. 48–54. Copyright 1974, Association for Investment Management and Research. Reproduced and republished from *Financial Analysts Journal* with permission from the Association for Investment Management and Research. All rights reserved.

If the world economy were so intimately linked that stock markets in different countries moved together, there would be little to gain from diversifying abroad. Fortunately, this sort of perfect positive correlation of markets does not occur. Exhibit 7.52 shows that the correlation coefficients between national stock markets are significantly less than +1. The correlations between the European and the Asian markets tend to be lower than the correlations within Europe. This makes intuitive sense given the degree of economic integration within Europe.[2] The correlation between the USA and Canada (0.7) is quite strong because their economies are closely linked.

Exhibit 7.52 Correlation matrix stock markets, January 1971–December 1998

	Fr.	*Ger.*	*It.*	*Ne.*	*Sp.*	*Swe.*	*Swz.*	*U.K.*	*Au.*	*H.K.*	*Ja.*	*Si.*	*Ca.*	*U.S.*
France	**1.00**													
Germany	0.61	**1.00**												
Italy	0.44	0.40	**1.00**											
Netherlands	0.61	0.69	0.38	**1.00**										
Spain	0.43	0.42	0.42	0.43	**1.00**									
Sweden	0.38	0.46	0.36	0.50	0.44	**1.00**								
Switzerland	0.60	0.67	0.35	0.69	0.39	0.50	**1.00**							
U.K.	0.54	0.44	0.34	0.64	0.35	0.43	0.54	**1.00**						
Australia	0.37	0.30	0.25	0.41	0.33	0.38	0.37	0.46	**1.00**					
Hong Kong	0.27	0.27	0.19	0.40	0.25	0.27	0.32	0.35	0.36	**1.00**				
Japan	0.39	0.36	0.35	0.42	0.38	0.36	0.40	0.35	0.28	0.26	**1.00**			
Singapore	0.29	0.28	0.21	0.41	0.23	0.35	0.37	0.48	0.42	0.52	0.33	**1.00**		
Canada	0.44	0.34	0.30	0.56	0.31	0.38	0.46	0.51	0.57	0.34	0.28	0.42	**1.00**	
U.S.A.	0.45	0.38	0.26	0.59	0.33	0.41	0.48	0.52	0.48	0.32	0.27	0.46	0.70	**1.00**

Source: Solnik, B.H. (2000) *International Investments*, 4th edn. Reading, Mass: Addison Wesley Longman.

Note: Based on monthly returns in US dollars.

Plainly, risk can be reduced by international diversification but some risk remains even for the broadest portfolio. There is an increasing degree of economic integration across the globe. The linkages mean that the economic independence of nations is gradually being eroded and there is some evidence that stock markets are becoming more correlated. A poor performance on Wall Street often ricochets across the Pacific to Tokyo and other Far East markets and causes a wave of depression on the European exchanges – or vice versa.

Despite the long-term trend to higher correlation there is still much to be gained from spreading investments internationally. Karen Lewis (1996) estimates that an American who invested globally between 1969 and 1993 would have been 10 per cent to 50 per cent better off than an individual who invested in the US domestic market. It is perhaps surprising to find that, typically US investors assign only 15 per cent of their individual equity portfolios to foreign shares.[3] This contrasts with the fact that US shares now constitute about 50 per cent of the total world equity capitalisation ($23,000 billion worldwide).[4] For UK institutional investors (pension funds, insurance companies, etc.) the proportion of their portfolio in foreign equities rose substantially through the 1980s and early 1990s as a number of restrictions were removed and now typically stands at over 25 per cent of their equity funds.

However around the world there is still a bias towards home investment. This disinclination to buy abroad is the result of many factors. These include: a lack of knowledge of companies and markets in faraway places; exchange rate problems; legal restrictions; cost; political risk. Many of these barriers can be, and are being, overcome and so the trend towards increasing internationalisation of security investment should continue.

THE CAPITAL MARKET LINE

Consider Portfolio A on the efficiency frontier of a multi-asset portfolio feasibility set in Exhibit 7.53. An investor could elect to place all funds into such a portfolio and achieve a particular risk-return trade-off. Alternatively, point B could be selected. Here the investor places half the funds invested in an efficient portfolio, C, and half in a risk-free asset such as bonds or Treasury bills issued by a reputable government. These bonds are represented by point r_f which demonstrates a relatively low return but a corresponding zero standard deviation. By purchasing government bonds the investor is effectively lending to the government. If the risk-free asset has a zero standard deviation then any combination containing a proportion of a share portfolio, such as C, and the risk-free asset will have an expected return which is a simple weighted average of the expected return of the share portfolio C and the risk-free asset r_f. More significantly, the standard deviation will also be a simple weighted average. This results in the straight line between C and r_f representing all the possible allocations of a fund between these two types of investment.

Exhibit 7.53 Combining risk-free and risky investments

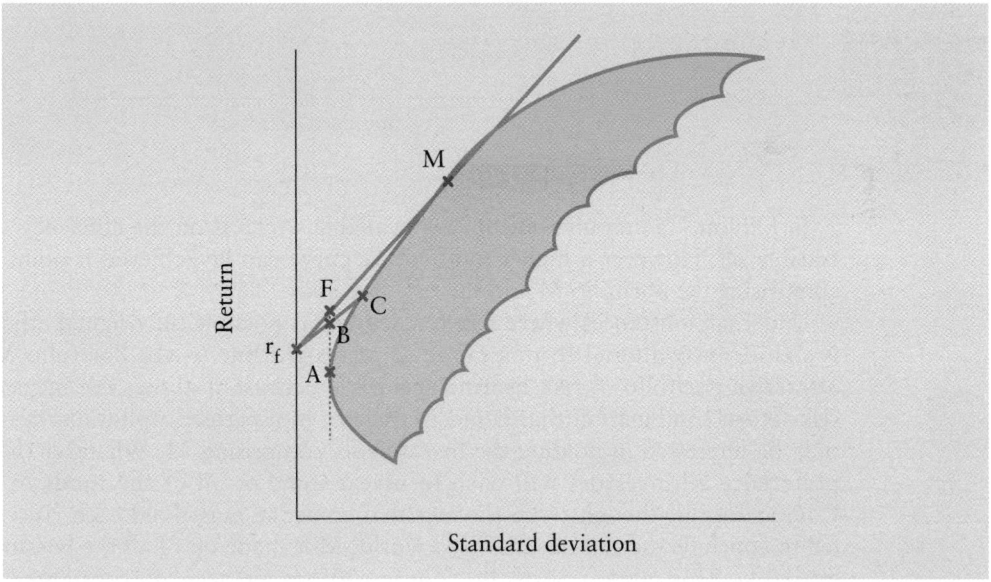

Point B in Exhibit 7.53 is obviously a more efficient combination of investments than point A because for the same level of risk a higher return is achievable. However this is not the best result possible. If a fund were split between a portfolio of shares represented by M and the risk-free investment then all possible allocations between r_f and M would dominate those on the line r_fC. If the fund were divided so that risk-free lending absorbed most of the funds, with approximately one-quarter going into shares of portfolio M, then point F would be reached. This dominates points B and A and is therefore more efficient. The schedule r_fM describes the best possible risk-return combinations. No other share portfolio when combined with a riskless asset gives such a steep slope as Portfolio M. Therefore the investor's interests will be best served by choosing investments comprising Portfolio M and selecting an optimum risk-return combination, by allocating appropriate proportions of a fund between M and the risk free asset, r_f. This is demonstrated in Exhibit 7.54.

Exhibit 7.54 Indifference curves applied to combinations of the market portfolio and the risk-free asset

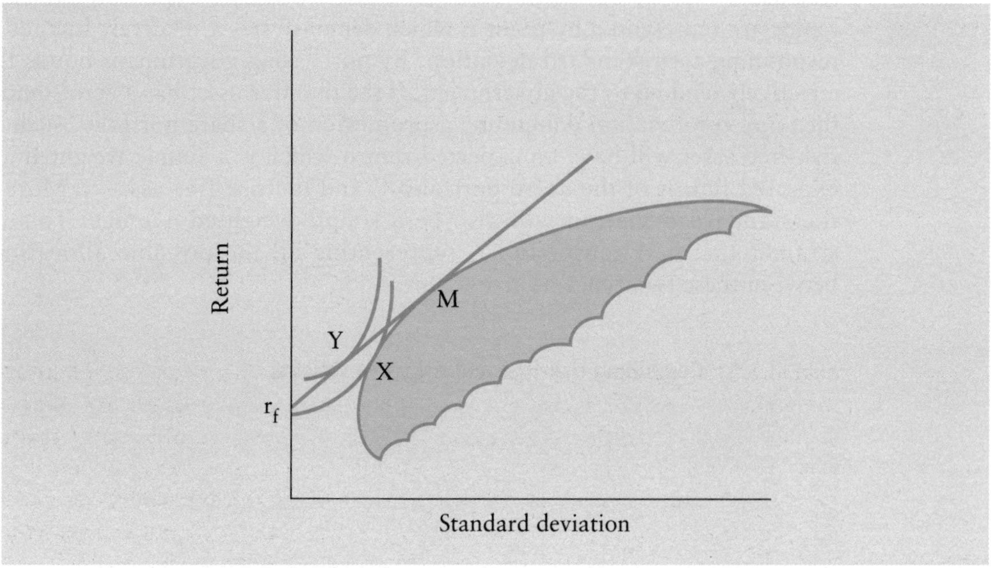

In Exhibit 7.54 an investment X is available which is on the efficiency frontier of the feasible set. However a higher indifference curve can be achieved if point Y is selected, comprising the portfolio M and the risk-free asset.

Under circumstances where risk-free lending is possible the original efficiency frontier is significantly altered from a curve to a straight line (r_fM). Portfolio M is the most attractive portfolio of risk-bearing securities because it allows the investor to select a risk-return combination that is most efficient. In a perfect capital market investors will only be interested in holding the investments comprising M. Whatever their risk-return preference all investors will wish to invest some or all of the funds in Portfolio M. Combining this thought with the fact that someone must hold each risky asset, we are led to conclude that, in this idealised world, M is made up of all the possible risky assets available. This market portfolio contains all traded securities weighted according to their market capitalisations.

To complete the model we need to consider the possibility of an investor borrowing rather than lending, that is, purchasing assets in Portfolio M to a value greater than the amount of money the investor has available from the existing fund. Borrowing to fund investment in risky assets is bound to lead to an overall increase in risk; but the corollary is that a higher return can be anticipated. This is shown in the line MN in Exhibit 7.55.

Exhibit 7.55 The capital market line

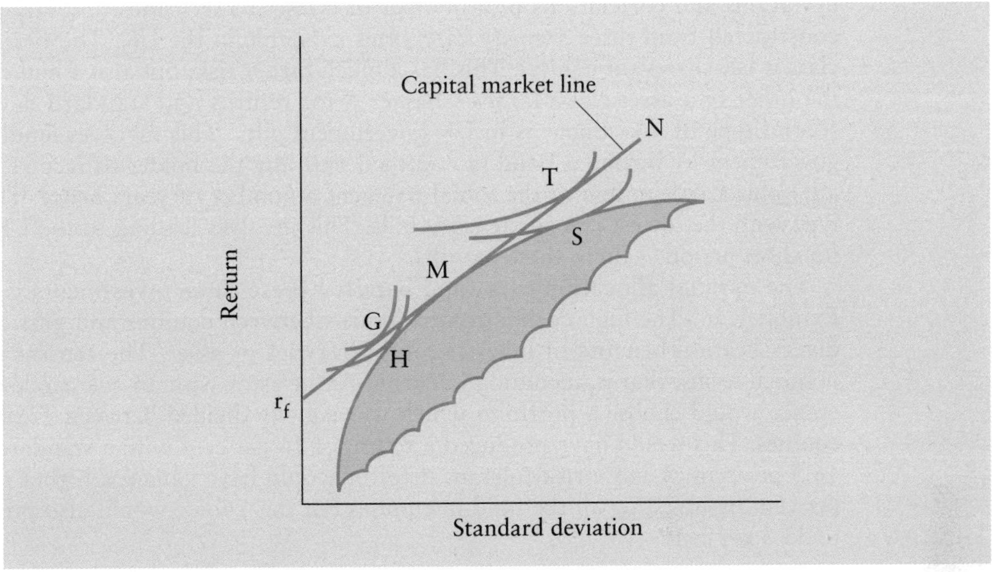

All the risk-return combinations along MN in Exhibit 7.55 dominate those along the original efficiency frontier. An investor who was only mildly risk averse might select point T, purchasing the market portfolio and being financed in part by borrowing at the risk-free rate. This is preferable to Portfolio S purchased without borrowing. The line r_fMN is called the capital market line; it describes the expected return and risk of all efficient portfolios. This idealised model shows that even though investors have differences in their tolerance of risk all will purchase the market portfolio. The degree of risk aversion of individuals expresses itself by the investors either placing some of the fund into risk-free securities, as in the case of the relatively risk-intolerant investor who selects point G, or borrowing (at the risk-free rate of return) to invest in the market portfolio, thereby raising both risk and return, as in the case of the investor who selects point T. This is the Separation Theorem (after Tobin),[5] that is, the choice of the optimal Portfolio M is separated from the risk/return choice. Thus the investor, according to the model, would have two stages to the investment process. First, find the point of tangency on the original efficiency frontier and thereby establish M; secondly, borrow or lend to adjust for preferred risk and return combinations.

This theory is founded on a number of major (some say dubious) assumptions, for example:

1 There are no transaction costs or taxes.
2 Investors can borrow or lend at the risk-free rate of return.
3 Investors have all relevant information regarding the range of investment opportunities. They make their choices on the basis of known expected returns and standard deviations.
4 Maximisation of utility is the objective of all investors.

A PRACTICAL APPLICATION OF PORTFOLIO THEORY

Calculated in BZW's *Equity-Gilt Study* 1996 are a number of optimal portfolios for individuals who have different risk tolerances, ranging from 'minimum risk tolerances' to 'maximum risk tolerances'. The BZW analysis examines the past returns, standard deviations and correlations of a number of classes of securities. Initially portfolios are constructed from three security categories available in the UK. The first type of asset class is UK shares (or equity). This has a much higher risk, but also a higher return, than the other two asset classes. (*See* Chapter 8 for returns and standard deviations.) The second type of investment is in UK government gilts. This involves lending to the UK government by buying a bond (a contract) entitling the holder to receive interest (usually) plus a redemption of the initial payment a number of years hence. The investment type with the lowest risk is Treasury bills. This involves lending to the UK government for short periods – up to three months.

The optimal allocation of a fund between these three investments is presented in Exhibit 7.56. The high correlation of returns between equities and gilts eliminates the diversification benefits of investing in both types of asset. The returns shown are in nominal terms, that is, including inflation. An investor with an average level of risk tolerance would choose a portfolio which was equally divided between Treasury bills and equities. This would have produced a return of 16 per cent with a standard deviation of 16.5 per cent. A more risk-tolerant investor would have gained a higher return at 21.8 per cent by investing all the fund in equities but this choice would also push up the risk to 33.8 per cent.

Exhibit 7.56 Optimal weights (%) for UK portfolio (1970–95)

	Levels of risk tolerance				
Asset class	*Min.*	*Low*	*Average*	*High*	*Max.*
Treasury bills	97.2	78.0	51.3	24.6	0.0
Gilts	2.5	0.0	0.0	0.0	0.0
Equities	0.3	22.0	48.7	75.4	100.0
Total portfolio	100.0	100.0	100.0	100.0	100.0
Portfolio return (%)	10.6	13.0	16.0	19.0	21.8
Portfolio risk (%)	3.1	7.7	16.5	25.5	33.8

Source: BZW (1996) *Equity-Gilt Study 1996*.

The optimal allocation exercise presented in Exhibit 7.56 was repeated with the inclusion of 12 more asset classes. These were the government bonds and equity markets of the other countries of the G7 – USA, Canada, Japan, Germany, France and Italy. The results in Exhibit 7.57 show optimal portfolios consisting of Japanese equities and German bonds combined with UK equities and Treasury bills. The main diversification benefits for high risk-tolerant investors have been obtained through Japanese equities rather than North American and European bond and equity markets. The average-risk investor is able to both increase return (from 16 per cent to 17.7 per cent) and reduce risk (from 16.5 per cent to 13.8 per cent) by holding assets from other countries in a portfolio. International diversification has proved beneficial over long periods in the past. However the BZW analysis is based on historical returns, standard deviations and correlations. It would be unwise to assume that these precise relationships will persist into the future. Indeed, between 1995 and 2001, Japanese equities, which feature strongly in Exhibit 7.57, have performed very badly, falling by over 50 per cent.

Exhibit 7.57 Optimal weights (%) for G7 equity and bond portfolio (1970–95)

	Levels of risk tolerance				
Asset class	*Min.*	*Low*	*Average*	*High*	*Max.*
Treasury bills	89.6	65.4	14.6	0.0	0.0
UK gilts	0.0	0.0	0.0	0.0	0.0
UK equities	0.0	4.8	15.5	29.4	0.0
Canadian equities	0.5	0.0	0.0	0.0	0.0
Japanese equities	1.5	7.6	18.8	50.7	100.0
French bonds	3.9	0.0	0.0	0.0	0.0
German bonds	2.3	18.7	47.1	19.9	0.0
Japanese bonds	2.3	3.4	3.9	0.0	0.0
Total portfolio	100.0	100.0	100.0	100.0	100.0
Portfolio return (%)	10.9	13.0	17.7	21.0	23.7
Portfolio risk (%)	2.6	5.3	13.8	24.9	37.7

Source: BZW (1996) *Equity-Gilt Study 1996*.

PROBLEMS WITH PORTFOLIO THEORY

The portfolio theory model is usually implemented using *historic* returns, standard deviations and correlations to aid decision making about *future* investment. Generally, there is the implicit assumption that key statistical relationships will not alter over the life of the investment. The model relies on the predictability and stability of the probability profile of returns. If the returns have, historically, been volatile then the probability distribution for the anticipated returns will be given a correspondingly wide range; if they have been confined to small fluctuations in the past, then the forecasted variability will be similarly small. Predicting returns, standard deviations and covariances is a difficult and imprecise art. The past may guide to some degree, but there remain large margins for error. As well as standard deviations and covariances changing significantly over time, we have the problem that they change depending on whether the historic data used for their calculation are based on daily, weekly, monthly or quarterly observations. The article in Exhibit 7.58 shows the variability of standard deviations for the group of UK shares in the FTSE All-Share Index.

In addition, the volume of computations for large portfolios can be inhibiting. If there are n securities then n expected returns have to be calculated along with n standard deviations and $n\ (n-1)/2$ covariances. Thus a portfolio of 30 shares will require 495 data items to be calculated.

Also, the accurate estimation of indifference curves is probably an elusive goal and therefore the techniques used in this chapter can be criticised for trying to use unobtainable information. However to counter this criticism it should be pointed out that utility analysis combined with an approximation of the efficiency frontier provides a framework for thinking through the implications of portfolio selection. It is perhaps true that people cannot express their indifference curves exactly, but they will probably be able to

Exhibit 7.58

In search of risk

Measuring risk is a much tougher job than you might think

The simplest measure of risk is the standard deviation of an asset's returns over some chosen period. The chart above shows this for daily returns on the FTSE All-Share. Each point on the line represents the standard deviation of returns over the previous 151 days.

A quick glance, however, reveals a problem. Risk can change dramatically. Had you used this measure in the early summer of 1997 you might have inferred that the market was quite stable.

Within a few weeks, however, the Asian currency crisis caused risk to almost double.

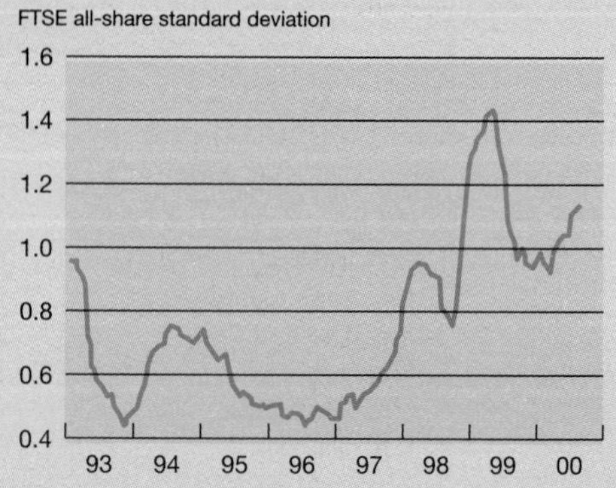

Source: Synergy/sequencer

Source: *Investors Chronicle*, 30 June 2000, p. 50. Reprinted with permission.

state their risk preferences within broad categories, such as 'highly risk averse' or 'moderately risk averse' and so on. Through such approximate methods more appropriate portfolio selection can be made than would be the case without the framework. The model has been particularly useful in the fund management industry for constructing portfolios of different risk-return characters by weighting classes of investment assets differently, for example domestic shares, cash, bonds, foreign shares, property. Theorists have gone a stage further and developed 'portfolio optimisers'. These are mathematical computer programs designed to select an optimal portfolio. Relatively few investment managers have adopted these models, despite their familiarity with the principles and technical aspects of portfolio theory. It appears that traditional approaches to investment selection are valued more highly than the artificial precision of the optimisers. The problem seems to stem from the difficulty of finding high-quality data to put into the system on expected returns, standard deviations, covariances and so on – because of the necessity to rely on past returns. Extreme historical values such as an extraordinarily low standard deviation can lead the program to suggest counter-intuitive and uninvestable portfolios. They have a tendency to promote a high turnover of shares within the portfolio by failing to take into account transaction costs. Also there is a tendency to recommend the purchasing of shares in very small firms having impossibly poor liquidity. The use of portfolio optimisers fits a pattern in finance: entirely substituting mathematics for judgement does not pay off.

CONCLUDING COMMENTS

The criticisms levelled at portfolio theory do strike at those who would use it in a dogmatic, mathematically precise and unquestioning manner. However they do not weaken the fundamental truths revealed. Selecting shares (or other types of securities, projects or assets) on the basis of expected returns alone is inadequate. The additional dimensions of risk and the ability to reduce risk through diversification must be taken into account.

In trying to achieve a low standard deviation it is not enough to invest in a large number of securities. The fundamental requirement is to construct a portfolio in which the securities have low covariance between them. Thus to invest in the shares of 100 different engineering firms will not bring about as many benefits of diversification as the same sized portfolio spread between the sectors of paper manufacturers, retailers, media companies, telecommunications operators and computer software producers. Returns on firms in the same industry are likely to respond in similar ways to economic and other events, to greater or lesser degrees, and so may all do badly at the same time. Firms in different industries are likely to have lower covariances than firms within an industry.

KEY POINTS AND CONCEPTS

- The one-year holding period return:

$$R = \frac{D_1 + P_1 - P_0}{P_0}$$

- With **perfect negative correlation** the risk on a portfolio can fall to zero if an appropriate allocation of funds is made.

- With **perfect positive correlations** between the returns on investments, both the expected returns and the standard deviations of portfolios are weighted averages of the expected returns and standard deviations, respectively, of the constituent investments.

- In cases of **zero correlation** between investments risk can be reduced through diversification, but it will not be eliminated.

- The **correlation coefficient** ranges from –1 to +1. Perfect negative correlation has a correlation coefficient of –1. Perfect positive correlation has a correlation coefficient of +1.

- **The degree of risk reduction** for a portfolio depends on:

  a the extent of statistical interdependency between the returns on different investments; and

  b the number of securities in the portfolio.

- *Portfolio expected returns* are a weighted average of the expected returns on the constituent investments:

$$R_P = aR_A + (1 - a)R_B$$

- Portfolio standard deviation is less than the weighted average of the standard deviation of the constituent investments (except for perfectly positively correlated investments):

$$\sigma_P = \sqrt{a^2\sigma_C^2 + (1 - a)^2\sigma_D^2 + 2a(1 - a)\ \text{cov}\ (R_C, R_D)}$$

$$\sigma_P = \sqrt{a^2\sigma_C^2 + (1 - a)^2\sigma_D^2 + 2a(1 - a)\ R_{CD}\sigma_C\sigma_D}$$

- **Covariance** means the extent to which the returns on two investments move together:

$$\text{cov}\ (R_A, R_B) = \sum_{i=1}^{n}\{(R_A - \bar{R}_A)(R_B - \bar{R}_B)p_i\}$$

- **Covariance and the correlation coefficient** are related. Covariance can take on any positive or negative value. The correlation coefficient is confined to the range –1 to +1:

$$R_{AB} = \frac{\text{cov}\,(R_A, R_B)}{\sigma_A\,\sigma_B}$$

or $\text{cov}\,(R_A, R_B) = R_{AB}\sigma_A\sigma_B$

- **Efficient portfolios** are on the **efficiency frontier**. These are combinations of investments which maximise the expected returns for a given standard deviation. Such portfolios **dominate** all other possible portfolios in an **opportunity set** or **feasible set.**

- To find the proportion of the fund, *a*, to invest in investment C in a two-asset portfolio to achieve **minimum variance on standard deviation:**

$$a = \frac{\sigma_D^2 - \text{cov}\,(R_C, R_D)}{\sigma_C^2 + \sigma_D^2 - 2\,\text{cov}\,(R_C, R_D)}$$

- **Indifference curves** for risk and return:
  - are upward sloping;
  - do not intersect;
  - are preferred if they are closer to the 'north-west';
  - are part of an infinite set of curves;
  - have a slope which depends on the risk aversion of the individual concerned.

- **Optimal portfolios** are available where the highest attainable indifference curve is tangential to the efficiency frontier.

- **Most securities** have correlation coefficients in the range of 0 to +1.

- The feasible set for **multi-asset portfolios** is an area that resembles an umbrella.

- **Diversification within a home stock market** can reduce risk to less than one-third of the risk on a typical single share. Most of this benefit is achieved with a portfolio of 15–20 securities.

- **International diversification** can reduce risk even further than domestic diversification.

- **Problems with portfolio theory:**
  - relies on past data to predict future risk and return;
  - involves complicated calculations;
  - indifference curve generation is difficult;
  - few investment managers use computer programs because of the nonsense results they frequently produce.

REFERENCES AND FURTHER READING

Barclays Capital (2001) *Equity-Gilt Study*. London: Barclays Capital. An example of a risk return line is shown.

Barry, C.B., Peavy J.W. (III) and Rodriguez, M. (1998) 'Performance characteristics of emerging capital markets', *Financial Analysts Journal*, January/February, pp. 72–80. Some useful evidence/data of relevance to international diversification.

Blake, D. (2000) *Financial Market Analysis*. Chichester: Wiley. A more detailed and mathematical treatment.

BZW (1996) *Equity-Gilt Study*, Barclays De Zoete Wedd, London.

Cooper, I. and Kaplanis, E. (1994) 'Home bias in equity portfolios, inflation hedging and international capital market equilibrium', *The Review of Financial Studies*, 7(1), pp. 45–60. Examines the general bias of investors toward investing in their domestic stock market.

Divecha, A.B., Drach, J. and Stefek, D. (1992) 'Emerging markets: a quantitative perspective', *Journal of Portfolio Management*, Fall, pp. 41–50. An investigation of the risk-reducing benefits of international diversification.

Economist, The (1991) 'School brief: risk and return', 2 February. Concise and clear discussion of portfolio theory.

Economist, The (1996) 'Economic focus: stay-at-home shareholders', 17 February. Discusses the attractions and problems of international diversification.

Elton, E.J. and Gruber, M.J. (1995) *Modern portfolio theory and investment analysis*, 5th edn. Chichester: Wiley. From introductory to advanced portfolio theory.

Fama, E.F. and Miller, M.H. (1972) *The Theory of Finance*. Orlando, Florida: Holt, Rinehart & Winston. Utility analysis and indifference curve theory.

Frost, P.A. and Savarino, J.E. (1986) 'Portfolio size and estimation risk', *Journal of Portfolio Management*, 12, Summer, pp. 60–4. Discussion of portfolio theory.

Jorion, P. (1992) 'Portfolio optimisation in practice', *Financial Analysts Journal*, 48, January/February, pp. 68–74. The use of portfolio theory investigated.

Kaplanis, E. (1996) 'Benefits and costs of international portfolio investments', *Financial Times Mastering Management*, January. Short article summarising the attractions of international diversification.

Kaplanis, E. and Schaefer, S. (1991) 'Exchange risk and international diversification in bond and equity portfolios', *Journal of Economics and Business*, 43, pp. 287–307. Considers the problem of exchange-rate risk on internationally diversified portfolios.

Lewis, K. (1996) 'Consumption, stock returns, and the gains from international risk-sharing', *NBER Working Paper*, No. 5410, January. Advanced theoretical discussion of the gains from international diversification.

Lintner, J. (1965) 'The valuation of risky assets and the selection of risky investments in stock portfolios and capital budgets', *Review of Economics and Statistics*, 47, February, pp. 13–37. Theoretical paper contributing to the development of portfolio theory.

Markowitz, H.M. (1952) 'Portfolio selection', *Journal of Finance*, 7, pp. 77–91. Pioneering theory

Markowitz, H.M. (1959) *Portfolio Selection: Efficient Diversification of Investments*. New York: Wiley (1991) 2nd edn. Basil Blackwell, Cambridge, MA. The Nobel Prize winner explains his ideas.

Markowitz, H.M. (1991) 'Foundations of portfolio theory', *Journal of Finance*, June. Markowitz describes some of his thinking in the development of portfolio theory. Plus some advanced utility theory.

Michaud, R.O. (1989) 'The Markowitz optimization enigma: Is "optimized" optimal?', *Financial Analysts Journal*, 45, January–February, pp. 31–42. Discusses reasons for the low rate of adoption of portfolio optimiser programmes by the investment community.

Michaud, R.O., Bergstorm, G.L., Frashure, R.D. and Wolahan, B.K. (1996) 'Twenty years of international equity investment', *Journal of Portfolio Management*, Fall, pp. 9–22. Diversifying into well-developed markets did not reduce risk substantially.

Mossin, J. (1966) 'Equilibrium in a capital asset market', *Econometrica*, 34, October, pp. 768–83. Theoretical paper taking forward portfolio theory and discussing the 'market line'.

Sharpe, W.F. (1963) 'A simplified model for portfolio analysis', *Management Science*, 9, pp. 277–93. Builds on Markowitz's work, focusing on the determination of the efficient set.

Sharpe, W.F., Alexander, G.J. and Bailey, J.V. (1999) *Investments*. 6th edn. Upper Saddle River, NJ: Prentice-Hall. Chapters 6, 7, 8 and 9 contain expositions of portfolio theory.

Solnik, B.H. (1974) 'Why not diversify internationally rather than domestically?', *Financial Analysts Journal*, July–August, pp. 48–54. Empirical investigation on the effect of diversification for eight countries.

Solnik, B. (2000) *International Investments*, 4th edn. Reading, Mass.: Addison Wesley Longman. The benefits of international diversification are discussed in an accessible manner – some good data.

Spiedell, L.S. and Sappenfield, R. (1992) 'Global diversification in a shrinking world', *Journal of Portfolio Management*, Fall, pp. 57–67. Diversifying into emerging markets enables significant risk reduction.

Tobin, J. (1958) 'Liquidity preference as behaviour toward risk', *Review of Economic Studies,* February, 26, pp. 65–86. The first discussion of the separation of the selection of the efficient market portfolio and the individual's risk return choice.

Wagner, W.H. and Lau, S. (1971) 'The effects of diversification on risk', *Financial Analysts Journal*, November–December. Empirical evidence of the effect on standard deviation of increasing portfolio size.

WEBSITE

Morgan Stanley Captial International www.msci.com. Recent correlation coefficients are available as well as a mass of other data.

SELF-REVIEW QUESTIONS

1 How do you calculate the risk on a two-asset portfolio?

2 What is a dominant portfolio?

3 What are indifference curves and why can they never intersect?

4 How are holding-period returns calculated?

5 Show how the covariance and correlation coefficient are related.

6 Explain the necessary conditions for the standard deviation on a portfolio to be zero.

7 Illustrate the efficiency frontier and explain why all portfolios on the frontier are not necessarily optimal.

8 A risk-averse investor currently holds low-risk shares in one company only. In what circumstances would it be wise to split the fund by purchasing shares in a high-risk and high-return share?

9 'The objective of portfolio investment is to minimise risk.' Do you agree?

10 Why is the standard deviation on a portfolio not a weighted average of the standard deviations of the constituent securities?

11 Describe why investors do not routinely calculate portfolio standard deviations and indifference curves.

12 How are the gains from diversifications linked to correlation coefficients?

QUESTIONS AND PROBLEMS

1 What is the holding-period return for a share which cost £2.50, was held for a year and then sold for £3.20, and which paid a dividend at the end of the holding period of 10p?

2 Calculate the holding-period return for a share which is held for three months and sold for £5. The purchase price was £4.80 and no dividend is payable. Now compare the return on this share with the return earned on the share described in Question 1.

3 Shares in Whitchat plc can be purchased today for £1.20. The expected dividend in one year is 5p. This is expected to be followed by annual dividends of 6p and 7p respectively in the following two years. The shares are expected to be sold for £2 in three years. What is the three-year holding-period return? What is the average annual rate of return?

4* The probability of a hot summer is 0.2. The probability of a moderately warm summer is 0.6, whereas the probability of a wet and cold summer is 0.2. If a hot summer occurs then the return on shares in the Ice Cream Manufacturing Company will be 30 per cent. If moderately warm the return will be 15 per cent, and if cold 2 per cent.

a What is the expected return?

b What is the standard deviation of that return?

5* Splash plc owns a swimming pool near to a major seaside resort town. Holidaymakers boost the turnover of this firm when they are unable to use the beach on cold and wet days. Thus Splash's returns are best when the weather is poor. The returns on the shares are shown in the table below, together with the probability of when a particular weather 'event' may occur.

Event	*Probability*	*Returns on shares in Splash plc (%)*
Hot weather	0.2	5
Modestly warm	0.6	15
Cold weather	0.2	20
	1.0	

Calculate

a The expected return for a share in Splash plc.

b The standard deviation of a share in Splash plc.

6* a Given the data on the Ice Cream Manufacturing Company (ICMC) in Question 4 and Splash plc in Question 5, now calculate the expected returns and standard deviation of the following portfolios.

Portfolio	*Proportion of funds invested in ICMC*	*Proportion of funds invested in Splash*
A	0.80	0.20
B	0.50	0.50
C	0.25	0.75

b Calculate the correct allocation of resources between ICMC and Splash which will give the minimum standard deviation. Draw a risk-return line on graph paper using the data you have generated from Questions 4, 5 and 6a.

7 Given the following expected returns and standard deviations for shares X and Y,

$$\bar{R}_X = 25\%, \bar{R}_Y = 35\%, \sigma_X = 15\%, \sigma_Y = 20\%$$

a What is the expected return and standard deviation for a portfolio composed of 50 per cent of X and 50 per cent of Y assuming X and Y have a correlation coefficient of –0.7?

b What is the expected return and standard deviation for a portfolio composed of 30 per cent of X and 70 per cent of Y, assuming X and Y have a correlation coefficient of +0.5?

8† The returns on shares S and T vary depending on the state of economic growth.

State of economy	*Probability of economic state occurring*	*Returns on S if economic state occurs (%)*	*Returns on T if economic state occurs (%)*
Boom	0.15	45	18
Growth	0.70	20	17
Recession	0.15	–10	16

Required

a Calculate the expected return and standard deviation for share S.

b Calculate the expected return and standard deviation for share T.

c What are the covariance and the correlation coefficient between returns on S and returns on T?

d Determine a portfolio expected return and standard deviation if two-thirds of a fund are devoted to S and one-third devoted to T.

9† Using the results generated in Question 8 and three or four additional calculations, display the efficiency frontier for a two-asset portfolio consisting of S and T.

Show a set of indifference curves for a highly risk-averse investor and select on optimal portfolio on the assumption that the investor can only invest in these two shares.

10† An investor has £100,000 to invest in shares of Trent or Severn the expected returns and standard deviations of which are as follows.

	$\bar{R}$	σ
Trent	10	5
Severn	20	12

The correlation coefficient between those two shares is –0.2.

Required

a Calculate the portfolio expected returns and standard deviations for the following allocations.

Portfolio	*Trent (%)*	*Severn (%)*
A	100	0
B	75	25
C	50	50
D	25	75
E		100

b Calculate the minimum standard deviation available by varying the proportion of Trent and Severn shares in the portfolio.

c Create a diagram showing the feasible set and the efficiency frontier.

d Select an optimal portfolio for a slightly risk-averse investor using indifference curves.

11† Big Trucks plc is considering two major projects. The first is to expand production at the Midlands factory. The second is to start production in East Asia. The returns in terms of internal rates of return depend on world economic growth. These are as follows.

World growth	*Probability of growth occurring*	*IRR for Midlands project (%)*	*IRR for Far East project (%)*
High	0.3	20	50
Medium	0.4	18	30
Low	0.3	16	0

Calculate

a The expected return and standard deviation of each project.

b An alternative to selecting one project or the other is to split the available investment funds between the two projects. Now calculate the expected return and standard deviation if half of the funds were devoted to the Midlands project and half to the Far East. Assume returns per pound invested remain constant regardless of the size of the investment.

c Calculate the expected return and standard deviation for a series of four other possible allocations of the funds and construct a risk-return line.

d Suggest an approach for choosing the optimal allocation of funds assuming a highly risk-averse management.

12† Shares in F and G are perfectly negatively correlated.

	$\bar{R}$	σ
F	17	6
G	25	10

a Calculate the expected return and standard deviation from a portfolio consisting of 50 per cent of F and 50 per cent of G.

b How would you allocate the fund to achieve a zero standard deviation?

13 Suppose that Mrs Qureshi can invest all her savings in shares of Ihser plc, or all her savings in Resque plc. Alternatively she could diversify her investment between these two. There are two possible states of the economy, growth or recession, and the returns on Ihser and Resque depend on which state will occur.

State of the economy	*Probability of state of the economy occurring*	*Ihser return (%)*	*Resque return (%)*
Growth	0.7	30	15
Recession	0.3	–10	20

Required

a Calculate the expected return, variance and standard deviation for each share.

b Calculate the expected return, variance and standard deviation for the following diversifying allocations of Mrs Qureshi's savings:

(i) 50% in Ihser, 50% in Resque;

(ii) 11% in Ihser, 89% in Resque.

c Explain the relationship between risk reduction and the correlation between individual financial security returns.

14* (*Examination level*) **Horace Investments**

Your Uncle Horace is a wealthy man with investments in a variety of businesses. He is also a generous person, especially to his nieces and nephews. He has written explaining that he will be distributing some of his shareholdings amongst the next generation. To your surprise, he has offered you £100,000 of shares in two firms of great sentimental value to him; Ecaroh and Acehar. You may allocate the £100,000 in any one of four ways. The first two options are to put all of the money into one of the firms. An alternative is to allocate half to Ecaroh and half to Acehar. Finally you may have £90,000 of Ecaroh shares and £10,000 of Acehar shares. During the week you are given to make your decision you contact a friend who is a corporate analyst with access to extensive brokers' and other reports on firms. The information he provides could help you to allocate this generous gift. He tells you that the market consensus is that Ecaroh is a relatively unexciting but steady, reliable firm producing profits which do not vary in an erratic fashion. If the economy is growing strongly then the returns on Ecaroh are expected to be 10 per cent per year. If normal economic growth occurs then the returns will be 15 per cent and if poor growth is the outcome the returns will be 16 per cent.

Acehar, a consumer electronics firm, is a much more exciting and dynamic but risky firm. Profits vary in dramatic ways with the general level of activity in the economy. If growth is strong then Acehar will return 50 per cent; if normal, 25 per cent; and, if poor, there will be no return. You generate your own estimates of the probabilities of particular economic growth rates occurring by amalgamating numerous macroeconomic forecasts and applying a dose of scepticism to any one estimate. Your conclusions are that there is a 30 per cent chance of strong growth, a 40 per cent chance of normal growth and the probability of slow growth is put at 30 per cent.

Because of Horace's emotional attachment to these firms he insists that these are the only investment(s) you hold, as he puts it, to 'engender commitment and interest in the success of his corporate babies'.

Required

a For each of the alternatives on offer calculate returns and standard deviation.

b Draw a risk and return diagram on graph paper displaying the four options and then add a reasonable risk-return line for all possible allocations between Acehar and Ecaroh. (This is hypothetical – no further calculations are required.)

State which of the four options are efficient portfolios and which are inefficient given your risk-return line.

c You are young and not as risk averse as most people, because you feel you will be able to bounce back from a financial disaster should one occur. Draw indifference curves on the diagram for a person who is only slightly risk averse. Demonstrate an optimal risk-return point on the risk-return line by labelling it point 'J'.

d Briefly discuss the benefits of greater diversification. Do these benefits continue to increase with ever greater diversification?

15 (*Examination level*) You have been bequeathed a legacy of £100,000 and you are considering placing the entire funds either in shares of company A or in shares in company B.

When you told your stock broker about this plan he suggested two alternative investment approaches.

a Invest some of the money in A and some in B to give you at least a small degree of diversification. The proportions suggested are given in Table 2 below.

b Invest the entire sum in a broad range of investments to reduce risk. This portfolio is expected to produce a return of 23 per cent per year with a standard deviation of 6 per cent.

To assist your final decision the broker provides you with forecasts by expert City analysts for shares in A and B given various states of the economy – *see* Table 1.

Table 1

State of the economy	*Probability of that state of the economy*	*Returns on A (%)*	*Returns on B (%)*
Recession	0.25	10	15
Growth	0.50	20	55
Boom	0.25	30	–10

Table 2

Portfolio	*Proportion of portfolio invested in A (%)*	*Proportion of portfolio invested in B (%)*
1	25	75
2	75	25
3	90	10

Required

a Compare the risk and return of the alternatives (including your original intention of putting all the money into either A or B).

b Display the results on graph paper and draw an estimated portfolio risk-return line based on the plot points for the two-share portfolio. (There is no requirement to calculate the minimum risk portfolio.)

c Describe the efficient and inefficient region.

d Use indifference curves to select the optimal portfolio to give the highest utility.

e Define the Market Portfolio in Modern Portfolio theory.

ASSIGNMENTS

1 If you have access to information on financial security return probability profiles then draw up a report showing the efficiency frontier for a two-asset portfolio. Draw indifference curves based on canvassed opinion and/or subjective judgement and select an optimal portfolio.

2 If you have access to the estimated probability distribution of returns for some projects within the firm, consider the impact of accepting these projects on the overall risk-return profile of the firm. For instance, are they positively or negatively correlated with the existing set of activities?

CHAPTER NOTES

1 See Appendix 2.1 for mathematical tools.

2 These correlation coefficients have to be treated with great caution as they tend to vary enormously from one study to another.

3 Solnik (2000).

4 Solnik (2000).

5 Tobin's Separation Theorem was first discussed in his 1958 article.

Chapter 8

THE CAPITAL ASSET PRICING MODEL AND MULTI-FACTOR MODELS

INTRODUCTION

One financial theory has dominated the academic literature and influenced greatly the practical world of finance and business for over three decades since it was first expounded by the Nobel prizewinner William Sharpe and other theoreticians.[1] This is the Capital Asset Pricing Model (CAPM). At its heart the CAPM (pronounced cap-em) has an old and common observation – the returns on a financial asset increase with risk. The 'breakthrough' in the 1960s was to define risk in a very precise way. It was no longer enough to rely on standard deviation after the work of Markowitz and others (*see* Chapter 7) had shown the benefits of diversification. The argument goes that it is illogical to be less than fully diversified so investors tend to create large portfolios. When a portfolio is formed one type of risk factor is eliminated – that which is specifically associated with the fortunes and misfortunes of particular companies. This is called unsystematic risk or unique risk. Once this is taken from the scene the investor merely has to concentrate on risks which cannot be eliminated by holding ever larger portfolios. This is systematic risk, an element of risk common to all firms to a greater or lesser extent.

A central tenet of the CAPM is that systematic risk, as measured by beta, is the *only* factor affecting the level of return required on a share for a completely diversified investor. For practical use this risk factor is considered to be the extent to which a particular share's returns move when the stock market as a whole moves. What is more, the relationship between this beta factor and returns is described by a straight line (it is linear). This neat and, at first sight, apparently complete model changed the way people viewed the world of finance and influenced their actions.

Its far-reaching consequences changed the way in which portfolios were constructed for many pension and insurance funds of millions of people. It contributed to the strengthening of the notions of stock market efficiency – the idea that the stock market 'correctly' prices shares (*see* Chapter 14). It has affected the investment philosophies of large numbers of investors. It has influenced the calculation of the cost of capital for a firm, or to express it another way, the required rate of return on projects. By providing a target figure of the return required by shareholders the CAPM has enabled management to vary the discount rate by which project cash flows were discounted, depending on the perceived level of systematic risk as defined by beta. Thus countless investment proposals have been accepted or rejected on the strength of what the CAPM has to say about the minimum return demanded by shareholders. In the view of many this is regrettable.

Some see the CAPM as artificially restricting the investment opportunities undertaken by firms in national economies and has led to charges of under-investment, economic backwardness and short-termism.

Far more damning criticism was to come for the CAPM in the 1980s and 1990s when researchers looked at the relationship between the CAPM's systematic risk measure, beta, and the returns on shares over the period since the mid-1960s. They discovered either that there was absolutely no relationship at all or that beta had only a weak influence on the return shares produced. They commented that there were other factors determining the returns on shares. This opened up a raging debate within the academic community, with some saying beta was dead, some saying that it was only wounded, and some saying it was alive and well.

The irony is that just as the academic community is having serious doubts about the model, in the outside world CAPM is reaching new heights of popularity. Hundreds of thousands, if not millions, have studied the CAPM in universities over the past three decades and are now placed in important positions around the world ready to make key decisions often under the subliminal influence of the CAPM. Indeed, a new industry has been built selling data and information which can be plugged into CAPM-based decision-making frameworks in the workplace.

Partly in response to the empirical evidence, and partly from theoretical doubts about the CAPM, academics began exploring models which were based on a number of explanatory factors influencing the returns on shares rather than the one solitary variable considered in the CAPM. The most prominent is the Arbitrage Pricing Theory (APT) which permits factors other than beta to explain share returns. But wait! We are running ahead of the story. First we have to understand the workings of the CAPM, its theoretical underpinnings and the various items of jargon that have grown up within this area of finance. Only then will a full appreciation of its limitations be possible, along with a consideration of alternative risk-return approaches.

Learning objectives

The ideas, frameworks and theories surrounding the relationship between the returns on a security and its risk are pivotal to most of the issues discussed in this book. At times it may seem that this chapter is marching you up to the top of the hill only to push you down again. But remember, sometimes what you learn on a journey and what you see from new viewpoints are more important than the ultimate destination. By the end of this chapter the reader should be able to:

- describe the fundamental features of the Capital Asset Pricing Model (CAPM);
- show an awareness of the empirical evidence relating to the CAPM;
- explain the key characteristics of multi-factor models, including the Arbitrage Pricing Theory (APT) and the three-factor model;
- express a reasoned and balanced judgement of the risk-return relationship in financial markets.

CASE STUDY 8.1

Pigs might fly

During the winter of 1995–96 a visitor to Birmingham, England might have seen an enticing advertisement on the local buses. This promised 'Stock market performance without any risk'. This amazing offer was available by purchasing a financial product sold by one of the major UK building societies, which has its headquarters in Birmingham. After using the freephone number potential investors receive a leaflet which informs them that they can purchase a 'No-risk stock market linked investment' with an 'Unlimited capital growth opportunity' and a 'GUARANTEED minimum return'. They were urged to 'Act Today' and invest between £5,000 and £500,000. This seems to defy the logic of both common sense and the theories described in this chapter. A basic law of finance is that more return comes with more risk. This investment product apparently offered the proverbial 'free lunch'. (By the way, the building society's literature on this product was decorated with numerous images of flying pigs.) On reading the small print they find that they are not dealing with a bunch of charlatans, nor do they have to reject the time-honoured relationship between risk and return. The society was not offering a stock market *return* with zero risk but offering a *performance* linked to the growth of FTSE 100 share index. This represents the capital gain on shares *only* and excludes a vital part of stock market returns which is the dividend income, then around 4 per cent a year. The only guarantee was that, at worst, after five years the investor's original capital will be returned plus 10 per cent. Thus if the FTSE 100 index were to fall the returns would be less than 2 per cent per year before tax (assuming the absence of a default by the guarantor). If the FTSE 100 index were to rise the investor would receive less than the return available by straightforward investment in shares. Thus in reality this product offered a lower risk than investing directly in shares but it also offered a lower return and so complies with the rule of a positive relationship between risk and return.

A SHORT HISTORY OF SHARES, BONDS AND BILLS

We begin with an examination of the rate of return earned on shares and other classes of financial securities over the period since the end of 1899. Elroy Dimson, Paul Marsh and Mike Staunton from the London Business School, in collaboration with the bank ABN Amro, produced an analysis of the returns earned on shares, bonds (lending to the UK government by buying long-term financial investments, often called 'gilts') and Treasury bills (short-term lending to the UK government – usually three months) for the entire period from the end of 1899 to the present. As can be seen from Exhibit 8.1 shares have produced a much better return than the other two classes of investment.

Exhibit 8.1 What a £100 investment in January 1900 would be worth at the end of 2000 with all income reinvested

	If invested in Equities (shares)	*If invested in Bonds (gilts)*	*If invested in Treasury bills*
Money (nominal) return	£1,611,200	£20,300	£14,900
Real return	£29,060	£370	£270

Even if the effects of inflation are removed, an investor placing £100 in a portfolio of shares at the end of 1899 will, by the beginning of 2001, be able to purchase 290.6 times as many goods and services as could be purchased in 1899 with the initial amount invested.[2]

The Dimson, Marsh and Staunton research shows that equities (shares) have produced average annual real returns (after reinvestment of dividends) much higher than that on gilts or Treasury bills (*see* Exhibit 8.2).

The study shows an extra return for equities compared with gilts of 4.5 per cent (5.8 per cent – 1.3 per cent) on the basis of geometric means and 5.3 per cent on the basis of arithmetic means. (For a discussion on geometric and arithmetic means consult Appendix 8.1). Over 101 years, under an alternative study conducted by Barclays, shares gave an annual average return of 4.4 per cent (5.5 per cent – 1.1 per cent) greater than gilts and 4.6 per cent greater than Treasury bills.

If a 50-year history of financial security returns is examined then the premium received by share investors rises. According to Dimson *et al.* the extra annual return over gilts is 6.9 per cent (8.6 per cent – 1.7 per cent). The premium over Treasury bills is even larger at 7.2 per cent. The Barclays study shows the extra annual return for equity investors received over the 50-year period to the end of 2000 amounted to 6.5 per cent over gilts and over Treasury bills it was 6.3 per cent. Clearly the size of the additional return achieved by equity investors compared with government bond or Treasury bill investors has varied over time. Indeed during 2000 the premium became negative as investors lost money on shares while gilts increased in value in addition to paying coupons.

To state definitively the return premium share investors received over gilt and Treasury bill investors is obviously impossible as it depends on the period of time studied. What we can do is apply a principle when trying to establish a usable figure for the equity risk premium. We would look at data for a long time period because the relationship between the returns on shares and bonds (or bills) is subject to a great deal of fluctuation in the short term (witness 2000 when shares fell). If we used the two longest periods in Exhibit 8.2 we would say the extra return on shares is under 5 per cent (based on geometric means). However, some observers may object and say that to use data from the first half of the last century is going back too far: the returns back then were influenced by many factors that no longer apply. For these objectors the last 50 years of observation are sufficient. For the remainder of this book we will, for practical

Exhibit 8.2 Real returns on UK financial securities (per cent per annum)

Geometric means (arithmetic means in brackets)	*101 years (1900–1.1.2001)*	*75 years (1926–1.1.2001)*	*50 years (1956–1.1.2001)*	*25 years (1976–1.1.2001)*
Equities	5.8 (7.6)	6.9	8.6	10.9
Gilts	1.3 (2.3)	2.3	1.7	7.1
Treasury bills	1.0 (1.2)	1.1	1.4	3.4
Inflation	4.1 (4.3)			

Source: Dimson, E., Marsh, P. and Staunton, M. (2001) *The Millennium Book II: 101 Years of Investment Returns*. © 2001 Elroy Dimson, Paul Marsh and Mike Staunton. London: London Business School/ABN Amro.

purposes, assume an historic premium for shares over reputable government band securities of 5 per cent – roughly in the middle of the above estimates, with a bias toward the longer-term studies.[3]

Exhibit 8.3 shows that investors in other countries' shares have received higher returns than if they had opted to invest in government securities. Generally the extra return on shares over government bonds is in the region 4.5 per cent to 6 per cent.

Exhibit 8.3 Real returns on equities and government bonds and bills: an international comparison, 1900–2000, 101 years (geometic means)

	Annualised percentage returns		
	Equity	*Bonds*	*Bills*
Sweden	8.0	2.4	2.0
Australia	7.5	1.1	0.4
USA	6.7	1.6	1.1
Canada	6.4	1.8	1.7
Netherlands	5.8	1.1	0.7
UK	5.8	1.3	1.0
Ireland	5.6	1.5	1.3
Denmark (equity from 1915)	5.2	2.8	2.9
Switzerland (equity from 1911)	5.0	2.8	1.1
Japan	4.6	−1.6	−2.0
Spain	4.5	1.2	0.4
France	3.9	−1.0	−3.3
Germany (equity 99 years excl. 1922/3)	3.6	−2.2	−0.6
Italy	2.7	−2.2	−4.1
Belgium	2.6	−0.4	−0.3

Sources: Dimson, E., Marsh, P. and Staunton, M. (2001) *The Millennium Book II: 101 Years of Investment Returns*. © 2001 Elroy Dimson, Paul Marsh and Mike Staunton. London: London Business School/ABN Amro.

Treasury bills are regarded as the safest possible investment. It is highly unlikely that the UK government will default and the fact they mature in a matter of days means that their prices do not vary a great deal.

Long-term government bonds also have a low risk of default but they do suffer from uncertainty concerning the price that can be achieved in the market when selling to another investor prior to the maturity date. The prices fluctuate inversely to interest rates. If interest rates rise due to, say, a perceived increase in inflation, then the price of bonds will fall, producing a capital loss. Often these capital losses over a period of a year outweigh the gain from the interest paid, producing an overall negative annual return. (*See* Chapter 11 for a more detailed discussion of bonds.) Despite these yearly ups and downs, for practical purpose bonds issued by a reputable government may be viewed as being risk free if a long-term (to maturity) perspective is taken. This is because the promised payments by the government are highly unlikely to be missed, therefore the nominal return is guaranteed (unexpected inflation may be a problem for real returns, but government bonds and bills are the nearest we are going to get to risk-free securities). Shares carry the highest risk because their payouts of dividends and capital gains and losses depend on the performance of the underlying businesses. We now examine the extent to which total returns (dividends or interest plus capital gain or loss) have varied over the years.

A general impression of the degree of volatility associated with each class of investment can be found by examining Exhibits 8.4, 8.5 and 8.6. An investor in Treasury bills in any year is unlikely to experience a real (after inflation) loss greater than 5 per cent. The investor in gilts, on the other hand, has a fairly high chance of making a significant negative return over the period of a year. There is also the possibility of large gains, many of which are over 10 per cent. Shares can show spectacular year-on-year gains and equally extraordinary losses. Take the years 1973 and 1974: a purchaser of shares at the start of 1973 lost 35 per cent in the first year followed by 58.1 per cent in 1974. The pain was offset by the bounce-back of 1975 but the fear and dislike of sharp stock market collapse is bound to haunt the experienced equity investor, given the history of stock market returns.

The frequency distribution of returns for the three asset classes is shown in Exhibits 8.7, 8.8 and 8.9. These show the number of years that each type of investment had a return within a particular range. For Treasury bills (cash) the returns vary from a negative 16 per cent to a positive 14 per cent (if we ignore the outlier at 41.5 per cent). The range for bonds is much wider, and for equities wider still. (The two most extreme returns for shares –58.1 per cent in 1974 and +99.6 per cent in 1975 were excluded as outliers.)

Exhibit 8.4 Annual real cash (Treasury bills) returns (per cent), 1900–2000

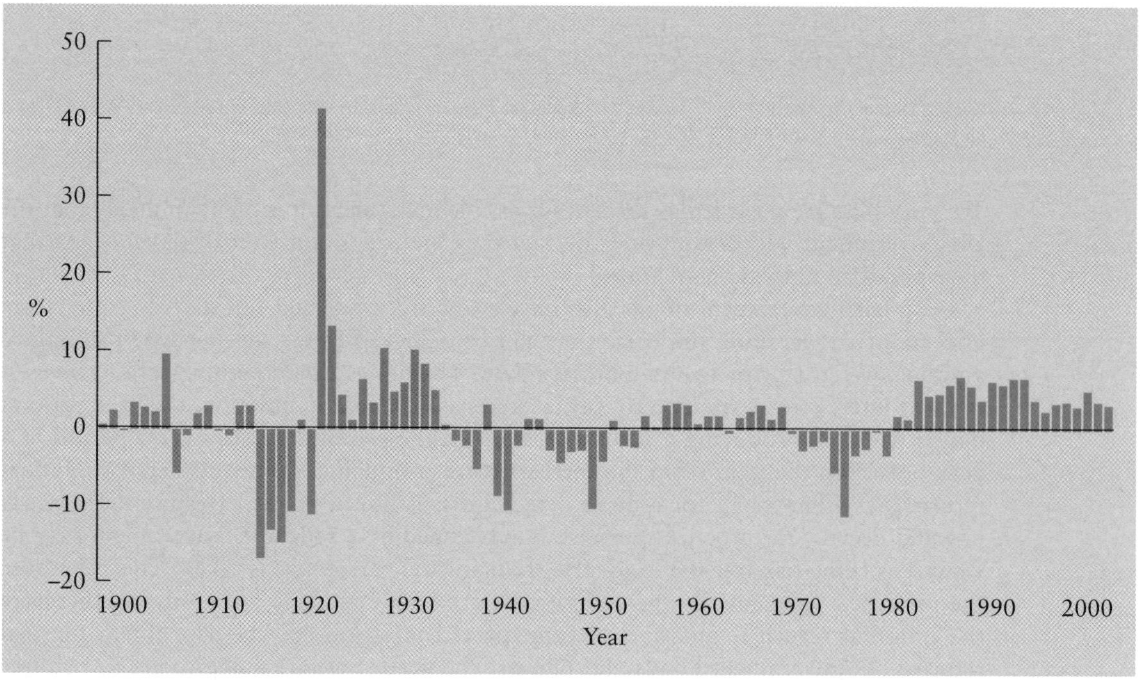

Source: Barclays Capital (2001) *Equity-Gilt Study*. London: Barclays Capital.

Exhibit 8.5 Annual real gilt returns (per cent), 1900–2000

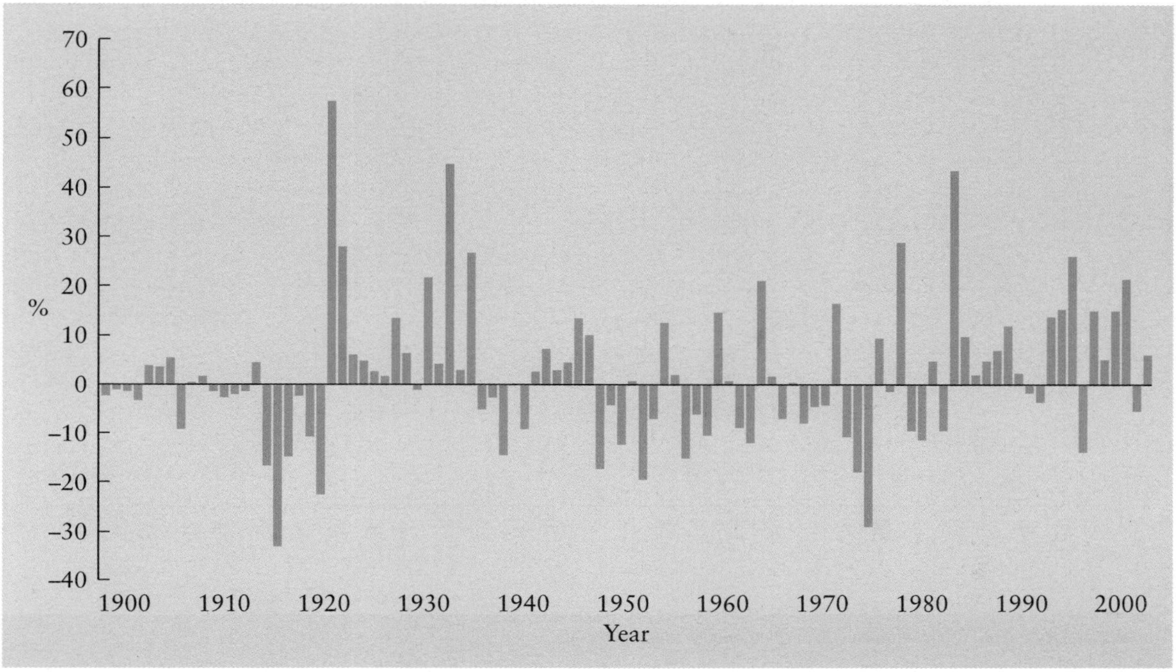

Source: Barclays Capital (2001) *Equity-Gilt Study*. London: Barclays Capital.

Exhibit 8.6 Annual real equity returns (per cent), 1900–2000

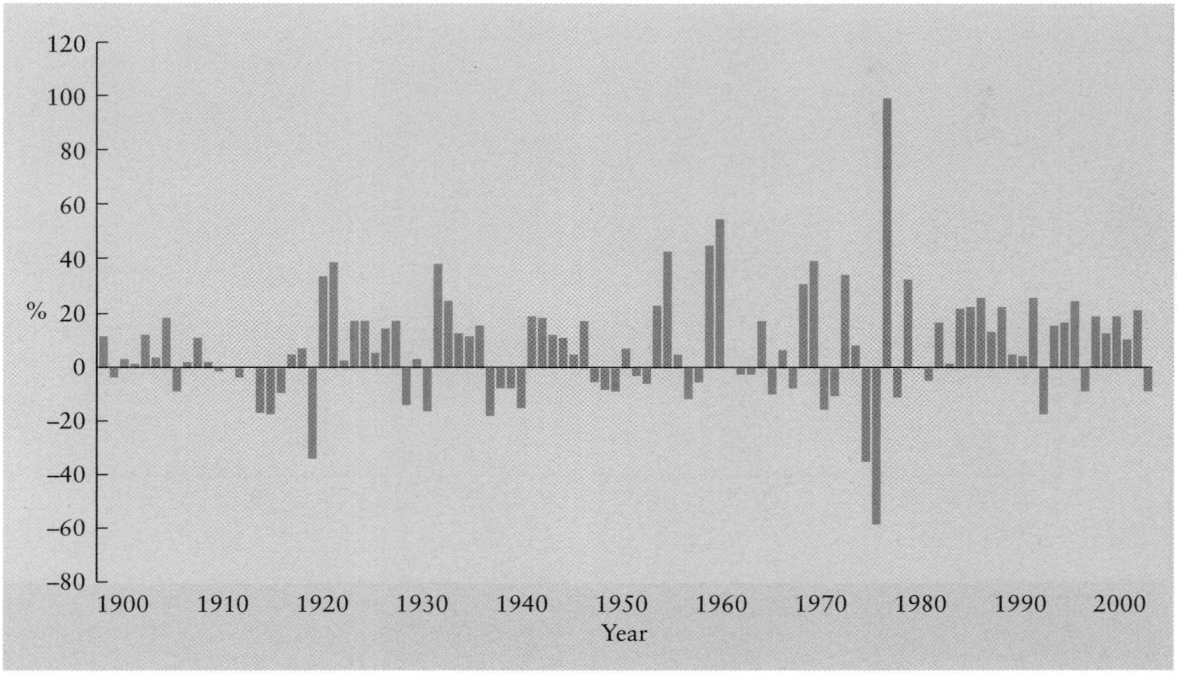

Source: Barclays Capital (2001) *Equity-Gilt Study*. London: Barclays Capital.

Exhibit 8.7 Distribution of real annual cash (Treasury bill) returns, 1900–2000

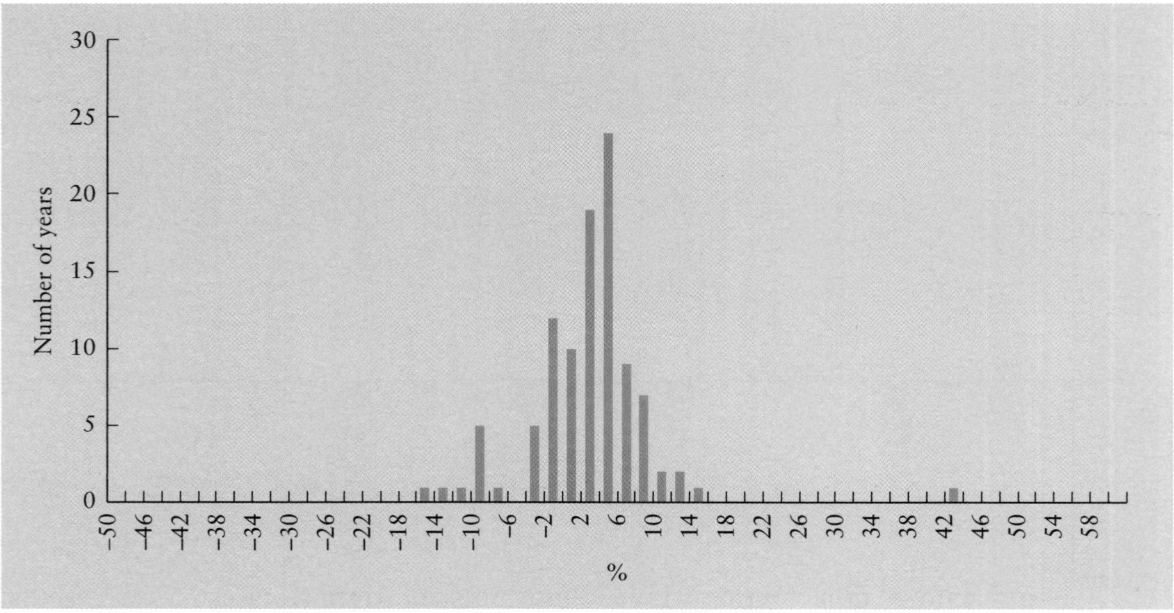

Source: Barclays Capital (2001) *Equity-Gilt Study*. London: Barclays Capital.

Exhibit 8.8 Distribution of real annual gilt returns, 1900–2000

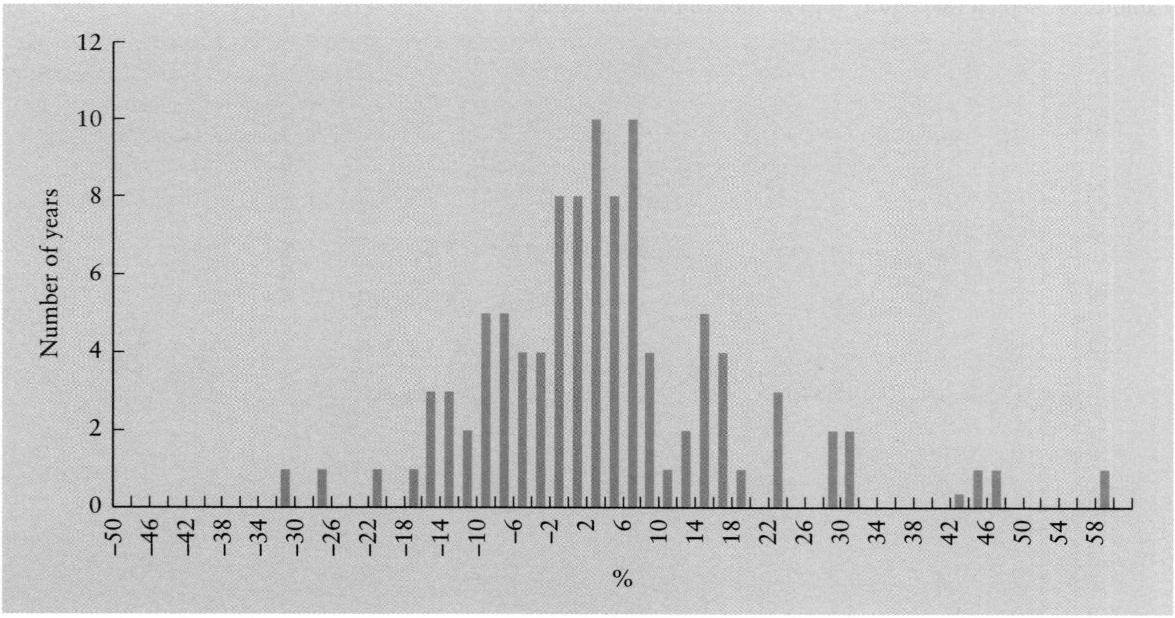

Source: Barclays Capital (2001) *Equity-Gilt Study*. London: Barclays Capital.

Exhibit 8.9 Distribution of real annual equity return, 1900–2000

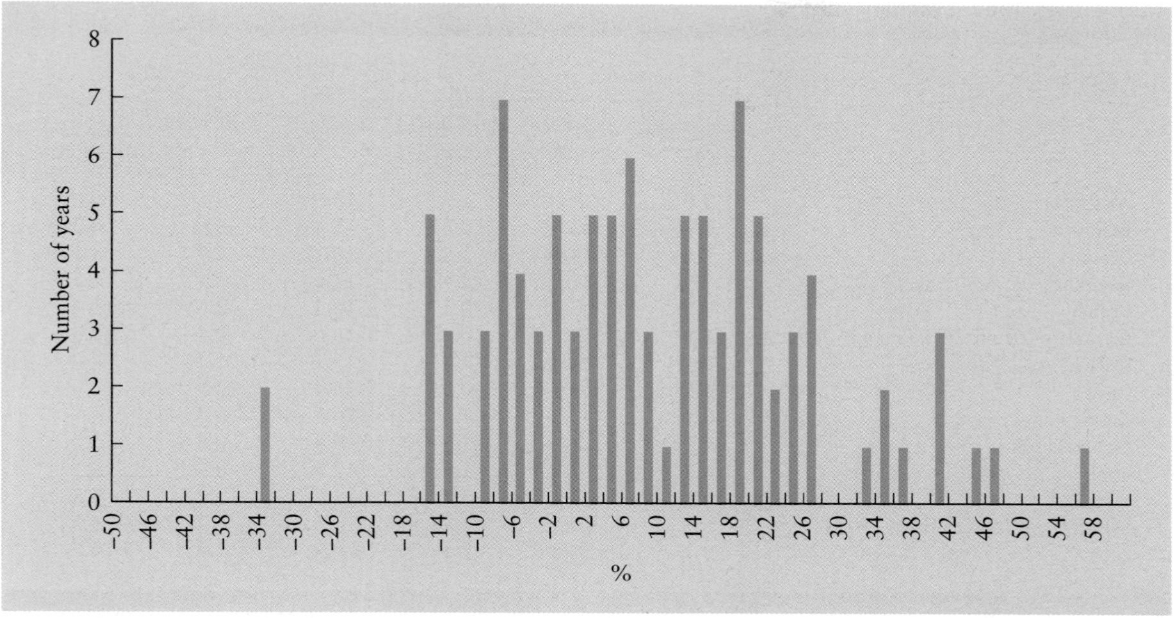

Source: Barclays Capital (2001) *Equity-Gilt Study*. London: Barclays Capital.

We now have data for the average annual return on each class of asset, and some impression of the annual variability, of those returns. These two characteristics are brought together in Exhibit 8.10, where standard deviation provides a measure of volatility. This confirms that equities are the most risky asset class of the three. The standard deviation of equities is much larger than that for bonds, and at least three times that for Treasury bills over the 101-year period. The exhibits examined so far endorse the belief in a positive relationship between return and risk. This is confirmed to be the case for a number of other countries in Exhibit 8.11.

Exhibit 8.10 Return and risk on financial securities, 1900–2000[a]

	Arithmetic mean returns %	*Standard deviation %*
Equities	7.7	20.0
Gilts	2.3	14.5
Treasury bills	1.2	6.6
Inflation	4.3	6.9

Note: *a* Based on real returns after inflation.

Source: Dimson, E., Marsh, P. and Staunton, M. (2001) *The Millennium Book II: 101 Years of Investment Returns*. © 2001 Elroy Dimson, Paul Marsh and Mike Staunton. London: London Business School/ABN Amro.

Exhibit 8.11 Means (arithmetic) and standard deviations of annual real returns for financial securities in 14 countries, 1900–1 January 2001

Country	*Equities*		*Bonds*		*Bills*	
	Arithmetic mean %	*Standard deviation*	*Arithmetic mean %*	*Standard deviation*	*Arithmetic mean %*	*Standard deviation*
Australia	9.0	17.7	1.9	13.0	0.6	5.6
Belgium	4.8	22.4	0.3	12.1	0.0	8.2
Canada	7.8	16.9	2.4	10.7	1.9	5.1
Denmark (equity from 1915)	7.0	21.4	3.4	11.6	3.1	6.5
France	6.4	23.2	0.1	14.4	–2.6	11.4
Germany (equity 99 years excl. 1922/3)	8.8	32.2	0.3	16.0	0.1	10.6
Ireland	8.3	24.3	2.4	13.3	1.4	6.0
Italy	6.8	29.4	–0.8	14.4	–2.9	12.0
Japan	9.4	30.3	1.3	20.9	–0.3	14.5
Netherlands	7.7	21.0	1.5	9.4	0.8	5.2
Spain	6.6	21.7	1.9	12.0	0.6	6.1
Sweden	10.3	23.1	3.1	12.7	2.2	6.8
Switzerland (equity from 1911)	6.9	20.4	3.1	8.0	1.2	6.2
USA	8.7	20.4	2.1	9.9	1.2	4.9

Source: Dimson, E., Marsh, P. and Staunton, M. (2001) *The Millennium Book II: 101 Years of Investment Returns*. © 2001 Elroy Dimson, Paul Marsh and Mike Staunton. London: London Business School/ABN Amro.

The article in Exhibit 8.12 describes the remarkable rewards for accepting additional risk by investing in shares (American, this time) rather than something safer.

Exhibit 8.12

Big bequest: Former Chicago secretary Gladys Holm, who never earned more than $15,000 (£9,202) a year, left $18m to a hospital in her will. She used to invest any spare earnings on the stock market.

FT

Source: *Financial Times*, 1 August 1997. Reprinted with permission.

The article from *Investors Chronicle* in Exhibit 8.13 gives some reasons why investors require a higher return on shares than on bonds. The author takes the line that the equity risk premium is too high.

Exhibit 8.13

The long-term charms of equities

History suggests the recent fall in equities could be a great buying opportunity. But is history a good guide? To see the answer, we must remember, says John Cochrane of the University of Chicago, that 'high average returns are only earned as a compensation for risk'. The equity premium has only existed because some people have shunned equities, believing them to be too risky. As a result, other investors have reaped high rewards.

Fortunately, there are reasons why some may continue to shy away from equities, allowing the rest of us to get good returns.

- *Misjudging risk* 'An investor who computed the value of her portfolio every day would find stocks very unattractive,' says Jeremy Siegel of the University of Pennsylvania. That's because, on any given day, even in good times, shares are almost as

Exhibit 8.13 **continued**

likely to fall as to rise. And if people suffer more pain from losses than they get pleasure from gains, they'll be keener to avoid equities.

- *Equities let you down when you need them* Financial assets are useful because they allow us to spend money even when our income has fallen. Equities, however, are a poor way of protecting our spending power, because they often fall in recessions – which is precisely when our salaries are falling. 'Consumers are afraid of holding stocks not because they fear the wealth volatility *per se*, but because bad stock returns tend to happen in recessions, and times of belt-tightening,' says Professor Cochrane.
- *Nervousness* In theory, high returns on equities could simply reflect the fact that people are so averse to short-term risk that they need huge returns to compensate for holding equities. Most economists believe people in general are not that risk-averse. But some might be.
- *Barriers to entry* Some people would like to own shares, but can't afford them. Even now, after recent building society flotations and the spread of private pensions, about 60 per cent of the adult population do not own shares.

Some people, therefore, will continue to perceive equities as inaccessible, or too risky. As a result, the rest of us should, over the long run, continue to enjoy an equity premium.

There is, as always, the small chance of a catastrophe that will hit long-run equity returns. Professor Siegel believes one reason for the equity premium in the past is precisely that investors have attached a small probability to such a calamity, and so avoided shares.

It's easy to imagine such disasters: deflation; the collapse of global capitalism; or entry into a Japanese-style stationary state, in which earning growth ceases for many years.

These, however, are remote possibilities – and the likeliest, deflation, isn't always bad for shares, as the experience of the 1920s teaches. So chances are the equity premium will continue.

Source: *Investors Chronicle*, 23 October 1998, p. 21. Reprinted with permission.

THE CAPITAL ASSET PRICING MODEL

From the Capital Market Line (CML) to the Security Market Line (SML)

The Capital Market Line was described in Chapter 7 as an expression of the relationship between risk and return for a fully diversified investor. If an investor is able to first identify and invest in the *market portfolio*; and secondly, be able to lend or borrow at the risk-free rate of return then the alternative risk-return combinations available to the investor lie on a straight line – there is a positive linear association. An example of this relationship is shown in Exhibit 8.14.

Exhibit 8.14 **A hypothetical Capital Market Line**

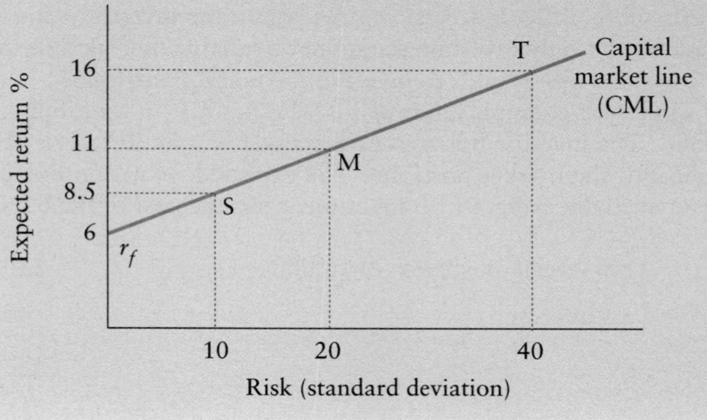

Ideally, when referring to the market portfolio, we should include all assets, ranging from gold through to bonds, property and shares. In practice, to make the CAPM workable, we use a proxy for the market portfolio, usually a broadly based index of shares such as the FTSE Actuaries All-Share Index which contains nearly 800 shares.

At least two possible options are open to a potential investor. The first is to place all funds into risk-free securities.[4] In the example given in Exhibit 8.14 this would result in a return of 6 per cent per year. The second option is to invest all the funds in the market portfolio. The share index proxies studied in empirical work such as the Barclays Capital and Dimson *et al.* studies generally show that over the past 50–101 years investors in shares have received a return ranging from 4.4 to 7.2 per cent more than if they had invested in risk-free securities.[5] We will use an 'average' figure of 5 per cent – an average with a slight bias toward the 101-year returns data. Thus an investor in the market portfolio will expect, in this assumed model, a return of 6 per cent plus, say, 5 per cent. Having established the two benchmarks, of 11 per cent return for a risk level with a standard deviation of 20 per cent and a return of 6 per cent for zero risk in this hypothetical but representative model, we can now calculate alternative risk-return combinations constructed by varying the amount of a fund going into each of these two types of investment. For example if half of the fund were placed in the market portfolio and half in the risk-free asset, the standard deviation on this new portfolio would be a weighted average of the two constituent standard deviations:

$$0.5 \times (\text{standard deviation of risk-free asset}) + 0.5 \times (\text{standard deviation of market portfolio})$$

$$0.5 \times 0 + 0.5 \times 20 = 10$$

For calculating the expected return a slightly more complicated formula is needed because the CML does not start at a zero expected return. This is as follows:

$$\text{expected return} = \text{risk-free return} + \begin{matrix}\text{risk premium}\\ \text{for market}\\ \text{portfolio}\end{matrix} \times \left[\frac{\text{risk of new portfolio, S}}{\text{risk of market portfolio}}\right]$$

$$r_j = 6 + (5 \times 10/20) = 8.5\%$$

These two formulae can be used to calculate any potential new portfolio along the capital market line. Between points r_f, the risk-free rate of return, and point M, the intuitive understanding of the creation of alternative risk-return conditions is fairly straightforward. Such conditions are created by using part of a fund to lend to a safe borrower (for example the UK government) and part for investment in risky assets as represented by the market portfolio. To the right of point M intuitive understanding is a little more difficult at first. In this region the investor achieves higher return and higher risk by not only investing the money available in a fund in the market portfolio but also borrowing more funds to invest in the market portfolio.

Take, for example, an investor who has a £1m fund fully invested in the market portfolio. The investor borrows at the risk-free rate of return of 6 per cent another £1m to put into the market portfolio. The expected return on this investment will be twice the rate available from a £1m investment less the cost of the borrowing:

11% return on shares (£110,000 × 2)	220,000
Less interest	60,000
	£160,000

This is a return of 16 per cent for a fund belonging to the investor of £1m. Before everyone rushes out to gear up their portfolios in this way, note that this is the expected return – the statistical mean. We saw in the last section how volatile share returns can be. It could be that the investor will receive no return from the market portfolio at all and yet will still have to pay the interest. Investors such as this one expose themselves to a greater variation in possible outcomes, that is, risk. The standard deviation for portfolio T is:

$$\frac{(2{,}000{,}000 \times 20\%) - (1{,}000{,}000 \times 0\%)}{1{,}000{,}000} = 40\%$$

Exhibit 8.15 The market portfolio

A linchpin of the CAPM is the market portfolio, because all investors are assumed to hold this in combination with risk-free lending and borrowing. In theory the market portfolio consists of a portion of all the potential assets in the world weighted in proportion to their respective market values. In practice, just identifying, let alone obtaining, the market portfolio is pretty well impossible. Consider what you would need to do. It would be necessary to identify all possible assets: that is, all the securities issued by firms in every country of the world, as well as all government debt, buildings and other property, cash and metals. Other possibilities for inclusion would be consumer durables and what is called human capital – the skills and knowledge of people. The value of these assets is clearly very difficult to assess. Because of these difficulties practitioners of the CAPM use market portfolio proxies such as broad share indices. Richard Roll (1977) has put forward the argument that the impossibility of obtaining or even identifying the market portfolio means that the CAPM is untestable. Using proxies can lead to conflicting results and the CAPM is not being properly employed.

From this section we can conclude that if the conditions leading to the establishment of the CML are fulfilled (such as a perfect capital market with no taxes, no transaction costs, full information about future return distributions disclosed to all investors and the ability to borrow and lend at the risk-free rate of interest) then an investor can achieve any point along the CML simply by varying the manner in which the portfolio is constructed from the two components of the market portfolio and the risk-free asset.

To get to a full understanding of the CAPM the reader is recommended to temporarily suspend disbelief. Of course the simplifying assumptions do not match reality, but such extraordinary artificiality is necessary to make a model intelligible and usable. What matters is whether the CAPM explains and predicts reality accurately and this is something examined much later in the chapter. For now we need to introduce the concept of beta in order to provide a bridge between the capital market line analysis and the capital asset pricing model.

Beta

In the previous chapter a number of graphs demonstrated the risk-reducing effect of adding securities to a portfolio. If there is only one company's shares in a 'portfolio' then risk is very high. Adding a second reduces risk. The addition of a third and fourth continues to reduce risk but by smaller amounts. This sort of effect is demonstrated in Exhibit 8.16. The reason for the risk reduction is that security returns generally do not vary with perfect positive correlation. At any one time the good news about one share is offset to some extent by bad news about another.

Exhibit 8.16 Systematic and unsystematic risk

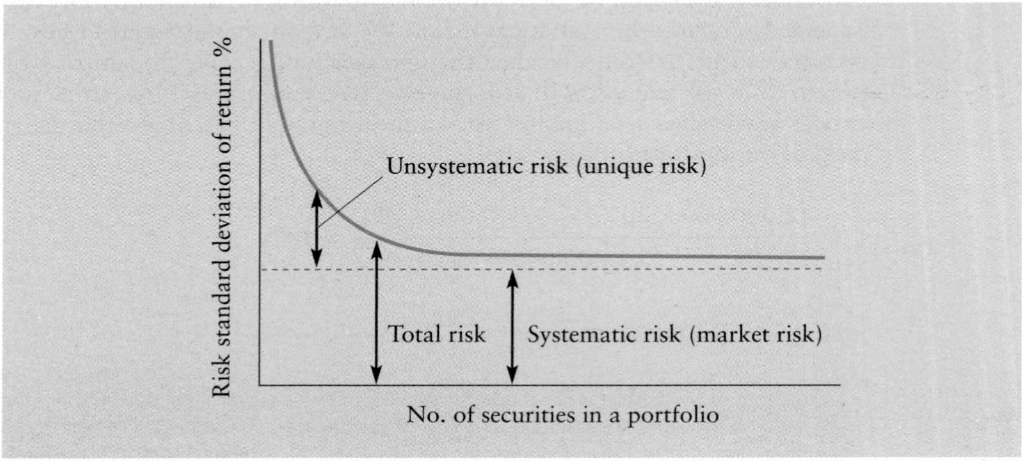

So, despite the fact that returns on individual shares can vary dramatically, a portfolio will be relatively stable. The type of risk that is being reduced through diversification is referred to as unique or unsystematic risk. This element of variability in a share's return is due to the particular circumstances of the individual firm. For instance one firm might have recently hired a very good chief executive, another has very poor industrial relations or a wasteful research and development programme, yet another might experience equipment failure or a sudden drop in demand. In a portfolio these individual ups and downs tend to cancel out. Another piece of jargon applied to this type of risk is that it is 'diversifiable'. That is, it can be eliminated simply by holding a sufficiently large portfolio.

However, no matter how many shares are held, there will always be an element of risk that cannot be cancelled out by broadening the portfolio. This is called systematic or market risk. There are some risk factors that are common to all firms to a greater or lesser extent. These include macroeconomic movements such as economic growth, inflation and exchange rate changes. No firm is entirely immune from these factors. For example, a deceleration in gross domestic product (GDP) growth or a rise in tax rates is likely to impact on the returns of all firms within an economy. Some shares will exhibit a greater sensitivity to these systematic risk elements than others. The revenues of the consumer and luxury goods sectors, for example, are particularly sensitive to the ups and downs of the economy. Spending on electrical goods and sports cars rises when the economy is in a strong growth phase but falls off significantly in recession. On the other hand, some sectors experience limited variations in demand as the economy booms and shrinks; the food-producing and retailing sector are prime examples here. People do not cut down significantly on food bought for home consumption even when their incomes fall.

It is assumed, quite reasonably, that investors do not like risk. If this is the case, then the logical course of action is going to be to eliminate as much unsystematic risk as possible by diversifying. Most of the shares in UK companies are held by highly diversified institutional investors such as pension funds, insurance funds, unit trusts and investment trusts. While it is true that many small investors are not fully diversified, it is equally true that the market, and more importantly market returns, are dominated by the actions of fully diversified investors. These investors ensure that the market does not reward investors for bearing some unsystematic risk. To understand this imagine that by some freak accident a share offered a return of, say, 50 per cent per annum which includes compensation for both unsystematic and systematic risk. There would be a mad scramble to buy these shares, especially by the major diversified funds which are not concerned about the unsystematic risk on this share – they have other share returns to offset the oscillations of this new one. The buying pressure would result in a rise in the share price. This process would continue until the share offered the same return as other shares offering that level of systematic risk. Let us assume that the price doubles and therefore the return falls to 25 per cent. Undiversified investors will be dismayed that they can no longer find any share which will compensate for what they perceive as the relevant risk for them, consisting of both unsystematic and systematic elements.

This is leading to a new way of measuring risk. For the diversified investor, the relevant measure of risk is no longer standard deviation, it is systematic risk.

The CAPM defined this systematic risk as beta.[6] Beta (β) measures the covariance between the returns on a particular share with the returns on the market as a whole (usually measured by a market index).

In the CAPM model, because all investors are assumed to hold the market portfolio, an individual asset (e.g. a share) owned by an investor will have a risk that is defined as the amount of risk that it adds to the market portfolio. Assets that tend to move a lot when the market portfolio moves will be more risky to the fully diversified investor than those assets that move a little when the market portfolio moves. To the extent that asset movements are unrelated to the market portfolio's movement they can be ignored by the investor because, with full diversification, this unsystematic risk element will be eliminated when the asset is added to the portfolio. Therefore only co-movements with the market portfolio count. Statistically, risk is measured by the covariance of the asset with the market portfolio:

$$\text{Beta of asset, } j = \frac{\text{Covariance of asset } j \text{ with the market portfolio}}{\text{Variance of the market portfolio}}$$

$$\beta_j = \frac{\text{Cov}\,(R_j, R_M)}{\sigma^2_M}$$

The beta value for a share indicates the sensitivity of that share to general market movements. A share with a beta of 1.0 tends to have returns which move broadly in line with the market index. A share with a beta greater than 1.0 tends to exhibit amplified return movements compared to the index. For example, Barclays has a beta of 1.55 and, according to the CAPM, when the market index return rises by say 10 per cent, the returns on Barclays shares will tend to rise by 15.5 per cent. Conversely, if the market falls by 10 per cent, the returns on Barclays shares will tend to fall by 15.5 per cent.

Shares with a beta of less than 1.0, such as Great Universal Stores (GUS) with a beta of 0.39, will vary less than the market as a whole. So, if the market is rising, shares in GUS will not enjoy the same level of upswing. However, should the market ever suffer a downward movement, for every 10 per cent decline in shares generally, GUS will give a return decline of only 3.9 per cent. Note that these co-movements are to be taken as statistical expectations rather than precise predictions. Thus, over a large sample of return movements GUS's returns will move by 3.9 per cent for a 10 per cent market movement if beta is a correct measure of company to market returns. On any single occasion the co-movements may not have this relationship. Exhibit 8.17 displays the betas for some large UK companies.

Exhibit 8.17 Betas as measured in 2000

Share	*Beta*	*Share*	*Beta*
BOC Group	0.59	Barclays Bank	1.55
Sainsbury's (J)	0.19	Marks and Spencer	0.44
Great Universal Stores	0.39	BT	0.94

Source: Thomson Financial Datastream.

The basic features of Beta are:

When

$\beta = 1$ A 1 per cent change in the market index return leads to a 1 per cent change in the return on a specific share.

$0 < \beta < 1$ A 1 per cent change in the market index return leads to a less than 1 per cent change in the returns on a specific share.

$\beta > 1$ A 1 per cent change in market index return leads to a greater return than 1 per cent on a specific company's share.

The Security Market Line (SML)

Risk has been redefined for a fully diversified investor in an efficient market as beta. The relationship between risk as measured by beta and expected return is shown by the *security market line* as in Exhibit 8.18. Shares perfectly correlated with the market return (M) will have a beta of 1.0 and are expected to produce an annual return of 11 per cent in the circumstances of a risk-free rate of return at 6 per cent and the risk premium on the market portfolio of shares over safe securities at 5 per cent. Shares which are twice as risky, with a beta of 2.0, will have an expected return of 16 per cent; shares which vary half as much as the market index are expected to produce a return of 8.5 per cent in this particular hypothetical risk-return line.

Exhibit 8.18 A hypothetical Security Market Line (SML)

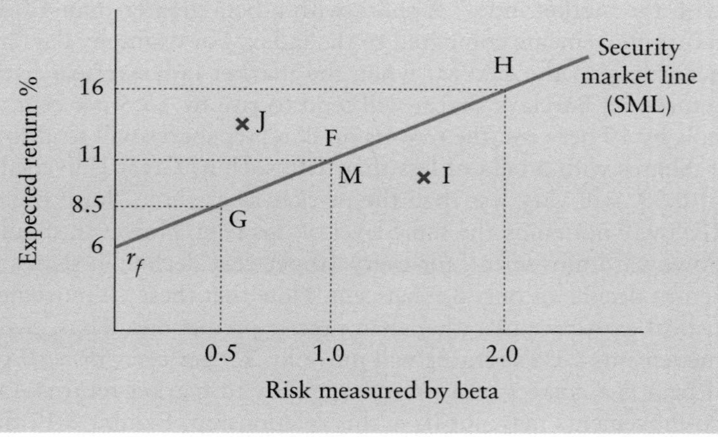

To find the level of return expected for a given level of beta risk the following equation can be used:

Expected return	=	risk-free rate	+ beta ×	Expected return on the market minus the risk-free rate (the average risk premium for a share)

or $r_j = r_f + \beta\,(r_m - r_f)$

Thus for a share with a beta of 1.31 the expected return will be:

$$r_j = 6 + 1.31\,(11 - 6) = 12.55\%$$

At any one time the position of the SML depends primarily on the risk-free rate of return.[7] If the interest rate on government securities rises by, say, four percentage points, the SML lifts upwards by 4 per cent (*see* Exhibit 8.19).

Exhibit 8.19 Shifts in the SML: a 4 percentage point rise in the risk-free rate

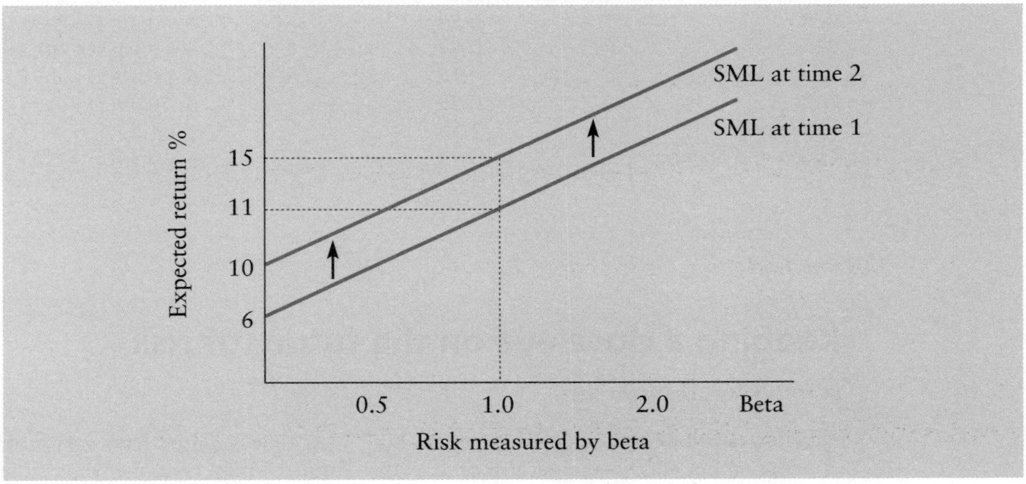

The market risk premium $(r_m - r_f)$ is fairly stable over time as it is taken from a long-term historical relationship. Indeed, taking a short period to estimate this would result in wild fluctuations from year to year (e.g. shares lost value in 2000). None of such fluctuations would reflect the premiums investors demand for holding a risky portfolio of shares compared with a risk-free security. It is only over long periods that the true extra returns required by shareholders as an acceptable premium are revealed.

According to the CAPM all securities lie on the security market line, their exact position being determined by their beta. But what about shares J and I in Exhibit 8.18? These are shares that are not in equilibrium. J offers a particularly high level of return for the risk its holders have to bear. This will not last for long in an efficient market because investors are constantly on the prowl for shares like this. As they start to buy in large quantities the prices will rise and correspondingly the expected return will fall. This will continue until the share return is brought on to the SML. Conversely, share I will be sold until the price falls sufficiently to bring about equilibrium, that is, I is placed on the SML.

Estimating some expected returns

To calculate the returns investors require from particular shares it is necessary to obtain three numbers using the CAPM: (a) the risk-free rate of return, r_f, (b) the risk premium for the market portfolio (or proxy index), $(r_m - r_f)$, and (c) the beta of the share. Betas are available from commercial information suppliers such as Datastream or the London Business School Risk Measurement Service. Exhibit 8.20 calculates the return required on shares of 10 leading UK firms using beta as the only risk variable influencing returns (assuming a risk-free rate of return of 6 per cent and a risk premium for shares over the risk-free rate of 5 per cent). We will discuss later the application of this knowledge as promoted by the proponents of the CAPM.

Exhibit 8.20 Returns expected by investors based on the capital asset pricing model

Share	*Beta (β)*	*Expected returns* $r_f + \beta(r_m - r_f)$
BOC	0.59	6 + 0.59(5) = 8.95
BT	0.94	6 + 0.94(5) = 10.7
Sainsbury's (J)	0.19	6 + 0.19(5) = 6.95
GUS	0.39	6 + 0.39(5) = 7.95
Barclays Bank	1.55	6 + 1.55(5) = 13.75
Marks and Spencer	0.44	6 + 0.44(5) = 8.2

Exhibit 8.21

Keeping a close eye on the future of risk

FT

By Barry Riley, Investment Watch

The forward-looking equity risk premium is a tempting but elusive analytical tool. It plays a crucial role in, for instance, pension fund long-term asset allocation models, and yet there is no way in which it can be directly observed in the stock market . . .

Perceived risk, according to investment theory, must be matched by higher expected returns. The equity risk premium can be defined as the additional return expected from stocks over and above the risk-free return from long-term government bonds.

The concept has triggered extensive academic arguments, mainly focusing on the oddly high level of historical premia.

At times equities have very strongly outperformed bonds. Over the whole 20th century the risk premium in the UK averaged 4.7 per cent, according to Barclays Capital.

Alternative UK estimates by Credit Suisse First Boston are on a 30-year rolling average basis, showing that the premium peaked at a formidable 9 per cent around 1970 but has since subsided to 4 per cent. In Japan, incidentally, the premium was *negative* during the 1990s.

Source: *Financial Times*, 6 December 2000, p. 39. Reprinted with permission.

Calculating beta

In order that the capital asset pricing model is workable for making decisions concerning the future it is necessary to calculate the *future* beta. Obviously, the future cannot be foreseen, and so it is difficult to obtain an estimate of the likely co-movements of the returns on a share and the market portfolio. One approach is to substitute subjective probability beliefs, but this has obvious drawbacks. The most popular method is to observe the historic relationship between returns and to assume that this covariance will persist into the future. This is called *ex-post* analysis because it takes place after the event.

Exhibit 8.22 shows a simplified and idealised version of this sort of analysis. Here are shown 12 monthly observations for, say, 2000. (Commercially supplied beta calculations are usually based on at least 60 monthly observations stretching back over five years.) Each plot point in Exhibit 8.22 expresses the return on the market index portfolio for a particular month and the return on the specific shares being examined in that same month.

Exhibit 8.22 The characteristic line: no unsystematic risk

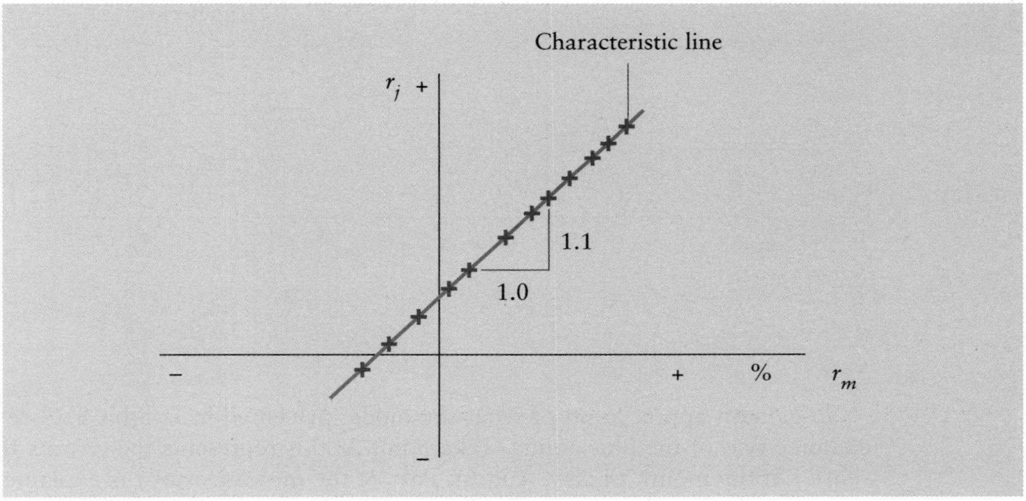

In an analysis such as that presented in Exhibit 8.22 the market portfolio will be represented by some broad index containing many hundreds of shares. In this highly idealised example the relative returns plot along a straight line referred to as the *characteristic line*. Exhibit 8.22 shows a perfect statistical relationship, in that there is no statistical 'noise' causing the plot points to be placed off the line. The characteristic line has a form described by the following formula:

$$r_j = \alpha + \beta_j r_m + e$$

where: r_j = rate of return on the jth share;
r_m = rate of return on the market index portfolio;
α = regression line intercept;
e = residual error about the regression line (in this simple case this has a value of zero because all the plot points are on a straight line);
β_j = the beta of security j.

Thus the slope of the characteristic line is the beta for share j. That is:

$$\frac{\text{Change in } r_j}{\text{Change in } r_m} = \frac{\Delta r_j}{\Delta r_m} = \beta$$

In this case the slope is 1.1 and therefore $\beta = 1.1$.

A more realistic representation of the relationship between the monthly returns on the market and the returns on a specific share is shown in Exhibit 8.23. Here very few of the plot points fall on the fitted regression line (the line of best fit). The reason for this scatter of points is that the unsystematic risk effects in any one month may cause the returns on a specific share to rise or fall by a larger or smaller amount than they would if the returns on the market were the only influence.

Exhibit 8.23 The characteristic line: with unsystematic risk

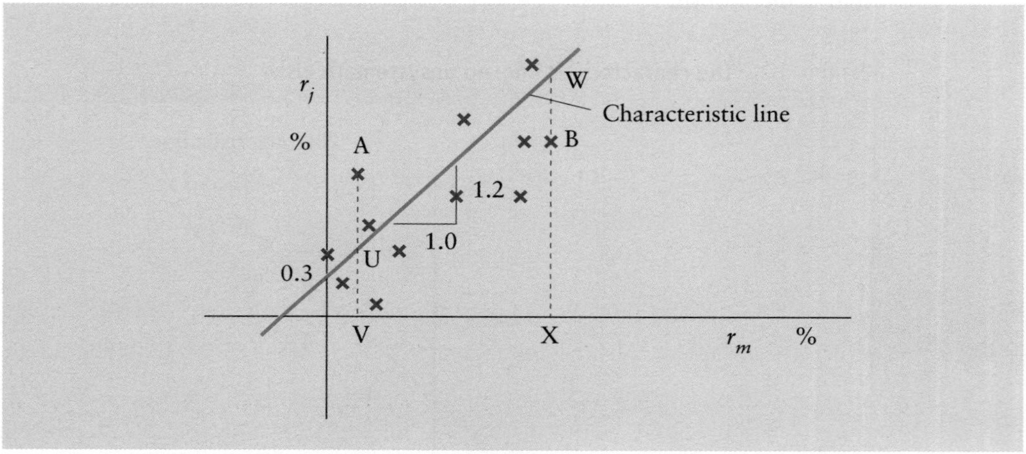

To gain an appreciation of what the model presented in Exhibit 8.23 reveals, we will examine two of the plot points. Take point A: this represents the returns for the market share j in the month of, say, August. Part of the movement of j is explained by the general market changes – this is the distance UV. However a large element of j's returns in that month was attributable to unsystematic risk factors – this is represented by the distance AU. Now consider point B for the month of November. If systematic risk was the only influence on the return of a single share then we would expect the change in j's return to be XW. However unsystematic risk influences have reduced the extent of variation to only BX. The distance AU and WB make up part of the error term e in the market model formula.

Different writers in this field use different terms for the two types of risk:

Total risk = undiversifiable risk + diversifiable risk
= systematic risk + unsystematic risk
= market risk + specific risk

Classifying shares by their betas

Shares classified by their betas may be aggressive, defensive or neutral.

Aggressive shares

If a share has a beta greater than the market average (this is, $\beta > 1$) it will be classified as an 'aggressive' share. Such shares tend to go up faster in a 'bull' market and fall more in a 'bear' market[8] than the average share. For example Barclays shares have tended to move by a greater proportion than the market as a whole.

Defensive shares

If a share has a beta which is less than the market (that is, $\beta < 1$) then it is known as a 'defensive' share. In a 'bull' market phase it will enjoy less of a rise but conversely it will be safer in a market downturn. Great Universal Stores is an example of a defensive share.

Neutral shares

If a share has a beta of 1 it is expected to fluctuate in line with the market.

Applications of the CAPM

In this section we present a few examples of how the CAPM has been employed.

Investment in the financial markets

Portfolio selection

The aggressive-defensive classificatory system has been used to construct different types of portfolio. For highly risk-averse investors a portfolio consisting of low beta securities may be chosen. If the average beta of the portfolio is 0.7 then for every 1 per cent change in the index the portfolio is expected to change by only 0.7 per cent. Similarly a high-risk portfolio could be created which consisted of high beta stocks and this will be expected to outperform the market in an upswing but underperform in a market correction. If the investor preferred a return which had similar returns to the market as a whole then one of the many 'tracker' funds might be useful (*see* Chapter 14).

Mispriced shares

Investors have used beta estimates to identify shares with anomalous risk-return characteristics. A share with an unusually attractive expected return for its beta level would be a 'buy' opportunity and one with an unusually low anticipated return a 'sell'. Getting this analysis correct is easier said than done, even if the CAPM worked perfectly.

Measuring portfolio performance

If a fund manager produces a high annual return of, say, 15 per cent how do you judge if this is due to good share selection? Well, one of the elements to consider is the systematic risk of the fund. If the 15 per cent return has been achieved because particularly risky shares were selected then perhaps you would hesitate to congratulate the manager. For example, if the beta risk is 1.7, the risk-free rate of return is 8 per cent and the historic risk premium for the market index over the risk-free investment ($r_m - r_f$) has been 5 per cent then you would expect a return of 16.5 per cent:

$$r_j = r_f + \beta\,(r_m - r_f) = 8 + 1.7(5) = 16.5\%$$

On the other hand, if the beta of the portfolio is only 0.8 you might be willing to agree to that promotion the fund manager has been pushing for (expected return on the fund would be 8 + 0.8(5) = 12%).

Calculating the required rate of return on a firm's investment projects

If it is true that shareholders price a company's shares on the basis of the perceived beta risk of the firm as a whole, and the firm may be regarded as a collection of projects, then investors will require different rates of return depending on the systematic risk of each new project that the company embarks upon. Consider a firm which at present has a beta of 1.1 because its existing projects produce returns which are vulnerable to systematic risk only slightly more than market average. If this firm now begins a major investment programme in a new area with a systematic risk of 1.8, shareholders will demand higher levels of return to compensate for the increased risk. The management team cannot rely on the same rate of return for all projects because each has a different risk level. This application of the CAPM is discussed later in this chapter and in Chapter 16.

This is a good point at which to recap, and to point out those issues that are generally accepted and those that are controversial.

- Shareholders demand a higher return for riskier assets – **uncontroversial.**
- Risk-averters are wise to diversify – **uncontroversial.**
- The risk of securities (for example shares) has two elements: (a) unsystematic risk factors specific to firms which can be diversified away; and (b) systematic risk caused by risk factors common to all firms – **uncontroversial.**
- Investors will not be rewarded for bearing unsystematic risk – **uncontroversial.**
- Different shares have different degrees of sensitivity to the systematic risk elements – **uncontroversial.**
- Systematic risk is measured by beta which, in practice, is calculated as the degree of co-movement of a security's return with a market index return – **highly controversial.** As we will see later, some researchers believe beta has no effect on the level of returns earned on shares (that is, there is no relationship, and the SML does not exist); others believe that beta is one of a number of systematic risk factors influencing share returns.
- Beta, as calculated by examining past returns, is valid for decision making concerned about the future – **controversial.**

Technical problems with the CAPM

There are two issues that need to be addressed if the CAPM is to be a valid and useful tool in the commercial world. First, the CAPM has to be workable from the technical point of view. Secondly, the users have to be reassured that the CAPM, through its emphasis on beta, does accurately describe the returns witnessed on shares and securities. This second issue has been examined in scores of market-place studies. The results of some of them are discussed in the next section; here we concentrate on the technical problems.

Measuring beta

The mathematics involved in obtaining a historic beta are straightforward enough; however it is not clear whether it is more appropriate to use weekly or monthly data, or whether the observation period should be three, five or ten years. Each is likely to provide a different estimate of beta. Even if this issue is resolved, the difficulty of using a historic measure for estimating a future relationship is very doubtful. Betas tend to be unstable over time. This was discovered as long ago as the early 1970s. Both Blume and Levy carried out extensive testing and discovered that the beta for a share tends to change from one period to another. Blume (1971) stated: 'assessments for individual securities derived from historical data can explain roughly 36% of the variation in the future estimated values, leaving about 64% unexplained. This large magnitude of unexplained variation may make the beta coefficient an inadequate measure of risk for analysing the cost of equity for an individual firm.' During the 1990s Glaxo's beta varied from less than zero (a negative beta!) to more than 1.6. For the first edition of this book Marks and Spencer's beta was obtained from Datastream. They used data for the five years to 1997 and M&S's beta was 0.95. A mere three years later Datastream calculated (based on the five years to 2000) its value at less than half that, at 0.44. For Sainsbury's the change is even more dramatic: 0.60 in 1997, 0.19 in 2000. Blume also showed that betas tended to change toward a value of 1 over time (M&S and Sainsbury's are exceptions, perhaps). The explanation he offered for this is that high-risk firms' new projects tend to have less extreme risk characteristics than existing projects. One potential explanation for the shifting betas is that the risk of the security changes – firms change the way they operate and the markets they serve. A company that was relatively insensitive to general market change two years ago may now be highly responsive, for example. Alternatively, the explanation may lie in measurement error – large random errors cause problems in producing comparable betas from one period to another. To add to this problem there is a wide variety of market indices (e.g. FT All-Share, FTSE-100) to choose from when calculating the historical co-variability of a share with the market (its beta). This problem of inferring from past observation future relationships links into the second technical problem.

Ex ante theory with *ex post* testing

Applications of the CAPM tend to be focused on the future, for example, deciding whether a share will provide a sufficiently high return to compensate for its risk level. Thus, it is investors' *expectations* that drive share prices. The CAPM follows this *ex ante* (before the event) line of reasoning; it describes *expected* returns and *future* beta. However, when it comes to testing the theory, we observe what has already occurred – these are *ex post* observations. There is usually a large difference between investors' expectations and the outcome.

The market portfolio is unobtainable

Roll's (1977) criticism of the CAPM as untestable, because the benchmark market indices employed, such as the FTSE All-Share Index, are poor substitutes for the true market portfolio, strikes at the heart of the CAPM. If the beta being used to estimate returns is constructed from an inferior proxy then the relationship revealed will not be based on the theoretically true CAPM. Even if all the shares in the world were included in the index this would exclude many other relevant assets, from stamp collections to precious metals.

One-period model

Investments usually involve a commitment for many years, whether the investment is made by a firm in real assets or by investors purchasing financial assets. However the CAPM is based on parameters measured at one point in time. Key variables such as the risk-free rate of return might, in reality, change.

Unrealistic assumptions

The CAPM is created on the foundation of a number of assumptions about the behaviour of investors and the operation of capital markets. Here are some of them:

- Investors are rational and risk averse.
- Investors are able to assess returns and standard deviations. Indeed they all have the same forecasts of returns and risk because of the free availability of information.
- There are no taxes or transaction costs.
- All investors can borrow or lend at the risk-free rate of interest.
- All assets are traded and it is possible to buy a fraction of a unit of an asset.

Clearly some of these assumptions do not reflect reality. But then, that is the way of economic modelling – it is necessary to simplify in order to explain real-world behaviour. In a sense it is not of crucial importance whether the assumptions are realistic. The important consideration is whether the model describes market behaviour. If it has some degree of predictive power about real-world relationships then it would be reasonable to overlook some of its technical problems and absurd assumptions.

Does the CAPM work in practice?

Researchers have sidestepped or ignored the technical and theoretical problems to try to see if taking on higher risk, as measured by beta, is rewarded by higher return, as described by the CAPM. More significantly, they have tried to establish if beta is the *only* factor influencing returns.

Empirical research carried out in the twenty years or so following the development of the CAPM tended to support the model. Work by Black *et al.* (1972) and Fama and MacBeth (1973), amongst dozens of others,[9] demonstrated that risk when measured by beta did have an influence on return. Eugene Fama and James MacBeth, for instance, allocated all the shares listed on the New York Stock Exchange between 1926 and 1968 to 20 portfolios. For each five-year period, portfolio 1 contained the 5 per cent of shares with the lowest betas. Portfolio 2 consisted of the second-lowest 5 per cent of shares as measured by their betas, and so on. Then a comparison was made for each subsequent five-year period between the calculated betas and the rate of return earned on each portfolio. If beta explained returns completely then the expectation is that the graphical plot points of beta and returns would be described by a straight line. The results did not show a perfect relationship. However, the plot points were generally placed around a market line and Fama and MacBeth felt able to conclude that 'there seems to be a positive trade off between returns and risk'.

While the early empirical work helped to spread the acceptance of the CAPM a few nagging doubts remained because, in general, the results gave only limited support to the notion that beta completely explains returns. An overview of these studies (presented in diagram form in Exhibit 8.24) gives the following conclusions. First, the intercept value for the security market line (SML) tends to be higher than the risk-free rate of return, r_f; perhaps this indicates other risk factors at play, or perhaps investors expected to be compensated for accepting unsystematic risk. Second, the slope of the SML is much flatter than theory would imply – that is, low-risk shares tend to show rates of return higher than theory would suggest and high beta shares show lower returns than the CAPM predicts. Third, when individual shares are examined, the R^2 (coefficient of determination) of the characteristic line is low, suggesting that systematic risk as meas-

Exhibit 8.24 A summary of early empirical work on the CAPM

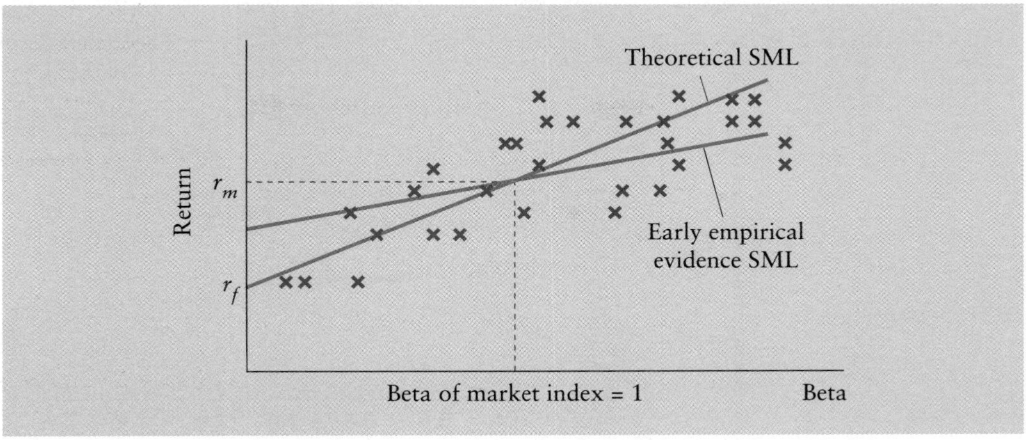

ured by beta is only a very small part of the explanation of the overall variability in share returns. Unsystematic risk and other types of systematic risk have far more significant effects on returns.

Work carried out in more recent years has generally caused more problems for the CAPM. For example Fischer Black (1993) discovered major differences in the strength of the beta-return relationship in the period 1931–65 compared with the period 1966–91. Ironically, up until the time of the development of the CAPM in the mid-1960s, the model seems to work reasonably well; but following its development and subsequent implementation the relationship breaks down. In his paper published in 1993 Black simulates a portfolio strategy that investors might adopt. The shares of quoted US companies (on the New York Stock Exchange) are allocated on an annual basis to 10 categories of different beta levels. Each year the betas are recalculated from the returns over the previous 60 months. The first investment portfolio is constructed by hypothetically purchasing all those shares within the top 10 per cent of beta values. As each year goes by the betas are recalculated and shares that are no longer in the top 10 per cent are sold and replaced by shares which now have the highest levels of beta. The second portfolio consists of the 10 per cent of shares with the next highest betas and this is reconstituted each year.

If ten portfolios with different levels of beta are created it should be possible to observe the extent to which beta risk is related to return. This is shown in Exhibit 8.25. The relationship is not exactly as described by the SML for these ten portfolios held over the period 1931–91. The plot points are not placed precisely on the SML but it would be reasonable to conclude that higher-beta portfolios produce higher returns than lower-beta portfolios. The portfolio with a beta of 1.52 produces a return above the risk-free rate of 17 per cent per annum compared with 9 per cent for a portfolio having a beta of only 0.49. Also note that if a regression line was fitted to the observed data its shape would be flatter than the SML passing through the market portfolio plot point.

The problems start when the data are split into two time periods. The pre-1965 data confirm a risk-return relationship roughly corresponding to the CAPM but with a flatter line. However the post-1965 data (in Exhibit 8.26) shows a complete absence of a relationship. Both the high-beta portfolio and the low-beta portfolio show average annual returns over the risk-free rate of 6 per cent.

Exhibit 8.25 Beta and returns, 1931–91

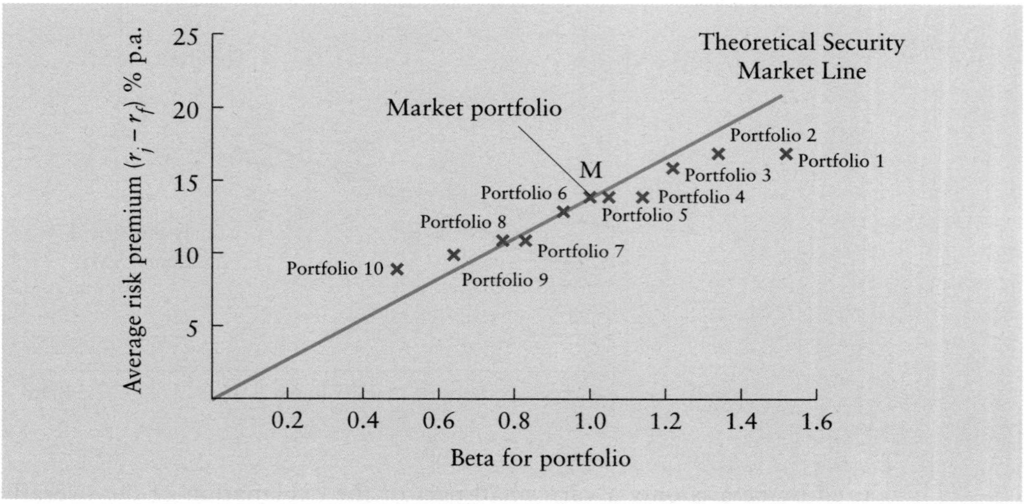

Source: Black, F. (1993) 'Beta and Returns', *Journal of Portfolio Management*, 20, Fall, pp. 8–18.

Exhibit 8.26 Beta and returns, 1966–91

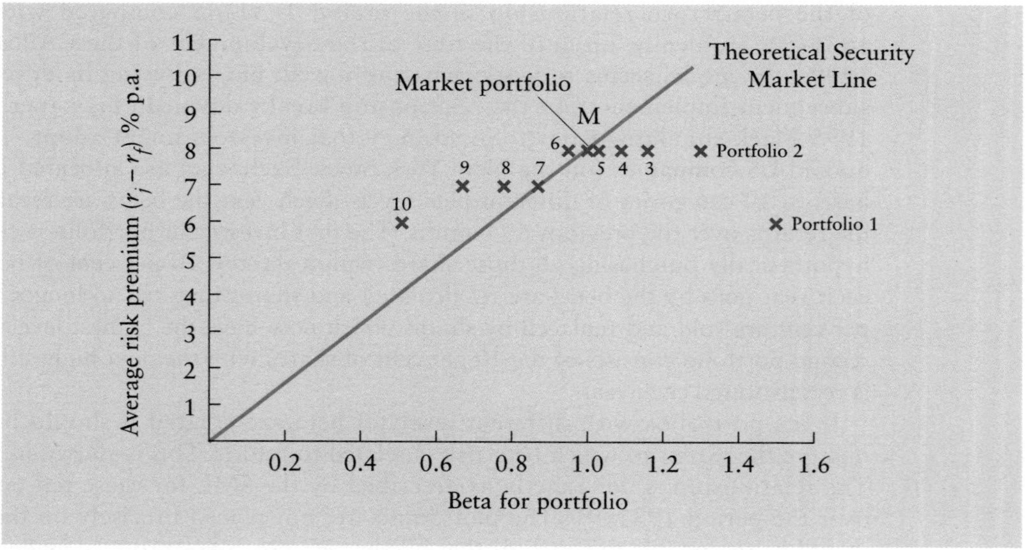

Source: Black, F. (1993) 'Beta and Returns', *Journal of Portfolio Management*, 20, Fall, pp. 8–18.

A further blow to the CAPM came with the publication of Eugene Fama and Kenneth French's (1992) empirical study of US share returns over the period 1963–90. They found 'no reliable relation between β and average return'.[10] They continue:

> The asset-pricing model of Sharpe (1964), Lintner (1965), and Black (1972) [the CAPM] has long shaped the way academics and practitioners think about average return and risk. . . In short, our tests do not support the most basic prediction of the SLB model, that average stock returns are positively related to market *β*s. . . Our bottom-line results are: (a) *β* does not seem

to help explain the cross-section of average stock returns, and (b) the combination of size and book-to-market equity [does].

In other words, beta has not been able to explain returns whereas two other factors have. A firm's total market value has had some effect on returns: the larger the firm, the lower the return. Also the ratio of the firm's book (balance sheet) value to its market value (total value of all shares issued on the exchange) has had some explanatory power: if book value is high *vis-à-vis* market value, then returns tend to be higher. This particular onslaught on the CAPM has caused great consternation and reaction in the academic world.

Another line of attack has come from Burton Malkiel (1990) who found that the returns on US mutual funds (collective investments similar to unit trusts in the UK) in the 1980s were unrelated to their betas. Louis Chan and Josef Lakonishok (1993) breathed a little life into the now dying beta. They looked at share returns over the period 1926–91 and found a faint pulse of a relationship between beta and returns, but were unable to show statistical significance because of the 'noisy' data. More vibrant life can be witnessed if the share return data after 1982 are excluded – but, then, shouldn't it work in all periods? They also argued that beta may be a more valid determinant of return in extreme market circumstances, such as a stock market crash, and therefore should not be written off as being totally 'dead'.

Beta has been brought to its knees by the punches delivered by American researchers, it was kicked again while it was down by the damaging evidence drawn from the European share markets. For example Albert Corhay and co-researchers Gabriel Hawawini and Pierre Michel (1987) found that investors in stocks (shares) trading in the United States, the United Kingdom and Belgium were not compensated with higher average returns for bearing higher levels of risk (as measured by beta) over the 13-year sample period. Investors in stocks trading on the Paris Stock Exchange were actually penalised rather than rewarded, in that they received below-average rates of return for holding stocks with above-average levels of risk. Strong and Xu (1997) show that UK shares during the period 1973–1992 displayed evidence consistent with a *negative* relationship between average returns and beta! Adedeji (1997) again found that beta has no influence on returns in his study of about 600 UK firms over the period 1990–6.

It is plain that even if the CAPM is not dead it has been severely wounded. Beta may or may not have strong explanatory power for returns. That debate will rage for many years yet. What we can conclude from the evidence presented is that there appears to be more to risk than beta.

FACTOR MODELS

The capital asset pricing model assumes that there is a single factor influencing returns on securities. This view has been difficult to sustain over recent years given the empirical evidence and theoretical doubts. It also seems to defy common sense; for example, it seems reasonable, and is observed in practice, that the returns on a share respond to industry or sector changes as well as to the general market changes.

Multi-factor models are based on the notion that a security's return may be sensitive to a variety of factors. Using these models the analyst attempts to first identify the important influences within the business and financial environment, and second, measure the degree of sensitivity of particular securities to these factors. We will see how this works by considering a one-factor model and building from there.

A one-factor model

Let us assume that we believe the main influence on the returns of shares in Rose plc (*see* Exhibit 8.27) is the economy-wide industrial output growth rate. To test this hypothesis we have gathered data for the past six years.

Exhibit 8.27 Returns on Rose and changes in a single potential explanatory factor

Year	*Growth rate of industrial output (%)*	*Return on a share in Rose plc (%)*
1	4	22.5
2	3.4	22.5
3	3.1	20.0
4	5.0	32.5
5	2.6	21.25
6	2.2	12.5

The fitted line in Exhibit 8.28 has a positive slope of 5, indicating a positive relationship between Rose's returns and industrial output growth. The relationship is not perfect (in that the plot points do not lie on the line), indicating that there are other influences on the return.

Exhibit 8.28 Rose plc returns and industrial output growth

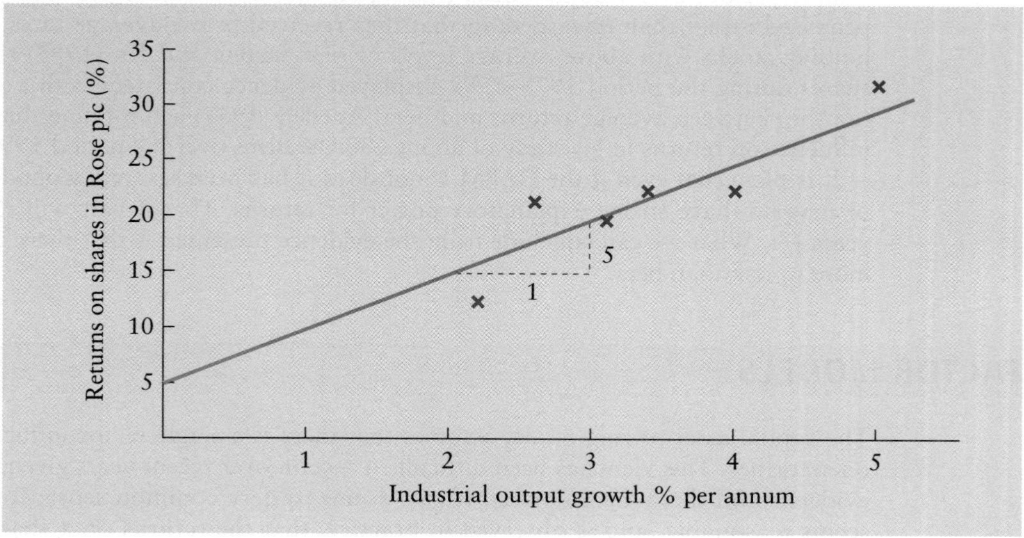

The kind of one-factor model shown in Exhibit 8.28 can be expressed in mathematical form:

$$r_j = a + b\,F_1 + e$$

where: r_j = return on share j
a = intercept term when the Factor F_1 is zero
F_1 = the factor under consideration
b = the sensitivity of the return to the factor
e = error term caused by other influences on return, e.g. unsystematic risk

In the example shown in Exhibit 8.28 the expected return on a share in Rose is given by

$$r_j = 5 + 5 \times F_1$$

so, if industrial output growth is 1 per cent the expected return on Rose will be 10 per cent; if it is 2 per cent, Rose is expected to return 15 per cent.

Of course, the CAPM is a type of one-factor model where F_1 is defined as the risk premium on the market index and b equates to beta (representing sensitivity to the determining factor):

$$r_j = a + b\,F_1 + e$$

In the CAPM: $a = r_f$, $b = \beta$, $F_1 = (r_m - r_f)$. Thus:

$$r_j = r_f + \beta\,(r_m - r_f) + e$$

However the useful characteristic of this factor model is that it permits F_1 to be any one of a number of explanatory influences, and does not restrict the researcher or practitioner to the market index.

An investment in Rose is an investment in a single company's shares; therefore both systematic and unsystematic risk will be present – or in the language of factor models, *factor risk* and *non-factor risk*. By diversifying, an investor can eliminate non-factor risk. Most factor model analysis takes place under the assumption that all non-factor (unsystematic) risk can be ignored because the investors are fully diversified and therefore this type of risk will not be rewarded with a higher return.

A two-factor model

The returns on Rose may be influenced by more than simply the growth of industrial output. Perhaps the price of oil products has an effect. A two-factor model can be represented by the following equation:

$$r_j = a + b_1\,F_1 + b_2\,F_2 + e$$

where: F_1 = industrial output growth
b_1 = sensitivity of j to industrial output growth
F_2 = price of oil
b_2 = sensitivity of j to price of oil

To establish the slope values of b_1 and b_2 as well as a, a multiple regression analysis could be carried out. The relationship of the returns on Rose and the influencing factors can no longer be represented by a two-dimensional graph. The level of return in any one period is determined by the following formula, which has been constructed on the assumption that for every $1 on the price of oil expected return increases by 0.3 of a percentage point and every 1 per cent increase in industrial output growth generates an extra 5 per cent of return . . .

$$r_j = a + b_1 F_1 + b_2 F_2$$
$$r_j = 3 + 5 F_1 + 0.3 F_2$$

If we assume the industrial output growth to be 3 per cent and the oil price to be \$18, the expected returns on a share in Rose will be:

$$r_j = 3 + 5 \times 3 + 0.3 \times 18 = 23.4\%$$

Multi-factor models

No doubt the reader can think of many other systematic risk factors that might influence the returns on a share, ranging from GDP growth to the inflation level and the exchange rate. These relationships have to be presented in a purely mathematical fashion. So, for a five-factor model the equation could look like this:

$$r_j = a + b_1 F_1 + b_2 F_2 + b_3 F_3 + b_4 F_4 + b_5 F_5 + e$$

where F_3 might be, say, the industrial group that firm j belongs to, F_4 is the growth in national GDP and F_5 is the size of the firm. This particular share will have a set of sensitivities (b_1, b_2, b_3, b_4 and b_5) to its influencing factors which is likely to be different from the sensitivity of other shares, even those within the same line of business.

THE ARBITRAGE PRICING THEORY

As the CAPM has come under attack the arbitrage pricing theory (APT) has attracted more attention (at least in the academic world) since it was developed by Stephen Ross in 1976. In similar fashion to the CAPM it assumes that investors are fully diversified and therefore factor risks (systematic risk) are the only influence on long-term returns. However the systematic factors permissible under the APT are many and various, compared with the CAPM's single determining variable. The returns on a share under the APT are found through the following formula:

$$\text{Expected returns} = \text{risk-free return} + \beta_1(r_1 - r_f) + \beta_2(r_2 - r_f) + \beta_3(r_3 - r_f) + \beta_4(r_4 - r_f) \ldots + \beta_n(r_n - r_f) + e$$

where β_1 stands for the security's beta with respect to the first factor, β_2 stands for the security's beta with respect to the second factor, and so on. The terms in brackets are the risk premiums for each of the factors in the model – $(r_1 - r_f)$ is the risk premium for the first factor for a security whose beta with respect to the first factor is 1 and whose beta with respect to all other factors is zero.

Arbitrage pricing theory does not specify what will be a systematic risk factor, nor does it state the size or the sign (positive or negative) of the 'βs'. Each share or portfolio will have a different set of risk factors (and risk premiums) and a different degree of sensitivity to each of them.

Researchers have tried to identify the most frequently encountered systematic risk factors. Some studies have shown these to be changes in the macroeconomic environment such as inflation, interest rates, industrial production levels, personal consumption and money supply. This seems to make sense given that future profits are likely to be influenced by the state of the economy. All firms are likely to react to a greater or lesser extent to changes in those macroeconomic variables. Also, most firms will respond in the same way. For instance, if the economy is growing strongly then most firms' profits will rise; therefore these factors cannot be diversified away. However some firms will be more sensitive to changes in the factors than others – this is measured by the 'βs'. Each of these risk factors has a risk premium because investors will only accept the risk if they are adequately rewarded with a higher return. It is the sum of these risk premiums when added to the risk-free rate that creates the return on a particular share or portfolio.

A major problem with the APT is that it does not tell us in advance what the risk factors are. In practice there have been two approaches to find these. The first is to specify those factors thought most likely to be important and then to test to see if they are relevant. The drawback here is that it is rather *ad hoc* and there will always be the nagging doubt that you failed to test some of the crucial factors. The second approach employs a complex statistical technique that simultaneously determines which factors are relevant in a data set as well as their coefficients.

Empirical research has demonstrated the value of the APT in highlighting where there is more than one factor influencing returns. Unfortunately there is disagreement about the key variables as the identified factors vary from study to study. This lack of specificity regarding the crucial factors has meant that the APT has not been widely adopted in the investment community despite its intuitive appeal. Investors are generally left to themselves to discover the risk factors if they can. Even if they are able to identify relevant factors and the degree of sensitivity is carefully worked out, the analyst is forced to recognise that the outcomes only explain past returns. The focus of most investors and business people is on the future and so judgement is needed to make these models valuable in a predictive role. Using historical information in a mechanical fashion to predict future returns may produce disappointing results.

THE THREE-FACTOR MODEL

Fama and French have developed a three-factor model, in which returns are determined by the risk-free rate plus:

- the excess return on a broad market portfolio $(r_m - r_f)$;
- the difference between the return on a portfolio of small shares and the return on a portfolio of large shares (SMB, small minus big);
- the difference between the return on a portfolio of high-book-to-market shares and the return on a portfolio of low-book-to-market shares (HML, high minus low).

$$\text{Expected return} = \text{risk-free rate} + \beta_1(r_m - r_f) + \beta_2(\text{SMB}) + \beta_3\,(\text{HML})$$

The model is attempting to pick up systematic risk factors not captured by the simple CAPM. In the Fama and French model, as well as being influenced by the general risk premium for shares $(r_m - r_f)$, the average small share is taken to be more risky than the average large stock and so offers an additional risk premium, SMB. Also the share with a high balance sheet (book) value per share relative to the market value of each share is more risky than a share with a low book value compared with the share price, and so offers a risk premium, HML. Fama and French tested this model on US shares and concluded that 'the model is a good description of returns' (Fama and French, 1996).

To make the model useful you need to establish the risk premium associated with each factor $(r_m - r_f)$, (SMB) and (HML). For the purposes of illustration let us assume that the risk premium on the market portfolio $(r_m - r_f)$ is 5 per cent and the annual risk premium for a small company share compared with a large company share is 3 per cent and the extra return received on a share with a high-book-to-market ratio compared with a low-book-to-market ratio is 5 per cent.

These are the risk premiums for averagely sensitive shares. Individual shares are more or less sensitive to the fluctuations in the returns on the three factors.

So, if we take the shares of an imaginary company, A, with a high sensitivity to market movements ($r_m - r_f$), they will be observed to have a high β_1, say, 1.5. If the sensitivity to size (SMB) is small then β_2 will be, say, 0.5. If the sensitivity to HML is average then $\beta_3 = 1$.

Thus:

$$\begin{aligned}\text{Expected risk premium} &= \beta_1(r_m - r_f) + \beta_2(\text{SMB}) + \beta_3(\text{HML}) \\ &= 1.5(5) + 0.5(3) + 1(5) \\ &= 14\%\end{aligned}$$

If the risk-free rate of return is 4 per cent the expected return is 18 per cent.

Arbitrage pricing theory and the three-factor model show promise but our quest to find an easy and workable model of risk and return is not yet over. Perhaps it will be useful to step back from high academic theory and observe the techniques that some market practitioners use to see if they have greater predictive power.

AN ALTERNATIVE APPROACH TO THE RISK–RETURN RELATIONSHIP

Our forefathers, long before the development of the APT and the CAPM, had to grapple with the problem of quantifying risk. Perhaps some of these more traditional approaches based on common-sense risk influences provide greater insight and predictive power than the fancy theoretical constructs. For example, you do not need knowledge of high finance to realise that a firm that has a large amount of borrowing relative to its equity base will be subject to more risk than one with a lower level of borrowing (assuming all other factors are the same). Furthermore, if the geared-up firm is in a particularly volatile industry it will be subject to even more risk.

Russell Fuller and Wenchi Wong (1988) carried out an investigation to see which of three approaches to measuring risk had the most predictive power over the rate of return witnessed on shares. The first two are now very familiar to us; they are beta and standard deviation. The third is a traditional risk measure called the Value Line Safety Rank. Under this popular US system shares are placed into one of five categories. A ranking of 1 indicates the lowest risk and a ranking of 5 indicates the highest. Two major sub-categories of risk are combined to produce the final ranking:

a the *price stability index*: this is merely the standard deviation of the share returns measured over the most recent five-year period; and

b the *financial strength rating*: this is an amalgam of risk factors which include, amongst others, debt-coverage ratios (a measure of proportion of profit absorbed by interest), fixed-charge coverage, accounting methods, the quick ratio (proportion of liquid short-term assets to short-term liabilities) and company size.

The Value Index Line Investment Survey provides a weekly advisory service for US shares. It reviews 1,700 shares and places them into the five risk categories for subscribers to enable them to make investment decisions. Fuller and Wong looked at the returns over the period 1974–85. To make the comparison between the alternative risk measures easier the shares were also placed in five beta categories (rank of 1 = lowest beta, rank of 5 = highest beta) and in five standard deviation categories (1 = lowest, 5 =

Exhibit 8.29 Return on shares categorised by risk measured in the ways, 1974–85

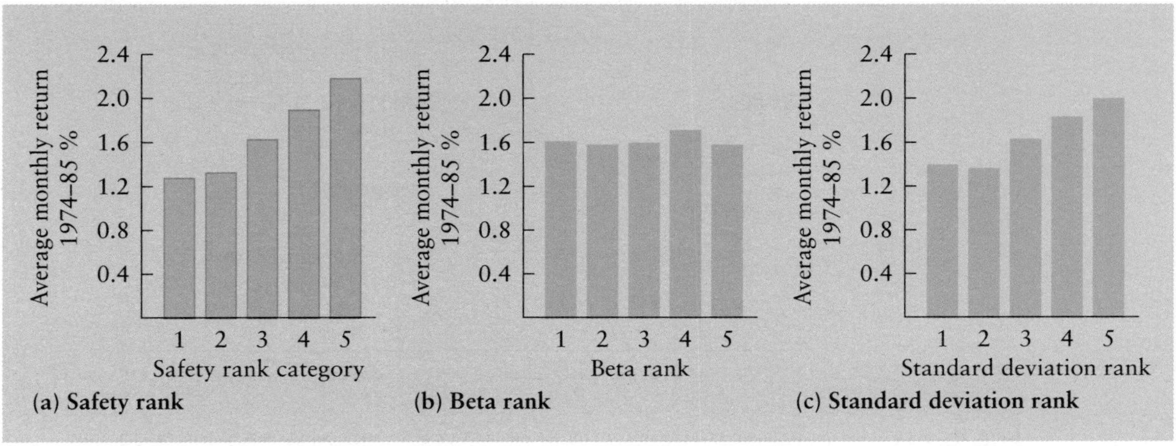

Source: Fuller R. and Wong G.W. (1988) 'Traditional versus Theoretical Risk Measures', *Financial Analysts Journal*, 44, March–April, pp. 52–7. Copyright 1988, Association for Investment Management and Research®. Reproduced and republished from *Financial Analysts Journal* with permission from the Association for Investment Management and Research. All rights reserved.

highest). The results are presented in Exhibit 8.29. The safety ranks show a strong positive relationship between risk and return. Standard deviation also shows a strong relationship, but beta is shown as having a very low correlation with the returns. These observations led to the conclusion that 'Safety rank is the most powerful explanatory risk measure, sigma rank [standard deviation] the second most powerful: beta rank is a distant third'. This evidence has not helped the revival of the CAPM.

PROJECT APPRAISAL AND SYSTEMATIC RISK

Senior managers are generally aware that the returns on their company's shares are set at a particular level by the collective buying and selling actions of shareholders adjusting the share price. They are further aware that adjustment continues until the investors are content that the prospective returns reflect the riskiness of the share. What determines the systematic risk of a share is the underlying activities of the firm. Some firms engage in high-risk ventures and so shareholders, in exchange for accepting the possibility of a large loss, will expect a high return. Other firms undertake relatively safe activities and so shareholders will be prepared to receive a lower return.

The overall return on the equity finance of a firm is determined by the portfolio of projects and their associated systematic risk. If a firm undertook an additional capital investment which had a much higher degree of risk than the average in the existing set then it is intuitively obvious that a higher return than the normal rate for this company will be required. On the other hand, if an extraordinarily low-risk activity is contemplated this should require a lower rate of return than usual.

Situations of this type are illustrated in Exhibit 8.30 for a representative all-equity financed firm. Given the firm's normal risk level the market demands a return of 15 per cent. If another project were started with a similar level of risk then it would be reasonable to calculate NPV on the basis of a discount rate of 15 per cent. This is the opportunity cost of capital for the shareholders – they could obtain 15 per cent by investing their money in shares of other firms in a similar risk class. If, however, the firm were to invest in project A with a risk twice the normal level, management would be doing

Exhibit 8.30 Rates of return for projects of different systematic risk levels

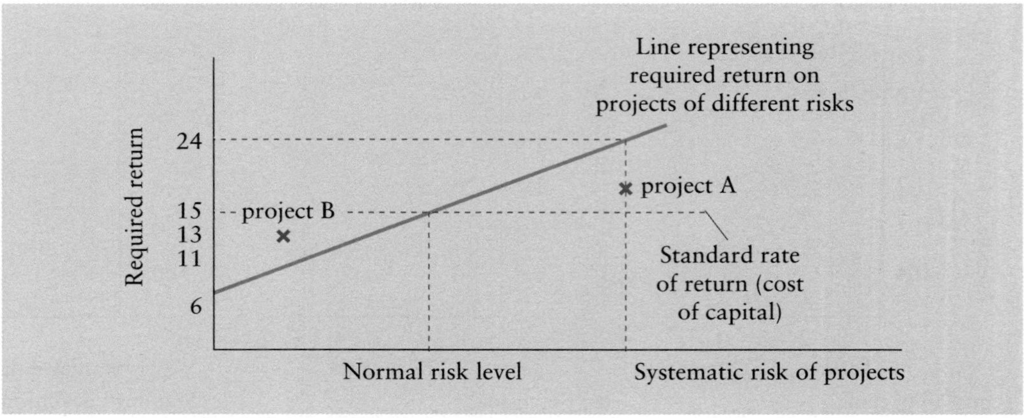

Note: The slope of the line is shown as being straight for the sake of simplicity; some people may dispute this linearity.

their shareholders a disservice if they sought a mere 15 per cent rate of return. At this risk level shareholders can get 24 per cent on their money elsewhere. This sort of economic decision making will result in projects being accepted when they should have been rejected. Conversely project B, if discounted at the standard rate of 15 per cent, will be rejected when it should have been accepted. It produces a return of 13 per cent when all that is required is a return of 11 per cent for this risk class. It is clear that this firm should accept any project lying above the sloping line and reject any project lying below this line.

The rule taught in Chapter 2 that a firm should accept any project that gives a return greater than the firm's opportunity cost of capital now has to be refined. This rule can only be applied if the marginal project has the same risk level as the existing set of projects. Projects with different risk levels require different levels of return.

While the logic of adjusting for risk is impeccable a problem does arise when it comes to defining risk. The traditional approach, before the use of the CAPM, was to exercise judgement. It was, and still is, popular to allocate projects to three or more categories (low, medium and high) rather than to precisely state the risk level. Then the CAPM presented a very precise linear relationship between beta risk as measured by the covariance of returns against the market index. Calculating the historical beta for a share quoted on a stock market is relatively straightforward because the analyst has access to share return data to construct the characteristic line. However the estimation of the risk on a *proposed* project that is merely one part of a firm's suite of activities is more problematic. A suggested solution is the use the beta values of quoted firms in a similar line of business. Thus if the new project were in food retailing, the betas from all the firms in the food retailing industry could be averaged to establish an estimate of this project's beta. Adjustments might have to be made to this to allow for differences in the riskiness of the average peer group firms and this particular project but the fundamental techniques will not change.

The doubts surrounding the CAPM have led to a questioning of this approach. An alternative is to factor-in a range of macroeconomic influences. Here we would try to estimate the sensitivity of the project's cash flows to changes in the economy such as taxation rates, inflation and industrial output. Some projects will be highly sensitive to macroeconomic forces and so will be regarded as more risky, others will be relatively stable. It is possible that an amalgamation of all three approaches – judgement, the CAPM and factor analysis – might provide the most robust methodology in practice, even if it will be criticised on theoretical grounds.

SCEPTICS' VIEWS – ALTERNATIVE PERSPECTIVES ON RISK

David Dreman, an experienced investor, does not have a great deal of respect for the financial economists' models. The following is a quotation from his book, *Contrarian Investment Strategies: The Next Generation*, pp. 297–311:

> **What is risk?**
>
> What then is risk? To the academics who built the efficient market hypothesis (EMH) and modern portfolio theory (MPT) the answer is obvious. Risk is an A-B-C commodity. According to this theory, investors are risk-averse: they are willing to take more risk for higher payoffs and will accept lower returns if they take less risk. A simple but elegant theory.
>
> How does one measure risk? That too is simple . . . The greater the volatility of a stock or portfolio, whether measured by standard deviation or beta, the greater the risk. A mutual fund of common stock that fluctuates more than the market is considered to be more risky and has a higher beta. One that fluctuates less is less risky and has a lower beta. How did these professors know that investors measured risk strictly by the volatility of the stock? They didn't, nor did they do any research to find out, other than the original studies of the correlation between volatility and return, with results which were mixed at best. The academics simply declared it as fact. Importantly, this definition of risk was easy to use to build complex market models, and that's what the professors wanted to do. Economists find this view of risk compelling, if not obsessional, because it is the way the rational man *should* behave according to economic theory . . . Whether unrealistic or not, an entire generation has been trained to believe risk is volatility.
>
> . . .
>
> In the first place it has been known for decades that there is no correlation between risk, as the academics define it, and return. Higher volatility does not give better results, nor lower volatility worse . . . The lack of correlation between risk and return was not the only problem troubling academic researchers. More basic was the failure of volatility measures to remain constant over time, which is central to both the efficient market hypothesis and modern portfolio theory. Although beta is the most widely used of all volatility measures, a beta that can accurately predict future volatility has eluded researchers since the beginning. The original betas constructed by Sharpe, Linter, and Mossin were shown to have no predictive power, that is, the volatility in one period had little or no correlation with that in the next. A stock that could pass from violent fluctuation to lamb like docility.
>
> . . .
>
> Fama and French found that stocks with low betas performed roughly as well as stocks with high betas. Fama stated that 'beta as the sole variable in explaining returns on stocks . . . is dead.'* Write this on the tombstone: 'What we are saying is that over the last 50 years, knowing the volatility of an equity doesn't tell you much about the stock's return'. Yes, make it a large stone, maybe even a mausoleum.
>
> . . .
>
> Beta gives the appearance of being a highly sophisticated mathematical formula, but is constructed while looking into the rearview mirror. It takes inputs that seemed to correlate with volatility in the past, then states it will work again in the future. This is not good science. Because some variables moved in step with volatility for a number of years, does not mean they initiated it. Most often, such correlations are sheer coincidence.
>
> I wrote almost two decades ago that betas, built as they were on spurious correlations with past inputs, were unlikely to work in the future. This is precisely what happened.

This is not just ivory tower stuff, as we've seen. Beta and other forms of risk measurement decide how hundreds of billions of dollars are invested by pension funds, and other institutional investors. High betas are no-nos while the money manager who delivers satisfactory returns with a low-beta portfolio is lionized.

. . .

We have seen that risk, as the academics defined it, was eventually rejected by efficient market types themselves. Higher volatility did not provide the promised returns, nor lower volatility lower results. This leads us back to square one.

. . .

What then is a better way of measuring your investment risk? . . .

. . .

A realistic definition of risk recognizes the potential loss of capital through inflation and taxes, and would include at least the following two factors:

1 The probability that the investment you choose will preserve your capital over the time you intend to invest your funds.
2 The probability the investments you select will outperform alternative investments for this period.

These measures of risk tell us the probabilities that we will both maintain our purchasing power and do better than alternative investments for the period we chose. Unlike the academic volatility measures, these risk measures look to the appropriate time period in the future – 5, 10, 15, 20, or 30 years – when the funds will be required. Market risk may be severe in a period of months or even for a few years, but . . . it diminishes rapidly over longer periods.

* *See* Eric N. Berg, 'Market Place: A Study Shakes Confidence in Volatile-Stock Theory', *New York Times*, 18 Feb 1992, p. 3.

Warren Buffett, the world's richest man (or the second richest, depending on the relative performance of the shares of Microsoft and Buffett's company, Berkshire Hathaway), has little respect for the CAPM, as the following extract indicates. Note that these comments come from a man who started with very little capital and made all his money by selecting company shares for purchase:

In our opinion, the real risk that an investor must assess is whether his aggregate after-tax receipts from an investment (including those he receives on sale) will, over his prospective holding period, give him at least as much purchasing power as he had to begin with, plus a modest rate of interest on that initial stake. Though this risk cannot be calculated with engineering precision, it can in some cases be judged with a degree of accuracy that is useful. The primary factors bearing upon this evaluation are:

1 The certainty with which the long-term economic characteristics of the business can be evaluated;
2 The certainty with which management can be evaluated, both as to its ability to realize the full potential of the business and to wisely employ its cash flows;
3 The certainty with which management can be counted on to channel the rewards from the business to the shareholders rather than to itself;
4 The purchase price of the business;
5 The levels of taxation and inflation that will be experienced and that will determine the degree by which an investor's purchasing-power return is reduced from his gross return.

These factors will probably strike many analysts as unbearably fuzzy, since they cannot be extracted from a data base of any kind. But the difficulty of precisely quantifying these matters does not negate their importance nor is it insuperable. Just as Justice Stewart found it impossible to formulate a test for obscenity but nevertheless asserted, 'I know it when I see it', so also can investors – in an inexact but useful way – 'see' the risks inherent in certain investments without reference to complex equations or price histories.

Is it really so difficult to conclude that Coca-Cola and Gillette possess far less business risk over the long-term than, say, *any* computer company or retailer? Worldwide, Coke sells about 44% of all soft drinks, and Gillette has more than a 60% share (in value) of the blade market. Leaving aside chewing gum, in which Wrigley is dominant, I know of no other significant businesses in which the leading company has long enjoyed such global power.

Moreover, both Coke and Gillette have actually increased their worldwide shares of market in recent years. The might of their brand names, the attributes of their products, and the strength of their distribution systems give them an enormous competitive advantage, setting up a protective moat around their economic castles. The average company, in contrast, does battle daily without any such means of protection. As Peter Lynch says, stocks of companies selling commodity-like products should come with a warning label: 'Competition may prove hazardous to human wealth.'

The competitive strengths of a Coke or Gillette are obvious to even the casual observer of business. Yet the beta of their stocks is similar to that of a great many run-of-the-mill companies who possess little or no competitive advantage. Should we conclude from this similarity that the competitive strength of Coke and Gillette gains them nothing when business risk is being measured? Or should we conclude that the risk in owning a piece of a company – its stock – is somehow divorced from the long-term risk inherent in its business operations? We believe neither conclusion makes sense and that equating beta with investment risk also makes no sense.

The theoretician bred on beta has no mechanism for differentiating the risk inherent in, say, a single-product toy company selling pet rocks or hula hoops from that of another toy company whose sole product is Monopoly or Barbie. But it's quite possible for ordinary investors to make such distinctions if they have a reasonable understanding of consumer behavior and the factors that create long-term competitive strength or weakness. Obviously, every investor will make mistakes. But by confining himself to a relatively few, easy-to-understand cases, a reasonably intelligent, informed and diligent person can judge investment risks with a useful degree of accuracy.

Buffett, W. (1993) Letter accompanying the Annual Report for Berkshire Hathaway Inc. for 1993.

CONCLUDING COMMENTS

So, where does all this grand theory leave people of a more practical persuasion, who simply want a tool that will help them to make better investment decisions? It is clear that we are far from the end of the road of discovery in this area. We have not yet reached *the* answer. However, the theoretical and empirical work has helped to clarify some important matters. The distinction between systematic and unsystematic risk is an important one. It seems reasonable to focus on the former when describing the relationship between risk and return. It also seems reasonable that one of the systematic risk factors is the general movement of the securities market.

Going right back to basics, investors do reveal a positive relationship between systematic risk and return required. Investors' buying and selling actions have given us two benchmarks by which to judge returns; if the investment is without systematic risk then the risk-free rate of return, approximated by the returns on government-issued securities, gives us the marker at the lower end of risk spectrum; we also have a revealed demand for a risk premium of around 5 per cent for investors accepting a risk level equivalent to that on the average ordinary share. The problem is that we cannot unequivocally, given the recent empirical evidence, draw a straight line between these two plot points with beta values placed on the x-axis. The relationship appears to be far more complex – the 'x-axis' probably consists of numerous risk factors. Investors appear to demand additional reward for accepting risk related to a range of macro-economic and other influences causing variability of return, ranging from the growth of GDP to the level of oil prices.

Nevertheless a finding of sorts emerges: higher risk, however defined, requires higher return. Therefore, for a company trying to estimate the rate of return a shareholder will require from a project, it is right that the estimate is calculated after taking account of some measure of systematic risk. If the project has a systematic risk which is lower than that on the average share then it would seem sensible that the returns attributable to shareholders on this project should be somewhere between the risk-free rate and the risk-free rate plus say 5 per cent. If the project has a systematic risk greater than that exhibited by shares generally then the returns required for shareholders will be more than the risk-free rate plus, say, 5 per cent.

The tricky part is calculating the systematic risk level. In the heyday of the CAPM this was simple: beta was all that was necessary. Today we have to allow for a multiplicity of systematic risk factors. Not unnaturally, many business people shrug their shoulders at the prospect of such a burdensome approach and fall back on their 'judgement' to adjust for the risk of a project. In practice it is extremely difficult to state precisely the riskiness of a project – we are dealing with future uncertainties about cash flows from day-to-day business operations subject to sudden and unforeseen shocks. The pragmatic approach is to avoid precision and simply place each proposed project into one of three risk categories: low, medium or high. This neatly bypasses the complexities laid on by the theorists and also accurately reflects the fact that decisions made in the real world are made with less than complete knowledge. Mechanical decision making within the firm based on over-simplistic academic models is often a poor substitute for judgement recognising the imperfections of reality. Analogously, informed judgement is a very important part of successful stock market investment.

Having been so critical of the theoretical models we have to be careful not to 'throw out the baby with the bathwater'. The academic debate has enabled us to ask the right questions and to focus on the key issues when enquiring what it is we should be doing to enhance shareholder value. It has also enabled a greater understanding of price setting in the financial markets and insight into the behaviour of investors.

The road is long and winding but the vistas revealed along the way provide enlightenment, if only of the kind captured in the following phrase: 'The fool says he is knowledgeable and has the answers, the wise man says he has much to learn.'

APPENDIX 8.1 NOTE ON ARITHMETIC AND GEOMETRIC MEANS

To understand the difference between arithmetic and geometric means, consider the case of an investment that only has capital gains and losses (there are no dividends).

At Time 0 the investment is worth £100. One year later (Time 1) it has risen to £200, an annual rate of return of 100 per cent. In the next year the investment falls back to £100, a loss of 50 per cent for the year. In the third year the value rises to £130, a 30 per cent gain.

The arithmetic average rate of return is 26.67 per cent:

$$\begin{array}{r} +\ 100\% \\ -\ \ 50\% \\ +\ \ 30\% \\ \hline 80\% \end{array} \qquad 80/3 = 26.67\%$$

The arithmetic mean is the average of the annual returns. The geometric mean, on the other hand is the compound annual return.

The geometric mean is the rate at which the beginning sum grows through the period of study. It depends on the initial and final values for the investment and not on any intermediate values.

So for our example:

$$\text{Geometric annual rate of return} = \sqrt[n]{(1 + \text{the first return})(1 + \text{the second return})(1 + \text{the third return})} - 1$$

$$= \sqrt[3]{(1 + 1.0)(1 - 0.5)(1 + 0.3)} - 1$$

$$= 0.0914 \text{ or } 9.14\%$$

Alternatively:

$$F = P(1 + r)^n$$

$$r = \sqrt[n]{(F/P)} - 1$$

$$= \sqrt[3]{(130/100)} - 1$$

$$= 0.0914 \text{ or } 9.14\%$$

For one-year periods arithmetic and geometric means will be identical. But over longer periods the geometric return is always less than the average returns (except when individual yearly returns are the same).

When examining past returns the geometric mean is more appropriate. However, for short-term forward-looking decisions the historic arithmetic mean is the more appropriate because it represents the mean of all the returns that may possibly occur over the investment holding period. For long-term forward-looking decisions the geometric mean is the more appropriate:

> Those who use the arithmetic mean argue that it is much more consistent with the mean-variance framework of the CAPM and a better predictor of the premium in the next period. The geometric mean is justified on the grounds that it takes into account compounding and that it is a better predictor of the average premium in the long term.
>
> (Damodaran (1999) p. 69.)

So, if the future-orientated decision is a short-term one (one year) then the arithmetic mean-based risk premium is appropriate. If the future-orientated decision is for more than one year then the geometric mean is more appropriate.

KEY POINTS AND CONCEPTS

- Risky securities, such as shares quoted on the London Stock Exchange, have produced a much higher average annual return than relatively risk-free securities. However, the annual swings in returns are much greater for shares than for Treasury bills. **Risk and return** are positively related.
- **Total risk** consists of two elements:
  - **systematic risk** (or market risk, or non-diversifiable risk) – risk factors common to all firms;
  - **unsystematic risk** (or specific risk, or diversifiable risk).
- **Unsystematic risk can be eliminated by diversification.** An efficient market will not reward unsystematic risk.
- **Beta** measures the covariance between the returns on a particular share with the returns on the market as a whole.
- The **Security Market Line (SML)** shows the relationship between risk as measured by beta and expected returns.
- The equation for the **capital asset pricing model** is:

  $$r_j = r_f + \beta_j (r_m - r_f)$$

- The slope of the **characteristic line** represents beta:

  $$r_j = \alpha + \beta_j r_m + e$$

- Aggressive shares, $\beta > 1$
  Defensive shares, $\beta < 1$
  Neutral shares, $\beta = 1$
- Some examples of the **CAPM's application**:
  - portfolio selection;
  - identifying mispriced shares;
  - measuring portfolio performance;
  - rate of return on firm's projects.
- **Technical problems with the CAPM:**
  - measuring beta;
  - *ex ante* theory but *ex post* testing and analysis;
  - unobtainability of the market portfolio;
  - one-period model;
  - unrealistic assumptions.
- **Early research** seemed to confirm the **validity of beta** as *the* measure of risk influencing returns. **Later work cast serious doubt** on this. Some researchers say beta has no influence on returns.
- **Beta is not the only determinant of return.**
- **Multi-factor models** allow for a variety of influences on share returns.
- Factor models refer to diversifiable risk as **non-factor risk** and non-diversifiable risk as **factor risk.**

- **Major problems with multi-factor models** include:
  - the difficulty of finding the influencing factors;
  - once found, the influencing factors only explain past returns.
- The **Arbitrage Pricing Theory (APT)** is one possible multi-factor model:

  Expected returns = risk-free return + $\beta_1(r_1 - r_f)$ + $\beta_2(r_2 - r_f)$ + $\beta_3(r_3 - r_f)$ + $\beta_4(r_4 - r_f)$ . . . + $\beta_n(r_n - r_f)$ + e
- Fama and French have developed a three-factor model:

  Expected return = risk-free rate + $\beta_1(r_m - r_f)$ + β_2(SMB) + β_3(HML)
- **Traditional common-sense based measures of risk** seem to have more explanatory power over returns than beta or standard deviation.
- Projects of differing risks should be appraised using different discount rates.

REFERENCES AND FURTHER READING

Adedeji, A. (1997) 'A test of the CAPM and the Three Factor Model on the London Stock Exchange', paper presented to the British Accounting Association Northern Accounting Group 1997 Annual Conference, 10 Sept. 1997, Loughborough University. Evidence of beta's poor relationship with returns.

Barclays Capital (2001) *The Equity-Gilt Study*. London: Barclays. Excellent data and discussion.

Black, F. (1972) 'Capital market equilibrium with restricted borrowing', *Journal of Business* (July), pp. 444–55. Showed how the CAPM charges when there is no risk-free asset or investors face restrictions on, or extra cost of, borrowing.

Black, F. (1993) 'Beta and returns', *Journal of Portfolio Management*, 20, Fall, pp. 8–18. Estimating the relationship between beta and return on US shares 1926–91. Relationship is poor after 1965.

Black, F., Jensen, M.C. and Scholes, M. (1972) 'The Capital Asset Pricing Model: some empirical tests', in M. Jensen (ed.), *Studies in the Theory of Capital Markets*. New York: Praeger. Early empirical work supporting the CAPM.

Blake, D. (2000) *Financial Market Analaysis*, 2nd edn. Chichester: Wiley. A thorough treatment of asset pricing models – for the mathematically able.

Blume, M.E. (1971) 'On the assessment of risk' *Journal of Finance*, 26(1), March, pp. 1–10. Betas change over time.

Blume, M.E. (1975) 'Betas and their regression tendencies', *Journal of Finance*, 30(3), June, pp. 785–95. Betas tend to 1 over time.

Blume, M. and Friend, I. (1973) 'A new look at the Capital Asset Pricing Model', *Journal of Finance*, March, pp. 19–33. The evidence in this paper seems to require a rejection of the capital asset pricing theory as an explanation of the observed returns on all financial assets.

Bower, D.H., Bower, R.S. and Logue, D.E (1986) 'A primer on arbitrage pricing theory', in J.M. Stern and D.H. Chen (eds), *The Revolution in Corporate Finance*. Oxford: Basil Blackwell. Well-written introduction to APT. Suitable for the beginner.

Chan, L.K.C. and Lakonishok, J. (1993) 'Are the reports of beta's death premature?', *Journal of Portfolio Management*, 19, Summer, pp. 51–62. Reproduced in S. Lofthouse (ed.), *Readings in Investment*. Chichester: Wiley (1994). Readable discussion of the CAPM's validity in the light of some new evidence.

Corhay, A., Hawawini, G. and Michel, P. (1987) 'Seasonality in the risk-return relationship: some international evidence', *Journal of Finance*, 42, pp. 49–68. Evidence on the validity of the CAPM in the UK, France, Belgium and the USA. Not good news for the CAPM.

Damodaran, A. (1999) *Applied Corporate Finance: A User's Manual*. New York: Wiley. A writer prepared to address the difficult practical issues rather than stay on the (often barren) high ground of theory – easy to read as well!

Dhrymes, P.J., Friend, I. and Gultekim, N.B. (1984) 'A critical reexamination of the empirical evidence on the arbitrage pricing theory', *Journal of Finance*, 39, June, pp. 323–46. Attacks APT as not being markedly superior to the CAPM in explaining relevant empirical evidence.

Dimson, E., Marsh, P. and Staunton, M. (2001) *The Millennium Book II: 101 Years of Investment Returns*. London: London Business School and ABN Amro. A joint study. Fascinating new evidence on risk premiums.

Dreman, D. (1998) *Contrarian Investment Strategies: The Next Generation*. New York: Wiley. A down-to-earth discussion of investment and the nature of risk and return.

Elton, E.J. and Gruber, M.J. (1995) *Modern Portfolio Theory and Investment Analysis*, 5th edn. New York: Wiley. Detailed but clear description of the CAPM, APT and empirical evidence.

Elton, E.J., Gruber, M.J. and Mei, J. (1994) 'Cost of capital using arbitrage pricing theory: a case study of nine New York utilities', *Financial Markets, Institutions and Instruments*, 3, August, pp. 46–73. Interesting application.

Fama, G. and French, K. (1992) 'The cross-section of expected stock return', *Journal of Finance*, 47, June, pp. 427–65. The relationship between beta and return is flat. Size and book-to-market equity ratio are better predictors of share returns.

Fama, E.F. and French, K.R. (1993) 'Common risk factors in the returns on stocks and bonds', *Journal of Financial Economics*, 33, pp. 3–56. Three-factor model.

Fama, E.F. and French, K.R. (1995) 'Size and book-to-market factors in earnings and returns', *Journal of Finance*, 50(1), March, pp. 131–55. The relationship of stock prices, size and book-to-market equity with earnings behaviour.

Fama, E.F. and French, K.R. (1996) 'Multifactor explanations of asset pricing anomalies', *Journal of Finance*, 50(1), March, pp. 55–84. The three-factor model is discussed.

Fama, E.F. and MacBeth, J. (1973) 'Risk, return and equilibrium: empirical test', *Journal of Political Economy*, May/June, pp. 607–36. Early empirical research. Shares on the NYSE grouped by beta and subsequent return is compared.

Friend, I. and Blume, M. (1970) 'Measurement of portfolio performance under uncertainty', *American Economic Review*, September, pp. 561–75. A discussion of the usefulness of market-line theory and its ability to explain market behaviour.

Friend, I., Westerfield, R. and Granito, M. (1978) 'New evidence on the Capital Asset Pricing model', *Journal of Finance*, 33, June, pp. 903–20. Empirical testing of the CAPM.

Fuller, R.J. and Wong, G.W. (1988) 'Traditional versus theoretical risk measures', *Financial Analysts Journal*, 44, March–April, pp. 52–7. Reproduced in S. Lofthouse (ed.), *Readings in Investment*. Chichester: Wiley (1994). A comparison of three explanatory models describing the relationship between risks and returns – the CAPM, standard deviation and Value Line Safety Rank. Value Line is best.

Lakonishok, J. and Shapiro, A.C. (1984) 'Stock returns, beta, variance and size: an empirical analysis', *Financial Analysts Journal*, 40, July–August, pp. 36–41. Technical paper.

Lakonishok, J. and Shapiro, A.C. (1986) 'Systematic risk, total risk and size as determinants of stock market returns', *Journal of Banking and Finance*, 10, pp. 115–32. Technical paper.

Levy, H. (1978) 'Equilibrium in an imperfect market: a constraint on the number of securities in the portfolio', *American Economic Review*, September, pp. 643–58. The CAPM cannot be accepted since it performs quite poorly in explaining price behaviour.

Levy, H. and Sarnat, M. (1994) *Capital Investment and Financial Decisions*, 5th edn. Upper Saddle River, NJ: Prentice-Hall. Chapter 12 presents a detailed consideration of the CAPM.

Levy, R.A. (1971) 'On the short-term stationarity of beta coefficients', *Financial Analysts Journal*, Nov–Dec, pp. 55–62. Betas change over time.

Lintner, J. (1965) 'The valuation of risky assets and the selection of risky investments in stock portfolios and capital budgets', *Review of Economics and Statistics*, Feb, 47, pp. 13–37. Major contributor to the development of CAPM theory.

Lowenstein, L. (1991) *Sense and Nonsense in Corporate Finance*. Reading, Mass: Addison Wesley. A sceptic's view of finance theory.

Macqueen, J. (1986) 'Beta is dead! Long live Beta!', in J.M. Stern and D.H. Chen (eds), *The Revolution in Corporate Finance*. Oxford: Basil Blackwell. Entertaining, easy-to-read introduction to the CAPM. The main argument is somewhat dated given the 1990s evidence.

Malkiel, B.G. (1990) *A Random Walk Down Wall Street*. New York: W.W. Norton & Co. A fascinating guide to financial markets.

Mossin, J. (1966) 'Equilibrium in a capital asset market', *Econometrica*, 34, October, pp. 768–83. Important early paper – technical.

Myers, S.C. (1996) 'Fischer Black's contributions to corporate finance', *Financial Management*, 25(4), Winter, pp. 95–103. Acceptance of the CAPM: disillusionment expressed.

Nichols, N.A. (1993) 'Efficient? Chaotic? What's the New Finance?', *Harvard Business Review*, March–April, pp. 50–8. Highly readable account of the 1990s disillusionment with the CAPM and Market Efficiency Theory.

Reinganum, M.R. (1982) 'A direct test of Roll's conjecture on the firm size effect', *Journal of Finance*, 37, pp. 27–35. Small firms' shares earn higher average rates of return than those of large firms, even after accounting for beta risk.

Ritter, J.R. and Chopra, N. (1989) 'Portfolio rebalancing and the turn-of-the-year effect', *Journal of Finance*, 44, pp. 149–66. Empirical study investigating the 'January effect' for share returns. Makes use of beta.

Roll, R. (1977) 'A critique of the Asset Pricing Theory's tests: Part 1: On past and potential testability of the theory', *Journal of Financial Economics*, 4 March, pp. 129–76. Important, theoretical attack on CAPM testing methods.

Roll, R. and Ross, S.A. (1980) 'An empirical investigation of the Arbitrage Pricing Theory', *Journal of Finance*, 35, December, pp. 1073–103. Testing of APT leads to at least three, possibly four, factors generating returns.

Roll, R.W. and Ross, S.A. (1983) 'Regulation, the Capital Asset Pricing Model and the Arbitrage Pricing Theory', *Public Utilities Fortnightly*, 111, 26 May, pp. 22–8. Reproduced in S. Lofthouse (ed.), *Readings in Investment*. Chichester: Wiley (1994). Summary of the CAPM and outline guide to APT. Argues against the CAPM in favour of APT.

Rosenberg, B. and Rudd, A. (1986) 'The corporate uses of Beta', in J.M. Stern and D.H. Chew (eds), *The Revolution in Corporate Finance*. Oxford: Basil Blackwell. Using the CAPM to find discount rate for projects. Incorporates other risk factors: growth, earnings variability, leverage and size. Easy-to-read article aimed at the novice.

Ross, S.A. (1974) 'Return, risk and arbitrage', in I. Friend and J.L. Bicksler (eds), *Risk and Return in Finance*. New York: Heath Lexington. The arbitrage pricing theory – the early days.

Ross, S.A. (1976) 'The arbitrage theory of capital asset pricing', *Journal of Economic Theory*, 13, December, pp. 341–60. Originator of the APT.

Ross, S.A., Westerfield, R.W. and Jaffe, J. (1999) *Corporate Finance*, 5th edn. Chicago: Irwin. Good chapter on the APT.

Sharpe, W.F. (1964) 'Capital asset prices: a theory of market equilibrium under conditions of risk', *Journal of Finance*, 19, Sept., pp. 425–42. Pioneering paper – technical.

Sharpe, W.F., Alexander, G.J. and Bailey, J.V. (1999) *Investments*, 6th edn. Upper Saddle River, NJ: Prentice-Hall. Chapters 10, 11 and 12 give a clear exposition of the CAPM, factor models and APT.

Strong, N. and Xu, X.G. (1997) 'Explaining the cross-section of UK expected stock returns', *British Accounting Review*, 29(1), pp. 1–23. more evidence of the poor relationship between beta and returns.

Treynor, J. (1965) 'How to rate management of investment funds', *Harvard Business Review*, Jan–Feb. Early theory.

SELF-REVIEW QUESTIONS

1 Outline the difference between systematic and unsystematic risk.

2 Explain the meaning of beta.

3 State the equation for the security market line.

4 If a share lies under the security market line is it over- or under-valued by the market (assuming the CAPM to be correct)? What mechanism will cause the share return to move towards the security market line?

5 What problems are caused to the usefulness of the CAPM if betas are not stable over time?

6 What influences the beta level for a particular share?

7 Describe how the characteristic line is established.

8 What are the fundamental differences between the CAPM and the APT?

9 Is the firm's existing cost of capital suitable for all future projects? If not, why not?

10 List the theoretical and practical problems of the CAPM.

11 Discuss the potential problems with the implementation of the arbitrage pricing theory.

12 In 2000 the return on UK shares was 14.7 per cent less than the return on UK Government bonds. Why don't we take the most recent returns for $r_m - r_f$ in the CAPM rather than the long-term historical average $r_m - r_f$?

QUESTIONS AND PROBLEMS

1 Company X has a beta value of 1.3, the risk-free rate of return is 8 per cent and the historic risk premium for shares over the risk-free rate of return has been 5 per cent. Calculate the return expected on shares in X assuming the CAPM applies.

2 'Last year I bought some shares. The returns have not been as predicted by the CAPM'. Is this sufficient evidence to reject the CAPM?

3 Share A has a beta of 2, share B has a beta of 0.5 and C a beta of 1. The riskless rate of interest is 7 per cent and the risk premium for the market index has been 5 per cent. Calculate the expected returns on A, B and C (assuming the CAPM applies).

4 The risk-free return is 9 per cent, Company J has a beta of 1.5 and an expected return of 20 per cent. Calculate the risk premium for the share index over the risk-free rate assuming J is on the security market line.

5 Shares in M and N lie on the security market line.

	Share M	*Share N*
Expected return	18%	22%
Beta	1	1.5
(assume the CAPM holds)		

a What is the riskless rate of return and the risk premium on the market index portfolio?

b Share P has an expected return of 30 per cent and a beta of 1.7. What is likely to happen to the price and return on shares in P?

c Share Q has an expected return of 10 per cent and a beta of 0.8. What is likely to happen to the price and returns on share in Q?

6 Explain from first principles the CAPM and how it may be used in financial markets and within a firm for determining the discount used in project appraisal. Why might you have doubts about actually using the model?

7† The directors of Frane plc are considering a project with an expected return of 23 per cent, a beta coefficient of 1.4 and a standard deviation of 40 per cent. The risk-free rate of return is 10 per cent and the risk premium for shares generally has been 5 per cent. (Assume the CAPM applies.)

a Explain whether the directors should focus on beta or the standard deviation given that the shareholders are fully diversified.

b Is the project attractive to those shareholders? Explain to the directors unfamiliar with the jargon of the CAPM the factors you are taking into account in your recommendation.

8 The risk-free rate of return is 7 per cent and the annual premium received on shares over Treasury bills has been 5 per cent. A firm is considering the following investments (the CAPM applies):

Project	*Beta*	*Expected return (%)*
1	0.6	10
2	0.9	11
3	1.3	20
4	1.7	21

a Which projects should be accepted?

b Why doesn't the firm simply use its overall discount rate of 13 per cent for all project appraisal?

9† True or false?

a A £1,000 investment in the market portfolio combined with a £500 investment in the risk-free security will have a beta of 2.

b The risk premium on the market portfolio of shares has always been 5 per cent.

c The CAPM states that systematic risk is the only factor influencing returns in a diversified portfolio.

d Beta has proved to be an excellent predictor of share returns over the past thirty years.

e Investors expect compensation for risk factors other than beta such as macroeconomic changes.

f The arbitrage pricing theory assumes unsystematic risk as a key input factor.

10† Mr Gill has inherited the following portfolio:

Share	*Share price*	*No. of shares*	*Beta*
ABC plc	£1.20	20,000	0.80
DEF plc	£2.00	10,000	1.20
GHI plc	£1.80	20,000	1.10

a What is the beta on this portfolio?

b If the risk-free rate of return is 6.5 per cent and the risk premium on shares over Treasury bills has been 5 per cent what is the expected return on this portfolio over the next year?

c Why might the outcome be significantly different from the expected return?

11† 'The arbitrage pricing theory has solved all the problems of estimating the relationship between risk and return.' Do you agree?

ASSIGNMENTS

1 Find out your firm's beta from published sources and calculate the rate of return expected from your firm's shares on the assumption that the CAPM holds.

2 Investigate how systematic risk factors are taken into account when setting discount rates for projects of different risk levels in a firm you know well. Write a report detailing how this process might be improved.

CHAPTER NOTES

1 Sharpe (1964), Lintner (1965), Mossin (1966), Treynor (1965) and Black (1972).

2 Barclays (2001) put the figure at 228 rather than 290.6.

3 Five per cent would be well within the confidence interval for the equity risk premium range shown in the most recent serious studies.

4 Real returns on government Treasury bills have not had a zero standard deviation when measured on a year-to-year basis. However, over the three-months life of a Treasury bill the rate of return is fixed and the risk of default is virtually zero. Returns on government bonds may fluctuate from year to year, but the government is highly unlikely to default, and so they may be regarded as risk free for practical purposes (in nominal terms, at least) if they are held to maturity.

5 For illustrative purposes we are using data supplied by Barclays Capital and Dimson *et al.* while also referring to the FTSE All-Share Index. These data, while being based on share returns, are not identical. Also they are mere proxies for the true market portfolio (*see* the discussion of the market portfolio later in this chapter).

6 Other models of risk and return define systematic risk in other ways. These are discussed later in the chapter.

7 We generally focus on a risk-free rate derived from long-term government bonds and a risk premium for shares above the government bond rate (rather than the Treasury bill rate) because in most applications we are concerned with rates of returns for projects with medium-term or long lives. The risk-free rate used should match the time horizon of the analysis. The risk-free rate is a completely certain return. For complete certainty two conditions are needed:

- The risk of default is zero.
- When intermediate cash flows are earned on a multi-year investment there is no uncertainty about reinvestment rates.

The return available on zero-coupon reputable government bond which has a time horizon equal to the cash flow (of a project, share investment, etc.) being analysed is the closest we are going to get to the theoretically correct risk-free rate of return. Business projects usually involve cash flows arising at intervals, rather than all at the end of an investment. Theoretically, each of these separate cash flows should be discounted using different risk-free rates. So, for the cash flows arising after one year on a multi-year project, the rate on a one-year zero-coupon government bond should be used as part of the calculation of the cost of capital. The cash flows arising in Year 5 should be discounted on the basis of a cost of capital calculated using the five-year zero-coupon rate, and so on. However, this approach is cumbersome, and there is a practical alternative that gives a reasonable approximation to the theoretical optimum. It is considered acceptable to use a long-term government rate on all the cash flows of a project that has a long-term horizon. Furthermore, the return on a government bond with coupons, rather than a zero-coupon bond, is generally taken to be acceptable. The rule of thumb is to use the return available on a reputable government security having the same time horizon as the project under consideration – so a short-term project should use the discount rate that incorporates the short-term government security rate, for a 10-year project use the 10-year gilt rate.

8 A bull market is one with a rising trend, whereas a bear market is one with a falling trend.

9 See Reading list and References at the end of this chapter for empirical studies.

10 There is some controversy over their interpretation of the data, but nevertheless this is a very serious challenge to the CAPM.

Part IV

SOURCES OF FINANCE

9 Stock markets

10 Raising equity capital

11 Long-term debt finance

12 Short-term and medium-term finance

13 Treasury and working capital management

14 Stock market efficiency

Chapter 9

STOCK MARKETS

CASE STUDY 9.1 Using the stock market both to create wealth and to treat disease

Oxford BioMedica

Alan and Sue Kingsman started an Oxford University-backed company called Oxford BioMedica in 1995. This company develops technologies to treat diseases including cancer, cystic fibrosis, Parkinson's disease and AIDS using gene therapy. The aim is to replace faulty genes.

Alan and Sue are biochemistry academics who lacked the finance needed for future research and development. They raised seed finance in June 1996 (small amounts of start-up money) and then sought several millions by floating on the Alternative Investment Market in December 1996.

Oxford BioMedica was upgraded to the Official List of the London Stock Exchange in April 2001 following a successful £35.5 million fund-raising. The company has two products in trial: MetXia(R) is in clinical trial for late stage breast cancer and ovarian cancer; TroVaxTM is in clinical trial for late stage colorectal cancer. The company has never made a profit, but shareholders are willing to wait. The potential rewards are huge, running into billions of pounds if a successful vaccine is produced. The rewards to patients could be beyond price.

Sources: Based on articles in the *Financial Times*, 3 June 1996, 18 August 1999 and 3 January 2001 and *Investors Chronicle*, 8 November 1996, and on Oxford BioMedica news releases, available at www.hemscott.com.

INTRODUCTION

This chapter is concerned with the role and value of stock markets in the modern economy. It also looks more specifically at the workings of the London Stock Exchange. Imagine the difficulties Sue and Alan Kingsman would have getting their venture off the ground in a world without some form of market where long-term risk capital can be raised from investors, and where those investors are able to sell on their holdings to other risk takers whenever they wish. There would certainly be a much smaller pool of money made available to firms with brilliant ideas and society would be poorer.

Learning objectives

An appreciation of the rationale and importance of a well-organised stock market in a sophisticated financial system is a necessary precursor to understanding what is going on in the world around us. To this end the reader will, having read this chapter, be able to:

- describe the scale of stock market activity around the world and explain the reasons for the widespread adoption of stock exchanges as one of the foci for a market-based economy;
- explain the functions of stock exchanges and the importance of an efficiently operated stock exchange;
- give an account of the stock markets available to UK firms and describe alternative share trading systems;
- demonstrate a grasp of the regulatory framework for the UK financial system;
- be able to understand many of the financial terms expressed in the broadsheet newspapers (particularly the *Financial Times*);
- outline the UK corporate taxation system.

STOCK EXCHANGES AROUND THE WORLD

Stock exchanges are markets where government and industry can raise long-term capital and investors can buy and sell securities. Stock exchanges grew in response to the demand for funds to finance investment and (especially in the early days) ventures in overseas trade. The risky sea-voyage trading businesses of the sixteenth, seventeenth and eighteenth centuries often required the raising of capital from large numbers of investors. Until the Napoleonic Wars the Dutch capital markets were pre-eminent, raising funds for investment abroad, loans for governments and businesses, and developing a thriving secondary market in which investors could sell their financial securities to other investors. This transferability of ownership of financial assets was an important breakthrough for the development of sophisticated financial systems. It offered the investor liquidity, which encouraged the flow of funds to firms, while leaving the capital in the business venture untouched.

The Napoleonic Wars led to a rapid rise in the volume of British government debt sold to the public. Trading in this debt tended to take place in coffee houses in London and other cities. Much of the early industrialisation was financed by individuals or partnerships, but as the capital requirements became larger it was clear that joint-stock enterprises were needed, in which the money of numerous investors was brought together to give joint ownership with the promise of a share of profits. Canal corporations, docks companies, manufacturing enterprises, railways and insurance companies were added to the list of shares and bonds traded on the London Stock Exchange in the first half of the nineteenth century.

The second major breakthrough was the introduction of limited liability for shareholders in 1855.[1] This meant that the owners of shares were not responsible for the debts of the firm – once they had handed over the money to purchase the shares they could not be called on to contribute any further, regardless of the demands of creditors to a failed firm. This encouraged an even greater flow of funds into equity (ownership) capital and aided the spectacular rise of Victorian Britain as an economic powerhouse. Similar measures were taken in other European and North American countries to boost the flow of funds for investment. Outside the Western economies the value of a stock exchange was quickly recognised – for example, Bombay and Johannesburg opened stock markets in the nineteenth century.

Today the important contribution of stock exchanges to economic well-being has been recognised from Moldova to Shanghai. There are now over 90 countries with officially recognised exchanges and many of these countries have more than one exchange. Exhibit 9.1 focuses on the share trading aspect of a number of these markets. Shares will be the main concern of this and the following chapter, but it is important to note that stock markets often do much more than trade shares. Many also trade government debt securities and a wide array of financial instruments issued by firms, for example corporate bonds, convertibles, preference shares, warrants and eurobonds. (These will be examined in later chapters.) Total (or market) capitalisation is the total value, at market prices, of all the shares in issue of the companies quoted on the stock market.

The 1990s was a dynamic period for global financial markets. The shift in political and economic philosophies and policies towards free markets and capitalism produced a growing demand for capital. Following the successful example of the West and the 'Tiger' economies of Asia, numerous emerging markets promoted stock exchanges as a major pillar of economic progress. The liberalisation and the accelerating wave of privatisation pushed stock markets to the forefront of developing countries' tools of economic progress. The collapse of communism and the adoption of pro-market policies led to the rise of share exchanges in dozens of former anti-capitalist bastions. Even countries which still espouse communism, such as China and Vietnam, now have thriving and increasingly influential stock exchanges designed to facilitate the mobilisation of capital and its employment in productive endeavour, with – 'horror-of-horrors' to some hard-line communists – a return going to the capital providers. In the emerging countries alone there are now over 26,000 companies quoted on stock exchanges worth over £1,500,000,000. The total value of all companies quoted on all the stock exchanges in the world amounts to more than £25,000 billion.

Clearly stock markets are an important element in the intricate lattice-work of a modern and sophisticated society. Not only are they a vital meeting place for investors and a source of investment capital for businesses, they permit a more appropriate allocation of resources within society – that is, a more optimum mix of goods and services produced to satisfy people. Peruvians see a 'Shareholder mentality' as a worthy objective since this may help in 'boosting low levels of domestic savings' – *see* Exhibit 9.2.

There has been a remarkable increase in the number of officially recognised stock exchanges around the globe in the last five to ten years. As well as an increase in the significance of stock exchanges in the economies of developing countries, there has also been a notable increase in the size and importance of the older exchanges. This is illustrated by the fact that the market value of all the ordinary shares issued by companies (market capitalisation) listed on some exchanges exceeds the total output of goods and services produced by that country's citizens in a year (Gross Domestic Product). This applies to Canada, France, Japan, Sweden, the UK and the USA. In some countries (e.g. Finland, the Netherlands and Switzerland, and in Hong Kong) market capitalisation of quoted companies is more than double annual national output.

China is a wholehearted convert to the virtues of stock markets. Over 50 million Chinese hold shares in over 1,000 companies quoted either on the stock exchange in Shanghai or on the one in Shenzhen. The president of China, Jiang Zemin, no less, speaks with the fervour of the recent convert – *see* Exhibit 9.3.

Exhibit 9.1 Stock exchanges around the world

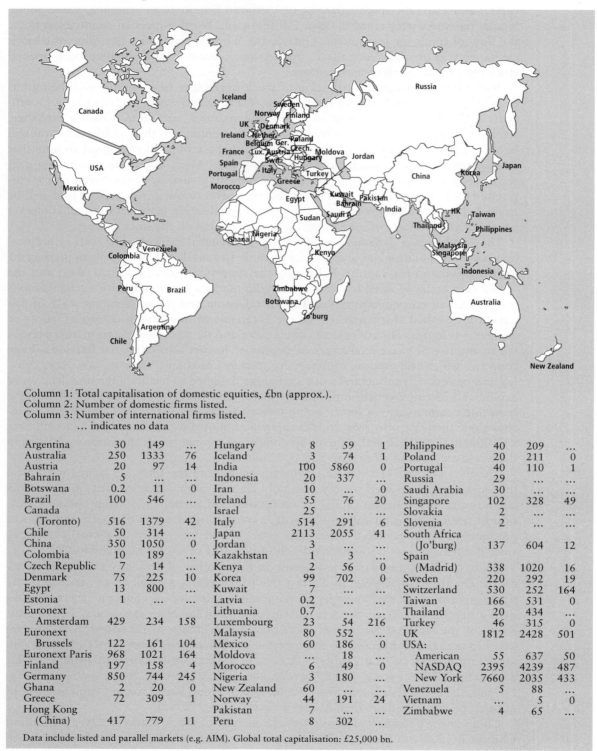

Column 1: Total capitalisation of domestic equities, £bn (approx.).
Column 2: Number of domestic firms listed.
Column 3: Number of international firms listed.
... indicates no data

Argentina	30	149	...	Hungary	8	59	1	Philippines	40	209	...
Australia	250	1333	76	Iceland	3	74	1	Poland	20	211	0
Austria	20	97	14	India	100	5860	0	Portugal	40	110	1
Bahrain	5	...	...	Indonesia	20	337	...	Russia	29	...	...
Botswana	0.2	11	0	Iran	10	...	0	Saudi Arabia	30	...	...
Brazil	100	546	...	Ireland	55	76	20	Singapore	102	328	49
Canada				Israel	25	...	...	Slovakia	2	...	...
(Toronto)	516	1379	42	Italy	514	291	6	Slovenia	2	...	...
Chile	50	314	...	Japan	2113	2055	41	South Africa			
China	350	1050	0	Jordan	3	...	...	(Jo'burg)	137	604	12
Colombia	10	189	...	Kazakhstan	1	3	...	Spain			
Czech Republic	7	14	...	Kenya	2	56	0	(Madrid)	338	1020	16
Denmark	75	225	10	Korea	99	702	0	Sweden	220	292	19
Egypt	13	800	...	Kuwait	7	...	...	Switzerland	530	252	164
Estonia	1	...	...	Latvia	0.2	...	...	Taiwan	166	531	0
Euronext				Lithuania	0.7	...	...	Thailand	20	434	...
Amsterdam	429	234	158	Luxembourg	23	54	216	Turkey	46	315	0
Euronext				Malaysia	80	552	...	UK	1812	2428	501
Brussels	122	161	104	Mexico	60	186	0	USA:			
Euronext Paris	968	1021	164	Moldova	...	18	...	American	55	637	50
Finland	197	158	4	Morocco	6	49	0	NASDAQ	2395	4239	487
Germany	850	744	245	Nigeria	3	180	...	New York	7660	2035	433
Ghana	2	20	0	New Zealand	60	...	...	Venezuela	5	88	...
Greece	72	309	1	Norway	44	191	24	Vietnam	...	5	0
Hong Kong				Pakistan	7	...	...	Zimbabwe	4	65	...
(China)	417	779	11	Peru	8	302	...				

Data include listed and parallel markets (e.g. AIM). Global total capitalisation: £25,000 bn.

Sources: *London Stock Exchange Fact File 2001*; *Financial Times*, various issues.

Exhibit 9.2

Peru's small investors given sell-off call

FT

'Treat me with a bit of respect, my friend,' an oil-stained though cheery garage mechanic tells his customer. 'I'm going to be a shareholder.'

The television advertisement forms part of a multi-million dollar publicity campaign in Peru designed to persuade tens of thousands of middle-income Peruvians to buy shares this month in Telefónica del Perú, the former state telecommunications monopoly in which Telefónica Internacional of Spain acquired a controlling stake in February 1994.

Now Peru is putting the bulk of its retained 28.6 per cent stake, worth up to $1.4bn (£915m), on the market. Offers for the domestic tranche began last Monday, with applications from Peruvian institutional investors – mainly insurance companies and private pension funds – and individuals.

The complementary but larger international offering kicked off this weekend with a road show, orchestrated by J.P. Morgan and Merrill Lynch, making presentations in 23 cities in the US, Europe and Japan. The price per share will be announced on July 1, but it is expected to prove one of Latin America's biggest equity offerings this year.

Citizen participation is geared to creating a shareholder mentality and boosting low levels of domestic savings. To encourage this, Peruvians who hang on to their investment for 18 months will get one free share for every 20 held.

'This is Peru's first large-scale privatisation and will form the basis for similar operations in the future,' says Mr Raimundo Morales, general manager of the Banco de Credito, Peru's largest bank and domestic co-ordinator of the offering. 'It will give the liberal economic model a permanence which is extremely important.'

Source: Sally Bowen, *Financial Times*, 10 June 1996. Reprinted with permission.

Exhibit 9.3

Jiang 'strongly endorses stock markets'

FT

Jiang Zemin, China's president, has given an unprecedented, ringing endorsement of the country's stock markets and their role in fostering the development of an efficient private sector, witnesses said yesterday . . .

'He spoke at great length about the development of the local stock markets,' said one person who heard him speak.

'I did not expect him to be so animated on this subject but he was very animated indeed.'

Mr Jiang made the point that robust stock markets were a vital component of a modern economy. He said that development of China's stock markets was important, adding that it would help foster the country's non-state sector, according to a summary of his comments provided by witnesses.

He also seemed to advocate the introduction of a culture of risk within the Chinese economy, saying at one point that Chinese people are inherently risk-takers. The president also mentioned his own role in helping to create the Shanghai stock market during his time as Communist party secretary of China's biggest city in the late 1980's . . .

Mr Jiang's comments represented the first time since Asia began to recover from the financial crisis that struck in 1997 that a top Chinese leader is known to have endorsed the promotion of the national stock markets.

His endorsement adds considerable weight to several indications over the past few weeks that Beijing is on the threshold of a crucial five years of financial reform . . .

The number of financial institutions, including foreign joint ventures, that will be permitted to invest in local stock markets is set to rise significantly. The stock markets are also expected to offer an expanded range of investment options, including new indices and new boards oriented towards younger and more high-tech companies.

Source: James Kynge, *Financial Times*, 15 June 2000, p. 12. Reprinted with permission.

Traditionally many European countries, such as France and Germany, were less focused on equity capital markets than the Anglo-Saxon economies (the UK, the USA, Australia, etc.), but this is starting to change. Privatisation and a greater concern for generating shareholder value is leading to an increasing appreciation of equity markets. Exhibit 9.4 shows that, in France, shares are seen as having a role in the provision of pensions and in encouraging employees to take an interest in their company's profitability.

Exhibit 9.4

France joins the stakeholder revolution

FT

The popularity of employee shareholding schemes at French companies is establishing an equity culture, says **Samer Iskandar**

Suez Lyonnaise des Eaux, the French utilities and environmental services group, yesterday joined the growing list of companies encouraging employees to invest in their shares.

Gérard Mestrallet, Suez Lyonnaise's chairman, is aiming to raise the share of the group's capital held by its 120,000 employees from less than 1 per cent to more than 5 per cent. Staff at Vivendi, Suez Lyonnaise's main domestic rival, increased their stake in the company from 2.5 per cent to more than 4 per cent in a similar scheme this year.

Equity investment has been relatively unpopular in France where, until recently, money market funds benefited from favourable tax treatment. Investors have started turning to shares only in the past few years, as interest rates fell to historic lows in the run-up to January's launch of the euro, reducing the risk-free returns previously available on cash and treasury bonds.

The fiscal treatment of shares, relative to bonds, has also been gradually relaxed by Dominique Strauss-Khan, finance minister, in an attempt to both tackle the country's pensions shortfall (by encouraging personal investment) and to encourage 'productive investment' – investment leading to job creation.

Analysts are optimistic that the growing popularity of employee shareholding schemes will play a significant role in establishing an 'equity culture' in continental Europe – and in France, in particular.

French law is especially supportive of employee share ownership. As part of the 1986 privatisation laws, the government, led by the prime minster Jacques Chirac, allowed privatised companies to offer employees discounts of up to 20 per cent on their shares' market price. The aim was to soften trade union opposition to the privatisation programme and thereby avoid social unrest.

Source: Samer Iskandar, *Financial Times*, 21 May 1999, p. 35. Reprinted with permission.

Thailand too is keen to develop an 'equity culture' – *see* Exhibit 9.5.

It can be seen from the world map (*see* Exhibit 9.1) that the dominant financial centres form a 'golden triangle' in three different time zones: USA, London and Tokyo. America is the largest source of equity capital, providing over one-third of the world's total, but the finance raised is split between three exchanges. The New York Stock Exchange (NYSE) is the largest in terms of market capitalisation. However, the NASDAQ (National Association of Securities Dealers Automated Quotations) market has over twice as many companies listed, but its market capitalisation is much less. The laggard is the American Stock Exchange (which is now owned by NASDAQ). In terms of domestic company share trading the NASDAQ is the world leader. However, in terms of trading in non-domestic (foreign) shares, London is pre-eminent. This is shown in Exhibit 9.6.

There is great rivalry between London and the American exchanges in attracting companies from other countries to list shares on their exchanges. In addition to 500 or so

Exhibit 9.5 **Thai Stock Exchange**

A market appeals to the sceptical masses

FT

Thailand wants to build an 'equity culture', especially among the young. But doubts about the standards of corporate governance mean it faces an uphill struggle, says Amy Kazmin.

During the recent school break, 15-year-old Soramon Prasirtphun spent three days at the Thai stock exchange.

It is all part of a campaign to create an 'equity culture' in Thailand, where less than 1 per cent of Thailand household savings are invested in stocks. As exchange officials struggle to breathe new life into a market valued at less than half of its 1994 all-time high, they say that attracting new money – and expanding the narrow domestic investor base – is crucial if the exchange is to be a viable venue for companies to raise capital.

So despite the market's seven-year downward slide – including a 44 per cent plunge last year – the exchange is out to convince a sceptical Thai public that buying stocks is not necessarily a losing gamble. A new Bt30m ($660,000) television advertising blitz contends that, like lighting a match, buying a diamond or growing a bonsai tree, investing in stocks can bring benefits if it is done properly. The exchange will also host its first 'Investor Fair' next month, where brokers and mutual fund companies will attempt to woo new money into the market.

'There is an abundance of people out there who are potential investors, who may have a sense that it is too risky to come in,' says Vicharat Vichit-Vadakan, president of the Stock Exchange of Thailand . . .

Thailand's equity market has always been a secondary part of the country's story of economic growth. As elsewhere in Asia, Thailand's boom during the 1980s and early 1990s was largely financed by corporate debt: Thais entrusted about 95 per cent of their savings into banks.

Although plenty of companies listed on the exchange during the growth years, many offerings were driven more by a desire for the status of being listed than by a real need for capital. Often, only small amounts of equity in family-run companies were sold and most controlling share-owners continued to view their companies as private domain, even if they were listed.

But since the Asian crisis, Thai banks have shunned new lending, focusing instead on digging themselves out from beneath a pile of bad loans. That has put the spotlight on the need to strengthen the equity market as a forum for raising capital. Investors, too, are looking for new things to do with their savings, given the historically low deposit rates at banks now flush with unwanted liquidity.

While the stock exchange mounts its charm offensive, the government of Thaksin Shinawatra, the prime minister, has laid out plans to support the market by offering new tax incentives for companies that agree to list and by accelerating Thailand's stagnant privatisation programme.

Source: Amy Kazmin, *Financial Times*, 21 May 2001, p. 11. Reprinted with permission.

international companies with a listing in London, hundreds more are listed and regulated on their home exchanges are traded via the London international share dealing service, Stock Exchange Automated Quotation International (SEAQI). The essential features of this are an electronic market-place where share prices are quoted in the home currency and the transactions are settled (that is, the legal rights to shares are transferred from one investor to another) through the local settlement system, not through London. Trading in these shares can take place 24 hours a day. Over one-half of equity turnover in the UK is in non-UK equities (£1,767 billion compared with £1,231 billion for domestic shares in 2000).

When SEAQI was created in the mid-1980s most European markets were relatively inaccessible, and SEAQI was well received as a way of helping to satisfy Europe's investment needs and it expanded rapidly. By the mid-1990s many of these markets had matured, so the significance of SEAQI in creating a market to establish a share's price and permit share exchange was lessened. However, SEAQI is now turning to the needs of emerging markets (developing economies) for investment capital.

Exhibit 9.6 Domestic and foreign equity turnover on major exchanges, 2000

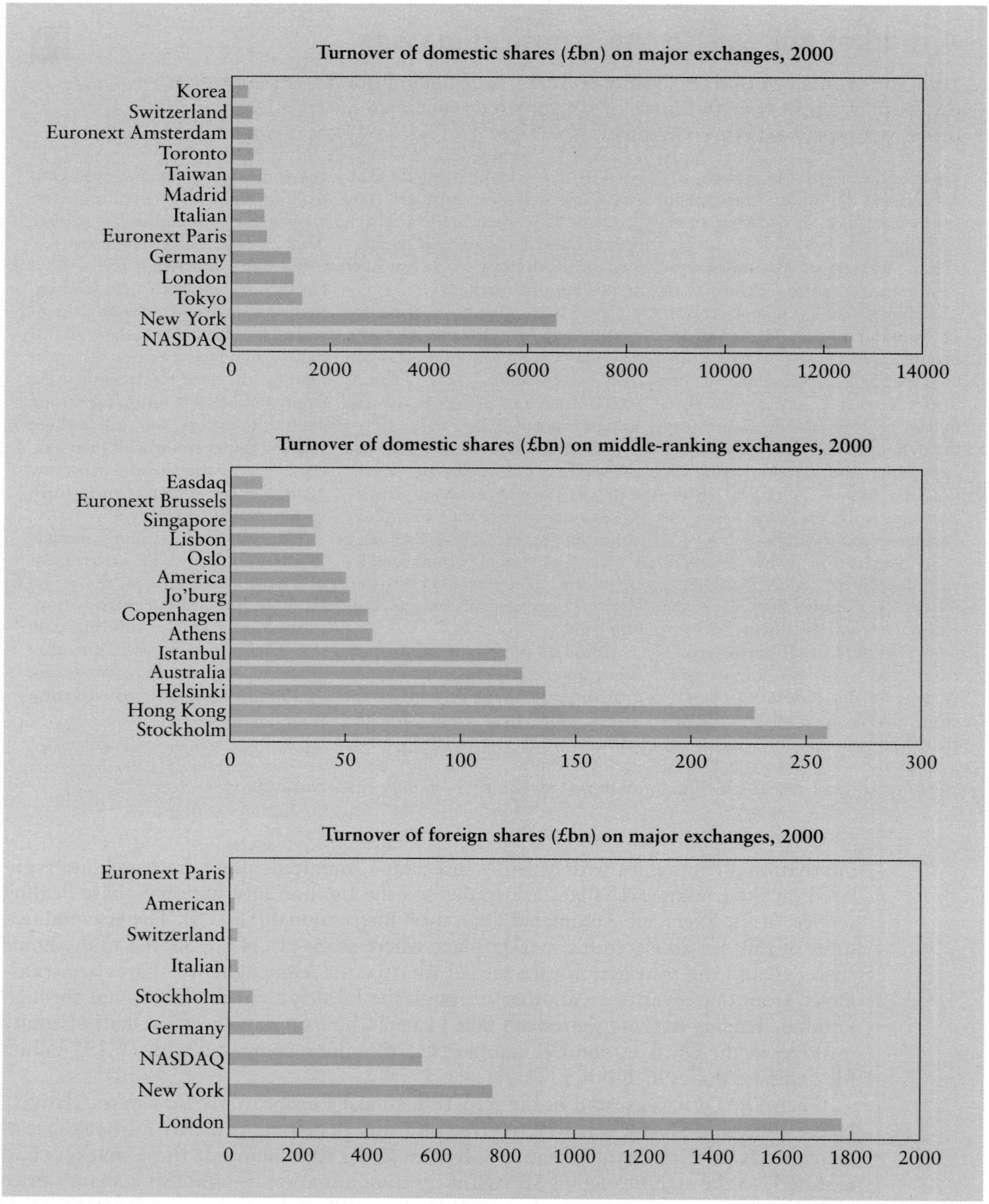

Note: London figures have been halved for comparison purposes for non-order book trading.

Source: *London Stock Exchange Fact File 2001*.

European stock exchanges

In Europe the trend is for stock exchanges to merge together or to form alliances. This is being encouraged by the major financial institutions which desire a seamless, less costly way of trading shares across borders. The ultimate ambition for some visionaries is a single highly liquid equity market allowing investors to trade and companies to raise capital, wherever it suits them. Ideally there would be no distortions in share price, costs of trading or regulation as investors cross from one country to another. Whether it is necessary to merge Europe's disparate stock exchanges to achieve frictionless pan-European trading is a matter that is currently hotly debated. Some argue that the absence of a single securities market damages the EU's competitive position *vis-à-vis* the huge, streamlined and highly liquid US capital market. Furthermore, they say, it prevents European companies and investors enjoying the full benefits of the euro.

On the other hand the cost of actually trading shares in Europe is extremely low. The major costs (90 per cent) arise in the processing of the transaction *after* the deal is done ('the back office'). These clearing and settlement activities (*see* later in the chapter for a definition) are usually carried out by organisations separate from the exchanges. The critics of the drive to merge argue that what is needed is pan-European transaction processing rather than one giant stock exchange.

Whatever the long-run outcome of the current arguments the state of play as in 2001 is as shown in Exhibit 9.7.

The most significant move toward integration has been the merger of the Brussels, Amsterdam and Paris markets to form Euronext. It is the largest market in the Eurozone with a market capitalisation of over £1,500 billion, only slightly lower than that for London. The merger creates a genuine cross-border exchange with enhanced liquidity and lower cost for investors. It also promotes three exchanges from the second rank to a more prominent role in the European financial structure. Already Euronext is wooing other leading stock exchanges ('bourses'), notably Luxembourg, Milan and Zurich, to join. The Lisbon bourse has even entered talks with Euronext.

The Deutsche Börse is the third most significant stock exchange in Europe. With 989 companies listed and a growing interest in share investment among the German people the Deutsche Börse is in a strong position – and it is also ambitious. It has attempted to form mergers and alliances to create a dominant pan-European exchange. So far it has failed, most notably in the attempt to merge with the London Stock Exchange in 2000. In 1997 the Deutsche Börse created a market for shares in young, innovative and generally more risky companies, called Neuer Market. This has been very successful: it is the largest of its kind in Europe with 339 companies.

Neuer Markt has joined with a number of other stock markets aimed at risky growth companies to form a European network called Euro.NM. Its members are Le Nouveau Marché (of the Paris Stock Exchange), Nuovo Mercato (of Italy), Euro.NM Amsterdam and Euro.NM Belgium. The market capitalisation of the 400 or so Euro.NM companies is about €250 billion, and the combined daily turnover of shares is about €1 billion. The Neuer Markt accounts for the vast majority of this.

An important rival to Euro.NM for the listing and trading of innovative, young and fast-growing companies is Nasdaq Europe. This was created in 1999 but it did not become a serious competitor until, in 2001, it took 58 per cent ownership of the ailing pan-European exchange for technology companies, EASDAQ. The American exchange clearly has ambitions to create a global 24-hour stock market and the expansion of its presence in Europe will help achieve its aim (there is also a Nasdaq Japan). With only 62

Exhibit 9.7 Stock exchanges in Europe

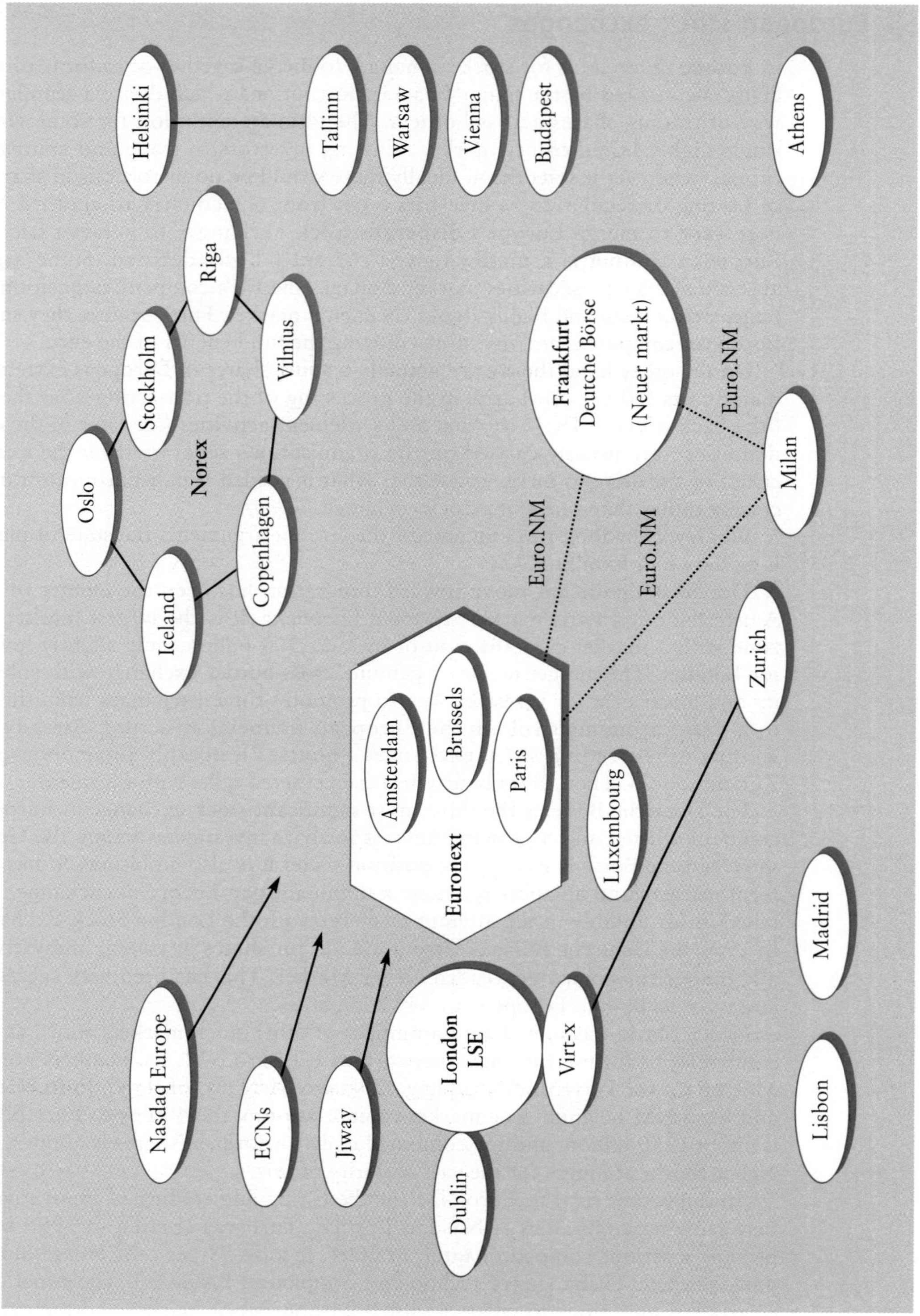

companies listed on Nasdaq Europe it starts from a low base but it has the resources and brand name to expand rapidly. This is a serious threat to the European exchanges. Angela Knight, chief executive of the London-based Association of Private Client Investment Managers and Stockbrokers, said Nasdaq Europe will increase competition between exchanges to the benefit of investors: 'Europe's exchanges are losing their national franchises, becoming listed companies, and now are facing an aggressive trading operation with a strong brand name. We are after a battle royal here'. (*Financial Times*, 28 March 2001, p. 36).

In 1998 the Stockholm and Copenhagen Exchanges formed the Norex Alliance. This was later to embrace Norway and Iceland. Latvia and Lithuania hope to join soon. The individual exchanges remain independent, and continue listing companies and supervising trading. However, the general rules and regulations are being harmonised to make cross-border trading simpler and cheaper. The larger market gives the smaller countries access to larger pools of capital and improves liquidity. Helsinki has chosen to remain outside the alliance. It has bought control of the Tallinn Stock Exchange and has increased its links with Deutsche Börse instead.

Tradepoint, started in 1995, became the second stock exchange permitted to trade shares in the UK. At first, it was thought to be a serious threat to the London Stock Exchange. However, in the 1990s it failed to take more than a 1 per cent of share transactions. In 2000 the Swiss stock exchange took a major stake and its name was changed to Virt-x. This is a London-based exchange, supervised by London's Financial Services Authority, that deals in all the large European company shares across the continent. The issuers of shares traded on Virt-x will remain listed in their chosen jurisdictions (e.g. on the Official List of the London Stock Exchange or the Deutsche Börse) and subject to the corporate governance and listing requirements of that jurisdiction. All trading in Swiss blue chips (leading companies), e.g. Nestlé, has been transferred to Virt-x together with 2,000 UK shares and the 230 largest European company shares. It plans to capture 20 per cent of European cross-border trading.

A major challenge to the traditional stock exchanges is the development of sophisticated electronic networks linking buyers and sellers of shares. Electronic Communication Networks (ECNs), such as Instinet and Island, have taken a considerable amount of share trading from NASDAQ and the NYSE in the USA. Some 30 per cent of trading in NASDAQ shares now takes place outside its organised market (the figure is 5 per cent for the NYSE).

So far ECNs have had little impact on European share trading. This is attributed to the efficiency of the traditional exchanges and, therefore, the low cost of trading. However, there is no room for complacency: Paul Walker-Duncalf, head of dealing in Europe of Merrill Lynch Investment Managers, said: 'It makes little difference where we trade. Most exchanges look the same. If I'm dealing in Paris, or London or Frankfurt, there are just a few visual differences and a few minor market differences. What matters is having a pool of liquidity' (*Financial Times Special Report on World Stocks and Derivative Exchanges,* 28 March 2001).

Another attempt to move share trading away from traditional exchanges is Jiway, launched in 2000. It does not list any shares; it merely offers a trading service across Europe and the USA for private investors (through their brokers). Instead of trading in ten different exchanges investors can execute trades in 6,000 shares (and transaction process) through Jiway. It is hoped that broker costs can be cut in half.

GLOBALISATION OF FINANCIAL FLOWS

Over the past twenty years there has been an increasing emphasis placed on share (equity) finance and stock exchanges. It seems that an 'equity culture' is spreading around the world. This trend toward equity has been given a name: 'equitisation'. Given that stock markets have been around for centuries, what has happened in the last twenty years to spark such a widespread interest? The first explanation is that a greatly increased number of companies have sought a stock market quotation for their shares and there have been deliberate attempts by governments to stimulate interest in share ownership. Following the Thatcher and Reagan privatisations, and the push for wider share ownership in 1980s Britain and the USA, hundreds of state-owned or privately held companies worldwide have floated their shares on stock exchanges. The issue of new shares globally has reached over £200 billion per year. Secondly, it became apparent that equities had provided good long-term returns over the first eighty years of the twentieth century – returns significantly ahead of inflation and those on bonds. So, increasingly, those with responsibility for providing pensions decades from now concentrated on buying shares. Thirdly, the 1980s and 1990s were one of the best periods ever for share returns. The bull market stimulated great interest from millions of investors who previously preferred to hold less risky, lower-return, securities, such as bonds. In America, for instance, almost one-half of all households now own shares (either directly or indirectly through mutual funds and self-select pension funds). In Australia, the level of ownership is higher still. One-quarter of British households own shares. The equity culture has grown so strongly in Germany that almost one-fifth of households hold shares (now, there are more share holders than trade union members). In the five years to mid-2001 there were more new companies joining the Deutsche Börse than in the previous fifty put together and there are over 10,000 German investment clubs. The Scandinavian countries and the Netherlands are even more 'equitised' than Germany.

Financial globalisation means the integration of capital markets throughout the world. The extent of the internationalisation of the equity markets is illustrated by the volume of foreign equity trades in the major financial centres (*see* Exhibit 9.6). It is also evident in the fact that a substantial proportion of pension fund and insurance fund money is invested in foreign equities (*see* Chapter 1). Also, today a corporation is not limited to raising funds in a capital market where it is domiciled. Three of the major elements encouraging cross-border financial activity are shown in Exhibit 9.8.

Exhibit 9.8 Globalisation of financial flows

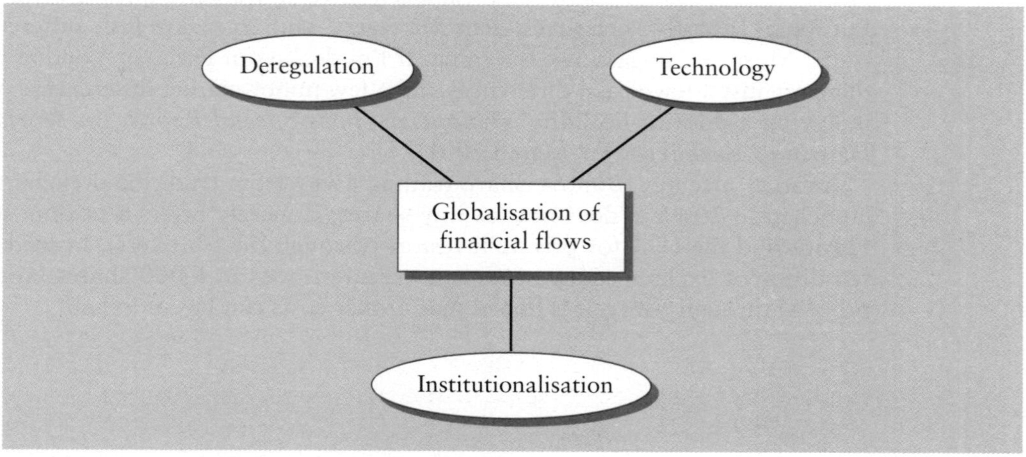

Deregulation

The 1980s and 1990s was a period when government deregulation of financial markets was seen as a way of enabling financial and corporate entities to compete in the global market-place and benefit consumers. The limits placed on the purchase and sale of foreign currency (foreign exchange controls) have been eliminated or lowered in most advanced economies. This has encouraged the flow of investment capital. Cartel-like arrangements for fixing the minimum commissions paid by investors for buying and selling shares have been eroded, as have the restrictions on ownership of financial firms and brokers by foreigners. Now, more than ever, domestic securities can be purchased by individuals and institutional funds from another country. Commercial banks have found the barriers preventing participation in particular markets being demolished. Tax laws have been modified so as not to discourage the flow of funds across borders for investment, and the previously statutorily enforced 'single-activity' financial institutions (in which, for example, banks did banking, building societies did mortgage lending) have ventured into each others' markets, increasing competition and providing a better deal for the consumer.

Technology

The rapid transmission of vast quantities of financial information around the globe has transformed the efficiency of financial markets. Securities can be monitored, analysed and dealt in on hundreds of share, bond, commodity and derivative exchanges at the touch of a button from almost anywhere in the world. The combination of powerful computers and extensive telecommunication networks allows accelerated integration, bringing with it complex trading strategies and enormous daily capital flows.

Institutionalisation

Thirty years ago most shares were owned by individuals. Today, the markets are dominated by financial institutions (pension funds, insurance companies and the 'mutual funds' such as unit and investment trusts). Whereas the individual, as a shareholder, tended to be more parochial and to concentrate on national company shares, the institutions have sufficient knowledge and strength to seek out the rewards from overseas investments. They also appreciate the diversification benefits which accrue due to the low level of correlation between some financial markets (*see* Chapter 7).

Why do companies list their shares on more than one exchange?

There are hundreds of companies which pay for the privilege of having their shares listed for trading on stock exchanges in other countries as well as on their local exchange. Exhibit 9.1 shows that the most popular secondary listings locations are the USA and the UK. There are also substantial numbers of foreign shares listed on most of the northern European exchanges, as well as on those of Canada, Australia, Japan and Singapore. This dual or triple listing can be a costly business and the regulatory environment can be stringent so there must be some powerful motivating factors driving managers to globalise their investor base. For British Telecom the costs and hassle of listing in four countries – the UK, the USA, Canada and Japan – when it floated in 1984 must have been a deterrent (the costs of maintaining a listing in Tokyo are over £100,000 per year alone).[2] Here are some reasons for listing abroad:

- *To broaden the shareholder base* By inviting a larger number of investors to subscribe for shares it may be possible to sell those shares for a higher price and thus raise capital more cheaply (that is, a lower return will be required per £ invested).
- *The domestic stock exchange is too small or the firm's growth is otherwise constrained* Some companies are so large relative to their domestic stock markets that they have no choice but to obtain equity finance from abroad. Ashanti Goldfields, the Ghanaian gold-mining company, was privatised in April 1994. It was valued at about $1.7 billion, which was more than ten times the capitalisation of the Accra stock market. A listing in London was a great success and the company has now expanded its activities in other African countries – it is now listed in New York, Toronto, Zimbabwe, Ghana and London. South African Breweries can raise money on a global basis and escape restrictions placed on it in South Africa by listing in London – *see* Exhibit 9.9.

Exhibit 9.9

SAB plans to raise up to £200m in London listing

FT

South African Breweries, the world's fourth largest brewing group, plans to raise between £150m and £200m in a placing of new shares when it lists on the London Stock Exchange next month.

SAB is the latest in a flood of South African companies moving to London. They are seeking to escape the constraints of exchange controls at home and to gain access to global capital markets to fund growth outside South Africa where most have reached market saturation.

The cash SAB is raising will be used to finance the group's switch to London and to find expansion in emerging markets.

SAB, which controls more than 98 per cent of the South African beer market with brands such as Castle and Lion, has operations in 18 countries countries, including China, Russia, Poland and Ghana ...

Other South African groups that have announced their intention to seek a London listing include Anglo American, another mining group, and Old Mutual, the country's largest life assurance group.

Source: John Willman, *Financial Times*, 11 February 1999, p. 29. Reprinted with permission.

- *To reward employees* Many employees of foreign-owned firms are rewarded with shares in the parent company. If these shares are locally listed these share-ownership plans can be better managed and are more appealing to employees.
- *Foreign investors may understand the firm better* This point is illustrated with the case of Eidos (Exhibit 9.10).

Exhibit 9.10 'My shareholders don't understand me.'

Eidos

In November 1996 Eidos, a UK software developer, decided to offer its shares to US investors by obtaining a quotation on the NASDAQ market. It expected to raise an additional £50 million. The reason the company gave for this snub to UK investors is the 'knowledge and understanding of computer software companies by US investor groups'. On the NASDAQ market US computer games developers' shares are usually valued at least at double their turnover, whereas Eidos is valued at only 1.5 expected sales in London.

Source: Based on *Investors Chronicle*, 1 November 1996.

- ***To raise awareness of the company*** For example, African Lakes listed on the Nairobi Stock Exchange as well as in London – *see* Exhibit 9.11.

Exhibit 9.11

African Lakes dips into Nairobi Stock Exchange

FT

African Lakes, the internet services, information technology and automotive distribution group, yesterday became the first London listed company to raise money through a secondary listing on the Nairobi Stock Exchange.

The company, which owns Africa Online, the continent's most broadly based internet service provider, is raising Ks378m (£3.2m) through an open offer of 4m shares at Ks94.5 (80p) each.

Lesley Davey, finance director, said the company was still cash rich after raising £17.7m through a placing and open offer at 55p a share in London last September. It had gone to Nairobi's exchange to enable African institutions to participate in the growth of the company and to raise its profile in eastern Africa.

Already operating in seven countries, Ms Davey said Africa Online was looking to double that number by the end of this year ...

The move will also give African Lakes substantial influence as the country's third-largest listed company

Source: David Blackwell and Mark Turner, *Financial Times*, 17 February 2000. Reprinted with permission.

- ***Discipline*** This is illustrated through the example of Chinese banks (*see* Exhibit 9.12). The value of stock market discipline has reached the heart of a previously totalitarian centrally controlled economy. Not only have Chinese companies seen the benefit of tapping Western share capital, they have also been made aware of the managerial rigour demanded by stock markets and their investors.

Exhibit 9.12 **'We need the discipline of the market.'**

Plan mooted to list 'big four' Chinese banks

FT

A senior Chinese state banker yesterday made the boldest official proposal yet for the listing of the 'big four' state banks, a move that would revolutionise the country's banking system and hasten the reform of China's socialist-era industries.

Fang Xinghai, general manager of the group co-ordination office at the China Construction Bank, one of the 'big four' banks that dominate the country's financial system, said that stock market flotations would be the only sure way to improve corporate governance at the banks.

'To establish a good governance and incentive system in banks, I see no other way but to list these banks on well functioning stock markets,' Mr Fang said in a statement seen by the Financial Times ...

A listing by one of the big four would have enormous consequences for China's economic reforms. The four banks are the pillars of the socialist economy, providing the loans that keep the inefficient but politically important state industrial sector in business.

Stock market listings could force the big four to apply commercial criteria to their lending, spelling an end to the indulgence that allows the state sector to swallow at least two-thirds of all bank loans to finance just one-third of industrial output.

Source: James Kynge, *Financial Times*, 19 April 2000, p. 10. Reprinted with permission.

- ***To understand better the economic, social and industrial changes occurring in major product markets.*** This is illustrated by the Toyota article – *see* Exhibit 9.13.

Exhibit 9.13

Toyota to list in New York and London

FT

Automotive effort to increase investor base will involve issuing 45m shares worth about Y162bn

Toyota, Japan's third-largest company by market capitalisation, plans to list its shares in New York and London this month.

The issue is aimed at attracting international investors, meeting the needs of the increasingly global industry and boosting Toyota's image, said Yuji Araki, senior managing director.

The move is the latest in a series of global offers by Japanese companies, which are aimed at increasing the international element of their shareholder base . . .

Mr Araki said the company decided to list in New York and London not only to increase its investor base but also to be able to judge whether Toyota's performance met western standards.

'If they don't, we will have to change ourselves', he said.

Listing in the two cities would also help Toyota sense the changes in foreign stock markets more quickly and from those changes, the economic, social and industrial changes occurring in those markets, Mr Araki said.

Foreigners own a relatively low proportion of Toyota – just 8.8 per cent. But Mr Araki emphasised that the company had no fixed target for foreign shareholders . . .

In addition to New York, Toyota decided to list in London because 'in order to attract international investors it is essential to list in London' he added . . .

However, over the next two to three years, changes would be introduced in Japanese reporting requirements, which would bring them much closer to SEC standards, Mr Araki said.

Source: Michiyo Nakamoto and Paul Abrahams, *Financial Times*, 8 September 1999, p. 26. Reprinted with permission.

THE IMPORTANCE OF A WELL-RUN STOCK EXCHANGE

A well-run stock exchange has a number of characteristics. It is one where a 'fair game' takes place; that is, where some investors and fund raisers are not able to benefit at the expense of other participants – all players are on 'a level playing field'. It is a market which is well regulated to avoid abuses, negligence and fraud in order to reassure investors who put their savings at risk. It is also one on which it is reasonably cheap to carry out transactions. In addition, a large number of buyers and sellers are likely to be needed for the efficient price setting of shares and to provide sufficient liquidity, allowing the investor to sell at any time without altering the market price. There are six main benefits of a well-run stock exchange.

1 Firms can find funds and grow

Because investors in financial securities with a stock market quotation are assured that they are, generally, able to sell their shares quickly, cheaply and with a reasonable degree of certainty about the price, they are willing to supply funds to firms at a lower cost than they would if selling was slow, or expensive, or the sale price was subject to much uncertainty. Thus stock markets encourage investment by mobilising savings. As well as stimulating the investment of domestic savings, stock markets can be useful for attracting foreign savings and for aiding the privatisation process.

2 Allocation of capital

One of the key economic problems for a nation is finding a mechanism for deciding what mixture of goods and services to produce. An extreme solution has been tried and shown to be lacking in sophistication – that of a totalitarian directed economy where bureaucratic diktat determines the exact quantity of each line of commodity produced. The alternative method favoured in most nations (for the majority of goods and services) is to let the market decide what will be produced and which firms will produce it.

An efficiently functioning stock market is able to assist this process through the flow of investment capital. If the stock market was poorly regulated and operated then the mis-pricing of shares and other financial securities could lead to society's scarce capital resources being put into sectors which are inappropriate given the objective of maximising economic well-being. If, for instance, the market priced the shares of a badly managed company in a declining industrial sector at a high level then that firm would find it relatively easy to sell shares and raise funds for further investment in its business or to take over other firms. This would deprive companies with better prospects and with a greater potential contribution to make to society of essential finance.

To take an extreme example: imagine the year is 1910 and on the stock market are some firms which manufacture horse-pulled carriages. There are also one or two young companies which have taken up the risky challenge of producing motor cars. Analysts will examine the prospects of the two types of enterprise before deciding which firms will get a warm reception when they ask for more capital in, say, a rights issue. The unfavoured firms will find their share prices falling as investors sell their shares, and will be unable to attract more savers' money. One way for the older firm to stay in business would be to shift resources within the firm to the production of those commodities for which consumer demand is on a rising trend.

A more recent transfer of finance is discussed in Exhibit 9.14. A dramatic shift in resources occurred in the late 1990s as financial markets supplied hundreds of billions of dollars to high-technology industries.

Exhibit 9.14

Rebuilt by Wall Street

FT

The US's dynamic stock market has directed resources into high-tech industries, giving the economy a huge advantage that other countries must strive to match, says David Hale.

The stock market boom has been part of a much larger process of reallocation of global resources resulting from the end of the cold war, the increasing role of information technology in the economy, and the leadership of US companies in utilising this technology.

Despite public perceptions to the contrary, there has not been a broad-based asset inflation in the US equity market during the past few years. The majority of the companies in the S & P 500 have experienced share price declines or only small gains since 1998. Nor has there been a visible expansion of margin debt or bank lending to finance stock market speculation ...

Rather, the stock market rise systems overwhelmingly from the take-off in the market capitalisation of the technology sector. It has mushroomed to $4,500bn (£2,700bn) from $300bn during the early 1990s. The resulting wealth creation has, in turn, redefined the US business cycle by combining a significant expansion of business investment with falling output prices. Moreover, the expansion – now the longest peacetime business cycle in US history – is unlikely to end in the foreseeable future because the technology revolution has helped it to develop several self-reinforcing growth characteristics that are apparent in both financial markets and the real economy.

First, there has been a dramatic improvement in the ability of small companies in the technology sector to obtain capital. In 1999 initial public offerings raised $69.2bn, compared with a previous peak of $49.9bn in 1996 and a grand total of $350.8bn since 1989. Second, the ability of small companies to go public has encouraged a dramatic expansion of the US venture capital industry. It raised funds at an annualised rate of $25bn during the first

►

Exhibit 9.14 continued

half of 1999, nearly twice as much as during all of 1998. About 66 per cent of the funds were placed in the information technology sector while 73 per cent of the IT component was placed with internet companies.

As a result, the technology share of the US stock market has expanded from 10 per cent in the early 1990s to about 33 per cent today. The US technology sector now has a market capitalisation of over $3,000bn, compared with $350bn for the entire global mining industry. Microsoft, alone has a market capitalisation of $535bn, making it the first US company to have a value larger than the GDP of Canada.

By contrast, the IT sector represents only 5.1 per cent of stock market capitalisation in Germany, 9.4 per cent in France, 4.9 per cent in Britain and 15 per cent in Japan. The countries that have IT sectors comparable to the stock market capitalisation of the US are Canada (29 per cent), Taiwan (21.9 per cent) Sweden (38.2 per cent) and Finland (more than 50 per cent).

As a result of the dramatic changes in the composition of the US stock market and the surge of IPO activity, the US economy has been able to reallocate resources on a large scale from traditional industries to new high-growth sectors linked to IT and the internet. But the impact of the technology revolution is also increasingly apparent in the real economy. Spending on research and development in the US has rebounded to 2.7 per cent of GDP after declining to 2.4 per cent during the mid-1990s. The number of patents issued during 1989 was about 140,000 – 29 per cent higher than during 1997 and 55 per cent higher than during 1990.

Human talent is flocking to the IT sector too: almost half the doctorates awarded in the US today are in technical subjects, up from a trough of 36 per cent during the late 1970s. Business investment has represented about one-third of the economy's growth since 1990, compared with only about one-sixth for all the output growth since 1950. The information technology share of output has increased to 5.8 per cent from 3.3 per cent in 1992.

The impact of technology on the real economy has enhanced productivity to such an extent that higher rates of non-inflationary growth are now possible. Most Federal Reserve governors now perceive that the economy's optimal non-inflationary growth rate is $3–3\frac{1}{2}$ per cent, compared with only $2–2\frac{1}{2}$ per cent a few years ago . . .

It would have been difficult for the US to finance the rapid growth of the IT sector without a buoyant stock market because companies in this field need equity capital, not debt finance. The US has been able to play a leading role because of its ratio of stock market capitalisation to bank assets is almost 3 to 1, whereas in Japan and continental Europe bank assets are typically three to five times larger than stock market capitalisation. The rise of the Neuer Markt in Germany and companies such as Softbank in Japan suggests that other countries could catch up with the US in the future, but the gap is still large today. In 1998 venture capital funding in Europe was only $6.8bn while in Japan the total value of all venture capital funds is about $6.7bn, compared with more than $100bn in the US.

It is not difficult to construct scenarios in which the US stock market could experience a correction and dampen the economy's momentum. The Federal Reserve will raise interest rates at least two or three times this year to slow the economy's growth rate to 3 per cent. As a result of the stock market boom, there is so much competition in America's high-tech sector that many companies may experience earnings disappointments and decline sharply.

But the main lesson of the US experience of the late 1990s is that a dynamic stock market can be a valuable national asset for mobilising capital and reallocating resources from low- to high-growth sectors. The stock market boom has given the US economy a huge advantage that will be difficult for other countries to follow until their stock markets promote entrepreneurial energy and creative destruction.

The author is global chief economist at Zurich Financial Services.

Source: David Hale, *Financial Times*, 25 January 2000, p. 22. Copyright © David Hale. Reprinted with permission.

3 For shareholders

Shareholders benefit from the availability of a speedy, cheap secondary market if they want to sell. Not only do shareholders like to know that they can sell shares when they want to, they may simply want to know the value of their holdings even if they have no intention of selling at present. By contrast, an unquoted firm's shareholders often find it very difficult to assess the value of their holding.

Founders of firms may be particularly keen to obtain a quotation for their firms. This will enable them to diversify their assets by selling a proportion of their holdings. Also, venture capital firms which fund unquoted firms during their rapid growth phase often press the management to aim for a quotation to permit the venture capitalist to have the option of realising the gains made on the original investment, or simply to boost the value of their holding by making it more liquid.

4 Status and publicity

The public profile of a firm can be enhanced by being quoted on an exchange. Banks and other financial institutions generally have more confidence in a quoted firm and therefore are more likely to provide funds at a lower cost. Their confidence is raised because the company's activities are now subject to detailed scrutiny. The publicity surrounding the process of gaining a quotation may have a positive impact on the image of the firm in the eyes of customers, suppliers and employees and so may lead to a beneficial effect on their day-to-day business.

5 Mergers

Mergers can be facilitated better by a quotation. This is especially true if the payments offered to the target firm's shareholders for their holdings are shares in the acquiring firm. A quoted share has a value defined by the market, whereas shares in unquoted firms are difficult to assess.

The stock exchange also assists what is called 'the market in managerial control'. That is a mechanism in which teams of managers are seen as competing for control of corporate assets. Or, to put it more simply, mergers through the stock market permit the displacement of inefficient management with a more successful team. Thus, according to this line of reasoning, assets will be used more productively and society will be better off. This 'market in managerial control' is not as effective as is sometimes claimed (it tends to be over-emphasised by acquiring managers) (*see* Chapter 20 for further discussion).

6 Improves corporate behaviour

If a firm's shares are traded on an exchange, the directors may be encouraged to behave in a manner conducive to shareholders' interests. This is achieved through a number of pressure points. For example, to obtain a quotation on a reputable exchange, companies are required to disclose a far greater range and depth of information than is required by accounting standards or the Companies Acts. This information is then disseminated widely and can become the focus of much public and press comment. In addition, investment analysts ask for regular briefings from senior managers and continuously monitor the performance of firms. Before a company is admitted to the Stock Exchange the authorities insist on being assured that the management team are sufficiently competent and, if necessary, additional directors are appointed to supplement the board's range of knowledge and skills. Directors are required to consult shareholders on important decisions, such as mergers, when the firm is quoted. They also have to be very careful to release price-sensitive information in a timely and orderly fashion and they are strictly forbidden to use inside information to make a profit by buying or selling the firm's shares.

THE LONDON STOCK EXCHANGE

The London Stock Exchange (LSE) started in the coffee houses of eighteenth-century London where the buying and selling of shares in joint stock companies took place. In 1773 the volume of trade was sufficiently great for the brokers to open a subscription room in Threadneedle Street. They called the building the Stock Exchange. (It began trading in its present form in 1801.) During the nineteenth century, over twenty other stock exchanges were formed in the rapidly expanding industrial towns of Britain. They amalgamated in 1973 to become a unified Stock Exchange. All of the old trading floors of the regional exchanges and in London, where market members would meet face to face to exchange shares, are now obsolete. Today, there is no physical market-place. The dealing rooms of the various finance houses are linked via telephone and computer, and trading takes place without physical contact.

Securities traded

The volume of trade has expanded enormously in recent years. There are three types of *fixed-interest securities* traded in London: gilts, sterling corporate bonds and Eurobonds. The government bond or 'gilts' market (lending to the UK government) is enormous, with an annual turnover in the secondary market of £1,595 billion in 2000. In that year the UK government raised a total of £8.2bn through gilt-edged securities. Sterling bonds issued by companies (corporate bonds) comprise a relatively small market – just a few billion. Specialist securities, such as warrants, are normally bought and traded by a few investors who are particularly knowledgeable in investment matters. (Warrants are discussed in Chapter 10.) During 2000, 1,826 new Eurobonds were listed in London, raising a total of £185.7 billion.

In addition foreign governments raised £2 billion by selling bonds on the LSE.

Exhibit 9.15 Types of financial securities sold on the London Stock Exchange

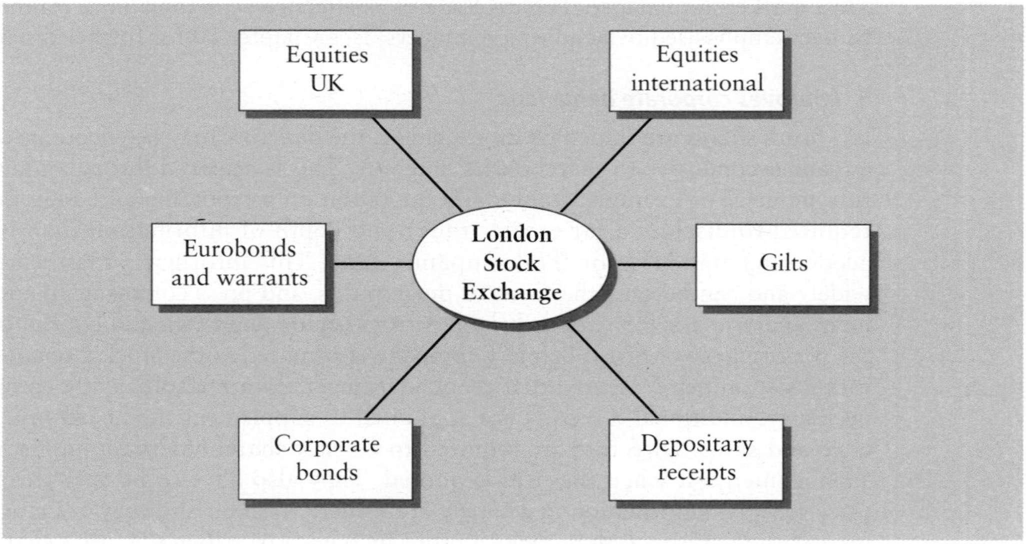

There has been the rapid development of the *depositary receipt* market since 1994. These are certificates which can be bought and sold, which represent evidence of ownership of a company's shares held by a depositary. Thus, an Indian company's shares could be packaged in, say, groups of five by a depositary (usually a bank) which then sells a certificate representing the bundle of shares. The depositary receipt can be denominated in a currency other than the corporation's domestic currency and dividends can be received in the currency of the depositary receipt rather than the currency of the original shares. These are attractive securities for sophisticated international investors because they may be more liquid and more easily traded than the underlying shares. They may also be used to avoid settlement, foreign exchange and foreign ownership difficulties which may exist in the company's home market. This market is large: for example, the China Petroleum and Chemical Corporation raised £2,435.9m when it issued its depositary receipts in London in 2000. Exhibit 9.16 discusses depositary receipts.

Exhibit 9.16

Stock markets are booming, call for the DRs

FT

A natural beneficiary of the booming stock market is the business in depositary receipts, which has experienced a strong start this year thanks to the high numbers of European initial public offerings from the technology, media and telecommunications sectors.

Depositary receipts allow companies to list on foreign stock exchanges, usually in the US, through the sale of repackaged shares. But they are not just a recent product of globalisation. The first DR programme was set up for the UK department store Selfridges by J.P. Morgan in 1927.

The most common form is the American Depositary Receipt, whereby companies from the rest of the world can tap the demand from US equity investors.

For a foreign company to list in the US it must also have an ADR programme, although many companies use ADRs to raise cash without having to go through a complete listing.

Companies hope that by broadening the range of investors who take part in its IPO, there will be a greater demand for their shares and a higher valuation for stock. 'An ADR brings higher visibility, attracts higher valuation and brings the greater liquidity associated with the US market,' says Akbar Poonawala, global head of the client management group at Deutsche Bank in New York.

European companies have been the heaviest users of DRs, though emerging market companies have also been keen to broaden their investor base internationally through Global Depositary Receipts . . .

The role of the depositary receipt is expanding. When UK internet company e-bookers launched its IPO, it listed ADRs on the Nasdaq as well as the German Neuer Markt without a listing of any ordinary shares. The ADRs, despite being denominated in dollars, can now be traded on the Neuer Markt in euros thanks to an arrangement between the clearing systems in the US and Germany. 'It is one of the first ever cases of a global ADR,' say Patrick Colle, head of ADRs for Europe, Middle East and Africa at J.P. Morgan. Another development has been the use of ADRs as an acquisition currency. In the cases of BP's takeover of Amoco and Vodafone's purchase of AirTouch, the UK companies paid the US companies' shareholders with ADRs. But despite the potential of ADRs in these situations, there have not been as many cases as expected . . .

But as other bankers point out, the number of new programmes is less important than their characteristics. Of the approximately 2,000 ADRs in existence, 50 account for 80 per cent of the value of the market. The others are dormant and illiquid programmes, the result of over-zealous marketing from depositary banks.

Source: Rebecca Bream, *Financial Times*, 3 April 2000, p. 35. Reprinted with permission.

Our main concern in this chapter is with the market in ordinary shares and it is to this we now turn. The London Stock Exchange is both a *primary market* and a *secondary market*. The primary market is where firms can raise new finance by selling shares to investors. The secondary market is where existing securities are sold by one investor to another (*see* Exhibit 9.17).

The primary market (equities)

Large sums of money flow from the savers in society via the Stock Exchange to firms wanting to invest and grow. At the beginning of 2001 there were 2,405 companies on the Official List (1,904 UK, and 501 foreign). There were also 524 companies on the Exchange's new market for smaller and younger companies, the Alternative Investment

Exhibit 9.17 Primary and secondary share markets

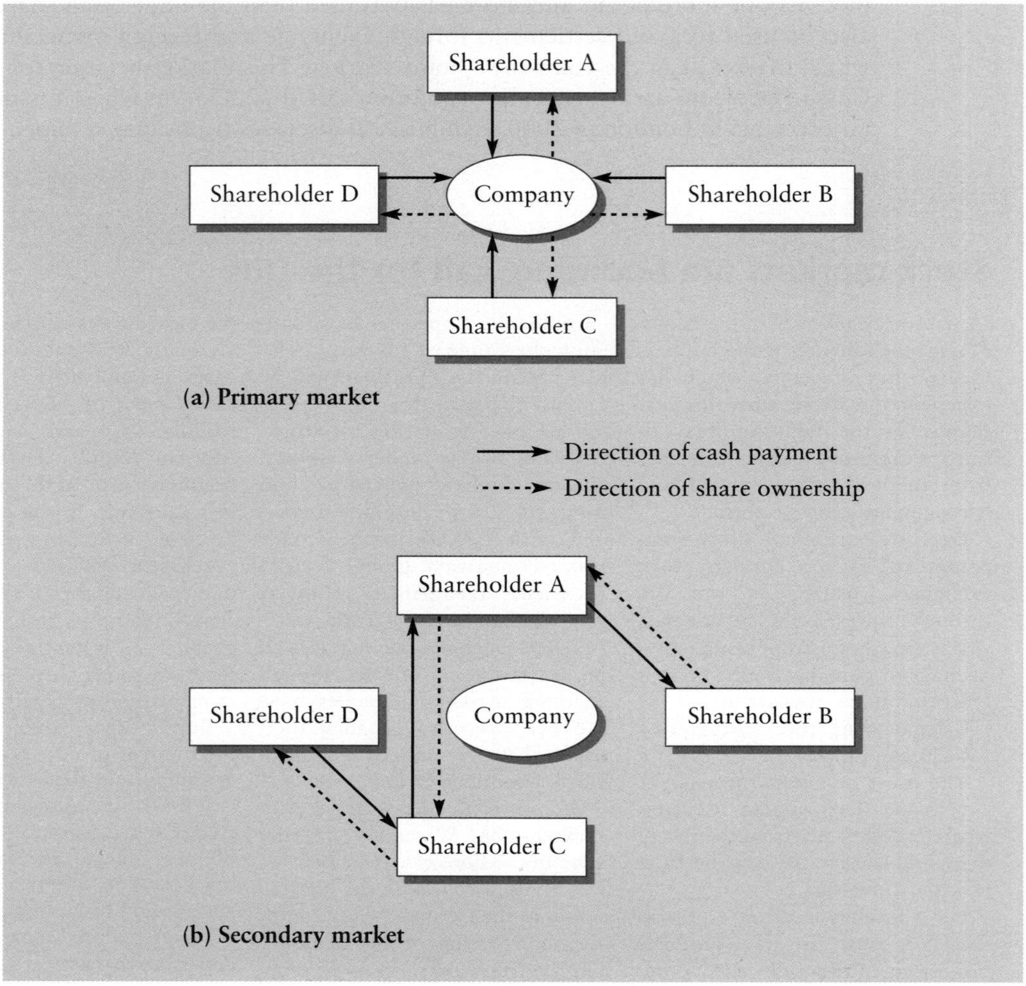

Market (AIM). During 2000, UK-listed firms raised new capital amounting to £125.9 billion by selling equity and fixed interest securities on the LSE. Included in this figure was £11 billion raised by companies coming to the stock exchange for the first time by selling shares. Companies already quoted on the Official List sold a further £10.1 billion of shares. AIM companies new to the market sold £1.75 billion of shares, while those AIM companies that had been quoted for some time sold £1.3 billion. UK companies also raised £0.3 billion by selling convertible bonds, £1.4 billion by selling debentures and loans and £2.5 billion by selling preference shares (*see* Chapters 10 and 11 for discussion on these securities). In addition international companies listed on the Official List raised £99.7 billion through the sale of equities (£10.3 billion) and fixed interest securities, including preference shares, eurobonds and warrants (£89.4 billion). Also, UK companies raised another £97 billion by selling Eurobonds.

Each year there is great interest and excitement inside dozens of companies as they prepare for flotation. The year 2000 was a watershed year for 163 UK companies and 37 foreign companies which joined the Official List and 277 which joined AIM. The requirements for joining the Official List are stringent. The listing particulars should

Exhibit 9.18 Money raised by UK companies on the Official List (OL) and by UK and international companies on the Alternative Investment Market (AIM), 1996–2000

Year	*Companies floating on OL during Year* No.	*Amount raised selling shares £bn*	*Companies already listed selling more shares, e.g. rights issue £bn*	*Companies floating on AIM during year* No.	*Amount raised selling shares £bn*	*Companies already on AIM Amount raised by selling more shares £bn*	*Convertible bond issues (OL) £bn*	*Debentures and loans (OL) £bn*	*Preference shares (OL) £bn*	*Eurobonds (UK companies only) £bn*
1996	230	10.6	8.9	145	0.5	0.3	n/a	n/a	n/a	35.7
1997	132	6.9	4.2	107	0.3	0.4	0.7	1.2	0.6	43.6
1998	122	4.1	5.8	75	0.3	0.3	0.2	0.6	0.3	46.0
1999	96	4.9	8.9	102	0.3	0.6	0.2	0.5	0.7	82.4
2000	163	11.0	10.1	277	1.8	1.3	0.3	1.4	2.5	97.0

Sources: *London Stock Exchange Fact File*, 1997, 1998, 1999, 2000, 2001

give a complete picture of the company; its trading history, financial record, management and business prospects. It should (normally) have at least a three-year trading history and has to make at least 25 per cent of its ordinary shares publicly available. Given the costs associated with gaining a listing, it may be surprising to find that the total value of the ordinary shares of the majority of quoted companies is less than £100 million – *see* Exhibit 9.19.

The LSE is clearly an important source of new finance for UK corporations. However, it is not the most significant source. The most important source of funds is from within the firm itself (internal finance). This is the accumulated profits retained within the firm and not distributed as dividends. In an average year retained profits account for about one half of the new funds for UK firms. The sale of ordinary shares rarely accounts for a

Exhibit 9.19 Distribution of UK companies by equity market value at 31 December 2000

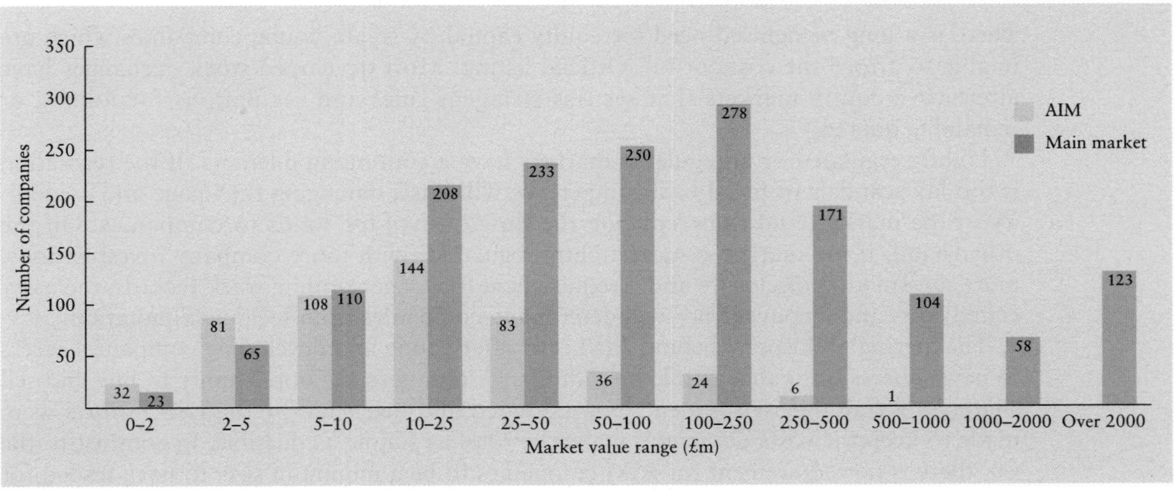

Source: *London Stock Exchange Fact File*, 2001. Reproduced with permission.

significant proportion of capital raised (it is usually less than 15 per cent of funds raised). Firms tend to vary greatly the proportion of finance obtained from bank loans. This is a form of finance that is most attractive when interest rates are low and retained earnings are insufficient to finance expansion. However, when interest rates are high and companies are reluctant to invest (as in the recession of the early 1990s) companies tend to repay loans rather than borrow more. The sale of bonds and preference shares combined generally accounts for less than 5 per cent of new capital put into UK companies.

The secondary market in equities

The LSE operates and regulates a secondary market for the buying and selling of UK shares between investors in which an average of 116,775 bargains, worth £7.5 billion, were completed in an average day in 2000 (average bargain value: £64,414). In addition to these domestic equities a further 44,845 bargains, worth £14.0 billion, of foreign shares were traded on a typical day (average bargain value: £311,457). The secondary market turnover far exceeds the primary market sales. This high level of activity ensures a liquid market enabling shares to change ownership speedily, at low cost and without large movements in price – one of the main objectives of a well-run exchange.

THE UK EQUITY MARKETS AVAILABLE TO COMPANIES

The Official List

Companies wishing to be listed have to sign a Listing Agreement which commits directors to certain high standards of behaviour and levels of reporting to shareholders. This is a market for medium and large established firms with a reasonably long trading history. The costs of launching even a modest new issue runs into hundreds of thousands of pounds and therefore small companies are unable to justify a full main market listing. Companies wishing to float are expected to have a trading history of three years and to put 25 per cent of the ordinary shares in public hands (that is, not in the hands of dominant shareholders or connected persons).

The Alternative Investment Market (AIM)

There is a long-recognised need for equity capital by small, young companies which are unable to afford the costs of full Official listing. Most developed stock exchanges have alternative equity markets that set less stringent rules and regulations for joining or remaining quoted.

Lightly regulated or unregulated markets have a continuing dilemma. If the regulation is too lax scandals of fraud or incompetence will arise, damaging the image and credibility of the market, and thus reducing the flow of investor funds to companies. On the other hand, if the market is more tightly regulated, with more company investigations, more information disclosure and a requirement for longer trading track records, the associated costs and inconvenience will deter many companies from seeking a quotation.

The driving philosophy behind AIM is to offer young and developing companies access to new sources of finance, while providing investors with the opportunity to buy and sell shares in a trading environment run, regulated and marketed by the LSE. Efforts were made to keep the costs down and make the rules as simple as possible. In contrast to the OL there is no requirement for AIM companies to be a minimum size, to have traded for a minimum period or for a set proportion of their shares to be in public hands. However, investors have some degree of reassurance about the quality of companies coming to the market. These firms have to appoint, and retain at all times, a nominated adviser and nominated broker. The nominated adviser ('nomad') is selected by the corporation from a Stock Exchange approved register of firms. These advisers have demonstrated to the Exchange that they have sufficient experience and qualifications to act as a 'quality controller', confirming to the LSE that the company has complied with the rules. Nominated brokers have an important role to play in bringing buyers and sellers of shares together. Investors in the company are reassured that at least one broker is ready to trade or do its best to match up buyers and sellers. The adviser and broker are to be retained throughout the company's life in AIM. They have high reputations and it is regarded as a very bad sign if either of them abruptly refuses further association with a firm. AIM companies are also expected to comply with strict rules regarding the publication of price-sensitive information and the quality of annual and interim reports. Upon flotation a detailed prospectus is required. This even goes so far as to state the directors' unspent convictions and all bankruptcies of companies where they were directors. The LSE charges companies £5,000 per year to maintain a quotation on AIM. If to this is added the cost of financial advisers and of management time spent communicating with institutions and investors the annual cost of being quoted on AIM runs into tens of thousands of pounds. This can be a deterrent for some companies.

Exhibit 9.20 The AIM market attracts the Moomins and Kenny Dalglish

Aim trickle becomes a torrent

FT

A surge in companies listing on Aim last week suggested the gloom that has been hanging over the new issues market since the beginning of the year may be lifting . . .

Aim bucked the main board trend with a steady trickle of small offerings. Last week, however, that flow of issues grew into a stream with a spurt of offerings in sectors ranging from media to window manufacturing.

The Moomins landed on Aim on Monday, with the listing of Maverick Entertainment, which owns the intellectual property of children's characters and toys.

It is run by John Howson and Michael Diprose, who were involved in marketing Mr Blobby and Wallace and Gromit at the BBC. Shares were issued at 3p and the company, which had a market capitalisation of £4.3m at listing, raised £1.96m. They closed at $3\frac{3}{4}$p on Friday.

Proactive Sports, which manages footballers such as Andrew Cole and Stuart Pearce, listed on Aim on Thursday at 25p.

Shares in the company – 3 per cent of which is owned by Kenny Dalglish who also acts as a consultant – rose 62 per cent on Thursday and closed at $40\frac{1}{2}$p on Friday, valuing the company at £40m.

Proactive was founded in 1990 by Paul Stretford, chief executive, and manages 150 professional footballers . . .

Shares in Send Group, which was formed following TT Group's decision to demerge its Beatson Group and James Gibbons Format operations, rose from 40p to $68\frac{1}{2}$p on its first day of listing on Aim on Tuesday an closed at 67p on Friday, valuing the company at £8.5m.

Send has four operating companies – Beatson Clark, which makes glass packaging, James Gibbons Format, a manufacturer of architectural ironmongery, James Gibbons, which manufactures and supplies aluminium windows and shop fronts and Rollalong, which makes modular accommodation for clients including the Ministry of Defence and NHS Trusts.

In 2000, these four businesses made pre-tax profits of £3.2m on turnover of £92.6m . . .

Clover Corporation, which takes the oil out of tuna so it can be added to other food for those who don't like the taste of fish, listed at 10p on Wednesday. The company's market capitalisation was £14m and shares closed unchanged at 10p on Friday.

Dutch company Vema, which makes electro-magnetic locking devices for European banks and hospitals, raised £2.9m when it listed on Thursday. It had a market capitalisation at listing of £5.8m and shares were issued at 4p. By Friday's close they had risen to $4\frac{3}{4}$p.

Imprint Search & Selection, the recently established recruitment consultancy, raised £5m last Monday when it listed on Aim at 80p per share. Trading will begin on May 23.

Source: Sarah Ross, *Financial Times*, 21 May 2001, p. 23. Reprinted with permission.

Exhibit 9.20 continued

Recent issues

Name	Business	Date of first trading	Latest market capitalisation	Issue price	High	Low	Latest price
PC Medics Group	IT support	May-08	£2.9m	2p	3p	2p	2.5p
MoneyGuru	Wealth management	May-08	£8.7m	3.5p	4p	3.5p	4p
Maverick Entertainment	Intellectual property	May-14	£5.4m	3p	3.75p	3.75p	3.75p
Send	Packaging/building products	May-15	£8.5m	40p*	68.5p	40p	67p
Clover Corporation	Natural oils	May-16	£10m	8.5p	10p	8.5p	10p
Proactive Sports	Sports management	May-17	£40m	25p	40.5p	25p	40.5p
Vema	Security products	May-17	£5.9m	4p	4.75p	4p	4.75p
Wincanton	Logistics	May-18	£241m	225p	n.a.	n.a.	210p

Impending issues

Name	Business	Sponsor	Issue method	Market debut	Expected market capitalisation	Issue price	Market
Imprint Search & Selection	Recruitment	Altium Capital	Placing	May-23	£14m	80p	Aim
Pursuit Dynamics	Engineering	Numis	Placing	May-23	£20m	n.a.	Aim
Capcon Holdings	Private investigation	Charles Stanley	Placing	May-25	£6m	n.a.	Aim
Cytomyx	Biotechnology	Corporate Synergy	Placing	May-29	n.a.	n.a.	Aim
Akaei	Computer games	Hoodless Brennan	Placing	May	n.a.	n.a.	Aim
Atlantic Global	Software developer	Seymour Pierce	Placing	May	£5m	25p	Aim
Oxus Resources	Gold mining	Old Mutual Securities	Placing	June	£50m	n.a.	Aim
Photo Therapeutics	Medical equipment	Investec Hend. Crosth.	TBA	Q2 2001	£75m	n.a.	Main
Friends Provident	Financial services	Merrill Lynch	Offer	Jul-09	£3.7bn–£4.2bn	n.a.	Main

Sources: companies; FT   Compiled by Jamie Chisholm   e-mail: jamie.chisholm@ft.com   *opening price

techMARK

At the end of 1999, at the height of high technology fever, the London Stock Exchange launched a 'market-within-a-market' called techMARK. This is part of the Official List and is therefore technically not a separate market. It is a grouping of technology companies on the Official List. One of the reasons for its creation was that many companies lacking the minimum three-year account history required to join the Official List had relatively high market values and desired the advantages of being on a prestigious market. The LSE relaxed its rule and permitted a listing if only one year of accounts are available for techMARK companies. This allowed investors to invest through a well-regulated exchange in companies at an early stage of development, such as Freeserve and lastminute.com. The LSE does insist that all companies joining techMARK have a market capitalisation of at least £50m and they must sell at least £20m worth of new or existing shares when floating. Also at least 25 per cent of their shares must have a free float and they must publish quarterly reports of the company's activities, including financial and non-financial (e.g. number of visitors to the company website for dot.com companies) operating data.

Another reason for creating techMARK as a separate segment of the Official List is to give technology companies a higher profile and visibility, resulting in more attention from investors and research analysts, and enticing more technology-led companies to go for a public quote. The intention is to emulate the success of the NASDAQ in the USA, and to challenge the Neuer Markt in Germany in attracting these young fast-moving companies. Most of the companies on techMARK are firms that were previously on the general part of the Official List, such as Vodafone and AstraZeneca (no AIM companies were transferred). However it has attracted a few dozen young, fast-growing companies. In March 2001 there were 232 UK companies listed on techMARK and 12 international companies.

Critics say it is less like a market than an index (see a discussion on indices later in the chapter), and it has done little to address the issues to stimulate investment in technology. It was also seen as a competitor to AIM which is the home of some exciting technological companies – *see* Exhibit 9.21.

Exhibit 9.21

Companies' nursery shrugs off rival

FT

The launch of Techmark at the end of last year posed a threat to Aim but the LSE is optimistic that the two markets will complement each other

Just as the future had started to look brighter for the Alternative Investment Market (Aim), Britain's long-suffering junior market, a fresh menace appeared on the horizon.

The potential competitor was Techmark – a new forum for technology companies set up by the London Stock Exchange at the end of last year.

Having been the main victim of investors' dislike of small companies, Aim had started to establish itself as the nursery for promising UK companies – shedding its traditional image as the repository for small old-economy groups. As a result the exchange enjoyed the most successful 12 months in its five-year history, with the FTSE Aim index rising 141 per cent in 1999 – a performance bettered only by the Turkish stock market.

Techmark, some thought at the time, threatened to take Aim back to square one.

Although not a separate exchange, Techmark has more lenient listing requirements than the main exchange.

Techmark, therefore, appeared to threaten Aim's growing orientation towards high-tech stocks.

Aim currently plays host to some of the UK's best known and most promising technology companies, including Infobank International and Affinity International – both of which are capitalised at more than £1bn. Sixteen out of the top 20 companies on the market are technology companies.

The initial fear of some analysts when Techmark was launched was that promising high-tech companies would by-pass Aim and that some of the exchange's brightest lights would jump ship. Some even feared that Aim would be consigned to the dustbin of history, like the USM, its ill-fated predecessor.

In the event, neither appears to have happened and the London Stock Exchange is optimistic that Techmark and Aim will prove complementary to each other.

Theresa Wallis, chief operating officer of Aim, is convinced that the junior exchange will retain its appeal.

'Techmark should actually be good for Aim, providing a better branded environment for Aim's high-tech stocks to move on to,' she says.

Companies do not need the three-year record normally required of listed stocks.

'Insofar as Techmark has stimulated investor interest in technology shares it has actually been good for the exchange.'

Many companies, she argues, will continue to choose the more relaxed regulatory regime offered by Aim.

Although companies floating on Techmark do not need a three-year trading record, they do need to have a market capitalisation of £50m. Many extremely promising companies, Ms Wallis says, are likely to fall short of this requirement.

Aspiring Techmark companies will also have to meet tougher disclosure requirements.

An Aim listing also allows founders to hold on to a larger share of the business than Techmark, which requires a free-float of at least 25 per cent of the company's shares.

This is not all, says Ms Wallis.

Other burdens of a full listing, she says, include the rules on takeovers, which require companies to seek shareholder approval for acquisitions which represent more than 25 per cent of their market capitalisation.

The differentiation between a Techmark listing and an Aim listing, she argues, should prevent Aim going the way of the USM . . .

So far so good, Aim has continued to attract companies. Since Techmark's birth in early November about 35 companies have come to the exchange.

►

Exhibit 9.21 continued

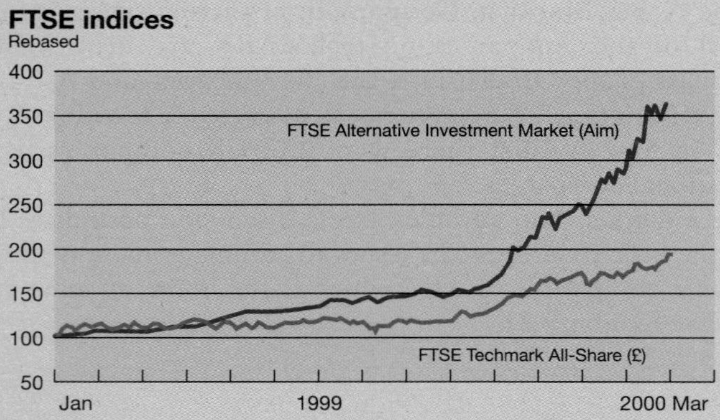

Investment bankers say there are many more in the pipeline.

Analysts, too, are now much more upbeat about the future of the exchange.

'Aim has been remarkably successful at rebranding as the home of young high-tech companies,' says Drew Edmonstone, editor of Durlacher's Aim Bulletin.

'While there will no doubt be companies that bypass it for Techmark, it would be wrong to think that Techmark has sounded the death knell for Aim,' he added.

His views are echoed by other Aim-watchers.

'Aim's recent success has given it a scale which now makes it more of a force to be reckoned with,' argues Peter Ashworth, at Teather and Greenwood.

'The market is now capitalised at £16bn and is made up of 362 companies,' he adds.

But the future is unlikely to be plain sailing for Aim.

The battle to win the listings of Europe's high-tech companies is hotting up.

The field of combatants – comprising Euro NM, an alliance of small-cap bourses, and Easdaq – has recently been joined by Nasdaq-Europe.

Richard Donner, managing director of information technology investment banking at Granville, says the future looks bleak both for Techmark and Aim.

'Most of Aim's recent success has been due to buoyant market conditions, which has put a premium on speed for companies wishing to come to the market,' he argues.

'As the froth subsides companies may think longer and harder about where they want to list.'

Nasdaq's association to the deepest and most liquid market in the world should give it an edge, he says.

'Techmark may prove little more than a short-term distraction.'

Source: Christopher Swann, *Financial Times*, 10 March 2000 (Special Survey: UK middle market companies). Reprinted with permission.

Ofex

Companies that do not want to pay the costs of an initial float (this can range from £100,000 to £1m) and the annual costs on AIM could go for a listing on Ofex. Ofex was set up by broker J.P. Jenkins in 1995. This is a dealing facility with few of the rules that apply to the OL or AIM. However, the annual fee for UK companies is £3,500. Ofex companies are generally very small and often brand new. However, some long-established and well-known firms also trade on Ofex, e.g. Weetabix and Arsenal Football Club.

J.P. Jenkins uses its electronic small company news service, Newstrack, as the basis for 'trading'. This runs on four of the City's main financial news services and acts as a noticeboard for company news. Jenkins makes a market in a company's share by posting on Newstrack two prices: a price at which it is willing to buy and a price at which it will sell. The spread between these prices is normally a maximum of around 5 per cent.

Ofex is a way for untried companies to gain access to capital without submitting to the rigour and expense of a listing on AIM. The only regulations are the basic requirements of company law and of the stockbroking watchdog, the Securities and Futures Authority (discussed later in this chapter) and the restrictions under the European Union's market abuse directive. However, companies raising fresh capital on Ofex must have a sponsor (e.g. a stockbroker, accountant or lawyer) and must produce a prospectus. In late 2001 Ofex asked the Treasury to amend the Financial Services and Markets Act so that it would be regulatd by the Financial Services Authority. That will generally cost between £25,000 and £50,000. Exhibits 9.22 and 9.23 discuss the demand for the Ofex Facility.

Exhibit 9.22

Record demand for internet shares swamps Ofex market

FT

The normally sleepy Ofex over-the-counter market for tiny company shares has been struggling to cope with record dealing levels after private investors discovered the high-risk internet shares quoted on it.

Stockbrokers trying to deal on Ofex faced long telephone waits this week after the unprecedented demand exposed flaws in the telephone system at J P Jenkins, the marketmaker that runs Ofex.

Ofex shares frequently go for months with no dealing at all, but more shares were dealt this week – almost all in internet companies – than in the whole of December 1998. This year's first day of trading, on Tuesday, was Ofex's busiest ever, despite the telephone problems.

The surge of interest has allowed Ofex internet shares to avoid the bloodletting in the internet sector, with many showing rises yesterday despite further falls in 'dot com' stocks listed on the main market ...

Stockbrokers are confounded by the interest in companies which many of them admit to never having heard of before, and are warning private investors that shares in tiny companies, particularly on the unregulated Ofex, are high risk.

But investors have ignored such warnings and acted on share tips in newspapers and on bulletin boards, driving huge leaps in the share prices of companies that few brokers can identify.

'Not only do we [brokers] not know much about these companies, but it is hard to see how anybody knows much about them,' said Justin Urquhart-Stewart, marketing director of Barclays Stockbrokers.

The biggest beneficiary is Silicon Valley, which saw its shares soar from 61.5p to £3.40 after a newspaper tip.

Mr Urquhart-Stewart said investors were looking for volatile internet shares. Because of the normally low levels of dealing on Ofex a few trades could move the share price sharply, so Ofex companies fitted their criteria perfectly.

However, there seems to be little risk of a consumer backlash if the internet bubble bursts, even though Ofex investors stand to lose the most. Private investors are not putting in large sums, with typical trades around £1,500–£2,000, described by one broker as 'punt money'.

Source: James Mackintosh, *Financial Times*, 7 January 2000, p. 2. Reprinted with permission.

Exhibit 9.23 **Junior market breweries, breakfast and bulls add the 'bricks and mortar'**

Exchange with eclectic tradition

FT

Although the upsurge of interest in Ofex has been driven mainly by its high-tech stocks, the unregulated junior market also plays host to some household names from the 'bricks and mortar' world.

The biggest by market capitalisation is Weetabix, the breakfast cereals maker, at £389m, followed by two football clubs, Rangers and Arsenal, and brewing companies Daniel Thwaites and Shepherd Neame. But the majority of the companies are valued at less than £10m.

Overall, Ofex, set up in 1995, now lists 191 constituent companies and 205 tradeable securities with a total market capitalisation of £2.81bn.

The range of activity lower down the list is broad – extending as far as Genus, Britain's largest supplier of bulls' semen – and the companies that came to the market last year continued the eclectic tradition.

They included Saregama, a music distributor spun off by India's RPG Group and the first Indian company on the exchange; Accidentcare, which provides a service to keep motorists on the road after a crash or other mishap; Wing Kong (Holdings), a Liverpool-based producer of frozen Chinese meals; and Mills Technology, which makes floor lighting strips for passenger aircraft.

During last year, 49 companies floated on Ofex – three up on 1998 – of whom the star performer was Easy-screen, the financial software provider that produces one of the leading computer interfaces used for trading electronically on the London International Financial Futures and Options Exchange.

Barry Hocken of J P Jenkins, the main marketmaker to Ofex, said that nine out of 10 inquiries about possible listings were now from companies with internet links. 'We have a very healthy potential flow of new companies – we should be quite busy in the first quarter in comparison with last year.'

He attributed much of the renewed interest in Ofex to the relaunch of its web site in June to provide real-time prices. 'The private investor can now see the same information as the professional – that has made a huge difference.'

Source: David Blackwell, *Financial Times*, 7 January 2000, p. 2. Reprinted with permission.

TASKS FOR STOCK EXCHANGES

Traditionally, exchanges perform the following tasks in order to play their valuable role in a modern society:

- Supervision of trading to ensure fairness and efficiency
- The authorisation of market participants such as brokers and marketmakers
- Creation of an environment in which prices are formed efficiently and without distortion
- Organisation of the settlement of transactions (after the deal has been struck the buyer must pay for the shares and the shares must be transferred to the new owners)
- The regulation of the admission of companies to the exchange and the regulation of companies on the exchange
- The dissemination of information, e.g. trading data, prices and company announcements

In recent years there has been a questioning of the need for stock exchanges to carry out all these activities. In the case of the LSE the settlement of transactions was long ago handed over to CREST (discussed later in this chapter). In 2001 the responsibility for authorising the listing of companies was transferred to the Financial Services Authority (the principal UK regulator). Also in 2001 the LSE's Regulatory News Service (which distributes important company announcements) was told that it will have to compete with other distribution platforms outside the LSE's control. Listed companies are now able to choose between competing providers of news dissemination platforms. However the LSE still retains an important role in the distribution of trading and pricing information. In response to some of these changes, and the threat to its position as the leading European stock exchange, from the competitive actions of other exchanges, the LSE went through a modernisation process: in 2000 it ceased to be an organisation owned by its members (a few hundred marketmakers, brokers and financial institutions) to being a company with shares. In 2001 it floated this company on its own Official List so anyone can now own a portion of the LSE. This move also makes mergers with other stock exchanges easier – not least, because the vested interests of the old members will not weigh so heavily in any future deal; shareholder value will be placed ahead of, say, marketmakers' loss of business. Exhibit 9.24 discusses the changing role of stock exchanges.

TRADING SYSTEMS

Quote-driven systems

A few stock exchanges use a quote-driven system for trading shares. NASDAQ in the USA is the most notable.

Following the stock market reforms known as 'Big Bang' in 1986, the LSE adopted a quote-driven system, which remains the main method of buying or selling shares. At the centre of this system are about 40 *marketmakers* who post on the computerised system called SEAQ (Stock Exchange Automated Quotation) the prices at which they are willing to trade shares. These competing marketmakers feed in two prices. The 'bid' price is the price at which they are willing to buy. The 'offer' price is the price at which they will sell. Thus, for Tesco, one marketmaker might quote the bid–offer prices of 335p–338p, while another quotes 336p–339p. The spread between the two prices represents a hoped-for return to the marketmaker.

The SEAQ computer gathers together the bid–offer quotes from all the marketmakers that make a market in that particular share. These competing quotations are then avail-

Exhibit 9.24

Trading places

FT

After four centuries of providing a range of services for the business world, Europe's stock markets must be prepared to share their role

Europe's stock markets are engaged in a thinly disguised war for survival: against each other, against their customers and against their US rivals. But the struggle is frequently misunderstood.

The threat is not that Paris will beat London; or that Frankfurt plus the Nasdaq will beat them both; or that the New York Stock Exchange will triumph over all. Nor does the threat come from the euro or the arrival of rival high-technology exchanges.

Instead, the risk is of an unbundling of the clutch of services an exchange provides. Exchanges will continue to exist, but as humble performers of routine duties. The real action – and the real added value – will have moved elsewhere.

Stock exchanges have been a part of business life for nearly four centuries, their role unquestioned until recent decades. Now, forced at last to justify their existence, exchanges struggle to provide a simple answer. Perhaps the truth is that they have no single *raison d'être*. Instead, their importance lies in the way they have bundled together a range of services, wrapping them in a layer of respectability or legal authorisation.

These services include the provision of price-information mechanism; the supervision of trading; the settlement of transactions; the authorisation of market participants; the administration and regulation of company listings; and the publication of trade data, prices and stock market indices.

Not all exchanges have performed all these functions. In some countries governments or private-sector bodies perform one or more of these tasks. But everywhere, surviving stock exchanges combine enough of these roles to give them a central status in the country's equity markets.

It is this bundling-up that is under threat: from governments, from technology, and from the increasing power of participants on buy and sell sides. Other groups, usually operating on a cross-border basis, are performing the individual functions of the traditional exchange. They are acquiring scale and skills that exchanges – organised on a national basis – cannot match.

Here are some examples. The US Securities and Exchange Commission is in effect setting listing criteria for the world's big companies, using US accounting principles. Settlement consortia and global custodians are taking over the back-office functions that exchanges historically provided. Bodies such as the European Union, the Iosco group of securities regulators or the Basle committee of the Bank for International Settlements are setting standards for market participants

Trading behaviour is increasingly supervised by government-sponsored bodies, not exchanges. Even the exchanges' most sacred role, providing a home for prices to be set and orders to be executed, is slipping from their hands. Traders can be linked electronically, without a physical floor. Many trades are matched automatically. Others are carried out off-market, or handled internally by big broker-dealers and investment managers.

There is a remaining role for exchanges in most of these areas, for example in ensuring that the standards set by external regulators are observed. But it is much less rewarding – and less well rewarded ...

Within five years, it is likely that Europe's top tier of companies will have found a common home on an electronic exchange. Whether the technology is inherited from Frankfurt or Paris, London or Washington is unimportant. So is the location of this new Euro-bourse's head office. So is the language of its statutes, the nationality of its governing board. Above all, it does not matter which of today's European exchanges leads the coalition from which the new bourse emerges.

Of course, some individuals will be winners or losers. Some national *amour-propre* will be affected. But that is all. The real struggle, the one with economic impact, is over the location of the value-added services that surround the exchange. Where will the main regulatory decisions be made: Brussels, London, Paris, Berlin or Washington? Who will host the settlement process? Where will the dealers who handle complex trades be located? Which city will have the critical mass of analysts and corporate financiers? Which region will host the bulk of the programmers who write the software market participants require? Where will the intellectual content of the new pan-European indices come from?

In deciding these issues, the site of incorporation of the Euro-bourse, or the location of its computers and officials, will carry only a little weight. Much more important will be the imagination, depth of human resources, and diplomatic skills and leadership of Europe's financial community. Exploiting those assets properly will ensure that Europe retains the economic role its individual exchanges are losing.

Source: Peter Martin, *Financial Times*, 2 July 1998, p. 24. Reprinted with permission.

able to brokers and other financial institutions linked up to the SEAQ system. For frequently traded shares, such as those of Tesco, there may be 15–20 marketmakers willing to 'make a book' in those shares. For an infrequently traded share there may be only two or three marketmakers willing to quote prices.

The marketmakers are obliged to deal (up to a certain number of shares) at the price quoted, but they have the freedom to adjust prices after deals are completed. The investor or broker (on behalf of an investor) is able to see the best price available on their computer terminals linked up to SEAQ and is able to make a purchase or sale.

Transactions are generally completed by the broker speaking to the marketmaker on the telephone. All trades are reported to the central electronic computer exchange and are disseminated to market participants (usually within three minutes) so that they are aware of the price at which recent trades were completed (*see* Exhibit 9.26).

The large investing institutions (pension funds, etc.) have SEAQ screens in their offices. This allows them to see the best prices being offered by marketmakers and to trade without necessarily going through a broker, thus cutting out commission.

The underlying logic of the quote-driven system is that through the competitive actions of numerous marketmakers, investors are able to buy or sell at any time at the best price. A problem arises for some very small or infrequently traded firms. Marketmakers are reluctant to commit capital to holding shares in such firms, and so for some there may be only one marketmaker's quote, for others there may be none. The LSE has developed SEATS plus, the Stock Exchange Alternative Trading Service, on which a single marketmaker's quote can be displayed. If business is so infrequent that no marketmaker will make a continuous quote the computer screen will act as a 'bulletin board' on which member firms can display their buy and sell orders. If more than one marketmaker registers in a share on SEATS plus the security is transferred to SEAQ (except for AIM shares which remain on SEATS plus). Huntingdon Life Sciences shareholders faced the prospect of trading through SEATS plus in 2001 – *see* Exhibit 9.25.

Exhibit 9.25

Shareholders take stock at a testing time

FT

The animal rights campaign against Huntindon Life Sciences now threatens to leave the drug-testing company's shareholders feeling isolated. With no marketmakers left offering trades in the shares yesterday, investors faced a trading system that resembled a lonely hearts column.

Those wishing to deal in the shares at the start of the week could have done so using the London Stock Exchange's computerised platform – Seaq. Some 3,000 companies are traded on the system, with each share requiring at least two brokers so that the price is formed through competing quotes.

When Winterflood Securities stepped down on Tuesday as one of HLS's two remaining marketmakers, the company was left with 10 days to find a replacement broker or be moved to the Seats Plus trading system. This platform lists some 600 shares, including Aim-listed companies regardless of the number of marketmakers and all other companies with only one or no broker.

Effectively, a sole marketmaker can set the prevailing share price, leaving investors with less choice and less liquidity.

If investors do not have confidence in this price-setting mechanism, they can resort to a virtual notice-board on their Seats Plus system, on which they can post an offer to buy or sell at their own price in the hope of eventually attracting a match.

These transactions would lack the immediacy offered by marketmakers and it is not impossible that share dealings could take weeks, depending on the number of orders posted.

This was the situation faced by HLS shareholders yesterday after Dresdner Kleinwort Wasserstein followed Winterflood in withdrawing because of a policy of not acting as the sole marketmaker. Dresdner's move not only forced HLS on to the Seats Plus platform but make it one of the 30 to 60 companies at any one time with no marketmaker at all.

Source: Gautam Malkani, *Financial Times*, 29 March 2001, p. 3. Reprinted with permission.

Exhibit 9.26 The SEAQ quote-driven system

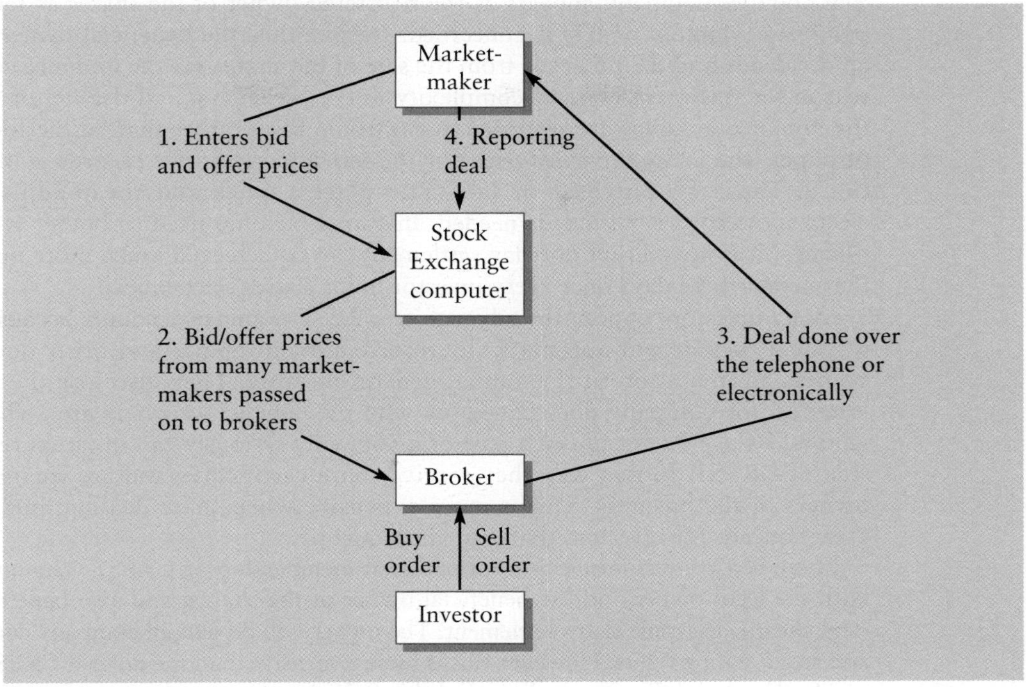

When a trade has been completed and reported to the exchange it is necessary to 'clear' the trade. That is, the exchange ensures that all reports of the trade are reconciled to make sure all parties are in agreement as to the number of shares traded and the price. Later the transfer of ownership from seller to buyer has to take place; this is called settlement (*see* Exhibit 9.27).

Exhibit 9.27 Settlement

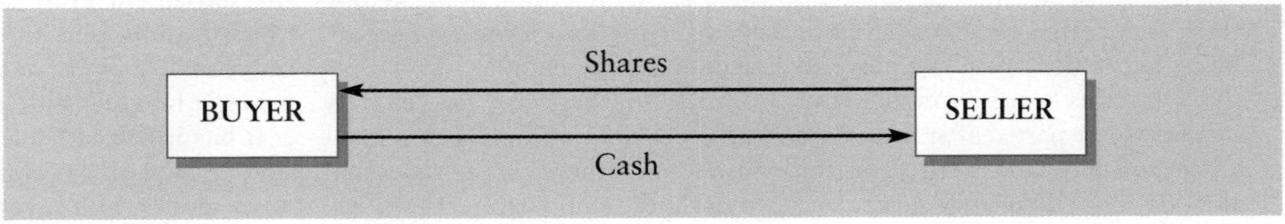

In 2001 the exchange moved to 'three-day rolling settlement' (Trading day +3, or T+3), which means that investors normally pay for shares three working days after the transaction date. Prior to 1996 the transfer of shares involved a tedious paper-chase between investors, brokers, company registrars, marketmakers and the Exchange. The new system, called CREST provides an electronic means of settlement and registration. This 'paperless' system is cheaper and quicker – ownership is transferred with a few strokes of a keyboard.

Under the CREST system shares are usually held in the name of a nominee company rather than in the name of the beneficial owner (i.e. the individual or organisation that actually bought them). Brokers and investment managers run these nominee accounts.

There might be dozens of investors with shares held by a particular nominee company. The nominee company appears as the registered owner of the shares as far as the company (say Marconi or BT) is concerned. Despite this, the beneficial owners will receive all dividends and the proceeds from the sale of the shares via the nominee company. One reason for this extra layer of complexity in the ownership and dealing of shares is that the nominee holdings are recorded in electronic form rather than in the form of a piece of paper (the inelegant word used for the move to electronic records is 'dematerialisation'). Thus, if a purchase or sale takes place a quick and cheap adjustment to the electronic record is all that is needed. Investors have no need to bother with share certificates. It is hoped that one day settlement can be achieved much more quickly than in the current three days once every investor holds shares electronically.

Many investors oppose the advance of CREST nominee accounts because under such a system they do not automatically receive annual reports and other documentation, such as an invitation to the annual general meeting. They also lose the right to vote (after all the company does not know who the beneficial owners are). Those investors who take their ownership of a part of a company seriously can insist on remaining outside of CREST. In this way they receive share certificates and are treated as the real owners of the business. This is more expensive when share dealing, but that is not a great concern for investors that trade infrequently.

There is a compromise position: personal membership of CREST. The investor is then both the legal owner and the beneficial owner of the shares, and also benefits from rapid (and cheap) electronic share settlement. The owner will be sent all company communications and retain voting rights. However, this is more expensive than the normal CREST accounts.

The *Financial Times* article in Exhibit 9.28 puts forward a case for reducing settlement delay to just one day.

Exhibit 9.28

Time running out for 'buy now, pay later'

FT

If you are an investor in UK equities, you will be aware by now that, from today, the settlement cycle is being shortened from five days to three. In other words, you and your money will be parted after three days when you buy stocks listed on the London Stock Exchange, instead of five. Are you ready for this?

You should be. The stock market is one of the few places that still works on the 'buy now, pay later' principle. That is slowly changing. Across the world, the trend is towards ever-shorter time lags between buying shares and paying for them (or selling them and getting paid, which is just as important).

This trend is generally held to be a Good Thing. After all, the shorter the settlement cycle, the less risk there is of something going wrong between the execution and settlement of a transaction.

Stock markets are not exactly super-efficient, high-tech businesses. So there is a risk that something could go wrong, especially in cross-border equity trading, which is all the rage these days. The sharp rise in trading volumes also increases risk factors

According to industry estimates, some 15 per cent of all cross-border trades fail. That means a buyer fails to pay up for shares on time (or at all), or a seller is not paid, or the shares go missing. A shorter settlement cycle is a good way to reduce the risk inherent in such trading.

In the US and much of Europe, the settlement cycle is three days (T+3: trading plus three days). So today's move by the London market brings it into line with its peers.

It has involved some reorganisation of back offices in the City. This costs money, and investors will no doubt be asked to pick up the bill. The argument, though, is that whatever the cost, it is outweighed by a parallel reduction in failed transactions and therefore in the risk inherent in exposure to a market.

Now that a certain global harmonisation has been achieved, the debate is about how far this process of shorter settlement cycles should go.

In theory, there is no reason why stock markets should not operate

Exhibit 9.28 continued

as other markets do. When you buy most goods you pay and go. Stock markets are not corner shops, however.

A particular problem in many markets is the need for paper share certificates to provide proof of ownership. Getting these bits of paper through the system is the reason for much of the grief of failed transactions.

The US, which has an efficient settlement and clearing infrastructure, had a plan to introduce T+1 settlement next year, at the urging of the Securities and Exchange Commission. But it has been put off until 2004 at the earliest.

In Europe, where the clearing and settlement infrastructure is not so joined up, there is no concerted push towards T+1, although there is an aspiration ...

Source: Vincent Boland, *Financial Times*, 5 February 2001, p. 25. Reprinted with permission.

The London Stock Exchange has a third quotation system sharing its Sequence platform along with SEAQ and SEATS plus. SEAQ International provides a linkage for quotations from competing international marketmakers in London. The 44 marketmakers, generally departments of major international securities houses, quote continuous two-way prices, usually in the home currency of the company. This is a market for professionals with an average bargain size in 2000 of £311,457 (compared with £64,414 for UK equities on SEAQ).

Order-driven systems

Most of the stock exchanges in the world operate order-driven markets, which do not require marketmakers to act as middlemen. These markets allow buy and sell orders to be entered on a central system, and investors are automatically matched (they are sometimes called matched-bargain systems). Shock-waves went through the financial markets when Tradepoint began and dozens of eminent City institutions signed up to take the service. Tradepoint (now renamed Virt-x) was designed to allow investors to avoid having to pay the marketmaker a spread for acting as an intermediary. It allowed institutional investors, in particular, to deal directly with each other at lower cost. Order-driven systems generally work as follows: All the buyers and sellers enter a price limit at which they are willing to deal (for most investors, without the computer systems, a broker would do this, for a commission). The computer calculates the price that permits the maximum quantity of sellers' and buyers' prices to be matched. So, in the stylised example shown in Exhibit 9.29, the equilibrium price is 98. At this price the sellers are willing to provide 9,000 shares (2,500 + 2,500 + 4,000). Some of these sellers would be content with 95 Euros, but set this merely as their price limit. At 98 euros there are buyers for 10,000 shares (3,000 + 2,000 + 5,000). At the market price of 98 as many orders as possible have been filled (9,000 shares). The unfilled orders at the market price are carried forward with 98 as the limit price.

The buyers and sellers orders and the recent market prices are continuously shown on the screen so a new buyer (or seller) can pitch the price they demand appropriately (*see* Exhibit 9.30).

The LSE initially responded to the Tradepoint threat by pointing out that a marketmaker-centred system provides more liquidity than an order-driven system where investors may not be able to trade on demand. However, in October 1997 the Stock Exchange introduced its own order-driven service for the largest 100 quoted UK firms – this is called SETS (the Stock Exchange Trading Service). This now trades 189 large company shares. A typical screen is shown in Exhibit 9.31.

Exhibit 9.29

Buyers		*Sellers*	
Quantity of shares	*Price limit (Euros)*	*Price limit (Euros)*	*Quantity of shares*
3000	100	95	2500
2000	99	97	2500
5000	98	98	4000
1000	96	99	2000
2000	95	100	4000
6000	94	101	10,000

Exhibit 9.30 A Virt-x screen

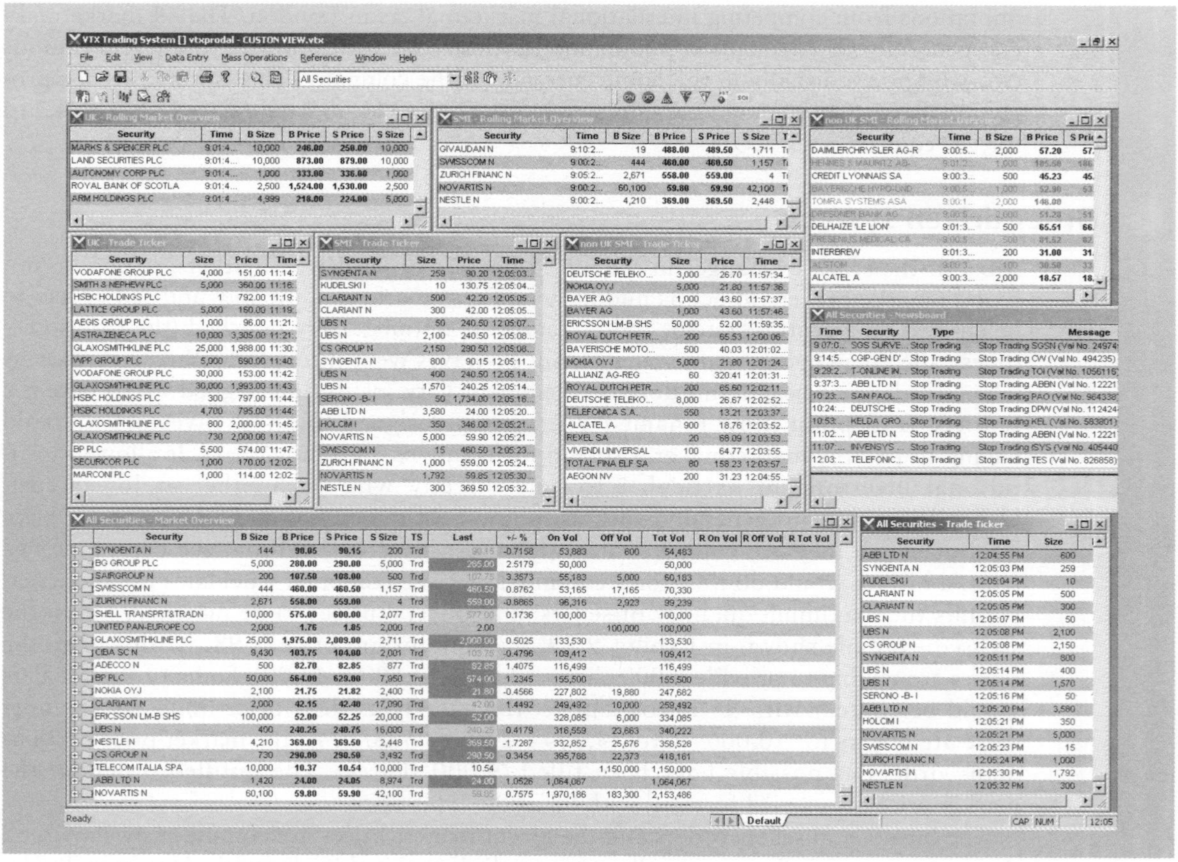

Source: Reproduced by courtesy of Virt-x Investment Exchange

The SETS system runs alongside the marketmaker system for the largest companies' shares. However, the medium-sized and small firms' shares are dealt with entirely through the marketmaker (quote-driven) system.

For SETS shares the London Stock Exchange has delegated clearing to the London Clearing House (LCH). The LCH has also become the counter-party in every SETS transaction. This means that it acts as the buyer to every seller and the seller to every buyer, thus guaranteeing that shares will be delivered against payment and vice versa. It also means that investors can trade anonymously. The article in Exhibit 9.32 discusses the introduction of the central counter-party (CCP).

Exhibit 9.31 SETS screen

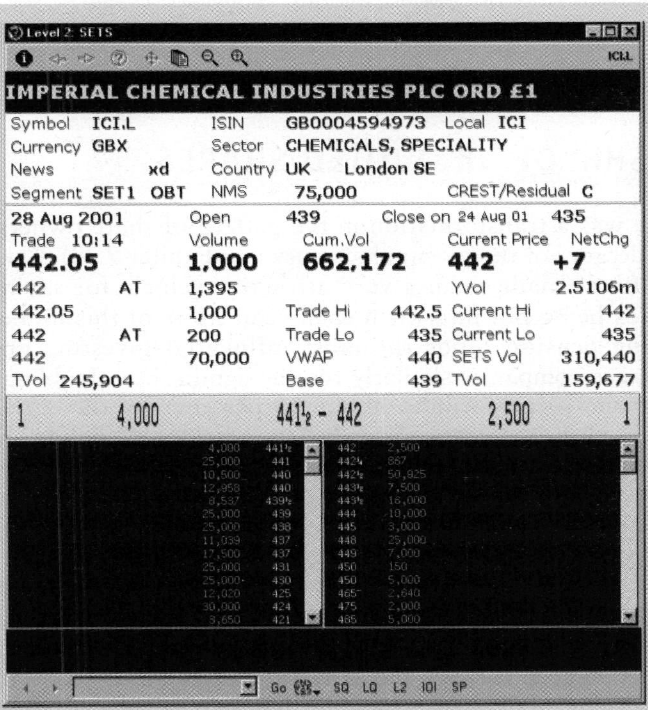

Source: Reproduced by courtesy of Thomson Financial.

Exhibit 9.32

LSE revamps trading structure

Intermediary service expected to provide strategic boost

The biggest shake-up in the structure of the UK equity market since the introduction of electronic trading – to be announced today – is expected to give a strategic boost to the London Stock Exchange.

The change involves the start of a 'central counter-party' (CCP) service to act as intermediary between buyers and sellers of shares.

Investors have been clamouring for years for the service, which offers enhanced risk management and guaranteed anonymity in trading. It will give the LSE a competitive advantage over Deutsche Börse. The LSE will be the second large European exchange to provide a CCP service, putting it on par with Euronext, the Euopean exchange operator. Deutsche Börse and other European exchanges either do not have one or are developing the service.

The CCP is a joint initiative by the three institutions at the heart of London's financial markets – the stock exchange, the London Clearing House and Crest, which processes equity market transactions . . .

Bankers and fund managers said the introduction of CCP was the most significant change to the way the stock market works since the Sets electronic trading system for

Exhibit 9.32 continued

blue-chip UK stocks was launched in 1997 ...

The CCP works by putting itself between the two parties involved in a stock market transaction – the buyer and the seller. It assumes the risk involved by becoming the buyer to every seller and the seller to every buyer. It also means buyers and sellers do not know each other's identity.

Large institution such as investment banks and fund management firms see this anonymity as an important advantage because it reduces the 'market impact cost' of other investors knowing that their competitors are active in the market at a particular time.

Source: Vincent Boland, *Financial Times*, 26 February 2001, p. 23. Reprinted with permission.

THE OWNERSHIP OF UK QUOTED SHARES

There was a transformation in the pattern of share ownership in Britain over the last four decades of the twentieth century (*see* Exhibit 9.33). The tax-favoured status of pension funds made them a very attractive vehicle for savings, resulting in billions of pounds being put into them each year. Most of this money was invested in equities, making pension funds the most influential investing group on the stock market. Insurance companies similarly rose in significance, doubling their share of quoted equities from 10 per cent to about 20 per cent by the early 1990s. The group which decreased in importance is ordinary individuals holding shares directly. They used to dominate the market, with 54 per cent of quoted shares in 1963. By the late 1980s this had declined to about 20 per cent. Investors tended to switch from direct investment to collective investment vehicles. They gain benefits of diversification and skilled management by putting their savings into unit and investment trusts or into endowment and other savings schemes offered by the insurance companies. Another factor was the increasing share of equities held by overseas investors: only 7 per cent in 1963, but over 16 per cent by the mid-1990s. While the proportion of the stock market owned by individuals plunged between the early 1960s and late 1980s, it has been broadly stable since then. A contributing factor to this halt is probably the spread of personal equity plans (PEPs) and Individual Savings Accounts (ISAs), which give some of the tax benefits available to pension schemes directly to individuals. Another major element has been the success of privatisation and building society conversions to public company status.

In 1980 only three million individuals held shares. After the privatisation programme, which included British Gas, British Telecom and TSB, the figure rose to nine million by 1988. By 1991 the flotations of Abbey National, the water companies and regional electricity companies had taken the numbers to 11 million. The stampede of building societies to market in 1997 produced a record 16 million individual shareholders.

Exhibit 9.33 Share ownership in Britain, distribution by sector (quoted shares) (%)

Sector	*1963*	*1975*	*1989*	*1997*
Individuals	54.0	37.5	17.7	20.5
Pension funds	6.4	16.8	34.2	27.9
Insurance cos.	10.0	15.9	17.3	23.1
Others (banks, public sector, unit trusts, overseas, etc.)	29.6	29.6	30.8	28.5

Source: Office for National Statistics. Crown Copyright 1997. Reproduced by permission of the Controller of HMSO and the Office for National Statistics.

Although the mode of investment has changed from direct to indirect, Britain remains a society with a deep interest in the stock market. Very few people are immune from the performance of the Exchange. The vast majority have a pension plan or endowment savings scheme, an ISA or a unit trust investment. Some have all four.

REGULATION

Financial markets need high-quality regulation in order to induce investors to place their trust in them. There must be safeguards against unscrupulous and incompetent operators. There must be an orderly operation of the markets, fair dealing and integrity. However, the regulations must not be so restrictive as to stifle innovation and prevent the markets from being competitive internationally.

London's financial markets have a unique blend of law, self-regulation and custom to regulate and supervise their members' activities. The Financial Services Act 1986 the Banking Act 1987 and the Financial Services and Markets Act 2000 created the present structure. The main burden of regulation falls upon self-regulatory bodies, but within a statutory (legal) framework. The Self-Regulatory Organisations (SROs) have the task of policing the investment business carried out by their members. Overseeing the SROs is the Financial Services Authority (FSA). The FSA has strong statutory powers. All individuals or organisations wishing to undertake 'investment business' have to be authorised to do so. The SROs have the duty to scrutinise their members to ensure their fitness to operate. It is a criminal offence to undertake investment business without being authorised.

There are three SROs reporting to the FSA:

- ***The Securities and Futures Authority (SFA)*** This covers dealing in securities (for example shares) as well as dealing in financial and commodity futures and dealing in international bonds from London. Thus, members of the LSE, the LIFFE futures and options market, the commodity markets and London Eurobond dealers are regulated by the SFA.
- ***The Investment Management Regulatory Organisation (IMRO)*** This regulates institutions managing pooled investments, for example managers of investment trusts, unit trusts and pension funds.
- ***The Personal Investment Authority (PIA)*** This covers insurance brokers, independent investment advisers and the marketing of pooled investment products (for example life assurance or unit trusts).

The FSA also recognises certain professional bodies whose members undertake investment business, primarily accountants and lawyers. A further responsibility of the FSA is the supervision of Recognised Investment Exchanges (RIE). A recognised exchange is exempt from the requirement of authorisation for anything done in its capacity as an RIE. However, the members of an exchange will need authorisation under, say, the SFA. To gain and retain the exalted status of an RIE an exchange has to convince the FSA that high standards are maintained through constant monitoring and enforcement of the rules of the exchange. The LSE is an RIE and, as such, it aims for the highest standards of integrity, fairness, transparency, efficiency and protection of shareholders.

For an overview of the regulation of the financial service industry, *see* Exhibit 9.34.

Outside the FSA structure there are numerous ways in which the conduct of firms and financial institutions is put under scrutiny and constraint. The media keep a watchful stance – always looking to reveal stories of fraud, greed and incompetence. There is legislation prohibiting insider dealing, fraud and negligence. Companies Acts regulate the

Exhibit 9.34 Financial service industry regulation

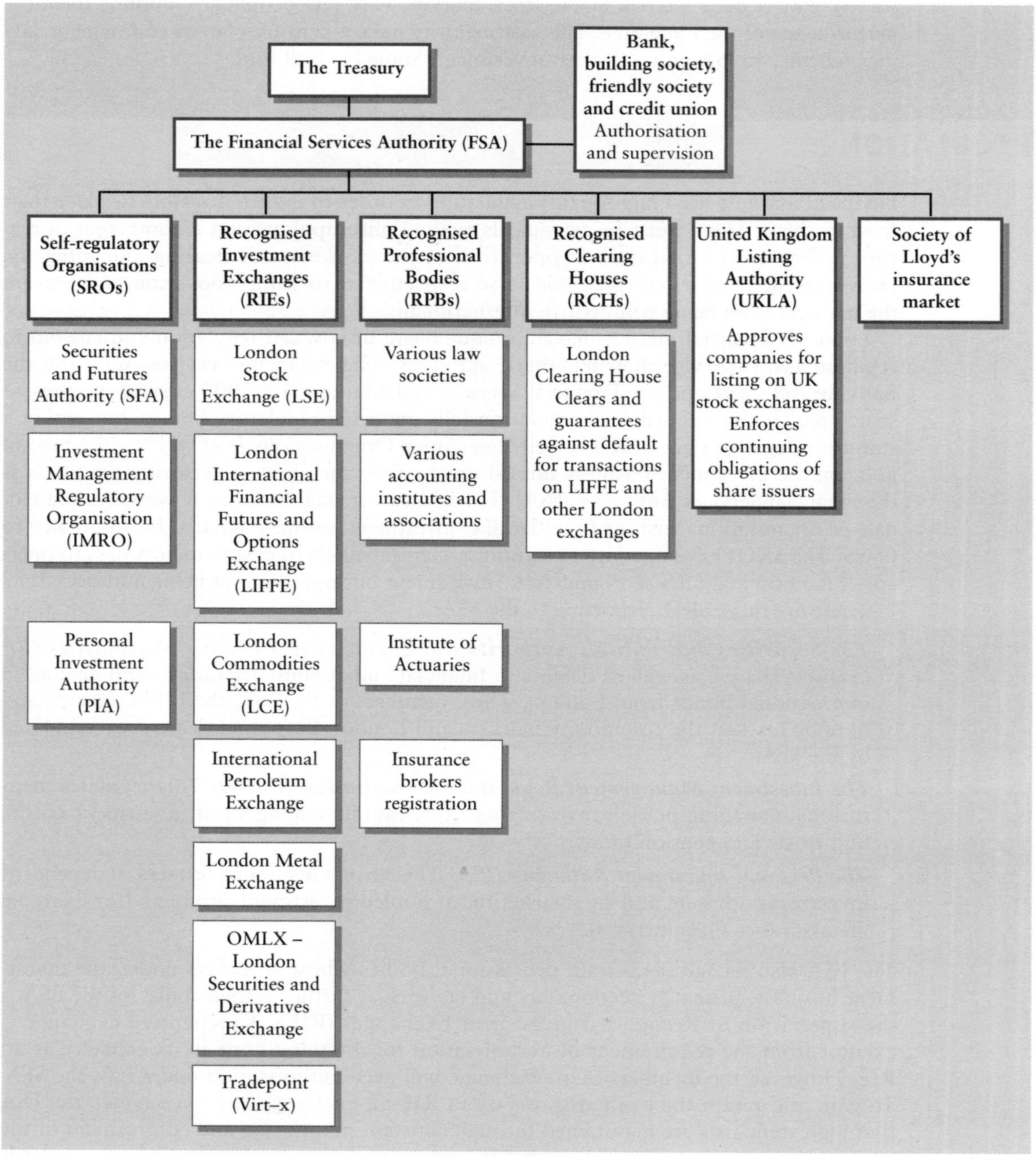

formation and conduct of companies and there are special Acts for building societies, insurance companies and unit trusts. The Competition Commission (CC) and the Office of Fair Trading (OFT) attempt to prevent abuse of market power. The Panel on Takeovers and Mergers determines the manner in which acquisitions are conducted for public companies (*see* Chapter 20). In addition European Union regulations are an increasing feature of corporate life. Accountants also function, to some extent, as regulators helping to ensure companies do not misrepresent their financial position. In addition any member of the public may access the account of any company easily and cheaply at Companies House (or via Companies House's website or the postal system).

UNDERSTANDING THE FIGURES IN THE FINANCIAL PAGES

Financial managers and investors need to be aware of what is happening on the financial markets, how their shares are affected and which measures are used as key yardsticks in evaluating a company. The financial pages of the broadsheet newspapers, particularly the *Financial Times*, provide some important statistics on company share price performance and valuation ratios. These enable comparisons to be made between companies within the same sector and across sectors. Exhibit 9.35 shows extracts from two issues of the *Financial Times* from the same week. The information provided in the Monday edition is different from that provided on the other days of the week.

Indices

Information on individual companies in isolation is less useful than information set in the context of the firm's peer group, or in comparison with quoted companies generally. For example, if ICI shares fall by 1 per cent on a particular day, an investor might be keen to learn whether the market as a whole rose or fell on that day, and by how much. The *Financial Times* (FT) joined forces with the Stock Exchange (SE) to create FTSE International in November 1995, which has taken over the calculation (in conjunction with the Faculty and Institute of Actuaries) of a number of equity indices. These indicate the state of the market as a whole or selected sectors of the market and consist of 'baskets' of shares so that the value of that basket can be compared at different times. Senior managers are often highly sensitive to the relative performance of their company's share price. One reason for this is that their compensation package may be linked to the share price and in extreme circumstances managers are dismissed if they do not generate sufficiently high relative returns.

The indices shown in Exhibit 9.36 are arithmetically weighted by market capitalisation. Thus, a 2 per cent movement in the share price of a larger company has a greater effect on an index than a 2 per cent change in a small company's share price. The characteristics of some of these indices are as follows.

- ***FTSE 100*** The 'Footsie™' index is based on the 100 largest companies (generally over £3bn market capitalisation). Large and relatively safe companies are referred to as 'blue chips'. This index has risen six-fold since it was introduced at the beginning of 1984 at a value of 1,000. This is the measure most watched by international observers. It is calculated in real time (every 15 seconds) and so changes can be observed throughout the day. The other international benchmarks are: for the USA, the Dow Jones Industrial average (DJIA) (30 share) index, the Standard and Poors 500 index and the NASDAQ 100; for the Japanese market the Nikkei 225 index; for France the CAC-40; for Hong Kong the Hang Seng index and for Germany the Dax index. For Europe as a whole there is FTSE Eurotop 300 and for the world FTSE All-World Index.
- ***FTSE All-Share*** This index is the most representative in that it reflects the average movements of nearly 800 shares representing 98 per cent of the value of the London market. This index is broken down into a number of industrial and commercial

Exhibit 9.35 London Share Service extracts: general retailers

FT

Market price: This is the mid-price (midway between the best buying and selling prices) quoted by marketmakers at 4.30 p.m. on the previous day; 'xd' (ex-dividend) means that new buyers of the share will not receive a recently announced dividend (it will go to the existing shareholders).

Change in closing price on Thursday compared with previous trading day.

The highest and lowest prices during the previous 52 weeks.

FRIDAY MAY 25 2001
GENERAL RETAILERS

	Notes	Price	+ or −	52 week high	52 week low	Volume '000s	yield	P/E
Alexon		126½	−8½	138½	47½	332	1.6	9.5
Allders	♣	161½	...	163	90	876	5.3	10.2
Arcadia		276½	−5½	299½	36	315	–	79.1
Arnotts 1£	♣	428¾	+11¾	457	364½	–	4.0	Φ
Ashley (Laura)		25½	...	27½	16¾	99	–	34.4
Austin Reed	♣	153½	+2½	157	82½	81	5.2	9.9
Beale	♣	112½	−1½	127½	69	20	4.7	10.0
Beattie (J)	♣	180xd	+½	186½	118½	144	6.4	11.1
Bentalls	♣	99xd	+4½	100	59½	344	4.1	41.7
Blacks Leisure	♣	179	+4	318½	136½	339	3.8	Φ
Body Shop		93½	...	132½	71½	7	6.4	11.6
Boots	†	585	+5	650	474	1,810	4.4	12.9
Brown & Jcksn		40½	−2	157½	27½	87	8.6	4.3
Brown (N)	q	291½	...	360	231½	304	1.8	21.9
Carpetright	♣†	600	...	682	428	61	4.1	16.6
Carphone Warehouse		140½	+4½	237½	110½	1,456	–	50.0
Cash Converters Units		1	...	5½	1	–	–	–
Clinton Cards		135xd	...	141	83½	292	4.4	6.7
Courts	♣†	327½	+5½	417½	272½	16	1.7	9.1
DFS Furniture	ts	487½xd	−1	490	297½	647	3.9	15.4
Debenhams	†	462	−2	485½	154	1,223	2.4	17.9
Dixons	tsP	250	+½	359	176	13,726	1.9	30.3
ebrokers.com		149	...	161½	97½	8	–	–
Electronics Boutique		92	+¾	95	30	1,299	0.7	Φ
Falkland Islands		146½	...	178½	130	4	3.0	12.1
Findel		276	+8½	288½	200½	203	4.2	Φ
Flying Brands Uts	♣q	130	...	132½	71½	4	5.7	15.8
Forminster		27	...	38½	24½	3	–	–
French Connect		857½xd	...	872½	642½	2	0.8	15.6
Gieves & Hawkes		20	...	25½	15½	3	–	–
Grampian	♣	75	+2	85	54½	242	11.5	Φ
Great Universal	♣	605	+14	607½	366½	5,280	3.4	18.2
Hamleys	a	127½	−3	168	112½	28	6.4	18.8
Harvey Nichols Grp	†	231	...	233½	116	3	3.2	11.6
Heal's		216	+1	217½	150	1	3.5	9.0
Homestyle	♣	459	−1	465	260	1,108	4.2	Φ

MONDAY MAY 21 2001
GENERAL RETAILERS

	Notes	Price	W'K% ch'nge	Div	Div cov.	Mkt cap£m	Last xd	City line
Alexon		118	13.5	2.0	6.6	73.9	11'93	1565
Allders	♣	155	4.7	8.4	1.6	120.4	15.1	2745
Arcadia		287½	4.5	–	–	544.0	1'0	2020
Arnotts 1£	♣	423¼	−.6	27.3c	Φ	76.8	18.9	–
Ashley (Laura)		26	2.0	–	–	155.2	5'97	1664
Austin Reed	♣	145	−2.4	7.75	1.9	45.5	30.10	3798
Beale	♣	114	...	5.3	2.1	23.2	28.2	5027
Beattie (J)	♣	177½xd	2.5	11.5	1.4	70.8	16.5	1784
Bentalls	♣	84xd	−4.0	4.05	0.6	34.4	9.5	1808
Blacks Leisure	♣	172½	...	6.65	Φ	71.4	18.12	1846
Body Shop		95	0.5	5.7	Φ	184.3	4.12	1864
Boots	†	583	−7.3	25.5	1.8	5,247	13,11	1876
Brown & Jcksn		42½	−24.8	3.5	2.7	71.3	13.11	1984
Brown (N)	q	280½	−1.9	5.2	2.5	820.7	27.11	1985
Carpetright	♣†	600	4.2	24.5	1.5	453.0	7.2	2464
Carphone Warehouse		128	1.6	–	–	1,048	–	2833
Cash Converters Units		1	...	–	–	1.51	11'98	2445
Clinton Cards		134½xd	3.5	5.88	3.4	92.4	9.5	4978
Courts	♣†	321	...	5.6	6.4	196.8	7.3	2256
DFS Furniture	ts	480xd	5.1	19.2	1.7	496.3	16.5	3588
Debenhams	†	478	2.4	11.1	2.3	1,769	20.11	2936
Dixons	tsP	244	0.1	4.8	1.7	4,672	29.1	2355
ebrokers.com		137½	...	–	–	63.9	–	–
Electronics Boutique		88	−4.3	0.66	Φ	306.0	30.10	3368
Falkland Islands		144	...	4.4	2.8	8.78	9.10	1615
Findel	†	251½	−1.4	10.65	1.3	182.6	18.12	2563
Flying Brands Uts	♣q	129	−1.9	7.35	1.1	34.7	28.2	2789
Forminster		27	...	–	–	8.94	11'99	2618
French Connect		865xd	0.6	6.5	8.4	163.5	21.3	2633
Gieves & Hawkes		20	−2.4	–	–	6.22	5.6	2694
Grampian	♣	72½	1.4	8.0	Φ	84.3	30.10	2751
Great Universal	♣	569	2.9	20.6	1.6	5,724	2.1	2740
Hamleys	a	122	0.4	8.15	1.1	25.6	18.12	4304
Harvey Nichols Grp	†	213½	3.6	7.5	2.6	117.4	8.1	1744
Heal's		205	6.5	7.6	3.2	25.0	7.2	2819

Price/earnings ratio (PER): Share price divided by the company's earnings (profits after tax) per share in the latest twelve-month period. A much examined and talked about measure (see Chapter 17):

$$\text{PER} = \frac{\text{share price}}{\text{earnings per share}}$$

Share price change over the previous week.

Dividend is the dividend paid in the company's last full year – it is the cash payment in pence per share.

Dividend cover: Profit after tax divided by the dividend payment, or earnings per share divided by dividend per share:

$$\text{Dividend cover} = \frac{\text{earnings per share}}{\text{dividend per share}}$$

Dividend yield: The dividend divided by the current share price expressed as a percentage:

$$\frac{\text{dividend per share}}{\text{current share price}} \times 100$$

Market capitalisation is calculated by multiplying the number of shares issued by their market price.

Ex-dividend date is the last date on which the share went ex-dividend.

City line: up-to-the-second share prices available by telephone (call 0906 003 plus 4-digit code).

Source: Financial Times, 21 and 25 May 2001. Reprinted with permission.

sectors, so that investors and companies can use sector-specific yardsticks, such as those for mining or chemicals. Companies in the FTSE All-Share index have market capitalisations above £35m.

- ***FTSE 250*** This index is based on 250 firms which are in the next size range after the top 100. Capitalisations are generally £350m–£3bn. (It is also calculated with investment trusts excluded.)
- ***FTSE 350*** This index is based on the largest 350 quoted companies. It combines the FTSE 100 and the FTSE 250. This cohort of shares is also split into two to give high and low dividend yield groups.
- ***FTSE SmallCap*** This index covers approximately 500–600 companies included in the FTSE All-Share but excluded from the FTSE 350, with a market capitalisation of between £35m and £350m.
- ***FTSE Fledgling*** This includes over 700 companies too small to be in the FTSE All-Share Index. This index is a mixture of Ordinary List and AIM shares.
- ***FTSE AIM*** Index of all AIM companies.
- ***FTSE techMARK 100*** Includes 100 techMARK companies with capitalisation less than £4bn.
- ***FTSE techMARK All share*** Includes all companies on the techMARK.

Exhibit 9.36 FTSE Actuaries Share Indices

FTSE Actuaries Share Indices UK series
Produced in conjunction with the Faculty and Institute of Actuaries

	£ Stlg May 24	Day's chge%	Euro Index	£ Stlg May 23	£ Stlg May 22	Year ago	Actual yield%	Cover	P/E ratio	Xd adj. ytd	Total Return
FTSE 100	5915.9	+0.3	7594.8	5897.8	5976.6	6231.1	2.25	1.98	22.44	67.86	2772.16
FTSE 250	6635.8	−0.4	8519.7	6663.7	6672.5	6153.8	2.59	1.89	20.37	74.18	3071.24
FTSE 250 ex Inv Co	6742.7	−0.4	8656.3	6773.1	6780.1	6173.4	2.73	1.97	18.60	80.19	3144.23
FTSE 350	2918.3	+0.2	3746.5	2912.1	2946.4	3020.6	2.30	1.97	22.14	33.35	2797.35
FTSE 350 ex Inv Co	2909.8	+0.2	3735.6	2903.4	2938.1	3014.5	2.32	1.98	21.83	33.69	1431.41
FTSE 350 Higher Yield	3279.4	+0.5	4210.1	3263.5	3282.5	2842.5	3.12	1.93	16.64	53.22	2762.38
FTSE 350 Lower Yield	2514.5	−0.2	3228.1	2519.0	2569.4	3231.4	1.15	2.11	41.36	11.47	1908.30
FTSE SmallCap	3146.56	+0.2	4039.55	3139.67	3142.88	3157.88	2.34	1.55	27.65	31.85	2965.82
FTSE SmallCap ex Inv Co	3118.80	+0.3	4003.91	3108.84	3111.92	3117.83	2.36	1.73	24.48	31.64	2982.76
FTSE All-Share	2864.51	+0.2	3677.46	2858.36	2890.91	2961.20	2.30	1.95	22.31	32.59	2787.74
FTSE All-Share ex Inv Co	2855.45	+0.2	3665.82	2849.03	2882.14	2954.66	2.32	1.97	21.90	32.92	1430.62
FTSE All-Share ex Multinational	984.09	+0.3	1047.11	981.07	991.50	1025.22	2.44	1.77	23.19	12.28	1025.82
FTSE Fledgling	2283.00	+0.1	2930.91	2280.50	2278.43	2073.45	3.13	0.49	65.82	24.52	2745.32
FTSE Fledgling ex Inv Co	2411.00	+0.1	3095.24	2408.09	2404.54	2128.66	3.06	0.41	79.97	24.76	2920.89
FTSE All-Small	1904.47	+0.2	2444.95	1900.74	1901.91	1873.00	2.50	1.27	31.52	19.51	2291.72
FTSE All-Small ex Inv Co	1937.24	+0.3	2487.03	1931.80	1932.79	1894.22	2.50	1.42	28.24	19.69	2355.81
FTSE AIM	1226.3	−0.2	1574.4	1228.8	1228.4	1609.8	0.55	‡	‡	2.69	1141.04
FTSE Actuaries Industry Sectors											
RESOURCES(15)	6524.31	+0.6	8375.90	6487.35	6554.80	5661.41	2.33	2.79	15.39	83.29	3246.80
Mining(5)	6363.93	−0.4	8170.01	6387.02	6480.08	4019.66	2.63	2.46	15.47	104.64	2233.30
Oil & Gas(10)	7201.43	+0.8	9245.18	7146.40	7214.29	6608.48	2.27	2.87	15.37	86.31	3673.74
BASIC INDUSTRIES(51)	2484.23	−0.6	3189.26	2500.22	2510.80	2072.62	3.37	1.83	16.24	34.96	1625.35
Chemicals(10)	2484.35	−1.4	3189.41	2519.25	2548.51	2302.02	4.20	1.79	13.29	29.46	1422.02
Construction & Bid Matls(39)	2349.42	−0.1	3016.19	2352.80	2356.55	1811.50	3.15	2.43	13.03	37.23	1430.91
Forestry & Paper(1)	8079.61	+1.9	10372.60	7926.20	7900.63	8100.83	5.44	2.01	9.13	143.18	4184.20
Steel & Other Metals(1)	1871.61	−3.4	2402.77	1937.81	1937.81	2256.77	1.29	‡	‡	0.00	1321.65

►

Exhibit 9.36 continued

	£ Stlg May 24	Day's chge%	Euro Index	£ Stlg May 23	£ Stlg May 22	Year ago	Actual yield%	Cover	P/E ratio	Xd adj. ytd	Total Return
GENERAL INDUSTRIALS(52)	2107.06	−1.4	2705.04	2136.23	2113.61	2489.14	3.64	1.71	16.09	31.66	1365.23
Aerospace & Defence(9)	2181.93	−1.2	2801.16	2208.12	2169.08	2373.47	2.71	1.73	21.34	30.27	1537.14
Electronic & Elect Equip(21)	4623.38	−1.6	5947.05	4708.38	4747.52	7355.89	3.99	1.52	16.52	24.95	2733.98
Engineering & Machinery(22)	2356.70	−1.5	3025.52	2392.70	2360.59	2413.22	5.23	1.82	10.53	59.79	1732.46
CYCLICAL CONSUMER GOODS(7)	5393.57	−0.1	6924.26	5401.44	5447.76	6089.85	2.93	2.36	14.49	91.04	2287.47
Automobiles & Parts(4)	3781.51	−0.3	4854.70	3794.54	3829.07	4365.61	2.64	2.56	14.81	64.18	2206.96
Household Goods & Texts(3)	2351.24	+2.0	3018.52	2305.29	2311.97	2120.44	6.01	1.42	11.73	37.31	1181.60
NON-CYCLICAL CONS GOODS(70)	6407.68	+0.7	8226.17	6359.99	6397.79	5847.36	2.17	1.80	25.64	60.55	2723.01
Beverages(7)	4111.71	+0.1	5278.61	4107.17	4043.07	3286.14	3.14	1.85	17.24	40.51	1777.88
Food Producers & Processors(13)	3174.66	−0.2	4075.62	3180.19	3164.41	2981.32	2.82	1.85	19.13	48.85	1675.50
Health(17)	3073.96	−0.3	3964.34	3083.21	3091.03	2660.37	1.40	2.83	25.27	22.99	2078.45
Packaging(5)	2393.21	+1.4	3072.40	2361.10	2397.69	1963.03	4.93	1.44	14.06	15.58	1262.93
Personal Care & Hse Prods(2)	2605.75	−0.9	3345.25	2628.49	2645.64	2170.78	2.79	1.13	31.61	35.76	1223.31
Pharmaceuticals(23)	11874.35	+1.1	15244.29	11746.80	11897.19	11259.29	1.60	1.73	36.25	70.35	4489.72
Tobacco(3)	7173.50	+1.3	9209.33	7079.51	7071.12	5609.31	5.11	1.88	10.43	250.59	2387.99
CYCLICAL SERVICES(219)	3558.95	−0.6	4568.98	3579.08	3618.60	3743.85	2.16	1.86	24.80	30.74	2083.61
Distributors(15)	2567.00	−3.6	3295.52	2662.67	2667.81	2652.72	2.92	1.86	18.39	12.70	1101.72
General Retailers(42)	1865.72	+0.7	2395.21	1856.36	1851.36	1744.78	2.97	1.70	19.80	11.93	1236.71
Leisure Entermt & Hotels(39)	3167.86	−0.4	4066.99	3180.46	3204.43	3299.20	2.41	2.56	16.19	45.22	1933.51
Media & Photography(48)	5959.17	−1.0	7650.38	6019.43	6167.02	7097.46	1.29	1.37	56.24	41.61	2354.09
Support Services(48)	5264.10	−0.3	6758.04	5278.35	5344.41	4942.18	1.45	2.78	24.88	40.87	3637.26
Transport(27)	2647.28	−1.2	3398.58	2678.17	2663.80	2701.50	3.80	1.59	16.60	28.20	1287.34
NON-CYCLICAL SERVICES(23)	2923.45	−0.4	3753.12	2936.51	3021.87	4486.07	0.94	1.74	61.00	6.38	1673.52
Food & Drug Retailers(9)	3367.47	+0.2	4323.15	3359.37	3361.39	2745.22	2.31	1.90	22.75	33.65	2477.02
Telecommunication Services(14)	4307.31	−0.6	5529.73	4331.67	4478.67	7184.31	0.70	1.65	80.80†	3.22	2166.33
UTILITIES(16)	3914.37	+1.1	5025.27	3873.65	3883.63	3566.76	3.99	1.23	20.40	58.48	2085.44
Electricity(8)	3999.13	+1.1	5134.08	3956.47	3979.95	3487.55	3.76	0.91	29.07	67.44	2637.61
Gas Distribution(2)	4100.72	+0.5	5264.50	4081.58	4082.31	4226.05	2.51	2.17	18.34	55.02	2518.15
Water(6)	2680.17	+1.8	3440.80	2633.21	2617.22	2346.07	6.85	1.37	10.70	27.35	1914.30
INFORMATION TECHNOLOGY(90)	1634.00	−0.9	2097.72	1648.26	1701.13	3106.53	0.62	3.24	49.75	2.90	1659.03
Information Tech Hardware(18)	3129.27	−1.6	4017.35	3178.79	3278.50	6351.01	0.69	2.93	35.56	4.95	3173.00
Software & Computer Services(72)	1478.28	−0.4	1897.81	1484.16	1532.48	2719.49	0.39	3.75	67.86	2.75	1499.59
NON FINANCIALS(543)	2804.18	...	3600.00	2802.84	2837.86	3068.47	2.10	2.01	23.77	25.40	2439.87
FINANCIALS(218)	6367.61	+0.7	8174.73	6323.00	6374.60	5492.58	2.89	1.83	18.94	115.37	3214.00
Banks(12)	10066.79	+0.9	12923.74	9978.77	10059.23	8043.32	3.07	2.24	14.55	209.50	3875.96
Insurance(9)	2363.94	+0.4	3034.82	2355.48	2415.74	2095.28	4.81	0.12	80.00†	74.13	2193.84
Life Assurance(7)	6616.22	+1.6	8493.90	6510.29	6612.76	7325.43	3.53	0.63	45.23	151.80	3227.68
Investment Companies(126)	4941.12	−0.1	6343.41	4947.82	4963.15	4943.46	1.64	0.91	67.01	29.57	1889.67
Real Estate(35)	2310.95	−0.1	2966.79	2313.82	2302.17	1904.41	2.32	1.77	24.41	13.95	1633.89
Speciality & Other Finance(29)	5451.34	−0.6	6998.42	5483.62	5531.56	4425.26	1.71	2.53	23.15	45.59	3538.25

■ Hourly movements	8.03	9.00	10.00	11.00	12.00	13.00	14.00	15.00	16.00	High/day	Low/day
FTSE 100	5898.0	5939.0	5933.7	5943.0	5922.9	5924.8	5924.3	5937.5	5925.6	5950.0	5889.3
FTSE 250	6652.3	6648.3	6644.4	6642.9	6637.5	6638.9	6637.1	6640.6	6639.6	6654.1	6633.8
FTSE SmallCap	3136.33	3136.88	3138.15	3138.82	3140.99	3142.71	3144.13	3146.05	3146.36	3146.61	3136.33
FTSE All-Share	2857.84	2874.18	2871.86	2875.58	2867.24	2868.14	2867.90	2873.45	2868.65	2878.43	2854.20

Time of FTSE 100 Day's high:10:15:15 Day's low: 8:21:15. FTSE 100 2001 High: 6334.5 (30/01/2001) Low: 5314.8 (22/03/2001)
Time of FTSE 100 All-Share Day's high:10:15:00 Day's low: 8:21:00. FTSE All-Share 2001 High: 3045.55 (30/01/2001) Low: 2573.07 (22/03/2201)

Further information is available on http://www.ftse.co,. © FTSE International Limited 2001. All Rights reserved.
'FTSE', 'FT-SE' and 'Footsie' are trade marks of the London Stock Exchange and The Financial Times and are used by FTSE International under licence. † Sector P/E ratios greater that 80 are not shown. – Values are negative.

Source: *Financial Times*, 25 May 2001. Reprinted with permission.

TAXATION AND CORPORATE FINANCE

Taxation impacts on financial decisions in at least three ways.

1 *Capital allowances* At one time it was possible for a firm to reduce its taxable profit by up to 100 per cent of the amount invested in certain fixed assets. So if a firm made a profit of £10m, and in the same year bought £10m worth of approved plant and equipment, the Inland Revenue would not charge any tax because the capital allowance of £10m could be subtracted from the profit to calculate taxable profit. The idea behind this generosity was to encourage investment and thus stimulate economic growth. Today, the capital allowance is generally 25 per cent of the value of the investment in the first year and 25 per cent on a declining balance for subsequent years.

   Capital allowances in project appraisal were discussed in Chapter 5.

2 *Selecting type of finance* The interest paid on borrowed capital can be used to reduce the taxable profit and thus lower the tax bill. On the other hand, payments to shareholders, such as dividends, cannot be used to reduce taxable profit. This bias against share capital may have some impact on the capital structure decision – see Chapter 18.

3 *Distribution of profit* Companies pay corporation tax on profits. The profits are calculated after all costs have been deducted, including interest but excluding dividends. The proportion of taxable profit paid to the tax authorities is 30 per cent if taxable profit exceeds £1,500,000, and 20 per cent where it is less than £300,000 but above £50,000 (a sliding scale applies between £300,000 and £1.5 million). Very small companies with profits under £10,000 pay only 10 per cent tax, and a sliding scale applies between £10,000 and £50,000.

   Standard-rate taxpayers (those with a marginal tax rate of 22 per cent on normal income) are liable to pay 10 per cent income tax on dividends. The rate of income tax on dividends for higher taxpayers is 32.5 per cent. The 10 per cent rate is deemed to be paid by the company when it pays corporation tax. Therefore, standard-rate taxpayers do not have to pay tax on dividends received. The higher-rate taxpayer can offset the 10 per cent tax paid against the total tax they are due to pay on dividends.

CONCLUDING COMMENTS

Stock markets are major contributors to the well-being of a modern financially sophisticated society. They have great value to a wide variety of individuals and institutions. For savers they provide an environment in which savings can be invested in real productive assets to yield a return both to the saver and to society at large. The powerful pension and insurance funds rely on a well-regulated and broadly based stock exchange to enable the generation of income for their members. The mobilisation of savings for investment is a key benefit of a well-run exchange; so too is the improved allocation of scarce resources in society which results in a more satisfying mixture of goods and services being produced. The stock market has a part to play in directing investment to those parts of the economy which will generate the greatest level of utility for consumers. If people want cars rather than horse-drawn transport then savings will be directed to permit investment in factories and production lines for cars. If they demand word processors rather than typewriters then the computer firm will find it easier to raise fresh finance than will the typewriter firm.

Companies value stock markets for their capacity to absorb new issues of financial securities permitting firms to expand, innovate and produce wealth. Entrepreneurs can reap the rewards of their efforts by having access to a flourishing secondary share market and employees can be rewarded with shares which become more appealing because they can be quickly valued by examining reports in the financial press on market prices. Managers often acknowledge the disciplinary benefits of a stock market which insists on high levels of information disclosure, integrity, competence and the upholding of shareholder interests. Governments are aware of the range of social benefits listed above and so should value an exchange on these grounds alone. However, they also see more direct advantages in a fit and proper market. For example, they are able to raise finance to cover the difference between taxes and expenditure, and they are able to tap the market in privatisations and thereby not only fill government coffers but encourage wider share ownership and allow the market to pressurise managers to run previously state-owned businesses in a more efficient manner.

Having gained some background knowledge of the workings of the London Stock Exchange, we now need to turn to the question of how equity funds are actually raised on the Official List and on AIM. The next chapter will examine this. It will also describe sources of equity finance available to firms which are not quoted.

KEY POINTS AND CONCEPTS

- **Stock exchanges** are markets where government and industry can raise long-term capital and investors can buy and sell securities.
- **Two breakthroughs in the rise of capitalism:**
  - thriving secondary markets for securities;
  - limited liability.
- **Over 90 countries now have stock markets.** They have grown in significance due to:
  - disillusionment with planned economies combined with admiration for Western and the 'tiger' economies;
  - recognition of the key role of stock markets in a liberal pro-market economic system.
- The **largest** domestic stock markets are in the USA, Japan and the UK. The **leading international equity market** is the London Stock Exchange.
- The **globalisation** of equity markets has been driven by:
  - deregulation;
  - technology;
  - institutionalisation.
- Companies **list on more than one exchange** for the following reasons:
  - to broaden the shareholder base and lower the cost of equity capital;
  - the domestic market is too small or the firm's growth is otherwise constrained;
  - to reward employees;
  - foreign investors may understand the firm better;
  - to raise awareness of the company;
  - to discipline the firm and learn to improve performance;
  - to understand better the economic, social and industrial changes occurring in major product markets.

- **A well-run stock exchange:**
  - allows a 'fair game' to take place;
  - is regulated to avoid negligence, fraud and other abuses;
  - allows transactions to take place cheaply;
  - has enough participants for efficient price setting and liquidity.
- **Benefits** of a well-run stock exchange:
  - firms can find funds and grow;
  - society can allocate capital better;
  - shareholders can sell speedily and cheaply. They can value their financial assets and diversify;
  - increase in status and publicity for firms;
  - mergers can be facilitated by having a quotation. The market in managerial control is assisted;
  - corporate behaviour can be improved.
- The **London Stock Exchange** regulates the trading of **equities** (domestic and international) and **debt instruments** (e.g. gilts, corporate bonds and Eurobonds, etc.) and **other financial instruments** (e.g. warrants, depository receipts and preference shares).
- The **primary market** is where firms can raise finance by selling shares (or other securities) to investors.
- The **secondary market** is where existing securities are sold by one investor to another.
- **Internal funds** are generally the most important source of long-term capital for firms. **Bank borrowing** varies greatly and **new share or bond issues** account for a minority of the funds needed for corporate growth.
- The **Official List** (OL) is the most heavily regulated UK exchange.
- The **Alternative Investment Market** (**AIM**) is the lightly regulated exchange designed for small, young companies.
- **techMARK** is the sector of the Official List focused on technology-led companies. The rules for listing are different for techMARK companies than for other OL companies.
- **Ofex** is an unregulated market.
- Stock exchanges undertake most or all of the following **tasks** to play their role in a modern society:
  - supervise trading;
  - authorise market participants (e.g. brokers, marketmakers);
  - assist price formation;
  - clear and settle transactions;
  - regulate the admission of companies to and companies on the exchange;
  - disseminate information.
- A **quote-driven** share trading system is one in which **marketmakers** quote a bid and an offer price for shares. An **order-driven** system is one in which investors' buy and sell orders are matched without the intermediation of marketmakers.
- The **ownership of quoted shares** has shifted from dominance by individual shareholders in the 1960s to dominance by institutions, particularly pension and insurance

funds. This trend has been encouraged by the tax system and the recognition of the advantages of pooled investment vehicles, for example diversification and skilled investment management.

- **High-quality regulation** generates confidence in the financial markets and encourages the flow of savings into investment.
- The **Financial Services Authority** is at the centre of UK financial regulation. **Self-Regulatory Organisations** (SROs) supervise the activities of financial businesses. There are two **Recognised Investment Exchanges** (RIEs) trading shares in the UK – the London Stock Exchange and Virt-x.
- **Dividend yield:**

$$\frac{\text{Dividend per share}}{\text{Share price}} \times 100$$

- **Price-earnings ratio (PER):**

$$\frac{\text{Share price}}{\text{Earnings per share}}$$

- **Dividend cover:**

$$\frac{\text{Earnings per share}}{\text{Dividend per share}}$$

- **Taxation** impacts on financial decisions in at least three ways:
  - capital allowances;
  - selecting type of finance;
  - corporation tax.

REFERENCES AND FURTHER READING

Brett, M. (2000) *How to Read the Financial Pages*. 5th edn. London: Random House Business Books. An easy to read jargon-buster. Chapter 6 is particularly relevant.

Buckle, M. and Thompson, J. (1995) *The UK Financial System: Theory and Practice*. Manchester: Manchester University Press. Well written, succinct and clear account of the City.

Levine, R. and Zervos, S. (1996a) 'Capital control liberalisation and stock market development', *World Bank Policy Research Working Paper* No. 1622. World Bank. Some useful data.

Levine, R. and Zervos, S. (1996b) 'Stock markets, banks and economic growth', *World Bank Policy Research Working Paper*, World Bank. Background information with a worldwide perspective.

London Stock Exchange Annual Report. An excellent overview of the role and activities of the LSE. Great graphics and illustrations.

London Stock Exchange Fact File. (Annual.) This superbly produced book contains a wealth of useful information.

London Stock Exchange Publicity. A quarterly newsletter focused on AIM and techMARK.

London Stock Exchange quarterly magazine. Discusses recent events.

Vaitilingam, R. (2001) *The Financial Times Guide to Using the Financial Pages*. 4th edn. London: FT Prentice Hall. Excellent introduction to the mysteries of the financial pages.

Valdez, S. (2000) *An Introduction to Global Financial Markets*. 3rd edn. London: Macmillan Business. Chapter 7 discusses, in an easy to read fashion, many of the topics covered in this chapter.

WEBSITES

Companies House www.companieshouse.gov.uk
CREST www.crestco.co.uk
Financial Services Authority www.FSA.gov.uk
Financial Times www.ft.com
FTSE International www.ftse.com
Hemmington Scott www.hemscott.net
International Federation of Stock Exchanges www.FIBV.com
Investors Chronicle www.investorschronicle.co.uk
London Clearing House www.lch.co.uk
London Stock Exchange www.londonstockexchange.com
Morgan Stanley Capital www.MSCI.com
NASDAQ www.nasdaq.com
New York Stock Exchange www.nyse.com
OFEX www.ofex.co.uk
Office of National Statistics www.statistics.gov.uk
Proshare www.proshare.org

SELF-REVIEW QUESTIONS

1 Name the largest (by volume of share turnover on the secondary market) share exchanges in the USA, Europe and Asia.

2 What is SEAQI?

3 What is a depositary receipt and why are they created?

4 Explain why finance has been 'globalised' over the last 20 years.

5 What are the characteristics of, and who benefits from, a well-run exchange?

6 What securities, other than shares, are traded on the London Stock Exchange?

7 Why is a healthy secondary market good for the primary share market?

8 Explain the acronyms AIM, NASDAQ, SEAQ, OL, IMRO, SFA, PIA, SRO, RIE and FSA.

9 Does the origin of long-term finance for firms remain stable over time? If not, how does it change?

10 Why has it been necessary to have more share exchanges than simply the Official List in the UK?

11 Why is a nominated adviser appointed to a firm wishing to join AIM?

12 Why might you be more cautious about investing in a company listed by J.P. Jenkins on Ofex, than a company on the Official List of the London Stock Exchange?

13 What is SEATS plus?

14 What is CREST?

15 What have been the main trends in UK share ownership over the past 30 years?

16 Explain the following: FTSE 100, FT All-Share, FTSE Fledgling.

QUESTIONS AND PROBLEMS

1 'Stock markets are capitalist exploitative devices giving no benefit to ordinary people.' Write an essay countering this argument.

2 Describe what a badly run stock exchange would be like and explain how society would be poorer as a result.

3 Many countries, for example Peru and Germany, are encouraging small investors to buy quoted shares. Why are they doing this?

4 Explain why firms obtain a share listing in countries other than their own.

5 Describe the trading systems of the London Stock Exchange and outline the advantages and disadvantages of the alternative methods of trading shares.

6 In the USA some firms have completely bypassed the formal stock exchanges and have sold their shares directly to investors over the internet (e.g. Spring Street Brewing). What advantages are there to this method of raising funds compared with a regulated exchange? What are the disadvantages, for firms and shareholders?

7 Discuss some of the consequences you believe might follow from the shift in UK share ownership over the past 30 years.

8 Describe the network of controls and restraints on the UK financial system to prevent fraud, abuse, negligence, etc. Do you regard this system as preferable to a statutorily controlled system? Explain your answer.

9 Frame-up plc is considering a flotation on the Official List of the London Stock Exchange. The managing director has asked you to produce a 1,000-word report explaining the advantages of such a move.

10 Collasus plc is quoted on the London Stock Exchange. It is a large conglomerate with factories and sales operations in every continent. Why might Collasus wish to consider obtaining additional quotations in other countries?

11 'The City is still far too clubby and gentlemanly. They are not rigorous enough in rooting out wrongdoing. What we need is an American type of system where the government takes a lead in setting all the detailed rules of behaviour.' Consider the advantages and disadvantages of a self-regulatory system so decried by this speaker.

ASSIGNMENTS

1 Carry out a comparative study in your firm (or any quoted firm) using information provided by the *Financial Times*. Compare PERs, dividend yields, dividend cover and other key factors, with a peer group of firms and the stock market as a whole. Try to explain the differences.

2 If your firm has made use of the stock market for any reason, put together a report to explain the benefits gained and some estimate of the costs of membership.

CHAPTER NOTES

1 The first limited liability law was introduced in the USA in 1811.

2 BT delisted from the Tokyo Stock Exchange in 2001 as only a small proportion of its shares were held there.

Chapter 10

RAISING EQUITY CAPITAL

CASE STUDY 10.1

To float or not to float? ...

Some firms are keen to float on the London Stock Exchange ...

EasyJet is ambitious. In 2000 it had 18 aircraft providing low-cost flights between European cities. It plans to increase its fleet to 44 by 2004. The intention is to grow seat capacity by 25 per cent per year until it is the largest airline flying inside the European Union. The company expects this to take 10 years. The order for the new 737s has a list price of £890m. (This manufacturer's published price will be reduced for such a large order.) Despite the discount EasyJet still has to find a massive amount of money to fund its ambitions. In November 2000 it sold 63 million new shares to outside investors and became listed on the Official List of the London Stock Exchange. The shares were priced at 310p and £195m was raised for the company. The new shares represented 25.1 per cent of the enlarged equity capital. The remainder is held by EasyJet's chairman, Stelios Haji-Ioannou, his brother and sister Polys and Celia, and Ray Webster, the chief executive, who holds 1.04 per cent. Stelios Haji-Ioannou, the Greek entrepreneur, founded the airline in 1995 with backing from his father's shipping fortune. It made £22m pre-tax profit in the year to September 2000.

Some firms are desperate to leave the London Stock Exchange ...

Bernard Matthews, Richard Branson, Alan Sugar, Andrew Lloyd Webber and **Anita and Gordon Roddick** have demonstrated deep dissatisfaction with their companies' quotation. Mr Branson floated the Virgin Group in 1986, then bought it back in 1988. Lord Lloyd Webber bought back his Really Useful Theatre Group in 1990 four years after floating. Alan Sugar had made plain his dislike of the City and its ways, and was particularly annoyed when investors rejected his 1992 offer to buy the Amstrad group for £175m. Bernard Matthews concluded that his turkey business was paying too high a price for a quotation and so he bought back the company in 2000. Anita Roddick, co-founder of Body Shop which floated in 1984, for many years made no secret of her desire to free herself of the misunderstanding and constraints imposed by City Folk, who she once described as 'pin-striped dinosaurs'.

And some firms are content to raise equity finance without being quoted on an exchange.

Professor Steve Young, a specialist in information engineering at Cambridge University, became a millionaire recently. He had commercialised some speech recognition software in the early 1990s. His project proceeded very nicely without a stock market quotation.

▶

Initially his invention was licensed to a US company by Cambridge University. In 1995 the business was further developed by the creation of a UK company, half of which was owned by the US company. The other half was jointly held by the university, Professor Young and fellow academic Phil Woodland.

To grow further they needed 'venture money'. First, the US and UK companies combined and then the merged group took $3m from Amadeus Capital Partners (venture capitalists). By 1999, with 60 staff, the company, Entropic, was in need of more equity capital. Venture capitalists offered $20m, but here the story takes a strange twist. Young thought that it would be wise to have some of the shares bought by corporate investors. Microsoft was approached; they said they were not interested in making small corporate investments. A few weeks later, however, Microsoft telephoned and offered to buy the whole company instead. The deal is secret, but is thought to be worth tens of millions of pounds. Professor Young has returned to full-time academia a richer man and grateful for the existence of venture capital funds.

Sources: EasyJet: based on *Financial Times*, 1, 9 and 16 November 2000 and 25 October 2000; Bernard Matthews, etc.: based on *Financial Times*, 1 November 1995 and 17 May 2000; Prof. Young: based on *Financial Times*, 14 June 2001.

INTRODUCTION

There are many ways of raising money by selling shares. This chapter looks at the most important. It considers the processes that a firm would have to go through to gain a quotation on the Official List (OL) and raise fresh equity finance. We will examine the tasks and responsibilities of the various advisers and other professionals who assist a company like EasyJet to present itself to investors in a suitable fashion.

A firm wishing to become quoted may, in preference to the OL, choose to raise finance on the Alternative Investment Market (AIM), where the regulations and the costs are lower.

In addition to, or as an alternative to, a 'new issue' on a stock market, which usually involves raising finance by selling shares to a new group of shareholders, a company may make a rights issue, in which existing shareholders are invited to pay for new shares in proportion to their present holdings. This chapter explains the mechanics and technicalities of rights issues as well as some other methods, such as placings and open offers.

It is necessary to broaden our perspective beyond stock markets, to consider the equity finance-raising possibilities for firms which are not quoted on an exchange. There are over one million limited liability companies in the UK and only 0.2 per cent of them have shares traded on the recognised exchanges. For decades there has been a perceived financing gap for small and medium-sized firms which has to a large extent been filled by the rapidly growing venture capital industry. Venture capital firms have supplied share and debt capital to thousands of companies on fast-growth trajectories, such as the company established by Professor Young.

Many, if not most, companies are content to grow without the aid of either stock markets or venture capital. For example J.C. Bamford (JCB) which manufactures earth-moving machines, has built a large, export award winning company, without needing to bring in outside shareholders. This contentedness and absence of a burning desire to be quoted is reinforced by the stories which have emerged of companies which became disillusioned with being quoted. The pressures and strains of being quoted are considered by some (for example Richard Branson and Andrew Lloyd Webber) to be an excessively high price to pay for access to equity finance. So to round off this chapter we examine some of the arguments advanced against gaining a quotation and contrast these with the arguments a growing company might make for joining a market.

Learning objectives

By the end of this chapter the reader will have a firm grasp of the variety of methods of raising finance by selling shares and understand a number of the technical issues involved. More specifically the reader should be able to:

- contrast equity finance with debt and preference shares;
- explain the admission requirements and process for joining the Official List of the London Stock Exchange and for the AIM;
- describe the nature and practicalities of rights issues, scrip issues, vendor placings, open offers and warrants;
- give an account of the options open to an unquoted firm wishing to raise external equity finance;
- explain why some firms become disillusioned with quotation, and present balanced arguments describing the pros and cons of quotation.

WHAT IS EQUITY CAPITAL?

Ordinary shares

Ordinary shares represent the equity share capital of the firm. The holders of these securities share in the rising prosperity of a company. These investors, as owners of the firm, have the right to exercise control over the company. They can vote at shareholder meetings to determine such crucial matters as the composition of the team of directors. They can also approve or disapprove of major strategic and policy issues such as the type of activities that the firm might engage in, or the decision to merge with another firm. These ordinary shareholders have a right to receive a share of dividends distributed as well as, if the worst came to the worst, a right to share in the proceeds of a liquidation sale of the firm's assets. To exercise effective control over the firm the shareholders will need information; and while management are reluctant to put large amounts of commercially sensitive information which might be useful to competitors into the public domain, they are required to make available to each shareholder a copy of the annual report.

There is no agreement between ordinary shareholders and the company that the investor will receive back the original capital invested. What ordinary shareholders receive depends on how well the company is managed. To regain invested funds an equity investor must either sell the shares to another investor (or the company – firms are now allowed to repurchase their own shares under strict conditions) or force the company into liquidation, in which case all assets are sold and the proceeds distributed. Both courses of action may leave the investor with less than originally invested. There is a high degree of discretion left to the directors in proposing an annual or semi-annual dividend, and individual shareholders are often effectively powerless to influence the income from a share – not only because of the risk attached to the trading profits which generate the resources for a dividend, but also because of the relative power of directors in a firm with a disparate or divided shareholder body.

Debt

Debt is very different from equity finance. Usually the lenders to the firm have no official control; they are unable to vote at general meetings and therefore cannot choose directors and determine major strategic issues. However there are circumstances in which lenders have significant influence. For instance, they may insist that the company does not exceed certain liquidity or solvency ratio levels (see negative covenants in Chapter 11, p. 461), or they may take a charge over a particular building as security for a loan, thus restricting the directors' freedom of action over the use and disposal of that building. Debt finance also contrasts with equity finance in that it usually requires regular cash outlays in the form of interest and the repayment of the capital sum. The firm will be obliged to maintain the repayment schedule through good years and bad or face the possibility of action being taken by the lender to recover their money by forcing the firm to sell assets or liquidate.

Disadvantages of ordinary shares for investors

The main disadvantage for investors holding ordinary shares compared to other securities is that they are the last in the queue to have their claims met. When the income for the year is being distributed others, such as debenture holders and preference shareholders, get paid first. If there is a surplus after that, then ordinary shareholders may receive a dividend. Also when a company is wound up, employees, tax authorities, trade creditors and lenders all come before ordinary shareholders. Given these disadvantages there must be a very attractive feature to ordinary shares to induce individuals to purchase and keep them. The attraction is that if the company does well there are no limits to the size of the claim equity shareholders have on profit. There have been numerous instances of investors placing modest sums into the shares of young firms who find themselves millionaires. For example, if you had bought £1,000 shares in Racal in 1961, by 1999 your holding would have been worth £4.8m (Vodafone was one of Racal's creations).

Advantages and disadvantages of share issues

From the company's point of view there are two significant advantages of raising finance by selling shares.

1 ***Usually there is no obligation to pay dividends*** So when losses are made the company does not have the problem of finding money for a dividend. Equity acts as a kind of shock absorber.

2 ***The capital does not have to be repaid*** Shares do not have a redemption date, that is, a date when the original sum invested is repaid to the shareholder. The large sums which had to be paid out in a short space of time as capital repayment to the lenders to some major retailers in the late 1980s and early 1990s, such as Next and Burton, put a severe strain on cash flow, to the point where there were serious doubts about the ability of these firms to survive. They had expanded rapidly in the 1980s and were hit simultaneously by a deep recession and the requirement to pay back large capital sums to lenders. If they had chosen to finance expansion with equity they could have avoided the period of pain they went through.

There are, however, disadvantages of this form of finance.

1 ***High cost*** The cost of issuing shares is usually higher than the cost of raising the same amount of money by obtaining additional loans. There are two types of cost. First, there are the direct costs of issue such as the costs of advice from a merchant bank and/or broker, and the legal, accounting and prospectus costs, etc. These costs can absorb up to 10 per cent of the amount of money raised. Second, and by far the most important, there is the cost represented by the return required to satisfy shareholders, which is greater than that on safer securities such as bonds issued by the firm (*see* Chapter 16 on cost of capital).
2 ***Loss of control*** Entrepreneurs sometimes have a difficult choice to make – they need additional equity finance for the business but dislike the notion of inviting external equity investors to buy shares. The choice is sometimes between slow/no growth or dilution of the entrepreneurs' control. External equity providers may impose conditions such as veto rights over important business decisions and the right to appoint a number of directors. In many instances, founders take the decision to forgo expansion in order to retain control.
3 ***Dividends cannot be used to reduce taxable profit*** Dividends are paid out of after-tax earnings, whereas interest payments on loans are tax deductible. This affects the relative costs to the company of financing by issuing interest-based securities and financing through ordinary shares.

Authorised, issued and par values

When a firm is created the original shareholders will decide the number of shares to be *authorised* (the *authorised capital*). This is the maximum amount of share capital that the company can issue (unless shareholders vote to change the limit). In many cases firms do not issue up to the amount specified. For example, Green plc has authorised capital of £5m, split between £1m of preference shares and £4m of ordinary shares. The company has issued all of the preference shares (at par) but the issued ordinary share capital is only £2.5m, leaving £1.5m as *authorised but unissued ordinary share capital.* This allows the directors to issue the remaining £1.5m of capital without the requirement of asking shareholders for further permission.

Shares have a stated par value, say 25p or 5p. This nominal value usually bears no relation to the price at which the shares could be sold or their subsequent value on the stock market. So let us assume Green has 10 million ordinary shares issued, each with a par value of 25p (£2.5m total nominal value divided by the nominal price per share, 25p = 10m shares); these were originally sold for £2 each, raising £20m, and the present market value is £3.80 per share.

The par value has no real significance[1] and for the most part can be ignored. However, a point of confusion can arise when one examines company accounts because issued share capital appears on the balance sheet at par value and so often seems pathetically small. This item has to be read in conjunction with the *share premium account*, which represents the difference between the price received by the company for the shares and the par value of those shares. Thus, in the case of Green the premium on each share was 200p – 25p = 175p. The total share premium in the balance sheet will be £17.5m.

Limited companies, plcs and listed companies

Limited liability means that the ordinary shareholders are only liable up to the amount they have invested or have promised to invest in purchasing shares. Lenders and other creditors are not able to turn to the ordinary shareholder should they find on a liquidation that the company, as a separate legal 'person', has insufficient assets to repay them in full. This contrasts with the position for a partner in a partnership who will be liable for all the debts of the business to the point where personal assets such as houses and cars can be seized to be sold to pay creditors.

Private companies, with the suffix 'Limited' or 'Ltd', are the most common form of company (over 95 per cent of all companies). The less numerous, but more influential, form of company is a public limited company (or just public companies). These firms must display the suffix 'plc'. The private company has no minimum amount of share capital and there are restrictions on the type of purchaser who can be offered shares in the enterprise, whereas the plc has to have a minimum share capital of £50,000 but is able to offer shares to a wide range of potential investors. Not all public companies are quoted on a stock market. This can be particularly confusing when the press talks about a firm 'going public' – it may have been a public limited company for years and has merely decided to 'come to the market' to obtain a quotation. Strictly speaking, the term 'listed' should only be applied to those firms on the Official List but the term is used rather loosely and shares on AIM are often referred to as being quoted or listed.

PREFERENCE SHARES

Preference shares usually offer their owners a fixed rate of dividend each year. However if the firm has insufficient profits the amount paid would be reduced, sometimes to zero. Thus, there is no guarantee that an annual income will be received, unlike with debt capital. The dividend on preference shares is paid before anything is paid out to ordinary shareholders – indeed, after the preference dividend obligation has been met there may be nothing left for ordinary shareholders. Preference shares are attractive to some investors because they offer a regular income at a higher rate of return than that available on fixed interest securities, e.g. bonds. However this higher return also comes with higher risk, as the preference dividend ranks after bond interest, and upon liquidation preference holders are further back in the queue as recipients of the proceeds of asset sell-offs.

Preference shares are part of shareholders' funds but are not equity share capital. The holders are not usually able to benefit from any extraordinarily good performance of the firm – any profits above expectations go to the ordinary shareholders. Also preference shares usually carry no voting rights, except if the dividend is in arrears or in the case of a liquidation.

Exhibit 10.1 shows the basic division of shareholder funds.

Advantages to the firm of preference share capital

Preference share capital has the following advantages to the firm.

1 *Dividend 'optional'* Preference dividends can be omitted for one or more years. This can give the directors more flexibility and a greater chance of surviving a downturn in trading. Although there may be no legal obligation to pay a dividend every year the financial community is likely to take a dim view of a firm which missed a dividend –

Exhibit 10.1 Shareholder funds

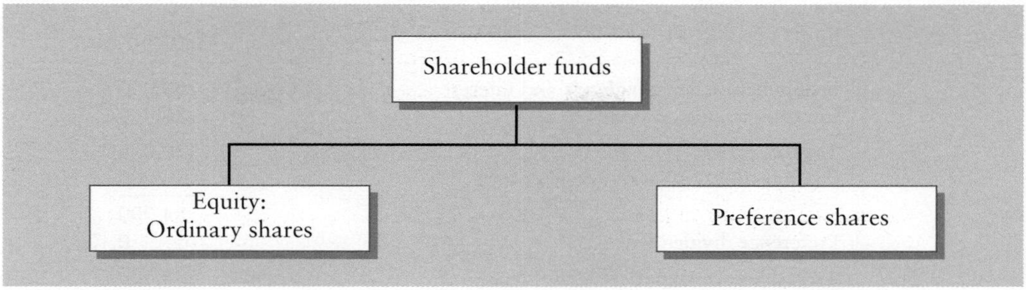

this may have a deleterious effect on the ordinary share price as investors become nervous and sell.

2 ***Influence over management*** Preference shares are an additional source of capital which, because they do not (usually) confer voting rights, do not dilute the influence of the ordinary shareholders on the firm's direction.

3 ***Extraordinary profits*** The limits placed on the return to preference shareholders means that the ordinary shareholders receive all the extraordinary profits when the firm is doing well.

4 ***Financial gearing considerations*** There are limits to safe levels of borrowing. Preference shares are an alternative, if less effective, shock absorber to ordinary shares because of the possibility of avoiding the annual cash outflow due on dividends. In some circumstances a firm may be prevented from raising finance by borrowing as this increases the risk of financial distress (*see* Chapter 18), and the shareholders may be unwilling to provide more equity risk capital. If this firm is determined to grow by raising external finance, preference shares are one option.

Disadvantages to the firm of preference share capital

Preference share capital also has disadvantages to the firm.

1 ***High cost of capital*** The higher risk attached to the annual returns and capital cause preference shareholders to demand a higher level of return than debt holders.

2 ***Dividends are not tax deductible*** Because preference shares are regarded as part of shareholders' funds the dividend is regarded as an appropriation of profits. Tax is payable on the firm's profit before the deduction of the preference dividend. In contrast, lenders are not regarded as having any ownership rights and interest has to be paid whether or not a profit is made. This cost is regarded as a legitimate expense reducing taxable profit. In recent years preference shares have become a relatively unpopular method of raising finance because bonds and bank loans, rival types of long-term finance, have this tax advantage. This is illustrated by the example of companies A and B. Both firms have raised £1m, but Company A sold bonds yielding 8 per cent, Company B sold preference shares offering a dividend yield of 8 per cent. (Here we assume the returns are identical for illustration purposes – in reality the return on preference shares might be a few percentage points higher than that on bonds.) *See* Exhibit 10.2.

Exhibit 10.2 Preference shares versus bonds

	Company A	*Company B*
Profits before tax, dividends and interest	200,000	200,000
Interest payable on bonds	80,000	0
Taxable profit	120,000	200,000
Tax payable @ 30% of taxable profit	36,000	60,000
	84,000	140,000
Preference dividend	0	80,000
Available for ordinary shareholders	84,000	60,000

Company A has a lower tax bill because its bond interest is used to reduce taxable profit, resulting in an extra £24,000 (£84,000 – £60,000) being available for the ordinary shareholders.

Types of preference shares

There are a number of variations on the theme of preference share. Here are some features which can be added:

- *Cumulative* If dividends are missed in any year the right to eventually receive a dividend is carried forward. These prior-year dividends have to be paid before any payout to ordinary shareholders.
- *Participating* As well as the fixed payment, the dividend may be increased if the company has high profits.
- *Redeemable* These have a finite life, at the end of which the initial capital investment will be repaid. Irredeemables have no fixed redemption date.
- *Convertibles* These can be converted into ordinary shares at specific dates and on preset terms (for example, one ordinary share for every two preference shares). These shares often carry a lower yield since there is the attraction of a potentially large capital gain.
- *Variable rate* A variable dividend is paid. The rate may be linked to general interest rates e.g. LIBOR (*see* Chapter 11) or to some other variable factor.

SOME UNUSUAL TYPES OF SHARES

In addition to ordinary shares and preference shares there are other, more unusual, types of shares.

1 **Non-voting shares** are sometimes issued by family-controlled firms which need additional equity finance but wish to avoid the diluting effects of an ordinary share issue. These shares are often called 'A' shares and usually get the same dividends, and the same share of assets in a liquidation as the ordinary shares. The issue of non-voting shares is contentious, with many in the City saying that everyone who puts equity into a company should have a vote on how that money is spent. On the other hand, investors can buy 'non-voters' for less than 'voters' and thereby gain a higher

yield. Also, without the possibility of issuing non-voting shares, many companies would simply prefer to forgo expansion. Despite this the number of non-voting share issues is now very low. The Savoy Hotel Group illustrated the takeover avoidance advantage of non-voting shares. When Granada took over Forte in early 1996 it acquired the 68 per cent of Savoy held by Forte. However, this gave Granada only 42 per cent of the voting shares, the remainder being held by the Wotner family.

2 **Preferred ordinary shares** rank higher than **deferred ordinary shares** for an agreed rate of dividend, so in a poor year the preferred ordinary holders might get their payment while deferred ordinary holders receive nothing. However in an exceptionally good year the preferred ordinary holders may only receive the minimum required while the deferred ordinary holders are entitled to all profits after a certain percentage has been paid to all other classes of shares.

3 **Golden shares** are shares with extraordinary special powers, for example the right to block a takeover. The UK government holds golden shares in a number of privatised firms. Golden shares are also useful if a company wishes to preserve certain characteristics it possesses (*see* Exhibit 10.3).

Exhibit 10.3

Golden share will corner Nottingham Forest buyer

FT

The owners of Nottingham Forest, the cash-strapped Premiership football club which has put itself up for sale, will retain a golden share after the club has been acquired by one of three potential buyers.

The golden share, which will be unique in football, will place tight restrictions on Forest's ultimate buyer. The most significant dictates that 80 per cent of revenues from transfer fees must be reinvested in new players.

This is aimed at deterring the club from selling players to get out of financial trouble.

The new owners will also be prevented from selling the club for five years, and will not be allowed to change the name or the colour of the team's red shirts.

If the new owners breach any of the rules, control of the club will automatically revert to Forest's current shareholders.

Mr Lance Darlaston, Forest's financial controller, said the golden share was designed to protect the integrity and traditions of the 131-year old club.

'This reflects the fact that our structure is based upon a private club, with 209 shareholders owning one share each. The golden share is being put into the memorandum of the articles of association to protect those rights against abuse,' he says.

Source: Patrick Haverson, *Financial Times*, 25 November 1996, p. 23. Reprinted with permission.

FLOATING ON THE OFFICIAL LIST

To 'go public' and become a listed company is a major step for a firm. The substantial sums of money involved can lead to a new, accelerated phase of business growth. Obtaining a quotation is not a step to be taken lightly; it is a major legal undertaking. The United Kingdom Listing Authority, UKLA (part of the Financial Services Authority)[2] rigorously enforces a set of demanding rules and the directors will be put under the strain of new and greater responsibilities both at the time of flotation and in subsequent years. As the example of Sports Division shows (*see* Exhibit 10.4), new issues can produce a greater availability of equity finance to fund expansion and development programmes. It may also allow existing shareholders to realise a proportion of their investment. In addition it can 'raise the profile' of a company both in the financial world and in its product markets, which may give it a competitive edge.

Exhibit 10.4

Running from foodstuff to footwear

FT

Patrick Harverson reports on Tom Hunter's plans to bring Sports Division to the market

Tom Hunter owes a debt to the contraction of Britain's coal industry, for his £300m fortune.

He was all set to become the fifth generation to run his family's grocery business in New Cumnock, Ayrshire, when the closure of the local pit hit the town's economy, persuading him he would never get rich selling food across the counter.

Instead, he began selling sports shoes. Starting in 1984 with a £10,000 loan and a concession in a small jeans store, Mr Hunter has built the UK's biggest specialist sports retailer.

When his Sports Division group floats on the stock market either this spring or early summer, the business should be valued at about £350m . . . The founder's stake will be worth more than £300m . . .

Sports Division's current expansion plans will see another 40 new outlets opened this year, taking the total to more than 300.

But with this growth comfortably funded out of cash flow, and no debt on the balance sheet, why does Mr Hunter feel the need to bring his company to the market?

He outlines several reasons: 'It will raise our profile – a London Stock Exchange listing is a great marketing tool. It will give us access to the capital markets to raise capital more efficiently. Also, we have a small shareholder who wants to cash out [the former Amber Day boss Philip Green, who owns 13 per cent of the group]. And I want financial security for myself.'

Mr Hunter admits he has not yet decided whether to raise any fresh capital from the flotation, which is being sponsored by UBS. NatWest are the brokers. He intends to keep 70 per cent of the group.

However, 'we're ambitious and we might need a fighting fund,' he says. He will not be drawn on the subject, but any money raised in the issue could well be used to finance expansion overseas.

Source: *Financial Times*, 13 February 1998, p. 25. Reprinted with permission.

Prospectus

In order to create a stable market and encourage investors to place their money with companies the UKLA tries to minimise the risk of investing by ensuring that the firms which obtain a quotation abide by high standards and conform to strict rules. For example the directors are required to prepare a detailed prospectus ('Listing particulars') to inform potential shareholders about the company. This may contain far more information about the firm than it has previously dared to put into the public domain. Even without the stringent conditions laid down by the UKLA the firm has an interest in producing a stylish and informative prospectus. A successful flotation can depend on the prospectus acting as a marketing tool as the firm attempts to persuade investors to apply for shares.

The content and accuracy of this vital document is the responsibility of the directors. Contained within it must be three years of audited accounts, details of indebtedness and a statement as to the adequacy of working capital. Statements by experts are often required: valuers may be needed to confirm the current value of property, engineers may be needed to state the viability of processes or machinery and accountants may be needed to comment on the profit figures. All major contracts entered into in the past two years will have to be detailed. Any persons with a shareholding of more than 3 per cent have to be named. A mass of operational data is required, ranging from an analysis of sales by geographic area and category of activity, to information on research and development and significant investments in other companies.

Conditions and responsibilities imposed

All companies obtaining a full listing must ensure that at least 25 per cent of their share capital is in public hands, to ensure that the shares are capable of being traded actively on the market. If a reasonably active secondary market is not established, trading may become stultified and the shares may become illiquid. 'Public' means people or organisations not associated with the directors or major shareholders.

Directors may find their room for discretion restricted when it comes to paying dividends. Stock market investors, particularly the major institutions, tend to demand regular dividends. Not only do they usually favour consistent cash flow, they also use dividend policy as a kind of barometer of corporate health (*see* Chapter 19). This can lead to pressure to maintain a growing dividend flow, which the unquoted firm may not experience.

There are strict rules concerning the buying and selling of the company's shares by its own directors. The Criminal Justice Act 1993 and the Model Code for Directors' Dealings have to be followed. Directors are prevented from dealing for a minimum period (normally two months) prior to an announcement of regularly recurring information such as annual results. They are also forbidden to deal before the announcement of matters of an exceptional nature involving unpublished information which is potentially price sensitive. These rules apply to any employee in possession of such information. All dealings in the company's shares by directors have to be reported to the market.

Suitability

The UKLA tries to ensure that the 'quality of the company' is sufficiently high to appeal to the investment community. The management team must have the necessary range and depth, and there must be a high degree of continuity and stability of management over recent years. Investors do not like to be over-reliant on the talents of one individual and so will expect a team of able directors, including some non-executives, and – preferably – a separation of the roles of chief executive and chairman. They also expect to see an appropriately qualified finance director.

The UKLA usually insists that a company has a track record (in the form of accounting figures) stretching back at least three years. However this requirement has been relaxed since 1993 for scientific research-based companies and companies undertaking major capital projects. In the case of scientific research-based companies there is the requirement that they have been conducting their activity for three years even if no revenue was produced. Some major project companies, for example Eurotunnel, have been allowed to join the market despite an absence of a trading activity or a profit record.

Companies can be admitted to the techMARK, part of the Official List with only one year of accounts so long as they have a market capitalisation of at least £50m and are selling at least £20m of new or existing shares when floating.

Another suitability factor is the timing of the flotation. Investors often desire stability, a reasonable spread of activities and evidence of potential growth in the core business. If the underlying product market served by the firm is going through a turbulent period it may be wise to delay the flotation until investors can be reassured about the long-run viability. Firms are also considered unsuitable if there is a dominant controlling shareholder as the presence of this shareholder could lead the company into a conflict of interest with its responsibilities to other shareholders. (A controlling shareholder is defined as one with 30 per cent or more of the voting capital, or any shareholder able to control the composition of the board.)

Other suitability factors are a healthy balance sheet, sufficient working capital, good financial control mechanisms and clear accounting policies.

The issuing process

The issuing process involves a number of specialist advisers (discussed below). The process is summarised in Exhibit 10.5.

The sponsor

Given the vast range of matters that directors have to consider in order to gain a place on the Official List (the 'main market') it is clear that experts are going to be required to guide firms through the complexities. The key adviser in a flotation is the sponsor. This may be a merchant bank, stockbroker or other professional adviser. Directors, particularly of small companies, often first seek advice from their existing professional advisers, for example accountants and solicitors. These may have the necessary expertise (and approval of the UKLA) themselves to act for the company in the flotation or may be able to recommend a more suitable sponsor. Sponsors have to be chosen with care as the relationship is likely to be one which continues long after the flotation. For large or particularly complex issues merchant banks are employed, although experienced stockbrokers have been frequently used.

The sponsor (sometimes called the issuing house) will first examine the company to assess whether flotation is an appropriate corporate objective by taking into account its structure and capital needs. The sponsor will also comment on the composition of the board and the calibre of the directors. The sponsor may even recommend supplementation with additional directors if the existing team do not come up to the quality expected. The sponsor will draw up a timetable, which can be lengthy – sometimes the planning period for a successful flotation may extend over two years. There are various methods of floating, ranging from a placing to an offer for sale, and the sponsor will advise on the most appropriate. Another important function is to help draft the prospectus and provide input to the marketing strategy. Throughout the process of flotation there will be many other professional advisers involved and it is vital that their activities mesh into a coherent whole. It is the sponsor's responsibility to co-ordinate the activities of all the other professional advisers.

Shortly before the flotation the sponsor will have the task of advising on the best price to ask for the shares, and, at the time of flotation, the sponsor will underwrite the issue. Most new issues are underwritten, because the correct pricing of a new issue of shares is extremely difficult. If the price is set too high, demand will be less than supply and not all the shares will be bought. The company is usually keen to have certainty that it will receive money from the issue so that it can plan ahead. To make sure it sells the shares it buys a kind of insurance called underwriting. In return for a fee the underwriter guarantees to buy the proportion of the issue not taken up by the market. A merchant bank sponsoring the issue will usually charge a fee of 2 per cent of the issue proceeds and then pays part of that fee, say 1.25 per cent of the issue proceeds, to sub-underwriters (usually large financial institutions such as pension funds) who each agree to buy a certain number of shares if called on to do so. In most cases the underwriters do not have to purchase any shares because the general public are keen to take them up. However occasionally they receive a shock and have to buy large quantities. This happened with the flop of the 1987 government sale of £7.2bn shares in BP. The October stock market crash caused the market share price to move below the offer price, resulting in very few shares being bought by the public. The underwriters really did earn their fees that day.[3]

Exhibit 10.5 The issuing process for the Official List

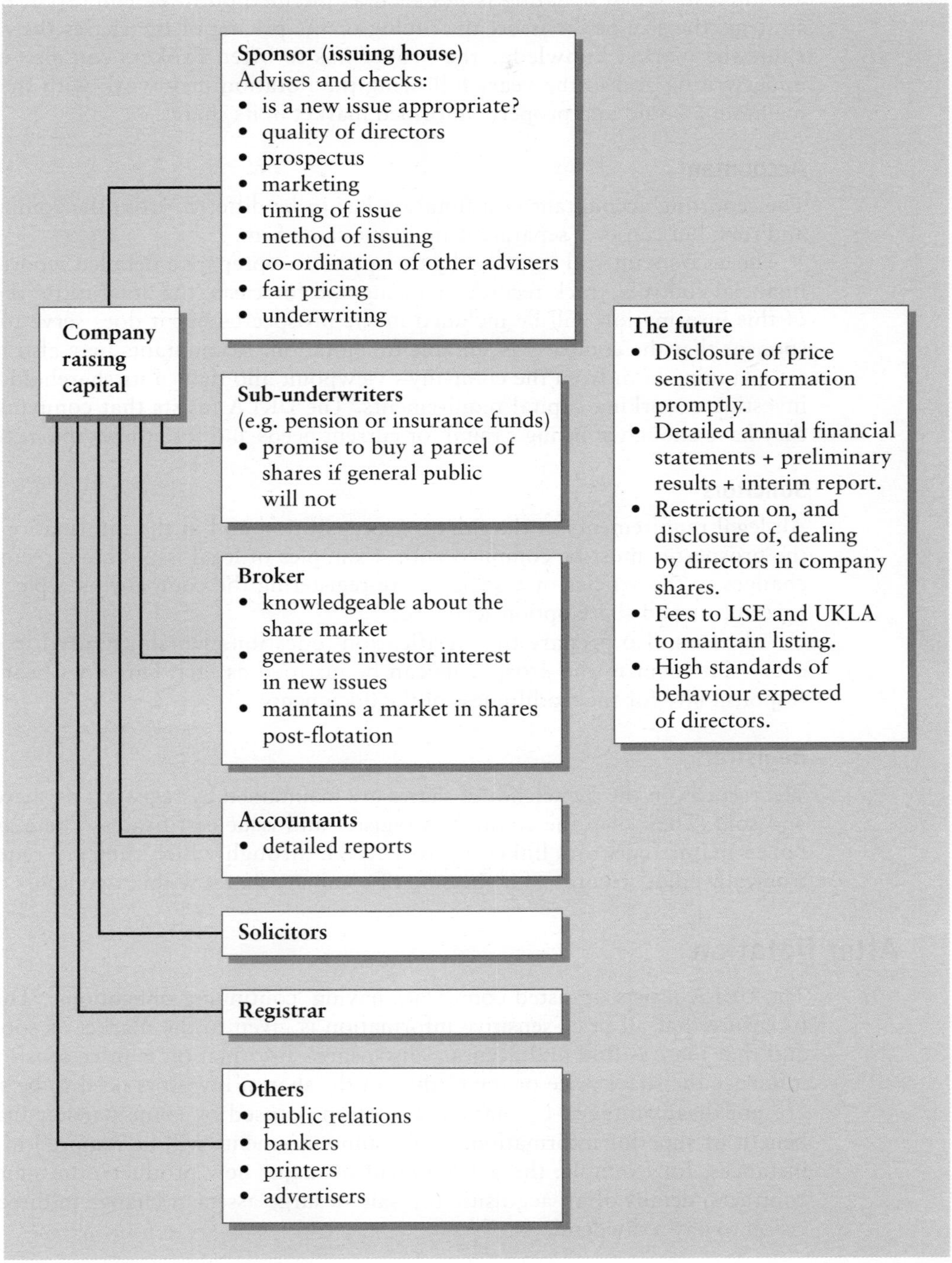

Sponsor (issuing house)
Advises and checks:
• is a new issue appropriate?
• quality of directors
• prospectus
• marketing
• timing of issue
• method of issuing
• co-ordination of other advisers
• fair pricing
• underwriting
Company raising capital
Sub-underwriters
(e.g. pension or insurance funds)
• promise to buy a parcel of shares if general public will not
Broker
• knowledgeable about the share market
• generates investor interest in new issues
• maintains a market in shares post-flotation
Accountants
• detailed reports
Solicitors
Registrar
Others
• public relations
• bankers
• printers
• advertisers
The future
• Disclosure of price sensitive information promptly.
• Detailed annual financial statements + preliminary results + interim report.
• Restriction on, and disclosure of, dealing by directors in company shares.
• Fees to LSE and UKLA to maintain listing.
• High standards of behaviour expected of directors.

The corporate broker

When a broker is employed as a sponsor the two roles can be combined. If the sponsor is, say, a merchant bank the UKLA requires that a broker is also appointed. Brokers play a vital role in advising on share market conditions and the likely demand from investors for the company's shares. They also represent the company to investors to try to generate interest. When debating issues such as the method to be employed, the marketing strategy, the size of the issue, the timing or the pricing of the shares the company may value the market knowledge the broker has to offer. Brokers can also organise sub-underwriting and in the years following the flotation may work with the company to maintain a liquid and properly informed market in its shares.

Accountant

The reporting accountant in a flotation has to be different from the company's existing auditors, but can be a separate team in the same firm.

The accountant will be asked by the sponsor to prepare a detailed report on the firm's financial controls, track record, financing and forecasts (the 'long form' report). Not all of this information will be included in the prospectus but it does serve to reassure the sponsor that the company is suitable for flotation. Accountants may also have a role in tax planning both from the company's viewpoint and that of its shareholders. They also investigate working capital requirements. The UKLA insists that companies show that they have enough working capital for current needs and for at least the next 12 months.

Solicitors

All legal requirements in the flotation preparation and in the information displayed in the prospectus must be complied with. Examples of legal issues are directors' contracts, changes to the articles of association re-registering the company as a plc, underwriting agreements and share option schemes.

Solicitors also prepare the 'verification' questions which are used to confirm that every statement in the prospectus can be justified as fact. Directors bear the ultimate responsibility for the truthfulness of the documents.

Registrars

The records on the ownership of shares are maintained by registrars as shares are bought and sold. They keep the company's register and issue certificates. There are about two dozen major registrars linked up to CREST through which they are required to electronically adjust records of ownership of company shares within two hours of a trade.

After flotation

The UKLA insists on listed companies having 'continuing obligations'. The intention is to ensure that all price-sensitive information is given to the market as soon as possible and that there is 'full and accurate disclosure'. Information is price sensitive if it might influence the share price or the trading in the shares. Investors need to be sure that they are not disadvantaged by market distortions caused by some participants having the benefit of superior information. Public announcements will be required in a number of instances, for example: the development of major new products; the signing of major contracts; details of an acquisition; a sale of large assets; a change in directors or a decision to pay a dividend.

Listed companies are also required to provide detailed financial statements within six months of the year-end. Firms usually choose to make preliminary profit announcements based on unaudited results for the year a few weeks before the audited results are published. Interim reports for the first half of each accounting year are also required (within four months of the end of the half year). The penalty for non-compliance is suspension from the exchange.

Other ongoing obligations include the need to inform the market about director dealings in the company's shares and the expectation that directors will conform to the standards of behaviour required by the UKLA and the Exchange, some of which are contained in the Cadbury, Greenbury and Hampel reports (now brought together in the Combined Code). While these standards of behaviour are encouraged they are not required by the UKLA.

New issue statistics

The number of companies joining the Official List varies greatly from one year to the next. But as Exhibit 10.6 shows the numbers are large and have not fallen below 80 per annum. The average amount raised by new issues is generally in the range £30m to £60m. The figures for the years 1986–91 were biased upward by privatisations.

Exhibit 10.6 Equity finance raised by listed UK companies (and Irish companies up to 1995) through the new issue market, 1985–2000

Year	*Number*	*Money raised (£m)*	*Average (£m)*
1985	80	1,462	18
1986	136	8,874	65
1987	155	5,002	32
1988	129	3,790	29
1989	110	7,578	69
1990	120	7,095	59
1991	101	7,474	74
1992	82	2,937	36
1993	180	5,966	33
1994	256	11,519	45
1995	190	2,962	16
1996	230	10,607	46
1997	132	6,940	53
1998	122	4,115	34
1999	96	4,869	51
2000	163	11,047	68

Source: *London Stock Exchange Fact Book*, 1996 and *Fact File* 1997, 1998, 1999, 2000 and 2001. Reproduced with permission.

METHODS OF ISSUE

The sponsor will look at the motives for wanting a quotation, at the amount of money that is to be raised, at the history and reputation of the firm and will then advise on the best method of issuing the shares. There are various methods, ranging from a full-scale offer for sale to a relatively simple introduction. The final choice often rests on the costs of issue, which can vary considerably. There are five main methods.

Offer for sale

The company sponsor offers shares to the public by inviting subscriptions from institutional and individual investors. Sometimes newspapers carry a prospectus and an application form. However, most investors will need to contact the sponsor or the broker to obtain an application form. (Exhibit 10.7 shows the telephone numbers to call for each company floating in the summer of 2001.) Normally the shares are offered at a fixed price determined by the company's directors and their financial advisers. A variation of this method is *an offer for sale by tender*. Here investors are invited to state a price at which they are willing to buy (above a minimum reserve price). The sponsor gathers the applications and then selects a price which will dispose of all the shares – the strike price. Investors who bid a price above this will be allocated shares at the strike price – not at the price of their bid. Those who bid below the strike price will not receive any shares. This method is useful in situations where it is very difficult to value a company, for instance, where there is no comparable company already listed or where the level of demand may be difficult to assess. Leaving the pricing to the public may result in a larger sum being raised. On the other hand it is more costly to administer and many investors will be put off by being handed the onerous task of estimating the share's value.

Introduction

Introductions do not raise any new money for the company. If the company's shares are already quoted on another stock exchange or there is a wide spread of shareholders, with more than 25 per cent of the shares in public hands, the Exchange permits a company to be 'introduced' to the market. This method may allow companies trading on AIM to move up to the Official List or for foreign corporations to gain a London listing. This is the cheapest method of flotation since there are no underwriting costs and relatively small advertising expenditures.

Offer for subscription

An offer for subscription is similar to an offer for sale, but it is only partially underwritten. This method is used by new companies which state at the outset that if the share issue does not raise a certain minimum the offer will be aborted. This is a particularly popular method for new investment trusts (*see* Chapter 1 for a description of investment trusts).

Placing

In a placing, shares are offered to the public but the term 'public' is narrowly defined. Instead of engaging in advertising to the population at large, the sponsor or broker handling the issue sells the shares to its own private clients – usually institutions such as pension and insurance funds. The costs of this method are considerably lower than those of an offer for sale. There are lower publicity costs and legal costs. A drawback of this method is that the spread of shareholders is going to be more limited. To alleviate this problem the Stock Exchange does insist on a large number of placees holding shares after the new issue.

In the 1980s the most frequently used method of new issue was the offer for sale. This ensured a wide spread of share ownership and thus a more liquid secondary market. It also permitted all investors to participate in new issues. Placings were only

Exhibit 10.7 Companies floating on the stock exchange

Company	Contact	Likely market	Trading expected	Main activity	Likely method of issue	Likely value
GQ Pharma	Collins Stewart	Aim	Late June	Drug development	Placing	£155m
	020 7283 1133	GW Pharma is developing cannabis-based pain relief applications. It is in phase III trials (see IC 18 May, page 45).				
Akaei	Hoodless Brennan	Aim	Late June	Computer games developer	Placing	TBA
	020 7538 1166	Company aims to use the funds raised to invest in licensing deals and increase in-house development.				
Ennex	Davy Stockbrokers	Aim	June	Mineral exploration	Introduction	£4.5m
	+353 1 679 7788	Ennex is already quoted on the Irish stock market. Its main interests are in mineral extraction in the former Soviet Union (see IC 2 March, page 60).				
Oxus Resources	Old Mutual Securities	Aim	June	Gold mining	Placing	£55m
	020 7489 4600	Oxus hopes to raise £10m to develop former Soviet mines in central Asia.				
Tikit	Williams de Broë	Aim	Early June	IT consultancy	TBA	£16m
	020 7588 7511	Tikit is raising £1.5m for existing shareholders and £2m of new funds to repay debt and provide extra working capital.				
Singer & Friedlander Aim 3 VCT	Teather & Greenwood	Main	4 June	Venture capital trust	Offer	£33m
	020 7426 9000	Investing 80 per cent in established Aim companies (though 15 per cent could be in Ofex) with 20 per cent in fixed interest.				
Atlantic Global	Seymour Pierce	Aim	4 June	Time and resource management	Placing	£5.2m
	0207 648 8700	Atlantic is joining Aim in an effort to boost sales and fund the development of new software (see IC 4 May, page 46).				
HiLife	Pinder, Fry and Benjamin	Aim	Q4 2001	Healthclub operator	Introduction	£18m
	020 7612 7650	Funds to be used in a joint venture with Luminar. Money is being raised from private investors as part of the EIS.				
Picardy Media	Brewin Dolphin	Aim	2001	Media group	Placing	£25m
	0141 221 7733	Float postponed. The company develops advertisements for the Internet and CD Roms. It plans to raise £7m by selling 28 per cent of its shares.				
Big Broadband	Rowan Dartington	Aim	2001	Web-based radio	Placing	TBA
	0117 925 3377	Float postponed. Big Broadband offers music from London-based unsigned bands.				
STG	Howard Kennedy	Main	2001	Hi-tech investment	Offer	£61m
	020 7493 7792	Company has raised the funds it needs and will list this year (see IC 18 Aug, page 45).				
Global Telematics	HSBC	Aim	2001	Telematics	Placing	£260m
	020 7621 0011	Float postponed. Company provides vehicle tracking to the commercial UK, South African and Australian markets.				
UbiNetics	Investec Hend Crosth	Main	2001	Telecoms technology	TBA	£800m
	020 7597 5000	UbiNetics, owned by PA Consulting, has developed 3G phone testing equipment and hand-held phone and internet device.				
theoilsite.com	Brewin Dolphin	Aim	2001	e-procurement exchange	Placing	£5m
	0113 241 0130	Group is moving to Aim after just seven months on Ofex (see IC 24 Nov, page 73).				
Web Orator	Graham H Wills	Aim	2001	Corporate information provider	Offer	£13.4m
	0117 910 5500	Currently trading on Ofex, Web Orator is raising money to expand (see IC 30 March, page 51).				
Independent Growth Finance	Charles Stanley	Aim	Autumn	Financial services	Placing	£18m
	020 7739 8200	Float postponed. Company specialises in providing factoring services to the SME market.				
London Stock Exchange	Cazenove	Main	Summer	Stock exchange	TBA	£1.2bn
	020 7588 2828	The LSE is Europe's biggest stock exchange. It demutualised, abandoned a merger and fought off a takeover last year.				
Friends Provident	Merrill Lynch	Main	9 Jul	Life assurance	Offer	£3.7bn–£4.2bn
	020 7772 1000	Friends Provident is demutualising and policyholders will receive a fixed issue of shares and a variable portion dependent on the value of their policies. In addition policyholders will also get preferential treatment in the share offer.				
Kinetic Information Systems Services	Dawnay Day	Main	H2 2001	Software	Placing	TBA
	020 7509 4570	Kinetic makes software for compiling financial market indices. It hopes to raise capital to accelerate growth.				
Photo Therapeutics	Investec Hend Crosth	Main	H2 2001	Medical equipment	TBA	£70–80m
	020 7597 5000	Photo Therapeutics has developed a lamp that is used with photo-sensitive drugs to treat skin conditions.				
Extreme	WestLB Panmure	Main	H1 2001	Sports programme distributor	Placing	£50m
	020 7638 4010	Group specialises in minority sports such as snowboarding. Proceeds likely to be used for US expansion.				
TV Travel	UBS Warburg	Main	H1 2001	Travel agency	Placing	£300m
	020 7567 8000	TV Travel sells holiday on TV. It wants to raise capital to fund overseas expansion.				

Source: *Investors Chronicle*, 1 June 2001, pp. 70 and 71. Reprinted with permission.

permitted for small offerings (< £15m) when the costs of an offer for sale would have been prohibitive. During the 1990s the rules were gradually relaxed and by 1997 any size of new issue could be placed. As this method is much cheaper and easier than an offer for sale, companies have naturally switched to placings. As you can see in the extract from the *Investors Chronicle* in Exhibit 10.7 the majority now choose to use the placing method, thus excluding small investors from most new issues. It is interesting to note that the London Stock Exchange now lists its own shares on its Official List. (TBA = To be advised.)

Intermediaries offer

Another method which is often combined with a placing is an intermediaries offer. Here the shares are offered for sale to financial institutions such as stockbrokers. Clients of these intermediaries can then apply to buy shares from them.

The Kier Group flotation, described in Exhibit 10.8, illustrates a number of points about new issues. First, note that in a new issue not all the shares sold come from the company itself. Frequently a high proportion (if not all) the shares are sold by the existing shareholders. Note also the motives for flotation: it will permit employees to sell their holdings at a later date should they wish and will also raise £2.7m to restructure its finances by redeeming preference shares. Staff who continue to hold shares will have the satisfaction of knowing the market price should they ever wish to sell in the future. The new issue comprises two parts: one is a sale to institutional investors through a placing and the second is an offer to sell more shares to employees.

Exhibit 10.8

Float tag of 170p values Kier at £53.8m

FT

The value of employee shares in Kier Group, Britain's largest unquoted construction company, has increased tenfold since 1992, based on a flotation price, announced yesterday, which values the group at £53.8m.

The average employee investment of £4,800 is now worth £48,000 at the 170p a share price.

Kier is floating by way of a placing and employee offer.

The company was bought four years ago by its employees from Hanson, the UK conglomerate.

Kier is issuing 1.6m new ordinary shares to raise £2.7m in order to redeem preference shares held by Hill Samuel.

The balance of the preference shares is held by Electra Fleming, which is redeeming its holdings in return for ordinary shares. These, together with other purchases, will leave Electra Fleming with a 9.8 per cent stake.

Employee shareholders representing 4.3 per cent of the enlarged capital have opted to sell their shares.

Staff, former employees and their families, however, would retain an 80.9 per cent stake in the company, said Mr Colin Busby, Kier's chairman and chief executive.

The placing price represented a multiple of about 11 times historic earnings per share of 15.5p in the 12 months to the end of June.

In that year, pre-tax profits increased 4 per cent to £7.3m (£7m). Turnover was up from £585.7m to £614.6m.

A notional dividend of 6.5p for the year represents a yield of 4.8 per cent at the placing price.

Mr Busby said: 'We are now seeing a significant improvement in the housebuilding market and encouraging signs in the UK construction market.

'We therefore believe it is a good time to join the stock market to position ourselves for the future.'

NatWest Markets organised the placing.

Source: Andrew Taylor, *Financial Times*, 6 December 1996, p. 24. Reprinted with permission.

Failure to float

Severe disruption can result if a company which planned to gain a quotation finds that circumstance forces the new issue to be scrapped. In the article 'Back to the Start' (*see* Exhibit 10.9), it can be seen that one effect of an aborted float is the demoralisation of employees who had anticipated a rise in future monetary compensation through share options to supplement their income as well as an outlet for their stored wealth in the company's shares. Growth plans often have to be cut back and venture capital backers are annoyed at not having an easy exit route.

Exhibit 10.9

Back to the start

FT

Private companies in the UK are having a miserable time trying to float. Business owners are not only having to swallow the disappointment of lower valuations, but in some cases the abandonment of planned share sales.

Given the market's recent unpredictability most private company shareholders will recognise that a flotation can be 'pulled' easily. Nevertheless, those who have done it say the disappointment has to be addressed early after a decision to postpone or cancel has been taken.

'We addressed all the issues in advance,' says John Hannah, managing director of New Look, the west of England-based retailer that has opened more than 250 shops in the last 25 years. 'We consider the motivation and aspirations of all our staff to make sure morale is maintained.'

The contingency plan New Look developed gave senior executives a profits-related bonus scheme to replace the share options they would have received on flotation.

Computer Management Group, one of Europe's largest private computer services groups, had a bigger problem. With a float planned for the spring, the company's advisers decided to pull the issue after McDonnell Information Systems – a computer service business in loosely related markets – issued two profit warnings shortly after coming to the market last year.

The scope for disappointment was great because of the large shareholder base. Since the company was formed 30 years ago, staff have spent £14m buying shares and reducing the stake of founder and chairman, Douglas Gorman, from 40 per cent to 15 per cent.

CMG shares have been tradeable on one day a year. A stock market quote would have greatly increased liquidity – and indeed was the prime reason for the float. CMG communicated with its employees and shareholders immediately after the issue was pulled and followed the letters with staff meetings at offices in the UK, the Netherlands and Germany.

Many companies coming to the market are, like CMG, seeking a quotation as an exit route for investors. But highly geared companies or those needing capital to maintain their growth have a more difficult problem to manage. Century Inns, which runs a cash generative chain of 300 pubs, postponed its flotation on February 7, the day after the Office of Fair Trading launched a surprise inquiry into the wholesale beer trade.

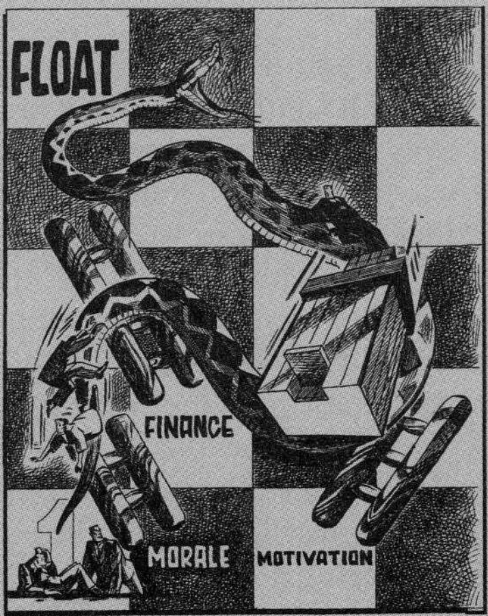

Hit by events beyond its control, Century Inns is facing a limited number of options. 'We will try to do as much of the business plan as we can given the capital constraints,' says Alistair Arkley, chief executive.

Those constraints are dictated by the way the Century Inns' buy-out from Bass in 1991 was structured. Century's bill for interest, debt repayment and the dividends it pays its venture backers has swallowed more than 75 per cent of the £23m cash it has generated over the last three years.

Century Inns will consequently have only £1m a year to spend on its estate instead of the £3.5m available had the float gone ahead.

On the other hand, cash generative businesses which decide to postpone a float but which are not desperate to reduce debt can also expect a welcome from the banks.

'The banking markets are quite positive about supporting businesses' capital expenditure,' says Michael Guthrie, founder of Brightreasons

►

Exhibit 10.9 continued

which owns the Pizzaland restaurant chain.

Guthrie postponed the Brightreasons flotation last year after the new issues market softened. He has since raised bank debt to supplement cash flow and says he has been able to continue expanding according to plan.

'In motivational terms, people were disappointed and wanted to be in the public arena,' says Guthrie. 'But I am not entirely shocked; I feel more concerned about the troops that are not so experienced.'

With the stock market in its current mood there are strong financial reasons for postponing a flotation and handling the resulting disappointment.

Source: Richard Gourlay, *Financial Times*, 21 February 1995. Reprinted with permission. Illustration © Jo Cummings. Reproduced with permission.

TIMETABLE FOR A NEW OFFER

The various stages of a new share issue will be explained using the example of the flotation of EasyJet on the Official List. This timetable is set out in Exhibit 10.10.

Railtrack

Pre-launch publicity

For many years before the flotation EasyJet raised its profile with the public with exciting news stories. It even allowed a television company to make a fly-on-the-wall documentary about the firm's operations. This was shown weekly for many weeks, almost like a soap opera.

Technicalities

UBS Warburg and Credit Suisse First Boston were co-leading sponsors, with Merrill Lynch and Schroder Salomon Smith Barney assisting as co-managers. It was decided to float by way of a placing, so having many leading City institutions managing the issue – their extensive range of contacts with fund managers was valuable. On 9 November a price range of 280p–340p was indicated. This was a narrowed range from that announced the previous week (250p–350p). By announcing a price range the sponsors and fund managers can gauge reaction from potential buyers before selecting the final single price.

It was decided that the company would sell 63 million shares (25.1 per cent of the enlarged capital). A further 9.45 million shares were put aside for a 'greenshoe' or over-allotment issue. This means that the company reserved the right to sell these additional shares if there was sufficient demand. Doing so would raise the final free float (shares not associated with a connected person) to 27.8 per cent of the enlarged capital. (These must be issued at the offer price within 30 days of the Official listing.)

During 2000 EasyJet had been gathering a distinguished group of non-executive directors to supplement its board. They have the task of looking after the interests of *all* the shareholders. Tony Illsley, the former chief executive of Telewest Communications, was hired in May, Colin Day, chief financial officer of Reckitt Benckiser, was appointed in September and John Quelch, dean of the London Business School, joined in November.

During the period up to Impact Day the auditors were very busy and the sponsoring banks marketed the issue forcefully.

Exhibit 10.10 Timetable of an offer for sale and a placing

Time relative to Impact Day	*1–2 years*	*Several weeks*	*A few days*	*IMPACT DAY*		*A few days*	*2 days to 2 weeks for offer for sale*	*2 weeks or so for an offer for sale*
Stage	Pre-launch publicity.	Sponsor and other advisers consider details such as price and method of issue. Also obtain underwriting, etc.	Pathfinder prospectus • to Press; • to major investors. No price	Prospectus published. Price announced in a fixed-price sale offer or placing.	Investors apply and send payments.	Offer closes.	Allotment.	Admission to the Exchange and dealing begins
Dates for EasyJet (placing)	1998 to 2000	Late 2000	31 October: price range of 250p–350p is announced.	15 November: a price is given: 310p.				22 November: first dealings.

'Auditors have been working hard to get the figures into shape for the prospectus, but in the meantime analysts from EasyJet's heavyweight investment banks have been intensely marketing this research to institutional investors.'

(*Financial Times*, 25 October 2000, p. 3).

It was decided that no shares were to be sold by existing shareholders.

Pathfinder prospectus

A few days before the sale the pathfinder prospectus is made available. This contains background information on the company but does not tell the potential investors the price at which the shares are to be offered. For EasyJet this was sent out on 31 October.

Impact Day

The prospectus is launched at this stage, together with the price. For EasyJet the price was set at 310p, valuing the company at £778m.

Offer closes

In an offer for sale up to two weeks is needed for investors to consider the offer price and send in payments. There is a fixed cut-off date for applications. In the case of a placing the time needed is much shorter as the share buyers have already indicated to the sponsors and managers their interest and transactions can be expedited between City institutions.

Allotment

More shares were applied for than were available and so they had to be allocated. This can be achieved in a number of different ways. A ballot means that only some investors receive shares. In a scaledown applicants generally receive some shares, but fewer than they applied for. EasyJet's share offer was over-subscribed by almost 10 times. It is not clear how the available shares were allocated.

Dealing begins

Formal dealing in the shares through the Stock Exchange started on 22 November for EasyJet. The shares traded 10 per cent above the placing price at 342p, giving investors an immediate profit. Between 15 November and 22 November share deals had been trading in a grey market off the exchange.

Financial Times statistics

The FT displays details of recent new issues daily (*see* Exhibit 10.11). These remain in the table for about six weeks after the flotation and then generally get transferred to the London Share service on the inside back page. The notation F.P. in the 'Amt paid up' column indicates that the investors have paid the full issue price. For some new issues including many privatisations the investors can pay in stages, in which case the shares will be partly paid.

Book-building

Selling new issues of shares through book-building is a popular technique in the USA. It is starting to catch on in Europe as Exhibit 10.12 demonstrates. Under this method the financial advisers to an issue contact major institutional investors to get from them bids for the shares. The investors' orders are sorted according to price, quantity and other factors such as 'firmness' of bid. This data may then be used to establish a price for the issue and the allocation of shares. EasyJet's sponsors used book-building.

Exhibit 10.11 Recent equity issues

Recent issues: Equities

Issue price p	Amt paid up	Mkt cap (£m.)	2001 High	Low	Stock	Close price p	+/–	Div	Div cov	Yld	P/E
§	F.P	6.11	31½	28½	†Atlantic Global	29½		–	–	–	–
§100	F.P.	27.7	103½	101	BC Prop ZDP	102¾		–	–	–	–
–	F.P	42.4	101½	61½	Blue Chip Value & Inc	62¾		–	–	–	–
–	F.P	0.60	7½	6	Do. Warrants	6		–	–	–	–
–	F.P	10.3	103¾	101½	Blue Chip Zero Dv Pf	103½		–	–	–	–
§80	F.P.	6.50	90½	82½	†Capcon	90½	+1	–	–	–	–
*	F.P.	0.60	4	4	†Clover Options	4		–	–	–	–
§	F.P.	13.5	7½	5½	†Cytomyx	7½		–	–	–	–
–	F.P.	8.58	81	80	Enterprise Captl	80½		–	–	–	–
150	F.P.	16.8	150	148	Do. Loan Notes	148		–	–	–	–
–	F.P.	16.9	105	86	†Imprint Search	97½		–	–	–	–
§100	F.P.	76.5	103½	100	Juniper Fin & In	102		–	–	–	–
§100	F.P.	19.7	110	101½	Do Zero Dv Pf	105		–	–	–	–
*100	F.P.	8.16	100	100	Leis & Media VCT	100		–	–	–	–
100	F.P.	33.5	101¾	100	Man Alt Invs	101½	+½	–	–	–	–
	F.P.	5.73	4	3¾	†Maverick Ent	4		–	–	–	–
–	F.P.	11.0	99½	99½	Media & Inc Pref Inc	99½		–	–	–	–
100	F.P.	8.95	100	100	Pennine Dwng AIM VCT 2	100		–	–	–	–
§25	F.P.	35.3	42½	32½	†Proactive Sports	36		–	–	–	–
§100	F.P.	82.2	102	100½	Prop Inc & Gth	101½		–	–	–	–
§50	F.P.	19.6	55½	54½	†Pursuit Dynamics	55½		–	–	–	–
§	F.P.	10.1	82½	38	†Send	80	+9	–	–	–	–
§115	F.P.	13.8	122½	122½	†Tikit Group	122½		–	–	–	–
§4	F.P.	3.42	4¾	4¾	†Vema	4¾					

New issues within the last six weeks. † Alternative Investment Market, § Placing price. *Introduction. For a full explanation of all other symbols please refer to The London Share Service notes. ‡ When issued.

Source: *Financial Times*, 11 June 2001, p. 30. Reprinted with permission.

Exhibit 10.12

Booking the bids in the power sale

This morning at 8.30 precisely, a small room on the second floor of a City office building will erupt in a flurry of activity as the international sale of the government's remaining 40 per cent stake in the UK's two big power generators – National Power and PowerGen – kicks off.

The 'book-building room' – the nerve centre of the operation – resembles the bridge of the Starship Enterprise, with a wall of computer screens displaying colour graphics that chart the progress of the sale by the minute. Thick blinds shield the action from inquisitive eyes.

Share orders from institutional investors across the globe will arrive here over the next week, indicating how much money they are prepared to invest at specific prices. The book-building period for the £4bn sale, one of Europe's largest privatisations this year, ends on March 3 at 5pm. The international offer price and allocation will be agreed over the weekend, and trading in the partly-paid shares begins on March 6.

Book-building, which has been used in previous UK privatisations, allows the Treasury to compile a comprehensive picture of the

Exhibit 10.12 continued

strength of institutional demand for the shares over a range of prices. The aim is to ensure that the shares will be spread across a wide range of high-quality investors.

The share offer, totalling about £4bn, is structured in two parts: a UK public offer, targeted at UK retail investors, and two separate international tender offers (one for shares in National Power and one for shares in PowerGen) aimed at institutional investors in the UK and around the world.

Roadshows for the international offer began last week, with both companies conducting separate roadshows in financial centres throughout Europe and the US.

The offers are being marketed through a syndicate of 17 investment banks with BZW and Kleinwort Benson acting as joint global co-ordinators and bookrunners.

The book-building process starts in the 'inputting room', where nine fax machines spew out forms detailing investors' orders. These show: how many shares in each company investors are willing to buy at what price, how much they would pay for a combination of shares in both at a ratio determined by the Treasury ('sector bid'), and whether the bid is firm or indicative.

The price and quality of investors' bids is crucial as it affects their final allocation. The Treasury will favour bids by investors considered to be likely buyers or holders of shares in the aftermarket; bids made at an early stage of the offer period; firm bids; bids at specific price levels (rather than market-relative or strike-price bids); and sector bids.

All the information is entered into a computer system by one of 15 input clerks and transmitted to the book-building room, where 24 screens throw up an instant graphic analysis of the data, highlighting strengths and weaknesses of distribution as the sale proceeds.

One monitor might show the build-up in demand for both companies over time. Another illustrates the value of demand at any given price. A pie chart represents the value of demand by country, and a bar chart shows it by syndicate member.

Yet another breaks down the orders into six different categories of investor quality, ranging from very serious, long-term investors to highly speculative accounts looking to play the deal over the very short term.

Source: Conner Middelmann, *Financial Times*, 23 February 1995. Reprinted with permission.

HOW DOES AN AIM FLOTATION DIFFER FROM ONE ON THE OFFICIAL LIST?

AIM's rules are kept as relaxed as possible to encourage a wide variety of companies to join and keep costs of membership and capital raising to a minimum. However it is felt necessary to have some vetting process for firms wishing to float on AIM. This policing role was given to nominated advisers who are paid a fee by the company to act as an unofficial 'sponsor' in investigating and verifying its financial health. When the cost of the nominated advisers' time is added to those of the stock exchange fees, accountants, lawyers, printers and so on, the (administrative) cost of capital raising can be as much as 10–12 per cent of the amount being raised. This, as a proportion, is comparable with the main market but the sums of money raised are usually much less on AIM and so the absolute cost is lower. AIM was designed so that the minimum cost of joining was in the region of £40,000–£50,000. But, as Exhibit 10.13 shows, it has now risen so that frequently more than £300,000 is paid. This sum is significantly higher than the originators of AIM planned. The nominated advisers argue that they are forced to charge firms higher fees because they incur more investigatory costs due to the emphasis put on their policing role by the Stock Exchange.

Exhibit 10.13

Property flotation highlights Aim fees

FT

Concerns among smaller companies over the costs of joining the Alternative Investment Market are likely to be heightened by news that most of the £300,000 being raised by a property company is to be spent on fees for the junior market.

Advisers to Inner City Enterprises said the cost of joining Aim would exceed £200,000; prospective institutional shareholders have been told by the company the cost is nearer the total being raised.

The average cost of joining Aim varies widely, but basic fees for the nominated adviser, nominated broker, solicitor, accountants and public relations company rarely top £100,000. Additional charges are usually associated with the raising of capital.

A survey last week from Neville Russell, the accountants, found that 20 per cent of companies joining Aim paid between £100,000 and £200,000, while a quarter paid more than £300,000. All had raised funds as part of their admission. Companies paying less than £100,000 had generally not raised any.

A third of the companies surveyed said their flotations had caused 'significant disruption'. Estimates for 'hidden' costs ranged between £50,000 and £2m.

Mr Stephen Goschalk, a corporate financier at English Trust, Inner City's adviser, said there were extenuating circumstances explaining the high costs it was incurring.

Among these were additional documentation required for its 60 existing institutional shareholders. Also, Inner City's property portfolio has had to be assessed and individually certified. However, both the company's adviser and Teather & Greenwood, its broker, said the costs were also a reflection of the rising price of joining Aim.

'Prices are going up because of pressure from the Aim authorities to tighten up on standards,' said Mr Ken Ford of Teather & Greenwood.

Last summer, Aim was hit by a series of corporate mishaps, such as profits warnings and delistings, which unnerved the authorities and led to monitoring of some advisers' behaviour. Under Aim rules, companies must retain a broker and an adviser. The latter has responsibility for a company's credentials in joining Aim and during membership.

'There is a move to improve standards and this has led to an increase in costs,' said Mr Goschalk. He added that the increases were such that it was uneconomical for a company with a market capitalisation of 'less than £7m' to come to the market.

Source: Christopher Price, *Financial Times*, 3 February 1997, p. 23. Reprinted with permission.

The cost of flotation on AIM varies significantly depending on the nature of the company and whether new capital is being raised, but a 'typical' breakdown in 2001 might be as set out in Exhibit 10.14.

Exhibit 10.14

	£
Nominated adviser	90,000–200,000
Nominated broker	60,000–200,000
Accountant's fees	40,000–150,000
Lawyers (company's and nominated adviser's)	40,000–120,000
Public relations	5,000–50,000
Printing	5,000–30,000
Registrars	2,500–20,000
	242,500–770,000

Companies floating on AIM need to be public limited companies and have accounts conforming to UK and other recognised international accounting standards. They need to produce a prospectus (or AIM document) but this is less detailed than the prospectus for an OL quotation and therefore cheaper. The real cost savings come in the continuing annual expense of managing the quotation. For example AIM companies do not have to disclose as much information as companies on the Official List. Price-sensitive information will have to be published but normally this will require only an electronic message from the adviser to the Exchange rather than a circular to shareholders.

The example of Firecrest (*see* Exhibit 10.15) demonstrates the risk attached to AIM companies and the role of the nominated adviser.

Exhibit 10.15

Aim makes Firecrest its first expulsion

FT

Firecrest, whose range of activities include the Internet and advertising, will today receive the ignominious title of becoming the first company to be delisted from the Alternative Investment Market.

The expulsion follows Firecrest's failure to appoint new advisers after the resignation of Singer & Friedlander last month. A nominated adviser is a prerequisite of Aim membership.

Firecrest said its attention had been focused on merger talks, which were ongoing, rather than finding new advisers. If the negotiations were to break down, the company would apply for membership of Ofex, the unregulated dealing facility, it said.

Its shares were suspended last month at 44½p following Singer & Friedlander's resignation.

Firecrest's removal from Aim closes one of the most colourful chapters in the market's short history. It joined the new market for junior companies in July 1995, a month after Aim's inception.

In the following months the company became famous for its appetite for publicity, issuing press releases sometimes on a weekly basis, often connected with its nascent Internet division.

Its shares rocketed: placed at 35p, they raced to 212p by the year-end, only to go into decline this year as the positive news flow dried up.

Firecrest was also hit by the Stock Exchange censure of its chief executive over failing to disclose an options package, as well as the unravelling of one of its main Internet deals.

Last week, two key members of its Internet team were dismissed and have threatened Firecrest with legal action.

Source: Christopher Price, *Financial Times*, 1 October 1996. Reprinted with permission.

THE COSTS OF NEW ISSUES

There are three types of cost involved when a firm makes an issue of equity capital:

- administrative/transaction costs;
- the equity cost of capital;
- market pricing costs.

The first of these has already been discussed earlier in this chapter. For both the Official List and AIM the costs as a proportion of the amount raised can be anywhere between 5 per cent and 12 per cent depending on the size of issue, and the method used (*see* Exhibit 10.16).

Some idea of the transaction costs associated with flotation are given in the example of Oasis, on which about £1.3m was spent (*see* Exhibit 10.17).

Exhibit 10.16 Costs of new issues

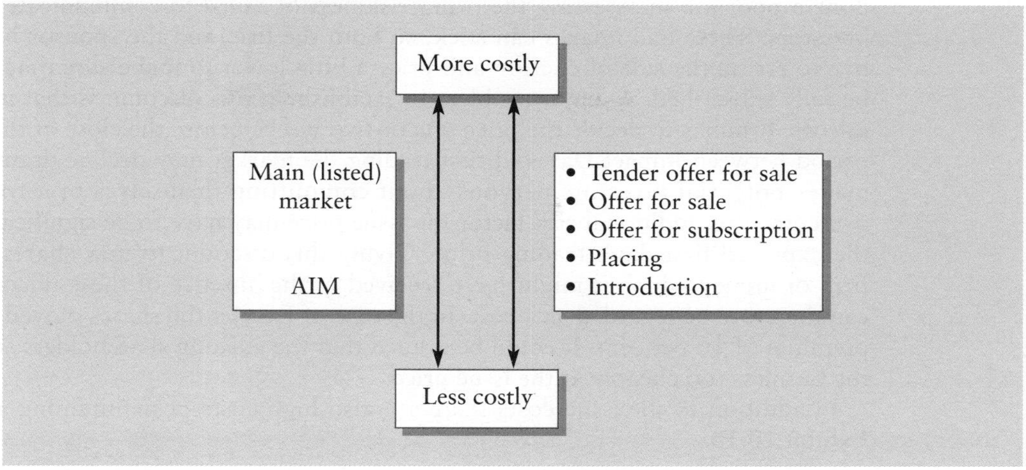

Exhibit 10.17

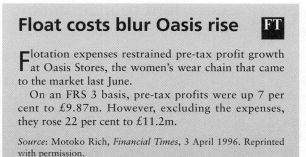

Float costs blur Oasis rise

FT

Flotation expenses restrained pre-tax profit growth at Oasis Stores, the women's wear chain that came to the market last June.

On an FRS 3 basis, pre-tax profits were up 7 per cent to £9.87m. However, excluding the expenses, they rose 22 per cent to £11.2m.

Source: Motoko Rich, *Financial Times*, 3 April 1996. Reprinted with permission.

The second cost is not something to be discussed in detail here – this can be left to Chapter 16. However we can say that shareholders suffer an opportunity cost. By holding shares in one company they are giving up the use of that money elsewhere. The firm therefore needs to produce a rate of return for those shareholders which is at least equal to the return they could obtain by investing in other shares of a similar risk class. Because ordinary shareholders face higher risks than debt or preference shareholders the rate of return demanded is higher. If the firm does not produce this return then shares will be sold and the firm will find raising capital difficult.

The market pricing cost is to do with the possibility of underpricing new issues. It is a problem which particularly affects offers for sale at a fixed price and placings. The firm is usually keen to have the offer fully taken up by public investors. To have shares left with the underwriters gives the firm a bad image because it is perceived to have had an issue which 'flopped'. Furthermore, the underwriters, over the forthcoming months, will try to offload their shares and this action has the potential to depress the price for a long time. The sponsor also has an incentive to avoid leaving the underwriters with large blocks of shares. These people are professional analysts and dealmakers and an issue which flops can be very bad for their image. It might indicate that they are not reading the market signals correctly and that they have overestimated demand. They might have done a poor job in assessing the firm's riskiness or failed to communicate its virtues to investors. These bad images can stick, so both the firm and the sponsor have an incentive to err on the side of caution and price a little lower to make sure that the issue will be fully subscribed. A major problem in establishing this discount is that in an offer for sale the firm has to decide the price one or two weeks before the close of the offer. In the period between Impact Day and first trading the market may decline dramatically. This makes potential investors nervous about committing themselves to a fixed price. To overcome this additional risk factor the issue price may have to be significantly less than the expected first day's trading price. Giving this discount to new shares deprives the firm of money which it might have received in the absence of these uncertainties, and can therefore be regarded as a cost. In the case of EasyJet the shares moved to a first-day premium of 10 per cent. It could be argued that the existing shareholders sold a piece of the business too cheaply at the issue price.

In addition to the issue costs there are also high costs of maintaining a listing – *see* Exhibit 10.18.

Exhibit 10.18

Professional expenses prove a deterrent to maintaining stock market exposure

FT

But costs of public-to-private deals can also be considerable. **Bertrand Benoit** reports

Ask Richard Johnson, chief executive of Wyko, what the industrial distribution and maintenance group gained in 10 years on the stock market and the answer is likely to be short.

Launched with a market value of about £50m in 1989, the group was performing honorably until investors began to pull out from the small company sector last year.

In less than six months, its shares fell from 190p to 64p. 'This happened as we were considering a £60m acquisition,' Mr Johnson says. 'But with a p/e of 5, we had suddenly become vulnerable to a takeover.'

Unable to expand in a market where size increasingly mattered, Wyko put an end to its turbulent relationship with the Stock Exchange last week by going private in a management buy-out valuing it at £92.2m, a 30 per cent discount to its peak price.

This is not an isolated case. So far this year, nearly 40 companies have pulled out of the exchange, against 25 last year and a mere seven in 1997.

Some deals might have been sparked by the 10.5 per cent fall in the small cap index in 1998, against a 10.9 per cent gain in the FTSE All-Share. But the fact that small companies have outperformed bigger ones this year suggests some are no longer prepared to bear the cost and bother maintaining a listing.

Although linked to the size of the company, the expense typically amounts to £250,000 a year. Businesses meeting the minimum requirements imposed by the exchange pay a lot less. However, Roy Hill, chief executive of Liberfabrica, the book manufacturer bought by a trade buyer this month, claims his company will save up to £400,000 a year in City-associated costs.

These include fees paid to stockbroker, registrars, lawyers, merchant banker and financial PR company, as well as the exchange fee and the auditing, printing and distribution of accounts.

Another problem has been the low rating experienced by some of the smaller companies that have virtually disappeared from investors' radar screens. As institutions have grown increasingly reluctant to invest in small caps, brokers have stopped following many of them, thus hastening share price declines.

'Some institutions have stopped investing in companies with a market capitalisation below £100m,' says Penny Freer, head of smaller companies research at Crédit Lyonnais in London. 'Some smaller companies that deliver good results may end up with a single digit p/e.'

For Tony Fry, partner at KPMG Transaction Services, 'being on the stock market is all about getting access to funding, if you are barred from such access, then the attraction disappears'.

In addition to the venture capital funding that can facilitate acquisitions, managers have been lured

Exhibit 10.18 continued

into public-to-private deals by the chance of raising their stake in the business. In a typical MBO backed by a private equity house, managers can end up owning up to 20 per cent of the bidding vehicle. One banker calculates that the value of such a stake can grow 10 times if the company is later sold for twice the price of the buy-out.

But because MBOs are highly geared operations, the risks involved are equally considerable. The same managers could lose all their investment if the company were sold below the original offer price.

Nor are the financial costs associated with a public-to-private transaction negligible. According to Richard Grainger, managing director at Close Brothers, the advisory firm, fees paid to bankers, registrars, venture capital funds and PR firms, can amount to 4 or 5 per cent of the purchase price.

The time spent in putting transactions together can also be consuming. 'The negotiations are so absorbing and involve so many parties that it can be very easy for management to take their eyes off the ball, especially if they do not have first class advisers,' says Mr Johnson, whose MBO of Wyko was concluded after seven months of talks.

In some instances, these efforts prove fruitless, as at Liberfabrica, whose management team was outbid by a trade buyer. Mr Hill reckons that £500,000 in fees was wasted in the exercise.

Source: Bertrand Benoit, *Financial Times*, 31 August 1999, p. 18. Reprinted with permission.

The cost of listing

Listed
Estimated annual cost of listing for a company with a market capitalisation of around £100m

Stockbroker	**£20,000 to £25,000**
Financial PR	**£20,000 to £25,000**
Financial reports and accounts	**around £30,000**
Registrars	**£5,000 to £25,000**
High profile merchant bank	**around £50,000**
Solicitors	**around £50,000**
Other costs	**around £50,000**
Total (per year)	**£250,000 to £350,000**

Private
Estimated cost of going private for a company with a purchase price of around £100m

Advisors to the bidders	**around 1% of purchase price**
Lawyers to the bidders	**£100,000 to £200,000**
Due diligence account	**£100,000 to £400,00**
Market report due diligence	**£30,000 to £50,000**
Stamp duty	**around 0.5% of purchase price**
Printers	**£15,000 to £20,000**
Receiving banks	**£10,000 to £15,000**
Takeover panel fee	**around £25,000**
Funders fee	**2% to 3% of purchase price**
Total	**£3,780,000 to £5,210,000**

Source: Industry estimates

RIGHTS ISSUES

A rights issue is an invitation to existing shareholders to purchase additional shares in the company. This is a very popular method of raising new funds. It is easy and relatively cheap (compared with new issues). Directors are not required to seek the prior consent of shareholders, and the London Stock Exchange will only intervene in larger issues (to adjust the timing so that the market does not suffer from too many issues in one period). The UK has particularly strong traditions and laws concerning *pre-emption rights*. These require that a company raising new equity capital by selling shares first offers those shares to the existing shareholders. The owners of the company are entitled to subscribe for the new shares in proportion to their existing holding. This will enable them to maintain the existing percentage ownership of the company – the only difference is that each slice of the company cake is bigger because it has more financial resources under its control.

The shares are usually offered at a significantly discounted price from the market value – typically 10–20 per cent per cent. Shareholders can either buy these shares themselves or sell the 'right' to buy to another investor. For further reassurance that the firm will raise the anticipated finance, rights issues are usually underwritten by institutions.

An example

Take the case of the imaginary listed company Swell plc with 100 million shares in issue. It wants to raise £25m for expansion but does not want to borrow it. Given that its existing shares are quoted on the stock market at 120p, the new rights shares will have to be issued at a lower price to appeal to shareholders because there is a risk of the market share price falling in the period between the announcement and the purchasing of new shares. (The offer must remain open for at least three weeks.) Swell has decided that the £25m will be obtained by issuing 25 million shares at 100p each. Thus the ratio of new shares to old is 25:100. In other words, this issue is a 'one-for-four' rights issue. Each shareholder will be offered one new share for every four already held. The discount on these new shares is 20p or 16.7 per cent. The market price of Swell shares will not be able to stay at 120p after the rights issue is complete. The *ex-rights price* is the price at which the shares should theoretically sell after the issue. This is calculated as follows:

Four existing shares at a price of 120p	480p
One new share for cash at 100p	100p
Value of five shares	580p
Value of one share ex-rights 580p/5	116p

An alternative way of viewing this is to focus on the worth of the firm before and after the rights. Prior to the issue the total capitalisation of the firm was £120m (£1.20 × 100 million shares). The rights issue put £25m into the company but also created 25 million additional shares. Therefore the price of each share should be (disregarding stock market fluctuations and revaluations of the company):

$$\frac{\text{Total market capitalisation}}{\text{Total shares available}} = \frac{£145\text{m}}{125\text{m}} = £1.16$$

The existing shareholders have experienced a decline in the price of their old shares from 120p to 116p. A fall of this magnitude necessarily follows from the introduction of new shares at a discounted price. However the loss is exactly offset by the gain in share value on the new rights issue shares. They cost 100p but have a market price of 116p. This can be illustrated through the example of Sid, who owned 100 shares worth £120 prior to the rights announcement. Sid loses £4 on the old shares – their value is now £116. However he makes a gain of £4 on the new shares.

Cost of rights shares (25 × £1)	£25
Ex-rights value (25 × £1.16)	£29
Gain	£4

In 2001 BT was a company in trouble. It had taken on too much debt relative to its equity base. To correct the situation it sold off assets around the world and raised equity capital from a rights issue – *see* Exhibit 10.19.

Exhibit 10.19

Institutions set to back BT

FT

British Telecommunications' £5.9bn rights issue closes at 9.30 this morning amid indications that the take-up by UK institutional investors has been strong.

But the interest is likely to focus on the level of enthusiasm among the company's army of 1.8m private shareholders for putting new cash into BT, whose value has fallen sharply since last year. They control about 17 per cent of the shares.

There are signs that private investors have been selling BT stock during the 30-day offer period. However, given the scale of the shareholder base, the registrars to the issue might not know the final result until the weekend.

The response of the non-UK shareholders, who control more than 7 per cent of the stock, has also been a source of uncertainty for the offer. BT management has been on an intensive roadshow to overseas institutions, particularly in the US where most of the non-UK shares are held.

The final outcome will be revealed next week when Cazenove and Merrill Lynch, the joint brokers, launch an international tender offer to sell off the rump of the shares that are not taken up by existing investors. The deep discount at which BT launched the record-breaking cash call – about 47 per cent below the then share price of 568½p – means it is almost certain to raise the money, even if demand from private investors is weak. But if there is a big overhang of shares for BT to dispose of next week, it could depress the shares.

Investors were offered the right to buy three new shares at 300p for every 10 they held. Those who do not take up their rights will still receive some cash to compensate for the fall in the shares caused by issuing new equity at 300p.

Source: Thorold Barker, *Financial Times*, 15 June 2001, p. 20. Reprinted with permission.

What if a shareholder does not want to take up the rights?

As owners of the firm all shareholders must be treated in the same way. To make sure that some shareholders do not lose out because they are unwilling or unable to buy more shares the law requires that shareholders have a third choice, other than to buy or not buy the new shares. This is to sell the rights on to someone else on the stock market (selling the rights nil paid). Take the case of impoverished Sid, who is unable to find the necessary £25. He could sell the rights to subscribe for the shares to another investor and not have to go through the process of taking up any of the shares himself. Indeed, so deeply enshrined are pre-emption rights that even if the shareholder does nothing the company will sell his rights to the new shares on his behalf and send the proceeds to him. (Hence the final sentence in the BT article.) Thus, Sid would benefit to the extent of 16p per share or a total of £4 (if the market price stays constant) which adequately compensates for the loss on the 100 shares he holds. But the extent of his control over the company has been reduced – his percentage share of the votes has decreased.

The value of a right on one old share in Swell is:

$$\frac{\text{Theoretical market value of share ex-rights} - \text{subscription price}}{\text{No. of old shares required to purchase one new share}}$$

$$= \frac{116 - 100}{4} = 4\text{p}$$

The value of a right on one new share is:

Theoretical market value of share ex-rights – subscription price = 116 – 100 = 16p

Ex-rights and cum-rights

Shares bought in the stock market which are designated cum-rights carry with them to the new owner the right to subscribe for the new shares in the rights issue. After a cut-off date the shares go ex-rights, which means that any purchaser of old shares will not have the right to the new shares.

The price discount decision

It does not matter greatly whether Swell raises £25m on a one-for-four basis at 100p or on a one-for-three basis at 75p per share, or on some other basis (*see* Exhibit 10.20).

Exhibit 10.20 Comparison of different rights bases

Rights basis	*Number of new shares (m)*	*Price of new shares (p)*	*Total raised (£m)*
1 for 4	25	100	25
1 for 3	33.3	75	25
1 for 2	50	50	25
1 for 1	100	25	25

As Exhibit 10.20 shows, whatever the basis of the rights issue, the company will receive £25m and the shareholders will see the price of their old shares decrease, but this will be exactly offset by the value of the rights on the new shares. However, the ex-rights price will change. For a one-for-three basis it will be £108.75:

Three shares at 120p	360p
One share at 75p	75p
Value of four shares	435p
Value of one share (435/4)	108.75p

If Swell chose the one-for-one basis this would be regarded as a *deep-discounted rights issue*. With an issue of this sort there is only a minute probability that the market price will fall below the rights offer price and therefore there is almost complete certainty that the offer will be taken up. It seems reasonable to suggest that the underwriting service provided by the institutions is largely redundant here and that the firm can make a significant saving. Yet 95 per cent of all rights issues are underwritten,[4] usually involving between 100 and 400 sub-underwriters. The underwriting fees are usually a flat 2 per cent of the offer. Of this the issuing house receives 0.5 per cent, the broker receives 0.25 per cent and the sub-underwriter 1.25 per cent (the same distribution as in a new issue). The reasons for the acceptance of the apparently high insurance cost of underwriting, as a constant proportion of the amount raised regardless of risk, remains something of a mystery. One suggestion is that there may be a capital gains tax liability for some investors in deeply discounted offers – but this does not apply to most investors. Another possibility is that 'underwriting is interpreted as a signal from the underwriting institutions that the issue is worthwhile'[5] and has the approval of the major institutions. The cynics amongst us have suggested that underwriting fees are a 'nice little earner' for City institutions and they are good at persuading firms to underwrite and not to simply discount rights issues deeply. Exhibit 10.21 shows the present system to be under attack.

Exhibit 10.21

The fight for rights

In the traditional British rights issue, new shares tend to be offered at a 15 per cent discount to the share price on the day of the issue. The shares usually remain on sale for three weeks. Provided that the price of new shares stays below that quoted in the stock market during that time, they will be snapped up by either existing or new investors.

But if the stock market price falls below the one at which new shares are offered, they will not be worth buying and the issue will fail. To avoid that risk, companies tend to insure themselves by asking a merchant bank to underwrite the issue. For a standard fee of 2 per cent, the bank guarantees to buy the shares if the market price falls too far.

The merchant bank itself keeps half a percentage point of the fee, and pays a quarter to a broker for distributing the issue. The remaining 1.25 per cent is paid to a group of 200 to 300 investment institutions who take on the underwriting risk from the merchant bank in the three-week offer period – a job known as sub-underwriting.

These fees have been fixed for three decades, except in rare cases such as privatisations or building society flotations. They have been applied for companies large and small, in every industrial sector. It was this fixing of standard fees in an apparently non-competitive manner that first raised alarms two years ago.

The OFT commissioned a study by Mr Paul Marsh, a professor at the London Business School, which found that the sub-underwriting fee was vastly in excess of the risks that institutions took, although Mr Marsh supported the principle of rights issues. Cases of sub-underwriters having to buy up shares at a loss – such as the 1987 British Petroleum flotation – were rare. In total, sub-underwriters had made what Mr Marsh described as an 'excess profit' of £490m between 1986 and 1994.

One unusual aspect of underwriting commissions is that lack of competition does not stem from a shortage of participants. There are several hundred sub-underwriters – mostly pension funds and life assurers – in the London market, but finance directors have not exerted much pressure on their merchant banks to strike a tough bargain.

Despite initial protests that Mr Marsh's sums were wrong, the sub-underwriters, represented by the National Association of Pension Funds and the Association of British Insurers, have retreated. In the face of OFT scepticism, and the threat of an MMC referral, big investors declared they were willing to see commissions trimmed.

The first results of this attitude change came a month ago, when

UK company rights issues June 1995 – May 1996

Price discount on underwritten right issues (%)

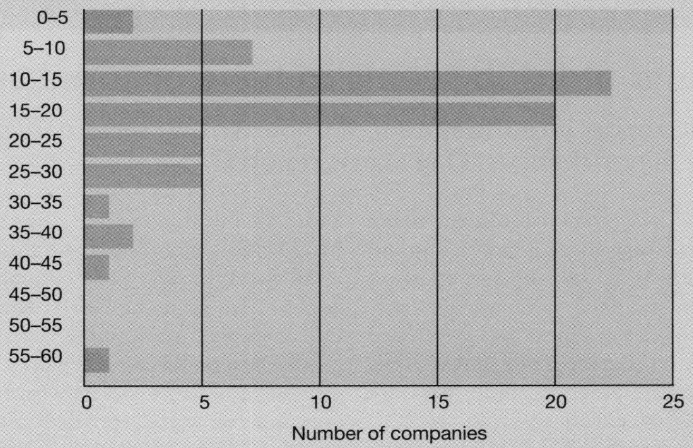

'Excess' returns to sub-underwriters

% of issues

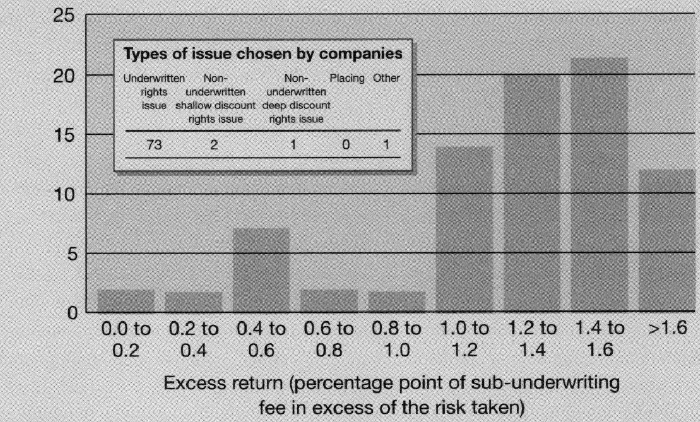

Source: *Underwriting of Equity Issues*, Office of Fair Trading, December 1996.

Exhibit 10.21 continued

the merchant bank Schroders launched a £222m rights issue for the hotels group Stakis in which sub-underwriting commissions were partially tendered. By putting about a third of the sub-underwriting up for auction, Schroders managed to knock some £400,000 off its bill.

One corporate financier at a US investment bank says pre-emptive rights are overly expensive because companies have to issue shares at an undue discount. He says that book-building is preferable because it allows a company to identify untapped sources of investment, and issue new shares at a higher price.

Supporters of rights issues insist that it is more expensive to raise equity capital in the US, where the commissions charged by big investment banks for raising new capital range between 3 and 6 per cent. They say the level of discount in a rights issue does not affect the cost of capital in itself – capital only becomes more expensive if a company fails to adjust its dividend to reflect the discount.

Source: John Gapper and William Lewis, 'The cost of raising equity: is it too high?', *Financial Times*, 11 December 1996, p. 23. Reprinted with permission.

The issue of excessive underwriting fees was referred to the Monopolies and Mergers Commission, MMC (now the Competition Commission), which reported in 1999 – *see* Exhibit 10.22.

Exhibit 10.22

Grand old club seems to have ensured survival

FT

MMC report into the system of underwriting secondary share issues has recommended only minor changes. Clay Harris reports.

The UK system of underwriting secondary share issues is a grand old club, based on pre-emption rights, standard fees, and – its critics say – a circle of privileged institutions. Like many clubs, it has relaxed its practices under pressure in order to ensure survival.

The approach appears to have paid off. Yesterday's report by the Monopolies and Mergers Commission endorsed by Stephen Byers, the trade and industry secretary, considered the evidence of a year-long inquiry and decided to recommend only minor changes.

The MMC recommended that any company not choosing to use a tender, rather than standard fees, for at least two-thirds of a rights offering should have to explain its reasons to shareholders.

It also wants financial advisers to tell clients of alternatives to underwriting at standard fees, an examination of the scope for cutting minimum rights period from 21 days and a favourable capital gains tax treatment of certain sales of rights.

All these, however, are peripheral issues. Although the MMC found two 'complex monopolies' existed in the provision of underwriting services, and expressed its wish that non-underwritten deeply discounted issues could be used more often, it came down against mandatory requirements of any kind because they would reduce flexibility and leave less scope for innovation.

This leaves intact the standard fee: 2 per cent of gross proceeds of an issue, with 0.5 per cent going to the lead underwriter, 0.25 per cent to the broker arranging the sub-underwriting and 1.25 per cent to sub-underwriters.

Ever since the system came under increasing criticism, tendering has played a bigger role in UK issues, but the MMC said it was not convinced the standard fee system had gone for good. Tendering had not opened sub-underwriting to competition because most issues used it only partially.

The MMC took comfort from evidence that 'fees in the UK are not that high compared with elsewhere'. Although figures had to be treated with 'great caution', it said fees ranged from 3–6 per cent in the US, 1–5 per cent in Germany, 2–4 per cent in France, 2–2.5 per cent in Australia and 3–5 per cent in Japan.

Issuing costs averaged 4.8 per cent in the US compared with 2.8 per cent for the UK rights issues that the MMC studied. Because US offers are non pre-emptive, moreover, any discount to the market price represented a cost to shareholders . . .

From 1986 to October 1996, based on research by Prof Paul Marsh, sub underwriters' losses on failed rights issues amounted to 0.53 per cent of the total amount raised over the period, a figure that dropped to 0.15 per cent when the 1987 crash was excluded.

Exhibit 10.22 continued

Even though this was less than the 1.25 per cent fee, a number of fund managers argued that fees were barely adequate to compensate for costs, including risk.

The MMC said deep discounting should be used more than it is, but said this appeared to be because of management preference.

Mr Byers supported the MMC recommendation that the Treasury consider giving special treatment in terms of capital gains tax to 'tail swallowing', the practice of selling just enough rights to pay to take up the rest.

Because rights are more valuable when issues are deeply discounted, potential CGT liability might be a disincentive to influential large shareholders agreeing to use that method. The Treasury's initial response was that there were good reasons of principle why CGT should continue to be charged on sale of rights, but it agreed to take representations on the issue.

Source: Clay Harris, *Financial Times*, 25 February 1999, p. 11. Reprinted with permission.

EXERCISE: Compel

To consolidate the knowledge gained from the rights issue section it is suggested that it be applied to the case of Fairey's one-for-six rights at 355p, which raised £55m after expenses.

Exhibit 10.23

Fairey funds deal with £125m rights issue

FT

Fairey, the process technology company that makes instruments for production lines, yesterday launched a rights issue to help fund the acquisition of a German instrument and controls maker for DM424m (£125m) . . .

The 1-for-6 rights issue will raise about £55m net of expenses at 355p a share. Yesterday the shares, trading above 500p at the beginnng of the year, closed up 40p at 479p.

Source: David Blackwell, *Financial Times*, 4 May 2000, p. 23. Reprinted with permission.

Calculate the following on the assumption that the market price of an old share is 479p:

a the ex-rights price;
b the value of a right of a new share;
c the value of a right of an old share;
d the amount a holder of £8,000 worth of shares could receive if the rights were sold.

OTHER EQUITY ISSUES

Some companies argue that the lengthy procedures and expense associated with rights issues (for example, a minimum three-week offer period) frustrate directors' efforts to take advantage of opportunities in a timely fashion. Firms in the USA have much more freedom to bypass pre-emption rights. They are able to sell blocks of shares to securities houses for distribution elsewhere in the market. This is fast and has low transaction costs. The worry for existing shareholders is that they could experience a dilution of their voting power and/or the share could be sold at such a low price that a portion of the firm is handed over to new shareholders too cheaply.

The UK authorities have produced a compromise. Here firms must obtain shareholders' approval through a special resolution (a majority of 75 per cent of those voting) at the company's annual general meeting or at an extraordinary general meeting to waive the pre-emption right. Even then the shares must not be sold to outside investors at more than a 5 per cent discount to the share price. This is an important condition. It does not make any difference to existing shareholders if new shares are offered at a deep discount to the market price as long as they are offered to them. If external investors get a discount there is a transfer of value from the current shareholders to the new.

Placings and open offers

In placings, new shares are sold directly to a narrow group of external investors. The institutions, wearing their hat of existing shareholders, have produced guidelines to prevent abuse, which normally only allow a placing of a small proportion of the company's capital (a maximum of 5 per cent in a single year and no more than 7.5 per cent is to be added to the company's equity capital over a rolling three-year period) in the absence of a *clawback*. Under clawback existing shareholders have the right to reclaim the shares as though they were entitled to them under a rights issue. They can buy them at the price they were offered to the external investors. With a clawback the issue becomes an 'open offer'. The major difference compared with a rights issue is that if they do not exercise this clawback right they receive no compensation for a reduction in the price of their existing shares – there are no nil-paid rights to sell. Vodafone raised £3.5bn in a placing to finance its purchase of assets being sold by BT – *see* Exhibit 10.24. Notice the fee received by the merchant banks.

Exhibit 10.24

How Operation Jam Jar filled one busy day

FT

The confirmation call from Chris Gent, Vodafone's chief executive, in Japan came at 5.30am. By 6am 'Operation Jam Jar' was well under way.

More than 300 salesmen gathered in the London office of UBS Warburg, the investment bank, connected by 48 telephone lines to their counterparts at Goldman Sachs.

The task of the two banks was to raise £3bn in less then 48 hours by placing Vodafone shares in the volatile market. Less than 12 hours later, the two banks not only captured enough investors in the jam jar to cover the books but increased the size of the placing to £3.5bn.

'I do not think we had the time or energy to be nervous,' one Goldman Sachs trader said.

[The] serious planning of the share issue started last month, according to one banker, when first reports appeared that BT was planning a rights issue.

The groundwork was laid on Tuesday night with telephone calls from Mr Gent to their top 10 investors. But the real work started at the crack of dawn yesterday.

There was a run on double espresso on the second floor of the London Offices of Goldman Sachs, which houses the bank's equity capital markets team. 'Normally everyone is ordering cappucino in the morning but today everyone has been asking for espresso,' said Goldman's coffee seller. Speed was of the essence.

A book-building in a normal public offering of shares takes between two and three weeks. But the placing of Vodafone shares had to be done at accelerated pace, given the volatility of the market.

'We did not want to expose Vodafone's shares to the vagaries of the market. If you have your books open for more than two days the risk of the market turning sour is too high. We had to finish book-building in one or two days,' said James Renwick, who led the equity capital markets team at UBS Warburg.

Exhibit 10.24 continued

Biggest accelerated share placings

May 2001	Vodafone	$5.1bn
Mar 2000	Hutchison/Vodafone	$5.0bn
Dec 1999	Equant	$4.2bn
May 1999	HSBC	$3.0bn
Sep 2000	ABN Amro	$2.7bn
Mar 1999	Cable & Wireless	$2.6bn
Feb 2001	Eni	$2.5bn

Source: Capital Data

The tricky part was to catch the upturn in the market to coincide with Vodafone's financing needs. 'These are tough markets but the sentiment has improved significantly over the past few weeks,' he said.

Yet the window of opportunity for the share placement was narrow. It could not be done on Tuesday because of possible disruption from May Day protests in London while today was ruled out because of a planned transport strike. The size of the placement also had to be carefully calculated not to overstretch the market. Given the constraints of the settlement deadline – three trading days in the case of the Vodafone share placement – investors do not have time to reallocate assets and banks mainly rely on the cash that investors have in hand, Mr Renwick explains.

The daily volume of trading in Vodafone shares is estimated at about $1bn. This means the market absorbed five days' worth of trading in Vodafone shares which is 'almost the limit'.

As for investors, they said several months with virtually no new shares issues had produced plenty of appetite for the deal.

For the banks, the reward for the busy morning was about £35m of fees.

Source: Arkady Ostrovsky, *Financial Times*, 3 May 2001, p. 21. Reprinted with permission.

Acquisition for shares

Shares are often issued to purchase businesses or assets. This is usually subject to shareholder approval.

Vendor placing

If a company wishes to pay for an asset such as a subsidiary of another firm or an entire company with newly issued shares, but the vendor does not want to hold the shares, the purchaser could arrange for the new shares to be bought by institutional investors for cash. In this way the buyer gets the asset, the vendors (for example shareholders in the target company in a merger or takeover) receive cash and the institutional investor makes an investment. (*See* Exhibit 10.25.)

There is usually a clawback arrangement for a vendor placing (if the issue is more than 10 per cent of market capitalisation of the acquirer). Again, the price discount can be no more than 5 per cent of the current share price.

Exhibit 10.25 Vendor placing

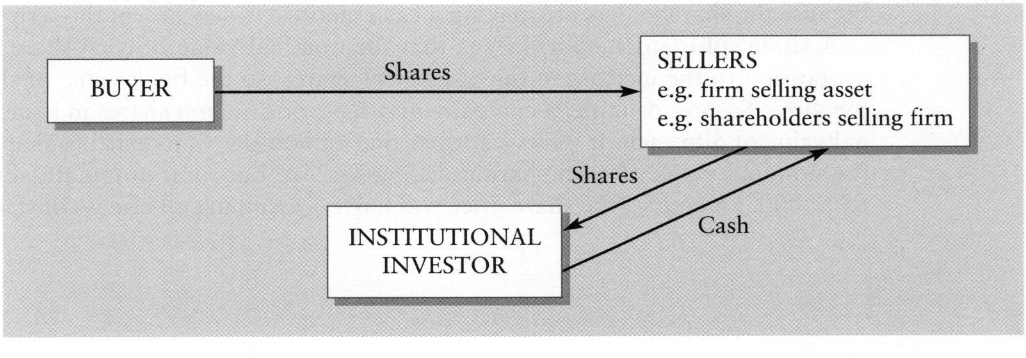

Bought deal

Instead of selling shares to investors companies are sometimes able to make an arrangement with a securities house whereby it buys all the shares being offered for cash. The securities house then sells the shares on to investors included in its distribution network, hoping to make a profit on the deal. Securities houses often compete to buy a package of shares from the company, with the highest bidder winning. The securities house takes the risk of being unable to sell the shares for at least the amount that they paid. Given that some of these bought deals are for over £100m, these securities houses need substantial capital backing.

SCRIP ISSUES

Scrip issues do not raise new money: a company simply gives shareholders more shares in proportion to their existing holdings. The value of each shareholding does not change, because the share price drops in proportion to the additional shares. They are also known as capitalisation issues or bonus issues. The purpose is to make shares more attractive by bringing down the price. British investors are thought to consider a share price of £10 and above as less marketable than one in single figures. So a company with shares trading at £15 on the Exchange might distribute two 'free' shares for every one held – a two-for-one scrip issue. Since the amount of money in the firm and its economic potential is constant the share price will theoretically fall to £5.

With a scrip issue there will be some adjustment necessary to the balance sheet. If we suppose that the pre-scrip issued share capital was £200m (25p par value × 800m shares) and the profit and loss account reserves accumulated from previous years amounted to £500m, then after the two-for-one scrip issue the issued share capital figure rises to £600m (25p par value × 2,400m shares) and the profit and loss account reserve (revenue reserve) falls to £100m. Thus £400m of profit and loss reserves are 'capitalised' into issued share capital.

A number of companies have an annual scrip issue while maintaining a constant dividend per share, effectively raising the level of profit distribution. For example, if a company pays a regular dividend of 20p per share but also has a one-for-ten scrip, the annual income will go up by 10 per cent. (A holder of 10 shares who previously received 200p now receives 220p on a holding of 11 shares.) Scrip issues are often regarded as indicating confidence in future earnings increases. If this new optimism is expressed in the share price it may not fall as much as theory would suggest.

Scrip dividends are slightly different: shareholders are offered a choice between receiving a cash dividend or receiving additional shares. This is more like a rights issue because the shareholders are making a cash sacrifice if they accept the scrip shares.

A **share split** (stock split) means that the nominal value of each share is reduced in proportion to the increase in the number of shares, so the book value of shares remains the same. So, for example, a company may have one million shares in issue with a nominal value of 50p each. It issues a further one million shares to existing shareholders with the nominal value of each share reducing to 25p, but total nominal value remains at £500,000. Of course, the share price will halve – assuming all else is constant.

WARRANTS

Warrants give the holder the right to subscribe for a specified number of shares at a fixed price at some time in the future. If a company has shares currently trading at £3 it might choose to sell warrants, each of which grants the holder the right to buy a share at, say, £4 in five years. If by the fifth year the share price has risen to £6 the warrant holders could exercise their rights and then sell the shares immediately, realising £2 per share, which is likely to be a considerable return on the original warrant price of a few pence. Warrants are frequently attached to bonds, and make the bond more attractive because the investor benefits from a relatively safe (but low) income on the bond if the firm performs in a mediocre fashion, but if the firm does very well and the share price rises significantly the investor will participate in some of the extra returns through the 'sweetener' or 'equity kicker' provided by the warrant.

EQUITY FINANCE FOR UNQUOTED FIRMS

We have looked at some of the details of raising money on the Stock Exchange. In the commercial world there are thousands of companies which do not have access to the Exchange. We now consider a few of the ways that unquoted firms can raise equity capital.

The financing gap

Small companies usually rely on retained earnings, capital injections from the founder family and bank borrowing for growth. More mature companies can turn to the stock market to raise debt or equity capital. In between these two, it is suggested, lies a financing gap. The intermediate businesses are too large or too fast growing to ask the individual shareholders for more funds or to obtain sufficient bank finance, and they are not ready to launch on the stock market (*see* Exhibit 10.26).

Exhibit 10.26 The financing gap

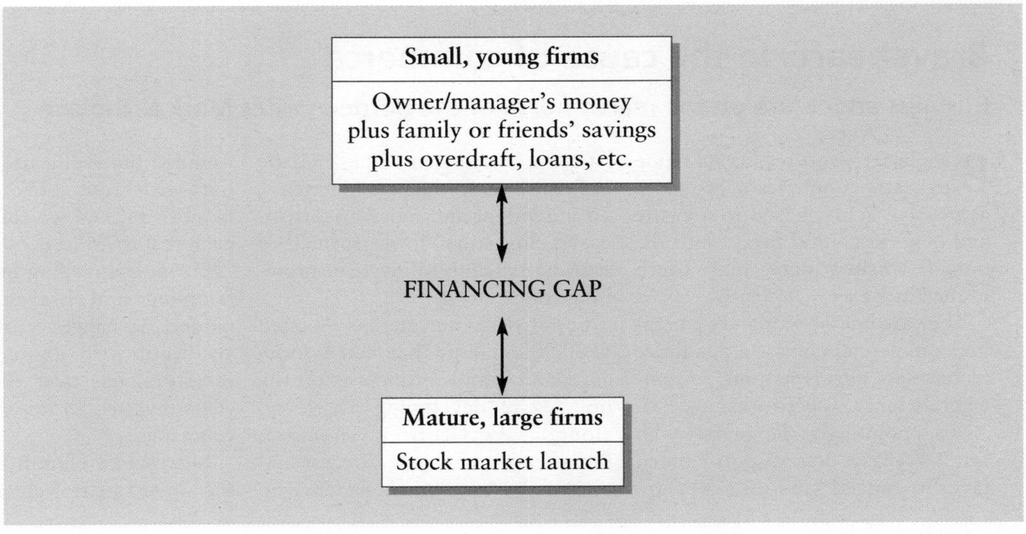

These companies may be frustrated in their plans to exploit market opportunities by a lack of available funds. To help fill this gap there has been the rapid development of the venture capital industry over the past 20 years. Today over £6bn per year[6] is supplied by formal venture capital suppliers to unquoted UK firms compared with just a few million in 1979. In Europe €34.9 billion was invested by venture capital organisations in 2000 to assist the vital small and medium-sized enterprise (SME) sector.[7] The tremendous growth of venture capital has to a large extent plugged the financing gap which so vexed politicians and business people alike in the 1970s and early 1980s.

Business angels

Business angels are wealthy individuals, generally with substantial business and entrepreneurial experience, who usually invest between £10,000 and £250,000 primarily in start-up, early stage or expanding firms. In 2000 73 per cent of the Business Angel investments monitored by the British Venture Capital Association (BVCA) were for sums of less than £100,000 and the average investment was £55,000. The majority of investments are in the form of equity finance but they do purchase debt instruments and preference shares. They usually do not have a controlling shareholding and they are willing to invest at an earlier stage than most formal venture capitalists. (They often dislike the term business angel, preferring the title informal venture capitalist.) They are generally looking for entrepreneurial companies which have high aspirations and potential for growth. A typical business angel makes one or two investments in a three-year period, often in an investment syndicate (with an 'archangel' leading the group). They generally invest in companies within a reasonable travelling distance from their homes because most like to be 'hands-on' investors, playing a significant role in strategy and management. Business angels are generally patient investors willing to hold their investment for at least a five-year period. The main way in which firms and angels find each other is through friends and business associates, although there are a number of formal networks.[8]

There are hundreds of groups of business angels throughout Europe. Exhibit 10.27 highlights some of the activity in Scotland.

Exhibit 10.27

Bravehearts in the cause of commerce

FT

Business angels are on the march north of the border, writes **Mark Nicholson**

Braveheart Ventures, as its name suggests, comprises a group of aggressive Scots, based in a castle and bent on gainful forays into the outside world – increasingly south of the border.

They are one of Scotland's emerging commercial clans – a syndicate of business angels helping to reinvigorate business networks.

Disappointingly, the quartet who run Braveheart do not sport painted faces or ragged kilts. But they are based, splendidly, in Fingask Castle in Perthshire. In the past four years, 30 individual and mostly Scottish-based investors have formed a semi-formal club to invest in promising companies.

So far the syndicate has invested £900,000 in more than half a dozen companies, and business is on the up. 'We're developing as we go along,' says Geoffrey Thomson, Braveheart's managing director and one of the four businessmen who founded the syndicate. 'We started out with four blokes, now we number 34, and we could probably push that to 75 or even 100.'

Business angelling in Scotland is booming and Braveheart is not unique. Archangel, another Scottish syndicate with about 30 private investors, has over the past nine years invested £15m in 40 Scottish companies.

Meanwhile Hamilton Portfolio, the investment vehicle of John

Exhibit 10.27 continued

Boyle, who founded and sold Direct Holidays to Airtours for £84m, has also invested £20m in just two years, partly on behalf of a syndicate of investors.

Just two weeks ago LINC, a Glasgow-based agency that marries angels and potential investees, and which has 500 angels on its books, was inducted on to the board of the European Business Angel Network, because it provided such a successful model.

In part this activity reflects growing opportunities for such investment, as smaller businesses, many of them burnt by experiences with bankers during the last recession, open themselves to private equity financing. A promising recent wave of Scottish software and technology-based start-up companies is also opening fresh territory.

Source: Mark Nicholson, *Financial Times*, 21 September 2000, p. 5. Reprinted with permission.

Venture capital

Venture capital funds provide finance for high-growth-potential unquoted firms. Venture capital is a medium- to long-term investment and can consist of a package of debt and equity finance. The equity element is often called 'private equity' because it is directed at companies that are not publicly quoted on an exchange. Venture capitalists take high risks by investing in the equity of young companies often with a limited (or no) track record. Many of their investments are into little more than a management team with a good idea – which may not have started selling a product or even developed a prototype. It is believed, as a rule of thumb in the venture capital industry, that out of ten investments two will fail completely, two will perform excellently and the remaining six will range from poor to very good.

As we discussed in Chapter 8, high risk goes with high return. Venture capitalists therefore expect to get a return of between five and ten times their initial equity investment in about five to seven years. This means that the firms receiving the equity finance are expected to produce annual returns of at least 26 per cent. Alongside the usual drawbacks of equity capital from the investors' viewpoint (last in the queue for income and on liquidation, etc.), investors in small unquoted companies also suffer from a lack of liquidity because the shares are not quoted on a public exchange. There are a number of different types of venture capital (VC):

- ***Seedcorn*** This is financing to allow the development of a business concept. Development may also involve expenditure on the production of prototypes and additional research.
- ***Start-up*** A product or idea is further developed and/or initial marketing is carried out. Companies are very young and have not yet sold their product commercially.
- ***Other early-stage*** Funds for initial commercial manufacturing and sales. Many companies at this stage will remain unprofitable. *See* Case study 10.2 on Paragon Software.
- ***Expansion (Development)*** Companies at this stage are on to a fast-growth track and need capital to fund increased production capacity, working capital and for the further development of the product or market. Professor Steve Young's company Entropic (*see* Case study 10.1 at the beginning of the chapter) provides an example of this.
- ***Management buy-outs (MBO)*** Here a team of managers make an offer to their employers to buy a whole business, a subsidiary or a section so that they own and run it for themselves. Large companies are often willing to sell to these teams, particularly if the business is under-performing and does not fit with the strategic core business. Usually the management team have limited funds of their own and so call on venture capitalists to provide the bulk of the finance.

CASE STUDY 10.2 Backers and founders

Confidence reaps a rich reward

FT

The charisma and enthusiasm of Paragon Software's boss gained him the crucial support of venture capitalist Michael Elias, writes **Fergal Byrne**

UK based Paragon Software was set up by Colin Calder in 1996 to develop a software product to synchronise personal data between mobile phones and personal computers. In 1997 the company won a £450,000 investment from venture capitalists 3i, through the *Sunday Times*/3i Business Catapult fundraising competition. A year later Michael Elias, of venture capital company Kennet Capital, acted as lead investor for a £1.25m investment in the business. In late 1999 a further $14m (£9.9m) was invested in a third round of funding by a consortium of investors, including 3i and Kennet Capital. Less than six months later the company was sold to US telecommunications company Phone.com for $540m, the largest sum ever paid for a European technology start-up company.

Michael Elias, investor, managing director of Kennet Capital.

I met Colin through a colleague, who had had an initial meeting with him in a New York bar and liked what he heard. Colin is extremely charismatic and knows how to put on a good show. When we met I could see he was driven: he had one unsuccessful company behind him and he lived and breathed the business. He also had a clear idea of what he was looking for from an investor. And as I got to know him personally, I realised we had a shared passion for fly fishing.

The idea for the business sounded deceptively simple. Often I would tell people about the business, only to see their eyes glaze over. When Colin spoke, however, it always sounded exciting. He had a clear strategic vision and would position data synchronisation software at the centre of a number of converging industries.

His enthusiasm was infectious: the employees exuded confidence and optimism. Paragon organised a lot of social events around the company's activities, many of which I attended. It felt like one big family.

The initial negotiations were tricky. Colin always felt the business was worth much more than we did. It was a classic confrontation between the enthusiastic entrepreneur and the slightly jaded venture capitalist who has heard it all before.

Throughout our relationship, Colin knew exactly what he was looking for. And he wanted to make sure he got his money's worth. He had no compunction about ringing whenever he needed something – an introduction, or information, whatever. We worked hard as Colin asked for a lot of assistance.

Colin was very good at managing relationships with the broader financial community, making sure that everyone felt that this was a must-have technology. Nonetheless we were amazed at the ultimate valuation he was able to realise for the business. I don't mind admitting he proved us all wrong.

Colin Calder, founder

I knew exactly what I was looking for from a VC investor: someone to help manage our relationship with the financial community, to help bring senior people on board and to help us develop relationships with key people in the industry. Most of all, I wanted someone willing to work really hard for the business.

Although we had several investors indicating that they wanted to do a deal, I chose Kennet because I could see Michael understood exactly what I needed, from his experience as a VC in Silicon Valley. On a personal level I liked him. He was tough but approachable. You knew where you stood: there was no hidden agenda.

My relationship with Michael was mainly good, not withstanding the inherently curious relationship that exists between VCs and entrepreneurs. For 95 per cent of the time you are a team heading in the same direction. The rest of the time you are negotiating face to face.

Sealing the initial deal was tough. I felt Michael was striking too hard a bargain, insisting on too much downside protection. But by the end of the due delligence process, I was running low on money and time; I felt my bargaining power was evaporating.

Once the deal was done, Michael delivered completely on his initial commitment. All Kennet's resources, and those of Broadview, its parent company, were made available when I needed them. Instantly. This responsiveness was crucial: where everyone is operating in internet time, days count. Michael made a vital contribution in terms of headhunting (he found our chief financial officer, who played a crucial role in building the business), introducing the company to strategic partners and helping to secure an A-list roster of investors for the third round of funding. And Broadview handled the sale of the company.

Interestingly, valuation was the one area where Michael and I had different views throughout. I always believed the business was worth far more than Michael thought. And I am glad to say I proved Michael wrong – and in the process made him a very happy man.

Source: Fergal Byrne, *Financial Times*, 24 May 2001, p. 17. Reprinted with permission.

- *Management buy-ins (MBI)* A new team of managers from outside an existing business buy a stake, usually backed by a venture capital fund. A combination of an MBO and MBI is called a BIMBO – buy-in management buy-out – where a new group of managers join forces with an existing team to acquire a business.
- *Public-to-private* The management of a company currently quoted on a stock exchange may return it to unquoted status with the assistance of venture capital finance being used to buy the shares. *See* the example of WT Foods in Exhibit 10.28.

Exhibit 10.28

Bid values WT Foods at £76m

FT

A bid for WT Foods valuing the ethnic foods maker at about £76m is being prepared by management led by Keith Stott, chief executive, and Rod Garland, finance director.

Backing for the bid is expected to come from Bridgepoint, the private equity firm. Including WT's debt, finance for the bid will have to top £100m.

WT announced late on Friday that it had received an approach that 'may lead to an offer' but refused to comment further. The news came after the market had closed with the shares up $1\frac{1}{2}$p at $39\frac{1}{2}$p. WT's results for the year to end March are due to be announced by the end of this month, when further details of the approach are likely to be released. The bid is subject to due diligence, which could take several weeks.

Analysts said WT's management had become frustrated by the company's poor share price performance, and wanted to take it private. 'It's no secret, they are brassed off,' said one. Although profits have grown at WT, helped by acquisitions such as the £50m purchase of Noon Group, the Indian ready-meal maker, in January 1999, its share price has not followed.

When it bought Noon it placed shares at 50p to finance the deal, and the bid price is expected to be around that level.

Although the shares topped 60p in 1999, they fell to a low of $27\frac{1}{2}$p by November last year. At Friday's close the whole company was valued at £57.8m, not much more than it paid for Noon. Last year WT bought Rio Pacific, a food-service company, for £7.5m.

Source: Maggie Urry, *Financial Times*, 11 June 2001, p. 23. Reprinted with permission.

Venture capital firms are less keen on financing seedcorn, start-ups and other early-stage companies than expansions, MBOs and MBIs (*see* Exhibit 10.29). This is largely due to the very high risk associated with early-stage ventures and the disproportionate time and costs of financing smaller deals. To make it worthwhile for a VC organisation to consider a company the investment must be at least £250,000 – the average investment is about £5m.

Exhibit 10.29

Stock market volatility fails to put off investors

FT

Last year saw a record £30bn flowing into private equity funds in Europe, an 89% rise on 1999, writes **Katharine Campbell**

Investors who poured money into private equity in Europe last year may be wondering where exactly their cash is heading.

Despite extreme stock market volatility, a record €48bn (£30bn) flowed into the industry in 2000, according to figures to be released today. This represents an increase of 89 per cent over 1999 levels, with pension funds overtaking banks as the primary source of funds.

Deploying the money, however, is proving something of a headache for private equity companies, following the collapse in confidence across the technology sector and uncertainty surrounding the extent and depth of the global economic slowdown.

Last year's figures – in a study for the European Private Equity and Venture Capital Association by PwC – depict an industry at a high-water mark.

New investment levels rose sharply – to €34.9bn – although the annual increase, at 39 per cent, was substantially lower than on the fund-raising slide.

High technology proved the main magnet for capital, with €11bn channelled into investments in the sector, 71 per cent more than in 1999.

PwC traces the growth in technology-related activity partly to the improving entrepreneurial climate in Europe, together with the increasing globalisation of small companies.

Germany, the most active private equity market after the UK and France, saw investments of €3.8bn in venture capital, 80 per cent of the country's total. Generous government subsidies, as well as the impetus from the creation of the Neuer Markt, the bourse for young companies, have provided fertile ground for start-ups.

While dotcom mania fuelled activity through to the second quarter of 2000, wireless developments – via first WAP and then third generation platforms – sustained momentum later in the year. Other important areas of investment included internet infrastructure, encryption and security software, optical technology and interactive TV.

In the buy-out sector, it was a case of fewer, larger deals, with a total of €14.4bn invested (up 9 per cent). But €24.3bn of the new funds raised are expected to be channelled into buy-outs (a 106 per cent increase), sparking fears of oversupply, particularly in the crowded German market.

Another big cloud over the industry relates to realisation of investments. These have become infinitely tougher – and not merely because public markets remain more or less closed to new issues. Exits via trade sales are also much harder, with large technology companies no longer able to use highly rated stock to pay inflated prices for start-ups. Debt-laden telecommunications operators are another category of potential buyer whose attentions are diverted elsewhere.

The rate of divestment fell already in 2000. The study records 318 initial public offerings, for a total of €573m, 36 per cent lower in amount than in 1999. The

Distribution of European equity investment

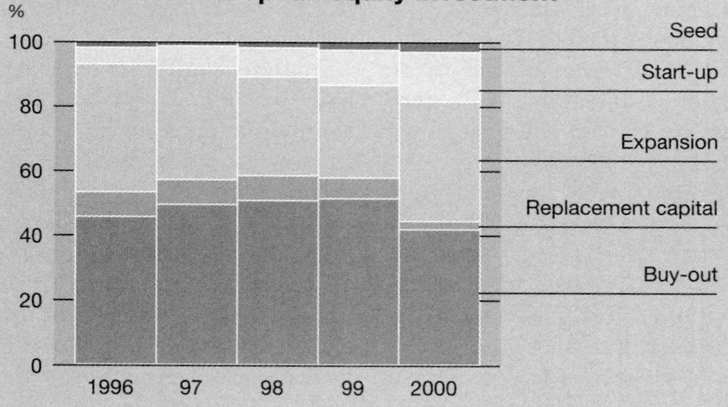

Source: European Private Equity and Venture Capital Association

Exhibit 10.29 continued

figures refer to original investment cost and do not reflect proceeds to investors. Trade sales fell slightly to €3bn.

High failure rates and a difficult exit environment suggest fund investors – including pension funds lured into the asset class for the first time – should brace themselves for considerably lower returns, industry watchers say.

Pension funds supplied almost a quarter of new money raised in 2000, with banks providing just over a fifth and insurance companies 13 per cent.

Funds of funds – vehicles that invest in other private equity groups rather than directly into companies – furnished 11 per cent of new money. Concerns are emerging about the longevity of this fast-growing sector.

US investors – who accounted for 22 per cent of new money in Europe last year – are scaling back following the collapse in value of their public equity portfolios.

'If you consider the US was putting roughly seven times as much into technology in 2000, then you see there is still quite a lot of catching up to do,' says Keith Arundale, director of business development and venture capital in PwC's global technology group.

Source: Katharine Campbell, *Financial Times*, 14 June 2001, p. 12. Reprinted with permission.

Because of the greater risks associated with the youngest companies, the VC funds may require returns of the order of 50–80 per cent per annum. For well-established companies with a proven product and battle-hardened and respected management the returns required may drop to the high 20s. These returns may seem exorbitant, especially to the managers set the task of achieving them, but they have to be viewed in the light of the fact that many VC investments will turn out to be failures and so the overall performance of the VC funds is significantly less than these figures suggest. In fact the British Venture Capital Association which represents 'every major source of venture capital in the UK' reports that returns on funds are not excessively high. Taken as a whole, the internal rate of return to investors net of costs and fees, for those funds which raise their money from institutional investors, was 16.4 per cent per annum to the end of 2000 for funds raised between 1980 and 1996.[9] (*See* Exhibit 10.30.)

Exhibit 10.30 Returns on funds raised from external investors for investment in venture capital, 1980–2000

Internal rates of return to investors, net of costs and fees since the inception of the fund

	Return to Dec. 2000 (% per annum)
Early stage	15.0
Development	10.0
Mid-MBO	16.3
Large MBO	18.7
Generalist fund	16.4
Total	16.4
Comparators	
FTSE All-Share (over 10 years)	15.4
Property (over 10 years)	8.9
Overseas equities (over 10 years)	14.2

Note: Excluding venture and development capital investment trusts and venture capital trusts.

Source: *British Venture Capital Association Performance Measurement Survey 2000*, conducted by PricewaterhouseCoopers (www.bvca.co.uk).

There are a number of different types of VC providers, although the boundaries are increasingly blurred as a number of funds now raise money from a variety of sources. The *independents* can be firms, funds or investment trusts, either quoted or private, which have raised their capital from more than one source. The main sources are pension and insurance funds, but banks, corporate investors and private individuals also put money into these VC funds. *Captives* are funds managed on behalf of a parent institution (banks, pension funds, etc.). *Semi-captives* invest funds on behalf of parent and also manage independently raised funds.

The largest UK venture capital firm is 3i (Investors in Industry) which is now a quoted public limited company with a wide range of shareholders. Since it was established by the Bank of England and the clearing banks in 1945 (as the ICFC) it has invested over £13.5bn. In the year ending March 2001, 3i invested £1bn in 328 UK companies, and a further £1bn in other companies around the world (an average of £7.8m each working day).

For the larger investments, particularly MBOs and MBIs, the venture capitalist may provide only a fraction of the total funds required. Thus, in a £50m buyout the venture capitalist might supply (individually or in a syndicate with other VC funds), say, £15m in the form of share capital (ordinary and preference shares). Another £20m may come from a group of banks in the form of debt finance. The remainder may be supplied as mezzanine debt – high-return and high-risk debt which usually has some rights to share in equity values should the company perform well (*see* Chapter 11). In the case of UniPoly (*see* Exhibit 10.31), of the £620m that was needed to buy this company and provide it with capital for expansion, 28 per cent was equity, 64 per cent bank debt (28 banks) and 8 per cent mezzanine finance (eight lenders).

Venture capitalists generally like to have a clear target set as the eventual 'exit' (or 'take-out') date. This is the point at which the VC can recoup some or all of the investment. The majority of exits are achieved by a sale of the company to another firm, but a popular method is a flotation on a stock market. Alternative exit routes are for the company to repurchase its shares or for the venture capitalist to sell the holding to an institution such as an investment trust.

Exhibit 10.31

Banks replace management at UniPoly

FT

The banks that backed the £620m management buy-out of UniPoly in 1997 have brought in a new management to improve the performance of the engineering business . . .

The 28 banks and eight mezzanine lenders in the syndicate have promised to support the business after 'a recent period of uncertainty', said Mr Teacher . . .

Unipoly makes industrial belting, fluid handling equipment and owns Schlegel, the US-based shielding equipment maker. It was sold by BTR, since renamed Invensys, in December 1997. At the time, UniPoly's diverse product range included water beds for cows and Wellington boots.

The original plan was that the business would be floated, or broken up and sold, within three to five years . . .

BTR received £515m for the company, which also raised a further £105m of capital for expansion.

Legal and General Ventures led the investors who put in £175m of equity and £50m of mezzanine finance, while Fuji Bank led the £395m debt finance.

Source: Maggie Urry, *Financial Times*, 12 June 2001, p. 30. Reprinted with permission.

Venture capital funds are rarely looking for a controlling shareholding in a company and are often content with a 20 or 30 per cent share. They may also provide funds by the purchase of convertible preference or preferred shares which give them rights to convert to ordinary shares – which will boost their equity holding and increase the return if the firm performs well. They may also insist, in an initial investment agreement, on some widespread powers. For instance, the company may need to gain the venture capitalist's approval for the issue of further securities, and there may be a veto over acquisition of other companies. Even though their equity holding is generally less than 50 per cent the VC funds frequently have special rights to appoint a number of directors. If specific negative events happen, such as a poor performance, they may have the right to appoint most of the board of directors and therefore take effective control. More than once the founding entrepreneur has been aggrieved to find him/herself removed from power. (Despite the loss of power, they often have a large shareholding in what has grown to be a multi-million pound company.) They are often sufficiently upset to refer to the fund which separated them from their creation as 'vulture capitalist'. But this is to focus on the dark side. When everything goes well, we have, as they say in the business jargon, 'a win-win-win situation': the company receives vital capital to grow fast, the venture capitalist receives a high return and society gains new products and economic progress.

The venture capitalist can help a company with more than money. Venture capitalists usually have a wealth of experience and talented people able to assist the budding entrepreneur. Many of the UK's most noteworthy companies were helped by the VC industry, for example Waterstones bookshops, Derwent Valley Foods (Phileas Fogg Crisps), Oxford Instruments (and in America: Apple computers, Sun Microsystems, Netscape, Lotus and Compaq).

Venture capital is most powerful in the United States (where would Silicon Valley be without it?) and in other Anglo-Saxon economies. However as Exhibit 10.32 shows, it is growing strongly across Europe.

Exhibit 10.32

Germany embraces venture capitalism

FT

The industry has mushroomed in the last few years with the help of the government but there are risks, writes **Bertrand Benoit**

Once a distinctly Anglo-Saxon pursuit, venture capitalism is growing roots across Europe and few countries are embracing the change with more enthusiasm than Germany.

Long reliant on banks for financing, the country has seen an explosion in the number of funds providing increasingly aggressive entrepreneurs with a pool of capital hard to imagine only five years ago.

According to the Berlin-based German venture capital association, private equity investment has trebled over the last five years to reach DM3.3bn (€1.68bn, $1.69bn) last year, a quarter of it going into early-stage finance.

Compared with neighbouring countries and particularly the UK, Germany remains a lightweight. Total funds available for investment account for a mere 0.07 per cent of its GDP, putting the country neck-and-neck with Portugal. Yet these funds are expected to grow nearly 80 per cent this year.

The key factor behind this increase has been the simultaneous rise in demand for, and supply of capital. 'Low interest rates, expensive stock markets, and dismal real estate returns mean people are looking for alternative investments,' says Falk Strascheg, co-founder of Technologieholding, Germany's largest venture capital fund based in Munich. 'At the same time, there is renewed confidence in entrepreneurs, who are no longer seen as evil bloodsuckers but as nice job-creators.'

►

Exhibit 10.32 continued

The German government has played a central role in kick-starting the industry. The state-sponsored EXIST programme, launched in 1997, has encouraged university-based networks to come up with high-technology ventures. Once concentrated around Munich – the 'laptop and Lederhosen' capital of Germany – high-tech companies are mushrooming all over the country, whether linked to universities, in the case of Freiburg, or on the rubble of older industries in the Ruhr and North-Rhine Westphalia regions.

Meanwhile, the state has also provided venture capitalists with the sort of financial support their British and US counterparts could only dream of. Federal agencies such as KFW, the development bank, and regional ones, such as Bayern Kapital in Bavaria, can provide up to two-thirds of venture capital investment in the form of loans, in addition to various guarantees protecting funds against losses.

'There is a snow-balling effect that increases the capital available to funds while considerably minimising their risks,' says Alexander Wessendorff, editor of Deutsche, a private equity newsletter. The most radical tranformation, however, has been the emergence of a viable exit route for funds, avoiding the disasters of the 1970s when banks bought into high-tech companies that later proved impossible to sell.

The creation in 1997 of the Neuer Markt, the Frankfurt-based high-growth/high-risk market, and its strong performance, have allowed funds to realise their investments through IPOs. These constituted 17 per cent of exits for private equity houses last year, against a mere 4 per cent in 1997. Trade sales, once the preferred exit route, now make up less than a third of the total. For venture capital funds, this has translated into handsome returns . . .

Germany's corporate giants have added to the pressure by setting up their own funds. These incubators give the companies access to products and innovations at a fraction of the cost of in-house research and development programmes, not to mention the recent entrance in the start-up market of large Anglo-Saxon equity houses with capital available for investment often in excess of DM2bn.

Source: Bertrand Benoit, *Financial Times*, 7 January 2000, p. 25. Reprinted with permission.

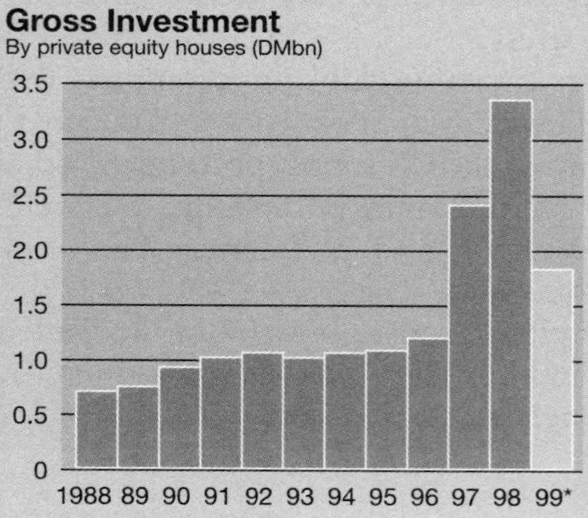

Exit routes

Buy-backs	%
1997	32.9
1998	43.5
Trade sales	
1997	52.0
1998	32.2
IPOs in Germany	
1997	4.1
1998	16.6
Others	
1997	11.0
1998	7.6

* First half

Source: German Venture Capital Association

Venture Capital Trusts (VCTs)

It is important to distinguish between venture capital trusts, an investment vehicle introduced in 1995 to encourage investment in small and fast-growing companies which have important tax breaks, and two other types of venture capital organisations: venture and development capital investment trusts, (VDCITs) which are standard investment trusts with a focus on more risky developing companies, and venture capital funds (described above).

There are four tax breaks for investors putting money into VCTs. There is an immediate relief on their current year's income at 20 per cent (by putting £10,000 into a VCT an investor will pay £2,000 less tax, so the effective cost is only £8,000). Also capital gains tax can be deferred on other investments if the gains are put into a VCT. The returns (income and capital gains) on a VCT are free of tax for investments up to £100,000 per year. These benefits are only available to investors buying new VCT shares who hold the investment for three years. The VCT managers can only invest in companies worth less than £15m and the maximum amount a VCT is allowed to put into each unquoted company's shares is limited to £1m per year. ('Unquoted' for VCT is used rather loosely and includes AIM companies.) A maximum of 15 per cent of the VCT fund can be invested in any one company. Up to half of the fund's investment in qualifying companies can be in the form of loans. VCTs are quoted on the London Stock Exchange.

These trusts offer investors a way of investing in a broad spread of small firms with high potential, but with greater uncertainty, in a tax-efficient manner.

Enterprise Investment Scheme (EIS)

Another government initiative to encourage the flow of risk capital to smaller companies is the Enterprise Investment Scheme. Income tax relief at 20 per cent is available for investments of up to £150,000 made directly into qualifying company shares. There is also capital gains tax relief, and losses within EISs are allowable against income tax. The tax benefits are lost if the investments are held for less than three years. To raise money from this source the firm must have been carrying out a 'qualifying activity' for three years – this generally excludes financial investment and property companies. The company must not be quoted on the Official List and the most it can raise under the EIS in any one year is usually £1m. The company must not have gross assets worth more than £15m. Funds which invest in a range of EIS companies are springing up to help investors spread risk.

Corporate venturing and incubators

Larger companies sometimes foster the development of smaller enterprises. This can take numerous forms, from joint product development work to an injection of equity finance. The small firm can thereby retain its independence and yet contribute to the large firm: perhaps its greater freedom to innovate will generate new products which the larger firm can exploit to the benefit of both. Intel uses corporate venturing to increase demand for its technology by, for example, investing in start-up companies in China. Shell uses it to promote innovation.

Incubators are places where a start-up company not only will gain access to finance, but will be able to receive support in many forms. This may include all humdrum operational managerial tasks being taken care of (e.g. accounting, legal, human resources), business planning, the supply of managers for various stages of the company's development, property management, etc. As a result the entrepreneurial team can concentrate on innovation and grow the business, even if they have no prior managerial experience. Incubators are large concerns in the USA and are catching on in Europe – *see* Exhibit 10.33.

Government sources

Some local authorities have set up VC-type funds in order to attract and encourage industry. Large organisations with similar aims include the Scottish Development Agency and the Welsh Development Agency. Equity, debt and grant finance may be available from these sources. Exhibit 10.34 shows that substantial sums are available from government agencies.

Exhibit 10.33

California dreams cross over

FT

All three of the US internet operations regarded as role models by European counterparts have now crossed the Atlantic, writes Katharine Campbell

When one UK venture capitalist recently learnt of plans by Idealab one of America's best known internet incubators, to expand into Europe, he was slightly sceptical: 'They will first have to work out how to clone Bill Gross.'

Mr Gross, who set up Idealab in Pasadena, California, in 1996, has made his name by hatching ideas – distinguishing him from most venture capitalists who back someone else's company at business-plan stage at the very earliest.

The outfit's bestknown investments – which are nurtured with a series of operational and financial support from cradle to initial public offering and beyond – include eToys, GoTo.com, and Tickets.com . . .

There has been an explosion of activity in Europe in the past nine months of vehicles loosely termed incubators. The more savvy among them say they want to emulate what they see as their US counterparts – with Idealab, CMGI and Internet Capital Group the most frequently cited role models . . .

Floated in 1994, CMGI still has a market capitalisation of about $24bn (£15bn) – after hitting a high of more than $40bn at the beginning of the year. Internet Capital Group, which went public last summer, was up at $50.6bn at one point although it is now at a more modest $18bn . . .

Internet Capital Group . . . set up in Europe last November – a market it believes is even more promising than the US on account of the fragmented nature of many of the region's supply chain.

Investing across most stages of a company's development, it likes to compare itself to an embryonic General Electric, distinguished by the 'depth' of its in-house resources. For instance, it has built what Stephen Duckett, joint European managing director, claims is the largest head-hunting firm in the business-to-business arena: 30 executives handling about 120 simultaneous searches worldwide.

It also stressed the operational experience it can offer its partner companies. Mary Coleman, former chief executive of Baan, the troubled Dutch software group, has for example popped up working for ICG in San Francisco.

Source: Katharine Campbell, *Financial Times*, 6 April 2000, p. 18. Reprinted with permission.

Exhibit 10.34

First regional venture capital funds expected soon

FT

Lack of access to adequate funding is the bane of small businesses, which is why a planned network of regional venture capital funds was announced by Gordon Brown, the chancellor, last year. However, the idea was blocked by the European Commission until recently on the grounds that the government's contribution could be unlawful state aid.

East Midlands Development Agency says it expects to be the first to get one of the funds under way, making a projected £30m available within the region for investments of up to £250,000, with further injections of £250,000 available later.

Derek Mapp, chairman of EMDA, welcomes the investment funds, observing that 'entrepreneurs seeking that level of money are neglected by big venture capital organisations'.

Companies receiving investment will have potential for high growth, says Mr Mapp. He says there is big demand for small equity developments and that other schemes have shown 'it is possible to get a commercial scheme going successfully'.

Source: Harriet Arnold, *Financial Times*, 14 June 2001, p. 14. Reprinted with permission.

DISILLUSIONMENT AND DISSATISFACTION WITH QUOTATION

Appendix 10.1 contains a number of newspaper articles about companies which either are dissatisfied with being quoted on a stock exchange or have never been quoted and feel no need to join. A reading of these will provide a wider understanding of the place of stock markets, their importance to some firms and how many companies are able to expand and produce wealth without them. Some of the main points are summarised in Exhibit 10.35. The arguments are taken directly from the articles and do not necessarily represent reasoned scientific argument.

Exhibit 10.35 Arguments for and against joining a stock exchange

For	*Against*
■ Access to new capital for growth. ■ Liquidity for existing shareholders. ■ Discipline on management to perform. ■ Able to use equity to buy businesses. ■ Allows founders to diversify. ■ Borrow more easily or cheaply. ■ Can attract better management. ■ Forces managers to articulate strategy clearly and persuasively. ■ Succession planning may be made easier – professional managers rather than family. ■ Increased customer recognition. ■ Allow local people to buy shares.	■ Dealing with 'City' folk is time consuming and/or boring. ■ City is short-termist. ■ City does not understand entrepreneurs. ■ Stifles creativity. ■ Focus excessively on return on capital. ■ Empire building through acquisitions on a stock exchange – growth for its own sake (or for directors) can be the result of a quote. ■ The stock market undervalues entrepreneur's shares in the entrepreneur's eyes. ■ Loss of control for founding shareholders. ■ Strong family-held companies in Germany, Italy and Asia where stock markets are used less. ■ Examples of good strong unquoted companies in UK: Bamford, Rothschilds, Littlewoods. ■ Press scrutiny is irritating. ■ Market share building (and short-term low profit margins) are more possible off exchange. ■ The temptation of over-rapid expansion is avoided off exchange. ■ By remaining unquoted, the owners, if they do not wish to put shareholder wealth at the centre of the firm's purpose, don't have to (environment or ethical issues may dominate). ■ Costs of maintaining a quote, e.g. SE fees, extra disclosure costs, management time.

CONCLUDING COMMENTS

There are a number of alternative ways of raising finance by selling shares. The advantages and problems associated with each method and type mean that careful thought has to be given to establishing the wisest course of action for a firm, given its specific circumstances. Failure here could mean an unnecessary loss of control, an unbalanced capital structure, an excessive cost of raising funds or some other destructive outcome. But getting the share question right is only one of the key issues involved in financing a firm. The next chapter examines another, that of long-term debt finance.

KEY POINTS AND CONCEPTS

- **Ordinary shareholders** own the company. They have the rights of control, voting, receiving annual reports, etc. They have no rights to income or capital but receive a residual after other claimants have been satisfied. This residual can be very attractive.
- **Debt capital holders** have no formal control but they do have a right to receive interest and capital.
- **Equity** as a way of financing the firm:

  Advantages

  1 No obligation to pay dividends – 'shock absorber'.
  2 Capital does not have to be repaid.

  Disadvantages

  1 High cost:
     a issue costs;
     b required rate of return.
  2 Loss of control.
  3 Dividends not tax deductible.

- **Authorised share** capital is the maximum amount permitted by shareholders to be issued.
- **Issued share** capital is the amount issued expressed at par value.
- **Share premium** The difference between the sale price and par value of shares.
- **Private companies** Companies termed 'Ltd' are the most common form of limited liability company.
- **Public limited companies** (plcs) can offer their shares to a wider range of investors, but are required to have £50,000 of share capital.
- **Preference shares** offer a fixed rate of return, but without a guarantee. They are part of shareholders' funds but not part of the equity capital.

  Advantages to the firm
  1 Dividend 'optional'.
  2 Usually no influence over management.
  3 Extraordinary profits go to ordinary shareholders.
  4 Financial gearing considerations.

  Disadvantages to the firm
  1 High cost of capital relative to debt.
  2 Dividends are not tax deductible.

- **Types of preference share:** cumulative, participating, redeemable, convertible.

- **Non-voting shares** provide returns without votes.
- **Preferred ordinary shares** rank higher than **deferred ordinary shares** for dividends.
- **Golden shares** have extraordinary special powers.
- **To float on the Official List** of the London Stock Exchange the following are required:
  - a prospectus;
  - an acceptance of new responsibilities (e.g. dividend policy may be influenced by exchange investors; directors' freedom to buy and sell may be restricted);
  - 25 per cent of share capital in public hands;
  - that the company is suitable;
  - usually three years of accounts;
  - competent and broadly based management team;
  - appropriate timing for flotation;
  - a sponsor;
  - a corporate broker;
  - underwriters (usually);
  - accountants' reports;
  - solicitors;
  - registrar.
- **Following flotation on the OL:**
  - greater disclosure of information;
  - restrictions on director share dealings;
  - annual fees to LSE;
  - high standards of behaviour.
- **Methods of flotation:**
  - offer for sale;
  - offer for sale by tender;
  - introduction;
  - offer for sale by subscription;
  - placing;
  - intermediaries' offer.
- **Stages in a flotation:**
  - pre-launch publicity;
  - decide technicalities, e.g. method, price, underwriting;
  - pathfinder prospectus;
  - launch of public offer – prospectus and price;
  - close of offer;
  - allotment of shares;
  - announcement of price and first trading.
- **Book-building** Investors make bids for shares. Issuers decide price and allocation in light of bids.
- **The Alternative Investment Market (AIM) differs** from the OL in:
  - nominated advisers, not sponsors;
  - lower costs;
  - no minimum capitalisation, trading history or percentage of shares in public hands needed;
  - lower ongoing costs.

- **Costs of new issues:**
  - administrative/transaction costs;
  - the equity cost of capital;
  - market pricing costs.
- **Rights issues** are an invitation to existing shareholders to purchase additional shares.
- **The theoretical ex-rights price** is a weighted average of the price of the existing shares and the new shares.
- The **nil paid rights** can be sold instead of buying new shares.
- **Value of a right on an old share:**

$$\frac{\text{Theoretical market value of share ex-rights} - \text{subscription price}}{\text{Number of old shares required to purchase one new share}}$$

- **Value of a right on a new share:**

  Theoretical market value of share ex-rights – Subscription price

- **The pre-emption right** can be bypassed in the UK under strict conditions.
- **Placings** New shares sold directly to a group of external investors. If there is a *claw-back* provision, so that existing shareholders can buy the shares at the same price instead, the issue may be termed an **open offer**.
- **Acquisition for shares** Shares are created and given in exchange for a business.
- **Vendor placing** Shares are given in exchange for a business. The shares can be immediately sold by the business vendors to institutional investors.
- **Scrip issues** Each shareholder is given more shares in proportion to current holding. No new money is raised.
- **Warrants** The holder has the right to subscribe for a specified number of shares at a fixed price at some time in the future.
- **Business angels** Wealthy individuals investing £10,000 to £250,000 in shares and debt of small young companies with high growth prospects. Also offer knowledge and skills.
- **Venture capital** (VC) Finance for high-growth-potential unquoted firms. Sums: £250,000 minimum, average £5m. Some of the investment categories of VC are:
  - seedcorn;
  - start-up;
  - other early-stage;
  - expansion (development);
  - management buyouts (MBO): existing team buy business from corporation;
  - management buy-in (MBI): external managers buy a stake in business and take over management;
  - BIMBO: combination of MBO and MBI;
  - Public-to-private.
- **Rates of return** demanded by VC range from 26 per cent to 80 per cent per annum depending on risk.

- **Exit** ('take-out') is the term used by venture capitalists to mean availability of a method of selling holding. The most popular method is a trade sale to another organisation. Stock market flotation, own-share repurchase and sale to an institution are other possibilities.
- Venture capitalists often strike **agreements** with entrepreneurs to give the venture capitalists **extraordinary powers** if specific negative event occurs, e.g. poor performance.
- **Venture Capital Trusts (VCTs)** are special tax-efficient vehicles for investing in small unquoted firms through a pooled investment.
- **Enterprise Investment Scheme (EIS)** Tax benefits are available to investors in small unquoted firms willing to hold the investment for five years.
- **Corporate venturing** Large firms can sometimes be a source of equity finance for small firms. **Incubators** provide finance and business services.
- **Government agencies** can be approached for equity finance.
- **Being quoted has significant disadvantages,** ranging from consumption of senior management time to lack of understanding between the City and directors and the stifling of creativity.

REFERENCES AND FURTHER READING

Breedon, F. and Twinn, I. (1996) 'The valuation of sub-underwriting agreements for UK rights issues', *Bank of England Quarterly Bulletin*, May, pp. 193–6. A discussion of the mystery of apparently high underwriting fees for rights issues.

British Venture Capital Association, London (www.bvca.co.uk). Variety of paper publications and online material which give an insight into a variety of aspects of venture capital.

Bruce, R. (1995) 'Parting from your parent', *Accounting*, September, pp. 38–9. An entertaining account of the trials and tribulations of a successful MBO.

Carty, P. (1995) 'Marriages made in heaven?', *Accounting*, September, p. 42. Overview of business angels with some interesting examples.

Cope, N. (1995) 'Cashing in on household prestige', *Accounting*, September, pp. 44–6. An example of a management buy-in is explained.

Jenkinson, T. and Ljungquist, A. (1996) *Going Public: The Theory and Evidence on How Companies Raise Equity Finance*. Oxford: Clarendon. A detailed and accessible description of the new issue market internationally.

Levis, M. (1990) 'The winner's curse problem, interest costs and the underpricing of initial public offerings', *Economic Journal*, 100, March, pp. 76–89. Underpricing for some issues is explained by fear on the part of uninformed investors, plus the cost of interest between application for shares and return of cheques in oversubscribed issues.

London Stock Exchange (2000) *A Practical Guide to Listing on the London Stock Exchange*. London: The Exchange. A clear and succinct guide to the essential issues.

Lowenstein, L. (1991) *Sense and Nonsense in Corporate Finance*. Reading, Mass: Addison-Wesley. Some important thoughts on LBOs and other financing issues.

Marsh, P. (1994) 'Underwriting of rights issues: a study of the returns earned by sub-underwriters from UK rights issues', *Office of Fair Trading Research Paper No. 6*. Conclusion: underwriting fees are excessive given the risk borne in rights issues.

Mason, C. and Harrison, R. (1997) 'Business angels – heaven-sent or the devil to deal with?' in Birley, S. and Muzyka, D.F. (eds) *Mastering Enterprise*, London: Pitman Publishing/Financial Times. Easy to read summary of business angel activity in the UK.

Massey, D. (1995) *New Issues: Profit From Flotations and Initial Public Offerings*. London: Pitman Publishing. The new issue market from the perspective of the investor – easy to read.

Osborne, A. (1996) 'Family firms place a price on a vote', *Investors Chronicle*, 22 November. A lively discussion of non-voting shares.

Rock, K. (1986) 'Why new issues are underpriced', *Journal of Financial Economics*, 15, January, pp. 187–212. Underpricing is explained by the winner's curse problem facing uninformed investors.

WEBSITES

British Venture Capital Association www.bvca.co.uk

Business Links www.businesslinks.co.uk

Enterprise zone www.enterprisezone.org.uk

European Private Equity and Venture Capital Associations www.evca.com

Financial Services Authority www.fsa.gov.uk

London Stock Exchange www.londonstockexchange.co.uk

United Kingdom Listing Authority www.fsa.gov.uk/ukla

APPENDIX 10.1 REASONS FOR AND AGAINST FLOATING

Exhibit 10.36

Small businesses shunning flotation

FT

Small and medium-sized private companies are rapidly losing interest in floating on the stock exchange as a way of raising funds for expansion because of indifference among institutional investors.

A survey by Manchester Business School found only 25 per cent of private companies said they would consider a flotation to raise funds for organic growth and acquisitions. A year ago the figure stood at 50 per cent . . .

AM Paper, the Lancashire-based soft tissues company bought last month by SCA of Sweden, opted for the trade sale after it became clear a flotation was 'not feasible'.

Steve Sealey, AM's chief executive, said: 'We were in an unsexy sector – pulp and paper – and it became evident that an institutional placing was not going to be feasible.'

Mr Poutziouris said: 'Large investors lack the appetite to invest in smaller companies, and policy-makers ought to consider drastic measures to close this equity gap.'

However, the study also showed smaller companies were reluctant to consider bringing in outside investors because of the dilution of their controlling interest. More than two-thirds of private companies in the survey said they would be unwilling to offer more than 49.9 per cent of their shares to the public.

Source: Sheila Jones, *Financial Times*, 29 September 1999, p. 12. Reprinted with permission.

Exhibit 10.37

Healthcall to go private via managers' £50m deal

FT

Healthcall, the medical company which specialises in handling night calls on behalf of general practitioners, is being taken private by its managers, who argue that political sensitivities make it hard to run as a public company.

Maurice Henchey, chief executive, said customers preferred dealing with a private company, adding 'every time the company makes a profit, doctors complain'.

He said that political changes resulted in considerable short term risk for the business.

Mr Henchey and the rest of the management team are offering £50.1m for the company with backing from NatWest Private Equity, which first proposed the deal.

NatWest Private Equity said that it was prepared to take a longer term view than institutional stock market investors and believed that in the medium term, political events would turn to Healthcall's favour.

Source: Roger Taylor, *Financial Times*, 17 February 1998, p. 23. Reprinted with permission.

Exhibit 10.38

'Too complex' Elliott to delist

FT

The directors of B Elliott are taking the specialist engineering group private with a £43.5m management buy-out backed by Deutsche Morgan Grenfell.

Michael Frye, chief executive, said the company was too small and complex for the stock market. It last year tried to raise £9m but was turned down by institutional investors.

'I am not anti-City, but I have to appreciate that we are too small and complicated for the market. It takes them too long to understand us – and why should they when there are plenty of bigger companies to look at,' he said . . .

'We have cleaned up our business and done what we said we would, but the share price has not responded,' Mr Frye said. The shares, which hit a low of 43p in 1993, were languishing below 75p for most of last year.

Source: Roger Taylor, *Financial Times*, 17 February 1998, p. 23. Reprinted with permission.

Exhibit 10.39

Two-tier market favouring high-tech

FT

A two-tier market is emerging for smaller quoted companies – with retail, engineering and food companies losing out to high-technology and service groups, according to a KPMG Corporate Finance report* published today.

Although more money is expected to flow into smaller quoted companies this year following sharp gains overall for small-cap indices last the amount going to the unfashionable, more traditional sectors looks set to decline.

A survey of more than 90 fund managers with a combined £1,000bn under management suggests there will be a net increase of 17 per cent in the money available for investment in smaller companies this year.

But the findings also show that while more than 60 per cent of those surveyed are planning to increase their investment in the software services sectors, 34 per cent are planning to cut investment in food producers and processors.

A further 28 and 26 per cent respectively are planning to reduce investment in engineering machinery and general retailing companies . . .

Meanwhile, as more traditional companies find it difficult to raise money or use shares to make acquisitions, further consolidation is likely in their sectors through trade buys or public-to-private transactions.

Last year there were 33 public-to-private transactions worth a total of £4.7bn.

Source: D Blackwell, *Financial Times*, 24 January 2000, p. 26. Reprinted with permission.

Exhibit 10.40

Cytomyx seeks a bypass route

FT

Cytomyx, a drug research company, is planning to raise £3m in a listing on Aim. It will be the first London listing of a biotechnology company since XTL Biopharmaceuticals, the Israel-based biotech company, listed on the London Stock Exchange in September last year. It is likely to be watched closely by other biotechnology companies for signs that investors are returning to the sector . . .

Cytomyx, which has been funded by its founders, Mike Kerins and Alan Seeley, is planning to bypass venture capital entirely. 'Aim appealed as a source of capital because it will give us a spread of investors,' said Mr Kerins, chief executive.

Analysts said the reporting requirements of listing seemed an onerous price to pay for such a small fund-raising. But Alan Kingsman, who floated Oxford BioMedica on Aim in 1995, before graduating to the main list in April, said the junior market route had some advantages over venture capital. 'By avoiding venture capital you can keep more control of your destiny,' he said.

Source: David Firn, *Financial Times*, 14 May 2001, p. 25. Reprinted with permission.

Exhibit 10.41

Small companies urged to think big in hunt for investment

FT

David Blackwell looks at why businesses with low market capitalisation are being neglected by institutions and asks how they can fight back.

Small companies – and there are 800 listed in London with a market capitalisation of less than £50m – are being increasingly marginalised by institutional investors.

At the same time, they are failing to excite the interest of private investors. Their options are limited: they can trundle along in obscurity on the Stock Exchange, move back into private ownership or sell themselves to a larger group.

The gulf between them and institutional investors is reflected in startling figures in the latest

Exhibit 10.41 continued

Department of Trade and Industry report on the sector.

Research showed that more than 60 per cent of small companies felt fund managers did not understand their business. Conversely, more than 70 per cent of fund managers said smaller companies had a poor grasp of what determined share value . . .

[Institutions] are increasing in size as the financial services industry consolidates. Fund managers are also taking a more pan-European view of smaller companies following the introduction of the euro. As a result many institutional investors are beginning to consider any company with a market capitalisation of less than £800m as 'small' . . .

In many ways the 800 companies valued below £50m risk being completely ignored, says Paul Myners, a NatWest executive director and part of the City and industry working group behind the DTI report. 'They have got to do something about it; they have got to get out there and beat the drum a bit,' he says.

Source: David Blackwell, *Financial Times*, 9 February 1999, p. 10. Reprinted with permission.

Exhibit 10.42

Ikea 'will never be listed'

FT

Ingvar Kamprad, founder and chairman of Ikea, the world's largest furniture retailer, yesterday ruled out ever taking the company public.

'I will never take the company public because we must be able to take long-term decisions,' he said.

He contrasted Ikea's approach to investments in Russia with those of other international retailers, claiming many had pulled out of the troubled country because of pressure to generate short-term returns.

'The advantage of not being a public company is that we can take decisions when we feel that in the long run they are good decisions,' Mr Kamprad said.

Source: Nicholas George, *Financial Times*, 23 March 1999, p. 37. Reprinted with permission.

Exhibit 10.43

MG Rover can stand alone, says chairman

FT

MG Rover is now capable of surviving indefinitely as an independent British car maker, John Towers, its chairman, said yesterday.

The presumption made by the Phoenix consortium of Midlands businessmen led by Mr Towers, when it bought Rover from BMW for £10 last May, was that it would be revived to the point where it could be seen as a worthwhile purchase or junior partner by a major carmaker . . .

MG Rover, which is wholly owned by its directors, employees and dealers, is to produce a shareholders' statement next month shortly after the first anniversary of the sale. It is expected to show sharply reduced losses and that MG Rover is on course to break even next year . . .

Declaring that MG Rover's cash situation continues to improve, Mr Towers said MG Rover has no need for any external financing.

Mr Towers also said that there was no prospect of a flotation, even if Rover was back in profits in a buoyant market.

'We need the freedom to make decisions on the basis of what we believe to be the long-term interests of the business and to hell with whether or not next month or the month after that is slightly adverse to what the optimum could be,' he said.

Source: John Griffiths, *Financial Times*, 27 April 2001, p. 3. Reprinted with permission.

Exhibit 10.44

Wainhomes to go private in £88m buy-out

FT

Wainhomes yesterday became the latest house-builder to take itself private out of frustration at investors' lack of appetite for smaller company shares . . .

'We feel unloved and unwanted,' Mr Ainscough said yesterday.

'There has been a lack of investor appetite for small company shares over the last two or three years. This made it difficult to fund expansion and acquisitions through the issue of new shares, which is one of the main reasons for going public in the first place.'

Wainhomes has not issued shares since floating in 1994.

Source: Charles Pretzlik, *Financial Times*, 4 March 1999, p. 28. Reprinted with permission.

Exhibit 10.45

Matthews family moves to buy back its turkey business

FT

Bernard Matthews, the Norfolk farmer who rose to fame after advertising his turkeys on television as 'bootiful, really bootiful', is planning to buy back the company that bears his name.

The Matthews family, which still controls almost 42 per cent of the shares, surprised most members of the board yesterday with an announcment that it was 'considering making an offer for the remaining shares in the company'. Mr Matthews, 70 remains executive chairman.

David McCall, a non-executive director, said the timing of the family's announcement had surprised him, although he could see why it would want to take the company private. He said that a quote could be inhibiting when there was no question of raising money in the market, something the company had never done . . .

Another analyst echoed the view that the approach could represent frustration at the low market rating. Over the past 12 months the shares had underperformed the FTSE All-Share index by 15 per cent – before yesterday's jump.

Source: David Blackwell, *Financial Times*, 17 May 2000, p. 25. Reprinted with permission.

Exhibit 10.46

Smaller quoted companies urged to quit market

FT

Smaller quoted companies should stop complaining about flagging share prices, recognise they deserve low ratings and leave the stock market, says a leading British venture capitalist.

Jon Moulton head of the £1bn Alchemy Partners fund, attacked executives and advisers who blamed the City, not internal problems, for poor stock market performance.

Speaking in Birmingham last night, Mr Moulton said many small listed companies should escape the burdens of stock market membership by going private. This would also give them far better access to debt facilities to fund expansion.

His speech – at an event hosted by Eversheds, the solicitors – comes as a direct challenge to smaller quoted companies, many of which argue that institutional investors are too concerned with big blue chip stocks and do not bother to understand them.

In an interview with the Financial Times, Mr Moulton said the best small companies did well and the rest, with some exceptions were correctly marked down.

'The shares will not grow much because the business will not grow much,' he said.

'If you take a typical Midlands traditional-industrial company, it's very unlikely they have good cash flow, profit growth or revenue growth. It's going to deserve a low valuation.'

In the past couple of years there has been a growing stream of companies leaving the stock market through buy-outs. Alchemy has

Exhibit 10.46 continued

backed 10 such public-to-private deals since the beginning of 1997.

Some companies did not follow that route because they believed their stock market ratings would pick up, others were attached to the status that went with running a public company while, in some cases, large shareholders did not want to crystallise capital gains tax liabilities by selling out. However, many small company bosses were frightened of having poor businesses examined in too much detail, he claimed.

'In some cases its down to very unattractive motivations: fat-happy management not wanting to be exposed to the pressures.'

Going private would save £500,000 a year in fees and wasted time on meeting corporate governance guidelines, and would enable long-term planning without the worry of share price fluctutations. Investors would still support good companies.

Many small companies believe they are unfairly tarnished because of their size and their presence in unglamorous sectors. This prejudice depressed their share price and made it difficult to fund expansion by issuing shares. But others in the City privately agree with Mr Moulton that most small companies' problems are of their own making. 'The market is not stupid,' said one corporate financier.

Source: Juliette Jowit, *Financial Times*, 10 October 1999, p. 8. Reprinted with permission.

Exhibit 10.47

Germany's growing listlessness

FT

No sooner have German companies started listing their shares than they are going private again, writes **Uta Harnischfeger**

The chairman of Rolf Benz, a Black Forest manufacturer of designer sofas, knew he had to do something when his company's shares refused to move. 'Even after the most positive piece of news, the stock would not even twitch – we had to ask ourselves about the meaning of being listed,' says Carsten Diercks, recalling the months before selling the business to 3i, the UK private equity company. About 12 months later, Rolf Benz has delisted from the Frankfurt Stock Exchange.

Contrary to the common view that Germany's equity culture is just beginning to develop, some German companies have already started to turn back the clock. Offended by investors' indifference, board members across the country have grown disillusioned with the bourse. As a result, rather than moving into the stock market, numerous companies have started to get out of it.

Estimates suggest that in the past two years about 14 German companies with a market value of about €4bn (£2.5bn) have gone private . . .

More and more companies are likely to go private. Not a week goes by without a German investor magazine printing a list of candidates who are pondering whether to take their publicly listed company private – and, in the long run, off the market altogether. The lists read like a who's who of mid-sized German companies, many of them in sectors such as construction, machinery, plant equipment or automotive supply. Typically such companies have a century-long business history but a relatively brief history on the stock market . . .

Jan Weidner, head of German M&A at Morgan Stanley, argues that small companies are the first to suffer when investors go for the quick money. 'We no longer see such large flows into value funds. In past years the classical value investor has been slaughtered or has pulled out of their type of investing,' says Mr Weidner. 'As a result, smaller companies don't see enough liquidity flowing into them.

'These companies are not even making mistakes – on the contrary, they are doing everything right from the operative point of view. But because their share price doesn't move, there's always the impression that they are doing something wrong.'

Take Honsel, a mid-sized 91-year-old automotive components maker. When customers such as DaimlerChrysler and BMW demanded increasingly large pre-production investments, it looked for a strong industry partner to shoulder such demands – its lagging share price ruled out a capital increase. When that search proved fruitless, it sold the family's 72 per cent stake to Carlyle, the private equity group, and abandoned its decade-old listing. 'Nobody was ever really interested in our share – it just traded along for years,' says Hans-Dieter Honsel, the former chairman. Several months after its delisting, Honsel bought a US components maker and more than doubled its market value to €1.7bn.

Source: Uta Harnischfeger, *Financial Times*, 1 May 2001, p. 14. Reprinted with permission.

Exhibit 10.48

In pursuit of a private life

FT

Richard Branson, Andrew Lloyd Webber, Alan Sugar, and Anita and Gordon Roddick: the roll-call of 1980s entrepreneurs who floated companies on the stock market then thought better of it is growing year by year.

Mr Branson, the bearded, balloon-piloting entrepreneur, floated his Virgin group in 1986, then bought it back in 1988. Mr Lloyd Webber . . . bought back his Really Useful Theatre Group in 1990, four years after floating.

Now the Roddicks' Body Shop, the cosmetics group whose entrepreneurial flair and 'green' products and image made it one of the most successful retail flotations of the 1980s, is in discussions with banks over turning itself into a charitable trust.

Such a move would free the Roddicks to run the business in their own, idiosyncratic way. Rather than paying out millions of pounds in dividends to shareholders, they could use more of their profits to invest in the business and support environmental and humanitarian causes – such as the campaign in support of the Ogoni people of Nigeria . . . Whether or not it is successful, this latest attempt to re-privatise a quoted company raises questions about whether flotation serves the best interests of entrepreneurial businesses, or stifles the initiative and spontaneity that allowed them to develop in the first place.

'When, as with Body Shop, you once had a majority of a company, but now whenever you want to do something you have to spend an inordinate amount of time explaining it to shareholders, you can imagine getting a bit fed up,' says Mr Rod Whitehead, retail analyst at SBC Warburg, the investment bank . . .

The reason behind the idea is a long-standing dissatisfaction with, and mistrust of, the City. Over the past five years, the feeling has become mutual.

Anita Roddick, founder and chief executive, has famously referred to city folk as 'pinstriped dinosaurs', and admits 'finance bores the pants off me'. Her husband Gordon, the chairman, is a shy man who, while admired by some City observers for his acumen, does not enjoy giving presentations . . .

Since flotation, however, Body Shop has faced increasing pressure from institutional investors to adopt a more 'conventional' structure and business approach. It has belatedly acceded to that pressure, appointing a managing director, three new directors, and two non-executive directors.

But the uneasy relationship between the Roddicks and the City has been made frostier by several setbacks in the 1990s, which provoked sharp criticism in the financial world and knocked its share price back to less than half its peak level . . .

Ms Roddick recently renewed her attack on the City's 'short-termism'.

'What is not understood is that companies need time for reflection and reinvention, which is what we have been trying to do for the past two years,' she said.

Analysts suggested yesterday, however, that Body Shop had discovered what several similar companies found before it: that the stock market views unconventional entrepreneurs rather like parents confronted by a prospective son-in-law with a skinhead haircut and tattoos. They may be accepted for a while but, at the first hint of trouble, the market throws up its hands and says: 'We told you so.'

The result is often a share price that languishes well below what the entrepreneur feels is the true worth of the company. It is hardly surprising some are tempted to buy back control.

A stock market shift – the crash of October 1987 – also blighted the quoted career of Mr Branson's Virgin group. But the buyback of Virgin also reflected Mr Branson's frustration that his desire to make decisions in the long-term interest of the business often conflicted with investors' wish for short-term profits and share price performance.

It is perhaps inevitable that entrepreneurs who have built up companies on the strength of their own personality and judgment resent the second-guessing and detailed questioning beloved by analysts and institutional investors.

Both Mr Branson and Mr Lloyd Webber, rather than their shareholders, had the last laugh. Mr Lloyd Webber floated his group for £36m in 1986, bought it back for £77.5m in 1990 and then sold 30 per cent to Polygram, the record company, for £78m a year later. Mr Branson floated Virgin for £242m at 140p a share and bought it back for the same share price, and then sold the music division to Thorn EMI for £510m.

In the short term, the reward for the Roddicks may not be so lucrative. But freedom from the 'pinstriped dinosaurs' may be a big enough incentive.

Source: Neil Buckley and Philip Coggan, *Financial Times*, 1 November 1995. Reprinted with permission.

Exhibit 10.49

JCB chief digs in to keep the business in the family

FT

Sir Anthony Bamford may be eyeing potential acquisitions but he is happy without external shareholders, Peter Marsh talks to him.

Joe Bamford, Sir Anthony's father, set up JCB in 1945 and it has become one of the few UK engineering companies to become a big global player in a sizeable industry. It has also bucked the trend by refusing to sell any of the company to outsiders.

Not having external shareholders to satisfy is 'a very big plus' in terms of being able to run JCB efficiently, according to Sir Anthony, whose father lives in Switzerland and occasionally calls in on Rocester to check on the business. Sir Anthony says the lack of external shareholders means he can 'concentrate on running the company', rather than spending time briefing analysts and other outsiders.

Source: Peter Marsh, *Financial Times*, 16 March 1999, p. 12. Reprinted with permission.

Exhibit 10.50

A simple story of success

FT

A decade or so before the Beatles were turned down for their first recording contract, Mr Joe Bamford had a similar experience at the hands of a credit finance house which decided he had 'little chance of expansion'.

The judgment was harsh even in the early 1950s – Mr Bamford, who had started his business on October 23 1945 at a rented lock-up garage in the Staffordshire town of Uttoxeter, was already expanding fast. Today, as J.C. Bamford Excavators (JCB) celebrates its 50th birthday, it seems singularly perverse.

JCB, still owned by the Bamford family, has grown into one of the few big success stories in postwar British engineering. It is by far the largest UK-owned producer of construction and agricultural equipment . . .

The company has consistently ploughed all its profits back into the business, with a very high rate of investment in products and facilities. It has stayed debt-free, relied almost totally on organic growth, and resisted any temptation to go public or diversify out of construction or agricultural equipment. . . .

The fact that the company has remained in family control has also helped its development, its founders say. This is because its unbureaucratic culture has helped it to react rapidly to changes in market needs.

Sir Anthony says JCB could still have been successful as a public company, but less so than it has been. 'Decision-making is quicker here, and executives do not have to spend 40 per cent of their time talking to the City.'

Going public would have given JCB access to equity capital, and might have enabled it to expand more quickly. But the Bamfords did not want to run the risk of being taken over.

**JCB – The First 50 Years, by John Mitchell. Special Event Books.*

Source: Andrew Baxter, *Financial Times*, 23 October 1995. Reprinted with permission.

Exhibit 10.51

The case for staying private

FT

At a time when the government and banks repeatedly encourage entrepreneurs to finance growth by raising equity, Allan Willett provides a powerful argument for doing exactly the opposite.

Remaining private, says the founder and owner of Willett International, is not only a benefit to the company concerned; it is crucial for the UK economy that dynamic private companies thrive as they do in Germany.

In little more than a decade, Willett has built his coding com-

▶

Exhibit 10.51 continued

pany's turnover to £58m – more than 80 per cent of which is export sales from the UK. He has sought market share, not bottom-line profit, though this is likely to be £3m this year. And apart from his own £711,000 investment, the company has grown entirely with bank debt and retained earnings.

'What I have shown is that you can build a £60m company in the UK and be self-financing,' says Willett. Not only is it possible, but financial self-reliance provides a freedom which high-technology companies actually need, he says.

The view is shared by Israel Wetrin, founder and managing director of Elonex, the UK manufacturer of personal computers and server systems, who is now reluctantly contemplating a flotation.

'Shareholders have a short-term interest in what is happening to the company but they do not understand the long term,' Wetrin says.

'If you decide to increase market share and have a very low margin – for instance to prepare the market for a new product launch in three or six months – shareholders will not understand.'

Low margins are not something Willett has had to suffer. Indeed the company's profitability probably explains how Willett has been able to grow so quickly on a diet of bank debt and retained profits . . .

Willett believes building the company with outside shareholders would have been more difficult. 'Our strategy is to grow sales at 20 per cent a year combined with a 5 per cent pre-tax profit on the bottom line and to pay a 20 per cent tax charge,' says Willett. 'Part of the problem in this country is the obsession with profit. What we are building is shareholder wealth not profit – half of which immediately gets paid away in tax.'

This approach requires strict financial discipline, Willett says. 'If you have a private company you have to accept that you have to live in a straitjacket,' he says.

One rule he has adopted is never to ask banks to provide more debt than the equity already in the company. Another is that group receivables should always be double borrowings. A third is never to capitalise anything – like R&D or the cost of setting up offices in new countries; write them off against profits.

The result is that expansion into new markets has been steady but not spectacularly fast. Typically when Willett moves into a new market, the group will provide up to £500,000 in 'seed money' to set up a new company. After two years a local bank is invited to provide the company with working capital, repaying some of the group's initial investment. The approach is then repeated elsewhere . . .

Domino may now be bigger – with annual sales of £90m – but Willett says there is no contest when comparing growth in shareholder value. 'Domino shareholders have put over £50m into their company which now has a market capitalisation of £139m,' says Willett. 'They have not had three times their money yet.' Linx raised £5m and is valued at about £13m and has given shareholders a torrid time.

For Willett, the sums are very different. 'I am not going to say what it's worth if I sold – which I don't want to do – but I can assure you it's a lot more than three times the £711,000 I put in,' he says.

Howard Whitesmith, Domino Printing Science's managing director since 1990, admires what Willett has achieved and does not argue with his analysis of the relative financial returns.

'He has reaped the benefits of being in a high-growth, high-margin market driven by the information revolution where everyone wants everything coded,' Whitesmith says. 'We have been able to fund a higher level of growth and we are still growing through acquisition. There are challenges to being public – like keeping shareholders informed – and challenges to being private. Both formulas work.'

Willett says there is one important area where being private provides crucial flexibility; the move into a difficult market. And none is more tricky than the US where Videojet has a stranglehold. While part of Willett's business is doing well in the US, the American company has taken a 'hard pounding' in the continuous inkjet market. But it plans to dedicate significant resources to cracking this market, and is preparing what will effectively be a relaunch.

Alan Barrell, Willett managing director and former managing director of Domino, says such a strategy would not wash with shareholders of many companies. 'When I was at Domino everyone was paranoid about half-year results,' says Barrell. He left Domino in 1990 after efforts to make ground in the US ran into trouble.

Where Willett is able to contemplate attacking the US armed only with the group's retained earnings and bank debt, no such luxury exists for Elonex. Wetrin recognises his company needs to sell in the US if it is to build on a significant local UK success and become a global computer manufacturer.

But to launch properly in the US will require £19m which Elonex does not have and which its banks are not prepared to lend. Wetrin is first of all seeking partners in the US or an investor. But he reluctantly accepts that if no deal can be struck with individual investors Elonex will have to float. Inevitably this will require dedication of valuable time to 'screaming shareholders'.

'If you float, you have to understand you have to satisfy shareholders all the time,' Wetrin says. 'It is particularly difficult with technology where markets and products are changing.'

Exhibit 10.51 continued

He wonders whether companies such as Willett can continue to grow without outside resources. 'There comes a time when expansion from own resources becomes very difficult,' says Wetrin. He has grown sales to £150m without substantial outside investment. 'Banks won't lend more and get nervous about further extending overdrafts.'

Willett disagrees and believes he has plenty more to go for. Steady growth, in line with the established pattern, can continue not only in the US but in Asia where sales are growing rapidly from a low base.

More fundamentally, Willett believes private hi-tech companies in the UK need to recognise there is an alternative to flotation. 'It's not that floating companies is wrong,' he says. 'It is just that while some companies should float, some companies definitely should not.'

Source: Richard Gourlay, *Financial Times*, 7 March 1995, p.14. Reprinted with permission.

Exhibit 10.52

Perils of entering the public arena

FT

Drew Scientific found that flotation was not all it was cracked up to be

Two years ago, Keith Drew took his medical diagnostic equipment company public and has since had to live with a string of problems.

Swept along by a wave of interest in biotechnology and diagnostic companies, Drew Scientific floated with a market valuation of £25m though it had a pre-tax profit of only £151,000.

That was the last reported profit. After discovering a faulty component on the only product it made – a machine to help control and manage diabetes – Drew's sole distributor, Siebe, froze all shipments.

Although they subsequently resumed, Drew says Siebe lost interest in a product that would have made a negligible impact on its earnings. The share price plunged, from a launch level of 105p to 19p today, and the company is now capitalised at a little over £4m.

There was, of course, an alternative to flotation in 1993. Drew says the company contemplated a collaboration or expansion through the use of its own resources before the flotation. But it was tempted by Siebe's interest in becoming Drew's global distributor.

'We had been doing business with Siebe in the UK and Europe,' says Drew. 'We had steadily built sales and here was someone saying here is a world market. We thought it was the turning point for the company.'

The company had previously been financed primarily by the families of the founders, Drew and Conor Maxwell, and was manufacturing in a small facility on the outskirts of London. Whereas Drew has been producing five machines a month, Siebe wanted 30. Drew therefore chose to raise £3.4m to build a new factory by selling about a quarter of the company.

'The alternative in hindsight was to go on producing at five or increase to 10 or 15 a month and manage with a slower launch,' Drew says. Instead the company expanded simultaneously in the US, Canada and East Asia, a path that proved disastrous when Siebe froze all shipments.

Drew recognises that the company's fundamental weakness has been its lack of product range and its reliance on only one distributor. Had the company remained private and grown from its own resources and bank finance it would have taken longer to expand into new markets.

But it would have developed relationships with more distributors. And it would also have ended up with more than one product.

Whether Drew Scientific would have survived its manufacturing problem at all had it remained private is a moot point. Without the cash raised in the float the company may not have survived the abrupt halt in the shipment of products.

On the other hand, had it been expanding more slowly, the impact of delayed shipments would have been less dramatic particularly if it was not reliant on one distributor.

Two years after flotation, Drew Scientific is in a financial limbo, bearing all the costs of maintaining a full share listing with no prospect of being able to issue shares to raise more capital in the short term.

Personally, Drew has benefited from flotation, raising £1.3m through the sale of shares. The company also has a new modern facility that meets US Food and Drug Administration standards.

'Probably we are much further on than had we remained private,' Drew says. 'The infrastructure to build and develop are far more advanced.'

But operationally Drew Scientific is behaving as if it had remained private. It is focusing on a few 'core' markets. It is slowly expanding its product range. And it is building a distributor chain – this time making sure that sales of Drew Scientific's machines will make a significant impact on that distributor.

Source: Richard Gourlay, *Financial Times*, 7 March 1995, p. 14. Reprinted with permission.

Exhibit 10.53

Product development vacuum

This is a cautionary tale. Mr James Dyson did the rounds of the banks, venture capital funds and development agencies three years ago to raise money to manufacture his new design for a vacuum cleaner. They all said 'no'.

Mr Dyson was already a millionaire from selling his previous designs to US and Japanese companies, and could afford to fund the launch himself. Three years later he owns 100 per cent of a company with an annual turnover of £55m, which employs 300 people and is about to create another 100 jobs having clinched a £30m export contract to Japan.

Ask venture capitalists why Mr Dyson could not persuade anyone to back him and, after groaning over what might have been their share of his profits, they say it is because they had no way of judging whether his new product would succeed.

Any financial institution must, of course, exercise caution in making investments. For every successful designer like Mr Dyson, there are dozens of crackpots trying to finance ill-fated inventions. But if the institutions cannot find a way of distinguishing the Dysons from the crackpots, they will continue to miss excellent investment opportunities – and the chance to help create new jobs.

It is difficult to see how anyone could have presented a more persuasive case for capital than Mr Dyson, who has a solid record as a designer and businessman.

The son of school teachers, he had studied product design at the Royal College of Art and worked in the engineering industry before starting his own business to manufacture the ballbarrow, a wheelbarrow he designed with a pneumatic ball instead of a wheel.

He became interested in vacuum cleaners when the cleaning machine in his factory broke down. He sold the ballbarrow rights to finance the development of the G-Force, a vacuum cleaner that used a cyclone system, rather than a filter, to separate dirt from air and collected it in a plastic container, not a bag.

Unable to persuade a European manufacturer to make the G-Force, he licensed his design to a Japanese company. It went on sale for £1,200 in 1983 and has since sold more than 300,000 models every year.

Mr Dyson set up a product development unit near his country house in Bath and spent £4.5m of his own money on developing a machine for the mass market, the Dual Cyclone. He needed another £1m to complete the launch, but none of the banks or venture capitalists he initially approached would give it to him.

'I couldn't believe it,' he recalls. 'I'd spent £4.5m of my own money. I had working prototypes with 10 years of research and development behind them. And I already owned a profitable product development company. But they said they didn't like backing designers.'

In the end, Mr Dyson financed the launch of the new model with a £600,000 loan from a bank. The first Dual Cyclone went on sale in spring 1993 for £199. By the end of 1994, Mr Dyson had recovered his investment and his company made pre-tax profits of £1.75m for that year on sales of £10m. By the beginning of 1995 Mr Dyson was ready to launch his second model, a cylinder version of the Dual Cyclone, and to invest another £11m in a new factory. The model is so successful he expects turnover to rise to £55m this year.

Why would no-one back Mr Dyson? Mr Christopher Tennant, a partner in Phildrew Ventures, says one reason may be that venture capitalists suspected they would have difficulty in negotiating good financial terms with him as he was providing such a high proportion of the cash.

However he believes the main reason was the difficulty of predicting whether Mr Dyson's design would succeed. 'If you're assessing a management buy-out, at least you've got the past results to go on,' he says. 'But you don't have that with a new product. Unless the venture capitalist really understands the market, they don't feel qualified to make a judgment.'

The Design Council is trying to find ways of helping innovators raise capital. 'There's a real problem,' says Ms Angela Dumas, research director. 'We want to encourage investment in product development, but we can't expect people to do it on a hunch.'

Other interested bodies include the Department of Trade and Industry's Innovation unit. But the main obstacle to improving access to finance for such people is the absence of precedents. There is no evidence to suggest that Mr Dyson would have found it easier to raise funds in other countries, even in the US.

Ms Dumas is considering commissioning research into why institutions are so unwilling to back product development and then to look at what they need to make them feel more confident about assessing the prospects for new products.

Until a solution is found there is a very real risk of the venture capital community rejecting another James Dyson, who might not be able to afford to go ahead and launch his own company to create a couple of hundred new jobs.

Source: Alice Rawsthorn, *Financial Times*, 22 November 1995. Reprinted with permission.

Exhibit 10.54

Valuable family heirlooms

FT

Propped up in the headquarters' foyer of Claas, Europe's biggest maker of combine harvesters, is an old bicycle. The bike, which belonged to August Claas, the farmer's son who started the business in 1913, is a symbol for staff and visitors to the northern German company of long-standing family ownership.

In a quiet corner of the English midlands is another such symbol – in this case of the family origins of JCB, Europe's biggest construction equipment supplier. A life-sized replica of the garage where Joe Bamford started the business in 1945 stands close to the company's giant factory.

Both companies illustrate the way in which continuity provided by long-standing family ownership – plus relative freedom from short-term shareholder pressures – can be important ingredients for success. These ingredients were also noted by others among the 20 middle-sized German and UK engineering companies studied in this series.

Both Claas and JCB have a second-generation family member at the helm – although in the case of Claas, Helmut Claas, son of the founder, retired two years ago from day-to-day management and now heads the company's supervisory board.

The companies have other similarities. Both are based in rural parts of their respective countries, away from the main industrial centres. They are a similar size, with annual sales of $830m (£512.3m) for Claas and $1.2bn for JCB, and in each case exports account for about two-thirds of turnover. Between them they employ 8,000 people. Each has built a management culture that focuses on product excellence and close links with customers.

Eckart Kottkamp, Claas chief executive, joined the company last year from Jungheinrich, the big German lift-truckmaker. He believes it is the company's private ownership which has enabled it to plan long-term for new products.

He cites as an example the family of Lexion combines, unveiled a year ago, with a development price tag of $35m. The machines use novel electronic systems to measure crop growth, adjusting cutting mechanisms accordingly. A publicly quoted company, continually looking to provide quick returns to shareholders, might have found such a project too risky, says Kottkamp . . .

At JCB, Joe's son, Sir Anthony Bamford, is chairman and managing director. He argues that outside shareholders would never have permitted JCB's long preoccupation with building up sales in the US. It took 13 years for the company to make a profit there, but the US now accounts for 25 per cent of sales.

He also says he can spend his time thinking about new products, rather than than having to worry about share prices and fronting meetings with shareholders and investment analysts. 'We can be single-minded and focused on the business.' . . .

There is a downside, it is often argued, to family ownership. Many such companies are criticised for being too inward-looking and failing to do enough to bring in new people, especially to top management positions.

Source: Peter Marsh, *Financial Times*, 20 June 1997, p. 14. Reprinted with permission.

Exhibit 10.55

Some keep things to themselves

FT

Iain Parker takes about three telephone calls a month from people interested in buying his company – but he always turns them down. 'We are determined to be our own masters. We'd rather invest long-term for the growth of the business than be beholden to an impersonal holding company,' says Parker, chairman of privately owned Otter Controls, which makes thermostats for the domestic appliance and automotive industries.

Parker says that if the 51-year-old company, based in Buxton, Derbyshire, had been publicly quoted, it might not have maintained its record of channelling 10 per cent of sales into new plant and equipment, in good years and bad.

As a result of such policies production volumes have more than tripled in the past 10 years without any changes in staff numbers, and the company is looking for a further doubling of volumes in the next five years while keeping employment stable at about 800.

About 85 per cent of Otter's $48m annual sales are exported.

Parker, who owns and controls the company with other directors and family members, scorns the

▶

Exhibit 10.55 continued

idea that his business needs prodding from outside shareholders to stop it becoming complacent.

'Every day we have customers here from around the world. The personal contact creates its own dynamic and keeps us on our toes,' he says.

Parker's comments illuminate the debate about whether businesses in 'niche' areas of the engineering industry will have a better chance of long-term growth under private or public ownership.

Of 20 companies of this type studied by the *Financial Times*, half in Germany and the rest in the UK, virtually all the German ones are privately owned. The overwhelming view from these companies is that publicly traded equity can hamper growth.

Hartmut Mehdorn, chairman of Heidelberger Druckmaschinen, the world's biggest supplier of printing machinery, says that accenting shareholder value is nothing more than a fashion trend that diverts managers from their customers and technical developments.

Mayer, a company based near Stuttgart, which with sales of $400m a year is the world's biggest maker of circular knitting machines, believes it might have followed many of its UK textile machinery rivals into liquidation in the early 1970s recession, had it not been for the stability and scope for long-term investment conferred by private ownership.

Private ownership is prized at Oxley, a UK-based leader in anti-interference circuitry in the electronics industry. The lack of outside shareholders means that the company can spend 10 per cent to 15 per cent of its $20m annual sales on research and development, much of it linked to manufacturing disciplines.

It has become one of Europe's leaders in the esoteric business of 'micro-machining', in which components such as optical switches are made to submicron accuracy using high-resolution sculpting with X-Rays.

'There is something compelling about this company that makes me want to carry on,' says Ann Oxley, the 61-year-old chairman and 90 per cent owner. She lives in a flat above the plant, tacked on to a converted mansion in Cumbria. On her death the company will automatically come under the control of Geoff Edwards, Oxley's long-serving managing director.

But private ownership is not the only way to success for the niche engineering manufacturer. The experience of a small number of publicly quoted British companies indicates that there is no fundamental block to such businesses becoming leaders in their field. Spirax-Sarco, the world's biggest maker of the steam control systems seen in a vast range of industries, from brewing to laundries, has built its business by channelling resources into informing customers of its capabilities . . .

Fortune says his company's stockmarket quotation has not been incompatible with long-term success. 'The stockmarket pressures have had a benign effect through helping us to focus and to improve,' he says.

The experience of German companies in these niche markets would suggest that private ownership has created the breadth and freedom they believe they need for strategic planning.

But British managements are showing that with a strong business focus it is possible to work within the potential strictures of public ownership.

Source: Peter Marsh, *Financial Times*, 30 May 1997. Reprinted with permission.

SELF-REVIEW QUESTIONS

1 What is equity capital? Explain the advantages to the firm of raising capital this way. What are the disadvantages?

2 Distinguish between authorised and issued share capital.

3 What is the par value of a share, and what is the share premium?

4 Are all plcs quoted? Describe both terms.

5 What is a preference share and why might a company favour this form of finance?

6 What would be the characteristics of a cumulative redeemable participating convertible preference share?

7 Why are non-voting shares disliked by the City investing institutions?

8 Why does the United Kingdom Listing Authority impose stringent rules on companies floating on the Official List?

9 Outline the contents of a prospectus in a new issue on the Official List.

10 How might the working lives of directors change as a result of their company gaining a quotation?

11 What does a sponsor have to do to help a company float?

12 Describe the role of each of the institutions and professional organisations that assist a company in floating on the Official List.

13 What are an offer for sale by tender and an introduction of a new issue? Which is the cheaper method of flotation?

14 List the differences between a flotation on AIM and the OL.

15 What are, and why do the UK authorities insist upon, pre-emption rights?

16 Why are placings surrounded by strict rules concerning the extent of price discount?

17 What adjustments need to be made to a balance sheet after a scrip issue?

18 Suggest circumstances when a firm may find the selling of warrants advantageous.

19 What do business angels bring to a firm?

20 What are the following: MBO, MBI, BIMBO, a venture capital fund, Seedcorn, 3i?

QUESTIONS AND PROBLEMS

1 (*Examination level*) Bluelamp plc has grown from a company with £10,000 turnover to one with a £17m turnover and £1.8m profit in the last five years. The existing owners have put all their financial resources into the firm to enable it to grow. The directors wish to take advantage of a very exciting market opportunity but would need to find £20m of new equity capital as the balance sheet is already over-geared (i.e. has high debt). The options being discussed, in a rather uninformed way, are flotation on the Official List of the London Stock Exchange, a flotation on the Alternative Investment Market and venture capital. Write a report to enlighten the board on the merits and disadvantages of each of these three possibilities.

2 In what circumstances would you advise a company to float on the Alternative Investment Market (AIM) in preference to the Official List (OL)?

3 Checkers plc is considering a flotation on the Official List of the London Stock Exchange. Outline a timetable of events likely to be encountered which will assist management planning.

4 Describe the three costs associated with gaining a flotation on a stock exchange by selling shares to new shareholders.

5 Discuss the merits and problems of the pre-emption right for UK companies.

6 Explain why failure to carry through a plan to raise capital by floating on the London Stock Exchange Official List might be highly disruptive to a firm.

7 There are a number of different methods of floating a company on the new issue market of the London Stock Exchange Official List (e.g. offer for sale). Describe these and comment on the ability of small investors to buy newly issued shares.

8* Mahogany plc has an ordinary share price of £3 and is quoted on the Alternative Investment Market. It intends to raise £20m through a one-for-three rights issue priced at £2.

a What will the ex-rights price be?

b How many old ordinary shares were in circulation prior to the rights issue?

c Patrick owns 9,000 shares and is unable to find the cash necessary to buy the rights shares. Reassure Patrick that he will not lose value. How much might he receive from the company?

d What is the value of a right on one old share?

e What do the terms cum-rights and ex-rights mean?

f Advise Mahogany on the virtues of a deep-discounted rights issue.

9 Venture capital funds made an internal rate of return of 16.4 per cent on investments up to the end of 2000. Describe the role of venture capitalists in the UK economy and comment on the rates of return they generally intend to achieve.

10 Examine the articles in Appendix 10.1 and write an essay advocating the case for avoiding flotation on a recognised investment exchange.

11 Write an essay advocating the case for flotation on a recognised investment exchange.

12 The shareholders of Yellowhammer plc are to offer a one-for-four rights issue at £1.50 when its shares are trading at £1.90. What is the theoretical ex-rights price and the value of a right per old share?

13 Explain the function of a prospectus in a new share issue.

14 What are the main advantages and disadvantages of raising finance through selling **a** ordinary shares, and **b** preference shares?

15 Discuss the main features of venture capital and explain the dangers to an unwary management.

16 Explain placings and offers for sale for new issues and comment on the reasons for the increased use of placings.

17 If business angels are not connected with divine intervention in business matters, seedcorn capital is not something to do with growing food and a captured fund is not theft, what are they and how might they assist a company?

18 If par values are not something to do with golf, bimbos is not an insulting term for women and a pathfinder prospectus is not something to do with scouting, what are they? Explain the context in which these terms are used.

19 (*Examination level*) Imagine that AM Paper (*see* Exhibit 10.56) have appointed you as adviser to the Board of directors. The directors have asked you to explain the relative merits and disadvantages of listing on the Official List of the London Stock Exchange and continuing to be financed by the venture capital. Write an essay to inform them.

Exhibit 10.56

AM Paper to examine options for a sale

FT

HSBC private equity may sell stake as Lancashire-based group heads for 'rapid growth'

AM Paper, the Lancashire-based soft tissues manufacturer, has appointed JP Morgan, the investment bank, to examine options that could lead to a sale.

HSBC Private Equity, which owns 54 per cent of AM, said AM was heading for rapid growth and had to consider ways of financing this.

HSBC may sell its stake to another venture capital investor, in a deal that might value the group at £200m–£250m.

Alan Murphy, AM's founder, stands to gain more than £50m if he sells his 27 per cent stake. It is understood Mr Murphy raised about £100m when he sold part of the business in a restructuring in 1997. AM's other managers own the remaining 19 per cent.

'HSBC Private Equity has received a number of approaches from organisations looking to acquire our investment or form strategic alliances,' said Phil Goodwin, HSBC's director in Manchester. 'We are considering these approaches along with all the other options available, that might include a future listing of the business or a bond issue,'

The private equity firm invested £40m in the company in 1997 as part of a £145m debt and equity package. It put in a further £20m to fund expansion last year . . .

Mr Goodwin said HSBC was delighted with its investment in the group so far, and it was 'far from clear' which route would be taken 'if indeed HSBC decides to realise its investment'. He added it was too early to say what value might be put on the business.

Steve Sealey, chief executive, said yesterday HSBC had been 'very supportive' in its involvement with the group.

'We feel that it is time to look at our options as to how to achieve future growth,' he added.

Source: Sheila Jones and Richard Rivlin, *Financial Times*, 21 May 1999, p. 24. Reprinted with permission.

ASSIGNMENT

Consider the equity base of your company, or one you are familiar with. Write a report outlining the options available should the firm need to raise further equity funds. Also consider if preference share capital should be employed.

CHAPTER NOTES

1 Except that it shows proportional voting and income rights.

2 Responsibility for governing admission to listing, the continuing obligations of issuers, the enforcement of those obligations and suspension and cancellation of listing was transferred from the LSE to the UKLA in 2000

3 Strictly speaking the BP issue was not a new issue because other BP shares were already trading on the market.

4 Breedon and Twinn (1996).

5 Breedon and Twinn (1996), p. 196.

6 *Source:* British Venture Capital Association.

7 *Source:* European Private Equity and Venture Capital Association.

8 See British Venture Capital Association at www.bvca.co.uk for a list of networks.

9 British Venture Capital Association, www.bvca.co.uk.

Chapter 11

LONG-TERM DEBT FINANCE

INTRODUCTION

The concept of borrowing money to invest in real assets within a business is a straightforward one, yet in the sophisticated capital markets of today with their wide variety of financial instruments and forms of debt, the borrowing decision can be a bewildering one. Should the firm tap the domestic bond market or the Eurobond market? Would bank borrowing be best? If so, on what terms, fixed or floating rate interest, a term loan or a mortgage? And what about syndicated lending, mezzanine finance and high-yield bonds? The variety of methods of borrowing long-term finance is infinite. This chapter will outline the major categories and illustrate some of the fundamental issues a firm may consider when selecting its finance mix. As you can see from the extract from the annual accounts of Boots plc (Exhibit 11.1) a firm may need knowledge and understanding of a great many different debt instruments. The terms bonds, notes, commercial paper and Eurobond mentioned in the extract are explained in this chapter. Lease finance and overdrafts are examined in Chapter 12. Swaps are discussed in Chapter 21.

Learning objectives

An understanding of the key characteristics of the main categories of debt finance is essential to anyone considering the financing decisions of the firm. At the end of this chapter the reader will be able to:

- explain the nature and the main types of bonds, their pricing and their valuation;
- describe the main considerations for a firm when borrowing from banks;
- give a considered view of the role of mezzanine and high-yield bond financing as well as convertible bonds, sale and leaseback, securitisation and project finance;
- demonstrate an understanding of the value of the international debt markets;
- explain the term structure of interest rates and the reasons for its existence.

Exhibit 11.1 Loans and other borrowings for Boots plc

Borrowings	Notes	**Group 2000 £m**
Bank loans and overdrafts repayable on demand		**103.1**
Other bank loans and overdrafts	a	**161.3**
Variable rate notes – Sterling	b	**11.8**
– Irish punts	b	**10.5**
Commercial paper		**–**
10.125% bond 2017	c	**47.6**
5.5% eurobond 2009	d	**300.0**
Net liability under currency swaps	e	**8.4**
Obligations under finance leases		**17.1**
		659.8
Amounts included above repayable by instalments		**187.4**
Repayments fall due as follows:		
Within one year:		
– Bank loans and overdrafts		**149.4**
– Obligations under finance leases		**6.9**
– Other borrowings		**54.5**
		210.8
After more than one year:		
– Within one to two years		**45.1**
– Within two to five years		**68.7**
– After five years		**335.2**
		449.0
		659.8

Source: The Boots Company Report and Accounts for the year ended 31st March 2000.

SOME FUNDAMENTAL FEATURES OF DEBT FINANCE

Put at its simplest, debt is something that has to be repaid. Corporate debt repayments have taken the form of interest and capital payments as well as more exotic compensations such as commodities and shares. The usual method is a combination of a regular interest, with capital (principal) repayments either spread over a period or given as a lump sum at the end of the borrowing. Debt finance is less expensive than equity finance, not only because the costs of raising the funds (for example arrangement fees with a bank or the issue costs of a bond) are lower, but because the annual return required to attract investors is less than for equity. This is because investors recognise that investing in a firm via debt finance is less risky than investing via shares. It is less risky because interest is paid out before dividends are paid so there is greater certainty of receiving a return than there would be for equity holders. Also, if the firm goes into liquidation, the holders of a debt type of financial security are paid back before shareholders receive anything.

Offsetting these plus-points for debt are the facts that lenders do not, generally, share in the value created by an extraordinarily successful business and there is an absence of voting power – although debt holders are able to protect their position to some extent through rigorous lending agreements.

When a company pays interest the tax authorities regard this as a cost of doing business and therefore it can be used to reduce the taxable profit. This lowers the effective cost to the firm of servicing the debt compared with servicing equity capital through dividends which are not tax deductible (see Chapters 9 and 10). Thus to the attractions of the low required return on debt we must add the benefit of tax deductibility.

There are dangers associated with raising funds through debt instruments. Creditors are often able to claim some or all of the assets of the firm in the event of non-compliance with the terms of the loan. This may result in liquidation. Institutions which provide debt finance often try to minimise the risk of not receiving interest and their original capital. They do this by first of all looking to the earning ability of the firm, that is, the pre-interest profits in the years over the period of the loan. As a back-up they often require that the loan be secured against assets owned by the business, so that if the firm is unable to pay interest and capital from profits the lender can force the sale of the assets to receive their legal entitlement. The matter of security has to be thought about carefully before a firm borrows capital. It could be very inconvenient for the firm to grant a bank a fixed charge on a specific asset – say a particular building – because the firm is then limiting its future flexibility to use its assets as it wishes. For instance, it will not be able to sell that building, or even rent it without the consent of the bank or the bondholders.

BONDS

A bond is a long-term contract in which the bondholders lend money to a company. In return the company (usually) promises to pay the bond owners a series of interest payments, known as coupons, until the bond matures. At maturity the bondholder receives a specified principal sum called the par, face or nominal value of the bond. This is usually £100 in the UK and $1,000 in the USA. The time to maturity is generally between seven and 30 years although a number of firms, for example Disney, IBM and Reliance of India, have issued 100-year bonds.

Bonds may be regarded as merely IOUs (I owe you) with pages of legal clauses expressing the promises made. These IOUs can usually be traded in the secondary market through securities dealers on the Stock Exchange so that the investor who originally provided the firm with money does not have to hold on to the bond until the maturity date (the redemption date). The amount the investor receives in the secondary market might be more or less than what he paid. For instance, imagine an investor paid £99.80 for a bond which promised to pay a coupon of 9 per cent per year on a par value of £100 and to repay the par value in seven years. If one year after issue interest rates on similar bonds are 20 per cent per annum no one will pay £99.80 for a bond agreement offering £9 per year for a further six years plus £100 on the redemption date. We will look at a method for calculating exactly how much they might be willing to pay later in the chapter.

These negotiable (that is tradeable in a secondary market) instruments come in a variety of forms. The most common is the type described above with regular (usually semi-annual) fixed coupons and a specified redemption date. These are known as straight, plain vanilla or bullet bonds. Other bonds are a variation on this. Some pay coupons every three months, some pay no coupons at all (called zero coupon bonds – these are sold at a large discount to the par value and the investor makes a capital gain by holding the bond), some bonds do not pay a fixed coupon but one which varies depending on the level of short-term interest rates (floating-rate or variable-rate bonds), some have interest rates linked to the rate of inflation. In fact, the potential for variety and innovation is almost infinite. Bonds issued in the last few years have linked the interest rates paid or the principal payments to a wide variety of economic events, such as the price of silver, exchange-rate movements, stock market indices, the price of oil, gold, copper – even to the occurrence of an earthquake. These bonds were generally designed to let companies adjust their interest payments to manageable levels in the event of the firm being adversely affected by some economic variable changing. For example, a copper miner pays lower interest on its finance if the copper price falls. In 1999 Sampdoria, the Italian football club, issued a €3.5m bond that paid a higher rate of return if the club won promotion to the 'Serie A' division. If the club rose to the top four in Serie A the coupon would rise to 14 per cent.

Debentures and loan stocks

The most secured type of bond is called a debenture. They are usually secured by either a fixed or a floating charge against the firm's assets. A fixed charge means that specific assets are used as security which, in the event of default, can be sold at the insistence of the debenture bondholder and the proceeds used to repay them. Debentures secured on property may be referred to as mortgage debentures. A floating charge means that the loan is secured by a general charge on all the assets of the corporation. In this case the company has a large degree of freedom to use its assets as it wishes, such as sell them or rent them out, until it commits a default which 'crystallises' the floating charge. If this happens a receiver will be appointed with powers to dispose of assets and to distribute the proceeds to the creditors. Even though floating-charge debenture holders can force a liquidation, fixed-charge debenture holders rank above floating-charge debenture holders in the payout after insolvency.

The terms bond, debenture and loan stock are often used interchangeably and the dividing line between debentures and loan stock is a fuzzy one. As a general rule debentures are secured and loan stock is unsecured but there are examples which do not fit this classification. If liquidation occurs the unsecured loan stockholders rank beneath the debenture holders and some other categories of creditors such as the tax authorities. In the USA the definitions are somewhat different and this can be confusing. There a debenture is an unsecured bond and so the holders become general creditors who can only claim assets not otherwise pledged. In the USA the secured form of bond is referred to as the mortgage bond and unsecured shorter-dated issues (less than 15 years) are called notes.

Trust deeds and covenants

Bond investors are willing to lower the interest they demand if they can be reassured that their money will not be exposed to a high risk. This reassurance is conveyed by placing risk-reducing restrictions on the firm. A trust deed sets out the terms of the contract between bondholders and the company. The trustees ensure compliance with the contract throughout the life of the bond and have the power to appoint a receiver. The loan agreement will contain a number of affirmative covenants. These usually include the requirements to supply regular financial statements, interest and principal payments. The deed may also state the fees due to the lenders and details of what procedures are to be followed in the event of a technical default, for example non-payment of interest.

In addition to these basic covenants are the negative covenants. These restrict the actions and the rights of the borrower until the debt has been repaid in full. Some examples are as follows.

- ***Limits on further debt issuance*** If lenders provide finance to a firm they do so on certain assumptions concerning the riskiness of the capital structure. They will want to ensure that the loan does not become more risky due to the firm taking on a much greater debt burden relative to its equity base, so they limit the amount and type of further debt issues – particularly debt which is higher (superior) ranking for interest payments and for a liquidation payment. Subordinated debt – with low ranking on liquidation – is more likely to be acceptable.
- ***Dividend level*** Lenders are opposed to money being taken into the firm by borrowing at one end, while being taken away by shareholders at the other. An excessive withdrawal of shareholder funds may unbalance the financial structure and weaken future cash flows.
- ***Limits on the disposal of assets*** The retention of certain assets, for example property and land, may be essential to reduce the lenders' risk.
- ***Financial ratios*** A typical covenant here concerns the interest cover, for example: 'The annual pre-interest pre-tax profit will remain four times as great as the overall annual interest charge'. Other restrictions might be placed on working capital ratio levels, and the debt to net assets ratio. In the case of Photobition the interest cover threshold is 3.25 – *see* Exhibit 11.2.

Exhibit 11.2

Photobition cautions on covenants

FT

Photobition, the Surrey-based graphics business, admitted yesterday it could breach banking covenants over the level of its interest cover if US advertising spending continued to slow down.

The company, which also reported a sharp fall in half-year profits, said net debt has risen to £103.5m (£77.3m) after a number of US acquisitions . . .

Analysts forecast that cover might fall to 2.43 times at the year-end in June, below the required minimum of 3.25.

'If they breach the bank covenants, they will be at the mercy of debt holders,' said one analyst. 'They could have to renegotiate their debt, or make some form of debt-equity conversion. They might also resort to a rights issue.'

Source: Florian Gimbel, *Financial Times*, 28 February 2001, p. 28. Reprinted with permission.

While negative covenants cannot provide completely risk-free lending they can influence the behaviour of the management team so as to reduce the risk of default. The lenders' risk can be further reduced by obtaining guarantees from third parties (for example guaranteed loan stock). The guarantor is typically the parent company of the issuer.

Despite a raft of safeguards the fact that bondholders are still exposed to some degree of risk was brought home painfully to the bondholders in Barings Bank in 1996. They had lent £100m on the understanding that the money would be used for standard merchant banking activities. When they lost their entire investment due to the extraordinary activities of Nick Leeson in the derivatives markets (*see* Chapter 21) their response was to issue writs for compensation from three stockbrokers and a dozen former Barings directors, claiming that misleading information was given about Barings' business when in January 1994 the bond issue was launched.

Repayments

The principal on many bonds is paid entirely at maturity. However, there are bonds which can be repaid before the final redemption date. One way of paying for redemption is to set up a sinking fund that receives regular sums from the firm which will be sufficient, with added interest, to redeem the bonds. A common approach is for the company to issue bonds where it has a range of dates for redemption; so a bond dated 2004–2008 would allow a company the flexibility to repay a part of the principal in cash in each of the four years. Another way of redeeming bonds is for the issuing firm to buy the outstanding bonds by offering the holder a sum higher than or equal to the amount originally paid. A firm is also able to purchase bonds on the open market.

Some bonds are described as 'irredeemable' as they have no fixed redemption date. From the investor's viewpoint they may be irredeemable but the firm has the option of repurchase and can effectively redeem the bonds.

Bond variations

Bonds which are sold at well below the par value are called deep discounted bonds, the most extreme form of which is the zero coupon bond. It is easy to calculate the rate of return offered to an investor on this type of bond. For example, if a company issues a bond at a price of £60 which is redeemable at £100 in eight years the annualised rate of return (r) is:

$$60(1 + r)^8 = 100$$

$$r = \sqrt[8]{\frac{100}{60}} - 1 = 0.066 \text{ or } 6.6\%$$

These bonds are particularly useful for firms with low cash flows in the near term, for example firms engaged in a major property development which will not mature for many years.

A major market has developed recently called the floating rate note (FRN) market (also called the variable-rate note market). Two factors have led to the rapid growth in FRN usage. First, the oscillating and unpredictable inflation of the 1970s and early 1980s caused many investors to make large real-term losses on fixed-rate bonds as the interest rate fell below the inflation rate. As a result many lenders became reluctant to lend at fixed rates on a long-term basis. Secondly, a number of corporations, especially financial institutions, hold assets which give a return that varies with the short-term interest rate level (for example bank loans and overdrafts) and so prefer to hold a similar floating-rate liability. These instruments pay an interest that is linked to a benchmark rate – such as the LIBOR (London Inter-Bank Offered Rate – the rate that banks charge each other for borrowed funds). The issuer will pay, say, 70 basis points (0.7 of a percentage point) over LIBOR. The coupon is set for (say) the first six months at the time of issue, after which it is adjusted every six months; so if LIBOR was 10 per cent, the FRN would pay 10.7 per cent for that particular six months.

There are many other variations on the basic vanilla bond, two of which will be examined later – high-yield bonds and convertible bonds. We now turn to another major source of long-term debt capital – bank borrowing.

BANK BORROWING

An alternative to going to the capital markets to raise money via a public bond issue or a private bond placement is to borrow directly from a bank. In this case a tradeable security is not issued. The bank makes the loan from its own resources and over time the borrowing company repays the bank with interest. Borrowing from banks is attractive to companies for the following reasons.

- ***Administrative and legal costs are low*** Because the loan arises from direct negotiation between borrower and lender there is an avoidance of the marketing, arrangement, regulatory and underwriting expenses involved in a bond issue.
- ***Quick*** The key provisions of a bank loan can be worked out speedily and the funding facility can be in place within a matter of hours.
- ***Flexibility*** If the economic circumstances facing the firm should change during the life of the loan banks are generally better equipped – and are more willing – to alter the terms of the lending agreement than bondholders. Negotiating with a single lender in a crisis has distinct advantages.
- ***Available to small firms*** Bank loans are available to firms of almost any size whereas the bond market is for the big players only.

Factors for a firm to consider

There are a number of issues a firm needs to address when considering bank borrowing.

Costs

The borrower may be required to pay an arrangement fee, say 1 per cent of the loan, at the time of the initial lending, but this is subject to negotiation. The interest rate can be either fixed or floating. If it is floating then the rate will generally be a certain percentage above the banks' base rate or LIBOR. For customers in a good bargaining position this may be 1 or 2 per cent 'over base'. For customers in a poorer bargaining position offering a higher risk proposal the rate could be 5 per cent or more over the base rate. The interest rate will be determined not only by the riskiness of the undertaking and the bargaining strength of the customer but also by the degree of security for the loan and the size of loan – economies of scale in lending mean that large borrowers pay a lower interest rate. A generation ago it would have been more normal to negotiate fixed-rate loans but sharp movements of interest rates in the 1970s and 1980s meant that banks and borrowers were less willing to make this type of long-term commitment. Most loans today are 'variable rate'.

Floating-rate borrowings have advantages for the firm over fixed-rate borrowings.

- If interest rates fall the cost of the loan falls.
- At the time of arrangement fixed rates are usually above floating rates (to allow for lenders' risk of misforecasting future interest rates).
- Returns on the firm's assets may be positively related to times when higher interest rates reign therefore the risk of higher rates is offset.

However floating rates have some disadvantages.

- The firm may be caught out by a rise in interest rates.
- There will be uncertainty about the precise cash outflow impact of the interest.

Security

When banks are considering the provision of debt finance for a firm they will be concerned about the borrower's competence and honesty. They need to evaluate the proposed project and assess the degree of managerial commitment to its success. The firm will have to explain why the funds are needed and provide detailed cash forecasts covering the period of the loan. Between the bank and the firm stands the classic gulf called 'asymmetric information' in which one party in the negotiation is ignorant of, or cannot observe, some of the information which is essential to the contracting and decision-making process. The bank is unable to accurately assess the ability and determination of the managerial team and will not have a complete understanding of the market environment in which they propose to operate. Companies may overcome bank uncertainty to some degree by providing as much information as possible at the outset and keeping the bank informed of the firm's position as the project progresses.

The finance director and managing director need to consider both the quantity and quality of information flows to the bank. An improved flow of information can lead to a better and more supportive relationship. Any firm which has significant bank financing requirements to fund growth will be well advised to cultivate and strengthen understanding and rapport with its bank(s). The time to lay the foundations for subsequent borrowing is when the business does not need the money so that when loans are required there is a reasonable chance of being able to borrow the amount needed on acceptable terms.

Another way for a bank to reduce its risk is to ensure that the firm offers sufficient collateral for the loan. Collateral provides a means of recovering all or the majority of the bank's investment should the firm fail. If the firm is unable to meet its loan obligations then holders of fixed-charge collateral can seize the specific asset used to back the loan. Also, on liquidation, the proceeds of selling assets will go first to the secured loan holders, including floating-charge bank lenders. Collateral can include stocks, debtors and equipment as well as land, buildings and marketable investments such as shares in other companies. In theory banks often have this strong right to seize assets or begin proceedings to liquidate. In practice they are reluctant to use these powers because the realisation of full value from an asset used as security is sometimes difficult and such Draconian action can bring adverse publicity. Banks are careful to create a margin for error in the assignment of sufficient collateral to cover the loan because, in the event of default, assigned assets usually command a much lower price than their value to the company as a going concern. A quick sale at auction produces bargains for the buyers of liquidated assets and usually little for the creditors.

Another safety feature applied by banks is the requirement that the firm abide by a number of loan covenants which place restrictions on managerial action in a similar fashion to bond covenants (*see* section on bonds earlier in this chapter).

Finally, lenders can turn to the directors of the firm to provide additional security. They might be asked to sign personal guarantees that the firm will not default. Personal assets (such as homes) may be used as collateral. This erodes the principle of limited liability status and is likely to inhibit risk-taking productive activity. However for many smaller firms it is the only way of securing a loan and at least it demonstrates the commitment of the director to the success of the enterprise.

Repayment

A firm must carefully consider the period of the loan and the repayment schedules in the light of its future cash flows. It could be disastrous, for instance, for a firm engaging in a capital project which involved large outlays for the next five years followed by cash inflows thereafter to have a bank loan which required significant interest and principal payments in the near term. For situations like these repayment holidays or grace periods may be granted, with the majority of the repayment being made once cash flows are sufficiently positive.

It may be possible for a company to borrow by means of a mortgage on freehold property in which repayments of principal plus interest may be spread over long periods of time. The rate charged will be a small margin over the base interest rate or LIBOR. The main advantage of a mortgage is that ownership of the property remains with the mortgagee (the borrowing firm) and therefore the benefits which come from the ownership of an asset, which may appreciate, are not lost.

A term loan is a business loan with an original maturity of more than one year and a specified schedule of principal and interest payments. It may or may not be secured and has the advantage over the overdraft of not being repayable at the demand of the bank at short notice (*see* Chapter 12). The terms of the loan are usually tailored to the specific needs of the individual borrower and these are capable of wide variation. A proportion of the interest and the principal can be repaid monthly or annually and can be varied to correspond with the borrower's cash flows. It is rare for there to be no repayment of the principal during the life of the loan but it is possible to request that the bulk of the principal is paid in the later years. Banks generally prefer self-amortising term loans with a high proportion of the principal paid off each year. This has the advantage of reducing risk by imposing a programme of debt reduction on the borrowing firm.

The repayment schedule agreed between bank and borrower is capable of infinite variety – four possibilities are shown in Exhibit 11.3.

Exhibit 11.3 Example of loan repayment arrangements

£10,000 borrowed, repayable over four years with interest at 10% p.a. (assuming annual payments, not monthly)

(a)	Time period (years)	1	2	3	4
	Payment (£)	3,155	3,155	3,155	3,155
(b)	Time period (years)	1	2	3	4
	Payment (£)	1,000	1,000	1,000	11,000
(c)	Time period (years)	1	2	3	4
	Payment (£)	0	0	0	14,641
(d)	Time period (years)	1	2	3	4
	Payment (£)	0	1,000	6,000	6,831

The retail and merchant banks are not the only sources of long-term loans. Insurance companies and other specialist institutions such as 3i will also provide long-term debt finance.

SYNDICATED LOANS

For large loans a single bank may not be able or willing to lend the whole amount. To do so would be to expose the bank to an unacceptable risk of failure on the part of one of its borrowers. Bankers like to spread their lending to gain the risk-reducing benefits of diversification. They prefer to participate in a number of syndicated loans in which a few banks each contribute a portion of the overall loan. So, for a large multinational company loan of, say, £500m, a single bank may provide £30m, with perhaps 100 other banks contributing the remainder. The bank originating the loan will usually manage the syndicate and is called the lead manager (there might be one or more lead banks). This bank (or these banks) may invite a handful of other banks to co-manage and underwrite the loan. They help the process of forming the syndicate group of banks in the general syndication. Syndicated loans are available at short notice and can be provided discreetly (helpful if the money is to finance a merger bid, for example). Syndicated loans generally offer lower returns than bonds, but as they rank above most bonds on liquidation payouts there is less risk. The loans carry covenants similar to those on bond agreements. The volume of new international syndicated loans now runs into hundreds of billions of pounds per year.

Pearson needed $6bn of bank loans to finance its purchase of Simon & Schuster in 1998; this is far too much for any one bank to provide. So Goldman Sachs and HSBC put together a syndicated loan package involving a number of banks – *see* Exhibit 11.4. A revolving credit facility gives Pearson the right to draw down short-term loans up to a maximum of $2bn as and when the need arises – this it can do at a number of points over a five-year period. Note that the loans are expected to be tradeable (bought and sold) in a secondary market so banks can sell off some of their loans if they wish to.

Exhibit 11.4

Pearson signs up facility to finance US acquisition

FT

Pearson, the UK media group which owns the *Financial Times*, has signed up $6bn of bank facilities to finance its acquisition of Simon & Schuster, the US publisher, and refinance outstanding syndicated loans. It is the latest in a line of substantial acquisitions to be financed through the syndicated loan market, following Texas Utilities' recent $11bn loan to fund its purchase of The Energy Group and jumbo loans from Imperial Chemical Industries and BAT Industries.

The new financing package has been put together by Goldman Sachs and HSBC and includes a $2.5bn five-year term loan, a $2bn five-year revolving credit and a $1.5bn 364-day loan. Investors expect the loans to be tradeable. This has become commonplace in the US but was only introduced to the euroloan market last year with the $8.5bn loan to ICI to finance its acquisition of Unilever's speciality chemicals business.

There has been considerable reluctance by European corporates to have bankers trading out of loans. The *quid pro quo*, in theory, is more attractive financing. Details of the terms of the loan were not available yesterday. A broader underwriting group will be put together in the next 10 days.

Pearson's credit rating from Standard & Poor's, the rating agency, has been put on negative outlook as a result of the acquisition, but its shares rose sharply yesterday.

Source: Simon Davies, *Financial Times*, 19 May 1998, p. 40. Reprinted with permission.

CREDIT RATING

Firms often pay to have their bonds rated by specialist credit-rating organisations. The debt rating depends on the likelihood of payments of interest and/or capital not being paid (that is, default) and on the extent to which the lender is protected in the event of a default by the loan contract (the recoverability of the debt). UK government gilts have an insignificant risk of default whereas unsecured subordinated corporate loan stock has a much higher risk. We would expect that firms which are in stable industries and have conservative accounting and financing policies and a risk-averse business strategy would have a low risk of default and therefore a high credit rating. Companies with a high total debt burden, a poor cash flow position, in a worsening market environment causing lower and more volatile earnings, will have a high default risk and a low credit rating. Several organisations provide credit ratings, including Moody's and Standard & Poor's (S&P) based in the USA and Fitch IBCA in Europe (owned by a French company). The highest rating is AAA or Aaa (triple-A rated). Such a rating indicates very high quality. The capacity to repay interest and principal is extremely strong. Single A indicates a strong capacity to pay interest and capital but there is some degree of susceptibility to impairment as economic events unfold. BBB indicates adequate debt service capacity but vulnerability to adverse economic conditions or changing circumstances. B and C rated debt has predominantly speculative characteristics. The lowest is D which indicates the firm is in default. Ratings of BBB– (or Baa3 for Moody's) or above are regarded as 'investment grade' – this is important because many institutional investors are permitted to invest in investment grade bonds only (*see* Exhibit 11.5). Bonds rated below this are called high-yield (or junk) bonds. The specific loan is rated rather than

Exhibit 11.5 A comparison of Moody's and Standard & Poor's rating scales

Standard & Poor's	*Moody's*	*Comments*
AAA	Aaa	Investment grade bonds
AA+	Aa1	
AA	Aa2	
AA–	Aa3	
A+	A1	
A	A2	
A–	A3	
BBB+	Baa1	
BBB	Baa2	
BBB–	Baa3	
BB+	Ba1	Non-investment grade high-yield 'junk' bonds
BB	Ba2	
BB–	Ba3	
B+	B1	
B	B2	
B–	B3	
CCC+	Caa1	
CCC	Caa2	
CCC–	Caa3	
CC	Ca	
C	C	

the borrower. If the loan does not have a rating it could be that the borrower has not paid for one, rather than implying anything sinister. Plus or minus signs, '+' or '–', may be appended to a rating to denote relative status within major rating categories.

The rating and re-rating of bonds is followed with great interest by borrowers and lenders and can give rise to some heated argument – *see* Exhibit 11.6.

Exhibit 11.6

UPC slams Moody's debt downgrade

FT

UPC, the European cable communications company, on Friday strongly disputed a downgrade in its debt rating, but investor worries over its funding brought falls in its share and bond prices . . .

The agency downgraded its senior notes, already carrying junk-bond status at B2, to Caa1 and said the outlook for the rating remained negative. The move affects $8.4bn of UPC debt.

Mark Schneider, UPC chairman, said: 'We are very disappointed, and fundamentally disagree with this analysis.' The company continued to meet all its financial targets, he maintained, and had 'significant liquidity in place' to fund its operations.

He added that the rating revision would not affect either its interest bill or other terms of its existing credit facilities. UPC shares, down 13 per cent at one stage, rallied to close 2.2 per cent lower at €6.32 on Friday. However, they remain below their flotation level of two years ago.

UPC's euro-denominated bonds reacted immediately to the downgrade, falling 9 points on Friday to approximately 55 per cent of their face value. Traders said prices then rose towards the end of the day, to around 60 per cent of face value.

UPC's bonds have been trading at relatively low levels for many months, reflecting worries about the company's credit quality. Analysts said the bond market had expected a downgrade, but not one as aggressive as Moody's announced.

Source: Gordon Cramb, *Financial Times*, 23 April 2001, p. 31. Reprinted with permission.

Credit ratings are of great concern to the borrowing corporation because bonds with lower ratings tend to have higher costs. Even enormous telecommunication concerns can run into difficulties and increase the risk for their lenders – *see* Exhibit 11.7. Examples of ratings on long-term instruments are given in Exhibit 11.8.

Exhibit 11.7

Credit rating agencies show their teeth

FT

Recent telecoms downgradings highlight more aggressive stance

Downgradings of the credit ratings of European telecommunications operators in the past six months has brought the work of Fitch, Moody's Investors Service and Standard & Poor's to the attention of a wider spectrum of spectators.

While fuelling demands for an insight into the agencies' inner workings and rating procedures, the downgradings have highlighted their shift towards a more aggressive ratings stance.

During the emerging market crisis of 1997/98, rating agencies were accused of being too slow to spot risks and were urged by the International Monetary Fund and others to change the way they rated countries.

Similar accusations were levelled last year about companies in the European telecoms sector, which took on tens of billions of new debt

Exhibit 11.7 continued

to pay the €100bn bill for acquiring third generation mobile phone licences in Europe.

But Chris Legge, head of corporate ratings at S&P, denies that agencies were not quick enough to downgrade telecoms companies during 2000.

'The two key elements of our work are to be right and to be early, but not necessarily to be first,' Mr Legge says . . .

Last September, Moody's downgraded companies including KPN and France Telecom and said it would give them 12–18 months to reduce their debt in line with their new ratings.

Soon after, equity markets became more hostile to telecoms companies and sensitive to their growing debt burdens, and the prospects of raising cash through asset disposals and initial public offerings receded.

After Orange's disappointing IPO, the rating agencies felt they could not wait any longer.

Further cuts from Fitch, Moody's and S&P have followed in the past few weeks, in some cases surprising the debt and equity markets.

When earlier this month Moody's cut France Telecoms rating just two days after assigning it a stable outlook, investors and bankers were angry that they were not given a warning.

Moody's say the cut was prompted by extra information from France Telecom but that the nature of the information had to be kept confidential . . .

The incident has led to accusations of opaqueness.

Although they pride themselves on their impartiality, agencies derive most of their income from the companies they rate. They frown on the practice of giving unsolicited ratings and depend on the fact that companies need to be rated to borrow in the corporate bond market.

Initial ratings are available for a standard cost in the region of €45,000. After that the cost of ratings coverage depends on its size.

One issue of concern to investors is the extent to which agency analysts are subject to intense pressure from companies to accept their version of events.

In the telecoms industry, company chairman and chief executives have been the ones telling ratings analysts their strategies.

'Rating agencies are subject to a powerful lobby from the companies they rate, which needs to be taken into account,' says Mark Wauton, executive director of fixed income at UBS Asset Management.

However many investors feel ratings only exist as a guide, and fund managers should be able to do their own analysis. 'Rating agencies can be wrong, and fund managers are paid to make up their own minds and spot investment opportunities,' says Marino Valensise at Baring Asset Management.

Source: Aline van Duyn and Rebecca Bream, *Financial Times*, 27 February 2001, p. 34. Reprinted with permission.

Long-term credit ratings history

BT	S&P	Moody's	**Deutsche Telekom**	S&P	Moody's
Feb 2000	**AA plus**	**Aa1**	Feb 2000	**AA minus**	**Aa2**
Apr 24 2000	**Put on neg watch**	–	Apr 28 2000	**Put on neg watch**	–
May 4 2000	–	**Put on neg watch**	Jun 22 2000	–	**Put on neg watch**
Aug 24 2000	**Cut to A**	–	Oct 5 2000	–	**Cut to A2**
Sep 6 2000	–	**Cut to A2**	Oct 6 2000	**Cut to A minus***	–
Feb 16 2001	**Put on neg watch**	–	**KPN**		
France Telecom			Feb 2000	**AA, with neg watch**	**Aa1***
Feb 2000	**AAminus**	**Aa2**	May 22 2000	–	**Cut to Aa2***
May 30 2000	–	**Put on neg watch**	Sep 1 2000	**Cut to A minus***	–
Aug 23 2000	**Cut to A***	–	Sep 7 2000	–	**Cut to A3**
Sep 18 2000	–	**Cut to A1**	Dec 13 2000	–	**Put on watch**
Feb 15 2001	–	**Cut to A3**	Jan 15 2001	**Cut to BBB plus***	–
Feb 16 2001	**Cut to A minus**	–	Feb 13 2001	–	**Cut to Baa2**

*With a negative outlook

The ratings in Exhibit 11.8 are for June 2001 and will not necessarily be applicable in future years because the creditworthiness and the specific debt issue can change significantly in a short period. This was illustrated in Exhibit 11.7, which describes the removal of BT's double-A rating to a single A in August 2000. This was to fall to A– in May 2001. In the late 1990s BT had a triple-A rating. As a consequence its cost of borrowing rose considerably, compounding its problems.

Exhibit 11.8 Examples of ratings on long-term instruments in June 2001

FT

	Currency of borrowing	*S&P*	*Moody's*
UK	€	AAA	Aaa
Spain (Kingdom of)	Yen	AA+	Aa2
Wal-Mart	US$	AA	Aa2
Halifax	£	AA	Aa1
Ford	US$	A	A2
GUS	£	A–	A2
Powergen	€	BBB+	A3
News Corp.	US$	BBB–	Baa3
NTL Comms	€	B–	B2
Argentina	US$	B–	Caa1
Jazztel	€	CCC+	Caa1

Source: *Financial Times*, 25 September 2001, p. 33. Reprinted with permission.

Exhibit 11.9 shows the default rates on bonds of different ratings over different time periods. Those bonds below investment grade have a much higher probability of default than high-grade bonds.

Before examining the data on default rates it is important to appreciate that default is a wide-ranging term, and could refer to any number of events from a missed payment to bankruptcy. For some of these events all is lost from the investor's perspective. For other events a very high percentage, if not all, of the interest and principal is recovered. Hickman (1958) observed that defaulted publicly held and traded bonds tended to sell for 40 cents on the dollar. This average recovery rate rule-of-thumb seems to have held over time. Standard & Poor's published a study of the recovery rates on defaulted bond issues in 1999. They obtained prices of defaulted bonds at the end of the default month for 533 S&P-rated straight-debt issues that defaulted between 1 January 1981 and 1 December 1997. Roughly, investors who liquidate a position in defaulted subordinated securities shortly after default can expect to recover, on average, 36–37 cents in the dollar.

Exhibit 11.9 Standard & Poor's average cumulative default rates by rating category (static pool), 1981–98 (percentage of bonds defaulting)

Rating	*After 1 year %*	*After 5 years %*	*After 10 years %*	*After 15 years %*
AAA	0.00	0.15	0.81	0.81
AA	0.00	0.24	0.78	0.87
A	0.04	0.48	1.53	1.98
BBB	0.22	1.75	3.52	4.06
BB	0.92	8.89	14.58	16.01
B	4.82	20.06	26.49	27.23
CCC	20.39	41.29	45.08	45.08
Investment grade	0.08	0.71	1.76	2.11
Speculative grade	3.83	16.08	22.01	23.03

Source: Standard & Poor's (1999) *Ratings Performance 1998: Stability and Transition*, January.

MEZZANINE DEBT AND HIGH-YIELD (JUNK) BONDS

Mezzanine debt is debt offering a high return with a high risk. It may be either unsecured or secured but ranking behind senior loans. This type of debt generally offers interest rates two to nine percentage points more than that on senior debt and frequently gives the lenders some right to a share in equity values should the firm perform well. It is a kind of hybrid finance ranking for payment below straight debt but above equity – it is thus described alternatively as *subordinated*, *intermediate*, or *low grade*. One of the major attractions of this form of finance for the investor is that it often comes with equity warrants (*see* Chapter 10) or share options attached which can be used to obtain shares in the firm – this is known as an 'equity kicker'. These may be triggered by an event such as the firm joining the stock market.

Mezzanine finance tends to be used when bank borrowing limits are reached and the firm cannot or will not issue more equity. The finance it provides is cheaper (in terms of required return) than would be available on the equity market and it allows the owners of a business to raise large sums of money without sacrificing control. It is a form of finance which permits the firm to move beyond what is normally considered acceptable debt : equity ratios (gearing or leverage levels).

Bonds with high-risk and high-return characteristics are called high-yield (junk) bonds (they are rated below investment grade by rating agencies with ratings of Bs and Cs). These may be bonds which started as apparently safe investments but have now become more risky ('fallen angels') or they may be bonds issued specifically to provide higher-risk finance instruments for investors. This latter type began its rise to prominence in the USA in the 1980s. The US junk bond market has grown from almost nothing in the early 1980s to over $120bn of new issues each year. This money has been used to spectacular effect in corporate America – the most outstanding event was the $25bn takeover of RJR Nabisco using primarily junk bonds. The rise of the US junk bond market meant that no business was safe from the threat of takeover, however large – *see* Case study 11.1 on Michael Milken.

CASE STUDY 11.1

The junk bond wizard: Michael Milken

While studying at Wharton Business School in the 1970s Michael Milken came to the belief that the gap in interest rates between safe bonds and high-yield bonds was excessive, given the relative risks. This created an opportunity for financial institutions to make an acceptable return from junk bonds, given their risk level. At the investment banking firm Drexel Burnham Lambert, Milken was able to persuade a large body of institutional investors to supply finance to the junk bond market as well as provide a service to corporations wishing to grow through the use of junk bonds. Small firms were able to raise billions of dollars to take over large US corporations. Many of these issuers of junk bonds had debt ratios of 90 per cent and above – for every $1 of share capital $9 was borrowed. These gearing levels concerned many in the financial markets. It was thought that companies were pushing their luck too far and indeed many did collapse under the weight of their debt. The market was dealt a particularly severe blow when Michael Milken was convicted of fraud, sent to jail and ordered to pay $600m in fines. Drexel was also convicted, paid $650m in fines and filed for bankruptcy in 1990. The junk bond market was in a sorry state in the early 1990s, with high levels of default and few new issues. However it did not take long for the market to recover. In 1993 $69.1bn was raised in junk bond issues and the annual amount raised has stayed well above $40bn since then.

The high-yield bond is much more popular in the USA than in Europe because of the aversion (constrained by legislation) to such instruments in the major financial institutions. The European high-yield bond market is in its infancy. The first high-yield bonds denominated in European currencies were issued as recently as 1997 when Geberit, a Swiss/UK manufacturer, raised DM 157.5m by selling 10-year bonds offering an interest rate which was 423 basis points higher than the interest rate on a 10-year German government bond (bund). Since then there have been over 100 issues. Nevertheless the European high-yield market remains about one-tenth the size of the US one. If the bond issue by Messer Griesheim (*see* Exhibit 11.10) is anything to go by, the European market will one day challenge the American one for leadership.

Exhibit 11.10

Messer Griesheim pulls off record high-yield bond

FT

Messer Griesheim, the German industrial gases group spun off from Aventis has completed the largest ever deal in the European high-yield bond market.

Proceeds from the €550m bond issue will help finance Messer's €1.8bn ($1.57m) leveraged buy-out by Allianz Capital Partners and Goldman Sachs Private Equity in January, one of Europe's biggest buy-outs to date.

Conditions are ripe for new junk bond deals, analysts say, as investors are cash-rich and the flow of new issues has dwindled after a hectic New Year . . .

The bonds were priced at a spread of 548 basis points over German government bonds, a yield of almost 10.4 per cent, and traders said that on Friday they were already trading well above their issue price. The B2/B plus-rated issue was arranged by Goldman Sachs.

Other large European high-yield deals, such as KPN Qwest's €500m issue in January this year, have so far been confined to the telecoms sector and issues from industrial borrowers tend to be small and illiquid. The telecoms sector, having been largely responsible for the market's dismal performance in 2000, remains out of favour with investors.

Source: Rebecca Bream, *Financial Times*, 14 May 2001, p. 28. Reprinted with permission.

Even though the high-yield bond market has not developed as strongly on this side of the Atlantic there has been a rapid growth in mezzanine finance. It has proved to be particularly useful to managers involved in a management buyout (MBO) which by necessity requires high levels of debt, that is, leveraged buyouts (LBOs). A typical LBO would have a financial structure as follows:

- 60 per cent from senior bank or other debt providers;
- 25–30 per cent from subordinated debt – for example, mezzanine finance, unsecured low-ranking bonds and/or preference shares;
- 10–15 per cent equity.

Fast-growing companies also make use of mezzanine finance. It has proved a particularly attractive source for cable television companies, telecommunications and some media businesses which require large investments in the near term but also offer a relatively stable profits flow in the long-term.

Exhibit 11.11 describes the importance of the mezzanine finance market in Europe.

Exhibit 11.11

Flexibility catches eye of investors

Mezzanine investors take higher risks than bond buyers but get higher returns

While bond markets have been buffeted by volatility in recent months, private markets such as mezzanine debt have come into their own and impressed investors with their flexibility.

Mezzanine debt has long been used by mid-cap companies in Europe and the US as a funding alternative to high yield bonds or bank debt. This product ranks between senior bank debt and equity in a company's capital structure, and mezzanine investors take higher risks than bond buyers but are rewarded with equity-like returns . . .

Sources of new funds raised

% (1999)

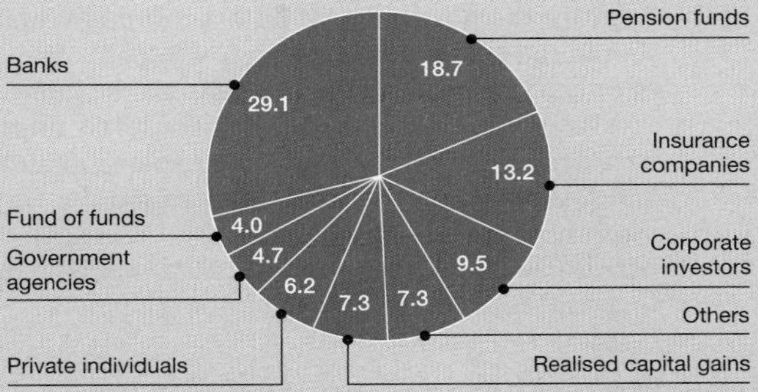

Source: Global Private Equity 2000

Companies that are too small to tap the bond markets have been the traditional users of mezzanine debt, but it is increasingly being used as part of the financing package for larger leveraged acquisition deals. Although mezzanine has been more expensive for companies to use than junk bonds, the recent spread widening in the high yield debt markets has closed this source of funding and has made mezzanine look better value . . .

'There has been a lot of hype over the past few years about high yield bonds crowding out mezzanine debt, but now the situation is reversing,' says Simon Collins, head of debt advisory services at KPMG . . .

The structures of leveraged finance transactions are evolving to cope with with the increased market volatility, and a greater use of mezzanine debt is part of this trend . . .

The characteristics of the mezzanine market make it well-suited to LBO deals – money can be raised quickly and discreetly as companies negotiate directly with mezzanine funds. 'There are inherent advantages to using mezzanine over high yield bonds. It is more flexible, offers better call protection and can be structured specifically for each deal,' says Mark Brunault, executive director at Pricoa.

New investors are being drawn to the European mezzanine market in search of higher returns, as illustrated by the burgeoning number of new funds established this year. In July, Mezzanine Management raised one of the largest independent mezzanine funds in the European market, worth $525m. Its first investment was a $12m mezzanine finance and equity injection into UK media monitoring company Xtreme Information . . .

Many of the funds in the mezzanine market are cash rich, because of the popularity of the product and due to the current lack of major investment opportunities . . .

Mezzanine fund managers are unlikely to rush into deals, though, having recently been reminded of the risks involved in the mezzanine market. At the start of October Finelist, the car parts distributor that was bought by French rival Autodis in March, went into receivership. The €505m buy-out had been financed with leveraged loans and €275m of mezzanine debt, and had one of the largest deals in the European mezzanine market.

Finelist's collapse was triggered when it broke financial covenants on its debt, and receivers Ernst & Young have since been readying the business for sale and looking into allegations of financial irregularities. While the bank lenders have a good chance of recovering their money, the mezzanine lenders risk losing their subordinated investment. Goldman Sachs, which arranged the buy-out's financing, is thought to hold more than half of the imperilled mezzanine debt in its Mezzanine Partners II fund.

New European funds raised

€bn

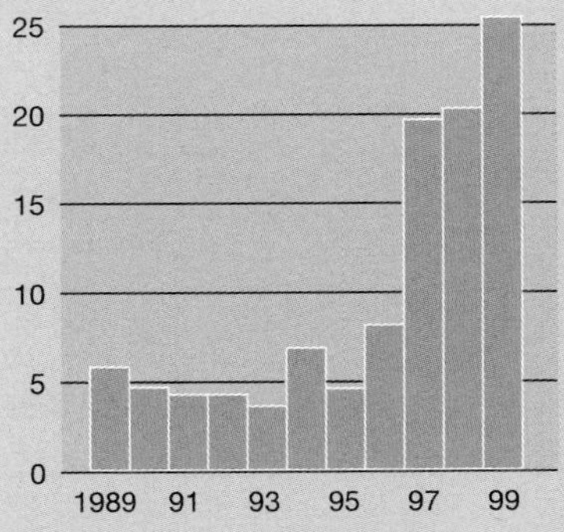

Source: Global Private Equity 2000

Source: Rebecca Bream, *Financial Times*, 3 November 2000, Leveraged Finance, p. 4. Reprinted with permission.

Mezzanine financing has been employed, not only by firms 'gearing themselves up' to finance merger activity, but also for leveraged recapitalisations. For instance, a firm might have run into trouble, defaulted and its assets are now under the control of a group of creditors, including bankers and bondholders. One way to allow the business to continue would be to persuade the creditors to accept alternative financial securities in place of their debt securities to bring the leverage to a reasonable level. They might be prepared to accept a mixture of shares and mezzanine finance. The mezzanine instruments permit the holders to receive high interest rates in recognition of the riskiness of the firm, and they open up the possibility of an exceptionally high return from warrants or share options should the firm get back to a growth path. The alternative for the lenders may be a return of only a few pence in the pound from the immediate liquidation of the firm's assets.

Mezzanine finance and high debt levels impose a high fixed cost on the firm and can be a dangerous way of financing expansion and therefore have their critics. On the other hand, some commentators have praised the way in which high gearing and large annual interest payments have focused the minds of managers and engendered extraordinary performance (*see* Chapter 18). Also, without this finance, many takeovers, buyouts and financial restructurings would not take place.

Financing a leveraged buyout

If the anticipated cash flows are reasonably stable then a highly leveraged buyout may give an exceptional return to the shareholders. Take the case of Sparrow, a subsidiary of Hawk plc. The managers have agreed a buyout price of £10m, equal to Sparrow's assets. They are able to raise £1m from their own resources to put into equity capital and have borrowed £9m. The debt pays an interest rate of 14 per cent and the corporate tax rate is 25 per cent (payable one year after year end). Profits before interest and tax in the first year after the buyout are expected to be £1.5m and will grow at 25 per cent per annum thereafter. All earnings will be retained within the business to pay off debt.

Exhibit 11.12 Sparrow – Profit and Loss Account and Balance Sheet (£000s)

		Years					
		1	2	3	4	5	6
Profit before interest and taxes (after depreciation)		1,500	1,875	2,344	2,930	3,662	4,578
Less interest		1,260	1,226	1,144	999	770	433
		240	649	1,200	1,931	2,892	4,145
Tax		0	60	162	300	483	723
Profits available to pay off debt		240	589	1,038	1,631	2,409	3,422
Balance Sheet				*Year*			
	Opening	1	2	3	4	5	6
Equity	1,000	1,240	1,829	2,867	4,498	6,907	10,329
Debt	9,000	8,760	8,171	7,133	5,502	3,093	0
Assets	10,000	10,000	10,000	10,000	10,000	10,000	10,329

Notes: Past tax liabilities have been accepted by Hawk. Money set aside for depreciation is used to replace assets to maintain £10m of assets throughout. Also depreciation equals capital allowances used for tax purposes.

In the first few years the debt burden absorbs a large proportion of the rapidly increasing profits. However it only takes six years for the entire debt to be retired. The shareholders then own a business with assets of over £10m, an increase of over tenfold on their original investment. The business is also producing a large annual profit which could make a stock market flotation attractive, in which case the value of the shares held by the management will probably be worth much more than £10m.[1]

CONVERTIBLE BONDS

Convertible bonds carry a rate of interest in the same way as vanilla bonds, but they also give the holder the right to exchange the bonds at some stage in the future into ordinary shares according to some prearranged formula. The owner of these bonds is not obliged to exercise this right of conversion and so the bond may continue until redemption as an interest-bearing instrument. Usually the *conversion price* is 10–30 per cent greater than the existing share price. So if a £100 bond offered the right to convert to 40 ordinary shares the conversion price would be £2.50 which, given the market price of the shares of, say, £2.20, would be a *conversion premium* of:

$$\frac{2.50 - 2.20}{2.20} = 0.136 \text{ or } 13.6\%$$

In a rising stock market it is reasonable to suppose that most convertible bonds issued with a small conversion premium will be converted to shares. However this is not always the case. Northern Foods (with the brand names Express Dairies, Eden Vale, Fox's Biscuits, Palethorpe Sausages, Pork Farms and Bowyers) issued convertible bonds in February 1993. The issue raised £91.28m. The bonds were to be redeemed in 15 years if they had not been converted before this and were priced at a par value of £100. The coupon was set at 6.75 per cent and the conversion price was at 326p per share. From this information we can calculate the *conversion ratio*:

$$\text{Conversion ratio} = \frac{\text{Nominal (par) value of bond}}{\text{Conversion price}} = \frac{£100}{£3.26} = 30.67 \text{ shares}$$

The conversion price was set at a premium of 18.11 per cent over the ordinary share price at the time of pricing which was 276p ((326 – 276)/276 = 18.11%). At the time of the issue many investors may have looked at the low interest rate on the convertible (for 15-year bonds in 1993) and said to themselves that although this was greater than the dividend yield on shares (4–5 per cent) it was less than that on conventional bonds, but offsetting this was the prospect of capital gains made by converting the bonds into shares. If the shares rose to, say, £4, each £100 bond could be converted to 30.67 shares worth 30.67 × £4 = £122.68. Unfortunately the share price by mid-2001 had fallen to about £1.54 and so the conversion right had not gained any intrinsic value – perhaps by the year 2008 it will be worthwhile exchanging the bonds for shares. In the meantime the investors at least have the comfort of a £6.75 coupon every year.

The value of a convertible bond (also called an 'equity-linked bond') rises as the value of ordinary shares increases, but at a lower percentage rate. If the share price rises above the conversion price the investor may exercise the option to convert if he/she anticipates that the share price will at least be maintained. If the share price rise is seen to be temporary the investor may wish to hold on to the bond. If the share price falls or rises by only a small amount the value of the convertible will be the same as a straight bond at maturity.

Exhibit 11.13 Summary of convertible bond technical jargon

- **Conversion ratio** This gives the number of ordinary shares into which a convertible bond may be converted:

$$\text{Conversion ratio} = \frac{\text{Nominal (par) value of bond}}{\text{Conversion price}}$$

- **Conversion price** This gives the price of each ordinary share obtainable by exchanging a convertible bond:

$$\text{Conversion price} = \frac{\text{Nominal (par) value of bond}}{\text{Number of shares into which bond may be converted}}$$

- **Conversion premium** This gives the difference between the conversion price and the market share price, expressed as a percentage:

$$\text{Conversion premium} = \frac{\text{Conversion price} - \text{Market share price}}{\text{Market share price}} \times 100$$

- **Conversion value** This is the value of a convertible bond if it were converted into ordinary shares at the current share price:

$$\text{Conversion value} = \text{Current share price} \times \text{Conversion ratio}$$

Most convertible bonds are unsecured but as the Case study on Greenhills shows, this is not always the case – a good thing for Hunter Ground.

CASE STUDY 11.2 Secured convertible debentures

Greenhills

The first AIM-traded company to go into receivership was Greenhills, the restaurant operator. A major investor, Hunter Ground, appointed administrative receivers on 4 December 1996. Hunter Ground held secured convertible debentures from Greenhills worth £506,000.

Source: *Investors Chronicle*, 20 December 1996, p. 11. Reprinted with kind permission of the *Investors Chronicle*.

Advantages to the company of convertible bonds

Convertible bonds have the following advantages to the company.

1 ***Lower interest than on a similar debenture*** The firm can ask investors to accept a lower interest on these debt instruments because the investor values the conversion right. This was a valuable feature for many dot.com companies in the late 1990s. Companies such as Amazon and AOL could pay 5–6 per cent on convertibles – less than half what they would have paid on straight bonds. In 1999 one-quarter of all US convertible issues were by internet companies.

2 ***The interest is tax deductible*** Because convertible bonds are a form of debt the coupon payment can be regarded as a cost of the business and can therefore be used to reduce taxable profit.

3 *Self liquidating* When the share price reaches a level at which conversion is worthwhile the bonds will (normally) be exchanged for shares so the company does not have to find cash to pay off the loan principal – it simply issues more shares. This has obvious cash flow benefits. However the disadvantage is that the other equity holders may experience a reduction in earnings per share and dilution of voting rights.

4 *Fewer restrictive covenants* The directors have greater operating and financial flexibility than they would with a secured debenture. Investors accept that a convertible is a hybrid between debt and equity finance and do not tend to ask for high-level security, impose strong operating restrictions on managerial action or insist on strict financial ratio boundaries – notwithstanding the case of Greenhills (*see* Case study 11.2).

5 *Underpriced shares* A company which wishes to raise equity finance over the medium term but judges that the stock market is temporarily underpricing its shares may turn to convertible bonds. If the firm does perform as the managers expect and the share price rises, the convertible will be exchanged for equity.

Advantages to the investor

The advantages of convertible bonds to the investor are as follows.

1 They are able to wait and see how the share price moves before investing in equity.

2 In the near term there is greater security for their principal compared with equity investment, and the annual coupon is usually higher than the dividend yield.

The terms associated with each issue of convertible bonds can vary considerably. In the case of BPB Industries, the plasterboard giant (*see* Case study 11.3) the bonds issued in 1993 offer the holders the right to convert between 1993 and 2008 while giving the company the power to redeem the bonds from 1998 to 2008.

CASE STUDY 11.3 Convertible subordinated bonds

BPB plc

'On 23 February 1993 the company issued £64 million 7.25 per cent convertible subordinated bonds, convertible at the bondholders' option into 24.8 million ordinary shares of the company at a price of 258p per share at any time from 27 April 1993 to 18 August 2008. The company may redeem the bonds, in full or in multiples of £5 million nominal, at any time from 8 September 1998 to 25 August 2008. The bonds are unsecured and rank after all creditors, but before ordinary shareholders.'

The reader may like to look up the current share price of BPB plc (formerly BPB Industries plc) and calculate a conversion value to gain some impression of the return made by the convertible bond investors in this instance.

Source: BPB Industries plc Annual Report 1996. Reprinted by permission of BPB plc. (Note that these bonds were withdrawn in 2000.)

The bonds sold may not give the right to conversion into shares of the issuers, but shares of another company held by the issuer – *see* the cases of Hutchison and Whampoa, Telecom Italia and France Telecom in Exhibit 11.14. Note that the term exchangeable bond is probably more appropriate in these cases.

Exhibit 11.14

Brakes applied to convertible bond market

FT

One of Europe's most active periods of issuance has been slowed by volatile equities, writes **Rebecca Bream**

The European convertible bond market kicked off the year with the most active period for new issues that many can remember. Not only were there high volumes of business but the deals were among the biggest the market had seen. But since March the volatility in the equity markets has taken its toll, and the hectic pace of new issues has slowed.

The first quarter saw €13.8bn of European equity-linked issuance, up almost 50 per cent from the first quarter of 2000's figure of €9.2bn. This compares to about €37bn of convertible issuance globally, and a 16 per cent decrease of issuance in the US . . .

In January Hong Kong conglomerate Hutchison Whampoa sold $2.65bn of bonds exchangeable into shares of Vodafone, the UK mobile phone operator. Hutchison had been gradually divesting its stake in the UK group since completing a $3bn exchangeable bond deal last September.

This was followed at the end of the month by Telecom Italia which sold €2bn of bonds exchangeable into shares of subsidiaries Telecom Italia Mobile and Internet operator Seat.

In February France Telecom sold €3.3bn of bonds exchangeable into shares of Orange, completed at the same time as the mobile unit's IPO, and one of the biggest exchangeable bond deals ever sold in Europe.

The deals were helped along by the fact that money had flowed into dedicated convertible bond funds at the end of 2000, both buy-and-hold accounts and arbitrage-driven hedge funds, and investor demand outstripped supply.

Source: Rebecca Bream, *Financial Times*, 6 April 2001, p. 35. Reprinted with permission.

VALUING BONDS

Bonds, particularly those which are traded in secondary markets such as the London Stock Exchange, are priced according to supply and demand. The main influences on the price of a bond will be the general level of interest rates for securities of that risk level and maturity. If the coupon is less than the current interest rate the bond will trade at less than the par value of £100. Take the case of an irredeemable bond with an annual coupon of 8 per cent. This financial asset offers to any potential purchaser a regular £8 per year for ever. When the bond was first issued general interest rates for this risk class may well have been 8 per cent and so the bond may have been sold at £100. However interest rates change over time. Suppose that the rate demanded by investors is now 10 per cent. Investors will no longer be willing to pay £100 for an instrument that yields £8 per year. The current market value of the bond will fall to £80 (£8/0.10) because this is the maximum amount needed to pay for similar bonds given the current interest rate of 10 per cent. If the coupon is more than the current market interest rate the market price of the bond will be greater than the nominal (par) value. Thus if markets rates are 6 per cent the irredeemable bond will be priced at £133.33 (£8/0.06).

The formula relating the price of an irredeemable bond, the coupon and the market rate of interest is:

$$P_D = \frac{i}{k_D}$$

where P_D = price of bond
i = nominal annual interest (the coupon rate × nominal value of the bond)
k_D = market discount rate, annual return required on similar bonds

Also:

$$V_D = \frac{I}{k_D}$$

where V_D = total market value of bonds
I = total annual nominal interest

We may wish to establish the market rate of interest represented by the market price of the bond. For example, if an irredeemable bond offers an annual coupon of 9.5 per cent and is currently trading at £87.50, with the next coupon due in one year, the rate of return is:

$$k_D = \frac{i}{P_D} = \frac{9.5}{87.5} = 0.1086 \text{ or } 10.86\%$$

Redeemable bonds

A purchaser of a redeemable bond buys two types of income promise; first the coupon, second the redemption payment. The amount that an investor will pay depends on the amount these income flows are worth when discounted at the rate of return required on that risk class of debt. The relationships are expressed in the following formulae:

$$P_D = \frac{i_1}{1 + k_D} + \frac{i_2}{(1 + k_D)^2} + \frac{i_3}{(1 + k_D)^3} + \ldots + \frac{R_n}{(1 + k_D)^n}$$

and:

$$V_D = \frac{I_1}{1 + k_D} + \frac{I_2}{(1 + k_D)^2} + \frac{I_3}{(1 + k_D)^3} + \ldots + \frac{R^*_n}{(1 + k_D)^n}$$

where i_1, i_2 and i_3 = nominal interest per bond in years 1, 2 and 3
I_1, I_2 and I_3 = total nominal interest in years 1, 2 and 3
R_n and R^*_n = redemption value of a bond, and total redemption of all bonds in year n

The worked example of Blackaby illustrates the valuation of a bond when the market interest rate is given.

Worked example 11.1 Blackaby plc

Blackaby plc issued a bond with a par value of £100 in September 2001, redeemable in September 2007 at par. The coupon is 8% payable annually in September. The facts available from this are:

- the bond might have a par value of £100 but this may not be what investors will pay for it;
- the annual cash payment will be £8 (8 per cent of par);
- in September 2007, £100 will be handed over to the bondholder.

Question 1

What is the price investors will pay for this bond at the time of issue if the market rate of interest for a security in this risk class is 7 per cent?

Answer

$$P_D = \frac{8}{1+0.07} + \frac{8}{(1+0.07)^2} + \frac{8}{(1+0.07)^3} + \ldots \frac{8}{(1+0.07)^6} + \frac{100}{(1+0.07)^6}$$

$$P_D = \text{£}8 \text{ annuity for 6 years @ 7 per cent} = 4.7665 \times 8 = 38.132$$

$$\text{plus } \frac{100}{(1+0.07)^6} = 66.634$$

$$\text{£}104.766$$

Question 2

What is the bond's value in the secondary market in September 2004 if interest rates rise by 200 basis points between 2001 and 2004? (Assume the next coupon payment is in one year.)

Answer

$$P_D = \text{£}8 \text{ annuity for 3 years @ 9 per cent} = 2.5313 \times 8 = 20.25$$

$$\text{plus } \frac{100}{(1+0.09)^3} = 77.22$$

$$\text{£}97.47$$

Note that as interest rates rise the price of bonds falls.

To calculate the rate of return demanded by investors from a particular bond we can compute the internal rate of return. For example Bluebird plc issued a bond many years ago which is due for redemption at par of £100 in three years. The coupon is 6 per cent and the market price is £91. The rate of return now offered in the market by this bond is found by solving for k_D:

$$P_D = \frac{i_1}{1+k_D} + \frac{i_2}{(1+k_D)^2} + \frac{R_n + i_3}{(1+k_D)^3}$$

$$91 = \frac{6}{1+k_D} + \frac{6}{(1+k_D)^2} + \frac{106}{(1+k_D)^3}$$

To solve this requires the skills learned in calculating internal rates of return in Chapter 2. At an interest rate (k_D) of 9 per cent, the right side of the equation amounts to £92.41. At an interest rate of 10 per cent the right-hand side of the equation amounts to £90.05. Using linear interpolation:

Interest rate	9%	?	10%
Value of discounted cash flows	£92.41	£91	£90.05

$$k_D = 9\% + \frac{92.41 - 91}{92.41 - 90.05} \times (10 - 9) = 9.6\%$$

The two types of interest yield

The *Financial Times* quotes two yields for fixed-interest securities. The *interest yield* (also known as the flat yield, income yield and running yield) is the gross (before tax) interest amount divided by the current market price of the bond expressed as a percentage:

$$\frac{\text{Gross interest (coupon)}}{\text{Market price}} \times 100$$

Thus for a holder of Bluebird's bonds the interest yield is:

$$\frac{£6}{£91} \times 100 = 6.59\%$$

This is a gross yield. The after-tax yield will be influenced by the investor's tax position.

Net interest yield = Gross yield $(1 - T)$,

where T = the tax rate applicable to the bondholder

At a time when interest rates are higher than 6.59 per cent it is obvious that any potential purchaser of Bluebird bonds in the market will be looking for a return other than from the coupon. That additional return comes in the form of a capital gain over three years of £100 – £91. A rough estimate of this annual gain is (9/91) ÷ 3 = 3.3 per cent per year. When this is added to the interest yield we have an approximation to the second type of yield, the yield to maturity (also called the redemption yield). The yield to maturity of a bond is the discount rate such that the present value of all the cash inflows from the bond (interest plus principal) is equal to the bond's current market price. The rough estimate of 9.89 per cent (6.59% + 3.3%) has not taken into account the precise timing of the investor's income flows. When this is adjusted for, the yield to maturity is 9.6 per cent – the internal rate of return calculated above. Thus the yield to maturity includes both coupon payments and the capital gain or loss on maturity.

Semi-annual interest

The example of Bluebird given above is based on the assumption of annual interest payments. This makes initial understanding easier and reflects the reality for many types of bond, particularly internationally traded bonds. However UK companies usually issue domestic sterling bonds with semi-annual interest payments. A bond offering a coupon of 9 per cent would pay £4.50 half-way through the year and the remainder at the end. The rate of return calculation on these bonds is slightly more complicated. For example Redwing plc has an 11 per cent bond outstanding which pays interest semi-annually. It will be redeemed in two years at £100 and has a current market price of £96, with the next interest payment due in six months. The redemption yield on this bond is calculated as follows:

Cash flows

Point in time (years)	0.5	1	1.5	2.0	2.0
Cash flow	£5.5	£5.5	£5.5	£5.5	£100

The nominal interest rate over a six-month period is 5.5% (11%/2):

$$96 = + \frac{5.50}{1 + k_D/2} + \frac{5.50}{(1 + k_D/2)^2} + \frac{5.50}{(1 + k_D/2)^3} + \frac{5.50}{(1 + k_D/2)^4} + \frac{100}{(1 + k_D/2)^4}$$

At a rate of 6% for $k_D/2$ the right-hand side equals:

$$5.50 \times 4\text{-period annuity @ } 6\% = 5.50 \times 3.4651 = 19.058$$

$$\text{plus } \frac{100}{(1 + 0.06)^4} = \underline{79.209}$$

$$\underline{\underline{£98.267}}$$

At a rate of 7% for $k_D/2$ the right-hand side equals:

$$5.50 \times 4\text{-period annuity @ } 7\% = 5.50 \times 3.3872 = 18.630$$

$$\text{plus } \frac{100}{(1 + 0.07)^4} = \underline{76.290}$$

$$\underline{\underline{£94.920}}$$

The IRR of the cash flow equals:

$$6\% + \frac{98.267 - 96}{98.267 - 94.92} \times (7 - 6) = 6.68\%$$

The IRR needs to be converted from a half-yearly cash flow basis to an annual basis:

$$(1 + 0.0668)^2 - 1 = 0.1381 \text{ or } 13.81\%$$

INTERNATIONAL SOURCES OF DEBT FINANCE

Larger and more creditworthy companies have access to a wider array of finance than small firms. These companies can tap the *Euro-securities markets* which are informal (unregulated) markets in money held outside its country of origin. For example there is a large market in *Eurodollars*. These are dollar credits and deposits managed by a bank not resident in the USA. This has the distinct advantage of transactions not being subject to supervision and regulation by the authorities in the USA. So, for example, an Italian firm can borrow dollars from a Spanish bank in the UK and the US regulatory authorities have no control over the transaction. There is a vast quantity of dollars held outside the USA and this money is put to use by borrowers. The same applies to all the major currencies – the money is lent and borrowed outside its home base and therefore is beyond the reach of the domestic regulators. Today it is not unusual to find an individual holding a dollar account at a UK bank – a *Eurodeposit* account – which pays interest in dollars linked to general dollar rates. This money can be lent to firms wishing to borrow in Eurodollars prepared to pay interest and capital repayments in dollars. There are large markets in Euromarks, Eurosterling and Euroyen. The title 'Euro' is misleading as this market is not limited to the European currencies or European banks (and is unconnected with the European single currency, the euro). Nowadays, there is daily Eurosecurities business transacted in all of the major financial centres.

The companies which are large enough to use the Eurosecurities markets are able to put themselves at a competitive advantage *vis-à-vis* smaller firms. There are at least four advantages:

- The finance available in these markets can be at a lower cost in both transaction costs and rates of return.

- There are fewer rules and regulations.
- There may be the ability to hedge foreign currency movements. For example, if a firm has assets denominated in a foreign currency it can be advantageous to also have liabilities in that same currency to reduce the adverse impact of exchange-rate movements (*see* Chapter 22).
- National markets are often not able to provide the same volume of finance. The borrowing needs of some firms are simply too large for their domestic markets to supply. To avoid being hampered in expansion plans large firms can turn to the international market in finance.

For these internationally recognised firms there are three sources of debt finance:

a the domestic or national market;

b the financial markets of other countries which make themselves open to foreign firms – *the foreign debt market;*

c the Eurosecurities market which is not based in any one country and is not therefore regulated by any country.

Thus, for example, there are three bond markets available to some firms – as shown in Exhibit 11.15.

Exhibit 11.15 Bond markets

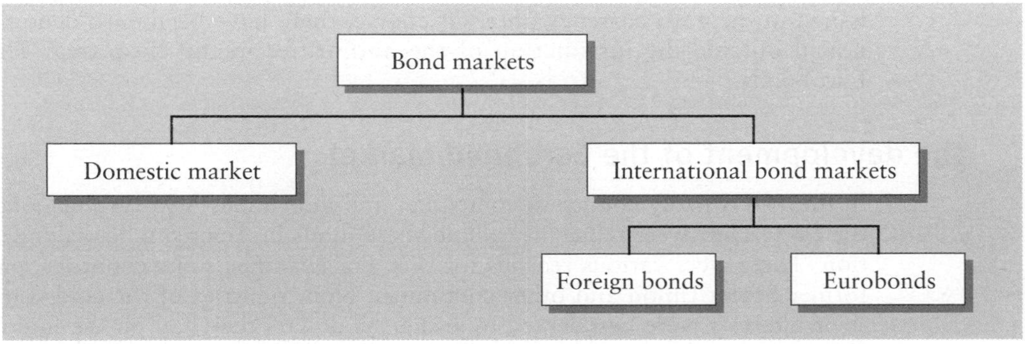

Foreign bonds

A foreign bond is a bond denominated in the currency of the country where it is issued when the issuer is a non-resident. For example, in Japan bonds issued by non-Japanese companies denominated in yen are foreign bonds. (The interest and capital payments will be in yen.) Foreign bonds have been given some amusing names: foreign bonds in Tokyo are known as Samurai bonds, foreign bonds issued in New York and London are called Yankees and Bulldogs respectively. The Netherlands allows foreigners to issue Rembrandt bonds and in Spain Matador bonds are traded. Foreign bonds are regulated by the authorities where the bond is issued. These rules can be demanding and an encumbrance to companies needing to act quickly and at low cost. The regulatory authorities have also been criticised for stifling innovation in the financial markets. The growth of the less restricted Eurobond market has put the once dominant foreign bond market in the shade.

Eurobonds

Eurobonds are bonds sold outside the jurisdiction of the country of the currency in which the bond is denominated. So, for example, the UK financial regulators have little influence over the Eurobonds denominated in Sterling, even though the transactions (for example interest and capital payments) are in pounds. They are medium- to long-term instruments. Eurobonds are not subject to the rules and regulations which are imposed on foreign bonds, such as the requirement to issue a detailed prospectus. More importantly they are not subject to an interest-withholding tax. In the UK most domestic bonds are subject to a withholding tax by which basic rate income tax is deducted before the investor receives interest. Interest on Eurobonds is paid gross without any tax deducted – which has attractions to investors keen on delaying, avoiding or evading tax. Moreover, Eurobonds are bearer bonds which means that the holders do not have to disclose their identity – all that is required to receive interest and capital is for the holder to have possession of the bond. In contrast, UK domestic bonds are registered, which means that companies and governments are able to identify the owners. Bearer bonds have to be kept in a safe place as a thief could benefit greatly from possession of a bearer bond.

Despite the absence of official regulation, the International Securities Market Association (ISMA), a self-regulatory body founded in 1969 and based in Switzerland, imposes some restrictions, rules and standardised procedures on Eurobond issue and trading.

Eurobonds are distinct from euro bonds, which are bonds denominated in euros and issued in the euro currency area. Of course, there have been euro-denominated bonds issued outside the jurisdiction of the authorities in the euro area. These are euro Eurobonds.

The development of the Eurobond market

In the 1960s many countries, companies and individuals held surplus dollars outside of the USA. They were reluctant to hold these funds in American banks under US jurisdiction. There were various reasons for this. For example, some countries, particularly the former Soviet Union and other communist bloc countries of the cold war era, thought their interests were best served by using the dollars they had on the international markets, away from the powers of the US authorities to freeze or sequestrate (seize) assets. More recently this sort of logic has applied to countries such as Iran, Iraq and Libya. Also in the 1960s the American authorities had some very off-putting tax laws and created a tough regulatory environment in their domestic financial markets. These encouraged investors and borrowers alike to undertake transactions in dollars outside the USA. London's strength as a financial centre, the UK authorities' more relaxed attitude to business, and its position in the global time zones, made it a natural leader in the Euro markets. The first Eurobond was issued in the early 1960s and the market grew modestly through the 1970s and then at a rapid rate in the 1980s. By then the Eurodollar bonds had been joined by bonds denominated in a wide variety of Eurocurrencies. The market was stimulated not only by the tax and anonymity benefits, which brought a lower cost of finance than for the domestic bonds, but also by the increasing demand from transnational companies and governments needing large sums in alternative currencies and with the potential for innovatory characteristics. It was further boosted by the recycling of dollars from the oil-exporting countries.

In 1979 less than $20bn worth of bonds were issued in a variety of currencies. As can be seen from Exhibit 11.16 the rate of new issuance is now over $1,900bn a year, with a

Exhibit 11.16 International bond issues

Year ($bn)	*1998*	*1999*	*2000*
Straights – fixed rate	846.9	1,231.5	1,252.7
Equity-related	47.1	52.1	56.5
Floating-rate issues	292.5	484.9	624.3
Total	1,186.4	1,768.5	1,933.5
Amount outstanding of fixed-rate bonds and floating-rate bonds	4,039.2	4,966.2	5,907.7

Source: Bank for International Settlements (BIS) *Quarterly Review,* www.BIS.org, November 2000, March 2001, June 2001, February 2000, March 1999.

total amount outstanding of over $5,900bn. In any one year approximately 30–50 per cent of new bonds are denominated in dollars. Euro-denominated issues account for 30–40 per cent of issues. The yen is the currency of issue for 10–20 per cent of international bonds. Sterling accounts for between 4 and 7 per cent. Even though the majority of Eurobond trading takes place through London, sterling is not one of the main currencies, and what is more, it tends to be large US and other foreign banks located in London which dominate the market.

Types of Eurobonds

The Eurobond market has been extraordinarily innovative in producing bonds with all sorts of coupon payment and capital repayment arrangements (for example, the currency of the coupon changes half-way through the life of the bond, or the interest rate switches from fixed to floating rate at some point). We cannot go into detail here on the rich variety but merely categorise the bonds into broad types.

1 ***Straight fixed-rate bond*** The coupon remains the same over the life of the bond. These are usually made annually, in contrast to domestic bond semi-annual coupons. The redemption of these bonds is usually made with a 'bullet' repayment at the end of the bond's life.

2 ***Equity related*** These take two forms:

   a *Bonds with warrants attached* Warrants are options which give the holder the right to buy some other asset at a given price in the future. An equity warrant, for example, would give the right, but not the obligation, to purchase shares. There are also warrants for commodities such as gold or oil, and for the right to buy additional bonds from the same issuer at the same price and yield as the host bond. Warrants are detachable from the host bond and are securities in their own right, unlike convertibles.

   b *Convertibles* The bondholder has the right (but not the obligation) to convert the bond into ordinary shares at a preset price.

3 ***Floating-rate notes (FRNs)*** Exhibit 11.16 shows the increasing importance of FRNs. These have a variable coupon reset on a regular basis, usually every three or six months, in relation to a reference rate, such as LIBOR. The size of the spread over LIBOR reflects the perceived risk of the issuer. The typical term for an FRN is about five to 12 years.

Within these broad categories all kinds of 'bells and whistles' can be attached to the bonds, for example *reverse floaters* – the coupon declines as LIBOR rises; *capped bonds* – the interest rate cannot rise above a certain level; *zero coupon* – a capital gain only is offered to the lender.

The majority of Eurobonds (more than 80 per cent) are rated AAA or AA and denominations are usually $1,000, $5,000 or $10,000 (or similar large sums in the currency of issue).

It is clear from Exhibit 11.17 that corporations account for a relatively small proportion of the international bond market. The biggest issuers are the banks. Issues by governments ('sovereign issues') and state agencies in the public sector account for about one-fifth of issues. Also strongly represented are governments and international agencies such as the World Bank, the International Bank for Reconstruction and Development and the European Investment Bank.

Exhibit 11.17 Issuers of international bond issues

	Year					
	1998		*1999*		*2000*	
	$bn	%	*$bn*	%	*$bn*	%
Banks and other financial institutions	596.1	50	896.8	51	1,021.4	53
Corporate issuers	261.2	22	476.5	27	478.5	25
Public sector	227.7	19	317.4	18	363.0	19
International institutions	101.4	9	77.8	4	70.7	3
Total	1,186.4	100	1,768.5	100	1,933.5	100

Source: Bank for International Settlements (BIS) *Quarterly Review*, www.BIS.org, November 2000, June 2001.

Issuing Eurobonds

The issuing of Eurobonds is similar to a placing. A bank (lead manager or book runner) or group of banks acting for the issuer invite a large number of other banks or other investors to buy some of the bonds. The managing group of banks is responsible for underwriting the issue and it may enlist a number of smaller institutions to use their extensive contacts to sell the bonds. Exhibit 9.18 on p. 357 in Chapter 9 gave some idea of the relative importance of the Eurobond market to UK-listed firms – in recent years the amount raised on the international market is greater than that raised through domestic debt and equity issues.

Eurobonds are traded on the secondary market through intermediaries acting as marketmakers. Most Eurobonds are listed on the London or Luxembourg stock exchanges but the market is primarily an over-the-counter one, that is, most transactions take place outside a recognised exchange. Deals are conducted using the telephone, computers, telex and fax. The ISMA set up Coredeal, an electronic trading platform for 6,000 international securities, in 2000. It is in competition with many other recently created electronic platforms. In 2002 ISMA plans to launch an internet-based market data service which will provide daily bid and offer quotes on more than 8,000 international debt issues. The extent to which electronic platforms will replace telephone dealing is as yet unclear. Exhibit 11.18 presents the advantages and disadvantages of Eurobonds.

Exhibit 11.18 Advantages and drawbacks of Eurobonds as a source of finance for corporations

Advantage	*Drawback*
1 Large loans for long periods are available. 2 Often cheaper than domestic bonds. The finance provider receives the interest without tax deduction and retains anonymity and therefore supplies cheaper finance. 3 Ability to hedge interest rate and exchange-rate risk. 4 The bonds are usually unsecured. The limitations placed on management are less than those for a secure bond. 5 The lower level of regulation allows greater innovation and tailor-made financial instruments.	1 Only for the largest companies – minimum realistic issue size is about £50m. 2 Bearer securities are attractive to thieves and therefore safe storage is needed. 3 Because interest and capital are paid in a foreign currency there is a risk that exchange-rate movements mean more of the home currency is required to buy the foreign currency than was anticipated. 4 The secondary market can be illiquid.

To conclude the discussion of Eurobonds we will consider a few examples and deal with some of the jargon. The article, 'Russian bond issue raises $1bn' (Exhibit 11.19) describes the history-making return of Russia to the international bond market after an absence of 79 years. Note the high rate of interest Russia has to pay compared with the US Treasury – an extra 3.45 per cent per year. Once trading was under way the buyers pushed the market price of the bond up so that any secondary-market purchasers would only achieve a 3.38 per cent premium over US Treasury notes.

Exhibit 11.19

Russian bond issue raises $1bn

FT

Chernomyrdin hails vote of confidence by international investors

Russia yesterday raised $1bn (£600m) in the bond markets, double the amount it originally thought it could raise, in its first international issue since the 1917 Bolshevik revolution . . .

J.P. Morgan and SBC Warburg, the investment banks that arranged the deal, said 44 per cent of the issue was placed with investors in the US, 30 per cent in Asia and 26 per cent in Europe.

The five-year bonds pay interest of 9.25 per cent semi-annually and were offered to investors at a yield of 9.36 per cent, 345 basis points more than the yield on US Treasury notes. That spread tightened to 338 basis points during trading yesterday on the high demand.

Source: Conner Middelmann and John Thornhill, *Financial Times*, 22 November 1996, p. 24. Reprinted with permission.

On Tuesday to Friday the *Financial Times* carries a small article giving a brief description of the new issues in the international bond market. The issues on Wednesday 13 June 2001 are described in Exhibit 11.20. Notice that a bond raising €800m is not regarded as particularly large (not a 'jumbo transaction'). The 'spread' mentioned is the yield to maturity above that on a government bond of similar maturity. So Washington

Exhibit 11.20

Accor launches €800m issue

FT

The primary market took a breather yesterday, with no jumbo transactions appearing, although preparations for large issues continued.

The deals that were launched focused on the corporate and the bank debt sector. Accor, the French hotel operator rated BBB/BBB+, launched a €800m five-year bond.

It was the company's first bond and the size reflects the growing acceptance of Triple B rated credits in the euro-zone bond markets.

In the secondary market spreads were a touch wider as investors continued to take profits, on renewed concern about the telecommunications sector and ahead of the large amount of new supply in coming weeks.

Roadshows for Deutsche Telekom's euro-dominated bond issue, which could total up to €8bn, will start on June 25 and be completed by June 29. It will be the company's only large international bond sale this year.

Also in telecoms, roadshows for a £500m high-yield bond issue to finance the purchase of Yell, the business directory services firm bought from British Telecommunications in May, will start on July 9.

Source: Aline van Duyn, *Financial Times*, 14 June 2001, p. 32. Reprinted with permission.

Total amount raised in currency shown at the top of each section

Coupon rate

Price of one bond

Fees payable to arrangers and underwriters

Yield spread (premium) compared with appropriate government bond

Lead manager (book runner)

Redemption date

New International bond issues

Borrower	Amount m.	Coupon %	price	Maturity	Fees %	Spread bp	Book-runner
■ US DOLLARS							
Washington Mutual Bk SA(S)	1bn	$6\frac{7}{8}$#(s)	99.816	Dec 2011	0.45	+162$\frac{1}{2}$(Feb 11)	Deutsche/M Stanley
Banc One Corp(a)	500	6.50#	102.118	Feb 2006	–	+114(May06)	Salomon Smith Barney
Rabobank Nederland(b)	250	5.50	97.759	Sep 2008	0.30	+100(May06)	Banc of America Secs
Kumgang Korea Chemical	100	7.625#	99.547R	Jun 2008	0.80R	+270(i)	JP Morgan
■ EUROS(e)							
Dexia Municipal Agency(p.f)	1bn	4.50	99.571R	Jun 2004	0.05R	+17(3$\frac{1}{2}$ Jul04)	Commerzbank/CA1/SSSB
Accor SA	800	(c)	(c)R	Jul 2006	–	+90(swaps)	CDC/JP Morgan/Natexis
BBVA Capital Funding(d,S)	500	5.50	99.829R	Jul 2011	0.35R	+90(5%Feb06)	CSFB/JP Morgan
Muenchener Hypo(g,p)	350	5.00	100.026R	Oct 2006	0.08R	+37(6$\frac{1}{4}$Apr06)	Deutsche/DG/Dresdner
Cartesio, 01–1, Trche B(h)‡	200	(h1)	100.00	Jan 2026	zero	–	Merrill Lynch
International Endesa BV‡	100	(i)	99.83	Jul 2006	0.10	–	Crdt Agricole Indosuez
■ STERLING							
Northern Rock plc‡	100	(k)	100.00	Jul 2003	undiscl	–	HSBC
■ SWISS FRANCS							
Holmes Financing(No4)(m)	850	3.50	100.35	Oct 2006	0.75	–	CSFB

Final terms, non-callable unless stated. Yield spread (over relevant government bond) at launch supplied by lead manager. ‡ Floating-rate note. #Semi-annual coupon. R: fixed re-offer price: fees shown at re-offer level. a) Fungible with $2bn. Plus 139 days accrued. b) Fungible with $500m. Plus 280 days accrued. c) Priced today. d) Callable from 4/7/06 at par. If not called coupon steps to 3ME +110bp. e) Spreads relate to German govt bonds unless stated. f) Spread re French govt bonds. g) Fungible with €2bn. Plus 259 days accrued. h) Secured on loan to TAV, Italian state railway. Av life: 15.73 yrs. h1) 3-mth Euribor +10bp. i) Over interpolated yield. j) 3-mth Euribor +30bp. k) 3-mth Libor +5bp. m) Secured on UK residential mortgages by Abbey National. Legal maturity: 15/10/09. p) Secured on loans to public sector. s) Short 1st. S) Subordinated.

Source: *Financial Times*, 14 June 2001, p. 32.

Mutual pays 1.62 per cent per annum more interest than a US government bond on its $10\frac{1}{2}$-year bond.

The *Financial Times* also publishes a table showing a selection of secondary-market bid prices of actively traded international and emerging market bonds. This gives the reader some idea of current market conditions and rates of return demanded for bonds of different maturities, currencies and riskiness.

Exhibit 11.21

World bond prices

FT

International bonds

Jun 11	Red date	Coupon	S&P* Rating	Moody's Rating	Bid price	Bid yield	Day's chge yield	Mth's chge yield	Spread vs Govts
■ US$									
Pac Bell	07/02	7.25	AA–	Aa3	102.8147	4.46	–0.03	–0.18	+4.46
NY Tel	08/25	7.00	A+	A1	92.3730	7.69	–0.06	–0.21	+2.00
CWE	05/08	8.00	A–	A3	105.7051	6.94	–0.07	–0.16	+1.65
GECC	05/07	8.75	AAA	Aaa	114.0138	5.91	–0.06	–0.14	+0.62
Banc One	08/02	7.25	A–	A1	103.1569	4.35	–0.02	–0.18	+4.35
CNA Fin	01/18	6.95	BBB	Baa1	85.4648	8.61	–0.05	–0.20	+2.92
Lucent	03/29	6.45	BBB–	Baa3	68.2678	9.79	–0.05	–0.49	+4.10
News Corp	10/08	7.38	BBB–	Baa3	100.8905	7.21	–0.06	–0.22	+1.92
TCI Comm	05/03	6.38	A	A3	101.4526	5.54	–0.06	–0.24	+1.45
FHLMC	04/09	5.86	N/A	Aaa	99.8138	5.88	–0.07	–0.21	+0.59
SLMA	05/04	7.01	N/A	Aaa	105.6619	4.88	–0.08	–0.21	+0.79
FNMA	08/28	6.16	N/A	Aaa	95.6238	6.50	–0.05	–0.18	+0.81
FFCB	05/02	5.25	N/A	Aaa	101.1131	3.95	–0.04	–0.24	+3.95
Charter Comm	04/09	8.63	B+	B2	95.5000	–	–	–	–
HMH Prop	08/08	7.88	BB	Ba2	96.5000	–	–	–	–
AMC Ent	02/11	9.50	CCC+	Caa3	90.0000	–	–	–	–
Jun 12									
IBRD	06/10	7.125	AAA	Aaa	107.9800	5.96	–0.07	–0.11	+0.72
Wal-Mart	08/09	6.875	AA	Aa2	104.9500	6.09	–0.05	–0.13	+0.89
Ford	06/10	7.875	A	A2	106.6700	6.87	–0.07	–0.15	+1.63
Viacom	07/10	7.700	A–	A3	106.4700	6.74	–0.04	–0.08	+1.50
■ C$									
Inter Am Dev Bk	06/09	5.625	AAA	Aaa	97.2800	6.06	–0.03	–0.13	+0.44
JP Morgan	03/04	6.875	A+	A2	101.7960	6.13	–0.02	–0.09	+1.03
Prov of Ontario	01/06	7.500	AA	Aa3	107.5900	5.60	–0.07	–0.05	+0.14
Quebec Hydro	07/22	9.625	A+	A2	133.7100	6.63	–0.03	–0.18	+0.72
■ £									
EIB	12/11	5.500	AAA	Aaa	97.4000	5.83	+0.09	+0.15	+0.61
GUS	07/09	6.375	A–	A2	97.0500	6.86	+0.12	+0.09	+1.53
Gallaher	05/09	6.625	BBB+	Baa2	97.3253	7.07	+0.13	+0.22	+1.74
Halifax	04/08	6.375	AA	Aa1	102.0000	6.00	+0.11	+0.23	+0.66
■ SFR									
EIB	01/08	3.750	AAA	Aaa	102.7654	3.27	–0.02	–	+0.03
Italy (REP)	07/10	3.125	AA	Aa3	96.3167	3.61	–0.01	+0.02	+0.27
JP Morgan	01/03	3.750	AA–	A1	100.6177	3.33	+0.01	+0.02	+0.30
Gen Elect.	07/09	3.125	AAA	Aaa	96.9906	3.56	–0.01	–	+0.24
■ YEN									
IBRD (World Bk)	03/03	4.500	AAA	Aaa	107.7810	0.08	–	–0.03	+0.02
Spain (Kingdom)	03/02	5.750	AA+	Aa2	104.3260	0.14	–	+0.03	+0.13
KFW Int	03/10	1.750	AAA	Aaa	107.2010	0.89	–0.02	–0.10	–0.18
Procter & Gamble	06/10	2.000	AA	Aa2	105.4580	1.35	–0.02	–0.09	+0.28
■ A$									
IBRD (World Bk)	02/08	6.000	AAA	Aaa	97.3890	6.49	–0.03	+0.37	+0.61
Queensland Trsy	06/05	6.500	AAA	Aaa	101.8678	5.97	–0.04	+0.44	+0.30
S. Aus Gov Fin	06/03	7.750	AA+	Aa2	103.5030	5.87	–0.03	+0.39	+0.57
Quebec, Provn of	10/02	9.500	A+	A2	104.5000	5.76	–	+0.27	+0.89
■ €									
UK	01/03	4.750	AAA	Aaa	100.557	4.37	+0.02	–0.04	–0.01
Denmark	09/08	4.625	AA+	Aaa	97.199	5.10	+0.02	+0.01	+0.29
Sweden	01/09	5.000	AA+	Aaa	98.869	5.18	+0.01	+0.00	+0.28
ADB	10/07	5.500	AAA	Aaa	101.582	5.20	+0.01	+0.01	+0.47
EIB	04/09	4.000	AAA	Aaa	91.971	5.28	+0.02	+0.05	+0.38
Eurofima	12/09	5.625	AAA	Aaa	101.711	5.36	+0.01	+0.00	+0.46
World Bank	04/05	7.125	AAA	Aaa	107.744	4.85	+0.02	–0.02	+0.27
EDF	10/10	5.750	AA+	Aaa	101.419	5.55	+0.02	+0.05	+0.56
TEPCO	05/09	4.375	AA–	Aa2	92.285	5.61	+0.01	–0.02	+0.71
Iberdrola	05/09	4.500	AA–	A1	91.166	5.93	+0.01	–0.01	+1.03
Powergen (UK)	07/09	5.000	BBB+	A3	94.067	5.95	+0.01	–0.03	+1.05
BNG	10/10	5.625	AAA	Aaa	101.685	5.39	+0.02	+0.00	+0.40
Fortis Fin	04/09	4.625	A+	Aa3	94.596	5.49	+0.01	–0.01	+0.59
Deutsche Finan	07/09	4.250	AA	Aa3	91.979	5.50	+0.01	–0.01	+0.60
Bayer Hypo	01/10	5.625	A+	Aa3	100.340	5.57	+0.01	–0.01	+0.58
Reseau Ferred	04/10	5.250	AAA	Aaa	99.037	5.39	+0.01	–0.01	+0.40
Statoil	06/11	5.125	AA–	A1	93.623	5.99	–0.01	+0.08	+0.91
Alcatel	02/09	4.375	A	A1	87.533	6.48	+0.01	–0.06	+1.58
Marconi	03/10	6.375	BBB+	A3	92.695	7.54	+0.01	–0.40	+2.55
Hypo in Essen	02/03	3.000	AAA	Aaa	97.840	4.39	+0.03	–0.05	+0.01
Euro Hypo	04/06	5.000	AAA	Aaa	100.348	4.91	+0.00	+0.00	+0.26
Depfa	07/08	4.750	AAA	Aaa	97.122	5.25	+0.01	+0.02	+0.44
Rhein Hypo	07/10	5.750	AAA	Aaa	102.090	5.45	+0.00	+0.02	+0.46
Jazztel	12/09	13.250	CCC+	Caa1	47.250	31.27	+0.77	+4.60	+26.37
Huntsman ICI	07/09	10.125	B	B2	101.250	9.89	–0.05	+0.40	+4.99
Kappa Beheer	07/09	10.625	B	B2	108.750	8.85	–0.27	–0.11	+3.95
NTL Comms	11/09	9.875	B	B2	69.750	16.69	+0.08	+2.24	+11.79

US $ denominated bonds NY latest; all other London closing. Yields: Local market standard.
*Standard & Poor's. *Source*: FT Interactive Data.

Emerging market bonds

Jun 12	Red date	Coupon	S&P* Rating	Moody's Rating	Bid price	Bid yield	Day's chge yield	Mth's chge yield	Spread vs Govts
■ EUROPE €									
Poland	03/10	6.000	BBB	Baa1	101.5842	5.76	+0.04	+0.06	+0.52
Slovenia	03/10	6.000	A	A2	101.7899	5.73	+0.01	+0.03	+0.49
Hungary	02/09	4.375	A–	A3	92.5859	5.59	+0.05	+0.09	+0.39
■ LATIN AMERICA $									
Argentina	07/03	10.250	B	B2	74.3136	13.89	–	–1.22	+8.24
Brazil	08/40	11.000	BB–	B1	77.0500	14.29	+1.10	–0.48	+8.62
Mexico	02/10	9.875	BB+	Baa3	110.4400	8.16	–	–0.55	+2.92
■ ASIA $									
China	12/08	7.300	BBB	A3	104.6850	6.50	+0.04	+0.10	+1.37
Philippines	01/19	9.875	BB+	Ba1	88.2900	11.43	–0.08	–0.93	+6.01
South Korea	04/08	8.875	BBB	Baa2	112.8225	6.52	–0.04	–0.08	+1.39
■ AFRICA/MIDDLE EAST $									
Lebanon	10/09	10.250	B+	B1	99.4758	10.34	–0.07	–0.44	+5.14
South Africa	05/09	9.125	BBB–	Baa3	108.0215	7.75	–0.07	–0.60	+2.55
Qatar	06/30	9.750	BBB+	Baa2	113.5097	8.49	–0.07	–0.59	+2.84
■ BRADY BONDS $									
Argentina	03/23	6.000	B	B2	68.2881	9.46	+0.08	–0.95	+3.96
Brazil	04/14	8.000	BB–	B1	76.2500	11.60	+0.02	–0.36	+6.28
Mexico	12/19	6.250	BB+	Baa3	93.1549	6.91	–0.08	–0.46	+1.49
Venezuela	03/20	6.750	B	B2	77.5000	9.30	–0.21	–0.39	+3.86

London closing. *Standard & Poor's. *Source*: FT Interactive Data

Redemption date March 2020

Yield to maturity

Yield spread (premium) on a Viacom bond above the US government rate

Yield spread (premium) above what the US government would have to pay in the yen Eurobond market

Source: *Financial Times*, 15 June 2001. Reprinted with permission.

Euro medium-term notes and domestic medium-term notes

By issuing a note a company promises to pay the holders a certain sum on the maturity date, and in many cases a coupon interest in the meantime. These instruments are unsecured and may carry floating or fixed interest rates. Medium-term notes (MTN) have been sold with a maturity of as little as nine months and as great as 30 years, so the term is a little deceiving. They can be denominated in the domestic currency of the borrower (MTN) or in a foreign currency (EMTN), and are usually sold in relatively small quantities on a continuous or an intermittent basis, as the need for fresh financing arises.

Eurocommercial paper and domestic commercial paper[2]

The issue and purchase of commercial paper is one means by which the largest commercial organisations can avoid paying the bank intermediary a middleman fee for linking borrower and lender. Commercial paper promises to the holder a sum of money to be paid in a few days. The lender buys these short-term IOUs, with an average life of about 40 days (normal range 30–90 days), and effectively lends money to the issuer. Normally these instruments are issued at a discount rather than the borrower being required to pay interest – thus the face value will be higher than the amount paid for the paper at issuance. Large corporations with temporary surpluses of cash are able to put that money to use by lending it directly to other commercial firms at a higher rate of effective interest than they might have received by depositing the funds in a bank. This source of finance is usually only available to the most respected corporations with the highest credit ratings, as it is usually unsecured lending. Standard & Poors and Moody's use a different grading system for short-term instruments (e.g. A–1 or P–1 are the highest ratings). While any one issue of commercial paper is short term it is possible to use this market as a medium-term source of finance by 'rolling over' issues. That is, as one issue matures another one is launched. A commercial paper programme can be set up by a bank whereby the bank (or a syndicate of banks) underwrites a specified sum for a period of five to seven years. The borrower then draws on this by the issue of commercial paper to other lenders. If there are no bids for the paper the underwriting bank(s) buys the paper at a specified price. Eurocommercial paper is issued and placed outside the jurisdiction of the country in whose currency it is denominated.

PROJECT FINANCE

A typical project finance deal is created by an industrial corporation providing some equity capital for a separate legal entity to be formed to build and operate a project, for example an oil pipeline, an electricity power plant. The project finance loan is then provided as bank loans or through bond issues direct to the separate entity. The significant feature is that the loan returns are tied to the cash flows and fortunes of a particular project rather than being secured against the parent firm's assets. For most ordinary loans the bank looks at the credit standing of the borrower when deciding terms and conditions. For project finance, while the parent company's (or companies') credit standing is a factor, the main focus is on the financial prospects of the project itself.

To make use of project finance the project needs to be easily identifiable and separable from the rest of the company's activities so that its cash flows and assets can offer the lenders some separate security. Project finance has been used across the globe to finance power plants, roads, ports, sewage facilities and telecommunications networks. A few recent examples are given in Exhibit 11.22.

Exhibit 11.22

Project finance has funded . . .

FT

A telephone infrastructure

In 2000 Hutchinson UK 3G raised £3bn by way of project finance to part-fund the building of the UK's fifth mobile network. This was three-year debt without recourse to shareholders (*see* below)

A power plant in Indonesia

In 1994 banks lent the developers of the $1.8bn Paiton 1 power plant project $180m with no government guarantees, repayable over eight years at a rate of 2.25 percentage points over LIBOR.

Electricity generating in Victoria

In 1996 banks agreed to lend A$2bn to PowerGen (the UK company) for the development of the coal-fired plant at Yallourn in Victoria, Australia despite the fact that there was no power purchase agreement in place – this is unusual as the lenders like to see reasonable certainty over the cash flows of the project before committing themselves. Here they are taking the risk that the price of electricity might fall.

Source: Based on *Financial Times*, 21 August 1996, p. 15 and *Financial Times*, 27 October 2000.

Project finance has grown rapidly over the last 25 years. Globally, about £50bn is lent in this form per year. A major stimulus has been the development of oil prospects. For the UK, the North Sea provided a number of project finance opportunities. Many of the small companies which developed fields and pipelines would not have been able to participate on the strength of their existing cash flow and balance sheet, but they were able to obtain project finance secured on the oil or fees they would later generate.

There is a spectrum of risk sharing in project finance deals. At one extreme the parent firm (or firms) accepts the responsibility of guaranteeing that the lenders will be paid in the event of the project producing insufficient cash flows. This is referred to as *recourse finance* because the lenders are able to seek the 'help' of the parent. At the other extreme, the lenders accept an agreement whereby, if the project is a failure, they will lose money and have no right of recourse to the parent company. If the project's cash flows are insufficient the lenders only have a claim on the assets of the project itself rather than on the sponsors or developers.

Between these two extremes there might be deals whereby the borrower takes the risk until the completion of the construction phase (for example, provides a completion guarantee) and the lender takes on the risk once the project is in the operational phase. Alternatively, the commercial firm may take some risks such as the risk of cost overruns and the lender takes others such as the risk of a government expropriating the project's assets.

The sums and size of projects are usually large and involve a high degree of complexity and this means high transaction and legal costs. Because of the additional risk to the lenders the interest rates charged tend to be higher than for conventional loans. Whereas a well-known highly creditworthy firm might pay 20 basis points (0.20 per cent) over LIBOR for a 'normal' parent company loan, the project company might have to pay 100 basis points (1 per cent) above LIBOR.

Advantages of project finance

Project finance has a number of advantages.

1 *Transfer of risk* By making the project a stand-alone investment with its own financing, the parent can gain if it is successful and is somewhat insulated if it is a failure, in that other assets and cash flows may be protected from the effects of project losses.

This may lead to a greater willingness to engage in more risky activities which may benefit both the firm and society. Of course, this benefit is of limited value if there are strong rights of recourse.

2 ***Off-balance-sheet financing*** The finance is raised on the project's assets and cash flows and therefore is not recorded as debt in the parent company's balance sheet. This sort of off-balance-sheet financing is seen as a useful 'wheeze' or ploy by some managers – for example, gearing limits can be bypassed. However, experienced lenders and shareholders are not so easily fooled by accounting tricks.

3 ***Political risk*** If the project is in a country prone to political instability, with a tendency towards an anti-transnational business attitude and acts of appropriation, a more cautious way of proceeding may be to set up an arm's length (separate company) relationship with some risk being borne by the banking community, particularly banks in the host country. An example of this sort of risk is given in Exhibit 11.23.

4 ***Simplifies the banking relationship*** In cases where there are a number of parent companies, it can be easier to arrange finance for a separate project entity than to have to deal with each of the parent companies separately.

Exhibit 11.23 'Regulatory risk' exists in many parts of the world . . .

Enron

In 1995 the state of Maharashtra in India suddenly revoked the contract it had with Enron for the construction of a power project, creating major problems for Enron and its bankers.

SALE AND LEASEBACK

If a firm owns buildings, land or equipment it may be possible to sell these to another firm (for example a bank, insurance company or specialised leasing firm) and simultaneously agree to lease the property back for a stated period under specific terms. The seller receives cash immediately but is still able to use the asset. However the seller has created a regular cash flow liability for itself. For example in 2000 Abbey National, the mortgage bank, sold its branch network and its Baker Street head office (221b Baker Street – the home of Sherlock Holmes) totalling 6.5m sq.ft. The 722 branches and head office will be occupied by Abbey National under leases as short as one year, and as long as 20. The objective was to obtain flexibility in accommodation so that the bank can change with its customers and with the industry. It allowed the firm to 'concentrate on banking rather than being property developers, which is not our job' (John Price, director of property, *Financial Times*, 20 October 2000, p. 27).

In 2001 Marks and Spencer planned to sell and then lease back £300m of its high street stores. This followed British Telecommunications £2bn, 7,000-property deal with Land Securities. These deals release cash tied up in assets, allowing the firms to concentrate on what they regard as their core businesses. A number of retailers have used their extensive property assets for sale and leaseback transactions so that they could plough the proceeds into further expansion.

In a number of countries the tax regime also propels sale and leaseback transactions. For example, some property owners are unable to use depreciation and other tax allowances (usually because they do not have sufficient taxable profits). The sale of the asset to an organisation looking to reduce taxable profits through the holding of depreciable assets enables both firms to benefit. Furthermore, the original owner's subsequent lease payments are tax deductible.

A sale and leaseback has the drawback that the asset is no longer owned by the firm and therefore any capital appreciation has to be forgone. Also long lease arrangements of this kind usually provide for the rental payments to increase at regular intervals, such as every three or five years. There are other factors limiting the use of sale and leaseback as a financial tool. Leasing can involve complex documentation and large legal fees, which often make it uneconomic to arrange leases for less than £20m. There is also a degree of inflexibility: for example, unwinding the transaction if, say, the borrower wanted to move out of the property can be expensive. Another disadvantage is that the property is no longer available to be offered as security for loans.

One of the attractions of sale and leaseback is the possibility of flattering the balance sheet. As Exhibit 11.24 makes clear, this practice is being curtailed.

Exhibit 11.24

Watchdog moves against off-balance sheet schemes FT

Listed companies face a crackdown on creative accounting after regulators yesterday signalled that they would not allow sale and leaseback transactions to flatter the performance of companies.

The Financial Reporting Review Panel, an investigative sister body of the Accounting Standards Board, yesterday agreed with Associated Nursing Services, the long-term care provider, that its accounts should be amended.

Sir Neil Macfarlane, chairman of ANS, said the panel's action had 'far reaching implications' for 'hundreds of companies in the UK which have entered into sale and leaseback transactions'.

Under such deals, companies sell fixed assets, such as buildings, to a financial institution or other purchaser, thereby removing the asset's value and any associated liabilities, such as mortgages, from their balance sheets. The purchaser then rents the asset back to the company so that it can go on using it.

In the ANS case, a nursing home was sold on this basis but the terms of the contract were such that the panel concluded that ANS retained many of the rights and risks associated with ownership.

The panel would not comment but it is known that its chairman, Mr Edwin Glasgow QC, wants the City to realise that such off-balance sheet schemes – which greatly reduce a company's gearing – can be in breach of the rules.

Merchant banks, accountants and auditors will see the panel's action as proof that it is prepared to defend the principle that a company's accounts should reflect the substance of a transaction, not just its legal form . . .

ANS entered into a complex sale and leaseback agreement involving a nursing home in which not all the rights and risks were transfered to the purchaser – Nursing Home Properties. The panel said the asset should therefore have stayed on the balance sheet.

Source: Jim Kelly, Accountancy Correspondent, *Financial Times*, 18 February 1997, p. 1. Reprinted with permission.

Hilton Group and Jarvis Hotels have negotiated interesting sale and leaseback deals – *see* Exhibit 11.25.

Exhibit 11.25

Jarvis goes for innovative style of financing

FT

Scheherazade Daneshkhu funds the hotels group opting for a new sale and leaseback

Jarvis Hotels, the midmarket operator, is expected today to return cash to shareholders with money released from a sale and leaseback deal with Royal Bank of Scotland.

It would be the third significant sale and leaseback transaction the bank has struck in the sector this year, following a £312m deal with Hilton Group and last month's £1.25bn deal to help Nomura International fund its £1.9bn purchase of the Le Méridien chain.

Sale and leasebacks, under which the hotel owner sells the freehold to an investor in exchange for a lease and then pays rent, are nothing new.

Charles Forte – now lord Forte – used them to finance his first hotel purchase, the Waldorf in London, in 1958. But the Royal Bank of Scotland deals were the hot topic at a recent London hotels conference because of an innovative type of contract.

The transactions differ from previous deals in that the lease payment is variable and linked to sales. The minimum guaranteed payment is also comparatively low.

In the case of Hilton, Royal Bank paid paid £312m for 11 hotels with a book value of £278m and granted Hilton 20- and 30-year leases.

Hilton is to pay 25 per cent of sales to Royal Bank, expected to total £22.5m this year.

The minimum payment is almost half this amount – £12.5m, or 5 per cent of sales. 'That's a lower turnover than during the Gulf War,' said David Michels, chief executive of Hilton Group.

'I've been around long enough to remember original leasebacks set at 15 per cent and you paid that whatever [the hotels trading conditions]. This arrangement is attractive because we keep our flag on the hotels yet it releases money for overseas expansion.'

The capital raised helped fund Hilton's subsequent £612m acquisition of Scandic Hotels.

The downside is that, unlike sale and leasebacks that give the operator an option to buy back a property if it rises in value above an agreed level, the hotel operator gives away capital appreciation of the assets.

Investors can be wary too of off-balance sheet liabilities but the terms of the Hilton contracts have been well disclosed.

Source: Scheherazade Daneshku, *Financial Times*, 12 June 2001, p. 30. Reprinted with permission.

SECURITISATION

In the strange world of modern finance you sometimes need to ask yourself who ends up with your money when you pay your monthly mortgage, or your credit card bill or the instalment payment on your car. In the old days you would have found that it was the organisation you originally borrowed from and whose name is at the top of the monthly statement. Today you cannot be so sure because there is now a thriving market in repackaged debt. In this market, a mortgage lender, for example, collects together a few thousand mortgage 'claims' it has (the right of the lender to receive regular interest and capital from the borrowers); it then sells those claims in a collective package to other institutions, or participants in the market generally. This permits the replacement of long-term assets with cash (improving liquidity and gearing) which can then be used to generate more mortgages. The borrower is often unaware that the mortgage is no longer owned by the original lender and everything appears as it did before, with the mortgage company acting as a collecting agent for the buyer of the mortgages. The mortgage company usually raises this cash by selling asset-backed securities to other institutions (the 'assets' are the claim on interest and capital) and so this form of finance is often called *asset securitisation*. These asset-backed securities may be bonds sold into a market with many players.

Asset backed securitisation involves the pooling and repackaging of a relatively small, homogeneous and illiquid financial assets into liquid securities.

The sale of the financial claims can be either 'non-recourse', in which case the buyer of the securities from the mortgage firm bears the risk of non-payment by the borrowers, or with recourse to the mortgage lender.

Securitisation has even researched the world of rock. Iron Maiden issued a long-dated $30m asset-backed bond securitised on future earnings from royalties in 1999. It followed David Bowie's $55m bond securitised on the income from his earlier albums and Rod Stewart's $15.4m securitised loan from Nomura. Apparently, some artistes are said to be worried about tarnishing their images by being seen to court the financial markets.

Tussauds has securitised ticket and merchandise sales, Keele University has securitised the rental income from student accommodation and Newcastle United has securitised its future ticket sales. The new issue market in asset-backed bonds in Europe in 2000 amounted to $81bn.

This form of securitisation is regarded as beneficial to the financial system, because it permits banks and other financial institutions to focus on those aspects of the lending process where they have a competitive edge. Some, for example, have a greater competitive advantage in originating loans than in funding them. This is illustrated in the example of Barclays' €1bn securities move (*see* Exhibit 11.26).

Exhibit 11.26

Barclays to issue bond securitised on card debt

FT

Move follows aggressive push by US providers

Barclays Bank is to break new ground in the UK by becoming the first British bank to launch a bond secured against debt owed by consumers to its credit card subsidiary.

The bond, which will total about €1bn (£643m), will also be comfortably the largest credit card securitisation to be arranged by a European bank.

It follows the aggressive move of US credit card providers, such as MBNA and Discover, into the UK and continental European market. A number of US credit card providers have also launched bonds in the European bond market this year.

A securitisation is a bond which is backed up by the collateral of future income streams such as credit card receivables, mortgages, autoloans and even film royalties. 'The Barclays deal is the first of what will probably be a large volume of UK credit card securitisations,' said Tamara Adler, a senior official at Deutsche Bank.

Under a securitisation, the bank removes assets from its balance sheet which allows it to free up regulatory capital originally set aside against those assets. The capital can then be put to more profitable uses without the bank losing its original customer base.

Source: Edward Luce, Capital Markets Editor, *Financial Times*, 12 October 1999, p. 27. Reprinted with permission.

THE TERM STRUCTURE OF INTEREST RATES

Until now we have assumed that the annual interest rate on a debt instrument remained the same regardless of the length of time of the loan. So, if the interest rate on a three-year bond is 7 per cent per year it would be 7 per cent on a five-year bond of the same risk class. However it is apparent that lenders in the financial markets demand different interest rates on loans of differing lengths of time to maturity – that is, there is a term structure of the interest rates. One of these relationships is shown in Exhibit 11.27 for lending to the UK government. This diagram, taken from a 2001 edition of the *Financial Times*, represents the rate of return that the UK government had to offer on its bonds. 'Years' means number of years to maturity. Note that default risk remains constant here; the reason for the different rates is the time to maturity of the bonds. Thus a one-year bond has to offer 5.3 per cent whereas a 20-year bond offers 5.1 per cent.

An upward-sloping yield curve occurs in most years but occasionally we have a situation where short-term interest rates (lending for, say, one year) exceed those of long-term interest rates (say, a 20-year bond). This downward-sloping term structure is shown in Exhibit 11.28(a). It is also possible to have a flat yield curve, like the one shown in Exhibit 11.28(b).

Exhibit 11.27 An approximation to the term structure of interest rates for UK government securities*

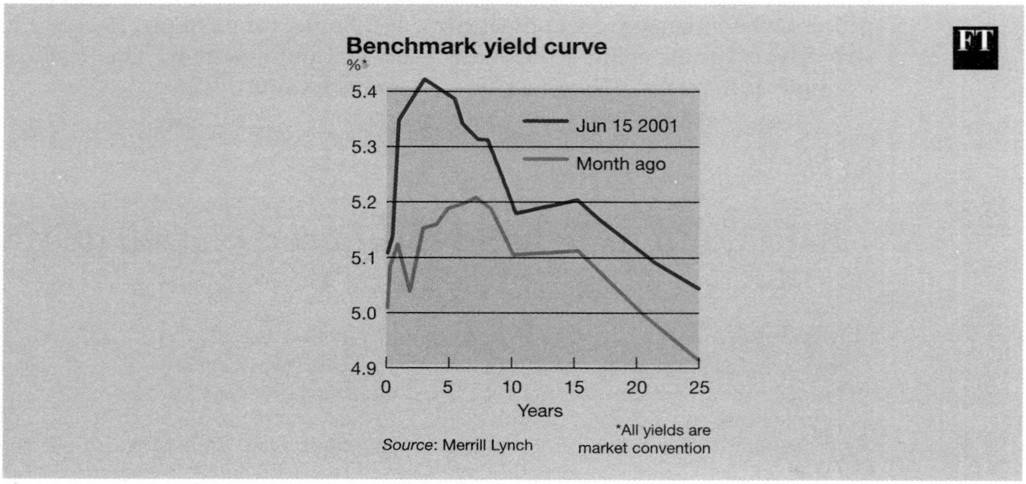

Note: *Using the benchmark yield curve as an example of term structures of interest rates may offend theoretical purity but it is a handy approximate measure and helps illustrate this section.

Source: *Financial Times*, 18 June 2001, p. 28. Reprinted with permission.

Exhibit 11.28 Downward-sloping and flat yield curves

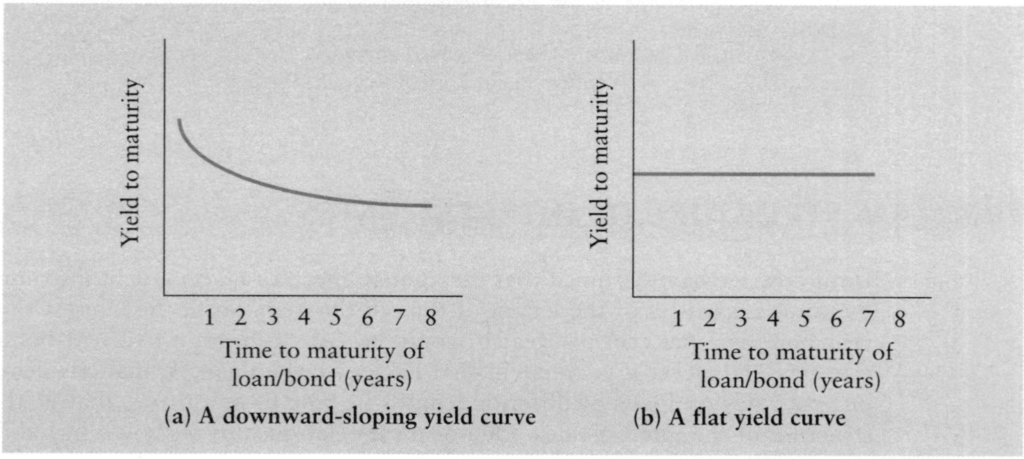

Three hypotheses have been advanced to explain the shape of the yield curve:

a the expectation hypothesis;
b the liquidity-preference hypothesis; and
c the market-segmentation hypothesis.

The expectation hypothesis

The expectation hypothesis focuses on the changes in interest rates over time. To understand the expectation hypothesis you need to know what is meant by a 'spot rate of interest'. The spot rate is an interest rate fixed today on a loan that is made today. So a corporation, Hype plc, might issue one-year bonds at a spot rate of, say, 8 per cent, two-year bonds at a spot rate of 8.995 per cent and three-year bonds at a spot rate of 9.5 per cent. This yield curve for Hype is shown in Exhibit 11.29. The interest rates payable by Hype are bound to be greater than for the UK government across the yield curve because of the additional default risk on these corporate bonds.

Exhibit 11.29 The term structure of interest rates for Hype plc at time 2001

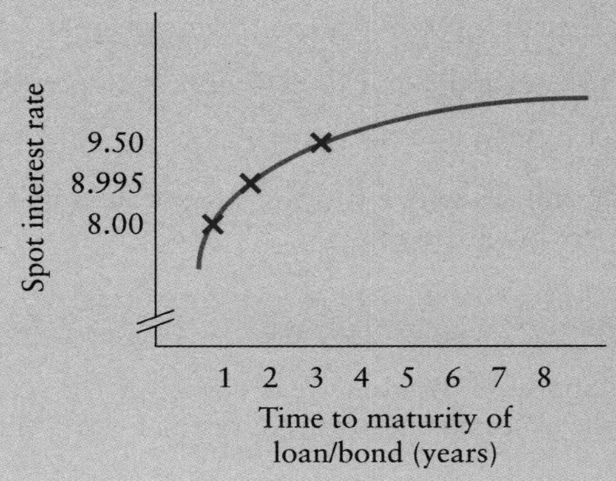

Spot rates change over time. The market may have allowed Hype to issue one-year bonds yielding 8 per cent at time 2001 but a year later (time 2002) the one-year spot rate may have changed to become 10 per cent. If investors expect that one-year spot rates will become 10 per cent at time 2002 they will have a theoretical limit on the yield that they require from a two-year bond when viewed from time 2001. Imagine that an investor (lender) wishes to lend £1,000 for a two-year period and is contemplating two alternative approaches:

1 Buy a one-year bond at a spot rate of 8 per cent; after one year has passed the bond will come to maturity. The released funds can then be invested in another one-year bond at a spot rate of 10 per cent, expected to be the going rate for bonds of this risk class at time 2002.
2 Buy a two-year bond at the spot rate at time 2001.

Under the first option the lender will have a sum of £1,188 at the end of two years:

$$£1{,}000\ (1 + 0.08) = £1{,}080$$

$$£1{,}080\ (1 + 0.1) = £1{,}188$$

Given the anticipated change in one-year spot rates to 10 per cent the investor will only buy the two-year bond if it gives the same average annual yield over two years as the first option of a series of one-year bonds. The annual interest required will be:

$$£1{,}000\ (1 + k)^2 = £1{,}188$$

$$k = \sqrt{(1{,}188/1{,}000)} - 1 = 0.08995 \text{ or } 8.995 \text{ per cent}$$

Thus, it is the expectation of spot interest rates changing which determines the shape of the yield curve according to the expectation hypothesis.

Now consider a downward-sloping yield curve where the spot rate on a one-year instrument is 11 per cent and the expectation is that one-year spot rates will fall to 8 per cent the following year. An investor considering a two-year investment will obtain an annual yield of 9.49 per cent by investing in a series of one-year bonds, viz:

$$£1{,}000\ (1.08)\ (1.11) = £1{,}198.80$$

With this expectation for movements in one-year spot rates, lenders will demand an annual rate of return of 9.49 per cent from two-year bonds of the same risk class.

$$k = \sqrt{(1198.8/1000)} - 1 = 0.0949 \text{ or } 9.49\% \text{ per year}$$

$$\text{or } \sqrt{(1.08)(1.11)} - 1 = 0.0949$$

Thus in circumstances where short-term spot interest rates are expected to fall, the yield curve will be downward sloping.

Worked Example 11.2 SPOT RATES

If the present spot rate for a one-year bond is 5 per cent and for a two-year bond 6.5 per cent, what is the expected one-year spot rate in a year's time?*

Answer

If the two-year rate is set to equal the rate on a series of one-year spot rates then:

$$(1 + 0.05)\ (1 + x) = (1 + 0.065)^2$$

$$x = \frac{(1 + 0.065)^2}{1 + 0.05} - 1 = 0.0802 \text{ or } 8.02\%$$

*In the financial markets it is possible to agree now to lend money in one year's time for, say, a year (or two years or six months, etc.) at a rate of interest agreed at the outset. This is a 'forward'.

The liquidity-preference hypothesis

The expectation hypothesis does not adequately explain why the most common shape of the yield curve is upward sloping. The liquidity-preference hypothesis helps explain the upward slope by pointing out that investors require an extra return for lending on a long-term basis. Lenders demand a premium return on long-term bonds compared with short-term instruments because of the risk of misjudging future interest rates. Putting your money into a ten-year bond on the anticipation of particular levels of interest exposes you to the possibility that rates will rise above the rate offered on the bond at some point in its long life. Thus, if five years later interest rates double, say because of a rise in inflation expectations, the market price of the bond will fall substantially, leaving the holder with a large capital loss. On the other hand, by investing in a series of one-year bonds, the investor can take advantage of rising interest rates as they occur. The ten-year bond locks in a fixed rate for the full ten years if held to maturity. Investors prefer short-term bonds so that they can benefit from rising rates and so will accept a lower return on short-dated instruments. The liquidity-preference theory focuses on a different type of risk attaching to long-dated debt instruments other than default risk – a risk related to uncertainty over future interest rates. A suggested reinforcing factor to the upward slope is that borrowers usually prefer long-term debt because of the fear of having to repay short-term debt at inappropriate moments. Thus borrowers increase the supply of long-term debt instruments, adding to the tendency for long-term rates to be higher than short-term rates.

Note that the word liquidity in the title is incorrectly used – but it has stuck so we still use it. Liquidity refers to the speed and ease of the sale of an asset. In the case of long-term bonds (especially government bonds) sale in the secondary market is often as quick and easy for short-term bonds. The premium for long bonds is compensation for the extra risk of capital loss; 'term premium' might be a better title for the hypothesis.

The market-segmentation hypothesis

The market segmentation hypothesis argues that the debt market is not one homogeneous whole, that there are, in fact, a number of sub-markets defined by maturity range. The yield curve is therefore created (or at least influenced) by the supply and demand conditions in each of these sub-markets. For example, banks tend to be active in the short-term end of the market and pension funds to be buyers in the long-dated segment. If banks need to borrow large quantities quickly they will sell some of their short-term instruments, increasing the supply on the market and pushing down the price and raising the yield. On the other hand pension funds may be flush with cash and may buy large quantities of 20-year bonds, helping to temporarily move yields downward at the long end of the market. At other times banks, pension funds and the buying and selling pressures of a multitude of other financial institutions will influence the supply and demand position in the opposite direction. The point is that the players in the different parts of the yield curve tend to be different. This hypothesis helps to explain the often lumpy or humped yield curve.

A final thought on the term structure of interest rates

It is sometimes thought that in circumstances of a steeply rising yield curve it would be advantageous to borrow short term rather than long term. However this can be a dangerous strategy because long-term debt may be trading at a higher rate of interest because of the expected rise in short-term rates and so when the borrower comes to refinance in, say, a year's time, the short-term interest rate is much higher than the long-term rate and this high rate has to be paid out of the second year's cash flows, which may not be convenient.

EUROTUNNEL

The sub-set of financial knowledge known as long-term debt finance is vast and daunting, as well as complex and challenging. Yet it is important that firms face up to the challenge because if mistakes are made there can be a heavy price to pay further down the line. To get an appreciation of the role of financial expertise in this area consider the following two articles (*see* Exhibits 11.30 and 11.31) about Eurotunnel's debt crisis in the mid-1990s:

Exhibit 11.30 By September 1995 shareholders had lost a fortune and the company was chronically overburdened with debt . . .

Still digging

FT

With characteristic bravado, Sir Alastair Morton has called his bankers' bluff; they have responded with characteristic inertia. Even though Eurotunnel suspended payments on its £8bn of junior debt yesterday, banks have not pulled the rug on the company. But Eurotunnel's problems are far from over: it is chronically overburdened with debt, and unable to trade its way out. Yesterday's drama has merely postponed the day of reckoning. The suspension of interest payments may last up to 18 months. But unpaid interest will continue to be added to Eurotunnel's pile of debt. The company is also about to draw down the second tranche of its senior debt facility.

Eurotunnel hopes that during this period the two parties will agree a restructuring plan. But the banks' do-nothing tendencies may mean that action comes later rather than sooner. There is some logic to this inertia. The banks do not want to take control of Eurotunnel since they do not believe the problem lies with the management of the company; they do not want to take possession of it because it would be hard to sell; and they do not want to force it into administration, partly because of France's unfavourable treatment of creditors – the company operates under both French and English law.

They may be hoping that a third rights issue will raise more cash from the company's long-suffering shareholders, but, given the company's admission that it cannot service existing debt, this is a long shot. Given also the company's failure to meet the targets set in the last rights issue prospectus, it might be difficult to find a bank to sign off the prospectus.

There is still only one long-term solution: a debt-for-equity swap, which would leave the company with a workable balance sheet. Eurotunnel currently has debt totalling more than £8bn and a market value of £700m. It could probably service around £4bn of debt. However, such a swap would effectively wipe out shareholders' capital.

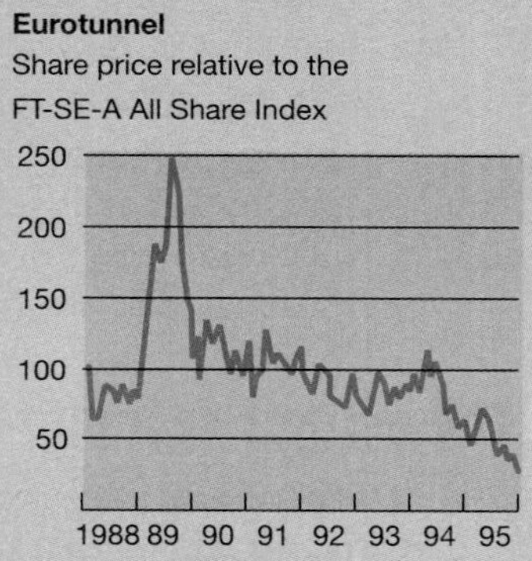

Sir Alastair is right to point out that the company's problems originated from the delays in building the tunnel and the overshoot on costs, as well as the shortfall in revenues. But whatever the injustices heaped upon Eurotunnel in the past, compensation from governments and contractors is unlikely to make up the shortfall in Eurotunnel's capacity to service its debt.

Source: *Financial Times*, 15 September 1995. Reprinted with permission.

Exhibit 11.31 In October 1996 an innovative and complex agreement was worked out with the bankers, creating new forms of debt instrument . . .

Eurotunnel stable, but still in intensive care

Is Eurotunnel dead? Not quite – if nothing else, the company and its bankers this week succeeded in fending off that day by several years. Shareholders are still left needing a miracle, though.

Eurotunnel this week returned from the land of the living dead when, in a complex deal with its banks, it restructured £4.7bn of its crippling £9.1bn debts, and dangled before investors the hope of a dividend within 10 years.

Acknowledging the necessity that the pain be shared by its shareholders and its 225 banks, outgoing co-chairman Sir Alastair Morton urged both sides to accept a 'fair and robust' deal. But although his brinkmanship may have saved Eurotunnel from imminent collapse, he has still left plenty of work for his successor.

'The deal's big and long-dated enough and has enough of a cushion to ensure Eurotunnel shouldn't need a second restructuring,' said Jeff Summers, an analyst with debt trader Klesch & Co. 'But for existing shareholders to get a dividend by about 2004, the company's got to achieve a Herculean rate of growth.'

Mark McVicar, analyst at NatWest Securities, said the restructuring had bought Eurotunnel time, 'Because Eurotunnel's capital is so hard to value – there's a mish-mash of financial instruments in the middle converting into either debt or equity depending on its future performance,' he said . . .

The deal means Eurotunnel's banks initially take 45.5 per cent of the company through a £1bn debt-for-equity swap in which the shares are valued at 130p. On top, there's a raft of financial instruments designed to reduce the interest burden from a current £600m–£650m a year to £400m from now until the end of December 2003. These are:

- £1bn of debt to be exchanged for equity notes, convertible into Eurotunnel units at 155p after December 2003;
- £1.5bn of debt swapped for resettable bonds (i.e. on which the interest rate may be subject to adjustment); and
- £1.2bn of debt exchanged for loan notes paying 1 per cent fixed interest plus 30 per cent of Eurotunnel's annual cash flow after operating costs, capital expenditure and financing costs.

For shareholders, Le Crunch comes in 2004 when the banks could convert their equity notes to give them 60.6 per cent of the company. To allow shareholders to maintain slim control, Eurotunnel is issuing them free warrants, exercisable at 150p until December 2003. If shareholders exercise these, they will redeem the bank's notes.

But the issue is complicated further because out of its present free cash flow of about £125m, Eurotunnel cannot pay even £400m a year in interest. To make up the shortfall, it has agreed £1.85bn of stabilisation notes which roll up interest-free until 2006 but can be converted into shares before then at 130p.

Sir Alastair believes the end of 'looney time' ferry pricing, thanks to the P&O/Stena-Sealink merger, and Eurotunnel's growing market share, should leave his company self-financing long before the £1.85bn runs out. But if he's wrong, the banks will end up with almost 76 per cent of Eurotunnel and it will need more-painful restructuring.

Source: Alastair Osborne, *Investors Chronicle*, 11 October 1996. Reprinted with kind permission of the *Investors Chronicle*.

CONCLUDING COMMENTS

So far this book has taken a fairly detailed look at a variety of ways of raising money by selling shares and has examined the main methods of raising funds through long-term debt. The decision to raise equity or debt finance is neither simple nor straightforward. In the next chapter we consider a wider array of financial sources and types, from leasing to factoring. Knowledge of these will enable the finance manager or other executives to select and structure the different forms of finance to maximise the firm's potential. Topics covered later in the book draw on the knowledge gained in Chapters 10, 11 and 12 to permit informed discussion of such crucial questions as: What is the appropriate mixture of debt and equity? How is the cost of various forms of finance calculated? How can the risk of certain forms of finance (for example a floating-interest-rate term loan) be reduced?

KEY POINTS AND CONCEPTS

- **Debt finance has a number of advantages:**
  - it has a lower cost than equity finance:
    a lower transaction costs;
    b lower rate of return;
  - debt holders generally do not have votes;
  - interest is tax deductible.
- **Drawbacks of debt:**
  - secured debt has the risk of forced liquidation;
  - the use of secured assets for borrowing may be an onerous constraint on managerial action.
- A **bond** is a long-term contract in which the bondholders lend money to a company. A straight 'vanilla' bond pays regular interest plus the capital on the redemption date.
- **Debentures** are generally more secure than **loan stock** (in the UK).
- A **trust deed** has **affirmative covenants** outlining the nature of the bond contract and **negative covenants** imposing constraints on managerial action to reduce risk for the lenders.
- A **floating rate note** (**FRN**) is a bond with an interest rate which varies as a benchmark interest rate changes (e.g. LIBOR).
- **Attractive features of bank borrowing:**
  - administrative and legal costs are low;
  - quick;
  - flexibility in troubled times;
  - available to small firms.
- **Factors for a firm to consider with bank borrowing:**

  Costs
  - fixed versus floating;
  - arrangement fees;
  - bargaining on the rate.

  Security
  - asymmetric information;
  - collateral;
  - covenants;
  - personal guarantees.

  Repayment arrangements:
  Some possibilities:
  - grace periods;
  - mortgage;
  - term loan.
- A **syndicated loan** occurs where a number of banks (or other financial institutions) each contribute a portion of a loan.

- A **credit rating** depends on **a** the likelihood of payments of interest and/or capital not being paid (i.e. default); and **b** the extent to which the lender is protected in the event of a default.

- **Mezzanine debt** is debt offering a high return with a high risk. It has been particularly useful in the following:
  - management buyouts (MBOs), especially leveraged management buyouts (LBOs);
  - fast-growing companies;
  - leveraged recapitalisation.

- **Convertible bonds** are issued as debt instruments but they also give the holder the right to exchange the bonds at some time in the future into ordinary shares according to some prearranged formula. They have the following advantages:
  - lower interest than on debentures;
  - interest is tax deductible;
  - self liquidating;
  - few negative covenants;
  - shares might be temporarily underpriced.

- A bond is **priced** according to general market interest rates for risk class and maturity:

  Irredeemable:

  $$P_D = \frac{i}{k_D}$$

  Redeemable:

  $$P_D = \frac{i_1}{1 + k_D} + \frac{i_2}{(1 + k_D)^2} + \frac{i_3}{(1 + k_D)^3} + \ldots + \frac{R_n}{(1 + k_D)^n}$$

- The **interest yield** on a bond is:

  $$\frac{\text{Gross interest (coupon)}}{\text{Market price}} \times 100$$

- The **yield to maturity** includes both annual coupon returns and capital gains or losses on maturity.

- The **Eurosecurities markets** are informal (unregulated) markets in money held outside its country of origin.

- A **foreign bond** is a bond denominated in the currency of the country where it is issued when the issuer is a non-resident.

- A **Eurobond** is a bond sold outside the jurisdiction of the country of the currency in which the bond is denominated.

- A **project finance** loan is provided as a bank loan or bond finance to an entity set up separately from the parent corporation to undertake a project. The returns to the lender are tied to the fortunes and cash flows of the project.

- **Sale and leaseback** Assets are sold to financial institutions or another company which releases cash. Simultaneously, the original owner agrees to lease the assets back for a stated period under specified terms.

- **Securitisation** Relatively small, homogeneous and illiquid financial assets are pooled and repackaged into liquid securities which are then sold on to other investors to generate cash for the original lender.

- The **term structure of interest rates** describes the manner in which the same default risk class of debt securities provides different rates of return depending on the length of time to maturity. There are three hypotheses relating to the term structure of interest rates:
  – the expectations hypothesis;
  – the liquidity-preference hypothesis;
  – the market-segmentation hypothesis.

REFERENCES AND FURTHER READING

Altman, E.I. and Kao D.L. (1992) 'Rating drift in high-yield bonds', *Journal of Fixed Income*, 1, March, pp. 15–20. Also reproduced in S. Lofthouse (ed.), *Readings in Investments*. New York: Wiley (1994). Investigates the re-rating of bonds on US markets over time.

Arnold, G. and Smith, M. (1999) *The European High Yield Bond Market: Drivers and Impediments*. London: Financial Times Finance Management Report. A comprehensive exploration of the potential of the junk bond market in Europe – a history of the US market is also given.

Association of Corporate Treasurers. *The Treasurer's Handbook*. An annual publication with up-to-date information on credit ratings and other financial matters.

Bank for International Settlements Quarterly Review. Available online – free (www.bis.org). Terrific source of information on the international debt market (and much else besides).

Bank of England Quarterly Bulletin. Comprehensible, illustrated and up-to-date discussions of financial markets events and statistics.

Blake, D. (2000) *Financial Market Analysis*. 2nd edn. Chichester: Wiley. A technical and detailed examination of long-term debt markets.

Brett, M. (2000) *How to Read the Financial Pages*. 5th edn. London: Random House: Business Books. An easy-to-read introductory text on the debt markets.

Brigham, E.F. (1966) 'An analysis of convertible debentures: Theory and some empirical evidence', *Journal of Finance*, March, pp. 35–54. Valuation of convertibles and the major factors influencing price. Evidence that most firms issue convertibles to raise equity finance.

Buckle, M. and Thompson, J. (1995) *The UK Financial System*. 2nd edn. Manchester: Manchester University Press. The Eurosecurities markets are discussed clearly and concisely. There are useful sections on the domestic bond market and the term structure of interest rates.

Buckley, A. (2000) *Multinational Finance*. 4th edn. London: FT Prentice Hall. Some additional detail on some of the issues discussed in this chapter – easy to read.

Corporate Finance Magazine. London: Euromoney. This monthly publication has some excellent articles describing corporate activity in the bond and other financial markets targeted at senior financial personnel.

The Economist. This excellent weekly publication has a section devoted to finance. A good way of keeping up to date.

Eiteman, D.K., Stonehill, A.I. and Moffett, M.H. (2001) *Multinational Finance: International Edition*. 9th edn. Reading, Mass: Addison Wesley. Some useful, easy-to-follow, material on international debt markets.

Financial Times. Details of recent syndicated loans, Eurobonds and bank lending can be found almost every day in the *Financial Times*.

Hickman, B.G. (1958) 'Corporate bond quality and investor experience', *National Bureau of Economic Research*, Princeton, 14. Early research into the returns and default rates on bonds.

Hicks, J.R. (1946) *Value and Capital: An Inquiry into some Fundamental Principles of Economic Theory*. 2nd edn. Oxford: Oxford University Press. Liquidity-preference hypothesis to explain the term structure of interest rates.

Lutz, F.A. and Lutz, V.C. (1951) *The Theory of Investment in the Firm*. Princeton, NJ: Princeton University Press. Expectations hypothesis of the term structure of interest rates.

Maude, D. (1996) 'Eurobond primary and secondary markets', in E. Gardener and P. Molyneux (eds), *Investment Banking: Theory and Practice*. London: Euromoney. A short introduction to the Eurobond markets.

Pilbeam, K. (1998) *International Finance*. 2nd edn. London: Macmillan Business. An introductory treatment of debt markets.

Standard & Poor's (1999) *Ratings Performance 1998: Stability and Transition*, January. Evidence on returns and defaults on bonds of different ratings.

Valdez, S. (2000) *An Introduction to Global Financial Markets*. 3rd edn. London: Macmillan Business. Easy-to-read background on international bond markets.

WEBSITES

Association of Corporate Treasurers www.corporate-treasurers.co.uk

Bank of England www.bankofengland.co.uk

The Economist www.economist.com

Financial Times www.FT.com

Fitch IBCA www.fitchibca.com

International Securities Market Association www.isma.co.uk

Moody's www.moodys.com

Standard & Poor's www.standardandpoors.com

SELF-REVIEW QUESTIONS

1 What are the relative advantages and drawbacks of debt and equity finance?

2 Explain the following (related to bonds):

a Par value.

b Trustee.

c Debenture.

d Zero-coupon bond.

e Floating-rate note.

3 The inexperienced finance trainee at Mugs-R-Us plc says that he can save the company money on its forthcoming issue of ten-year bonds. 'The rate of return required for bonds of this risk class in the financial markets is 10 per cent and yet I overheard our merchant banking adviser say, "We could issue a bond at a coupon of only 9 per cent." I reckon we could save the company a large sum on the £100m issue.' Do you agree with the trainee's logic?

4 In what circumstances would you recommend borrowing from a bank rather than a capital market bond issue?

5 What are the fundamental considerations to which you would advise a firm to give thought if it were contemplating borrowing from a bank?

6 Is securitisation something to do with anti-criminal precautions? If not, explain what it is and why firms do it.

7 In what ways does the tax regime encourage debt finance rather than equity finance?

8 Why does convertible debt carry a lower coupon than straight debt?

9 What is meant by asymmetric information in the relationship between banker and borrower?

10 What is a syndicated loan and why do banks join so many syndicates?

11 What are the differences between a domestic bond, a Eurobond and a foreign bond?

12 What is the credit rating on a bond and what factors determine it?

13 Why do bond issuers accept restrictive covenants?

14 What are high-yield bonds? What is their role in financing firms?

15 What is a bearer bond?

16 What is a debenture?

17 What is the difference between a fixed-rate and a floating-rate bond?

QUESTIONS AND PROBLEMS

1 Imagine that the market yield to maturity for three-year bonds in a particular risk class is 12 per cent. You buy a bond in that risk class which offers an annual coupon of 10 per cent for the next three years, with the first payment in one year. The bond will be redeemed at par (£100) in three years.

a How much would you pay for the bond?

b If you paid £105 what yield to maturity would you obtain?

2 A £100 bond with two years to maturity and an annual coupon of 9 per cent is available. (The next coupon is payable in one year.)

a If the market requires a yield to maturity of 9 per cent for a bond of this risk class what will be its market price?

b If the market price is £98, what yield to maturity does it offer?

c If the required yield to maturity on this type of bond changes to 7 per cent, what will the market price change to?

3 a If the government sold a 10-year gilt with a par value of £100 and an (annual) coupon of 9 per cent, what price can be charged if investors require a 9.5 per cent yield to maturity on such bonds?

b If yields to maturity on bonds of this risk class fall to 8.5 per cent, what could the bonds be sold for?

c If it were sold for £105, what yield to maturity is the bond offering?

d What is the flat yield on this bond?

4* The price of a bond issued by C & M plc is 85.50 per cent of par value. The bond will pay an annual 8.5 per cent coupon until maturity (the next coupon will be paid in one year). The bond matures in seven years.

a What will be the market price of the bond if yields to maturity for this risk class fall to 7.5 per cent?

b What will be the market price of the bond if yields to maturity for this risk class rise to 18 per cent?

5 A zero coupon bond with a par value of £100 matures in five years.

a What is the price of the bond if the yield to maturity is 5 per cent?

b What is the price of the bond if the yield to maturity is 10 per cent?

6 Bond 1 has an annual coupon rate of 6 per cent and Bond 2 has an annual coupon of 12 per cent. Both bonds mature in one year and have a par value of £100. If the yield to maturity on bonds of this risk class is 10 per cent at what price will the bonds sell? Assume that the next coupons are due in one year's time.

7* You are considering three alternative investments in bonds but would like to gain an impression of the extent of price volatility for each given alternative changes in future interest rates. The investments are:

i A two-year bond with an annual coupon of 6 per cent, par value of £100 and the next coupon payment in one year. The current yield to maturity on this bond is 6.5 per cent.

ii A ten-year bond with an annual coupon of 6 per cent, a par value of £100 and the next coupon payable in one year. The current yield to maturity on this bond is 7.2 per cent.

iii A 20-year bond with an annual coupon of 6 per cent, a par value of £100 and the next coupon due in one year. The current yield to maturity on this bond is 7.7 per cent.

a Draw an approximate yield curve.

b Calculate the market price of each of the bonds.

c Calculate the market price of the bonds on the assumption that yields to maturity rise by 200 basis points for all bonds.

d Now calculate the market price of the bonds on the assumption that yields to maturity fall by 200 basis points.

e Which bond price is the most volatile in circumstances of changing yields to maturity?

f Explain the liquidity-preference theory of the term structure of yields to maturity.

8 What are the factors that explain the difference in yields to maturity between long-term and short-term bonds?

9 Find the current yield to maturity on government securities with maturities of one year, five years and ten years in the *Financial Times*. How has the yield curve changed since 2001 as shown in the chapter? What might account for this shift?

10 If the yield to maturity on a two-year zero coupon bond is 13 per cent and the yield to maturity on a one-year zero coupon bond is 10 per cent what is the expected spot rate of one-year bonds in one year's time assuming the expectations hypothesis is applicable?

11 If the yield to maturity on a one-year bond is 8 per cent and the expected spot rate on a one-year bond, beginning in one year's time, is 7 per cent what will be the yield to maturity on a two-year bond under the expectations hypothesis of the term structure of interest rates?

12 In 2001 the term structure of interest rates for UK government securities was downward sloping and in 1996 it was upward sloping. Explain how these curves come about with reference to the expectations, liquidity and market-segmentation hypotheses.

13 Iris plc borrows £50m at 9.5 per cent from Westlloyds bank for five years. What cash flows will the firm have to find if the interest and principal are paid in the following ways?

a All interest and capital is paid at the end of the period.

b Interest only is paid for each of the years (at the year ends); all principal is paid at the end.

c £10m of the capital plus annual interest is paid on each anniversary date.

14 What factors should a firm consider when borrowing from a bank?

15 'Convertibles are great because they offer a lower return than straight debt and we just dish out shares rather than having to find cash to redeem the bonds' – executive at Myopic plc. Comment on this statement as though you were a shareholder in Myopic.

16 Lummer plc has issued £60m 15-year 8.5 per cent coupon bonds with a par value of £100. Each bond is convertible into 40 shares of Lummer ordinary shares, which are currently trading at £1.90.

a What is the conversion price?

b What is the conversion premium?

c What is the conversion value of the bond?

17 Explain the following terms and their relevance to debt-finance decision makers:

a Negative covenant.

b Conversion premium.

c Collateral.

d Grace periods.

18 Outline the main advantages and disadvantages of fixed and floating interest rates from the borrowing company's perspective.

19 (*Examination level*) Flying High plc plans to expand rapidly over the next five years and is considering the following forms of finance to support that expansion.

- **a** A five-year £10m floating-rate term loan from MidBarc Bank plc at an initial annual interest of 9 per cent
- **b** A five-year Eurodollar bond fixed at 8 per cent with a nominal value of US$15m.
- **c** A £10m convertible bond offering a yield to redemption of 6 per cent and a conversion premium of 15 per cent.

As the financial adviser to the board you have been asked to explain each of these forms of finance and point out the relative advantages and drawbacks. Do this in report form.

20 'We avoid debt finance because of the unacceptable constraint placed on managerial actions.' Explain what this executive means and suggest forms of long-term borrowing which have few constraints.

ASSIGNMENTS

1 Review the long-term debt instruments used by a company familiar to you. Consider the merits and drawbacks of these and explain alternative long-term debt strategies.

2 Write a report for the senior management of a company you know well explaining your views on the wisdom of using some of the firm's assets in a sale and leaseback transaction.

CHAPTER NOTES

1 This example is designed to show the effect of leverage. It does lack realism in a number of respects; for example it is unlikely that profits will continue to rise at 25 per cent per annum without further investment. This can be adjusted for – the time taken to pay off the debt lengthens but the principles behind the example do not alter.

2 This topic and the previous one do not sit perfectly in a chapter on long-term finance, but they help to give a more complete view of the Euromarkets.

Chapter 12

SHORT-TERM AND MEDIUM-TERM FINANCE

INTRODUCTION

Short-term and medium-term finance is presented in this textbook as the third major category of funding. This is not meant to imply that the forms of finance described in this chapter are any less important than the first two (equity and long-term debt finance). Indeed, for many firms, especially smaller ones, a combination of overdrafts and loans, trade credit, leasing and hire purchase make up the greater part of the funding needs. Large companies have access to stock markets, bond markets and syndicated loan facilities. These are often closed to the smaller firm, so, in order to achieve their expansion programmes, they turn to the local banks and the finance houses as well as their suppliers for the wherewithal to grow. The giants of the corporate world have access to dozens of different types of finance, but they also value the characteristics, cheapness and flexibility of the forms discussed here.

The definitions of short-term and medium-term finance are not clear-cut. Usually finance which is repayable within a year is regarded as short, whereas that due for

Exhibit 12.1 The main forms of short-term and medium-term finance

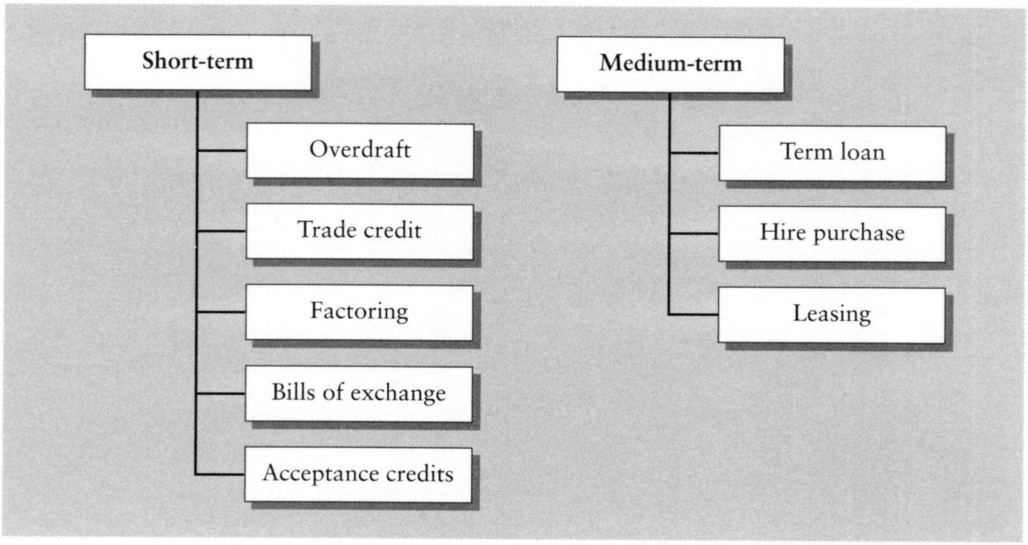

repayment between one and seven years is taken to be medium. But these cut-offs are not to be taken too seriously. Quite often an overdraft facility, which is due for repayment in, say, six months or one year, is regularly 'rolled over' and so may become relied upon as a medium- or even long-term source of funds. Leasing, which is usually classified as a medium-term source, can be used for periods of up to 15 years in some circumstances, in others it is possible to lease assets for a period of only a few weeks, for example, a computer or photocopier. The forms of finance we will examine in this chapter are listed in Exhibit 12.1.

Learning objectives

This chapter is largely descriptive and so it would be an achievement merely to understand the nature of each form of finance. However we will go further, and explore the appropriate use of these sources in varying circumstances. Specifically the reader should be able to:

- describe, compare and contrast the bank overdraft and the bank term loan;
- show awareness of the central importance of trade credit and good debtor management and be able to analyse the early settlement discount offer;
- explain the different services offered by a factoring firm;
- consider the relative merits of hire purchase and leasing.

BANK SOURCES

For most companies and individuals banks remain the main source of externally raised finance. Total bank lending to the small business sector in the UK was £37.1bn in 1999. Ten years earlier the most common form of bank borrowing was the overdraft facility. As we shall see there has been a remarkable shift, so that now the term loan has come to dominate.

Overdraft

Usually the amount that can be withdrawn from a bank account is limited to the amount put in. However business and other financial activity often requires some flexibility in this principle, and it is often useful to make an arrangement to take more money out of a bank account than it contains – this is an overdraft.

An overdraft is a permit to overdraw on an account up to a stated limit.

Overdraft facilities are usually arranged for a period of a few months or a year and interest is charged on the excess drawings.

Advantages of overdrafts

Overdrafts have the following advantages.

1 ***Flexibility*** The borrowing firm is not asked to forecast the precise amount and duration of its borrowing at the outset but has the flexibility to borrow up to a stated

limit. Also the borrower is assured that the moment the funds are no longer required they can be quickly and easily repaid without suffering a penalty.

2 *Cheapness* Banks usually charge two to five percentage points over base rate (or LIBOR) depending on the creditworthiness, security offered and bargaining position of the borrower. There may also be an arrangement fee of, say, 1 per cent of the facility. These charges may seem high but it must be borne in mind that overdrafts are often loans to smaller and riskier firms which would otherwise have to pay much more for their funds. Large and well-established borrowers with low gearing and plenty of collateral can borrow on overdraft at much more advantageous rates. For both large and small firms, however, the interest margin over the base rate or LIBOR is only one aspect of the benefits of an overdraft: a major saving comes from the fact that the banks charge interest on only the daily outstanding balance. So, if a firm has a large cash inflow one week it can use this to reduce its overdraft, temporarily lowering the interest payable, while retaining the ability to borrow more another week.

Overdraft interest can also be deducted from income to determine the profits to be subject to tax.

Drawbacks of an overdraft

A major drawback to an overdraft is that the bank retains the right to withdraw the facility at short notice. Thus a heavily indebted firm may receive a letter from the bank insisting that its account be brought to balance within a matter of days. This right lowers the risk to the lender because it can quickly get its money out of a troubled company which allows it to lower the cost of lending. However it can be devastating for the borrower and so firms are well advised to think through the use to which finance provided by way of an overdraft is put. It is not usually wise to use the money for an asset which cannot be easily liquidated; for example, it could be problematic if an overdraft is used for a bridge-building project which will take three years to come to fruition.

The age-old convention of attaching the right of the bank to withdraw the overdraft facility to a loan agreement was flouted by NatWest in 2000. (We are yet to see if the other banks will follow – *see* Exhibit 12.2.)

Exhibit 12.2

NatWest deletes overdraft clause

FT

Campaigners for small companies claimed a victory yesterday after NatWest bank abolished its right to remove a customer's overdraft at a moment's notice.

NatWest said it would turn current industry practice on its head by deleting the 'repayable on demand' clause from its small business overdrafts.

The bank said it would end the uncertainty faced by SMEs by ensuring that a three, six or 12 month overdraft meant exactly that. The conditions will apply to both secured and unsecured overdrafts.

Source: Jim Pickard, *Financial Times*, 21 November 2000, p. 6. Reprinted with permission.

Another major consideration for the borrower is the issue of security. Banks usually take a fixed charge (on a specific asset) or a floating charge ('floats' over the general assets of the firm). Alternatively, or in addition, the bank may require a personal guarantee of the directors or owners of the business. When Sir Richard Branson borrowed from Lloyds TSB the bank took shares owned by Sir Richard in Virgin Atlantic as security. Note also that a three-year overdraft facility was arranged – *see* Exhibit 12.3.

Exhibit 12.3

Branson wins £17m loan facility increase

FT

Sir Richard Branson can borrow a further £17m from Lloyds TBS under a loan facility backed by Virgin Group's controlling stake in Virgin Atlantic, the prize of his business empire.

Virgin said yesterday it had mortgaged his 51 per cent stake in the Virgin Atlantic in exchange for a £67m three-year facility from Lloyds.

Sir Richard's group has already used £50m of the overdraft facility on new businesses, including US and Australian mobile phone ventures and the acquisition of a chain of South African health clubs.

Source: Francesco Guerrera and Thorold Barker, *Financial Times*, 12 June 2001, p. 26. Reprinted with permission.

Conditions of lending

A bank will generally examine the following factors before lending to a firm:

1 ***Cash flow projections*** A healthy set of projected cash flows will usually be required showing sufficient profitability and liquidity to pay off the overdraft at the end of the agreed period.

2 ***Creditworthiness*** This goes beyond examining projected future cash flows and asset backing and considers important factors such as character and talents of the individuals leading the organisation.

3 ***The amount that the borrower is prepared to put into the project*** or activity, relative to that asked from the bank. If the borrower does not show commitment by putting their money into a scheme banks can get nervous and stand-offish.

4 ***Security*** The back-up of specific assets or a charge over a large body of general assets will help to reassure a lender that it will be repaid one way or another. Bankers may look at a firm or a project on two levels. First, they might consider a 'liquidation analysis' in which they think about their position in a scenario of bankruptcy. Secondly, they will look at a firm or project on the assumption that it is a 'going concern', where cash flows rather than assets become more important.

Overdrafts are particularly useful for seasonal businesses because the daily debit-balance interest charge and the absence of a penalty for early repayment mean that this form of finance can be cheaper than a loan. Take the case of Fruit Growers plc (*see* Worked example 12.1).

Worked example 12.1 Fruit growers plc

In the case of Fruit Growers plc the management are trying to decide whether to obtain financing from an overdraft or a loan. The interest on both would be 10 per cent per year or 2.5 per cent per quarter. The cash position for the forthcoming year is represented in Exhibit 12.4.

Exhibit 12.4 Monthly cash flow balance for Fruit Growers plc

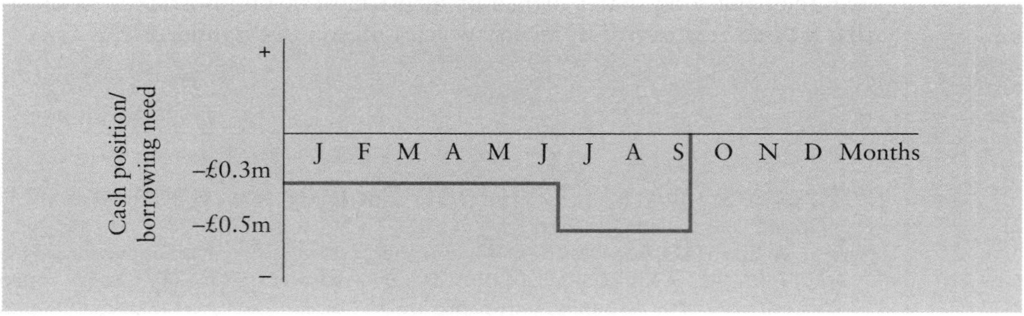

Option 1 A loan for the whole year

A loan for the whole year has the advantage of greater certainty that the lending facility will be in place throughout the year. A total loan of £0.5m will be needed, and this will be repaid at the end of the year with interest. At the beginning of the year Fruit Growers' account is credited with the full £500,000. For the months when the business does not need the £500,000 the surplus can be invested to receive a return of 2 per cent per quarter.

Exhibit 12.5 Cost of a loan for the whole year

Interest charged 500,000 × 10%	=	£50,000
Less interest receivable when surplus funds earn 2% per quarter		
January–June 200,000 × 4%	=	£8,000
October–December 500,000 × 2%	=	£10,000
Total cost of borrowing	=	£32,000

Option 2 An overdraft facility for £500,000

An overdraft facility for £500,000 has the drawback that the facility might be withdrawn at any time during the year. However it is cheaper, as Exhibit 12.6 shows.

Exhibit 12.6 Costs of an overdraft facility for £500,000

1st quarter (J, F & M) 300,000 × 2.5%	=	£7,500
2nd quarter (A, M & J) 300,000 × 2.5%	=	£7,500
3rd quarter (J, A & S) 500,000 × 2.5%	=	£12,500
4th quarter (O, N & D)	=	£0
Total cost of borrowing	=	£27,500

Note: We will ignore the complications of compounding intra-year interest.

The risk of a sudden withdrawal of an overdraft facility for most firms is very slight: banks do not generate goodwill and good publicity by capriciously and lightly cancelling agreed overdrafts. The high street banks came in for strong criticism in the early 1990s: 'In 1993 the best that could be said about the relationship between banks and their small firm customers was that both sides were in a state of armed neutrality' (Howard Davies, Deputy

Governor of the Bank of England, 1996). They were said to have failed to lower interest rates to small firms to the same extent as general base rates (a charge of which the Bank of England said they were not guilty), of not supporting start-ups, of having excessive fees, of being too ready to close down a business and being too focused on property-based security backing rather than looking at the cash flows of the proposed activity.

A number of these areas of contention have been addressed and matters are said to be improving. One particular problem with UK lending was said to be the excessive use of the overdraft facility when compared with other countries which used term loans more extensively. In the 1980s between one-half and two-thirds of bank lending to small firms was in the form of overdrafts. A high proportion of these were rearranged at the end of each year for another 12 months ('rolled over') and so, in effect, became a medium-term source of finance. The disadvantages of this policy are that each overdraft renewal involves arrangement fees as well as the risk of not reaching an agreement. It became obvious that a longer-term loan arrangement was more suitable for many firms and the banks pushed harder on this front. As a result, between 1993 and 1998, the proportion of bank lending to small firms represented by overdrafts declined from 49 per cent to 30 per cent, with term lending rising to 70 per cent.

The relationship between banks and small businesses is said to have improved during the 1990s – *see* Exhibit 12.7.

Exhibit 12.7

Banks boost links with small businesses

FT

Financing study expects switch to medium-term loans will bolster defences against economic swings

Small businesses are less vulnerable to the swings of the economic cycle than in the past because they rely less on bank overdrafts and more on medium-term bank loans with fixed repayments.

The slowdown will show the extent to which improvements have been made in small-business financing over the past 10 years, a Bank of England study says, 'Banks are now more locked into the provision of finance to the small-firm sector throughout the economic cycle.' Banks' codes of practice for small business and improved British Bankers' Association industry standards for dealing with small businesses, have led to 'a more open, two-way relationship' between banks and small companies.

Banks now have better warning systems to highlight businesses that are getting into difficulty, and small companies appear more prepared to share information. The study, The Financing of Small Firms in the UK, says: 'Better relations and a greater degree of co-operation should help to avoid some of the strains of the previous recession, which contributed to increased business failures and seriously affected the reputation of the banks.'

Better sharing of information also means banks are levying lower charges, requiring less collateral, and offering fixed-rate loans rather than overdraft facilities tied to short-term interest rates.

The balance between overdraft and term-lending was equally split in 1992. By 1998, term-lending accounted for 70 per cent of the total. Two thirds of banks' committed funds have maturities of more than five years.

As a percentage of total small-business finance, bank lending has fallen from 61 per cent in 1990 to 47 per cent in 1997. Hire purchasing and leasing has risen from 16 per cent to 27 per cent over the same period. Only 39 per cent of small businesses sought external finance in 1995–97, compared with 65 per cent in 1987–90. Small businesses are also relying more on internally generated funds than in the past, the Bank says.

The four main clearing banks have accounted for a stable 85 per cent share of lending to small businesses throughout the decade, the bulletin says. NatWest and Barclays together accounted for almost half the total, but have lost market share to Lloyds-TSB and Midland, particularly in lending to business start-ups.

Risk capital for technology-based small businesses is still limited. Venture capital finance has remained at 3 per cent of the total throughout the decade.

Source: Andrew Balls, *Financial Times*, 17 May 1999, p. 10. Reprinted with permission.

Term loans

A term loan is a loan of a fixed amount for an agreed time and on specified terms. These loans are normally for a period of between three and seven years, but they can range from one to 20 years. The specified terms will include provisions regarding the repayment schedule. If the borrower is to apply the funds to a project which will not generate income for perhaps the first three years it may be possible to arrange a grace period during which only the interest is paid, with the capital being paid off once the project has a sufficiently positive cash flow. Other arrangements can be made to reflect the pattern of cash flow of the firm or project: for example a 'balloon' payment structure is one when only a small part of the capital is repaid during the main part of the loan period, with the majority repayable as the maturity date approaches. A 'bullet' repayment arrangement takes this one stage further and provides for all the capital to be repaid at the end of the loan term.

Not all term loans are drawn down in a single lump sum at the time of the agreement. In the case of a construction project which needs to keep adding to its borrowing to pay for the different stages of development, an instalment arrangement might be required with, say, 25 per cent of the money being made available immediately, 25 per cent at foundation stage and so on. This has the added attraction to the lender of not committing large sums secured against an asset not yet created. From the borrower's point of view a drawdown arrangement has an advantage over an overdraft in that the lender is committed to providing the finance if the borrower meets prearranged conditions, whereas with an overdraft the lender can withdraw the arrangement at short notice.

The interest charged on term loans can be either at fixed or floating rates. The fixed rate is generally at a higher rate of interest than the floating rate at the time of arrangement because of the additional risk to the lender of being unable to modify rates as an uncertain future unfolds. In addition, the borrower will pay an arrangement fee which will largely depend on the relative bargaining strength of the two parties.

A term loan often has much more accompanying documentation than an overdraft because of the lengthy bank commitment. This will include a set of obligations imposed on the borrowing firm such as information flows to the bank as well as gearing and liquidity ratio constraints. If these financial ratio limits are breached or interest and capital is not paid on the due date the bank has a right of termination, in which case it could decide not to make any funds available, or, in extreme cases, insist on the repayment of funds already lent. Banks are unlikely to rush into declaring default, seizing assets and liquidating a firm because, even if they take such draconian action, they may not get much of their funds back, and the adverse publicity is a disincentive. Instead they will often try to reschedule or restructure the finance of the business. Usually the bank expects either a fixed or floating charge over the firm's assets and/or guarantees from third parties.

TRADE CREDIT

Perhaps the simplest and the most important source of short-term finance for many firms is trade credit. This means that when goods or services are delivered to a firm for use in its production they are not paid for immediately. These goods and services can then be used to produce income before the invoice has to be paid.

The writer has been involved with a number of small business enterprises, one of which was a small retail business engaged in the selling of crockery and glassware – Crocks. Reproduced as Exhibit 12.8 is an example of a real invoice (with a few modifications to hide the identity of the supplier). When we first started buying from this supplier we, as a matter of course, applied for trade credit. We received the usual response, that the supplier requires two references vouching for our trustworthiness from other suppliers that have granted us trade credit in the past, plus a reference from our bankers. Once these confidential references were accepted by the supplier they granted us normal credit terms for retailers of our type of product, that is, 30 days to pay from the date of delivery. One of the things you learn in business is that agreements of this kind are subject to some flexibility. We found that this supplier does not get too upset if you go over the 30 days and pay around day 60: the supplier will still supply to the business on normal credit terms even if you do this on a regular basis.

Each time supplies were delivered by this firm we had to make a decision about when to pay. Option 1 is to pay on the 14th day to receive $2\frac{1}{2}$ per cent discount. Option 2 is to take 60 days to pay. (Note: with Option 1 the $2\frac{1}{2}$ per cent deduction is on the 'nett goods' amount which is the value of the invoice before value added tax (VAT) is added, that is £217.30.)

Exhibit 12.8 A typical invoice

Supplier XYZ plc
54 West Street, Sussex

Invoice number 501360
Date 29/02/98

Invoice address
Crocks
Melton Mowbray
Leics
LE13 1XH

Branch address
Crocks
Grantham
Lincolnshire

INVOICE

Account	Customer order No.	Sales order	Carrier	AEP	Despatch No.	Due date	Page
T02251	81535	T01537		090	000067981	28/03/98	1

Item	Part code	Description	Unit of sale	Quantity despatched	Unit price	%	Amount	VAT code
1	1398973	Long glass	each	12	0.84	0.00	10.08	0
2	12810357	Tumbler	each	12	0.84	0.00	10.08	0
3	1395731	Plate	each	60	1.10	0.00	66.00	0
4	1258732	Bowls	each	30	4.23	0.00	126.90	0
5	1310102	Cup	each	1	4.24	0.00	4.24	0
		VAT 0: 217.30 @ 17.5%						

Note our settlement terms:

$2\frac{1}{2}$% discount may be deducted for payment within 14 days of invoice date; otherwise due 30 days strictly nett.

Nett goods	217.30
Charges	0.00
VAT	38.03
	255.33

Option 1

$$£217.30 \times 0.025 = £5.43$$

So, we could knock £5.43 off the bill if we paid it 14 days after delivery. This looks good but I do not yet know whether it is better than the second option.

Option 2
This business had an overdraft, so if we could avoid taking money from the bank account the interest charge would be less. How much interest could be saved by taking an additional 46 days (60 – 14) to pay this invoice? Assuming the annual percentage rate (APR) charged on the overdraft is 10 per cent the daily interest charge is:

$$(1 + \mathrm{d})^{365} = 1 + i$$

$$d = \sqrt[365]{(1 + i)} - 1$$

$$= \sqrt[365]{(1 + 0.1)} - 1 = 0.00026116$$

where

d = daily interest, and i = annual interest

Interest charge for 46 days:

$$(1 + 0.00026116)^{46} - 1 = 0.01208 \text{ or } 1.208\%$$

$$(255.33 - 5.43) \times 0.01208 = £3.02$$

Thus £3.02 interest is saved by delaying payment to the sixtieth day, compared with a saving of over £5 on the option of paying early.[1] In this particular case taking extended trade credit is not the cheapest source of finance; it is cheaper to use the overdraft facility.

Many suppliers to our business did not offer a discount for early settlement. This gives the impression that trade credit finance is a free source of funds and therefore the logical course of action is to get as much trade credit as possible. The system is therefore open to abuse. However the corrective to that abuse is that a supplier will become tired of dealing with a persistent late payer and will refuse to supply, or will only supply on a basis of payment in advance. Another point to be borne in mind is that gaining a bad reputation in the business community may affect relationships with other suppliers.

Advantages of trade credit

Trade credit has the following advantages.

1 ***Convenient/informal/cheap*** Trade credit has become a normal part of business in most product markets.

2 ***Available to companies of any size*** Small companies, especially fast-growing ones, often have a very limited range of sources of finance to turn to. Banks frequently restrict overdrafts and loans to the asset backing available.

Factors determining the terms of trade credit

Tradition within the industry

Customs have been established in many industries concerning the granting of trade credit. Individual suppliers may be unwise to step outside these traditions because they may lose sales. Exhibit 12.9 shows the number of days it takes customers of the firms in the listed industries to pay their bills. There is quite a large variation between industries; for retailers where most sales are completed on zero credit terms the average period is only a few days, whereas in the metal goods sector 11 weeks is considered the norm.

Exhibit 12.9 Credit period days taken by customers of East and West Midlands medium-sized firms, 1985–1994

		Credit period (days)	
		East Mids	*West Mids*
1	Chemicals	68	64
2	Metal goods	75	74
3	Mechanical engineering	74	77
4	Electrical and electronic engineering	72	78
5	Rubber and plastics	72	71
6	Textiles	49	60
7	Footwear and clothing	42	48
8	Food, drink and tobacco	37	39
9	Paper, print and publishing	68	66
10	Construction	44	46
11	Wholesale distribution	56	70
12	Retail distribution	19	20
13	Business services	80	64

Source: G.C. Arnold and P. Davis (1995) *Profitability trends in West Midlands Industries. A study for Lloyds Bowmaker.* Edinburgh: Lloyds Bowmaker. Reprinted with permission of Lloyds UDT Limited.

Bargaining strength of the two parties

If the supplier has numerous customers, each wanting to purchase the product in a particular region, and the supplier wishes to have only one outlet then it may decide not to supply to those firms which demand extended trade credit. On the other hand, if the supplier is selling into a highly competitive market where the buyer has many alternative sources of supply credit might be used to give a competitive edge.

Product type

Products with a high level of turnover relative to stocks are generally sold on short credit terms, for example food. The main reason is that these products usually sell on a low profit margin and the delay in payment can have a large impact on the profit margin.

TRADE DEBTOR MANAGEMENT

Trade credit is a two-edged sword for businesses. Firms usually benefit from being granted credit by their suppliers but because of the necessity of providing credit to their customers they are burdened with additional costs. To gain a true appreciation of trade credit we need to examine the subject from the other side of the fence and ask: 'What considerations does the credit provider have to take into account?'

Trade debtors are the sales made on credit as yet unpaid.

The management of debtors involves a trade-off (*see* Exhibit 12.10). On the one hand, the more generous a company is in allowing its customers to delay payment, the greater the sales. On the other hand, longer credit terms impose costs of financing those goods and services until they are paid for. There may also be a strain on the company's liquidity with a large proportion of the company's assets tied up in debtors (typically one-quarter to one-third of the company's assets are in the form of debtors). In addition there is the risk of the customer defaulting on the payment and there are also the sometimes considerable costs of administering an effective debtor management system.

Exhibit 12.10 The debtor trade-off

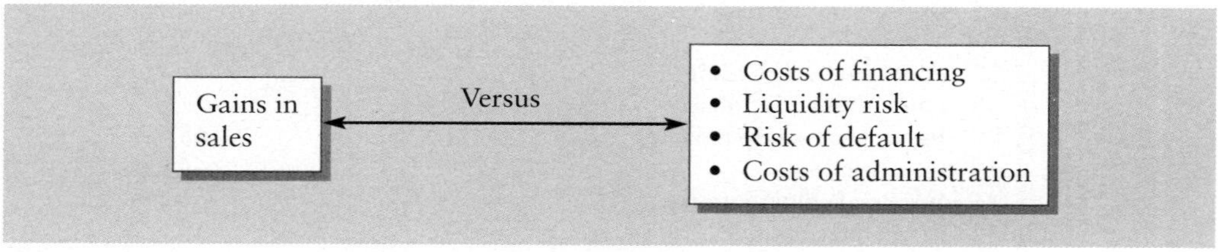

The solution to the debtor trade-off is to compare the incremental returns from a more accommodating credit stance with the incremental costs. The following points are relevant in trade credit management.

Credit policy

The first issue in the management of trade debtors is to decide whether to grant credit at all. Credit is not inevitable; many businesses, for example service-based organisations, from hairdressers to vehicle repairers, choose not to offer any credit. Some compromise and offer credit on sales above a certain value, say £100. If a firm decides that it is in its best interest to allow delayed payment then it needs to set up a system of rules and guidelines which will amount to a debtor policy.

Assessing credit risk

Granting credit is, in effect, the granting of a loan. It is important to assess the probability of either delayed payment or complete failure to pay. Information to make this judgement can come from a variety of sources. First, the customer's accounts could be examined. (All limited liability companies in the UK are required to submit their accounts to Companies House and these are then available for inspection by anyone.)

An analysis of the accounts could give some idea of the liquidity and solvency of the customer as well as its trading performance and growth trajectory. Much of this type of public information is now held in electronic form and can be quickly accessed, for example FAME on CD-ROM. If the credit provider does not wish to become involved in the detail of credit checking it could employ a credit reporting agency (such as Dun and Bradstreet) which uses accounting information combined with knowledge of the problems other companies have had with the customer and special enquiries to rate creditworthiness. In addition to trade references from existing suppliers and bank references the debtor management department could canvass the opinion and impressions of the salespeople. This can be a rich source of anecdotal evidence, as they are the individuals who are most likely to meet the customer in the work environment.

If the customer has been buying from an organisation for some time then that organisation will have a set of records on which to base an assessment of risk. Using this information, and keeping the corporate 'eyes and ears' open in day-to-day dealings for signs of customers experiencing liquidity problems, the supplier can take risk-reducing action early. For example if a customer has gradually increased the length of time between delivery and payment and the sales team report that the customer's shops are looking understocked, the firm might move the customer from 30-day credit period terms to payment on delivery.

Many companies allocate customers to different risk classes and treat each category differently. Some customers are allowed 60 days, while others are only permitted 10 days. Special discounts are available to some and not to others. Certain small, poorly capitalised companies present particular problems to the supplying firm as it is faced with the difficult choice of whether or not to sell. The first order from a company like this might be valued at only £1,000, the profit on which is only, say, £200. But the supplier has somehow to estimate the lost sales and profits for all future years if it refuses credit on this first purchase. These could mount up to a large present value. In addition, a lost customer will turn to a competitor firm for supplies and assist their expansion. On the other hand, there is a chance that the £1,000 will not be received or may be received months after the due date.

Once customers have been classified into risk categories it is possible to decide whether or not to trade with particular types of firms. For example, suppose that a group of customers have been assessed to have a one in eight probability of not paying:

Sales to these firms	100,000
Less bad debts (1/8 × 100,000)	–12,500
Income from sales	87,500
Costs of production, distribution, etc.	–80,000
Incremental profit	£7,500

Given the present costs of production and creditworthiness of the customers it is worthwhile selling goods on credit to these firms. However a careful watch will have to be placed on firms of this risk class as their position can deteriorate rapidly.

Assessing credit risk is an area of management which relies less on numerical frameworks than on sound and experienced judgement. There are two rules to bear in mind:

1 ***Focus effort on the most risky*** Some sales are to large, safe, regular customers with a good reputation for prompt payment. Do not put large resources into monitoring these accounts. Concentrate time and effort on the problematic customers.

2 *Accept some risk: it may lead to greater profit* The minimisation of bad debt is not the key objective. Poor risk may have to be accepted to make sales and generate profit. For example a risky small customer may be granted credit in the hope that one day it will become large and established.

Agreeing terms

Having decided to sell on credit to a particular firm the supplier has to agree the precise details with the customer. This is going to be heavily influenced by the factors discussed earlier: industry tradition, bargaining strength and product type. Firms usually adopt terms which require payment in a number of days from the invoice date or the delivery date (in theory these should be close together). An alternative system requires payment on or before the last day of the month following the date of invoice. Thus goods delivered on 5 August are paid for on 30 September. This approach can lead to almost two months' credit and customers quickly appreciate the advantage of making sure deliveries are made at the start of each month. Payment is usually by means of a cheque, but increasingly direct bank transfers are used, where the customer's bank automatically pays a certain number of days after receiving notification from the supplier.

Customers are generally given credit limits, that is, a maximum amount that can be outstanding at any one time. For example, suppose a customer has taken delivery of five consignments of goods over a three-week period from one supplier amounting to £2,000, which is equal to its credit limit with that supplier. That firm will be refused any more deliveries until it has paid off some of its arrears.

Goods are normally sold under a contract whereby the supplier can take repossession should the buyer fail to pay. This has the advantage that the supplier avoids becoming a lowly general creditor of the company and therefore being way down the pecking order in a liquidation.

The size of the orders may influence the terms of credit. Customers ordering small quantities are more expensive to manage than those that place large orders and therefore their credit period may be less generous. If the goods are perishable the supplier may grant only short credit terms because of the absence of good collateral.

Collecting payment

An effective administration system for debtors must be established. The firm needs clearly defined procedures and the customers need to be informed and/or warned that they are expected to conform to certain rules. Some profitable companies go bankrupt because they fail to collect the cash from customers that is vital to sustain production and satisfy their own creditors. The following list sets out some elements of a good system.

- *Be strict with the credit limit* Insist on payment for previous orders before dispatching more goods if the credit limit is breached.
- *Send invoices promptly* Ensure that there is no delay between delivery of the goods and dispatch of the invoice, so that the customer is made aware of the due date for payment as early as possible.
- *Systematically review debtors* One measure useful in reviewing debtors is the average collection period (ACP). For example, if a firm has £1.5m of outstanding debtors and an annual turnover of £20m, the average collection period is:

$$\frac{\text{Debtors outstanding}}{\text{Average daily sales}} = \frac{1{,}500{,}000}{20{,}000{,}000/365} = 27 \text{ days}$$

Note that if sales are seasonal the 'acceptable' ACP may vary through the year. Another guide to aid decision making and prompt action is the ageing schedule. The total debtor figure is broken down to show how long invoices have been outstanding. This is shown in Exhibit 12.11.

Exhibit 12.11 An ageing schedule

Period account has been outstanding (days)	*Total debtors (%)*
0–29	42
30–59	40
60–89	10
90–119	6
120+	2

- ***Slow payers have to be chased*** Any good system will call for a response immediately a debtor has failed to pay on time. This does not mean jumping to court action to recover the debt. There will be a sequence of actions before the drastic involvement of lawyers. Exhibit 12.12 shows a typical sequence.

A balance has to be struck when pressing for payment between the effort, expense and lost goodwill on the one hand and the cost of financing the loan to a customer on the other. The gain from receiving payment one day earlier is:

$$d = \sqrt[365]{(1+i)} - 1$$

where d = daily interest and i = annual cost of capital.

For example, the gain of receiving £100,000 one day earlier when the annual cost of capital is 12 per cent is:

$$d = \sqrt[365]{(1+0.12)} - 1 = 0.000310538$$

$$\pounds 100{,}000 \times 0.000310538 = \pounds 31.05$$

Despite improved credit controls late payment of bills is still a serious problem with a typical delay of 46 days in 2001. Exhibit 12.13 provides some more ideas on how to speed up payment.

Cash discounts are used as part of the collecting system due to two benefits they give *if* they stimulate early settlement. First, early settlement reduces the cost of carrying the loan, and second, the longer an account remains unpaid the greater the risk of eventual default. The level of discount has to be considered very carefully as the effective cost can be extremely high.

Exhibit 12.12 Stages in payment collection

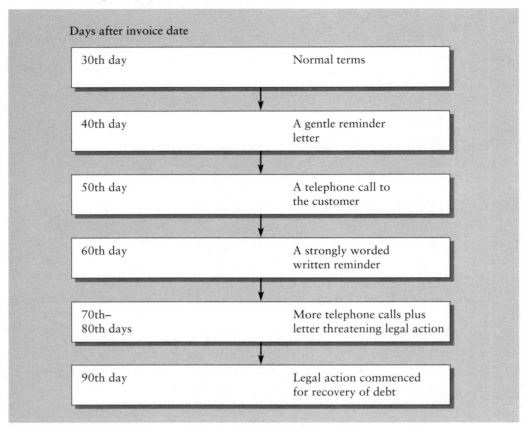

Days after invoice date	
30th day	Normal terms
40th day	A gentle reminder letter
50th day	A telephone call to the customer
60th day	A strongly worded written reminder
70th–80th days	More telephone calls plus letter threatening legal action
90th day	Legal action commenced for recovery of debt

Exhibit 12.13 Late payment

The subtle art of getting paid

FT

Many small businesses could be more effective at tackling unpaid bills. But an array of tactics are available, says David Baker

Some small businesses develop creative ways to pursue customers who are paying their bills late.

An antique fireplace shop in north London until recently kept on call a 6ft 3in ex-con who had two fingers missing on his left hand and halitosis. His job was simple: to persuade defaulting customers to pay up by going to their workplace and sitting quietly, but unpleasantly, in the lobby. He seldom had to stay long before the promised cheque appeared.

Another small businessman, this time in advertising, was owed money by a smart furniture shop. He took the afternoon off to stand in the customer's doorway telling people coming in that they would be ripped off. He had his cheque within the hour.

Neither approach would feature in a business school textbook on credit management, but both were effective . . .

Each year 10,000 UK businesses fail because their invoices are paid late, according to Dun & Bradstreet, the credit management consultancy. Out of £17bn owed to UK small businesses last year, £6.8bn was paid after the due date, costing them the equivalent of £78m in unpaid interest, according to the Credit Management Research Centre at Leeds University and the Federation of Small Businesses, the trade body. Yet few small businesses make use of legislation that penalises late payers, and most believe the law can be of little

Exhibit 12.13 continued

help when witholding payment appears to be becoming the norm . . .

To address this, the Late Payment of Commercial Debts (Interest) Act 1998 allows creditors to add interest to unpaid invoices without having to go to court. A European Community directive, for which the UK consultation period ends on Friday, would allow companies to claim compensation as well as interest from late paying customers.

But few businesses surveyed by the SBRT were confident that legislation could help, with more than half saying they were unlikely to use it. 'Late payment legislation is unworkable,' said one. They cited upsetting the customer and the sheer 'waste of time' as reasons for not going to court.

'Many companies are worried about losing their larger clients,' says Ms Low. 'The feeling is that if you want to do business with the big boys you have to play to their terms.' . . .

Trade credit is a loan to your customer, yet customer/supplier contracts can be surprisingly vague on the terms of payment. Mr Bosworth identifies three steps to managing trade credit:

- Sell the payment terms at the same time as you sell the product, agree those terms and get to know the person who actually signs the cheque.
- Eliminate 'own goals' such as delivering the product late or sending an invoice that does not match the delivery note.
- Be prepared to ask for the money you are owed . . .

Another option would be to look at factoring, where a financial institution pays you about 85 per cent of the money you are owed upfront and pursues the debtors itself. Factoring can be costly, but so is chasing debt yourself. As one SBRT respondent put it: 'We suffer little from late-payment problems but only because we devote much time and effort to chasing monies due and this is a expensive use of management time.'

Source: David Baker, *Financial Times*, 24 April 2001, p. 18. Reprinted with permission.

Outline guide to getting invoices paid on time

- **Get your attitude right**
  A sale is not a sale until it is paid for.
  Make enough time to send reminders at short intervals.
- **Cultivate large customers**
  Check their credit ratings, get to know the person who makes the payments, give these customers top priority, phone or fax for payments – don't send routine letters.
- **Make your payment terms very clear**
  Ask if any problems paying by agreed date, state terms boldly on quotation to inquiries, put date for payment in bold on invoice.
- **Open new accounts competently**
  The customer should sign a form agreeing payment terms.
  Only open the account when you are satisfied with the risk.
- **Invoice immediately and accurately**
  Do not give customers any grounds for non-payment through errors.
  Courier large invoices
- **Use the right methods to collect overdue debts**
  This can range from visiting in person (very large accounts), to phone, letters and fax. As a last resort consider issuing a statutory demand or taking legal action.
- **Set targets, deadlines and priorities**
  Decide total cash needed by month end. Chase large debts first. Plot your daily progress towards that target – may include wallchart and staff incentives to collect debt.
- **Use third parties sooner rather than later**
  If standard efforts fail, the customer won't pay until threatened. Use a collection agency for undisputed debts below a certain value and three months overdue, or a strong solicitor's letter to try to avoid proceedings.

Adapted from the Better Payment Practice Group website at www.payontime.co.uk

Take the case of a firm that normally collects debts after 40 days which introduces a 3 per cent discount for payment on the tenth day. If customers took advantage of this, the cost on an annual basis would be:

$$\text{Discount over 30 days is: } \frac{3}{100-3} = 0.0309278 \text{ or } 3.09\% \text{ for a 30-day period}$$

$$\text{The number of 30-day periods per year is: } \frac{365}{30} = 12.167$$

The annual interest rate is:

$$(1.0309278)^{12.167} - 1 = 44.9\%$$

The effective cost of the discount is very large and has to be offset against the improved cash flow, lowered bad debt risk and increased sales. The use of the cash discount has been further complicated by the fact that some customers abuse the system and take the discount even if they delay payment beyond the specified time.

Another way of encouraging payment at the contracted time is to make it clear that interest will be charged on overdue accounts. Suppliers are often reluctant to use this method as it has the disadvantage of creating resentment and blank refusals to pay the interest.

Firms that grant trade credit need to establish a policy on what to do when an invoice is highly unlikely to be paid, that is, it becomes a bad debt. In many cases there comes a stage when it is better to cease pursuing a debtor rather than to incur any more expense. The firm will need to work out a set of criteria for deciding when to write off a bad debt.

Integration with other disciplines

Customers sometimes see a glimpse of the conflict between the objectives of the sales team and the finance departments of suppliers. Sales representatives go out of their way to find new customers and to gain large orders from existing clients only to find that head office has vetoed the opening of a new account or is enforcing a strict credit limit. The sales personnel often spend years cultivating a relationship which can be seriously damaged by the harsh actions of the debtor collection department, ranging from unpleasant letters to court action. On the other hand, the debtor management department may complain that the sales representatives offer the customer excessively generous terms for the customer's risk class in order to meet a monthly sales target. Such conflicts need careful handling. Inter-function communication will help, as will an ethos of shareholder wealth enhancement with rewards and penalties directed at that goal in all departments.

FACTORING

Factoring (or 'invoice finance') companies provide three services to firms with outstanding debtors, the most important of which, in the context of this chapter, is the immediate transfer of cash. This is provided by the factor on the understanding that when invoices are paid by customers the proceeds will go to them. Factoring is increasingly used by companies of all sizes as a way of meeting cash flow needs induced by rising sales and debtor balances. A total of £77bn was factored in the UK in 2000. About 80 per cent of factoring turnover is handled by the clearing bank subsidiaries, e.g. HSBC Invoice Finance, Alex Lawrie (Lloyds TSB) and Royal Bank of Scotland Invoice Finance. However there are dozens of smaller factoring companies. Three closely related services are offered by factors. These are the provision of finance, sales ledger administration and credit insurance.

1 The provision of finance

At any one time a typical business can have a fifth or more of its annual turnover outstanding in trade debts: a firm with an annual turnover of £5m may have a debtor balance of £1m. These large sums create cash difficulties which can pressurise an otherwise healthy business. Factors step in to provide the cash needed to support stock levels, to pay suppliers and generally aid more profitable trading and growth. The factor will give an advanced payment on the security of outstanding invoices. Normally about 80 per cent of the invoice value can be made available to a firm immediately (with some factors this can be as much as 90 per cent). The remaining 20 per cent is transferred from the factor when the customer finally pays up. Naturally the factor will charge a fee and interest on the money advanced. The cost will vary between clients depending on sales volume, the type of industry and the average value of the invoices. According to HSBC the charge for finance is comparable with overdraft rates (2–3 per cent over base rate). As on an overdraft the interest is calculated on the daily outstanding balance of the funds that the borrowing firm has transferred to their business account. Added to this is a service charge that varies between 0.2 per cent and 3 per cent of invoiced sales. This is set at the higher end if there are many small invoices or a lot of customer accounts or the risk is high. Exhibit 12.14 shows the stages in a typical factoring transaction. First, goods are delivered to the customer and an invoice is sent. Secondly, the supplier sells the right to receive the invoice amount to a factor in return for, say, 80 per cent of the face value now. Thirdly, some weeks later the customer pays the sum owing, which goes to the factor and finally, the factor releases the remaining 20 per cent to the supplier less interest and fees.

Exhibit 12.14 Stages in a factoring deal

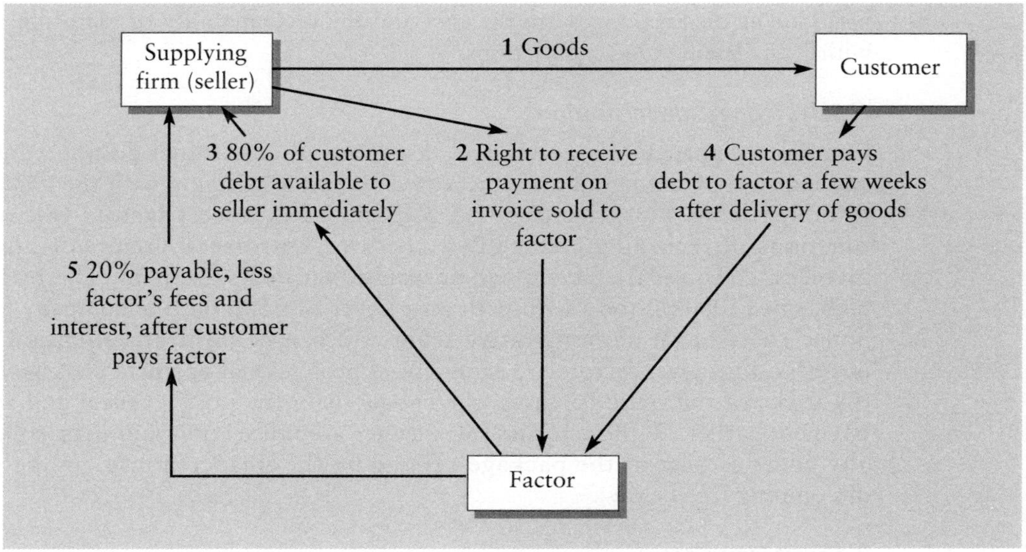

Exhibit 12.15 shows how a factor might calculate the amount to be advanced.

Exhibit 12.15

Amount available from a factor

A supplying firm has £1,000,000 of outstanding invoices, £40,000 are so old that the factor will not consider them, £60,000 are rejected as poor quality or are export sales and £30,000 are subject to a dispute between the supplier and the customer. The factor is prepared to advance 80 per cent of suitable invoices:

Total invoices		£1,000,000
Less:		
Debts excessively old	£40,000	
Non-approved	£60,000	
In dispute	£30,000	
		(130,000)
		£870,000

The amount the factor is willing to provide to the supplier immediately is 80 per cent of £870,000, or £696,000 (69.6 per cent of total invoices).

Factors frequently reject clients as unsuitable for their services. The factor looks for 'clean and unencumbered debts' so that it can be reasonably certain of receiving invoice payments. It will also want to understand the company's business and to be satisfied with the competence of its management.

This form of finance has some advantages over bank borrowing. The factor does not impose financial ratio covenants or require fixed asset backing. Also the fear of instant withdrawal of a facility (as with an overdraft) is absent as there is usually a notice period. The disadvantages are the cost and the unavailability of factoring to companies with many small-value transactions.

2 Sales ledger administration

Companies, particularly young and fast-growing ones, often do not want the trouble and expense of setting up a sophisticated system for dealing with the collection of outstanding debts. For a fee (0.5–2.5 per cent of turnover) factors will take over the functions of recording credit sales, checking customers' creditworthiness, sending invoices, chasing late payers and ensuring that debts are paid. The fees might seem high, say £100,000 for a firm with a turnover of £5m, but the company avoids the in-house costs of an administrative team and can concentrate attention on the core business. Moreover factors are experienced professional payment chasers who know all the tricks of the trade (such as 'the cheque is in the post' excuse) and so can obtain payment earlier. With factoring sales ledger administration and debt collection generally come as part of the package offered by the finance house, unlike with invoice discounting (*see* below).

3 Credit insurance

The third service available from a factor is the provision of insurance against the possibility that a customer does not pay the amount owed.

Recourse and non-recourse

Most factoring arrangements are made on a non-recourse basis, which means that the factor accepts the risk of non-payment by the customer firm. For accepting this risk the factor will not only require a higher return but also want control over credit assessment, credit approval and other aspects of managing the sales ledger to ensure payment. Some firms prefer recourse factoring in which they retain the risk of customer default but also continue to maintain the relationship with their customers through the debt collection function without the sometimes overbearing intervention of the factor. With confidential invoice factoring the customer is usually unaware that a factor is the ultimate recipient of the money paid over, as the supplier continues to collect debts, acting as an agent for the factor.

Invoice discounting

With invoice discounting, invoices are pledged to the finance house in return for an immediate payment of up to 90 per cent of the face value. The supplying company guarantees to pay the amount represented on the invoices and is responsible for collecting the debt. The customers are generally totally unaware that the invoices have been discounted. When the due date is reached it is to be hoped that the customer has paid in full. Regardless of whether the customer has paid, the supplying firm is committed to handing over the total invoice amount to the finance house and in return receives the remaining 10 per cent less service fees and interest. Note that even invoice discounting is subject to the specific circumstances of the client agreement and is sometimes made on a non-recourse basis. The key differences between invoice discounting and factoring are that the former is *usually* with recourse to the supplying company and collection from the customer is made by the supplying company.

The finance provider will usually only advance money under invoice discounting if the business is well established and profitable. There must be an effective and professional sales ledger administration system and turnover must be at least £500,000. Charges are usually lower than for factoring because the sales ledger administration is the responsibility of the supplying company.

HIRE PURCHASE

With hire purchase the finance company buys the equipment that the borrowing firm needs. The equipment (plant, machinery, vehicles, etc.) belongs to the hire purchase (HP) company. However the finance house allows the 'hirer' firm to use the equipment in return for a series of regular payments. These payments are sufficient to cover interest and contribute to paying off the principal. While the monthly installments are still being made the HP company has the satisfaction and security of being the legal owner and so can take repossession if the hirer defaults on the payments. After all payments have been made the hirer becomes the owner, either automatically or on payment of a modest option-to-purchase fee. Nowadays, consumers buying electrical goods or vehicles have become familiar with the attempts of sales assistants to also sell an HP agreement so that the customer pays over an extended period. Sometimes the finance is provided by the same organisation, but more often by a separate finance house. The stages in an HP agreement are as in Exhibit 12.16, where the HP company buys the durable good which is made available to the hirer firm for immediate use. A series of regular payments follows until the hirer owns the goods.

Exhibit 12.16 The hire purchase sequence

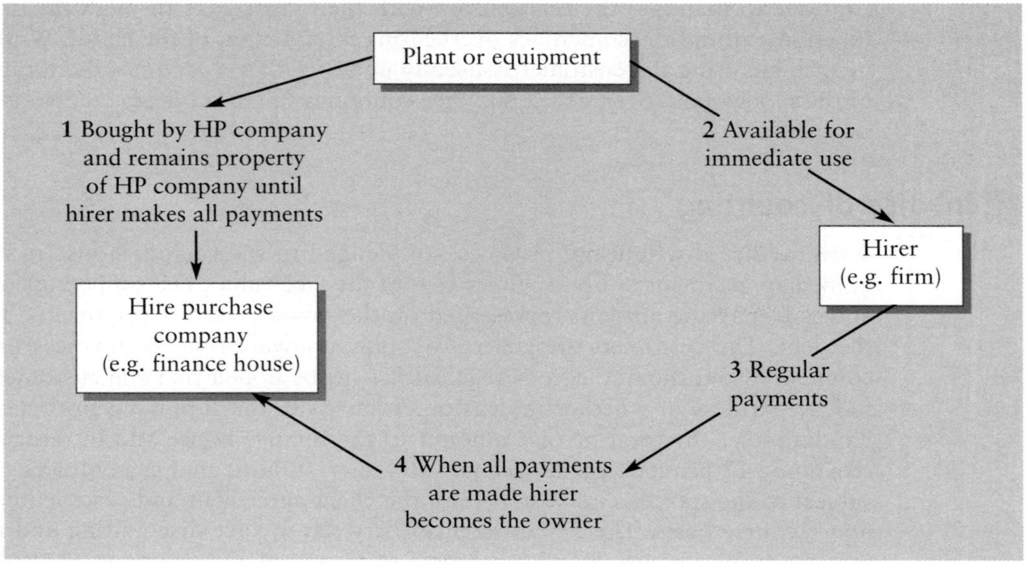

Some examples of assets that may be acquired on HP are as follows.

- Plant and machinery
- Business cars
- Commercial vehicles
- Agricultural equipment
- Hotel equipment
- Medical and dental equipment
- Computers, including software
- Office equipment

There are clearly some significant advantages of this form of finance, given the fact that over £7bn of new agreements are arranged each year for UK businesses alone. The main advantages are as follows.

1 ***Small initial outlay*** The firm does not have to find the full purchase price at the outset. A deposit followed by a series of instalments can be less of a cash flow strain. The funds that the company retains by handing over merely a small deposit can be used elsewhere in the business for productive investment. Set against this are the relatively high interest charges and the additional costs of maintenance and insurance.

2 ***Easy to arrange*** Usually at point of sale.

3 ***Certainty*** This is a medium-term source of finance which cannot be withdrawn provided contractual payments are made, unlike an overdraft. On the other hand the commitment is made for a number of years and it could be costly to terminate the agreement.

4 *HP is often available when other sources of finance are not* For some firms the equity markets are unavailable and banks will no longer lend to them, but HP companies will still provide funds as they have the security of the asset to reassure them.

5 *Fixed-rate finance* In most cases the payments are fixed throughout the HP period. While the interest charged will not vary with the general interest rate throughout the life of the agreement the hirer has to be aware that the HP company will quote an interest rate which is significantly different from the true annual percentage rate. The HP company tends to quote the flat rate. So, for example, on a £9,000 loan repayable in equal instalments over 30 months the flat rate might be 12.4 per cent. This is calculated by taking the total interest charged over the two and a half years and dividing by the original £9,000. The monthly payments are £401.85 and therefore the total paid over the period is £401.85 × 30 = £12,055.50. The flat interest is:

$$\sqrt[2.5]{(12{,}055.50/9{,}000)} - 1 = 0.1240 \text{ or } 12.4\%$$

This would be the true annual rate if the entire interest and capital were repaid at the end of the thirtieth month. However, a portion of the capital and interest is repaid each month and therefore the annual percentage rate (APR) is much higher than the flat rate. As a rough rule of thumb the APR is about double the flat rate. To calculate the APR more accurately annuity tables can be used. The present value (PV) is given as £9,000, the regular payments are £401.85 and we need to find the (monthly) interest rate which makes these 30 future inflows, when discounted, the same as the initial outflow.

$$\text{Present value} = \text{annuity} \times \text{annuity factor}$$

$$9{,}000 = 401.85 \times \text{annuity factor (af)}$$

$$\text{af} = \frac{9{,}000}{401.85} = 22.3964$$

Look along the 30 payments row of the annuity table (*see* Appendix III) to find the interest rate which corresponds with an annuity factor of 22.3964. This is very nearly 2 per cent per month. An interest rate of 2 per cent per month is equivalent to an annual percentage rate of 26.8 per cent, viz.:

$$(1 + m)^{12} = 1 - \text{i}$$

$$i = (1 + m)^{12} - 1$$

$$i = (1 + 0.02)^{12} - 1$$

$$i = 0.268 \text{ or } 26.8\%$$

If the writer's experience in buying a car on HP is anything to go by, obtaining the annual percentage rate (APR) from the sales representative is not easy – they tend to be much more interested in talking about the flat rate and emphasising the affordability of the monthly payments. The point is that you need to know the APR in order to compare alternative sources of finance.

6 *Tax relief* The hirer qualifies for tax relief in two ways:

a The asset can be subject to a writing-down allowance (WDA) on the capital expenditure. For example, if the type of asset is eligible for a 25 per cent WDA and originally cost £10,000 the using firm can reduce its taxable profits by £2,500 in the year of purchase; in the second year taxable profits will be lowered by £7,500 × 0.25 = £1,875. If tax is levied at 30 per cent on taxable profit the tax bill is reduced by £2,500 × 0.30 = £750 in the first year, and £1,875 × 0.3 = £562.50 in the second year. Note that this relief is available despite the hirer company not being the legal owner of the asset.

b Interest payments are deductible when calculating taxable profits.

The tax reliefs are valuable only to profitable companies. Many companies do not make sufficient profit for the WDA to be worth having. This can make HP an expensive form of finance. An alternative form of finance which circumvents this problem (as well as having other advantages) is leasing.

LEASING

Leasing is similar to HP in that an equipment owner (the lessor) conveys the right to use the equipment in return for regular rental payments by the equipment user (the lessee) over an agreed period of time. The essential difference is that the lessee never becomes the owner – the leasing company retains legal title. Subsidiaries of clearing banks dominate the UK leasing market, but the world's biggest leasing companies are Ford, GE Capital and GMAC (owned by General Motors).

Leasing, together with hire purchase, accounts for approximately one-quarter of all fixed capital investment by UK firms – rising to 50 per cent for small firms. Exhibit 12.17 shows that a typical lease transaction involves a firm wanting to make use of an asset approaching a finance house which purchases the asset and rents it to the lessee.

Exhibit 12.17 A leasing transaction

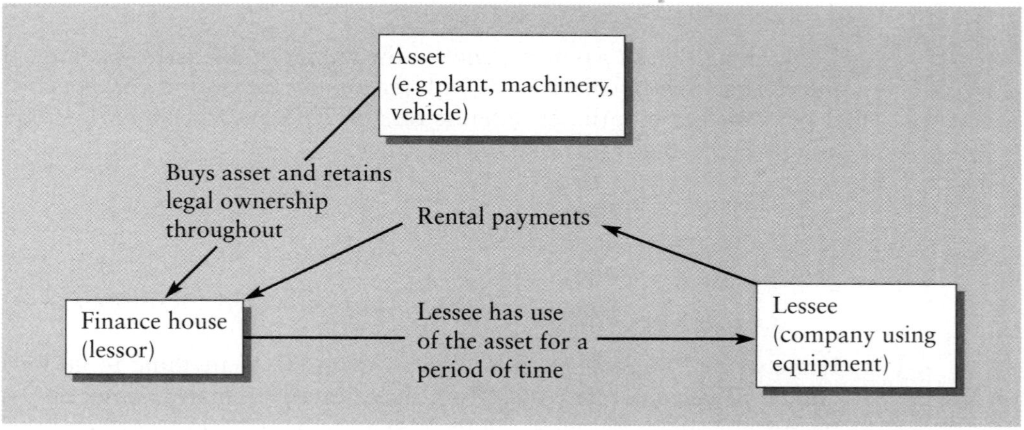

It is important to distinguish between operating leases and finance leases.

Operating lease

Operating leases commit the lessee to only a short-term contract or one that can be terminated at short notice. These are certainly not expected to last for the entire useful life of the asset and so the finance house has the responsibility of finding an alternative use for the asset when the lessee no longer requires it. Perhaps the asset will be sold in the secondhand market, or it might be leased to another client. Either way the finance house bears the risk of ownership. If the equipment turns out to have become obsolete more quickly than was originally anticipated it is the lessor that loses out. If the equipment is less reliable than expected the owner (the finance house) will have to pay for repairs. Usually, with an operating lease, the lessor retains the obligation for repairs, maintenance and insurance. It is clear why equipment which is subject to rapid obsolescence and frequent breakdown is often leased out on an operating lease. Photocopiers, for example, used by a university department are far better leased so that if they break down the university staff do not have to deal with the problem. In addition the latest model can be quickly installed in the place of an outdated one. The same logic applies to computers, facsimile machines and so on.

Operating leases are also useful if the business involves a short-term project requiring the use of an asset for a limited period. For example building firms often use equipment supplied under an operating lease (sometimes called plant hire). Operating leases are not confined to small items of equipment. There is a growing market in leasing aircraft and ships for periods less than the economic life of the asset, thus making these deals operating leases. Many of Boeing's aircraft go to leasing firms – *see* Exhibit 12.18 about Boeing selling to International Lease Finance Corporation which will then lease the aircraft to Virgin.

Exhibit 12.18

Branson orders new Boeings

FT

Richard Branson's Virgin has ordered 10 new generation Boeing 737 aircraft for A$540m (US$330m) as part of its plans to launch a no-frills airline to serve the Australian domestic market.

Virgin Australia, which aims to start operations before September's Sydney Olympics, said yesterday it had agreed the deal with International Lease Finance Corporation, the Los Angeles-based leasing group, earlier this week.

Delivery of the aircraft, which are to be paid for from operating cashflow, is due to begin in a year's time.

Source: Virginia Marsh, *Financial Times*, 24 March 2000, p. 16. Reprinted with permission.

Finance lease

Under a finance lease (also called a capital lease or a full payout lease) the finance provider expects to recover the full cost (or almost the full cost) of the equipment, plus interest, over the period of the lease. With this type of lease the lessee usually has no right of cancellation or termination. Despite the absence of legal ownership the lessee will have to bear the risks and rewards that normally go with ownership: the lessee will usually be responsible for maintenance, insurance and repairs and suffer the frustrations of demand being below expectations or the equipment becoming obsolete more rapidly than anticipated. Most finance leases contain a primary and a secondary period. It is during the primary period that the lessor receives the capital sum plus interest. In the secondary period the lessee pays a very small 'nominal', rental payment. Even the armed forces have turned to leasing as a method of funding: in 2001 the Ministry of Defence signed a 10-year deal worth £500m involving 8,500 vehicles being leased from Lex Vehicle Leasing.

Advantages of leasing

The advantages listed for hire purchase also apply to leasing: small initial outlay, certainty, available when other finance sources are not, fixed-rate finance and tax relief. There is an additional advantage of operating leases and that is the transfer of obsolescence risk to the finance provider.

The tax advantages for leasing are slightly different from those for HP. The rentals paid on an operating lease are regarded as tax deductible and so this is relatively straightforward. However, for financial leases the tax treatment is linked to the modern accounting treatment following SSAP 21. This was introduced to prevent some creative accounting which under the old system allowed a company to appear to be in a better gearing (debt/equity ratio) position if it leased rather than purchased its equipment. Prior to SSAP 21 a company could lower its apparent gearing ratio and therefore improve its chances of obtaining more borrowed funds by leasing. Take the two companies X and Y, which have identical balance sheets initially, as shown in Exhibit 12.19.

Exhibit 12.19 Balance sheets of companies X and Y

Shareholders' funds (net assets)	£1,000,000
Debt capital	£1,000,000
Total assets	£2,000,000

Now if X borrows a further £1m to buy equipment, while Y leases £1m of equipment the balance sheets appear strikingly different under the old accounting rules.

	Company X	*Company Y*
Shareholders' funds (net assets)	1,000,000	1,000,000
Debt capital	2,000,000	1,000,000
Total assets	3,000,000	2,000,000

Company X has a debt/equity ratio of 66.67 per cent whereas Y has obtained the use of the asset 'off-balance sheet' and so has an apparent gearing ratio of only 50 per cent. A superficial analysis of these two firms by, say, a bank lender, may lead to the conclusion that Y is more capable of taking on more debt. However in reality Y has a high level of fixed cash outflow commitments stretching over a number of years under the lease and is in effect highly geared. Company Y could also show a higher profit to asset ratio.

Today finance leases have to be 'capitalised' to bring them on to the balance sheet. The asset is stated in the balance sheet and the obligations under the lease agreement are stated as a liability. Over subsequent years the asset is depreciated and, as the capital repayments are made to the lessor, the liability is reduced. The profit and loss account is also affected: the depreciation and interest are both deducted as expenses.

The tax authorities apply similar rules and separate the cost of interest on the asset from the capital cost. The interest rate implicit in the lease contract is tax deductible in the relevant year. The capital cost for each year is calculated by allocating rates of depreciation (capital allowances) to each year of useful life.

These new rules apply only to finance leases and not to operating leases. A finance lease is defined (usually) as one in which the present value of the lease payments is at least 90 per cent of the asset's fair value (usually its cash price). This has led to some bright sparks engineering leasing deals which could be categorised as operating leases and therefore kept off-balance sheets – some are designed so that 89 per cent of the value is paid by the lessee. However the authorities are fighting back as Exhibit 12.20 shows. This discusses the impact of bringing operating lease liabilities on to the balance sheet for property companies. However, the proposed accounting changes will apply to all companies.

Exhibit 12.20

A tougher stand on leases

FT

The new accountancy rules being considered on leaseholds would not always make pleasant reading on the balance sheet

How is a lease different from a loan? Both require a steady stream of payments over a period of time, and failure to pay results in clear penalties.

So why then are corporations required to show the capital value of loans on their balance sheets, but not the capital value of most leases?

Accountancy bodies around the world are taking a tougher stand on off-balance sheet obligations . . .

For some years the accounting profession has been considering the ironic situation whereby companies are required to show their debt in stark detail while ignoring much of their leasehold obligations.

This anomoly has been troubling the G4 Plus One accountancy regulators – a group comprising the UK, US, Australia, Canada and New Zealand plus the International Accounting Standards Committee – for years.

In most countries, regulators have allowed a distinction between finance leases in which the economic benefits of ownership remain with the occupier, and operation leases in which the benefits and risks are largely transferred. This has allowed companies to disguise finance leases as operating leases and leave them off-balance sheet, an outcome about which none of the regulators are happy . . .

Next month, the UK's Accountancy Standards Board will issue a discussion paper on a proposed new rule that will require occupiers, for the first time, to show both the asset and liability values of their leaseholds.

Occupiers would be required to capitalise the value of future rental streams they will have to pay under all the leases they have entered into and disclose these as a liability. This would be matched by an asset of corresponding value representing the worth of the lease.

For countries with short-term lease structures, the new rules may not make much difference to corporate liabilities. But that is not the case in the UK where long-term leases prevail: the longer the lease, the greater the liability.

Even though the entry would be matched by an asset of corresponding value, it will force occupiers for the first time to focus on the true cost of long-term leases.

For this reason, the British property industry is concerned. No other member of the so-called G4 accountancy group has long-term leases with upward-only rent reviews in which the full costs of repair and insurance are borne by tenants . . .

The proposal under discussion, is logical on the face of it, and, indeed, is not even directed at the property industry, notes Andrew Lennard, assistant technical director at the UK's Accounting Standards Board. The impact of ignoring leasehold liabilities, according to a string of academic papers, distorts several key financial ratios for occupiers. A 1985 paper which looked at US corporate accounts, concluded that five accounting numbers are affected by leasehold recognition: interest charges, depreciation, fixed assets, accumulated depreciation and debt.

More recent studies by US-based professors Imhoff, Lipe and Wright in 1997, which looked at US companies, concluded that not only are numbers affected, but that key financial ratios, including returns on equity and debt to equity, are distorted by a decision to exclude the capital value of leases.

▶

Exhibit 12.20 continued

Most recently, professors Vivien Beattie, Keith Edwards and Alan Goodacre at the University of Stirling concluded that the impact of ignoring leasehold obligations is significant. On average, the unrecorded liability represented 39 per cent of long-term debt, while the unrecorded asset was 6 per cent of total assets. Perhaps even more critically, the effect on gearing ratios is substantial.

'The magnitude of the change astonished us, with gearing rising from 20 per cent to 72 per cent, an increase of 260 per cent,' the professors wrote, in a recent extract of their paper in Accountancy Magazine.

In particular, they found that the greatest impact on gearing was sustained by companies in the services sector, which includes retailers. There, average gearing goes from 24 per cent to 141 per cent.

Thus, it is not unreasonable that accounting professionals should be pressing to place unrecognised lease obligations on balance sheets.

Source: Norma Cohen, *Financial Times*, 29 October 1999, p. 24. Reprinted with permission.

A very important tax advantage can accrue to some companies through leasing because of the legal position of the asset not belonging to the lessee. Companies that happen to have sufficient profits can buy assets and then reduce their taxable profits by writing off a proportion of the assets' value (say 25 per cent on a reducing balance) against income each year. However companies with low profits or those which make a loss are unable to fully exploit these investment allowances and the tax benefit can be wasted. But if the equipment is bought by a finance company with plenty of profits, the asset cost can be used to save on the lessor's tax. This benefit can then be passed on to the customer (the lessee) in the form of lower rental charges. This may be particularly useful to start-up companies and it has also proved of great value to low- or no-profit privatised companies. For example, the railway operating companies often make losses and have to be subsidised by the government. They can obtain the services of rolling stock (trains, etc.) more cheaply by leasing from a profit-generating train-leasing company than by buying. Another advantage is that the leasing agreement can be designed to allow for the handing back of the vehicles should the operating licence expire or be withdrawn (as the train-operating licences are – after seven years or so). This is big business as you can see from Exhibit 12.21.

Exhibit 12.21

Staff reap £57m profit in rail deal

FT

Eversholt sale prompts claims leasing companies were disposed of too cheaply

Forward Trust, a leading UK leasing group, yesterday clinched a £788m takeover of the Eversholt train leasing company in a deal which netted a £57m profit for management and employees.

The deal, for £192m more than the buy-out team and its backers paid in January 1996, is the second sale of one of the recently created rolling stock leasing companies, or roscos, in less than nine months. It prompted renewed criticism from Labour, which said 10 'fat cat' managers of privatised rail companies had amassed fortunes totalling £103m in a little over a year.

The rolling stock companies were set up by the government to take over British Rail's fleet of trains and lease them to the 25 train operating companies. The three – Eversholt, Porterbrook and Angel Trains – were sold in January 1996 for a total of £1.8bn plus an £800m dividend payment to the government.

The largest gainer in the Eversholt sale is Mr Andrew Jukes, the managing director, who turns a £110,000 investment into £15.9m. Sixty-six employees who put up an average of £1,600 each will receive an average of £231,000. The seven financial groups which backed the buy-out, led by the Candover Investments development capital company, made £396m, a near six-fold return on investment of £69.6m.

Exhibit 12.21 continued

Forward Trust, the leasing arm of Midland Bank and part of HSBC Holdings, said the deal would make it a substantial participant in the rail vehicle market. The company, which has assets of £4.4bn, already finances or manages a fleet of 200,000 cars and trucks. Mr Graham Picken, chief executive, said: 'There will be opportunities to lease new trains and refurbish existing ones. We want to be part of that.'

Source: Charles Batchelor and George Parker, *Financial Times*, 20 February 1997, p. 8. Reprinted with permission.

To buy or to lease?

A comparison of the relative costs of leasing through a finance lease and purchase through a bank loan is in practice a very complicated calculation. It is necessary to allow for the cost of capital and the tax treatment of alternative sources of finance. These, in turn, depend on the precise circumstances of the company at the time. It is further complicated by the timing of the tax payments and reliefs, and the potential for a residual value of the asset at the end of the primary lease period. Added to all of that is the problem that the tax rules change frequently and so a method of calculation applicable at one time is quickly out of date. The point is that a proper comparison requires highly specialised knowledge and so is beyond the scope of this book. However if a few simplifying assumptions are made the general principles can be conveyed easily. The simplifying assumptions are:

a Taxation does not exist.

b There is no value in the asset at the end of the lease period.

c The cost of capital applicable to the equipment is the same as the term loan interest rate; this is only valid if investors regard the lease and the bank loan as being perfect substitutes for each other with respect to the capital structure (gearing, etc.) and the riskiness of the cash flows. Armed with these assumptions we can assess whether it is better for The Quissical Games Company to lease or to buy.

Worked example 12.2 Quissical Games Company

The Quissical Games Company needs £10m of equipment to increase its production capacity. A leasing company has offered to purchase the equipment and lease it to Quissical for three annual lease payments of £3.8m, with the first payable immediately, the second at the beginning of the second year and the third at the beginning of the third year. The equipment

Exhibit 12.22 Quissical's lease versus buy decision (£m)

	Points in time (yearly intervals)		
	0	*1*	*2*
Lease rentals	–3.80	–3.80	–3.80
Cash flows associated with buy option	10.00		
Incremental cash flows	+6.20	–3.80	–3.80
Present value of incremental cash flows at 10%	+6.20	–3.4545	–3.1405
Net present value	–0.395		

will have a three-year useful life at the end of which it will have a zero scrap value. A bank has offered to lend £10m on a three-year term loan at a rate of interest of 10 per cent p.a. Which form of finance should Quissical accept?

This problem may be analysed on an incremental cash flow basis, that is, focusing on the differences in the cash flows – as shown in Exhibit 12.22.

The cash flows associated with the lease option have a present value which is £395,000 more than £10m when discounted at 10 per cent and therefore the lease is the more expensive method of finance.

Of course, in reality the tax payments are likely to have a significant impact on the relative merits of a bank loan and leasing finance, but this depends on Quissical's tax position, the time delay in paying tax, the current tax rates, the capital allowance permitted and so on.

Exhibit 12.23 (Big ticket leasing) and Exhibit 12.24 (IFC) demonstrate the extent to which the availability of lease finance influences big business, at the macro end of the scale, and the working lives of millions of people even in the poorest countries on earth, on the micro scale, where it is seen as playing an important role in lifting people out of poverty.

Exhibit 12.23 Big ticket leasing

Big ticket leasing accounts for a third of the funds provided through leasing

Leasing is sometimes used for very large assets – often in excess of £100m – which range from entire production lines and ships to shopping centres and accommodation for university students. For example in the early 1990s NatWest Markets put together a £290m leasing facility for Humber Power for gas and electrical plant and machinery. Another example is Airstream Finances, which leases 200 commercial aircraft on six continents. Even the high street bank Abbey National provides lease finance – for example £150m for train rolling stock for Network South East. Abbey also plans to have £2bn of aircraft leases by 2004.

Exhibit 12.24

IFC extends leasing aid to Vietnam

FT

The International Finance Corporation, the private sector arm of the World Bank, has announced its first foray in Vietnam's financial sector – the establishment of a leasing company to enable small and medium-sized companies to procure capital goods.

On the surface the $15m loan and $750,000 equity investment looks modest. However, the corporation has been promoting leasing as one of the quickest, cheapest and most flexible ways of supporting business in emerging economies, where businesses desperately need machinery, office and plant equipment.

The IFC is planning to sign a joint venture deal on November 12 to set up the first leasing company in Egypt.

The new Vietnamese company, Vietnam International Leasing Company (VILC), is expected to write leases of $25,000–$30,000 for smaller or micro enterprises and $100,000–$150,000 for medium-sized companies. IFC says VILC will have 'a strong impact on Vietnam's financial sector by extending and improving credit delivery and introducing new financial products to the local market to encourage capital formation and investment' . . .

IFC has been working closely with governments, advising them on leasing regulations, recruiting sponsors and technical partners and investing in new leasing companies.

An IFC paper, issued in August, said one-eighth of the world's private investment was financed

Exhibit 12.24 continued

through leasing. Its share is soaring; in some countries it provides as much as one-third of the private investment.

IFC has helped set up leasing companies in over half of the developing countries. In August it provided $5.6m in financing to help establish Uzbek Leasing International, the first specialised leasing company in Uzbekistan.

The corporation also helps leasing companies, in which it has equity, to expand. Last March it guaranteed a local currency loan of $3m equivalent for the Industrial Development Leasing Company of Bangladesh, established in 1986.

IFC's involvement allows the company to borrow locally for a longer period than otherwise would be possible.

IFC's first leasing venture was in 1977 in Korea. The Korea Development Leasing Corporation is now the world's fifth largest leasing industry.

Source: Nancy Dunne, *Financial Times*, 1 November 1996, p. 5. Reprinted with permission.

BILLS OF EXCHANGE

A bill is a document which sets out a commitment to pay a sum of money at a specified point in time. The simplest example is an ordinary bank cheque which has been dated two weeks hence. The government borrows by selling Treasury bills which commit it to paying a fixed sum in, say, three months. Local authorities issue similar debt instruments, as do commercial organisations in the form of commercial bills (discussed in Chapter 11).

Bills of exchange are mainly used to oil the wheels of overseas trade. They have a long history helping to promote international trade, particularly in the nineteenth and twentieth centuries. The seller of goods to be transported to a buyer in another country frequently grants the customer a number of months in which to pay. The seller will draw up a bill of exchange – that is, a legal document is produced showing the indebtedness of the buyer. The bill of exchange is then forwarded to, and accepted by the customer, which means that the customer signs a promise to pay the stated amount and currency on the due date. The due date is usually 90 days later but 30, 60 or 180 days bills of exchange are not uncommon. The bill is returned to the seller who then has two choices, either to hold it until maturity, or to sell it to a bank or discount house (the bill is discounted). Under the second option the bank will pay a lower amount than the sum to be received in, say, 90 days from the customer. The difference represents the bank's interest.

For example, if a customer has accepted a bill of exchange which commits it to pay £200,000 in 90 days the bill might be sold immediately to a discount house or bank for £194,000. After 90 days the bank will realise a profit of £6,000 on a £194,000 asset, an interest rate of 3.09 per cent ((6,000/194,000) × 100) over 90 days. This gives an approximate annual rate of:

$$(1.0309)^4 - 1 = 0.1296 = 12.96\%$$

Through this arrangement the customer has the benefit of the goods on 90 days credit, the supplier has made a sale and immediately receives cash from the discount house amounting to 97 per cent of the total due. The discounter, if it borrows its funds at less than 12.9 per cent, turns in a healthy profit. The sequence of events is shown in Exhibit 12.25.

Bills of exchange are normally only used for transactions greater than £75,000. The effective interest rate charged by the discounter is a competitive 1.5 per cent to 4 per cent over interbank lending rates (for example, LIBOR) depending on the creditworthiness of the seller and the customer. The bank has recourse to both of the commercial

Exhibit 12.25 The bill of exchange sequence

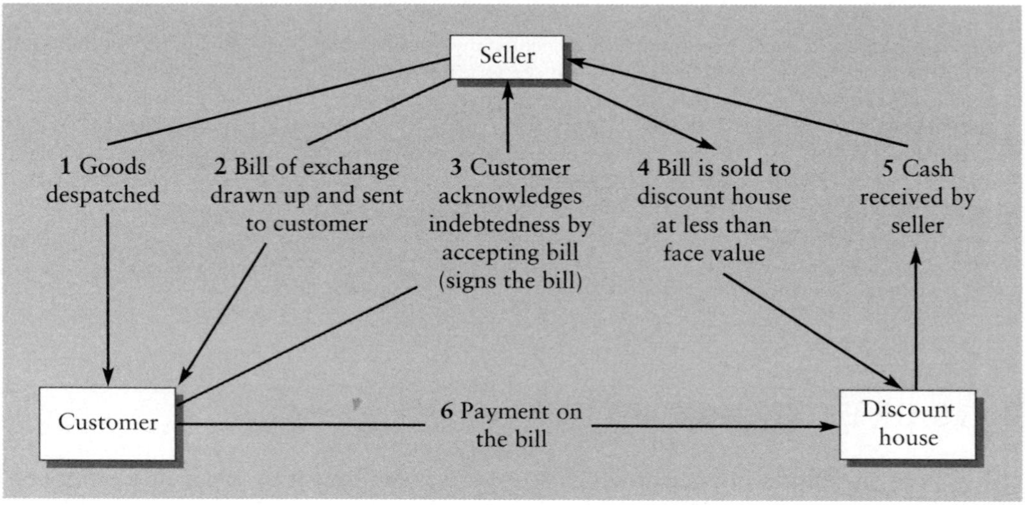

companies: if the customer does not pay then the seller will be called upon to make good the debt. This overhanging credit risk can sometimes be dealt with by the selling company obtaining credit insurance. Despite the simplification of Exhibit 12.25 many bills of exchange do not remain in the hands of the discounter until maturity but are traded in an active secondary market (the money market).

ACCEPTANCE CREDITS (BANK BILLS OR BANKER'S ACCEPTANCE)

In the case of acceptance credits (bank bills) the company which is in need of finance draws up a document agreeing to pay a sum of money at a set date in the future which is 'accepted' by a bank rather than by a customer. This bank commitment to pay the holder of the acceptance credit can then be sold in the money markets to, say, another bank (a discounter) by the firm to provide for its cash needs. (Alternatively an importing company could give the acceptance credit to its overseas supplier in return for goods – and the supplier can then sell it at a discount if required). The acceptance credit is similar to a bill of exchange between a seller and a buyer, but now the organisation promising to pay is a reputable bank representing a lower credit risk to any subsequent discounter. These instruments therefore normally attract finer discount rates than a trade bill. When the maturity date is reached the company pays the issuing bank the value of the bill, and the bank pays the ultimate holder of the bill its face value.

The company does not have to sell the acceptance credit immediately and so can use this instrument to plug finance gaps at opportune times. There are two costs of bank bill finance.

1 The bank charges acceptance commission for adding its name to the bill.
2 The difference between the discount price and the acceptance credit's due sum.

These costs are relatively low compared with those on overdrafts and there is an ability to plan ahead because of the longer-term commitment of the bank. Unfortunately this facility is only available in hundreds of thousands of pounds and then only to the most credit-worthy of companies.

Exhibit 12.26 An acceptance credit sequence

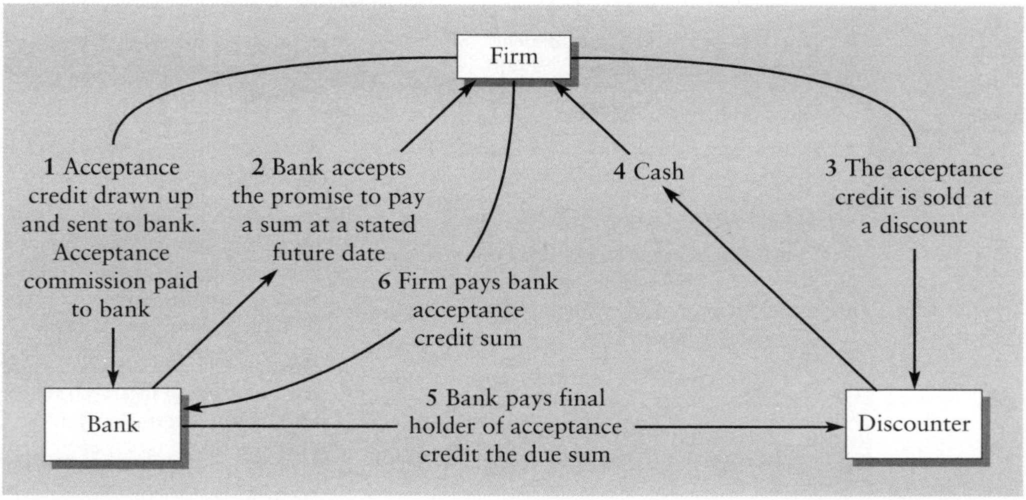

CONCLUDING COMMENTS

The modern corporation has a rich array of alternative sources of funds available to it. Each organisation faces different circumstances and so the most appropriate mixture will change from one entity to another. Of the dozens of forms of finance discussed in this chapter and Chapters 10 and 11 any organisation is unlikely to select more than five or six. However, the knowledge gained by reading these chapters and considering the relative merits of each type will, it is hoped, lead to a more informed choice and contribute to the achievement of the firm's objective. The quick revision sheet that follows, covering the sources of finance, shows how far we have come (*see* Exhibit 12.27).

Exhibit 12.27 Some of the types of finance available from the firm

Equity

1 **Ordinary shares** Owners of the firm. Full rights to vote at general meetings. Entitled to dividend and surplus on liquidation. High risk – residual income.

2 **Preferred ordinary and deferred ordinary** The former rank for payment of an agreed rate of dividend before the latter receive anything. The agreement may also permit the preferred holders to a share in the profits after they have received their priority percentage.

3 **Non-voting shares** Used to raise equity finance without losing control over the firm.

4 **Founders' shares** Dividends paid only after all other categories of equity shares have received fixed rates of dividend.

5 **Share warrants** Entitlement to buy a stated number of shares at a specific price up to a certain date. Often attached to loan stocks.

Preference shares

No voting rights (usually), except in liquidation. Entitled to a fixed and relatively certain dividend. Priority over ordinary shares in dividends and liquidation. Types:

- cumulative – if dividend is missed it is carried over and paid when firm is sufficiently profitable;
- participating – some or all of the dividend is related to corporate performance;
- redeemable – a fixed maturity date for capital repayment;
- convertible – can be converted into ordinary shares at a specific rate and price;

▶

Exhibit 12.27 continued

- variable rate – dividend depends on movements in benchmark, e.g. LIBOR.

Retained profits and reserves

The most important source of finance. Funds reinvested from previous years' profits.

Long-term debt

1 **Debenture (secured loan stock/bond)** A legal document showing the right to receive interest and a capital repayment. Often tradeable (negotiable). Types:

- 'fixed-charge debenture'– specific asset nominated as security;
- 'floating-charge debenture' – security is all the present and future assets of the firm;
- 'zero coupon' – no interest paid, but there is a large difference between initial payment for the bond and redemption value.

2 **Unsecured loan stock/bond** Legal document showing right to receive interest and capital repayment. Low down in pecking order for payment on liquidation. Coupon (interest) payment higher than debenture.

3 **Floating-rate note (FRN)** A bond on which the rate of interest is linked to short-term interest rates, e.g. three- or six-month London Interbank Offered Rate, LIBOR.

4 **Convertible unsecured loan stock/bond** Loan stock which can be converted into equity capital at the option of the holder. Lower rate of interest than debentures. Interest is tax deductible. Often self-liquidating.

5 **Bank loan** Term lending at fixed or floating rates (2–6 per cent above base rate). Arrangement fees at, say, 1 per cent of loan. Usually secured – guarantees by directors or charge over assets. Covenants usually required – e.g. target interest cover ratios or limits on further borrowing. Types:

- 'Bullet' loan – one final payment of capital.
- 'Balloon' loan – low repayments in early periods followed by high repayment rate in later period.
- 'Mortgage' style – regular repayment of equal amount.
- 'Grace periods' often available with low or no repayment.

6 **Syndicated lending** A group of banks provide a large loan.

Medium-term

1 **Bank loans** As above except period is one to seven years.

2 **Medium-term notes (MTNs)** A promise to pay a certain sum on a named date. Unsecured. Maturity: 9 months–20 years. Sold on to the financial markets. Fixed, floating or zero interest rates.

3 **Floating rate notes (FRNs)** Promissory notes with a floating interest rate, e.g. linked to LIBOR. Used particularly in the Euromarkets.

4 **Leasing** An equipment owner conveys the right to use the equipment in return for rental payments over an agreed period. Avoids up-front lump-sum payment. Available when other sources exhausted. Tax advantages.

- Finance (capital) lease – covers entire useful life of asset (or at least 90 per cent of the value of the asset); the finance house receives back at least 90 per cent of the outlay plus interest over lease period.
- Operating lease – only covers a proportion of the useful life of the asset, e.g. plant hire, photocopier, cars.

5 **Hire purchase** An HP company purchases an asset which is used by the hirer, who after a series of payments becomes the owner. Convenient and available when other finance is not.

Short-term

1 **Trade credit** Delaying payment for goods received. Very important source, convenient and informal. Not necessarily free: consider opportunity cost of losing discount for early settlement.

2 **Overdraft** Allowing a bank account to go into debit position. Easy to arrange, flexible, but repayable on demand.

3 **Factoring** Raising funds on the security of the company's debts. Services available:

- Provision of finance – factor advances up to 90 per cent of value of debts. When invoices are paid the remaining 10 per cent less charges is paid to firm by factor. Fee plus interest at 2–5 per cent over base.

Exhibit 12.27 continued

- Sales ledger administration, dispatching invoices and ensuring bills are paid. Fee: 0.5 to 3 per cent.
- Credit insurance.
- Confidential invoice factoring – customer is unaware that the debts have been sold. Customer sends payment to supplier, not to factor.

4 **Invoice discounting** Stages:
  1 Firm sends invoice to finance house (FH) and firm guarantees that invoice will be paid.
  2 FH pays up to 90 per cent of invoice amount to firm.
  3 Three months later (say) the firm collects debt from customer and pays FH.
  Cost: 2–6 per cent over base.

5 **Deferred tax payments** Interval between earning of profits and payment of taxes produces cash availability.

6 **Commercial paper** Paper (a legal document expressing loan terms) with a maturity of seven days to nine months.

7 **Bill of exchange** A buyer sends a promise to pay a sum of money at a future date to a supplier. The bill can then be sold before the set date to a bank or discount house for cash. Useful for overseas trade. (Analogy: post-dated cheque.)

8 **Acceptance credit (bank bills)** A bank promises to pay out the amount of a bill of exchange at a future date. The firm then sells the bill. On maturity the bank pays the holder and the firm pays the bank.

9 **Revolving underwriting facility (RUF)** A bank underwrites the borrower's access to funds at a specified rate in the short-term financial markets throughout an agreed period.

Other

1 **Mezzanine finance** High-yielding loan, usually with equity warrants attached. Low security/high risk. Useful for restructuring, buyouts and leveraged takeovers. Interest rate 2 to 9 per cent over LIBOR. Usually no secondary market. Types:

- strip financing – the firm obtains a variety of different types of mezzanine, with different costs, maturity and risk;
- stepped interest – lower repayments early on;
- junior mezzanine – ranking below senior mezzanine;
- high yield (junk) bonds – high-risk bonds.

The definition of mezzanine can be stretched to preference shares and convertible loans subordinate to the secured debt.

2 **Venture capital** Funding for new businesses or MBOs. Specialist funds, banks and 3i are principal suppliers. High failure rate, therefore high return required. Finance provider is usually looking for exit route in five to ten years.

3 **3i (Investors in industry)** Largest investor in unquoted companies in Europe.

4 **Sale and leaseback** Sale of property, etc. to investment institution and then renting back.

5 **Mortgaging property** Available from insurance companies, investment companies and pension funds.

6 **Eurobonds** International bonds sold outside the jurisdiction of the country of the currency in which the issue is denominated. No formal regulatory framework. Interest paid before tax. Usually bearer bonds. Usually cheaper than domestic bonds. Large sums available.

7 **Securitisation** A package of financial claims, e.g. the right to receive payments from 1,000 households for 25 years, is sold. Assets securitised include: commercial paper, mortgages, car loans, credit card receivables and export credits.

8 **Export finance** Documentary Letters of Credit. The purchaser's bank undertakes to pay at maturity on a bill of exchange. The exporter's bank discounts the bill. Also overdraft, loans, acceptance credits.

9 **Forfaiting** A bank purchases a number of sales invoices or promissory notes from an exporting company. Usually the importer's bank guarantees the invoices.

10 **Project finance** Medium-term borrowing for a particular purpose. The bank's security is the project itself, e.g. North Sea oil projects. Usually high risk/return for lender.

KEY POINTS AND CONCEPTS

- **Overdraft** A permit to overdraw on an account up to a stated limit.
  Advantages:
  – flexibility;
  – cheap.
  Drawbacks:
  – bank has right to withdraw facility quickly;
  – security is usually required.
- **A bank usually considers the following before lending:**
  – the projected cash flows;
  – creditworthiness;
  – the amount contributed by borrower;
  – security.
- **Term loan** A loan of a fixed amount for an agreed time and on specified terms, usually one to seven years.
- **Trade credit** Goods delivered by suppliers are not paid for immediately.
- The **early settlement discount** means that taking a long time to pay is not cost free.
- **Advantages of trade credit:**
  – convenient, informal and cheap;
  – available to companies of any size.
- **Factors determining the terms of trade credit:**
  – tradition within the industry;
  – bargaining strength of the two parties;
  – product type.
- **Trade debtors** are sales made on credit as yet unpaid. The management of debtors requires a trade-off between increased sales and costs of financing, liquidity risk, default risk and administration costs.
- **Debtor management** requires consideration of the following:
  – credit policy;
  – assessing credit risk;
  – agreeing terms;
  – collecting payment;
  – integration with other disciplines.
- **Factoring companies** provide at least three services:
  – providing finance on the security of trade debts;
  – sales ledger administration;
  – credit insurance.
- **Invoice discounting** is the obtaining of money on the security of book debts. Usually confidential and with recourse to the supplying firm. The supplying firm manages the sales ledger.
- **Hire purchase** is an agreement to hire goods for a specified period, with an option or an automatic right to purchase the goods at the end for a nominal or zero final payment.

The main advantages:
- small initial outlay;
- certainty;
- available when other sources of finance are not;
- fixed-rate finance;
- tax relief available.

- **Leasing** The legal owner of an asset gives another person or firm (the lessee) the possession of that asset to use in return for specified rental payments. Note that ownership is never transferred to the lessee.
- **An operating lease** commits the lessee to only a short-term contract, less than the useful life of the asset.
- **A finance lease** commits the lessee to a contract for the substantial part of the useful life of the asset.
- **Advantages of leasing:**
  - small initial outlay;
  - certainty;
  - available when other finance sources are not;
  - fixed rate of finance;
  - tax relief (operating lease: rental payments are a tax-deductible expense; finance lease: capital value can be written off over a number of years; interest is tax deductible. Capital allowance can be used to reduce tax paid on the profit of a finance house, which then passes on the benefit to the lessee);
  - avoid danger of obsolescence with operating lease.
- **Bills of exchange** A trade bill is the acknowledgement of a debt to be paid by a customer at a specified time. The legal right to receive this debt can be sold prior to maturity, that is discounted, and thus can provide a source of finance.
- **Acceptance credit** A financial institution or other reputable organisation accepts the promise to pay a specified sum in the future to a firm. The firm can sell this right, that is discount it, to receive cash from another institution.

REFERENCES AND FURTHER READING

Accounting Standards Committee (1984) *Accounting for leases and hire purchase contracts*, SSAP 21. London: Accounting Standards Committee. Details on the accounting regulations.

Arnold, G.C. and Davis, P. (1995) *Profitability trends in West Midlands industries. A study for Lloyds Bowmaker*. Edinburgh: Lloyds Bowmaker. Data and analysis combining accounting, finance and economics. Historical trends in ratios.

Arnold, G.C. and Davis, P. (1996) *Profitability trends in East Midlands industries. A study for Lloyds Bowmaker*. Edinburgh: Lloyds Bowmaker. Data and analysis combining accounting, finance and economics. Historical trends in ratios.

Bank of England Quarterly Bulletin. Up-to-date analysis of corporate financing methods.

Berry, A. *et al.* (1990) 'Leasing and the smaller firm', The Chartered Association of Certified Accountants, Occasional Research Paper No. 3. Empirical evidence on the use of leasing by small firms – discussion of the influences leading to the decision to lease.

Carty, P. (1994) 'The economics of expansion', *Accountancy*, March. Very interesting and clear article considering the sources of finance used by small UK firms.

Clark, T.M. (1978) *Leasing*. Maidenhead: McGraw-Hill. Old but still useful – easy to read.

Drury, J.C. and Braund, S. (1990) 'The leasing decision: A comparison of theory and practice', *Accounting and Business Research*, Summer, pp. 179–91. Survey evidence on the reasons why companies choose to lease assets.

Finance and Leasing Association (FLA) Annual Report. London: FLA. Gives some insight into HP and leasing in the UK, www.fla.org.uk.

James, A.N.G. and Peterson, P.P. (1984) 'The leasing puzzle', *Journal of Finance*, September. An investigation of the extent to which leases displace debt. An economic modelling approach.

Maness, T.S. and Zietlow, J.T. (1993) *Short-term financial management*. St Paul, MN: West Publishing Company. Debtor management is explained in greater detail than in this chapter.

Ross, S.A., Westerfield, R.W. and Jaffe, J. (1999) *Corporate Finance*. 5th edn. New York: McGraw-Hill. Chapter 28 gives consideration of debtor management.

Wynne, G.L. (1988) 'Sources of UK short-term and medium-term debt', in Rutterford, J. and Carter, D. (eds), *Handbook of Corporate Finance*. London: Butterworths. Short and well-written chapter on short- and medium-term finance.

WEBSITES

British Bankers Association www.bba.org.uk

Department of Trade and Industry www.dti.gov.uk

Federation of Small Businesses www.fsb.org.uk

Better Payments Practice Group www.payontime.co.uk

Finance and Leasing Association www.fla.org.uk

SELF-REVIEW QUESTIONS

1. What are the essential differences between an overdraft and a term loan?
2. What do banks take into account when considering the granting of an overdraft or loan?
3. Describe a circumstance in which an overdraft is preferable to a term loan from the borrower's point of view.
4. 'Taking a long time to pay suppliers' invoices is always a cheap form of finance.' Consider this statement.
5. What are the main determinants of the extent of trade credit granted?
6. In assessing whether to grant trade credit to a customer what would you take into account and what information sources would you use?
7. Discuss the advantages and disadvantages of offering an early settlement discount on an invoice from the supplier's point of view.
8. What are the main features of a good debtor collection system?
9. What is hire purchase and what are the advantages of this form of finance?
10. Explain the difference between the flat rate of interest on a hire purchase agreement quoted by a sales representative and the annual percentage rate.

11 How does hire purchase differ from leasing?

12 Explain the terms 'operating lease' and 'finance lease'.

13 How can lease finance be used to create off-balance-sheet debt? How are leases accounted for today?

14 What are the tax advantages of leasing an asset?

15 What is a bill of exchange and what does discounting a bill mean?

16 For what type of firms are acceptance credits useful?

QUESTIONS AND PROBLEMS

1 Ronsons plc, the jewellery retailer, has a highly seasonal business with peaks in revenue in December and June. One of Ronsons' banks has offered the firm a £200,000 overdraft with interest charged at 10% p.a. (APR) on the daily outstanding balance, with £3,000 payable as an arrangement fee. Another bank has offered a £200,000 loan with a fixed interest rate of 10% p.a. (APR) and no arrangement fee. Any surplus cash can be deposited to earn 4% APR. The borrowing requirement for the forthcoming year is as follows:

Month	J	F	M	A	M	J	J	A	S	O	N	D
£000s	0	180	150	180	200	0	150	150	180	200	200	0

Which offer should the firm accept?

2* Snowhite plc has taken delivery of 50,000 units of Dwarf moulds for use in its garden ornament business. The supplier has sent an invoice which states the following:

> *'£50,000 is payable if the purchaser pays in 30 days. However, if payment is within 10 days, a 1 per cent discount may be applied.'*

Snowhite has an unused overdraft facility in place, on which interest is payable at 12 per cent annual percentage rate on the daily outstanding balance. If Snowhite paid after 10 days the overdraft facility would have to be used for the entire payment.

a Calculate whether to pay on the 30th day or on the 10th day, on the basis of the information provided.

b Despite the 30-day credit limit on the contract Snowhite is aware that it is quite normal in this industry to pay on the 60th day without incurring a penalty legally, financially or in terms of reputation and credit standing. How does this alter your analysis?

3 (*Examination level*) Gordons plc has an annual turnover of £3m and a pre-tax profit of £400,000. It is not quoted on a stock exchange and the family which own all the shares have no intention of permitting the sale of shares to outsiders or providing more finance themselves. Like many small and medium-sized firms, Gordons has used retained earnings and a rolled-over overdraft facility to finance expansion. This is no longer seen as adequate, especially now that the bank manager is pushing the firm to move to a term loan as its main source of external finance.

You, as the recently hired finance director, have been in contact with some financial institutions. The Matey hire purchase company is willing to supply the £1m of additional equipment the firm needs. Gordons will have to pay for this over 25 months at a rate of £50,000 per month with no initial deposit.

The Helpful leasing company is willing to buy the equipment and rent it to Gordons on a finance lease stretching over the four-year useful life of the equipment, with a nominal rent thereafter. The cost of this finance is virtually identical to that for the term loan, that is, 13 per cent annual percentage rate.

Required

Write a report for the board of directors explaining the nature of the four forms of finance which may be used to purchase the new equipment: hire purchase, leasing, bank term loan and overdraft. Point out their relative advantages and disadvantages.

4 The Biscuit company has taken delivery of £10,000 of flour from its long-established supplier. Biscuit is in the habit of paying for flour deliveries 50 days after the invoice/delivery date. However things are different this time: the supplier has introduced an early settlement discount of 2 per cent if the invoice is paid within 10 days. The rate of interest being charged on Biscuit's overdraft facility is 11 per cent per annum. You may assume no tax to avoid complications.

Required

Calculate whether Biscuit should pay on the 10th day or the 50th day following the invoice date.

5* The Snack company is considering buying £30,000 of new kitchen equipment through a hire purchase agreement stretching over 18 months. £10,000 is paid as a deposit and the hire purchase company will require 18 monthly payments of £1,222.22 each to pay for the £20,000 borrowed, before the ownership of the equipment is transferred to the snack company. The rate of interest the Snack company would pay on an overdraft is 10 per cent per annum.

Required

a Calculate the annual percentage rate paid on the hire purchase contract.

b Discuss the relative merits and drawbacks of the two forms of finance mentioned in the question.

6 The Cable Company sells its goods on six months' credit which until now it has financed through term loans and overdrafts. Recently factoring firms have been pestering the managing director, saying that they can offer him immediate cash and the chance to get rid of the hassle of collecting debts. He is very unsure of factoring and has requested a report from you outlining the main features and pointing out the advantages and hazards. Write this report.

7 A small firm is considering the purchase of a photocopier. This will cost £2,000. An alternative to purchase is to enter into a leasing agreement known as an operating lease, in which the agreement can be terminated with only one month's notice. This will cost £60 per month. The firm is charged interest of 12 per cent on its overdraft.

Required

Consider the advantages and disadvantages of each method of obtaining the use of a photocopier.

8 Write an essay with the title: 'Small firms find it more difficult to raise finance than larger firms'.

9* (*Examination level*) A factoring company has offered a one-year agreement with Glub Ltd to both manage its debtors and advance 80 per cent of the value of all its invoices immediately a sale is invoiced. Existing invoices will be eligible for an immediate 80 per cent cash payment.

The annual sales on credit of Glub are £6m spread evenly through the year, and the average delay in payment from the invoice date is at present 80 days. The factoring company is confident of reducing this delay to only 60 days and will pay the remaining 20 per cent of invoice value to Glub immediately on receipt from the customer.

The charge for debtor management will be 1.7 per cent of annual credit turnover payable at the year-end. For the advance payment on the invoices a commission of 1 per cent will be charged plus interest applied at 10 per cent per annum on the gross funds advanced.

Glub will be able to save £80,000 during this year in administration costs if the factoring company takes on the debtor management. At the moment it finances its trade credit through an overdraft facility with an interest rate of 11 per cent.

Required

Advise Glub on whether to enter into the agreement. Discuss the relative advantages and disadvantages of overdraft, factoring and term loan financing.

10 Acorn presently sells on 60 days' credit. Is it financially attractive for a customer to accept a 1.5 per cent discount for payment on the 14th day, given an annual percentage rate of interest of 9 per cent, or continue to take 60 days with no discount?

11 (*Examination level*) Extracted data from Penguin plc's last accounts are as follows:

	£m
Annual sales	21
Profits before interest and tax	2
Interest	0.5
Shareholder funds	5
Long-term debt	4
Debtors	2.5
Stocks	2
Trade creditors	5
Bank overdraft	4

A major supplier to Penguin offers a discount of 2 per cent on all future supplies if payment is made on the seventh day following delivery rather than the present 70th day. Monthly purchases from this supplier amount to a regular £0.8m.

Penguin pays 15 per cent annual percentage rate on its overdraft.

Required

a Consider what Penguin should do with respect to this supplier.

b Suggest steps that Penguin could take to improve the balance sheet, profit and loss and cash flow position.

12* (*Examination level*) Oxford Blues plc has standard trade terms requiring its customers to pay after 30 days. The average invoice is actually paid after 90 days. A junior executive has suggested that a 2.5 per cent discount for payment on the 20th day following the invoice date be offered to customers.

It is estimated that 60 per cent of customers will accept this and pay on the 20th day, but 40 per cent will continue to pay, on average, on the 90th day.

Sales are £10m per annum and bad debts are 1 per cent of sales.

The company's overdraft facility costs 14 per cent per annum.

The reduced collection effort will save £50,000 per annum on administration and bad debts will fall to 0.7 per cent of turnover.

Required

a Should the new credit terms be offered to customers?

b What are the main considerations you would give thought to in setting up a good credit management system?

13 What sources of information would you access to assess the creditworthiness of a customer? What systems would you install to try to obtain prompt payment?

14 Explain some of the reasons for the growth in the hire purchase and leasing industry round the world over the past two decades.

15 Explain why a loss-making company is more likely to lease an asset than to buy it.

ASSIGNMENTS

1 Consider some of the items of equipment that your firm uses and investigate the possibility of alternative methods of obtaining the use of those assets. Write a report outlining the options with their advantages and disadvantages, fully costed (if possible) and make recommendations.

2 Investigate the debtor management policy of a firm with which you are familiar. Write a report contrasting current practice with what you consider to be best practice. Recommend action.

3 If a firm familiar to you is at present heavily reliant on bank finance, consider the relative merits of shifting the current balance from overdraft to term loans. Also consider the greater use of alternative forms of short-term or medium-term finance.

4 Obtain a representative sample of recently paid invoices. Examine the terms and conditions, calculate the benefit of paying early and recommend changes in policy if this seems appropriate.

CHAPTER NOTE

1 An alternative approach that is generally sufficiently accurate is:

$$\text{Interest rate for } n \text{ days} = \frac{i}{365} \times (n)$$

Chapter 13

TREASURY AND WORKING CAPITAL MANAGEMENT

INTRODUCTION

The majority of the issues discussed in this book are concerned with major long-term commitments where each individual investment or finance-raising act has profound consequences for the success of the organisation. There is, however, a class of decision which usually involves small and short-term commitments. Despite being individually small and often routine, they are collectively extremely important for the well-being of the firm and the achievement of its goals. It is to these issues that we now turn.

An example of the sort of question that needs to be addressed in this area is, what should the organisation do with any temporary surplus cash? Should it merely be deposited in a bank account or should the firm be more adventurous and try to obtain a higher return by placing the funds in the money market? But then, what about the increased risk and loss of liquidity associated with some forms of lending?

Another area for action is the creation of a system which does not allow cash to lie idle or be unnecessarily tied up in, say, inventories of partially finished goods or debtors. The firm, naturally, has to put money into these areas to permit production and gain sales, but this should be kept at an optimum level, bearing in mind that money has an opportunity cost. The estimation of that optimum is far from easy. For instance, managers know that raw material and work-in-progress inventory are needed at a sufficiently high level to prevent the problems associated with running out of stock, for example through production stoppages and lost sales, but they do not want to incur the excessive costs of storage, deterioration and interest charges associated with warehouses full of stock piled up to prevent all risks of a stock-out. The difficult management task is to strike a balance of risks and costs and work out a policy for appropriate stock levels and reordering.

The quality of day-to-day interaction with banks, shareholders and other finance providers is also vitally important. Thought and time have to be devoted to cultivating these relationships. Any one encounter with, or information flow to, these backers may be regarded as insignificant, but cumulatively an image of a business is created in the minds of some very influential people. Ideally that image needs to be professional and purposeful and to show a sound grasp of the competitive positioning and potential of the firm. A poor image can lead to increased cost of funds, the blocking of expansion and, in extreme cases, the removal of managers.

There are some other fundamental financing problems where the knowledge and experience of the corporate treasurer may also be drawn upon. For example, how does the firm obtain a balance between short-term and long-term borrowing, and how could the firm finance a merger?

The treasurer is additionally given the task of managing the risk associated with interest rate and exchange rate change. So a UK firm may sell £1m of goods to a Canadian importer on six months' credit invoiced in dollars. What the UK firm does not know is the quantity of sterling it will receive when in six months it converts the dollars into pounds. The treasury department will have a range of approaches available to remove the uncertainty and reassure other managers that the export deal will be a profitable one. Similarly, skilled individuals within the treasury will be able to hedge interest rate risk; that is, make arrangements which reduce the potential for interest rate movements to impact adversely on the firm.

These and many other duties involve small, short-term decisions in the main, but can make or break a company. *The Economist* described the treasury function as 'the financial engine room of companies',[1] meaning that these decisions do not necessarily have the grandeur and broad sweep of the decisions made on the bridge of the corporate ship but they are vital to maintaining its progress. This becomes all too tragically apparent when things go wrong in the engine room and companies founder due to poor working capital management, to running out of cash despite high profits or to losing a fortune on the derivative markets

Learning objectives

This chapter covers a wide range of finance issues, from cheque clearance to optimum inventory models. Matters such as the use of derivatives to reduce interest rate risk or foreign exchange risk have entire chapters devoted to them later in the book and so will be covered in a brief fashion here to give an overview. By the end of this chapter the reader should be able to:

- describe the main roles of a treasury department and the key concerns of managers when dealing with working capital;
- comment on the factors influencing the balance of the different types of debt in terms of maturity, currency and interest rates;
- show awareness of the importance of the relationship between the firm and the financial community;
- demonstrate how the treasurer might reduce risk for the firm, perhaps through the use of derivative products;
- understand the working capital cycle, the cash conversion cycle and an inventory model.

The need for good treasury management and working capital management has been with us ever since business began. They both focus on liquid resources (cash flow) and they both take into account risk. Few businesses, even the simplest, can afford to ignore the importance of the efficient planning and control of cash resources while allowing for risk. In small and medium-sized firms both functions will usually be undertaken by the chief accountant and his/her team. As firms grow it usually becomes necessary to appoint specialist staff skilled in treasury while maintaining a team dedicated to helping to ensure high-quality working capital decisions.

Working capital can be defined as the difference between current assets and current liabilities.

Working capital thus means net current assets, or net current liabilities (if current liabilities exceed current assets). It is the investment a company makes in assets which are in continual use and are turned over many times in a year. Working capital encompasses the following:

- Short-term resources
  - inventory;
  - debtors;
  - investments;
  - cash.

Less:
- Short-term liabilities
  - trade creditors;
  - short-term borrowing;
  - other creditors repayable within a year.

The way in which the organisation is structured, and roles assigned to individuals to undertake these kinds of decisions, varies tremendously but the fundamental questions and the need for action remain. These are illustrated in Exhibit 13.1, where the over-

Exhibit 13.1 The main areas of treasury and working capital management

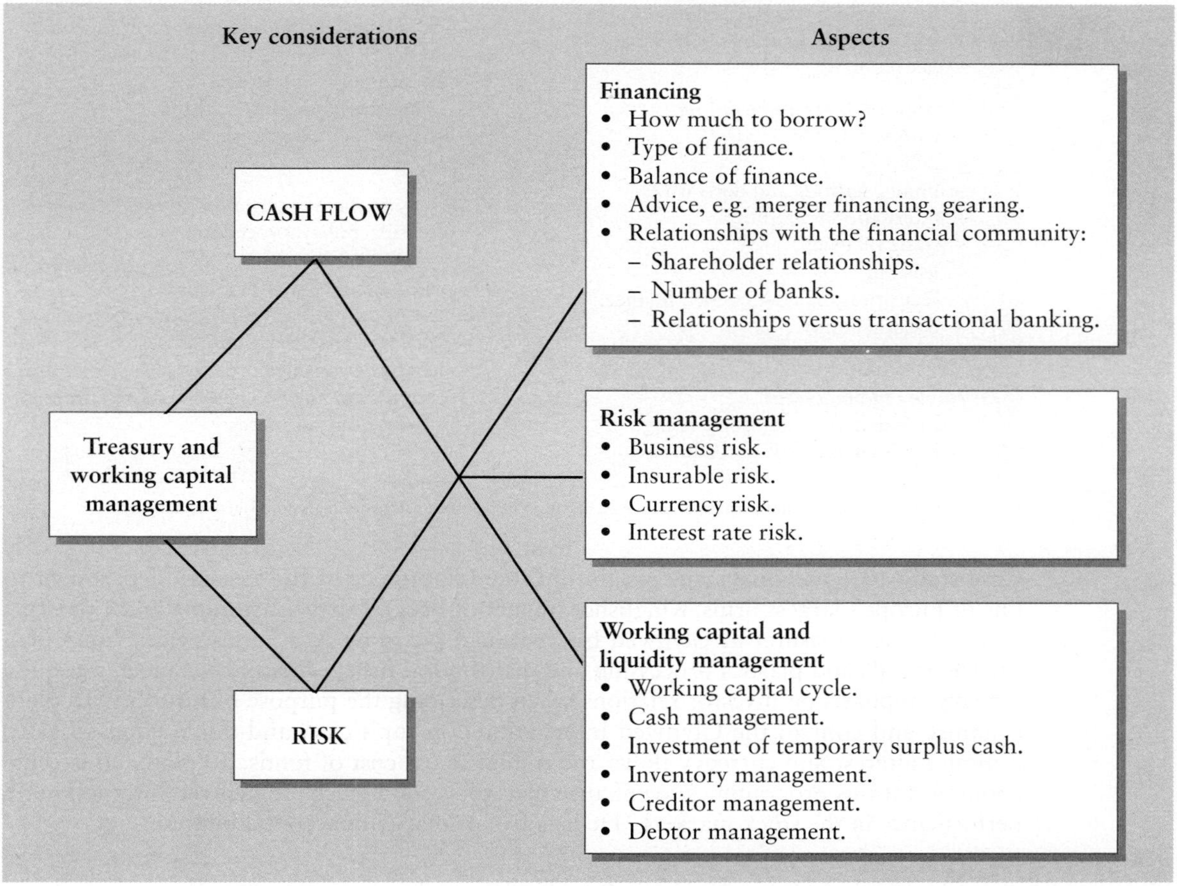

arching groups of issues to be addressed are shown. The first two, financing and risk management, are usually in the domain of the specialist treasury department, in collaboration with other senior managers, in large multinational firms. The third, working capital and liquidity management, will require some input from the treasury team, especially for the investment of temporary cash, but many of these issues will be examined by line managers with the assistance of the finance and accounting team. The areas of responsibilities covered by either the treasurer or the financial controller (the head of the group concerned more with accounting issues rather than finance) will be unique for every firm, and the list in Exhibit 13.1 is far from exhaustive, but at least it provides a framework for considering the myriad decisions in this area.

Exhibit 13.1 provides a guide for progress through this chapter but it must be noted that treasurers (leaving to one side the working capital specialists for the moment) must have knowledge of a wider range of corporate issues than those in Exhibit 13.1. The Association of Corporate Treasurers regard as key topics those listed in Exhibit 13.2.

Exhibit 13.2 Corporate treasury subjects

1 *Corporate financial management*
- financial aims, strategies and tactics;
- financial structuring;
- balance sheet management;
- dividend policy;
- investment appraisal and assessment;
- acquisitions, divestments and mergers;
- tax planning.

2 *Capital markets and funding*
- equity;
- debt;
- bonds, hybrids and derivatives;
- international funding;
- trade finance;
- leasing;
- securitisation/asset backed finance;
- documentation;
- tax issues.

3 *Money management*
- cash dynamics and forecasting;
- cash management procedures;
- international cash pooling systems;
- investment and borrowing objectives;
- tax issues.

4 *Risk management*
- business risk;
- risk management objectives and evaluation;
- currency exposure, interest rate risk and counterparty exposures;
- identification and forecasting;
- control and reporting;
- tax issues.

5 *Managing the treasury function*
- treasury policy, procedures and organisation;
- the control of treasury;
- use of technology and treasury systems;
- legal and regulatory issues;
- bank relationships;
- rating company and investor relationships;
- ethical responsibilities.

Source: Reprinted with the kind permission of the Association of Corporate Treasurers (unpublished document).

Case study 13.1 will give some insight into the importance of the treasury department to one of Europe's largest firms, Kingfisher (owner of B&Q, Darty, Castorama and Comet).

The former treasurer at Glynwed International plc (now Aga Foodservice Group plc), the UK metals and plastics processing and distribution firm, Christopher Purser, put quite a heavy emphasis on investor relations when describing the purpose of his job:[2] 'To plan, organise and control the Glynwed International group's cash and borrowings so as to optimise interest and currency flows and minimise the cost of funds. To plan and execute communications programmes to enhance investors' confidence in Glynwed International's performance in the stock markets.' He lists five primary job accountabilities:

CASE STUDY 13.1

Treasury policy at Kingfisher

'The main financial risks faced by the Group and managed by its Treasury function are funding risk, interest rate risk and currency risk. The Board regularly reviews these risks and approves written Treasury policies covering the use of financial instruments to manage these risks.

Treasury ensures that the Group has sufficient secure resources to meet its business objectives and manages the Group's exposure to liquidity risk by promoting a diversity of funding sources and debt maturities.

During 1999, the Group established a €2.5 billion Euro Medium Term Note Programme and a €750 million Euro Commercial Paper Programme . . .

The funding drawn under the securitisation programme, established in 1996, to finance part of the receivables of Time Retail Finance has averaged £239.5 million throughout the year.

The Group maintains a portfolio of committed and uncommitted bank facilities. Committed facilities of £400 million mature in January 2003, £18.4 million during 2002, £4.6 million during 2001, with £368.3 million maturing prior to January 2001 . . .

The Group's objective for debt maturities is to ensure that the amount of funding maturing in any year is not beyond the Group's means to repay or refinance . . . The Group's borrowings and investments were kept mainly at floating rates of interest during the year . . .

Interest rate and foreign currency policies provide a degree of flexibility, whilst ensuring that the overall level of risk is maintained within agreed limits. Treasury activity relates solely to the underlying cash flows and asset and liability positions of the Group.

The interest rate exposure of the Group arising from its borrowing and deposits is managed by the use of fixed and floating rate debt and investments, interest rate swaps, cross currency interest rate swaps and interest futures.

The Group's policy is to ensure that when a Group company enters into a commercial contract the Group is protected against the potential impact of adverse currency movements. Halcyon Finance Limited fulfils this policy objective by entering into currency instruments, generally comprising forward contracts and currency options to hedge the Group's net exposures.'

Note the statement that:

> 'Treasury activity relates solely to the underlying cash flows and asset and liability positions of the Group.'

In other words the treasury operation is not a profit centre. There have been a number of blunders by treasury departments using the derivative markets (futures, options, swaps, etc.) for speculative (risk-seeking) rather than hedging (risk-reducing) purposes because the treasury team was expected to generate a profit rather than simply control risk.

Source: Kingfisher Annual Report and Accounts 2000.

1 Manage the Group's cash and currency flows so as to:
   - minimise interest paid;
   - maximise interest earned;
   - minimise foreign currency exposure.
2 Ensure that sufficient funds are available at acceptable rates to meet the Group's cash flow requirements internationally.
3 Control, monitor and report the level of the Group's borrowings against available facilities and budgets.
4 Ensure that key financial analysts, fund managers and investors are aware of the Group's financial objectives and performance.
5 Ensure that investors' confidence in the Group is enhanced through knowledge of and contact with the Group's top management.

FINANCING

Obtaining the most appropriate mixture of finance is likely to be of great importance to most firms. In this section we first examine the most appropriate forms of borrowing in terms of maturity of that borrowing, for example a short-term overdraft or a 20-year loan, as well as considering the question of the currency of the borrowing and the choice of interest rates; secondly, we look at retained earnings as a source of finance; and thirdly, we consider the more 'strategic' type of financing issues for which a treasurer might be called upon to give advice. There follows a commentary on the importance of maintaining good relationships with the financial community.

Is it better to borrow long or short?

Once a company has decided to raise funds by borrowing, it then has to decide whether to raise the money through:

a short-term debt – a loan which has to be repaid within, say, one year;

b medium-term debt; or

c long-term debt – where the loan is paid over a 10-, 25- or even 100-year period.

There are a number of factors to be taken into consideration in making a decision of this nature.

- *Maturity structure* A company will usually try to avoid having all of its debts maturing at or near the same date. It could be disastrous if the firm was required to repay loan capital on a number of different instruments all within, say, a six-month period. Even if the firm is profitable the sudden cash outflow could lead to insolvency. A number of major UK retailers came perilously close to this in the early 1990s. In the late 1980s they had experienced a boom in sales and everything the management touched seemed to turn to gold. Buoyed up by overoptimism, they opened up dozens of new branches, funded to a large extent by medium-term finance. By the time these bank loans, bonds, etc. came to maturity in the early 1990s these shop chains were already suffering from a biting recession and an excessive cost base. Negotiations with bankers and others were necessary as loan covenants were broken and bankruptcy loomed. Most of the larger groups survived but they have learnt a hard lesson about the importance of spreading the dates for principal repayment.

  Thames Water plc regards this issue as sufficiently important for it to include a graph in its annual accounts showing the years in which its debt matures – *see* Exhibit 13.3.
- *Costs of issue/arrangement* It is usually cheaper to arrange an overdraft and other one-off short-term finance than long-term debt facilities, but this advantage is sometimes outweighed by the fact that if funds are needed over a number of years short-term debt has to be renewed more often than long-term debt. So over, say, a 20-year period, the issuing and arrangement costs of short-term debt may be much greater than a 20-year bond.
- *Flexibility* Short-term debt is more flexible than long-term debt. If a business has fluctuations in its needs for borrowed funds, for example it is a seasonal business, then for some months it does not need any borrowing funds, whereas at other times it needs large loans. A long-term loan may be inefficient because the firm will be paying interest even if it has surplus cash. True, the surplus cash could be invested but the

Exhibit 13.3 An example of a company conscious of the necessity for a range of maturity dates for debt – Thames Water plc

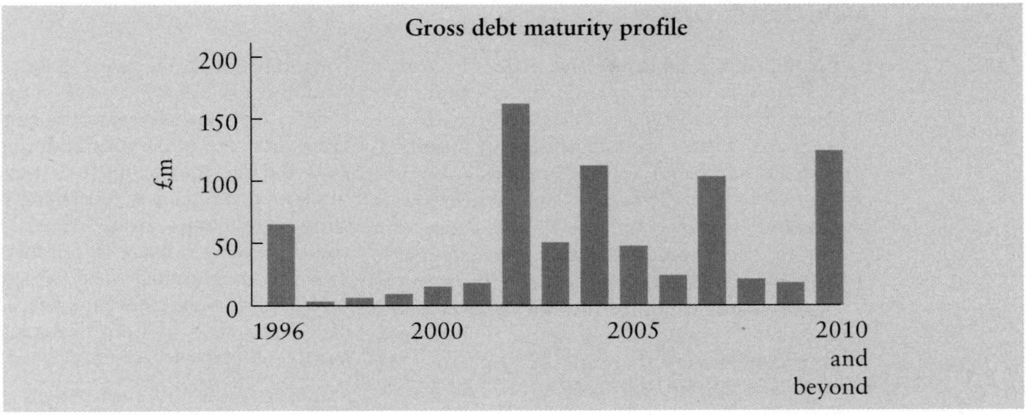

Source: Thames Water, Annual Report and Accounts 1995.

proceeds are unlikely to be as great as the cost of the loan interest. It is cheaper to take out short-term loans or overdrafts when the need arises which can be paid back when the firm has high cash inflows.

- ***The uncertainty of getting future finance*** If a firm is investing in a long-term project which requires borrowing for many years it would be risky to finance this project using one-year loans. At the end of each year the firm has to renegotiate the loan or issue a new bond. There may come a time when lenders will not supply the new money. There may, for example, be a change in the bank's policy or a reassessment of the borrower's creditworthiness, a crisis of confidence in the financial markets or an imposition of government restrictions on lending. Whatever the reason, the project is halted and the firm loses money.

  Thus, to some extent, the type of project or asset that is acquired determines the type of borrowing. If the project or asset is liquid and short term then short-term finance may be favoured. If it is long term then longer-term borrowing gives more certainty about the availability of finance, and (possibly) the interest rate.

  MobilCom faced a crisis in 2000 as doubts grew about its ability to refinance its short-term loans – *see* Exhibit 13.4.

- ***The term structure of interest rates*** The yield curve is described in Chapter 11. There it is stated that it is usual to find interest rates on short-term borrowing which are lower than on long-term debt. This may encourage managers to borrow on a short-term basis. In many circumstances this makes sense. Take the case of Myosotis plc, which requires £10m of borrowed funds for a ten-year project. The corporate treasurer expects long-term interest rates to fall over the next year. It is therefore thought unwise to borrow for the full ten years at the outset. Instead the firm borrows one-year money at a low interest rate with the expectation of replacing the loan at the end of the year with a nine-year fixed-rate loan at the then reduced rate.

  However there are circumstances where managers find short-term rates deceptively attractive. For example, they might follow a policy of borrowing at short-term rates while the yield curve is still upward sloping, only switching to long-term borrowing when short-term rates rise above long-term rates. Take the case of Rosa plc, which wishes to borrow money for five years and faces the term structure of interest rates shown in the lower line of Exhibit 13.5. If it issued one-year bonds the rate of return

Exhibit 13.4

MobilCom

FT

Will MobilCom be the first victim of Europe's mobile licence spree? Underwriters are struggling to syndicate bridging loans to the company, which suggests its days of independence are numbered. MobilCom is not about to go bust – a €5.7bn (£3.51bn) credit line is already in place. But €4.7bn is short-term money, repayable in August, and extendable only at a punitive rate. Unless conditions in the capital markets change radically between now and then, MobilCom will not be able to raise long-term money to refinance the loan. The odds are that it will have to sell to France Telecom at a firesale price early next year.

MobilCom is not alone. The sector faces a liquidity crisis. The weak link in the chain is the syndicated loan market, where banks and regulators are getting nervous about concentration risk. But the root problem is weakness in the stock market, which is preventing telecommunication companies from raising enough new equity, causing spreads on telecom debt to balloon. The average high-yield telecoms bond now trades at a staggering 14.4 percentage points over Treasuries – up from 11.8 a month ago and a mere 4.8 percentage points a year back.

Source: Lex column, *Financial Times*, 8 December 2000, p. 24. Reprinted with permission.

paid would be 7 per cent. The returns required on four-year and five-year bonds are 8 per cent and 8.3 per cent respectively. The company opts for a one-year bond with the expectation of issuing a four-year bond one year later. However by the time the financing has to be replaced, 365 days after the initial borrowing, the entire yield curve has shifted upwards due to general macroeconomic changes. Now Rosa has to pay an interest rate of 10 per cent for the remaining four years. This is clearly more expensive than arranging a five-year bond at the outset.

The case of Rosa shows that it can be cheaper to borrow long at low points in the interest rate cycle despite the 'headline' interest charge on long-term debt being greater than on short-term loans.

Exhibit 13.5 A shifting yield curve affects the relative cost of long- and short-term borrowing – the example of Rosa plc

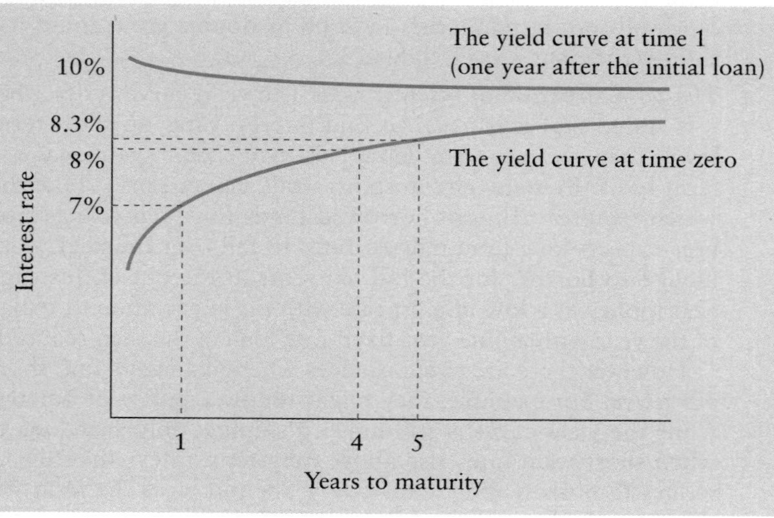

To 'match' or not to 'match'?

Firms usually come to the conclusion that there is a need for an appropriate mixture of debt finance with regard to length of time to maturity: some short-term borrowing is desirable alongside some long-term borrowing. The major factors which need to be taken into account in achieving the right balance are: **a** cost (interest rate, arrangement fee, etc.) and **b** risk (of not being able to renew borrowings, of the yield curve shifting, of not being able to meet a sudden outflow if the maturity is bunched, etc.). Some firms follow the 'matching' principle, in which the maturity structure of the finance matches the maturity of the project or asset. Here fixed assets and those current assets which are needed on a permanent basis (for example cash, minimum inventory or debtor levels) are financed through long-term sources, while current assets whose financing needs vary throughout the year are financed by short-term borrowings. Examples of the latter type of asset might be stocks of fireworks at certain times of the year, or investment in inventories of chocolate Easter eggs in the spring.

Thus there are three types of asset which need to be financed:

- fixed assets;
- permanent current assets;
- fluctuating current assets.

A firm taking the maturity matching approach is considered to be adopting a moderate stance. This is shown in Exhibit 13.6, where a rising level of total assets is financed principally through increases in long-term finance applied to fixed assets and permanent current assets. The fluctuating current assets, such as those related to seasonal variations, are financed with short-term funds.

A more aggressive approach is represented in Exhibit 13.7. This entails more risk because of the frequent need to refinance to support permanent current assets as well as fluctuating current assets. If the firm relied on an overdraft for this it will be vulnerable to a rapid withdrawal of that facility. If stocks and cash are reduced to pay back the overdraft the firm may experience severe disruption, loss of sales and output, and

Exhibit 13.6 Moderate financing policy stance – the matching principle

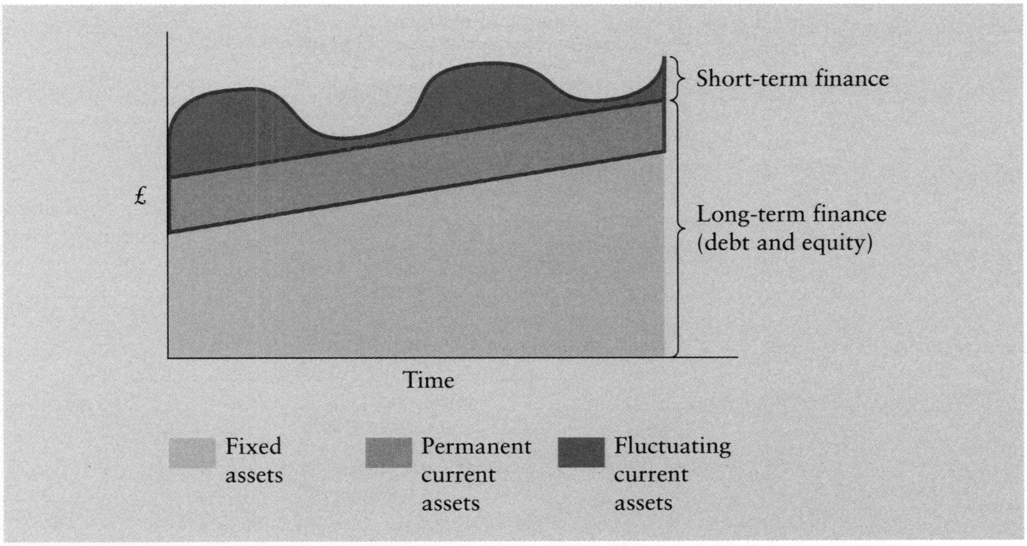

Exhibit 13.7 An aggressive financing policy

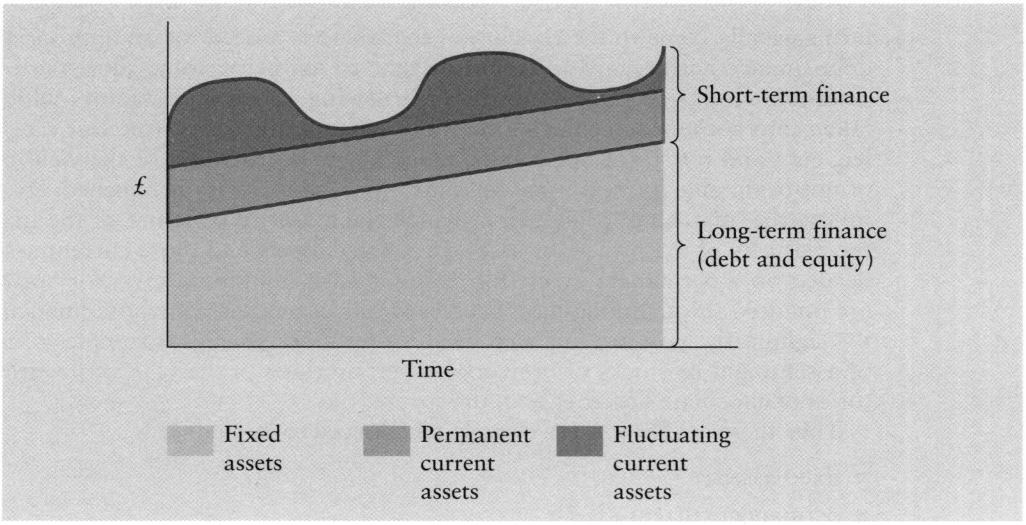

additional costs because of a failure to maintain the minimum required working capital to sustain optimum profitability.

The low-risk policy is to make sure that long-term financing covers the total investment in assets. If there are times of the year when surplus cash is available this will be invested in short-term instruments. This type of policy is shown in Exhibit 13.8.

Many managers would feel much happier under the conservative approach because of the lower risk of being unable to pay bills as they arise. However such a policy may not be in the best interests of the owners of the firm. The surplus cash invested in short-term securities is unlikely to earn a satisfactory return relative to the cost of the long-term

Exhibit 13.8 A conservative financing policy

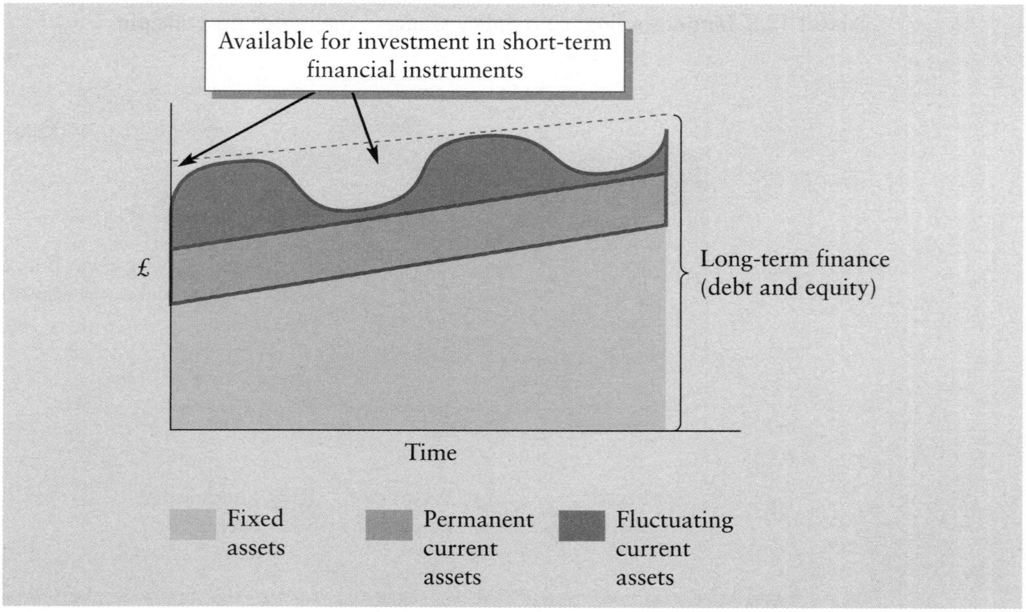

funds. In all likelihood shareholders would be better off if the firm reduced its long-term financing, by returning cash to shareholders or paying off some long-term loans.

There is no sound theoretical formula to help decide the balance between long- and short-term finance but many managers seem to follow a policy of matching the maturity of their assets and liabilities, thereby accepting a modest level of risk while avoiding excessive amounts of surplus investible funds. However this is far from universally accepted: for example, Microsoft has $23bn of cash and short-term investments.

The currency of borrowing

Deciding on the maturity structure of the firm's debt is one aspect of the financing decision. Another is selecting the currency in which to borrow. For transnational firms it is common to find borrowing in the currency of the country where the funds are to be invested. This can reduce exposure to foreign exchange rate changes. For example, suppose that Union Jack plc borrows £100m to invest in the USA. It exchanges the £100m into $150m at the exchange rate of $1.5 to the pound. The net cash flows in subsequent years are expected to be $30m per annum. If the exchange rate remained constant Union Jack would therefore receive £20m per year to pay for the financing costs and produce a surplus. However if the rate of exchange moved to $2 for every pound the annual cash inflow in sterling terms would be merely £15m.[3] The project is producing £5m less than originally anticipated despite generating the same quantity of dollars, and this is insufficient as a rate of return for Union Jack. The risk attached to this project can be reduced by ensuring that the liabilities are in the same currency as the income flow. So if Union Jack borrows $150m to invest in the project, even though the exchange rate may move to $2 : £1 the project remains viable. Currency risk is considered in more detail in Chapter 22.

The interest rate choice

Another consideration for the debt portfolio is the balance to be struck between fixed and floating interest-rate borrowings. In many circumstances it is thought advisable to have a mixture of the two types of borrowing. If all the borrowings are floating rate then the firm is vulnerable to rising interest rates. This often happens at the most unfortunate times: for example, at the start of recessions interest rates are usually high at the same time as sales are in decline.

Industries with high fixed-cost elements, which need a large volume of sales to maintain profitability, may be particularly averse to floating-rate borrowing as this may add to their cost base and create an additional source of risk. Even if they have to pay more for fixed-rate borrowing initially, the directors may sleep better knowing that one element of risk has been eliminated.

On the other hand, if all borrowing is fixed rate the firm is unable to take advantage of a possible decline in interest rates. Other aspects of the debate about fixed or floating rates were considered in Chapter 12.

Retained earnings as a financing option

Internally generated funds from previous years' profits is the most important source of long-term finance for the typical firm, and yet it is so easily overlooked while attention is focused on the more glamorous ways of raising funds in the financial markets. Internal funds account for between one-third and two-thirds of the capital invested by UK firms. These are the profits plus depreciation retained within the firm after the payment of dividends. The retained earnings level is therefore the inverse of the decision to pay dividends. The dividend decision is discussed in Chapter 19. We now consider the advantages and disadvantages of retained earnings as a source of finance.

One significant advantage of retained earnings is that there is no dilution of the existing shareholders' share of corporate control or share of returns. If the alternative of raising long-term funds by selling additional shares to outside shareholders were taken this would reduce the proportionate shareholdings of the existing owners. Even a rights issue might alter the relative position of particular shareholders if some chose not to take up their rights. Secondly, retaining earnings avoids the issuing costs associated with new shares or bonds and the arrangement fees on bank loans. Thirdly, management may value the fact that, in contrast to the position with a new equity or debt issue, they do not have to explain in such detail the use to which the funds will be put. This 'advantage' may not be in the shareholders' best interest, however.

A potential disadvantage of relying on internally generated funds is that they are limited by the firm's profits. Some firms wish to invest and grow at a much faster rate than would be possible through retained earnings. Indeed, some biotechnology firms are not expected to have profits for many years and yet have ambitious growth targets. Also, using retained earnings means reducing the dividend payout. Shareholders, on the whole, like to receive a steadily rising dividend stream. They may not be willing to forgo this simply because the management have a large number of projects in which they wish to invest. Retained earnings also have the drawback of being uncertain as they fluctuate with the ups and downs of the company's fortunes. Depending on this source of finance alone carries the risk of not being able to obtain finance at a vital stage in an investment programme.

Perhaps the most serious problem associated with retained earnings is that many managers regard them as essentially 'free capital'. That is, there is no cost to this capital – no opportunity cost of using these funds. This can encourage firms to invest to a greater extent than can be justified by the availability of positive NPV projects. There can be a resulting diminution of shareholders' wealth as the firm expands beyond a profitable size or diversifies into new areas, or acquires other firms. Forcing firms to raise funds externally subjects them to periodic scrutiny by critically minded investors who ask for a thorough justification. (*See* Chapters 15 and 16 on shareholder value.)

Retained earnings are not free. Shareholders, by allowing the firm to keep profits within the business, are making a significant sacrifice. They are forgoing dividends which could be invested in other financial securities. These other financial securities, for example shares in other firms of the same risk class, would have given a return. Thus shareholders have an opportunity cost and so the return required on retained earnings is the same as for any equity capital.

The treasurer at a strategic level

Treasurers may be asked to advise on matters of great significance to the future direction of the firm. For example, the decision to merge with another firm or to purchase a major business (a trade purchase) will require some assessment of the ability of the organisation to finance such activity. The treasurer will be able to advise on the sources of finance available, the optimum mixture and the willingness of the financial community to support the initiative. In a similar fashion a treasurer could help with disposals of subsidiaries.

Their knowledge of financial markets may permit treasurers to advise on the course of interest rates and exchange rates and so may aid vital decisions such as whether to establish a manufacturing facility or begin a marketing campaign in another country (*see* Chapters 21 and 22). Forecasting interest and exchange rates is notoriously difficult and even the greatest so-called experts frequently predict the future erroneously, and yet the treasurer may be the only person in the company able to make an informed guess.

Another major area of concern is the total amount of borrowing a firm should aim for. If it does not borrow at all then it will be losing the advantage of cheap finance. On the other hand, high levels of borrowing increase the chances of financial distress and the firm could be liquidated. Striking the appropriate balance is important and the treasurer may have some input in this area. Chapter 18 is devoted to the question of how much to borrow.

Relationships with the financial community

Neglecting to engender good relationships with shareholders, banks and other financial institutions can result in severe penalties for the firm. The typical treasurer and chief financial officer of a corporation will spend a great deal of time communicating with major finance providers on a weekly, or even a daily basis.

There will be a planned and sustained effort to maintain mutual understanding between shareholders and the organisation. The treasurer might be asked to create a detailed and up-to-date picture of who the shareholders are and then to follow through with a high-quality flow of information to enable shareholders to better appreciate the firm and its strategy in order to sustain their commitment. In the absence of informative communication to fill in gaps in their knowledge, shareholders may imagine all kinds of problems. If they are kept informed they are more likely to be supportive when the firm asks for additional finance, or asks for patience in times of difficulty, or appeals for the rejection of a merger bid. The point could be put even more simply: the shareholders own the firm and therefore both desire and deserve comprehensive information about its progress.

We turn now to banking relationships. Most firms make use of the services of more than one bank. A multinational firm may use over 100 banks. For example, Monsanto, the US chemical company, is proud of the fact that it has managed to cut the number down to 150 – it used to have 336. One reason for using so many banks is that large international firms have complex financial issues to deal with and any one bank may not have all the requisite skills and infrastructure to cope with them. Also banks have a tendency to join syndicates to make large loans to firms – an example here is Eurotunnel with 225 banks. In addition, some companies operate in dozens of countries and so may value the local network of the domestic banks in each of those markets.

The relationship between banks and large corporations has changed over the past decade. In the 1980s corporate treasurers, in an attempt to cut costs and boost investment returns, increasingly insisted on banks competing with each other to offer the lowest-cost services. The provision of credit, the arrangement of bonds, notes, loans and commercial paper were put out to tender, as were the foreign exchange and cash management services. This competitive method is called 'transactional banking'. For a time treasurers were content with the results but towards the end of the 1980s the drawbacks of this mercenary approach became apparent. Banks started to view some companies as one-off service takers interested in low cost only, and did not attempt to become knowledgeable about the firms. This led to complaints from corporations that banks were unable to provide more tailored advice and services which so many of them need. When crises arose firms found banks deserting them and this often posed a threat to their existence. The lack of two-way knowledge meant a greater tendency to pull out of a difficult situation rather than help develop imaginative plans for regeneration. Also, maintaining contact with more than 100 bankers can be very costly if the treasury system is not to become chaotic.

Today the emphasis is back on 'relationship banking' in which there is much more intimacy, with corporations being open with their banks and attempting to nurture a long-term relationship. As a result the quality of tailored service and the volume of consultancy type advice from banks have risen – *see* Exhibit 13.9. Companies have tended to

Exhibit 13.9

Treasurers resent paying for bank links

FT

Company treasurers may say they value a close relationship with their bankers – but hardly any are willing to pay for it.

A survey conducted for Wilde Sapte, the City law firm, showed that many treasurers thought their banks ought to pay them for the privilege of doing business with them by charging less interest on their loans.

The survey of 100 corprate treasurers drawn from the FTSE 300 companies showed that 81 per cent described 'relationship banking' as 'very important' to them, with a further 17 per cent considering it to be 'quite important'.

While most expected to pay exactly the same for services from their 'relationship banks' as from any other bank, 27 per cent said they would expect to pay less, with 11 per cent expecting to pay more. Even among those willing to pay more, most valued their relationship at just 10 basis points on the price of a loan.

On the other hand 65 per cent of the treasurers questioned said they were more likely to consider some of the complex financial structures that banks routinely try to market to them if the proposal came from their principal relationship bank.

Relationship banking has become a creed for many corporate bankers. They are willing to invest effort in getting to know a company's business and to provide it with low margin services such as basic loans or foreign exchange dealing in the hope that they will then be first in line when the company wants advice on more complicated financial products with higher fees.

Source: George Graham, Banking Editor, *Financial Times*, 26 January 1998, p. 7. Reprinted with permission.

reduce the number of core banks to a handful. Unilever, for example, has a 'golden circle' of 11 institutions which transact the majority of its business. Successful treasury management of banking relationships seems to demand high levels of openness, honesty and the maintenance of a long-term interaction. Philips has learnt this – *see* Case study 13.2.

CASE STUDY 13.2

Philips goes for relationship banking

In the early 1990s Philips' profits fell and a number of banks refused to supply more finance at a crucial time in the company's history. The reaction of the bankers made the survival of the recession more difficult than it might have been. To avoid future problems Jean-Pierre Lac, the treasurer of the Dutch electronics group, has developed a new approach to banking relationships. There is now a core group of 12 with a second tier of 20. Those that will act more like partners to the firm rather than one-off product providers will be given preference. These banks will be called upon to provide a range of services, from risk management to cash management, and become highly knowledgeable about Philips.

Source: *Corporate Finance*, July 1995, Euromoney Publications PLC. Reprinted with permission of Euromoney International Investor PLC. If you would like to subscribe to *Corporate Finance* please contact Esther Rodd at +44 20 7779 8062.

RISK MANAGEMENT

Running a business naturally entails taking risks – it is what business activity is about. Satisfactory profits rarely emerge from a risk-eliminating strategy; some risk is therefore inevitable. However it is up to managers of firms to select those risks the business might take and those which it should avoid. Take a company like GlaxoSmithKline which accepts high risks in its research and development programme. Should it also take a risk with exchange rates when it receives money from sales around the world, or should it try to minimise that particular type of risk? Risk reduction is often costly. For example, insurance premiums may be payable or transaction costs may be incurred in the derivative markets. Given the additional cost burden managers have to think carefully about the benefits to be derived from reducing or eliminating risk. There are at least three reasons firms sacrifice some potential profits in order to reduce the impact of adverse events.

- ***It helps financial planning*** Being able to predict future cash flows, at least within certain boundaries, can be advantageous and can allow the firm to plan and invest with confidence. Imagine trying to organise a business if the future cash flows can vary widely depending on what happens to the currency, the interest rate or the price of a vital raw material input.
- ***Reduce the fear of financial distress*** Some events can disrupt and damage a business to the point of threatening its existence. For example, massive claims have been made against firms involved in the production of asbestos. If it had not been for the passing on of this risk to the insurance companies many of these firms would now be liquidated. A similar logic applies to the insurance of super tankers against an ocean oil spillage. By limiting the potential damage inflicted on firms, not only will the managers and shareholders benefit, but other finance providers, such as banks, will have greater confidence which will lower the cost of capital.
- ***Some risks are not rewarded*** It is possible to reduce risk in situations where there are no financial rewards for accepting that extra risk. For example, if British Airways contracted to buy a dozen aircraft from Boeing for delivery over the next ten years and had to pay in dollars as each aeroplane was completed it would have to accept the risk of a recession in international flights and numerous other risks, but, in the sophisticated foreign exchange markets of today, at least it can eliminate one risk. It does not have to live with any uncertainty about the cost of the aeroplanes in terms of sterling because it could make an arrangement with a bank at the outset to purchase the required number of dollars for a specified number of pounds at set dates in the future. (This is a forward agreement.) British Airways would then know precisely how many pounds will be needed to buy the dollars to pay Boeing in each year of the next decade (*see* Chapter 22 for more currency risk-hedging strategies).

There are many different types of risk that a commercial organisation has to deal with and we will discuss the four most important: business risk, insurable risk, currency risk and interest-rate risk.

Business risk

Many of the risks of operating in a competitive business environment have to be accepted by management to a greater or lesser extent. Sales may fall because of, say, recession, or innovative breakthroughs by competitors. Costs may rise because of, say, strong union power or government-imposed tariffs. For some of these risk elements there is little that management can do. However in many areas management can take positive action to reduce risk. For example consider a bakery company heavily dependent on buying in wheat. The managers are likely to be worried that the price of wheat may rise over the forthcoming months, thereby making their operations unprofitable. On the other hand farmers may be worried by the possibility of wheat falling in price. Both would value certainty. One way of achieving this is for the baker and farmer to enter into a wheat futures agreement, in which the baker agrees to take delivery of wheat at a later date at a price which is agreed today. Both sides now know exactly how much the wheat will be sold for and so can plan ahead.

There are other ways of reducing business risk. For example, firms are often faced with a choice between two machines. The first is highly specialised to a particular task, for example, turning out a particular component. The second, slightly more expensive machine can turn out the same component, but can also be used in a more flexible fashion to switch production to other components. The option to use the machine in alternative ways can sometimes have a high value and so it is worthwhile paying the extra initial set-up costs and even higher production costs.

Consider also an electricity generator contemplating the construction of a power plant. The installation of a coal-fired station would be £100m. This would leave the generator dependent on coal price movements for future profitability. An alternative power plant can be switched from coal to gas but costs an additional £30m. The value of the option to switch is then for the management to evaluate and weigh against the extra cost of construction.

Likewise, a car production line may be more expensive if it is to be capable of being used for a number of different models. But the option to use the facility for more than one type of car reduces the firm's risk by making it less dependent on one model. These are examples of real options, which are considered further in Chapter 21.

Insurable risk

Many risks encountered by business can be transferred, through the payment of a premium, to insurance companies. These include factory fires, pollution damage and accidental damage to vehicles and machinery. Insurance companies are often better able to bear risk than ordinary commercial firms. The reasons for this are the following:

- experience in estimating probabilities of events and therefore 'pricing' risk more efficiently;
- knowledge of methods of reducing risk. They can pass on this knowledge to the commercial firms which may obtain lower premiums if they take precautionary measures;
- ability to *pool* risks, in other words, to diversify risk. The chance of an accident occurring in one firm is highly uncertain, but the probability of a particular proportion of a portfolio of insurance policies making a claim is fairly predictable.

Insurance can be an expensive option because of the tendency for insurance companies to charge for much more than the probability of having to pay out. For example, if there was a one in a hundred chance of your £10,000 car being stolen in a year and never recovered then for every 100 cars insured the insurance company will expect one £10,000 claim per year. The insurance premium to each owner to cover this specific type of risk would, justifiably, be slightly over £100 (£10,000/100), to allow for a modest profit. However, in reality, the premium may be much more than this. The insurance company is likely to have to bear significant administrative costs in setting up the policy in the first place and then dealing with subsequent claims. Anyone who has had to communicate with an insurance company quickly becomes aware of the mountain of paperwork they generate annually. Insurance companies also have to charge premiums sufficiently high to cover the problems of 'adverse selection'. Put it this way: you may be a sensible car owner, being cautious about where you park your car, never leave the doors unlocked and live in a good part of town, but many of the other purchasers of theft insurance may be less fastidious and fortunate. The grouping together of good and bad risks tends to increase the cost of insurance to relatively good policyholders. This is made worse for the good policyholders by the increased tendency of those in high-risk situations to buy insurance.

The third boost to insurance premiums comes from 'moral hazard' (the encouragement of bad behaviour) which causes holders of insurance to be less careful than they might otherwise be – the 'It's all right, don't worry, it's insured' syndrome. An extreme example of moral hazard has been created with the 'new-for-old' policies for electrical items in which a brand new video cassette recorder, for example, is provided should the old one suffer accidental damage – some have been tempted to 'accidentally' drop the video!

These three additional costs may push insurance premiums beyond acceptable levels for a firm. In some cases large corporations have taken the bold decision to bear many insurable risks. They may still pay insurance premiums to safeguard against major events which threaten the continuance of the firm but accept routine risks themselves such as machine breakdown, accidents at work, etc. There seems little point in paying premiums just to receive a regular, but lower, inflow in return. The treasurer may have an important role in deciding which risks to insure and which to accept in-house.

Currency risk

Another major area of responsibility for the corporate treasurer is in the management of risk which arises because exchange rates move. Take the case of Acarus plc which has sold electrical goods to an Australian importer on six months' credit. The importer is sent an invoice requiring payment of A$20m. The current exchange rate is two Australian dollars to one pound so if currency rates do not change in the subsequent six months Acarus will receive £10m. If the exchange moves to A$1.80 : £1 then Acarus will receive £11.11m, and will be very pleased with the extra £1.11m of income. However matters might turn out worse than expected. Say the rate of exchange moved to A$2.20 : £1. Then Acarus would receive only £9.09m. If the management team are risk averse they may say to themselves, 'While we like the possibility of making additional profit on the deal this is more than outweighed by the downside risk of making less than £10m'. There are various ways of ensuring that Acarus receives at least £10m and an entire chapter (Chapter 22) is devoted to the subject of exchange-rate risk management. Here we will have just a taster. One of the possibilities is for Acarus to buy an option giving the firm the right but not the obligation to exchange A$20m for sterling at a rate of A$2 : £1 in six months. If the dollar appreciates against the pound to A$1.80 then Acarus would choose not to exercise the option – to let it lapse – and then exchange the A$20m for £11.11m in the spot market in six months' time. Alternatively, if the dollar falls against sterling Acarus would insist on exercising the option to receive £10m rather than exchanging at the spot rate of A$2.20 : £1 and therefore achieving a mere £9.09m. By purchasing the option Acarus ensures that the lowest amount it will receive is £10m and the upside potential is unrestrained. However it would need to pay a hefty premium to the option seller for passing on this risk – perhaps 2 to 4 per cent of the amount covered. The difficult part is weighing the cost of risk-reducing action against the benefit.

Interest-rate risk

Interest rates cannot be predicted with any degree of accuracy. If a company has large amounts of floating-rate debt it could be vulnerable to interest-rate rises. Alternatively, a company with large fixed-rate debt could have to face living with regret, and higher debt costs than necessary, if interest rates fall.

There is a wide variety of arrangements and financial products which enable a treasurer to reduce the firm's exposure to the vicissitudes of interest rates. Chapter 21 explores a number of them. Here we examine one of the weapons in the treasurer's armoury – the cap.

Ace plc wishes to borrow £20m to finance a major expansion. It does so at a floating rate of LIBOR plus 150 basis points. LIBOR is currently 8 per cent and therefore Ace pays a rate of 9.5 per cent. This loan is a large sum relative to Ace's capital base and profits, and the management are concerned that if LIBOR rises above 10 per cent the firm will get into serious financial difficulty. To avoid this Ace purchases a cap agreement by which a bank promises to pay any interest charge above a LIBOR of 10 per cent. Thus, if two years later LIBOR rises to 11 per cent, without the cap Ace would pay 12.5 per cent. However, Ace can call upon the bank which made the cap agreement to pay the extra 1 per cent. Ace's interest charge cannot go beyond a total of (10 per cent + 1.5 per cent) = 11.5 per cent. What is more, Ace can benefit if interest rates fall because rates are linked to a variable LIBOR at any rate below the cap. The premium charged by the bank for this form of interest-rate insurance can be quite substantial but there are ways of offsetting this cost, for example by simultaneously selling a floor, but consideration of these will have to wait until Chapter 21. Suffice to say, the judicious management of interest-rate risk can be an important part of the treasurer's job description.

WORKING CAPITAL MANAGEMENT

A firm needs to invest in order to thrive. Major long-term investments in a new factory or new machinery are part of that investment. Another necessary element for expansion is additional resources devoted to current assets. Higher levels of output call for extra inventories of raw materials and work in progress (WIP) (partially finished goods). More sales volume often means that additional credit is granted to customers so that the investment in debtors increases. Greater sales usually means more inventory held in the form of finished goods. Also, a higher level of general business activity usually requires greater amounts of cash to oil the wheels. Some of the additional investment in inventories, debtors and cash may come from long-term sources of finance but in most cases short-term sources such as trade credit or a bank overdraft will cover much of the increased need.

The working capital cycle

The upper, circular, part of Exhibit 13.10 shows the working capital cycle for a typical firm. (This chain of events applies to the typical manufacturing firm rather than service businesses which often miss one or two stages.) It starts with the investment in raw material inventories which are then used in the production process and thereby become partially completed products. Eventually finished goods are produced which are held in inventory until sold. Some of these goods are sold for cash and others are sold on credit, with the customer paying days or weeks later. At each stage of the process expenditure is necessary on labour and other operational inputs. Helping to ease the cash burden of this cycle are suppliers, who provide credit.

The lower half of the diagram in Exhibit 13.10 shows non-working capital cash flows. These are generally infrequent events, involving large sums on each occasion and are of a long-term nature. They will not be considered any further in this chapter.

Money tied up in any stage in the working capital chain has an opportunity cost. In addition there are costs associated with storage and/or administration. The combined costs can be considerable and it is the art of good working capital management to so arrange the affairs of the business as to obtain a balance between the costs and benefits through raising or lowering stocks, cash, debtors and creditors to their optimum levels.

Exhibit 13.10 A typical working capital cycle and other cash flows

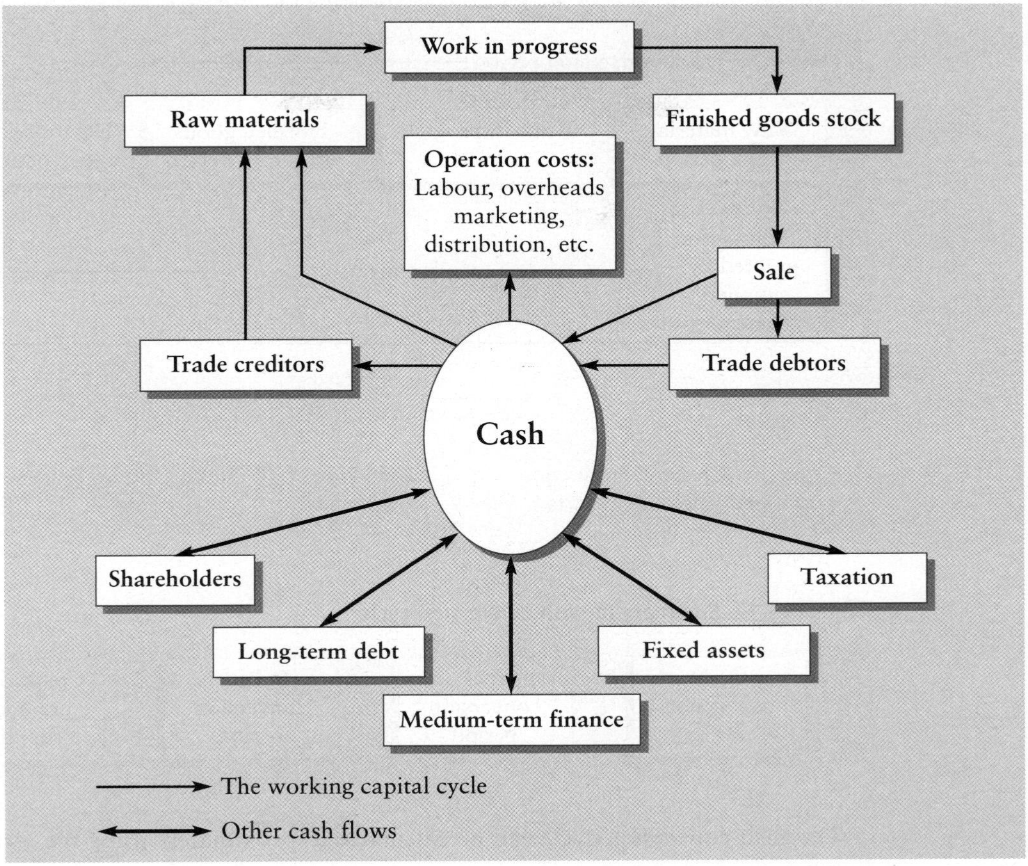

The amount invested by the average large UK firm in current assets is about 80 per cent of the amount devoted to fixed assets. The size and significance of working capital investment means that the success of an organisation may depend upon the wise implementation of well thought-out policies.

Cash-conversion cycle

The working capital cycle can be expressed in terms of the length of time between the acquisition of raw materials and other inputs and the inflow of cash from the sale of goods. As can be seen from Exhibit 13.11 this involves a number of intermediate stages.

The cash-conversion cycle focuses on the length of time between the company's outlay on inputs and the receipt of money from the sale of goods. For manufacturing firms it is the average time raw materials remain in stock, plus the time taken to produce the company's output, plus the length of time finished goods stay within the company as a form of inventory, plus the time taken for debtors to pay, less the credit period granted by suppliers. The shorter this cycle the fewer resources the company needs to tie up. The cash-conversion cycle can be summarised as the stock-conversion period plus the debtor-conversion period less the credit period granted by suppliers.

Exhibit 13.11 The cash-conversion cycle as part of the working capital cycle

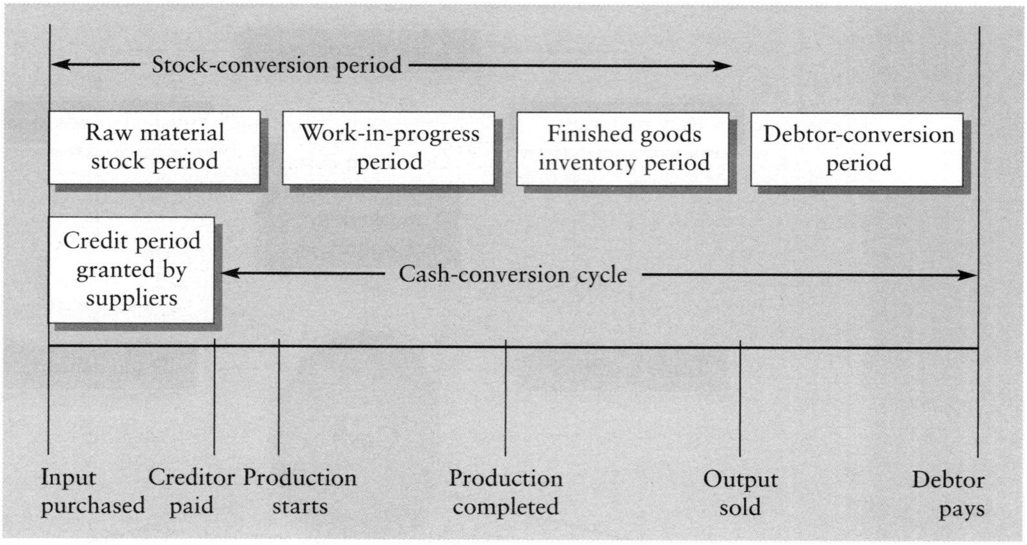

Exhibit 13.12 Summary of cash-conversion cycle

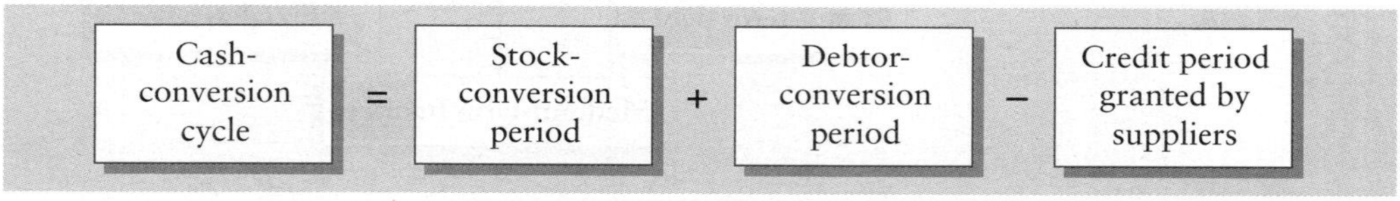

The cash-conversion cycle can be calculated approximately using the terms set out in Exhibit 13.13.

Exhibit 13.13 Calculation of cash-conversion cycle

- **Raw materials stock period** The average number of days raw materials remain unchanged and in stock:

$$\text{Raw materials stock period} = \frac{\text{Average value of raw materials stock}}{\text{Average purchase of raw materials per day}} = X \text{ days}$$

Less

- **Average credit period granted by suppliers** The average length of time between the purchase of inputs and the payment of them:

$$\text{Credit period} = \frac{\text{Average level of creditors}}{\text{Purchases on credit per day}} = X \text{ days.}$$

Add

- **Work-in-progress period** The number of days to convert raw materials into finished goods:

$$\text{Work-in-progress period} = \frac{\text{Average value of work in progress}}{\text{Average cost of goods sold per day}} = X \text{ days}$$

Exhibit 13.13 continued

Add

- **Finished goods inventory period** The number of days finished goods await delivery to customers:

$$\text{Finished goods inventory period} = \frac{\text{Average value of finished goods in stock}}{\text{Average cost of goods sold per day}} = X \text{ days}$$

Add

- **Debtor-conversion period** The average number of days to convert customer debts into cash:

$$\text{Debtor conversion period} = \frac{\text{Average value of debtors}}{\text{Average value of sales per day}} = X \text{ days}$$

The cash-conversion cycle can, perhaps, be better understood when some numbers are attached. The figures given in Exhibit 13.14 can be used to illustrate it.

Exhibit 13.14 Figures invented in order to calculate a cash-conversion cycle

	20X1 £m	*20X2 £m*	*Mean £m*	*Per day £000s*
Raw materials inventory	22	24	23	
Creditors	12	14	13	
Work-in-progress inventory	10	11	10.5	
Finished goods inventory	9	10	9.5	
Debtors	30	32	31	
Sales	150	170	160	438,356
Raw material purchases (annual)	100	116	108	295,890
Cost of goods sold (annual)	130	146	138	378,082

The cash-conversion cycle is the length of time a pound is tied up in current assets. For the figures given in Exhibit 13.14 it is:

$$\text{Raw materials stock period} = \frac{23{,}000{,}000}{295{,}890} = 78 \text{ days}$$

$$\textit{Less} \text{ creditor period*} = \frac{13{,}000{,}000}{295{,}890} = -44 \text{ days}$$

$$\text{Work-in-progress period} = \frac{10{,}500{,}000}{378{,}082} = 28 \text{ days}$$

$$\text{Finished goods inventory period} = \frac{9{,}500{,}000}{378{,}082} = 25 \text{ days}$$

$$\text{Debtor-conversion period} = \frac{31{,}000{,}000}{438{,}356} = 71 \text{ days}$$

$$\text{Cash-conversion cycle} = 158 \text{ days}$$

* This is simplified to the creditor period on a single input, raw materials – there will be other inputs and creditors in most firms.

After observing the length of time money is invested in working capital the management of the firm are likely to try to think of ways of shortening the cash-conversion cycle – so long as such shortening does not excessively damage operations. A number of actions could be taken: debtor levels could be cut by changing the conditions of sale or being more forceful in the collection of old debts; inventory levels can be examined to see if overstocking is occurring and whether the production methods can be altered to process and sell goods more quickly; perhaps creditors could be pushed into granting more credit. If these actions can be carried out without any adverse impact on costs or sales, then they should be implemented.

An extreme form of reducing the cash-conversion cycle has been achieved by Amazon.com. It sells goods and receives payment from customers *before* it has to pay suppliers. In the article in Exhibit 13.15 the term operating cycle is substituted for cash-conversion cycle (American phraseology).

Exhibit 13.15

Amazon spreads its risks

FT

The online retailer's expertise at fulfilment may vindicate its decision to sell PCs

In the early days of electronic commerce, . . . companies such as Amazon kept no inventories of the vast majority of books they sold: only when your order came in did they buy in the book you wanted from a wholesaler.

Thanks to the clever use of software, the process happened so quickly that the book arrived within a few days – just as fast as from a mail order retailer that was a little slower off the mark in shipping its orders.

And this way of doing business has a marvellous advantage: what accountants called a negative operating cycle. Because the retailer got credit, it could sell the books to customers and get paid before having to settle up with its suppliers. Instead of sucking a flow of cash out of the business, the products being sold provided working capital for other purposes.

As competition intensified, however, the customers expected more reliable fulfilment. Thus Amazon along with everybody else, was forced to keep more items in stock. That is why the company has ended up as one of the larger operators of centralised inventory in the US.

The attractions of the negative operating cycle are still in place. Amazon can still receive payment for its sales before paying its suppliers.

Source: Tim Jackson, *Financial Times*, 12 June 2001, p. 15. Copyright © Tim Jackson. Reprinted with permission.

The difficult decisions come when reducing the cash-conversion cycle entails costs as well as benefits – then a careful evaluation and balancing of cost and benefits is needed. These will be considered later in the chapter.

Exhibit 13.16 provides a brief overview of the tension with which managers have to cope. If there is too little working capital, it results in inventories, finished goods and customer credit not being available in sufficient quantity. On the other hand, if there are excessive levels of working capital, the firm has unnecessary additional costs: the cost of tying up funds, plus the storage, ordering and handling costs of being overburdened with stock. Running throughout is the risk of being temporarily short of that vital lifeblood of a business – cash (that is, suffering a liquidity risk).

Exhibit 13.16 Working capital tension

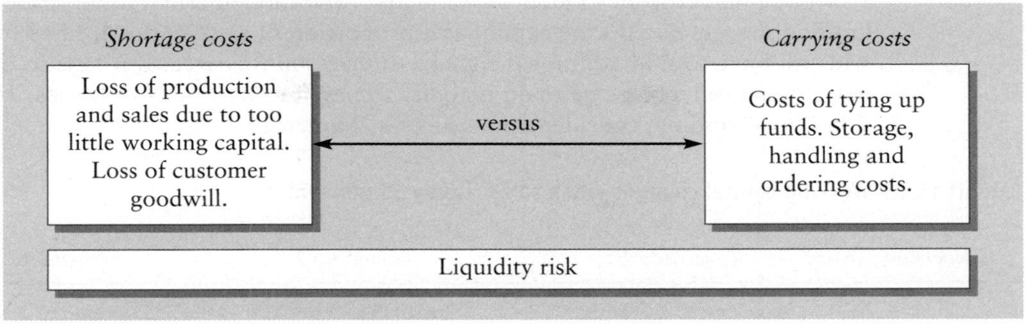

The dynamics of working capital

The level of activity of an organisation is likely to have an impact on the investment needed in working capital. Take a company with annual sales of £10m and the working capital periods set out in Exhibit 13.17.

Exhibit 13.17 Working capital periods

Stock-conversion period (raw material + work-in-progress + finished goods periods)	2 months
Debtor-conversion period	1.5 months
Creditor period	1 month

Assuming that the input costs are 60 per cent of sales the working capital investment will be £1,750,000:

Stock	60% × £10m × 2/12	1,000,000
Debtors	£10m × 1.5/12	1,250,000
Creditors	60% × £10m × 1/12	–500,000
		£1,750,000

As the level of sales increases there are three possible types of impact on the level of working capital (if we exclude the theoretical fourth possibility of a decline):

1 The investment in working capital increases in proportion to the increase in sales because the conversion periods remain constant.

2 A disproportionate rise in working capital is experienced. The conversion periods may be lengthened because of longer credit granted to customers to increase sales or higher raw materials, WIP and finished goods inventory to support the increased activity. These moves may make logical business sense in order to generate more sales and avoid stock-out costs, or they may be a result of poor working capital management. Much depends on the environment and the economics of the business concerned.

3 Working capital increases at a slower rate than the sales volume.

These three possibilities are shown in Exhibit 13.18.

What emerges from Exhibit 13.18 is that even though remarkable strides are made in limiting the rise in working capital as a proportion of sales in the third scenario, the firm will still have to find additional finance to invest in this area. If it fails to do so the firm may cease production due to an inability to pay for day-to-day expenses. This is a situation of overtrading, considered later in this chapter.

Exhibit 13.18 Working capital changes when sales rise by 50 per cent

Conversion periods	*Possibility 1*		*Possibility 2*		*Possibility 3*	
Stock	Constant @ 2 months		Increase to 3 months		Decrease to $1^1/_2$ months	
Debtors	Constant @ $1^1/_2$ months		Increase to 2 months		Decrease to 1 month	
Creditor	Constant @ 1 month		Increase to $1^1/_2$ months		Decrease to $^1/_2$ month	
		£m		£m		£m
Stock	60% × £15m × 2/12 =	1.5	60% × £15m × 3/12 =	2.25	60% × £15m × $1^1/_2$/12 =	1.125
Debtors	£15m × $1^1/_2$/12 =	1.875	£15m × 2/12 =	2.50	£15m × 1/12 =	1.250
Creditors	60% × £15m × 1/12 =	−0.750	60% × £15m × $1^1/_2$/12 =	−1.125	60% × £15m × $^1/_2$ /12 =	−0.375
Working capital investment		2.625		3.625		2.0
Absolute increase		0.875		1.875		0.25
Percentage increase over £1.75m		50%		107%		14%

Working capital policies

Exhibit 13.19 shows three alternative policies for working capital as sales rise. The top line represents a relatively relaxed approach with large cash or near-cash balances, more generous customer credit and/or higher inventories. This may be a suitable policy for a firm operating in a relatively uncertain environment where safety (or buffer) stocks of raw

Exhibit 13.19 Policies for working capital

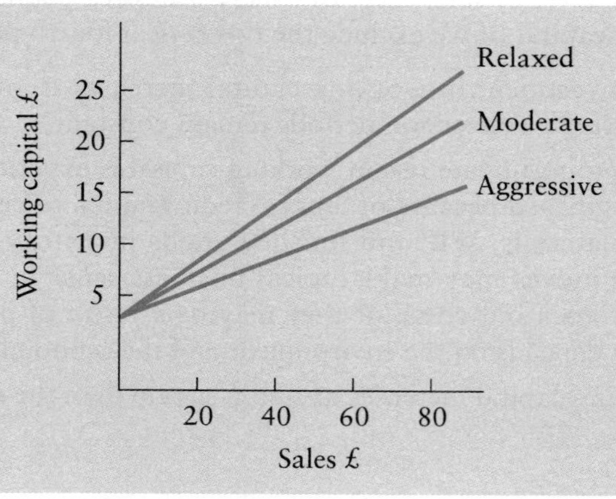

Note: The numbers are illustrative and do not imply a 'normal' relationship between sales and current assets.

materials, work in progress and finished goods are needed to avoid production stoppages and lost sales due to stock-outs. Customers may demand longer to pay and suppliers are less generous with credit. The aggressive stance is more likely to be taken in an environment of greater certainty over future flows which permits working capital to be kept to relatively low levels. Here the firm would hold minimal safety stocks of cash and inventories and/or would be able to press customers for relatively early settlement while pushing trade creditors to increase the time interval between receipt and payment for inputs. The aggressive policy approach will exhibit a shorter cycle for cash conversion.

Overtrading

A firm operating in a particular business environment and with a given level of activity will have certain levels of working capital needs. For example, a manufacturing firm with a stable level of annual sales will aim to invest an optimum amount in stocks and trade debtors. If sales should rise, by, say, 50 per cent, then it is likely that stocks of raw materials, WIP and finished goods will rise and the money devoted to support additional debtors will also increase. Perhaps the rise in investment in working capital will need to be more than 50 per cent, or perhaps the economics of the firm means that a lower proportionate rise in working capital is needed for each increase in total activity. Whatever the particular circumstance of each firm it is likely that additional working capital resources will be needed to permit judicious expansion without the fear of overtrading.

Overtrading occurs when a business has insufficient finance for working capital to sustain its level of trading.

A business is said to be overtrading when it tries to engage in more business than its working capital will allow. It could be that too much money is tied up in stocks and trade debtors, and cash is not coming in quickly enough to meet debts as they fall due. It could be that the firm failed to obtain sufficient equity finance when it was established to support its trading level, or it could be that the managers are particularly bad at managing the working capital resources that they have. The most common cause of overtrading (or under-capitalisation) is a failure to match increases in turnover with appropriate increases in finance for working capital.

It may seem odd that a firm could suffer from an increase in the demand for its products, but in the harsh world of business it is perfectly possible for a firm to double its sales, and its profits, and yet become insolvent. Managers can be sorely tempted by the lure of new sales opportunities and lead the firm to rapid expansion, believing that the additional revenue will more than cover the extra investment needed in working capital to pay day-to-day bills. However this sometimes does not work out because of the time delays involved in receiving cash from customers and the necessity to precede turnover increases with large payments for inventory, labour and other costs.

Thus the firm could find itself unable to pay short-term bills while at the same time anticipating great prosperity in the long run. This sort of problem arose in a number of information technology businesses in the UK in the 1990s as turnover doubled or tripled in a year. Take the case of (fictional) Bits and Rams Ltd which in 1999 had a turnover of £2m and a profit of £200,000:

	£000
Turnover	2,000
Cost of goods sold	1,800
Profit	200

All costs are variable for Bits and Rams and debtors generally take two and a half months to pay. Inventories for two months' worth of costs of sales are held and trade creditors are paid one and a half months after delivery.

In 2000 sales doubled but the company came close to collapse because it could not pay suppliers and the labour force on time. The cash flows for 2000 were as shown in Exhibit 13.20.

Exhibit 13.20 Cash flow for Bits and Rams Ltd

	£000
Turnover	4,000
Cost of goods sold	3,600
Profit	+400
Additional investment in debtors (2,000 × 2½/12)	–417
Additional investment in inventories (1,800 × 2/12)	–300
Tax bill from previous year's trading	–67
Increase in trade creditors (1,800 × 1½/12)	+225
Cash flow	–159

If Bits and Rams is unable to finance this large increase in working capital it could find itself insolvent. Even if it manages to avoid the worst fate management may have to engage in short-term crisis management to overcome the cash shortage (for example selling assets, chasing late payers) which is likely to distract them from the more important task of creating long-term shareholder wealth.

In an overtrading situation if it is not possible to increase the capital base of a firm, by borrowing finance or selling shares, and the management have done all they can to tighten up working capital management (for example, by reducing stock levels) then the only option left open is likely to be to reduce activity. This can be a very painful prescription psychologically for managers as they have to turn down profitable business.

Why is cash important?

Exhibit 13.10 shows the centrality of cash in the operations of firms. Many firms do not have stocks, particularly in the service sector, while others do not have debtors or creditors, but all have to use cash. So what is it about cash which causes all firms to need it? There are three categories of motives ascribed to the holding of cash:

1 *Transaction motive* Cash is often needed to pay for wages, buy materials and fixed assets, to pay taxes, service debts and for a host of other day-to-day transactions. This cash is necessary because the daily cash inflows do not match the cash outflows and so cash is needed to act as a buffer to permit activity to continue. This is particularly important in seasonal businesses or where long credit periods are granted to customers.

2 *Precautionary motive* The forecasting of future cash flows is subject to error. The more vulnerable cash flows are to unpredictable shocks the greater the cash balance needed to act as a safety stock. Future cash flows can vary from those originally anticipated for a wide variety of reasons, for example a sales shortfall, a strike or the failure of a supplier.

3 ***Speculative motive*** This simply means that any unexpected profitable opportunities can be taken immediately, for example, to purchase a competitor firm quickly when a fleeting opportunity presents itself.

The term cash is somewhat misleading in modern finance. Firms tend to hold liquid 'near-cash' assets which can quickly be converted (within hours or days), as a large constituent of their 'cash balances'. There may be, for example, holdings of commercial paper or Treasury bills which can be sold at short notice to plug a gap in cash needs. These near-cash assets carry a rate of interest but this is likely to be low relative to less liquid assets and so there is a disadvantage to holding these rather than longer-term investments.

Exhibit 13.21 shows the trade-off management have to take into account when considering the levels of cash to maintain.

Exhibit 13.21 The cash trade-off

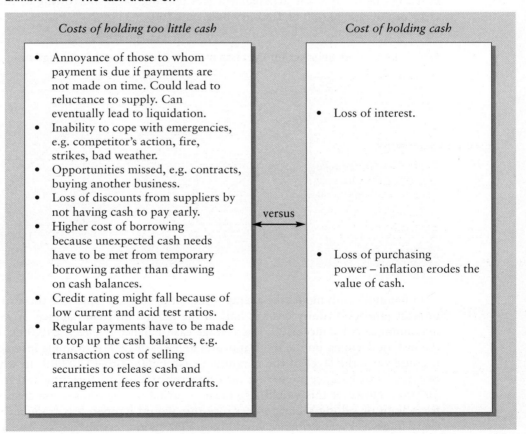

Costs of holding too little cash		*Cost of holding cash*
• Annoyance of those to whom payment is due if payments are not made on time. Could lead to reluctance to supply. Can eventually lead to liquidation. • Inability to cope with emergencies, e.g. competitor's action, fire, strikes, bad weather. • Opportunities missed, e.g. contracts, buying another business. • Loss of discounts from suppliers by not having cash to pay early. • Higher cost of borrowing because unexpected cash needs have to be met from temporary borrowing rather than drawing on cash balances. • Credit rating might fall because of low current and acid test ratios. • Regular payments have to be made to top up the cash balances, e.g. transaction cost of selling securities to release cash and arrangement fees for overdrafts.	versus ⟷	• Loss of interest. • Loss of purchasing power – inflation erodes the value of cash.

Cash management models

Models have been developed which attempt to set cash levels at a point, or within a range, which strikes the best balance between the costs outlined in Exhibit 13.21. All these models suffer from being over-simplistic and are heavily dependent on the accuracy of the inputs. There is also a danger of managers using them in a mechanical fashion, and neglecting to apply the heavy dose of judgement needed to allow for the less easily quantified variables ignored by the models.

Baumol's cash model

Baumol's model assumes that the firm operates in a steady state environment where it uses cash at a constant rate which is entirely predictable. Take the case of Cypressa plc which pays out £100,000 per week and receives a steady inflow of £80,000. The firm will have a need for additional cash of £20,000 per week. (This may sound like a disastrous pattern at first glance. However, it could be that Cypressa is highly profitable but has these cash flow shortages for the forthcoming months because of large capital expenditure. Eventually there will be a large cash inflow.) If it has a beginning cash balance of £80,000 then the pattern of cash balances over time will be as shown in Exhibit 13.22. It takes four weeks for the initial balance to be reduced to zero. At the end of Week 4 the cash balance is topped up to £80,000 by the firm, say, borrowing or selling some of its holdings of securities such as Treasury bills. Both of these actions involve costs. Let us say that the arrangement fees on £80,000 of borrowing or the transaction costs of selling £80,000 of Treasury bills are £500.

Exhibit 13.22 Cash balances for Cypressa plc with Baumol's model assumptions

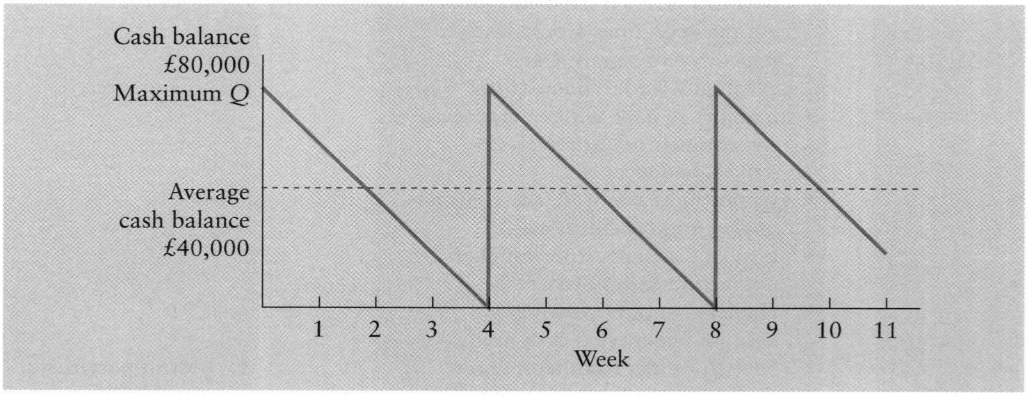

In Baumol's cash model the average amount of cash on hand and therefore earning no interest (an opportunity cost) is half of the maximum cash balance. If we denote the maximum cash balance as Q, the average cash balance is $Q/2$ = £40,000. The firm has the task of deciding on the most appropriate level of Q. For example instead of £80,000 it could raise the level of the maximum cash balance to £120,000, in which case the average cash balance incurring an opportunity cost of forgoing interest would be £60,000. However this would also mean a saving on the transaction costs of arranging for a loan or selling securities because this would happen less frequently. Instead of every four weeks new finance would be drawn upon every six weeks. The forgone interest opportunity cost of having large cash holdings has to be compared with the lower transaction costs. This is shown in Exhibit 13.23, where, as the amount of cash held is increased, the frequency (and therefore the transaction cost) of selling securities or borrowing declines while the cost of interest forgone rises.

We have the following factors to help establish the position of Q^* mathematically:

Exhibit 13.23 Finding the optimum cash balance

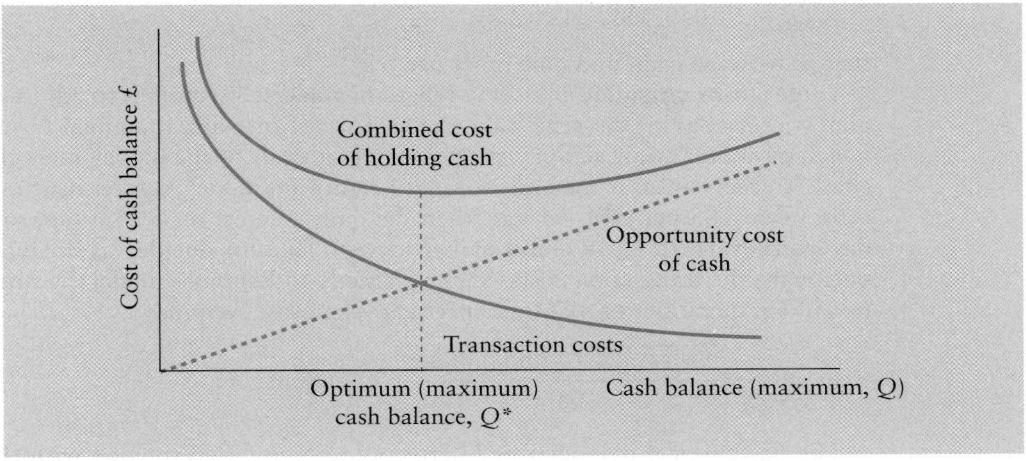

Q	=	maximum cash balance
$Q/2$	=	average cash balance
C	=	transaction costs for selling securities or arranging a loan
A	=	total amount of new cash needed for the period under consideration; this is usually one year
K	=	the holding cost of cash (the opportunity cost equal to the rate of return forgone)

The total cost line consists of the following:

$$\text{Average amount tied up} \times \text{Opportunity cost} + \text{Number of transactions} \times \text{Cost of each transaction}$$

$$\frac{Q}{2} \times K + \frac{A}{Q} \times C$$

The optimal cash balance Q^* is found as follows (the mathematics to derive this are beyond the scope of this book – the derivative of the above total cost function is set to zero):

$$Q^* = \sqrt{\frac{2CA}{K}}$$

If we assume the interest rate forgone, K, is 7 per cent then given the annual need for cash is (£20,000 × 52) = £1,040,000 for Cypressa, the optimal amount to transfer into cash on each occasion is:

$$Q^* = \sqrt{\frac{2 \times £500 \times £1{,}040{,}000}{0.07}} = £121{,}890$$

Given the assumptions of the model Cypressa should replenish its cash balances when they reach zero to the extent of £121,890.

We can also calculate the number of times replenishment will take place each year:

$$A/Q^* = £1{,}040{,}000 / £121{,}890$$

that is, between eight and nine times per year.

Larger firms often find it worthwhile to buy and sell securities to adjust cash balances almost every day of the year. Take the case of a firm with an annual turnover of £2bn which pays £600 transaction costs every time it deals in the money market to, say, purchase Treasury bills. If the annual rate of return on money market instruments is 7 per cent, or 0.0185 per cent per day, then the daily interest on £5.5m (approximately one day's turnover) is £1,018 and it makes sense to lend for one day as the interest received outweighs the transaction costs. Sticking strictly to Baumol's model the firm should deal in £5.86m quantities or 342 times per year – let's say, every day:

$$Q^* = \sqrt{\frac{2 \times £600 \times £2{,}000{,}000{,}000}{0.07}} = £5.86\text{m}$$

The basic model demonstrated here could be modified to cope with the need for a safety stock of cash to reduce the probability of cash shortages in a less than certain world. One drawback of the model is its inapplicability when finance is provided by way of an overdraft.

Some considerations for cash management

Create a policy framework

It is advisable for frequent and routine decisions to establish a set of policies. This will enable simpler and quicker decisions to be taken at lower levels in the organisation. Such a policy framework needs to retain some flexibility so that exceptional circumstances can bring forth a more detailed consideration. The framework should also be capable of change as the environment changes.

Plan cash flows

Good cash management requires good planning. Management need to know when cash is likely to be in surplus (so that it can be invested) and when it is necessary to borrow. Cash budgets allow for forward planning. For example, the company represented in Exhibit 13.24 with a constant monthly cash outflow and an undulating cash inflow has six months of the year when effort has to be devoted to investing surplus cash and six

Exhibit 13.24 Cash planning

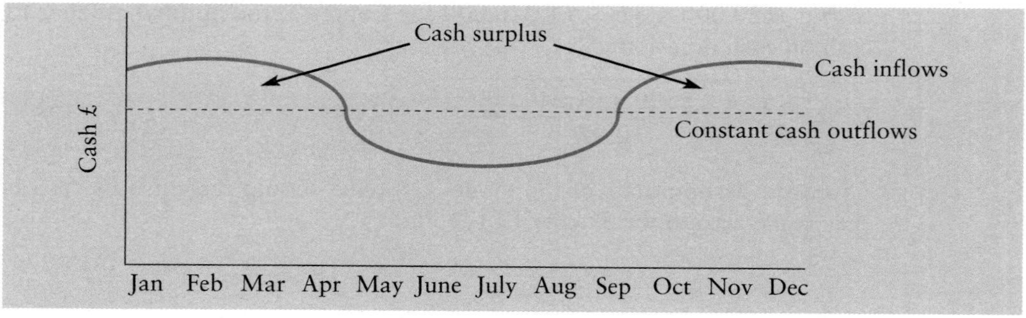

months to financing a cash shortfall. The volume and length of time of those surpluses or deficits need to be known in advance to obtain the best terms and select the most appropriate instruments. For example if £10m is available for investment over three months perhaps a portfolio of commercial and Treasury bills will be purchased; if only £10,000 is available for seven days an interest-bearing bank account might be best. Companies which do not expect a surplus at any time in the forthcoming months but rely on an overdraft facility will still need to plan ahead to ensure that the overdraft limit is not breached. If there is to be an exceptional cash need for a few months perhaps an increased overdraft limit will have to be negotiated.

The cash budget is an estimate of cash inflows and outflows at fixed intervals over a future period.

Cash budgets may be drawn up on a quarterly, monthly, weekly or daily basis. Generally a monthly budget for the next year plus a more detailed daily budget for the forthcoming month will be drawn up.

Exhibit 13.25 shows a cash budget for Cedrus plc over the next six months. Cedrus is a manufacturer of nutcrackers and so has a peak in its sales in December. One-third of sales in any month are paid for in the month of delivery, with the remainder paid after one month's credit.

Exhibit 13.25 Cedrus plc: sales

	Sales £000s		
	Total	*Paid for in month of delivery*	*Paid for 1 month later*
August	90	30	60
September	90	30	60
October	120	40	80
November	150	50	100
December	600	200	400
January	60	20	40

Note: Sales on credit outstanding at the end of July are £60,000.

Cedrus maintains a constant level of output through the year and so builds up stocks in the autumn and early winter. During October an old machine tool will be replaced at a cost of £100,000 payable upon installation. Also, in the November edition of a glossy food and drink magazine the range of nutcrackers will be promoted, costing the firm a further £50,000. In January £150,000 tax will be payable. At the beginning of August the cash balance will be a positive £50,000.

To calculate the cash budget we can split the problem into three stages:

1 Show the inflows from sales when the cash is actually received rather than when the sale is recorded.

2 List the cash outflows in the month of occurrence.

3 Display the opening cash balance for each month less the cash surplus (or deficit) generated that month to show a closing cash balance (*see* Exhibit 13.26).

Exhibit 13.26 Cedrus plc cash budget

£000s	*Aug*	*Sep*	*Oct*	*Nov*	*Dec*	*Jan*
Cash inflows						
Sales (delivered and paid for in same month)	30	30	40	50	200	20
Sales (cash received from prior month's sales)	60	60	60	80	100	400
Total inflows	90	90	100	130	300	420
Cash outflows						
Payments for materials	50	50	55	55	55	55
Wages	20	20	22	25	30	22
Rent	10	10	10	10	10	10
Other expenses	10	10	11	9	10	11
New machine			100			
Advertising				50		
Tax						150
Total outflows	90	90	198	149	105	248
Balances						
Opening cash balance for month	50	50	50	(48)	(67)	128
Net cash surplus (deficit) for month (i.e. inflows minus outflows)	0	0	(98)	(19)	195	172
Closing cash balance	50	50	(48)	(67)	128	300

Cedrus is likely to need some borrowing facility to cover its cash shortfall in October and November. For the other four months the management will have to give thought to the best use of surplus cash. Perhaps some will be paid out in the form of dividends, some used to repay long-term debt and some deposited to earn interest. Having considered the projected cash flows the management might also consider ways of boosting net cash inflows by shortening the cash-conversion cycle, for example holding less stock or offering early settlement discount to customers.

Two additional points need to be made about the use of cash budgets in practice. First, the figures represent the most likely outcome and do not allow for the risk of variability from these 'best guesses'. It is more sensible to examine a range of possible outcomes to gain a realistic picture of what might happen and the range of the cash needs. The projection of sales is particularly problematic and yet it has a profound impact on the budget. Secondly, the figures shown are the cash position at the end of each month. It is possible that cash needs or surpluses are much larger than these during some parts of the month.

Control cash flows

Many large firms have operations in a number of regions in one country or in a range of countries. Unilever, for example, manufactures and sells all over the world. To operate effectively Unilever has numerous bank accounts so that some banking transactions can take place near to the point of business. Sales receipts from America will be paid into local banks there, likewise many operating expenses will be paid for with funds drawn from those same banks. The problem for Unilever is that some of those bank accounts will have high inflows and others high outflows, so interest could be payable on one while funds are lying idle or earning a low rate of return in another. Therefore, as well as taking advantage of the benefit of having local banks carry out local transactions, large firms need to set in place a co-ordinating system to ensure that funds are transferred from where there is surplus to where they are needed.

Also, many payments are made centrally, such as dividends, taxes, bond interest, major new investments, and so an efficient mechanism is needed to funnel money to the centre.

Another aspect of good cash management is to try to reduce the level of cash balances needed by ensuring that cash outflows occur at the same time as cash inflows. This is known as cash flow synchronisation. For example, some firms insist on customer payment at the end of the month and pay their own suppliers at the same time. The reduced cash balances mean lower bank loans and therefore higher profit.

Managers can make use of the cash budget as a control device by regularly comparing the outcome with the original plan for a period. If there is a substantial deviation then this might prompt enquiries and action to correct any problems.

Management should also consider using the delays in the cheque-clearing system rather than becoming victims of them. There is often a substantial delay between the time that a cheque is written and the time that the ultimate recipient can use the money. In the UK it generally takes between two and four days to clear a cheque and, as Exhibit 13.27 shows, this is only one of the causes of delay.

Some firms are able to take advantage of this delay to boost their cash balances. Take a firm which writes, on average, cheques for £1,000 per day, where the managers know from experience that these cheques generally take five days to clear (that is, for the cheque to be received, paid into a bank account and for the cash to be drawn from the bank account). This means that the cheque book balance will be £5,000 less than the bank balance. If the firm also receives cheques of £1,000 per day from customers and takes three days to deposit and clear cheques, its cheque book balance will be £3,000 more than its bank balance. In total there will be a *net float* of £2,000 due to the delay in processing cheques. For large firms the float can run into millions of pounds and the resulting interest savings can be very large. If British Telecommunications, with a turnover of £21.9bn per year, can obtain its money one day earlier, the cash balance will increase by £60m.

Exhibit 13.27 The delays in clearing a cheque

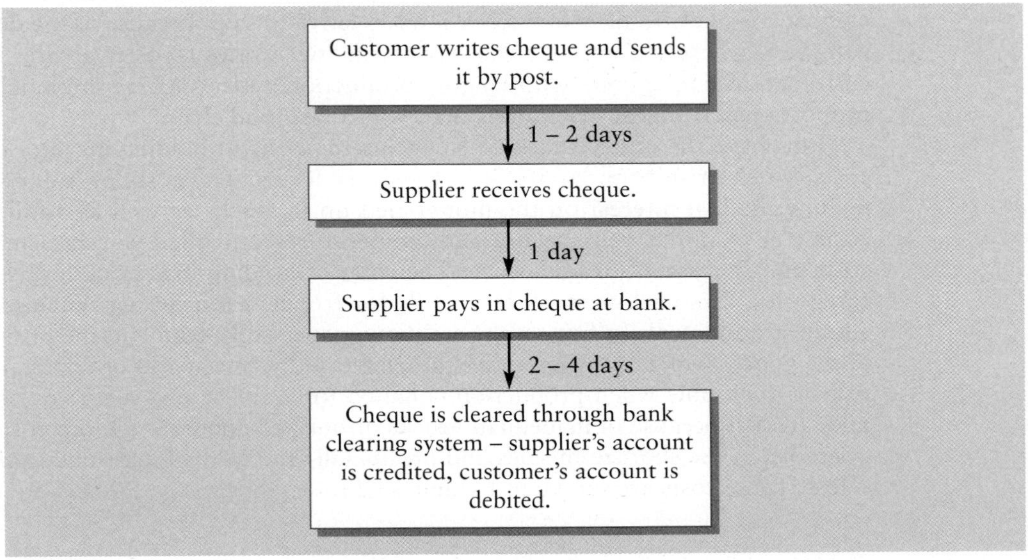

The *float* is the difference between the cash balance shown on the firm's cheque book and the bank account. The size of the float depends on the firm's ability to slow the cash transfer on cheques written and to accelerate the crediting of bank accounts with cheques received. Some firms are much more efficient at this than others and are capable of running accounts which are positive at the bank but are negative on the cheque book for lengthy periods.

The banking system has responded to the growing need to speed up the transfer of money from one firm to another. For example, the CHAPS system in the UK (Clearing House Automated Payments System) permits same-day cheque clearance and CHIPS (Clearing House Interbank Payment System), a computerised network, enables the electronic transfer of international dollar payments. These systems provide two benefits to the larger firms which use them. First, there is greater certainty as to when money will be received, and secondly, they can reduce the time that money is in the banking system.

Companies can take other action to create a beneficial float. They could bank frequently to avoid having cheques remaining in the accounts office for more than a few hours. They could also encourage customers to pay on time, or even in advance, of the receipt of goods and services by using the direct debit system through which money is automatically transferred from one account to another on a regular basis. Many UK consumers now pay for gas, telecommunications and electricity via a monthly direct debit. In return they often receive a small discount. From the producer's viewpoint this not only reduces the float but also avoids the onerous task of chasing late payers. Also retailers now have terminals which permit electronic funds transfer at the point of sale (EFTPOS) – money taken from customers' accounts electronically using a debit card.

Inventory management

The form of inventory varies from one firm to another. For a construction firm it may consist of bricks, timber and unsold houses, while for a retailer it is goods bought in for sale but as yet unsold.

The quantity of inventory held is determined by factors such as the predictability of sales and production (more volatility may call for more safety stocks), the length of time it takes to produce and the nature of the product. On the last point, note that a dairy company is likely to have low stock levels relative to sales because of the danger of deterioration, whereas a jeweller will have large inventories to offer greater choice to the customer. Manufacturers with lengthy production cycles such as shipbuilders will have proportionately higher inventories than, say, a fast food chain.

Firms have the difficult task of balancing the costs of holding inventories against the costs which arise from having low inventory levels. The costs of holding inventories include the lost interest on the money tied up in stocks as well as additional storage costs (for example, rent, secure and temperature-controlled warehousing), insurance costs and the risk of obsolescence. The costs of holding low stock levels fall into two categories. First, a low stock level calls for frequent reordering. Each order involves administration costs (office employees' time, paperwork, etc.) and the physical handling of the goods (warehouse employees' time). Secondly, in a world of uncertainty there is a risk of stock-outs when production is halted for want of raw materials or WIP and/or sales are lost because of inadequate stocks of finished goods. Stock-out costs can be considerable; in the short term sales and profits fall, and in the long run customer goodwill is lost. These costs are shown in Exhibit 13.28.

Exhibit 13.28 The inventory trade-off

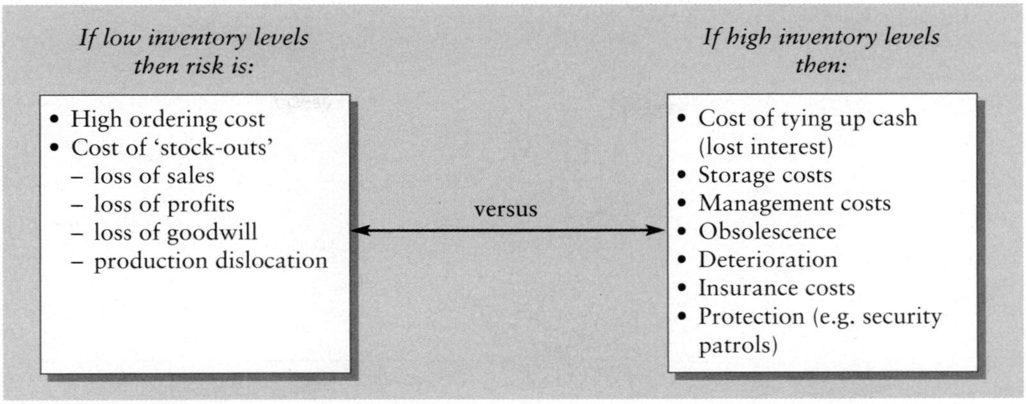

Inventory management modelling in a world of certainty

If the usage and delivery of stock can be predicted accurately management are likely to avoid stock-out costs and need only concern themselves with achieving the optimal balance between ordering costs (the first point in the left box of Exhibit 13.28) and 'holding costs' (the right box of Exhibit 13.28). Given a steady usage of raw materials we can calculate the optimum size of order to be placed with suppliers. Exhibit 13.29 shows a gradual rundown of stock levels until zero stock is reached, at which time there is an instant replenishment – taking stock back to the maximum level, *Q*. Each time stock is reordered there are ordering costs and so the firm naturally wishes to reduce this to a minimum, but on the other hand if it reorders very infrequently the average stock levels, *Q*/2, will be high and the holding costs will be excessive.

Exhibit 13.29 Stock levels over time in a predictable environment

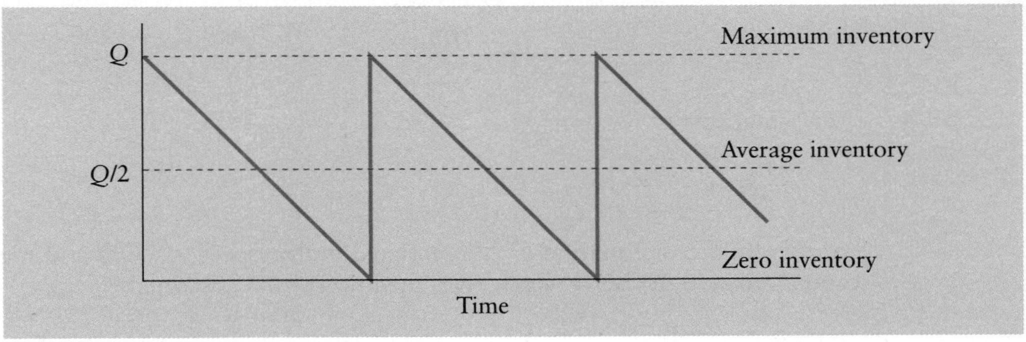

The holding costs are assumed to rise in proportion to the rise in the quantity ordered on each occasion (because of the rise in the average stock level) in Exhibit 13.30.

The ordering costs decline as the frequency of ordering declines and large orders are made on each occasion. There is an economic order quantity, EOQ, which minimises the combined costs.

Exhibit 13.30 Optimum inventory cost

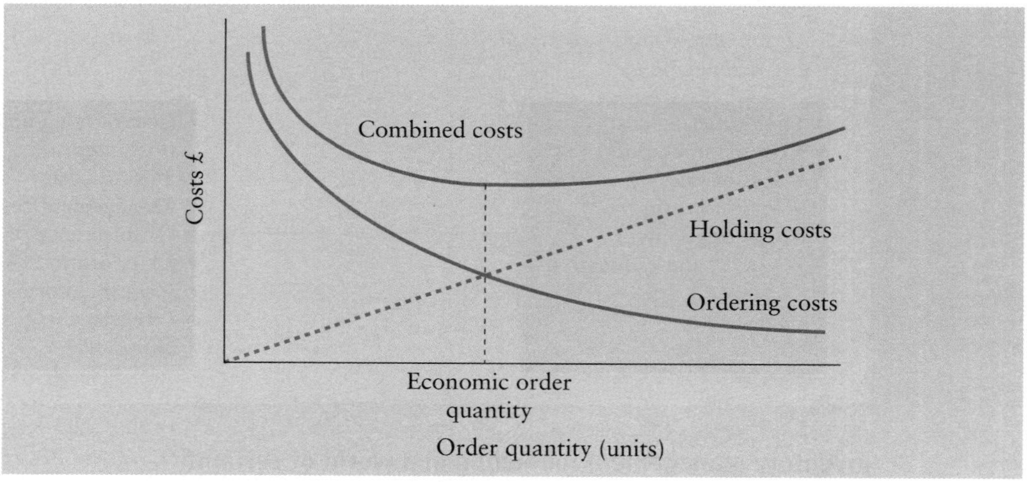

If C is the cost of placing each order, A is the annual usage of the inventory items, and H is the cost of holding one unit of stock for one year then:

$$\text{The annual ordering costs} = \text{Number of orders per year} \times \text{Cost of each order}$$
$$= A/Q \times C$$
$$\text{or} \quad \frac{AC}{Q}$$

and:

$$\text{The cost of holding stock} = \text{Average stock level (in units)} \times \text{Cost of holding each unit per year}$$
$$= Q/2 \times H$$
$$\text{or} \quad \frac{HQ}{2}$$

The total cost is:

$$\frac{AC}{Q} + \frac{HQ}{2}$$

If this total cost equation is differentiated with respect to EOQ and the derivative is set equal to zero the EOQ which gives the lowest total cost will be:

$$\text{EOQ} = \sqrt{\frac{2AC}{H}}$$

Worked example 13.1 Wicker plc

Wicker plc uses 20,000 units per year of a particular item of stock. It costs £28 for each order and the cost of holding each of the units is £1.20. What is the economic order quantity?

Answer

$$\text{EOQ} = \sqrt{\frac{2 \times 20{,}000 \times 28}{1.20}} = 966 \text{ units}$$

Each order will be for 966 units, which will cost an annual total of:

$$\frac{AC}{Q} + \frac{HQ}{2}$$

$$= (20{,}000 \times 28)/966 + (1.20 \times 966)/2 = £1{,}159.31$$

(This excludes the amount paid to the supplier for the particular inventory.)

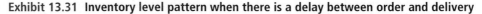

The EOQ model used above has failed to take account of two types of risk:

1 There may be uncertainty over the time it takes for an order to be delivered. That is, the 'lead time' is neither 0 (as assumed in Exhibit 13.29 where instant delivery takes place) nor necessarily predictable.
2 The rate at which inventory is used may not be as shown in Exhibit 13.29 – demand may be subject to fluctuations and the overall annual demand may be impossible to predict with accuracy.

To cope with these two risk elements the company will hold buffer (or safety) stocks. These buffer stock levels can be calculated by weighing up the costs of stock-outs and the cost of holding additional inventories. This can be done in complicated mathematical fashion using probability distribution and sophisticated statistics, but for most firms a more pragmatic approach is adopted, with some estimate of uncertainty gained by subjective assessment defining the most appropriate buffer level. Consider first a firm which has to wait one week between reordering and the delivery of stock. For now we will assume that the weekly usage is stable and certain at 2,000 units per week and that the lead time is predictable. The economic order quantity is set at 8,000 units. To avoid having any stock-outs this firm will need to reorder when the stock levels fall to 2,000 units. This is shown in Exhibit 13.31.

Exhibit 13.31 Inventory level pattern when there is a delay between order and delivery

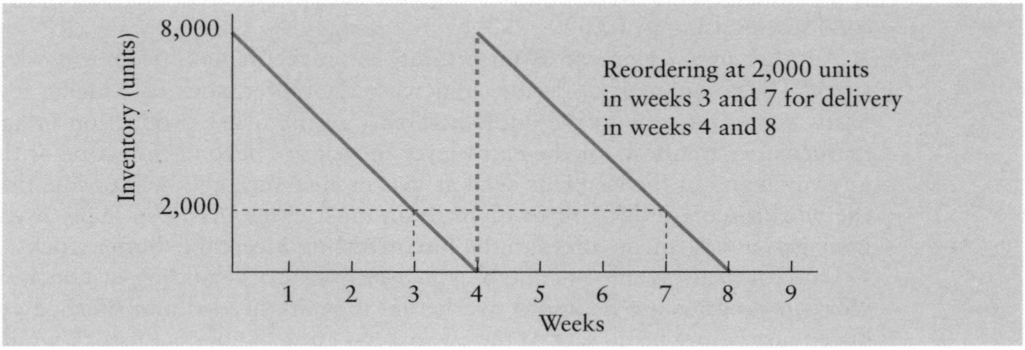

Now assume uncertainty over the lead time – it may be one week or it may be two – it is impossible to be precise because of the unreliability of the supplier. The firm will need to have a maximum inventory holding of 10,000 units with an EOQ of 8,000 units as shown in Exhibit 13.32.

Exhibit 13.32 Inventory level pattern when there is uncertainty over the lead time

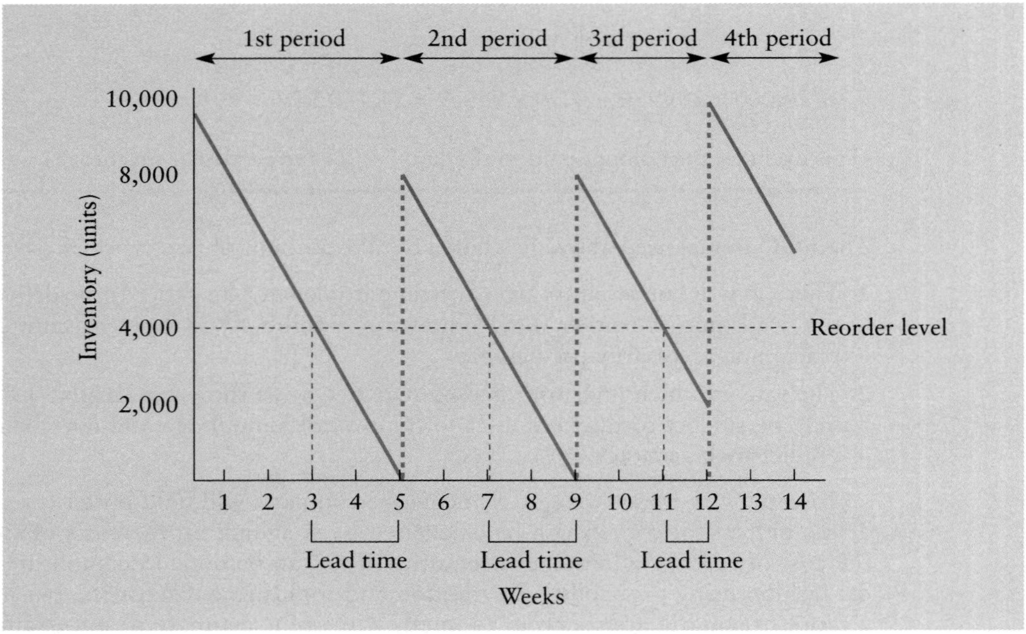

The firm has to ensure a maximum inventory level of 10,000 units just in case the supplier takes two weeks to deliver. Given the usage rate of 2,000 units per week the reorder level is set at 4,000 units and so in the first period, at the end of the third week, 8,000 units are ordered. It so happens that the supplier is slow with this order and delivery does not take place until the end of the fifth week. Again in the second period the supplier takes two weeks but the reorder level of 4,000 was reached in the seventh week and so the firm does not run out of stock. In the third period stocks are reordered at the end of the eleventh week and this time the supplier delivers one week later, resulting in total stocks rising to 10,000.

Another major element of uncertainty is on the demand side: the usage rate of the stock. The company may decide to increase the buffer stock to a higher level to prevent costly stock-outs due to the unpredictability of the firm's production or sales flow. The mathematics to allow for the extra layer of risk are beyond the scope of this book, and anyway many of the elements such as loss of customer goodwill or idle time of some of the workforce are difficult to quantify in most cases. As in so many areas of finance, managerial judgement comes to the fore in setting acceptable buffer stocks.

One form of inventory control is *just-in-time* stock holding in which materials and work in progress are delivered just before they are needed and finished goods are produced just before being sent to the customers. Large amounts of stock would never build up in such a system and there are obvious consequential savings. However such a system cannot be introduced in isolation. There will be a need, in many cases, for revolutionary change throughout the organisation ranging from improving relationships and the quality of information flows to suppliers to a 'right-first-time' culture and a flexible attitude on the part of the workforce. It may even require the relocation of factories so that supplier and customer can be close together.

Debtor and creditor management

Trade credit is both a source and a use of finance. Chapter 12 dealt with the management of trade debtors and creditors. Here we will focus on a summary of the trade-off a firm has to consider when judging whether to accept trade credit. This is shown in Exhibit 13.33.

Exhibit 13.33 The credit trade-off

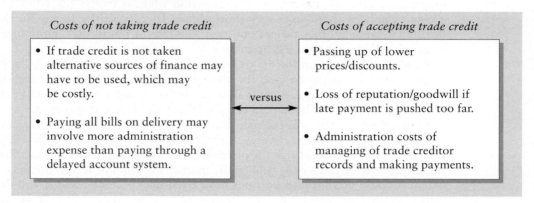

Costs of not taking trade credit		*Costs of accepting trade credit*
• If trade credit is not taken alternative sources of finance may have to be used, which may be costly. • Paying all bills on delivery may involve more administration expense than paying through a delayed account system.	versus	• Passing up of lower prices/discounts. • Loss of reputation/goodwill if late payment is pushed too far. • Administration costs of managing of trade creditor records and making payments.

INVESTMENT OF TEMPORARY SURPLUS FUNDS

Most companies generate occasional cash surpluses which need to be kept within the business to be used at a later date. In the meantime opportunities should be taken to generate a return on these funds by following the treasurer's maxim 'never let cash lie idle'.

Short-term cash surpluses arise for a number of reasons and for varying periods of time. If a business is seasonal or cyclical there may be a build-up of cash in certain periods. For example Chrysler, Ford and General Motors, the US car producers, were heavily criticised for their multibillion-dollar portfolio of near-cash financial instruments during 1997. Chrysler had \$6bn, Ford \$9bn and General Motors \$12bn. Some of the shareholding critics would have preferred the companies to pay out this money to them. The management however argued that the car industry is a cyclical one and they need large cash or near-cash balances in good times in order to maintain product development and capital spending through a downturn. Toyota had cash reserves of \$20bn in 2001!

Firms also build up cash reserves to be able to meet large outflow events such as major asset purchases, dividends, tax bills or bond redemptions. In addition, some firms may have sold an asset or raised fresh borrowing but have yet to direct that money to its final use. Alternatively, cash could be in surplus due to surprisingly good control of working capital. Sometimes cash builds up because the business is highly profitable and the management choose to hold on to it.

In 2000 Microsoft was generating cash at a rate of around \$3bn per quarter, totalling \$23bn by year-end.

Senior management, in conjunction with the treasurer, need to consider carefully what proportion of surplus cash is permanent and therefore is available for dividends or to repay debt and what proportion is really temporary.

The objective

A treasurer will set as an objective the maximisation of return from temporarily surplus cash, but this is subject to the constraints imposed by risk. One of those risk elements is the possibility of not having cash available at the right time to fund working capital – this is liquidity risk. There is a requirement to ensure that investments are sufficiently liquid to match anticipated cash flow needs and that there is a reserve (a safety margin) to provide a buffer against unpredictable events. Funds invested in a commercial bill may not be available for a three-month period whereas money placed in a 'sight' bank account can be withdrawn at very short notice. There is a price to pay for this degree of flexibility: keeping other factors constant, the rate of return on a more liquid financial asset is less than that on a less liquid one.

Another consideration for the treasurer is the risk of default. This is the risk that the borrower will be unable to meet the interest and principal payments. Lending to the UK government (for example, buying Treasury bills) carries a minute default risk whereas investment in shares or bonds can carry significant risk of non-payment.

Another risk factor is event risk. This is the probability that some events such as a change in capital structure (leverage) of the borrower will occur which will increase the risk of default. Valuation risk (or price risk) occurs because of the possibility that when the instrument matures or is sold in the market the amount received is less than anticipated. It could be that interest rates have risen unexpectedly, which will depress bond prices, or the firm may have to pay a penalty for early redemption. Inflation risk is the probability of a reduction in purchasing power of a sum of money.

The treasurer has the task of balancing return and acceptable risk when investing temporarily surplus funds, as shown in Exhibit 13.34.

Exhibit 13.34 The short-term investment trade-off

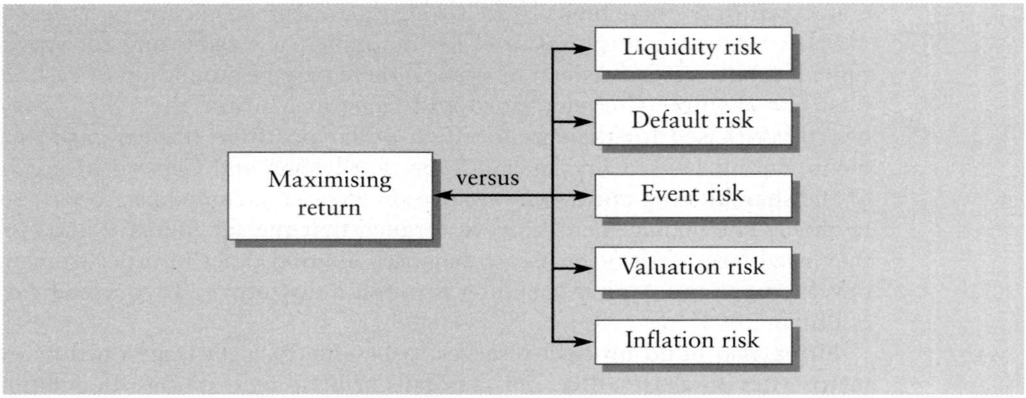

Investment policy

There are three crucial areas in which senior management need to set policy guidelines for treasurers:

1 *Defining the investable funds* Just how much of the firm's cash is to be available to invest is often a difficult decision. Subsidiaries will require minimum working capital and so cash has to be allocated to the units by the centre. But subsidiaries often lack the specialised personnel and economies of scale to carry out effective surplus cash investment so this is best done from the centre. It is therefore necessary to have policies and

mechanisms for transferring cash between the central treasury and the operating units. The centre will need to provide sufficient cash to the subsidiaries to avoid liquidity risk, that is, a shortage of cash to pay day-to-day bills. This is likely to be uppermost in the minds of subsidiary managers whereas the treasurer will want to keep a tight rein to ensure cash is not being kept idle. This tension needs clever resolution.

2 ***Acceptable investment*** The treasurer may be permitted a wide range of options for investment, from bank deposits to futures and options. Alternatively there may be limits placed on the type of investment. For example, foreign shares may be excluded because of the valuation risk and the risk of exchange rates moving adversely. All derivative instruments may be banned except for the purpose of hedging.
3 ***Limits on holdings*** Within the acceptable range of instruments it may be necessary to set maximum acceptable holdings. This may be in terms of total monetary amount or as a proportion of the total investable funds. For example, the treasurer may not be permitted to invest more than 30 per cent of funds in the Euromarkets.

Investment choice

The range of instruments open to the treasurer is large. Some idea of this can be gained by examining the money market table published daily in the *Financial Times*, one of which is reproduced in Exhibit 13.35. Descriptions of the instruments are given in Exhibit 13.36.

Exhibit 13.35

UK Interest Rates

FT

Jun 21	Over-night	7 days notice	One month	Three months	Six months	One year
Interbank Sterling	$4\frac{1}{2} - 4\frac{3}{32}$	$4\frac{5}{8} - 4\frac{3}{8}$	$5\frac{1}{8} - 5$	$5\frac{1}{4} - 5\frac{1}{8}$	$5\frac{3}{8} - 5\frac{1}{4}$	$5\frac{5}{8} - 5\frac{1}{2}$
BBA Sterling LIBOR	$4\frac{3}{8}$ –	$4\frac{5}{8}$ –	$5\frac{5}{32}$ –	$5\frac{1}{4}$ –	$5\frac{3}{8}$–	$5\frac{5}{8}$–
Sterling CDs	–	–	$5\frac{1}{4} - 5\frac{3}{16}$	$5\frac{1}{8} - 5\frac{3}{32}$	$5\frac{1}{8} - 5\frac{3}{32}$	$5\frac{3}{32} - 5\frac{1}{8}$
Treasury Bills	–	–	$5\frac{7}{32} - 5\frac{5}{32}$	$5\frac{3}{32} - 5\frac{1}{32}$	–	–
Bank Bills	–	–	$5\frac{7}{32} - 5\frac{5}{32}$	$5\frac{1}{8} - 5$	–	–
Local authority deps.	–	$5 - 4\frac{7}{8}$	$5\frac{3}{16} - 5\frac{1}{16}$	$5\frac{1}{4} - 5\frac{1}{8}$	$5\frac{3}{8} - 5\frac{1}{4}$	$5\frac{5}{8} - 5\frac{1}{2}$
Discount Market deps	$5\frac{3}{8} - 5\frac{1}{8}$	$5\frac{3}{8} - 5\frac{1}{3}$	–	–	–	–

UK clearing bank base lending rate $5\frac{1}{4}$ per cent from May 10, 2001

Note: The lower rate quoted is the rate applicable to lenders, the higher rate is payable by borrowers.

Source: *Financial Times*, 22 June 2001. Reprinted with permission.

The extent of marketability (or ability to sell in the secondary market) influences the interest paid. Lending to a bank via the interbank market and by depositing money in a bank via a certificate of deposit (CD) are very similar except that the certificate can be sold to raise cash and is therefore more liquid. The treasurer has not only a range of instruments to choose from but also a range of maturities, from overnight deposits to one-year commitments. It is also necessary to consider carefully the tax implications of each investment decision as well as the foreign exchange risk if non-sterling investments are made. One crucial final point is that the treasurer has to consider the administrative complexity and specialist skills needed to understand and use appropriately some of the more exotic instruments.

Exhibit 13.36 Some of the investments available to a corporate treasurer

'Sight' deposit at a bank, e.g. current account	Instant withdrawal – highly liquid but low interest rate.
Time deposit at a bank	Some notice is required to withdraw funds.
Interbank lending: (a) Sterling (b) Foreign currencies	Banks and others with a very high credit rating borrow from each other.
Certificate of deposit (CD)	A company agrees to lock away a sum (e.g. £500,000) in a bank deposit for a period of between three months and five years. The bank provides the company with a certificate of deposit stating that the bank will pay interest and the original capital to the holder. This is now a valuable instrument and the company can sell this to release cash. The buyer of the CD will receive the deposited money on maturity plus interest. Result: the bank has money deposited for a set period and the original lender can obtain cash by selling CD at any time.
Treasury bills	Sold by the government at a discount to face value to provide an effective yield. Tradeable in the secondary market.
Bank bills (acceptance credits) – *see* Chapter 12	A bill of exchange accepted by a bank. The bank is committed to pay the amount on the bill at maturity. A company with surplus cash could invest in such a bill.
Local authority deposits	Lending to a local authority (local government).
Discount market deposits	A deposit normally repayable at call (on demand) or made for a very short term with a London discount house.
Gilts	Purchase of UK government bonds, usually in the secondary market.
Corporate bonds	Secondary-market purchases of bonds issued by other firms.
Eurobonds, FRN, EMTN	Lending on an international bond – *see* Chapter 11.
Commercial paper	Unsecured promissory note: usually 60 days or less to maturity.
Shares	*See* Chapters 9 and 10.
Derivatives (futures, swaps, options, etc.)	*See* Chapter 21.

CONCLUDING COMMENTS

Considering the complexity of modern finance it is not surprising that treasury management has become a profession in its own right. The efficient management of short-term assets and liabilities gives the competitive edge needed for a firm to survive and thrive.

This chapter has highlighted the core issues in treasury and working capital management but, in all truth, it has only skimmed the surface. One major question left untouched is whether to centralise the treasury function. The Japanese group, Sony, for example, with operations in almost every country in the world is in the process of a significant reorganisation to concentrate its financial operations in only one centre – *see* Exhibit 13.37. The operating companies will be able to use the central treasury for foreign exchange and money market deals. In this way the best rates can be achieved on the market due to economies of scale and netting (combining subsidiary balances and simply dealing with the net amounts), control over risk levels can be exercised, skills can be concentrated and advantage can be taken of the sophisticated computerised treasury management systems.

Exhibit 13.37

Sony financial operations to shift to London

FT

Sony, the Japanese electronics group, is moving its currency hedging and fund-raising operations to London to cut costs.

The move – believed to be the first of its kind in the industry – affects about Y3,000bn ($25bn) worth of foreign exchange transactions annually. Sony believes it will lead to savings of Y6bn–Y7bn on commissions, interest payments and other costs each year.

The shift highlights Japanese companies' increased sensitivity to exchange rate fluctuations – more than 70 per cent of Sony's sales come from overseas – and a push to improve the efficiency of group finances. But it also underlines the corporate sector's mounting frustration with Japanese financial institutions and Tokyo as a financial centre . . .

Sony said the move was a natural extension of its plan, launched two years ago, to consolidate financial operations in four cities globally. Last autumn, it concluded that it would be more efficient to consolidate these functions in one place.

'In terms of market information, infrastructure, and people, London is the best city to consolidate our financial operations,' Sony said.

In December, it established Sony Global Treasury Services to oversee its exchange hedging and fund-raising activities in Europe. The company, capitalised at Y90bn with a staff of 90, will oversee commercial paper issuance, bank loans and medium-term notes as well as settlement for Sony's e-commerce operations.

Source: Alexandra Harney, *Financial Times*, 5 June 2001, p. 31. Reprinted with permission.

Another fundamental question is whether the treasury should act as a risk minimiser or a profit maximiser. Many companies make use of the derivative markets both to hedge (reduce risk) foreign exchange and interest rates, and for 'trading' purposes to try to make gains. Other firms, for example Pearson, are adamant that their treasury should not speculate: 'Risks are managed by the Group finance director . . . The treasury department is not a profit centre' (*Pearson plc Annual Report 1999*). The danger with instructing the treasury to act as a profit centre is that the managers may be tempted to take excessive risks. There have been some spectacular and well-publicised losses made by members of treasury teams. The embarrassment to ostensibly staid and low-risk firms such as Procter & Gamble (US$100m+ lost) can be considerable.

KEY POINTS AND CONCEPTS

- **Working capital** is net current assets or net current liabilities.
- In deciding **whether to borrow long or short** a company might consider the following:
  - maturity structure of debt;
  - cost of issue or arrangement;
  - flexibility;
  - the uncertainty of getting future finance;
  - the term structure of interest rates.

- Firms often strive to **match** the maturity structure of debt with the maturity structure of assets. However a more **aggressive financing policy** would finance permanent short-term assets with short-term finance. A more **conservative policy** would finance all assets with long-term finance.
- Firms need to consider the **currency in which they borrow**.
- A balance needs to be struck between **fixed and floating** interest-rate debt.
- Don't forget **retained earnings** as a financing option:

Advantages	*Disadvantages*
– No dilution of existing shareholders' returns or control	– Limited by firm's profits
– No issue costs	– Dividend payment reduced
– Managers may not have to explain use of funds (dubious advantage for shareholders)	– Subject to uncertainty
	– Regarded as 'free capital'

- **Treasurers** help decision making at a **strategic level**:

  e.g. mergers, interest and exchange-rate changes, capital structure.
- **Good relationships need to be developed with the financial community.**

  This requires effort – often the treasurer makes a major contribution:
  - flow of information;
  - number of banks;
  - transaction banking versus relationship banking.
- Some of the **risks** which can **be reduced or avoided** by a firm:
  - business risk;
  - insurable risk;
  - currency risk;
  - interest-rate risk.
- The **working capital cycle** flows from raw materials, to work in progress, to finished goods stock, to sales, and collection of cash, with creditors used to reduce the cash burden.
- **The cash-conversion cycle** is the length of time between the company's outlay on inputs and the receipt of money from the sale of goods. It equals the stock-conversion period plus the debtor-conversion period minus the credit period granted by suppliers.
- **Working capital tension** Too little working capital leads to loss of production, sales and goodwill. Too much working capital leads to excessive costs of tying up funds, storage, handling and ordering costs.
- **Working capital policies:**
  - relaxed – large proportional increases in working capital as sales rise;
  - aggressive – small proportional increases in working capital as sales rise.
- **Overtrading** occurs when a business has insufficient finance for working capital to sustain its level of trading.

- The **motives for holding cash:**
  - transactional motive;
  - precautionary motive;
  - speculative motive.
- **Baumol's cash management model:**

$$Q^* = \sqrt{\frac{2CA}{K}}$$

- **Some considerations for cash management:**
  - create a policy framework;
  - plan cash flows, e.g. cash budgets;
  - control cash flows.
- **Inventory management** requires a balance of the trade-off between the costs of high inventory (interest, storage, management, obsolescence, deterioration, insurance and protection costs) against ordering costs and stock-out costs.
- An **economic order quantity** in a world of certainty can be found:

$$\text{EOQ} = \sqrt{\frac{2AC}{H}}$$

With uncertainty buffer stocks may be needed.

- In **investing temporarily surplus cash** the treasurer has to consider the trade-off between return and risk (liquidity, default, event, valuation and inflation). Investment policy considerations:
  - defining the investable funds;
  - acceptable investments;
  - limits on holdings.

REFERENCES AND FURTHER READING

Ball, M., Brady, S. and Olivier, C. (1995) 'Getting the best from your banks', *Corporate Finance*, July, pp. 26–47. Fascinating insight into the world of high finance.

Baumol, W.J. (1952) 'The transactions demand for cash: An inventory theoretic approach', *Quarterly Journal of Economics*, November, pp. 545–56. Cash model is presented.

Brigham, E.F., Gapenski, L.C. and Ehrhardt, M.C. (1998) *Financial Management: Theory and Practice*. 9th edn. Fort Worth: Dryden Press. More detailed treatment of working capital issues.

Collier, P., Cooke, T. and Glynn, J. (1988) *Financial and Treasury Management*. Oxford: Heinemann CIMA series. Good coverage of the essential elements of treasury management.

Corporate Finance. Monthly journal. London: Euromoney. Provides insight into high-level corporate finance issues of a practical nature.

Davis, E.W. and Collier, P.A. (1982) 'Treasury management in the UK'. Association of Corporate Treasurers. Some interesting data on treasurers – their role and activities.

Howells, P. and Bain, K. (2000) *Financial Markets and Institutions*. 3rd edn. Harlow: Financial Times Prentice Hall. Includes a useful chapter introducing money market instruments.

Maness, T.S. and Zietlow, J.T. (1993) *Short-Term Financial Management*. St Paul, MN: West Publishing. A more detailed consideration of many of the issues discussed in this chapter.

Miller, M.N. and Orr, D. (1966) 'A model of the demand for money by firms', *Quarterly Journal of Economics*, August, pp. 413–35. A more sophisticated model than Baumol's.

Treasurer (a monthly journal). London: Euromoney. Up-to-date consideration of Treasurer matters.

The Treasurers Handbook. London: Association of Corporate Treasurers. An annual publication. A useful reference work.

WEBSITES

Association of Corporate Treasurers www.corporate-treasurers.co.uk

Financial Times www.ft.com

SELF-REVIEW QUESTIONS

1 Why do firms hold cash or near cash?

2 Why do firms need to make short-term financial investments?

3 Explain what is meant by liquidity, event and valuation risk.

4 What are the strengths and weaknesses of Baumol's cash management model?

5 Describe the advantages and disadvantages of retained earnings as a source of finance.

6 What are the main considerations when deciding whether to borrow long or short?

7 What are the main areas of risk a treasurer might help to manage?

8 What are relationship banking and transactional banking?

9 Describe the working capital cycle and the cash-conversion cycle.

10 What is overtrading?

11 Why do insurance companies exist?

12 What is an 'aggressive' working capital policy?

13 What is the 'float' in cash management?

14 What is a certificate of deposit?

15 What does it mean to make 'the treasury a profit centre'?

16 What are the main areas of 'control' of cash?

17 What is a cash budget?

18 What is the economic order quantity?

QUESTIONS AND PROBLEMS

1 Tollhouse plc has a large overdraft which is expected to continue. Its annual sales are £10m, spread evenly through the year – the same amount in each week. The interest rate on the overdraft is 11 per cent. The present policy is to pay into the bank the weekly receipts from customers each Friday. However a new director has raised the question of whether it would be better to pay in on Mondays as well as Fridays especially in the light of the fact that Monday's receipts are three times the level of those of the other days of the working week. No cash is received on Saturdays or Sundays. It costs £35 each time money is paid into the bank account and all daily cash inflows arrive before the regular paying-in time of 3 p.m. Ignore taxation and consider which of the following three policies is the best for Tollhouse:

a Continue to pay in on Fridays.

b Pay in on Mondays and Fridays.

c Pay in every day of the week.

Also discuss ways of reducing the 'float' of a company.

2 As the treasurer of Stokes plc you have been asked to write a report putting forward ideas for the use of temporarily surplus cash. These funds will be available for varying periods – from one week to four months.

Describe the main considerations or trade-offs for short-term cash management. Choose any four of the potential investment instruments, describe them and outline their advantages and disadvantages.

3* Rounded plc, a new retail business, has projected sales as follows:

	£m		£m		£m
Jan.	1.3	May	2.0	Sept.	2.0
Feb.	1.5	June	2.2	Oct.	1.8
March	1.6	July	2.3	Nov.	1.9
April	1.5	Aug.	2.0	Dec.	3.0

One-third of sales are for cash, one-third is received one month after sales, and one-third is received two months after sale. The cash balance at the beginning of January is £500,000.

A major investment in new shops will cost £2m in cash in May. Stock costs one-half of sales and is purchased and paid for in the same month it is sold.

Labour and other costs amount to £300,000 per month, paid for as incurred. Assume no tax is payable in this year.

Required

a Show the monthly cash balance for the first year.

b Recommend action to be taken based on these cash balances.

4 Bluebond uses 300,000 units of raw material per year. It costs £200 to process and receive delivery of this stock regardless of the size of order. It also costs £10 per year to hold a unit for a year. Assuming complete certainty over demand and instantaneous delivery when an order is made, what is the economic order quantity? How many orders will be made per year and what is the total inventory cost of this raw material?

5 Blackwide uses 10,000 items of stock per year. It costs £7 to hold an item of stock for a year and the reorder costs are £50 regardless of quantity.

a Find the economic order quantity in a completely certain world with instantaneous replenishment of stock.

b Determine the total inventory cost for this item and the number of orders per year.

c If there was a certain delay in delivery of this item from the time of order of one week, at what level will stock be reordered?

d If the delay between order and delivery can vary from one week to two weeks what is the maximum inventory holding if no stock-outs are to occur?

e What other factors might need to be allowed for in the real world of business?

6* Numerical example of treasury investment:
As the treasurer of a firm you anticipate the following cash position which will require either short-term borrowing or investment:

Cash flow forecast for an 11-day period

Opening balance £11,000,000

Day	*Net cash flow*	*Cumulative*
1.3.x1	–5,000,000	6,000,000
2.3.x1	–5,000,000	1,000,000
3.3.x1	–6,000,000	–5,000,000
4.3.x1	0	–5,000,000
5.3.x1	+20,000,000	+15,000,000
6.3.x1	–3,000,000	+12,000,000
7.3.x1	–2,000,000	+10,000,000
8.3.x1	+1,000,000	+11,000,000
9.3.x1	0	+11,000,000
10.3.x1	– 500,000	+10,500,000
11.3.x1	+2,000,000	+12,500,000

The interest rates available are:

	Borrowing rate	*Lending rate*
Interbank overnight	$5\frac{3}{4}$%	$5\frac{1}{4}$%
Interbank seven-day	$6\frac{1}{16}$%	$5\frac{13}{16}$%
Time deposit (seven-day)		5%
Sight deposit at bank		4%
Borrowing on overdraft	7%	

Describe how you would manage the firm's money over this 11-day period.
What are the risks inherent in your plan of action?

7 (*Examination level*) You have been asked to prepare a cash budget for Whitborrow plc for the next three months, October, November and December. The managers are concerned that they may not have sufficient cash to pay for a £150,000 investment in equipment in

December. The overdraft has reached its limit of £70,000 at the present time – the end of September. Sales during September were a total of £400,000, of which £55,000 was received in cash, £165,000 is expected to be paid in October, with the remainder likely to flow in during November. Sales for the next three months are as follows:

	Total sales	*Cash sales*	*Credit sales*
October	450,000	90,000	360,000
November	550,000	110,000	440,000
December	700,000	140,000	560,000

There is a gross profit margin of 40 per cent on sales. All costs (materials, labour and other) are paid for on receipt. Only 20 per cent of customer sales are expected to be paid for in the month of delivery. A further 70 per cent will be paid after one month and the remainder after two months. Labour and other costs amount to 10 per cent of sales. Debtor levels at the end of September are £400,000 and the investment in stock is £350,000.

Required

a Prepare a cash budget for October, November and December, and state if the firm will be able to purchase the new equipment.

b Recommend action that could be taken to improve the working capital position of Whitborrow.

8* Silk plc invests surplus cash in a range of money-market securities which earn a rate of return of 8 per cent per annum. It tries to hold the smallest cash balances possible while permitting the business to operate. For the next year there will be a need for cash taken from near-cash investments (money market investments) of £40,000 per week. There is a fixed cost of liquidating these securities of £200 regardless of amount (a combination of broker's fees and administration costs). Should Silk draw on these funds every week or at some other interval? Calculate the optimum level of cash balance.

9† It costs £20 in administration expenses and fees every time Davy Ltd pays funds into the bank to reduce its large overdraft on which it is charged 10 per cent annual percentage rate (APR). The company receives net cash from operations of £10,000 per day. How often should Davy pay into the bank?

10† Captain plc buys 100,000 widgets per year at a cost of £15 per widget for use in its production process. The cost of holding one widget in stock, in terms of interest, security, insurance, storage, etc. is £1.20 per year. The cost of reordering and taking delivery of widgets is £250 regardless of the size of the order.

Required

a Calculate the economic order quantity and the total cost of inventory management on the assumption that usage is predictable and even through the year and ordering and delivery of widgets is simultaneous.

b What buffer stock would you suggest if the firm is determined never to have a stock-out and the supplier of Widgets sometimes delivers one week and sometimes three weeks after an order – the lead time is unpredictable?

11 Christopher Purser said that Glynwed plc's treasury department had as one of its responsibilities to 'Manage the group's cash and currency flows so as to:

– minimise interest paid;
– maximise interest earned;
– minimise currency exposure risk'.

What do you understand by this statement?

12 'I run this business the way I want to. Shareholders and bankers are told once a year how we performed but I will not give them details or meet regularly with them. We have a business to run. Bankers should be treated like any supplier – make them compete to provide the lowest cost service and put everything out to tender and let them bid for each scrap of work.'

Consider this statement by a finance director and relate it to the efforts many treasurers and finance directors make in their relationships with finance providers.

13 (*Examination level*) Reraser plc has grown fast and has recently appointed you as its corporate treasurer. You have been asked by the board to write a report pointing out the ways in which the treasurer's department can help the firm to manage its various risks. Write this report.

14 Explain why firms sometimes have temporarily surplus funds. What considerations are relevant when choosing the type of financial instrument to be purchased with these funds?

15 Calumnor plc's board of directors is concerned that it may have an imbalance in its debt profile. You have been asked to write a report pointing out the main considerations in achieving the right mixture of debt.

16 (*Examination level*) 'The treasurer sits up there in his office, earning a salary three times my level, playing with his computer all day. At least I produce something useful for the firm' – a statement by a shopfloor worker.

Try to persuade this worker that the treasurer contributes to the well-being of the firm by illustrating the activities a typical treasurer might undertake (you do not have to justify the relative salary levels).

17 Describe the motives for holding cash. Why is it useful for a firm to draw up cash budgets?

18 (*Examination level*) Describe the cash operating cycle and suggest ways of making it smaller.

19 'How can we go bankrupt if we have a full order book and sales rising by 100 per cent per year. Don't be ridiculous.' Explain to this incredulous managing director the problem of overtrading and possible solutions to it.

20 Explain the tension managers have to cope with when judging the correct level of working capital. Also describe the alternative approaches to funding business growth.

21 What are the costs of holding too little or too much cash? Describe what is meant by a policy framework for cash management, planning of cash flow, and control of cash flow.

22 Companies go bankrupt if they get working capital management badly wrong. Describe two ways in which this might happen.

23* Rubel plc has the following figures:

	£000s	
	20X1	*20X2*
Finished goods inventory	50	55
Work-in-progress inventory	40	38
Raw material inventory	100	110
Debtors	300	250
Creditors	150	160
Sales (per annum)	1,000	1,200
Cost of goods sold (per annum)	600	650
Raw material purchases (per annum)	500	550

Calculate the cash-conversion cycle.

24 Texas plc, a large manufacturer of windscreen wipers, holds 100 days' stock. This contrasts with the 50 days' stock held by its main competitor. Describe what might explain this difference and suggest solutions to any problem areas.

25† (*Examination level*) Sheetly plc has an overdraft of £500,000 which the directors are alarmed about. Their concern is further aroused by the fact that in July a tax demand for £200,000 will be payable. Also the company expects to pay for replacement vehicles at a cost of £150,000 in August. The present time is the beginning of May and the following figures are projected for the next six months:

	May	*June*	*July*	*Aug*	*Sept*	*Oct*
	£000	*£000*	*£000*	*£000*	*£000*	*£000*
Anticipated sales	1,100	1,150	900	800	1,300	1,200
Purchases (materials)	800	810	660	600	950	850
Labour	100	110	90	90	110	100
Rent	50	50	50	50	50	50
Other costs	40	50	60	45	50	60

For each month's sales 30 per cent of the cash is received in the month of sale, 40 per cent is received one month later, with the remainder coming in two months after sale. Debtors at the beginning of May are £200,000 and it is expected that of this, £120,000 will be received in May and £80,000 in June.

Suppliers of materials grant one month's credit and at the beginning of May these suppliers were owed £820,000. All other costs are paid for as incurred.

Required

a Draw up a cash flow forecast for the next six months showing the monthly overdraft if Sheetly continues to rely on this source of finance.

b Suggest ways in which working capital management policy could be altered to reduce the cash flow strain over the forthcoming months.

c Consider the following alternatives to the overdraft and describe their advantages *vis-à-vis* the overdraft:

- factoring;
- hire purchase;
- leasing.

ASSIGNMENTS

1 Select an item of stock held by a firm familiar to you and estimate the total cost of holding one unit of that type of inventory for one year. Also obtain some estimate of the cost of placing and receiving an order from the supplier of that stock and the annual usage. Calculate the economic order quantity and appropriate buffer quantity under various assumptions concerning factors which are subject to uncertainty.

2 Consider the working capital cycle of a firm you know well. Try to estimate the length of time money is tied up in each stage. Suggest ways of improving the efficiency of working capital management.

3 If your firm does not yet have a designated treasurer write a report pointing out the value of such a role and recommend whether such an appointment should be made or other, less specialised managers should continue to carry out treasury-type functions.

4 Examine the annual reports of six large quoted UK firms and note the role of the treasury by reading the text and between the lines.

CHAPTER NOTES

1 *The Economist*, 16 November 1996, p. 131.

2 Given at a special lecture at Aston Business School, 'The Purpose of a Treasurer', 13 February 1997.

3 Assume no hedging in the derivative or money markets.

Chapter 14

STOCK MARKET EFFICIENCY

INTRODUCTION

The question of whether the stock market is efficient in pricing shares and other securities has fascinated academics, investors and businessmen for a long time. This is hardly surprising: even academics are attracted by the thought that by studying in this area they might be able to discover a stock market inefficiency which is sufficiently exploitable to make them very rich, or at least, to make their name in the academic community. In an efficient market undervalued or overvalued shares do not exist, and therefore it is not possible to develop trading rules which will 'beat the market' by, say, buying identifiable underpriced shares. However, if the market is inefficient it regularly prices shares incorrectly, allowing a perceptive investor to identify profitable trading opportunities. This is an area of research where millions, have been spent trying to find 'nuggets of gold' in the price movements of securities. A small amount of this money has been allocated to university departments, with the vast majority being spent by major securities houses around the world and by people buying investment advice from professional analysts offering to 'pick winners'. Money has also been taken from the computer literati paying for real-time stock market prices and analytical software to be piped into their personal computer, and by the millions of buyers of books which promise riches beyond imagining if the reader follows a few simple stock market trading rules.

They do say that a fool and his money are soon parted – never was this so true as in the world of stock market investment with its fringe of charlatans selling investment potions to cure all financial worries. This chapter may help the reader to discern what investment advice is, and is not, worth paying for. But this is too limited an ambition; the reader should also appreciate the significance of the discovery that for most of the people and for most of the time the stock market correctly prices shares given the information available (and it is extremely difficult to make more than normal returns). There are profound implications for businessmen and their interaction with the share markets, for professional fund managers, and for small investors.

Learning objectives

By the end of this chapter the reader should be able to:

- discuss the meaning of the random walk hypothesis and provide a balanced judgement of the usefulness of past price movements to predict future share prices (weak-form efficiency);
- provide an overview of the evidence for the stock market's ability to take account of all publicly available information including past price movements (semi-strong efficiency);
- state whether stock markets appear to absorb all relevant (public or private) information (strong-form efficiency);
- outline some of the behavioural-based arguments leading to a belief in inefficiencies;
- comment on the implications of the evidence for efficiency for investors and corporate management.

WHAT IS MEANT BY EFFICIENCY?

In an efficient capital market, security (for example shares) prices rationally reflect available information.

The efficient market hypothesis (EMH) implies that, if new information is revealed about a firm, it will be incorporated into the share price rapidly and rationally, with respect to the direction of the share price movement and the size of that movement. In an efficient market no trader will be presented with an opportunity for making a return on a share (or other security) that is greater than a fair return for the riskiness associated with that share. The absence of abnormal profit possibilities arises because current and past information is immediately reflected in current prices. It is only new information that causes prices to change. News is by definition unforecastable and therefore future price changes are unforecastable. Stock market efficiency does not mean that investors have perfect powers of prediction; all it means is that the current level is an unbiased estimate of its true economic value based on the information revealed.

In the major stock markets of the world prices are set by the forces of supply and demand. There are hundreds of analysts and thousands of traders, each receiving new information on a company through electronic and paper media. This may, for example, concern a technological breakthrough, a marketing success or a labour dispute. The individuals who follow the market are interested in making money and it seems reasonable to suppose that they will try to exploit quickly any potentially profitable opportunity. In an efficient market the moment an unexpected, positive piece of information leaks out investors will act and prices will rise rapidly to a level which gives no opportunity to make further profit.

Imagine that BMW has announced to the market that it has a prototype electric car which will cost £10,000, has the performance of a petrol driven car and will run for 500 miles before needing a low-cost recharge. This is something motorists and environmentalists have been demanding for many years. The profit-motivated investor will try to assess the value of a share in BMW to see if it is currently underpriced given the new information. The probability that BMW will be able successfully to turn a prototype into a mass market production model will come into the equation. Also the potential reaction of competitors, the state of overall car market demand and a host of other factors have to be weighed up to judge the potential of the electric car and the future returns on a BMW share. No analyst or shareholder is able to anticipate perfectly the commercial viability of BMW's technological breakthrough but they are required to think in terms of probabilities and attempt to make a judgement.

If one assumes that the announcement is made on Monday at 10 a.m. and the overwhelming weight of investor opinion is that the electric car will greatly improve BMW's returns, in an efficient market the share price will move to a higher level within seconds. The new higher price at 10.01 a.m. is efficient but incorporates a different set of information to that incorporated in the price prevailing at 10 a.m. Investors should not be able to buy BMW shares at 10.01 a.m. and make abnormal profits except by chance (50 per cent of efficiently priced shares turn out to perform better than the market as a whole and 50 per cent perform worse; the efficient price is unbiased in the statistical sense).

Most investors are too late

Efficiency requires that new information is rapidly assimilated into share prices. In the sophisticated financial markets of today the speedy dissemination of data and information by cheap electronic communication means that there are large numbers of informed investors and advisers. These individuals are often highly intelligent and capable of fast analysis and quick action, and therefore there is reason to believe many stock markets are efficient at pricing securities. However this belief is far from universal. Thousands of highly paid analysts and advisers maintain that they can analyse better and act more quickly than the rest of the pack and so make abnormally high returns for their clients. There is a famous story which is used to mock the efficient market theoreticians:

A lecturer was walking along a busy corridor with a student on his way to lecture on the efficient market hypothesis. The student noticed a £20 note lying on the floor and stooped to pick it up. The lecturer stopped him, saying, 'If it was really there, someone would have picked it up by now'.

With such reasoning the arch-advocates of the EMH dismiss any trading system which an investor may believe he has discovered to pick winning shares. If this system truly worked, they say, someone would have exploited it before and the price would have already moved to its efficient level.

This position is opposed by professional analysts: giving investment advice and managing collective funds is a multi-billion pound industry and those employed in it do not like being told that most of them do not beat the market. However, a *few* stock pickers do seem to perform extraordinarily well on a consistent basis over a long period of time. There is strong anecdotal evidence that some people are able to exploit inefficiencies – we will examine some performance records later.

Types of efficiency

Efficiency is an ambiguous word and we need to establish some clarity before we go on. There are three types of efficiency:

1 *Operational efficiency* This refers to the cost to buyers and sellers of transactions in securities on the exchange. It is desirable that the market carries out its operations at as low a cost as possible. This may be promoted by creating as much competition between marketmakers and brokers as possible so that they earn only normal profits and not excessively high profits. It may also be enhanced by competition between

exchanges for secondary-market transactions. In this context it is interesting to witness the London Stock Exchange's delayed but eventually forthright response to competitive threats from, for example, Tradepoint (virt-x), Neuer Markt, NASDAQ, and the New York Stock Exchange (*see* Chapter 9).

2 ***Allocational efficiency*** Society has a scarcity of resources (that is, they are not infinite) and it is important that we find mechanisms which allocate those resources to where they can be most productive. Those industrial and commercial firms with the greatest potential to use investment funds effectively need a method to channel funds their way. Stock markets help in the process of allocating society's resources between competing real investments. For example, an efficient market provides vast funds for the growth of the electronics, pharmaceuticals and biotechnology industries (through new issues, rights issues, etc.) but allocates only small amounts for slow-growth industries.

3 ***Pricing efficiency*** It is pricing efficiency that is the focus of this chapter, and the term efficient market hypothesis applies to this form of efficiency only. In a pricing efficient market the investor can expect to earn merely a risk-adjusted return from an investment as prices move instantaneously and in an unbiased manner to any news.

The black line in Exhibit 14.1 shows an efficient market response to BMW's (fictional) announcement of an electric car. The share price instantaneously adjusts to the new level. However, there are four other possibilities if we relax the efficiency assumption. First, the market could take a long time to absorb this information and it could be only after the tenth day that the share price approaches the new efficient level. This is shown in Line 1. Second, the market could anticipate the news announcement – perhaps there have been leaks to the Press, or senior BMW management has been

Exhibit 14.1 New information (an electric car announcement by BMW) and alternative stock market reactions – efficient and inefficient

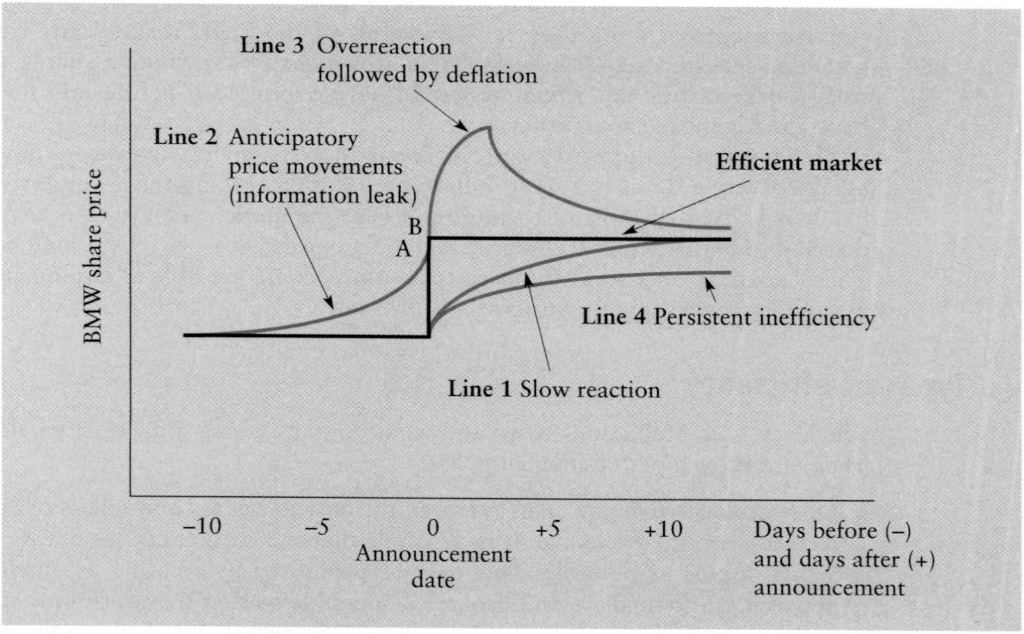

dropping hints to analysts for the past two weeks. In this case the share price starts to rise before the announcement (Line 2). It is only the unexpected element of the announcement that causes the price to rise further on the announcement day (from point A to point B). A third possibility is that the market overreacts to the new information (Line 3); the 'bubble' deflates over the next few days. Finally, the market may fail to get the pricing right at all and the shares may continue to be underpriced for a considerable period (Line 4).

The value of an efficient market

It is important that share markets are efficient for at least three reasons.

1 *To encourage share buying* Accurate pricing is required if individuals are going to be encouraged to invest in private enterprise. If shares are incorrectly priced many savers will refuse to invest because of a fear that when they come to sell the price may be perverse and may not represent the fundamental attractions of the firm. This will seriously reduce the availability of funds to companies and inhibit growth. Investors need to know they are paying a fair price and that they will be able to sell at a fair price – that the market is a 'fair game'.

2 *To give correct signals to company managers* In Chapter 1 it was stated, for the purposes of this book, that the objective of the firm was the maximisation of shareholder wealth. This can be represented by the share price in an efficient market. Sound financial decision making therefore relies on the correct pricing of the company's shares. In implementing a shareholder wealth-enhancing decision the manager will need to be assured that the implication of the decision is accurately signalled to shareholders and to management through a rise in the share price. It is important that managers receive feedback on their decisions from the share market so that they are encouraged to pursue shareholder wealth strategies. If the share market continually gets the pricing wrong, even the most shareholder-orientated manager will find it difficult to know just what is required to raise the wealth of the owners.

   In addition share prices signal the rate of return investors demand on securities of a particular risk class. If the market is inefficient the risk-return relationship would be unreliable. Managers need to know the rate of return they are expected to obtain on projects they undertake. If shares are wrongly priced there is a likelihood that in some cases projects will be wrongly rejected because an excessively high cost of capital (discount rate) is used in project appraisal. In other circumstances, if the share prices are higher than they should be the cost of capital signalled will be lower than it should be and projects will be accepted when they should have been rejected.

   Correct pricing is not just a function of the quality of the analysis and speed of reaction of the investment community. There is also an onus placed on managers to disclose information. Shares can only be priced efficiently if all relevant information has been communicated to the market. Managers neglect this issue at their peril.

3 *To help allocate resources* Allocation efficiency requires both operating efficiency and pricing efficiency. If a poorly run company in a declining industry has highly valued shares because the stock market is not pricing correctly then this firm will be able to issue new shares, and thus attract more of society's savings for use within its business. This would be wrong for society as the funds would be better used elsewhere.

RANDOM WALKS

Until the early 1950s it was generally believed that investment analysis could be used to beat the market. In 1953 Maurice Kendall presented a paper which examined security and commodity price movements over time. He was looking for regular price cycles, but was unable to identify any. The prices of shares etc. moved in a random fashion – one day's price change cannot be predicted by looking at the previous day's price change. There are no patterns or trends. An analogy has been drawn between security and commodity price changes and the wanderings of a drunken man placed in the middle of a field. Both follow a random walk, or to put it more technically, there is no systematic correlation between one movement and subsequent ones.

To many people this is just unacceptable. They look at a price chart of shares and see patterns; they may see an upward trend running for months or years, or a share price trapped between upper and lower resistance lines. They also point out that sometimes you get persistent movements in shares; for example a share price continues to rise for many days. The statisticians patiently reply that the same apparent pattern or trends can occur purely by chance. Readers can test this for themselves: try tossing a coin several times and recording the result. You will probably discover that there will be periods when you get a string of heads in a row. The apparent patterns in stock market prices are no more significant for predicting the next price movement than the pattern of heads or tails are for predicting what the next toss will produce. That is, they both follow a random walk.

To reinforce this look at Exhibit 14.2, which shows two sets of price movements. Many chartists (those who believe future prices can be predicted from past changes) would examine these and say that both display distinct patterns which may enable predictions of the future price movements. One of the charts follows the FTSE 100 index each week between March 1995 and April 1997 rebased to 100 in March 1995. The other was generated by the writer's six-year-old son. He was given a coin and asked to toss it 110 times. Starting at a value of 100, if the first toss was a head the 'weekly return' was 4 per cent, if a tail it was –3 per cent. Therefore the 'index' for this imaginary share portfolio has a 50 : 50 chance of ending the first week at either 104 or 97. These rules were applied for each of the imaginary 110 weeks. This chart has a positive drift of 1 per cent per week to imitate the tendency for share indices to rise over time. However, the price movements within that upward drift are random because successive movements are independent.

Dozens of researchers have tested security price data for dependence. They generally calculate correlation coefficients for consecutive share price changes or relationships between share prices at intervals. The results show a serial correlation of very close to zero – sufficiently close to prevent reliable and profitable forecasts being made from past movements.

Why does the random walk occur?

A random walk occurs because the share price at any one time reflects all available information and it will only change if new information arises. Successive price changes will be independent and prices follow a random walk because the next piece of news (by definition) will be independent of the last piece of news. Shareholders are never sure

Exhibit 14.2 Charts showing the movements on the FT 100 share index and a randomly generated index of prices. Which is which?

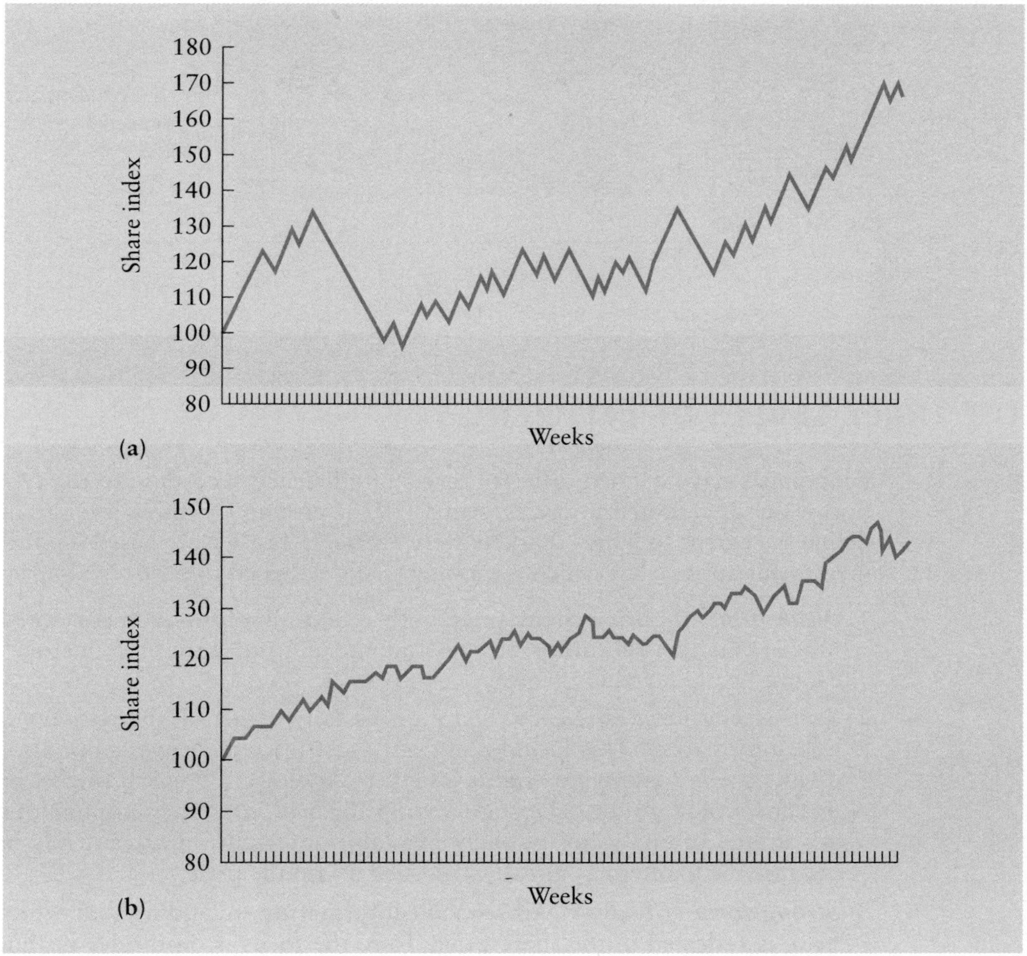

whether the next item of relevant information is going to be good or bad – as with the heads and tails on a coin there is no relationship between one outcome and the next. Also, there are so many informed market traders that as soon as news is released the share price moves to its new rational and unbiased level.

We can see how an efficient market will not permit abnormal profits by examining Exhibit 14.3. Here a chartist at time A has identified a cyclical pattern. The chartist expects that over the next six months the share price will rise along the dotted line and is therefore a 'buy'. However this chartist is not the only participant in the market and as soon as a pattern is observed it disappears. This happens because investors rush to exploit this marvellous profit opportunity. As a result of the extraordinary buying pressure the price immediately rises to a level which gives only the normal rate of return. The moment a pattern becomes discernible in the market it disappears under the weight of buy or sell orders.

Exhibit 14.3 A share price pattern disappears as investors recognise its existence

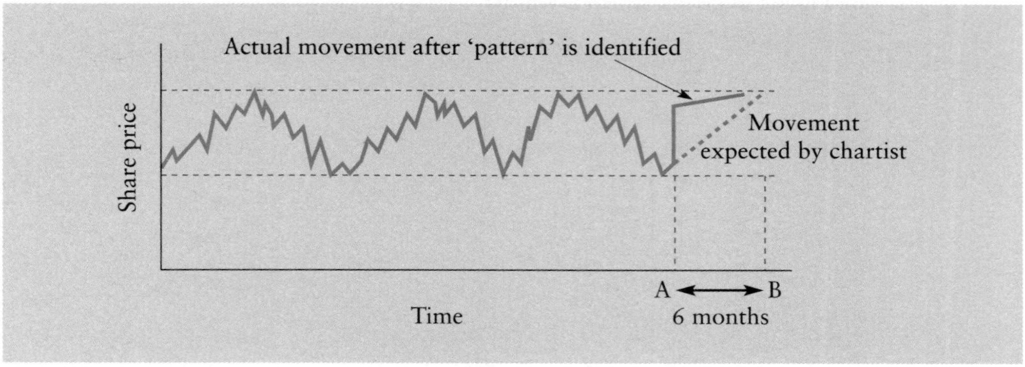

THE THREE LEVELS OF EFFICIENCY

Economists have defined different levels of efficiency according to the type of information which is reflected in prices. Fama (1970) produced a three-level grading system to define the extent to which markets were efficient. These were based on different types of investment approaches which were supposedly designed to produce abnormal returns.

1 *Weak-form efficiency* Share prices fully reflect all information contained in past price movements. It is pointless basing trading rules on share price history as the future cannot be predicted in this way.
2 *Semi-strong form efficiency* Share prices fully reflect all the relevant publicly available information. This includes not only past price movements but also earnings and dividend announcements, rights issues, technological breakthroughs, resignations of directors, and so on. The semi-strong form of efficiency implies that there is no advantage in analysing publicly available information after it has been released, because the market has already absorbed it into the price.
3 *Strong-form efficiency* All relevant information, including that which is privately held, is reflected in the share price. Here the focus is on insider dealing, in which a few privileged individuals (for example directors) are able to trade in shares, as they know more than the normal investor in the market. In a strong-form efficient market even insiders are unable to make abnormal profits – as we shall see the market is acknowledged as being inefficient at this level of definition.

WEAK-FORM TESTS

If weak-form efficiency is true a naïve purchase of a large, broadly based portfolio of shares typically produces returns the same as those purchased by a 'technical analyst' poring over historical share price data and selecting shares on the basis of trading patterns and trends. There will be no mechanical trading rules based on past movements which will generate profits in excess of the average market return (except by chance).

Consider some of the following techniques used by technical analysts (or chartists) to identify patterns in share prices.

A simple price chart

A true chartist is not interested in estimating the intrinsic value of shares. A chartist believes that a chart of the price (and/or volume of trading data) is all that is needed to forecast future price movements. Fundamental information, such as the profit figures or macroeconomic conditions, is merely a distraction from analysing the message in the chart. One of the early chartists, John Magee, was so extreme in trying to exclude any other influences on his 'buy' or 'sell' recommendations that he worked in an office boarded up so that he was not aware of the weather. Exhibit 14.4 shows one of the best known patterns to which chartists respond – it is called a head and shoulders formation.

Exhibit 14.4 The 'head and shoulders' pattern

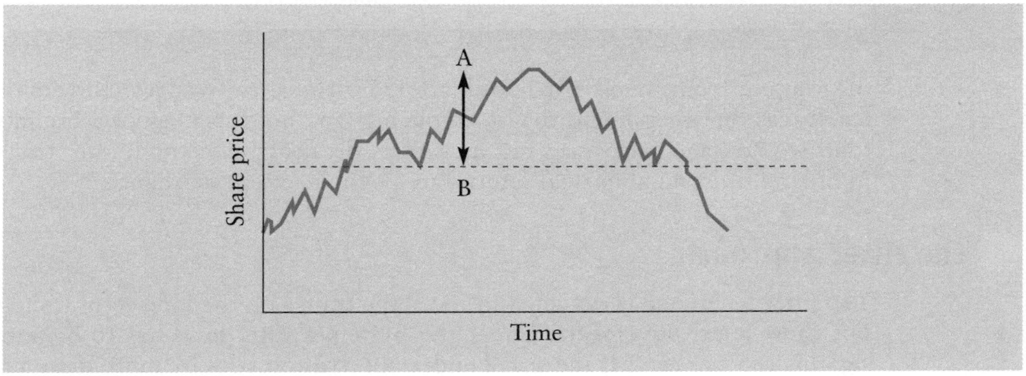

A head and shoulders pattern like the one shown in Exhibit 14.4 is supposed to herald the start of a major price drop. The left shoulder is formed, according to the chartists, by some investors taking profits after a large price rise, causing a minor price drop. The small fall encourages new buyers, hoping for a continuation of the price rally. They keep pushing the shares above the previous high, but prices soon drift down again, often to virtually the same level at which the left shoulder's decline ended. It drops to a support level called the neckline. Finally the right shoulder is formed by another wave of buying (on low volume). This peters out, and when the prices fall below the neckline by, say, 3 per cent, it is time to sell. Some chartists even go so far as to say that they can predict the extent of the fall below the neckline – this is in proportion to the distance AB.

Exhibit 14.5 provides another chart with a pattern, where the share price trades between two trend lines until it achieves 'breakout' through the 'resistance line'. This is a powerful 'bull signal' – that is, the price is expected to rise significantly thereafter.

Chartists have a very serious problem in that it is often difficult to see a new trend until after it has happened. Many critical voices say that it is impossible for the chartist to act quickly enough on a buy or sell signal because competition among chartists immediately pushes the price to its efficient level. To overcome this, some traders start to anticipate the signal, and buy or sell before a clear breakthrough is established. This leads other traders to act even earlier, to lock themselves into a trade before competition causes a price movement. This will lead to trends being traded away and prices adjusting to take into account all information regarding past price movements, leading us back to the weak form of stock market efficiency.

In academic studies modern high-powered computers have been used to simulate chartist trades. Researchers were instructed to find the classic patterns chartists respond

Exhibit 14.5 A 'line and breakout' pattern

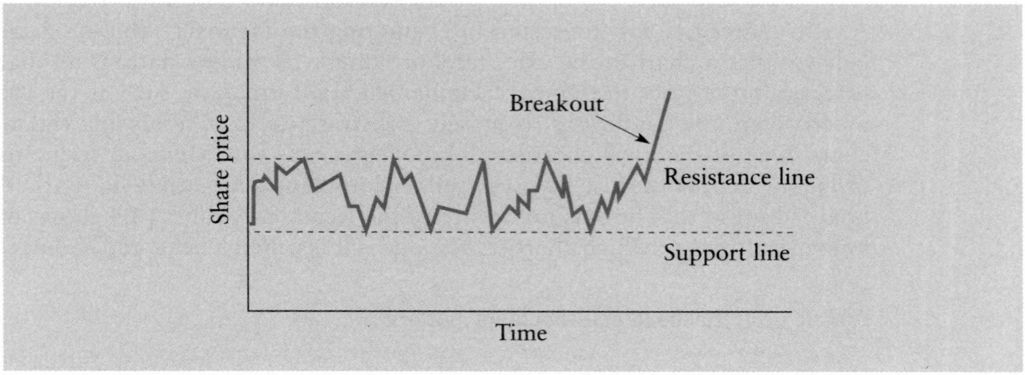

to, ranging from 'triple tops' and 'triple bottoms' to 'wedges' and 'diamonds'.[1] The result was that they found that a simple buy and hold strategy of a broadly based portfolio would have performed just as well as the chartist method, after transaction costs. In other words, no abnormal returns are possible except by chance.

The filter approach

The filter technique is designed to focus the trader on the long-term trends and to filter out short-term movements. Under this system a filter level has to be adopted – let us say this is 5 per cent. If the share under observation rises by more than 5 per cent from its low point the trader is advised to buy, as it is in an up-trend. If the share has peaked and has fallen by more than 5 per cent it should be sold. Price movements of less than 5 per cent are ignored. In a down-trend, as well as selling the share the trader owns, the trader should also 'sell short', that is, sell shares not yet owned in the anticipation of buying at a later date at a lower price. Again, there has been a considerable amount of academic research of various filter rules, and again the conclusion goes against the claims of the technical analysts – a simple buy and hold policy performs at least as well after transaction costs.

The Dow theory

Charles Dow, co-founder and editor of the Wall Street Journal, developed, along with others, the Dow theory in the early part of this century. According to the theory the stock market is characterised by three trends. The primary trend is the most important and refers to the long-term movement in share prices (a year or more). The intermediate trend runs for weeks or months before being reversed by another intermediate trend in the other direction. If an intermediate trend is in the opposite direction to the primary trend it is called a secondary reversal (or reaction). These reversals are supposed to retrace between one-third and two-thirds of the primary movement since the last secondary reversal. Tertiary trends, which last for a few days, are less important and need not concern us any further.

The left part of Exhibit 14.6 shows a primary up-trend interrupted by a series of intermediate reversals. In the up-trend the reversals always finish above the low point of the previous decline. Thus we get a zigzag pattern with a series of higher peaks and higher lows.

Exhibit 14.6 The Dow theory

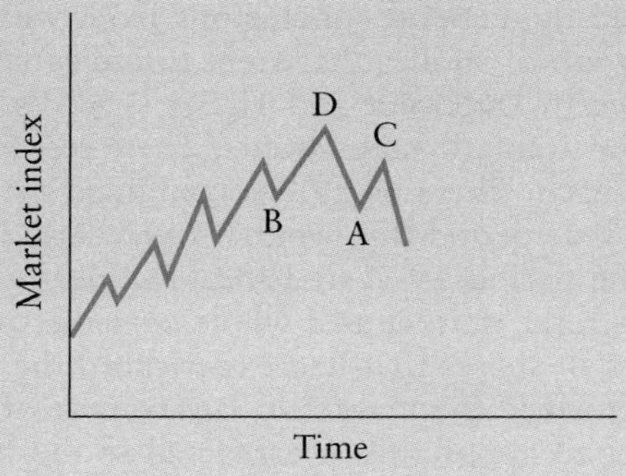

The primary up-trend becomes a down-trend (and therefore a sell signal) when an intermediate downward movement falls below the low of the previous reversal (A compared with B) and the next intermediate upward movement does not manage to reach the level of the previous intermediate upward spike (C compared with D).

In practice there is a great deal of subjectivity in deciding what is, or is not, an intermediate trend. Also primary trends, while relatively easy to identify with hindsight, are extremely difficult to identify at the moment they occur. The verdict of the academic researchers is that a simple buy and hold strategy produces better returns than those produced by the Dow theory.

Other strategies

Technical analysts employ a vast range of trading rules. Some recommend buying shares that have performed well relative to the rest of the market, maintaining that their performance will continue in that vein. Others advise a purchase when a share rises in price at the same time as an increase in trading volume occurs. More bizarrely, other investors have told us to examine the length of women's dresses to get a prediction of stock market moves. Bull markets are apparently associated with short skirts and bear markets (falling) with longer hemlines! Some even look to sunspot activity to help them select shares.

Overwhelmingly the evidence and the weight of academic opinion is that the weak form of the EMH is to be accepted. The history of share prices cannot be used to predict the future in any abnormally profitable way. Despite the continual outpouring of negative conclusions from independent researchers thousands, if not millions, of investors pay large sums to technical analyst gurus to guide them to riches. Investors would be better off saving on transaction costs and asking the proverbial monkey to select a broadly based portfolio!

One of the most respected investors and intellectuals of the twentieth century, Benjamin Graham, drew on his decades of experience to declare that technical analysts were making a mistake:

> The one principle that applies to nearly all these so-called 'technical approaches' is that one should buy *because* a stock or the market has gone up and should sell *because* it has declined. This is the exact opposite of sound business sense everywhere else, and it is most unlikely that it can lead to lasting success in Wall Street. In our own stock-market experience and observation extending over 50 years, we have not known a single person who has consistently or lastingly made money by thus 'following the market'. We do not hesitate to declare that this approach is as fallacious as it is popular. (Graham (1973), p. x.)

Exceptions?

Having stated the general conclusions from weak-form efficiency tests, we must also mention a group of studies that seem to indicate that the market might consistently fail to price properly. De Bondt and Thaler (1985) state that investors tend to overreact to unexpected or dramatic news events. These researchers selected a series of 16 portfolios of 35 shares each. These portfolios contained the shares which had fallen most in price over a three-year period (the worst 10 percent). The portfolios were drawn up from US data from the period 1926 to 1982. The performances of these portfolios were then compared with the market as a whole over the subsequent three years. They found that the portfolios of shares that had experienced the sharpest fall in prices in the first three years outperformed the market by an average of 19.6 per cent in the next 36 months. The market had apparently overreacted to the bad news and undervalued the shares. Moreover, when portfolios of shares which had risen the most in three years (the top 10 per cent of risers) were constructed and followed for a further three years, they underperformed the market by 5 per cent. De Bondt and Thaler[2] claim: 'Substantial weak form market inefficiencies are discovered', in their analysis.

Dissanaike (1997) studied the overreaction hypothesis (that is, the tendency for share prices to overshoot as a consequnce of excessive investor optimism or pessimism leading to predictable price reversals for a portfolio of shares) in the UK context. The results showed a very large outperformance of portfolios made up from 'loser' shares (those that had fallen the most over the four previous years) over a four-year period and a very poor performance for 'winner' shares (those that had previously performed well). 'The evidence appeared to be largely consistent with the overreaction hypothesis . . . In summary, the evidence would seem to suggest a stock market anomaly, if not an inefficiency . . . the EMH . . . is, at best, a highly simplified representation of the working of equity markets' (Dissanaike, 1997). In Chopra, Lakonishok and Ritter's (1992) study: 'In portfolios formed on the basis of prior five-year returns, extreme prior losers outperform extreme prior winners by 5–10% per year during the subsequent five years'. There is a growing literature attempting to supply explanations for the overreaction effect. This draws on behavioural science as much as finance: e.g. Daniel, Hirshleifer and Subrahmanyam (1998) and Hong and Stein (1999).

Examining the history of share prices and applying specific simple trading rules will produce abnormal returns according to Brock, Lakonishok and Le Baron (1992). They found that if investors (over the period 1897 to 1986) bought the 30 shares in the Dow Jones Industrial Average when the short-term moving average of the index (the average over, say, 50 days) rises above the long-term moving average (the average over, say, 200 days) they would have outperformed the buy-and-hold investor. Investors would also have achieved abnormal performance if they bought when a share 'broke out' from the trading range. 'However, transaction costs should be carefully considered before such strategies can be implemented' (Brock *et al.* 1992). Also it has been discovered that the trading rules did not work in the 10 years following the study period (Sullivan, Timmermann and White (1999)).

Chaos, neural networks and genetic algorithms

Recently, able individuals have searched for patterns in share prices by combining the number-crunching ability of high-powered computers with chaos theory, neural networks and genetic algorithms. These approaches are a touch more sophisticated than a hand-drawn resistance line on a chart but they have yet to prove that they can consistently lead to out-performance.

Chaos theory is a development in mathematics which describes systems that give a random appearance but which have underlying subsystems which can be modelled – that is, they are generated by relatively simple rules. Edgar Peters (1991) suggests that stock markets exhibit chaos and that there is some degree of dependence between price changes over time, but he fails to demonstrate an ability to make use of apparent non-randomness to produce abnormal profits after transaction costs.

Neural network computer programs learn to perform better as events unfold in a similar fashion to human learning in which errors produce an adaptive response and new ways of doing things. Genetic algorithms go a step further and model the market by following evolutionary laws.

Schoenburg (1990), Kamijo and Tanigawa (1990) and Baba and Kozaki (1992) have used neural networks to successfully predict share prices. The problem with neural networks, however, is that the results cannot be replicated because the output of the neural network is very sensitive to the precise way in which it has been calibrated – it is possible for two different networks to produce different results using the same input data. Neural networks are often dismissed as merely a complex version of data-mining.

SEMI-STRONG FORM TESTS

The semi-strong form of efficiency has the greatest fascination for most researchers and practitioners. It focuses on the question of whether it is worthwhile expensively acquiring and analysing publicly available information. If semi-strong efficiency is true it undermines the work of millions of fundamental (professional or amateur) analysts whose trading rules cannot be applied to produce abnormal returns because all publicly available information is already reflected in the share price.

Fundamental analysts try to estimate a share's true value based on future business returns. This is then compared with the market price to establish an over- or under-valuation. To estimate the intrinsic value of a share the fundamentalists gather as much relevant information as possible. This may include macroeconomic growth projections, industry conditions, company accounts and announcements, details of the company's personnel, tax rates, technological and social change and so on. The range of potentially important information is vast, but it is all directed at one objective: forecasting future profits and dividends.

There are thousands of professional analysts constantly surveying information in the public domain. Given this volume of highly able individuals examining the smallest piece of news about a firm and its environment, combined with the investigatory and investment activities of millions of shareholders, it would seem eminently reasonable to postulate that the semi-strong form of EMH describes the reality of modern stock markets.

The semi-strong form of EMH is threatening to share analysts, fund managers and others in the financial community because, if true, it means that they are unable to outperform the market average return except by chance or by having inside knowledge.

The great majority of the early evidence (1960s and 1970s) supported the hypothesis, especially if the transaction costs of special trading strategies were accounted for. The onus was placed on those who believed that the market is inefficient and misprices shares to show that they could perform extraordinarily well other than by chance. As Exhibit 14.7 makes clear most of these professionals have performed rather poorly.

Exhibit 14.7 How good are the professionals?

Index sets hard target

More than 70, or about 15 per cent, of UK unit trusts failed to outperform the FTSE All-Share index in any one of the last five years, according to new research by independent financial advisers, Chase de Vere . . .

Cumulative performance figures show little improvement – only 97 out of 342 funds (28 per cent) beat the index over the period as a whole.

Source: Investors Chronicle, 23 June 2000, p. 36. Reprinted with permission.

The fundamental analysts have not lost heart and have fought back with the assistance of some academic studies which appear to suggest that the market is less than perfectly efficient. There are some anomalies which may be caused by mispricing. For example, small firm shares have performed abnormally well (for certain periods) given their supposed risk class, and 'value investing' seems to produce unexpectedly high returns.

We will now discuss *some* of the evidence for and against semi-strong efficiency.[3]

Information announcements

Many of the early studies investigated whether trading in shares immediately following announcements of new information (for example announcements on dividends or profit figures) could produce abnormal returns. Overwhelmingly the evidence supports the EMH, and excess returns are nil.

It has been discovered that most of the information in annual reports, profit or dividend announcements are reflected in share prices before the announcement is made. Ball and Brown (1968), for example, found that share prices start to drift upwards or downwards 12 months before the annual report is published. Most of the information contained within it is anticipated because investors receive information through Press reports, statements and briefings by directors and interim reports and so on throughout the year. In the month the final report is produced less than 15 per cent of the information is unanticipated. The share price has already absorbed most of the relevant facts. The share price does tend to move by 10–15 per cent at the time of the announcement of the results, due to unanticipated information in the report. There is, therefore, some potential for investors to try to guess whether the new elements will be good or bad. But the direction of the movement is unpredictable (or unsystematic) and so there is an indication of efficiency.

Manipulation of earnings

Published accounts are an important source of information about companies. An efficient market will incorporate this information into share prices. But, as is well known, there is a great deal of leeway when it comes to drawing up accounts. One way of altering accounts is to openly and honestly reflect the changing underlying economics of the business by changing, say, the depreciation policy. If this is taken a stage further we have creative accounting, which obeys the letter of the law and accounting body rules but involves the manipulation of the accounts to show the most favourable profit figures and balance sheet. Finally, there is outright fraud and lies. Kaplan and Roll (1972) investigated US firms which switched from one depreciation policy to another and thereby boosted reported profits. The change did not alter the cash flows of the businesses (for example, taxes did not go up). Evidently shareholders were not fooled by the accounting change. The share price did not move in response to the superficial earnings modification. The conclusion of efficiency in this case seems reasonable because investors are aware of the nature of the accounting change, but doubts have been raised about market efficiency if there is wholesale creative accounting.

Terry Smith (1992) identified a number of UK companies using complex (and often disguised) techniques to create an impression of profit growth and/or balance sheet strength which was unjustified. Some of the companies he examined came to a sticky end – Coloroll, The Maxwell Group, Polly Peck and British and Commonwealth. Smith points out that basic financial weaknesses were hidden by creative accounting and that many investors were fooled. It is not entirely clear whether this is evidence of semi-strong stock market inefficiency. It could be that the inaccurate assessment by the market of those doomed companies was not due to inadequate analysis of publicly available information but was due to the failure of insiders to release important information. This would constitute a failure of strong-form efficiency rather than semi-strong efficiency.

George Foster (1979) has investigated the creative accounting effect in the US markets. He investigated the reaction of investors to pronouncements by a famous critic of creative accounting, Abraham Briloff. If the market is able to see through creative accounting gimmicks it should not react to Briloff's articles – which point out that this or that company has employed creative accounting techniques. In fact, Foster makes a remarkable finding: on the day of publication of a Briloff article, the prices of shares of the company concerned fall on average by 8 per cent. He concludes:

> I am unable (given existing data) to determine whether the magnitude of the price reaction is consistent with the capital market inefficiency explanation or the superior insight (information market) explanation.

Seasonal, calender or cyclical effects

Numerous studies have identified apparent market inefficiencies on specific markets at particular times. One is the weekend effect, in which there appear to be abnormal returns on Fridays and relative falls on Mondays. The January effect refers to the tendency for shares to give excess returns in the first few days of January in the USA. Some researchers have found an hour of the day effect in which shares perform abnormally at particular times in the trading day. For example, the first 15 minutes have given exceptional returns, according to some studies.

The problem with placing too much importance on these studies for practical investment is that the moment they are identified and publicised there is a good chance that they will cease to exist. Investors will buy in anticipation of the January effect and so cause the market to already be at the new higher level on 1 January. They will sell on Friday when the price is high and buy on Monday when the price is low, thus eliminating the weekend effect.

Even if the effects are not eliminated trading strategies based on these findings would be no more profitable than buying and holding a well-diversified portfolio. This is because of the high transaction costs associated with such strategies as, say, buying every Tuesday and selling every Friday. Also the research in this area is particularly vulnerable to the accusation of 'data-snooping'. Sullivan, Timmermann and White (1999) claim to demonstrate that calendar effects are illusory and findings obtained merely the result of extensive mining of the data until an (apparent) relationship is found:

> Data-snooping need not be the consequence of a particular researcher's efforts. It can result from a subtle survivorship bias operating on the entire universe of technical trading rules that have been considered historically. Suppose that, over time, investors have experimented with technical trading rules drawn from a very wide universe – in principle thousands of parameterizations of a variety of types of rules. As time progresses, the rules that happen to perform well historically receive more attention and are considered 'serious contenders' by the investment community, and unsuccessful trading rules are more likely to be forgotten. After a long sample period, only a small set of trading rules may be left for consideration, and these rules' historical track records will be cited as evidence of their merits. If enough trading rules are considered over time, some rules are bound by pure luck, even in a very large sample, to produce superior performance even if they do not genuinely possess predictive power over asset returns. Of course, inference based solely on the subset of surviving trading rules may be misleading in this context because it does not account for the full set of initial trading rules, most of which are likely to have underperformed.

Small firms

The searchers for inefficiency seem to be on firmer ground when examining smaller firms. The problem is that the ground only appears to be firm until you start to build. A number of studies in the 1980s found that smaller firms' shares have outperformed those of larger firms over a period of several decades. This was found to be the case in the USA, Canada, Australia, Belgium, Finland, The Netherlands, France, Germany, Japan and Britain.[4] Dimson and Marsh (1986) put the outperformance of small UK firms' shares at just under 6 per cent per year. These studies caused quite a stir in both the academic and the share-investing communities. Some rational explanations for this outperformance were offered: for example, perhaps the researchers had not adequately allowed for the extra riskiness of small shares – particularly the risk associated with lower liquidity. In most of these studies beta is used as the measure of risk and there are now doubts about its ability to capture all the risk-return relationship (*see* Chapter 8). Another explanation was that it is proportionately more expensive to trade in small companies' shares: if transaction costs are included, the net return of trading in small company shares comes down (but this does not explain the outperformance of a portfolio bought and held for a long period). There is also the issue of 'institutional neglect', by which analysts fail to spend enough time studying small firms, preferring to concentrate on the larger 100 or so. This may open up opportunities for the smaller investor who is prepared to conduct a more detailed analysis of those companies to which inadequate professional attention is paid.

The excitement about small companies' shares by investors and their advisers was much greater than in academe, but it was to end in tears. Investors who rushed to exploit this small firm effect in the late 1980s and early 1990s got their fingers burnt. As *The Economist*[5] put it: 'The supposedly inefficient market promptly took its revenge, efficiently parting investors from their money by treating owners of small stocks to seven years of under-performance.' This article refers to the US market but similar underperformance occurred on both the US and UK markets.

A UK study by Dimson, Marsh and Staunton in 2001 showed that small companies outperformed large companies by 5.2 per cent per annum between 1955 and 1988. However, in the period 1989 to 2000 the return premium in favour of small companies went into reverse: large companies produced a return 4.3 per cent greater than small companies. The researchers show that this kind of reversal occurred in many different countries in the late 1980s and 1990s.

Underreaction

Research evidence is building which shows that investors are slow to react to the release of information in some circumstances. This introduces the possibility of abnormal returns following the announcement of certain types of news. The first area of research has been into 'post-earnings-announcement drift'. That is, there is a sluggish response to the announcement of unexpectedly good or unexpectedly bad profit figures. Bernard and Thomas (1989) found that cumulative abnormal returns (CARs) continue to drift up for firms that report unexpectedly good earnings and drift down for firms that report unexpectedly bad figures for up to 60 days after the announcement. (The abnormal return in a period is the return of a portfolio after adjusting for both the market return in that period and risk). This offers an opportunity to purchase and sell shares after the information has been made public and thereby outperform the market returns. Shares were allocated to 10 categories of standardised unexpected earnings (SUE). The 10 per cent of shares with the highest positive unexpected earnings were placed in category 10. (The worst unexpected return shares were placed in category 1.) Exhibit 14.8 shows that after the announcement the shares of companies in category 10 continue to provide positive CARs. Investors did not move the share price to incorporate the new information in the earnings announcement on the day of the announcement. Those reporting bad surprises in earnings (the worst of which were in category 1) continued to show a falling return relative to the market in the period after the announcement day. Bernard and Thomas say that a strategy of buying shares in category 10 and selling shares in category 1 on the announcement day and selling (buying) 60 days later would have yielded an estimated abnormal return of approximately 4.2 per cent over 60 days, or about 18 per cent on an annualised basis. Similar results have been reported in studies by Foster, Olsen and Shevlin (1984), and Rendleman, Jones and Latané (1982). These studies suggest that all the news is not properly priced into the shares at the time of announcement as would be expected under EMH.

The second area of research into underreaction relates to the repurchase of shares. Ikenberry, Lakonishok and Vermaelen (1995) found that share prices rise on the announcement that the company will repurchase its own shares. This is to be expected as this is generally a positive piece of news. The suggestion of inefficiency arises because after the announcement the shares continue to provide abnormal returns over the next few years. Thirdly, Michaely, Thaler and Womack (1995) found evidence of share price drift following dividend initiations and omissions. Fourthly, Ikenberry, Rankine and Stice (1996) found share price drift after share split announcements. Fifthly, Jegadeesh and Titman (1993) found that trading strategies in which the investor buys shares that have risen in recent months produce significant abnormal returns. However, if these shares are held for two years the excess return dissipates. Chan, Jegadeesh and Lakonishok (1996) confirm an underreaction to past price movements (a 'momentum effect') and also identify a drift after earnings surprises.

Value investing

There is a school of thought in investment circles that investors should search for 'value' shares. Different sub-schools emphasise different attributes of an undervalued share but the usual candidates for inclusion are:

Exhibit 14.8 The cumulative abnormal returns (CAR) of shares in the 60 days before and the 60 days after an earnings announcement

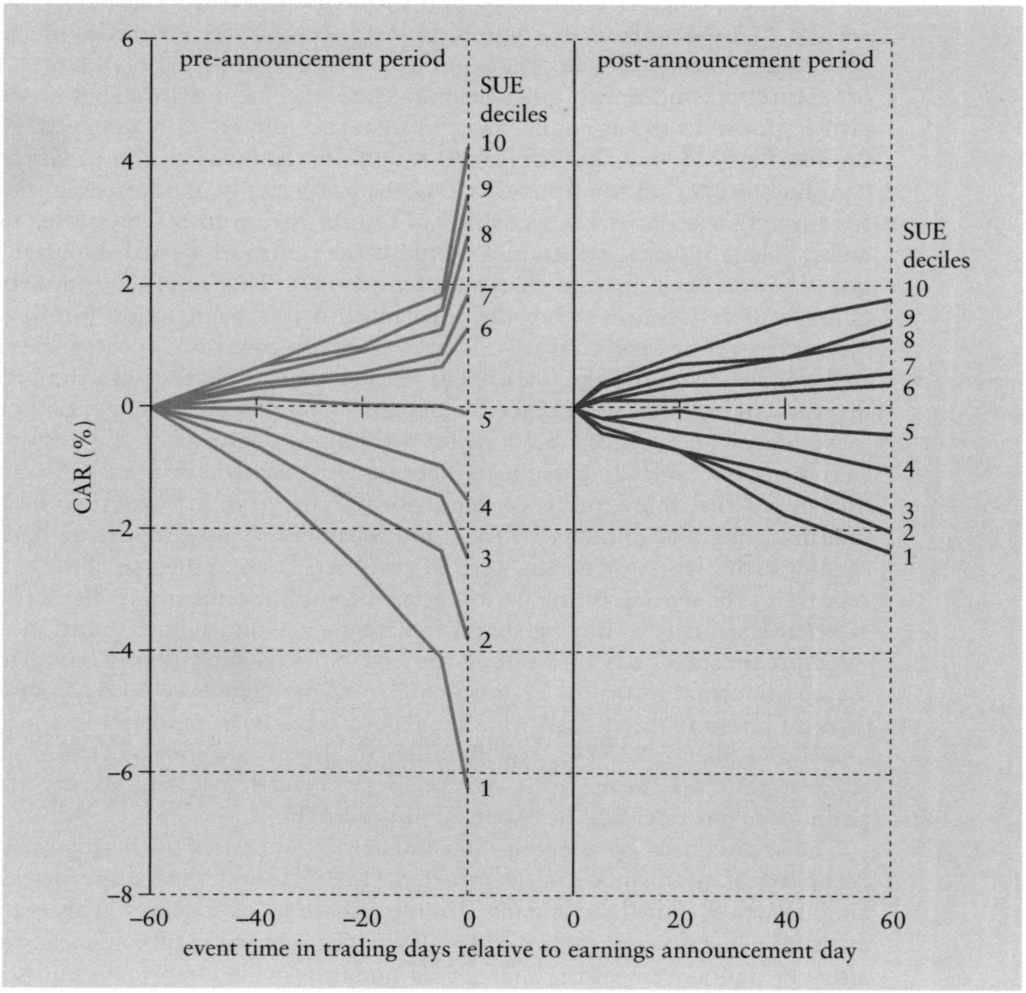

Source: V. Bernard and J. Thomas, 'Post-earnings-announcement drift: Delayed price response or risk premium', *Journal of Accounting Research*, 27 (1989, Supplement), p. 10.

Note: The 10 per cent of shares with the most positive unexpected news continued to produce abnormal returns after the announcement day, whereas the 10 per cent with the worst news continued to produce negative abnormal returns cumulating to over 2 per cent.

- a share with a price which is a low multiple of the earnings per share (low P/E ratios or PERs);
- a share price which is low relative to the balance sheet assets (book-to-market ratio);
- a share with high dividends relative to the share price (high-yield shares).[6]

We turn first to the purchase of low price-earning ratio shares as an investment strategy. The evidence generally indicates that these shares generate abnormal returns. Basu (1975, 1977, 1983) Keim (1988) Lakonishok et al. (1993) have produced evidence which appears to defy the semi-strong EMH, using US data. Mario Levis (1989) found exceptional performance of low PER shares in the UK, and for Japan, Chan *et al.* (1991) report similar findings. The academic literature tends to agree that low PER shares produce abnormal returns but there is some dispute whether it is the small-size effect that is really being observed; when this factor is removed the PER effect disappears, according to Reinganum (1981) and Banz and Breen (1986). Doubts were raised because small firm shares are often on low PERs and so it is difficult to disentangle the causes of outperformance. Jaffe *et al.* (1989), based on an extensive study of US shares over the period 1951–86, claimed that there was both a price-earnings ratio effect and a size effect. However the results were contradicted by Fama and French (1992), who claim that low PER shares offer no extra return but that size and book-to-market ratio are determining factors. On British shares Levis (1989) distinguished between the size and PER effects and concluded that low PERs were a source of excess returns.

One explanation for the low PER anomaly is that investors place too much emphasis on short-term earnings data and fail to recognise sufficiently the ability of many poorly performing firms to improve. Investors seem to put some companies on a very high price relative to their current earnings to reflect a belief in rapid growth of profits, while putting firms with modest growth on unreasonably low prices. The problem is that the market apparently consistently overprices the 'glamour' stocks and goes too far in assigning a high PER because of overemphasis on recent performance, while excessively depressing the share prices of companies with low recent earnings growth. To put it crudely: so much is expected of the 'glamour' shares that the smallest piece of bad news (or news that is less good than was expected) brings the price tumbling. On the other hand, so little is expected of the historically poor performers that good news goes straight into a share price rise.

The efficient market protagonists have countered the new evidence of inefficiency by saying that the supposed outperformers are more risky than the average share and therefore an efficient market should permit them to give higher returns. Lakonishok *et al.* (1993) examined this and found that low PER shares are actually less risky than the average.

Before everyone rushes out to buy low PER shares remember the lesson that followed the discovery of a small firm effect in the mid-1980s. In the case of the Lakonishok et al. study, the underpricing was observed over the period 1963 to 1990 – we do not know if it still exists.

Shares that sell at prices which are a low multiple of the net assets per share seem to produce abnormal returns.[7] This seems odd because (as we discuss in Chapter 17) the main influence on most share prices is the discounted value of their future income flows. Take BSkyB, the satellite television operator, which had negative net assets and is valued in the stock market at over £12bn. Its assets are largely intangible and not adequately represented in a balance sheet. In other words, there is very little connection between balance sheet asset figures and share price for many shares. The causes of the results of the empirical studies remain largely unexplained. Fama and French (1992) suggest there may be a systematic difference between companies which have high or low book-to-market value ratios. That is, companies with high book-to-market ratios are more risky. However, company shares have high market price-to-book value for different reasons – for some the nature of their industrial sector means they have few balance sheet recordable assets, for some the share price has risen because of projections of strong earnings growth.

Malkiel (1999) cautions against over-excitement: 'The results are not consistent over time, and stocks selling at very low multiples of book values may be fundamentally riskier. Moreover, some of the studies documenting a price-book value effect may suffer from survivorship bias by not including companies that actually went bankrupt.'

It has been suggested that investors underprice some shares in an overreaction to a series of bad news events about the company, while overpricing other shares that have had a series of good news events. Thus, the book-to-market ratio rises as share prices fall in response to an irrational extrapolation of a bad news trend.

Many studies have concluded that shares offering a higher dividend yield tend to outperform the market.[8] Explanations have been offered for this phenomenon ranging from the fact that dividend income is taxed at a higher rate than capital gains and so those investors keen on after-tax income will only purchase high-yielding shares if they offer a higher overall rate of return, to the argument that investors are bad at assessing growth prospects and may underprice shares with a high dividend yield because many have had a poor recent history. (For example, the dividend may be high relative to the share price because the latter has fallen due to disappointing news.)

Bubbles

Occasionally financial assets go through periods of boom and bust. There are explosive upward movements generating unsustainable prices, which may persist for many years, followed by a crash. These bubbles seem at odds with the theory of efficient markets because prices are not supposed to deviate markedly from fundamental value.

The tulip bulb bubble (tulipmania) in seventeenth-century Holland is an early example in which tulip bulb prices began to rise to absurd levels. The higher the price went the more people considered them good investments. The first investors made lots of money and this encouraged others to sell everything they had to invest in tulips. As each wave of speculators entered the market the prices were pushed higher and higher, eventually reaching the equivalent of £30,000 in today's money for one bulb. But the fundamentals were against the investors and in one month, February 1637, prices collapsed to one-tenth of the peak levels (by 1739 the price had fallen to 1/200th of one per cent of its peak value).

The South Sea Bubble which burst in 1720 was a British share fiasco in which investors threw money at the South Sea Company on a surge of over-optimism only to lose most or all of it. The increase in share prices in the 1920s and before the 1987 crash have also been interpreted as bubbles. The internet bubble of the late 1990s is merely the latest in a long series.

One explanation for this seemingly irrational behaviour of markets is what is called noise trading by naïve investors. According to this theory there are two classes of traders, the informed and the uninformed. The informed trade shares so as to bring them towards their fundamental value. However the uninformed can behave irrationally and create 'noise' in share prices and thereby generate bias in share pricing. They may be responding to frenzied expectations of almost instant wealth based on an extrapolation of recent price trends – perhaps they noted from the newspapers that the stock market made investors high returns over the past couple of years and so rush to get a piece of the action. This tendency to 'chase the trend' can lead to very poor performance because the dabbler in the markets often buys shares after a sharp rise and sells shares after being shocked by a sharp fall.

To reinforce the power of the uninformed investor to push the market up and up, the informed investor seeing a bubble developing often tries to get in on the rise. Despite knowing that it will all end in disaster for some the informed investor buys in the hope of selling out before the crash. This is based on the idea that the price an investor is willing to pay for a share today is dependent on the price the investor can sell for at some point in the future and not necessarily on fundamental value. Keynes (1936) as far back as the 1930s commented that share prices may not be determined by fundamentals but by investors trying to guess the value other investors will place on shares. He drew the analogy with forecasting the outcome of a beauty contest. If you want to win you are better off concentrating on guessing how the judges will respond to the contestants rather than trying to judge beauty for yourself. George Soros is an example of a very active (informed and successful) investor who is quite prepared to buy into an apparent irrational market move but makes every effort to get out before the uninformed investors. Note that the term informed investor does not equal professional investor. There are many professional fund managers and analysts who, on a close examination, fall into the category of ill-informed noise traders (*see* Arnold (2002) for more on the inadequacy of 'professional investors', also known as 'the oxymorons').

Comment on the semi-strong efficiency evidence

Despite the evidence of some work showing departures from semi-strong efficiency, for most investors most of the time the market may be regarded as efficient. This does not mean the search for anomalies should cease. The evidence for semi-strong efficiency is significant but not as overwhelming as that for weak-form efficiency.

While the volume of evidence of pockets of market inefficiencies is impressive, we need to be wary when placing weight on these results. Given the fact that there have been hundreds of researchers examining the data it is not a surprise that some of them find plausible looking statistical relationships indicating excess return opportunities. The research that actually gets published tends to be that which has 'found' an inefficiency. The research that does not show inefficiency receives much less publicity. Furthermore, the excess return strategies may be time-specific and may not continue into the future.

On the other hand consider this: suppose that you discover a trading strategy that produces abnormal returns. You could publish it in a respected journal or you could keep it to yourself. Most would select the latter option because publishing may result in the elimination of the inefficiency and with it the chance of high investment returns. So there may be a lot of evidence of inefficiency that remains hidden and is being quietly exploited.

There is a strange paradox in this area of finance: in order for the market to remain efficient there has to be a large body of investors who believe it to be inefficient. If all investors suddenly believed that shares are efficiently priced and no abnormal profits are obtainable they would quite sensibly refuse to pay for data gathering and analysis. At that moment the market starts to drift away from fundamental value. The market needs speculators and long-term investors continually on the prowl for under- or overpriced securities. It is through their buying and selling activities that inefficiencies are minimised and the market is a fair game.

There are some investors who have rejected the strictures of the EMH and have achieved astonishingly good returns. Here are some of them.[9]

Peter Lynch

Peter Lynch is the most outstanding fund manager of the latter part of the twentieth century. From May 1977 to May 1990 he was the portfolio manager of Fidelity's Magellan Fund. Over this 13-year period a $1,000 investment rose to be worth $28,000, a rate of return that is way ahead of the field at 29.2 per cent per annum. Furthermore, the Fund's performance was consistent – in only two of those years did it fail to beat the S&P 500. The fund grew from an asset base of $18 million to one of more than $14 billion. It was not only the best-performing fund in the world; it also became the biggest. There were one million shareholders in 1990, when Lynch quit, at the age of 46, to devote more time to his family. His experiences as a young man gave him a sceptical eye to what was being taught on his MBA course at Wharton:

> It seemed to me that most of what I learned at Wharton, which was supposed to help you succeed in the investment business, could only help you fail . . . Quantitative analysis taught me that the things I saw happening at Fidelity couldn't really be happening. I also found it difficult to integrate the efficient market hypothesis . . . It also was obvious that the Wharton professors who believed in quantum analysis and random walk weren't doing nearly as well as my new colleagues at Fidelity, so between theory and practice, I cast my lot with the practitioners . . . My distrust of theorizers and prognosticators continues to the present day.[10]

John Neff

When John Neff managed the Windsor Fund, his investment philosophy emphasised the importance of a low share price relative to earnings. However, his approach required a share to pass a number of tests besides the price-earnings criteria. These additional hurdles turn his approach from simple low price-earnings investing to a sophisticated one. John Neff was in charge of the Windsor Fund for 31 years. It beat the market for 25 of those 31 years. He took control in 1964, and retired in 1995. Windsor was the largest equity mutual in the United States when it closed its doors to new investors in 1985. Each dollar invested in 1964 had returned $56 by 1995, compared with $22 for the S&P 500. The total return for Windsor, at 5,546.5 per cent outpaced the S&P 500 by more than two to one. This was an additional return on the market of 3.15 percentage points a year after expenses. Before expenses the outperformance was 3.5 percentage points.[11] This is a very good performance, especially when you consider that the return on an average fund was less than on the S&P 500. He was always on the lookout for out-of-favour, overlooked or misunderstood stocks. These nuggets of gold always stood on low price-earnings ratios. Not only that; their prospects for earnings growth were good. He believes that the market tends to allow itself to be swept along with fads, fashions and flavours of the month. This leads to overvaluation of those stocks regarded as shooting stars, and to the undervaluation of those which prevailing wisdom deems unexciting, but which are fundamentally good stocks. Investors become caught in the clutch of group-think and en masse ignore solid companies. Bad news tends to weigh more heavily than good news as the investor's malaise deepens. The way Neff saw it, if you could buy a stock where the negatives were largely known, then any good news that comes as a surprise can have a profoundly positive effect on the stock price. On the other hand if you buy into a growth story where great things are expected and built in to the price, the slightest hint of bad news can take the sizzle out of the stock.

Benjamin Graham

Benjamin Graham is regarded as the most influential of investment philosophers. Graham was the leading exponent of the value investing school of thought. By this I do not mean the simplistic, distorted and crude 'analysis' which passes for much value investing today. The methods often promoted in the financial press have no greater intellectual foundation than to buy stocks with high dividends, or buy those with low price-earnings ratios, or with low book-to-equity ratios. No, Graham's value investing was far more sophisticated than that. He looked for bargain prices but was aware that following a one-criterion philosophy could be damaging. Over twenty years (from 1936) the Graham-Newman Corporation achieved an abnormally high performance for its clients: 'The success of Graham-Newman Corporation can be gauged by its average annual distribution. Roughly speaking, if one invested $10,000 in 1936, one received an average of $2,100 a year for the next twenty years and recovered one's original $10,000 at the end.'[12] Graham in testimony to the US Senate[13] in 1955 put a slightly different figure on it: 'Over a period of years we have tended to earn about 20 per cent on capital per year'. This is much better than the return available on the market as a whole. For example, Barclays Capital[14] show the annual average real (excluding inflation) rate of return on US stocks with gross income reinvested of 7.4 per cent for those years. Even if we add back average annual inflation of 3.8 per cent[15] to the Barclays' figures to make them comparable, the Graham-Newman figures are much better than the returns received by the average investor. According to Graham market prices are not determined by any necessarily rational or mathematical relationship to fundamental factors (at least, not in the short run) 'but through the minds and decisions of buyers and sellers'.[16]. . . 'The prices of common stock are not carefully thought out computations, but the resultants of a welter of human reactions. The stock market is a voting machine rather than a weighing machine. It responds to factual data not directly, but only as they affect the decisions of buyers and sellers.'[17]

Plainly, he did not believe the efficient markets hypothesis:

> Evidently the processes by which the securities market arrives at its appraisals are frequently illogical and erroneous. These processes . . . are not automatic or mechanical, but psychological for they go on in the minds of people who buy and sell. The mistakes of the market are thus the mistakes of groups of masses of individuals. Most of them can be traced to one or more of three basic causes: exaggeration, oversimplification, or neglect.[18]

Warren Buffett and Charles Munger

Warren Buffett is the most influential investment thinker of our time; he is also the wealthiest. Charles Munger is Buffett's partner, both intellectually and in the running of one of the world's largest companies. They each started with very little capital. At first, they developed their investment philosophies independently. They were far away from each other, both in their investment approach and geographically (Munger in California and Buffett in Nebraska). Despite the different approaches to stock picking they each created highly successful fund management businesses before coming together. Buffett took managerial control of Berkshire Hathaway in 1965 when the book value per share was $19.46 (as measured at the prior year-end 30 September 1964). By year-end 2000 the book value, with equity holdings carried at market value, was $40,442 per share. The gain in book value over 36 years came to 23.6 per cent compounded annually. At this rate of return an investment of $100 becomes worth over $200,000 over 36 years. There are people who are multimillionaires today because in the 1960s or 1970s they invested a few thousand dollars in Berkshire Hathaway. Warren Buffett and his wife Susan own around 40 per cent of Berkshire Hathaway, a company with a market capitalisation of approximately $100 billion (it was valued at a mere $20m in 1965). Exhibit 14.9 shows the truly outstanding performance of Berkshire Hathaway. There have been only four years in which the rise in book value was less than the return on the S&P 500. It is even better than it looks – the S&P 500 numbers are pre-tax whereas the Berkshire numbers are after-tax!

Exhibit 14.9 Berkshire Hathaway's corporate performance vs. the S&P 500

	Annual percentage change		
Year	*In per-share book value of Berkshire (1)*	*In S&P 500 with dividends included (2)*	*Relative results (1) – (2)*
1965	23.8	10.0	13.8
1966	20.3	(11.7)	32.0
1967	11.0	30.9	(19.9)
1968	19.0	11.0	8.0
1969	16.2	(8.4)	24.6
1970	12.0	3.9	8.1
1971	16.4	14.6	1.8
1972	21.7	18.9	2.8
1973	4.7	(14.8)	19.5
1974	5.5	(26.4)	31.9
1975	21.9	37.2	(15.3)
1976	59.3	23.6	35.7
1977	31.9	(7.4)	39.3
1978	24.0	6.4	17.6
1979	35.7	18.2	17.5
1980	19.3	32.3	(13.0)
1981	31.4	(5.0)	36.4
1982	40.0	21.4	18.6
1983	32.3	22.4	9.9
1984	13.6	6.1	7.5
1985	48.2	31.6	16.6
1986	26.1	18.6	7.5
1987	19.5	5.1	14.4
1988	20.1	16.6	3.5
1989	44.4	31.7	12.7
1990	7.4	(3.1)	10.5
1991	39.6	30.5	9.1
1992	20.3	7.6	12.7
1993	14.3	10.1	4.2
1994	13.9	1.3	12.6
1995	43.1	37.6	5.5
1996	31.8	23.0	8.8
1997	34.1	33.4	0.7
1998	48.3	28.6	19.7
1999	0.5	21.0	(20.5)
2000	6.5	(9.1)	15.6

Source: Berkshire Hathaway, Annual Report, 2000 (www.berkshirehathaway.com). Copyrighted material. Reprinted with permission.

Berkshire owns shares in publicly traded companies worth $37.6 billion. These holdings include approximately 11.4 per cent of American Express, 8.1 per cent of Coca-Cola, 9.1 per cent of Gillette, 18.3 per cent of the *Washington Post* and 3.2 per cent of Wells Fargo. Some investors have been with Buffett long before he took control of Berkshire. An investor who placed $100 in one of his investment partnerships in the late 1950s, and placed it in Berkshire after the partnership was dissolved, would find that investment worth more than $2 million today. In the 13 years of the partnership funds (1957–69) investors made annual returns greater than that on Berkshire, at almost

30 per cent per year. The funds managed by the young Buffett outperformed the Dow Jones Industrial Average in every year and made money even when the market was sharply down. If you put the two phases of his career – first the partnership, then Berkshire – together then you have a quite remarkable performance record, one that, to my knowledge, has not been beaten.

Buffett himself has become the richest or second richest man in the world, depending on the relative performance of Microsoft and Berkshire shares in any one year. He is the only person ever to make it to the Forbes billionaire list by stock market investing. Imagine being one of the lucky people to have trusted Buffett in the early days. It is what investors' dreams are made off. Apparently, the following conversation between two Berkshire shareholders was overheard at the annual meeting in 1996: 'What price did you buy at ?' The reply: 'Nineteen' says the first. 'You mean nineteen hundred?' 'No, nineteen.'[19] These shares are now worth $69,000 each!

Warren Buffett said:

> I'm convinced that there is much inefficiency in the market . . . When the price of a stock can be influenced by a 'herd' on Wall Street with prices set at the margin by the most emotional person, or the greediest person, or the most depressed person, it is hard to argue that the market always prices rationally. In fact, market prices are frequently nonsensical . . . There seems to be some perverse human characteristic that likes to make easy things difficult. The academic world, if anything, has actually backed away from the teaching of value investing over the last 30 years. It's likely to continue that way. Ships will sail around the world but the Flat Earth Society will flourish.[20]

The question is: are these performances possible through chance? Just to muddy the waters, consider the following situation. You give dice to 100 million investors and ask them each to throw 30 sixes in a row. Naturally most will fail, but some will succeed. You follow up the exercise with a series of interviews to find out how the masters of the dice did it. Some say it was the lucky cup they use, others point to astrological charts. Of course we all know that it was purely chance that produced success but try telling that to the gurus and their disciples.

Warren Buffett has countered this argument – *see* Exhibit 14.10. It is very difficult to prove either way whether excellent stock picking performance is due to superior analysis in an inefficient environment or merely good fortune. Ultimately you have to make a subjective judgement given the weight of evidence.

Exhibit 14.10

The superinvestors of Graham-and-Doddsville by Warren E. Buffett

Many of the professors who write textbooks . . . argue that the stock market is efficient: that is, that stock prices reflect everything that is known about a company's prospects and about the state of the economy. There are no undervalued stocks, these theorists argue, because there are smart security analysts who utilize all available information to ensure unfailingly appropriate prices. Investors who seem to beat the market year after year are just lucky. 'If prices, fully reflect available information, this sort of investment adeptness is ruled out,' writes one of today's textbook authors. Well, maybe, but I want to present to you a group of investors who have, year in and year out, beaten the Standard & Poor's 500 stock index. The hypothesis that they do this by pure chance is at least worth examining. Crucial to this examination is the fact that these winners were all well known to me and pre-identified as superior

►

Exhibit 14.10 continued

investors, the most recent identification occurring over fifteen years ago. Absent this condition – that is, if I had just recently searched among thousands of records to select a few names for you this morning – I would advise you to stop reading right here. I should add that all these records have been audited. And I should further add that I have known many of those who have invested with these managers, and the checks received by those participants over the years have matched the stated records.

Before we begin this examination, I would like you to imagine a national coin-flipping contest. Let's assume we get 225 million Americans up tomorrow morning and we ask them all to wager a dollar. They go out in the morning at sunrise, and they all call the flip of a coin. If they call correctly, they win a dollar from those who called wrong. Each day the losers drop out, and on the subsequent day the stakes build as all previous winnings are put on the line. After ten flips on ten mornings, there will approximately 220,000 people in the United States who have correctly called ten flips in a row. They each will have won a little over $1,000.

Now this group will probably start getting a little puffed up about this, human nature being what it is. They may try to be modest, but at cocktail parties they will occasionally admit to attractive members of the opposite sex what their technique is, and what marvellous insights they bring to the field of flipping.

Assuming that the winners are getting the appropriate rewards from, the losers, in another ten days we will have 215 people who have successfully called their coin flips 20 times in a row and who, by this exercise, each have turned one dollar into a little over $1 million. $225 million would have been lost; $225 million would have been won.

By then, this group will really lose their heads. They will probably write books on 'How I Turned a Dollar into a Million in Twenty Days Working Thirty Seconds a Morning'. Worse yet, they'll probably start jetting around the country attending seminars on efficient coin-flipping and tackling sceptical professors with, 'If it can't be done, why are there 215 of us?'.

But then some business school professor will probably be rude enough to bring up the fact that if 225 million orangutans had engaged in a similar exercise, the results would be much the same – 215 egotistical orangutans with 20 straight winning flips.

I would argue, however, that there *are* some important differences in the examples I am going to present. For one thing, if (a) you had taken 225 million orangutans distributed roughly as the U.S. population is; if (b) 215 winners were left after 20 days; and if (c) you found that 40 came from a particular zoo in Omaha, you would be pretty sure you were on to something. So you would probably go out and ask the zookeeper about what he's feeding them, whether they had special exercises, what books they read, and who knows what else. That is, if you found any really extraordinary concentrations of success, you might want to see if you could identify concentrations of unusual characteristics that might be causal factors.

Scientific inquiry naturally follows such a pattern. If you were trying to analyse possible causes of a rare type of cancer – with, say, 1,500 cases a year in the United States – and you found that 400 of them occurred in some little mining town in Montana, you would get very interested in the water there, or the occupation of those afflicted, or other variables. You know that it's not random chance that 400 come from a small area. You would not necessarily know the causal factors, but you would know where to search.

I submit to you that there are ways of defining an origin other than geography. In addition to geographical origins, there can be what I call an *intellectual* origin. I think you will find that a disproportionate number of successful coin-flippers in the investment world came from a very small intellectual village that could be called Graham-and-Doddsville. A concentration of winners that simply cannot be explained by chance can be traced to this particular intellectual village.

Conditions could exist that would make even that concentration unimportant. Perhaps 100 people were simply imitating the coin-flipping call of some terribly persuasive personality. When he called heads, 100 followers automatically called that coin the same way. If the leader was part of the 215 left at the end, the fact that 100 came from the same intellectual origin would mean nothing. You would simply be identifying one case as a hundred cases. Similarly, let's assume that you lived in a strongly patriarchal society and every family in the United States conveniently consisted of ten members. Further assume that the patriarchal culture was so strong that, when the 225 million people went out the first day, every member of the family identified with the father's call. Now, at the end of the 20-day period, you would have 215 winners. and you would find that they came from only 21.5 families. Some naive types might say that this indicates an enormous hereditary factor as an explanation of successful coin flipping. But, of course, it would have no significance at all because it would simply mean that you didn't have 215 individual winners, but

Exhibit 14.10 continued

rather 21.5 randomly distributed families who were winners.

In this group of successful investors that I want to consider, there has been a common intellectual patriarch, Ben Graham. But the children who left the house of this intellectual patriarch have called their 'flips' in very different ways. They have gone to different places and bought and sold different stocks and companies, yet they have had a combined record that simply can't be explained by random chance. It certainly cannot be explained by the fact that they are all calling flips identically because a leader is signalling the calls to make. The patriarch has merely set forth the intellectual theory for making coin-calling decisions, but each student has decided on his own manner of applying the theory.

The common intellectual theme of the investors from Graham-and-Doddsville is this: they search for discrepancies between the *value* of a business and the price of small pieces of that business in the market. Essentially, they exploit those discrepancies without the efficient market theorist's concern as to whether the stocks are bought on Monday or Thursday, or whether it is January or July, etc. Incidentally, when businessmen buy businesses – which is just what our Graham & Dodd investors are doing through the medium of marketable stocks – I doubt that many are cranking into their purchase decision the day of the week or the month in which the transaction is going to occur. If it doesn't make any difference whether all of a business is being bought on a Monday or a Friday, I am baffled why academicians invest extensive time and effort to see whether it makes a difference when buying small pieces of those same businesses. Our Graham & Dodd investors, needless to say, do not discuss beta, the capital asset pricing model, or covariance in returns among securities. These are not subjects of any interest to them. In fact, most of them would have difficulty defining those terms. The investors simply focus on two variables, price and value.

. . . I think the group that we have identified by a common intellectual home is worthy of study. Incidentally, despite all the academic studies of the influence of such variables as price, volume, seasonality, capitalization size, etc., upon stock performance, no interest has been evidenced in studying the methods of this unusual concentration of value-oriented winners.

I begin this study of results by going back to a group of four of us who worked at Graham-Newman Corporation from 1954 through 1956. There were only four – I have not selected these names from among thousands. I offered to go to work at Graham-Newman for nothing after I took Ben Graham's class, but he turned me down as overvalued. He took this value stuff very seriously! After much pestering he finally hired me. There were three partners and four of us at the 'peasant' level. All four left between 1955 and 1957 when the firm was wound up, and it's possible to trace the record of three.

The first example is that of Walter Schloss. Walter never went to college, but took a course from Ben Graham at night at the New York Institute of Finance. Walter left Graham-Newman in 1955 and achieved the record shown here over 28 years. [A compound rate of return of 21.3 per cent compared with a market return of 8.4 per cent from 1956 to 1984].

. . . Walter has diversified enormously, owning well over 100 stocks currently. He knows how to identify securities that sell at considerably less than their value to a private owner. *And that's all he does* . . . He simply says, if a business is worth a dollar and I can buy it for 40 cents, something good may happen to me. and he does it over and over and over again. He owns many more stocks than I do – and is far less interested in the underlying nature of the business; I don't seem to have very much influence on Walter. That's one of his strengths; no one has much influence on him.

The second case is Tom Knapp, who also worked at Graham-Newman with me. Tom was a chemistry major at Princeton before the war; when he came back from the war, he was a beach bum. And then one day he read that Dave Dodd was giving a night course in investments at Columbia. Tom took it on a noncredit basis, and he got so interested in the subject from taking that course that he came up and enrolled at Columbia Business School, where he got the MBA degree. He took Dodd's course again, and took Ben Graham's course. Incidentally, 35 years later I called Tom to ascertain some of the facts involved here and I found him on the beach again. The only difference is that now he owns the beach!

In 1968 Tom Knapp and Ed Anderson, also a Graham disciple, along with one or two other fellows of similar persuasion, formed Tweedy, Browne Partners, and their investment results appear in Table 2 [showing an annual compound rate of return of 20 per cent compared with the market's return of 7 per cent, 1968–83]. Tweedy, Browne built that record with very wide diversification. They occasionally bought control of businesses, but the record of the passive investments is equal to the record of the control investments.

Table 3 describes the third member of the group who formed the Buffett Partnership in 1957. Table 3 [not reproduced here] shows a compound rate of nearly 30 per cent against the market rate

Exhibit 14.10 continued

of 7.4 per cent, 1957–69.] The best thing he did was to quit in 1969. Since then, in a sense, Berkshire Hathaway has been a continuation of the partnership in some respects. There is no single index I can give you that I would feel would be a fair test of investment management at Berkshire. But I think that any way you figure it, it has been satisfactory.

Table 4 shows the record of the Sequoia Fund, which is managed by a man whom I met in 1951 in Ben Graham's class, Bill Ruane. [Table 4, not reproduced here, shows compound annual return of 17.2 per cent against a market return of 10 per cent, 1970–84.] After getting out of Harvard Business School, he went to Wall Street. Then he realized that he needed to get a real business education so he came up to take Ben's course at Columbia, where we met in early 1951. Bill's record from 1951 to 1970, working with relatively small sums, was far better than average. When I wound up Buffett Partnership I asked Bill if he would set up a fund to handle all our partners, so he set up the Sequoia Fund. He set it up at a terrible time, just when I was quitting.

He went right into the two-tier market and all the difficulties that made for comparative performance for value-oriented investors. I am happy to say that my partners, to an amazing degree, not only stayed with him but added money, with the happy result shown.

There's no hindsight involved here. Bill was the only person I recommended to my partners, and I said at the time that if he achieved a four-point-per-annum advantage over the Standard & Poor's, that would be solid performance. Bill has achieved well over that, working with progressively larger sums of money.

. . . I should add that in the records we've looked at so far, throughout this whole period there was practically no duplication in these portfolios. These are men who select securities based on discrepancies between price and value, but they make their selections very differently . . . The overlap among these portfolios has been very, very low. These records do not reflect one guy calling the flip and fifty people yelling out the same thing after him.

. . . A friend of mine who is a Harvard Law graduate, . . . set up a major law firm. I ran into him in about 1960 and told him that law was fine as a hobby but he could do better. He set up a partnership quite the opposite of Walter's. His portfolio was concentrated in very few securities and therefore his record was much more volatile but it was based on the same discount-from-value approach [average annual compound rate of return of 19.8 per cent compared with market return of 5 per cent p.a., 1962–75]. He was willing to accept greater peaks and valleys of performance, and he happens to be a fellow whose whole psyche goes toward concentration, with the results shown [not reproduced]. Incidentally, this record belongs to Charlie Munger, my partner for a long time in the operation of Berkshire Hathaway. When he ran his partnership, however, his portfolio holdings were almost completely different from mine and the other fellows mentioned earlier.

Table 6 [not reproduced here] is the record of a fellow who was a pal of Charlie Munger's another non-business school type – who was a math major at USC. He went to work for IBM after graduation and was an IBM salesman for a while. After I got to Charlie, Charlie got to him. This happens to be the record of Rick Guerin. Rick, from 1965 to 1983, against a compounded gain of 316 percent for the S&P, came off with 22,200 percent which, probably because he lacks a business school education, he regards as statistically significant.

One sidelight here: it is extraordinary to me that the idea of buying dollar bills for 40 cents takes immediately with people or it doesn't take at all. It's like an inoculation. If it doesn't grab a person right away, I find that you can talk to him for years and show him records, and it doesn't make any difference. They just don't seem able to grasp the concept, simple as it is. A fellow like Rick Guerin, who had no formal education in business, understands immediately the value approach to investing and he's applying it five minutes later. I've never seen anyone who became a gradual convert over a ten-year period to this approach. It doesn't seem to be a matter of IQ or academic training. It's instant recognition, or it is nothing.

. . . Stan Perlmeter . . . was a liberal arts major at the University of Michigan who was a partner in the advertising agency of Bozell & Jacobs. We happened to be in the same building in Omaha. In 1965 he figured out I had a better business than he did, so he left advertising. Again, it took five minutes for Stan to embrace the value approach. [Performance: 23 per cent p.a. compared with market return of 7 per cent 1966–83.]

Perlmeter does not own what Walter Schloss owns. He does not own what Bill Ruane owns. These are records made *independently*. But every time Perlmeter buys a stock it's because he's getting more for his money than he's paying. That's the only thing he's thinking about. He's not looking at quarterly earnings projections, he's not looking at next year's earnings, he's not thinking about what day of the week it is, he doesn't care what investment research from any place says, he's not interested in price momentum, volume, or anything. He's simply asking: What is the business worth?

Exhibit 14.10 continued

. . . So these are . . . records of 'coin-flippers' from Graham-and-Doddsville. I haven't selected them with hindsight from among thousands. It's not like I am reciting to you the names of a bunch of lottery winners – people I had never heard of before they won the lottery. I selected these men years ago based upon their framework for investment decision-making. I knew what they had been taught and additionally I had some personal knowledge of their intellect, character, and temperament. It's very important to understand that this group has assumed far less risk than average; note their record in years when the general market was weak. While they differ greatly in style, these investors are, mentally, *always buying the business, not buying the stock*. A few of them sometimes buy whole businesses. Far more often they simply buy small pieces of businesses. Their attitude, whether buying all or a tiny piece of a business, is the same. Some of them hold portfolios with dozens of stocks; others concentrate on a handful. But all exploit the difference between the market price of a business and its intrinsic value.

I'm convinced that there is much inefficiency in the market. These Graham-and-Doddsville investors have successfully exploited gaps between price and value.

. . . In conclusion, some of the more commercially minded among you may wonder why I am writing this article. Adding many converts to the value approach will perforce narrow the spreads between price and value, I can only tell you that the secret has been out for 50 years, ever since Ben Graham and Dave Dodd wrote *Security Analysis*, yet I have seen no trend toward value investing in the 35 years that I've practiced it . . . There will continue to be wide discrepancies between price and value in the marketplace, and those who read their Graham and Dodd will continue to prosper.

Source: Warren Buffett (1984), An edited transcript of a talk given at Columbia University in 1984. Reproduced in *Hermes*, magazine of Columbia Business School, Fall 1984 and in the 1997 reprint of Graham (1973).

STRONG-FORM TESTS

It is well known that it is possible to trade shares on the basis of information not in the public domain and thereby make abnormal profits. The mining engineer who discovers a rich seam of silver may buy the company shares before the market is told of the likely boost to profits. The director who becomes aware of lost orders and declining competitive position may quietly sell shares to 'diversify his interests' or 'pay for school fees', you understand. The merchant banker who hears of a colleague assisting one firm to plan a surprise takeover bid for another has been known to purchase shares (or options) in the target firm. Stock markets are not strong-form efficient.

Trading on inside knowledge is thought to be a 'bad thing'. It makes those outside of the charmed circle feel cheated. A breakdown of the fair game perception will leave some investors feeling that the inside traders are making profits at their expense. If they start to believe that the market is less than a fair game they will be more reluctant to invest and society will suffer. To avoid the loss of confidence in the market most stock exchanges attempt to curb insider dealing. It was made a criminal offence in the UK in 1980 where insider dealing is considered to be, besides dealing for oneself, either counselling or procuring another individual to deal in the securities or communicating knowledge to any other person, while being aware that he or she (or someone else) will deal in those securities. The term 'insider' now covers anyone with sensitive information not just a company director or employee. Most modern economies have rules on insider dealing and the EU has a directive on the subject. Despite the complex legislation and codes of conduct it is hard to believe that insider trading has been reduced significantly in the last two decades. It would appear that the lawyers have great difficulty obtaining successful prosecutions. The article in Exhibit 14.11, shows one conviction but many more go undetected or at least, unpunished.

Exhibit 14.11

Grouse farmer guilty of insider dealing

FT

By Harvey Morris

In a rare successful prosecution for insider dealing, a Cheshire grouse farmer was found guilty yesterday of an illicit deal, based on information he picked up while he was arranging a shooting weekend, that netted more than £25,000.

Christopher Williams, 58, learnt from Peter Korniotis, his shooting partner, in October 1997, that Visual Action Holdings, the entertainment services company, was about to be taken over by Caribiner of the US. Mr Korniotis's wife worked for the British company and faced redundancy if the take-over went ahead.

Acting on the tip, Mr Williams bought 35,000 shares in Visual Action and sold on shares worth £6,000 to Mr Korniotis. Mr Williams bought at 197p and sold at 275p when the takeover bid was announced. He was said to have told Mr Korniotis that the authorities would not bother chasing insider deals on small investments. The trade, however, was to spark a Stock Exchange investigation.

The farmer said he invested heavily in the mid-1990s before turning to refurbishing properties but acknowledges this was his largest investment.

Mr Williams denied he knew that Mr Korniotis's wife worked for Visual Action and that he knew it was about to be taken over. Asked why he was prepared to invest so heavily in a company he did not know, he said: "I think my investing criteria were totally flawed. With hindsight, I would have been much more careful."

Under legislation introduced in 1993, the maximum penalty for insider trading is seven years in jail. Since insider trading was outlawed in that year, only a handful of successful prosecutions have been brought by the Department of Trade and Industry.

Source: H. Morris, *Financial Times*, 26 June 2001, p. 3. Reprinted with permission.

Another weapon in the fight against insiders is to raise the level of information disclosure: making companies release price sensitive information quickly. The London Stock Exchange and the United Kingdom Listing Authority have strict guidelines to encourage companies to make announcements to the market as a whole as early as possible, on such matters as current trading conditions and profit warnings.

A third approach is to completely prohibit certain individuals from dealing in the company's shares for crucial time periods. For example, directors of quoted firms are prevented by the 'Model Code for Director Dealings' from trading shares for a minimum period (two months) before an announcement of regularly recurring information such as annual results. The Code also precludes dealing before the announcement of matters of an exceptional nature involving unpublished information which is potentially price sensitive. These rules apply to other employees in possession of price-sensitive information.

There is a grey area which stands between trading on inside knowledge and trading purely on publicly available information. Some investment analysts, though strictly outsiders, become so knowledgeable about a firm that they have some degree of superior information. Their judgement or guesstimates about future prospects are of a higher order than that of other analysts and certainly beyond anything the average shareholder is capable of. They may make regular visits to the company head office and operating units. They may discuss the opportunities and potential problems for the firm and the industry with the directors and with competitors' employees. Despite the strict rules concerning directors briefing one analyst better than the generality of shareholders it may be possible to 'read between the lines' and gather hints to give an informed edge. The hypothesis that there are some exceptional analysts has limited empirical backing and relies largely on anecdotal evidence and so this point should not be overemphasised. It is clear from previous sections of this chapter that the vast majority of professional analysts are unable to outperform the market.

BEHAVIOURAL FINANCE

There has been a forceful attack on the EMH by finance specialists drawing on a combination of human behavioural literature and their knowledge of markets. The EMH rests on the assumption that all investors are rational, or, even if there are some irrational investors, that the actions of rational informed investors will eliminate pricing anomalies through arbitrage. The behavioural finance proponents argue that investors frequently make systematic errors and these errors can push the prices of shares (and other financial securities) away from fundamental value for considerable periods of time.

This is a field of intellectual endeavour that is attracting increasing numbers of adherents as the evidence on apparent inefficiencies grows. Behavioural finance models offer plausible reasoning for the phenomena we observe in the pattern of share prices. They offer persuasive explanations for the outperformance of low PER, high dividend yield and low book-to-market ratio shares as well as the poor performance of 'glamour' shares. They can also be drawn on to shed light on both underreaction and the overreaction effects. In addition, behavioural science has a lot to offer when it comes to understanding stock market bubbles and irrational pessimism.

Many of the investors who made a fortune in the twentieth century have been saying all along that to understand the market you must understand the psychology of investors. In the 1960s, 1970s and even the 1980s, they were denounced as naïve at best by the dyed-in-the-wool quantitative financial economist – the economists had 'scientific proof' of the market's efficiency. They insisted that even if investors were generally irrational the market had inherent mechanisms to arrive at the efficient price, leaving no abnormal returns to be had. The successful investors were merely lucky. Worse! They were lucky and had the nerve to go against the scientific 'evidence' and publicly declare that they believed that there are sound investment principles which permit outperformance.

The successful investors continued to believe in the irrationality and exploitability of markets despite the onslaught from many university economists who were characterised as believing that 'It might work in practice, but it'll never work in theory'. Eventually a growing band of respected academics provided theoretical and empirical backing to the behavioural view of financial markets (e.g. Robert Shiller at Yale, Hersh Shefrin at Santa Clara, Richard Thaler at Chicago and Andrei Shleifer at Harvard). Now the debate has reached a fascinating point with high-quality modelling and empirical evidence on both sides.

The three lines of defence for EMH

To defend the EMH its adherents have three progressively stronger arguments which have to be surmounted if the behavioural finance advocates are to be able to attack the core.[21]

1 Investors are rational and hence value securities rationally.

2 Even if some investors are not rational, their irrationally inspired trades of securities are random and therefore the effects of their irrational actions cancel each other out without moving prices away from their efficient level.

3 If the majority of investors are irrational in similar ways and therefore have a tendency to push security values away from the efficient level this will be countered by rational arbitrageurs who eliminate the influence of the irrational traders on prices.

Under the first condition all investors examine securities for their fundamental value. That is, they calculate the present value of the future income flow associated with the security using an appropriate discount rate given the risk level (*see* Chapter 17). If any new information comes along which will increase future flows or decrease the discount rate then the price will rise to the new efficient level instantly. Likewise, bad news results in a lower efficient price. This barrier is easy to attack and demolish. It is plain from anecdotal evidence and from empirical study that the majority of investors do not assess fundamental value – just ask those who were day-traders in the dotcom boom or those who buy on the basis of a tip from a friend, or a newspaper or broker.

The second barrier is more of a challenge. It accepts individual irrational behaviour but the result is collective rationality in pricing because the irrational trades are evenly balanced and so the effect is benign. This may explain the large volume of trades as irrational investors exchange securities with each other, but this does not lead to inefficient pricing away from fundamental value. The key assumption to be attacked here is the absence of correlation in the actions of irrational investors. There is growing evidence that investors do not deviate from rationality randomly but most deviate in the same way (that is, there is correlation between their deviations) and therefore they lead prices away from fundamental value. The next section of this chapter provides an outline of some of the psychological biases that are being studied to try to explain apparent inefficiencies in pricing.

The third argument says that the actions of rational arbitrageurs are strong enough to restore efficiency even in the presence of numerous investors making cognitive errors. Arbitrage is the act of exploiting price differences on the same security or similar securities by simultaneously selling the overpriced security and buying the underpriced security. If a security did become overpriced because of the combined actions of irrational investors, smart investors would sell this security (or if they did not own it, 'sell it short') and simultaneously purchase other 'similar securities' to hedge their risks. In a perfect arbitrage they can make a profit without any risk at all (and even without money). The arbitrageurs' selling action brings down the security's price to its fundamental value in the EMH. If a security became underpriced arbitrageurs would buy the security and, to hedge risk, would sell short essentially similar securities, lifting the price of the security to its efficient level.

The arbitrage argument is impressive and forms a strong bulwark against the financial behaviourists. However, there are some weaknesses. Shleifer (2000) points out a number of reasons why arbitrage does not work well in the real world and therefore prices are not returned to fundamental value. To be effective the arbitrageur needs to be able to purchase or sell a close-substitute security. Some securities, e.g. futures and options, usually have close substitutes, but in many instances there is no close substitute and so locking in a safe profit is not possible. For example, imagine that you, as a rational investor, discover that Unilever's shares are undervalued. What other security(securities) would you sell at the same time as you purchase Unilever's shares to obtain a risk-free return when the price anomaly is detected? If we were talking about the price of a tonne of wheat of the same quality selling on two different markets at different prices we could buy in the low-price market and simultaneously sell in the high-price market and make a profit (guaranteed without risk and probably without the need for capital) even if the price difference was only 10p. But what can you use in arbitrage trade that is the same as a Unilever share? Well, you might consider that Procter & Gamble shares are close enough and so you sell these short. You expect that in six months the pricing anomaly will correct itself and you can close your position in Unilever by selling and close your position in P&G by buying its shares. But this strategy is far from the risk-free arbitrage of economists' ideal. You face the risk of other fundamental factors influencing the shares of Unilever and P&G (e.g. a strike, a product flop). You also face the risk that the irrational investors push irrationality to new heights. That is, the price does not gradually move towards the fundamental value over the next six months, but away from it. If this happens you lose money as a buyer of Unilever shares and have no offsetting gain on P&G shares. There is growing evidence of the problem of continued movement away from the fundamental value even after an anomaly has been spotted by arbitrageurs, (e.g. Froot and Dabora (1999)). For anecdotal evidence we need only remember back to 1999 and the pricing of dotcom stocks where arbitrageurs sold at high prices only to see the price climb higher as thousands of ill-informed investors piled in. This type of risk facing the arbitrageur is called 'noise trader risk' (De Long *et al.* (1990)) because it is the actions of the poorly informed investors that create noise in the price series; and this can get worse rather than better. So, in the real world 'with a finite risk-bearing capacity of arbitrageurs as a group, their aggregate ability to bring prices of broad groups of securities into line is limited' (Shleifer (2000), p. 14).

Trading in overvalued or undervalued stocks and using imperfect substitutes to offset a position is termed 'risk arbitrage' and is a completely different kettle of fish from risk-free arbitrage. Risk arbitrage entails a calculation of the statistical likelihood of the convergence of relative prices and does not deal with certainties.

Shleifer builds a behaviourally based model on the foundation of two observations of real-world markets:

1 Many securities do not have perfect, or even good substitutes, making arbitrage risky.
2 Even if a good substitute is available arbitrage remains risky because of noise trader risk, and the possibility that prices will not converge to fundamental values quickly enough to suit the arbitrageur's time horizon.

He concludes that market efficiency will only be an extreme special case and financial markets in most scenarios are not expected to be efficient.

Some cognitive errors made by investors

Investors are subject to a variety of psychological tendencies that do not fit with the economists' 'rational man' model. This, it is argued, can lead to markets being heavily influenced by investor sentiment. The combination of limited arbitrage and investor sentiment pushing the market leads to inefficient pricing. Both elements are necessary. If arbitrage is unlimited then arbitrageurs will offset the herd actions of irrational investors so prices quickly and correctly move to incorporate relevant news. In the absence of investor sentiment prices would not move from fundamental value in the first place. Listed below are some of the psychological tendencies that are thought to impact on investor' buying and selling decisions and thus to create sentiment.

Overconfidence

When you ask drivers how good they are relative to other drivers research has shown that 65–80 per cent will answer that they are above average. Investors are as overconfident about their trading abilities as about their driving abilities. People significantly overestimate the accuracy of their forecasts. So, when investors are asked to estimate the profits for a firm one year from now and to express the figures in terms of a range where they are confident that the actual result has a 95 per cent chance of being within the projected range, they give a range that is far too narrow. Investors make bad bets because they are not sufficiently aware of their informational disadvantage. This line of research may help explain the underreaction effect. Investors experience unanticipated surprise at, say, earnings announcements because they are overconfident about their earnings predictions. It takes a while for them to respond to new information in the announcement (due to conservatism – *see* below) and so prices adjust slowly.

Overconfidence may be caused, at least in part, by self-attribution bias. That is, investors ascribe success to their own brilliance, but failures in stock picking to bad luck. Overconfidence may be a cause of excessive trading because investors believe they can pick winners and beat the market. Inexperienced investors are, apparently, *more* confident that they can beat the market than experienced investors.

Representativeness

Representativeness is the making of judgements based on stereotypes. It is the tendency to see identical situations where none exist. For example, if Michael is an extrovert – the life and soul of the party, highly creative and full of energy, people are more likely to judge that he is an advertising executive rather than a postman. Representativeness can be misleading. Michael is more likely to be a postman, rather than an advertising executive, even though he 'sounds' to be typical of advertising executives: there are far more postmen than advertising executives. People overweight the representative description and underweight the statistical base evidence.

If there is a sharp decline in the stock market, as in 1987 or 2001, you will read articles pointing out that this is 1929 all over again. These will be backed up by a chart showing the index movement in 1929 and recent index movements. The similarities can be striking, but this does not mean that the Great Depression is about to be repeated, or even that share prices will fall for the next three years. The similarities between the two situations are superficial. The economic fundamentals are very different. Investors tend to give too much weight to representative observation (e.g. share price movements) and underweight numerous other factors.

Representativeness may help explain the overreaction effect. People look for patterns. If a share has suffered a series of poor returns investors assume that this pattern is representative for that company and will continue in the future. They forget that their conclusion could be premature and that a company with three bad years can produce several good quarterly profit figures. Similarly investors overreact in being too optimistic about shares that have had a lot of recent success. It may also explain why unit trust and investment trusts with high past performance attract more of investors' capital even though studies have shown that past performance is a poor predictor of future performance – even poor quality managers can show high returns purely by chance.

Conservatism

Investors are resistant to change an opinion, even in the presence of pertinent new information. So, when profits turn out to be unexpectedly high they initially underreact. They do not revise their earnings estimates enough to reflect the new information and so one positive earnings surprise is followed by another positive earnings surprise.

Narrow framing

Investors' perceptions of risk and return are highly influenced by how the decision problems are framed. Many investors 'narrow frame' rather than look at the broader picture. For example, an investor aged under 35 saving for retirement in 30 years pays too much attention to short-term gains and losses on a portfolio. Another investor focuses too much on the price movements of a single share, although it represents only a small proportion of total wealth. This kind of narrow framing can lead to an overestimation of the risk investors are taking, especially if they are highly risk averse. The more narrow the investor's focus, the more likely he is to see losses. If the investor took a broad frame he would realise that despite short-term market fluctuations and one or two down years the equity market rises in the long term and by the time of retirement a well-diversified portfolio should be worth much more than today. Likewise, by viewing the portfolio as a whole the investor does not worry excessively about a few shares that have performed poorly. Benartzi and Thaler (1995) show evidence suggesting that framing errors caused investors to avoid equities in favour of risk-free government securities, thus missing out on the much better returns on equities. Investors evaluated the riskiness of shares on a time horizon that was too short.

Ambiguity aversion

People are excessively fearful when they feel that they do not have very much information. On the other hand they have an excessive preference for the familiar in which they feel they have good information: as a result they are more likely to gamble. For example, ambiguity aversion may explain the avoidance of overseas shares despite the evidence of the benefits of international diversification.

Positive feedback and extrapolative expectations

Stock market bubbles may be, at least partially, explained by the presence of positive feedback traders who buy shares after prices have risen and sell after prices fall. They develop extrapolative expectations about prices. That is, simply because prices rose (fell) in the past and a trend has been established investors extrapolate the trend and anticipate greater future price appreciation (falls). This tendency has also been found in house prices and in the foreign exchange markets. George Soros describes in his books (1987, 1998) his exploitation of this trend-chasing behaviour in a variety of financial and real asset markets. Here the informed trader (e.g. Soros) can buy into the trend thus pushing it along, further away from fundamental values, in the expectation that uninformed investors will pile in and allow the informed trader to get out at a profit. Thus the informed trader creates additional instability instead of returning the security to fundamental value through arbitrage.

Regret

Experimental psychologists have observed that people will forgo benefits within reach in order to avoid the small chance of feeling they have failed. They are overly influenced by the fear of feeling regret.

Cognitive dissonance

If a belief has been held for a long time people continue to hold it even when such a belief is plainly contradicted by the evidence.

Availability heuristic

People may focus excessively on a particular fact or event because it is more visible, fresher in the mind or emotionally charged, at the expense of seeing the bigger picture. The bigger picture may incorporate soundly-based probabilities. For example, following a major train crash, people tend to avoid train travel and use their cars more. However, the bigger picture based on the statistical evidence reveals that train travel is far safer than road transport. In financial markets, if some particularly high-profile companies in an industrial sector (e.g. IT) have produced poor results, investors might abandon the whole sector, ignoring the possibility that some excellent companies may be selling at low prices. They overweight the prominent news.

Miscalculation of probabilities

Experiments have shown that people attach too low a probability to likely outcomes and too high a probability to quite unlikely ones. Can this explain the low valuations of 'old economy' shares in the late 1990s as the technological revolution was in full swing? Did investors underestimate these companies' prospects for survival and their ability to combine the new technology with their traditional strengths? At the same time did investors overestimate the probability of all those dotcom start-ups surviving and becoming dominant in their segments?

There is some meeting of the ways between the rational and the irrational school of thought, so that investors are viewed as flawed rationalists rather than hopelessly irrational beings. These quasi-rational humans try hard to be rational but are susceptible to repeating the same old mistakes.

MISCONCEPTIONS ABOUT THE EFFICIENT MARKET HYPOTHESIS

There are good grounds for doubting some aspects of the EMH and a reasoned debate can take place with advocates for efficiency and inefficiency stating their cases with rigorous argument and robust empirical methodology. However the high-quality debate has sometimes been overshadowed by criticism based on a misunderstanding of the EMH. There are three classic misconceptions:

1 **Any share portfolio will perform as well as or better than a special trading rule designed to outperform the market** A monkey choosing a portfolio of shares from the *Financial Times* for a buy and hold strategy is nearly, but not quite, what the EMH advocates suggest as a strategy likely to be as rewarding as special inefficiency-hunting approaches. The monkey does not have the financial expertise needed to construct broadly based portfolios which fully diversify away unsystematic risk. A selection of shares in just one or two industrial sectors may expose the investor to excessive risk. So it is wrong to conclude from the EMH evidence that it does not matter what the investor does, and that any portfolio is acceptable. The EMH says that after first eliminating unsystematic risk by holding broadly based portfolios and then adjusting for the residual systematic risk, investors will not achieve abnormal returns.

2 **There should be fewer price fluctuations** If shares are efficiently priced why is it that they move every day even when there is no announcement concerning a particular company? This is what we would expect in an efficient market. Prices move because new information is coming to the market every hour which may have some influence on the performance of a specific company. For example, the governor of the Bank of England may hint at interest rate rises, the latest industrial output figures may be released and so on.

3 **Only a minority of investors are actively trading, most are passive, therefore efficiency cannot be achieved** This too is wrong. It only needs a few trades by informed investors using all the publicly available information to position (through their buying and selling actions) a share at its semi-strong-form efficient price.

IMPLICATIONS OF THE EMH FOR INVESTORS

If the market is efficient there are a number of implications for investors. Even if it is merely efficient most of the time, for most participants a sensible working assumption is that pricing is based on fundamental values and the following implications apply.

1 **For the vast majority of people public information cannot be used to earn abnormal returns** (that is, returns above the normal level for that systematic risk class). The implication is that fundamental analysis is a waste of money and that so long as efficiency is maintained the average investor should simply select a suitably diversified portfolio, thereby avoiding costs of analysis and transaction. This message has struck a chord with millions of investors and thousands of billions of pounds have been placed with fund managers who merely replicate a stock market index (Index funds) rather than try to pick winners in an actively managed fund. About 25 per cent of UK financial assets managed by professional investors (e.g. unit trusts) is in indexed funds. For the USA the figure is 35 per cent. As the article in Exhibit 14.12 makes clear, the active fund managers generally underperform the All Share Index – so do the 'trackers', but at least they have lower costs.

Exhibit 14.12

Index tracking funds

There is no point in paying high unit trust management charges for indifferent returns. This view has increased interest in low cost funds with a modest ambition. They aim to produce returns which reflect the performance of a particular stock market index.

Index-tracking funds have become popular. They will not suit investors who want to study form and select a fund on the basis that it has the prospect of outperforming the pack. But for those bewildered by the sheer choice of unit trusts, an index-tracking fund could be a sensible option.

The disappointing record of active fund management increases the appeal of passive fund management through an index-tracking fund. In an index-tracking fund, the stocks pick themselves on the basis of their inclusion and weighting in a particular index.

What is ultimately of importance to investors is the actual investment return they receive. If less money goes in management charges, more can go back to the investor. Most tracker funds have low charges because running costs are relatively low.

For example, the much publicised Virgin Direct fund has no initial charge, a 1 per cent annual charge and an exit fee of 0.5 per cent in the first five years.

River & Mercantile's FT-SE 100 is the cheapest, with no load and an annual charge of just 0.35 per cent.

Source: Anthony Bailey, *Investors Chronicle*, 19 January 1996. Reprinted with kind permission of the *Investors Chronicle*.

Another trend has been for small investors to trade shares through execution-only brokers. These brokers do not provide their clients with (nor charge them for) analysis of companies, 'hot tips' and suggestions for purchases. They merely carry out the client's buy or sell orders in the cheapest manner possible.

2 **Investors need to press for a greater volume of timely information** Semi-strong efficiency depends on the quality and quantity of publicly available information, and so companies should be encouraged by investor pressure, accounting bodies, government rulings and stock market regulation to provide as much as is compatible with the necessity for some secrecy to prevent competitors gaining useful knowledge.

3 **The perception of a fair game market could be improved by more constraints and deterrents placed on insider dealers.**

IMPLICATIONS OF THE EMH FOR COMPANIES

The efficient market hypothesis also has a number or implications for companies.

1 **Focus on substance, not on short-term appearance** Some managers behave as though they believe they can fool shareholders. For example creative accounting is used to show a more impressive performance than is justified. Most of the time these tricks are transparent to investors, who are able to interpret the real position, and security prices do not rise artificially.

There are some circumstances when the drive for short-term boosts to reported earnings can be positively harmful to shareholders. For example, one firm might tend to overvalue its inventory to boost short-term profitability, another might not write off bad debts. These actions will result in additional, or at least earlier, taxation payments which will be harmful to shareholder wealth. Managers, aware that analysts often pay a great deal of attention to accounting rate of return, may, when facing a choice between a project with a higher NPV but a poor short-term ARR, or one with a lower NPV but higher short-term ARR, choose the latter. This principle of short-termism can be extended into areas such as research and development or marketing spend. These can be cut to boost profits in the short term but only at a long-term cost to shareholders.

One way to alleviate the short-term/long-term dilemma is for managers to explain why longer-term prospects are better than the current figures suggest. This requires a diligent communications effort.

2 **The timing of security issues does not have to be fine-tuned** Consider a team of managers contemplating a share issue who feel that their shares are currently underpriced because the market is 'low'. They opt to delay the sale, hoping that the market will rise to a more 'normal level'. This defies the logic of the EMH – if the market is efficient the shares are already correctly priced and the next move in prices is just as likely to be down as up. The past price movements have nothing to say about future movements.

The situation is somewhat different if the managers have private information that they know is not yet priced into the shares. In this case if the directors have good news then they would be wise to wait until after an announcement and subsequent adjustment to the share price before selling the new shares. Bad news announcements are more tricky – to sell the shares to new investors while withholding bad news will benefit existing shareholders, but will result in loss for the new shareholders.

3 **Large quantities of new shares can be sold without moving the price** A firm wishing to raise equity capital by selling a block of shares may hesitate to price near to the existing share price. Managers may believe that the increase in supply will depress the price of the shares. This is generally not the case. In empirical studies (e.g. Scholes. (1972)), if the market is sufficiently large (for example the London or New York

Stock Exchange) and investors are satisfied that the new money will generate a return at least as high as the return on existing funds, the price does not fall. This is as we would expect in an efficient market: investors buy the new shares because of the return offered on them for their level of risk.[22] The fact that some old shares of the same company already exist and that therefore supply has risen does not come into the equation. The key question is: what will the new shares produce for their holders? If they produce as much as an old share they should be priced the same as an old share. If they are not, then someone will spot that they can gain an abnormal return by purchasing these shares (which will push up the price).

4 **Signals from price movements should be taken seriously** If, for instance, the directors announce that the company is to take over another firm and its share price falls dramatically on the day of the announcement this is a clear indication that the merger will be wealth destroying for shareholders – as the majority of mergers are (*see* Chapter 20). Managers cannot ignore this collective condemnation of their actions. An exception might be allowed if shareholders are dumping the shares in ignorance because the managers have special knowledge of the benefits to be derived from the merger – but then shouldn't the directors explain themselves properly?

CONCLUDING COMMENTS

While modern, large and sophisticated stock markets exhibit inefficiencies in some areas, particularly at the strong-form level, it is reasonable to conclude that they are substantially efficient and it is rare that a non-insider can outperform the market. One of the more fruitful avenues of future research is likely to concern the influence of psychology on stock market pricing. We have seen how many of the (suggested) semi-strong inefficiencies, from bubbles to underpricing low PER shares, have at their base a degree of apparent 'non-rationality'.

Another line of enquiry is to question the assumption that all investors respond in a similar manner to the same risk and return factors and that these can be easily identified. Can beta be relied upon to represent all relevant risk? If it cannot, what are the main elements investors want additional compensation for? What about information costs, marketability limits, taxes and the degree of covariability with human capital returns for the investor (e.g. earnings from employment)? These are factors disliked by shareholders and so conceivably a share with many of these attributes will have to offer a high return. For some investors who are less sensitive to these elements the share which gives this high return may seem a bargain. A problem for the researcher in this field is that abnormal returns are calculated after allowance for risk. If the model used employs a risk factor which is not fully representative of all the risk and other attributes disliked by investors then efficiency or inefficiency cannot be established.

One way of 'outperforming' the market might be to select shares the attribute of which you dislike less than the other investors do, because it is likely to be underpriced for you – given your particular circumstances. Another way is through luck – which is often confused with the third way, that of possessing superior analytical skills.

A fourth method is through the discovery of a trading rule which works (but do not tell anybody, because if it becomes widespread knowledge it will probably stop working). A fifth possibility is to be quicker than anyone else in responding to news – George Soros and his teams may fall into this category occasionally. The last, and the most trustworthy method, is to become an insider – the only problem with this method is that you may end up a different kind of insider – in prison.

To conclude: the equity markets are generally very efficient, but the person with superior analytical ability, knowledge, dedication and creativity can be rewarded with abnormally high returns.

KEY POINTS AND CONCEPTS

- **In an efficient market security prices rationally reflect available information.** New information is **a** rapidly and **b** rationally incorporated into share prices.
- **Types of efficiency:**
  - operational efficiency;
  - allocational efficiency;
  - pricing efficiency.
- **The benefits of an efficient market are:**
  - it encourages share buying;
  - it gives correct signals to company managers;
  - it helps to allocate resources.
- Shares, other financial assets and commodities move with a **random walk** – one day's price change cannot be predicted by looking at previous price changes. Security prices respond to news which is random.
- **Weak-form efficiency** Share prices fully reflect all information contained in past price movements.

  Evidence: overwhelmingly in support.
- **Semi-strong form efficiency** Share prices fully reflect all the relevant, publicly available information.

  Evidence: substantially in support.
- **Strong-form efficiency** All relevant information, including that which is privately held, is reflected in the share price.

  Evidence: stock markets are strong-form inefficient.
- **Insider dealing** is trading on privileged information. It is profitable and illegal.
- **Behavioural finance studies** offer insight into anomalous share pricing.
- **Implications of the EMH for investors:**
  - for the vast majority of people public information cannot be used to earn abnormal returns;
  - investors need to press for a greater volume of timely information;
  - the perception of a fair game market could be improved by more constraints and deterrents placed on insider dealers.
- **Implications of the EMH for companies:**
  - focus on substance, not on short-term appearances;
  - the timing of security issues does not have to be fine-tuned;
  - large quantities of new shares can be sold without moving the price;
  - signals from price movements should be taken seriously.

REFERENCES AND FURTHER READING

Abraham, A. and Ikenberry, D. (1994) 'The individual investor and the weekend effect', *Journal of Financial and Quantitative Analysis*, June. An examination of a particular form of inefficiency.

Arnold, G.C. (2002) *Valuegrowth Investing*. London: Financial Times Prentice Hall. Brings together the insights from successful investors, finance theory and strategic analysis.

Atkins, A.B. and Dyl, E.A. (1993) 'Reports of the death of the efficient markets hypothesis are greatly exaggerated', *Applied Financial Economics*, 3, pp. 95–100. A consideration of some key issues.

Baba, N. and Kozaki, M. (1992) 'An intelligent forecasting system of stock prices using neural networks', *Proceedings of International Joint Conference on Neural Networks*, Baltimore, MD, vol. 1, pp. 371–7. Evidence on a possible inefficiency.

Ball, R. (1995) 'The theory of stock market efficiency: Accomplishments and limitations', *Journal of Applied Corporate Finance*, Winter and Spring, pp. 4–17. Interesting discussion.

Ball, R. and Brown, P. (1968) 'An empirical evaluation of accounting income numbers', *Journal of Accounting Research*, Autumn, pp. 159–78. The stock market turns to other sources of information to value shares so that when the annual report is published it has little effect on prices.

Ball, R. and Kothari, S.P. (1989) 'Nonstationary expected returns: Implications for tests of market efficiency and serial correlation in returns', *Journal of Financial Economics*, 25, pp. 51–94. Negative serial correlation in relative returns is due largely to changing relative risks and thus changing expected returns.

Ball, R., Kothari, S.P. and Shanken, J. (1995) 'Problems in measuring portfolio performance: An application to contrarian investment strategies', *Journal of Financial Economics*, May, vol. 38, pp. 79–107. Performance measurement problems cast doubt on the overreaction study results.

Banz, R. (1981) 'The relationship between return and market value of common stock', *Journal of Financial Economics*, 9, pp. 3–18. Important early paper on small small firm effect.

Banz, R.W. and Breen, W.J. (1986) 'Sample-dependent results using accounting and market data: Some evidence', *Journal of Finance*, 41, pp. 779–93. A technical article concerned with the problem of bias when using accounting information (earnings). The bias in the data can cause the low PER effect.

Barclays Capital (2001) *Equity-Gilt Study*. London: Barclays Capital. Important source of data on share and other security returns and risks.

Basu, S. (1975) 'The information content of price-earnings ratios', *Financial Management*, 4, Summer, pp. 53–64. Evidence of a market inefficiency for low PER shares. However transaction costs, search costs and taxation prevent abnormal returns.

Basu, S. (1977) 'Investment performance of common stocks in relation to their price/earnings ratios: A test of the efficient market hypothesis', *Journal of Finance*, 32(3), June, pp. 663–82. Low PER portfolios earn higher absolute and risk-adjusted rates of return than high PER shares. Information was not fully reflected in share prices.

Basu, S. (1983) 'The relationship between earnings' yield, market value and return for NYSE stocks – Further evidence', *Journal of Financial Economics*, June, pp. 129–56. The PER effect subsumes the size effect when both variables are considered jointly.

Benartzi, S. and Thaler, R. (1995) 'Myopic loss aversion and the equity premium puzzle', *Quarterly Journal of Economics*, 110(1), pp. 73–92. Narrow framing leads to unreasonable risk aversity and too little investment in equities.

Bernard, V. (1993) 'Stock price reaction to earnings announcements', in Thaler, R. (ed.) *Advances in Behavioural Finance*. New York: Russell Sage Foundation. Sluggish response.

Bernard, V.L. and Thomas, J.K. (1989) 'Post-earnings-announcement drift: Delayed price response or risk premium?', *Journal of Accounting Research*, 27 (Supplement 1989), pp. 1–36. A study showing slow reaction to unexpected earnings figures indicating inefficiency.

Black, F. (1986) 'Noise', *Journal of Finance*, 41(3), July, pp. 529–34. A large number of small events is often a causal factor much more powerful than a small number of large events.

Blake, D. (2000) *Financial Market Analysis*. 2nd edn. Chichester: Wiley. A more technical approach. Useful as an introduction to empirical research methodology in this area.

Brock, W., Lakonishok, J. and LeBaron, B. (1992) 'Simple technical trading rules and the stochastic properties of stock returns', *Journal of Finance*, 47, December, pp. 1731–64. Some interesting evidence suggesting weak-form inefficiency.

Buffett, W.E. (1984) 'The superinvestors of Graham-and-Doddsville', an edited transcript of a talk given at Columbia University in 1984. Reproduced in *Hermes*, the magazine of Columbia Business School, Fall 1984 and in the 1997 reprint of Graham (1973).

Buffett, W.E. (2000) Letter to shareholders included with the 2000 Annual Report of Berkshire Hathaway Inc: www.berkshirehathaway.com. High-quality thinking and writing from the world's most successful investor.

Capaul, C., Rowley, I. and Sharpe, W.F. (1993) 'International value and growth stock returns', *Financial Analysts Journal*, 49, January–February, pp. 27–36. Evidence on returns from a book-to-market ratio strategy for France, Germany, Switzerland, the UK and Japan.

Chan, L.K.C., Jegadeesh, N. and Lakonishok, J. (1996) 'Momentum strategies', *Journal of Finance*, 51, December, pp. 1681–713. Underreaction to both past share returns and earnings surprises.

Chan, L.K.C., Hamao, Y. and Lakonishok, J. (1991) 'Fundamentals and stock returns in Japan', *Journal of Finance*, 46, pp. 1739–64. The book-to-market ratio and cash flow yield have influences on the returns. There is a weak size effect and a doubtful PER effect.

Chew, D.H. (ed.) (1993) *The New Corporate Finance*. New York: McGraw-Hill. Contains a number of easy-to-read articles on efficiency.

Chopra, N., Lakonishok, J. and Ritter, J.R. (1992) 'Measuring abnormal performance: Do stocks overact?', *The Journal of Financial Economics*, 31, pp. 235–68. Overreaction effect observed.

Clare, A. and Thomas, S. (1995) 'The overreaction hypothesis and the UK stock market', *Journal of Business Finance and Accounting*, 22(7), October, pp. 961–73. Overreaction occurs, but it is a manifestation of the small firm effect.

Cuthbertson, K. (1996) *Quantitative Financial Economics*. Chichester: Wiley. Contains a more rigorous mathematical treatment of the issues discussed in this chapter.

Daniel, K., Hirshleifer, D. and Subrahmanyam, A. (1998) 'Investor psychology and security market under- and overreactions', *Journal of Finance*, 53(6), pp. 1839–85. Behavioural explanation of inefficiencies. Under- and overreaction is due to the psychological biases of investor overconfidence and biased self-attributes.

De Bondt, W.F.M. and Thaler, R.H. (1985) 'Does the stock market overreact?', *Journal of Finance*, 40(3), July, pp. 793–805. An important paper claiming weak-form inefficiency.

De Bondt, W.F.M. and Thaler, R.H. (1987) 'Further evidence on investor overreaction and stock market seasonality', *Journal of Finance*, 42(3), pp. 557–81. Overreaction effect observed.

De Long, J.B., Shleifer, A., Summers, L.H. and Waldmann, R.J. (1989) 'The size and incidence of the losses from noise trading', *Journal of Finance*, 44(3), July, pp. 681–96. Noise trading by naïve investors can lead to costs for society.

De Long, J.B., Shleifer, A., Summers, L.H. and Waldmann, R.J. (1990) 'Noise trader risk in financial markets', *Journal of Political Economy*, 98, pp. 703–38. Discussing the risk that irrational ill-informed investors may push prices further away from fundamental value thus throwing the arbitrageurs trading strategies.

Dimson, E. (ed.) (1988) *Stock Market Anomalies*. Cambridge: Cambridge University Press. A collection of 19 important articles questioning stock market efficiency.

Dimson, E. and Marsh, P. (1986) 'Event study methodologies and the size effect: The case of UK press recommendations', *Journal of Financial Economics*, 17, pp. 113–42. UK small firm shares outperformed those of larger firms.

Dimson, E., Marsh, P. and Staunton, M. (2001) *The Millennium Book II: 101 Years of Investment Returns*. London: ABN Amro/LBS. An important study showing returns on shares and other securities over the twentieth century. The section on small firms shows a reversal of the small-firm effect.

Dissanaike, G. (1997) 'Do stock market investors overreact?', *Journal of Business Finance and Accounting*, 24(1), January, pp. 27–49. Buying poor-performing shares gives abnormal returns as they are underpriced due to investor overreaction (UK study).

Dreman. D. (1998) *Contrarian Investment Strategies: The next generation*. New York: Simon & Schuster. A sceptic's view on efficiency.

Dreman, D. and Berry, M. (1995) 'Overreaction, underreaction, and the low P/E effect', *Financial Analysts Journal*, 51, July/August, pp. 21–30. Overreaction and underreaction shown.

Economist, The (1992) Beating the market: Yes – it can be done' *The Economist*, 5 December. Good survey of the evidence on the EMH and CAPM. Easy to read.

Elton, E.J. and Gruber, M.J. (1995) *Modern Portfolio Theory and Investment Analysis*. New York: Wiley. A more technical treatment that in this chapter.

Elton, E.J., Gruber, M.J. and Rentzler, J. (1983) 'A simple examination of the empirical relationship between dividend yields and deviations from the CAPM', *Journal of Banking and Finance*, 7, pp. 135–46. Complex statistical analysis leads to the conclusion: 'We have found a persistent relationship between dividend yield and excess returns.'

Fama, E.F. (1965) 'The behaviour of stock market prices', *Journal of Business*, January, pp. 34–106. Leading early article.

Fama, E.F. (1970) 'Efficient capital markets: A review of theory and empirical work', *Journal of Finance*, May, pp. 383–417. A review of the early literature and a categorisation of efficiency.

Fama, E.F. (1991) 'Efficient capital markets II', *Journal of Finance*, 46(5), December, pp. 1575–1617. A review of the market efficiency literature.

Fama, E.F. (1998) 'Market efficiency, long-term returns, and behavioural finance', *Journal of Financial Economics*, 49, September, pp. 283–306. Anomalies are explained and efficiency is championed.

Fama, E.F. and French, K.R. (1988) 'Permanent and temporary components of stock prices', *Journal of Political Economy*, 96, pp. 246–73. Useful.

Fama, E.F. and French, K.R. (1992) 'The cross-section of expected stock returns', *Journal of Finance*, 47, pp. 427–65. An excellent study casting doubt on beta and showing size of company and book-to-market ratio affecting returns on shares.

Fama, E.F. and French, K.R. (1995) 'Size and book-to-market factors in earnings and returns', *Journal of Finance*, 50(1), pp. 131–55. Efficiency is retained – are risk factors as above.

Fama, E.F. and French, K.R. (1996) 'Multifactor explanations of asset pricing anomalies', *Journal of Finance*, 50(1), March pp. 55–84. Efficiency is retained – size and book-to-market are risk factors.

Fama, E.F. and French, K.R. (1998) 'Value versus growth: The international evidence', *Journal of Finance*, 53(6), December, pp. 1975–99. An average return on global portfolios of high and low book-to-market shares is 7.68 per cent per year. Explanation: additional distress risk.

Fama, E.F., Fisher, L., Jensen, M.C. and Roll, R. (1969) 'The adjustment of stock prices to new information', *International Economic Review*, 10(1), February, pp. 1–21. Investigates the adjustment of share prices to the information which is implicit in share splits. Evidence of semi-strong EMH.

Firth, M.A. (1977a) 'An empirical investigation of the impact of the announcement of capitalisation issues on share prices', *Journal of Business, Finance and Accounting*, Spring, p. 47. Scrip issues in themselves have no impact on share prices. Evidence that the stock market is efficient.

Firth, M.A. (1977b) *The Valuation of Shares and the Efficient Markets Theory*. Basingstoke: Macmillan. An early discussion of stock market efficiency.

Foster, G. (1979) 'Briloff and the capital markets', *Journal of Accounting Research*, 17, pp. 262–74. An elegantly simple investigation of the effect of one man's pronouncement on stock market prices.

Foster, G., Olsen, C. and Shevlin, T. (1984) 'Earnings releases, anomalies, and the behaviour of security returns', *Accounting Review*, 59(4), October, pp. 574–603. A delayed response of share prices to earnings surprise news.

Froot, K.A. and Dabora, E. (1999) 'How are stock prices affected by the location of trade?', *Journal of Financial Economics*, 53, pp. 189–216. Evidence of noise trader risk.

Graham, B. (1973) *The Intelligent Investor*. Revised 4th edn. New York: Harper Business (reprinted 1997). Regarded by many as the best book written on investment.

Graham, B. and Dodd, D. (1934). *Security Analysis*. New York: McGraw-Hill. The foundation stone for value investors.

Harris, A. (1996) 'Wanted: Insiders', *Management Today*, July, pp. 40–1. A short and thought-provoking article in defence of insider dealing.

Hawawini, G.A. and Michel, P.A. (eds.) (1984) *European Equity Markets, Risk, Return and Efficiency*. Garland Publishing. A collection of articles and empirical work on the behaviour of European equity markets.

Hawawini, G. and Klein, D.B. (1994) 'On the predictability of common stock returns: Worldwide evidence', in Jarrow, R.A., Maksinovic, V. and Ziembas, W.T. (eds) (1994) *Finance*. Amsterdam: North-Holland. More evidence on inefficiency.

Hong, H. and Stein, J.C. (1999) 'A unified theory of underreaction, momentum trading and overreaction in asset markets', *Journal of Finance*, 54(6), pp. 2143–84. Behavioural explanation of inefficiencies. A model in which information diffuses gradually across the investing population is used to provide an explanation for underreaction and then overreaction.

Ikenberry, D., Lakonishok, J. and Vermaelen, T. (1995) 'Market under reaction to open market share repurchases', *Journal of Financial economics*, October–November, pp. 181–208. Share price drift after share repurchase announcements.

Ikenberry, D., Rankine, G. and Stice, E. (1996) 'What do stock splits really signal?', *Journal of Financial and Quantitative Analysis*, 31, pp. 357–75. Share price drift evidence.

Jaffe, J., Keim, D.B. and Westerfield, R. (1989) 'Earnings yields, market values and stock returns', *Journal of Finance*, 44, pp. 135–48. US data, 1951–86. Finds significant PER and size effects (January is a special month).

Jegadeesh, N. and Titman, S. (1993) 'Returns to buying winners and selling losers: Implications for stock market efficiency', *Journal of Finance*, 48, March, pp. 65–91. Holding shares which have performed well in the past generates significant abnormal returns over 3–12 month holding periods.

Jensen, M.C. (1968) 'The performance of mutual funds in the period 1945–64', *Journal of Finance*, 23, May, pp. 389–416. Mutual funds were poor at predicting share prices and underperformed the market.

Kahnemann, D. and Tversky, A. (2000) *Choices, Values and Frames*. Cambridge: Cambridge University Press. An important book on behavioural finance.

Kamijo, K.-I. and Tanigawa, T. (1990) 'Stock price recognition – approach', International Joint Conference on Neural Networks. San Diego, CA, vol. 1, pp. 215–21. Evidence on a potential inefficiency.

Kaplan, R. and Roll, R. (1972) 'Investor evaluation of accounting information: Some empirical evidence', *Journal of Business*, 45, pp. 225–57. Earnings manipulation through accounting changes has little effect on share prices.

Keim, D. (1983) 'Size-related anomalies and stock return seasonality: Further empirical evidence', *Journal of Financial Economics*, 12, pp. 13–32. Small-firm effect.

Keim, D.B. (1988) 'Stock market regularities: A synthesis of the evidence and explanations', in Dimson, E. (ed.), *Stock Market Anomalies*, Cambridge: Cambridge University Press, and in Lofthouse, S. (ed.) (1994) *Readings in Investment*, Chichester: Wiley. A non-technical, easy to understand consideration of some evidence of market inefficiencies.

Kendall, M. (1953) 'The analysis of economic time-series prices', *Journal of the Royal Statistical Society*, 96, pp. 11–25. Classic founding article on random walks.

Keynes, J.M. (1936) *The General Theory of Employment, Interest and Money*. London: Harcourt, Brace and World. A classic economic text with some lessons for finance.

Kindleberger, C.P. (1996) *Manias, Panics and Crashes: A History of Financial Crises*. 3rd edn. New York: Macmillan. Study of the history of odd market behaviour.

Kothari, S.P., Shanken, J. and Sloan, R.G. (1995) 'Another look at the cross-section of expected stock returns', *Journal of Finance*, March, 50(1), pp. 185–224. Apparent excess returns disappear if risk is allowed for.

Lakonishok, J., Shleifer, A. and Vishny, R. (1994) 'Contrarian investment extrapolation and risk', *Journal of Finance*, 49, pp. 1541–78. Value share outperformance.

Lakonishok, J., Vishny, R.W. and Shleifer, A. (1993) 'Contrarian investment, extrapolation and risk', *National Bureau of Economic Research Working Paper*, May, No. 4360. Important evidence on 'value' shares outperforming 'glamour' shares, Defying EMH with regard to PERs, book-to-market ratios, size and sales growth rates. Easy to read.

La Porta, R. (1996) 'Expectations and the cross-section of stock returns', *Journal of Finance*, 51(5), December, pp. 1715–42. 'I show that investment strategies that seek to exploit errors in analysts' forecasts earn superior returns'.

La Porta, R., Lakonishok, J., Shleifer, A. and Vishny, R. (1997) 'Good news for value stocks: Further evidence on market efficiency', *Journal of Finance*, 52(2), pp. 859–74. Earnings surprises are more positive for value shares: 'The evidence is inconsistent with risk-based explanation for the return differential.'

Lee, D.R. and Verbrugge, J.A. (1996) 'The efficient market theory thrives on criticism', *Journal of Applied Corporate Finance*, 9(1), pp. 3–11. An overview of efficiency evidence.

Levis, M. (1989) 'Stock market anomalies: A reassessment based on UK evidence', *Journal of Banking and Finance*, 13, pp. 675–96. Shows that strategies based on dividend yield, PE ratios and share prices appear to be as profitable as (if not more so than) a strategy of concentrating on firm size.

Litzenberger, R.H. and Ramaswamy, K. (1979) 'The effect of personal taxes and dividends on capital asset prices: Theory and empirical evidence', *Journal of Financial Economics*, 7, pp. 163–95. Technical paper with the conclusion: 'There is a strong positive relationship between dividend yield and expected return for NYSE stocks'.

Lofthouse, S. (1994) *Equity Investment Management*. Chichester: Wiley. Great for those interested in financial market investment. Transparently clear explanations of complex material.

Lofthouse, S. (ed.) (1994) *Readings in Investment*. Chichester: Wiley. A superb book for those keen on understanding stock market behaviour. A collection of key papers introduced and set in context by Stephen Lofthouse.

Lowe, J. (1997) *Warren Buffett Speaks*. New York: Wiley. Terrific quotations from Buffett.

Lowe, J. (1999) *The Rediscovered Benjamin Graham*. New York: Wiley. Some observations from the most respected practitioner/intellectual, complied by Janet Lowe.

Lynch, P. (1990) *One Up on Wall Street* (with John Rothchild). New York: Penguin Books. (Originally published by Simon & Schuster, 1989.) Fascinating insight into the world of stock picking. Presents sound investment principles.

Lynch, P. (1994) *Beating the Street* (with John Rothchild). New York: Simon & Schuster. Revised version of 1993 hardback publication. Fascinating insight into the world of stock picking. Presents sound investment principles.

Malkiel, B.G. (1999) *A Random Walk Down Wall Street*. New York: W.W. Norton & Co. A superb introduction to the theory and reality of stock market behaviour. A witty prose description of the arguments for and against EMH, presented in a balanced fashion.

Martikainen, T. and Puttonen, V. (1996) 'Finnish days-of-the-week effects', *Journal of Business, Finance and Accounting*, 23(7), September, pp. 1019–32. There is evidence of a day-of-the-week effect in the cash and derivative markets.

Michaely, R., Thaler, R. and Womack, K. (1995) 'Price reaction to dividend initiations and omissions: Overreaction or drift?', *Journal of Finance*, 50, pp. 573–608. Share price drift evidence.

Neff, J. (1999) *John Neff on Investing* (with S.L. Mintz). New York: Wiley. Decades of investing experience create a very interesting book to guide aspiring investors. Insight into investor/market behaviour.

Peters, E.E. (1991) *Chaos and Order in the Capital Markets*. New York: Wiley. A comprehensible account of a difficult subject. The evidence is not powerful enough to demolish the EMH.

Pontiff, J. and Schall, L.D. (1998) 'Book-to-market ratios as predictors of market returns', *Journal of Financial Economics*, 49, pp. 141–60. Book-to-market ratios predict market returns and small-firm excess returns.

Poterba, J.M. and Summers, L.H. (1988) 'Mean reversion in stock prices: Evidence and implications', *Journal of Financial Economics*, 22, pp. 27–59. The idea that share returns eventually revert to the average.

Reinganum, M.R. (1981) 'Misspecification of capital asset pricing: Empirical anomalies based on earnings' yields and market values', *Journal of Financial Economics*, 9, pp. 19–46. The PER effect disappears when size is simultaneously considered.

Reinganum, M.R. (1988) 'The anatomy of a stock market winner', *Financial Analysts Journal*, March–April, pp. 272–84. More on inefficiencies due to low net assets.

Rendleman, R.J., Jones, C.P. and Latané, H.E. (1982) 'Empirical anomalies based on unexpected earnings and the importance of risk adjustments', *Journal of Financial Economics*, November, pp. 269–87. Abnormal returns could have been earned by exploiting the slow response to unexpected earnings figures.

Ridley, M. (1993) 'Survey of the frontiers in finance', *The Economist*, 9 October. A series of excellent easy-to-read articles on the use of mathematics for predicting share prices.

Roberts, H.V. (1959) 'Stock market "patterns" and financial analysis: Methodological suggestions', *Journal of Finance*, March, pp. 1–10. Describes chance-generated price series to cast doubt on technical analysis.

Roll, R. (1981) 'A possible explanation for the small firm effect', *Journal of Finance*, September. Interesting consideration of the issue.

Roll, R. (1994) 'What every CFO should know about scientific progress in financial economics: What is known and what remains to be resolved', *Financial Management*, 23(2) (Summer), pp. 69–75. A discussion, in straightforward terms, of Roll's views on the state of play in the efficiency/inefficiency debate.

Rosenberg, B., Reid, K. and Lanstein, R. (1985) 'Persuasive evidence of market inefficiency', *Journal of Portfolio Management*, 11, Spring, pp. 9–16. Reports the identification of two market inefficiencies.

Schoenburg, E. (1990) 'Stock price prediction using neural networks', *Neurocomputing*, 2, pp. 17–27. Some evidence of predictability.

Scholes, M. (1972) 'The market for securities: Substitution versus price pressure effects of information on share prices', *Journal of Business*, April, pp. 179–211. Evidence that the issue of more shares does not depress share prices.

Shefrin, H. (2000) *Beyond Greed and Fear*. Boston, MA: Harvard Business School Press. An important book in the field of behavioural finance.

Shiller, R.J. (2000) *Irrational Exuberance*. Princeton, NJ: Princeton University Press. Behavioural finance applied to the bubble at the turn of the millennium.

Shleifer, A. (2000) *Inefficient Markets: An Introduction to Behavioural Finance*. Oxford: Oxford University Press. A landmark presentation of the case for the impact of human (irrational) behaviour in financial markets.

Smith, C. (1986) 'Investment banking and the capital acquisition process', *Journal of Financial Economics*, 15, pp. 3–29. Lists numerous studies that report a decrease in the share price when a share issue is announced.

Smith, T. (1992) *Accounting for Growth*. London: Century Business. A modern classic on creative accounting. Easy to read. (Now in a second edition.)

Soros, G. (1987) *The Alchemy of Finance*. New York: Wiley. (Reprinted in 1994 with a new preface and a new foreword.) Provides insight into the investment approach of a highly successful investor.

Soros, G. (1995) *Soros on Soros*. New York: Wiley. Financial theory and personal reminiscence interwoven.

Soros, G. (1998) *The Crisis of Global Capitalism*. New York: Public Affairs. More on market irrationality.

Sullivan, R., Timmermann, A. and White, H. (1999) 'Data-snooping, technical trading rule performance, and the bootstrap', *Journal of Finance*, 54(5), pp. 1647ff. A demonstration of false inferences being drawn from data. Many technical trading rules that had been shown to 'work' in other academic studies are shown to be false when data-snooping is eliminated.

'Symposium on some anomalous evidence on capital market efficiency' (1977). A special issue of the *Journal of Financial Economics*, 6, June. Generally technical articles, but useful for those pursuing the subject in depth.

Thaler, R. (ed.) (1993) *Advances in Behavioural Finance*. New York: Russell Sage Foundation. An important book in the development of this developing discipline.

Train, J. (1980) *The Money Masters*. New York: Harper Business (reprinted 1994). Some insights into successful trading strategies.

Train, J. (1987) *The Midas Touch*. New York: Harper & Row. Some insights into successful trading strategies.

Urry, M. (1996) 'The $45bn man makes his pitch' *Financial Times*, *Weekend Money*, 11/12 May, p. 1. An article on Buffett.

US Office of Business Economics (1966) *The National Income and Product Accounts of the United States 1929–1965*. Washington: Government Printing Office.

West, K.D. (1988) 'Bubbles, fads and stock price volatility tests: A partial evaluation', *Journal of Finance*, 43(3), pp. 639–56. A summary and interpretation of some of the literature on share price volatility. Noise trading by naïve investors is discussed.

SELF-REVIEW QUESTIONS

1 Explain the three forms of market efficiency.

2 Does the EMH imply perfect forecasting ability?

3 What does 'random walk' mean?

4 Reshape plc has just announced an increase in profit of 50 per cent. The market was expecting profits to double. What will happen to Reshape's share price?

5 Can the market be said to be inefficient because some shares give higher returns than others?

6 What use is inside information in the trading of shares?

7 Why is it important for directors and other managers to communicate to shareholders and potential shareholders as much information as possible about the firm?

8 What are the implications of the EMH for investors?

9 What are the implications of the EMH for managers?

10 What are allocative, operational and pricing efficiency?

11 What are 'technical analysis' and 'fundamental analysis'?

QUESTIONS AND PROBLEMS

1 Manchester United plc, the quoted football and leisure group, wins the cup and therefore can anticipate greater revenues and profits. Before the win in the final the share price was 640p.

a What will happen to the share price following the final whistle of the winning game?

b Which of the following suggests the market is efficient? (Assume that the market as a whole does not move and that the only news is the football match win.)

i The share price rises slowly over a period of two weeks to reach 700p.

ii The share price jumps to 750p on the day of the win and then falls back to 700p one week later.

iii The share price moves immediately to 700p and does not move further relative to the market.

2 If Marks and Spencer has a 1 for 1 scrip issue when its share price is 550p what would you expect to happen to its share price in theory (no other influences) and in practice?

3 (*Examination level*) 'The paradox of the efficient market hypothesis is that large numbers of investors have to disbelieve the hypothesis in order to maintain efficiency.' Write an essay explaining the EMH and explain this statement.

4 (*Examination level*) 'Of course the market is not efficient. I know lots of people from technical analysts to professional fundamental analysts who have made packets of money on the market.' Describe the terms technical and fundamental analyst. Explain how some individuals might generate a satisfactory return from stock market investment even if it is efficient.

5 (*Examination level*) It could be said that insufficient attention has been paid to psychological factors when explaining stock efficiency anomalies. Outline the efficient stock market hypothesis (EMH) and describe some of the evidence which casts doubts on the semi-strong level of the efficient market hypothesis for which psychological explanations might be useful.

6 (*Examination level*) The efficient market hypothesis, if true, encourages managers to act in shareholder wealth enhancing ways. Discuss this.

7 If the efficient market hypothesis is true an investor might as well select shares by sticking a pin into the *Financial Times*. Explain why this is not quite true.

8 Arcadia plc has been planning a major rights issue to raise £300m. The market has fallen by 10 per cent in the past four days and the merchant bank adviser suggests that Arcadia wait another three or four months before trying to sell these new shares. Given that the market is efficient, evaluate the merchant banker's suggestion.

9 Chartism and fundamental analysis are traditional methods used by stock market investors to make buy or sell decisions. Explain why modern finance theory has contributed to the growing popularity of share index funds which have a simple strategy of buying and holding a broadly based portfolio.

10 (*Examination level*) 'The world's well developed stock markets are efficient at pricing shares for most of the people most of the time.' Comment on this statement and explain what is meant by stock market efficiency.

11 (*Examination level*) The following statements are extracts from the detailed minutes taken at a Board meeting of Advance plc. This company is discussing the possibility of a new flotation on the main listed market of the London stock market.

Mr Adams (Production Director): 'I have been following the stock market for many years as a private investor. I put great value on patterns of past share prices for predicting future movements. At the moment my charts are telling me that the market is about to rise significantly and therefore we will get a higher price for our shares if we wait a few months. This will benefit our existing shareholders as the new shareholders will not get their shares artificially cheap.'

Mr Cluff: 'I too have been investing in shares for years and quite frankly have concluded that following charts is akin to voodoo magic, and what is more, working hard analysing companies is a waste of effort. The market cannot be predicted. I now put all my money into tracker funds and forget analysis. Delaying our flotation is pointless, the market might just as easily go down.'

Required

Consider the efficient stock markets theory and relate it to Mr Adams' and Mr Cluff's comments.

12 'A number of companies were put off flotation on the London Stock Exchange in 1994 because the market was too low.' Explain the efficient market hypothesis and assess the logic of such postponements.

13 The chief geneticist at Adams Horticultural plc has discovered a method for raising the yield of commercial crops by 20 per cent. The managing director will make an announcement to the Stock Exchange in one week which will result in a sharp rise in the share price. Describe the level of inefficiency this represents. Is the geneticist free to try to make money on the share price issue by buying now?

14 Rapid Growth plc has recently changed the methods of accounting for depreciation, stock and research and development, all of which have the effect of improving the reported profit figures. Consider whether the share price will rise as a result of these actions.

15 A famous and well-respected economist announces in a Sunday newspaper that the growth phase of the economy is over and a recessionary trend has begun. He bases his evidence on the results of a dozen surveys which have been conducted and made public by various economic institutes over the past three months. Should you sell all your shares? Explain the logic behind your answer with reference to the efficient market hypothesis.

16 Explain why professional and highly paid fund managers generally produce returns less than those available on a broadly based market index.

17 (*Examination level*) Describe the extent to which the evidence supports the efficient market hypothesis.

ASSIGNMENT

Consider the actions of the directors of a stock market quoted company you know well. Do they behave in such a way as to convince you they believe in the efficiency of the stock market? In what ways could they take steps to ensure greater efficiency of stock market pricing of the company's shares?

CHAPTER NOTES

1 For explanations of these terms, the reader is referred to one of the populist 'how to get rich quickly' books.

2 Another paper on this area is Jegadeesh and Titman's 1993 study, which fails to support De Bondt and Thaler.

3 This is an area with an enormous literature. The References and Further Reading at the end of the chapter contain some of the EMH papers.

4 Key studies in the area are Banz (1981), Keim (1983) and Fama and French (1992).

5 *The Economist*, 26 March 1994.

6 The doyen of the value investing school, Benjamin Graham, regarded the use of a single measure in isolation as a very crude form of value investing. In fact, he would condemn such an approach as not being a value strategy at all. *See Security Analysis* by Graham and Dodd (1934) and *The Intelligent Investor* (1973) by Graham (reprinted 1997)

7 For example Lakonishok *et al.* (1994), Chan *et al.* (1991), De Bondt and Thaler (1987), Rosenberg *et al.* (1985), Fama and French (1992), Capaul *et al.* (1993), Pontiff and Schall (1998) and Reinganum (1988).

8 For example Litzenberger and Ramaswamy (1979), Elton *et al.* (1983) and Levis (1989).

9 These performances are explored more fully in Arnold (2002).

10 Lynch (1990), pp. 34–5.

11 Neff (1999), pp. 62 and 71.

12 Train (1980), p. 98.

13 Reproduced in Lowe (1999), p. 116.

14 Barclays Capital (2000).

15 Implicit price deflation for GNP. US Office of Business Economics, *The National Income and Product Accounts of the United States 1929–1965*.

16 Graham and Dodd (1934), p. 12

17 Graham and Dodd (1934), p. 452.

18 Graham and Dodd (1934), p. 585

19 Urry (1996), p. 1.

20 Warren Buffett (1984).

21 These three arguments are identified by Andrei Shleifer in his excellent book *Inefficient Markets* (2000).

22 Although some studies have shown a decrease in share price when the sale of shares is announced (e.g. *see* Smith (1986) for a list of studies).

Part V

CORPORATE VALUE

15 Value-based management

16 Managing a value-based company and the cost of capital

17 Valuing shares

18 Capital structure

19 Dividend policy

20 Mergers

Chapter 15

VALUE-BASED MANAGEMENT

INTRODUCTION

The first few chapters of this book linked together the objective of shareholder wealth maximisation and acceptance or otherwise of proposed projects. This required a knowledge of the concepts of the time value of money and the opportunity cost of investors' funds placed into new investm\anagers fail to achieve returns at least as high as those available elsewhere for the same level of risk then, as agents for investors, they are failing in their duty. If a group of investors place £1m in the hands of managers who subsequently generate annual returns of 10 per cent those managers would in effect be destroying value for those investors if, for the same level of risk, a 14 per cent return is available elsewhere. With a future project the extent of this value destruction is summarised in the projected negative NPV figure.

This technique, and the underlying concepts, are well entrenched throughout modern corporations (*see* Chapter 4 for a description of a survey of practice by Arnold and Hatzopoulos (2000)). However the full potential of their application is only now dawning on a few particularly progressive organisations. Applying the notion of opportunity cost of capital and focusing on the cash flow of new projects rather than profit figures is merely skimming the surface. Since the mid-1980s a growing band of corporations, ranging from Pepsi in the USA to Lloyds TSB bank in the UK, have examined their businesses in terms of the following questions:

- How much money has been placed in this business by investors?
- What rate of return is being generated for those investors?
- Is this sufficient given the opportunity cost of capital?

These questions can be asked about past performance or about future plans. They may be asked about the entire organisation or about a particular division, strategic business unit or product line. If a line of business does not create value on the capital invested by generating a return greater than the minimum required then managerial attention can be directed to remedying the situation. Ultimately every unit should be contributing to the well-being of shareholders.

The examination of an organisation to identify the sources of value may not seem particularly remarkable to someone who has absorbed the concepts discussed in

Chapters 1 to 8, but to many managers steeped in the traditions of accounting-based performance measures such as profits, return on investment and earnings per share, they have revolutionary consequences.

The ideas themselves are not revolutionary or even particularly new. It is the far-reaching application of them to create a true shareholder-value-orientated company that can revolutionise almost everything managers do.

- Instead of working with ***plans*** drawn up in terms of accounting budgets, with their associated distorted and manipulable view of 'profit' and 'capital investment', managers are encouraged to think through the extent to which their new strategies or operational initiatives will produce what shareholders are interested in: a discounted inflow of cash greater than the cash injected.
- Instead of being ***rewarded*** in terms of accounting rates of return (and other 'non-value' performance measures, such as earnings per share and turnover) achieved in the short term, they are rewarded by the extent to which they contribute to shareholder value over a long time horizon. This can radically alter the incentive systems in most firms.
- Instead of directors accepting a low ***cash flow on the (market value of) assets tied up*** in a poorly performing subsidiary because the accounting profits look satisfactory, they are forced to consider whether greater wealth would be generated by either closure and selling off the subsidiary's assets or selling the operation to another firm which can make a more satisfactory return.

  There then follows a second decision: should the cash released be invested in other activities or be given back to shareholders to invest elsewhere in the stock market? The answers when genuinely sought can sometimes be uncomfortable for executives who prefer to expand rather than contract the organisation.

Dealing with such matters is only the beginning, once an organisation becomes value based. Mergers must be motivated and evaluated on the criterion of the extent to which a margin above the cost of capital can be achieved given the purchase price. Strategic analysis does not stop at the point of often vague and woolly qualitative analysis, it goes on to a second phase of valuation of the strategies and quantitative sensitivity analysis. The decisions on the most appropriate debt levels and the dividend payout ratios have as their core consideration the impact on shareholder wealth. In the field of human resources, it is accepted that all organisations need a committed workforce. But committed to what? Shareholder value-based management provides an answer but also places an onus on managers to communicate, educate and convert everyone else to the process of value creation. This may require a shift in culture, in systems and procedures as well as a major teaching and learning effort.

Value-based management brings together the way in which shares are valued by investors with the strategy of the firm, its organisational capabilities and the finance function – *see* Exhibit 15.1.

Value-based management is much more than a technique employed by a few individuals 'good with numbers'. The principles behind it must pervade the organisation; it touches almost all aspects of organisational life.

> Value-based management is a managerial approach in which the primary purpose is long-run shareholder wealth maximisation. The objective of the firm, its systems, strategy, processes, analytical techniques, performance measurements and culture have as their guiding objective shareholder wealth maximisation.

Exhibit 15.1 Components of shareholder value-based management

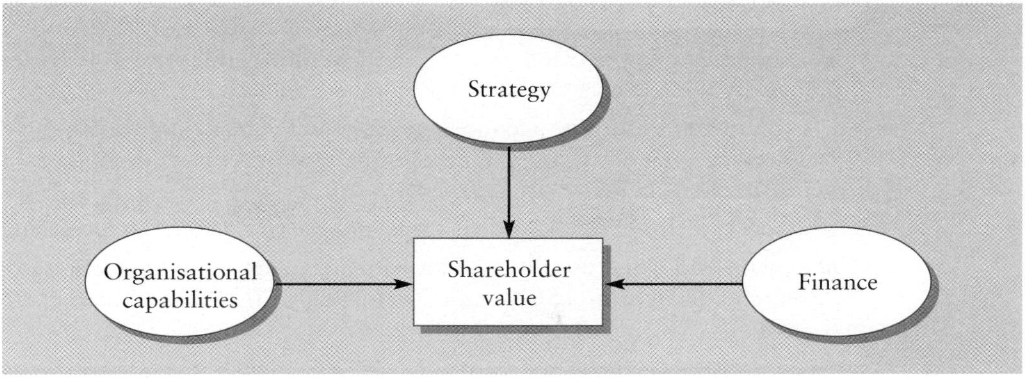

This chapter will concentrate on some of the finance-based techniques that have been developed to assist investors and managers to focus on value creation. Chapter 16 examines the management of value-based organisations.

The example of German companies (*see* Exhibit 15.2) shows that a switch to shareholder value-based management can have dramatic consequences.

Exhibit 15.2

The monoliths stir

A wave of corporate restructuring is sweeping across Germany in response to the growing pressures of global competition, writes **Haig Simonian**

'Shareholder value' has become a driving force in German boardrooms. Conglomerates could once justify unwieldy structures, poor earnings and cross subsidisation between profitable and loss-making businesses by saying they were pursuing long-term goals. This stance tended to be compared favourably with the 'short termism' of industrial rivals in the UK or US.

The argument sometimes had merits, but it was also used as an excuse for inactivity. It has been harder to make the same claim in the face of rising shareholder pressure. This has partly come from German investors, but has been led by the US and UK institutions that have increasingly diversified investments outside their domestic stock market.

The pressure for improved profitability and consistency of dividends has led to greater pressure on operations within larger underperforming industrial groups. At Daimler-Benz, Mr Schrempp has required every business to make a return of 12 per cent on capital employed or face closure. Mr Esser of Mannesmann has set an internal target of 15 per cent return on capital for his group next year.

The demand for higher profits has forced many company chairmen to reassess the breadth of their activities. Not all have been as Draconian as Mr Schrempp, but there has been a widespread move to identify activities with the most potential, and try either to improve or to sell less promising ones.

'We have to think what is best for business, and of creating value for the shareholders,' says Mr Esser about Mannesmann's demerger plan . . .

Heinrich von Pierer, Siemens chairman, wants to shed the group's reputation for conservatism by divesting almost one-seventh of its businesses, with sales of about DM17bn. Earlier this year, he said three of its four lossmaking operations would break even within a year, and launched plans to float a number of subsidiaries. 'It's only in the past year that they have started to take shareholder value really seriously,' says Mr Berger.

Source: Haig Simonian, *Financial Times*, 28 September 1999, p. 25. Reprinted with permission.

Learning objectives

This chapter demonstrates the rationale behind value-based management techniques. By the end of it the reader should be able to:

- explain the failure of accounts-based management (e.g. profits, balance sheet assets, earning per share and accounting rate of returns) to guide value maximising decisions in many circumstances;
- describe the four key drivers of value and the five actions to increasing value;
- explain and make use of value-based management measurement yardsticks: total shareholder return (TSR), market value added (MVA) and market to book ratio (MBR).

VALUE CREATION AND VALUE DESTRUCTION

We will start by taking a brief look at three companies. One has successfully created vast amounts of value for shareholders, one has destroyed shareholder value over a long period and one is trying to convert itself from a value destroyer to a value creator.

GlaxoSmithKline (GSK) has been a terrific share over 10, 20 and 30 years. If you had bought £1,000 of shares in Glaxo in 1966 your holding would have grown to be over £60m by 2000. Ian White, pharmaceutical analyst at Robert Fleming, says of Glaxo, 'It had the combination of good commercial management, vibrancy and the drive to succeed, and the right products. You often get two of the three, but rarely the whole package.'[1] The return on Glaxo shares relative to the *FTSE All-Share Index* is shown in Exhibit 15.3.

Exhibit 15.3 GSK total return performance

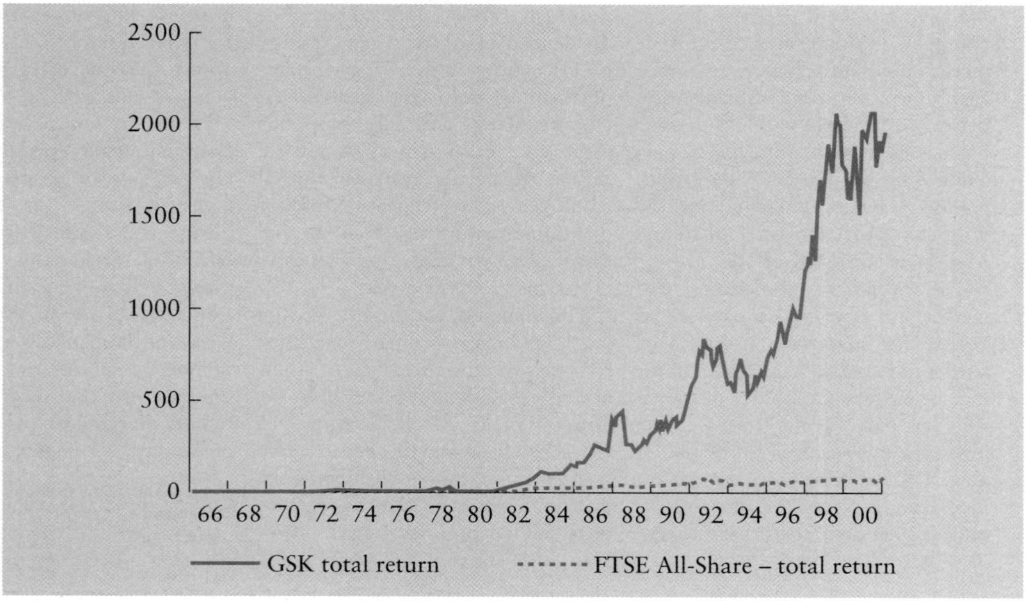

Source: Thomson Financial Datastream

Take another company, the UK-based industrial firm T & N. In 1982 investors realised that T & N would suffer as a result of asbestosis-related litigation. During August the market value of its shares fell to £37m as the shareholders realised that T & N would be forced to pay out vast sums to the victims of asbestosis. In November 1996 the company estimated that past and future compensation and other payments would amount to between £800m and £1.6bn.

> From where [the *Investors Chronicle*[2] asked] did a £37m basket case get £1.6bn? From its shareholders. Since 1986 T & N has issued around £700m of new equity via five rights issues, one placing and the 1987 takeover of AE . . . All this is to the good of the asbestosis sufferers, but it's a fair bet the shareholders who put it up aren't normally so generous with their donations to charity which is what in effect all T & N's capital raisings have been . . . The best course of action for T & N at any date in the 1980s would have been to hand the company over to the asbestos litigants lock, stock and barrel.

In 1998 T & N was taken over by the US company Federal Mogul.

Exhibit 15.4 Relative total return performance of T & N

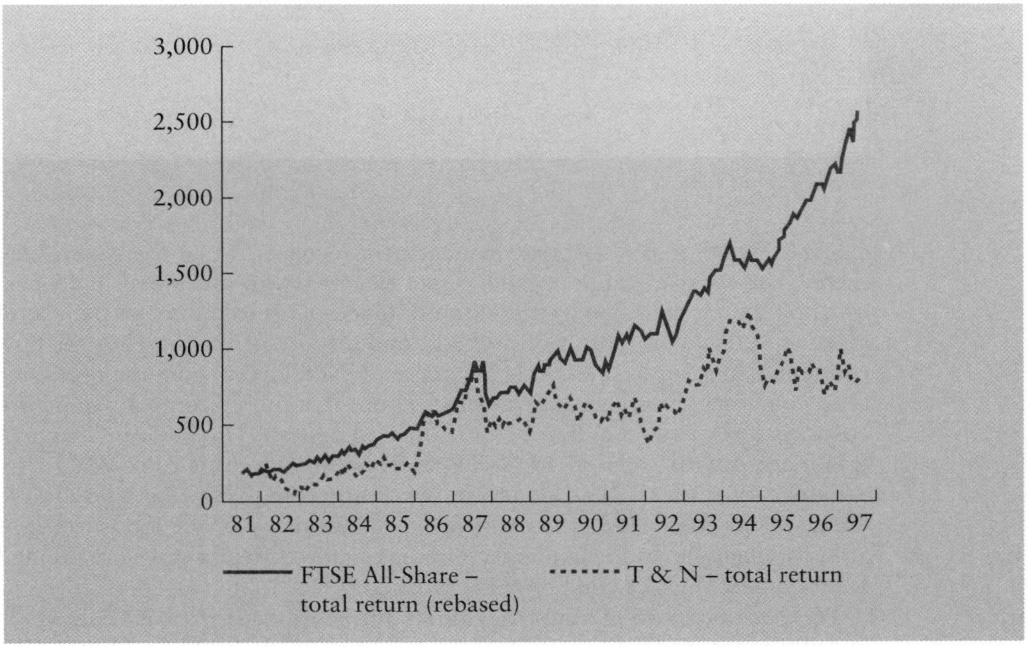

Source: Thomson Financial Datastream

Perhaps we can gain a glimpse of what shareholder value is by considering the mid-1990s crisis at the transport property conglomerate P&O. Lord Sterling, the chairman, was facing a shareholders revolt and was battling to keep his job. As Exhibit 15.5 makes clear P&O had under performed the FTSE All-Share Index for ten years.

The management were judged to have destroyed shareholder value by putting resources into activities which 'have not produced enough return to cover the cost of using the money'.[3] When they began to shake themselves up the change was noticeable to outside observers such as David Court, a fund manager at Scottish Amicable: 'When we met P&O in early 1996 it was regarded by its management as a national institution holding the flag for UK plc. When we met again six months later there were some interesting

Exhibit 15.5 P&O total return relative to the FTSE All-Share Index

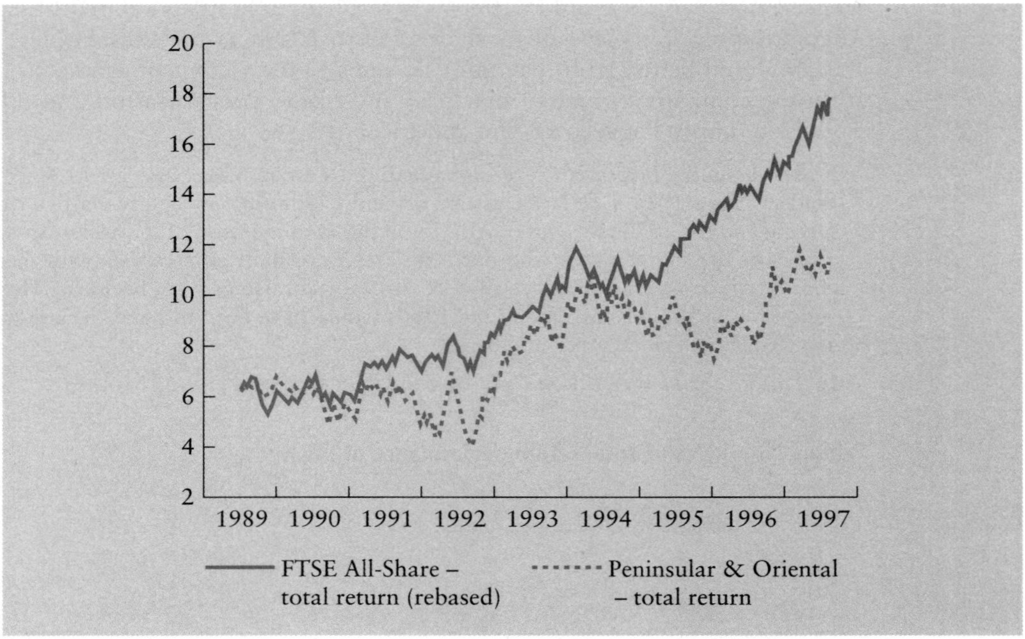

Source: Thomson Financial Datastream

changes. Much to our surprise, management recognised that there were shareholders out there.' The company announced a target rate of return on capital of 15 per cent for each of its operating divisions by 1998 and outlined plans to reduce its exposure to bulk shipping, sell off £500m worth of property and dispose of its housebuilder Bovis Homes. Its container shipping business was merged with Nedlloyd to gain the necessary critical mass (112 container ships and a turnover of £4bn) in a highly competitive market and to gain cost savings estimated at between £120m and £400m. The English Channel ferry business was merged with Stena in 1998. These two shipping deals took P&O closer to making satisfactory returns. Many analysts were not convinced that these moves could save P&O, mainly because of the unattractiveness of many of the industries in which it operates; for example, in the container shipping market, freight rates are falling because there are too many ships chasing too little work.

P&O formed a joint venture with a Chinese company for its bulk shipping unit and in 1999 Bovis was sold to an Australian company. By 2000 P&O was achieving returns of nearly 15 per cent, but the share price had not risen very much over the three years of managerial effort (total shareholder returns on shares had averaged 2.6 per cent per year). The company pushed on with its search for shareholder value. This included investing in new capital items as well as disposals. For example it ordered nine ships for delivery during 2000–4 at a total cost of £2.3bn. The directors judged that more shareholder value could be achieved if the company split inself into two. In October 2000 it demerged the cruise business from the ports, ferries and logistics business – a radical move as most of the company's value was in cruising. In 2001 it went even further, selling its 50 per cent stake in the bulk shipping operations and planning to achieve a stock market quotation for the container business with Nedlloyd.

Exhibit 15.6 shows that the 'weird Anglo-American concept' of shareholder value is starting to have an impact in many European countries.

Exhibit 15.6

Shareholder value

FT

Buybacks, demergers and the like are expressions of a single philosophy – shareholder value. The notion that companies should be run in the interests of shareholders, for long considered a weird Anglo-American concept, is taking root in continental Europe, especially Germany. Daimler-Benz, in the past decade one of the world's great destroyers of value, has this year slaughtered herds of sacred cows – letting Fokker go bust and dismantling AEG. Meanwhile, Hoechst has engaged in a whirlwind of restructuring that has lifted its share price by over 80 per cent.

But even in Germany, the roots are not deep. Such has been the political backlash to 'shareholder value' that Daimler now uses a German word *Unternehmenswertsteigerung*, which means improving the company's value.

Elsewhere, progress is patchy. Though many French chairmen pay lip-service to *le shareholder value*, the government often meddles in private-sector decisions. It was ministers who climbed down in the truck drivers' strike, which should have been employers' business.

Italy, too, has a long way to go. The Olivetti affair was at best a partial victory for shareholder activism. Mr Carlo De Benedetti did resign as chairman, but only after trillions of lire had been wasted. And international investors shied away from the confrontation that was needed to ensure a clean break with the past.

Though shareholders have too often been shrinking violets in 1996, they have chalked up some wins: P&O pulled off a couple of excellent deals after investor pressure; and shareholder disquiet pushed General Electric Company into modifying the undemanding performance element of its new managing director's pay packet.

Of course, it is much better if companies pursue wealth creation of their own accord. There is no substitute for raw competitive spirit. And the year has seen few more aggressive exponents of that than Microsoft's Mr Bill Gates. By embracing the Internet, which threatened his software monopoly, he has potentially opened up new frontiers to colonise – enriching his investors in the process.

Source: Lex column, *Financial Times*, 28–29 December 1996. Reprinted with permission.

The shareholder wealth maximising goal

It is clear that many commercial companies put shareholder value in second or third place behind other objectives. So why should we feel justified in holding up shareholder wealth maximisation as the banner to follow? Isn't growth in sales or market share more worthy? And what about the return to the labour force and to society generally?

Here is provided a brief recap and extension of some of the comments made in Chapter 1 about the objectives of the firm in a competitive market environment which has responsibilities to shareholders.

There are several reasons why shareholder value is gaining momentum. One of these is the increasing threat of takeover by teams of managers searching for poorly managed businesses. Perhaps these individuals are at present running a competitor firm or are wide-ranging 'corporate raiders' ready to swoop on undermanaged firms in any industry which, through radical strategic change, divestiture and shifting of executive incentives, can create more value for shareholders.

The owners of businesses have a right to demand that directors act in their best interests, and are increasingly using their powers to remove the stewards of their savings if they fail to do their utmost. To feel truly safe in their jobs managers should aim to create as much wealth as possible.

Arguably society as a whole will benefit if shareholder-owned firms concentrate on value creation. In this way scarce resources can be directed to their most valuable uses.

There are many reasons why earnings can mislead in the measurement of value creation, some of which are:[6]

- accounting is subject to distortions and manipulations;
- the investment made is often inadequately represented;
- the time value of money is excluded from the calculation;
- risk is not considered.

Accounting methods

In drawing up profit and loss accounts and balance sheets accountants have to make judgements and choose a basis for their calculations. They try to match costs and revenues. Unfortunately for the users of the resulting 'bottom line' figures, there can be many alternative approaches, which give completely different results and yet all follow accounting body guidelines.

Take the example of the identical companies X and Y. These have just started up and in the first three years annual pre-depreciation profits of £3m are expected. Both companies invested their entire initial capital of £10m in plant and machinery. The accountant at X takes the view that the machinery has a useful life of ten years and that a 25 per cent declining balance depreciation is appropriate. The accountant at Y, after reviewing the information on the plant and machinery, is more pessimistic and judges that a seven-year life with straight-line depreciation more truly reflects the future reality. The first three years' profits are shown in Exhibit 15.9.

The underlying economic position is the same for both company X and company Y, but in the first two years company X appears to be less profitable. Outside observers and management comparing the two companies may gain a distorted view of quality of stewardship and the potential of the firm. Investment decisions and incentive schemes based on profit figures can lead to suboptimal decisions and behaviour. They may also lead to deliberate manipulation. There are several arbitrary accounting allocations which make comparisons and decisions difficult. These concern, for example, goodwill and provisions, extraordinary and exceptional items and the treatment of research and development expenditure.

Exhibit 15.9 Companies X and Y: Profits for first three years

		Years (£000s)	
	1	*2*	*3*
Company X			
Pre-depreciation profit	3,000	3,000	3,000
Depreciation	2,500	1,875	1,406
Earnings	500	1,125	1,594
Company Y			
Pre-depreciation profit	3,000	3,000	3,000
Depreciation	1,429	1,429	1,429
Earnings	1,571	1,571	1,571

Investment

Examining earnings per share growth as an indicator of success fails to take account of the investment needed to generate that growth. Take the case of companies A and B (see Exhibit 15.10), both of which have growth in earnings of 10 per cent per year and are therefore equally attractive to an earnings-based analyst or manager.

Exhibit 15.10 Companies A and B: Earnings

		Year (£000s)	
	1	*2*	*3*
Earnings of A	1,000	1,100	1,210
Earnings of B	1,000	1,100	1,210

To a value-orientated analyst A is much more interesting than B if we allow for the possibility that less additional investment is needed for A to create this improving profits pattern. For example, both firms have to offer credit terms to their customers: however B has to offer much more generous terms than A to gain sales; therefore it has to invest cash in supporting higher debtor balances. B is also less efficient in its production process and has to invest larger amounts in inventory for every unit increase in sales.

When B's accounts are drawn up the additional debtors and inventory are included as an asset in the balance sheet and do not appear as a cost element in the profit and loss account. This results in the costs shown in the profit and loss account understating the cash outflow during a period.

If we examine the cash flow associated with A and B (Exhibit 15.11) we can see immediately that A is generating more shareholder value (assuming the pattern continues and all other factors are the same).

Exhibit 15.11 illustrates the conversion from earnings to cash flow figures.

Exhibit 15.11 Companies A and B: Earnings and cash flow

	Company A £000s			*Company B £000s*		
Year	1	2	3	1	2	3
Profit (earnings)	1,000	1,100	1,210	1,000	1,100	1,210
Increase in debtors	0	20	42	0	60	126
Increase in inventory	0	30	63	0	50	105
Cash flow before tax	1,000	1,050	1,105	1,000	990	979
Percentage change		+5%	+5.2%		–1%	–1.1%

If B also has to invest larger amounts in vehicles, plant, machinery and property for each unit increase in sales and profit than A the difference in the relative quality of the earnings growth will be even more marked.

Time value

It is possible for growth in earnings to destroy value if the rate of return earned on the additional investment is less than the required rate. Take the case of a team of managers trying to decide whether to make a dividend payment of £10m. If they retained the money within the business both earnings and cash flow would rise by £1,113,288 for each of the next ten years. Managers motivated by earnings growth might be tempted to omit the dividend payment. Future earnings would rise and therefore the share price would also rise on the announcement that the dividend would not be paid. Right? Wrong! Investors in this firm are likely to have a higher annual required rate of return on their £10m than the 2 per cent offered by this plan.[7] The share price will fall and shareholder value will be destroyed. What the managers forgot was that money has a time value and investors value shares on the basis of *discounted* future cash flows.

Risk

Focusing purely on the growth in earnings fails to take account of another aspect of the quality of earnings, risk. Increased profits which are also subject to higher levels of risk require a higher discount rate. Imagine a firm is contemplating two alternative growth options with the same expected earnings, of £100,000 per year to infinity. Each strategy is subject to risk but S has a wider dispersion of possible outcomes than T (see Exhibit 15.12).

Investors are likely to value strategy T more highly than strategy S. Examining crude profit figures, either historic or projected, often means a failure adequately to allow for risk. In a value-based approach it is possible to raise the discount rate in circumstances of greater uncertainty.

Exhibit 15.12 Probabilities of annual returns on strategies S and T

	Strategy S		*Strategy T*	
	Outcome earnings (profits) £	*Probability*	*Outcome earnings (profits)* £	*Probability*
	–100,000	0.10	80,000	0.10
	0	0.20	90,000	0.15
	100,000	0.40	100,000	0.50
	200,000	0.20	110,000	0.15
	300,000	0.10	120,000	0.10
Expected outcome	£100,000		£100,000	

Worked example 15.1 Earnings growth and value

Earnings and eps growth can lead to higher shareholder value in some circumstances. In others it can lead to value destruction. Shareholder value will rise if the return obtainable on new investment is at least as great as the required rate of return for the risk class. Consider EPSOS plc, financed entirely with equity capital and with a required rate of return of 15 per cent. To make the example simple we assume that EPSOS does not need to invest in higher levels of working capital if sales are expanded. EPSOS pays shareholders its entire earnings after tax every year and is expected to continue doing this indefinitely. Earnings amount to £100m per year. (The amount charged as depreciation is just sufficient to pay for investment to maintain sales and profits.) The value of the company given the opportunity cost of shareholders' money of 15 per cent is £100m/0.15 = £666.67m.

	£m
Sales	300.00
Operating expenses	155.07
Pre-tax profit	144.93
Taxes @ 31 per cent	44.93
Profits and cash flow after tax	100.00

Now imagine that EPSOS takes the decision to omit this year's dividend. Shareholders are made poorer by £100m now. However, as a result of the additional investment in its operations for the next year and every subsequent year sales, earnings and cash flows after tax will rise by 20 per cent. This is shown below.

	£m
Sales	360.00
Operating expenses	186.08
Pre-tax profit	173.92
Taxes @ 31 per cent	53.92
Profits and cash flow after tax	120.00

Earnings have grown by an impressive 20 per cent. Also value has been created. The extra £20m per annum stretching into the future is worth £20m/0.15 = £133.33m. This is achieved with a £100m sacrifice now. Here a growth in earnings has coincided with an increase in value.

Now consider a scenario in which sales growth of 20 per cent is achieved by using the £100m to expand the business, but this time the managers, in going for sales growth, push up operating expenses by 35 per cent. Earnings increase but value falls.

	£m
Sales	360.00
Operating expenses 155.07 × 1.35	209.34
Pre-tax profit	150.66
Taxes @ 31 per cent	46.70
Profits and cash flow after tax	103.96

The incremental perpetual cash flow is worth a present value of £3.96m/0.15 = £26.4m. But the 'cost' of achieving this is the sacrifice of £100m of income now. Therefore overall shareholder value has been destroyed despite earnings and eps growth.

Accounting rates of return (ARR) revisited

It is becoming clear that simply examining profit figures is not enough for good decision making and performance evaluation. Obviously the amount of capital invested has to be considered alongside the income earned. This was recognised long before the development of value-based management, as signified by the widespread use of a ratio of profits to assets employed. There are many variations on this theme: return on capital employed (ROCE), return on investment (ROI) and return on equity (ROE), but they all have the same root. They provide a measure of return as a percentage of resources devoted. The major problem with using these metrics of performance is that they are still based on accounting data. The profit figure calculations are difficult enough but when they are combined with balance sheet asset figures we have a recipe for unacceptable distortion. The *Financial Times* [8] puts it this way:

> Unfortunately, the crude figures for return on capital employed – operating profit/capital employed – that can be derived from a company's accounts are virtually useless. Here the biggest problem is not so much the reported operating profit as the figures for capital employed contained in the balance sheet. Not only are assets typically booked at historic cost, meaning they can be grossly undervalued if inflation has been high since they were acquired; the capital employed is also often deflated by goodwill write-offs.

Added to the list of problems is the issue of capitalisation. That is the extent to which an item of expenditure is written off against profits as an expense or taken on to the balance sheet and capitalised as an asset. For example, firms differ in their treatment of research and development; companies which spend significant sums on R&D and then have a policy of writing it off immediately are likely to have lower asset value than those which do not write it off against profits in the year of expenditure. Cross-company comparisons of profits/assets can therefore be very misleading.

Focusing on accounting rates of return can lead to short-termism. Managers who are judged on this basis may be reluctant to invest in new equipment as this will raise the denominator in the ratio, producing a poor ARR in the short term. This can destroy value in the long run. Fast-growing companies needing extensive investment in the near term with the expectation of reaping rich rewards in the long term should not be compared with slow-growth and low-investing firms on the basis of ARR because, despite their low profit returns on assets in the short term, they are more likely to outperform in terms of value in the long term.

Focus on eps and ARR

One of the most pervasive myths of our time is: **'But our shareholders do focus on eps and ARR, don't they?'** – and it is easy to see why. Senior executives when talking with institutional shareholders and analysts often find the conversation reverting to a discussion of short-term earnings forecasts. If a merger is announced directors feel the need to point out in press releases that the result will not be 'earnings dilutive' in the forthcoming year.

This surface noise is deceiving. Shareholders and analysts are primarily interested in the long-term cash flow returns on shares. The earnings attributable to the next couple of years are usually an insignificant part of the value of a share. Over two-thirds of the value of a typical share is determined by income to be received five or more years hence (see Chapter 17 for these calculations). Knowledge of this or next year's earnings is not particularly interesting in itself. It is sought because it sheds light on the medium- and long-term cash flows.

There are hundreds of quoted companies which do not expect to report any earnings at all in the next two to five years and yet often these shares are amongst the most highly valued in the market. There are dozens of biotechnology companies that have tapped shareholders for funds through rights issues and the like for years. Some have become massive concerns and yet have never made a profit or paid a dividend. The same applies to cable companies, and, in the past it was true of satellite television operators (for example BSkyB) as well as cellular telephone service providers, both of which have now reached the phase of high cash generation. Other evidence that shareholders are not primarily concerned with accounting earnings includes empirical studies which have shown that earnings changes are not very well correlated with share prices.[9] It has also been pointed out that the deliberate 'window dressing' or creative accounting of earnings figures does not, in most cases, influence share prices.[10]

Exhibit 15.13 shows what investors are looking for.

Exhibit 15.13

Investment community piles on pressure for better returns

FT

Companies need increasingly to develop medium-term corporate strategies which will enable them meet the rising expectations of those who provide their equity capital

Tapping into the booming liquidity of global capital markets is the corporate ideal – but the gatekeepers of that liquidity, the global investor and analyst communities, are basing their investment strategies on increasingly focused information. In this environment, the historical reporting model is living on borrowed time – investors, who typically base share price valuations on their forecasts of future cash flows, demand forward-looking information to feed into their valuation models.

Management is increasingly sensitive to the stark fact that the use of equity capital is not 'free' – it has been invested in the hope of earning a return. It is this required return . . . that defines the company's cost of equity capital. Management can only create value for shareholders if the company consistently generates a return on capital greater than its cost of capital . . .

For companies, the challenge must be to use this escalating value focus in their strategic planning, and in measuring performance. Once the internal systems are in place, the priority is to establish effective communication into the marketplace. Ken Lever, chairman of the ICAEW steering group, and finance director for Tomkins, the industrial conglomerate, says: 'Companies are increasingly recognising that earning a return on capital in excess of its cost is essential to long-term creation.

'Historical cost accounting measures are becoming less relevant, with more companies using value-based information and non-financial indicators to judge performance internally. Greater disclosure in these areas will allow investors to make more informed decisions on the potential future of companies.'

The international investment community is well aware of the limitations of annual reports, which provide emphasis on accounting profit – itself no real indicator of the creation of economic value . . .

Analysts and institutional investors focus much of their research on company strategy and the 'value platforms' underlying that strategy and recent surveys of investors' demand for, and use of, information confirm their desire for more forward-looking information, as well as the importance of drivers of future performance to their investment decisions.

Source: Nigel Page, *Financial Times*, 10 December 1999, FT Director (special section), p. VIII. Reprinted with permission.

HOW A BUSINESS CREATES VALUE

Value is created when investment produces a rate of return greater than that required for the risk class of the investment. Shareholder value is driven by the four factors shown in Exhibit 15.14.

Exhibit 15.14 The four key elements of value creation

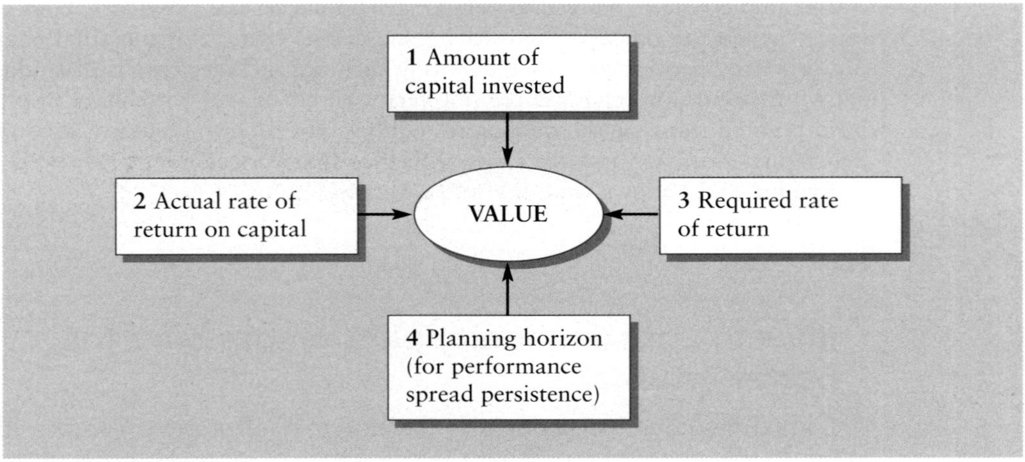

The difference between the second and third elements in Exhibit 15.14 creates the *performance spread*. Value is destroyed if 3 is greater than 2, and is created when 2 is greater than 3. The performance spread is measured as a percentage spread above or below the required rate of return, given the finance provider's opportunity cost.

The absolute amount of value generated is determined by the quantity of capital invested multiplied by the performance spread. So, for example, if Black plc has a required rate of return of 14 per cent per annum and actually produces 17 per cent on an investment base of £1,000,000 it will create £30,000 of value per year:

$$\begin{aligned}\text{Annual value creation} &= \text{Investment} \times (\text{actual return} - \text{required return})\\ &= \text{I}\,(r-k)\\ &= £1{,}000{,}000 \times (0.17 - 0.14) = £30{,}000\end{aligned}$$

The fourth element in Exhibit 15.14 needs more explanation. It would be unreasonable to assume that positive or negative return spreads will be maintained for ever. If return spreads are negative, presumably managers will (eventually) take the necessary action to prevent continued losses. If they fail to respond then shareholders will take the required steps through, say, sackings or the acceptance of a merger offer. Positive spreads arise as a result of a combination of the attractiveness of the industry and the competitive strength of a firm within that industry (*see* Chapter 16). High returns can be earned because of market imperfections. For example, a firm may be able to prevent competitors entering its market segment because of economies of scale, brand strength or legal exclusion through patents. However most firms will sooner or later experience increased competition and reduced margins. The higher the initial performance spread the more attractive market entry seems to potential competitors (or substitute product developers). Examples of industries that were at one time extremely profitable and which were penetrated to the point where they have become highly competitive include personal computers and silicon chip manufacture in the 1980s and 1990s.

In shareholder value analysis it is usually assumed that returns will, over time, be driven towards the required rate of return. At some point in the future (the planning horizon) any new investment will, on average, earn only the minimum acceptable rate of return. Having said this, we do acknowledge that there are some remarkable businesses that seem to be able to maintain positive performance spreads for decades. Their economic franchises are protected by powerful barriers preventing serious competitive attack, e.g. Coca-Cola, Disney. Warren Buffett calls such companies 'Inevitables' because there is every reason to believe they will be dominating their industries decades from now – see Arnold (2002). If we leave Inevitables to one side, we see that for the majority of businesses their value consists of two components, as shown in Exhibit 15.15.

Exhibit 15.15 Corporate value

Corporate value	=	Present value of cash flows within planning horizon	+	Present value of cash flows after planning horizon

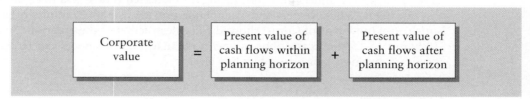

In the second period (after the planning horizon), even if investment levels are doubled, corporate value will remain constant, as the discounted cash inflows associated with that investment exactly equal the discounted cash outflows.

If it is assumed that Black plc can maintain its 3 per cent return spread for ten years and pays out all income as dividends then its future cash flows will look like this:

Years 1 → 10	11 → ∞
Cash flow £170,000	£140,000

The value of the firm is the discounted value of these cash flows.

The discounted cash flow within the planning horizon is:

£170,000 × annuity factor (10 years, 14 per cent) = 170,000 × 5.2161 = £886,737

plus the discounted cash flow after the planning horizon:

£140,000/0.14 = 1,000,000

This is then discounted back 10 years:

$$\frac{1,000,000}{(1 + 0.14)^{10}} = £269,744$$

Present value of future cash flows (886,737 + 269,744)	£1,156,481
Less initial investment	£1,000,000
Value created	£156,481

The value of the firm is equal to the initial investment in the firm (£1,000,000) plus the present value of all the values created annually.

Investment	+	Value created within planning horizon	+	Value created after planning horizon
£1,000,000	+	£30,000 × 5.2161 £30,000 × Annuity factor (10 years, 14%)	+	£1,000,000 (0.14 – 0.14)

£1,000,000 + £156,481 + 0 = £1,156,481

The five actions for creating value

Good growth occurs when a business unit or an entire corporation obtains a positive spread. Bad growth, the bane of shareholders, occurs when managers invest in strategies which produce negative return spreads. This can so easily happen if the focus of attention is on sales and earnings growth. To managers encouraged to believe that their job is to expand the business and improve the bottom line, acceptance of the notion of bad growth in profits is a problem. But, as we have seen, it is perfectly possible to show growing profits on a larger investment base producing an increased return less than the incremental cost of capital. While Reuters and Vodaphone provide us with examples of good growth, British Steel (now part of Corus) showed value destruction of the order of £3bn.[11]

Exhibit 15.16 shows the options open to managers. This model can be applied at the corporate, business unit or product line level.

Exhibit 15.16 To expand or not to expand?

	Grow	Shrink
Positive performance spread	Value creation	Value opportunity forgone
Negative performance spread	Value destruction	Value creation

It has already been demonstrated that overall Black plc produces a more than satisfactory return on investment. Now assume that the firm consists of two divisions: a clothing factory and a toy import business. Each business is making use of £500,000 of assets (at market value). The clothing division is expected to produce an 11 per cent return per annum over the next ten years whereas the toy division will produce a 23 per cent per annum return over the same period. After the ten-year planning horizon both divisions will produce returns equal to their risk-adjusted required return: for the clothing division this is 13 per cent and for the more risky toy division this is 15 per cent.

The cash flows are:

Year	$1 \rightarrow 10$	$11 \rightarrow \infty$
Clothing	£55,000	£65,000
Toys	£115,000	£75,000

The annual value creation within the planning horizon is:

$I \times (r - k)$

Clothing	£500,000 × (0.11 – 0.13) = –£10,000
Toys	£500,000 × (0.23 – 0.15) = +£40,000

Thus despite the higher return required in the toy division it creates value. For the next ten years a 15 per cent return is achieved plus a shareholder bonus of £40,000. This division would fit into the top left box of Exhibit 15.16. The management team may want to consider further investment in this unit so long as the marginal investment can generate a return greater than 15 per cent. To pass up positive return spread investments would be to sacrifice valuable opportunities and enter the top right box of Exhibit 15.16.

The clothing operation does not produce returns sufficient to justify its present level of investment. Growth in this unit would only be recommended if such a strategy would enable the division to somehow transform itself so as to achieve a positive spread. If this seems unlikely then the best option is probably retrenchment, a scaling down or withdrawal from the market. This will release resources to be more productively employed elsewhere, either within or outside of the firm. Such a shrinkage would create value by reducing the drag this activity has on the rest of the firm.

This line of thought can assist managers at all levels to allocate resources. At the corporate level knowledge of potential good growth and bad growth investments will help the selection of a portfolio of businesses. At the business unit level, product and customer groups can be analysed to assess the potential for value contribution. Lower down, particular products and customers can be ranked in terms of value. A simplified example of corporate level value analysis is shown in Exhibit 15.17.

In Exhibit 15.17, strategic business unit A (SBU_A) is a value destroyer due to its negative return spread. Perhaps there is over investment here and shareholders would be better served if resources were transferred to other operations. SBU_B produces a small positive spread and decisions on its future will depend on the expected longevity of its contribution. SBU_C produces a lower return spread than SBU_E but manages to create more value because of its higher future investment levels. Some businesses have greater potential than others for growth while maintaining a positive spread. For example, SBU_E might be a niche market player in fine china where greatly expanded activity would reduce the premium paid by customers for the exclusivity of the product – quickly producing negative spread on the marginal production. Strategic business unit C might be in

Exhibit 15.17 Value creation and Strategic Business Unit (SBU) performance spreads

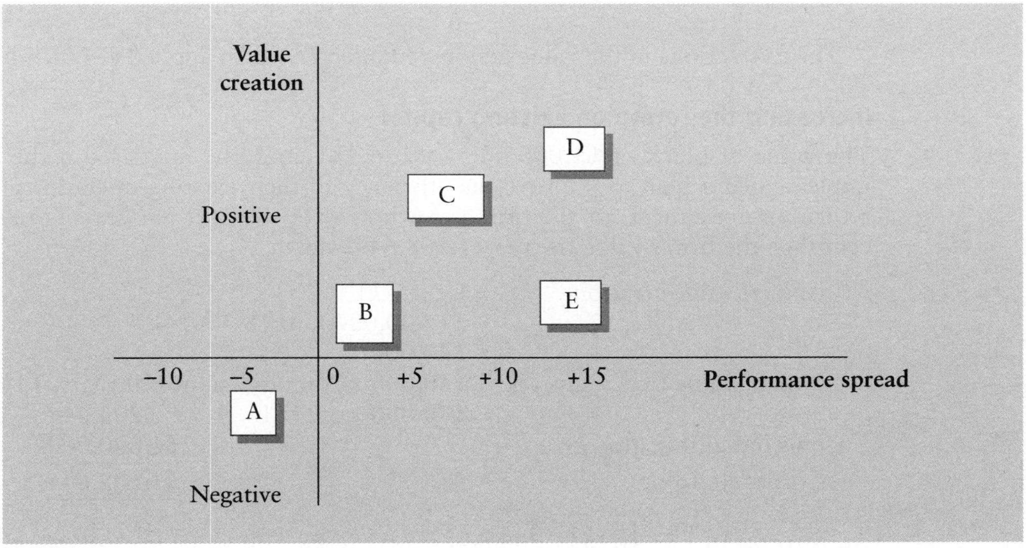

mid-priced tableware competing on design where investment in the design and marketing teams might produce positive spread growth. Strategic business unit D is capable of high spreads and high investment producing the largest overall gain in value. The anti-ulcer drug, Zantac, when still under patent, produced large spreads and was sold in high volumes around the world, producing billions of pounds of value for GlaxoSmithKline.

The five actions available for increasing value are shown in the value action pentagon (Exhibit 15.18).

Exhibit 15.18 The value action pentagon

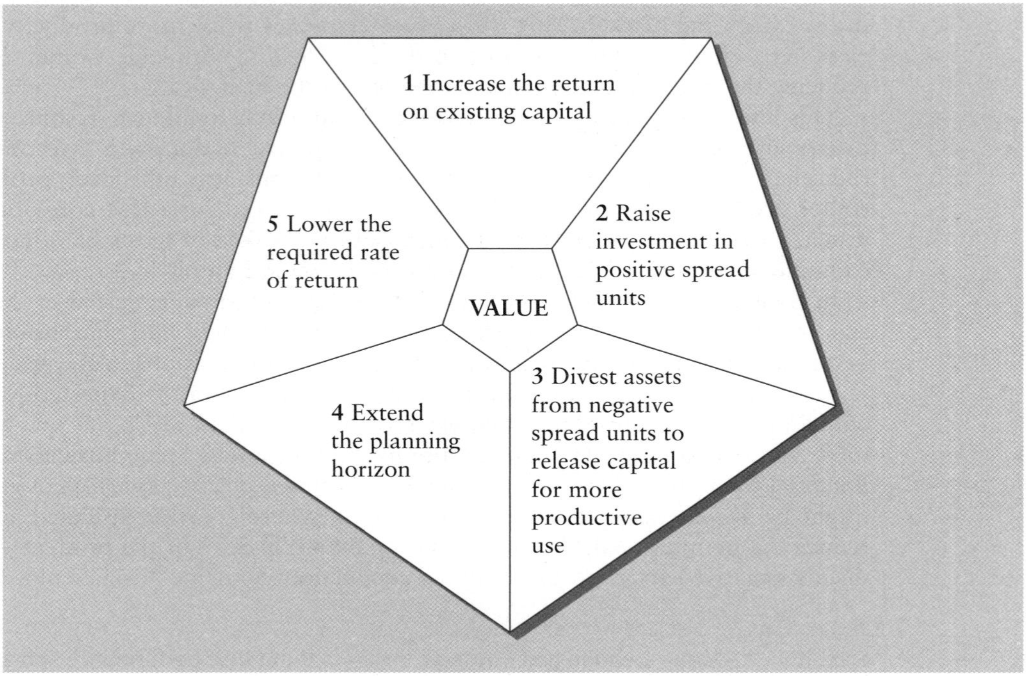

The five actions in the value action pentagon could be applied to Black plc.

Increasing the return on existing capital

The value of Black of £1,000,000 + £156,481 could be increased if the management implemented a plan to improve the efficiency of their existing operations. If the rate of return on investment for the firm as a whole over the next ten years is raised to 18 per cent then the firm's value rises to £1,208,644, viz:

Annual value creation	$= I \times (r - k)$	
	= £1,000,000 × (0.18 – 0.14)	
	= £40,000	
Present value over ten years	= £40,000 × Annuity factor (10 years, 14%)	
	= £40,000 × 5.2161 =	£208,644
plus initial investment		£1,000,000
Corporate value		£1,208,644

An increase of £52,163 (£1,208,644 – £1,156,481) in value is available for every 1 per cent improvement in return spread.

Raise investment in positive spread units

If Black could obtain a further £500,000 from investors with a required rate of return of 15 per cent to invest in the toy division to produce a 23 per cent return the value of the firm would rise to £1,860,521 (of this £204,040 would be additional value created, the remaining increase of £500,000 being the new capital invested).

Annual value creation on clothing	=	–£10,000
Annual value creation on toys = £40,000 × 2	=	£80,000
		£70,000

Over ten years = £70,000 × Annuity factor (10 years, 14.33%)[12]

= £70,000 × 5.1503 =	£360,521
plus the initial investment	1,500,000
Corporate value	£1,860,521

Divest assets

If Black could close its clothing division, release £500,000 to expand the toy division and achieve returns of 23 per cent on the transferred investment then value increases dramatically:

Annual value creation	$= I \times (r - k)$	
	= £1,000,000 × (0.23 – 0.15)	
	= £80,000	
Present value over ten years	= £80,000 × Annuity factor (10 years, 15%)	
	= £80,000 × 5.0188 =	£401,504
plus initial investment		£1,000,000
Corporate value		£1,401,504

Extend the planning horizon

Sometimes there are steps which can be taken to exploit a competitive advantage over a longer period than originally expected. For example, perhaps the toy division could negotiate a long-term exclusive import licence with the supplier of an established premium-priced product, thus closing the door on the entry of competitors. If we suppose that the toy division will now produce a return spread of 23 per cent for a 15-year period the value of the company rises to £1,179,634, viz:

Annual value creation on clothing	=	–£10,000
Annual value creation on toys	=	£40,000

Present value over 10 years (clothing)

= – £10,000 × Annuity factor (10 years, 13%)
= –£10,000 × 5.4262
= –£54,262

Present value over 15 years (toys)	= £40,000 × Annuity factor (15 years, 15%)	
	= £40,000 × 5.8474 =	£233,896
Total value creation	= £233,896 – £54,262 =	£179,634
plus initial investment		£1,000,000
Corporate value		£1,179,634

Lower the required rate of return

It may be possible to lower the required rate of return by adjusting the proportion of debt to equity in the capital structure or by reducing business risk. (Capital structure is examined in more detail in Chapter 18.) Suppose that Black can lower its required rate

Exhibit 15.19 The chief financial officers' role is evolving so that they spend increasing amounts of time on shareholder value initiatives and focusing on strategy

Finance role change

FT

Diane Summers

The traditional role of the finance function, overseeing and controlling internal corporate resources, is evolving. The trend is for chief financial officers to spend increasing amounts of time leading shareholder value initiatives and focusing on strategy.

Evidence of the trend comes from The Conference Board, the business network and research organisation, in a report published today. The research was sponsored by Price Waterhouse, the accountants and consultants.

Of 300 chief financial officers in the US, Europe and Asia surveyed as part of the study, 75 per cent said they led shareholder value initiatives in their companies. These included: corporate restructuring and cost reduction; important capital investments; and shareholder communication.

Cedric Read, Price Waterhouse partner in London, says the study shows chief financial officers are taking 'ever more strategic responsibilities in their companies and becoming true partners to the chief executive officer'. He adds: 'it is clear that managing and meeting shareholder expectations is becoming the primary role of top financial executives around the world.'

The senior finance staff surveyed said that, over the past three years, over 24 per cent of their time had been taken up with financial operations; this was projected to drop to about 18 per cent. Time spent on financial strategy and shareholder initiatives was projected to rise from 13 per cent to over 17 per cent (see chart).

Chief financial officers whose company's shares outperformed the competition were: most likely to spend more than 20 per cent of their time with the heads of business units; make the development of systems to support decision-making a top priority; and rank re-engineering finance processes as the most effective way of reducing costs.

(CFO, 2000: 'The global CFO as strategic business partners', by Stephen Gates.)

Source: Diane Summers, *Financial Times*, 23 June 1997, p. 12. Reprinted with permission.

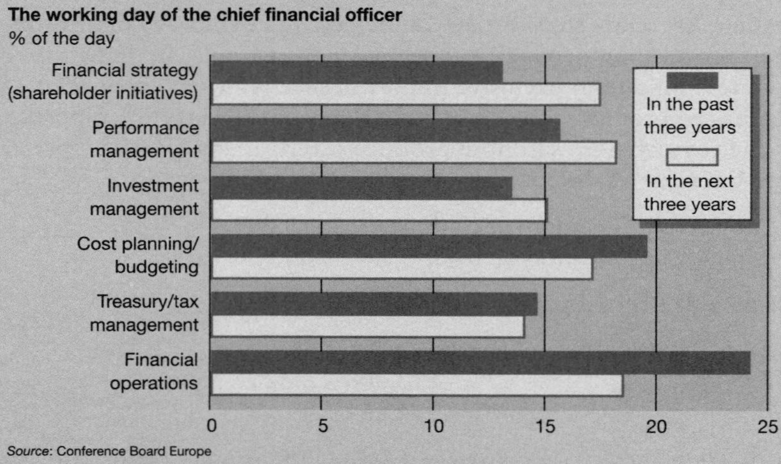

of return by shifting to a higher proportion of debt, so that the overall rate falls to 12 per cent. Then the value of the firm rises to £1,282,510.

Annual value creation	$= I \times (r - k)$	
	$= 1{,}000{,}000 \times (0.17 - 0.12)$	
	= £50,000	
Present value over ten years	= £50,000 × Annuity factor (10 years, 12%)	
Total value creation	= £50,000 × 5.6502 =	£282,510
plus initial investment		£1,000,000
Corporate value		£1,282,510

MEASURING VALUE CREATION: EXTERNAL METRICS

This section will examine the use of stock market-based measures of value. These are:

- Total shareholder return, TSR;
- Market value added, MVA;
- Market to book ratio, MBR.

Total shareholder return (TSR)

What is of interest to shareholders is the total return earned on their investment relative to a peer group of firms, or the market as a whole. Total returns includes dividend returns and share price changes over a specified period. For one-period TSR:

$$\text{TSR} = \frac{\text{Dividend per share} + (\text{share price at end of period} - \text{initial share price})}{\text{Initial share price}} \times 100$$

Consider a share which rises in price over a period of a year from £1 to £1.10 and a 5p dividend is paid at the end of the year. The TSR is 15 per cent.

$$\text{TSR} = \frac{d_1 + (P_1 - P_0)}{P_0} \times 100$$

$$\text{TSR} = \frac{0.05 + (1.10 - 1.00)}{1.00} \times 100 = 15\%$$

When dealing with multi-period TSRs we need to account for the dividends received in the interim years as well as the final dividend. The TSR can be expressed either as a total return over the period or as an annualised rate.

So, for example if a share had a beginning price of £1, paid annual dividends at the end of each of the next three years of 9p, 10p and 11p and had a closing price of £1.30, the total return (assuming dividends are reinvested in the company's shares immediately on receipt) is calculated via internal rate of return:

Time	0	1	2	3
Price/cash flow(p)	–100	9	10	11+130

$$-100 + \frac{9}{1+r} + \frac{10}{(1+r)^2} + \frac{141}{(1+r)^3} = 0$$

At:
r = 19%: –1.7038
r = 18%: 0.6259

The internal rate of return =

$$18 + \frac{0.6259}{0.6259 + 1.703} = 18.27\%$$

The annualised TSR is 18.27%.

The total shareholder return over the 3 years = $(1 + 0.1827)^3 - 1 = 65.4\%$.

TSRs for a number of periods are available from financial data organisations, such as Datastream.

TSR has become an important indicator of managerial success:

> Performance against this type of measure is now used as the basis for calculating the major component of directors' bonuses in over half of FTSE 100 companies . . . TSR reflects the measure of success closest to the hearts of a company's investors: what they have actually gained or lost from investing in one set of executives rather than in another. (*Management Today*, March 1997, p. 48.)

The 'dividend yield plus capital gain' metric needs to be used in conjunction with a benchmark to filter out economy-wide or industry-wide factors. In Exhibit 15.20 the TSRs of the ten largest UK companies are shown for one year and for five years. Some perform better than their industry averages, while others perform far worse (e.g. British Telecommunications). The industry averages are constructed using all the major quoted firms in Europe in a particular sector.

Exhibit 15.20 TSRs for the 10 largest UK quoted companies over 1 year and 5 years to March 2001 FT

	Company TSR 1 year %	*Industry TSR 1 year %*	*Company TSR 5 years %*	*Industry TSR 5 years %*
Shell T&T	5.2	5.9	195.5	205.6
BP Amoco	–0.2	5.9	225.3	205.6
Vodafone	–46.1	–54.2	498.4	255.8
GlaxoSmithKline	1.7	19.9	257.5	187
HSBC	13.3	12.6	317.9	250.9
AstraZeneca	33.7	19.9	306	187
Royal Bank of Scotland	85.4	12.6	482	250.9
Lloyds TSB	5.2	12.6	266.6	250.9
British Telecom	–57.1	–54.2	160.1	255.8
Barclays	31.4	12.6	395.3	250.9

Source: *Financial Times* in conjunction with FTSE, the global equity index provider. These figures were shown in a special section of the *Financial Times*, 'European Performance League', 29 June 2001. http://specials.ft.com/europerformance/index.html

TSR has taken off as a key performance measure. For example in 1999 HSBC announced that its 'overall aim is to beat the average total shareholder returns of a peer group of nine leading international financial institutions – such as rival Citigroup

– with a minimum objective of doubling shareholder returns over five years'[13] and Ford said it was 'setting a new objective of providing a total shareholder return – dividend plus share price appreciation – in the top quartile of the S&P500 group of companies over time'.[14] In 2000 Pilkington became the first UK company to pay its non-executive directors in shares only, in an attempt to align the management's interests to that of shareholders.

There are three issues to be borne in mind when making use of TSR:

1 ***Relate return to risk class*** Two firms may have identical TSRs and yet one may be subject to more risk due to the greater volatility of earnings as a result, say, of the economic cycle. The risk differential must be allowed for in any comparison. This may be particularly relevant in the setting of incentive schemes for executives. Managers may be tempted to try to achieve higher TSRs by taking greater risk.

2 **Assumes efficient share pricing** It is difficult to assess the extent to which share return outperformance is due to management quality and how much is due to exaggerated (or pessimistic) expectations of investors at the start and end of the period being measured. If the market is not efficient in pricing shares and is capable of being swayed by irrational optimism and pessimism then TSRs can be an unreliable guide to managerial performance. (*See* Chapter 14 for a discussion on share pricing efficiency.)

3 ***TSR is dependent on the time period chosen*** A TSR over a three-year period can look very different from a TSR measured over a one-year or ten-year period. Consider the annual TSRs for Company W in Exhibit 15.21.

Exhibit 15.21 Annual TSRs for company W

	Annual TSR	*Value of £1m investment made at the end of 2002*
2003	+10%	£1,100,000
2004	–20%	£880,000
2005	–40%	£528,000
2006	+30%	£686,400
2007	+50%	£1,029,600

Measured over the last two years the TSR of company W is very good. However over five years a £1,000,000 investment grows to only £1,029,600, an annual rate of return of 0.6 per cent. Exhibit 15.20 showed that while GlaxoSmithKline outperformed its industry peer group over five years it underperformed over one year.

TSRs must be used carefully. If, for example, performance bonuses are dependent on one-year TSRs there may be some encouragement for executives to manipulate TSRs through, say, the selective release of information.

Market Value Added (MVA)

The consulting firm Stern Stewart & Co has developed the concept of Market Value Added (MVA). This looks at the difference between the total amount of capital put into the business by finance providers (debt and equity) and the current market value of the company's shares and debt. It gives a measure of how executives have performed with the capital entrusted to them. A positive MVA indicates value has been created. A negative MVA indicates value has been destroyed.

MVA = Market value – Capital

where:

Market value	=	Current value of debt, preference shares and ordinary shares.
Capital	=	All the cash raised from finance providers or retained from earnings to finance new investment in the business, since the company was founded.

Managers are able to push up the conventional yardstick, total market value of the business, simply by investing more capital. MVA, by subtracting capital injected or retained from the calculation, measures net value generated for shareholders.

Illustration of MVA

MerVA plc was founded 20 years ago with £15m of equity finance. It has no debt or preference shares. All earnings have been paid out as dividends. The shares in the company are now valued at £40m. The MVA of MerVA is therefore £25m:

MVA = Market value – Capital
MVA = £40m – £15m = £25m

If the company now has a rights issue raising £5m the market value of the firm must rise to at least £45m in order for shareholder wealth to be maintained. If the market value of the shares rose to only £44m because shareholders are doubtful about the returns to be earned when the rights issue money is applied within the business (that is, a negative NPV project) shareholders will lose £1m of value. This is summarised below:

	Before rights issue	*After rights issue*
Market value	£40m	£44m
Capital	£15m	£20m
MVA	£25m	£24m

According to Stern Stewart & Co, if a company pays a dividend, both the 'market value' and the 'capital' parts of the equation are reduced by the same amount and MVA is unaffected. Imagine an all-equity financed company with an equity market value of £50m at the start of the year, which increased to £55m by the end of the year (after the payment of a £6m dividend). The capital put into the firm by shareholders over the company's life by purchasing shares and retained earnings amounted to £20m at the start of the year. If the firm earns £10m post-tax profit and pays the dividend of £6m on the last day of the year the effect is as follows:

	At start of year		*At end of year*
Market value	£50m		£55m
Capital	£20m	£20m	
	plus earnings	£10m	
	less dividend	–£6m	
			£24m
MVA	£30m		£31m

If the company had not paid the dividend then, according to Stern Stewart[15] both the market value and the capital rise by £6m and MVA would remain at £31m. Thus:

	At start of year	*At end of year*
Market value	£50m	£61m
Capital	£20m	£30m
MVA	£30m	£31m

In the practical application of MVA analysis it is often assumed that the market value of debt and preference shares equals the book value of debt and preference shares. This permits the following version of MVA:

MVA = Ordinary shares market value – Capital supplied by ordinary shareholders

Stern Stewart produces annual MVA rankings for quoted companies. Some of these have been published in the *Sunday Times*. Of the UK's 200 largest quoted firms the ten best and ten worst MVA performers are shown in Exhibit 15.22.

Exhibit 15.22 The ten UK companies with the highest MVA and the ten UK companies with the lowest MVA (from the 200 largest UK companies) to 2000

Company	*MVA(£m)*	*Company*	*MVA(£m)*
1. BP Amoco	88,393	191. Iceland	122
2. BT	78,497	192. Laporte	97
3. Shell	57,631	193. Thistle Hotels	92
4. Glaxo Welcome	54,465	194. First Choice Holidays	89
5. HSBC	42,585	195. Glynwed	66
6. Unilever	42,169	196. David S. Smith	61
7. SmithKline Beecham	41,239	197. Millenium & Copthorne	29
8. AstraZeneca	36,393	198. Northern Foods	16
9. Vodafone	33,417	199. Lasmo	1
10. Lloyds TSB	26,713	200. Enodis	–13

Source: www.sunday-times.co.uk/news/pages/sti/2000/09/24/stibusnws.01010.html

The absolute level of MVA is perhaps less useful for judging performance than the change in MVA over a period. Alistair Blair, writing in *Management Today*,[16] is quite scathing about crude MVA numbers:

> An MVA includes years old and now irrelevant gains and losses aggregated on a pound-for-pound basis with last year's results and today's hope or despair, as expressed in the share price. Surely, what we are interested in is current performance, or if we're going to be determinedly historic, performance since the current top management team got its hands on the controls.

By converting MVA into a period measure of performance we can isolate the value-creating contribution of a particular span of years under the leadership of a team of managers.

Problems with MVA

There are a number of problems with MVA.

- **Estimating the amount of cash invested** Measuring the amount of capital put into and retained within a business after it has been trading for a few years is fraught with problems. For example, does R&D expenditure produce an asset or is it an expense? How do you treat goodwill on acquisitions? The accountants' balance sheet is not designed for measuring capital supplied by finance providers, but at least it is a starting point. Stern Stewart make use of a proxy measure called 'economic book value'. This is based on the balance sheet capital employed figure, subject to a number of adjustments. It has been pointed out by critics that these adjustments are rather arbitrary and complex, making it difficult to claim that economic book value equals the theoretically correct 'capital' in most cases.
- **When was the value created?** As Ian Cornelius and Matt Davies (1997) in their excellent review of shareholder-value-based management analysis techniques point out, MVA 'does not explain when value was created, whether it is still being created, or whether it will be created in the future'. The present share price may reflect value-creating decisions taken a generation ago rather than by present management.
- **Is the rate of return high enough?** If it is not specified when value is created, it is difficult to know whether the amount generated is sufficiently in excess of capital used to provide a satisfactory return relative to the risk-adjusted time value of money. Positive MVA companies can produce poor rates of return. Take company B in the following example.

	A	*B*
MVA	£50m	£50m
Market value	£100m	£100m
Capital	£50m	£50m
Age of firm	3 years	30 years

(Both firms have paid out profits each year as dividends, therefore the capital figure is the starting equity capital.) Firm B has a much lower rate of return on capital than A and yet they have the same MVA.

- **Inflation distorts MVA** If the capital element in the equation is based on a balance sheet figure then during times of inflation the value of capital employed may be understated. If capital is artificially lowered by inflation *vis-à-vis* current market value for companies where investment took place a long time ago then MVA will appear to be superior to that for a similar firm with recently purchased assets.
- **MVA is an absolute measure** Judging companies on the basis of absolute amounts of pounds means that companies with larger capital bases will tend to be at the top (and bottom) of the league tables of MVA performance. Size can have a more significant impact on MVA than efficiency. This makes comparison between firms of different sizes difficult. The next metric examined, the market to book ratio, is designed to alleviate this problem.

Market to book ratio (MBR)

Rather than using the arithmetical difference between the capital raised and the current value, as in MVA, the MBR is the market value divided by the capital invested. If the market value of debt can be taken to be the same as the book value of debt then a version of the MBR is the ratio of the market value of the company's ordinary shares to the amount of capital provided by ordinary shareholders (if preference share capital can be regarded as debt for the purpose of value-based management).

There is, of course, the problem of estimating the amount of capital supplied, as this is usually dependent on adjusted balance sheet net asset figures. For example, goodwill write-offs and other negative reserves are reinstated, as in MVA. It is also suggested that asset values be expressed at replacement cost so that the MBR is not too heavily distorted by the effects of inflation on historic asset figures.

Illustration of MBR

MaBaR plc has an equity market value of £50m, its book debt is equal to the market value of debt, and the adjusted replacement cost of assets attributable to ordinary shareholders amounts to £16m.

Market value	£50m
Capital	£16m
MVA	£34m
MBR £50m/£16	= 3.125

MaBaR has turned every pound put into the firm into £3.125.

The rankings provided by MBR and MVA differ sharply. The largest companies dominating the MVA ranks generally have lower positions when ordered in terms of MBR.

Care must be taken when using MBR for performance measurement and target setting because if it is wrongly applied it is possible for positive NPV projects to be rejected in order for MBR to be at a higher level. Take the case of a company with an MBR of 1.75 considering fundraising to make an investment of £10m in a project estimated to produce a positive NPV of £4m. Its market to book ratio will fall despite the project being shareholder wealth enhancing.

		Before project		*After project acceptance*
Value of firm		£70m	(70 + 10 + 4)	£84m
Capital		£40m		£50m
MVA		£30m		£34m
MBR	70/40 =	1.75	84/50 =	1.68

The new project has an incremental MBR of 1.4 (14/10 = 1.4). This is less than the firm's original overall MBR of 1.75, which is therefore dragged down by the acceptance of the project. This effect should be ignored by managers motivated by shareholder wealth enhancement. They will focus on NPV.

TSR, MVA and MBR should be seen not as competitors, but as complementary. Relying on one indicator is unnecessarily restrictive. It is perfectly possible to use all three measures simultaneously and thereby overcome many of the weaknesses of each individually.

Shareholders are right to concentrate on these external measures. Also those within the firm who are involved in managerial decision making need to take heed of these market-based metrics. However, these are long-term measures which span years, if not decades. For day-to-day and year-to-year management within the organisation more immediate tools to guide management target setting and performance monitoring on a regular basis are needed.

Exhibit 15.23 Summary table of market-based performance metrics

	Merits	*Problems*
TSR	■ Very easy to understand and calculate. ■ Not affected by the problems of having to rely on accounting balance sheet values. Subjective and complex adjustments are avoided. ■ Better able to identify when value is created than are MVA and MBR. ■ Not affected by relative size of firms.	■ Vulnerable to distortion by the selection of time period over which it is measured. ■ Need to express TSR relative to a peer group to obtain impression of performance. ■ It fails to relate risk to TSR. ■ Assumes stock market efficiency in share pricing.
MVA	■ Assesses wealth generated over entire business life. ■ Managers judged on MVA have less incentive to invest in negative NPV projects than those judged on earnings growth. ■ Measures in absolute amounts of money.	■ Many doubts about the validity of the capital invested figure used, e.g. to what extent should R&D be regarded as an asset, or goodwill, or brands? ■ Size of business not allowed for in inter-firm comparisons. ■ Do not know in which part of the firm's history the value was created. ■ Inflation can distort MVA. ■ Do not know if rate of return obtained is higher or lower than the required rate of return given the opportunity cost of capital. ■ Assumes stock market efficiency in share pricing.
MBR	■ Assesses wealth generated over entire business life. ■ Adjusts for size of business.	■ Over-reliance on MBR for performance measurement and incentive schemes can lead to bad investment decisions. ■ Accurate capital invested figure is very difficult to obtain. ■ Do not know if rate of return obtained is higher or lower than the required rate of return given the opportunity cost of capital. ■ Do not know when value was created. ■ Inflation can distort MBR. ■ Assumes stock market efficiency in share pricing.

A further point to bear in mind is that TSR, MVA and MBR are applied to the organisation as a whole. What management often needs are measures which can be used for individual business units (or product lines or projects) to provide an indication of the contribution to overall shareholder value from the component parts of the business. Senior managers at head office, as well as those operating each potential value centre, need to know where action is necessary to maximise the value potential of all parts of the firm. The next chapter concerns measurements developed to assist managers in identifying value-destroying and value-creating operations on a unit-by-unit basis, as well as for the entire business.

CONCLUDING COMMENTS

The switch from management by accounting numbers to management using financial concepts such as value, the time value of money and opportunity cost is only just beginning. Some highly successful firms are leading the way in insisting that each department, business unit and project add value to shareholders' investment. This has required a re-examination of virtually all aspects of management, ranging from performance measurement systems and strategic planning to motivational schemes and training programmes. The next chapter looks at some of the techniques being used by managers at the cutting edge of their craft to create a value-based organisation.

KEY POINTS AND CONCEPTS

- **Value-based management** is a managerial approach in which the primacy of purpose is long-run shareholder-wealth maximisation. The objective of the firm, its systems, strategy, processes, analytical techniques, performance measurement and culture have as their guiding objective shareholder-wealth maximisation.
- **Shareholder-wealth maximisation** is the superior objective in most commercial organisations operating in a competitive market for many reasons. For example:
  - managers not pursuing this objective may be thrown out (e.g. via a merger);
  - owners of the business have a right to demand this objective;
  - society's scarce resources can thereby be better allocated.
- **Non-shareholder wealth-maximising goals** may go hand in hand with shareholder value, for example market share targets, customer satisfaction and employee benefits. But, sometimes the two are contradictory and then shareholder wealth becomes paramount.
- **Mission statements** have to be more than business school jargon. A sincere shareholder value statement must be followed with practical steps to achieve the goal. Do not confuse the objective of the organisation (value) with strategic targets (for example to be the world's number one widget maker) to achieve the objective:
- **Earnings (profit) based management is flawed**:
  - profit figures are drawn up following numerous subjective allocations and calculations relying on judgement rather than science;
  - profit figures are open to manipulation and distortion;
  - the investment required to produce earnings growth is not made explicit;
  - the time value of money is ignored;
  - the riskiness of earnings is ignored.
- **Bad growth** is when the return on the marginal investment is less than the required rate of return, given the finance providers' opportunity cost of funds. This can occur even when earnings-based figures are favourable.
- **Accounting rates of return** (ROCE, ROI, ROE, etc.) attempt to solve some of the problems associated with earnings or earnings per share metrics especially with regard to the investment levels used to generate the earnings figures. However balance sheet figures are often too crude to reflect capital employed. Using ARRs can also lead to short-termism.

- **That shareholders are interested solely in short-term earnings and eps is a myth** These figures are only interesting to the extent that they cast light on the quality of stewardship over fund providers' money by management and therefore give an indication of long-term cash flows. Evidence:
  - most of the value of a share is determined by income to be received five or more years hence;
  - hundreds of quoted firms produce zero or negative profits with high market values.
  - earnings changes are not correlated with share price changes; for example, earnings can fall due to a rise in R&D spending and yet share prices may rise;
  - the window dressing of accounts (creative accounting) does not, in most cases, influence share prices.

- **Value is created** when investment produces a rate of return greater than that required for the risk class of investment.

- **Shareholder value is driven by four key elements:**
  1 Amount of capital invested.
  2 Required rate of return.
  3 Actual rate of return on capital.
  4 Planning horizon (for performance spread persistence).

- **Performance spread**

  Actual rate of return on capital – required return

  $$r - k$$

- **Corporate value**

=	Present value of cash flows within planning horizon	+	Present value of cash flows after planning horizon

- **To expand or not to expand?**

	Grow	**Shrink**
Positive performance spread	Value creation	Value opportunity forgone
Negative performance spread	Value destruction	Value creation

- **The value action pentagon**

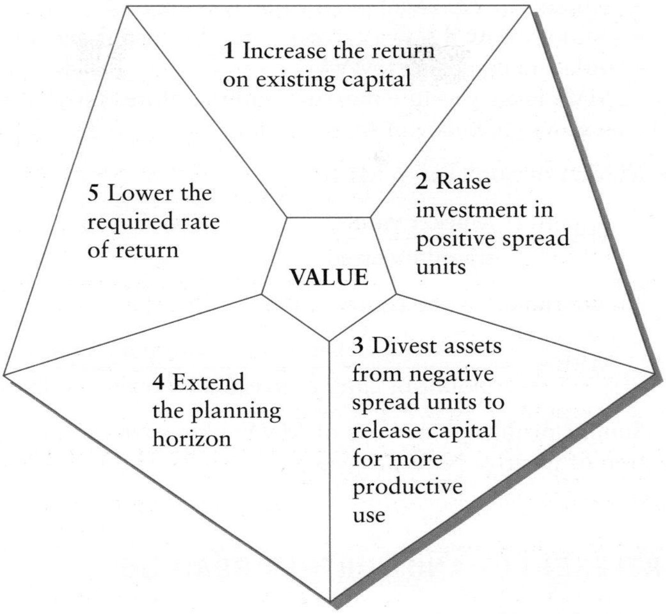

- **Total shareholder returns (TSR)**

Single period:

$$\text{TSR} = \frac{\text{Dividend per share} + (\text{share price at end of period} - \text{initial share price})}{\text{Initial share price}}$$

Multi-period:

Allow for intermediate dividends in an internal rate of return calculation.
- TSR is most useful when used in comparison with a benchmark of a peer group of firms or a market index;
- it is important to relate the TSR to risk class of share;
- a percentage return (eg. TSR) may not be as useful as an absolute return (e.g. MVA) in some circumstances;
- TSR is dependent on the time period chosen;
- Assumes stock market efficiency in pricing.

- **Market value added (MVA)**

MVA = Market value – capital

or, if market value of debt (and preference shares) equals book value of debt (and preference shares):

Equity MVA = Ordinary shares market value
– Capital supplied by ordinary shareholders

- **Problems with MVA:**
  - difficult to estimate the amount of cash invested;
  - difficult to establish when value was created;
  - do not know if a satisfactory rate of return is generated even with positive MVA;
  - inflation can distort MVA;
  - MVA is an absolute measure and therefore is biased in favour of larger firms;
  - assumes efficiency in share pricing.

- **Market to book ratio, MBR:**

$$\text{MBR} = \frac{\text{Market value}}{\text{Capital invested}}$$

An alternative is the equity MBR:

$$\text{MBR} = \frac{\text{Market value of ordinary shares}}{\text{Amount of capital invested by ordinary shareholders}}$$

Similar problems to those of MVA, plus over-reliance on MBR, can lead to the rejection of positive NPV projects.

REFERENCES AND FURTHER READING

Arnold, G.C. (2000) 'Tracing the development of value-based management', in G.C. Arnold and M. Davis, (eds), *Value-Based Management*. London: Wiley. More detail on the intellectual foundations of VBM.

Arnold, G.C. (2002) *Valuegrowth Investing*. London: Financial Times Prentice Hall. An investment book that considers corporate strategy and the potential for value creation.

Arnold G.C. and Davies, M (eds) (2000) *Value-Based Management*. London: Wiley. A collection of research monographs focuses on this emerging field.

Arnold, G.C. and Hatzopoulos, P.D. (2000) 'The theory-practice gap in capital budgeting: Evidence from the United Kingdom', *Journal of Business Finance & Accounting*, 27(5) and (6), June/July, pp. 603–26. Shows the extent of use of discounted cash flow analysis in UK companies.

Biddle, G. and Lindahl, F. (1982) 'Stock price reactions to LIFO adoptions: The association between excess returns and LIFO tax savings', *Journal of Accounting Research*, 20(2), Autumn, pp. 551–88. Share price movements are related to underlying cash flow changes and not to earnings figures.

Boston Consulting Group (1996) *Shareholder Value Metrics*. Shareholder Value Management Series. Builds on TSR to suggest some other value metrics.

Braxton Associates (1991) *The Fundamentals of Value Creation*. Insights: Braxton on Strategy. Boston, Mass: DRT International. Discusses accounting-based performance metrics and then goes on to describe a value-based metric, CFROI.

Braxton Associates (1993) *Managing for Value*. Insights: Braxton on Strategy. Boston, Mass: DRT International. The basics of value-based management are discussed.

Copeland, T., Koller, T. and Murrin, J. (1996) *Valuation*. 2nd edn. New York: Wiley. The management of value-based organisations and the principles behind the techniques are explained extremely well.

Cornelius, I. and Davies, M. (1997) *Shareholder Value*. London: Financial Times: Financial Publishing. An excellent account of value-based management and the metrics used.

Davies, M., Arnold, G.C., Cornelius, I. and Walmsey, S. (2000) *Managing For Shareholder Value*. London: Informa Publishing Group. An introductory overview of VBM.

Financial Times (Lex Column) (1996) 'Return on Investment', 7 May. Criticism of earnings and EPS figures as performance measures.

Hong, H., Kaplan, R. and Mandelker, G. (1978) 'Pooling vs. purchase: The effects of accounting for mergers on stock prices', *Accounting Review*, 53, January, pp. 31–47. Investors are not fooled by boosts to earnings caused by changes in accounting methods.

Investors Chronicle (1997) 'A week in the markets' 18 April, p. 10. The value destruction by T & N is discussed.

Jackson, T. (1997) 'A serving of added value', *Financial Times*, 13 January, p. 12. Considers MVA, EVA, VCQ and Realised Economic Value (REV), another value metric.

Jebb, F. (1997) 'Who's delivered the goods?', *Management Today*/William M. Mercer, March, pp. 48–52. Total shareholders' return rankings for the FTSE 350.

Knight, R.F. (1996) *Value Creation among Britain's Top 500 Companies*. The Oxford Executive Research Briefings. Oxford: Templeton College. A league table of the top 500 UK firms ranked by VCQ.

Lynn, A. (1995) 'Creating Wealth', *Sunday Times*, 10 December. Uses Stern Stewart's MVA figures to compare the value created by the UK companies.

Lynn, M. 'Creating value: The best and the worst', *Sunday Times*, 27 September 1998.

McConnell, J. and Muscarella, C. (1985) 'Corporate capital expenditure decisions and the market value of the firm', *Journal of Financial Economics*, March, pp. 399–422. Despite short-term earnings depression caused by high investment, firms' share prices perform well.

McTaggart, J.M., Kontes, P.W. and Mankins, M.C. (1994) *The Value Imperative*. New York: Free Press. A superb book showing the application of value-based techniques to strategy and other disciplines.

Myers, R. (1996) 'Keeping score: Metric wars', *CFO*, October, pp. 41–50. Describes the battle amongst rival consultancies to sell their value metrics.

Rappaport, A. (1998) *Creating Shareholder Value*. New York: Free Press. (Revised and updated version.) A landmark book. Presents an important value metric – shareholders' value analysis (SVA).

Reimann, B.C. (1989) *Managing for Value*. Oxford: Basil Blackwell. Useful because it brings together strategy and value.

Rushe, D. (2000) 'Winners and losers in the drive to add value', *Sunday Times*, 24 September 2000. Market Value Added statistics shown for the largest 200 UK firms.

Stern Stewart and Co (1995) 'Creating wealth', *Sunday Times*, 10 December.

Stewart, G.B. (1991) *The Quest for Value*. New York: Harper Business. Written by a founding partner in Stern Stewart and Co., the US consultancy which has so successfully promoted MVA and EVA. Some useful insights.

Watts, R. (1986) 'Does it pay to manipulate E.P.S.?', in J.M. Stern and D.M. Chew (eds), *Revolution in Corporate Finance*. Oxford: Blackwell. 'The stock market is not systematically misled by accounting changes'.

SELF-REVIEW QUESTIONS

1 In what ways are accounting-based performance measures inadequate for guiding managerial decisions?

2 Define value-based management.

3 What are the four key drivers of shareholder value creation?

4 What are the five actions available to increase value?

5 Describe at least three arguments for managers putting shareholder wealth maximisation as the firm's objective.

6 Invent a mission statement and strategic objectives which comply with value-based management principles.

7 Outline the evidence against the popular view that shareholders judge managerial performance on the basis of short-term earnings figures.

8 What is 'good growth' and what is 'bad growth'?

9 In what circumstances would you reduce investment in a strategic business unit even if its profits are on a rising trend?

10 What is total shareholder return (TSR) and what are its advantages and problems as a metric of shareholder wealth creation?

11 Describe market value added (MVA) and note the problems in its practical use.

12 Outline the market-to-book ratio (MBR) and state why it is superior to MVA for some purposes.

QUESTIONS AND PROBLEMS

1 (*Examination level*) 'Thirty years ago we measured the success of our divisional managers on the basis of market share growth, sales and profits. In the late 1970s we switched to return on capital employed because the old system did not take account of the amount of capital invested to achieve growth targets. Now you are telling me that we have to change again to value-based performance metrics. Why?' Explain in the form of an essay to this chief executive what advantages value-based management has over other approaches.

2 Describe three of the ways in which accounts can be manipulated and distorted.

3 Gather some more data on T & N, GSK, and P&O from newspapers, industry sources, annual reports, etc. and give a more detailed account than that given in this chapter of the ways in which value was created or destroyed.

4 Shareholder value management has been described as a 'weird Anglo-American concept'. Describe this philosophy and consider whether it has applicability outside the Anglo-American world.

5 Do you feel comfortable with the notion that commercial organisations acting in a competitive environment should put shareholders' wealth creation as their first priority? If not, why not? Explain your reasoning.

6 'EPS (earnings per share) is not a holy grail in determining how well a company is performing': Lex column of the *Financial Times*, 7 May 1996. Describe and explain the reasons for dissatisfaction with eps for target setting and increasing performance.

7* Which of the following two companies creates most value, assuming that they are making the same initial investment?

Company A's projected profits

Year	*Profit (£000s)*
Last year	1,000
1	1,000
2	1,100
3	1,200
4	1,400
5	1,600
6 and all subsequent years	1,800

Company B's projected profits

Year	*Profit (£000s)*
Last year	1,000
1	1,000
2	1,080
3	1,160
4	1,350
5	1,500
6 and all subsequent years	1,700

Profits for both companies are 20 per cent of sales in each year. With company A, for every £1 increase in sales 7p has to be devoted to additional debtors because of the generous credit terms granted to customers. For B, only 1p is needed for additional investment in debtors for every £1 increase in sales. Higher sales also mean greater inventory levels at each firm. This is 6p and 2p for every extra £1 in sales for A and B respectively.

Apart from the debtor and inventory adjustments the profit figures of both firms reflect their cash flows. The cost of capital for both firms is 14 per cent.

8 Ready plc is financed entirely by equity capital with a required return of 13 per cent. Ready's business is such that as sales increase, working capital does not change. Under current policy, post-tax earnings of £10m per year are expected to continue indefinitely. All earnings are paid out as dividends in the year of occurrence.

Calculate

a The value of the company under this policy.

b The value of the company if the current dividend (time 0) is missed and the retained earnings are put into investments yielding an extra £2m per year to infinity in addition to the current policy's earnings. What happens to earnings and cash flow? Is this good or bad investment?

c The value of the company if half of the current dividend is missed and the retained earnings are put into investment yielding £0.5m per year to infinity. What happens to earnings and cash flows? Is this good or bad investment?

9 What is the annual value creation of Sheaf plc which has an investment level of £300,000 and produces a rate of return of 19 per cent per annum compared with a required rate of return of 13 per cent?
What is the performance spread?
Assuming that the planning horizon for Sheaf plc is 12 years, calculate the value of the firm. (Assume the investment level is constant throughout.)

10* Busy plc, an all equity-financed firm, has three strategic business units. The polythene division has capital of £8m and is expected to produce returns of 11 per cent for the next five years. Thereafter it will produce returns equal to the required rate of return for this risk level of 14 per cent. The paper division has an investment level of £12m and a planning horizon of 10 years. During the planning horizon it will produce a return of 22 per cent compared with a risk-adjusted required rate of return of 15 per cent. The cotton division uses £2m of capital, has a planning horizon of seven years and a required rate of return of 16 per cent compared with the anticipated actual rate of 17 per cent over the first seven years.

a Calculate the value of the firm.

b Draw a value-creation and strategic business unit performance spread chart.

c Develop five ideas for increasing the value of the firm. State your assumptions.

11 Tear plc has not paid a dividend for 20 years. The current share price is 580p and the current index level is 3,100. Calculate total shareholder returns for **a** the past three years, **b** the past five years and **c** the past ten years, given the following data:

Time before present	*Share price (pence)*	*Share index*
1 year	560	3,000
2 years	550	2,400
3 years	600	2,500
4 years	500	2,000
5 years	450	1,850
6 years	400	1,700
7 years	250	1,300
8 years	170	1,500
9 years	130	1,300
10 years	125	1,000

Comment on the problems of total shareholders' returns as a metric for judging managerial performance.

12* Sity plc has paid out all earnings as dividends since it was founded with £15m of equity finance 25 years ago. Today its shares are valued on the stock market at £90m and its long-term debt has a market value and book value of £20m.

a How much market value added (MVA) has Sity produced?

b What is Sity's market to book ratio (MBR)?

c Given that another company, Pity plc, was founded with £15m of equity capital five years ago and has paid out all earnings since its foundation and is now worth (equity and debt) £110m (£90m equity, £20m debt), discuss the problems of using MVA and MBR for inter-firm comparison.

ASSIGNMENTS

1 Using data on a company you know well try to calculate TSR, MVA and MBR. Point out the difficult judgements you have had to make to calculate these figures.

2 Apply the four key elements of value creation, the 'expand or not to expand?' model and the value action pentagon to a firm you are familiar with. Write a report for senior executives.

CHAPTER NOTES

1 Quoted in *Investors Chronicle*, 26 July 1996, p. 20.

2 *Investors Chronicle*, 18 April 1997, p. 10.

3 *Investors Chronicle*, 31 January 1997, p. 16.

4 This conclusion is based on evidence from R.F. Knight (1996), Stern Stewart and Co (1995) and *Sunday Times*, 27 September 1998, 'Creating value: the best and the worst'. The basis of the calculation is described later in the chapter.

5 *Financial Times*, 7 May 1996, Lex column.

6 Rappaport (1998) and Cornelius and Davies (1997) go into more detail on these issues.

7 A ten-year annuity of £1,113,288 per year for a £10m investment at time 0 has an effective annual rate of return of about 2 per cent.

8 *Financial Times*, 7 May 1996, Lex column.

9 For example see: Copeland *et al.* (1996), p. 80 where PE ratios in 1991 are shown to have little relation to eps growth between 1987 and 1991, and McConnell and Muscarella's (1985) study of the effect on share prices of announcements of major capital expenditures between 1975 and 1981: short-term earnings are depressed but share prices rise due to higher longer-term cash flows.

10 That the market is generally not fooled by the employment of accounting techniques to improve the appearance of earnings has been shown by Biddle and Lindahl (1982), who showed that the market was able to see through attempts to raise earnings by changing the inventory valuation method, and by Hong, Kaplan and Mandelker (1978), who found the market unresponsive to changes in the method of accounting for mergers. Watts (1986) states that manipulating reported earnings through accounting changes to increase the corporation stock prices will in most cases be a futile exercise.

11 Source: *Sunday Times*, 27 September 1998, 'Creating value: the best and the worst'.

12 A weighted average of the required returns for the toy and clothing divisions.

13 George Graham, 'HSBC's new guiding light aims to outshine peer group', *Financial Times*, 23 February 1999, p. 25.

14 Nikki Tait, 'Ford aims to slash $1bn from cash base this year', *Financial Times*, 8 January 1999, p. 17.

15 Dividend policy and its effect on value are considered in Chapter 19.

16 Alistair Blair, *Management Today*, January 1997, p. 44.

Chapter 16

MANAGING A VALUE-BASED COMPANY AND THE COST OF CAPITAL

INTRODUCTION

The transforming of a corporation from one which is earnings based to one which is focused on value has profound effects on almost all aspects of organisational life. New light is cast on the most appropriate portfolio of businesses making up the firm, and on the strategic thrust of individual business units. Acquisition and divestment strategies may be modified to put shareholder wealth creation at centre stage. Capital structure and dividend policy are predicated on the optimal approach from the shareholders' point of view, not by 'safety first' or earnings growth considerations. Performance measures, target setting and managerial compensation become linked to the extent that wealth is created rather than the vagaries of accounting numbers.

To unite the organisation in pursuit of wealth creation an enormous educational and motivational challenge has to be met. A culture change is often required to ensure that goals at all levels are set to ensure that congruence around value is achieved. Retraining and new reward systems are needed to help lift eyes from the short term to long-term achievements.

This chapter gives a taste of the pervading nature of value-based managerial thinking. Later chapters consider some specific aspects of finance such as the debt–equity ratio debate, dividend policy and mergers. First we provide an overview of value management and this is followed by a discussion of metrics which can be employed for internal decision making. Then we look in more detail at the calculation of the required rate of return, which has been used throughout the book so far, but without an explanation of where it comes from.

Learning objectives

By the end of this chapter the reader will be able to:

- explain the extent of the ramifications of value-based management;
- describe, explain and use shareholder value analysis and economic profit analysis (including EVA);
- explain the calculation of the cost of equity, debt and preference share capital, and calculate a weighted average cost of capital for a firm.

AN OVERVIEW OF THE APPLICATION OF THE VALUE PRINCIPLES

Exhibit 16.1 summarises some of the most important areas where value-based management impacts on the firm. To describe them all fully would require a book as long as this one, so only a short discussion of some of the most important points is given.

The firm's objective

The firm has first to decide what it is that is to be maximised and what will merely be satisficed. In value management the maximisation of sales, market share, employee satisfaction, customer service excellence, and so on, are rejected as the objective of the firm. All of these are important and there are levels of achievement for each which are desirable in so far as they help the achievement of maximising shareholder wealth, but they are not *the* objective. It is important that there is clarity over the purpose of the firm and crystal-clear guiding principles for managers making strategic and operational decisions. Objectives stated in terms of a vague balance of interests are not appropriate for a commercial organisation in a competitive environment. The goal of maximising discounted cash flows to shareholders brings simplicity and direction to decision making.

Strategic business unit management

A strategic business unit (SBU) is a business unit within the overall corporate entity which is distinguishable from other business units because it serves a defined external market in which management can conduct strategic planning in relation to products and markets.

Large corporations often have a number of SBUs which each require strategic thought and planning. Put simply, this means selecting which product or market areas to enter/exit and how to ensure a good competitive position in those markets/products. This requires a consideration of issues such as price, service level, quality, product features, methods of distribution, etc.

The managers of an SBU are the individuals who come into regular contact with customers in the competitive market environment and it is important that SBU strategy be developed largely by those managers who will be responsible for its execution. By doing this, by harnessing these managers' knowledge and encouraging their commitment through a sense of 'ownership' of a strategy the firm is more likely to prosper.

Before the creation of new strategic options it is advisable to carry out a review of the value creation of the present strategy. This can be a complex task but an example will demonstrate one approach. Imagine that the plastic products division of Red plc is a defined strategic business unit with a separable strategic planning ability servicing markets distinct from Red's other SBUs. This division sells three categories of product, A, B and C to five types of customer, (a) UK consumers, (b) UK industrial users, (c) UK government, (d) European Union consumers and (e) other overseas consumers. Information has been provided showing the value expected to be created from each of the product/market categories based on current strategy. These are shown in Exhibits 16.2 and 16.3.

Product line C is expected to destroy shareholder value while absorbing a substantial share of the SBU's resources. Likewise this analysis has identified sales to UK industry and government as detrimental to the firm's wealth. This sort of finding is not unusual: many businesses have acceptable returns at the aggregate level but hidden behind these figures are value-destructive areas of activity. The analysis could be made even more revealing by showing the returns available for each product and market category; for

Exhibit 16.1 Value management principles influence most aspects of management

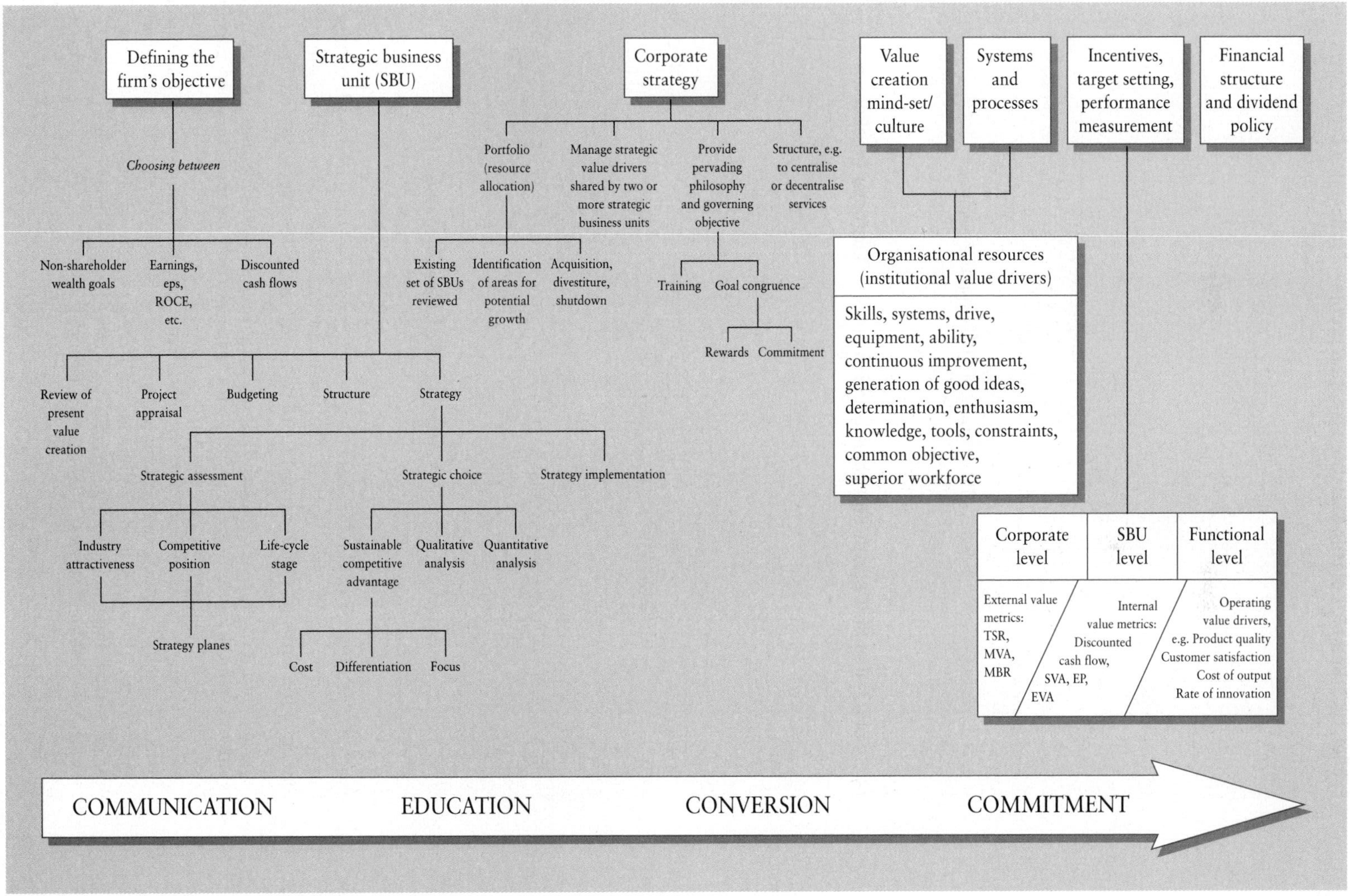

Exhibit 16.2 Red plc's plastic SBU value creation profile – Product line breakdown

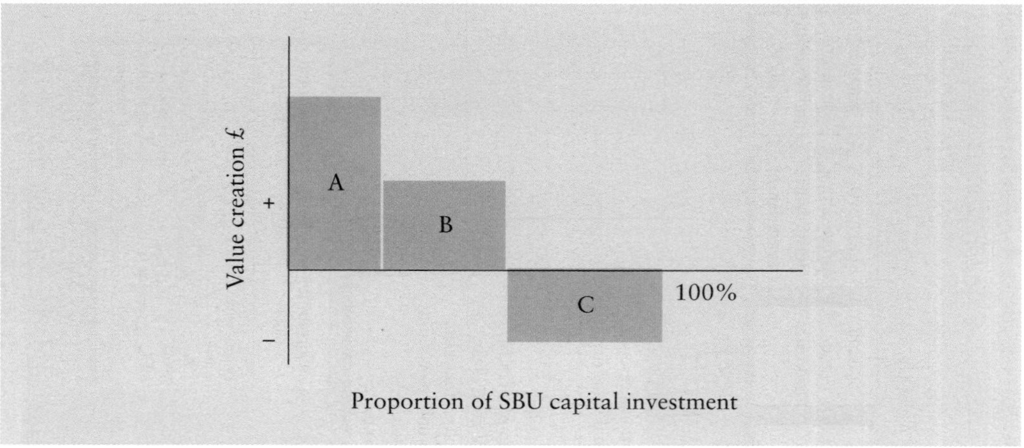

Exhibit 16.3 Red plc's plastic SBU value creation profile – Customer breakdown

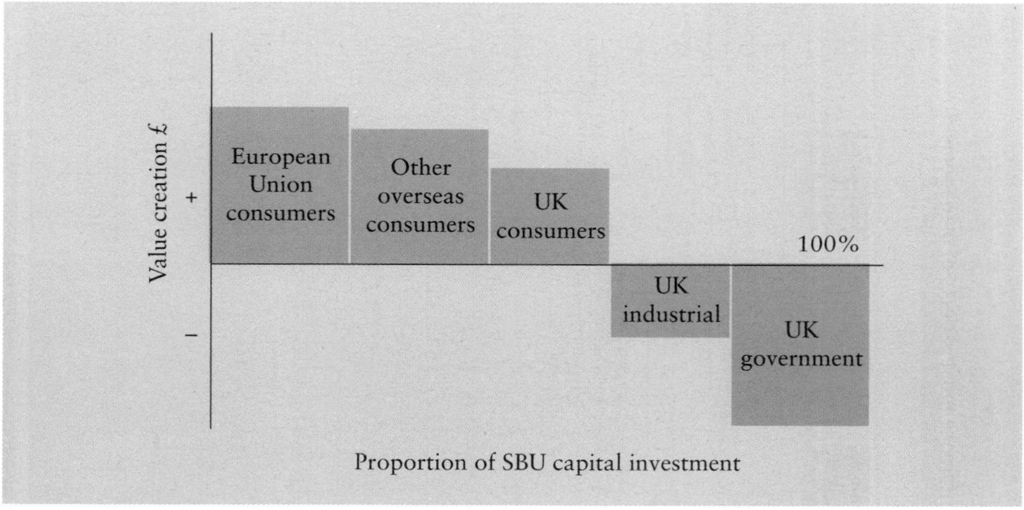

example, product A in the UK consumer market can be compared with product A in the European market. Warren Buffett, the financier, has made some pithy comments on the tendency for firms to fail to identify and root out value-destructive activities:

> Many corporations that consistently show good returns both on equity and on overall incremental capital have, indeed, employed a large portion of their retained earnings on an economically unattractive, even disastrous, basis. Their marvellous core businesses, however, whose earnings grow year after year, camouflage repeated failures in capital allocation elsewhere (usually involving high-priced acquisitions of businesses that have inherently mediocre economics). The managers at fault periodically report on the lessons they have learned from the latest disappointment. They then usually seek out future lessons. (Failure seems to go to their heads.) (Berkshire Hathaway 1984 Annual Report.)

Project appraisal, budgeting systems and the organisational structure of each SBU must be in harmony with the principle of value-based management. Project appraisal will be carried out using discounted cash flow techniques. Budgeting will not rely solely on accounting considerations, but will have value-based metrics (methods of measurement). The lines of decision-making authority and communication will be the most appropriate given the market environment in order to achieve greatest returns. For example in a dynamic unpredictable market setting it is unwise to have a bureaucratic, hierarchical type structure with decision making concentrated at the top of long chains of command. Devolved power and responsibility are likely to produce a more flexible response to change in the market-place, and initiative with self-reliance are to be highly prized and rewarded.

Strategy for SBUs

Strategic analysis can be seen as having three parts.[1]

1 ***Strategic assessment*** – in which the external environment and the internal resources and capability are analysed to form a view on the key influences on the value-creating potential of the organisation.
2 ***Strategic choice*** – in which strategic options are developed and evaluated.
3 ***Strategic implementation*** – action will be needed in areas such as changes in organisational structure and systems as well as resource planning, motivation and commitment.

Strategic assessment

There are three primary strategic determinants of value creation.

1 Industry attractiveness

The economics of the market for the product(s) have an enormous influence on the profitability of a firm. In some industries firms have few competitors, and there is low customer buying power, low supplier bargaining power and little threat from new entrants or the introduction of substitute products. Here the industry is likely to be attractive in terms of the returns accruing to the existing players, which will on average exhibit a positive performance spread. Other product markets are plagued with overcapacity, combined with a reluctance on the part of the participants to quit and apply resources in another product market. Prices are kept low by the ability of customers and suppliers to 'put the squeeze on' and by the availability of very many close-substitute products. Markets of this kind tend to produce negative performance spreads.[2]

2 Competitive resource strength

Identifying a good industry is only the first step. Value-based companies aim to beat the average rates of return on capital employed. To beat the averages, companies need something special. That something special comes from the bundle of resources that the firm possesses. Most of the resources are ordinary. That is, they give the firm competitive parity. However, the firm may be able to exploit one or two extraordinary resources – those that give a competitive edge. An extraordinary resource is one which, when combined with other (ordinary) resources enables the firm to outperform competitors and create new value-generating opportunities. Critical extraordinary resources determine what a firm can do successfully. It is the ability to generate value for customers that is crucial for superior returns. High shareholder returns are determined by the firm either being able to offer the same benefits to customers as competitors, but at a lower price; or being able to offer unique benefits that more than outweigh the associated higher price. Ordinary resources provide a threshold competence. They are vital to ensure a company's survival. In the food retail business, for example, most firms have a threshold competence in basic activities, such as purchasing, human resource management, accounting control and store layout. However, the large chains have resources that set them apart from the small stores: they are able to obtain lower-cost supplies because of their enormous buying power; they can exploit economies of scale in advertising and in the range of produce offered.

Despite the large retailers having these advantages it is clear that small stores have survived, and some produce very high returns on capital invested. These superior firms provide value to the customer significantly above cost. Some corner stores have a different set of extraordinary resources compared with the large groups: personal friendly service could be valued highly; opening at times convenient to customers could lead to acceptance of a premium price; the location may make shopping less hassle than traipsing to an out-of-town hypermarket. The large chains find emulation of these qualities expensive. If they were to try and imitate the small store they could end up losing their main competitive advantages, the most significant of which is low cost.

The extraordinary resources possessed by the supermarket chains as a group when compared with small shops are not necessarily extraordinary resources in the competitive rivalry *between* the chains. If the focus is shifted to the 'industry' of supermarket chains factors like economies of scale may merely give competitive parity – scale is needed for survival. Competitive advantage is achieved through the development of other extraordinary resources, such as the quality of the relationship with suppliers, a very sophisticated system for collecting data on customers combined with target marketing, ownership of the best sites. However, even these extraordinary resources will not give superior competitive position forever. Many of these can be imitated. Long-term competitive advantage may depend on the capabilities of the management team to continually innovate and thereby shift the ground from under the feet of competitors. The extraordinary resource is then the coherence, attitude, intelligence, knowledge and drive of the managers in the organisational setting.

Many successful companies have stopped seeing themselves as bundles of product lines and businesses. Instead they look at the firm as a collection of resources. This helps to explain the logic behind some companies going into apparently unconnected product areas. The connection is the exploitation of extraordinary resources. So, for example, Honda has many different product areas: motor boat engines, automobiles, motorcycles, lawn mowers and electric generators. These are sold through different distribution channels in completely different ways to different customers. The common root for all these products is Honda's extraordinary resource which led to a superior ability to produce engines. Likewise, photocopiers, cameras and image scanners are completely different product sectors and sold in different ways. Yet, they are all made by Canon – which has extraordinary capabilities and knowledge of optics, imaging and microprocessor controls.

The analyst should not be looking for a long list of extraordinary resources in any one firm. If one can be found, that is good – it only takes one to leap ahead of competitors and produce super-normal returns. If two are found then that is excellent. It is very unusual to come across a company that has three or more extraordinary resources.

Coca-Cola is an exception with an extraordinary brand, a distribution system with connected relationships and highly knowledgeable managers. To assist the thorough analysis of a company's extraordinary resource I have developed the TRRACK system. This classifies extraordinary resources into six categories – *see* Exhibit 16.4.

Exhibit 16.4 The TRRACK system

T	Tangible
R	Relationships
R	Reputation
A	Attitude
C	Capabilities
K	Knowledge

Notice that the vast majority of extraordinary resources are intangible. They are qualities that are carried within the individuals that make up organisations, or are connected with the interaction between individuals. They are usually developed over a long time rather than bought. These qualities cannot be scientifically evaluated to provide objective quantification. Despite our inability to be precise it is usually the case that these people-embodied factors are the most important drivers of value creation and we must pay most attention to them.

- ***Tangible*** Occasionally physical resources provide a sustainable competitive advantage. These are assets that can be physically observed and are often valued (or misvalued) in a balance sheet. They include real estate, materials, production facilities and patents. They can be purchased, but if they were easily purchased they would cease to be extraordinary because all competitors would go out and buy. There must be some barrier preventing other firms from acquiring the same or similar assets for them to be truly valuable in the long run. In many countries the dominant, usually previously state-owned, telephone company has a valuable physical resource in the copper wire linking up millions of houses and businesses. It would be uneconomic for a competitor to replicate such a network (however, this advantage is being eroded as alternative telecommunication systems are developed, e.g. cable, mobile phones). Microsoft's ownership of its operating system and other standards within the software industry gives it a competitive edge. McDonald's makes sure that it takes the best locations on the busiest highways, rather than settle for obscure secondary roads. Many smaller businesses have found themselves, or have made smart moves to ensure they are, the owners of valuable real estate adjacent to popular tourist sites. Pharmaceutical companies, such as Merck, own valuable patents giving some protection against rivalry – at least temporarily. The port in Hong Kong owned by Hutchinson Whampoa has the extraordinary resource of being the major entry and exit point for goods in the region.
- ***Relationships*** Over time companies can form valuable relationships with individuals and organisations that are difficult or impossible for a potential competitor to emulate. Relationships in business can be of many kinds. The least important are the contractual ones. The most important are informal or implicit. These relationships are usually based on a trust that has grown over many years. The terms of the implicit contract are enforced by the parties themselves rather than through the court

– a loss of trust can be immensely damaging. It is in all the parties' interests to co-operate with integrity because there is the expectation of reiteration leading to the sharing of collective value created over a long period. South African Breweries (SAB) has 98 per cent, of the beer market in South Africa. It has kept out foreign and domestic competitors because of its special relationships with suppliers and customers. It is highly profitable, and yet, for the last two decades it has reduced prices every year – the price of beer has halved in real terms. Most of South Africa's roads are poor and electricity supplies are intermittent. To distribute its beer it has formed some strong relationships. The truck drivers, many of whom are former employees, are helped to set up their small trucking businesses by SAB. *Shebeens* sell most of the beer. These are unlicensed pubs. Often, they are tiny – no more than a few benches. SAB cannot sell directly to the illegal *shebeens*. Instead it maintains an informal relationship via a system of wholesalers. SAB makes sure that distributors have refrigerators and, if necessary, generators. A new entrant to the market would have to develop its own special relationship with truck drivers, wholesalers and retailers. In all likelihood it would have to establish a completely separate and parallel system of distribution. Even then it would lack the legitimacy that comes with a long-standing relationship. Relationships between employees, and between employees and the firm, can give a competitive edge. Some firms seem to possess a culture that creates wealth through the co-operation and dynamism of the employees. Information is shared, knowledge is developed, innovative activity flows, rapid response to market change is natural and respect for all pervades. The quality of the relationships with government can be astonishingly important to a company. Many the defence contractors concentrate enormous resources to ensure a special relationship with various organs of government. The biggest firms often attract the best ex-government people to take up directorships or to head liaison with the government department. Their contacts and knowledge of the inside workings of purchasing decisions, with the political complications, can be very valuable. A similar logic often applies to pharmaceutical companies, airlines and regulated companies.

- ***Reputation*** Reputations are normally made over a long period. Once a good reputation is established it can be a source of very high returns (assuming that all the necessary ordinary resources are in place to support it). Sony's reputation gives it the edge in the minds of consumers. The Sony offer carries more than a similar offer by a company with an obscure brand. With car hire in a foreign country the consumer is unable to assess quality in advance. Hertz provide certification for local traders under a franchise arrangement. These local car hirers would see no benefit to providing an above-average service without the certification of Hertz because they would not be able to charge a premium price.[3] It is surprising how much more consumers are willing to pay for the assurance of reliable and efficient car hire when they travel abroad compared with the hiring of a car from an unfranchised local. Companies pay a large premium to hire Goldman Sachs when contemplating an issue of securities or a merger. They are willing to pay for 'emotional reassurance'.[4] The CEO cannot be sure of the outcome of the transaction. If it were to fail the penalty would be high – executives may lose bonuses, and, perhaps their jobs, shareholders lose money. The CEO therefore hires the best that is available for such once-in-a-lifetime moves. The cost of this hand-holding is secondary. Once an adviser has a history of flawless handling of large and complex transactions it can offer a much more effective 'emotional comfort-blanket'[5] to CEOs than smaller rivals. This principle may apply to pension fund advisers, management consultants and advertising agencies as well as top investment bankers. Branding is designed to represent and enhance reputations.

- *Attitude* Attitude refers to the mentality of the organisation. It is the prevalent outlook. It is the way in which the organisation views and relates to the world. Terms such as disposition, will and culture are closely connected with attitude.[6] Every sports coach is aware of the importance of attitude. The team may consist of players with the best technique in the business or with a superb knowledge of the game, they may be the fastest and the most skilful, but without a winning attitude they will not succeed. There must be a will to win. Attitude can become entrenched within an organisation. It is difficult to shake off a negative attitude. A positive attitude can provide a significant competitive edge. Some firms develop a winning mentality based on a culture of innovation, others are determinedly orientated towards customer satisfaction while some companies are quality driven. 3M, has a pervasive attitude of having a go. Testing out wild ideas is encouraged. Employees are given time to follow up a dreamed-up innovation, and they are not criticized for failing. Innovations such as 'Post-it' notes have flowed from this attitude. Canon has the attitude of *Tsushin* – 'heart-to-heart and mind-to-mind communication' between the firm and its customers. In this way trust is developed.
- *Capabilities* Capabilities are derived from the company's ability to undertake a set of tasks. The term skill can be used to refer to a narrow activity or a single task. Capability is used for the combination of a number of skills.[7] For example, a company's capability base could include abilities in narrow areas such as market research, innovative design and efficient manufacturing that, when combined, result in a superior capability in new product development. Some firms have a superior ability to efficiently produce value for the customer. A capability is more than the sum of the individual processes – the combination and co-ordination of individual processes may provide an extraordinary resource. Sony developed a capability in miniaturisation. This enabled it to produce a string of products from the Walkman to the Playstation.
- *Knowledge* Knowledge is the awareness of information, and its interpretation, organisation, synthesis and prioritisation, to provide insights and understanding. The retention, exploitation and sharing of knowledge can be extremely important in the achievement and maintenance of competitive advantage. All firms in an industry share basic knowledge. For example, all publishers have some knowledge of market trends, distribution techniques and printing technology. It is not this common knowledge that I am referring to in the context of extraordinary resources. If a publisher builds up data and skills in understanding a particular segment of the market, say investments books, then its superior awareness, interpretation, organisation, synthesis, and prioritisation of information can create competitive advantage through extraordinary knowledge. The company will have greater insight than rivals into this segment of the market. There are two types of organisational knowledge. The first, *explicit* knowledge, can be formalised and passed on in codified form. This is objective knowledge that can be defined and documented. The second, *tacit* knowledge, is ill-defined or undefined. It is subjective, personal and context specific. It is fuzzy and complex. It is hard to formalise and communicate. Examples of explicit knowledge include costing procedures written in company accounting manuals, formal assessment of market demand, customer complaint data and classification. Explicit knowledge is unlikely to provide competitive advantage: if it is easily defined and codified it is likely to be available to rivals. Tacit knowledge, on the other hand, is very difficult for rivals to obtain. Consider the analogy of a baseball: explicit knowledge of tactics is generally available; what separates the excellent from the ordinary player is the application of tacit knowledge, e.g. what becomes an instinctive ability to recognise types of pitches and the appropriate response to them. Tacit knowledge is

transmitted by doing, the main means of transferring knowledge from one individual to another is through close interaction to build understanding, as in the master-apprentice relationship.

For more detail on competitive resource analysis consult Chapter 11 of Arnold (2002).

3 Life-cycle stage of value potential

A competitive advantage in an attractive industry will not lead to superior long-term performance unless it provides a *sustainable* competitive advantage and the economics of the industry *remain* favourable. Rival firms will be attracted to an industry in which the participants enjoy high returns and sooner or later competitive advantage is usually whittled away. The longevity of the competitive advantage can be represented in terms of a life cycle with four stages: development, growth, maturity and decline (*see* Exhibit 16.5). In the development phase during which competitive advantage (and often the industry) is established perhaps through technological or service innovation, the sales base will be small. As demand increases a growth phase is entered in which competitive strength is enhanced by factors such as industry leadership, brand strength and patent rights. A lengthy period of competitive advantage and high return can be expected. Eventually the sources of advantage are removed, perhaps by competitor imitation, or by customers and suppliers gaining in bargaining power. Other possibilities pushing towards the maturity stage are technological breakthroughs by competitors able to offer a superior product, or poor management leading to a loss of grip on cost control. Whatever the reason for the reduction in the performance spread, the firm now faces a choice of three routes, two of which can lead to a repositioning on the life cycle; the third is to enter a period of negative performance spreads. The two positive actions are (**a**) to erect barriers to the entry of firms to the industry, and (**b**) to continually innovate and improve the SBU's product offering so as to stay one step ahead of the competitors. An example of the simultaneous use of those two actions is provided by Microsoft, able to dominate the operating software market and the application market via close working relationships with hardware producers and continual innovation. But even Microsoft will find its business units eventually fall into a terminal decline phase of value creation because of a loss of competitive advantage. When it does, even though it will be extremely difficult for it to do so, the

Exhibit 16.5 The life-cycle stages of value creation

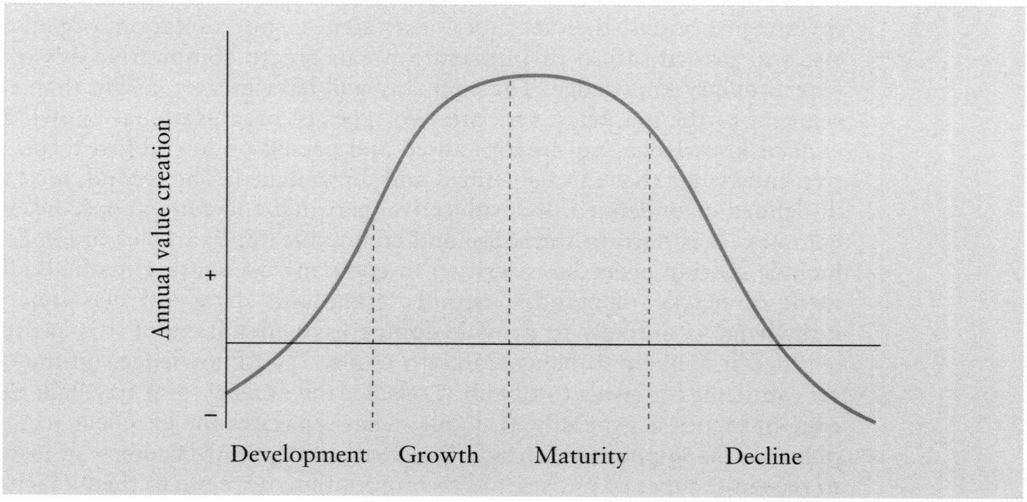

Exhibit 16.6 Strategy planes

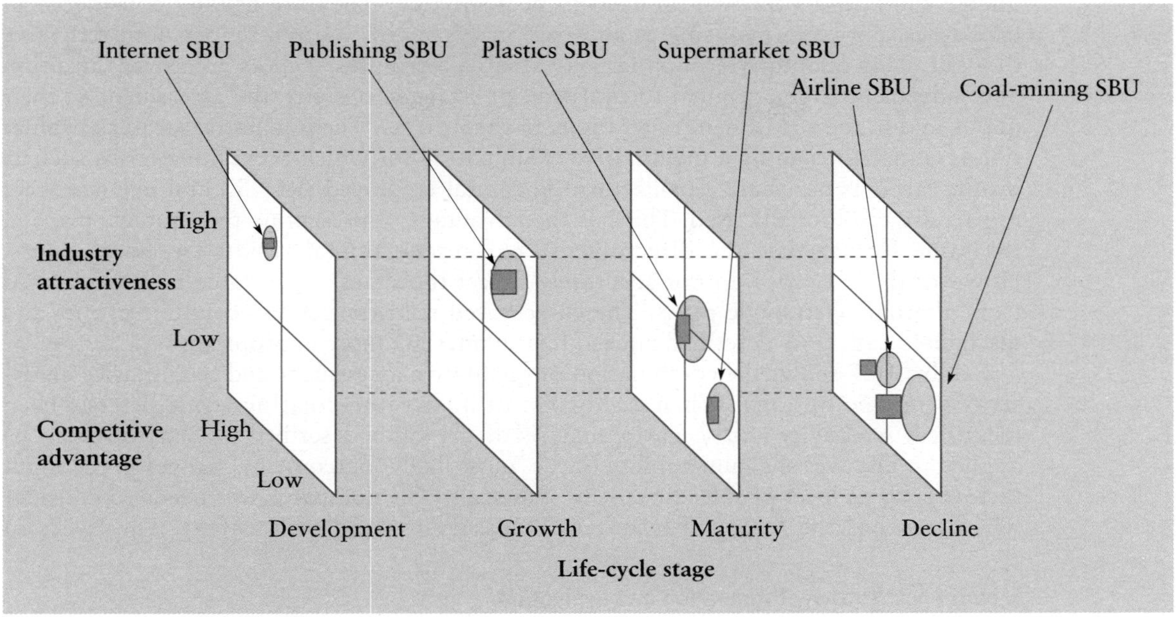

Note: The size of the circle represents the proportion of the firm's assets devoted to this SBU. The size of the rectangle represents the current performance spread. If the spread is negative it is shown outside the circle.

company must withdraw from value-destructive activities and plough the capital retrieved into positive performance-spread SBUs.

The three elements of strategic assessment can be summarised on a strategic planes chart like the one shown in Exhibit 16.6 for Red plc which, besides the plastics SBU, also has a young Internet games division, a coal-mining subsidiary, a publishing group with valuable long-term copyrights on dozens of best sellers, a supermarket chain subject to increasingly intense competition in an over-supplied market and a small airline company with an insignificant market share.

The strategy planes can be used at the SBU level or can be redrawn for product/customer segments within SBUs.

Strategic choice

Managers need to consider a wide array of potential strategic options. The process of systematic search for alternative market product entry/exit and competitive approaches is a vital one. The objective of such a search is to find competitive advantage in attractive markets sustainable over an extended period of time yielding positive performance spreads.

Michael Porter suggests that there are three ways in which firms can achieve sustainable competitive advantage:

- *A cost leadership strategy* – a standard no-frills product. The emphasis here is on scale economies or other cost advantages.
- *A differentiation strategy* – the uniqueness of the product/service offering allows for a premium price to be charged.
- *A focus strategy* – the selection of a segment in the industry to serve to the exclusion of others.

Once a sufficiently wide-ranging search for possible strategic directions has been conducted the options thrown up need to be evaluated. They are usually considered in broad descriptive terms using qualitative analysis with written reports and reflective thought. This qualitative thinking has valuable attributes such as creativity, intuition and judgement in the original formulation of strategic options, the assessment of their merits and in the subsequent reiterations of the process. The qualitative strategy evaluation is complemented by a quantitative examination for which accounting terms such as profit, earnings per share (eps), return on capital employed (ROCE) and balance sheet impact are traditionally used. This has the advantage of presenting the strategic plans in the same format that the directors use to present annual results to shareholders. However these metrics do not accurately reflect the shareholder value to be generated from alternative strategic plans. The value-based metrics such as economic profits and discounted cash flow described later in this chapter are more appropriate.

Exhibit 16.7 shows the combination of qualitative assessment and quantitative analysis of strategic options. When a shortlist of high-value-creating strategies has been identified, sensitivity and scenario analysis of the kinds described in Chapter 6 can be applied to discover the vulnerability of the 'most likely' outcome to changes in the input factors such as level of sales or cost of materials. The company also needs to consider whether it has the financial resources necessary to fund the strategy. The issues of

Exhibit 16.7 Strategy formulation and evaluation

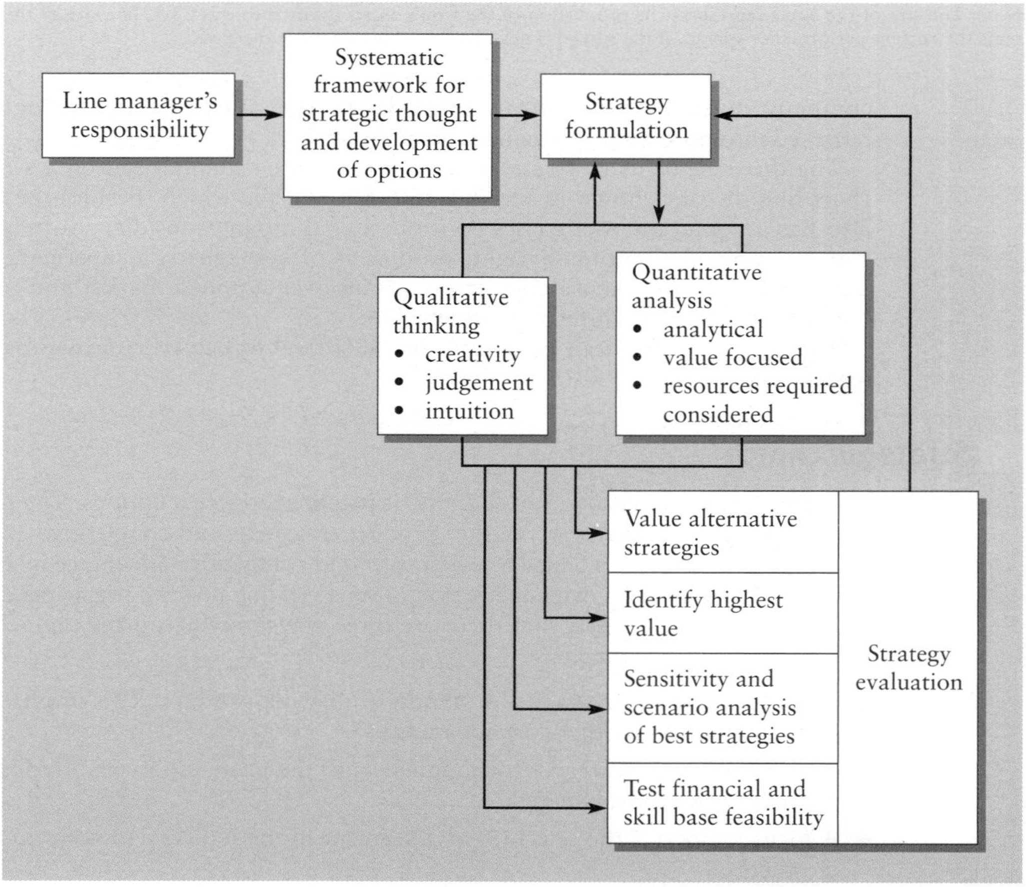

finance raising, debt levels and dividend policy come into the equation at this point. Other aspects of feasibility include whether the organisation has the skill base necessary to provide the required quality of product or service, whether it is able to gain access to the required technology, materials, or services and so on.

Strategy implementation

Making the chosen strategy work requires the planned allocation of resources and the reorganisation and motivation of people. Changing the firm to value-based principles has an impact on these implementation issues. Resources are to be allocated to units or functions if it can be shown that this part of the organisation will contribute to value creation after taking into account the resources used. Managers are given responsibilities and targets set in accordance with value creation.

Corporate strategy

In a value-based company the role of the corporate centre (head office) has four main aspects:

1. ***Portfolio planning*** – allocating resources to those SBUs and product and/or customer areas offering the greatest value creation while withdrawing capital from those destroying value.
2. ***Managing strategic value drivers shared by two or more SBUs*** – these crucial organisational capabilities, giving the firm competitive advantage, may need to be centrally managed or at least co-ordinated by the centre to achieve the maximum benefit. An example here could be strong brand management or technological knowledge. The head office needs to ensure adequate funding of these and to achieve full, but not over-exploitation.
3. ***Provide the pervading philosophy and governing objective*** – training, goal setting, employee rewards and the engendering of commitment are all focused on shareholder value. A strong lead from the centre is needed to avoid conflict, drift and vagueness.
4. ***The overall structure of the organisation*** needs to be appropriate for the market environment and designed to build value. Roles and responsibilities are clearly defined with clear accountability for value creation.

We can apply the principles of portfolio planning to Red plc. The corporate centre could encourage and work with the plastics division in developing ideas for reducing or eliminating the value losses being made on some of its products and markets. Once these have been fully evaluated head office could ensure that resources and other services are provided to effectively implement the chosen strategy. For example, if the highest value-creating option is to gradually withdraw capital from product line C and to apply the funds saved to product line A, the management team at C are likely to become demotivated as they reduce the resources under their command and experience lower sales (and profit) rather than, the more natural predisposition of managers, a rising trend. The centre can help this process by changing the targets and incentives of these managers away from growth and empire building towards shareholder value.

On the level of corporate-wide resource allocation, the directors of Red plc have a great deal of work to do. The publishing division is already creating high value from its existing activities and yet it is still in the early growth phase. The management team at the subsidiary believe that significant benefits would flow from buying rights to other

Exhibit 16.8 Using strategy plane analysis. Red plc's shifting strategic plan

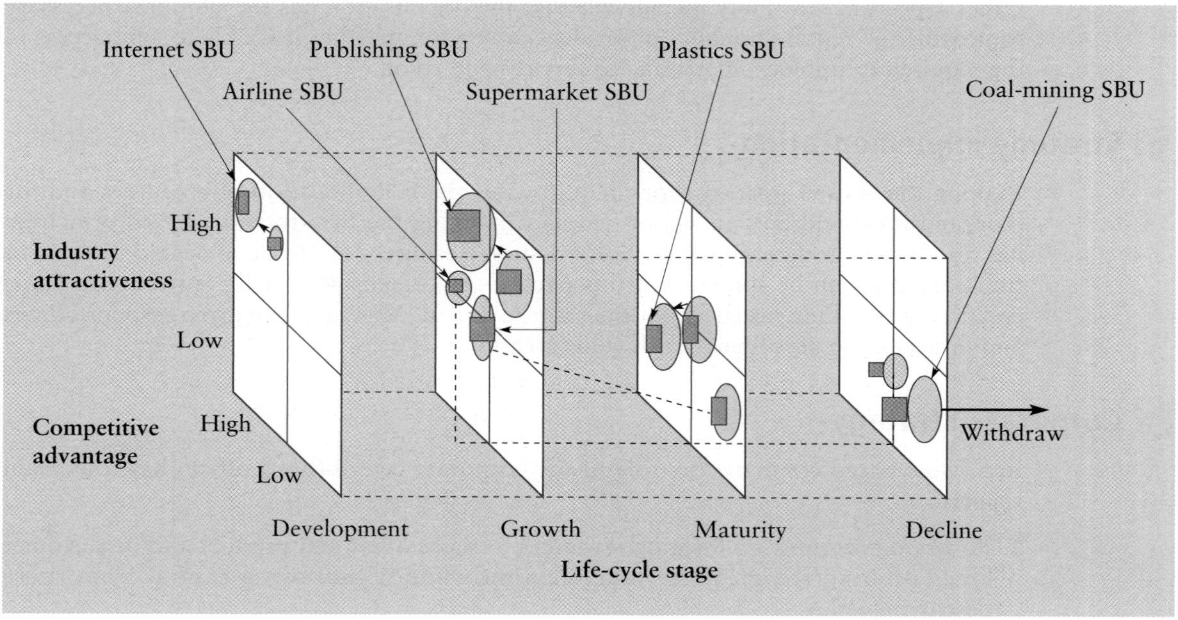

Note: The size of the circle represents the proportion of the firm's assets devoted to this SBU. The size of the rectangle represents the current performance spread. If the spread is negative it is shown outside the circle.

novels and children's stories. By combining these with its present 'stable' it could enter more forcefully into negotiations with book retailers, television production companies wishing to make screen versions of its stories and merchandising companies intending to put the image of some of the famous characters on articles ranging from T-shirts to drink cans. This strategy will involve the purchase of rights from individual authors as well as the acquisition of firms quoted on the stock exchange. It will be costly and require a substantial shift of resources within the firm. But, as can be seen from Exhibit 16.8, the value created makes the change attractive.

The Internet division has been put on a tight rein in terms of financial resources for its first three years because of the high risk attached to businesses involved in speculative innovation in this market. However, the energetic and able managers have created a proven line of services which have a technological lead over competitors, a high market share and substantial barriers to entry in the form of copyrights and patents. The directors decide to expand this area.

The plastics division as a whole is in a mature market with positive but gradually declining performance spreads. Here the strategic approach is to reduce the number of product lines competing on cost and transfer resources to those niche markets where product differentiation allows a premium price to be charged. The intention is to move gradually to a higher competitive advantage overall but accept that industry attractiveness will decline. Overall resources dedicated to this division will remain approximately constant, but the directors will be watching for deterioration greater than that anticipated in the current plan.

The supermarket division is currently producing a positive performance spread but a prolonged price war is forecast for the industry, to be followed by a shake-out, leading to a withdrawal of many of the current firms. Some directors are in favour of supporting this division vigorously through the troublesome times ahead in the expectation that when many of the weaker players have left the field, margins will rise to abnormally high levels – producing large performance spreads and high value in the long run. In terms of the value-creating life cycle this SBU would be shifted from the maturity strategy plane to the growth plane (shown in Exhibit 16.8). Other directors are not willing to take the risk that their firm will not be one of the survivors from the battle for market share. Furthermore, they argue that even if they do win, the enormous resources required, over the next five years, will produce a value return less than that on the publishing or Internet SBUs. Therefore, if financial resources are to be constrained, they should put money into these 'star' divisions.

The coal-mining division is haemorrhaging money. The industry is in terminal decline because of the high cost of coal extraction and the increasing tendency for the electricity-generating companies to source their coal needs from abroad. Moreover Red is a relatively small player in this market and lacks the economies of scale to compete effectively. To add insult to injury a large proportion of the corporation's capital is tied up in the coal stockpiles required by the electricity firms. The decision is taken to withdraw from this industry and the best approach to achieve this is investigated – sale to a competitor or liquidation.

The airline operation has never made a satisfactory return and is resented by the managers in other divisions as a drain on the value they create. However, the recent deregulation of air travel and especially the opening up of landing slots at major European airports has presented a major new opportunity. Despite being one of the smallest operators and therefore unable to compete on price it provides a level of service which has gained it a high reputation with business travellers. This, combined with its other major value driver, the strength of its marketing team, leads the divisional managers and the once sceptical directors to conclude that a sufficiently high premium ticket price can be charged to produce a positive performance spread. The new European rules enable the division to be placed on the growth plane as the spread is thought to be sustainable for some time.

The analysis in Exhibit 16.8 of Red's corporate strategy is an extremely simplified version of strategy development in large corporations where thousands of man-hours are needed to develop, evaluate and implement new strategic plans. Strategy is a complex and wide-ranging practical academic discipline in its own right and we can only scratch the surface in this chapter.

The remaining aspects of management affected by a switch from an earnings-based approach to a value-based approach shown in Exhibit 16.1 have already been touched on and, given the scope of this textbook, will not be explained any further here. The interested reader can consult some of the leading writers in this area (*see* Rappaport (1998), McTaggart *et al.* (1994), Copeland *et al.* (1996), Stewart (1991) and Reimann (1989)). The financial structure debate concerning the proportion of debt in the overall capital mix of the firm is discussed in Chapter 18 and the dividend payout ratio debate is described in Chapter 19.

One final point to note with regard to Exhibit 16.1 is the importance of having different types of value-creating targets at different levels within the organisation. At the board room and senior executive level it seems reasonable that there should be a concern with overall performance of the firm as seen from the shareholders' perspective and so TSR, MVA and MBR would be important guides to performance, and incentive schemes would be (at least partially) based upon them. Moving down the organisation, target setting and rewards need to be linked to the level of control and responsibility over outcomes. Strategic business unit performance needs to be expressed in terms of internal value metrics (discussed in the next section). Outcomes are usually under the control of divisional and other middle-ranking managers and so the reward system might be expressed in terms of shareholder value analysis (SVA), and/or economic profit (EP). At the operating level where a particular function contributes to value creation but the managers in that function have no control over the larger value centre itself, perhaps the emphasis should shift to rewarding high performance in particular operational value drivers such as throughput of customers, reduced staff turnover, cost of production, faster debtor turnover, etc.

CASE STUDY 16.1

Strategy, planning and budgeting at Lloyds TSB

Although business units are responsible for their own strategy development, the Lloyds TSB group provides guidelines on how strategy should be developed. . . . These unit plans are then consolidated into an aggregate plan for the value centre. The process undertaken is then subjected to scrutiny by the centre. The strategic planning process consists of five stages:

(1) ***Position assessment.*** Business units are required to perform a value-based assessment of the economics of the market in which the business operates and of the relative competitive position of the business within that market. Market attractiveness and competitive position must include a numerical rather than a purely qualitative assessment.
(2) ***Generate alternative strategies.*** Business units are required to develop a number of realistic and viable alternatives.
(3) ***Evaluate alternative strategies.*** Business units are required to perform shareholder value calculations in order to prioritise alternatives. Even if a potential strategy has a high positive net present value, this does not necessarily mean that it will be accepted. An assessment of project risk or do-ability is overlaid across the net present value calculations.
(4) ***Agree chosen strategy with the centre.*** Whilst it is perceived to be vital that the managers who best understand their business are given sufficient authority to develop strategies which they consider to be most appropriate, it is nevertheless considered equally important that there is a challenge mechanism at the centre to ensure that appropriate analyses have been performed and assumptions made are credible.
(5) ***The chosen strategy becomes a contract.*** Once the preferred strategy has been agreed with the centre, resource allocation and milestones are agreed. Budgetary performance targets are derived from the projections included within the strategic plan. Beyond this, however, business unit managers are free to choose whatever structures and performance indicators are considered to be relevant and appropriate.

Source: M. Davies (2000), 'Lessons from practice: VBM at Lloyds TSB', in G. Arnold and M. Davies (eds), *Value-Based Management*. Chichester: Wiley.

MEASURING VALUE CREATION: INTERNAL METRICS

Cash flow

In Chapters 2 and 3 the value of an investment is described as the sum of the discounted cash flows (NPV). This principle was applied to the assessment of a new project: if the investment produced a rate of return greater than the finance provider's opportunity cost of capital it is wealth enhancing. The same logic can be applied to a range of different categories of business decisions, including:

- resource allocation;
- business unit strategies;
- corporate level strategy;
- motivation, rewards and incentives.

Consider the figures for Gold plc in Exhibit 16.9. These could refer to the entire company. Alternatively the figures could be for business unit returns predicated on the assumption of a particular strategy being pursued. By examining the discounted cash flow the SBU management and the firm's managing director can assess the value contribution to be gained by allocating the required resources to the SBU. The management team putting forward these projected cash flows could then be judged and rewarded on the basis of performance targets expressed in cash flow terms. On the other hand, the

Exhibit 16.9 Gold plc forecast cash flows.

Required rate of return = 12% per annum.

Year	*1*	*2*	*3*	*4*	*5*	*6*	*7*	*8 and subsequent years*
	£	£	£	£	£	£	£	£
Forecast profits	1,000	1,100	1,100	1,200	1,300	1,450	1,500	1,600
Add book depreciation	500	600	800	800	850	900	950	1,000
Less fixed capital investment	−500	−3,000	−600	−600	−300	−500	−500	−600
Less additional investment in working capital*								
Inventory	50	−100	−70	−80	−50	−50	−50	−50
Debtors	−20	−20	−20	−20	−20	−20	−20	−20
Creditors	10	20	10	10	20	20	30	30
Cash	−10	−10	−10	−10	−10	−10	−10	−10
Add interest charged to profit and loss account	100	150	200	200	200	200	200	200
Taxes	−300	−310	−310	−420	−450	−470	−520	−550
Cash flow	830	−1,570	1,100	1,080	1,540	1,520	1,580	1,600
Discounted cash flow	$\frac{830}{1.12}$	$-\frac{1,570}{(1.12)^2}$	$+\frac{1,100}{(1.12)^3}$	$+\frac{1080}{(1.12)^4}$	$+\frac{1,540}{(1.12)^5}$	$+\frac{1,520}{(1.12)^6}$	$+\frac{1,580}{(1.12)^7}$	$+\frac{1,600}{0.12}\times\frac{1}{(1.12)^7}$
	741	−1,252	783	686	874	770	715	6,031

*A positive figure for inventory, debtors and cash indicates cash released from these forms of investment. A negative figure indicates additional cash devoted to these areas. For creditors a positive figure indicates higher credit granted by suppliers and therefore a boost to cash flows.

cash flows may refer to a particular product line or specific customer(s). At each of these levels of management a contribution to overall corporate value is expected.

The planning horizon is seven years and so the present value of the future cash flows is:

Present value of cash flows within planning horizon	+	Present value of cash flows after planning horizon		
741 – 1,252 + 783 + 686 + 874 + 770 + 715	+	6,031		
£3,317		£6,031	=	£9,348

Worked example 16.1 Investment after the planning horizon

After the planning horizon cash flows may well differ from the figure of £1,600 due to additional investment but this will make no difference to present *value* as any new investment made (when discounted) will be the same as the discounted value of the future cash inflows from that investment. In other words, the company is able to earn merely the required rate of return from Year 8 onwards so no new investment can create value. For example, suppose that Gold raised additional funds of £1,000 and at the end of Year 9 invested this in a project generating a perpetual annual cash flow of £120 starting at time 10. When these figures are discounted to time 0 the NPV is zero:

Present value of cash outflow $\frac{£1{,}000}{(1.12)^9} = -360.61$

Present value of cash inflows $\frac{£120/0.12}{(1.12)^9} = +360.61$

Thus incremental investment beyond the planning horizon generates no incremental value.

The kind of discounted cash flow analysis illustrated in Exhibit 16.9 is used by financial institutions to value shares. (In these cases interest paid to lenders is subtracted to determine the cash flow attributable to shareholders and the total remaining cash flow is divided by the number of shares in issue to provide the cash flow per share – *see* Chapter 17.) Given the emphasis by the owners of the firm on cash flow generation it would make sense for managers when evaluating strategies, projects, product lines and customers to use a similar method.

Shareholder value analysis

Alfred Rappaport (1998) has taken the basic concept of cash flow discounting and developed a simplified method of analysis. In the example of Gold plc (*see* Exhibit 16.9) the component elements of the cash flow did not change in a regular pattern. For example, fixed capital investment was ten times as great in Year 2 as in Year 5. Rappaport's shareholder value analysis assumes relatively smooth change in the various cash flow elements from one year to the next as they are all taken to be related to the sales level. Rappaport's seven key factors (value drivers) which determine value are as set out in Exhibit 16.10.

Rappaport calls the seven key factors value drivers, and this can be confusing given that other writers describe a value driver as a factor which enables some degree of competitive advantage. To distinguish the two types of value driver the quantitative seven

Exhibit 16.10 Rappaport's value drivers

1	Sales growth rate
2	Operating profit margin
3	Tax rate
4	Fixed capital investment
5	Working capital investment
6	The planning horizon (forecast period)
7	The required rate of return

listed in Exhibit 16.10 will be referred to as Rappaport's value drivers. To estimate future cash flows Rappaport assumes a constant percentage rate of growth in sales. The operating profit margin is a constant percentage of sales. The tax rate is a constant percentage of the operating profit. Fixed capital and working capital investment are related to the *increase* in sales.

So, if sales for the most recent year amount to £1,000,000 and are rising by 12 per cent per year, the operating profit margin on sales[8] is 9 per cent, taxes are 31 per cent of operating profit, the incremental investment in fixed capital items is 14 per cent of the change in sales, and the incremental working capital investment is 10 per cent of the change in sales, the cash flow for the next year will be as set out in Exhibit 16.11.

Using shareholder value analysis to value an entire company

Corporate value is the combined value of the debt portion and equity portion of its overall capital structure:

Corporate value = Debt + Shareholder value

The debt element is the market value of debt, such as long-term loans and overdrafts, plus the market value of quasi-debt liabilities, such as preference shares. In practical shareholder value analysis the balance sheet book value of debt is often used as a reasonable approximation to the market value. The above equation can be rearranged to derive shareholder value:

Shareholder value = Corporate value – Debt

Rappaport's corporate value has three elements, due to his separation of the discounted cash flow value of marketable securities (that is, their current market price) from the cash flows from operations (*see* Exhibit 16.12).

Free cash flow is the operating cash flow after fixed and working capital investment; that which comes from the *operations* of the business. It therefore excludes cash flows arising from, say, a rights or bond issue. It also excludes payments of interest or dividends (*see* Exhibit 16.13).

Exhibit 16.11 Silver plc: Sales, operating profit and cash outflows for next year

Sales in year 1		
= Sales in prior year × (1 + Sales growth rate)		
	= 1,000,000 × 1.12	
		1,120,000
Operating profit		
= Sales × Operating profit margin		
	= 1,120,000 × 0.09	
		100,800
Taxes		
= Operating profit × 31%		
	= 100,800 × 0.31	
		–31,248
Incremental investment in fixed capital		
= Increase in sales × Incremental fixed capital investment rate		
	= 120,000 × 0.14	
		–16,800
Incremental investment in working capital		
= Increase in sales × Working capital investment rate		
	= 120,000 × 0.10	
		–12,000
Operating free cash flow		£40,752

Exhibit 6.12 Rappaport's corporate value

Corporate value	=	Present value of operating cash flows within the planning horizon (forecast period)	+	Present value of operating cash flows after the planning horizon (forecast period)	+	The current value of marketable securities and other non-operating investments, e.g. government bonds

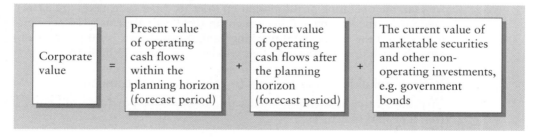

A closer look at depreciation and investment in fixed capital

Investment in plant, machinery, vehicles, buildings, etc. consists of two parts.

1 Annual investment to replace worn-out equipment and so on, leaving the overall level of assets constant.

2 Investment which adds to the stock of assets, presumably with the intention of permitting growth in productive capacity. This is called incremental fixed-capital investment.

A simplifying assumption often employed in shareholder value analysis is that the 'depreciation' figure in the profit and loss account is equal to the type 1 investment. This avoids the necessity of first adding back depreciation to operating profit and then deducting type 1 capital investment. It is only necessary to account for that extra cash outflow associated with incremental fixed capital investment. Free cash flow therefore is as illustrated in Exhibit 16.13.

Exhibit 16.13 Rappaport's free cash flow

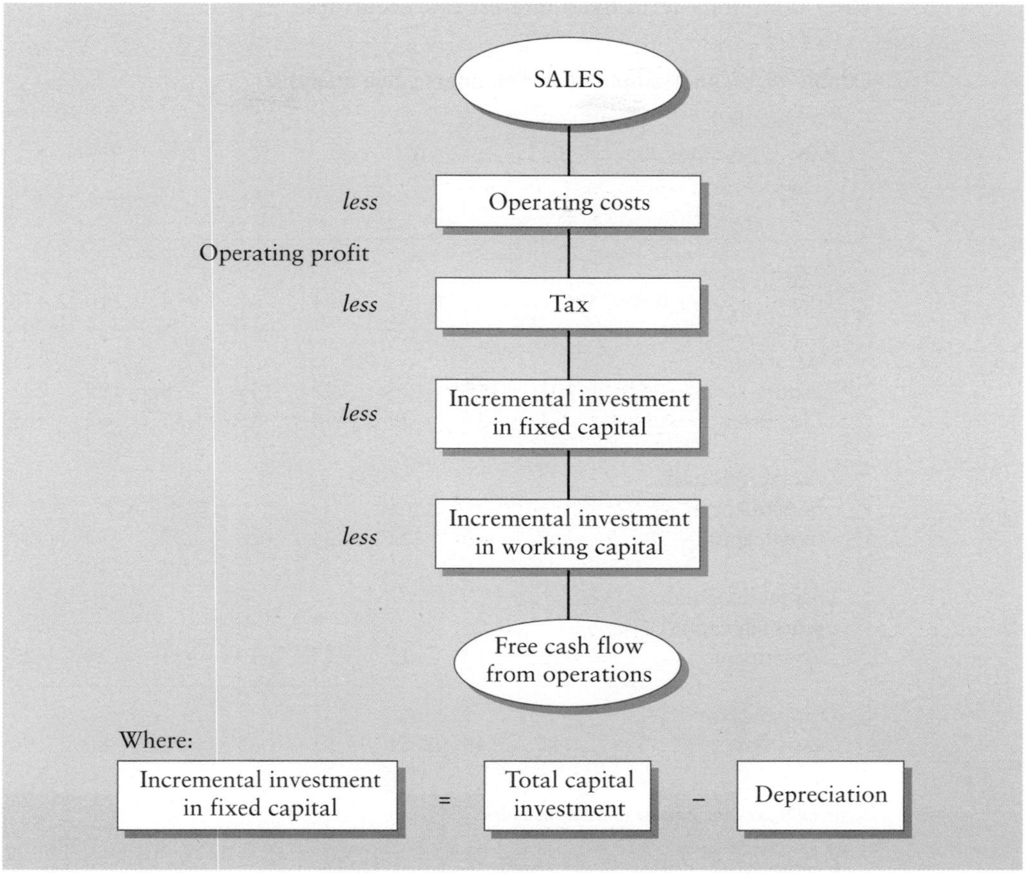

Illustration

We can calculate the shareholder value of Silver plc by using Rappaport's seven value drivers if we assume a planning horizon of eight years and a required rate of return of 15 per cent (*see* Exhibits 16.14 and 16.15).

Exhibit 16.14 Rappaport's value drivers applied to Silver plc

1	Sales growth	12% per year
2	Operating profit margin	9% of sales
3	Taxes	31% of operating profit
4	Incremental fixed capital investment	14% of the change in sales
5	Incremental working capital investment	10% of the change in sales
6	The planning horizon (forecast period)	8 years
7	The required rate of return	15% per year

The company also has £60,000 of investments in foreign and domestic shares and £50,000 in long-term fixed interest rate securities.

Exhibit 16.15 An example of shareholders value analysis

Year	*0*	*1*	*2*	*3*	*4*	*5*	*6*	*7*	*8*	*9 and subsequent years*
£000s										
Sales	1,000	1,120	1,254	1,405	1,574	1,762	1,974	2,210	2,476	2,476
Operating profits		101	113	126	142	159	178	199	223	223
Less taxes		−31	−35	−39	−44	−49	−55	−62	−69	−69
Less incremental investment in fixed capital		−17	−19	−21	−24	−26	−30	−33	−37	0
Less incremental working capital investment		−12	−13	−15	−17	−19	−21	−24	−27	0
Operating free cash flow		41	46	51	57	65	72	80	90	154

Note: All figures are rounded to whole numbers.

Corporate value is as set out in Exhibit 16.16.

The required rate of return in shareholder value analysis is the weighted average required return on debt and equity capital which allows for a return demanded by the debt holders and shareholders in proportion to their provision of capital. This explains why pre-interest cash flows are discounted rather than just those attributable to shareholders: some of those cash flows will go to debt holders. (The derivation of the weighted average cost of capital is explained later in the chapter.) The discounted cash flows derived in this way are then summed to give the corporate value: when debt (say, £200,000) is deducted, shareholder value is obtained.

Shareholder value = Corporate value – Debt
Shareholder value = £705,000 – £200,000 = £505,000

This kind of analysis can be used at a number of different levels:

- whole business;
- division;
- operating unit;
- project;
- product line or customer.

Exhibit 16.16 **Corporate value**

Present value of operating cash flows within the planning horizon (forecast period)	$\frac{41}{1.15} + \frac{46}{(1.15)^2} + \frac{51}{(1.15)^3} + \frac{57}{(1.15)^4} + \frac{65}{(1.15)^5} + \frac{72}{(1.15)^6} + \frac{80}{(1.15)^7} + \frac{90}{(1.15)^8}$	= 259
+		
Present value of operating cash flows after the planning horizon (forecast period)	$\frac{154}{0.15} = 1{,}027$ $\frac{1{,}027}{(1.15)^8}$	= 336
+		
The current value of marketable securities and other non-operating investments	60 + 50	= 110
	Corporate value	= 705
		or £705,000

Strategy valuation

The quantitative evaluation of alternative strategies in terms of value creation can assist strategic choice. It is advisable when applying shareholder value analysis to a business unit or corporate level strategy formulation and evaluation to consider at least four alternative strategic moves:

- a continuation of current strategy – 'base-case' strategy;
- liquidation;
- trade sale or spin-off;
- new operating strategy.

Imagine that the company we have been using to explain shareholder value analysis is involved in the production of plastic guttering for houses and the shareholder value figure of £505,000 represents the base-case strategy, consisting of relatively low levels of incremental investment and sales growing at a slow rate. The company has recently been approached by a property developer interested in purchasing the company's depot and offices for the sum of £400,000. Other assets (vehicles, inventory, machinery) could be sold to raise a further £220,000 and the marketable securities could be sold for £110,000. This liquidation would result in shareholders receiving £530,000 (£400,000 + £220,000 + £110,000 – £200,000). This liquidation option produces slightly more than the base-case strategy.

The third possibility is a trade sale or spin-off. Companies can sell separable businesses to other firms or float off strategic business units or groups of SBUs on the stock market. Thorn EMI split itself in 1996 into a music company and an electrical goods company, each with a separate quotation. P&O split the Princess cruise business from the ports, logistics and ferry businesses in 2000. In the case of the fictional guttering firm, it is too small to obtain a separate quotation for component parts, and its operations are too well integrated to allow a trade sale of particular sections. However, the shareholders have been approached by larger competitors in the past to discuss the possibility of a take-over. The three or four major industry players are trying to build up market share with the stated aim of achieving 'economies of scale and critical mass' and there is the distinct impression that they are being over-generous to selling shareholders in smaller firms – they are paying 'silly prices'. The management feel that if they could get a bidding war going between these domineering larger firms they could achieve a price of about £650,000 for shareholders.

The fourth possibility involves an expansion into a new product area of multicoloured guttering. This will require large-scale investment but should result in rapidly rising sales and higher operating margins. The expected Rappaport value drivers are as set out in Exhibit 16.17.

Exhibit 16.17 Rappaport's value drivers applied to an expansion of Silver plc

1	Sales growth	25% per year
2	Operating profit margin	11% of sales
3	Taxes	31% of operating profit
4	Incremental fixed capital investment	15% of the change in sales
5	Incremental working capital investment	10% of the change in sales
6	The planning horizon (forecast period)	8 years
7	The required rate of return	16% per year

The guttering firm's shareholder value under the new strategy is as set out in Exhibit 16.18.

Exhibit 16.18 shows that there are lower cash flows in the first three years with this strategy compared with the base-case strategy, yet the overall expected shareholder value rises from £505,000 to £1,069,000. Of course, to make the analysis more sophisticated we could consider the possibility of Rappaport's value drivers which were not fixed percentage rises throughout.

Sensitivity and scenario analysis

To make a more informed choice the directors may wish to carry out a sensitivity and scenario analysis (*see* Chapter 6 for details of this). A worst-case and a best-case scenario could be constructed and the sensitivity to changes in certain variables could be scrutinised. For example, alternative discount rates and incremental investment in fixed capital rates could be examined for the multicoloured product strategy as shown in Exhibit 16.19.

One observation that may be made from Exhibit 16.19 is that even if the amount of incremental capital investment required rises to 20 per cent of incremental sales and the discount rate moves to 17 per cent this strategy produces the highest value of all the options considered. The management team may wish to consider the consequences and the likelihood of other variables changing from the original expected levels.

Exhibit 16.18 The guttering firm's shareholder value under the new strategy

Year	*0*	*1*	*2*	*3*	*4*	*5*	*6*	*7*	*8*	*9 and subsequent years*
£000s										
Sales	1,000	1,250	1,563	1,953	2,441	3,052	3,815	4,768	5,960	5,960
Operating profits		138	172	215	269	336	420	524	656	656
Less taxes		−43	−53	−67	−84	−104	−130	−162	−203	−203
Less incremental investment in fixed capital		−38	−47	−59	−73	−92	−114	−143	−179	0
Less incremental working capital investment		−25	−31	−39	−49	−61	−76	−95	−119	0
Operating free cash flow		32	41	50	63	79	100	124	155	453

Discounted cash flows within planning horizon

$$\frac{32}{1.16}+\frac{41}{(1.16)^2}+\frac{50}{(1.16)^3}+\frac{63}{(1.16)^4}+\frac{79}{(1.16)^5}+\frac{100}{(1.16)^6}+\frac{124}{(1.16)^7}+\frac{155}{(1.16)^8}=295$$

Discounted cash flow beyond planning horizon

$$\frac{453}{0.16}=2{,}831 \text{ then } \frac{2{,}831}{(1.16)^8}=864$$

Marketable securities	= 110
Corporate value	1,269

Shareholder value = Corporate value − Debt
= £1,269,000 − £200,000
= £1,069,000

Exhibit 16.19 Shareholder value for the guttering firm under different discount and capital investment rates

£000s		*Discount rate*		
		15%	16%	17%
Incremental fixed capital investment rates	15%	1,205	1,069	951
	20%	1,086	955	843

Merits of shareholder value analysis

There are a number of advantages of using shareholder value analysis. These are as follows:

- relatively easy to understand and apply;
- consistent with the valuation of shares on the basis of discounted cash flow;
- makes explicit the (Rappaport) value drivers for managerial attention. This creates awareness of key variables and, enables performance measurement and target setting;
- the value drivers may be used to benchmark the firm against competitors.

Problems with shareholder value analysis

There are, however, some disadvantages to the use of shareholder value analysis.

- constant percentage increases in value drivers lack realism in some circumstances;
- can be misused in target setting, for example if managers are given a specific cash flow objective for a 12-month period they may be dissuaded from necessary value-enhancing investment in order to achieve the short-term target;
- data availability – many firms' accounting systems are not equipped to provide the necessary input data. The installation of a new system may be costly.

Economic profit

Economic profit (EP) has an advantage over shareholder value analysis because it uses the existing accounting and reporting systems of firms by focusing on profit rather than cash flow information. This not only reduces the need to implement an overhaul of the data collecting and reporting procedures but also provides evaluatory and performance measurement tools which use the familiar concept of profit. Thus, managers used to 'bottom line' figures are more likely to understand and accept this metric than one based on cash flow information.

Economic profit for a period is the amount earned by a business after deducting all operating expenses and a charge for the opportunity cost of the capital[9] employed.

A business only produces an economic profit if it generates a return greater than that demanded by the finance providers given the risk class of investment.

To calculate EP take profit before interest and subtract the cost of capital employed.[10] There are two ways to calculate EP.

1 *The 'performance spread' approach* The difference between the return achieved on invested capital and the weighted average cost of capital (WACC) is the performance spread. This percentage figure is then multiplied by the quantity of invested capital to obtain EP:

$$\text{Economic profit} = \text{Performance spread} \times \text{Invested capital}$$
$$\text{Economic profit} = (\text{Return on capital} - \text{WACC}) \times \text{Invested capital}$$

The WACC allows for an appropriate risk-adjusted return to each type of finance provider (debt and equity) – *see* later section of this chapter for calculation of this.

2 *The profit less capital charge approach* Here a capital charge equal to the invested capital multiplied by the return required by investors is deducted from the operating profits after tax:

Economic profit = Operating profit before interest and after tax – Capital charge
Economic profit = Operating profit before interest and after tax – (Invested capital × WACC)

As can be seen from the following illustration either method leads to the same EP.

Illustration

EoPs plc has a weighted average cost of capital of 12 per cent and has used £1,000,000 of invested capital to produce an operating profit of £180,000 during the past year.

Performance spread approach:

EP = (Return on capital – WACC) × Invested capital
= (18% – 12%) × £1,000,000
= £60,000

Profit less capital charge:

EP = Operating profits before interest and after tax – (Invested capital × WACC)
= £180,000 – (£1,000,000 × 0.12)
= £60,000

A short history of economic profit

The principles behind economic profit have a long antecedence. For at least a century economists (notably Alfred Marshall) have been aware of the need to recognise the

CASE STUDY 16.2

The use of economic profit is becoming more widespread

For over a decade major US firms, including Walt Disney, Quaker Oats and AT&T, have been switching to using economic profit as a guiding concept. The focus of economic profit on the productive use of capital can have profound consequences. Roberto Goizueta, CEO of Coca-Cola, put the basic philosophy this way: 'We raise capital to make concentrate, and sell it at an operating profit. Then we pay the cost of that capital. Shareholders pocket the difference'. Barclays Bank adopted the technique in 2000 declaring their aim to double economic profit every four years.† Bass stated that 'any acquisition must clear three hurdles: create value in net present value terms; enhance earnings in year one; and produce returns above the weighted average cost of capital by year three'.**

Using economic profit can alter shareholders' perception of firms. For example *Investors Chronicle* asked, 'Which company created more value for its shareholders last year: BAT or Carlton Communications? That's easy isn't it? After all, Michael Green's TV and video production group has a glowing track record. Its profits have improved annually for the past five years. BAT, by contrast, is a conglomerate that has a large exposure to the dying tobacco industry. It lacks the critical mass to compete in financial services, its other business'.‡ Carlton, despite its more glamorous image, destroyed value in 1996 and produced a return of 8 per cent on capital when it needed to produce 14 per cent to match the opportunity cost of investors' funds. BAT, on the other hand, generated a 19 per cent return against a required rate of 11 per cent.

Sources: *Quoted in Tully (1993), p. 93. † *The Economist* Newspaper, London, 18 November 2000. ** *Financial Times*, 8 December 2000. ‡ *Investors Chronicle*, 17 January 1997, p. 18.

minimum return to be provided to the finance provider as a 'cost' of operating a business. Enlightened chief executives have for decades, if not centuries, taken account of the amount of capital used by divisional managers when setting targets and measuring performance, with some sort of implicit, or explicit, cost being applied. David Solomons (1965) formalised the switch from return on capital employed (ROCE) and other accounting rates of return measures to 'the excess of net earnings over the cost of capital as the measure of managerial success'. But even he drew on practical innovation which had taken place in a number of large US companies.

Usefulness of economic profit

Economic profit can be used to evaluate strategic options which produce returns over a number of years. For example, Spoe plc is considering the investment of £2,000,000 in a new division which is expected to produce a constant operating profit after tax of £300,000 per year to infinity without the need for any further investment in fixed capital or working capital in subsequent years. The company has a required rate of return on capital of 13 per cent. The extra value created on top of the initial investment of £2m is:

$$\begin{aligned}\text{Economic profit per year} &= (\text{Return on capital} - \text{WACC}) \times \text{Invested capital}\\ &= (15\% - 13\%) \times £2{,}000{,}000\\ &= £40{,}000\end{aligned}$$

The present value of this perpetuity is:

$$£40{,}000/0.13 = £307{,}692$$

This £307,692 is the additional value, in present terms, of operational cash flow. To obtain total value of this division we add the initial investment:

$$\begin{aligned}\text{Value of new division} &= \text{Present value of economic profit} + \text{Initial investment}\\ &= £307{,}692 + £2{,}000{,}000 = £2{,}307{,}692\end{aligned}$$

Economic profit can also be used for the evaluation of particular product lines or customers and for managerial reward schemes.

Drawbacks of economic profit

There are, however, some disadvantages to the use of economic profit.

1 ***The balance sheet does not reflect invested capital*** Balance sheets are not designed to provide information on the present economic value of assets being used in a business. Assets are generally recorded at original cost less depreciation. With or without inflation it does not take many years for these balance sheet values to deviate dramatically from the theoretically correct capital employed figures for most firms. Generally balance sheets significantly understate the amount of capital employed, and this understatement therefore causes EP to appear high. A possible solution is to value assets on a replacement cost or market value basis, but this is not always easy or accurate. Moreover, many businesses invest in assets which never find their way to a balance sheet. For example, some firms pour vast sums into building up brand images and do so with the often correct belief that shareholders' money is being well invested, with the pay-off arising years later. Nevertheless, accounting convention insists on such expenditures being written off against profits rather than being taken into the balance sheet. The same problem applies to other 'investments' such as business reputation and management training.

2 ***Manipulation and arbitrariness*** The difficulties caused by relying on accounting data are exacerbated by the freedom available to manipulate such figures as well as the degree of subjectivity involved in arriving at some of the figures in the first place. For example, if a business has sold goods on credit some customers are likely to fail to pay on the due date. The problem for the accountant (and managers) is to decide when to accept that particular debts will never be paid; is it after three months, six months or a year? Until they are declared 'bad debts' they are recorded as an asset – perhaps they will turn out to be worth something, perhaps they won't. At each balance sheet date judgement is required to establish an estimate of the value of the debtor balance to the firm. Similar problems of 'flexibility' and potential for manipulation are possible with the estimate of the length of life of an asset (which has an effect on annual depreciation), and with R&D expenditure or inventory valuation.

   Having a wide range of choice of treatment of key inputs to the profit and loss account and balance sheets makes comparability over time, and between companies, very difficult.

3 ***High economic profit and negative NPV can go together*** There is a danger of over-reliance on EP. For example, imagine a firm has become a convert to economic profit and divisional managers are judged on annual economic profit. Their bonuses and promotion prospects rest on good performance spreads over the next 12 months. This may prompt a manager to accept a project with an impressive EP over the short term whether or not it has a positive NPV over its entire life. Projects which produce poor or negative EPs in the first few years, for example biotechnology investments, will be rejected even if they will enhance shareholder wealth in the long term.

   Also, once a project has been started within a particular year managers given specific EP targets may be tempted to ensure the profit target is met by cutting down on certain expenditures such as training, marketing and maintenance. The target will be achieved but long-term damage may be inflicted.

   A third value-destroying use of EP occurs when managers are demotivated by being set EP targets. For example, if managers have no control over the capital employed in their part of the business, they may become resentful and cynical of value-based management if they are told nevertheless to achieve certain EP targets.

4 ***Difficult to allocate revenues, costs and capital to business units, products, etc.*** To carry out EP analysis at the sub-firm level it is necessary to measure profit and capital invested separately for each area of the business. Many costs and capital assets are shared between business units, product lines and customers. It is very difficult in some situations to identify the proportion of the cost or asset that is attributable to each activity. It can also be expensive.

Economic value added (EVA®)

EVA, developed and trademarked by the US consultants Stern Stewart and Co., is a variant of EP which attempts to overcome some of the problems outlined above. Great energy has been put into its marketing and it is probably the most widely talked about value metric.

EVA = Adjusted invested capital × (Adjusted return on capital – WACC)
or
EVA = Adjusted operating profits after tax – (Adjusted invested capital × WACC)

The adjustments to profit and capital figures are meant to refine the basic EP. Stern Stewart suggest that up to 164 adjustments to the accounting data may be needed. For example, spending on marketing and R&D helps build value and so these are added back to the balance sheet as assets (and amortised over the period expected to benefit from these expenditures). Goodwill on acquisitions previously written off is also returned and is expressed as an asset, thus boosting both profits and the balance sheet.

There are a number of difficulties with these adjustments – for example, over what period should these reconstituted 'assets' be amortised? Should you make adjustments for events up to five years ago, ten years ago, or the whole life of the firm?

EVA, like the generic EP, has the virtue of being based on familiar accounting concepts and it is arguably more accurate than taking ordinary accounting figures. However critics have pointed out that the adjustments can be time-consuming and costly, and many are based on decisions that are as subjective as the original accountant's numbers. There also remains the problem of poorly, if enthusiastically, implemented EVA reward systems producing results which satisfy targets for EVA but which produce poor decisions with regard to NPV. Furthermore, the problem of allocating revenue, costs and capital to particular business units and products is not solved through the use of EVA.

Despite the outstanding problems companies are seeing benefits from introducing EVA.

> It's not rocket science, but it is good lingua franca that does indeed get everyone back to basics, makes them understand better the cash consequences of their own actions and, further, makes them address other departments' problems, not just their own. Within each of our businesses we don't incentivise, for example, the sales director on sales and we don't incentivise the finance director on cash generation. The whole management team is incentivised on EVA and that means they are all pulling in the same direction and have to liaise better. (Mike Ashton, finance director of BWI).[11]

At Burtons, the UK clothing retailer (now Arcadia), Martin Clifford-King says:

> We've been running EVA for just the first 12 weeks of our financial year. We see it as an operational tool. In the past, stores used to be targeted on sales, then we moved to profit, and EVA is a further refinement of this approach, taking into account the cost of capital tied up in the business.[12]

Exhibit 16.20 shows one attempt at the calculation of EVA for an entire company. Note the high degree of judgement required. Another analyst would have produced different figures. (The error in the use of the capital asset pricing model needs to be looked at with a blind eye.)

Comments on internal value metrics

Rather than selecting one metric a better approach for both strategic investment discussion and performance targeting and measurement is to set both cash flow and economic profit objectives. To do so can help to alleviate the problem of managers taking action to achieve particular short-term targets at the expense of long-term wealth.

A major issue to be resolved for both the cash flow (for example shareholder value added) and the EP approach is the need for an accurate estimate of the cost of capital. It is to this that we now turn.

Exhibit 16.20

What's it all about, EVA®

EVA may look interesting in theory. But how easy is it to apply? Here we show how to calculate Glaxo Wellcome's EVA for the year to December 1995.

To begin with, we have to get a better idea of Glaxo's economic value by bringing its balance sheet up to date. The two largest adjustments are goodwill and R&D. Following its acquisition of Wellcome, Glaxo wrote off over £5bn of **goodwill**. Since that reflects what Wellcome is really worth, we added it back to Glaxo's shareholders' funds.

Glaxo also spends over £1bn a year on R&D, which it writes off against profits. Since this is aimed at developing new drugs, EVA suggests it should be treated as an asset. So we worked out Glaxo's **R&D spending for the past four years**, and added it back.

Finally, since a company's employed capital is put to work regardless of how it is funded, we also added Glaxo's **total debt** and its **minority interests** to its capital.

Now we can work out what Glaxo's assets earned in 1995. This is defined as its **operating profit after tax**. However, profit figures can be distorted by charges. In 1995, Glaxo set aside over £1.2bn to fund Wellcome's integration. But the lion's share was merely added to provisions, and was not spent in 1995. So we added the **movement in provisions** back to profits. Similarly, we have already capitalised past **R&D costs** as an asset on the balance sheet. So Glaxo's 1995 outlay has to be added back as well.

Now we can calculate Glaxo Wellcome's return on capital. In 1995, we find it earned a healthy 29.5 per cent return.

But working out the return on capital is only the first step. We now have to find out how much Glaxo's capital costs. That means looking at the cost of debt and equity.

The cost of debt is simply the average interest rate the company pays. Glaxo Wellcome pays an average interest rate of just 7 per cent.

EVA uses the capital asset pricing model to work out the cost of equity . . . Applying the model to Glaxo produces a cost of equity of 13.8 per cent. That's cheap because historically Glaxo's shares have been pacific relative to the market.

Finally, we have to weight the costs of equity and debt relative to their use by Glaxo. About 70 per cent of its capital is equity and the rest debt, so the weighting produces a cost of 11.5 per cent.

From these figures, we can see that Glaxo's return on capital exceeded its cost of capital by 18 per cent in 1995. That year, it certainly suceeded in creating value for its shareholders.

Return on capital

£m	
Shareholders' equity	91
+ Goodwill written off	5,197
+ Past R&D written off	3,322
+ Minority interests	130
+ Total debt	4,347
	13,087
Operating profit	2,126
+ Movement in provisions	1,169
+ R&D costs	1,130
– Tax	564
Total:	**3,861**

Return on capital = (3,861/13,087) × 100 = 29.5%

Cost of capital

Average interest rate of debt:	7%
Cost of equity:	
(Bond yield + Equity risk) × Glaxo beta	
(7.7 + 6.0) × 1.01 =	13.8%
Weighted cost of capital:	11.5%
Economic value added =	18.0%

Source: *Investors Chronicle*, 17 January 1997, p. 19. Reprinted with kind permission of the *Investors Chronicle*.

THE COST OF CAPITAL

Until this point a cost of capital (required rate of return) has been assumed for, say, a project or a business unit strategy, but we have not gone into much detail about how an appropriate cost of capital is calculated.

The cost of capital is the rate of return that a company has to offer finance providers to induce them to buy and hold a financial security.

Using the correct cost of capital as a discount rate is important. If it is too high investment will be constrained, firms will not grow as they should and shareholders will miss out on value-enchancing opportunities. There can be a knock-on effect to the macroeconomy and this causes worry for politicians. For example in November 1994 the then President of the Board of Trade, Michael Heseltine, complained:

> Businesses are not investing enough because of their excessive expectations of investment returns . . . The CBI tells me that the majority of firms continue to require rates of return above 20 per cent. A senior banker last week told me his bank habitually asked for 30 per cent returns on capital.[13]

The main point we need to clear up in this section is the degree of vagueness about the hurdle rate of return applied in businesses.

Two sides of the same coin

The issues of the cost of capital for managerial use within the business and the value placed on a share (or other financial security) are two sides of the same coin. They both depend on the level of return. The holders of shares make a valuation on the basis of the returns they estimate they will receive. Likewise, from the firm's perspective, it estimates the cost of raising money through selling shares as the return that the firm will have to pay to shareholders to induce them to buy and hold the shares. The same considerations are in the minds of bondholders, preference shareholders and so on. If the cash flows are expected to go down then the selling price of the share, bond, etc. goes down until the return is at the level dictated by the returns on financial securities of a similar type and risk. Different types of finance have different levels of systematic risk for the purchaser. The returns on

Exhibit 16.21 Two sides of the same coin

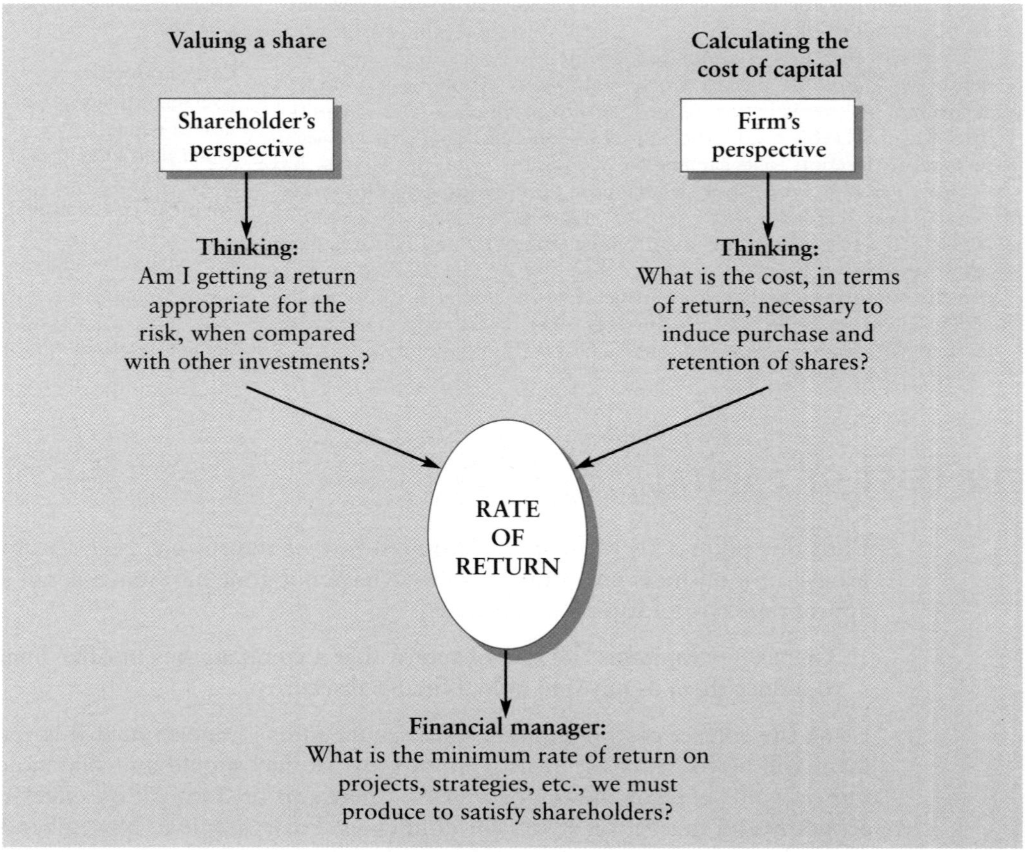

securities are likely to reflect these differences in systematic risk. If a company fails to achieve returns which at least compensate finance providers for their opportunity cost it is unlikely to survive for long. Exhibit 16.21, taking shares as an example, illustrates that valuing a share and the cost of capital are two sides of the same coin.

Calculating the cost of equity capital

A shareholder has in mind a minimum rate of return determined by the returns available on other shares of the same risk class. Managers, in order to maximise shareholder wealth, must obtain this level of return for shareholders from the firm's activities. If a company does not achieve the rate of return to match the investor's opportunity cost it will find it difficult to attract new funds and will become vulnerable to take-over or liquidation.

With debt finance there is generally a specific rate payable for the use of capital. In contrast, ordinary shareholders are not explicitly offered specific payments. However, there is an implicit rate of return that has to be offered to attract investors.

With equity capital the investor is accepting a fairly high probability of receiving no return at all on the investment. The firm has no obligation to pay annual dividends, and other forms of capital have prior claims on annual cash flows. If the firm does less well than expected then it is, generally, ordinary shareholders who suffer the most. On the other hand, if the firm performs well a £1,000 stake can grow to be worth millions. It is the expectation of high returns that causes ordinary shareholders to accept high risk – a large dispersion of returns.

Investors have a range of risk levels to choose from in selecting a home for their money, from virtually risk-free government securities to junk bonds, blue chip ordinary shares and venture capital. To take on more risk investors must be offered more return. Assuming they are fully diversified this relationship is shown in Exhibit 16.22. (*See* Chapter 8 for more on systematic risk and the security market line – SML.)

Investors in shares require a return which provides for two elements. First, they need a return equal to the risk-free rate (usually taken to be that on government securities). Second, there is the risk premium, which rises with the degree of systematic risk.

Rate of return on shares = Risk-free rate + Risk premium

$$k_E = r_f + RP$$

Exhibit 16.22 The relationship between rate of return and systematic risk

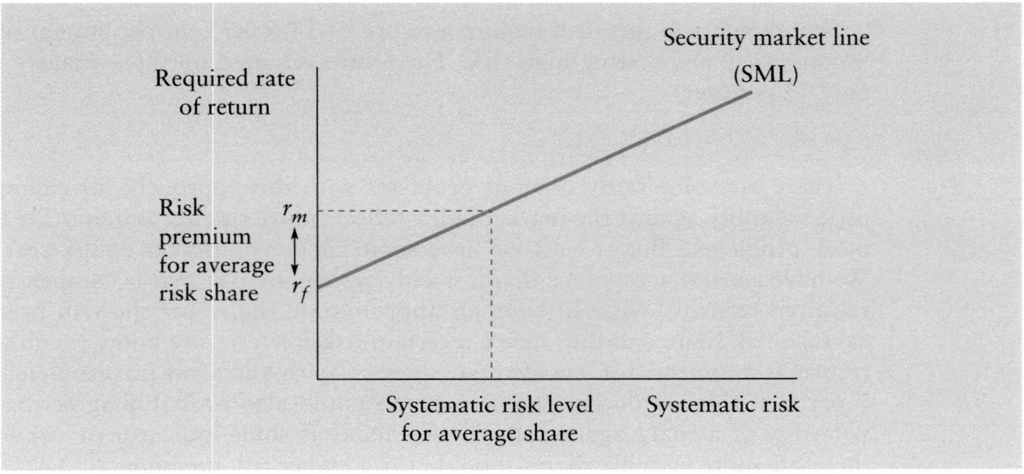

The risk-free rate gives a return sufficient to compensate for both impatience to consume and inflation. To estimate the relevant risk premium on a company's equity there are two steps. Stage one is to estimate the average extra return demanded by investors over the risk-free return to induce them to buy a portfolio of average-risk level shares. The risk premium actually obtained by shareholders can only be observed over an extended period of time as short-term returns on shares can be distorted (they are often negative, for example). This is expressed as the difference between the market return, r_m, and the risk-free return, r_f, that is $(r_m - r_f)$.

The second stage is to adjust the risk premium for a typical (average-risk level) share to suit the risk level for the particular company's shares. If the share is more risky than the average then $(r_m - r_f)$ is multiplied by a systematic risk factor greater than 1. If it is less risky it may be multiplied by a systematic risk factor of, say, 0.8 to reduce the risk premium.

Using the data examined in Chapter 8 we could take the extra return required by investors on an average-risk level share as 5 per cent per year. This was derived from data for the whole of the twentieth century and included periods of war, depression and boom. Some analysts have suggested that this extra return for risk is too high, being biased by the extreme events in the first half of the twentieth century. However it would not be the first time that commentators have been proved wrong after saying that the skies were now much bluer and that unpleasant surprises would never occur again. Taking a long period has the virtue of reflecting a diverse set of economic and political circumstances.

The capital-asset pricing model

In the thirty years following the development of the CAPM, in practical cost of capital calculations, the risk premium was generally adjusted by a beta based on the extent to which a share had moved when a market index moved (its covariance with the market), say over a five-year period. If a share tended to rise by 1.5 per cent for a 1 per cent upward market movement over a five-year period it would be assigned a beta value of 1.5. This more volatile share would then be regarded as more risky than the average in future periods and therefore would have a high risk premium and a greater cost of equity capital. Thus if the risk-free rate of return is 7 per cent and the average risk premium is 5 per cent, the return required on this share is 14.5 per cent.

$$k_E = r_f + \beta(r_m - r_f)$$
$$k_E = 7 + 1.5(5) = 14.5\%$$

Shareholders in this firm require a return of 14.5 per cent per annum on their shares because they are bearing high risk. The return required on the averagely risky share is only 12 per cent.

$$k_E = 7 + 1.0\ (5) = 12\%$$

There are some fairly obvious problems with this approach; for example, does historic volatility against the market index reflect future risk accurately? (*See* Chapter 8 for more problems.) But at least we have some anchor points for equity cost calculations. We have general acceptance that it is only systematic risk that is compensated for in the required returns. We also have an approximate figure for the risk premium on the average-risk share and thus, given a certain risk-free rate, we know roughly what rate of return is required for an average share – with rates on government securities at 7 per cent this would be 12 per cent. We could also probably agree that the relative volatility of a share against the market index is some indicator of riskiness, and that therefore more variable shares should bear a higher risk premium.

Despite this progress we are still left with some uncertainty over how to adjust the average risk premium for specific shares. The systematic risk adjustment factor, in practical employment, needs to be made more sophisticated. One route has been to describe a number of beta factors through the arbitrage pricing theory (APT), which takes into account key economic factors – some firms are more sensitive to, say, overall economic output levels for the general economy, while others respond more to interest rate changes. The degree of sensitivity and therefore riskiness of specific shares is measured by a number of betas. Unfortunately, making use of the APT is time consuming and difficult.

Fama and French in their 1992 paper stated that equity returns (and therefore risk premiums) are related to firm size and the ratio of the book value of the company's equity to its market value. Smaller firms' shareholders have received a higher return than larger firms' shareholders, and the higher the book value relative to market value the greater the return. Perhaps the adjustment to the risk premium demanded on the average risk share should take account of these two risk factors.

Gordon growth model method for estimating the cost of equity capital

The most influential model for calculating the cost of equity in the early 1960s (and one which is still used today) was created by Gordon and Shapiro (1956), and further developed by Gordon (1962). Suppose a company's shares priced at P produce earnings of E per share and pay a dividend of d per share. The company has a policy of retaining a fraction, b, of its earnings each year to use for internal investments. If the rate of return (discount or capitalisation rate) required on shares of this risk class k_E then, under certain restrictive conditions, it can be shown that earnings, dividends and reinvestment will all grow continuously, at a rate of $g = br$, where r is the rate of return on the reinvestment of earnings, and we have:

$$P = \frac{d_1}{k_E - g}$$

Solving for k_E we have:

$$k_E = \frac{d_1}{P} + g$$

where d_1 is the dividend to be received next year.

That is, the rate of return investors require on a share is equal to the prospective dividend yield *plus* the rate at which the dividend stream is expected to grow.

Gordon and Shapiro said that there are other approaches to the estimation of future dividends than the extrapolation of the current dividend on the basis of the growth rate explicit in b and r, so we can derive g in other ways and still the k_E formula remains valid,

A major problem in the practical employment of this model is obtaining a trustworthy estimate of the future growth rate of dividends to an infinite horizon. Gordon and Shapiro (1956) told us to derive this figure from known data in an objective manner, using common sense and with reference to the past rate of growth in a corporation's dividend. This advice does not get us very far – the cost of equity capital is very sensitive to the figure put in for g, and yet there is no reliable method of estimating it for the *future*, all we can do is make reasoned estimates and so the resulting k_E is based merely on an informed guess. Using past growth rates is one approach, but it means that it is assumed that the future growth of the company's earnings and dividends will be exactly the same as in the past – often an erroneous supposition. Professional analysts' forecasts could be examined, but their record of predicting the future is generally a poor one – especially for more than two years ahead.

The cost of retained earnings

There are many large companies which rarely, if ever, go to their shareholders to raise new money. These companies often rely on the most important source of long-term finance, retained earnings. There is a temptation to regard these funds as 'costless' because it was not necessary for the management to go out and persuade investors to invest by offering a rate of return. However, retained earnings should be seen as belonging to the shareholders. They are part of the equity of the firm. The shareholders could make good use of these funds by investing in other firms and obtaining a return. These funds therefore have an opportunity cost. We should regard the cost of retained earnings as being equal to the expected returns required by shareholders buying new shares in a firm. There is a slight modification to this principle in practice because new share issues involve costs of issuance and therefore are required to give a marginally higher return to cover the costs of selling the shares.

The cost of debt capital

When a finance provider chooses to supply finds in the form of debt finance, there is a deliberate attempt to reduce risk. This can be achieved in a number of ways: by imposing covenants on management, for example, to restrict the gearing level or maintain an interest cover ratio, by accepting assets as security, by ensuring that the lenders are ahead of other finance providers (particularly ordinary and preference holders) in terms of annual payouts and in the event of liquidation. A lender to a corporation cannot expect to eliminate all risk and so the required rate of return is going to be above that of leading to a reputable government, r_f. Perhaps, for a corporate bond with a high credit rating (low risk of default) 100 basis points will be the risk premium:

Then, the cost of debt capital, k_D, is:

$$k_D = r_f + \text{RP}$$

If the current risk free rate is 6 per cent, then k_D = 7 per cent.

If the firm already has a high level of debt and wishes to borrow more it may need to offer, say, 400 basis points above the risk-free rate. The credit rating is likely to be below investment grade (below BBB- by Standard & Poor's and Baa3 by Moody's) and therefore will be classified as a high-yield (or junk) bond. So the required return might be 10 per cent.

$$k_D = r_f + \text{RP} = 6 + 7 = 10\%$$

There are two types of debt capital. The first is debt which is traded, that is, bought and sold in a secondary market. The second is debt which is not traded.

Traded debt

In the UK bonds are normally issued with a nominal value of £100. Vanilla bonds carry an annual coupon rate until the bonds reach maturity when the nominal or par value of £100 is paid to the lender (*see* Chapter 11 for more details). The rate of return required by the firm's creditors, k_D, is represented by the interest rate in the following equation which causes the future discounted cash flows payable to the lenders to equal the current market price of the bond P_D:

$$P_D = \sum_{t=1}^{n} \frac{i}{(1 + k_D)^t} + \frac{R_n}{(1 + k_D)^n}$$

where:

i = annual nominal interest (coupon payment) receivable from year 1 to year n;
R_n = amount payable upon redemption;
k_D = cost of debt capital (pre-tax).

For example, Elm plc issued £100m of bonds six years ago carrying an annual coupon rate of 8 per cent. They are due to be redeemed in four years for the nominal value of £100 each. The next coupon is payable in one year and the current market price of a bond is £93. The cost of this redeemable debt can be calculated by obtaining the internal rate of return, imagining that a new identical set of cash flows is being offered to the lenders from a new (four-year) bond being issued today. The lenders would pay £93 for such a bond (in the same risk class) and receive £8 per year for four years plus £100 at the end of the bond's life:

Year	0	1	2	3	4
	+£93	–£8	–£8	–£8	–£108

Thus the rate of return being offered is calculated from:

$$+93 - \frac{8}{1 + k_D} - \frac{8}{(1 + k_D)^2} - \frac{8}{(1 + k_D)^3} - \frac{108}{(1 + k_D)^4} = 0$$

With k_D at 11 per cent the discounted cash flow = + £2.307.
With k_D at 10 per cent the discounted cash flow = –£0.66.
Using linear interpretation the IRR can be found:

$$k_D = 10\% + \frac{0.66}{2.307 + 0.66}(11 - 10) = 10.22\%$$

The total market value of the bonds, V_D, is calculated as follows:

$$V_D = £100\text{m} \times \frac{£93}{£100} = £93\text{m}$$

We are concerned with finding the cost to a company of the various types of capital it might use to finance its investment projects, strategic plans, etc. It would be wrong to use the coupon rate of 8 per cent on the bond. This was the required rate of return six years ago (assuming the bond was sold for £100). A rate of 10.22 per cent is appropriate because this is the rate of return bond investors are demanding in the market today. The cost of capital is the best available return available elsewhere for the bondholders for the same level of risk. Managers are charged with using the money under their command to produce a return at least equal to the opportunity cost. If the cash flows attributable to these lenders for a project or SBU are discounted at 8 per cent then a comparison of the resulting net present value of the investment with the return available by taking the alternative of investing the cash in the capital markets at the same risk is not being made. However using 10.22 per cent for the bond cost of capital this can be compared with the alternatives available to the lenders in the financial markets.

Irredeemable bonds have interest payments which form a perpetuity:

$$k_D = \frac{i}{P_D}$$

Tax effects

A firm is able to offset debt interest against a corporation tax liability. This reduces the effective cost of this form of finance. It is the after-tax cost of debt capital which is of interest to firms – assuming they have taxable profits which can be reduced by the interest charge.

In the calculation for Elm plc taxation has been ignored and so the above calculation of 10.22 per cent should be properly defined as the cost of debt before tax, k_{DBT}. An adjustment is necessary to establish the true cost of the bond capital to the firm.

If T is the rate of corporate tax, 30 per cent, then the cost of debt after tax, k_{DAT} is:

$$k_{DAT} = k_{DBT}\,(1 - T)$$

$$k_{DAT} = 10.22\,(1 - 0.30) = 7.15\%$$

Untraded debt

Most debt capital, such as bank loans, is not quoted on a financial market. We need to find a rate of interest which is the opportunity cost of lenders' funds – the current 'going rate' of interest for the risk class. This is most easily done by looking at the rate being offered on similar tradeable debt securities.

Floating-rate debt

Most companies have variable-rate debt in the form of either bonds or bank loans. Usually the interest payable is set at a margin over a benchmark rate such as LIBOR (*see* Chapter 11). For practical purposes the current interest payable can be taken as the before-tax rate of return (k_{DBT}) because these rates are the market rates. There is a theoretical argument against this simple approach based on the difference between short- and long-term interest rates. For example, it may be that a firm rolls over a series of short-term loans – in this case the theoretically correct approach is to use the long-term interest rate.

The cost of preference share capital

Preference share capital

Preference shares have some characteristics in common with debt capital (e.g. a specified annual payout of higher ranking than ordinary share dividends) and some characteristics in common with equity (dividends may be missed in some circumstances, and the dividend is not tax deductible). If the holders of preference shares receive a fixed annual dividend and the shares are irredeemable the perpetuity formula may be used, where:

$$P_p = \frac{d_1}{k_p}$$

where P_p is the price of preference shares, d_1 is the annual preference dividend, k_p, is the investors' required rate of return. The cost of this type of preferred share is given by:

$$k_p = \frac{d_1}{P_p}$$

Hybrid securities

Hybrid securities can have a wide variety of features – e.g. a convertible bond is a combination of a straight bond offering regular coupons and a conversion option. It is usually necessary to calculate the cost of capital for each of the component elements separately. This can be complex and is beyond the scope of this chapter.

The weighted average cost of capital

The weighted average cost of capital (WACC) is the discount rate used in value management, including project appraisal. The capital structure of companies can be classified into two types:

- all equity;
- mixed, where debt and equity are held in varying proportions.

In an all-equity firm the current cost of equity capital could be used as the discount rate because it represents the opportunity cost of the shareholders' capital. This is acceptable if any new investment would not alter the company's overall level of risk.

For the more common type of capital structure, a mixed one, the discount rate is calculated by weighting the cost of debt and equity in proportion to their contribution to the total capital of the firm. Consider the example of Poise plc.

Worked example 16.2 Poise plc

The before tax rate of return on debt, k_{DBT}, is 10 per cent, whereas the required return on equity is 20 per cent. The total amount of capital in use (equity + debt), V, is £2m. Of that, £1.4m represents the market value of its equity, V_E, and £600,000 equals the market value of its debt, V_D.

Thus:

$$k_{DBT} = 10\%$$
$$k_E = 20\%$$
$$V = £2m$$
$$V_E = £1.4m$$
$$V_D = £0.6m$$

The weight for equity capital is:

$$W_E = \frac{V_E}{V} = \frac{1.4}{2.0} = 0.7$$

The weight for debt is:

$$W_D = \frac{V_D}{V} = \frac{0.6}{2.0} = 0.3$$

The corporate tax rate is 30 per cent and therefore the after-tax cost of debt is:

$$k_{DAT} = k_{DBT}\,(1–T)$$

$$k_{DAT} = 10\,(1 - 0.30) = 7\%$$

The weighted average cost of capital for Poise is:

$$\begin{aligned} \text{WACC} &= k_E W_E + k_{DAT} W_D \\ &= 20\% \times 0.7 + 7\% \times 0.3 \\ &= 16.1\% \end{aligned}$$

This is the rate of return demanded by Poise's finance providers given the firm's existing set of risky projects.

What the WACC tells you

Imagine that a corporation obtained one-half of its £1,000 million of capital from lenders. The cost of this debt capital is 8 per cent after account has been taken of the ability of the firm to offset interest against taxable profits (after the company has benefited from the 'tax shield'). One-half of its capital is from shareholders, who require a 12 per cent rate of return. Thus we have the following facts:

Cost of debt after tax:		$k_{DAT} = 8\%$
Cost of equity:		$k_E = 12\%$
Weight of debt	(£500 million / £1 billion)	$W_D = 0.5$
Weight of equity	(£500 million / £1 billion)	$W_E = 0.5$

We need to calculate the weighted average cost of capital (WACC) to establish the minimum return needed on an investment within the firm, that will produce enough to satisfy the lenders and leave just enough to give shareholders their 12 per cent return. Anything less than this WACC and the shareholders will receive less than 12 per cent. They will quickly recognise that 12 per cent is available elsewhere for that level of risk and remove money from the firm.

$$\text{WACC} = k_E W_E + k_{DAT} W_D$$
$$\text{WACC} = 12 \times 0.5 + 8 \times 0.5 = 10\%$$

If the firm invested £100,000 in a project that produced a net cash flow per year of £10,000 to infinity (assuming a perpetuity makes the example simple), the first call on that cash flow is from the debt holders, who effectively supplied £50,000 of the funds for this project. The cost to the firm of satisfying them is £4,000 per annum. That leaves £6,000 for equity holders – an annual rate of return of 12 per cent on the £50,000 they provided.

If a return of £11,000 is generated then debt holders still cost the firm only £4,000, but the equity holders get a 14 per cent rate of return (£7,000 / £50,000).

If a return of £8,500 is generated then the lenders cost the firm £4,000, leaving £4,500 for the equity providers. This rate of return of merely 9 per cent is clearly inadequate for shareholders who could obtain 12 per cent elsewhere in the financial markets for the same level of risk.

The weighted average cost of capital (WACC) with three or more types of finance

The formula becomes longer, but not fundamentally more difficult when there are three (or more) types of finance. For example, if a firm has preference share capital as well as debt and equity the formula becomes:

$$\text{WACC} = k_E W_E + k_{DAT} W_D + k_p W_p$$

where W_p is the weight for preference shares.

The weight for each type of capital is proportional to market values – and, of course, $W_E + W_D + W_p$ totals to 1.0.

Do not use the cost of the latest capital raised to discount projects, SBUs etc.

The latest capital raised by a company might have been equity at 12 per cent, or debt at a cost of 8 per cent. If the firm is trying to decide whether to go ahead with a project which will produce an IRR of, say, 10.5 per cent the project will be rejected if the latest capital-raising exercise was for equity and the discount rate used was 12 per cent. On the other hand the project will be accepted if, by chance, the latest funds raised happen to be debt with a cost of 8 per cent. The WACC should be used for all projects – at least, for all those of the same risk class as the existing set of projects. The reason is that a firm cannot move too far away from its optimal debt to equity ratio level. If it does its WACC will rise (*see* Chapter 18). So, although it may seem attractive for a subsidiary manager to promote a favoured project by saying that it can be financed with borrowed funds and therefore it needs only to achieve a rate of return in single figures it must be borne in mind that the next capital-raising exercise after that will have to be for equity to maintain an appropriate financial gearing level.[14]

Applying WACC to SBUs and projects

Different projects or different activities can have different degrees of risk. For example, a firm could take a very conservative stance and invest all its money in government bonds where the risk would be very low. Alternatively it could set up a division to develop a cure for cancer: the rewards will be large if successful drugs and treatments are found, but the risks are high that all the investment will be lost.

Projects and SBUs with a higher risk than the existing set should be discounted at a higher rate. Using Exhibit 16.23 it would be inappropriate to use 16 per cent as the discount rate for a new project to develop a computer game as well as for the well-established division which produces matches. Given the higher risk of computer game development a 20 per cent rate of return is required whereas the value created from the match division is calculated using a 12 per cent rate of return.

Exhibit 16.23 Higher-risk activities are discounted at higher rates

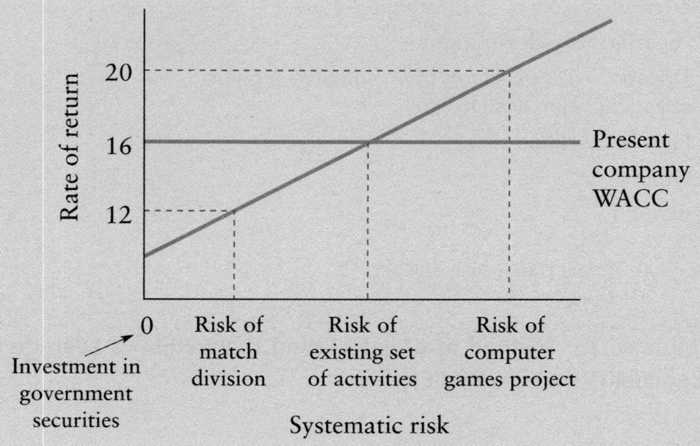

EMPIRICAL EVIDENCE OF CORPORATE PRACTICE

Academic literature promotes the use of a weighted average cost of capital. This section considers the extent to which United Kingdom firms have adopted the recommended methods. In 1983 Richard Pike expressed a poor opinion of the techniques used by businessmen to select the cost of capital: 'the methods commonly applied in setting hurdle rates are a strange mixture of folk-lore, experience, theory and intuition'. In 1976 Westwick and Shohet reported that less than 10 per cent of the firms they studied used a WACC. The position has changed significantly over the last two decades. Arnold and

Hatzopoulos (2000), in a study of 96 UK firms, found that the majority now calculate a WACC – *see* Exhibit 16.24.

Despite years of academic expounding on the virtues of WACC and extensive managerial education, a significant minority of firms do not calculate a WACC for use in capital investment appraisal. Furthermore, as Exhibits 16.25 and 16.26 show, many firms that calculate a WACC do not follow the prescribed methods. Some of the statements made by respondents showed that many fail to follow a textbook procedure:

> above is a minimum [WACC]. A hurdle rate is also used which is the mid-point of the above [WACC] and the lowest rate of return required by venture capitalists.
>
> WACC + safety margin.
>
> Weighted average cost of capital plus inflation.

Exhibit 16.24 Replies to the question: How does your company derive the discount rate used in the appraisal of major capital investments? (percentage of respondents)

	Category of company			
Method used	*Small (%)*	*Medium (%)*	*Large (%)*	*Composite (%)*
WACC	41	63	61	54
The cost of equity derived from the capital asset pricing model is used	0	8	16	8
Interest payable on debt capital is used	23	8	1	11
An arbitrarily chosen figure	12	4	3	6
Dividend yield on shares plus estimated growth in capital value of share	0	0	3	1
Earnings yield on shares	3	0	0	1
Other	12	8	11	10
Blank	9	8	5	7

Source: Arnold and Hatzopoulos (2000).

Exhibit 16.25 Method of of calculating the weighted average cost of capital (percentage of respondents that use WACC)

	Category of company			
Method	*Small (%)*	*Medium (%)*	*Large (%)*	*Composite (%)*
Using the capital asset pricing model for equity and the market rate of return on debt capital	50	68	79	70
Cost of the equity calculated other than through the capital asset pricing model with the cost of debt derived from current market interest rates	50	32	18	29
Other	0	0	3	1

Source: Arnold and Hatzopoulos (2000).

Exhibit 16.26 If the weighted average cost of capital is used, then how are the weights defined? (percentage of respondents)

	Category of company			
Method of defining weights	*Small* (%)	*Medium* (%)	*Large* (%)	*Composite* (%)
A long-term target debt and equity ratio	19	26	39	30
The present market values of debt and equity	44	47	42	44
Balance sheet ratios of debt and equity	37	26	19	26

Source: Arnold and Hatzopoulos (2000).

Gregory and Rutterford (1999) and Rutterford (2000) carried out a series of in-depth interviews with 18 FTSE-100 company finance directors or heads of corporate finance in 1996. They found that 14 of the companies made use of the capital asset pricing model to estimate the equity cost of capital, five used the dividend yield plus growth method (Gordon's growth model), four used the historic real rate of return on equity and five used more than one method.

In terms of the risk-free rate most firms (12 out of 14 using the CAPM) used the yield on UK government bonds – they generally chose a maturity of between seven and 20 years. The remainder used a real rate of interest with an implicit or explicit inflation rate. None used the Treasury bill rate.

Betas were sourced from financial databases, such as that of the London Business School, or from financial advisers – most firms used more than one source. Many interviewees felt that any fine-tuning of the beta estimate would have less impact on the k_E estimate than would the choice of the equity risk premium.

Two out of the 13 firms which estimated an equity risk premium chose a figure from a mid-1990s Barclays Capital Equity-Gilt Study. This was based on a different time period to the recent Barclays Capital report (2001) we have used in Chapter 8 (the mid-1990s studies track returns from 1918 only) – the figure reported (7.5 per cent) is much higher than that used earlier in this chapter. The other 11 firms chose a number in a narrow range of 4.5 per cent to 6 per cent. The firms concerned admitted that their estimates were a 'gut feel' choice 'that came from our planning manager. He's an MBA and a lot of his MBA work was on the cost of capital. 5 per cent is a figure he's plucked out of the air based on his experience and knowledge' (Company O: Gregory and Rutterford, 1999, p. 43). Alternatively managers tended to rely on advice from their bankers that the current equity risk premium was lower than at any time in the past – this had the effect of reducing the WACC estimate by almost two percentage points (compared with using a risk premium of 7.5 per cent) in most cases. This intuitive approach has subsequently been borne out by the downward revision of historic risk premiums in empirical studies, such as Barclays' 2001 Equity-Gilt Study.

All 11 firms that explicitly consider the cost of debt allowed for the marginal corporate tax rate to reduce the effective cost. All the companies used the cost of long-term debt. The majority chose to base the cost of debt on the cost of government debt and either take this as the cost of debt or add a credit risk premium. Three companies took the yield on their own outstanding bonds and the remainder chose a long-term bond yield 'based on experience'. 'We do not put in our real cost of debt. There are certain, for example tax driven, vehicles which give us actually quite a low cost of debt . . . So we tend to ignore those. That does build up a nice margin of safety within the target (cost of capital) of course.' (Company C: Gregory and Rutterford, 1999, p. 46).

Ten out of 15 firms that calculated the WACC used a long-run target debt/equity ratio, five used the actual debt/equity ratio and one used both. For firms using a target ratio, this was taken as 20 per cent, 25 per cent or 30 per cent, and was at least as high as the current actual debt/equity ratio, in some cases substantially higher – one firm with a cash surplus nevertheless chose a ratio of 20 per cent.

Ten companies chose to estimate a nominal WACC (average value of 11.67 per cent). Five used a real (excluding inflation) WACC (average value of 8.79 per cent) and three used both a nominal and a real WACC. Rutterford (2000) comments: 'differences in data inputs for the equity risk premium (from 4 per cent to 7.5 per cent) and the choice of debt/equity ratio (from 0 per cent to 50 per cent) meant that the final WACC estimate was a fairly subjective estimate for each firm'.

Corporations seem to make a distinction between WACC and the hurdle rate. Gregory and Rutterford found that the average *base* hurdle rate was 0.93 per cent higher than the average WACC. The base hurdle rate is defined as the rate for standard projects, before any adjustments for divisional differences in operating risk, financial risk or currency risk. Most of the firms had a range of hurdle rates, depending on project or the risk factors. However there was no consensus among the firms on how to adjust the differential project risk. Fourteen out of 18 made some adjustment for different levels of risk, with nine of those 14 making some adjustment for country risk or foreign exchange risk as well as for systematic risk. Note however that in 17 out of 18 cases the adjustment was made to the base hurdle rate and not to the more theoretically appropriate WACC. There was a general impression of sophistication in attaining the WACC in the first place, followed by a rule-of-thumb-type approach when making risk adjustments: 'The comment I make in terms of the hurdle rates for investment purposes is that we do it relatively simplistically in terms of low risk, high risk, country-specific risk' (Company P: Gregory and Rutterford, 1999, p. 53). Methods range from adding two percentage point increments, to having two possible hurdle rates, say, 15 per cent and 20 per cent. Fifteen firms had premiums of zero per cent to 8 per cent over the base hurdle rate, while three firms added more than 10 percentage points for the highest-risk projects.

Even when the textbook model is accepted a range of WACCs can be estimated for the same firm: 'for example, altering the choice of target debt/equity ratio or equity risk premium can have an impact of 2 per cent or more on the resulting WACC figure. Furthermore, little work has yet been done to extend the complex analysis for the firm's WACC to the divisional level' (Rutterford, 2000, p. 149). This lack of sophistication was confirmed in another study, carried out by Francis and Minchington (2000) that discovered 24 per cent of firms (of varied sizes) used a divisional cost of capital that reflects the cost of debt capital only. Furthermore, 69 per cent did not use a different rate for different divisions to reflect levels of risk.

IMPLEMENTATION ISSUES

How large is the equity risk premium?

To understand the controversy over the equity risk premium we need to appreciate that it can only ever be a subjective estimate. The reason for this is that we are trying to figure out how much additional annual return investors in an averagely risky share require above the risk-free rate today. Investors when deciding this are looking at the future, not the past. Each investor is likely to have a different assessment of the appropriate extra return compared with the risk-free investment. We need to assess the weighted average of investors' attitudes.

Using historical returns to see the size of the premium actually received may be a good starting point, but we must be aware that we are making a leap of faith to then assume that the past equity risk premium is relevant for today's analysis with its future focus. In using historic data we are making at least two implicit assumptions:

- There has been no systematic change in the risk aversion of investors over time.
- The index being used as a benchmark has had an average riskiness that has not altered in a systematic way over time.

Some City analysts believe that things have changed so radically in terms of the riskiness of ordinary shares for a fully diversified investor that the risk premium is now very small – some plump for 2 per cent while extremists say that over the long run shares are no more risky than gilts, and therefore say that the premium is zero. To justify their beliefs they point to the conquest of inflation, the lengthening of economic cycles, the long bull market and the increasing supply of risk capital as ageing industrial societies start to save more for retirement.

Even Barclays Capital dramatically revised the figure in their annual equity-gilt study in the last four years or so. In the 1997 study they showed annual equity returns of more than seven percentage points greater than gilts. As a result of improved analysis and an extension of the analysis back to 1899 their estimate for the risk premium falls to 4.4 per cent. The Competition Commission tends to take a range of between 3.5 and 5 per cent. OFWAT (the UK water industry regulator) prefers not to use historic premiums as they 'all significantly overstate the current expectations of actual equity investors'; OFWAT uses a range of between 3 and 4 per cent. OFGEM (the UK gas and electricity regulator) states that a range of between 3 and 4.2 per cent 'appears appropriate' (based on forward-looking averages of market predictions). Note that in their negotiating stance the regulators are likely to take a range that is as low as possible.[15]

In my view, equities have not become as safe as gilts. For equities the last two decades have been an unusually charmed period. If long-term history is guide shareholders will eventually learn the hard way that one can lose a great deal of money in stock markets. It is possible for returns to be negative for an entire decade or more. Turbulence and volatility will be as present in the twenty-first century as in the last. I believe the prudent investor needs to examine a long period of time, in which rare, but extreme, events have disrupted the financial system (wars, depressions, manias and panics) to gain an impression of the riskiness of shares.

What is clear is that obtaining the risk premium is not as scientific as some would pretend. The range of plausible estimates is wide and the effect of choosing 2 per cent rather than 4.4 per cent, or even 7.5 per cent can have a significant effect on the acceptance or rejection of capital investment projects within the firm, or the calculation of value performance metrics. One of the respondents to the Arnold and Hatzopoulos survey expressed the frustration of practitioners by pointing out that precision in the WACC method is less important than to have reliable basic data: 'The real issue is one of risk premium on equity. Is it 2% or 8%?!'

Which risk-free rate?

The risk-free rate is a completely certain return. For complete certainty two conditions are needed:

- The risk of default is zero.
- When intermediate cash flows are earned on a multi-year investment there is no uncertainty about reinvestment rates.

The return available on a zero coupon government bond which has a time horizon equal to the cash flow (of a project, an SBU, etc.) being analysed is the closest we are going to get to the theoretically correct risk-free rate of return.

Business projects usually involve cash flows arising at intervals, rather than all at the end of an investment. Theoretically, each of these separate cash flows should be discounted using different risk-free rates. So, for the cash flows arising after one year on a multi-year project, the rate on a one-year zero-coupon government bond should be used as part of the calculation of the cost of capital. The cash flows arising in year five should be discounted on the basis of a cost of capital calculated using the five-year zero-coupon rate and so on. However, this approach is cumbersome, and there is a practical alternative that gives a reasonable approximation to the theoretical optimum. It is considered acceptable to use a long-term government rate on all the cash flows of a project that has a long-term horizon. Furthermore, the return on a government bond with coupons, rather than a zero coupon bond, is generally taken to be acceptable. The rule of thumb seems to be to use the return available on a reputable government security having the same time horizon as the project under consideration – so for a short-term project one should use the discount rate which incorporates the short-term government security rate, for a 20-year project use the 20-year government bond yield-to-maturity.

How reliable are the CAPM and beta?

There are many problems with the use of beta in the cost of equity capital calculation. We will consider two of them here:

1 **The use of historic betas for future analysis** Should betas be calculated using weekly or monthly data? Should the observation period be three, five or ten years? Each is likely to provide a different estimate of beta. Even if this question is resolved the difficulty of using an historic measure for estimating a future relationship is very doubtful. As we saw in Chapter 8 betas tend to be unstable over time. Exhibit 16.27 gives an impression of the variability of the betas for some UK firms – some have been stable, while others have changed significantly.

Exhibit 16.27 Betas as measured for the five years to 1997 and 2000

	1997	*2000*
BOC	0.65	0.59
Barclays Bank	1.22	1.55
BT	0.91	0.94
GUS	0.59	0.39
Marks and Spencer	0.95	0.44
J. Sainsbury	0.60	0.19

Source: Thomson Financial Datastream

2 **The breakdown in the relationship between beta and returns** The fundamental point about the CAPM is that investors demand higher returns on more volatile shares (beta > 1). Recent evidence has cast considerable doubt on the strength of the relationship between the CAPM's beta and return.

FUNDAMENTAL BETA

Instead of using historical betas calculated through a regression of the firm's returns against a proxy for the market portfolio some analysts calculate a 'fundamental beta'. This is based on the intuitive underpinning of the risk-return relationship: if the firm (or project) cash flows are subject to more (systematic) variability then the required return should be higher. What causes greater systematic variability? Three factors have been advanced:

1 **The type of business that the company (SBU or project) is engaged in** Some businesses are more sensitive to market conditions than others. The turnover and profits of cyclical industries change a great deal with macroeconomic fluctuations. So, for example, the sale of yachts, cars or designer clothes rises in a boom and crashes in decline. On the other hand, non-cyclical industries, such as food retailing or tobacco, experience less variability with the economic cycle. Thus, in a fundamental beta framework cyclical businesses would be allocated a higher beta than non-cyclical businesses. If the purchase of the product can be delayed for months, years or even indefinitely (i.e. it is discretionary) then it is more likely to be vulnerable to an economic downturn.
2 **Degree of operating gearing** If the firm has high fixed costs compared with variable costs of production its profits are highly sensitive to output levels. A small percentage fall in output and revenue can result in a large percentage change in profits. The higher variability in profit means that a higher beta should be allocated.
3 **Degree of financial gearing** If the company has high borrowings, with a concomitant requirement to pay interest regularly, then profits attributable to shareholders are likely to be more vulnerable to shocks. So the beta will rise if the company has higher financial gearing (or leverage). The obligation to meet interest payments increases the variability of after-interest profits. In a recession profits can more easily turn into losses. Financial gearing exacerbates the underlying business risk.

The obvious problem with using the fundamental beta approach is the difficulty of deriving the exact extent to which beta should be adjusted up or down depending on the strength of the three factors.

SOME THOUGHTS ON THE COST OF CAPITAL

There have been a number of significant advances in theory and in practice over the last 40 years. No longer do most firms simply use the current interest rate, or adjust for risk in an entirely arbitrary manner. There is now a theoretical base to build on, both to determine a cost of capital for a firm, and to understand the limitations (or qualities) of the input data and modelling.

It is generally accepted that a weighted average of the costs of all the sources of finance is to be used. It is also accepted that the weights are to be based on market values (rather than book values), as market values relate more closely to the opportunity cost of the finance providers.

Even before the development of modern finance it was obvious that projects (or collections of projects, as firms are) that had a risk higher than that of investing in government securities require a higher rate of return. A risk premium must be added to the risk-free rate to determine the required return. However, modern portfolio theory has refined the definition of risk, so the analyst need only consider compensation (additional return) for systematic risk.

Despite the progress, considerable difficulties remain. Practitioners need to be aware of both the triumphs of modern financial theory as well as its gaps. The area of greatest controversy is the calculation of the cost of equity capital. In determining the cost of equity capital we start with the following facts.

- The current risk-free rate is the bedrock. It is acceptable to use the rate on a government bond with the same maturity as the project, SBU, etc.
- One increases the return to allow for the risk on a share with average systematic risk. (Add a risk premium to the risk-free rate return.) As a guide, investors have received a risk premium of around 4–5 per cent for accepting the risk level equivalent to that on the average ordinary share over the past 100 years.
- A particular company's shares do not carry average equity risk, therefore the risk premium should be increased or decreased depending on the company's systematic risk level.

So, if the project or SBU under examination has a systematic risk which is lower than that on the average share then it would seem sensible that the returns attributable to shareholders on this project should be somewhere between the risk-free rate and the risk-free rate plus, say, 5 per cent. If the project has a systematic risk greater than that exhibited by shares generally then the returns required for shareholders will be more than the risk-free rate plus, say, 5 per cent.

The main difficulty is in calculating the systematic risk level. In the heyday of the CAPM this was simple: beta was all you needed. Today we have to allow for a multiplicity of systematic risk factors. Not unnaturally many business people are unwilling to adopt such a burdensome approach and fall back on their 'judgement' to adjust for the risk of a project. In practice it is extremely difficult to state precisely the riskiness of a project – we are dealing with future uncertainties about cash flows from day-to-day business operations subject to sudden and unforeseen shocks. The pragmatic approach is to avoid precision and simply place each proposed project into one of three risk categories: low, medium or high. This neatly bypasses the complexities laid out by the theorists and also accurately reflects the fact that decisions made in the real world are made with less than complete knowledge. Mechanical decision making within the firm based on over-simplistic academic models is often a poor substitute for judgement recognising the imperfections of reality.

One thing is certain: if anyone ever tells you that they can unequivocally state a firm's cost of capital to within a tenth of a percentage point, you know you are talking to someone who has not quite grasped the complexity of the issue.

CONCLUDING COMMENTS

A commercial organisation that adopts value principles is one that has an important additional source of strength. The rigorous thought process involved in the robust application of these principles will force managers to review existing systems and product and market strategies and to bring an insistence on a contribution to shareholder value from all parts of the company. A firm that has failed to ask the right questions of its operating units and to use the correct metrics in measuring performance will find its position deteriorating *vis-à-vis* its competitors. One that asks an unreasonably high rate of return will be denying its shareholders wealth-enhancing opportunities and ceding valuable markets to competitors. One that employs an irrationally low cost of capital will be wasting resources, setting managers targets that are unduly easy to reach and destroying wealth.

KEY POINTS AND CONCEPTS

- **Switching to value-based management principles affects many aspects of the organisation.** These include:
  - strategic business unit strategy and structure;
  - corporate strategy;
  - culture;
  - systems and processes;
  - incentives and performance measurement;
  - financial strategy.
- A **strategic business unit** (SBU) is a business unit within the overall corporate entity which is distinguishable from other business units because it serves a defined external market in which management can conduct strategic planning in relation to products and markets.
- **Strategy** means selecting which product or market areas to enter/exit and how to ensure a good competitive position in those markets or products.
- **SBU managers** should be involved in strategy development because **a** they usually have great knowledge to contribute, and **b** they will have greater 'ownership' of the subsequently chosen strategy.
- A **review of current SBU** activities using **value-creation profile charts** may reveal particular product or customer categories which destroy wealth.
- **Strategic analysis** has three stages:
  - strategic assessment;
  - strategic choice;
  - strategic implementation.
- **Strategic assessment** focuses on the three determinants of value creation:
  - industry attractiveness;
  - competitive resources;
  - life-cycle stage of value potential.
- **Competitive resource analysis** can be conducted using the **TRRACK system:**
  - Tangible
  - Relationships
  - Reputation
  - Attitude
  - Capabilities
  - Knowledge

- A company's SBU positions with regard to the three value creation factors could be represented in a **strategy planes diagram**. The product and/or market segment within SBUs can also be shown on strategy planes.

- To make good **strategic choices** a wide search for alternatives needs to be encouraged.

- **Sustainable competitive advantage** is obtainable in three ways (according to Porter):
  - cost leadership;
  - differentiation;
  - focus.

- In the **evaluation of strategic options** both qualitative judgement and quantitative valuation are important. The short-listed options can be tested in sensitivity and scenario analysis as well as for financial and skill-base feasibility.

- **Strategy implementation** is making the chosen strategy work through the planned allocation of resources and the reorganisation and motivation of people.

- The **corporate centre** has four main roles in a value-based firm:
  - portfolio planning;
  - managing strategic value drivers shared by SBUs;
  - providing and inculcating the pervading philosophy and governing objective;
  - structuring the organisation so that rules and responsibilities are clearly defined, with clear accountability for value creation.

- **Targets, incentives and rewards** should be based on metrics appropriate to the level of management within the firm as shown in Exhibit 16.28.

Exhibit 16.28

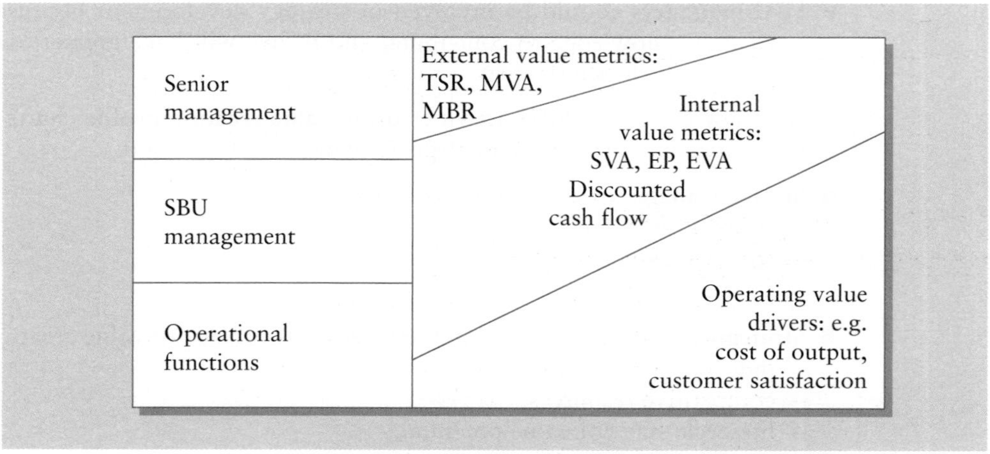

- **Shareholder Value Analysis** simplifies discounted cash flow analysis by employing (**Rappaport's**) **seven value drivers**, the first five of which change in a consistent fashion from one year to the next.
  Rappaport's seven value drivers:
  1. Sales growth rate.
  2. Operating profit margin.
  3. Tax rate.

4 Fixed capital investment.
5 Working capital investment.
6 The planning horizon.
7 The required rate of return.

Corporate value = Shareholder value + Debt value

- **At least four strategic options should be considered** for a SBU or product and/or market segment:
  - base-case strategy;
  - liquidation;
  - trade sale or spin-off;
  - new operating strategy.

- **Merits of shareholder value analysis**
  - easy to understand and apply;
  - consistent with share valuation;
  - explicit value drivers;
  - able to benchmark.

- **Problems with shareholder value analysis**
  - constant percentages unrealistic;
  - can lead to poor decisions if misused;
  - data often unavailable.

- **Economic profit** (EP) is the amount earned after deducting all operating expenses *and* a charge for the opportunity cost of the capital employed. A major advantage over shareholder value analysis is that it uses accounting data.

- **Performance spread method of calculating EP:**

  Economic profit = Performance spread × Invested capital
  = (Return on capital – WACC) × Invested capital

- **The profits less capital charge approach to calculating EP:**

  Economic profit = Operating profit before interest and after tax – Capital charge
  = Operating profit before interest and after tax – Invested capital × WACC

- **Drawbacks of EP:**
  - the balance sheet does not reflect invested capital;
  - open to manipulation and arbitrariness;
  - high economic profit and negative NPV *can* go together;
  - problem with allocating revenues, costs and capital to business units.

- **Economic value added (EVA®)** is an attempt to overcome some of the accounting problems of standard EP.

  EVA = Adjusted invested capital × (Adjusted return on capital – WACC)
  or
  EVA = Adjusted operating profit after tax – (Adjusted invested capital × WACC)

- The **cost of capital** is the rate of return that a company has to offer finance providers to induce them to buy and hold a financial security.

- **Investors in shares** require a return, k_E, which provides for two elements:
  - a return equal to the risk-free rate; plus
  - a risk premium.

The risk premium calculation has two stages:
– estimate the average risk premium for shares $(r_m - r_f)$; and:
– adjust the average premium to suit the risk on a particular share.

The CAPM using a beta based on the relative co-movement of a share with the market has been used for the second stage but other risk factors appear to be relevant.

- An alternative method for calculating the required rate of return on equity is to use the **Gordon growth model:**

$$k_E = \frac{d_1}{P} + g$$

- The **cost of retained earnings** is equal to the expected returns required by shareholders buying new shares in a firm.
- The **cost of debt capital,** k_D, is the current market rate of return for a risk class of debt. The cost to the firm is reduced to the extent that interest can be deducted from taxable profits.

$$k_{DAT} = k_{DBT}(1 - T)$$

- The **cost of irredeemable constant dividend preference share capital** is:

$$k_p = \frac{d_1}{P_P}$$

- The **weighted average cost of capital (WACC)** is calculated by weighting the cost of debt and equity in proportion to their contribution to the total capital of the firm:

$$WACC = k_E W_E + k_{DAT} W_D$$

For projects, etc. with similar risk to that of the existing set, use WACC, which is based on the target debt to equity ratio. Do not use the cost of the latest capital raised.

- For projects, SBUs, etc. of a **different risk level to that of the firm,** raise or lower the discount rate in proportion to the risk.
- Companies use a mixture of theoretically correct techniques with rules-of-thumb to calculate hurdle rates of return.
- Calculating a cost of capital relies a great deal on judgement rather than scientific precision. But there is a theoretical framework to guide that judgement.

REFERENCES AND FURTHER READING

Allen, D. (1991) 'The whiching hour has arrived', *Management Accounting*, November, pp. 48–53. Contrasts shareholder value analysis with a technique called strategic financial management.

Arnold, G. (2000) 'Tracing the development of value-based management', in G.C. Arnold and M. Davies (eds.) *Value-Based Management*. London: Wiley. Shows the synthesis of the insights from a number of disciplines to create VBM.

Arnold, G. (2002) *Valuegrowth Investing*. London: FT Prentice Hall. An integration of strategic analysis with equity market investment principles.

Arnold, G.C. and Davies, M. (eds) (2000) *Value-Based Management*. London: Wiley. A collection of research monographs.

Arnold, G.C. and Hatzopoulos, P.D. (2000) 'The theory practice gap in capital budgeting: evidence from the United Kingdom', *Journal of Business Finance and Accounting*, 27(5) and (6), June/July, pp. 603–26.

Barclays Capital (2001) *The Equity-Gilt Study*. London: Barclays. Source of data on historic returns.

Blair, A. (1997a) 'EVA fever', *Management Today*, January, pp. 42–5. A critical appraisal of EVA and in particular Stern Stewart's advocacy of high debt levels.

Blair, A (1997b) 'Watching the new metrics', *Management Today*, April, pp. 48–50. Discusses the marketing behind the new value metrics.

Boston Consulting Group (1996) *Shareholder value metrics*. Shareholder Value Management Series. Builds on TSR to suggest some other value metrics.

Braxton Associates (1991) *The Fundamentals of Value Creation*. Insights: Braxton on Strategy. Boston, Mass: DRT International. Discusses accounting-based performance metrics and then goes on to describe a value-based metric, CFROI.

Braxton Associates (1993) *Managing for Value*. Insights: Braxton on Strategy. Boston, Mass: DRT International. The basics of value-based management are discussed.

Buffett, W. (1984) *Berkshire Hathaway Annual Report*. Omaha, Nebraska: Berkshire Hathaway. As with all reports by Buffett, this one is full of profound and witty insight. www.berkshirehathaway.com.

Collis, D.J. and Montgomery, C.A. (1997) *Corporate Strategy: Resources and the Scope of the Firm*. New York: McGraw Hill. A very important and easy to read book on the subject of resources of companies.

Copeland, T., Koller, T. and Murrin, J. (1996) *Valuation*. 2nd edn. New York: Wiley. The management of value-based organisations and the principles behind the techniques are explained extremely well.

Cornelius, I. and Davies, M. (1997) *Shareholder Value*. London: *Financial Times*: Financial Publishing. An excellent account of value-based management and the metrics used.

Damodaran, A. (1999) *Applied Corporate Finance: A User's Manual*. New York: Wiley. An excellent book prepared to deal with the difficult practical issues of WACC calculation and employment.

Davies, M. (2000) 'Lessons from Practice: VBM at Lloyds TSB', in G.C. Arnold and M. Davies (eds) *Value-Based Management*. London: Wiley. Insights into a company making use of VBM principles.

Davies, M., Arnold, G., Cornelius, I. and Walmsley, S. (2001) *Managing for Shareholder Value*. London: Informa. An overview of shareholder value management for practitioners.

De Wit, B. and Meyer, R. (1998) *Strategy: Process, Content, Context*. 2nd edn. London: International Thomson Business Press. Some interesting sections in a very long book.

Dimson, E., Marsh, P. and Staunton, M. (2001) *The Millennium Book II: 101 Years of Investment Returns*. London: London Business School and ABN Amro. Fascinating new evidence on risk premiums.

Fama, E.F. and French, K.R. (1992) 'The cross-section of expected stock returns', *Journal of Finance*, 47, pp. 427–65. A study casting doubt on beta and showing size of company and book-to-market ratio affecting returns on shares.

Francis, G. and Minchington, C. (2000) 'Value-based Metrics as Divisional Performance Measures', in G.C. Arnold and M. Davies (eds.) *Value-Based Management*. London: Wiley. Empirical evidence and discussion.

Gordon, M.J. (1962) *The Investment, Financing and Valuation of the Corporation*. Homewood, IL: Irwin. Dividend growth model.

Gordon, M.J. and Shapiro, E. (1956) 'Capital equipment analysis: the required rate of profit', *Management Science*, III pp. 102–10. Dividend growth model.

Gregory, A and Rutterford, J. (1999) 'The cost of capital in the UK: a comparison of industry and the city'. CIMA monograph, May. Evidence on UK practice.

Jackson, T. (1997) 'A serving of added value', *Financial Times*, 13 January, p. 12. Considers MVA, EVA, VCQ and Realised Economic Value (REV), another value metric.

Johnson, G. and Scholes, K. (2002) *Exploring Corporate Strategy*. 6th edn. Harlow: Financial Times Prentice Hall. A well-regarded introductory textbook to the strategic management of firms.

Kay, H. (1994) 'Capital city', *Director*, October, pp. 34–40. An easy-to-follow description of EVA and its application.

Kay, J. (1993) *Foundations of Corporate Success*. New York: Oxford University Press. A study of corporate strategy.

Knight, R.F. (1996) *Value Creation among Britain's Top 500 Companies*. Templeton College, Oxford: The Oxford Executive Research Briefings. A league table of the top 500 UK firms ranked by VCQ.

Lynn, A. (1995) 'Creating wealth', *Sunday Times*, 10 December. Uses Stern Stewart's MVA figures to compare the value created by UK companies.

McTaggart, J.M., Kontes, P.W. and Mankins, M.C. (1994) *The Value Imperative*. New York: Free Press. A superb book showing the application of value-based techniques to strategy and other disciplines.

Martin, P. (1998) 'Goldman's goose', *Financial Times*, 11 August, p. 14. Why Goldman Sachs can charge a large amount for advice.

Mills, R. and Print, C. (1995) 'Strategic value analysis', *Management Accounting*, February, pp. 35–7. Contrasts and points out the connection between shareholder value analysis and EVA.

Myers, R. (1996) 'Keeping score: Metric wars', *CFO*, October, pp. 41–50. Describes the battle amongst rival consultancies to sell their value metrics.

OFGEM (1999) 'Review of Public Electricity Suppliers, 1998–2000. Distribution Price control review: Consultation Paper', May. www.ofgem.gov.uk/public/pqarc.htm. Discussion of cost of capital.

Pike, R.H. (1983) 'A review of recent trends in formal capital budgeting processes', *Accounting and Business Research* (Summer), pp. 201–8. Evidence of practitioner approaches.

Porter, M.E. (1985) *Competitive Advantage*. New York: Free Press. One of the most important books on strategy ever written.

Rappaport, A. (1998) *Creating Shareholder Value*. Revised and updated edition. New York: Free Press. A landmark book. Presents an important value metric – shareholder value analysis.

Reimann, B.C. (1989) *Managing for Value*. Oxford: Basil Blackwell. Useful because it brings together strategy and value.

Rutterford, J. (2000) 'The cost of capital and shareholder value', in G.C. Arnold and M. Davies (eds) *Value-Based Management*. London: Wiley. Some fascinating evidence of UK practice.

Solomon, E. (1963) *The Theory of Financial Management*. New York: Columbia University Press. WACC presented for the first time.

Solomons, D. (1985) *Divisional Performance, Measurement and Control*. 2nd edn. (1st edn 1965) Connecticut: Weiner Publishing. An early use of the concept of economic profit.

Stewart, G.B. (1991) *The Quest for Value*. New York: Harper Business. Written by a founding partner in Stern Stewart & Co., the US consultancy, which has so successfully promoted MVA and EVA. Some useful insights.

Thal Larsen, P. (1997) 'EVA: Nice figures, but what do they mean?', *Investors Chronicle*, 17 January, pp. 18–19. An easy introduction to EVA.

Tully, S. (1993) 'The real key to creating wealth', *Fortune*, 20 September, pp. 38–50. The application of EVA to US corporations is described in an accessible style.

Westwick, C.A. and Shohet P.S.D. (1976) 'Investment Appraisal and Inflation', ICAEW Research Committee, Occasional Paper, No. 7. Early evidence of techniques used in practice.

SELF-REVIEW QUESTIONS

1 List the main areas in which value principles have an impact on the managerial process. Write a sentence explaining each one.

2 What is an SBU and how can a value-creation profile chart be used to improve on an SBU's performance?

3 List the three stages of strategic analysis and briefly describe the application of value-based management ideas to each one.

4 Invent a company and show how the strategic planes diagram can be used to enhance shareholder wealth. Explain each dimension of the planes as you do so.

5 Briefly describe the main roles of the corporate centre in a value-led organisation.

6 What types of value metrics are useful for achieving motivation and goal congruence at different levels within the firm?

7 List the stages in the conversion of profit and loss accounts to cash flow figures.

8 What is shareholder value analysis and what are the seven value drivers as described by Rappaport?

9 What is economic profit (EP)? Describe the alternative ways of measuring it.

10 Describe the relative merits and problems of shareholder value analysis and EP.

11 Why does 'the cost of capital' equal 'the required rate of return' for a company?

12 Explain how you might calculate the cost of equity capital.

13 Why can we not always take the coupon rate on a bond issued years ago as the cost of bond capital?

14 Describe the weighted average cost of capital and explain why a project SBU or product line should not be evaluated using the cost of finance associated with the latest portion of capital raised.

15 Should the WACC be used in all circumstances?

QUESTIONS AND PROBLEMS

1 (*Examination level*) Imagine you are an expert on finance and strategy and have been asked by a large company with subsidiaries operating in a variety of industrial sectors to explain how the organisation might be changed by the adoption of value principles. Write a report to convince the managerial team that the difficulties and expense of transformation will be worth it.

2 In the form of an essay discuss the links between strategy and finance with reference to value-based management principles.

3* Blue plc is a relatively small company with only one SBU. It manufactures wire grilles for the consumer markets, cooker manufacturers and for export. Following a thorough investigation by the finance department and customer line heads some facts emerged about the returns expected in each of these customer sectors. The consumer sector uses £1m of the firm's capital and is expected to produce a return of 18 per cent on this capital, for the next five years, after which it will return the same as its risk-adjusted cost of capital, 15 per cent.

The cooker sales sector uses £2m of capital and will return 14 per cent per annum for seven years when its planning horizon ends. Its WACC is 16 per cent.

The export sector has a positive performance spread of 2 per cent for the next six years. The required rate of return is 17 per cent. From Year 7 the performance spread becomes zero. This division uses £1.5m of capital.

Required

a Calculate the annual economic profit of each sector.

b What is the total value creation from each?

c Display a value-creation profile chart and suggest possible action.

4 Payne plc has six SBUs engaged in different industrial sectors:

	Proportion of firm's capital	*Annual value creation (£m)*
1 Glass production	0.20	3
2 Bicycles retailing	0.15	10
3 Forestry	0.06	2
4 Electrical goods manufacture	0.20	5
5 Car retailing	0.25	–1
6 Road surfacing	0.14	–10

Make assumptions (and explain them) about the industry attractiveness and competitive position of Payne and its stage in the life cycle of value potential. Place the SBUs on a strategic planes diagram. Explain and show how you would alter the portfolio of the company.

5 'The corporate centre in most firms is an expensive drag on the rest of the organisation.' Explain to this sceptical head of an SBU how the corporate centre can contribute to value creation.

6* Apply shareholder value analysis to an all-equity firm with the following Rappaport value drivers, assuming that the last reported annual sales were £25m.

Sales growth rate	13%
Operating profit margin before tax	10%
Tax rate	31%
Incremental fixed capital investment (IFCI)	11% of the change in sales
Incremental working capital investment (IWCI)	8% of the change in sales
Planning horizon	4 years
Required rate of return	15%

Marketable securities amount to £5m and depreciation can be taken to be equal to the investment needed to replace worn-out equipment.

7* Regarding the answer obtained in Question 6 as the 'base-case' strategy, make a judgement on the best strategic option given the following:

- If the firm were liquidated the operating assets could be sold, net of the repayment of liabilities, for a total of £20m.
- If the firm separated its A division from its B division then A could be sold for £10m and the B division would have the following Rappaport value drivers:

Sales growth rate	15%
Operating profit margin before tax	12%
Tax rate	31%
Incremental fixed capital investment (IFCI)	13% of the change in sales
Incremental working capital investment (IWCI)	10% of the change in sales
Planning horizon	6 years
Required rate of return	14%

The B division had sales in the last year of £15m.

- If both divisions are retained and a new product differentiation strategy is attempted then the following Rappaport value drivers will apply:

Sales	18%
Operating profit margin before tax	12%
Tax rate	31%
(IFCI)	15%
(IWCI)	9%
Planning horizon	5 years
Required rate of return	17%

8* a Conduct sensitivity analysis on the shareholder value analysis of Question 6, changing the required rate of return to 14 per cent and 16 per cent, and changing the planning horizon to Year 5 and Year 6. Present the results in a table and comment on them briefly.

b Discuss the advantages and disadvantages of using shareholder value analysis.

9 Last year Tops plc produced an accounting operating profit of £5m. Its WACC is 14 per cent and the firm has £50m of capital. What was the economic profit?

10* (*Examination level*) Burgundy plc is expected to have an operating profit of £1.5m this year. It is financed through bonds and ordinary shares. The bonds were issued five years ago at a par value of £100 (total funds raised £5m). They carry an annual coupon of 10 per cent, are due to be redeemed in four years and are currently trading at £105.

The company's shares have a market value of £4m, the return on risk-free government securities is 8 per cent and the risk premium for an average-risk share has been 5 per cent. Burgundy's shares have a lower than average risk and its historic beta as measured by the co-movement of its shares and the market index correctly reflects the risk adjustment necessary to the average risk premium – this is 0.85. The corporate tax rate is 31 per cent. Burgundy has a net asset figure of £3.5m showing in its balance sheet.

Required

a Calculate the cost of debt capital.

b Calculate the cost of equity capital.

c Calculate the weighted average cost of capital.

d Calculate the economic profit for Burgundy.

e Should Burgundy use the WACC for all future projects and SBUs? Explain your answer.

11 Explain and contrast economic profit and shareholder value analysis.

12 (*Examination level*) Petalt plc wishes to carry out a shareholder value analysis for which it has gathered the following information:

Latest annual sales	£1m
Sales growth rate	10%
Operating profit margin before tax	10%
Tax rate	31%
Incremental fixed capital investment	17% of sales change
Incremental working capital investment	6% of sales change
Planning horizon	5 years

The managers do not yet know the cost of capital but do have the following information. The capital is in three forms:

1 A floating-rate bank loan for £1m at 2 per cent over bank base rate. Base rates are currently 9 per cent.

2 A 25-year vanilla bond issued 20 years ago at par (£100) raising £1m. The bond has an annual coupon of 5 per cent and is currently trading at £80. The next coupon is due in one year.

3 Equity capital with a market value of £2m.

The rate of return available by purchasing government securities is currently 6 per cent and the average risk premium for shares over the risk-free rate has averaged 5 per cent. Petalt's shares have an above-average risk and its historic beta as measured by the co-movement of its shares and the market index correctly reflects the risk adjustment necessary to the average risk premium – this is 1.3.

Required

a Calculate the cost of bond finance.

b Calculate the cost of equity finance.

c Calculate the weighted average cost of capital.

d Calculate shareholder value.

e Conduct sensitivity analysis on the calculated shareholder value by altering the operating profit margin and the number of years in the planning horizon. Show a table containing three alternative profit margin assumptions and two planning horizon assumptions.

13† (*Examination level*) Diversified plc is trying to introduce an improved method of assessing investment projects using discounted cash flow techniques. For this it has to obtain a cost of capital to use as a discount rate.

The finance department has assembled the following information:

- The company has an equity beta of 1.50 which may be taken as the appropriate adjustment to the average risk premium. The yield on risk-free government securities is 7 per cent and the historic premium above the risk-free rate is estimated at 5 per cent for shares. Share prices and dividends per share over the past five years are as follows:

Year	Share price (pence)	Dividend per share (pence)
2001	270	29
1999	255	27
1998	243	24
1997	221	23
1996	205	18

– The 2002 dividend has just been declared at 32p per share and the company's market share price is 310p.
– The market value of the firm's equity is twice the value of its debt.
– The cost of borrowed money to the company is estimated at 12 per cent (before tax shield benefits).
– Corporation tax is 30 per cent.

Assume: No inflation.

Required

a Estimate the equity cost of capital using the capital asset pricing model (CAPM). Create an estimate of the weighted average cost of capital (WACC).

b Comment on the appropriateness of using this technique for estimating the cost of capital for project appraisal purposes for a company with many subsidiaries in different markets.

c Describe some of the evidence on the calcuation of WACC in practice by UK firms and comment on the justification for using rules-of-thumb rather than theoretically precise methods.

ASSIGNMENTS

1 Identify an SBU in a company you know well. Conduct a value-based analysis and write a report showing the current position and your recommendations for change. Include in the analysis value-creation profile charts, strategy planes diagrams, sources of competitive advantage (value drivers), qualitative evaluation of strategies, shareholder value analysis and EP.

2 Write a report for senior managers pointing out how incentive schemes within the firm should be changed to achieve goal congruence around shareholder wealth maximisation.

CHAPTER NOTES

1 See Johnson and Scholes (1999) for more detail.

2 For more detail on market attractiveness analysis consult any major textbook on strategy. Michael Porter is a leading writer in the field of strategy.

3 Kay (1993).

4 Martin (1998).

5 *Ibid.*

6 Collis and Montgomery (1997).

7 De Wit and Meyer (1998).

8 Operating profit margin on sales is sales revenue *less* cost of sales and all selling and administrative expenses before tax and interest.

9 The meaning of the word 'capital' used here is different from its meaning in accounting. 'Capital' in accounting is a part of the shareholders' equity of the company ('capital issued', 'paid-in capital', etc.). 'Capital' in the present context means the sum of shareholders' equity and of the borrowings of the company.

10 There are a few technical complications ignored here, but this is the essence or EP. For more detail consult either Cornelius and Davies (1997) or Stewart (1991).

11 Quoted in *Management Today*, January 1997, p. 45.

12 Quoted in *Management Today*, January 1997, p. 45.

13 Quoted in Philip Coggan and Paul Cheeseright, *Financial Times*, 8 November 1994.

14 Short-term debt should be included as part of the overall debt of the firm when calculating WACC. The lenders of this money will require a return. However, to the extent that this debt is temporary or is offset by cash and marketable securities, it may be excluded.

15 An excellent discussion of the calculation of the cost of capital by regulators is to be found in Lockett, M. (2001) 'Calculating the Cost of Capital for the Regulated Electricity Distribution Companies', Aston University MBA Project Dissertation.

Chapter 17

VALUING SHARES

INTRODUCTION

Knowledge of the main influences on share prices is important from the perspective of two groups. The first group is managers, who, if they are to be given the responsibility of maximising the wealth of shareholders, need to know the factors influencing that wealth, as reflected in the share price. Without this understanding they will be unable to determine the most important consequence of their actions – the impact on share value. Managers need to appreciate share price derivation because it is one of the key factors by which they are judged. It is also useful for them to know how share prices are set if the firm plans to gain a flotation on a stock exchange, or when it is selling a division to another firm. In mergers an acquirer needs good valuation skills so as not to pay more than necessary, and a seller needs to ensure that the price is fair.

The second constituency for whom the ideas and models presented in this chapter will be of practical use is investors, who risk their savings by buying shares.

This chapter describes the main methods of valuing shares: net asset value, dividend valuation model, price earnings ratio model, cash flow model and the owner earnings model. There is an important subsection in the chapter which shows that the valuation of shares which give managerial control over the firm is somewhat different to the valuation of shares which provide only a small minority stake.

Learning objectives

By the end of this chapter the reader should be able to:

- describe the principal determinants of share prices and be able to estimate share value using a variety of approaches;
- demonstrate awareness of the most important input factors and appreciate that they are difficult to quantify;
- use valuation models to estimate the value of shares when managerial control is achieved.

Two skills are needed to be able to value shares. The first is analytical ability, to be able to understand and use mathematical valuation models. Second, and most importantly, good judgement is needed, because most of the inputs to the mathematical calculations are factors, the precise nature of which cannot be defined with absolute certainty, so great skill is required to produce reasonably accurate results. The main problem is that the determinants of value occur in the future, for example future cash flows, dividends or earnings.

The monetary value of an asset is what someone is prepared to pay for it. Assets such as cars and houses are difficult enough to value with any degree of accuracy. At least corporate bonds generally have a regular cash flow (coupon) and an anticipated capital repayment. This contrasts with the uncertainties associated with shares, for which there is no guaranteed annual payment and no promise of capital repayment.

The difficulties of share valuation are amply represented by the cases of Amazon.com and Orange.

CASE STUDY 17.1

Amazon.com

Amazon, the internet retailer, has never made a profit. In fact it lost over \$700m in 1999 and offered little prospect of profits in the near term. So, if you were an investor in early 2000 what value would you give to a company of this calibre? Anything at all? Amazingly, investors valued Amazon at over \$30 billion in early 2000 (more than all the traditional book retailers put together). The brand was well established and the numbers joining the online community rose by thousands every day. Investors were confident that Amazon would continue to attract customers and produce a rapid rate of growth in revenue. Eventually, it was thought, this revenue growth would translate into profits and high dividends. When investors had calmed down after taking account of the potential for rivalrous competition in this business and the fact that by 2001 Amazon was still not producing profits they reassessed the value of Amazon's likely future dividends. In mid-2001, they judged the company to be worth only \$4bn – it had run up losses of \$1.4bn in 2000, indicating that profits and dividends were still a long way off.

Orange

When France Telecom first contemplated selling 15 per cent of Orange and floating the company it valued the firm at €150bn. That was in May 2000. As the flotation drew nearer in January 2001 Orange was valued by analysts at less than half this amount at between €55bn and €65bn. Much had changed in the mobile telephone industry in 2000. The prospect for continued high growth was beginning to look suspect. Even if large numbers of new customers bought mobile phones the operators had agreed to pay so much to obtain third-generation mobile licences and to set up the required infrastructure that future profit projections were rapidly marked down. When the shares were floated in February, France Telecom sold them at €10, valuing the entire company at a mere €43bn. Worse was to follow: the share price immediately declined to €8.96.

These companies are not the worst casualties of the new economy bubble-burst. There is a so-called club, the 99% Club, for companies which are now valued at less than 1 per cent of their previous valuation.

VALUATION USING NET ASSET VALUE (NAV)

The balance sheet seems an obvious place to start when faced with the task of valuation. In this method the company is viewed as being worth the sum of the value of its net assets. The balance sheet is regarded as providing objective facts concerning the company's ownership of assets and obligations to creditors. Here fixed assets are recorded along with stocks, debtors, cash and other liquid assets. With the deduction of long-term and short-term creditors from the total asset figure we arrive at the net asset value (NAV).

An example of this type of calculation is shown Exhibit 17.1 for the retailer Boots.

Exhibit 17.1 Boots plc Abridged Balance Sheet 31 March 2000

		£m
Fixed assets		2,002.5
Current assets		
Stocks	689.5	
Debtors falling due within one year	404.5	
Debtors falling due after more than one year	4.0	
Investments and deposits	379.2	
Cash at bank and in hand	43.0	
		1,520.2
Creditors: Amounts falling due within one year		(1,153.2)
Creditors: Amounts falling due after more than one year		(489.2)
Provisions for liabilities and charges		(26.8)
Net assets		1,853.5
Equity shareholders' funds		1,851.6
Equity minority interests		0.5
Non-equaity minority interests		1.4
		1,853.5

Source: Boots plc *Annual Report 2000*

The NAV of £1,853.5m of Boots plc compares with a market value placed on all the shares when totalled of £6,000m (market capitalisation). This great difference makes it clear that the shareholders of Boots are not rating the firm on the basis of balance sheet net asset figures. This point is emphasised by an examination of Exhibit 17.2.

Some of the firms listed in Exhibit 17.2 have a very small balance sheet value in comparison with their total market capitalisation. For most companies, investors look to the income flow to be derived from a holding. This flow is generated when the balance sheet assets are combined with assets impossible to quantify: these include the unique skills of the workforce, the relationships with customers and suppliers, the value of brands, the reservoir of experience within the management team, and the competitive positioning of the firms' products. Thus assets, in the crude sense of balance sheet values, are only one dimension of overall value. Investors in the market generally value intangible, unmeasurable assets more highly than those which can be identified and recorded by accountants.

Exhibit 17.2 Net asset values and total capitalisation of some firms

Company (Accounts year)	*NAV £m*	*Total capitalisation (market value of company's shares) £m*
British Telecom (2001)	14,069	38,858
Cadbury Schweppes (2000)	2,927	9,540
EMI (2001)	660	3,262
Kingfisher (2001)	3,556.7	5,580
Marks and Spencer (2000)	4,921.8	7,187
Oxford BioMedica (2000)	12.98	91

Source: Annual reports and accounts; *Financial Times*, 23 July 2001.

Exhibit 17.3 What creates value for shareholders?

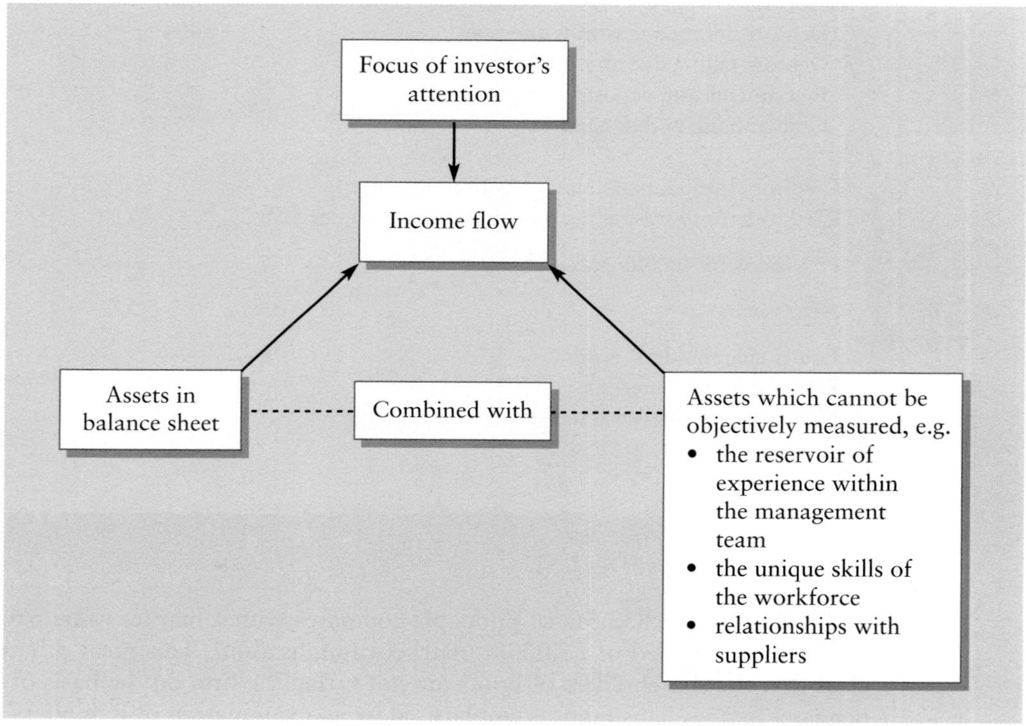

Criticising accountants for not producing balance sheets which reflect the true value of a business is unfair. Accounts are not usually designed to record up-to-date market values. Land and buildings are frequently shown at cost rather than market value; thus the balance sheet can provide a significant over- or under-valuation of the assets' current value. Plant and machinery is shown at the purchase price less a depreciation amount. Stock is valued at the lower of cost or net realisable value – this can lead to a significant under-estimate, as the market value can appreciate to a figure far higher than either of these. The list of balance sheet entries vulnerable to subjective estimation, arbitrary method and even cynical manipulation is a long one: goodwill, provisions, merger accounting, debtors, intangible brand values and so on.

The slippery concept of balance sheet value is demonstrated in the article about Hanson reproduced in Exhibit 17.4.

Exhibit 17.4

Hanson cuts asset value by £3.2bn

FT

Hanson, the industrial conglomerate, yesterday marked the latest stage of its four-way demerger by announcing a £3.2bn reduction in assets following accounting changes and write-downs in the value of its US mineral reserves.

The write-downs at Peabody, the largest coal producer in the US, and Hanson's Cornerstone aggregates subsidiary will bring the company into line with US accounting standards on the treatment of 'long lived assets'.

Mr Derek Bonham, chief executive, said the move would have no impact on operational cash flow and added: 'It in no way reflects on the accuracy of previous accounts.'

Some industry analysts, however, suggested Hanson might have overvalued the assets of both Peabody and Cornerstone in the past – a charge rejected by the company.

In total, the book value of mineral reserves at Cornerstone have been reduced by £2.3bn to £1.3bn and by £600m at Peabody to £1.5bn. A further £300m charge is being made against Peabody's reserves to cover accounting changes over industry liabilities.

As part of the accounting changes, Hanson has removed £1.2bn of its £1.5bn provisions from Peabody's balance sheet and plans to charge £300m of previous payments to profit and loss reserves. Mr Bonham said this move would cut the carrying value of Peabody's coal reserves by £1.5bn.

Source: Tim Burt, *Financial Times*, 9 July 1996, p. 17. Reprinted with permission.

When asset values are particularly useful

The accounts-based approach to share value is fraught with problems but there are circumstances in which asset backing is given more attention.

Firms in financial difficulty

The shareholders of firms in financial difficulty may pay a great deal of attention to the asset backing of the firm. They may weigh up the potential for asset sales or asset-backed borrowing. In extreme circumstances they may try to assess the break-up value.

Takeover bids

In a takeover bid shareholders will be reluctant to sell at less than NAV even if the prospect for income growth is poor. A standard defensive tactic in a takeover battle is to revalue balance sheet assets to encourage a higher price.

When discounted income flow techniques are difficult to apply

For some types of company there is no straightforward way of employing income-flow based methods:

1 ***Property investment companies*** are primarily valued on the basis of their assets. It is generally possible to put a fairly realistic up-to-date price on the buildings owned by such a company. These market values have a close link to future cash flows. That is, the future rents payable by tenants, when discounted, determine the value of property

assets and thus the company. If higher rent levels are expected than were previously anticipated, chartered surveyors will place a higher value on the asset, and the NAV in the balance sheet will rise, forcing up the share price. For such companies, future income, asset values and share values are all closely linked.

2 *Investment trusts* The future income of investment trusts comes from the individual shareholdings. The shareholder in a trust would find it extremely difficult to calculate the future income to be received from each of the dozens or hundreds of shares held. An easier approach is simply to take the current share price of each holding as representing the future discounted income. The share values are aggregated to derive the trusts' NAV and this has a strong bearing on the price at which the trust shares are traded.

3 *Resource-based companies* For oil companies, mineral extractors, mining houses and so on, the proven or probable reserves have a significant influence on the share price (*see* Exhibit 17.5).

Exhibit 17.5

NAV valuation sparks dispute

A row had broken out between oil company LASMO and HSBC Securities over the broker's sharp cut in its estimation of LASMO's net asset value from 132p to 89p a share. It knocked £48m off LASMO's stock market value driving its shares down 5p to 123p. This is a particularly sensitive time because LASMO is in the middle of an all-share offer for Monument Oil & Gas – whose former broker is HSBC . . .

Most of the dispute over the valuation centres on Algeria where LASMO has a 12 per cent stake in 14 oil fields operated by US group Anadarko. Mr Perry does not accept LASMO's valuation of between £300m and £500m for its Algerian interests, putting a price of just £210m on them.

Source: Timon Day, *Investors Chronicle*, 11 June 1999. Reprinted with permission.

VALUATION USING INCOME-FLOW METHODS

The value of a share is usually determined by the income flows that investors expect to receive in the future from its ownership. Information about the past is only of relevance to the extent that it contributes to an understanding of expected future performance. Income flows will occur at different points in the future and so they have to be discounted. There are three classes of income valuation models:

- dividend-based models;
- earnings-based models;
- cash flow-based models.

THE DIVIDEND VALUATION MODELS

The dividend valuation models (DVMs) are based on the premise that *the market value of ordinary shares represents the sum of the expected future dividend flows, to infinity, discounted to present value.*

The only cash flows that investors ever receive from a company are dividends. This holds true if we include a 'liquidation dividend' upon the sale of the firm or on formal liquidation, and any share repurchases can be treated as dividends. Of course, an individual shareholder is not planning to hold a share forever to gain the dividend returns to an infinite horizon. An individual holder of shares will expect two types of return:

a income from dividends, and

b a capital gain resulting from the appreciation of the share and its sale to another investor.

The fact that the individual investor is looking for capital gains as well as dividends to give a return does not invalidate the model. The reason for this is that when a share is sold, the purchaser is buying a future stream of dividends, therefore the price paid is determined by future dividend expectations.

To illustrate this, consider the following: A shareholder intends to hold a share for one year. A single dividend will be paid at the end of the holding period, d_1.

$$\text{Total shareholder return} = \frac{\text{Dividend} + \text{Capital gain}}{\text{Original investment}} \times 100$$

$$= \frac{d_1 + (P_1 - P_0)}{P_0} \times 100$$

P_0 = share price at time 0 $\quad$ P_1 = share price at time 1

To derive the value of a share at time 0 to this investor (P_0), the future cash flows, d_1 and P_1 , have to be discounted at a rate which includes an allowance for the risk class of the share, k_E.

$$P_0 = \frac{d_1}{1 + k_E} + \frac{P_1}{1 + k_E}$$

Example

An investor is considering the purchase of some shares in Willow plc. At the end of one year a dividend of 22p will be paid and the shares are expected to be sold for £2.43. How much should be paid if the investor judges that the rate of return required on a financial security of this risk class is 20 per cent?

Answer

$$P_0 = \frac{d_1}{1 + k_E} + \frac{P_1}{1 + k_E}$$

$$P_0 = \frac{22}{1 + 0.2} + \frac{243}{1 + 0.2} = 221\text{p}$$

The dividend valuation model to infinity

The relevant question to ask in order to understand DVMs is: Where does P_1 come from? The buyer at time 1 estimates the value of the share based on the present value of future income given the required rate of return for the risk class. So if the second investor expects to hold the share for a further year and sell at time 2 for P_2, the price P_1 will be:

$$P_1 = \frac{d_2}{1 + k_E} + \frac{P_2}{1 + k_E}$$

Returning to the P_0 equation we are able to substitute discounted d_2 and P_2 for P_1. Thus:

$$P_0 = \frac{d_1}{1 + k_E} + \frac{P_1}{1 + k_E}$$

$$P_0 = \frac{d_1}{1 + k_E} + \frac{d_2}{(1 + k_E)^2} + \frac{P_2}{(1 + k_E)^2}$$

If a series of one-year investors bought this share, and we in turn solved for P_2, P_3, P_4, etc., we would find:

$$P_0 = \frac{d_1}{1 + k_E} + \frac{d_2}{(1 + k_E)^2} + \frac{d_3}{(1 + k_E)^3} + \dots + \frac{d_n}{(1 + k_E)^n}$$

Even a short-term investor has to consider events beyond his or her time horizon because the selling price is determined by the willingness of a buyer to purchase a future dividend stream. If this year's dividends are boosted by short-termist policies such as cutting out R&D and brand-support marketing the investor may well lose more on capital value changes than the gains in dividend income.

Example

If a firm is expected to pay dividends of 20p per year to infinity and the rate of return required on a share of this risk class is 12 per cent then:

$$P_0 = \frac{20}{1 + 0.12} + \frac{20}{(1 + 0.12)^2} + \frac{20}{(1 + 0.12)^3} + \dots + \frac{20}{(1 + 0.12)^n}$$

$$P_0 = 17.86 + 15.94 + 14.24 + \dots + \dots +$$

Given this is a perpetuity there is a simpler approach:

$$P_0 = \frac{d_1}{k_E} = \frac{20}{0.12} = 166.67\text{p}$$

The dividend growth model

In contrast to the situation in the above example, for most companies dividends are expected to grow from one year to the next.[1] To make DVM analysis manageable simplifying assumptions are usually made about the patterns of growth in dividends. Most managers attempt to make dividends grow more or less in line with the firm's long-term earnings growth rate. They often bend over backwards to smooth out fluctuations, maintaining a high dividend even in years of poor profits or losses. In years of very high profits they are often reluctant to increase the dividend by a large percentage for fear that it might have to be cut back in a downturn. So, given management propensity to make dividend payments grow in an incremental or stepped fashion it seems that a reasonable model could be based on the assumption of a constant growth rate. (Year to year deviations around this expected growth path will not materially alter the analysis.)

What is a normal growth rate?

Growth rates will be different for each company but for corporations taken as a whole dividend growth will not be significantly different from the growth in nominal gross national product (real GNP plus inflation) over the long run. If dividends did grow in a long-term trend above this rate then they would take an increasing proportion of national income – ultimately squeezing out the consumption and government sectors. This is, of course, ridiculous. Thus in an economy with inflation of 3 per cent per annum and growth of 2.5 per cent we might expect the long-term growth in dividends to be about 5.5 per cent. Also, it is unreasonable to suppose that a firm can grow its earnings and dividends forever at a rate significantly greater than that for the economy as a whole. To do so is to assume that the firm eventually becomes larger than the economy. There will be years, even decades, when average corporate dividends do grow faster than the economy as a whole and there will always be companies with much higher projected growth rates than the average for periods of time. Nevertheless the real GNP + inflation growth relationship provides a useful benchmark. Exhibit 17.6 provides some earnings growth figures over a relatively short run of years. Please note that these figures can be heavily influenced by the stage in the economic cycle.

Worked example 17.1 A constant dividend growth valuation: Shhh plc

If the last dividend paid was d_0 and the next is due in one year, d_1, then this will amount to $d_0\ (1 + g)$ where g is the growth rate of dividends.

For example, if Shhh plc has just paid a dividend of 10p and the growth rate is 7 per cent then:

d_1 will equal $d_0\ (1 + g) = 10\ (1 + 0.07) = 10.7\text{p}$

and

d_2 will be $d_0\ (1 + g)^2 = 10\ (1 + 0.07)^2 = 11.45\text{p}$

The value of a share in Shhh will be all the future dividends discounted at the risk-adjusted discount rate of 11 per cent:

$$P_0 = \frac{d_0\ (1+g)}{(1+k_E)} + \frac{d_0\ (1+g)^2}{(1+k_E)^2} + \frac{d_0\ (1+g)^3}{(1+k_E)^3} + \dots + \frac{d_0\ (1+g)^n}{(1+k_E)^n}$$

$$P_0 = \frac{10\ (1+0.07)}{1+0.11} + \frac{10\ (1+0.07)^2}{(1+0.11)^2} + \frac{10\ (1+0.07)^3}{(1+0.11)^3} + \dots + \frac{d_0\ (1+g)^n}{(1+k)^n}$$

Using the above formula could require a lot of time. Fortunately it is mathematically equivalent to the following formula[2] which is much easier to employ.

$$P_0 = \frac{d_1}{k_E - g} = \frac{d_0\ (1+g)}{k_E - g} = \frac{10.7}{0.11 - 0.07} = 267.50\text{p}$$

Note that, even though the shortened formula only includes next year's dividend all the future dividends are represented.

A further illustration is provided by the example of Pearson plc.

Exhibit 17.6

British companies' soaring profits outpace many rivals

FT

By Ed Crooks, Economics Editor

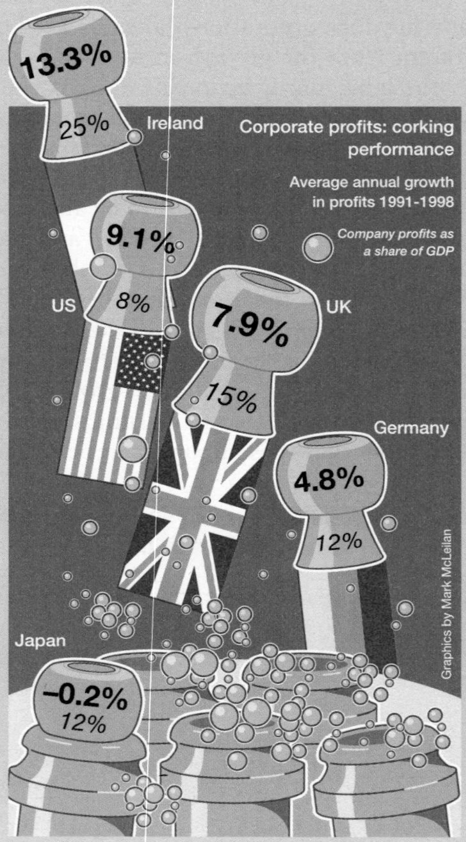

Source: ONS

The UK saw some of the fastest profits growth in the developed world during the 1990s, according to official figures released for the first time yesterday.

The profits of UK companies grew from £67.1bn in 1991 to £114.2bn in 1998, an annual average growth rate of 7.9 per cent.

Over the same period in the US, profits grew at a rate of 9.1 per cent, in Germany at an average of 4.8 per cent, and in Japan they actually declined, despite a recovery in the mid-1990s.

Ireland has had spectacular corporate profits in the 1990s as a result of a booming economy. It also has a high share of profits in the national economy, reflecting the attractiveness of its low tax regime.

Comparisons between countries are difficult because of differences in industrial structure and accounting, but the Office for National Statistics says the figures are the most reliable yet published.

For Britain, they show poor profitability in the 1970s being raised sharply during the 1980s, and to a lesser extent in the 1990s.

Businesses say the demands imposed by shareholders, who were increasingly able to move their money around the world in search of the best return, forced managers to become more profitable.

'In the 1970s the return on capital was pathetic,' said Ruth Lea of the Institute of Directors. 'Now fund managers are so much more aggressive. If you don't deliver, you will be out,' she said.

But some economists said aspects of the figures were puzzling. 'The trend is very welcome – we were clearly not making enough money before,' said Kate Barker, chief economist of the Confederation of British Industry.

'Business needs profits invest. But Germany has invested more than the UK in the 1990s, even though they have apparently had lower profits.'. . .

Analysts do not expect that profits growth in the UK will necessarily outpace the rest of Europe in the next decade. Many forecasters believe that for the next couple of years, economic growth in the euro-zone may be stronger than in Britain.

The strategists at Credit Suisse First Boston, for example, are expecting UK corporate earnings to rise by 8 per cent this year followed by 7 per cent in 2001. But they expect corporate earnings for Europe as a whole to grow by 13 per cent this year and again in 2001.

In the longer term, there is more scope to raise profitability in continental Europe. The single currency the deregulation of labour, product and financial markets, corporate reorganisation and tax reform may deliver the sort of growth seen in the UK during the 1980s and 1990s.

Source: Ed Crooks, Economics Editor, *Financial Times*, 20 January 2000, p. 4. Reprinted with permission.

Worked example 17.2 Pearson plc

Pearson plc, the publishing, media and education group, has the following dividend history:

Year	*Net dividend per share (p)*
1996	16.1
1997	17.4
1998	18.8
1999	20.1
2000	21.4

The average annual growth rate, g, over this period has been:

$$g = \sqrt[4]{\frac{21.4}{16.1}} - 1 = 0.074 \text{ or } 7.4\%$$

If it is assumed that this historic growth rate will continue into the future and 10 per cent is taken as the required rate of return, the value of a share can be calculated.

$$P_0 = \frac{d_1}{k_E - g} = \frac{21.4\ (1 + 0.074)}{0.10 - 0.074} = 884\text{p}$$

In fact, in the summer of 2001 Pearson's shares stood at over 940p. Perhaps analysts were anticipating a faster rate of growth in future than in the past. Perhaps we employed an excessively high discount rate. Or perhaps the market consensus view of Pearson's growth prospects was over-optimistic.

Non-constant growth

Firms tend to go through different phases of growth. If they have a strong competitive advantage in an attractive market they might enjoy super-normal growth. Eventually, however, most firms come under competitive pressure and growth becomes normal. Ultimately, many firms fail to keep pace with the market environmental change in which they operate and growth falls to below that for the average company.

To analyse companies which will go through different phases of growth a two-, three- or four-stage model may be used. In the simplest case of two-stage growth the share price calculation requires the adding together of the results of the following:

1 Discount each of the forecast annual dividends in the first period to time 0.

2 Estimate the share price at the point at which the dividend growth shifts to the new permanent rate. Discount this share price to time 0.

Worked example 17.3 Noruce plc

You are given the following information about Noruce plc.

The company has just paid an annual dividend of 15p per share and the next is due in one year. For the next three years dividends are expected to grow at 12 per cent per year. This rapid rate is caused by a number of favourable factors: for example an economic upturn, the fast acceleration stage of newly developed products and a large contract with a government department.

After the third year the dividends will grow at only 7 per cent per annum, because the main boosts to growth will, by then, be absent.

Shares in other companies with a similar level of systematic risk to Noruce produce an expected return of 16 per cent per annum.

What is the value of one share in Noruce plc?

Answer

Stage 1 Discount dividends for the super-normal growth phase.

$$d_1 = 15(1 + 0.12) = 16.8$$

$$d_2 = 15(1 + 0.12)^2 = 18.8$$

$$d_3 = 15(1 + 0.12)^3 = 21.1$$

Stage 2 Calculate share price at time 3 when the dividend growth rate shifts to the new permanent rate.

$$P_3 = \frac{d_3(1+g)}{k_E - g} = \frac{21.1\ (1+0.07)}{0.16-0.07} = 250.9$$

Stage 3 Discount and sum the amounts calculated in Stages 1 and 2.

$$\frac{d_1}{1+k_E} = \frac{16.8}{1+0.16} = 14.5$$

$$+\frac{d_2}{(1+k_E)^2} = \frac{18.8}{(1+0.16)^2} = 14.0$$

$$+\frac{d_3}{(1+k_E)^3} = \frac{21.1}{(1+0.16)^3} = 13.5$$

$$+\frac{P_3}{(1+k_E)^3} = \frac{250.9}{(1+0.16)^3} = 160.7$$

$$\underline{202.7\text{p}}$$

Companies that do not pay dividends

Some companies, for example Warren Buffett's Berkshire Hathaway, do not pay dividends. This is a deliberate policy as there is often a well-founded belief that the funds are better used within the firms than they would be if the money was given to shareholders. This presents an apparent problem for the DVM but the measure can still be applied because it is reasonable to suppose that one day these companies will start to pay dividends. Perhaps this will take the form of a final break-up payment, or perhaps when the founder is approaching retirement he/she will start to distribute the accumulated resources. At some point dividends must be paid, otherwise there would be no attraction in holding the shares.

Some companies do not pay dividends for many years due to regular losses. Often what gives value to this type of share is the optimism that the company will recover and that dividends will be paid in the distant future.

Problems with dividend valuation models

Dividend valuation models present the following problems.

1 They are highly sensitive to the assumptions. Take the case of Pearson above. If we change the growth assumption to 8 per cent and reduce the required rate of return to 9.5 per cent, the value of the share leaps to 1,540.8p.

$$P_0 = \frac{d_0\,(1+g)}{k_E - g} = \frac{21.4\,(1+0.08)}{0.095-0.08} = 1{,}540.8\text{p}$$

2 The quality of input data is often poor. The problems of calculating an appropriate required rate of return on equity were discussed in the last chapter. Added to this is great uncertainty about the future growth rate.

3 If g exceeds k_E a nonsensical result occurs. This problem is dealt with if the short-term super-normal growth rate plus the lower rate after the super-normal period is replaced with a g which is some weighted average growth rate reflecting the return expected over the long run. Alternatively, for those periods when g is greater than k, one may calculate the specific dividend amounts and discount them as in the non-constant growth model. For the years after the super-normal growth occurs, the usual growth formula may be used.

The difficulties of using the DVMs are real and severe and yet they are to be favoured, less for the derivation of a single number than for the understanding of the principles behind the value of financial assets that the exercise provides. They demand a disciplined thought process that makes the analyst's assumptions about key variables explicit.

Forecasting dividend growth rates – *g*

The most influential variable, and the one subject to most uncertainty, on the value of shares is the growth rate expected in dividends. Accuracy here is a much sought-after virtue. While this book cannot provide readers with perfect crystal balls for seeing future dividend growth rates, it can provide a few pointers.

Determinants of growth

There are three factors which influence the rate of dividend growth.

1 ***The quantity of resources retained and reinvested within the business*** This relates to the percentage of earnings not paid out as dividends. The more a firm invests the greater its potential for growth.

2 ***The rate of return earned on those retained resources*** The efficiency with which retained earnings are used will influence value.

3 *Rate of return earned on existing assets* This concerns the amount earned on the existing baseline set of assets, that is, those assets available before reinvestment of profits. This category may be affected by a sudden increase or decrease in profitability. If the firm, for example, is engaged in oil exploration and production, and there is a worldwide increase in the price of oil, profitability will rise on existing assets. Another example would be if a major competitor is liquidated, enabling increased returns on the same asset base due to higher margins because of an improved market position.

There is a vast range of influences on the future return from shares. One way of dealing with the myriad variables is to group them into three categories: at the firm, the economy and the industry level.

Focus on the firm

A dedicated analyst would want to examine dozens of aspects of the firm, and its management, to help develop an informed estimate of its growth potential. These will include the following.

1 *Evaluation of management* Usually the most important determinant of a firm's value is the quality of its management. A starting point for analysis might be to collect factual information such as age of the key managers, their level of experience and education. But this has to be combined with far more important evaluatory variables which are unquantifiable, such as judgement, and even gut-feeling about issues such as integrity, intelligence and so on. Warren Buffett has spent a lifetime observing managers and selecting which of them should be trusted with his money. He likes owner-orientated managers – in 1994 he said: 'I always picture myself as owning the whole place. And if management is following the same policy that I would follow if I owned the whole place, that's a management I like.'[3]

2 *Using the historical growth rate of dividends* For some firms the past growth may be extrapolated to estimate future dividends. If a company demonstrated a growth rate of 6 per cent over the past ten years it might be reasonable to use this as a starting point for evaluating its future potential. This figure may have to be adjusted for new information such as new strategies, management or products – that is the tricky part.

3 *Financial statement evaluation and ratio analysis* An assessment of the firm's profitability, efficiency and risk through an analysis of accounting data can be enlightening. However, adjustments to the published figures are likely to be necessary to view the past clearly, let alone provide a guide to the future. Warren Buffett again:

> When managers want to get across the facts of the business to you, it can be done within the rules of accounting. Unfortunately when they want to play games, at least in some industries, it can also be done within the rules of accounting. If you can't recognise the differences, you shouldn't be in the equity-picking business.[4]

   Accounts are valuable sources of information but they have three drawbacks: **a** they are based in the past when it is the future which is of interest, **b** the fundamental value-creating processes within the firm are not identified and measured in conventional accounts, and **c** they are frequently based on guesses, estimates and judgements, and are open to arbitrary method and manipulation.

   Armed with a cynical and questioning frame of mind the analyst can adjust accounts to provide a truer and fairer view of a company. The analyst may wish to calculate three groups of ratios to enable comparisons:

a Internal liquidity ratios permit some judgement about the ability of the firm to cope with short-term financial obligations – quick ratios, current ratios, etc.

b Operating performance ratios may indicate the efficiency of the management in the operations of the business – asset turnover ratio, profit margins, debtor turnover, etc.

c Risk analysis concerns the uncertainty of income flows – sales variability over the economic cycle, operational gearing (fixed costs as a proportion of total), financial gearing (ratio of debt to equity) cash flow ratios, etc.

Ratios examined in isolation are meaningless. It is usually necessary to compare with the industry, or the industry sub-group comprising the firm's competitors. Knowledge of changes in ratios over time can also be useful.

4 ***Strategic analysis*** The analyst needs to consider the attractiveness of the industry, the competitive position of the firm within the industry and the firm's position on the life cycle of value creation to appreciate the potential for increased dividends (*see* Chapter 16 and Arnold (2002)).

Focus on the economy

All firms, to a greater or lesser extent, are influenced by macroeconomic changes. The prospects for a particular firm can be greatly affected by sudden changes in government fiscal policy, the central bank's monetary policy, changes in exchange rates, etc. Forecasts of macroeconomic variables such as GNP are easy to find (for example *The Economist* publishes a table of forecasts every week). Finding a forecaster who is reliable over the long term is much more difficult. Perhaps the best approach is to obtain a number of projections and through informed judgement develop a view about the medium-term future. Alternatively, the analyst could recognise that there are many different potential futures and then develop analyses based on a range of possible scenarios – probabilities could be assigned and sensitivity analysis used to provide a broader picture.

Focus on the industry prospects

Firms differ in the extent of the reaction of their earnings to general economic fluctuations.

1 ***Cyclical industries*** Some companies are in cyclical industries in which an 'up' phase of the economic cycle produces large percentage rises in turnover and profits, and a 'down' phase can cut margins dramatically. Sectors vulnerable to customers deferring spending on goods and services when economic conditions worsen include vehicles, construction, furniture, carpets and white electrical goods. Recognition of the phase of the industry cycle can be important to accurate forecasting of dividends.

2 ***Defensive industries*** Consumers and industrial buyers cannot, or choose not to, postpone the purchase of particular products despite poor economic conditions – for example food, heating, health care and water. The returns for these firms fluctuate less than those for firms in cyclical industries.

3 ***Growth industries*** These tend to experience growth almost regardless of the state of the economy – for example biotechnology, telemedia, Internet software, pharmaceuticals.

The newspaper article reproduced in Exhibit 17.7 demonstrates the practical difficulties of estimating growth in earnings (and by implication dividends) from one year to the next – let alone many years ahead. Analysts had to rapidly alter their projections for 1998 earnings growth. At the start of the year it was expected to be 10 per cent, by December a decline of 2 or 5 per cent was forecast.

Exhibit 17.7

Series of corporate warnings bring an icy chill to market forecasts

FT

Share prices have fallen along with profits in 1998 but nobody really knows whether the trend is over, says **Maggie Urry**

Hardly a trading day has passed in the past few weeks without a profit warning from a big company. The trickle of warnings in the early autumn has become a spate that has swept away forecasts for earnings growth from the totality of UK quoted companies this year.

Rising corporate profits are one of the most powerful forces that push stock markets higher. As expectations of improving earnings erode, market strategists expect share prices to come under further pressure.

The message of the recent stream of warnings is that analysts of UK stocks have seriously underestimated the impact on company profits of the Asian and Russian economic troubles, and of the fall in domestic consumer confidence.

Bob Semple, equity market analyst at BT Alex Brown, says: 'The spate of warnings will continue for the next few months. Nobody knows quite how bad the economy is.'

When the year began, he says, the broking firm's forecasts suggested UK corporate earnings would rise by 10 per cent this year.

Now, he says, the forecast shows an earnings decline of 2 per cent for the market. 'Profit warnings have killed this year's numbers,' he says.

Similarly, Richard Kersley, the market strategist at CSFB, reckons earnings from the market as a whole will fall 5 per cent in 1998.

The burning question is over profit forecasts for 1999. While expectations for 1998 earnings growth have slipped, hopes for 1999 have remained high.

According to The Estimate Directory, which aggregates analysts' consensus earnings forecasts, while predictions for 1998 have fallen away, those for 1999 have remained steady, forecasting growth of 12 per cent.

Source: Maggie Urry, *Financial Times*, 4 December 1998, p. 24. Reprinted with permission.

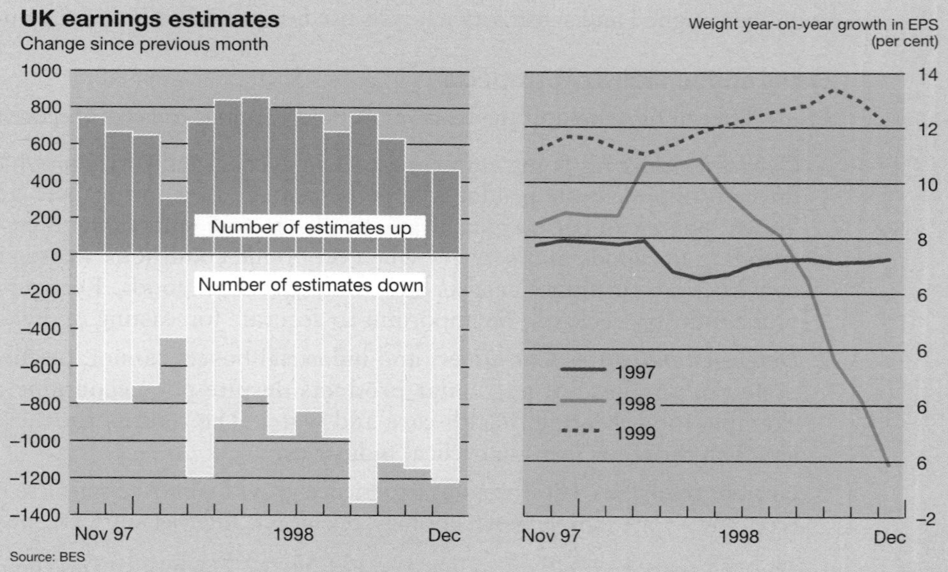

PRICE–EARNINGS RATIO (PER) MODEL

The most popular approach to valuing a share is to use the price-to-earnings (PER) ratio. This compares a firm's share price with its latest earnings (profits) per share. Investors estimate a share's value as the amount they are willing to pay for each unit of earnings. If a company produced earnings per share of 10p in its latest accounts and investors are prepared to pay 20 times historic earnings for this type of share it will be valued at £2.00. The historic PER is calculated as follows:

$$\text{Historic PER} = \frac{\text{Current market price of share}}{\text{Last year's earnings per share}} = \frac{200\text{p}}{10\text{p}} = 20$$

So, the retailer Kingfisher which reported earnings per share of 26.8p for the year ending in February 2001 with a share price of 389.5p in July 2001 had a PER of about 14.5 (389.5/26.8). PERs of other retailers are shown in Exhibit 17.8.

Exhibit 17.8 PERs for retailers FT

Retailer	*PER*
Ashley (Laura)	40.2
Body Shop	12.4
Dixons	24.4
Marks and Spencer	22.5
Next	20.0

Source: Financial Times, 26 July 2001. Reprinted with permission.

Investors are willing to buy Next shares at 20.0 times last year's earnings compared with only 12.4 times last year's earnings for Body Shop. One explanation for the difference in PERs is that companies with higher PERs are expected to show faster growth in earnings in the future. Next may appear expensive relative to Body Shop based on historical profit figures but the differential may be justified when forecasts of earnings are made. If a PER is high investors expect profits to rise. This does not necessarily mean that all companies with high PERs are expected to perform to a high standard, merely that they are expected to do significantly better than in the past. Few people would argue that Laura Ashley has performed, or will perform, well[5] in comparison with Dixons and yet it stands at a higher historic PER, reflecting the market's belief that Laura Ashley has more growth potential from its low base than Dixons.

Using the historic PER can be confusing because a company can have a high PER because it is usually a high-growth company or because it has recently had a reduction of profits from which it is expected soon to recover.

PERs are also influenced by the uncertainty of the future earnings growth. So, perhaps, Dixons and Kingfisher might have the same expected growth rate but the growth at Kingfisher is subject to more risk and therefore the market assigns a lower earnings multiple.

PERs over time

There have been great changes over the years in the market's view of what is a reasonable multiple of earnings to place on share prices. What is excessive in one year is acceptable in another. This is illustrated in Exhibits 17.9 and 17.10.

Exhibit 17.9 PERs for the UK stock market 1971–2001

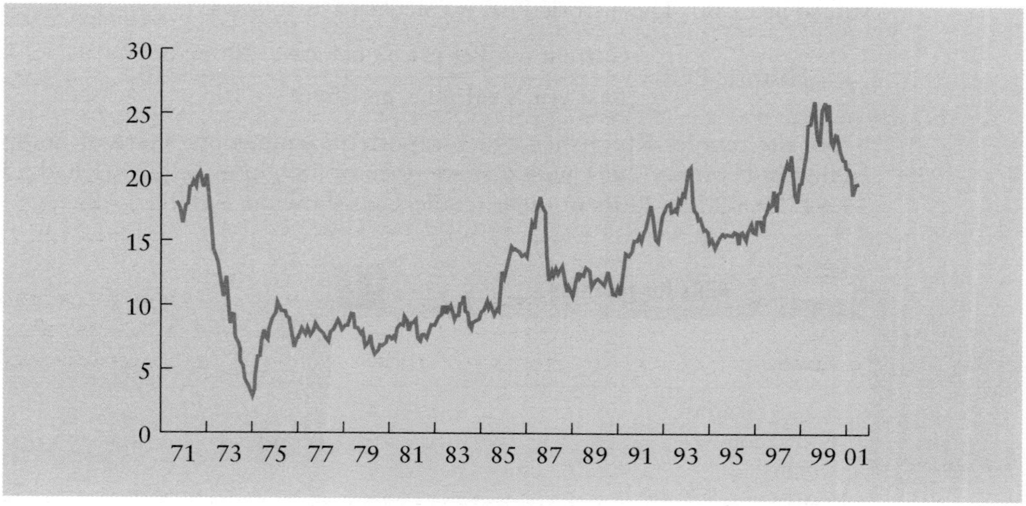

Source: Thomson Financial Datastream

Exhibit 17.10 PERs for the US stock market 1971–2001

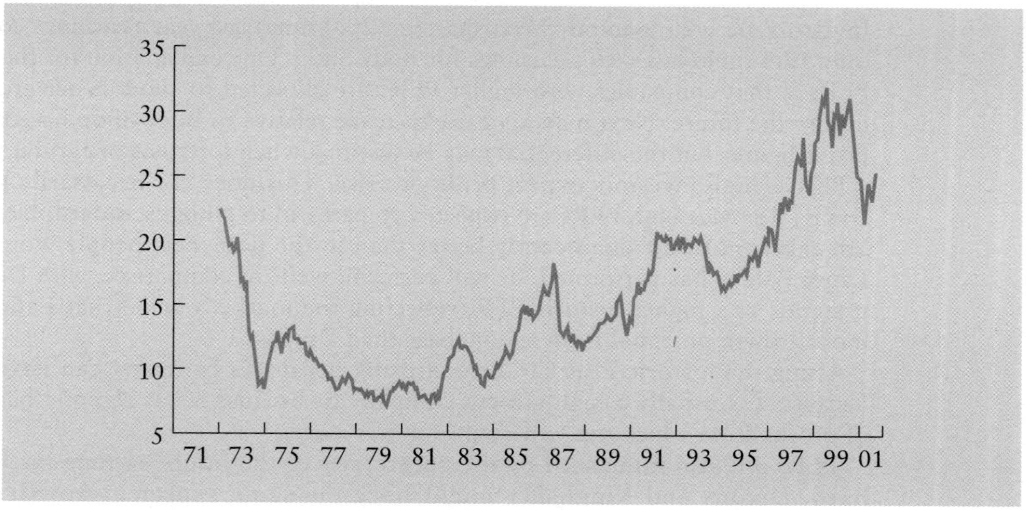

Source: Thomson Financial Datastream

The crude and the sophisticated use of the PER model

Some analysts use the historic PER (P_0/E_0), to make comparisons between firms without making explicit the considerations hidden in the analysis. They have a view of an appropriate PER based on current prevailing PERs for other firms in the same industry. So, for example, in 2001 Tesco with a PERs of 20.9 may be judged to be priced correctly relative to similar firms – Sainsbury had a PER of 22.6, Morrison 22.9 and Safeway 16.1. Analysing through comparisons lacks intellectual rigour. First, the assumption that the 'comparable' companies are correctly priced is a bold one. It is easy to see how the market could be pulled up (or down) by its own bootstraps and lose touch with fundamental considerations by this kind of thinking. Second, it fails to provide a framework for the analyst to test the important implicit input assumptions – for example, the growth rate expected in earnings in each of the companies, or the difference in required rate of return given the different risk level of each. These elements are probably in the mind of the analyst, but there may be benefits in making these more explicit. This can be done with the more complete PER model which is forward-looking and recognises both risk levels and growth projections.

The infinite dividend growth model can be used to develop the more complete PER model because they are both dependent on the key variables of growth, g (in dividends or earnings), and the required rate of return, k_E. The dividend growth model is:

$$P_0 = \frac{d_1}{k_E - g}$$

If both sides of the dividend growth model are divided by the expected earnings for the next year, E_1, then:

$$\frac{P_0}{E_1} = \frac{d_1/E_1}{k_E - g}$$

Note this is a *prospective* PER because it uses next year's earnings, rather than an historic PER, which uses E_0.

In this more complete model the appropriate multiple of earnings for a share rises as the growth rate, g, goes up; and falls as the required rate of return, k_E, increases. The relationship with the ratio d_1/E_1 is more complicated. If this payout ratio is raised it will not necessarily increase the PER because of the impact on g – if more of the earnings are paid out less financial resource is being invested in projects within the business, and therefore future growth may decline.

Worked example 17.4 Ridge plc

Ridge plc is anticipated to maintain a payout ratio of 48 per cent of earnings. The appropriate discount rate for a share for this risk class is 14 per cent and the expected growth rate in earnings and dividends is 6 per cent.

$$\frac{P_0}{E_1} = \frac{d_1/E_1}{k_E - g}$$

$$\frac{P_0}{E_1} = \frac{0.48}{0.14 - 0.06} = 6$$

The spread between k_E and g is the main influence on an acceptable PER. A small change can have a large impact. Taking the case of Ridge, if we now assume a k_E of 12 per cent and g of 8 per cent the PER doubles.

$$\frac{P_0}{E_1} = \frac{0.48}{0.12 - 0.08} = 12$$

If k_E becomes 16 per cent and g 4 per cent then the PER reduces to two-thirds its former value:

$$\frac{P_0}{E_1} = \frac{0.48}{0.16 - 0.04} = 4$$

Worked example 17.5 **Whizz plc**

You are interested in purchasing shares in Whizz plc. This company produces high-technology products and has shown strong earnings growth for a number of years. For the past five years earnings per share have grown, on average, by 10 per cent per annum.

Despite this performance and analysts' assurances that this growth rate will continue for the foreseeable future you are put off by the exceptionally high prospective price earnings ratio (PER) of 25.

In the light of the more complete forward-looking PER method, should you buy the shares or place your money elsewhere?

Whizz has a beta of 1.8 which may be taken as the most appropriate systematic risk adjustment to the risk premium for the average share (*see* Chapter 16).

The risk premium for equities over government bills has been 5 per cent over the past few decades, and the current risk-free rate of return is 7 per cent.

Whizz pays out 50 per cent of its earnings as dividends.

Answer

Stage 1 Calculate the appropriate cost of equity.

$$k_E = r_f + \beta\,(r_m - r_f)$$

$$k_E = 7 + 1.8\,(5) = 16\%$$

Stage 2 Use the more complete PER model.

$$\frac{P_0}{E_1} = \frac{d_1/E_1}{k_E - g} = \frac{0.5}{0.16 - 0.10} = 8.33$$

The maximum multiple of next year's earnings you would be willing to pay is 8.33. This is a third of the amount you are being asked to pay, therefore you will refuse to buy the share.

With the market propensity to focus on the future it can appear to provide strange valuations if historic relationships are examined. Take the case of Jefferson Smurfit, the Irish paper and packaging company which announced a fivefold jump in interim profits in August 1995 to IR£200.6m. The company was optimistic about its prospects, yet the consensus view on the stock exchange was that Jefferson Smurfit should be valued at a PER which was one-third of that for the average quoted firm, six compared with 18.

The market was concerned about future earnings and was far less sanguine than the company. The Lex column of the *Financial Times* summed up the market view (*see* Exhibit 17.11).

Exhibit 17.11

Jefferson Smurfit

FT

The world's paper companies have a reputation for being like the Bible's Gadarene swine which, in a fit of madness, charged down a cliff. Paper groups are enjoying sharp increases in profitability, as shown by Jefferson Smurfit's interim results yesterday; but shareholders believe the industry will bring disaster on itself through over-investment in new capacity just as demand turns down. Hence, the sector's lowly ratings: Smurfit trades on little over six times next year's projected earnings; its US and European rivals trade on multiples of about seven or eight.

But, according to Smurfit, the industry is not about to repeat the destructive behaviour of previous cycles. New capacity is coming on stream less quickly than demand is growing. Some groups, notably Smurfit itself, have put plans for new plants on the back-burner. Instead, the industry has embarked on a wave of takeovers, since it is cheaper to buy old capacity than build new plants. Such consolidation is healthy since it should lead to a more disciplined market. A further healthy development is the trend, joined by Smurfit yesterday, for share buy-backs and large dividend increases. The more cash channelled into buy-backs, dividend increases and takeovers, the less will be left over for new capacity. While it is hard to believe that the industry's suicidal tendencies are permanently in check, current moves towards self-control are positive.

Source: Lex column, *Financial Times*, 24 August 1995. Reprinted with permission.

By April 1996 Smurfit had to admit that increasing output capacity, particularly in America, had led to a flooding of Europe with cheap imports and to poorer profit prospects. The company warned that the downturn in the market could be extended because of 'poor demand, volatile prices and over-capacity'.[6]

Prospective PER varies with g and k_E

If an assumption is made concerning the payout ratio, then a table can be drawn up to show how PERs vary with k_E and g.

Exhibit 17.12 Prospective PERs for various risk classes and dividend growth rates

Assumed payout ratio $= \frac{d_1}{E_1} = 0.5$

		Discount rate, k_E			
		10	12	14	16
Growth rate, g	0	5.0	4.2	3.6	3.1
	4	8.3	6.3	5.0	4.2
	6	12.5	8.3	6.3	5.0
	8	25.0	12.5	8.3	6.3

Exhibit 17.13 shows that a payout ratio of 40–50 per cent has been common for UK shares in the 1990s.

Exhibit 17.13

An upbeat season with ominous signs for the next

There is a perceptible sense of relief among City analysts and investors as the 1996 financial reporting season draws to a close.

On average, according to analysis by BZW, corporate post-tax profits increased by 6 per cent. Dividends increased 50 per cent faster, by 9 per cent, lifting the pay-out ratio for the market as a whole to 48 per cent.

A survey by NatWest Securities of results monitored by its traders shows a broadly upbeat picture. Of the 167 companies monitored during February and March, 60 reported results ahead of market expectations, whereas 23 disappointed. The remainder were in line with City predictions.

But the 1996 results season may turn out to be a turning point in another respect. The proportion of company profits distributed to investors as dividends started to grow again.

The dividend pay-out ratio in the UK last surged during the early 1990s, when falling profits left companies distributing a bigger proportion of their earnings to shareholders.

It then slumped sharply as companies were cautious with their pay-outs, while earnings were recovering rapidly.

Source: Ross Tieman, *Financial Times*, 10 April 1997, p. 33. Reprinted with permission.

Pay-out ratio for UK market (%)

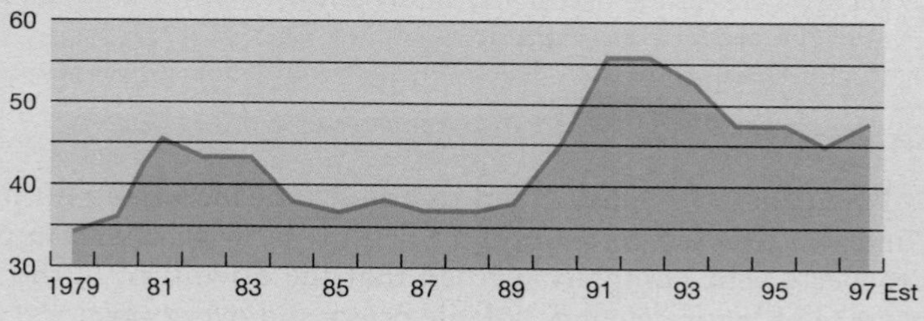

Source: Thomson Financial Datastream, BZW.

The more complete model can help explain the apparently perverse behaviour of stock markets. If there is 'good' economic news such as a rise in industrial output or a fall in unemployment the stock market often falls. The market likes the increase in earnings that such news implies, but this effect is often outweighed by the effects of the next stage. An economy growing at a fast pace is vulnerable to rises in inflation and the market will anticipate rises in interest rates to reflect this. Thus the r_f and the rest of the SML are pushed upward. The return required on shares, k_E, will rise, and this will have a depressing effect on share prices. The article reproduced in Exhibit 17.15 expresses this well.

VALUATION USING CASH FLOW

The third and perhaps most important income-based valuation method is cash flow. In business it is often said that 'cash is king'. From the shareholders' perspective the cash flow relating to a share is crucial – they hand over cash and are interested in the ability of the business to return cash to them. John Allday, head of valuation at Ernst and Young, says that discounted cash flow 'is the purest way. I would prefer to adopt it if the information is there.[7]

Exhibit 17.14 **A comparison of the crude PER and the more complete model**

Crude PER P_0/E_1

The assumptions here are implicit, e.g:

1 Valuation (P_0) consists of two parts:
  a value of earnings assuming no growth,
  b value of growth in earnings.
2 No explicit recognition of the need for different required rates of return (k_E) for shares in different risk classes.

The more complete model

$$\frac{P_0}{E_1} = \frac{d_1/E_1}{k_E - g}$$

Payout ratio
Superficially P_0 relative to E_1 could be raised by increasing payout ratio. However a lower retention ratio may reduce g to leave the overall value lower.

Growth rate, g
A complex composite of myriad influences on a firm's future growth of earnings and dividends, e.g.:

- proportion of profit retained;
- efficient use of resources;
- market opportunities;
- quality of management;
- strategy.

Required return for risk class, k_E, related to risk class of share

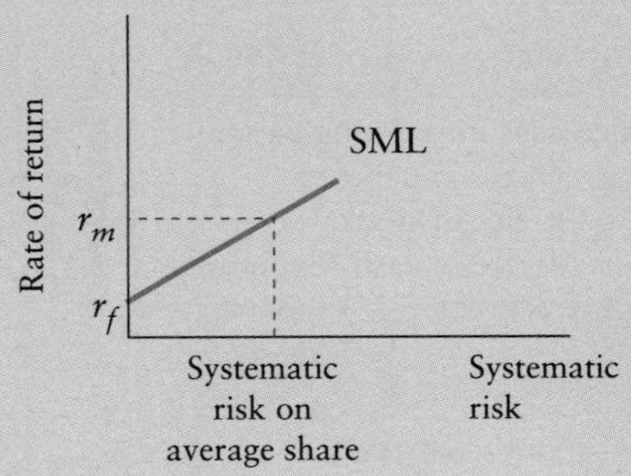

Note the influences on this: e.g. if prospective inflation rises, interest rates (probably) rise and SML shifts upwards thus increasing k_E. Also the risk profile of the firm may change with a new strategy; therefore altering k_E.

Exhibit 17.15

Why policymakers should take note

FT

One issue which always mystifies the novice investor is why the financial markets always react so joyously to bad economic news. A rise in unemployment or a fall in industrial production seems to be worth a point on bonds and a jump in the stock market index.

Experienced global investors explain patiently that the key determinant of short term financial market performance is interest rates. Slower growth prompts monetary authorities to lower rates; this in turn reduces corporate costs, reduces the appeal of holding cash, and in the case of falling long term yields, by lowering the rate at which future income streams are discounted, increases the present value of shares.

Conversely, of course, faster economic growth causes governments and central banks to fear higher inflation, prompting them to increase interest rates, with consequent adverse effects on share prices.

Source: Philip Coggan, 'Global Investors', *Financial Times*, 5 February 1996, p. 20. Reprinted with permission.

The interest in cash flow is promoted by the limited usefulness of published accounts. Scepticism about the accuracy of earnings figures, given the flexibility available in their construction, prompts attempts to find a purer valuation method than PER.

The cash flow approach involves the discounting of future cash flows, that is, the cash generated by the business after investment in fixed assets and working capital (to maintain the existing asset base *and* create new assets for future growth) and tax payments. To derive the cash flow attributable to shareholders, any interest paid in a particular period is deducted. The process of the derivation of cash flow from profit figures is shown in Exhibit 17.16.

A stylised example of a cash flow calculation is shown in Exhibit 17.17. Note that the earnings figures for 2003 are very different from the cash flow because of the large capital investment in fixed assets – earnings are positive because only a small proportion of the cost of the new fixed assets is depreciated in that year.

Exhibit 17.16 Cash flow approach: one possibility

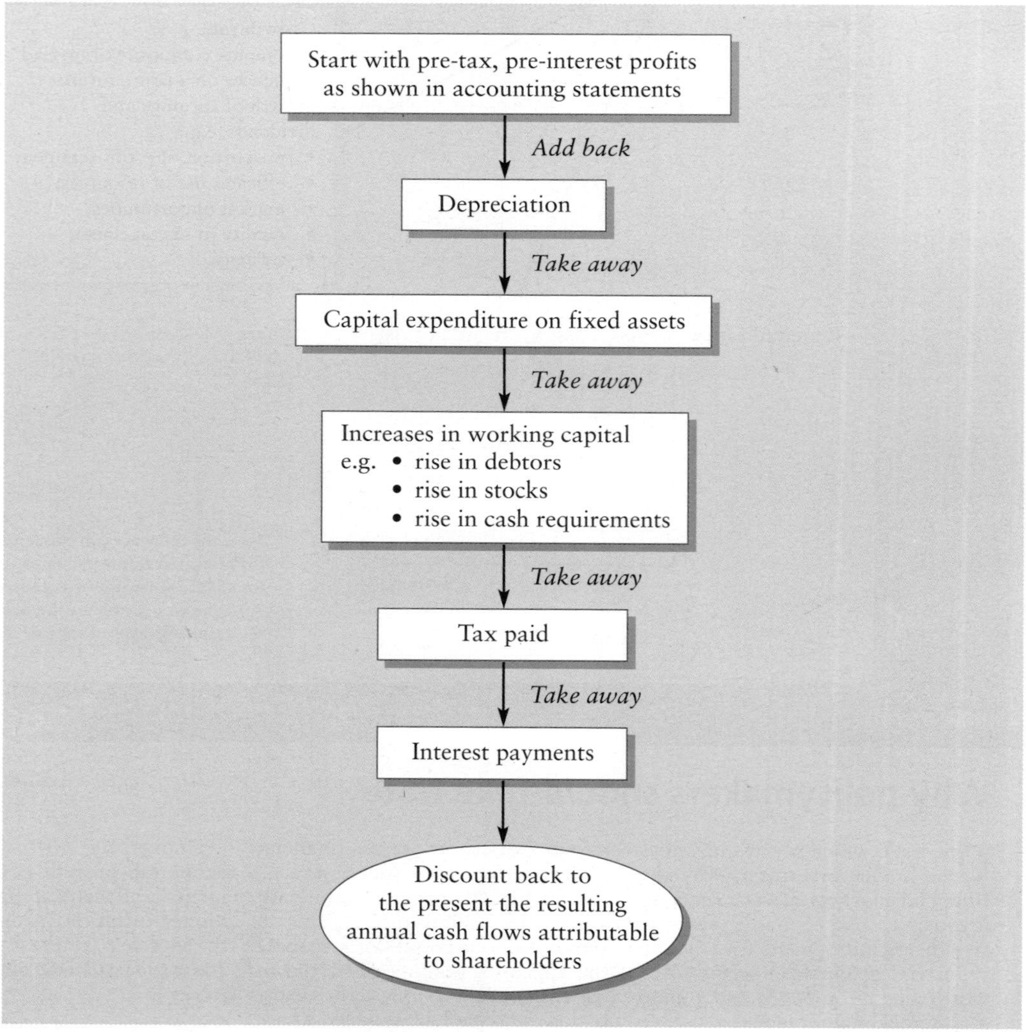

Exhibit 17.17 Cash flow-based share valuation

£m	*2002*	*2003*	*2004*	*2005*	*2006*	*Estimated average annual cash flow for period beyond planning horizon 2007–infinity*
Forecast pre-tax, pre-interest profits	+11.0	+15.0	+15.0	+16.0	+17.0	
Add depreciation	+1.0	+2.5	+5.5	+4.5	+4.0	
Working capital increase (–) decrease (+)	+1.0	–0.5	0.0	+1.0	+1.0	
Tax (paid)	–3.3	–5.0	–5.0	–5.4	–5.8	
Interest on debt capital	–0.5	–0.5	–0.5	–0.6	–0.7	
Fixed capital investment	–1.0	–16.0	0.0	–1.2	–1.8	
Cash flow	+8.2	–4.5	+15.0	+14.3	+13.7	+14.0
Cash flow per share (assuming 100m shares)	8.2p	–4.5p	15p	14.3p	13.7p	14p
Discounted cash flow $k_E = 14\%$	$\frac{8.2}{1.14}$	$-\ \frac{4.5}{(1.14)^2}$	$+\ \frac{15}{(1.14)^3}$	$+\ \frac{14.3}{(1.14)^4}$	$+\ \frac{13.7}{(1.14)^5}$	$+\ \frac{14}{0.14} \times \frac{1}{(1.14)^5}$
Share value =	7.20	–3.5	+10.1	+8.5	+7.1	+51.9
						= 81.3p

Note also that there is a subtle assumption in this type of analysis. This is that all annual cash flows are paid out to shareholders rather than reinvested. If all positive NPV projects have been accepted using the money allocated to additional capital expenditures on fixed assets and working capital, then to withhold further money from shareholders would be value destructive because any other projects would have negative NPVs. An alternative assumption, which amounts to the same effect in terms of share value, is that any cash flows that are retained and reinvested generate a return that merely equals the required rate of return for that risk class; thus no additional value is created. Of course, if the company knows of other positive value projects, either at the outset or comes across them in future years, it should take them up. This will alter the numbers in the table and so a new valuation is needed.

VALUATION USING OWNER EARNINGS

For shares, intrinsic value is the discounted value of the owner earnings that can be taken out of a business during its remaining life. Future owner earnings are determined by the strength and durability of the economic franchise (attractiveness of the industry plus competitive positions of the firm in the industry), the quality of management and the financial strength of the business. In the following analysis we make use of Buffett's definition of owner earnings, but with the additional factor in (**c**) and (**d**) of 'investment in all new value-creating projects'.[8] Owner earnings are defined as:

(**a**) reported earnings after tax; *plus*

(**b**) depreciation, depletion, amortisation and certain other non-cash charges; *less*

(**c**) the amount of capitalised expenditures for plant and machinery, etc. that a business requires to fully maintain its long-term competitive position and its unit volume and to make investment in all new value-creating projects; *less*

(**d**) any extra amount for working capital that is needed to maintain the firm's long-term competitive position and unit volume and to make investment in all new value-creating projects.

Thus, there are two types of investment. First that which is needed to permit the firm to to continue to maintain its existing competitive position at the current level of output. Second, investment in value-creating growth opportunities beyond the current position.

So, for example, Cotillo plc has reported earnings after tax for the most recent year of £16.3 million. In drawing up the income (profit and loss) account deductions of £7.4 million were made for depreciation, £152,000 for the amortisation of intangible assets and £713,000 of goodwill was written off. It is estimated that an annual expenditure of £8.6 million on plant, machinery, etc. will be required for the company to maintain its long-term competitive position and unit volume. For the sake of simplicity we will assume that no further monies will be needed for extra working capital to maintain long-term competitive position and unit volume. Also, Cotillo has no new value-creating projects.

The trading record of Cotillo plc has been remarkably stable in the past and is unlikely to alter in the future. It is therefore reasonable to use the above figures for all the future years. This would result in an estimated annual owner earnings of £15.965 million (see Exhibit 17.18).

The discounted value of this perpetuity = £159.65m, if we take the discount rate to be 10 per cent:

$$\text{Intrinsic value} = \frac{\pounds 15.965\text{m}}{0.10} = \pounds 159.65\text{m}$$

Intrinsic value is determined by the owner earnings that can be *taken out* of the business during its remaining life. Logically the management of Cotillo should pay out the full £15.956m each year to shareholders if the managers do not have investment projects within the firm that will generate returns of 10 per cent or more because shareholders can get 10 per cent return elsewhere for the same level of risk as holding a share in Cotillo. If the managers come across another project that promises a return of exactly 10 per cent shareholder wealth will be unchanged whether the company invests in this

Exhibit 17.18 Cotillo plc, owner earnings

		£000s
(a)	Reported earnings after tax	16,300
	Plus	
(b)	Depreciation, depletion, amortisation and other non-cash charges (7,400 + 152 + 713)	8,265
		24,565
	less	
(c) and (d)	Expenditure on plant, equipment, working capital, etc. required to maintain long-term competitive position, unit volume and investment in new projects	8,600
		15,965

or chooses to ignore the project and continues with the payment of all owner earnings each year. If the management discover, in a future year, a value-creating project that will produce, say, a 15 per cent rate of return (for the same level of risk as the existing projects) then shareholders will welcome a reduction in dividends during the years of additional investment. The total value of discounted future owner earnings will rise and intrinsic value will be greater than £159.65m if such a project is undertaken.

Now let us assume that Cotillo has a series of new value-creating (i.e. generating returns greater than 10 per cent) projects it can invest in. By investing in these projects owner earnings will rise by 5 per cent year on year (on the one hand owner earnings are decreased by the need for additional investment under (**c**) and (**d**), but, on the other hand reported earnings are boosted under (**a**), to produce a net 5 per cent growth). The intrinsic value becomes £335.26m viz:

$$\text{Intrinsic value} = \text{next year's owner earnings}/k_E - g = \frac{16.763}{0.10 - 0.05} = £335.26\text{m}$$

VALUING UNQUOTED SHARES

The principles of valuation are the same for companies with a quoted share price on an exchange and for unquoted firms. The methods of valuation discussed above in relation to shares quoted on an exchange may be employed, but there may be some additional factors to consider in relation to unquoted firms' shares.

1 *There may be a lower quality and quantity of information* The reporting statements tend to be less revealing for unquoted firms. There may also be a managerial reluctance to release information – or managers may release information selectively so as to influence value, for example, in merger discussions.
2 *These shares may be subject to more risk* Firms at an early stage in their life cycle are often more susceptible to failure than are established firms.

3 *The absence of a quotation usually means the shares are less liquid*, that is, there is a reduced ability to sell quickly without moving the price. This lack of marketability can be a severe drawback and often investors in unquoted firms, such as venture capitalists, insist on there being a plan to provide an exit route within say five years, perhaps, through a stock market float. But that still leaves a problem for the investor within the five years should a sale be required.
4 *Cost of tying-in management* When a substantial stake is purchased in an unquoted firm, in order for the existing key managers to be encouraged to stay they may be offered financial incentives such as 'golden hand-cuffs' which may influence value. Or the previous owner-managers may agree an 'earn-out' clause in which they receive a return over the years following a sale of their shares (the returns paid to these individuals will be dependent on performance over a specified future period).

Unquoted firms' shares tend to sell at significantly lower prices than those of quoted firms. Philip Marsden, deputy managing director of corporate finance at 3i, discounts the price by anything from one-third to a half[9] and the BDO Stoy Hayward/ Acquisitions Monthly Private Company Price Index shows unquoted firms being sold at an average PER of under two-thirds that for quoted shares.

UNUSUAL COMPANIES

Obtaining information to achieve accuracy with discounted income flow methods is problematic for most shares. But in industries subject to rapid technological innovation it is extraordinarily difficult. While discounted income flow remains the ultimate method of valuation some analysts use more immediate proxies to estimate value. (A less scientific-sounding description is 'rules of thumb'.) For example, Gerry Stephens and Justin Funnell, media and telecoms analysts at NatWest Markets, describe the approach often adopted in their sector:[10]

> Rather than DCF (discounted cash flow), people are often more comfortable valuing telemedia project companies using benchmarks that have evolved from actual market prices paid for similar assets, being based on a comparative measure or scale such as per line, per subscriber, per home or per pop (member of population). For example, an analyst might draw conclusions from the per-pop price that Vodaphone trades at to put a price on the float of Telecom Italia Mobile. The benchmark prices will actually have originated from DCF analysis and the price paid can give an element of objective validation to the implied subjective DCF.

This sort of logic has been employed in the valuation of internet companies. In their attempt to value future profits that were far from certain 'analysts' became more and more extreme in clutching at straws to value internet companies in the late 1990s – *see* Exhibit 17.19.

Other sectors difficult to value directly on the basis of income flow include: advertising agencies, where a percentage of annual billings is often used as a proxy; fund managers, where value of funds under management is used; and hotels, where star ratings may be combined with number of rooms and other factors.

Valuing and buying shares in a well-regulated, stable environment with a flow of factual information is one thing. As the article reproduced in Exhibit 17.20 shows, buying in some emerging markets is another – innovative valuation techniques may be called for.

Exhibit 17.19

The internet revolution

FT

Lies, damned lies and web valuations

Internet fever gripped the world and led credulous investors to think dotcom companies were sure-fire winners. We show how scarce data, high hopes and fast-talking 'rock star' analysts fuelled a frenzy of speculation that eventually ended in tears

The internet has turned out to be one of the most powerful forces shaping business for decades. But it has also proved to be fertile ground for speculation. Entirely new markets have been promised, with entirely new ways of doing business and new ways of making money.

With so much of this potential untested, financial analysts have developed new tools in order to be able to value businesses whose financial success will not be clear for years, if ever. Previously cautious professional forecasters have become accustomed to taking leaps in the dark to describe a future that seems almost limitless in its potential. And an army of boosters and spin doctors has been on hand to take up these predictions and trumpet them, aided by journalists and commentators, themselves struggling to keep up with the extraordinary changes that appeared to be under way . . .

In a market where many internet companies had little in the way of revenues to show, let alone profits, their ability to attract the attention of growing online audience became one of the only ways of measuring their performance.

Investors began to focus on the number of unique users (the number of different people who visited its site) and page views (the number of web pages these visitors clicked on) claimed by a site.

Bob Davis, chief executive of Lycos, the US portal, defends the methods that have been developed for measuring internet audiences, while adding: 'It's working on being a science, but it isn't a science yet.' Of the audience numbers produced by such research, he adds: 'I wouldn't want to look at them on an absolute basis – but on a relative basis, they probably do a good job.' . . .

But companies did not always make it clear where they were using gross revenue, before subtracting cost of sales, and where they were referring to net revenue. Some omitted to point out how much of their advertising revenues derived from barter advertising with other websites, where money did not actually change hands. This backdrop of scarce data and high hopes provided an ideal environment for a number of quick-thinking, fast-talking analysts to make a name for themselves . . .

Indeed, credibility was sometimes conferred by the amount of press attention the stocks had generated. Internet analysts joked about a 'price-to-press-cuttings ratio'.

Source: *Financial Times*, 13 October 2000, p. 16. Reprinted with permission.

Exhibit 17.20

Analysts grapple with Russian valuations

FT

With few companies producing western-style accounts, alternative methodologies are called for

Markets have often experienced speculative frenzies, be it the explosion of tulip bulb prices in seventeenth century Holland or Florida real estate in the 1920s.

Observers of the Russian stock market may wonder if they are not watching a similar phenomenon.

'People may argue they are buying cheap assets, but at the end of the day it is earnings which drive prices. If you cannot see what those earnings are and the company is not adhering to shareholder rights, then you risk buying a pig in the poke,' Mr Mobius [president of Templeton Emerging Markets Fund] says. 'You are just creating conditions for people to gamble.'

To date, only a handful of Russia's 110,000 companies produce accounts that would survive the scrutiny of a diligent investor; almost none make dividend payouts on ordinary shares. That makes valuing Russian companies extremely difficult, heightening the dangers of speculative bubbles.

However, some analysts have invented alternative valuation methodologies to assess a company's worth. One of the earliest was to compare crude asset prices in Russia and abroad. So, for example, the implied value of a barrel of oil in the ground in Siberia would be compared with one in Texas by dividing an oil company's market value by its proven reserves.

▶

Exhibit 17.20 continued

Comparisons were made between an electricity generator's market value per kilowatt of output in Moscow and in Berlin, for instance.

The problem here is that a company's earnings are not always linked to output. Some prices are still subsidised, non-payments between companies are rife, and even big enterprises receive much of their income in bartered goods. Enterprises could be increasing output but bleeding cash.

Analysts therefore turned to market capitalisation-to-turnover valuations. But Russian companies use cash-based accounts rather than the accruals method used in the west. That means sales are only booked when a company receives the cash, making comparative sales figures look extremely erratic.

That prompted the most diligent analysts to reconstruct a company's accounts on an internationally-recognisable basis. Taking its annual output and guessing the market price of its goods, they made an attempt to forecast sales.

Unpicking stated tax accounts and adding back unrecognised factors such as depreciation charges, they then estimated earnings and cash flow.

But even for the most transparent companies, such estimates vary wildly. One investment bank has calculated Mosenergo, Moscow's electricity utility, stands on a price/earnings ratio of five; a rival bank suggests the true figure is 16. Many of these valuation techniques also contradict each other.

'On an asset basis Russian companies always look incredibly cheap. On a production basis they still look quite cheap. On a price to sales basis they begin to look like they might be priced about right. But on a p/e basis, taking account of corrected earnings, they all look blatheringly expensive,' Mr Nail [head of research at Deutsche Morgan Grenfell's Moscow office] says.

Source: John Thornhill, *Financial Times*, 31 January 1997. Reprinted with permission.

MANAGERIAL CONTROL AND VALUATION

The value of a share can change depending on whether the purchaser gains a controlling interest in the firm. The purchase of a single share brings a stream of future dividends without any real influence over the level of those dividends. However, control of a firm by, say, purchasing 50 per cent or more of the shares, permits the possibility of changing the future operations of the firm and thus enhancing returns. A merger may allow economies of scale and other synergies, or future earnings may be boosted by the application of superior management skills.

The difference in value between a share without management control and one with it helps to explain why we often witness a share price rise of 30–50 per cent in a takeover bid battle. There are two appraisals of the value of the firm, both of which may be valid depending on the assumption concerning managerial control. Exhibit 17.21 shows that extra value can be created by merging the operations of two firms.

Exhibit 17.21 is not meant to imply that the acquiring firm will pay a bid premium equal to the estimated merger benefits. The price paid is subject to negotiation and bargaining. The acquirer is likely to try to offer significantly less than the combined amount of the target firm's value 'as is' and the merger benefits. This will enable it to retain as much as possible of the increased value for itself rather than pass value on to the target shareholders. (*See* Chapter 20 for more detail.)

Valuation models and managerial control

The merger of Glaxo Wellcome and SmithKline Beecham will provide a framework for illustrating possible use of the income flow model when managerial control is obtained. In 2000 the two companies claimed that by merging they could save £1,300m annually by combining projects, R&D synergies and by cost cutting in manufacturing and supply operations.

Exhibit 17.21 Value creation through merger

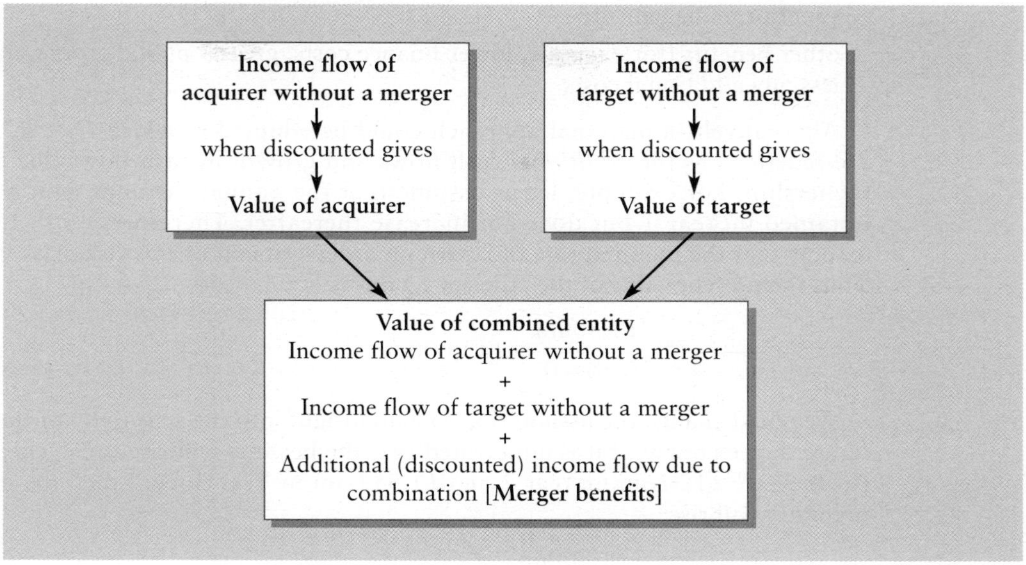

In the absence of a takeover the value of a share in either company is:

$$P_0 = \frac{d_1}{k_E - g}$$

This is where d_1 and g are generated by the existing structure and strategy.

Alternatively, we could examine the entire cash flow of the company rather than a single share.

$$V = \frac{C_1}{k_E - g_c}$$

where:

V = value of the entire firm;
C_1 = total cash flows at time 1 expected to continue growing at a constant rate of g_c in future years.

If there is a new strategy the values in the equations change:

$$P_0 = \frac{d_1^*}{k_E - g^*}$$

or, for the entire cash flow:

$$V = \frac{C_1^*}{k_E - g_c^*}$$

d_1^*, C_1^*, g^*, g_c^* allow for the following:

- synergy;
- cutting out costs;

- tax benefits;
- superior management;
- other benefits (for example, lower finance costs, greater public profile, market power) less any additional costs.

Alternatively, a marginal approach could be adopted in which C_1^*, d_1^*, g^* and g_c^* are redefined as the *additional* cash flows and growth in cash flows due to changes in ownership. For example, let us assume that the annual earnings gain of £1,300m is obtained in Year 1 but does not increase thereafter. Therefore $g = 0$. Let us further assume that the required rate of return on an investment of this risk class is 10 per cent. Thus the present value of the efficiency gains is:

$$V = \frac{C_1^*}{k_E - g_c^*} = \frac{£1{,}300\text{m}}{0.10 - 0} = £13{,}000\text{m}$$

We could change the assumption to gain insight into the sensitivity of the added value figure. For example, if it is anticipated that the benefits will rise each year by 2 per cent (so they are £1,326m in Year 2 and £1,352.5m in Year 3, etc.) then the maximum bid premium will rise:

$$V = \frac{C_1^*}{k_E - g_c^*} = \frac{£1{,}300\text{m}}{0.10 - 0.02} = £16{,}250\text{m}$$

On the other hand, the management of the two companies might have been carried away with the excitement of the bid battle and the £1,300m quoted might have come from hype or hubris, and, in fact, the difficulties of integration produce negative incremental cash flows. (*See* Chapter 20 for a discussion on the problems of post-merger integration, and hubris as a driver of merger activity.)

In July 2001 GlaxoSmithKline managers were very pleased with themselves: they announced that cost synergies have been revised upwards – they now expect £1.8bn by 2003.

Worked example 17.6 Thingamees

Big plc has made it clear to the widget industry that it is willing to sell its subsidiary, Little plc, a manufacturer of thingamees. You are a member of the strategy management team at Thingamees International plc, the largest producers of thingamees in the UK. Your firm is interested in acquiring Little and as a first step has obtained some information from Big plc.

Little plc Balance Sheet		*£m*
Fixed assets		10
Current assets		
Cash	0.5	
Stock	1.5	
Debtors	3.0	
		5
Current liabilities		(6)
Bank loan		(4)
Net assets		5

Trading record	
Year	*Total earnings, £m*
2001	1.86
2000	1.70
1999	1.65
1998	1.59
1997	1.20
1996	1.14
1995	1.01

Additional information

By combining the logistical departments you estimate that transport costs could be lowered by £100,000 per annum, and two secretarial posts eliminated, saving £28,000 p.a.

The closure of Little's head office would save £400,000 p.a. in staffing and running costs, but would also mean an additional £250,000 of administration costs at Thingamees plc to undertake some crucial tasks. The office building is situated in a good location and would raise a net £5m if sold immediately. A potential liability not displayed in Little's balance sheet is a possible legal claim of £3m relating to an earlier disposal of an asset. The plaintiff and Little's board have not yet reached agreement (Little's board is adamant that there is no liability).

Your appraisal of Little's management team is that it is a mixed bunch – some good, some very bad. Profits could be raised by £500,000 per year if you could impose your will quickly and remove poor managers. However, if you have to take a more gradual 'easing out' approach, operating profits will rise by only £300,000 per year.

The problems connected with a quick transition are: a sacking left, right and centre may cause disaffection among the good managers, encouraging hostility, departures and (**a**) profits collapse, and (**b**) Big plc is keen that you provide a commitment to avoid large-scale redundancies.

Big, Little and Thingamees International all have a beta of 1.5, which is representative of the appropriate adjustment to the risk premium on the average share given the systematic risk. The risk-free rate of return is 8 per cent and the historical risk premium of share portfolios over safe securities has been 5 per cent.

The increased market power available to Thingamees International after purchasing Little would improve margins in Thingamees International's existing business to provide an additional £100,000 per annum.

Assume that tax is irrelevant. Earnings may be treated as equivalent to cash flows.

Required

a Calculate the value of Little plc in its present form, assuming a continuation of its historic growth rate.

b Calculate the value of Little plc if you were unable to push for maximum management redundancies and Little continued with its historical growth rate for its profits (that is, the profits before merger benefits). Assume that the annual merger benefits are constant for all future years to an infinite horizon, that is, there is no growth.

c Calculate the value of Little plc on the assumption that you are able to push through the rapid management changes and the pre-acquisition earnings continue on their historic growth path. (Again, the annual merger savings are fixed).

d Discuss the steps you would take to get around the obstacles to profit maximisation.

Answers

a First calculate the required rate of return:

$$k_E = r_f + \beta\,(r_m - r_f)$$
$$= 8 + 1.5\,(5) = 15.5\%$$

Then calculate growth rate of cash flows:

$$g = \sqrt[6]{\frac{1.86}{1.01}} - 1 = 10.71\%$$

Then calculate the value of Little plc:

$$V = \frac{C_1}{k_E - g} = \frac{1.86\,(1 + 0.1071)}{0.155 - 0.1071} = £42.990\text{m}$$

The value of Little to its shareholders under its present strategy and managers is £42.990m.

b Calculate the present value of the future cash flows. These come in three forms.

i Those cash flows available immediately from selling assets, etc., less the amount due on a legal claim (taking the most conservative view):

Time 0 cash flows	
Sale of head office	£5m
less legal claim	£3m
	£2m

ii Merger benefit cash flow – constant for all future years:

	£m
Transport	0.100
Secretaries	0.028
Head office	0.150
Managerial efficiency	0.300
Market power	0.100
Boost to cash flow	0.678

This is a perpetuity which has a present value of:

$$\frac{0.678}{0.155} = £4.374\text{m}$$

iii The present value of Little under its existing strategy, £42.990m.
Add these values together:

i	£2.000m
ii	£4.374m
iii	£42.990m
Total value	£49.364m

c

Value of business in existing form	£42.990m
plus value of annual savings and benefits	
$\frac{678{,}000 + 200{,}000}{0.155}$	£5.665m
plus Time 0 cash flows	£2.000m
Total value	£50.655m

Thingamees International now has a bargaining range for the purchase of Little. Below £42.99m the existing shareholders will be reluctant to sell. Above £50.665m, Thingamees may destroy value for its own shareholders even if all poor managers can be removed.

d Some ideas: One possible step to reduce risk is to insist that Big plc accepts all liability relating to the legal claim.

Another issue to be addressed in the negotiation phase is to avoid being hamstrung by redundancy commitments.

Also plan the process of merger integration. In the period before the merger explain your intentions to Little's employees. After the transfer do not alienate the managers and other employees by being capricious and secretive – be straight and honest. If pain is to be inflicted for the good of the firm, be quick, rational and fair, communicate and explain. (See Chapter 20 for more detail.)

CONCLUDING COMMENTS

There are two points about valuation worth noting. First going through a rigorous process of valuation is more important than arriving at *an* answer. It is the understanding of the assumptions and an appreciation of the nature of the inputs to the process which give insight, not a single number at the end. It is the recognition of the qualitative, and even subjective, nature of key variables in a superficially quantitative analysis that leads to knowledge about values. We cannot escape the uncertainty inherent in the valuation of a share – what someone is willing to pay depends on what will happen in the future – and yet this is no excuse for rejecting the models as unrealistic and impractical. They are better than the alternatives: guessing, or merely comparing one share with another with no theoretical base to anchor either valuation. At least the models presented in this chapter have the virtue of forcing the analyst to make explicit the fundamental considerations concerning the value of a share. As the sage of finance, Warren Buffett, says, 'Valuing a business is part art and part science'.[11]

The second point leads on from the first. It makes sense to treat the various valuation methods as complementary rather than as rivals. Obtain a range of values in full knowledge of the weaknesses of each approach and apply informed judgement to provide an idea of the value region.

KEY POINTS AND CONCEPTS

- **Knowledge of the influences on share value** is needed by:
  a managers seeking actions to increase that value;
  b investors interested in allocating savings.

- **Share valuation requires a combination of two skills:**
  a analytical ability using mathematical models;
  b good judgement.

- The **net asset value** (NAV) approach to valuation focuses on balance sheet values. These may be adjusted to reflect current market or replacement values.
  Advantage: 'objectivity'.
  Disadvantages: – excludes many non-quantifiable assets;
  – less objective than is often supposed.

- **Asset values are given more attention in some situations:**
  – firms in financial difficulty;
  – takeover bids;
  – when discounted income flow techniques are difficult to apply, for example in property investment companies, investment trusts, resource-based firms.

- **Income flow valuation methods** focus on the future flows attributable to the shareholder. The past is only useful to the extent that it sheds light on the future.
- **The dividend valuation models (DVM)** are based on the premise that the market value of ordinary shares represents the sum of the expected future dividend flows to infinity, discounted to a present value.
- A **constant dividend valuation model:**

$$P_0 = \frac{d_1}{k_E}$$

- The **dividend growth model:**

$$P_0 = \frac{d_1}{k_E - g}$$

  This assumes constant growth in future dividends to infinity.

- **Problems with dividend valuation models:**
  - highly sensitive to the assumptions;
  - the quality of input data is often poor;
  - g cannot be greater than k_E, but then, on a long-term view, this would not happen.
- **Factors determining the growth rate of dividends:**
  - the quantity of resources retained and reinvested;
  - the rate of return earned on retained resources;
  - the rate of return earned on existing assets.
- **How to calculate** g, some pointers:
  a Focus on the firm:
    - evaluate the management;
    - extrapolate historic dividend growth;
    - financial statement evaluation and ratio analysis;
    - evaluate strategy.

  b Focus on the economy.
  c Focus on the industry prospects.
- **The historic price earnings ratio (PER)** compared with PERs of peer firms is a crude method of valuation (it is also very popular):

$$\text{Historic PER} = \frac{\text{Current market price of share}}{\text{Last year's earnings per share}}$$

- **Historic PERs may be high for two reasons:**
  - the company is fast growing and a stock market 'darling';
  - the company has been performing poorly, has low historic earnings, but is expected to improve.

  The linking factor is the anticipation of high future growth in earnings. Risk is also reflected in differences between PERs.

- The **more complete PER model:**

  $$\frac{P_0}{E_1} = \frac{d_1/E_1}{k_E - g}$$

  This is a prospective PER model because it focuses on next year's dividend and earnings.

- The **discounted cash flow method:**

  $$P_0 = \sum_{t=1}^{t=n} C/(1 + k_E)^t$$

  For constant cash flow growth:

  $$P_0 = \frac{C_1}{k_E - g_c}$$

- The **owner earnings model** requires the discounting of the company's future owner earnings which are standard reported earnings plus non-cash charges less the amount of expenditure on plant, machinery, working capital needed for the firm to maintain its long-term competitive position and its unit volume and to make investment in all new value-creating projects.

- Additional factors to consider when **valuing unquoted shares:**
  - lower quality and quantity of information;
  - more risk;
  - less marketable;
  - may involve 'golden hand-cuffs' or 'earn-outs'.

- Some companies are extraordinarily **difficult to value;** therefore **proxies are used for projected cash flow,** such as:
  - telemedia valuations: multiply the number of lines, homes served or doors passed;
  - advertising agencies: annual billings;
  - fund managers: funds under control;
  - hotels: star ratings and bedrooms.

- **Control over a firm** permits the possibility of changing the future cash flows. Therefore a share may be more highly valued if control is achieved.

- **A target company could be valued on the basis of its discounted future cash flows,** e.g.:

  $$V = \frac{C_1^*}{k_E - g_c^*}$$

- Alternatively the **incremental flows** expected to flow from the company under new management could be discounted to estimate the bid premium (d_1^*, C_1^*, and g^* are redefined to be incremental factors only):

  $$P_0 = \frac{d_1^*}{k_E - g^*} \text{ or } V = \frac{C_1^*}{k_E - g_c^*}$$

REFERENCES AND FURTHER READING

Arnold, G.C. (1996) 'Equity and corporate valuation', in E. Gardener and P. Molyneux (eds), *Investment Banking: Theory and Practice*. 2nd edn. London: Euromoney. A more succinct version of valuation methods.

Arnold, G. (2002) *Valuegrowth Investing*. London: Financial Times Prentice Hall. An integration of strategic analysis with equity market investment principles.

Blake, D. (2000) *Financial Market Analysis*. 2nd edn. New York: Wiley. Chapter 6 contains a valuable discussion on share valuation.

Copeland, T., Koller, T. and Murrin, J. (1996) *Valuation*. 2nd edn. New York: Wiley. Some valuation issues are presented in an accessible style.

Damodaran, A. (1999) *Applied Corporate Finance: A User's Manual*. New York: Wiley. Chapter 12 of this excellent book is particularly useful for share valuation.

Gordon, M.J. (1962) *The Investment, Financing and Valuation of the Corporation*. Homewood, IL: Irwin. An early statement of a dividend growth model.

Gordon, M.J. and Shapiro, E. (1956) 'Capital equipment analysis: the required rate of profit', *Management Science*, III, pp. 102–10. Dividend growth model presented.

Lofthouse, S. (1994) *Equity Investment Management*. Chichester: Wiley. A practitioner assesses the theoretical models and empirical evidence on investment issues, including valuation.

Lowe, J. (1997) *Warren Buffett Speaks*. New York: Wiley. A knowledgeable, witty and wise financier's comments are collected and presented. An excellent antidote to theoretical purism.

Outram, R. (1997) 'For what it's worth', *Management Today*, May, pp. 70–1.

Rappaport, A. (1999) *Creating Shareholder Value*. New York: Free Press. Revised and updated. Describes cash flow valuation models clearly.

Sharpe, W.F., Alexander, G.J. and Bailey, J.V. (1999) *Investments*. 6th edn. Upper Saddle River, NJ: Prentice-Hall. A wider range of valuation issues is discussed in an accessible introductory style.

Solomon, E. (1963) *The Theory of Financial Management*. New York: Columbia University Press. An early discussion of the Gordon and Shapiro dividend growth model.

Stephens, G. and Funnell, J. (1995) 'Take your partners . . .', *Corporate Finance*, London: Euromoney monthly journal, July. Discusses the difficult issue of valuation of telemedia companies.

SELF-REVIEW QUESTIONS

1 What are the problems of relying on NAV as a valuation method? In what circumstances is it particularly useful?

2 Why do analysts obtain historic information on a company for valuation purposes?

3 Name the three types of future income flows which may be examined to value shares.

4 Explain why the dividend valuation model discounts all dividends to infinity and yet individual investors hold shares for a shorter period, making capital gains (and losses).

5 The dividend growth model takes the form:

$$P_0 = \frac{d_1}{k_E - g}$$

Does this mean that we are only valuing next year's dividend? Explain your answer.

6 What are the main investigatory routes you would pursue to try to establish the likely range of future growth rates for a firm?

7 What are the differences between the crude PER model and the more complete PER model?

8 Why do PERs vary over time, and between firms in the same industry?

9 What additional factors might you consider when valuing an unquoted share rather than one listed on a stock exchange?

10 Why might a share have a different value to someone who was able to exercise control over the organisation compared with someone who had a small, almost powerless, stake?

QUESTIONS AND PROBLEMS

1 'Valuing shares is either a simple exercise of plugging numbers into mathematical formulae or making comparisons with shares in the same sector.' Explain the problems with this statement.

2 'Some companies do not pay dividends, in others the growth rate is higher than the required rate of return, therefore the dividend valuation models are useless.' Explain your reasons for agreeing or disagreeing with this statement.

3 Shades plc has the following dividend history:

Year	*Dividend per share*
Recently paid	21p
Last year	19p
Two years ago	18p
Three years ago	16p
Four years ago	14p
Five years ago	12p

The rate of return required on a share of this risk class is 13 per cent. Assuming that this dividend growth rate is unsustainable and Shades will halve its historic rate in the future, what is the value of one share?

4 ElecWat is a regulated supplier of electricity and water. It is expected to pay a dividend of 24p per share per year for ever. Calculate the value of one share if a company of this risk class is required to return 10 per cent per year.

5* Tented plc has developed a new tent which has had rave reviews in the camping press. The company paid a dividend of 11p per share recently and the next is due in one year. Dividends are expected to rise by 25 per cent per year for the next five years while the company exploits its technological and marketing lead. After this period, however, the growth rate will revert to only 5 per cent per year.

The rate of return on risk-free securities is 7 per cent and the risk premium on the average share has been 5 per cent. Tented is in a systematic risk class which means that the average risk premium should be adjusted by a beta factor of 1.5.

Calculate the value of one share in Tented plc.

6* (*Examination level*) The current share price of Blueberry plc is 205p. It recently reported earnings per share of 14p and has a policy of paying out 50 per cent of earnings in dividends each year. The earnings history of the firm is as follows:

Last reported	14p
One year ago	13p
Two years ago	12p
Three years ago	11p
Four years ago	10p
Five years ago	9p

The rate of growth in earnings and dividends shown in the past is expected to continue into the future.

The risk-free rate of return is 6.5 per cent and the risk premium on the average share has been 5 per cent for decades. Blueberry is in a higher systematic risk class than the average share and therefore the risk premium needs to be adjusted by a beta factor of 1.2.

Required

a Calculate the historic price earnings ratio.

b Calculate the future growth rate of dividends and earnings.

c Calculate the required rate of return on a share of this risk class.

d Use the more complete PER model to decide if the shares at 205p are over- or underpriced.

e Describe and explain the problems of using the crude historic PER as an analytical tool.

f What additional factors would you need to allow for when valuing an unquoted share rather than one listed on a stock exchange?

7* (*Examination level*) The following figures are extracted from Tesco plc's Annual Report and Accounts 1996:

Balance sheet

24 February 1996	*Group 1996 £m*
Fixed assets	
Tangible assets	5,466
Investments	19
	5,485
Current assets	
Stocks	559
Debtors	80
Investments	54
Cash at bank and in hand	38
	731
Creditors: falling due within one year	(2,002)
Creditors: falling due after more than one year	
Convertible capital bonds	–
Other	(598)
Provisions for liabilities and charges	(22)
	3,594
Capital and reserves	
Called-up share capital	108
Share premium account	1,383
Other reserves	40
Profit and loss account	2,057
Equity shareholders' funds	3,588
Minority equity interests	6
	3,594

Dividend and earnings history	*Dividends per share*	*Earnings per share*
1980	0.82p	3.51p
1996	9.60p	21.9p

The average risk premium over risk-free securities is 5 per cent. The risk-free rate of return is 6.25 per cent and Tesco's beta of 0.77 represents the appropriate adjustment to the average risk premium.

Required

a Calculate a revised net asset value (NAV) for the Tesco group assuming the following:
- buildings are overvalued in the balance sheet by £100m;
- 20 per cent of the debtors figure will never be collected;
- the stock figure includes £30m of unsaleable stock;
- 'Current investments' now have a market value of £205m.

b The total market capitalisation of Tesco in late 1996 was in the region of £8bn. Provide reasons for the great difference between the value that the market placed on Tesco and the NAV.

c For what type of company and in what circumstances does NAV provide a good estimate of value?

d If you assume that the dividend growth rate between 1980 and 1996 is unsustainable, and that in the future the rate of growth will average half the rate of the past, at what would you value one share in 1996 using the dividend growth model?

e Give some potential explanatory reasons for the difference between the value given in **d** and the value placed on a share in the London Stock Market in 1996 of about 355p.

f Given the answer in **d** for share price, what is the *prospective* price earnings ratio (PER) if future earnings grow at the same rate as future dividends?

g What would be the PER if, **i** $k = 14$, $g = 12$; **ii** $k = 15$, $g = 11$ and next year's dividend and earnings are the same as calculated in **d** and **f**?

h If you assumed for the sake of simplicity that all the long-term debt in the balance sheet is a debenture issued in 1990 which is due for redemption in 1999 at par value of £100, what was the weighted average cost of capital for this firm in 1996?

Other information

- The debenture pays a coupon of 9 per cent on par value.
- The coupons are payable annually – the next is due in 12 months.
- The debenture is currently trading at 105.50.
- The balance sheet shows the nominal value, not the market value.
- Tax is payable at 30 per cent (relevant to question **h** only).
- Use the capitalisation figure given in **b** for the equity weight.

8* Lanes plc, the retail butchers, is considering the purchase of ten shops from Roberts plc, the conglomerate. The information gathered on the ten shops trading as a separate subsidiary company is as follows:

Balance sheet

		£m
Fixed assets		2
Current assets		
Cash	0.1	
Stock	0.6	
Debtors	0.1	
		0.8
Current liabilities		(0.5)
Long-term loan		(1.0)
Net assets		1.3

Trading history

Year	*Earnings (£m)*
2001	1.4
2000	1.3
1999	1.1
1998	1.2
1997	1.0
1996	1.0

If the shops remain part of Roberts the earnings growth is expected to continue at the average historical rate to infinity.

The rate of return required on a business of this risk class is 13 per cent per annum.

Required

a Calculate the value of the shops to Roberts' shareholders.

b Lanes' management believe that the ten shops will be a perfect fit with their own. There are no towns in which they both trade, and economies of scale can be obtained. Suppliers will grant quantity discounts which will save £1m per annum. Combined transportation costs will fall by £200,000 per year and administration costs can be cut by £150,000 per year. These savings will remain constant for all future years. In addition, the distribution depot used by the ten shops could be closed and sold for £1.8m with no adverse impact on trading. Calculate the value of the ten shops to Lanes' shareholders on the assumption that the required return remains at 13 per cent and underlying growth continues at its historic rate.

9† (*Examination level*) Green plc is a conglomerate quoted on the main London market. The latest set of accounts have just been published. The balance sheet is summarised below:

Green plc	*Balance Sheet*	*1 June 2001*
		£m
Fixed assets		
Tangible fixed assets		140
Investments		40
		180
Current assets		
Stocks	180	
Debtors	120	
Cash	30	
	330	330
Creditors (amounts falling due within one year)		(200)
Creditors (amounts falling due after more than one year)		(100)
Net assets		210

Other information

Dividend history

1993	*1994*	*1995*	*1996*	*1997*	*1998*	*1999*	*2000*	*2001*
5p (dividend per share)	5.3	6	6.2	7	7.5	8	8.5	9.2p

Green plc have demonstrated an equity beta of 1.3 over the past five years (and this can be taken as an appropriate adjustment factor to the average risk premium for shares over risk-free securities). The risk-free return is currently 6.5 per cent and the risk premium for equities over risk-free securities has averaged 5 per cent per annum.

Shares in issue: 300 million (constant for the last ten years).

Required

a Calculate a net asset value for each of Green's shares after adjusting the balance sheet for the following:
- tangible assets are worth £50m more than shown in the balance sheet;
- one-half of the debtors figure will never be collected; and
- in your judgement Green's directors have overestimated the stock value by £30m.

b Comment on some of the problems associated with valuing a share or a corporation using net asset value. For what type of company is net asset value particularly useful?

c Use a dividend valuation model to calculate the value of one share in Green plc. Assume that future dividend growth will be the same as the average rate for recent years.

d Calculate the weighted average cost of capital (WACC) for Green plc on the assumptions that the share price calculated in question **c** is the market share price and the entry 'creditors (amount falling due after more than one year)' consists entirely of a debenture issued at a total par value of £100m five years ago. The debenture will pay a coupon of 8 per cent in one year, followed by a similar coupon in two years from now. A final coupon will be paid in three years upon redemption of the debenture at par value. The debenture is currently trading in the secondary market at £103 per £100 nominal.

For the purpose of calculating the weighted average cost of capital the tax rate may be assumed to be 30 per cent.

10* (*Examination level*) You have been asked to carry out a valuation of Dela plc, a listed company on the main London market.

At the last year-end Dela's summarised balance sheet is as shown in Table 1.

Table 1 Dela 1 May 2001

		£m
Fixed assets		300
Current assets		
Stocks	70	
Debtors	120	
Cash at bank	90	280
Liabilities		
Creditors: trade creditors falling due within one year		(400)
Creditors falling due after more than one year		(50)
Shareholders' funds (Net assets)		130

Table 2 Dela plc trading history

Year-end	*Earnings per share (pence)*	*Dividend per share (pence)*
2001	20	10
2000	18	9.5
1999	17	9
1998	16	8
1997	13	7
1996	12	6
1995	10	5.5
1994	10	5

Datastream has calculated a beta for Dela of 1.2 and this may be used as the appropriate adjustment to the risk premium on the average share. The risk-free rate of return on UK Treasury bills is 6.5 per cent and the latest study shows an annual equity risk premium over the yield on UK government bonds of 5 per cent for the period 1900–2001.

The impressive average annual growth in Dela's earnings and dividends over the last few years is likely to persist.

Additional information

- You have obtained an independent valuation of Dela's fixed assets at £350m.
- You believe that Dela has overstated the value of stocks by £30m and one-quarter of its debtors are likely to be uncollectable.
- There have been no new issues of shares in the past eight years.
- Dela has 1,000 million shares in issue.

Required

a Value Dela using the net asset value (NAV) method.

b Briefly explain why balance sheets generally have limited usefulness for estimating the value of a firm.

c Briefly describe two circumstances where balance sheet net asset values become very important for corporate valuation.

d Value one of Dela's shares using the dividend valuation model. (Assume the dividend of 10p has just been paid and the next dividend is due in one year.)

e What is the prospective price to earnings ratio (P/E ratio) given the share price in **d**?

f Calculate a weighted average cost of capital given that the balance sheet entry 'creditors falling due after more than one year' consists entirely of the nominal value of a debenture issue. The debenture will be redeemed at par in three years, it carries an annual coupon of 8 per cent (the next payment will be in one year) and it is presently trading in the market at 96.50 per £100 nominal. The total nominal value is £50m.

Assume for the purpose of **f** that the shares are valued at your valuation in **d** and that Dela is taxed at a rate of 30 per cent.

ASSIGNMENTS

1 Estimate the value of a share in your company (or one you know well) using the following approaches:
- net asset value;
- dividend valuation model;
- crude price – earnings ratio – comparing with peer firms;
- more complete price – earnings ratio model;
- cash flow model;
- owner earnings model.

In a report make clear your awareness of the sensitivity of the results to your assumptions.

2 If your company has recently acquired a business or is considering such a purchase obtain as much data as you can to calculate a possible bargain range. The upper boundary of this is fixed by the value of the business to your firm, given the implementation of a plan to change the future cash flows. The lower boundary is fixed by the value to the present owner.

CHAPTER NOTES

1 *See* discussion in Chapter 19 based on evidence from Lintner (1956) and 3i (1993) – details of these sources are in Chapter 19 References and Further Reading.

2 If the dividends continue to grow at the rate *g* in perpetuity.

3 Quoted by Jim Rasmussen, 'Billionaire talks strategy with students', *Omaha – World Herald*, 2 January 1994, p. 175. Also in Janet Lowe (1997).

4 Warren Buffett seminar held at Columbia University Business School, 'Investing in equity markets', 13 March 1985, transcript, p. 23. Reproduced in Janet Lowe (1997).

5 Laura Ashley had many years of losses in the late 1990s.

6 *Financial Times*, 11 April 1996.

7 Quoted by Robert Outram (1997), p. 70.

8 This form of analysis is set out in Arnold (2002).

9 *Source*: Robert Outram (1997), p. 71.

10 Stephens and Funnell (1995), p. 20.

11 Quoted by Adam Smith, 'The modest billionaire', *Esquire*, October 1988, p. 103. Reprinted in Janet Lowe (1997), p. 100.

Chapter 18

CAPITAL STRUCTURE

INTRODUCTION

Someone has to decide what is an appropriate level of borrowing for a firm given its equity capital base. To assist this decision it would be useful to know if it is theoretically possible to increase shareholder wealth by changing the gearing (debt–equity ratio) level. That is, if future cash flows generated by the business are assumed to be constant, can managers simply by altering the proportion of debt in the total capital structure increase shareholder value? If this is possible then surely managers have a duty to move the firm towards the optimal debt proportion.

The traditional view was that it would be beneficial to increase gearing from a low (or zero) level because the firm would then be financed to a greater extent by cheaper borrowed funds, therefore the weighted average cost of capital (WACC) would fall. The discounting of future cash flows at this lower WACC produces a higher present value and so shareholder wealth is enhanced. However, as debt levels rise the firm's earnings attributable to shareholders become increasingly volatile due to the requirement to pay large amounts of interest prior to dividends. Eventually the burden of a large annual interest bill can lead the firm to become financially distressed and, in extreme circumstances, liquidated. So the traditional answer to the question of whether there was an optimum gearing level was 'yes'. If the gearing level is too low, shareholder value opportunities are forgone by not substituting 'cheap' debt for equity. If it is too high the additional risk leads to a loss in shareholder value through a higher discount rate being applied to the future cash flows attributable to ordinary shareholders. This is because of the higher risk and, at very high gearing, the penalty of complete business failure becomes much more of a possibility.

Then, in the late 1950s a theory was developed by Franco Modigliani and Merton Miller (1958) which said that it did not matter whether the firm had a gearing level of 90 per cent debt or 2 per cent debt – the overall value of the firm is constant and shareholder wealth cannot be enhanced by altering the debt–equity ratio. This conclusion was based on some major assumptions and required the firm to operate in a perfect world of perfect knowledge, a world in which individual shareholders can borrow and lend at the same rate as giant corporations, and in which taxation and cost of financial distress do not exist.

Later Modigliani and Miller (MM) modified the no-taxation assumption. This led to a different conclusion: the best gearing level for a firm interested in shareholder wealth maximisation is, generally, as high as possible. This was an astonishing result; it means that a company financed with £99m of debt and £1m of equity serves its shareholders better than one funded by £50m of debt and £50m of equity. Within academic circles thousands of hours of thinking and research time has been spent over the past four decades building on the MM foundations, and millions of hours of undergraduates' and postgraduates' precious time has been spent learning the intricacies of the algebraic proofs lying behind MM conclusions. Going through this process has its virtues: the models provide a systematic framework for evaluating the capital structure question and can lead to some rigorous thought within the confines of the models.

However, this chapter will not dwell on algebra (the interested reader is referred to some more advanced reading at the end of the chapter). Emphasis will be given to explanations which have been advanced to explain actual gearing levels. A conclusion will be drawn which fits neither the MM first conclusion, that there is not an optimal gearing level, nor their modified theory with taxes, in which there is an optimum at the most extreme level of debt.

Learning objectives

The level of debt relative to ordinary share capital is, for most firms, of secondary consideration behind strategic and operational decisions. However, if wealth can be increased by getting this decision right managers need to understand the key influences. By the end of the chapter the reader should be able to:

- discuss the effect of gearing, and differentiate business and financial risk;
- describe the underlying assumptions, rationale and conclusions of Modigliani and Miller's models, in worlds with and without tax;
- explain the relevance of some important, but often non-quantifiable, influences on the optimal gearing level question.

A fundamental question for any chapter of this book is: does this subject have any relevance to the real world? Perhaps Case Study 18.1 will help. Senior managers frequently consider the balance between debt and ordinary share capital in a company's financial make-up.

Clearly there is a perception amongst directors, analysts and financial commentators that there is an optimal gearing level, or at least a range of gearing levels which help to maximise shareholder wealth and this lies at neither extreme of the spectrum.

Debt finance is cheaper and riskier (for the company)

Financing a business through borrowing is cheaper than using equity. This is, first, because lenders require a lower rate of return than ordinary shareholders. Debt financial securities present a lower risk than shares for the finance providers because they have prior claims on annual income and in liquidation. In addition security is often provided and covenants imposed.

A profitable business effectively pays less for debt capital than equity for another reason: the debt interest can be offset against pre-tax profits before the calculation of the corporation tax bill, thus reducing the tax paid.

Third, issuing and transaction costs associated with raising and servicing debt are generally less than for ordinary shares.

CASE STUDY 18.1

The balance between debt and ordinary share capital

In 2001 BT management was in serious trouble. The company had accumulated debt of over £30bn following a worldwide acquisition spree and infrastructure investment. The net assets of the company were roughly half the debt level, at £14bn. The City institutions were desperately concerned by the high level of debt. Sir Peter Bonfield, the chief executive, recognised that he had allowed the debt to rise too high. 'We identified the need to introduce new equity capital into the business to support the reduction in the unsustainable level of group debt' (BT Annual Report 2001). The company raised £5.9bn through a rights issue, sold off property, slashed investment and sold stakes in telecom businesses around the world. It also stopped paying a dividend.

In 2000 Shell expressed its intention to borrow in order to buy back shares: 'This is a way of managing our balance sheet'.[1]

In March 1996 Iceland, the frozen food retail chain, spent £42m buying back 27m of its own shares at 156p, representing 10 per cent of its equity. Gearing was expected to rise to about 25 per cent from 14 per cent by the end of 1996 as a result of this action. Mr Bernard Leigh, Finance Director, said, 'We are throwing off cash – the last thing our shareholders want is to see us ungeared'.[2] Iceland continued in this vein and one year later announced plans to distribute £118m to shareholders and cancel more than a third of its equity. However, investment analysts were worried that the capital restructuring was going too far. Peggy Hollinger wrote in the Financial Times,[3] 'The borrowings needed to finance the deal would leave Iceland weakened in a declining market, with gearing of 125 per cent'.

Severn Trent, the water company, returned £121.5m to shareholders by buying back 5 per cent of its shares in 1996. This was part of a plan to raise gearing to 30 per cent. The Group Finance Director, Mr Alan Costin, explained the rationale behind the decision. 'We are replacing expensive equity with less expensive debt.'[4]

A key question for senior management.

There are some valuable benefits from financing a firm with debt. So why do firms tend to avoid very high gearing levels? One reason is financial distress risk. This could be induced by the requirement to pay interest regardless of the cash flow of the business. If the firm hits a rough patch in its business activities it may have trouble paying its bondholders, bankers and other creditors their entitlement. Exhibit 18.1 shows that, as gearing increases, the risk of financial failure grows.

Exhibit 18.1 At low gearing levels the risk of financial distress is low, but the cost of capital is high; this reverses at high gearing levels

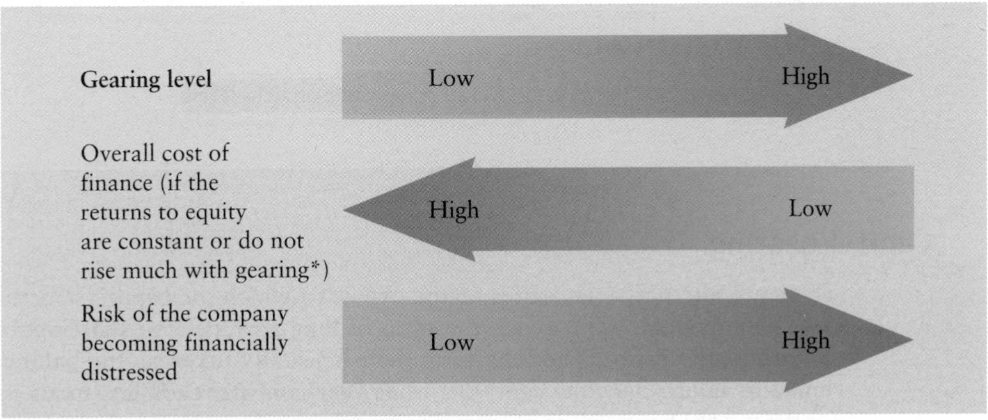

Note: *This assumption is considered in the text.

Note the crucial assumption in Exhibit 18.1 – if the returns to equity are constant, or do not rise much, the overall cost of finance declines. This is obviously unrealistic because as the risk of financial distress rises ordinary shareholders are likely to demand higher returns. This is an important issue and we will return to it after a discussion of some basic concepts about gearing.

WHAT DO WE MEAN BY 'GEARING'?

We need to avoid some confusion which is possible when using the word 'gearing'. First, we should make a distinction between operating gearing and financial gearing.

Operating gearing refers to the extent to which the firm's total costs are fixed. the profits of firms with high operating gearing, such as car or steel manufacturers, are very sensitive to changes in the sales level. They have high break-even points (the turnover level at which profits are achieved) but when this level is breached a large proportion of any additional sales revenue turns into profit because of the relatively low variable costs.

Financial gearing is the focus of this chapter and concerns the proportion of debt in the capital structure. Net income to shareholders in firms with high financial gearing is more sensitive to changes in operating profits.

Second, the terms gearing and leverage are used interchangeably by most practitioners, although leverage is used more in America.

Third, there are many different ways of calculating financial gearing (to be called simply 'gearing' throughout this chapter). Financial analysts, the Press and corporate managers usually measure gearing by reference to balance sheet (book) figures, but it is important to recognise that much of finance theory concentrates on the market values of debt and equity. Both book and market approaches are useful, depending on the purpose of the analysis.

There are two ways of putting in perspective the levels of debt that a firm carries. *Capital gearing* focuses on the extent to which a firm's total capital is in the form of debt. *Income gearing* is concerned with the proportion of the annual income stream (that is, the pre-interest profits) which is devoted to the prior claims of debtholders, in other words, what proportion of profits is taken by interest charges.

Exhibit 18.2 A firm's financial gearing can be measured in two ways

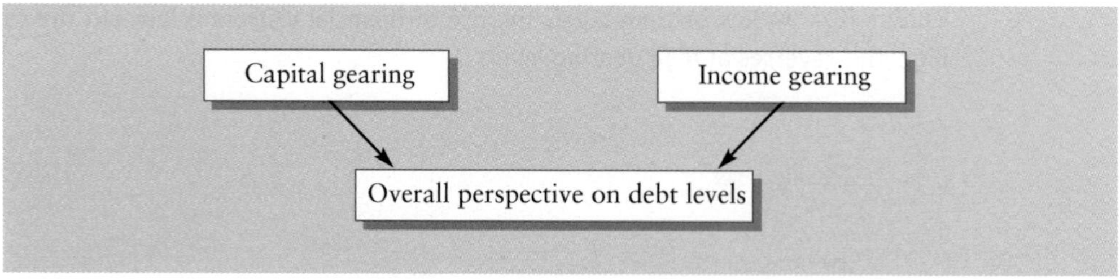

Capital gearing

There are alternative measures of the extent to which the capital structure consists of debt. One popular approach is the ratio of long-term debt to shareholders' funds (the debt to equity ratio). The long-term debt is usually taken as the balance sheet items 'amounts falling due after more than one year' and shareholders' funds is the net asset (or net worth) figure in the balance sheet.

$$\text{Capital gearing (1)} = \frac{\text{Long-term debt}}{\text{Shareholders' funds}}$$

This ratio is of interest because it may give some indication of the firm's ability to sell assets to repay debts. For example, if the ratio stood at 0.3, or 30 per cent, lenders and shareholders might feel relatively comfortable as there would be, apparently, over twice as many net (that is after paying off liabilities) assets as long-term debt. So, if the worst came to the worst, the company could sell assets to satisfy its long-term lenders.

There is a major problem with relying on this measure of gearing. The book value of assets can be quite different from the saleable value. This may be because the assets have been recorded at historical purchase value (perhaps less depreciation) and have not been revalued over time. It may also be due to the fact that companies forced to sell assets to satisfy creditors often have to do so at greatly reduced prices if they are in a hurry.[5]

Second, this measure of gearing can have a range of values from zero to infinity and this makes inter-firm comparisons difficult. The measure shown below puts gearing within a range of zero to 100 per cent as debt is expressed as a fraction of all long-term capital.[6]

$$\text{Capital gearing (2)} = \frac{\text{Long-term debt}}{\text{Long-term debt + Shareholders' funds}}$$

These ratios could be further modified by the inclusion of 'provisions' and deferred taxation. Provisions are sums set aside in the accounts for anticipated loss or expenditure, for example a bad debt or costs of merger integration. Deferred tax likewise may be included as an expected future liability.

The third capital gearing measure, in addition to allowing for long-term debt, includes short-term borrowing.

$$\text{Capital gearing (3)} = \frac{\text{All borrowing}}{\text{All borrowing + Shareholders' funds}}$$

Many firms rely on overdraft facilities and other short-term borrowing, for example commercial bills. Technically these are classified as short term. In reality many firms use the overdraft and other short-term borrowing as a long-term source of funds. Furthermore, if we are concerned about the potential for financial distress, then we must recognise that an inability to repay an overdraft can be just as serious as an inability to service a long-term bond.

To add sophistication to capital gearing analysis it is often necessary to take into account any cash (or marketable securities) holdings in the firm. These can be used to offset the threat that debt poses.

A measure of gearing which is gaining prominence is the ratio of debt to the total market value of the firm's equity (also called the debt to equity ratio (market value)).

$$\text{Capital gearing (4)} = \frac{\text{Long-term debt}}{\text{Total market capitalisation}}$$

This has the advantage of being closer to the market-value-based gearing measures (assuming book long-term debt is similar to the market value of the debt). It gives some indication of the relative share of the company's total value belonging to debtholders and shareholders.

It is plain that there is a rich variety of capital gearing measures and it is important to know which measure people are using – it can be very easy to find yourself talking at cross-purposes.[7]

Income gearing

The capital gearing measures rely on the appropriate valuation of net assets either in the balance sheet or in a revaluation exercise. This is a notoriously difficult task to complete with any great certainty. Try valuing a machine on a factory floor, or a crate of raw material. Also the capital gearing measures focus on a worst case scenario: 'What could we sell the business assets for if we had to, in order to pay creditors?'

It may be erroneous to focus exclusively on assets when trying to judge a company's ability to repay debts. Take the example of a successful advertising agency. It may not have any saleable assets at all, apart from a few desks and chairs, and yet it may be able to borrow hundreds of millions of pounds because it has the ability to generate cash to make interest payments. Thus, quite often, a more appropriate measure of gearing is one concerned with the level of a firm's income relative to its interest commitments:

$$\text{Interest cover} = \frac{\text{Profit before interest and tax}}{\text{Interest charges}}$$

The lower the interest cover ratio the greater the chance of interest payment default and liquidation. The inverse of interest cover measures the proportion of profits paid out in interest – this is called income gearing.

The ratios considered above are now calculated for BT. The data in Exhibit 18.3 and in the following calculations are taken from the 2001 Annual Report and Accounts.

Exhibit 18.3 BT Balance Sheet and profit figures 2001

	£m	£m
Fixed assets		45,209
Current assets		
Stocks	361	
Debtors	6,260	
Investments	2,557	
Cash and bank balances	412	
		9,590
Creditors due within one year		(20,733)
of which:		
Loans and other borrowings	12,136	
Other creditors	8,597	
Creditors due after one year: loans and other borrowings		(18,775)
Provisions for liabilities and charges		(723)
Minority interests		(499)
Total net assets (shareholders' funds)		14,069
Profit before interest and taxation		£3,373m
Interest		£1,243m
Market capitalisation		£39,000m

We now calculate the ratios using the data in Exhibit 18.3:

$$\text{Capital gearing (1)} = \frac{\text{Long-term debt}}{\text{Shareholders' funds}} \times 100$$

$$= \frac{£18{,}775\text{m}}{£14{,}069\text{m}} \times 100 = 133\%$$

$$\text{Capital gearing (2)} = \frac{\text{Long-term debt}}{\text{Long-term debt + Shareholders' funds}} \times 100$$

$$= \frac{£18{,}775\text{m}}{£18{,}775\text{m} + £14{,}069\text{m}} \times 100 = 57\%$$

$$\text{Capital gearing (3)} = \frac{\text{All borrowing}}{\text{All borrowing + Shareholders' funds}} \times 100$$

$$= \frac{£18{,}775\text{m} + £12{,}136\text{m}}{£18{,}775\text{m} + £12{,}136\text{m} + £14{,}069\text{m}} \times 100 = 69\%$$

$$\text{Capital gearing (4)} = \frac{\text{Long-term debt}}{\text{Total market capitalisation}} \times 100$$

$$= \frac{£18{,}775\text{m}}{£39{,}000\text{m}} \times 100 = 48\%$$

$$\text{Interest cover} = \frac{\text{Profit before interest and taxation}}{\text{Interest charges}}$$

$$= \frac{£3{,}373\text{m}}{£1{,}243\text{m}} = 2.7 \text{ times}$$

$$\text{Income gearing} = \frac{\text{Interest charges}}{\text{Profit before interest and taxation}} \times 100$$

$$= \frac{£1{,}243\text{m}}{£3{,}373\text{m}} \times 100 = 37\%$$

Exhibit 18.4 presents an extract from a report designed to assist managers. It gives some idea of the typical gearing ratios for medium-sized firms (turnover £1m–£50m) in Britain's East and West Midlands regions. This draws on data from over 1,200 firms and provides average figures for a ten-year period.

The Lex column of the *Financial Times* commented on the most appropriate measures of gearing for modern industry (*see* Exhibit 18.5).

Exhibit 18.4 Solvency/liquidity averages 1985–1994

	Quick ratio		*Total debt/ Net worth (%)*		*Long-term debt/Net worth (%)*		*Interest/ Pre-interest profit (%)*	
	East Mids	*West Mids*	*East Mids*	*West Mids*	*East Mids*	*West Mids*	*East Mids*	*West Mids*
1 Chemicals	2.24	1.00	140	67	137	24	28	23
2 Metal goods	1.08	1.00	90	175	40	70	19	27
3 Mechanical engineering	1.08	0.94	76	145	28	55	18	29
4 Electrical and Electronic engineering	0.87	0.90	118	186	35	83	27	20
5 Rubber and Plastics	0.86	0.85	131	108	45	37	30	36
6 Textiles	0.85	0.80	131	86	51	23	38	28
7 Footwear and Clothing	1.00	0.66	89	80	21	15	24	42
8 Food, Drink and Tobacco	0.95	0.67	76	164	32	34	33	29
9 Paper, Print and Publishing	0.96	1.05	109	84	63	30	29	24
10 Construction	0.78	0.88	75	81	23	18	23	20
11 Wholesale distribution	0.89	0.79	145	206	27	32	33	38
12 Retail distribution	0.56	0.54	158	132	40	26	51	40
13 Business services	1.06	1.09	125	166	40	98	24	19

Solvency and liquidity ratios

Quick ratio (acid test) is the ratio of current assets less stock to total current liabilities. It measures the extent to which short-term assets are adequate to settle short-term liabilities. The stock figure is excluded on the grounds that stock may take several months to turn into cash.

Total debt/Net worth as a ratio expresses total debt (formal long- and short-term loans) as a percentage of net worth (a measure of shareholders' funds). It shows the extent to which lenders have financed the firm's assets. It is often called the borrowing ratio, a type of gearing ratio. A firm can be dangerously susceptible to a decline in trading volumes and profits if this ratio is at a high value.

Long-term debt/Net worth expresses long-term debt as a percentage of net worth (shareholders' funds). It is a narrower measure of gearing than the total debt–net worth ratio. By comparing the two ratios, it is possible to establish the relative proportions of long-term and short-term debt. Relying too heavily on short-term debt can lead to difficulties. For example, bank overdrafts can be recalled at very short notice.

Interest/Pre-interest profit expresses gross interest payable as a percentage of pre-interest and pre-tax profit. It gives an indication of ability to cover interest payments. The greater the proportion of profits that have to be paid out in interest payments, the riskier the firm's position. A ratio of 100 per cent means that all pre-interest profit is used to pay interest to lenders, leaving nothing to add to shareholder wealth. The inverse of this ratio is known as 'Interest cover'.

Source: Arnold, G.C. and Davis P. (1995) *Profitability Trends in West Midlands Industries*, Lloyds Bowmaker Corporate Finance. Reprinted with permission of Lloyds UDT Limited.

Exhibit 18.5

Goodbye gearing

FT

Investors have long used balance-sheet gearing as the main yardstick of a company's indebtedness. In the past, this was appropriate as the balance sheet offered a reasonable guide to a company's value. But balance sheets are now scarcely relevant as a measure of corporate worth. As the world economy shifts from manufacturing to services, value is increasingly the product of human brains. Companies like Microsoft, Disney and Marks & Spencer owe their success to intellectual property, media creations and brands. Unlike physical property or machines, such products of the mind do not typically appear on balance sheets. Even in manufacturing, inflation and arbitrary depreciation policies make balance sheets a misleading guide to value.

If balance-sheet gearing is no longer useful, what yardsticks should be employed instead? One option is to look at interest cover – either operating profit or operating cash flow divided by interest payments. Such ratios measure how easy it is for companies to service their debts. Different levels of interest cover are appropriate for different types of company; clearly, cyclicals need higher ratios than utilities.

Another option is to divide a company's debt by its market capitalisation. Market capitalisation overcomes the inadequacies of balance-sheet measures of equity. But in other ways this ratio is similar to traditional gearing: a higher figure means shareholders' returns are more leveraged to the enterprise's underlying performance and so more risky. In future, debt/market capitalisation and interest cover will be Lex's preferred yardsticks.

Source: *Financial Times*, 9 October 1995. Reprinted with permission.

THE EFFECT OF GEARING

The introduction of interest-bearing debt 'gears up' the returns to shareholders. Compared with those of the ungeared firm the geared firm's returns to its owners are subject to greater variation than underlying earnings. If profits are high, the geared firm's shareholders will experience a more than proportional boost in their returns compared to the ungeared firm's shareholders. On the other hand, if profits turn out to be low the geared firm's shareholders will find their returns declining to an exaggerated extent.

The effect of gearing can best be explained through an example. Harby plc is shortly to be established. The prospective directors are considering three different capital structures which will all result in £10m of capital being raised.

1 All equity – 10 million shares sold at a nominal value of £1.
2 £3m debt (carrying 10 per cent interest) and £7m equity.
3 £5m debt (carrying 10 per cent interest) and £5m equity.

To simplify their analysis the directors have assigned probabilities to three potential future performance levels (*see* Exhibit 18.6).

We can now examine what will happen to shareholder returns for each of the gearing levels.

Note, in Exhibit 18.7, what happens as gearing increases: the changes in earnings attributable to shareholders is magnified. For example, when earnings before interest rise by 500 per cent from £0.5m to £3.0m the returns on the 30 per cent geared structure rises by 1,200 per cent from 3 per cent to 39 per cent. This magnification effect

Exhibit 18.6 Probabilities of performance levels

Customer response to firm's products	*Income before interest**	*Probability (%)*
Modest success	£0.5m	20
Good response	£3.0m	60
Run-away success	£4.0m	20

* Taxes are to be ignored.

Exhibit 18.7 The effect of gearing

Customer response	*Modest*	*Good*	*Run-away*
Earnings before interest	£0.5m	£3.0m	£4.0m
All-equity structure			
Debt interest at 10%	0.0	0.0	0.0
Earnings available for shareholders	£0.5m	£3.0m	£4.0m
Return on shares	$\frac{£0.5m}{£10m}$ = 5%	$\frac{£3.0m}{£10m}$ = 30%	$\frac{£4.0m}{£10m}$ = 40%
30% gearing (£3m debt, £7m equity)			
Debt interest at 10%	£0.3m	£0.3m	£0.3m
Earnings available for shareholders	£0.2m	£2.7m	£3.7m
Return on shares	$\frac{£0.2m}{£7m}$ = 3%	$\frac{£2.7m}{£7m}$ = 39%	$\frac{£3.7m}{£7m}$ = 53%
50% gearing (£5m debt, £5m equity)			
Debt interest at 10%	£0.5m	£0.5m	£0.5m
Earnings available for shareholders	0.0	£2.5m	£3.5m
Returns on shares	$\frac{£0.0m}{£5m}$ = 0%	$\frac{£2.5m}{£5m}$ = 50%	$\frac{£3.5m}{£5m}$ = 70%

works in both positive and negative directions – if earnings before interest are only £0.5m the all-equity structure gives shareholders some return, but with the 50 per cent geared firm they will receive nothing. Harby's shareholders would be taking a substantial risk that they would have no profits if they opted for a high level of gearing.

The data for the ungeared and the 50 per cent geared capital structure are displayed in Exhibit 18.8. The direction of the effect of gearing depends on the level of earnings before interest. If this is greater than £1m, the return to shareholders is increased by gearing. If it is less than £1m, the return is reduced by gearing. Note that the return on the firm's overall assets at this pivot point is 10 per cent (£1m/£10m). If a return of more than 10 per cent on assets is achieved, shareholders' returns are enhanced by gearing.

Exhibit 18.8 Changes in shareholder returns for ungeared and geared capital structures

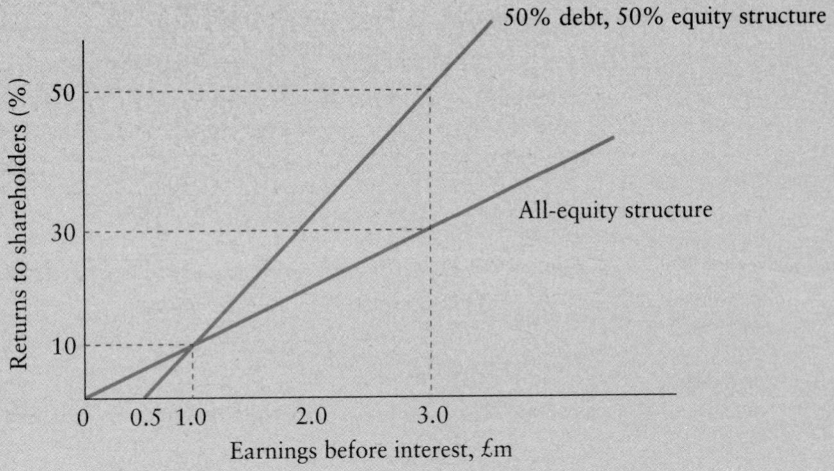

Expected returns and standard deviations for Harby plc

It makes intuitive sense to say that year-to-year variations in income will be greater for a more highly geared firm as it experiences good and bad trading years. We can be more precise for Harby if we calculate the standard deviation of the return to shareholders under the three gearing levels (*see* Exhibit 18.9).

Exhibit 18.9 Expected returns and standard deviations of return to shareholders in Harby plc

All equity

Return, R (%)	*Probability, p_i*	*Return × probability*	
5	0.2	1	
30	0.6	18	
40	0.2	8	
		27	Expected return, $\bar{R}$ = 27%

Return, R (%)	*Expected return, $\bar{R}$*	*Probability*	*$(\bar{R} - R)^2 p_i$*
5	27	0.2	96.8
30	27	0.6	5.4
40	27	0.2	33.8
		Variance σ^2 =	136.0

▶

Exhibit 18.9 continued

30% gearing

Return, R (%)	*Probability, p_i*	*Return × probability*	
3	0.2	0.6	
39	0.6	23.4	
53	0.2	10.6	
		34.6	Expected return, $\bar{R}$ = 34.6%

Return, R (%)	*Expected return, $\bar{R}$*	*Probability*	*$(\bar{R} - R)^2\, p_i$*
3	34.6	0.2	199.71
39	34.6	0.6	11.62
53	34.6	0.2	67.71
			Variance σ^2 = 279.04
			Standard deviation σ = 16.7%

50% gearing

Return, R (%)	*Probability, p_i*	*Return × probability*	
0	0.2	0	
50	0.6	30	
70	0.2	14	
		44	Expected return, $\bar{R}$ = 44%

Return, R (%)	*Expected return, $\bar{R}$*	*Probability*	*$(\bar{R} - R)^2\, p_i$*
0	44	0.2	387.2
50	44	0.6	21.6
70	44	0.2	135.2
			Variance σ^2 = 544.0
			Standard deviation σ = 23.3%

As Exhibit 18.9 indicates, as the gearing levels rise for Harby, the expected return also rises, but this is accompanied by a rising level of risk. Management have to weigh up the relative importance of the 'good' resulting from the increase in expected returns and the 'bad' from the wider dispersion of returns attributable to shareholders.

Business risk and financial risk

Business risk is the variability of the firm's operating income, that is, the income before interest. In the case of Harby this is found by examining the dispersion of returns for the all-equity capital structure. This dispersion is caused purely by business-related factors, such as the characteristics of the industry and the competitive advantage possessed by the firm within that industry. This risk will be influenced by factors such as the variability of sales volumes or prices over the business cycle, the variability of input costs, the degree of market power and the level of growth.

The business risk of a monopoly supplier of electricity, gas or water is likely to be significantly less than that for, say, an entrepreneurial company trying to gain a toehold in the internet optical switch market. The range of possible demand levels and prices is likely to be less for the utilities than for the hi-tech firm. Business risk is determined by general business and economic conditions and is not related to the firm's financial structure.

Financial risk is the additional variability in returns to shareholders that arises because the financial structure contains debt. In Exhibit 18.10 the standard deviation gives the total risk. If a 50 per cent geared structure is selected the returns to shareholders would have a high dispersion, that is, a standard deviation of 23.3 per cent. Of this overall risk roughly half is caused by underlying business risk and half by financial risk. The increasing proportion of debt raises the firm's fixed financial costs. At high gearing levels there is an increased probability of the firm not only failing to make a return to shareholders, but also failing to meet the interest cost obligation, and thus raising the likelihood of insolvency.

Exhibit 18.10 Business and financial risk

Gearing (%)	*Expected return to shareholders (%)*	*Standard deviation (total risk) (%)*	*Business risk (%)*	*Remaining total risk due to financial risk* (%)*
0 (all-equity)	27	11.7	11.7	0
30	34.6	16.7	11.7	5
50	44	23.3	11.7	11.6

*This is a simplified representation of the relationship between total risk, financial risk and business risk. It should be: Variance of total risk = (Business risk standard deviation)^2 + (Financial risk standard deviation)^2.

Exhibit 18.11 implies that firms with low business risk can take on relatively high levels of financial risk without exposing their shareholders to excessive total risk. The increased expected return more than compensates for the higher variability resulting in climbing share prices.

It is appropriate at this point to remember that, until now we have focused primarily on accounting values for debt and equity – book debt, net assets in the balance sheet, etc. In the models which follow the correct bases of analysis are the market values of debt and equity. This is because we are interested in the effect of the capital structure decision on share values in the market-place, not on accounting entries.

Exhibit 18.11

Power of debt

FT

The imminent demerger of the National Grid will be good for regional electricity company (Rec) shareholders not simply because they will receive shares in the group; the flotation will also trigger another round of financial restructuring. Once the remaining independent Recs have a clear picture of the effect of the demerger on their balance sheets, they will have no excuse to postpone gearing themselves up. As utilities with steady cash flows, they can support high levels of indebtedness. Excess capital can be handed back to shareholders.

Yorkshire Electricity started the ball rolling last week with a £180m special dividend. But only one of the companies, Northern Electric, has yet taken the process to its logical conclusion. Northern's pay-out of nearly £5 a share – dating from its scorched earth defence against Trafalgar House's bid – was initially viewed as excessively risky by some investors. But shareholders are rightly recognising that its projected balance-sheet gearing of about 175 per cent is irrelevant. With operating profits more than three times interest plus preference dividend payments, the business is well able to finance its borrowings.

Source: Financial Times, 23 October 1995. Reprinted with permission.

THE VALUE OF THE FIRM AND THE COST OF CAPITAL

Recall from Chapters 16 and 17 that the value of the firm is calculated by estimating its future cash flows and then discounting these at the cost of capital. For the sake of simplification we will assume, in the following theoretical discussion, that the future cash flows are constant and perpetual (at annual intervals to an infinite horizon) and thus the value of the firm is:

$$V = \frac{C_1}{WACC}$$

where:

V = value of the firm;
C_1 = cash flows to be received one year hence;
$WACC$ = the weighted average cost of capital.

The same logic can be applied to cash flows which are increasing at a constant rate, or which vary in an irregular fashion. The crucial point is this: if the cash flows are assumed to be fixed then the value of the firm depends on the rate used to discount those cash flows. If the cost of capital is lowered the value of the firm is raised.

What is meant by the value of the firm, V, is the combination of the market value of equity capital, V_E (total capitalisation of ordinary shares), plus the market value of debt capital, V_D.

$$V = V_E + V_D$$

DOES THE COST OF CAPITAL (WACC) DECREASE WITH HIGHER DEBT LEVELS?

The question of whether the cost of capital decreases with higher debt levels is obviously crucial to the capital structure debate. If the WACC is diminished by increasing the proportion of debt in the financial structure of the firm then company value will rise and shareholders' wealth will increase.

The firm's cost of capital depends on both the return needed to satisfy the ordinary shareholders given their opportunity cost of capital, k_E, and the return needed to satisfy lenders given their opportunity cost of capital k_D. (We will ignore taxes for now.)

$$WACC = k_E\, W_E + k_D\, W_D$$

where:

W_E = proportion of equity finance to total finance;
W_D = proportion of debt finance to total finance.

If some numbers are now put into this equation, conclusions might be possible about the optimal debt level and therefore the value of the firm. If it is assumed that the cost of equity capital is 20 per cent, the cost of debt capital is 10 per cent, and the equity and debt weights are both 50 per cent the overall cost of capital is 15 per cent.

$$WACC = 20\% \times 0.5 + 10\% \times 0.5 = 15\%$$

If it is further assumed that the firm is expected to generate a perpetual annual cash flow of £1m, then the total value of the firm is:

$$V = \frac{C_1}{WACC} = \frac{£1\text{m}}{0.15} = £6.667\text{m}$$

This whole area of finance revolves around what happens next, that is, when the proportion of debt is increased. So, let us assume that the debt ratio is increased to 70 per cent through the substitution of debt for equity. We will consider four possible consequences.

Scenario 1 The cost of equity capital remains at 20 per cent

If shareholders remain content with a 20 per cent return, the WACC decreases:

$$WACC = k_E\, W_E + k_D\, W_D$$

$$WACC = 20\% \times 0.3 + 10\% \times 0.7 = 13\%$$

If the cost of capital decreases, the value of the firm (and shareholder wealth) increases:

$$V = \frac{C_1}{WACC} = \frac{£1\text{m}}{0.13} = £7.69\text{m}$$

Under this scenario the debt proportion could be increased until it was virtually 100 per cent of the capital. The *WACC* would then approach 10 per cent (assuming that the cost of debt capital remains at 10 per cent).

***Scenario 2** The cost of equity capital rises due to the increased financial risk to exactly offset the effect of the lower cost of debt*

In this case the *WACC* and the firm's value remain constant.

$$WACC = k_E \, W_E + k_D \, W_D$$

$$WACC = 26.67\% \times 0.3 + 10\% \times 0.7 = 15\%$$

***Scenario 3** The cost of equity capital rises, but this does not completely offset all the benefits of the lower cost of debt capital*

Let us assume that equity holders demand a return of 22 per cent at a 70 per cent gearing level:

$$WACC = k_E \, W_E + k_D \, W_D$$

$$WACC = 22\% \times 0.3 + 10\% \times 0.7 = 13.6\%$$

In this case the firm, by increasing the proportion of its finance which is in the form of debt, manages to reduce the overall cost of capital and thus to increase the value of the firm and shareholder wealth.

$$V = \frac{C_1}{WACC} = \frac{£1\text{m}}{0.136} = £7.35\text{m}$$

***Scenario 4** The cost of equity rises to more than offset the effect of the lower cost of debt*

Here the equity holders are demanding much higher returns as compensation for the additional volatility and risk of liquidation. Let us assume that shareholders require a return of 40 per cent.

$$WACC = k_E \, W_E + k_D \, W_D$$

$$WACC = 40\% \times 0.3 + 10\% \times 0.7 = 19\%$$

$$V = \frac{C_1}{WACC} = \frac{£1\text{m}}{0.19} = £5.26\text{m}$$

The first of the four scenarios presented above is pretty unrealistic. If the proportion of debt that a firm has to service is increased, the riskiness of the shares will presumably rise and therefore the shareholders will demand a higher return. Thus, we are left with the three other scenarios. It is around these three possibilities that the capital structure debate rumbles.

MODIGLIANI AND MILLER'S ARGUMENT IN A WORLD WITH NO TAXES

The capital structure decision was first tackled in a rigorous theoretical analysis by the financial economists Modigliani and Miller in 1958. MM created a simplified model of the world by making some assumptions. Given these assumptions they concluded that the value of a firm remains constant regardless of the debt level. As the proportion of debt is increased, the cost of equity will rise just enough to leave the *WACC* constant. If the *WACC* is constant then the only factor which can influence the value of the firm is its cash flow generated from operations. Capital structure is irrelevant. Thus, according to MM, firms can only increase the wealth of shareholders by making good investment decisions. This brings us to MM's first proposition.

Proposition 1

The total market value of any company is independent of its capital structure

The total market value of the firm is the net present value of the income stream. For a firm with a constant perpetual income stream:

$$V = \frac{C_1}{WACC}$$

WACC is constant because the cost of equity capital rises to exactly offset the effect of cheaper debt and therefore shareholder wealth is neither enhanced nor destroyed by changing the gearing level.

The assumptions

Before going any further, some of the assumptions upon which this conclusion is reached need to be mentioned.

1 There is no taxation.
2 There are perfect capital markets, with perfect information available to all economic agents and no transaction costs.
3 There are no costs of financial distress and liquidation (if a firm is liquidated, shareholders will receive the same as the market value of their shares prior to liquidation).
4 Firms can be classified into distinct risk classes.
5 Individuals can borrow as cheaply as corporations.

Clearly, there are problems relating some of these assumptions to the world in which we live. For now, it is necessary to suspend disbelief so that the consequences of the MM model can be demonstrated. Many of the assumptions will be modified later in the chapter.

An example to illustrate the MM no-tax capital structure argument

In the following example it is assumed that the WACC remains constant at 15 per cent regardless of the debt–equity ratio.

A company is shortly to be formed, called Pivot plc. It needs £1m capital to buy machines, plant and buildings. The business generated by the investment has a given systematic risk and the required return on that level of systematic risk for an all-equity firm is 15 per cent.

The expected annual cash flow is a constant £150,000 in perpetuity. This cash flow will be paid out each year to the suppliers of capital. The prospective directors are considering three different finance structures.

- **Structure 1** All-equity (1,000,000 shares selling at £1 each).
- **Structure 2** £500,000 of debt capital giving a return of 10 per cent per annum. Plus £500,000 of equity capital (500,000 shares at £1 each).
- **Structure 3** £700,000 of debt capital giving a return of 10 per cent per annum. Plus £300,000 of equity capital (300,000 shares at £1 each).

Exhibit 18.12 shows that the returns to equity holders, in this MM world with no tax, rises as gearing increases so as to leave the *WACC* and the total value of the company constant. Investors purchasing a share receive higher returns per share for a more highly geared firm but the discount rate also rises because of the greater risk, to leave the value of each share at £1.

Exhibit 18.12 Pivot plc capital structure and returns to shareholders

	Structure 1 £	*Structure 2* £	*Structure 3* £
Annual cash flows	150,000	150,000	150,000
less interest payments	0	50,000	70,000
Dividend payments	150,000	100,000	80,000
Return on debt, k_D	0	50,000/500,000 = 10%	70,000/700,000 = 10%
Return on equity, k_E	150,000/1m = 15%	100,000/500,000 = 20%	80,000/300,000 = 26.7%
Price of each share, $\frac{d_1}{k_E}$	$\frac{15p}{0.15}$ = 100p	$\frac{20p}{0.20}$ = 100p	$\frac{26.7p}{0.267}$ = 100p
WACC ($k_E W_E + k_D W_D$)	15 × 1.0 + 0 = 15%	20 × 0.5 + 10 × 0.5 = 15%	26.7 × 0.3 + 10 × 0.7 = 15%
Total market value of debt, V_D	0	500,000	700,000
Total market value of equity, V_E	$\frac{150,000}{0.15}$ = 1m	$\frac{100,000}{0.2}$ = 0.5m	$\frac{80,000}{0.267}$ = 0.3m
Total value of the firm, $V = V_D + V_E$	£1,000,000	£1,000,000	£1,000,000

The relationship given in the tabulation in Exhibit 18.12 can be plotted as a graph (*see* Exhibit 18.13). Under the MM model the cost of debt remains constant at 10 per cent, and the cost of equity capital rises just enough to leave the overall cost of capital constant.

Exhibit 18.13 The cost of debt, equity and WACC under the MM no-tax model

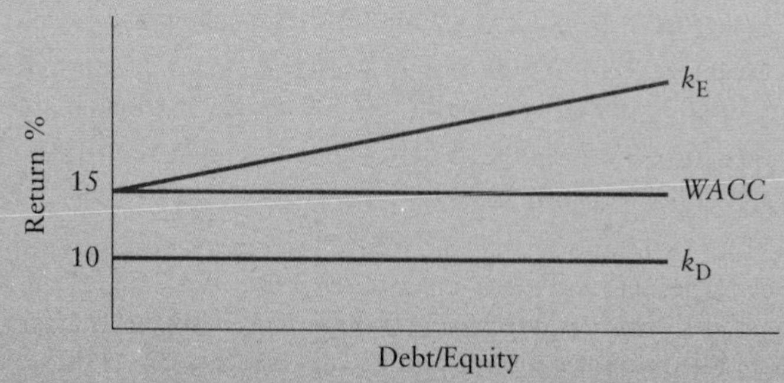

If the WACC is constant and cash flows do not change, then the total value of the firm is constant:

$$V = V_E + V_D = £1\text{m}$$

$$V = \frac{C_1}{WACC} = \frac{£150{,}000}{0.15} = £1\text{m}$$

This is presented in Exhibit 18.14.

Exhibit 18.14 Value of the firm under the MM no-tax model

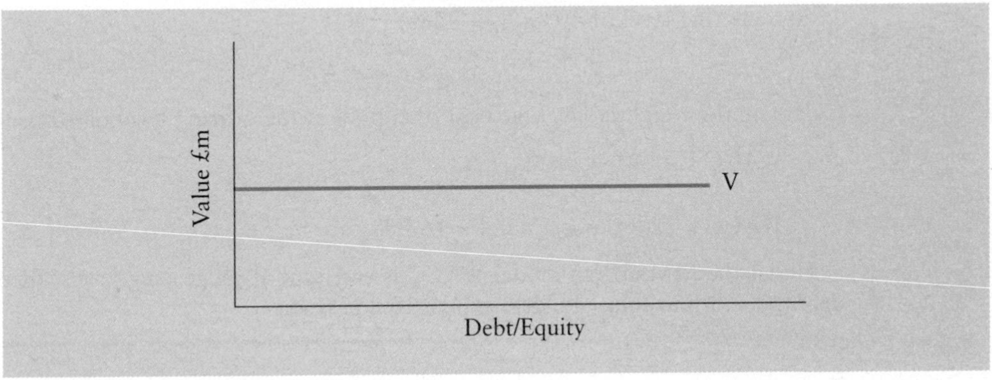

Pivot also illustrates the second and third propositions put forward by MM.

Proposition 2

The expected rate of return on equity increases proportionately with the gearing ratio

As shareholders see the riskiness of their investment increase because the firm is taking on increasing debt levels they demand a higher level of return. The geared firm pays a risk premium for financial risk. The increase in the cost of equity exactly offsets the benefit to the *WACC* of 'cheaper' debt. (Modigliani and Miller actually expressed Proposition 2 in a more technical way requiring a knowledge of the full theoretical proof to understand that 'the expected yield of a share of stock is equal to the appropriate capitalisation rate, ρ_k, for a pure equity stream in the class, plus a premium related to financial risk equal to the debt-to-equity ratio times the spread between ρ_k and r' (MM (1958), p. 271). ρ_k can be taken as being equal to our k_E, and r equals k_D.)

Proposition 3

The cut-off rate of return for new projects is equal to the weighted average cost of capital – which is constant regardless of gearing

MM expressed Proposition 3 differently: 'the cut-off point for investment in the firm will in all cases be ρ_k and will be completely unaffected by the type of security used to finance the investment. Equivalently, we may say, that regardless of the financing used, the marginal cost of capital to a firm is equal to the average cost of capital, which is in turn equal to the capitalisation rate for an unlevered stream in the class to which the firm belongs' (MM (1958), p. 288).

Worked example 18.1 Cost of equity capital for an all-equity financed firm in a world with no taxes

Assume that the world is as described by MM with no taxes to answer the following.

What would the cost of equity capital be if the firm described below is all-equity financed?

Perpetual future cash flow of £2.5m

$$\frac{\text{Market value of debt}}{\text{Market value of debt + Market value of equity}} = 0.40$$

k_D = 9% regardless of gearing ratio.
At a gearing level of 40%, k_E = 22%.

Answer

Calculate the weighted average cost of capital at the gearing level of 40 per cent.

$$WACC = k_E\ W_E + k_D\ W_D$$

$$WACC = 22 \times 0.6 + 9 \times 0.4 = 16.8\%$$

Under the MM no-tax model WACC is constant at all gearing levels; therefore, at zero debt the return to equity holders will be 16.8 per cent.

THE CAPITAL STRUCTURE DECISION IN A WORLD WITH TAX

The real world is somewhat different from that created for the purposes of MM's original 1958 model. One of the most significant differences is that individuals and companies *do* have to pay taxes. MM corrected for this assumption in their 1963 version of the model – this changes the analysis dramatically.

Most tax regimes permit companies to offset the interest paid on debt against taxable profit. The effect of this is a tax saving which reduces the effective cost of debt capital.

In the previous no-tax analysis the advantage of gearing-up (a lower cost of debt capital) was exactly matched by the disadvantage (the increased risk for equity holders and therefore an increased k_E). The introduction of taxation brings an additional advantage to using debt capital: it reduces the tax bill. Now value rises as debt is substituted for equity in the capital structure because of the tax benefits (or tax shield). The WACC declines for each unit increase in debt so long as the firm has taxable profits. This argument can be taken to its logical extreme, such that WACC is at its lowest and corporate value at its highest when the capital of the company is almost entirely made up of debt.

In Exhibit 18.15 the cost of equity rises but the extent of the rise is insufficient to exactly offset the cheaper debt. Thus the overall cost of capital falls throughout the range of gearing. In a 30 per cent corporate tax environment a profitable firm's cost of debt falls from a pre-tax 10 per cent to only 7 per cent after the tax benefit:

$$10\%\ (1 - T) = 10\%\ (1 - 0.30) = 7\%$$

For a perpetual income firm, the value is $V = C_1/WACC$. As $WACC$ falls, the value of the company rises, benefiting ordinary shareholders.

The conclusion from this stage of the analysis, after adjusting for one real-world factor, is that companies should be as highly geared as possible.

Exhibit 18.15 MM with tax

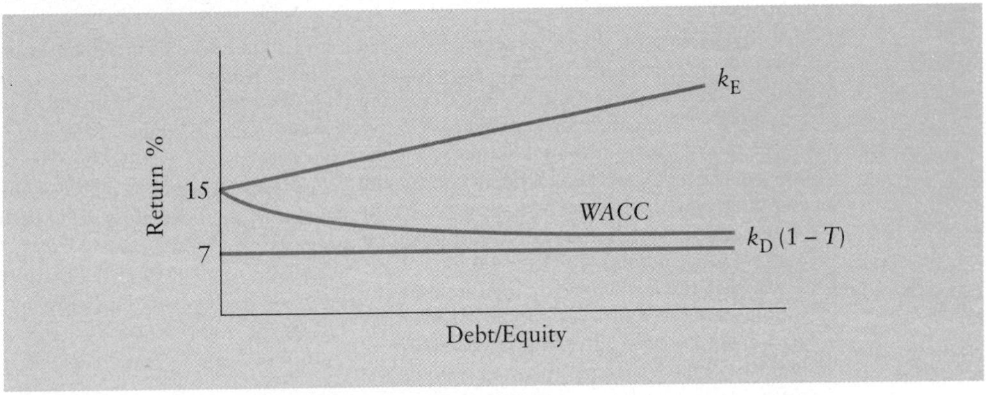

Exhibit 18.16 Value of the firm, MM with tax

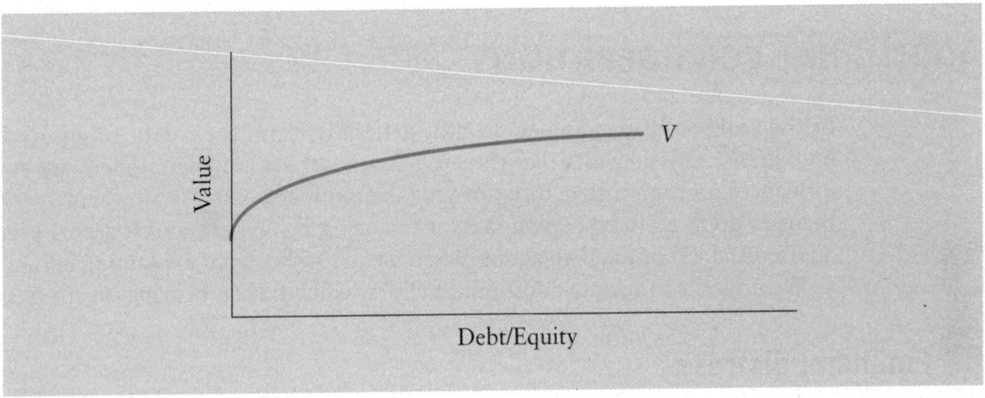

The following newspaper article (Exhibit 18.17) shows a company that has structured itself so that it can take on an extreme capital structure – Glas Cymru is financed entirely by debt. Note that this is possible only because the risk of financial distress has been substantially reduced. The bond offerings were eagerly taken up by lenders.

Exhibit 18.17

Glas Cymru launches bond campaign

FT

Water marketing drive in plan to raise £2bn for purchase of Dwr Cymru

By Aline van Duyn and Andrew Taylor

Glas Cymru, the self-styled "Welsh people's company" which has agreed to buy the principality's water supplier, will today launch a £2bn bond marketing campaign to turn the company into the UK's first fully debt-financed water utility . . .

The bond issues, if successful, will reduce Glas Cymru's cost of capital to between 4 and 4.5 per cent, compared with a 6.5 per cent industry threshold set by the regulator.

Glas Cymru, a non-profit making company led by Lord Burns, former permanent secretary at the Treasury, will buy Dwr Cymru (Welsh Water) in return for taking on debts of £1.8bn. It will be fully debt financed and switch from shareholder ownership . . .

Exhibit 18.17 continued

Bond investors in the water sector have seen prices on their holdings fall after rating downgrades following the regulatory price cuts and concern over diversification strategies.

The Glas Cymru deal aims to address these concerns by giving bondholders full control and ensuring that they are exposed purely to the water sector, which is a monopoly business with stable cash flows.

Most of the bonds will be denominated in sterling, although euro and dollar tranches are also being considered. About £1bn worth of bonds will have a Triple A rating, the highest rating category, due to a guarantee from an insurance company.

Just under £700m worth will be rated A minus. About £250m is rated Triple B, with £100m worth of unrated bonds also sold.

The Glas Cymru structure is possible because the assets are bought for less than their regulatory asset value, giving a £150m cushion. Between now and the next regulatory price review in 2004–2005, Glas Cymru can lock in a lower cost of capital and accumulate the excess, boosting its reserves to £350. It expects to tap the markets for £100m–£150m a year.

Source: Aline van Duyn and Andrew Taylor, *Financial Times*, 9 April 2001, p. 26. Reprinted with permission.

ADDITIONAL CONSIDERATIONS

In the real world companies do not, generally, raise their debt-to-equity ratios to very high levels. This suggests that the models are not yet complete. There are some important influences on capital structure not yet taken into account. As Stewart Myers[8] wrote, 'Our theories don't seem to explain actual financing behaviour, and it seems presumptuous to advise firms on optimal structure when we are so far from explaining actual decisions'.

We now turn to some additional factors which have a bearing on the gearing level.

Financial distress

A major disadvantage for a firm taking on higher levels of debt is that it increases the risk of financial distress, and ultimately liquidation. This may have a detrimental effect on both the equity and the debt holders.

Financial distress: where obligations to creditors are not met or are met with difficulty.

The risk of incurring the costs of financial distress has a negative effect on a firm's value which offsets the value of tax relief of increasing debt levels. These costs become considerable with very high gearing. Even if a firm manages to avoid liquidation its relationships with suppliers, customers, employees and creditors may be seriously damaged. Suppliers providing goods and services on credit are likely to reduce the generosity of their terms, or even stop supplying altogether, if they believe that there is an increased chance of the firm not being in existence in a few months' time. The situation may be similar with customers. Many customers expect to develop close relationships with their suppliers, and plan their own production on the assumption of a continuance of that relationship, for example motor manufacturers. If there is any doubt about the longevity of a firm it will not be able to secure high-quality contracts. In the consumer markets customers often need assurance that firms are sufficiently stable to deliver on promises, for example package holiday companies taking bookings six months in advance. Employees may become demotivated in a struggling firm as they sense increased job insecurity and few prospects for advancement. The best staff will start to move to posts in safer companies. Bankers and other lenders will tend to look upon a request for further finance from a financially distressed company with a prejudiced eye – taking a safety-first approach – and this can continue for many years after the crisis has passed. Management find that much of their time is spent 'fire fighting' – dealing with day-to-day liquidity problems – and focusing on short-term cash flow rather than long-term shareholder wealth.

The indirect costs associated with financial distress can be much more significant than the more obvious direct costs such as paying for lawyers and accountants and for refinancing programmes. Some of these indirect and direct costs are shown in Exhibit 18.18.

The article in Exhibit 18.19 shows that Daewoo suffered severe distruption because some suppliers, nervous about the company's ability to pay, refused to deliver.

As the risk of financial distress rises with the gearing ratio shareholders (and lenders) demand an increasing return in compensation. The important issue is at what point does the probability of financial distress so increase the cost of equity and debt that it outweighs the benefit of the tax relief on debt? Exhibit 18.20 shows that there is an optimal level of gearing. At low levels of debt the major influence on the overall cost of capital is

Exhibit 18.18 Costs of financial distress

Indirect examples

- Uncertainties in customers' minds about dealing with this firm – lost sales, lost profits, lost goodwill.
- Uncertainties in suppliers' minds about dealing with this firm – lost inputs, more expensive trading terms.
- If assets have to be sold quickly the price may be very low.
- Delays, legal impositions, and the tangles of financial reorganisation may place restrictions on management action, interfering with the efficient running of the business.
- Management may give excessive emphasis to short-term liquidity, e.g. cut R&D and training, reduce trade credit and stock levels.
- Temptation to sell healthy businesses as this will raise the most cash.
- Loss of staff morale, tendency to examine possible alternative employment.
- To conserve cash, lower credit terms are offered to customers, which impacts on the marketing effort.

Direct examples

- Lawyers' fees.
- Accountants' fees.
- Court fees.
- Management time.

the cheaper after-tax cost of debt. As gearing rises investors become more concerned about the risk of financial distress and therefore the required rates of return rise. The fear of loss factor becomes of overriding importance at high gearing levels.

Exhibit 18.19

Daewoo's main plant halts output as supplies dry up FT

By John Burton in Seoul

Daewoo Motor yesterday suspended production at its biggest and oldest assembly plant in South Korea as suppliers refused to deliver components following the appointment of court receivers.

The Pupyong plant, outside Seoul, has an annual capacity of 500,000 cars – about half the carmaker's production in Korea – but has been operating at 50 per cent of capacity because of falling sales.

Daewoo's two other main domestic plants, at Changwon and Kunsan, were operating normally but they will also have to stop production once their stock of parts is exhausted, since suppliers are worried about not being paid. . . .

Daewoo said it hoped delivery of parts would resume once suppliers received cash payments. Creditors and the government have proposed giving payment guarantees to subcontractors. . . .

Analysts say Pupyong has little chance of survival if creditors break up Daewoo Motor and sell assets piecemeal to foreign investors. Closure of Pupyong would affect 185 main subcontractors, which employ 100,000 workers, and thousands of smaller suppliers.

Source: John Burton, *Financial Times*, 10 November 2000, p. 29. Reprinted with permission.

Exhibit 18.20 The cost of capital and the value of the firm with taxes and financial distress, as gearing increases

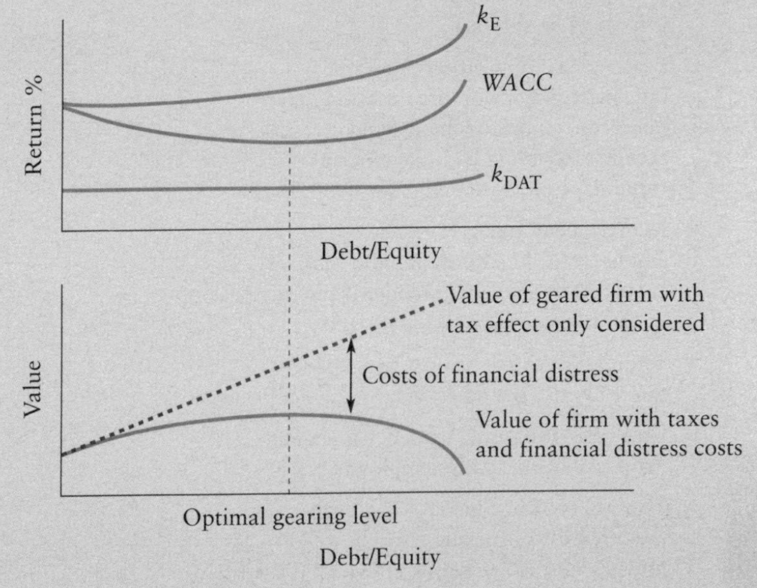

Some factors influencing the risk of financial distress costs

The susceptibility to financial distress varies from company to company. Here are some influences:

1 *The sensitivity of the company's revenues to the general level of economic activity* If a company is highly responsive to the ups and downs in the economy, shareholders and lenders may perceive a greater risk of liquidation and/or distress and demand a higher return in compensation for gearing compared with that demanded for a firm which is less sensitive to economic events.

2 *The proportion of fixed to variable costs* A firm which is highly operationally geared, and which also takes on high borrowing, may find that equity and debt holders demand a high return for the increased risk.

3 *The liquidity and marketability of the firm's assets* Some firms invest in a type of asset which can be easily sold at a reasonably high and certain value should they go into liquidation. This is of benefit to the financial security holders and so they may not demand such a high risk premium. A hotel chain, for example, should it suffer a decline in profitability, can usually sell hotels in a reasonably active property market. On the other hand investors in an advertising agency, with few saleable assets, would be less sanguine about rises in gearing.

4 *The cash-generative ability of the business* Some firms produce a high regular flow of cash and so can reasonably accept a higher gearing level than a firm with lumpy and delayed cash inflows.

Exhibit 18.21 illustrates that the optimal gearing level for firms shifts along the spectrum depending on key characteristics of the underlying business.

Exhibit 18.21 The characteristics of the underlying business influences the risk of liquidation/distress, and therefore WACC, and the optimal gearing level

Characteristic	*Food retailer*	*Steel producer*
Sensitivity to economic activity	Relatively insensitive to economic fluctuations	Dependent on general economic prosperity
Operational gearing	Most costs are variable	Most costs are fixed
Asset liquidity	Shops, stock, etc., easily sold	Assets have few/no alternative uses. Thin secondhand market
Cash-generative ability	High or stable cash flow	Irregular cash flow
Likely acceptable gearing ratio	**HIGH**	**LOW**

Agency costs

Another restraining influence on the decision to take on high debt is the agency cost of doing so. Agency costs arise out of what is known as the 'principal–agent' problem. In most large firms the finance providers (principals) are not able to actively manage the firm. They employ 'agents' (managers) and it is possible for these agents to act in ways which are not always in the best interests of the equity or debt holders.

Agency costs are the direct and indirect costs of ensuring that agents act in the best interest of principals.

We are concerned in this chapter with the issue of debt so we will assume there is no potential conflict of interest between shareholders and the management. If management are acting for the maximisation of shareholder wealth debt holders may have reason to fear agency problems, because there may be actions which potentially benefit the owners at the expense of lenders. It is possible for lenders to be fooled or misled by managers. For example, management might raise money from bond holders saying that this is low-risk lending (and therefore paying a low interest rate) because the firm has low gearing and the funds will be used for a low-risk project. In the event the managers invest in high-risk ventures, and the firm becomes more highly geared by borrowing more. As a result the original lenders do not receive a return sufficient for the level of risk and the firm has the benefit of low-interest financing.

Alternatively, consider a firm already in financial distress. From the shareholders' point of view there is little to lose from taking an enormous gamble by accepting very high-risk projects. If the gamble pays off the shareholders will win but the debt holders will gain no more than the obligated fixed interest. If it fails, the shareholders are no worse off but the lenders experience default on their securities.

The problem boils down to one of *information asymmetry* – that is, the managers are in possession of knowledge unavailable to the debt providers. One of the solutions is to spend money on monitoring. The lenders will require a premium on the debt interest to compensate for this additional cost. Also restrictions (covenants) are usually built into a lending agreement. For example, there may be limits on the level of dividends so that shareholders do not strip the company of cash. There may be limits placed on the overall level of indebtedness, with precise capital and income-gearing ratios. Managers may be restricted in the disposal of major assets or constrained in the type of activity they may engage in.

Extensive covenants imposed by lenders can be costly for shareholders because they reduce the firm's operating freedom and investment flexibility. Projects with a high NPV may be forgone because of the cautiousness of lenders. The opportunity costs can be especially frustrating for firms with high growth potential.

Thus agency costs include monitoring costs passed on as higher interest rates and the loss of value caused by the inhibition of managerial freedom to act. These increase with gearing, raising the implicit cost of debt and lowering the firm's value.[9]

There may also be a psychological element related to agency costs; managers generally do not like restrictions placed on their freedom of action. They try to limit constraints by not raising a large proportion of capital from lenders. This may help to explain why, in practice, we find companies generally have modest gearing levels.

Borrowing capacity

Borrowing capacity has a close connection with agency costs. Lenders prefer secured lending, and this often sets an upper limit on gearing. They like to have the assurance that if the worst happened and the firm was unable to meet its interest obligations they could seize assets to sell off in order that loans could be repaid. Thus, high levels of gearing are unusual because companies run out of suitable assets to offer as security against loans. So, the gearing level may not be determined by a theoretical, informed and considered management decision, but by the limits to total borrowing imposed by lenders.

Firms with assets which have an active secondhand market, and which do not tend to depreciate, such as property, are likely to have a higher borrowing capacity than firms that invest in assets with few alternative uses.

Managerial preferences

Liquidation affects not only shareholders, but managers and other employees. Indeed, the impact on these people can be far greater than the impact on well-diversified investors. It may be argued that managers have a natural tendency to be cautious about borrowing.

Pecking order

There is a 'pecking order' for financing. Firms prefer to finance with internally generated funds. If a firm has potentially profitable investments it will first of all try to finance the investments by using the store of previous years' profits, that is, retained earnings. If still more funds are needed, firms will go to the capital markets. However, the debt market is called on first, and only as a last resort will companies raise equity finance. The pecking order of financing is in sharp contrast to the MM plus financial distress analysis, in which an optimal capital structure is targeted. Myers (1984, p. 581) puts it this way: 'In this story, there is no well-defined target debt–equity mix, because there are two kinds of equity, internal and external, one at the top of the pecking order and one at the bottom.'

One reason for placing new issues of equity at the bottom is supposedly that the stock markets perceive an equity issue as a sign of problems – an act of desperation. Myers and Majluf (1984) provide a theoretical explanation of why an equity issue might be bad news – managers will only issue shares when they believe the firm's shares are overpriced. Bennett Stewart (1990, p. 391) puts it differently: 'Raising equity conveys doubt. Investors suspect that management is attempting to shore up the firm's financial resources for rough times ahead by selling over-valued shares.' The pecking order idea helps to explain why the most profitable companies often borrow very little. It is not that they have a low target debt ratio, but because they do not need outside finance. If they are highly profitable they will use these profits for growth opportunities and so end up with very little debt and no need to issue shares.

Less profitable firms issue debt because they do not have internal funds sufficient for their capital investment programme and because debt is first in the pecking order of externally raised finance.

There is an argument that firms do not try to reach the 'correct' capital structure as dictated by theory, because managers are following a line of least resistance. Internal funds are the first choice because using retained earnings does not involve contact with outside investors. This avoids the discipline involved in trying to extract investors' money. For example, the communication process required to raise equity finance is usually time consuming and onerous, with a formal prospectus, etc., and investors will scrutinise the detailed justifications advanced for the need to raise additional finance. It seems reasonable to suppose that managers will feel more comfortable using funds they already have in their hands. However, if they do have to obtain external financing then debt is next in the line of least resistance. This is because the degree of questioning and publicity associated with a bank loan or bond issue is usually significantly less than that associated with a share issue.

Another reason for a pecking order is that ordinary shares are more expensive to issue than debt capital, which in turn is more expensive than simply applying previously generated profits. The costs of new issues and rights issues of shares can be very expensive, whereas retained earnings are available without transaction costs.

Exhibit 18.22 shows that rights issues (particularly 'rescue' rights issues designed to save the company from the danger of liquidation) can be accompanied by pain for the management. The resignation of Sir Iain Vallance as chairman of BT was a price the board of BT agreed to pay to induce institutional investor acceptance of an equity capital raising exercise.

Exhibit 18.22

Institutions expect rights issue

FT

By Simon Targett, Thorold Barker and Charles Batchelor

British Telecommunications' institutional investors are expecting Sir Iain Vallance's downfall to trigger the biggest rights issue in UK corporate history. . . .

Investors, who only recently were warning that a rights issue would be poorly received, are expecting an issue of about £5bn. But several want proof that the strategy to break-up the company remains intact. . . .

History suggests that rescue rights issues have a mixed record. They have often coincided with reshuffles of both management and advisers – a precedent that would tally with Sir Iain's departure yesterday. Some, such as British Aerospace, now known as BAE Systems, have failed spectacularly to convince shareholders to back the issue. In 1991, the defence group's £432m rights issue was taken up by just 4.9 per cent of shareholders.

Source: Simon Targett, Thorold Barker and Charles Batchelor, *Financial Times*, 27 April 2001, p. 32. Reprinted with permission.

Financial slack

Operating and strategic decisions are generally the prime determinants of company value, not the financing decision. Being able to respond to opportunities as they fleetingly appear in business is important. If a firm is already highly geared it may find it difficult to gain access to more funds quickly as the need arises. Financial slack means having cash (or near-cash) and/or spare debt capacity. This slack can be extremely valuable and firms may restrict debt levels below that of the 'optimal' gearing level in order that the risk of missing profitable investments is reduced.

Financial slack is also valuable for meeting unforeseen circumstances. Managers may wish to be cautious and have a reserve of cash or spare borrowing capacity to cope with a 'rainy day'.

Signalling

Managers and other employees often have a very powerful incentive to ensure the continuance of the business. They are usually the people who suffer most should it become insolvent. Because of this, it is argued, managers will generally increase the gearing level only if they are confident about the future. Shareholders are interested in obtaining information about the company's prospects, and changes in financing can become a signal representing management's assessment of future returns. Ross (1977) suggests that an increase in gearing should lead to a rise in share price as managers are signalling their increased optimism. Managers, therefore, need to consider the signal transmitted to the market concerning future income whenever it announces major gearing changes.

Control

The source of finance chosen may be determined by the effect on the control of the organisation. For example, if a shareholder with 50 per cent of a company's shares is unable to pay for more shares in a rights issue, he or she may be reluctant to allow the company to raise funds in this way, especially if shares are sold to a rival. This limits the range of sources of finance and may lead to a rise in debt levels. If we broaden the definition of control beyond shareholder voting rights, the article reproduced in Exhibit 18.23 provides yet another incentive for keeping debt levels low.

Exhibit 18.23 An aversion to dependency on men's institutions

Matriarch in a waxed jacket

FT

Margaret Barbour enjoys undeserved obscurity. As the highest-earning business woman in Britain, she shuns publicity, believing renown based on her wealth would be misleading and dangerous.

In her eyes, her multi-million income is no more than a number on a balance sheet. Most of it is locked up in the assets of Barbour, the waxed jacket manufacturer.

When she took charge of the business, in 1968, Barbour was no more than a tiny mail-order company, set up at the end of the last century to make oilskins for lighthouse men, and since developed as a manufacturer of motor cycle gear.

Today the company has nine factories, 800 employees and turnover of about £75m, compared with £500,000 in 1968.

She characterises her approach as the woman's way of doing business. 'The Barbour family has never lived in any great style,' she says, and the Barbour women have never required huge dividends. That has left the company with plenty of cash. It did once have some debt, after a sharp rise in demand in the early 1980s triggered a rapid expansion into more factories. But the loans are long since repaid.

An aversion to dependency on men's institutions is a recurring theme. She describes the textile and clothing industry associations as 'too male-dominated'. Barbour belongs to none of them.

Source: Jenny Luesby, *Financial Times*, 25 June 1997, p. 10. Reprinted with permission.

Industry group gearing

Suppose you are a financial manager trying to decide on an appropriate gearing ratio and have absorbed all the above theories, ideas and models. You might have concluded that there is no precise formula which can be employed to establish the *best* debt–equity ratio for firms in all circumstances. It depends on so many specific, and often difficult to measure, factors. One must consider the tax position of the firm, the likelihood of financial distress, the type of business the firm is in, the saleability of its assets, the level of business risk and the 'psychology' of the market. (For example, are rights issues perceived as bad signals, and debt issues a sign of confidence, or not?)

Given all these difficulties about establishing the theoretically 'correct' gearing level that will maximise shareholder wealth, managers may be tempted to take the safest route and to simply follow the crowd, to look at what other similar firms are doing, to find out what the financial markets seem to regard as a reasonable level of gearing, and to follow suit.

SOME FURTHER THOUGHTS ON DEBT FINANCE

There are some intriguing ideas advanced to promote the greater use of debt in firms' capital structure. Three of them will be considered here.

Motivation

High debt will motivate managers to perform better and in the interests of shareholders. Consider this thought: if an entrepreneur (an owner-manager) wishes to raise finance for expansion purposes, debt finance is regarded as the better choice from the perspective of entrepreneurs and society. The logic works like this: if new shares are sold to outside investors, this will dilute the entrepreneur's control and thus the level of interest of the entrepreneur in the success of the business. The firm will be run less efficiently because less effort is provided by the key person.

Or consider this argument: Bennett Stewart argues that in firms without a dominant shareholder and with a diffuse shareholder base, a recapitalisation which substitutes debt for equity can result in the concentration of the shares in the hands of a smaller, more proactive group. These shareholders have a greater incentive to monitor the firm. (If managers are made part of this shareholder owning group there is likely to be a greater alignment of shareholder and managers' interests.) Large quoted firms often have tens of thousands of shareholders, any one of whom has little incentive to go to the expense of opposing managerial action detrimental to shareholders' interests – the costs of rallying and co-ordinating investors often outweigh the benefits to the individuals involved. However, if the shareholder base was shrunk through the substitution of debt for equity, the remaining shareholders would have greater incentive to act against mismanagement. An extreme form of this switch to concentration is when a management team purchases a company through a leveraged buy-out or buy-in. Here a dispersed, divided and effectively powerless group of shareholders is replaced with a focused and knowledgeable small team, capable of rapid action and highly motivated to ensure the firm's success.

Reinvestment risk

High debt forces the firm to make regular payments to debt holders, thereby denying 'spare' cash to the managers. In this way the firm avoids placing a temptation in the manager's path which might lead to investment in negative NPV projects and to making destructive acquisitions. Deliberately keeping managers short of cash avoids the problem that shareholders' funds may be applied to projects with little thought to returns. If funds are needed, instead of drawing on a large pot held within the firm, managers have to ask debt and equity finance providers. This will help to ensure that their plans are subject to the scrutiny and discipline of the market.

The problem of managers over-supplied with money, given the limited profitable investment opportunities open to them, seems to be widespread, but specific examples are only clearly seen with hindsight. For example, shortly after the Trustee Savings Bank (TSB) was privatised in the 1980s leaving an enormous pile of cash burning a hole in the directors' pockets, it was decided to purchase Hill Samuel, the merchant bank, at a price that many analysts considered excessive. This marriage in haste was repented at leisure, and much money was lost. Now TSB is part of Lloyds TSB.

The danger of poor investment decisions is at its worst in firms that are highly profitable but which have few growth opportunities. The annual surplus cash flow is often squandered on increasingly marginal projects within existing SBUs or wasted in a diversification effort looking to buy growth opportunities: unfortunately these often cost more than they are worth (*see* the evidence on merger failure in Chapter 20). It is far better, say Stewart (1990), Hart (1995), Jensen (1986) and others, that managers are forced to justify the use of funds by having to ask for it at regular intervals. This process can be assisted by having high debt levels which absorb surplus cash through interest and principal payments and deposit it out of the reach of empire-building, perk-promoting, lazy managers.

These are some of the arguments put forward, particularly in America in the era of massive leveraged buy-outs (LBOs), junk bonds and share repurchase programmes (in the 1980s and 1990s), in support of high debt. They seem to make some sense but the downside of excessive debt must be balanced against these forcefully advanced ideas. Turning back to Exhibit 18.18, which shows the costs of financial distress, can help to give some perspective. In addition, many firms have found themselves crippled and at a competitive disadvantage because of the burden of high debt. These include the Campeau Group in America, following its acquisition of the Federated and Allied department stores and a number of UK retailers (for example Next) in the early 1990s following the expansion binge in the late 1980s.

Operating and strategic efficiency

'Equity is soft; debt is hard. Equity is forgiving; debt is insistent. Equity is a pillow; debt is a dagger.' This statement by Bennett Stewart (1990, p. 580) emphasises that operating and strategic problems and inefficiencies are less likely to be attended to and corrected with a capital base which is primarily equity. However, the managers of a highly geared company are more likely to be attuned to the threat posed by falling efficiency and profitability. The failing is the same under both a high equity and a high debt structure: it just seems more of a crisis when there is a large interest bill each month. The geared firm, it is argued, simply cannot afford to have any value-destructive activities (SBUs or product lines). Managers are spurred on by the pressing need to make regular payments, to reform, dispose or close – and quickly.

Exhibit 18.24 shows that the level of debt relative to net assets and earnings can vary tremendously – it would appear to be related to the economic cycle. Times of optimism encourage more borrowing, as in 1997–9 (the post-boom recession leaving companies with high debt levels to pay off, as in 1990–3).

Exhibit 18.24

Mid-caps have 'sharply raised gearing'

FT

By Charles Batchelor

Mid-sized quoted companies have sharply increased their borrowing levels over the past three years, a study by Close Brothers Corporate Finance shows.

The average level of net debt to net assets among 120 established "old economy" companies including Amec, the construction group, sugar company Tate & Lyle, and ABP, the ports operator, more than doubled from 25 per cent in 1997 to 52 per cent in 1999.

This was partly the result of a decline in interest rates but also reflected a more relaxed view of what was an acceptable level of gearing.

An influx of US private equity providers that were prepared to take on high levels of debt to finance acquisitions also played a role in changing the financial culture of UK companies, Close said.

However, gearing levels among quoted companies remain modest by private equity standards and the standards of US quoted companies, it noted.

The rise since 1997 is particularly marked, but after a dip in early and mid-1990s, borrowing is also at a higher level than in 1990.

This might be taken as an indication that gearing is dangerously high, the study said. But in contrast with the early 1990s, when the economy was in recession and interest rates peaked at 15 per cent, the

▶

Exhibit 18.24 continued

UK currently has stable economic growth and low interest rates.

Gearing levels are expected to rise further as result of share buy-backs, with listed companies set to spend a record £8.8bn buying their own shares in the first half of this year alone, according to one estimate.

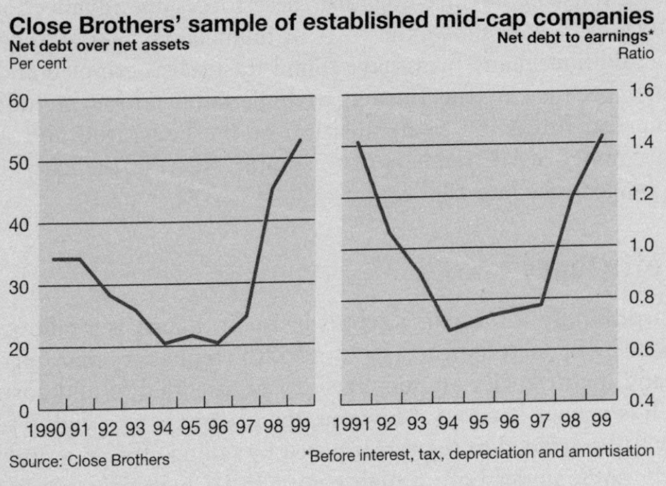

In addition, illiquidity in equity markets for non-technology companies has prompted a rise in the use of debt, while managements are increasingly aware of the benefits of higher gearing. Credit analysis of the debt markets has also become more sophisticated.

The engineering sector has undergone a particularly sharp rise with gearing levels rising fourfold from 40 per cent of net assets to nearly 160 per cent between 1997 and 1999.

The low market rating of the sector has meant debt has often been the only method of raising capital, Close said.

Source: Charles Batchelor, *Financial Times*, 9 May 2000, p. 30. Reprinted with permission.

CONCLUDING COMMENTS

The proportion of debt in the total capital of a firm can influence the overall cost of capital and therefore the value of the firm and the wealth of shareholders. If, as a result of increasing the gearing ratio, it is possible to lower the weighted average cost of capital, then all the future net cash flows will be discounted at a lower rate. It is generally observed that as gearing increases the WACC declines because of the lower cost of debt. This is further enhanced by the tax relief available on debt capital.

But as gearing rises the risk of financial distress causes shareholders (and eventually debt holders) to demand a greater return. This eventually rises to such an extent that it outweighs the benefit of the lower cost of debt, and the WACC starts to rise. This risk factor is difficult, if not impossible, to quantify and therefore the exact position and shape of the WACC curve for each firm remains largely unknown. Nevertheless, it seems reasonable to postulate there is a U-shaped relationship like that shown in Exhibit 18.25.

We cannot scientifically establish a best debt–equity ratio. There are many complicating factors which determine the actual gearing levels adopted by firms. These cloud the picture sufficiently for us to say that while we accept that the WACC is probably U-shaped for firms generally, we cannot precisely calculate a best gearing level.

This explains why there is such a variation in gearing levels. Some firms are under the influence of particular factors to a greater extent than other firms: some may have very low borrowing capacity, and others may have management keen on signalling confidence in the future; some may have very cautious management unwilling to borrow and a diffuse uncoordinated shareholder body; some may be in very volatile product markets with high liquidation probabilities and others in stable industries with marketable tangible assets; other companies may be dominated by leaders steeped in the high gearing

Exhibit 18.25 WACC is U-shaped and value can be altered by changing the gearing level

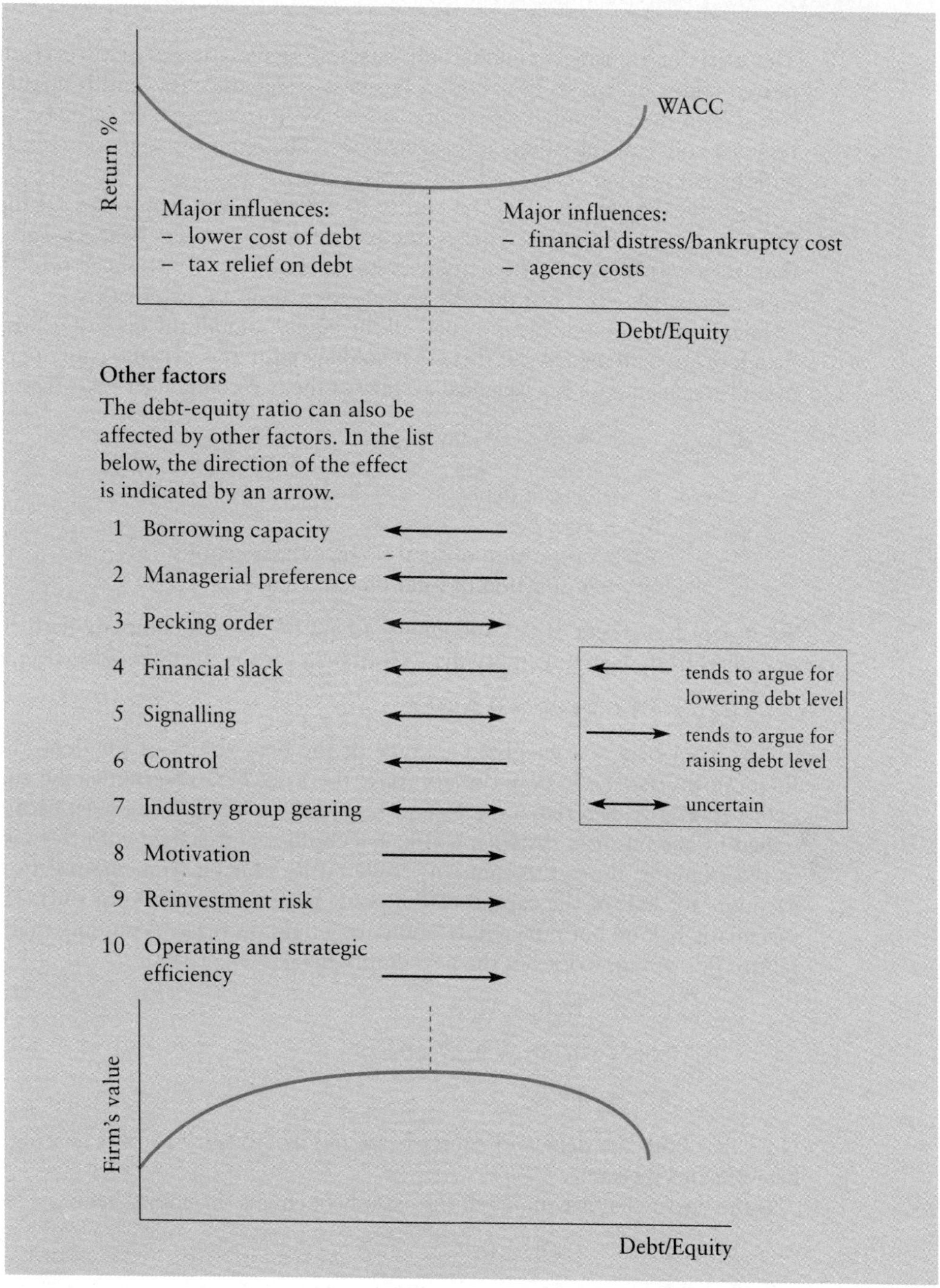

thinking of the late 1980s and early 1990s, believing that managers are better motivated and less likely to waste resources if the firm is highly indebted.

So, to the question of whether a firm can obtain a level of gearing which will maximise shareholder wealth the answer is 'yes'. The problem is finding this level in such a multifaceted analysis.

APPENDIX 18.1 ASSET BETA

The assets of a business contain only business systematic risk. However, the equity of a geared company has to bear both **a** business systematic risk, and **b** financial systematic risk due to the additional variability caused by borrowing. The business systematic risk remains constant regardless of gearing level. The equity systematic risk, however, rises with higher gearing

In the CAPM the beta of the equity (β_E) rises as the firm takes on higher gearing. Debt can also have a beta. That is, the returns to the lenders has a co-variability greater than zero with the market portfolio's returns. Both types of finance providers, debt and equity, bear risk – it is just that the shareholders bear a greater risk.

Imagine that an individual owned all the equity and all the debt of a firm. This person therefore bears all the risks. If these two holdings form this person's entire portfolio then the overall systematic risk is a weighted average of the two component betas (ignoring taxes).

$$\beta_{portfolio} = W_E \beta_E + W_D \beta_D = \beta_A$$

where β_D = beta of debt
β_A = asset beta
W_E = proportion of total finance that is equity
W_D = proportion of total finance that is debt

So, if debt has a beta of 0.3 and equity a beta of 1.3 in a company with equal amounts of capital from debt and equity the overall beta for the firm, the asset beta, β_A, is:

$$\beta_A = 0.5 \times 1.3 + 0.5 \times 0.3 = 0.8$$

The asset beta is a weighted average of the beta values of the debt and equity that financed the assets. To be more accurate, the asset beta determines the equity beta and debt beta. Asset beta remains constant regardless of the gearing level because it is determined by the business systematic risk, which does not change with the debt level. So, if in the example above the company lowered its gearing from the position where debt accounts for half of the capital to the point where it accounts for only 25 per cent the systematic risk on both the equity and debt would decrease. Assuming that the debt beta falls to 0.2 we can work out the new equity beta:

$$\beta_A = 0.8 = W_E\beta_E + W_D\beta_D$$
$$0.8 = 0.75\beta_E + 0.25 \times 0.2$$
$$\beta_E = 1$$

Note that both the debt and equity betas fall as a result of lower gearing but the asset beta remains the same.

If the borrowing is eliminated the asset beta equals the equity beta:

$$\beta_A = 0.8 = 1 \times \beta_E + 0$$
$$\beta_A = \beta_E = 0.8$$

Asset beta is the equity beta of the ungeared company given its underlying business systematic risk.

It is often assumed that the beta of debt is zero. This makes useable the following formulas:

$$\beta_A = \beta_E \times W_E$$

and

$$\beta_E = \beta_A \times 1/W_E$$

or

$$\beta_E = \beta_A \times W_D$$

or

$$\beta_E = \beta_A(1 + D/E)$$

where D = amount of borrowing
E = amount of equity finance

In this case equity beta rises in direct proportion to the gearing level.

If we now switch to a world where there are taxes, then (keeping the assumption of debt beta of zero) the tax shield on debt results in the following relationship:

$$\beta_E = \beta_A[1 + (1 - T)(D/E)]$$

where T = corporation tax rate.

The equity beta is reduced because the tax relief (shield) on debt capital effectively lowers the financial risk borne by the equity holders at all gearing levels.

Users of this formula should never forget the major assumption that the lenders bear no systematic risk (debt beta is zero). There is also the assumption that the CAPM is the right model for risk. If it is not the betas estimated may not reflect the true market risk exposure for the equity. In addition, the model excludes the possibility that β_E might rise in a non-linear fashion with gearing.

Perhaps the most useful point to make about asset beta analysis is that it is good to be aware that the beta obtained from commercial sources is an equity beta dependent on the gearing levels for the firms at the time that the beta was estimated. This gearing level may not be the gearing level applicable to WACC calculations and so some adjustment is needed. The equity beta can be *ungeared* by using the above formulas, and then calculated for a variety of gearing levels (if a few bold assumptions are made).

APPENDIX 18.2 ADJUSTED PRESENT VALUE (APV)

In the adjusted present value approach the value of financial gearing is separated from the value of the firm (project) without debt. The APV is equal to the value of the firm or project at zero debt (the NPV) plus the present value of the benefits (costs) of debt financing.

APV = NPV + PV of effects of gearing.

Or,

APV = value with all equity financing + PV of the effects of gearing.

Start by calculating the NPV of a project (or firm) as though it was to be financed entirely by equity. For example, a project is being considered that will produce annual cash flows of £1m for every future year to infinity. The project's business risk is such that the appropriate discount rate for this all-equity financed project is 10 per cent. The initial investment required is £10.5m.

NPV = –£10.5m + £1m/0.1 = –£0.5m

Under this all-equity capital the project produces a negative NPV and the managers would be inclined to reject it.

Now consider the same project in the circumstances where one half of the firm's (and project's) finance is debt and one half is equity. The debt finance carries with it a tax shield due to the ability to reduce taxable profit, and therefore the amount of tax paid, by the amount of interest. In other words, interest payments on debt are tax deductible, while cash flows on equity have to be paid out of after-tax cash flows.

If we make a few assumptions we can value the tax shield. if the interest rate on the £5.25m of debt is 6 per cent, and the tax rate, T, on income is 30 per cent, the annual tax savings from being able to deduct interest from taxable profits are:

$$\text{Annual interest on the debt} = k_D \times D$$
$$= 0.06 \times £5.25\text{m} = £315{,}000$$
$$\text{Annual tax savings due to interest payments} = T \times k_D \times D$$
$$= 0.3 \times 0.06 \times £5.25\text{m} = £94{,}500$$

If we make the following four assumptions we can calculate the present value of all the future tax savings due to interest payments:

- The debt remains at the same level forever, therefore the tax savings are a perpetuity.
- The discount rate to be used to obtain the present value of all the future tax savings is the interest rate on debt (because it reflects the riskiness of debt).
- The tax rate will be the same for all future periods.
- The company will always be in tax paying position. There are always annual taxable profits that can be decreased by the payment of interest.

In these circumstances the present value of the savings is:

$$\text{Present value of tax savings due to debt} = \frac{Tk_D D}{k_D} = TD$$
$$= 0.3 \times £5.25\text{m}$$
$$= £1{,}575\text{m}$$

Thus, the tax rate multiplied by the amount of debt gives us the present value of the effects of gearing in this simple case where there is only one effect of gearing: the tax shield benefit. We will introduce other effects later.

We can now add together the value of the project in the all-equity case and the value of the tax shield.

$$\text{APV} = \text{value with all-equity finance} + \text{PV of the effects of gearing.}$$
$$= -£0.5\text{m} + £1.575\text{m} = £1.075\text{m}$$

As a result of changing the financing structure the project generates positive value and should be accepted.

In separating the value of gearing the APV approach has the suggested advantage that we can more easily calculate overall value at a variety of debt levels than by using WACC. For example, in a leveraged buy-out where there is rapid pay-down of the debt, so that the ratio changes from year to year, the APV provides a computationally easier way of calculating value than WACC.

However, some caution is needed when employing APV. It assumes, for instance, that the firm can fully benefit from the tax shield at all debt levels. In reality tax shields will often be unused and therefore not adding value because the firm is not paying taxes. There may be periods of the future when the company is not making profits. Also very high debt levels need very high taxable income to gain all the benefit from the deductibility of interest. The tax shield value may be much less than that calculated using the simple formula above.

In addition, to use APV you need to be able to predict debt ratio levels for each of the future years with some considerable accuracy.

Most importantly, the APV formula used so far has ignored the disbenefits of higher debt. It implicitly assumes that the benefits of debt increase as the gearing level rises (as in MM's world with tax model). The logical extreme outcome of this would be to select a capital structure that was virtually all debt. In reality, there are some drawbacks of higher debt, the most important of which are financial distress, agency costs and loss of financial slack. So, the APV formula needs to be modified to allow for the disadvantages of debt:

$$\text{APV} = \begin{array}{c}\text{Value with}\\\text{all-equity}\\\text{financing}\end{array} + \begin{array}{c}\text{PV of tax}\\\text{benefits of}\\\text{debt}\end{array} - \begin{array}{c}\text{PV of expected}\\\text{disbenefits}\\\text{of debt}\end{array}$$

At low levels of debt the tax benefits will outweigh the disbenefits. But at high gearing it will be the other way around and the APV will fall with an increasing proportion of debt.

In this more realistic model the valuation of the financially geared company at different debt levels is far more complex, not least because it is very difficult to put numerical values on the disbenefits. To add to the complexity, there are a number of other factors we should allow for: for example, the benefit of higher debt leading to more highly motivated managers, the benefit of government loan subsidies, the transaction costs of issuing debt.

KEY POINTS AND CONCEPTS

- **Financial gearing** concerns the proportion of debt in the capital structure.
- **Operating gearing** refers to the extent to which the firm's total costs are fixed.
- **Capital gearing** can be measured in a number of ways. For example:

  1 $\dfrac{\text{Long-term debt}}{\text{Shareholders' funds}}$

  2 $\dfrac{\text{Long-term debt}}{\text{Long-term debt + Shareholders' funds}}$

  3 $\dfrac{\text{All borrowing}}{\text{All borrowing + Shareholders' funds}}$

  4 $\dfrac{\text{Long-term debt}}{\text{Total market capitalisation}}$

- **Income gearing** is concerned with the proportion of the annual income stream which is devoted to the prior claims of debt holders.

- The **effect of financial gearing** is to magnify the degree of variation in a firm's income for shareholders' returns.
- **Business risk** is the variability of the firm's operating income (before interest).
- **Financial risk** is the additional variability in returns to shareholders due to debt in the financial structure.
- In **Modigliani and Miller's perfect no-tax world** three propositions hold true:
  1. The total market value of any company is independent of its capital structure.
  2. The expected rate of return on equity increases proportionately with the gearing ratio.
  3. The cut-off rate of return for new projects is equal to the weighted average cost of capital – which is constant regardless of gearing.
- In an **MM world with tax** the optimal gearing level is the highest possible.
- The **risk of financial distress** is one factor which causes firms to moderate their gearing levels. Financial distress is where obligations to creditors are not met, or are met with difficulty.
- The **indirect costs of financial distress**, such as deterioration in relationships with suppliers, customers and employees, can be more significant than the direct costs, such as legal fees.
- **Financial distress risk is influenced by the following:**
  - the sensitivity of the company's revenues to the general level of economic activity;
  - the proportion of fixed to variable costs;
  - the liquidity and marketability of the firm's assets;
  - the cash-generative ability of the business.
- **Agency costs** are the direct and indirect costs of ensuring that agents (e.g. managers) act in the best interests of principals (e.g. shareholders, lenders), for example monitoring costs, restrictive covenants, loss of managerial freedom of action and opportunities forgone.
- **Financial distress and agency costs eventually outweigh the lower cost of debt** as gearing rises causing the WACC to rise and the firm's value to fall.
- **Borrowing capacity** is determined by the assets available as collateral – this restricts borrowing.
- There is often a **managerial preference** for a lower risk stance on gearing.
- **The pecking order** of finance:
  1. internally generated funds;
  2. borrowings;
  3. new issue of equity.

  The reasons for the pecking order:
  - equity issue perceived as 'bad news' by the markets;
  - line of least resistance;
  - transaction costs.

- **Financial slack** means having cash (or near-cash) and/or spare debt capacity so that opportunities can be exploited quickly (and trouble avoided) as they arise in an unpredictable world and to provide a contingency reserve – it tends to reduce borrowing levels.
- **Signalling** An increased gearing level is taken as a positive sign by the financial markets because managers would only take the risk of financial distress if they were confident about future cash flows.
- The source of finance chosen may be determined by the effect on the **control** of the organisation.
- Managers may be tempted to adopt the **industry group gearing** level.
- It is suggested that high gearing **motivates** managers to perform if they have a stake in the business, or if a smaller group of shareholders are given the incentive to monitor and control managers.
- **Reinvestment risk** is diminished by high gearing.
- It is argued that **operating and strategic efficiency** can be pushed further by high gearing.

REFERENCES AND FURTHER READING

Arnold, G.C. and Davis, P. (1995) *Profitability Trends in West Midlands Industries. A study for Lloyds Bowmaker*. Edinburgh: Lloyds Bowmaker.

Brealey, R.H. and Myers, S.C. (2000) *Principles of Corporate Finance*. 6th edn. New York: McGraw-Hill. A more detailed treatment of the theoretical material is provided.

Damodaran, A. (1999) *Applied Corporate Finance*. New York: Wiley. An accessible introduction to the practical estimation of optimum capital structure.

Donaldson, G. (1961) *Corporate debt policy and the determination of corporate debt capacity*. Boston: Harvard Graduate School of Business Administration. A study of the financing practices of large corporations: discussion of pecking order theory.

Fama, E.G. (1978) 'The effects of a firm's investment and financing decisions', *American Economic Review*, 68(3), June, pp. 272–84. A development of the economic modelling approach.

Harris, M. and Raviv, A. (1991) 'The theory of capital structure', *Journal of Finance*, 46, pp. 297–355. A helpful review of the subject.

Hart, O. (1995) *Firms, Contracts and Financial Structure*. Oxford: Oxford University Press. High debt helps to align the interests of owners and managers.

Jensen, M.C. (1986) 'Agency costs of free cashflow, corporate finance and takeovers', *American Economic Review*, 26 May, p. 323. Discusses the problem of encouraging managers to pay to shareholders cash above that needed for all positive NPV projects.

Jensen, M.C. (1989) 'Eclipse of the public corporation', *Harvard Business Review*, September–October, pp. 61–74. High debt levels impose a discipline on managers. In particular they are forced to distribute cash, reducing the potential waste of free cash flow investment. Also in LBOs managers are incentivised by becoming owners.

Journal of Economic Perspectives (1988) Fall. A collection of review articles on MM propositions.

Lowenstein, L. (1991) *Sense and Nonsense in Corporate Finance*. Reading, MA: Addison-Wesley. A sceptical approach to the over-elaborate algebraic examination of financial structure.

Luehrman, T.A. (1997) 'Using APV: A better tool for valuing operations', *Harvard Business Review*, 75 (May–June), pp. 145–54. An easy-to-read introduction to adjusted present value.

Marsh, P. (1982) 'The choice between equity and debt: An empirical study', *Journal of Finance*, 37, March, pp. 121–44. Evidence that companies appear to have target debt levels. These targets are a function of company size, bankruptcy risk and asset composition.

Miller, M.H. (1977) 'Debt and taxes', *Journal of Finance*, 32, May, pp. 261–75. A further contribution to the theoretical debate – technical and US focused.

Miller, M.H. (1991) 'Leverage', *Journal of Finance*, 46, pp. 479–88. An interesting article by a leader in the field.

Modigliani, F. and Miller, M.H. (1958) 'The cost of capital, corporation finance and the theory of investment', *American Economic Review*, 48, June, pp. 261–97. The classic original economic modelling approach to this subject.

Modigliani, F. and Miller, M.H. (1963) 'Corporate income taxes and the cost of capital: A correction', *American Economic Review*, 53, June, pp. 433–43. A technical account of the important correction to the 1958 article – allows for taxes.

Modigliani, F. and Miller, M.H. (1969) 'Reply to Heins and Sprenkle', *American Economic Review*, 59, September, pp. 592–5. More on the economic model approach.

Myers, S.C. (1974) 'Interaction of corporate financing and investment decisions – implications for capital budgeting', *Journal of Finance*, 29 (March), pp. 1–25. The adjusted-present-value method is developed in this article.

Myers, S.C. (1984) 'The capital structure puzzle', *Journal of Finance*, 39, July, pp. 575–82. Easy-to-read consideration of capital structure theory – particularly of pecking order theory.

Myers, S. and Majluf, N. (1984). 'Corporate financing and investment decisions when firms have information investors do not have', *Journal of Financial Economics*, June, pp. 187–221. Pecking order theory is advanced as an explanation for capital structure in practice.

Ross, S. (1977) 'The determination of financial structure: The incentive-signalling approach', *Bell Journal of Economics*, 8, pp. 23–40. The signalling hypothesis of debt increases is advanced.

Stern, J. (1998) 'The capital structure puzzle', *Journal of Applied Corporate Finance*, II(I), Spring, pp. 8–23. A round-table discussion between Joel Stern, Stewart Myers and other capital structure specialists. It focuses particularly on managerial performance and incentives. There is also a discussion of financial slack by the Treasurer of Sears – very interesting.

Solomon, E. (1963) *The Theory of Financial Management*. New York: Columbia University Press. An early discussion of WACC.

Stewart, G.B. (1990) *The Quest for Value*, New York: Harper Business. Chapter 13 is written in praise of capital structures with high debt levels.

SELF-REVIEW QUESTIONS

1 What was the traditional (pre-MM) view on optimal gearing levels?

2 Explain how debt finance is 'cheaper and riskier' for the firm.

3 Explain the terms operating gearing, financial gearing, capital gearing, income gearing.

4 What are business risk and financial risk?

5 Modigliani and Miller's original model resulted in three propositions. Describe them. Also, what are the major assumptions on which the model was built?

6 Describe how MM analysis changes if taxes are allowed into the model.

7 What is financial distress and how does it affect the gearing decision?

8 What are agency costs and how do they affect the gearing decision?

9 Describe the following ideas which are advanced to explain the low levels of gearing in some companies:

a Borrowing capacity.

b Managerial preferences.

c Pecking order.

d Financial slack.

e Control.

10 Some writers advocate the increased use of debt because of its beneficial effect on (a) managerial motivation, (b) reinvestment risk, and (c) operating and strategic efficiency. Explain these ideas.

QUESTIONS AND PROBLEMS

1* Calculate and comment upon some gearing ratios for Marks and Spencer plc.

Marks and Spencer plc Balance sheet and profit figures, 2000

	£m	*£m*
Fixed assets		4,298.4
Current assets:		
Stocks	474.4	
Debtors	2,555.2	
Investments	386.4	
Cash	301.1	
		3,717.1
Creditors due within one year		(2,162.8)
of which:		
Bank loans and overdraft	1,169.4	
Creditors due after more than one year		(804.3)
of which: borrowings	686.1	
Provisions for liabilities and charges		(126.6)
Net assets		4,921.8
Profit before interest and taxation		557.2
Interest received		14.2
Market capitalisation		5,000.0

2* (*Examination level*) Eastwell plc is to be established shortly. The founders are considering their options with regard to capital structure. A total of £1m will be needed to establish the business and the three ways of raising these funds being considered are:

a Selling 500,000 shares at £2.00.

b Selling 300,000 shares at £2.00 and borrowing £400,000 with an interest rate of 12 per cent.

c Selling 100,000 shares at £2.00 and borrowing £800,000 at an interest rate of 13 per cent.

There are three possible outcomes for the future annual cash flows before interest:

Success of product	*Cash flow before interest*	*Probability*
Poor	£60,000	0.25
Good	£160,000	0.50
Excellent	£300,000	0.25

Note: Taxes may be ignored.

Required

a Calculate the expected annual return to shareholders under each of the capital structures.

b Calculate the standard deviation of the expected annual return under each of the capital structures.

c Separate out business risk and financial risk and explain what these terms mean.

d Some writers have advocated the high use of debt because of the positive effect on managerial actions. Describe these ideas and consider some counter-arguments.

3* a (*Examination level*) Hose plc presently has a capital structure which is 30 per cent debt and 70 per cent equity. The cost of debt (i.e borrowings) before taxes is 9 per cent and that for equity is 15 per cent. The firm's future cash flows, after tax but before interest, are expected to be a perpetuity of £750,000. The tax rate is 30 per cent.

Calculate the WACC and the value of the firm.

b The directors are considering the partial replacement of equity finance with borrowings so that the borrowings make up 60 per cent of the total capital. Director A believes that the cost of equity capital will remain constant at 15 per cent; Director B believes that shareholders will demand a rate of return of 23.7 per cent; Director C believes that shareholders will demand a rate of return of 17 per cent and Director D believes the equity rate of return will shift to 28 per cent. Assuming that the cost of borrowings before income taxes remains at 9 per cent, what will the WACC and the value of the firm be under each of the directors' estimates?

c Relate the results in question **3b** to the capital structure debate. In particular draw on Modigliani and Miller's theory, financial distress and agency theory.

4 (*Examination level*) 'It is in management's interest to keep the financial gearing level as low as possible, while it is in shareholders' interests to keep it at a high level.' Discuss this statement.

5 (*Examination level*) In 1984 Stewart Myers wrote, 'our theories do not seem to explain actual financing behaviour', when referring to the capital structure debate. In what ways do the main MM economic models of gearing fail? Discuss some alternative explanations for the actual gearing levels of companies.

6 a (*Examination level*) Hickling plc has estimated the cost of debt and equity for various financial gearing levels:

Proportion of debt $\frac{V_D}{(V_D + V_E)}$	*Required rate of return* *Debt,* k_{DAT} %	*Equity,* k_E %
0.80	9.0	35.0
0.70	7.5	28.0
0.60	6.8	21.0
0.50	6.4	17.0
0.40	6.1	14.5
0.30	6.0	13.5
0.20	6.0	13.2
0.10	6.0	13.1
0.00	–	13.0

What is the optimal capital structure?

b Describe and explain the factors which might lead to a rise in the overall cost of capital for Hickling.

7 (*Examination level*) The managing director of your firm is thinking aloud about an appropriate gearing level for the company:

The consultants I spoke to yesterday explained that some academic theorists advance the idea that, if your objective is the maximisation of shareholder wealth, the debt to equity ratio does not matter. However, they did comment that this conclusion held in a world of no taxes. Even more strangely, these theorists say that in a world with tax it is best to 'gear-up' a company as high as possible. Now I may not know much about academic theories but I do know that there are limits to the debt level which is desirable. After listening to these consultants I am more confused than ever.

You step forward and offer to write a report for the managing director both outlining the theoretical arguments and explaining the real-world influences on the gearing levels of firms.

8 (*Examination level*) Within a given industry, wide variations in the degree of financial gearing of firms is observed. What might explain this?

9 Given the following facts about Company X, what would the equity cost of capital be if it had no debt, if Modigliani and Miller's model with no tax applied?

$$k_E = 30\%$$

$$k_D = 9\%$$

$$\frac{V_D}{(V_D + V_E)} = 0.6$$

ASSIGNMENTS

1 Obtain accounting and other information on a company of interest to you and calculate gearing ratios. Point out in a report the difficulties involved in this process.

2 Analyse a company you know well in the light of the various ideas, theories and models regarding capital structure. Write up your findings in a report, and include implications and recommendations for action.

CHAPTER NOTES

1 *Financial Times*, 11 February 2000, p. 21.

2 Quoted in *Financial Times*, 28 March 1996.

3 *Financial Times*, 13 March 1997, p. 23.

4 Quoted by Leyla Boulton, *Financial Times*, 18 December 1996.

5 These problems also apply to capital gearing measures (2) and (3).

6 To make this discussion easier to follow it will be assumed that there are only two types of finance, debt and ordinary shares. However, the introduction of other types of finance does not fundamentally alter the analysis.

7 In many countries there is another capital gearing ratio in use:

Net worth (or Shareholders' equity)/Debt + Equity.

8 Myers (1984), p. 575.

9 On the other hand Jensen (1986) has argued that if managers have less free cash flow they are less likely to invest in negative NPV projects, and this restraint is better for shareholders.

Chapter 19

DIVIDEND POLICY

'Dividend policy is often reported to shareholders, but seldom explained. A company will say something like, "Our goal is to pay out 40% to 50% of earnings and to increase dividends at a rate at least equal to the rise in the CPI."[1] And that's it – no analysis will be supplied as to why that particular policy is best for the owners of the business. Yet, allocation of capital is crucial to businesses and investment management. Because it is, we believe managers and owners should think hard about the circumstances under which earnings should be retained and under which they should be distributed.'

Source: Warren Buffett, a letter to shareholders attached to the *Annual Report of Berkshire Hathaway Inc* (1984). Reprinted with kind permission of Warren Buffett. © Warren Buffett.

INTRODUCTION

No one has more right to speak on dividend policy than Warren Buffett, who has become a multi-billionaire by putting his money where his mouth is and backing managers who agree with, and implement, his approach to management. After fifty years of observing managers his comments may be viewed as a sad indictment of the quality of managerial thought. On the central issue of whether to retain profits, or distribute them to shareholders to use elsewhere, there appears to be vagueness and confusion. He has suggested that the issue is addressed at a superficial level with the employment of simple rules of thumb and no analysis. This conclusion may or may not be unfair – this chapter is not designed to highlight managerial failings in the depth of thought department. What it can do, however, is point out the major influences on the level of the dividend decision in any one year. Some of these are fully 'rational' in the sense of the economist's model, others are less quantifiable, and stem more from the field of psychology.

The conclusion reached is that managers have to weigh up a range of forces – some pulling them in the direction of paying out either a high proportion of earnings or a low one; other forces pulling them to provide a stable and consistent dividend, and yet others pulling them to vary the dividend from year to year.

These are, of course, merely the range of forces influencing managers who are fully committed to shareholder wealth maximisation and thinking 'hard about the circumstances under which earnings should be retained'. If we admit the possibility that managers have other goals, or that they make little intellectual effort, the possible outcomes of the annual or semi-annual boardroom discussion on the dividend level can range widely.

Learning objectives

This area of finance has no neat over-arching theoretical model to provide a simple answer. However, there are some important arguments which should inform the debate within firms. By the end of this chapter the reader should be able to:

- explain the rationale and conclusion of the ideas of Modigliani and Miller's dividend irrelevancy hypothesis, as well as the concept of dividends as a residual;
- describe the influence of particular dividend policies attracting different 'clients' as shareholders, the effect of taxation and the importance of dividends as a signalling device;
- outline the hypothesis that dividends received now, or in the near future, have much more value than those in the far future because of the resolution of uncertainty and the exceptionally high discount rate applied to more distant dividends;
- discuss the impact of agency theory on the dividend decision;
- discuss the role of scrip dividends and share repurchase.

DEFINING THE PROBLEM

Dividend policy is the determination of the proportion of profits paid out to shareholders – usually periodically. The issue to be addressed is whether shareholder wealth can be enhanced by altering the *pattern* of dividends not the *size* of dividends overall. Naturally, if dividends over the lifetime of a firm are larger, value will be greater. So in the forthcoming analysis we will assume that:

a the underlying investment opportunities and returns on business investment are constant; and

b the extra value that may be created by changing the capital structure (debt–equity ratio) is constant.

Therefore only the pattern of dividend payments may add or subtract value. For example, perhaps a pattern of high payouts in the immediate future, with a consequential reduction in dividend growth thereafter, may be superior to a policy of zero or small dividends now followed by more rapid growth over time.

Another aspect of the pattern question is whether a steady, stable dividend growth rate is better than a volatile one which varies from year to year depending on the firm's internal need for funds.

Some background

UK-quoted companies usually pay dividends every six months. In each financial year there is an *interim* dividend related to the first half year's trading, followed by the *final* dividend after the financial year-end. The board of directors are empowered to recommend the final dividend level but it is a right of shareholders as a body to vote at the annual general meeting whether or not it should be paid. Not all companies follow the typical cycle of two dividends per year: a few pay dividends quarterly and others choose not to pay a dividend at all.

Dividends may only be paid out of accumulated profits and not out of capital. This means that companies which have loss-making years may still pay dividends, but only up to the point that they have retained profits from previous years. This rule is designed to provide some protection to creditors by putting a barrier in the way of shareholders looking to remove funds from the firm, and thereby withdrawing the cushion of capital originally provided by shareholders. Further restrictions may be placed on the firm's freedom of action with regard to dividend levels by constraints contained in bond, preference share and bank-loan agreements.

MODIGLIANI AND MILLER'S DIVIDEND IRRELEVANCY PROPOSITION

According to an important 1961 paper by Modigliani and Miller (MM) (1961), if a few assumptions can be made, dividend policy is irrelevant to share value. The determinant of value is the availability of projects with positive NPVs and the pattern of dividends makes no difference to the acceptance of these. The share price would not move if the firm declared either a zero dividend policy or a policy of high near-term dividends. The conditions under which this was held to be true included:

1. There are no taxes.
2. There are no transaction costs; for example:
   - a investors face no brokerage costs when buying or selling shares;
   - b companies can issue shares with no transaction costs.
3. All investors can borrow and lend at the same interest rate.
4. All investors have free access to all relevant information.

Given these assumptions, dividend policy can become irrelevant. For example, a firm which had plentiful positive NPV projects but nevertheless paid all profits each year as dividends would not necessarily be destroying shareholder wealth because in this ideal world any money paid out could quickly be replaced by having a new issue of shares.[2] The investors in these shares would willingly pay a fair price because of their access to all relevant information. The shares can be issued by the firm without costs of underwriting or merchant banks' fees, etc., and bought by the shareholders without brokers' fees or costs associated with the time spent filling in forms, etc. That is, there are no transaction costs.

If a company chose not to pay any dividends at all and shareholders required a regular income then this could be achieved while leaving the firm's value intact. 'Homemade dividends' can be created by shareholders selling a portion of their shares to other investors – again, as there are no costs of transactions and no taxation the effect is identical to the receipt of cash in the form of an ordinary dividend from the firm.

Take the example of Belvoir plc, an all-equity company which has a policy of paying out all annual net cash flow as dividend. The company is expected to generate a net cash flow of £1m to an infinite horizon. Given the cost of equity capital is 12 per cent we can calculate the value of this firm using the dividend valuation model (with zero growth – see Chapter 17 for details).

$$P_0 = d_0 + \frac{d_1}{k_E} = £1\text{m} + \frac{£1\text{m}}{0.12} = £9.333\text{m}$$

This includes £1m of dividend due to be paid immediately, plus the £1m perpetuity.

Now suppose that the management have identified a new investment opportunity. This will produce additional cash flows of £180,000 per year starting in one year. However the company will be required to invest £1m now. There are two ways in which this money for investment could be found. First, the managers could skip the present dividend and retain £1m. Second, the company could maintain its dividend policy for this year and pay out £1m, but simultaneously launch a new issue of shares, say a rights issue, to gain the necessary £1m.

It will now be demonstrated that in this perfect world, with no transaction costs, shareholder value will be the same whichever dividend policy is adopted.

What *will* increase shareholder value is the NPV of the project.

$$\text{NPV} = -\text{£}1\text{m} + \frac{\text{£}180{,}000}{0.12} = \text{£}500{,}000$$

The value of the firm is raised by £500,000, by the acceptance of the project and not because of the dividend policy. If the project is financed through the sacrifice of the present dividend the effect on shareholder wealth is:

Year	*0*	*1*	*2*	*3 etc.*
Cash flow to shareholders	0	1,180,000	1,180,000	1,180,000

$$\text{Shareholders' wealth} = \frac{1{,}180{,}000}{0.12} = \text{£}9.833\text{m}$$

Thus shareholders' wealth is increased by £500,000.

If the project is financed through a rights issue while leaving the dividend pattern intact the effect on shareholder wealth is the same – an increase of £500,000.

Year	*0*	*1*	*2*	*3 etc.*
Cash flow to shareholders				
Receipt of dividend	+ £1,000,000			
Rights issue	– £1,000,000			
	0	1,180,000	1,180,000	1,180,000

$$\text{Shareholders' wealth} = \frac{1{,}180{,}000}{0.12} = \text{£}9.833\text{m}$$

Shareholders' wealth is enhanced because £1m of shareholders' money is invested in a project which yields more than 12 per cent. If the incremental cash inflows amounted to only £100,000 then the wealth of shareholders would fall, because a 10 per cent return is insufficient given the opportunity cost of shareholders' money:

$$\frac{\text{£}1{,}100{,}000}{0.12} = \text{£}9.167\text{m}$$

If the new investment produces a 12 per cent return shareholders will experience no loss or gain in wealth. The critical point is that in this hypothetical, perfect world the pattern of dividend makes no difference to shareholders' wealth. This is determined purely by the investment returns. If a firm chose to miss a dividend for a year, because it had numerous high-yielding projects to invest in, this would not decrease share values, because the perfectly well-informed investors are aware that any cash retained will be going into positive NPV projects which will generate future dividend increases for shareholders.

DIVIDENDS AS A RESIDUAL

Now we take another extreme position. Imagine that the raising of external finance (for example rights issues) is so expensive that to all intents and purposes it is impossible. The only source of finance for additional investment is earnings. Returning to the example of Belvoir, it is obvious that under these circumstances, to pay this year's dividend will reduce potential shareholder value by £500,000 because the new project will have to be abandoned.

In this world dividends should only be paid when the firm has financed all its positive NPV projects. Once the firm has provided funds for all the projects which more than cover the minimum required return, investors should be given the residual. They should receive this cash because they can use it to invest in other firms of the same risk class which provide an expected return at least as great as the required return on equity capital, k_E. If the firm kept all the cash flows and continued adding to its range of projects the marginal returns would be likely to decrease, because the project with the highest return would be undertaken first, followed by the one with the next highest return, and so on, until returns became very low.

In these circumstances dividend policy becomes an important determinant of shareholder wealth:

1 If cash flow is retained and invested within the firm at less than k_E, shareholder wealth is destroyed; therefore it is better to raise the dividend payout rate.

2 If retained earnings are insufficient to fund all positive NPV projects shareholder value is lost, and it would be beneficial to lower the dividend.

What about the world in which we live?

We have discussed two extreme positions so far and have reached opposing conclusions. In a perfect world the dividend pattern is irrelevant because the firm can always fund itself costlessly if it has positive NPV projects, and shareholders can costlessly generate 'homemade dividends' by selling some of their shares. In a world with no external finance the pattern of dividends becomes crucial to shareholder wealth, as an excessive payout reduces the take-up of positive NPV projects; and an unduly low payout means value destruction because investors miss out on investment opportunities elsewhere in the financial securities market.

In our world there are transaction costs to contend with. If a firm pays a dividend in order to keep to its avowed dividend pattern and then, in order to fund projects, takes money from shareholders through a rights issue, this is not frictionless: there are costs. The expense for the firm includes the legal and administrative cost of organising a rights issue or some other issue of shares; it may be necessary to prepare a prospectus and to incur advertising costs; underwriting fees alone can be as much as 2 per cent of the amount raised. The expense for the shareholder of receiving money with one hand only to give it back with the other might include brokerage costs and the time and hassle involved. Taxes further complicate the issue by imposing additional costs.

It is plain that there is a powerful reason why dividend policy might make some difference to shareholder wealth: the investment opportunities within the firm obviously have some effect. This may help to explain why we witness many young rapidly growing firms with a need for investment finance having a very low dividend (or zero) payouts, whereas mature 'cash cow' type firms choose a high payout rate.

The relationship between investment opportunity and dividend policy is a far from perfect one and there are a number of other forces pulling on management to select a particular policy. These will be considered after some more down-to-earth arguments from Warren Buffett (*see* Exhibit 19.1).

Wassall (*see* Exhibit 19.2) is trying to 'treat its shareholders like grown-ups' and hand cash back to shareholders when it has cash surplus to requirements.

Exhibit 19.1 Buffett on dividends

Berkshire Hathaway Inc

'Earnings should be retained only when there is a reasonable prospect – backed preferably by historical evidence or, when appropriate by a thoughtful analysis of the future – *that for every dollar retained by the corporation, at least one dollar of market value will be created for owners* [italics in original]. This will happen only if the capital retained produces incremental earnings equal to, or above, those generally available to investors.'

Warren Buffett says that many managers think like owners when it comes to demanding high returns from subordinates but fail to apply the same principles to the dividend payout decision:

'The CEO of multi-divisional company will instruct Subsidiary A, whose earnings on incremental capital may be expected to average 5%, to distribute all available earnings in order that they may be invested in Subsidiary B, whose earnings on incremental capital are expected to be 15%. The CEO's business school oath will allow no lesser behaviour. But if his own long-term record with incremental capital is 5% – and market rates are 10% – he is likely to impose a dividend policy on shareholders of the parent company that merely follows some historic or industry-wide payout pattern. Furthermore, he will expect managers of subsidiaries to give him a full account as to why it makes sense for earnings to be retained in their operations rather than distributed to the parent-owner. But seldom will he supply his owners with a similar analysis pertaining to the whole company . . . shareholders would be far better off if earnings were retained only to expand the high-return business, with the balance paid in dividends or used to repurchase stock.'

Source: Warren Buffett, A letter to shareholders attached to the *Annual Report of Berkshire Hathaway Inc* (1984). Reprinted with kind permission of Warren Buffett. © Warren Buffett.

Exhibit 19.2

Wassall plans £150m payout for investors

FT

Wassall yesterday outlined plans to float 70 per cent of its General Cable Corporation subsidiary in the US and distribute £150m of the proceeds to shareholders.

The payout represents the amount invested by the conglomerate in buying General Cable almost three years ago, net of dividends.

It is part of a new strategy under which Wassall aims to come to shareholders when it needs funds for expansion, and hand the cash back when it is surplus to requirements.

Mr Chris Miller, the chief executive, said: 'We are trying to treat shareholders like grown-ups.'

Shares in Wassall rose 22p to 376p as brokers and investors responded with enthusiasm to the announcement.

Source: Ross Tieman, *Financial Times*, 11 March 1997, p. 21. Reprinted with permission.

CLIENTELE EFFECTS

Some shareholders prefer a dividend pattern which matches their desired consumption pattern. There may be natural clienteles for shares which payout a high proportion of earnings, and another clientele for shares which have a low payout rate. For example, retired people, living off their private investments, may prefer a high and steady income, so they would tend to be attracted to firms with a high and stable dividend yield. Likewise, pension funds need regular cash receipts to meet payments to pensioners.

Shareholders who need a steady flow of income, could, of course, generate a cash flow stream by selling off a proportion of their shares on a regular basis as an alternative to investing in firms with a high payout ratio. But this approach will result in transaction costs (brokerage, marketmakers' spread and loss of interest while waiting for cash after sale). Also it is time consuming and inconvenient regularly to sell off blocks of shares; it is much easier to receive a series of dividend cheques through the post.

Another type of clientele are people who are not interested in receiving high dividends in the near term. These people prefer to invest in companies with good growth potential – companies which pay low dividends and use the retained money to invest in projects with positive NPVs within the firm. The idea behind such practices is that capital gains (a rising share price) will be the main way in which the shareholder receives a return. An example of such a clientele group might be wealthy middle-aged people who have more than enough income from their paid employment for their consumption needs. If these people did receive large amounts of cash in dividends now they would probably only reinvest it in the stock market. A cycle of receiving dividends followed by reinvestment is very inefficient.

Thus, it seems reasonable to argue that a proportion of shareholders choose to purchase particular shares at least partially because the dividend policy suits them. This may place pressure on the management to produce a stable and consistent dividend policy because investors need to know that a particular investment is going to continue to suit their preferences. Inconsistency would result in a lack of popularity with any client group and would depress the share price. Management therefore, to some extent, target particular clienteles.[3]

The clientele force acting on dividend policy at first glance seems to be the opposite of the residual approach. With the clientele argument, stability and consistency are required to attract a particular type of clientele, whereas with the residual argument, dividends depend on the opportunities for reinvestment – the volume of which may vary in a random fashion from year to year, resulting in fluctuating retentions and dividends. Most firms seem to square this circle by having a consistent dividend policy based on a medium or long-term view of earnings and investment capital needs. The shortfalls and surpluses in particular years are adjusted through other sources of finance: for example, borrowing or raising equity through a rights issue in years when retained earnings are insufficient; paying off debt or storing up cash when retentions are greater than investment needs. There are costs associated with such a policy, for example the costs of rights issues and these have to be weighed against the benefit of stability.

The clientele effect is often reinforced by the next factor we will examine, taxation. The consistent dividend pattern is encouraged by the information aspect of dividends – discussed after that.

TAXATION

The taxation of dividends and capital gains on shares is likely to influence the preference of shareholders for receiving cash either in the form of a regular payment from the company (a dividend) or by selling shares. If shareholders are taxed more heavily on dividends than on capital gains they are more likely to favour shares which pay lower dividends. In the past, UK and US dividends were taxed at a higher rate than that which applied to the capital gains made on the sale of shares for those shareholders subject to these taxes. However, in recent years, the difference has been narrowed significantly. In the UK, for example, capital gains are now taxed at the individual's marginal tax rate. Capital gains still, however, have tax advantages. Investors are allowed to make annual capital gains of £7,500 (in 2001–2) tax free, and they only pay tax on realised gains (when the shares are sold). Therefore they can delay payment by continuing to hold the shares until they can, say, take advantage of a future year's capital allowance of £7,500. In addition, if shares are held for a few years the tax falls significantly.

Elton and Gruber (1970) found evidence that there was a statistical relationship between the dividend policy of firms and the tax bracket of their shareholders – shareholders with higher income tax rates were associated with low-dividend shares and those with lower income tax rates with high-dividend shares.

In July 1997 a major change in the tax position of UK pension funds (owners of over 30 per cent of UK shares) was introduced. Before that date dividend income received was exempt from tax. If a firm paid a gross dividend of 10p the government would take 2p as advanced corporation tax; therefore the tax-liable shareholder would receive only 8p. Pension funds in receipt of the 8p could reclaim the 2p from the government. Gordon Brown, the Chancellor, put a stop to the reclamation of this money, effectively reducing the income of pension funds. He said:

> The present system of tax credits encourages companies to pay out dividends rather than reinvest their profits. This cannot be the best way of encouraging investment for the long term as was acknowledged by the last government. Many pension funds are in substantial surplus and at present many companies are enjoying pension holidays, so this is the right time to undertake long-needed reform. So, with immediate effect, I propose to abolish tax credits paid to pension funds and companies.[4]

Thus we have a clear attempt by the UK government to use the tax system to try to encourage lower dividends and greater reinvestment.

DIVIDENDS AS CONVEYORS OF INFORMATION

Dividends appear to act as important conveyors of information about companies. An unexpected change in the dividend is regarded as a sign of how the directors view the future prospects of the firm. An unusually large increase in the dividend is often taken to indicate an optimistic view about future profitability. A declining dividend often signals that the directors view the future with some pessimism.

The importance of the dividend as an information-transferring device occurs because of a significant market imperfection – information asymmetry. That is, managers know far more about the firm's prospects than do the finance providers. Investors are continually trying to piece together scraps of information about a firm. Dividends are one source that the investor can draw upon. They are used as an indicator of a firm's sustainable level of income. It would seem that managers choose a target dividend payout ratio based on a long-term earnings trend.[5] It is risky for managers' career prospects for them to increase the dividend above the regular growth pattern if they are not expecting improved business prospects. This sends a false signal and eventually they will be found out when the income growth does not take place.

It is the increase or decrease over the *expected* level of dividends that leads to a rise or fall in share price. This phenomenon can be illustrated from the article on British Airways reproduced in Exhibit 19.3. Here, BA produced very poor profit figures and yet the share price rose because the management signalled its optimism by raising the dividend. (That optimism proved to be unfounded, especially in the light of the transatlantic travel decline following the terrorist attack on 11 September 2001.)

Exhibit 19.3

BA profits plunge 61% to £225m

FT

By Michael Skapinker, Aerospace Correspondent

British Airways yesterday revealed its worst pre-tax profits for six years but vowed to win back business class passengers who have moved to economy cabin or to other airlines.

BA said the poor 1998-1999 result – down 61 per cent to £225m – was the result of fierce competition on north Atlantic routes. The airline said it planned to improve performance by reducing the number of cut-price economy passengers it carried.

The shares rose 12p to 469½p in spite of the profits fall. The market was cheered by BA's decision to raise the full-year dividend 7.8 per cent to 17.9p.

Derek Stevens, chief financial officer, said the increased dividend – on earnings per share of 19.2p – was an indication of BA's confidence in its future. "We don't expect profits to stay down," he said.

Source: Michael Skapinker, *Financial Times*, 26 May 1999, p. 21. Reprinted with permission.

Generally company earnings fluctuate to a far greater extent than dividends. This smoothing of the dividend flow is illustrated in Exhibit 19.4 where Kingfisher has shown a rise and a fall in earnings per share but a steadily rising dividend.

Exhibit 19.4 Kingfisher earnings and dividend, five-year record (pence)

	1997	*1998*	*1999*	*2000*	*2001*
Kingfisher					
Earnings per share	21.3	27.5	29.3	30.0	26.8
Dividends per share	9.5	11.5	13.0	14.5	15.5

A reduction in earnings is usually not followed by a reduction in dividends, unless the earnings fall is perceived as likely to persist for a long time. Researchers, ever since Lintner's (1956) survey on managers' attitudes to dividend policy in the 1950s, have shown that directors are aware that the market reacts badly to dividend downturns and they make strenuous efforts to avoid a decline. Almost every day the financial press reports firms making losses and yet still paying a dividend. By continuing the income stream to shareholders the management signal that the decline in earnings is temporary and that positive earnings are expected in the future.

When times are good and profits are bounding ahead directors tend to be cautious about large dividend rises. To double or treble dividends in good years increases the risk of having to reduce dividends should the profit growth tail off and losing the virtue of predictability and stability cherished by shareholders.

RESOLUTION OF UNCERTAINTY

Myron Gordon (1963) has argued that investors perceive that a company, by retaining and reinvesting a part of its current cash flow, is replacing a certain dividend flow to shareholders now with an uncertain more distant flow in the future. Because the returns from any reinvested funds will occur in the far future they are therefore subject to more risk and investors apply a higher discount rate than they would to near-term dividends. Thus the market places a greater value on shares offering higher near-term dividends. Investors are showing a preference for the early resolution of uncertainty. Under this model investors use a set of discount rates which rise through time to calculate share values; therefore the dividend valuation model becomes:

$$P_0 = \frac{d_1}{1 + k_{E1}} + \frac{d_2}{(1 + k_{E2})^2} + \dots \frac{d_n}{(1 + k_{En})^n} + \dots$$

where:

$$k_{E1} < k_{E2} < k_{E3} \dots$$

The dividends received in Years 2, 3 or 4 are of lower risk than those received seven, eight or nine years' hence.

The crucial factor here may not be actual differences in risk between the near and far future, but *perceived* risk. It may be that immediate dividends are valued more highly because the investors' perception of risk is not perfect. They overestimate the riskiness of distant dividends and thus undervalue them. However, whether the extra risk attached to more distant dividends is real or not, the effect is the same – investors prefer a higher dividend in the near term than they otherwise would and shareholder value can be raised by altering the dividend policy to suit this preference – or so the argument goes.

There have been some impressive counter-attacks on what is described as the 'bird-in-the-hand fallacy'. The riskiness of a firm's dividend derives from the risk associated with the underlying business and this risk is already allowed for through the risk-adjusted discount rate, k_E. To discount future income even further would be excessive. Take a company expected to produce a dividend per share of £1 in two years and £2 in ten years. The discount rate of, say, 15 per cent ensures that the £2 dividend is worth, in present value terms, less than the dividend received in two years, and much of this discount rate is a compensation for risk.

$$\text{Present value of £1 dividend} = \frac{£1}{(1.15)^2} = 75.6\text{p}$$

$$\text{Present value of £2 dividend} = \frac{£2}{(1.15)^{10}} = 49.4\text{p}$$

Alternatively, take a company which pays out all its earnings in the hope of raising its share price because shareholders have supposedly had resolution of uncertainty. Now, what is the next move? We have a company in need of investment finance and shareholders wishing to invest in company shares – as most do with dividend income. The firm has a rights issue. In the prospectus the firm explains what will happen to the funds raised: they will be used to generate dividends in the future. Thus shareholders buy shares on the promise of future dividends; they discount these dividends at a risk-adjusted discount rate determined by the rate of return available on alternative, equally risky investments, say, 15 per cent (applicable to *all* the future years). To discount at a higher rate would be to undervalue the shares and pass up an opportunity of a good investment.

OWNER CONTROL (AGENCY THEORY)

As Exhibit 19.5 shows, politicians have taken the view that UK firms pay out an excessive proportion of their earnings as dividends. The argument then runs that this stifles investment because of the lower retention rate.

Exhibit 19.5

Treasury drops dividends probe after pressure

FT

The Treasury has abandoned its review of whether companies' dividend payments are too high and there will be no measures in the Budget next week aimed at controlling dividends.

Mr Stephen Dorrell, as financial secretary to the Treasury, initiated an inquiry a year ago into whether the tax structure encourages companies to allocate an excessive proportion of retained profits to dividends compared with funds for investment. It was part of a wider review of the financing of industry.

Mr Dorrell disclosed details of the probe in a speech to a Confederation of British Industry conference in the spring.

He was immediately attacked by Mr Paddy Linaker, then chief executive of M&G, the fund management group. But a far greater embarrassment was the leak of a letter to Mr Dorrell from Lord Hanson, accusing the minister of 'sounding like a socialist'.

A government official said yesterday that since then the probe has been quietly shelved.

• Companies are making artificially high dividend payments to keep pension funds happy and protect themselves against hostile takeovers, a study by the School of Business and Economics at Leeds University said yesterday.

All 700 respondents said companies were pressured by City opinion to be more generous with dividend payments than they would like.

Source: Robert Peston, *Financial Times*, 24 November 1994. Reprinted with permission.

Set alongside the concern expressed in the article in Exhibit 19.5 should go the observation that many firms seem to have a policy of paying high dividends, and then, shortly afterwards, issuing new shares to raise cash for investment. This is a perplexing phenomenon. The cost of issuing shares can be burdensome and shareholders generally pay tax on the receipt of dividends. One possible answer is that it is the signalling (information) value of dividends that drives this policy. However, the costs are so high that it cannot always be explained by this. A second potential explanation lies with agency cost.

Managers may not always act in the best interests of the owners. One way for the owners to regain some control over the use of their money is to insist on relatively high payout ratios. Then, if managers need funds for investment they have to ask. A firm that wishes to raise external capital will have its plans for investment scrutinised by a number of experts, including:

- investment bankers who advise on the issue;
- underwriters who, like investment bankers, will wish to examine the firm and its plans as they are attaching their good name to the issue;
- analysts at credit-rating agencies;
- analysts at stockbroking houses who advise shareholders and potential shareholders;
- shareholders.

In ordinary circumstances the firm's investors can only influence managerial action by voting at a general meeting (which is usually ineffective due to apathy and the use of proxy votes by the board), or by selling their shares. When a company has to ask for fresh capital investors can tease out more information and can examine managerial action and proposed actions. They can exercise some control over their savings by refusing to buy the firm's securities if they are at all suspicious of managerial behaviour. Of particular concern might be the problem of investment in projects with negative NPV for the sake of building a larger managerial empire.

SCRIP DIVIDENDS

A scrip dividend gives shareholders an opportunity to receive additional shares in proportion to their existing holding instead of the normal cash dividend. The shareholders can then either keep the shares or sell them for cash. From the company's point of view scrip dividends have the advantage that *cash does not leave the company*. This may be important for companies going through difficult trading periods or as a way of adjusting the gearing ratio. Shareholders may be attracted to a scrip dividend because they can increase their holdings without brokerage costs and other dealing costs.

An enhanced scrip dividend is one where the shares offered are worth substantially more than the alternative cash payout. Such an offer is designed to encourage the take-up of shares and is like a mini-rights issue.

SHARE BUY-BACKS AND SPECIAL DIVIDENDS

An alternative way to return money, held within the company, to the owners is to repurchase issued shares. In 2000 Shell was concerned that the retention of profits was causing the gearing level to become too low. The directors chose to return more cash by way of a buy-back scheme – *see* Exhibit 19.6.

Buy-backs may also be a useful alternative when the company is unsure about the sustainability of a possible increase in the normal cash dividend. A stable policy may be pursued on dividends, then, as and when surplus cash arises, shares are repurchased. This two-track approach avoids sending an over-optimistic signal about future growth through underlying dividend levels.

A second possible approach to returning funds without signalling that all future dividends will be raised abnormally is to pay a special dividend. This is the same as a normal dividend but usually bigger and paid on a one-off basis.

Share repurchases have been permitted in the UK since the 1981 Companies Act came into force, subject to the requirement that the firm gain the permission of share-

Exhibit 19.6

Shell set to launch share buybacks

FT

Changes to tax laws may allow oil group to start multi-billion dollar programme next year

By Robert Corzine

Royal Dutch/Shell, the Anglo-Dutch energy group, yesterday gave its strongest signal yet that it will be allowed to embark on a regular, multiple year, multi-billion dollar share buyback programme as early as 2001.

Mark Moody-Stuart, chairman, said he expected the necessary legislative framework for such a programme to be in place in the Netherlands by January 1, 2001.

Punitive tax laws in the Netherlands have prevented Shell from emulating rivals such as ExxonMobil of the US, in returning significant surplus cash to shareholders.

"I am delighted to say that it now seems likely [that the necessary legal changes] are about to happen," he said.

Lawmakers this month approved legislation that will permit Shell to buy back its shares "without dividend withholding tax from any shareholder". The Dutch Senate is expected to give its final approval to allow for implementation next January.

Regular share buybacks are increasingly seen as a vital competitive tool among the three companies that dominate the international oil industry's "super league" – ExxonMobil, BP Amoco and Shell.

Exxon has long used buybacks to enhance its overall shareholder return, and BP Amoco is expected to launch a multi-billion dollar programme later this year.

The Dutch legislation permits buybacks equivalent to 25 per cent to 80 per cent of a company's annual cash dividend, which in the case of Shell is about $5.6bn to $5.7bn.

The surge in oil prices over the past year, which has boosted Shell's cash flow and sharply reduced capital expenditure as a result of strict new investment controls at the group, should give Shell scope for an extensive buyback programme, although Mr Moody-Stuart said the aim was to implement "a regular, disciplined" scheme.

Shell ended the year with a cash surplus of about $4bn, and gearing of just 18 per cent, a figure that some analysts say could fall to as low as 10 per cent or so this year if oil prices stay at relatively high levels.

Stephen Hodge, group treasurer, said: "We are making profits, generating cash and doing more with less money. We see the dividend as a long-term commitment, so to lob our surplus cash into that would ratchet up the base level. This is a way of managing our balance sheet and equity effectively."

Full-year group profits calculated on a current cost of supplies basis were up 38 per cent to just over $7bn.

Shell also announced that it achieved $2bn in cost savings last year, and said that it was "well on the way towards the new $4bn annual target by 2001".

Source: Robert Corzine, *Financial Times*, 11 February 2000, p. 21. Reprinted with permission.

holders as well as warrant holders, option holders or convertible holders. The rules of the London Stock Exchange (and especially the Takeover Panel) must also be obeyed. These are generally aimed at avoiding the creation of an artificial market in the company's shares.

A special dividend has to be offered to all shareholders. However a share repurchase may not always be open to all shareholders as it can be accomplished in one of three ways:

a purchasing shares in the stock market;

b all shareholders are invited to tender some or all of their shares;

c an arrangement with particular shareholders.

Exhibit 19.7 discusses Woolwich's decision to return cash to shareholders via both a special dividend and a share buy-back.

Exhibit 19.7

Woolwich payout boosts bank shares

FT

Former building society announces special £104m dividend and stock buy-back

By Christopher Brown-Humes

Woolwich yesterday ignited shares in the banking sector when it announced a £104m special dividend and plans to buy back some of its shares later this year.

Woolwich shares surged 6.5 per cent to a record 395¼p. Hopes of payouts from other banks fuelled rises across the sector, led by Alliance & Leicester, up 5.46 per cent, and Bank of Scotland, up 5.18 per cent.

Woolwich plans a special dividend of 6.5p per share on top of a 6.5p final and a 3p interim, taking the total 1997 payout to 16p per share. This is worth £105 to an average small shareholder with 650 shares.

It also plans to ask shareholders for permission to buy back up to 10 per cent of its shares later this year.

Robert Jeens, finance director, said the total value of the special dividend and the share buy-back would be 'between £200m and £300m'.

'We will hand back as much as we can as long as it is tax efficient and provided we can find shares in the market at the right price,' he said.

But he implied that the company would be reluctant to buy back its shares at much more than 400p a share.

'It is a very unusual position for a bank to be rated so highly that a share buy-back might not enhance earnings,' he said.

After the cost of the special dividend, Woolwich estimates it has £671m of surplus capital.

John Stewart, chief executive, struck a cautious note on cash acquisitions in the UK, saying prices were so high they were 'likely to destroy shareholder value'. But he did not rule out moves to expand in continental Europe, and said the company was still open to 'mergers and joint ventures' in the UK.

Source: Christopher Brown-Humes, *Financial Times*, 19 February 1998, p. 19. Reprinted with permission.

A ROUND-UP OF THE ARGUMENTS

There are two questions which are at the core of the dividend policy debate.

- *Question 1* Can shareholder wealth be increased by changing the pattern of dividends over a period of years?
- *Question 2* Is a steady, stable dividend growth rate better than one which varies from year to year depending on the firm's internal need for funds?

The answer to the first question is 'yes'. The accumulated evidence suggests that shareholders for one reason or another value particular patterns of dividends across time. But there is no neat, simple, straightforward formula into which we can plug numbers in order to calculate the best pattern. It depends on numerous factors, many of which are unquantifiable, ranging from the type of clientele shareholder the firm is trying to attract to changes in the taxation system.

Taking the residual theory alone the answer to Question 2 is that the dividend will vary from year to year because it is what is left over after the firm has retained funds for investment in all available projects with positive NPV. Dividends will be larger in years of high cash flow and few investment opportunities, and will be reduced when the need for reinvestment is high relative to internally generated cash flow. However, in practice, shareholders appear to prefer stable, consistent dividend growth rates. Many of them rely on a predictable stream of dividends to meet (or contribute to) their consumption needs. They would find an erratic dividend flow inconvenient. Investors also use dividend policy changes as an indication of a firm's prospects. A reduced dividend could send an incorrect signal and depress share prices.

There are so many factors influencing dividend policy that it is very difficult to imagine that someone could develop a universally applicable model which would allow firms to identify an optimal payout ratio. Exhibit 19.8 shows the range of forces pulling managers towards a high payout rate, and other forces pulling towards a low payout rate. Simultaneously, there are forces encouraging a fluctuating dividend and other factors promoting a stable dividend.

Most of the factors in Exhibit 19.8 have already been explained, but there are two which need a comment here: liquidity and credit standing. Dividends require an outflow of cash from firms; therefore companies with plentiful liquid assets, such as cash and marketable securities, are more able to pay a dividend. Other firms, despite being highly profitable, may have very few liquid assets. For example, a rapidly growing firm may have a large proportion of its funds absorbed by fixed assets, inventory and debtors. Thus some firms may have greater difficulty paying cash dividends than others.

Lenders generally prefer to entrust their money to stable firms rather than ones that are erratic, as this reduces risk. Therefore it could be speculated that a consistent dividend flow helps to raise the credit standing of the firm and lowers the interest rates payable. Creditors suffer from information asymmetry as much as shareholders and may therefore look to this dividend decision for an indication of managerial confidence about the firm's prospects.

Exhibit 19.8 The forces pulling management in the dividend decision

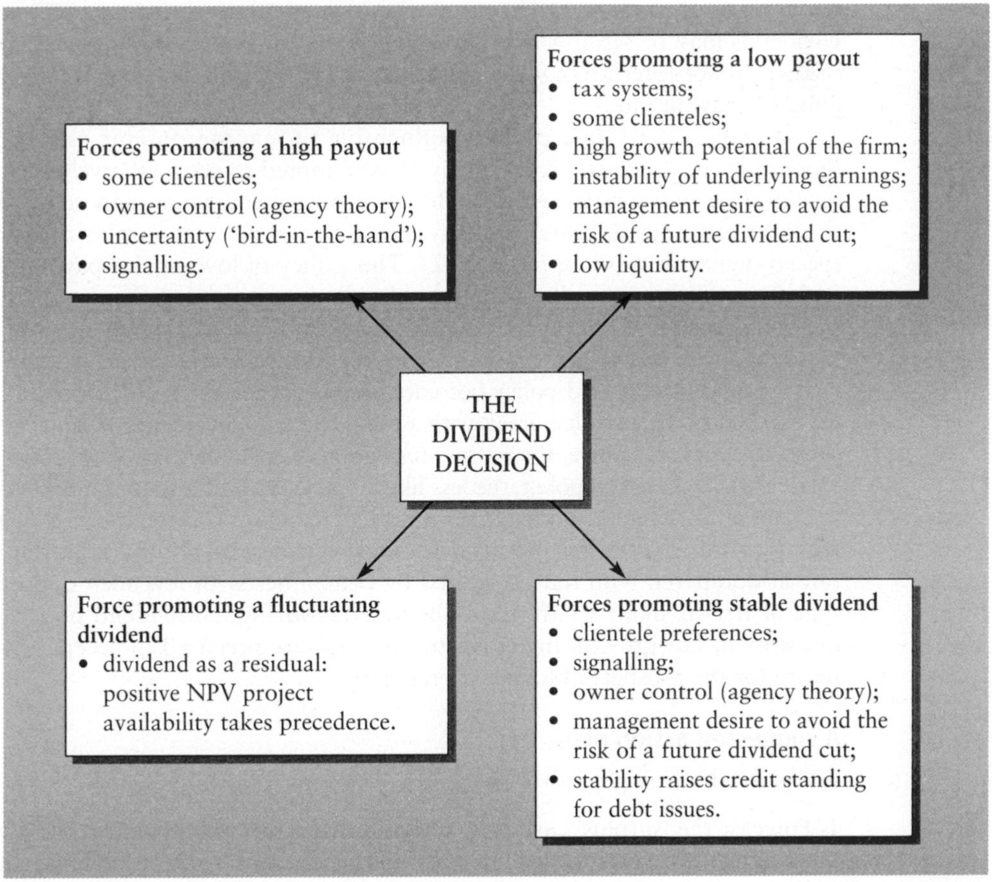

CONCLUDING COMMENTS

This section considers a possible practical dividend policy, taking into account the various arguments presented in the chapter.

Most large firms forecast their financial position for a few years ahead. Their forecasts will include projections for fixed capital expenditure and additional investment in working capital as well as sales, profits, etc. This information, combined with a specified target debt to equity ratio, allows an estimation of medium- to long-term cash flows.

These companies can then determine a dividend level that will leave sufficient retained earnings to meet the financing needs of their investment projects without having to resort to selling shares. (Not only does issuing shares involve costs of issue but, as described in Chapter 18, investors sometimes view share issues as a negative omen.) Thus a *maintainable regular dividend* on a growth path is generally established. This has the virtue of providing some certainty to a particular clientele group and provides a stable background, to avoid sending misleading signals. At the same time the residual theory conclusions have been recognised, and (over, say, a five-year period) dividends are intended to be roughly the same as surplus cash flows after financing all investment in projects with a positive NPV. Agency costs are alleviated to the extent that managers do not, over the long run, store up (and misapply) cash flows greater than those necessary to finance high-return projects.

The future is uncertain and so companies may consider their financial projections under various scenarios. They may focus particularly on the negative possibilities. Dividends may be set at a level low enough that, if poorer trading conditions do occur, the firm is not forced to cut the dividend. Thus a margin for error is introduced by lowering the payout rate.

Companies that are especially vulnerable to macroeconomic vicissitudes, such as those in cyclical industries, are likely to be tempted to set a relatively low maintainable regular dividend so as to avoid the dreaded consequences of a reduced dividend in a particularly bad year. In years of plenty directors can pay out surplus cash in the form of special dividends or share repurchases. This policy of low regular payouts supplemented with irregular bonuses allows shareholders to recognise that the payouts in good years might not be maintained at the extraordinary level. Therefore they do not interpret them as a signal that profits growth will persist at this high level.

If a change in dividend policy becomes necessary then firms are advised to make a gradual adjustment, as a sudden break with a trend can send an erroneous signal about the firms' prospects. And, of course, the more information shareholders are given concerning the reasons behind a change in policy, the less likelihood there is of a serious misinterpretation.

Firms in different circumstances are likely to exhibit different payout ratios. Those with plentiful investment opportunities will, in general, opt for a relatively low dividend rate as compared with that exhibited by companies with few such opportunities. Each type of firm is likely to attract a clientele favouring its dividend policy. For example investors in fast-growth, high-investment firms are prepared to accept low dividends in return for the prospect of higher capital gains.

A suggested action plan

A suggested action plan for a dividend policy is as follows.

1 Forecast the 'surplus' cash flow resulting from the subtraction of the cash needed for investment projects from that generated by the firm's operations over the medium to long term.

2 Pay a maintainable regular dividend based on this forecast. This may be biased on the conservative side to allow for uncertainty about future cash flows.

3 If cash flows are greater than projected for a particular year, keep the maintainable regular dividend fairly constant, but pay a special dividend or initiate a share repurchase programme. If the change in cash flows is permanent, gradually shift the maintainable regular dividend while providing as much information to investors as possible about the reasons for the change in policy.

KEY POINTS AND CONCEPTS

- **Dividend policy** concerns the pattern of dividends over time and the extent which they fluctuate from year to year.
- UK quoted companies generally pay dividends every six months – an **interim** and a **final**. They may only be paid out of accumulated profits.
- **Modigliani and Miller** proposed that, in a perfect world, the policy on dividends is irrelevant to shareholder wealth. Firms are able to **finance investments** from retained earnings or new share sales at the same cost (with no transaction costs). Investors are able to manufacture **'homemade dividends'** by selling a portion of their shareholding.
- In a world with **no external finance dividend policy should be residual.**
- In a world with some transaction costs associated with issuing dividends and obtaining investment finance through the sale of new shares, dividend policy will be **influenced by**, but not exclusively determined by, the **'dividends as a residual approach'** to dividend policy.
- The **clientele effect** is the concept that shareholders are attracted to firms that follow dividend policies consistent with their objectives. The clientele effect encourages stability in dividend policy.
- **Taxation** can influence the investors' preference for the receipt of high dividends or capital gains from their shares.
- **Dividends can act as conveyors of information.** An unexpected change in dividends is regarded as a **signal** of how directors view the future prospects of the firm.
- It has been argued (e.g. by Myron Gordon) that **investors perceive more distant dividends as subject to more risk**, therefore they prefer a higher near-term dividend – a bird in the hand. This **'resolution of uncertainty'** argument has been attacked on the grounds that it implies an extra risk premium on the rate used to discount cash flows.
- The **owner control** argument says that firms are encouraged to distribute a high proportion of earnings so that investors can reduce the **principal–agent problem** and achieve greater goal congruence. Managers have to ask for investment funds; this subjects their plans to scrutiny.
- A **scrip dividend** gives the shareholders an opportunity to receive additional shares in proportion to their existing holding instead of the normal cash dividend.
- A **share repurchase** is when the company buys a proportion of its own shares from investors.
- A **special dividend** is similar to a normal dividend but is usually bigger and paid on a one-off basis.

REFERENCES AND FURTHER READING

Black, F. (1976) 'The dividend puzzle', *Journal of Portfolio Management*, 2, pp. 5–8. A consideration of the issue by a leading writer in the field.

Brealey, R.H. (1986) 'Does dividend policy matter?', in J.M. Stern and D.H. Chew (eds), *The Revolution in Corporate Finance*. Oxford: Basil Blackwell. Argues that dividend policy is irrelevant to wealth except that this is affected by taxes. Also acknowledges the information effect.

Brennan, M. (1971) 'A note on dividend irrelevance and the Gordon valuation model', *Journal of Finance*, December, pp. 1115–21. A technical discussion of the opposing theories of MM and Gordon.

Crossland, M., Dempsey, M. and Moizer, P. (1991) 'The effect of cum- to ex-dividend changes on UK share prices', *Accounting and Business Research*, 22(85), pp. 47–50. 'Our statistical analysis provides evidence of the clientele effect in the UK stock market' – shareholders in the high income, low capital gains tax bracket hold shares in high-growth companies and shareholders with low income and in the high capital gains tax bracket hold shares in low-growth companies.

Damodaran, A. (1999) *Applied Corperate Finance*, New York: Wiley. Chapters 10 and 11 consider dividend policy in a practical exposition.

Elton, E.J. and Gruber, M.J. (1970) 'Marginal stockholder tax rates and the clientele effect', *Review of Economics and Statistics*, February, pp. 68–74. Evidence is found which supports the clientele effect – shareholders in higher tax brackets prefer capital gains to dividend income.

Gordon, M.J. (1959) 'Dividends, earnings and stock prices', *Review of Economics and Statistics*, 41, May, pp. 99–105. Discusses the relationship between dividends, earnings and share prices.

Gordon, M.J. (1963) 'Optimal investment and financing policy', *Journal of Finance*, May. A refutation of the MM dividend irrelevancy theory based on the early resolution of uncertainty idea.

Keane, S. (1974) 'Dividends and the resolution of uncertainty', *Journal of Business Finance and Accountancy*, Autumn. Discusses the bird in the hand theory of dividend policy.

Lewellen, W.G., Stanley, K.L., Lease, R.C. and Schlarbaum, G.G. (1978) 'Some direct evidence of the dividend clientele phenomenon', *Journal of Finance*, December, pp. 1385–99. An investigation of the clientele effect.

Lintner, J. (1956) 'Distribution of income of corporations among dividends, retained earnings and taxes', *American Economic Review*, 46, May, pp. 97–113. An empirical study and theoretical model of dividend policy practices.

Litzenberger, R. and Ramaswamy, K. (1982) 'The effects of dividends on common stock prices: tax effects or information effects?', *Journal of Finance*, May, pp. 429–43. A technical paper which presents 'evidence consistent with the Tax-Clientele CAPM'.

Miller, M.H. and Modigliani, F. (1961) 'Dividend policy, growth and the valuation of shares', *Journal of Business*, 34, October, pp. 411–33. In an ideal economy dividend policy is irrelevant – algebraic proofs.

Pettit, R.R. (1977) 'Taxes, transaction costs and clientele effects of dividends', *Journal of Financial Economics*, December. Discusses the clientele effect.

Porterfield, J.T.S. (1965) *Investment Decisions and Capital Costs*. Upper Saddle River, NJ: Prentice-Hall. Chapter 6 discusses the dividend decision in a readable fashion with an emphasis on theory.

Rozeff, M. (1986) 'How companies set their dividend payout ratios'. Reprinted in J.M. Stern and D.H. Chew (eds), *The Revolution in Corporate Finance*. Oxford: Basil Blackwell. A discussion of the information effect of dividends, the agency problems, industry rules of thumb. Easy-to-follow arguments.

Smith, T. (1995) 'Many happy returns', *Management Today*, May, pp. 56–9. An easy-to-read consideration of dividend policy in practice.

Solomon, E. (1963) *The Theory of Financial Management*. New York: Columbia University Press. Chapter 11 contains an interesting early discussion of the dividend policy debate.

3i (1993) 'Dividend Policy'. Reported in *Bank of England Quarterly Review* (1993), August, p. 367. The most important factor influencing dividend policy is long-term profit growth. Cuts in dividends send adverse signals.

SELF-REVIEW QUESTIONS

1 What are the two fundamental questions in dividend policy?

2 Explain MM's dividend irrelevancy hypothesis.

3 Explain the idea that dividends should be treated as a residual.

4 How might clientele effects influence dividend policy?

5 What is the effect of taxation on dividend payout rates?

6 What is meant by 'asymmetry of information' and 'dividends as signals'?

7 Explain the 'resolution of uncertainty' argument supporting high dividend payout rates. What is the counter-argument?

8 In what ways does agency theory influence the dividend debate?

9 When are share repurchases and special dividends particularly useful?

10 Outline a dividend policy for a typical fast growth and high investment firm.

QUESTIONS AND PROBLEMS

1 (*Examination Level*) 'These days we discuss the dividend level for about an hour a year at board meetings. It changes very little from one year to the next – and it is just as well if you consider what happened to some of the other firms on the stock exchange which reduced their dividend' – director of a large company.

Explain, with reference to dividend theory, how this firm may have settled into this comfortable routine. Describe any problems that might arise with this approach.

2 (*Examination Level*) 'We believe managers and owners should think hard about the circumstances under which earnings should be retained and under which they should be distributed.'

Use the above sentence together with the following one written in the same letter to shareholders by Warren Buffett (1984), plus dividend policy theory, to explain why this is an important issue: 'Nothing in this discussion is intended to argue for dividends that bounce around from quarter to quarter with each wiggle in earnings or in investment opportunities.'

3 Re-examine the article about Wassall's payout policy (see Exhibit 19.2). Discuss the advantages and disadvantages of this approach.

4 (*Examination Level*) Sendine plc has maintained a growth path for dividends per share of 5 per cent per year for the past seven years. This was considered to be the maintainable regular dividend. However the company has developed a new product range which will require major investment in the next 12 months. The amount needed is roughly equivalent to the proposed dividend for this year. The project will not provide a positive net cash flow for three to four years but will give a positive NPV overall.

Required

Consider the argument for and against a dividend cut this year and suggest a course of action.

5* (*Examination Level*) Vale plc has the following profit-after-tax history and dividend-per-share history:

Year		*Profit after tax* £	*Dividend per share*
This year	(t_0)	10,800,000	5.4
Last year	($t-1$)	8,900,000	4.92
2 years ago	($t-2$)	6,300,000	4.48
3 years ago	($t-3$)	5,500,000	4.083
4 years ago	($t-4$)	3,500,000	3.71
5 years ago	($t-5$)	2,600,000	3.38

Two years ago the number of issued ordinary shares was increased by 30 per cent (during the financial year $t-1$). Four years ago a rights issue doubled the number of shares (during the financial year $t-3$). Today there are 100 million ordinary shares in issue with a total market value of £190m. Vale is quoted on the Alternative Investment Market. Vale's directors are committed to shareholder wealth maximisation.

Required

a Explain the following dividend theories and models and relate them to Vale's policy:

i dividends as a residual;

ii signalling;

iii clientele preferences.

b The risk-free return on government securities is currently 6.5 per cent, the risk premium for shares above the risk-free rate of return has been 5 per cent per annum and Vale is in a risk class of shares which suggests that the average risk premium of 5 should be adjusted by a factor of 0.9. The company's profits after tax per share are expected to continue their historic growth path, and dividends will remain at the same proportion of earnings as this year.

Use the dividend valuation model and state whether Vale's shares are a good buying opportunity for a stock market investor.

6* (*Examination Level*) Tesford plc has estimated net cash flows from operations (after interest and taxation) for the next five years as follows:

Year	*Net cash flows* £
1	3,000,000
2	12,000,000
3	5,000,000
4	6,000,000
5	5,000,000

The cash flows have been calculated before the deduction of additional investment in fixed capital and working capital. This amounts to £2m in each of the first two years and £3m for each year thereafter. The firm currently has a cash balance of £500,000 which it intends to maintain to cope with unexpected events. There are 24 million shares in issue. The directors are committed to shareholder wealth maximisation.

Required

a Calculate the annual cash flows available for dividend payments and the dividend per share if the residual dividend policy was strictly adhered to.

b If the directors chose to have a smooth dividend policy based on the maintainable regular dividend what would you suggest the dividends in each year should be? Include in your consideration the possibility of a special dividend or share repurchase.

c Explain why companies tend to follow the policy in **b** rather than **a**.

7 (*Examination Level*) The retailers, Elec Co and Lighting are competitors in the electrical goods market. They are similar firms in many respects: profits per share have been very similar over the past 10 years, and are projected to be the same in the future; they both have (and have had) 50 per cent debt to equity ratio; and they have similar investment needs, now and in the future. However they do differ in their dividend policies. Elec Co pays out 50 per cent of earnings as dividends, whereas Lighting has adopted a stable dividend policy. This is demonstrated in the following table.

Year	*Elec Co*		*Lighting*	
	Earnings per share	*Dividend per share*	*Earnings per share*	*Dividend per share*
× 1	11p	5.5p	11p	5.5p
× 2	16p	8.0p	17p	6.25p
× 3	13p	6.5p	11p	7.11p
× 4	20p	10.0p	21p	8.1p
× 5	10p	5.0p	9p	9.2p
× 6	0	0	0	10.5p
× 7	15p	7.5p	17p	11.9p
× 8	25p	12.5p	24p	13.5p
× 9	30p	15.0p	31p	15.4p
× 10	35p	17.5p	35p	17.5p

The managing director of Elec Co has asked you to conduct a thorough review of dividend policy and to try to explain why it is that Lighting has a market value much greater than Elec Co. (Both companies have, and have had, the same number of shares in issue.)

Write a report detailing the factors that influence dividend policy and recommend a dividend policy for Elec Co based on your arguments.

8 (*Examination Level*) Guff plc, an all-equity firm, has the following earnings per share and dividend history (paid annually).

Year	*Earnings per share*	*Dividend per share*
This year	21p	8p
Last year	18p	7.5p
2 years ago	16p	7p
3 years ago	13p	6.5p
4 years ago	14p	6p

This year's dividend has just been paid and the next is due in one year. Guff has an opportunity to invest in a new product, Stuff, during the next two years. The directors are considering cutting the dividend to 4p for each of the next two years to fund the project. However the dividend in three years can be raised to 10p and will grow by 9 per cent per annum thereafter due to the benefits from the investment. The company is focused on shareholder wealth maximisation and requires a rate of return of 13 per cent for its owners.

Required

a If the directors chose to ignore the investment opportunity and dividends continued to grow at the historical rate what would be the value of one share using the dividend valuation model?

b If the investment was accepted, and therefore dividends were cut for the next two years, what would be the value of one share?

c What are the dangers associated with dividend cuts and how might the firm alleviate them?

ASSIGNMENTS

1 Consider the dividend policy of your firm or one you know well. Write a report detailing the factors contributing to the selection of this particular policy. Make recommendations on the decision-making process, range of influences considered and how a change in policy could be executed.

2 Write a report which relates the dividend frameworks and theories discussed in this chapter to the evidence provided by the following UK companies.

Year	*British Telecom*		*EMI*		*Kingfisher*	
	Earnings	*Dividends*	*Earnings*	*Dividends*	*Earnings*	*Dividends*
	(Pence per share)		*(Pence per share)*		*(Pence per share)*	
1997	32.2	54.85*	26.9	15	21.3	9.5
1998	26.2	19.0	24.9	16	27.5	11.5
1999	45.3	20.4	18.5	16	29.3	13.0
2000	30.9	21.9	19.2	16	30.0	14.5
2001	(27.7)	8.7	22.3	16	26.8	15.5

Note: figures in brackets indicate a loss.
* Includes special dividend of 35p.

CHAPTER NOTES

1 The CPI, consumer price index, is the main US measure of inflation.

2 The complicating effect of capital structure on firms' value is usually eliminated by concentrating on all-equity firms.

3 The following researchers present evidence on the clientele effect: Elton and Gruber (1970), Pettit (1977), Lewellen, Stanley, Lease and Schlarbaum (1978), Litzenberger and Ramaswamy (1982), Crossland, Dempsey and Moizer (1991).

4 Gordon Brown, Chancellor of the Exchequer, Budget Speech, 2 July 1997.

5 Lintner (1956) and 3i (1993) survey, in which 93 per cent of finance directors agreed with the statement that 'dividend policy should follow a long-term trend in earnings'.

Chapter 20

MERGERS

INTRODUCTION

The topic of mergers is one of those areas of finance which attracts interest from the general public as well as finance specialists and managers. There is nothing like an acrimonious bid battle to excite the Press, where one side is portrayed as 'David' fighting the bullying 'Goliath', or where one national champion threatens the pride of another country by taking over a key industry. Each twist and turn of the campaign is reported on radio and television news broadcasts, and, finally, there is a victor and a victim. So many people have so much hanging on the outcome of the conflict that it is not surprising that a great deal of attention is given by local communities, national government, employees and trade unionists. The whole process can become emotional and over-hyped to the point where rational analysis is sometimes pushed to the side.

This chapter examines the reasons for mergers and the ways in which they are financed. Then the merger process itself is described, along with the rules and regulations designed to prevent unfairness. A major question to be addressed is: Who gains from mergers? Is it shareholders, managers, advisers, society, etc.? Evidence is presented which suggests that in less than one half of corporate mergers do the shareholders of the acquiring firm benefit. To help the reader understand the causes of this level of failure the various managerial tasks involved in achieving a successful (that is, a shareholder wealth-enhancing) merger, including the 'soft' science issues, such as attending to the need to enlist the commitment of the newly acquired workforce, are discussed.

Learning objectives

The study of mergers is a subject worthy of a textbook in its own right. This chapter provides an overview of the subject and raises the most important issues. By the end of the chapter the reader will be able to:

- describe the rich array of motives for a merger;
- express the advantages and disadvantages of alternative methods of financing mergers;
- describe the merger process and the main regulatory constraints;
- comment on the question: 'Who benefits from mergers?'
- discuss some of the reasons for merger failure and some of the practices promoting success.

THE MERGER DECISION

Expanding the activities of the firm through acquisition involves significant uncertainties. Very often the acquiring management seriously underestimate the complexities involved in merger and post-merger integration.

Theoretically the acquisition of other companies should be evaluated on essentially the same criteria as any other investment decision, that is, using NPV. As Rappaport states: 'The basic objective of making acquisitions is identical to any other investment associated with a company's overall strategy, namely, to add value'.[1]

In practice, the myriad collection of motivations for expansion through merger, and the diverse range of issues such an action raises, means that mergers are usually extremely difficult to evaluate using discounted cash flow techniques. Consider these two complicating factors.

1 The benefits from mergers are often difficult to quantify. The motivation may be to 'apply superior managerial skills' or to 'obtain unique technical capabilities' or to 'enter a new market'. The fruits of these labours may be real, and directors may judge that the strategic benefits far outweigh the cost, and yet these are difficult to express in numerical form.

2 Acquiring companies often do not know what they are buying. If a firm expands by building a factory here, or buying in machinery there, it knows what it is getting for its money. With a merger information is often sparse – especially if it is a hostile bid in which the target company's managers are opposed to the merger. In Chapter 17 it was stated that most of the value of many firms is in the form of assets which cannot be expressed on a balance sheet, for example the reservoir of experience within the management team, the reputation with suppliers and customers, competitive position and so on. These attributes are extremely difficult to value, especially from a distance, and when there is a reluctance to release information. Even the quantifiable elements of value, such as stock, buildings and free cash flow, can be miscalculated by an 'outsider'.

DEFINITIONS AND SEMANTICS

Throughout this book the word merger will be used to mean the *combining of two business entities under common ownership*.

Many people, for various reasons, differentiate between the terms merger, acquisition and takeover – for example, for accounting and legal purposes. However, most commentators use the three terms interchangeably, and with good reason. It is sometimes very difficult to decide if a particular unification of two companies is more like a merger, in the sense of being the coming together of roughly equal-sized firms on roughly equal terms and in which the shareholders remain as joint owners, or whether the act of union is closer to what some people would say is an acquisition or takeover – a purchase of one firm by another with the associated implication of financial and managerial domination. In reality it is often impossible to classify the relationships within the combined entity as a merger or a takeover. The literature is full of cases of so-called mergers of equals which turn out to be a takeover of managerial control by one set of managers at the expense of the other.[2] Jürgen Schrempp, the chairman of DaimlerChrysler, shocked the financial world with his honesty on this point. At the time of the union of Chrysler with Daimler Benz in 1998 it was described as a merger of equals. However, in 2000

Schrempp said, 'The structure we have now with Chrysler [as a standalone division] was always the structure I wanted. We had to go a roundabout way but it had to be done for psychological reasons. If I had gone and said Chrysler would be a division, everybody on their side would have said: "There is no way we'll do a deal."'[3] Jack Welch, the well-respected industrialist, supports Schrempp: 'This was a buy-out of Chrysler by Daimler. Trying to run it as a merger of equals creates all kinds of problems . . . There is no such thing as a merger of equals . . . There has to be one way forward and clear rules.'[4] This book will use the terms merger, acquisition and takeover interchangeably.

Economic and/or strategic definitions of mergers

Mergers have been classified into three categories: horizontal, vertical and conglomerate.

1 *Horizontal* In a horizontal merger two companies which are engaged in similar lines of activity are combined. Recent examples include the merger of Royal Bank of Scotland with NatWest, Glaxo Wellcome with SmithKline Beecham and BP with Amoco and Arco. One of the motives advanced for horizontal mergers is that economies of scale can be achieved. But not all horizontal mergers demonstrate such gains. Another major motive is the enhancement of market power resulting from the reduction in competition. Horizontal mergers often attract the attention of government competition agencies such as the Office of Fair Trading and the Competition Commission in the UK.

2 *Vertical* Vertical mergers occur when firms from different stages of the production chain amalgamate. So, for instance, if a manufacturer of footwear merges with a retailer of shoes this would be a (downstream) vertical merger. If the manufacturer then bought a leather producer (an upstream vertical merger) there would be an even greater degree of vertical integration. The major players in the oil industry tend to be highly vertically integrated. They have exploration subsidiaries, drilling and production companies, refineries, distribution companies and petrol stations. Vertical integration often has the attraction of increased certainty of supply or market outlet. It also reduces costs of search, contracting, payment collection, advertising, communication and co-ordination of production. An increase in market power may also be a motivation: this is discussed later.

3 *Conglomerate* A conglomerate merger is the combining of two firms which operate in unrelated business areas. For example, in 1996 Tomkins bought The Gates Corporation (a manufacturer of power transmission belts, wellington boots and carpet underlay) for US$1,160m to add to its interests in Hovis Bread, Lyons Cakes, Robertsons Jams, Smith and Wesson Guns and Murray Motor Mowers.

   Some conglomerate mergers are motivated by risk reduction through diversification; some by the opportunity for cost reduction and improved efficiency. Others have more complex driving motivations – many of which will be discussed later.

MERGER STATISTICS

The figures in Exhibit 20.1 show that merger activity has occurred in waves, with peaks in the early 1970s, late 1980s, and late 1990s. The vast majority (over 95 per cent) of these mergers were agreed ('friendly'), rather than opposed by the target (acquired) firm's management ('hostile'). It is only a small, but often noisy, fraction which enter

Exhibit 20.1 UK merger activity, 1970–2000

Year	*Number of UK companies acquired*	*Expenditure (£m)*	*Method of payment*		
			Cash (%)	*Ordinary shares (%)*	*Preference shares and loan stock %*
1970	793	1,122	22	53	25
1971	884	911	31	48	21
1972	1,210	2,532	19	58	23
1973	1,205	1,304	53	36	11
1974	504	508	68	22	9
1975	315	291	59	32	9
1976	353	448	72	27	2
1977	481	824	62	37	1
1978	567	1,140	57	41	2
1979	534	1,656	56	31	13
1980	469	1,475	52	45	3
1981	452	1,144	68	30	3
1982	463	2,206	58	32	10
1983	447	2,343	44	54	2
1984	568	5,474	54	33	13
1985	474	7,090	40	52	8
1986	842	15,370	26	57	17
1987	1,528	16,539	35	60	5
1988	1,499	22,839	70	22	8
1989	1,337	27,250	82	13	5
1990	779	8,329	77	18	5
1991	506	10,434	70	29	1
1992	432	5,939	63	36	1
1993	526	7,063	81	16	3
1994	674	8,269	64	34	2
1995	505	32,600	78	20	2
1996	584	30,457	63	36	1
1997	506	26,829	41	58	1
1998	635	29,525	53	45	2
1999	493	26,166	62	37	1
2000	587	106,916	38	61	1

Source: Office for National Statistics, *Financial Statistics*. © Crown Copyright 2001. Reproduced by the permission of the Controller of HMSO and the Office for National Statistics.

Note: The figures include all industrial and commercial companies quoted or unquoted which reported the merger to the press (small private mergers are excluded).

into a bid battle stage. In the late 1990s shares became a more important means of payment as the stock market boomed. In the first part of the 1980s merger boom (1985–89) ordinary shares tended to be the preferred method of payment. However after the October 1987 stock market decline there was a switch to cash. There was a similar pattern in the early 1970s: when share prices were on the rise (1970–72) shares were used most frequently. Following the collapse in 1973–74 cash became more common.

On a worldwide scale merger activity grew dramatically through the 1990s. In the early part of the decade the value of companies merging rarely totalled more than

$400bn during a year. However, in 1999 and 2000 a staggering $3,300bn and $3,500bn respectively was achieved.

It is not entirely clear why merger activity has boom periods, but some relationships have been observed and ideas advanced: companies go through confident expansion phases organically (that is, by internal growth) and through acquisitions, as the economy prospers, and corporate profitability and liquidity are high; there is also a deregulation effect which allows increased innovation in financial markets, and access to finance, especially debt, permitting even the largest firms to be threatened with takeover; perhaps some managers become over-confident after a few good years, and, impatient with internal growth, decide to grow in big steps through acquisition. The hubris hypothesis and other managerial explanations of mergers are discussed in the next section. The article in Exhibit 20.2 shows the extent of European merger activity over the last few years.

Exhibit 20.2

European M&A

FT

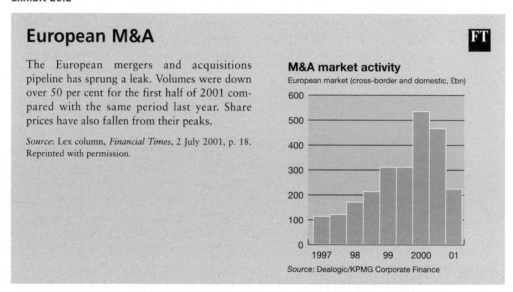

The European mergers and acquisitions pipeline has sprung a leak. Volumes were down over 50 per cent for the first half of 2001 compared with the same period last year. Share prices have also fallen from their peaks.

Source: Lex column, *Financial Times*, 2 July 2001, p. 18. Reprinted with permission.

M&A market activity

European market (cross-border and domestic, £bn)

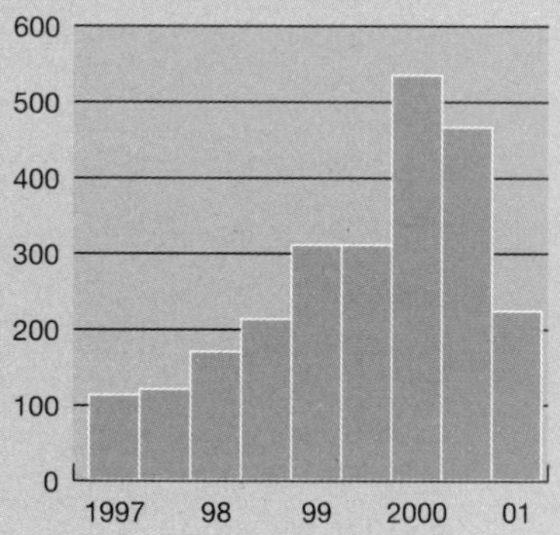

Source: Dealogic/KPMG Corporate Finance

MERGER MOTIVES

Firms decide to merge with other firms for a variety of reasons. Exhibit 20.3 identifies four classes of merger motives. This may not be complete but at least it helps us to focus.

Synergy

In the first column of Exhibit 20.3 we have the classic word associated with merger announcements – synergy. The idea underlying this is that the combined entity will have a value greater than the sum of its parts. The increased value comes about because of boosts to revenue and/or the cost base. Perhaps complementary skills or complementary market outlets enable the combined firms to sell more goods. Sometimes the ability to share sources of supply or production facilities improves the competitive position of the firm. Some of the origins of synergy are listed in the exhibit. Before discussing these we will look at the concept of synergy in more detail.

If two firms, A and B, are to be combined a gain may result from synergistic benefits to provide a value above that of the present value of the two independent cash flows:

Exhibit 20.3 Merger motives

Synergy

The two firms together are worth more than the value of the firms apart.

- $PV_{AB} = PV_A + PV_B + \text{gains}$
- Market power
- Economies of scale
- Internalisation of transactions
- Entry to new markets and industries
- Tax advantages
- Risk diversification.

Bargain buying

Target can be purchased at a price below the present value of the target's future cash flow when in the hands of new management.

- Elimination of inefficient and misguided management
- Under-valued shares: strong form or semi-strong form of stock market inefficiency.

Managerial motives

- Empire building
- Status
- Power
- Remuneration
- Hubris
- Survival: speedy growth strategy to reduce probability of being takeover target
- Free cash flow: management prefer to use free cash flow in acquisitions rather than return it to shareholders.

Third party motives

- Advisers.
- At the insistence of customers or suppliers.

$$PV_{AB} = PV_A + PV_B + \text{gains}$$

where:

PV_A = discounted cash flows of company A;
PV_B = discounted cash flows of company B;
PV_{AB} = discounted cash flows of the merged firm.

Synergy is often expressed in the form 2 + 2 = 5. The above equation for present value simply expresses this intuitive approach in slightly more scientific terms.

Value is created from a merger when the gain is greater than the transaction costs. These usually comprise advisers' fees, underwriters' fees, legal and accounting costs, stock exchange fees, public relations bills and so on. So if we assume that A and B as separate entities have present values of £20m and £10m respectively, the transaction costs total £2m and the value of the merged firms is £40m (£42m before paying transaction costs), then the net (after costs) gain from merger is £10m:

$$£40m = £20m + £10m + \text{gain}$$

But who is going to receive this extra value? The incremental value may be available for the acquirer or the target, or be split between the two. If company A is the acquirer, it might pay a price for B which is equal to the PV of B's cash flows (£10m), in which case all of the gain from the merger will accrue to A. However, this is highly unlikely. Usually an acquiring firm has to pay a price significantly above the pre-bid value of the target company to gain control – this is called the acquisition premium, bid premium or control premium.

If it is assumed that before the bid B was valued correctly on the basis of its expected future cash flows to shareholders then the bid premium represents the transferring of some of the gains to be derived from the created synergy. For example, if A paid £15m for B then B's shareholders receive £5m of the gain. If A has to pay £20m to acquire B then A receives no gain.

In 2000 Royal Bank of Scotland (RBS) paid £20.7bn to take over NatWest. Prior to the bidding period NatWest was valued at £16bn (market capitalisation). RBS expected

Exhibit 20.4

No longer ripping the shirt from M&S's back

FT

There have been a few changes at Brooks Brothers, the most conservative of US clothing store chains. ...

Profits have taken a turn for the better – to the immense relief of Marks and Spencer, Brooks Brothers' British parent, which bought the company for an eye-popping $750m (£493.4m) in 1988.

As M&S now concedes, it paid far too much. Ever since, Brooks Brothers has staggered from one year of poor profitability to the next as M&S sought unsuccessfully to make the best of a bad investment.

This week, however, M&S declared that Brooks Brothers' operating profit had risen by 81 per cent to £10.7m in the year to March. Sales, it said, rose 11 per cent to £286.1m.

The latest figure falls far short of what would be necessary to justify the purchase price. Even so, the trend is in the right direction and it comes at a time when other US retailers are struggling to cope with weak demand and cut-throat competition.

Source: Richard Tomkins, *Financial Times*, 24 May 1996. Reprinted with permission.

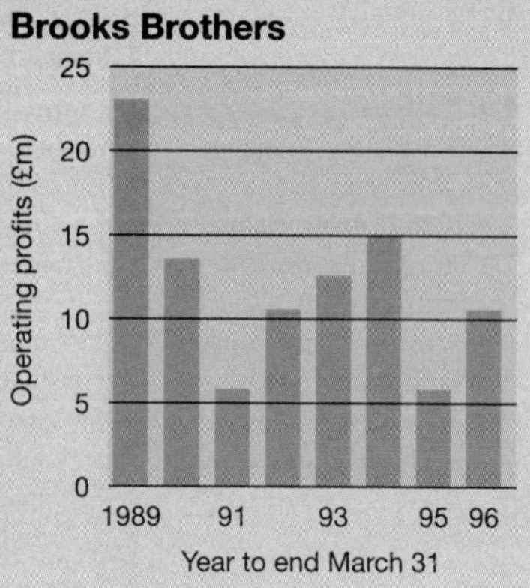

to make annualised revenue gains of £120m – by 2001 it had delivered £147m. It promised that £550m of annualised cost savings would be made – it found £653m of savings. Qualitative benefits were greater than expected. NatWest gained retail and corporate customers, and customer complaints were down by 15 per cent. Even allowing for the 'costs of integration' of £1.6bn RBS is confident that it has generated shareholder value from the deal.

Also, note another possibility known as the 'winner's curse' – the acquirer pays a price higher than the combined present value of the target and the potential gain. The winner's curse is illustrated by Marks & Spencer's admission that it overpaid for Brooks Brothers (*see* Exhibit 20.4).

Market power

One of the most important forces driving mergers is the attempt to increase market power. This is the ability to exercise some control over the price of the product. It can be achieved through either **a** monopoly, oligopoly or dominant producer positions, etc., or **b** collusion.

If a firm has a large share of a market it often has some degree of control over price. It may be able to push up the price of goods sold because customers have few alternative sources of supply. Even if the firm does not control the entire market, a reduction in the number of participating firms to a handful makes collusion easier. Whether openly or not, the firms in a concentrated market may agree amongst themselves to charge customers higher prices and not to undercut each other. The regulatory authorities are watching out for such socially damaging activities and have fined a number of firms for such practices, for example in the cement, steel and chemicals industries.

Market power is a motivator in vertical as well as horizontal mergers. Downstream mergers are often formed in order to ensure a market for the acquirer's product and to shut out competing firms. Upstream mergers often lead to the raising or creating of barriers to entry or are designed to place competitors at a cost disadvantage.

Even conglomerate mergers can enhance market power. For example, a conglomerate may force suppliers to buy products from its different divisions under the threat that it will stop buying from them if they do not comply. It can also support each division in turn as it engages in predatory pricing designed to eliminate competitors. Or it may insist that customers buy products from one division if they want products from another.

According to the European Commission General Electric, in trying to merge with Honeywell, was attempting to put competitors at a disadvantage. In the end the Competition Commissioner blocked the bid, much to the annoyance of GE and US politicians, including George W. Bush – *see* Exhibit 20.5.

Exhibit 20.5

GE to face call for Gecas separation

FT

European Commission sees aircraft leasing arm as possible obstacle to Honeywell deal

By Deborah Hargreaves in Brussels

The European Commission is expected to press General Electric to separate the accounts and management of Gecas, its aircraft leasing arm, as a condition of giving the go-head to its $41bn (£29bn) deal to buy Honeywell.

The Commission is also believed to be looking for some divestment of part of Honeywell's avionics business and its regional jet engines business . . .

Gecas offers aircraft financing, leasing and fleet management. Brussels has been concerned about GE's ability to bundle products when offering equipment to airlines – for example, by offering a cheaper engine if an airline agrees to take Honeywell avionics – and its use of Gecas' market power to kit out airlines with GE products.

The Commission's statement of objections to the deal says: 'Gecas is therefore used by GE to influence the outcome of airlines' airframe purchasing decisions and act as a promoter of GE-powered airframes to the detriment of GE's engine manufacturer competitors and eventually results, through the use of its disproportionate power, in excluding competing engine sales.'

Gecas will specify the use of a GE engine in aircraft it wants buy. Brussels is worried that the leasing arm will do the same for Honeywell's avionics and other aircraft equipment.

Source: Deborah Hargreaves, *Financial Times*, 6 June 2001, p. 23. Reprinted with permission.

Economies of scale

An important contributor to synergy is the ability to exploit economies of scale. Larger size often leads to lower cost per unit of output. Rationalising and consolidating manufacturing capacity at fewer, larger sites can lead to economies of production utilising larger machines. Economies in marketing can arise through the use of common distribution channels or joint advertising. There are also economies in administration, research and development, purchasing and finance.

Even with mergers of the conglomerate type managers claim achievable economies of scale. They identify savings from the sharing of central services such as administrative activities and accounting. Also the development of executives might be better at a large firm with a structured programme of training and access to a wider range of knowledgeable and experienced colleagues. Financial economies, such as being able to raise funds more cheaply in bulk, are also alluded to.

Many businesses possess assets such as buildings, machinery or peoples' skills which are not used to their full limits. For example, banks and building societies own high street sites. In most cases neither the buildings nor the employees are being used as intensively as they could be. Hence we have one of the motivating forces behind bank and building society mergers. Once a merger is completed, a number of branches can be closed, to leave one rather than two in a particular location. Thus the customer flow to the remaining branch will be, say, doubled, with the consequent saving on property and labour costs.

Another synergistic reason for financial service industry mergers is the ability to market successful products developed by one firm to the customers of the other. Also when two medium-size banks or building societies become large, funds borrowed on the capital market are provided at a lower cost per unit of transaction and at lower interest rates.

Case study 20.1 on the oil industry demonstrates the importance of even greater size in an industry that already had giants.

CASE STUDY 20.1

Economies of scale in oil

Around the turn of the millennium there was a great deal of merger activity in the oil industry. Exxon and Mobil merged; as did Chevron and Texaco; Total, Fina and Elf; and B.P., Amoco and Arco, to name a few. The financial markets encouraged the trend, seeing the benefits from economies of scale. Greater size allows the possibility of cutting recurring costs, particularly in overlapping infrastructure. It also means access to cheaper capital. However, the most important advantage it gives is the ability to participate in the difficult game of twenty-first-century exploration and production. The easily accessible oil of the world has long been tapped. Today's oil companies have to search in awkward places like the waters off West Africa and in China. The capital costs are enormous and risks are high. It is only very large companies that can put up the required money and absorb the risk of a series of failed explorations. In addition, bigger oil companies have more political clout, particularly in George W. Bush's Washington, but also in developing country capitals around the world.

Internalisation of transactions

By bringing together two firms at different stages of the production chain an acquirer may achieve more efficient co-ordination of the different levels. The focus here is on the costs of communication and the costs of bargaining. Vertical integration reduces the uncertainty of supply or the prospect of finding an outlet. It also avoids the problems of having to deal with a supplier or customer in a strong bargaining position. Naturally, the savings have to be compared with the extra costs which may be generated because of the loss of competition between suppliers – managers of units may become complacent and inefficient because they are assured of a buyer for their output.

Across Europe the heavy building materials industry is vertically integrated. The manufacturers of cement also own ready-mix concrete divisions and/or aggregates businesses. 'Cement represents the main cost item in the production of ready mix concrete, so there are powerful incentives for ready mix suppliers to secure access to supplies of cement to add to their existing supplies of aggregates.'[5]

Entry to new markets and industries

If a firm has chosen to enter a particular market but lacks the right know-how, the quickest way of establishing itself may be through the purchase of an existing player in that product or geographical market. To grow into the market organically, that is, by developing the required skills and market strength through internal efforts alone, may mean that the firm, for many years, will not have the necessary critical size to become an effective competitor. During the growth period losses may well be incurred. Furthermore, creating a new participant in a market may generate over-supply and excessive competition, producing the danger of a price war and thus eliminating profits. An example of a market-entry type of merger is Nestlé's takeover of Rowntree. As a result Nestlé quickly established a position in the toffee and boiled sweet market and captured an effective distribution operation without creating additional capacity.

Many small firms are acquired by large ones because they possess particular technical skills. The small firm may have a unique product developed through the genius of a small team of enthusiasts, but the team may lack the interest and the skills to produce the product on a large scale, or to market it effectively. The purchaser might be aware that its present range of products are facing a declining market or are rapidly becoming obsolescent. It sees the chance of applying its general managerial skills and experience to a cutting-edge technology through a deal with the technologically literate enthusiasts. Thus the two firms are worth more together than apart because each gains something it does not already have.

The media, electronic and entertainment industries went through a phase of acquisition activity due to the search by small entrepreneurial companies for partnership with an established group (see Exhibit 20.6).

Exhibit 20.6

Media and electronic deals jump

FT

'Digital media, and its delivery over the World Wide Web, is forcing content owners to rethink pricing and delivery strategies and to "own" their end customers,' said Broadview.

'As a result, boardrooms are awash with corporate restructuring as media groups recognise the need for business focus.

'Focus means divesting non-core activities and acquiring or investing in businesses and technologies that are going to be strategic in the future.

'The nimblest media giants are staking out their territory by making strategic, fill-in acquisitions, the brave are investing in new technologies and others seem to be struggling to find "true north",' it said.

According to Broadview, there is no shortage of targets because of the new generation of entrepreneurial media companies eager for the funding and market access that a deal with an established group can bring . . .

Among the deals in the first half, 137 were Internet-related. In particular there was a spate of investments by large media groups in companies such as Yahoo! of the US which operate Web search engines – systems to help people find their way around the World Wide Web.

'Becoming aligned with one or more Web search engines ensures a place at the Internet table,' said Broadview.

Looking ahead, Broadview predicts the global battle over the delivery of digital entertainment services by satellite 'cannot fail to drive M&A activity over the next few years. The opportunity is just too big, and the risk/reward ratio too acute for even the most bullish to consider going alone.'

Source: Paul Taylor, *Financial Times*, 19 August 1996. Reprinted with permission.

Another reason for acquiring a company at the forefront of technology might be to apply the talent, knowledge and techniques to the parent company's existing and future product lines to give them a competitive edge. Consider the Daewoo purchase of Lotus (*see* Exhibit 20.7).

Exhibit 20.7

Daewoo ready to pay premium for Lotus

FT

Daewoo, the Korean industrial group, is poised to pay a substantial premium to acquire Group Lotus, the UK sports car and engineering concern.

Daewoo urgently needs to double its motor vehicle engineering staff to 8,000. It has been determined to outbid other potential investors in the financially pressed UK concern to gain access to the 1,000-strong engineering staff at Lotus, considered among the world's most talented.

Daewoo is keen to expand its design and engineering capabilities to rush into production the much wider vehicle range needed to meet its ambitious target of joining the world's top 10 car makers . . .

Daewoo is expected to pay some \$75m (£48m) to Mr Romano Artioli, the Italian entrepreneur and current owner of Lotus.

Source: John Griffiths, *Financial Times*, 1 October 1996, p. 22. Reprinted with permission.

Tax advantages

In some countries, notably the USA, if a firm makes a loss in a particular year these losses can be used to reduce taxable profit in a future year. More significantly, for this discussion about mergers, not only can past losses be offset against current profits within one firm in one line of business, past losses of an acquired subsidiary can be used to reduce present profits of the parent company and thus lower tax bills. Thus there is an incentive to buy firms which have accumulated tax losses.

In the UK the rules are more strict. The losses incurred by the acquired firm before it becomes part of the group cannot be offset against the profits of another member of the group. The losses can only be set against the future profits of the acquired company. Also that company has to continue operating in the same line of business.

Risk diversification

One of the primary reasons advanced for conglomerate mergers is that the overall income stream of the holding company will be less volatile if the cash flows come from a wide variety of products and markets. At first glance the pooling of unrelated income streams would seem to improve the position of shareholders. They obtain a reduction in risk without a decrease in return.

The problem with this argument is that investors can obtain the same risk reduction in an easier and cheaper way. They could simply buy a range of shares in the independent separately quoted firms. In addition, it is said that conglomerates lack focus – with managerial attention and resources being dissipated.

A justification which is on more solid theoretical grounds runs as follows. A greater stability of earnings will appeal to lenders, thus encouraging lower interest rates. Because of the reduced earnings volatility there is less likelihood of the firm producing negative returns and so it should avoid defaulting on interest or principal payments. The other group that may benefit from diversification is individuals who have most of their income eggs in one basket – that is, the directors and other employees.

Bargain buying

The first column of Exhibit 20.3 deals with the potential gains available through the combining of two firms' trading operations. The second column shows benefits which might be available to an acquiring company which has a management team with superior ability, either at running a target's operations, or at identifying undervalued firms which can be bought at bargain prices.

Inefficient management

If the management of firm X is more efficient than the management of firm Y then a gain could be produced by a merger if X's management is dominant after the unification. This type of merger can result in a rise in the welfare of society generally as well as the welfare of the firms involved. Inefficient management may be able to survive in the short run but eventually the owners will attempt to remove them by, say, dismissing the senior directors and management team through a boardroom coup. Alternatively the shareholders might invite other management teams to make a bid for the firm, or simply accept an offer from another firm which is looking for an outlet for its perceived surplus managerial talent.

A variation on the above theme is where the target firm does have talented management but they are directing their efforts in their own interests and not in the interests of shareholders. In this case the takeover threat can serve as a control mechanism limiting the degree of divergence from shareholder wealth maximisation.

Undervalued shares

Many people believe that stock markets occasionally underestimate the true value of a share. It may well be that the potential target firm is being operated in the most efficient manner possible and productivity could not be raised even if the most able managerial team in the world took over. Such a firm might be valued low by the stock market because the management are not very aware of the importance of a good stock market image. Perhaps they provide little information beyond the statutory minimum and in this way engender suspicion and uncertainty. Investors hate uncertainty and will tend to avoid such a firm. On the other hand, the acquiring firm might be very conscious of its stock market image and put considerable effort into cultivating good relationships with the investment community.

This line of thinking does not automatically reject semi-strong-form efficiency. This requires that share prices fully reflect all publicly available information. In many of these situations the acquiring firm has knowledge which goes beyond that which is available to the general public. It may be intimately acquainted with the product markets, or the technology, of the target firm and so can value the target more accurately than most investors. Or it may simply be that the acquirer puts more resources into information searching than anyone else. Alternatively they may be insiders, using private information, and may buy shares illegally.

Managerial motives

The reasons for merger described in this section are often just as rational as the ones which have gone before, except, this time, the rational objective may not be shareholder wealth maximisation.

One group which seems to do well out of merger activity is the management team of the acquiring firm.[6] When all the dust has settled after a merger they end up controlling a larger enterprise. And, of course, having responsibility for a larger business means that the managers *have* to be paid a lot more money. Not only must they have higher monthly pay to induce them to give of their best, they must also have enhanced pension contributions and myriad perks. Being in charge of a larger business and receiving a higher salary also brings increased status. Some feel more successful and important, and the people they rub shoulders with tend to be in a more influential class.

As if these incentives to grow rapidly through mergers were not enough, some people simply enjoy putting together an empire – creating something grand and imposing gives a sense of achievement and satisfaction. To have control over ever-larger numbers of individuals appeals to basic instincts: some measure their social position and their stature by counting the number of employees under them. Warren Buffett comments, 'The acquisition problem is often compounded by a biological bias: many chief executive officers attain their positions in part because they possess an abundance of animal spirit and ego. If an executive is heavily endowed with these qualities, they won't disappear when he reaches the top.'[7]

Exhibit 20.8

Weaning Simon off an addiction

FT

Colleagues of Mr Maurice Dixson say his hair was already white when he became chief executive of Simon Engineering.

What is surprising is that he has any hair at all, given the difficulties facing the storage, process engineering and mobile platform group.

For Mr Dixson, turning Simon round has been like trying to rehabilitate a drug addict. When he arrived three years ago, he found himself in charge of an acquisition junkie that had spent £124.4m on often unrelated businesses.

To feed that habit, Simon had run up debts of £145.3m and had breached its banking covenants. Sales halved to £386.1m between 1989 and 1993 – the year in which losses reached £160.3m.

'When I arrived this company had about £10m of net worth and almost £150m of debt. It was a great big mess,' recalls Mr Dixson.

Three years into the treatment, Simon has been weaned off acquisitions and made more than a dozen disposals, raising some £40m.

It has abandoned the flawed diversification strategy and refocused on three core divisions: Simon Storage, Carves – mainly process engineering – and Access, making mobile platforms.

Source: Tim Burt, *Financial Times*, 12 November 1996, p. 23. Reprinted with permission.

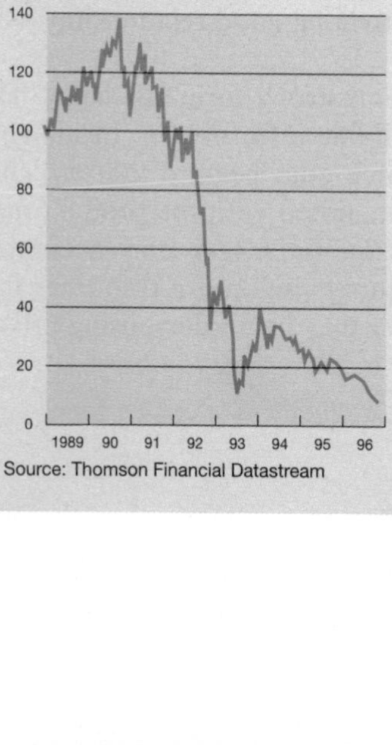

Source: Thomson Financial Datastream

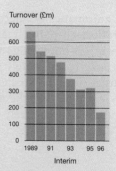

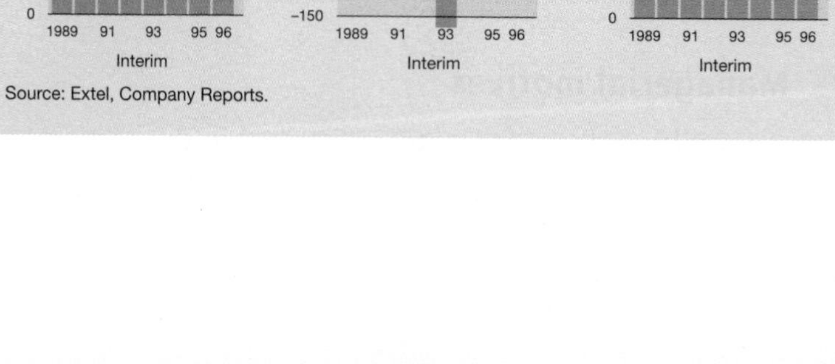

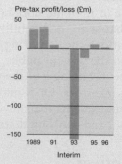

Source: Extel, Company Reports.

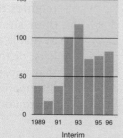

John Kay points out that many managers enjoy the excitement of the merger process itself:

> For the modern manager, only acquisition reproduces the thrill of the chase, the adventures of military strategy. There is the buzz that comes from the late-night meetings in merchant banks, the morning conference calls with advisers to plan your strategy. Nothing else puts your picture and your pronouncements on the front page, nothing else offers so easy a way to expand your empire and emphasise your role.[8]

Exhibit 20.8 reproduces an article about a company which seems to have suffered from a badly executed merger strategy.

These first four managerial motives for merger – empire building, status, power and remuneration – can be powerful forces impelling takeover activity. But, of course, they are rarely expressed openly, and certainly not shouted about during a takeover battle.

Hubris

The fifth reason, hubris, is also very important in explaining merger activity. It may help particularly to explain why mergers tend to occur in greatest numbers when the economy and companies generally have had a few good years of growth, and management are feeling rather pleased with themselves.

Richard Roll in 1986 spelt out his hubris hypothesis for merger activity. Hubris means over-weaning self-confidence, or less kindly, arrogance. Managers commit errors of over-optimism in evaluating merger opportunities due to excessive pride or faith in their own abilities. The suggestion is that some acquirers do not learn from their mistakes and may be convinced that they can see an undervalued firm when others cannot. They may also think that they have the talent, experience and entrepreneurial flair to shake up a business and generate improved profit performance (*see* Exhibit 20.9).

Exhibit 20.9 Warren Buffett on hubris

On toads and princesses

'Many managements apparently were overexposed in impressionable childhood years to the story in which the imprisoned, handsome prince is released from the toad's body by a kiss from the beautiful princess. Consequently, they are certain that the managerial kiss will do wonders for the profitability of Company T(arget). Such optimism is essential. Absent that rosy view, why else should the shareholders of Company A(cquisitor) want to own an interest in T at the 2X takeover cost rather than at the X market price they would pay if they made direct purchases on their own? In other words, investors can always buy toads at the going price for toads. If investors instead bankroll princesses who wish to pay double for the right to kiss a toad, those kisses had better pack some real dynamite. We've observed many kisses, but very few miracles. Nevertheless, many managerial princesses remain serenely confident about the future potency of their kisses – even after their corporate backyards are knee-deep in unresponsive toads.'

Source: Warren Buffett, Berkshire Hathaway, Annual Report, 1981. Reprinted by kind permission of Warren Buffett. © Warren Buffett.

Note that the hubris hypothesis does not require the conscious pursuit of self-interest by managers. They may have worthy intentions but can make mistakes in judgement.

Survival

It has been noticed by both casual observers and empiricists that mergers tend to take place with a large acquirer and a smaller target. Potential target managements may come to believe that the best way to avoid being taken over, and then sacked or dominated, is to grow large themselves, and to do so quickly. Thus, mergers can have a self-reinforcing mechanism or positive feedback loop – the more mergers there are the more vulnerable management feel and the more they are inclined to carry out mergers – *see* Exhibit 20.10.

Exhibit 20.10 The self-reinforcement effect of mergers

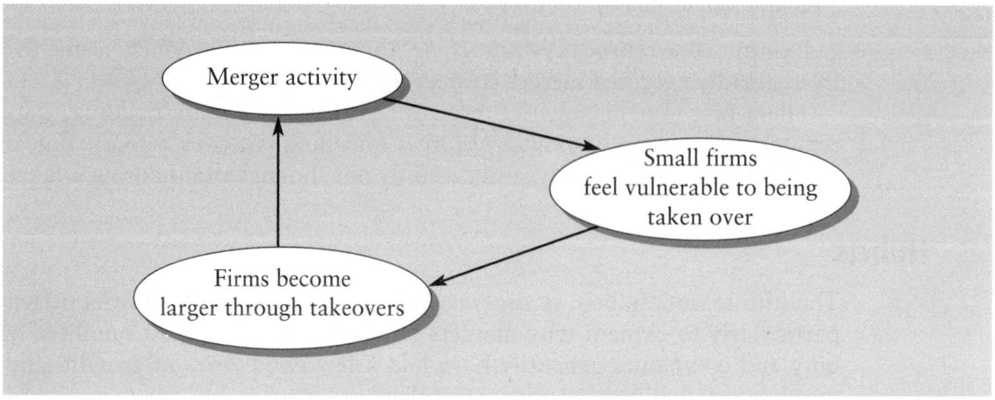

Firms may merge for the survival of the management team and not primarily for the benefit of shareholders.

Free cash flow

Free cash flow is defined here as cash flow in excess of the amount needed to fund all projects that have positive NPVs. In theory firms should retain money within the firm to invest in any project which will produce a return greater than the investors' opportunity cost of capital. Any cash flow surplus to this should be returned to shareholders (*see* Chapter 19).

However Jensen (1986) suggests that managers are not always keen on simply handing back the cash which is under their control. This would reduce their power. Also, if they needed to raise more funds the capital markets will require justification concerning the use of such money. So instead of giving shareholders free cash flow the managers use it to buy other firms. Peter Lynch is more blunt: '[I] believe in the bladder theory of corporate finance, as propounded by Hugh Liedtke of Pennzoil: The more cost that builds up in the treasury, the greater the pressure to piss it away.'[9]

Third party motives

Advisers

There are many highly paid individuals who benefit greatly from merger activity.

Advisers charge fees to the bidding company to advise on such matters as identifying targets, the rules of the takeover game, regulations, monopoly references, finance, bidding tactics, stock market announcements, and so on. Advisers are also appointed to the target firms.

Other groups with a keen eye on the merger market include accountants and lawyers. Exhibit 20.11 gives some impression of the level of fees paid.

Exhibit 20.11 Advisers don't come cheap

A lucrative business for some

The amount of money spent on advisers during merger battles is truly astonishing. In 2000 Klaus Esser, the chairman of Mannesmann, felt compelled to put an upper limit on the cost of advisers assisting the company trying to fend off a bid from Vodafone. What would you regard as a reasonable limit? £10m? or maybe £15m at a push? Surely that would buy a lot of merchant bankers', lawyers', and PR advisers' time? Well, Esser set the limit at €200m (£140m). Mannesmann employed four investment banks, four legal firms and a host of other consultants. The bidder spent even more – it was reckoned that the cost of the bid (including the transaction costs of setting up a joint venture with Bell Atlantic) amounted to £400m. Admittedly some of these costs are related to raising funds, but even so we are looking at handsome take-home pay for advisers.

Royal Bank of Scotland incurred £93m of advisory fees in bidding for NatWest. Bank of Scotland bid for NatWest at the same time. Even though it failed it spent £56m on advisory fees. In 2001 Bank of Scotland eventually found a partner in Halifax. The investment banks charged £40m to assist the marriage – and this was despite the fact that it was an agreed merger. The total cost of the deal was £76m, including financial advice, printing, postage and legal fees. This means that Barclays got a 'bargain' from its advisers: for its 2000 friendly merger with Woolwich the total transaction costs were a mere £30.5m, of which £21m went to advisers.

There is also the Press, ranging from tabloids to specialist publications. Even a cursory examination of them gives the distinct impression that they tend to have a statistical bias of articles which emphasise the positive aspects of mergers. It is difficult to find negative articles, especially at the time of a takeover. They like the excitement of the merger event and rarely follow up with a considered assessment of the outcome. Also the Press reports generally portray acquirers as dynamic, forward-looking and entrepreneurial.

It seems reasonable to suppose that professionals engaged in the merger market might try to encourage or cajole firms to contemplate a merger and thus generate turnover in the market. Some provide reports on potential targets to try and tempt prospective clients into becoming acquirers.

Of course, the author would never suggest that such esteemed and dignified organisations would ever stoop to promote mergers for the sake of increasing fee levels alone. You may think that, but I could not possibly comment.

Suppliers and customers

In 1999 British Steel and Hoogovens merged to form Corus. One of the key drivers of the merger was the forecast that the number of carmakers will continue to decline, meaning fewer buyers insisting steel makers should supply car plants anywhere in the world. A similar logic applied to the mergers of Bosch with American Allied Signal and Lucas with Varity in the late 1990s. There was pressure from the customers – the car producers. They were intent on reducing the number of car-parts suppliers and to put more and more responsibility on the few remaining suppliers. Instead of buying in small mechanical parts from dozens of suppliers and assembling them themselves into, say, a braking system, the assemblers wanted to buy the complete unit. To provide a high level of service Bosch, which is skilled in electronics, needed to team up with Allied Signal for its hydraulics expertise. Similarly Lucas, which specialises in mechanical aspects of braking, needed Varity's electronic know-how. Ford announced that it was intent on reducing its 1,600 suppliers to about 200 and is 'even acting as marriage broker to encourage smaller suppliers to hitch-up with bigger, first-tier suppliers'.[10] These suppliers would then be world players with the requisite financial, technical and managerial muscle.

An example of suppliers promoting mergers is at the other end of the car production chain. Motor dealers in the UK in the late 1990s were sent a clear message from the manufacturers that a higher degree of professionalism and service back-up is required. This prompted a flurry of merger activity as the franchisees sought to meet the new standards.

Exhibit 20.3 provided a long list of potential merger motives. This list is by no means complete. Examining the reasons for merger is far from straightforward. There is a great deal of complexity, and in any one takeover, perhaps half a dozen or more of the motives discussed are at play.

FINANCING MERGERS

Exhibit 20.1 showed the relative importance of alternative methods of paying for the purchase of shares in another company over three decades. The relative popularity of each method has varied considerably over the years but in most years cash is the most attractive option, followed by shares, and finally the third category, comprising mostly debentures, loan stocks, convertibles and preference shares.

The figures given in the table in Exhibit 20.1 tend to give a slightly distorted view of the financial behaviour of acquiring firms. In many cases where cash is offered to the target shareholders the acquirer does not borrow that cash or use cash reserves. Rather, it raises fresh funds through a rights issue of shares before the takeover bid.

The table may also be misleading in the sense that a substantial proportion of mergers do not fall neatly into the payment categories. Many are mixed bids, providing shareholders of the target firms with a variety of financial securities or offering them a choice in the consideration they wish to receive, for example cash or shares, shares or loan stock. This is designed to appeal to the widest range of potential sellers.

Cash

One of the advantages of using cash for payment is that the acquirer's shareholders retain the same level of control over their company. That is, new shareholders from the target have not suddenly taken possession of a proportion of the acquiring firm's voting rights, as they would if the target shareholders were offered shares in the acquirer. Sometimes it is very important to shareholders that they maintain control over a company by owning a certain proportion of the firm's shares. Someone who has a 50.1 per cent stake may resist attempts to dilute that holding to 25 per cent even though the company may more than double in size.

The second major advantage of using cash is that its simplicity and preciseness give a greater chance of success. The alternative methods carry with them some uncertainty about their true worth. Cash has an obvious value and is therefore preferred by vendors, especially when markets are volatile.

From the point of view of the target's shareholders, cash has the advantage – in addition to being more certain in its value – that it also allows the recipients to spread their investments through the purchase of a wide-ranging portfolio. The receipt of shares or other securities means that the target shareholder either keeps the investment or, if diversification is required, has to incur transaction costs associated with selling the shares.

A disadvantage of cash to the target shareholders is that they may be liable for capital gains tax. This is payable when a gain is 'realised'. If the target shareholders receive cash on shares which have risen in value they may pay tax at their marginal rate: in the UK if they are 22 per cent tax payers on the last pound earned they will pay 22 per cent on the gain; if they are 40 per cent tax payers they pay 40 per cent on the gain (although the amount payable can be reduced by holding shares for a long period). If, on the other hand, the target shareholders receive shares in the acquiring firm then their investment gain is not regarded as being realised and therefore no capital gains tax is payable at that time. The tax payment will be deferred until the time of the sale of the new shares – assuming an overall capital gain is made.

Shares

There are two main advantages to target shareholders of receiving shares in the acquirer rather than cash. First, capital gains tax can be postponed because the investment gain is not realised. Second, they maintain an interest in the combined entity. If the merger offers genuine benefits the target shareholders may wish to own part of the combined entity.

To the acquirer, an advantage of offering shares is that there is no immediate outflow of cash. In the short run this form of payment puts less pressure on cash flow. However the firm may consider the effect on the capital structure of the firm and the dilution of existing shareholders' positions – *see* Exhibit 20.12.

Exhibit 20.12

Vodafone's winning formula is now seen as a recipe for producing wrong numbers

FT

£113bn takeover was once hailed as a smart move. Not any more, says **Dan Roberts**

The end of telecommunications investment bubble has put many of last year's takeovers and mergers under the spotlight.

Now attention is turning towards the biggest of them all – Vodafone's £113bn takeover of Mannesmann.

It had looked smart compared with deals struck by rivals such as British Telecommunications because it used highly-rated shares as currency rather than saddling Vodafone with unsustainable debt as a result of paying cash.

Assembling the world's biggest mobile phone company to provide mobile internet access seemed a winning formula.

But renewed scepticism about the growth potential of mobile internet services has led investors to question whether Mannesmann, and Vodafone's string of other acquisitions over the last 18 months, were worth the fourfold dilution of existing shareholders' holdings.

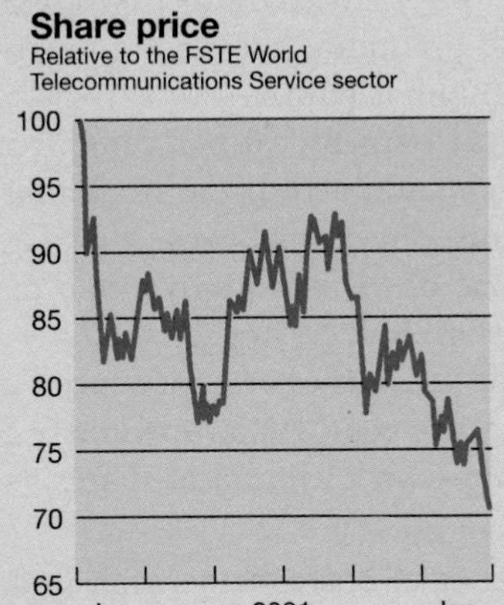

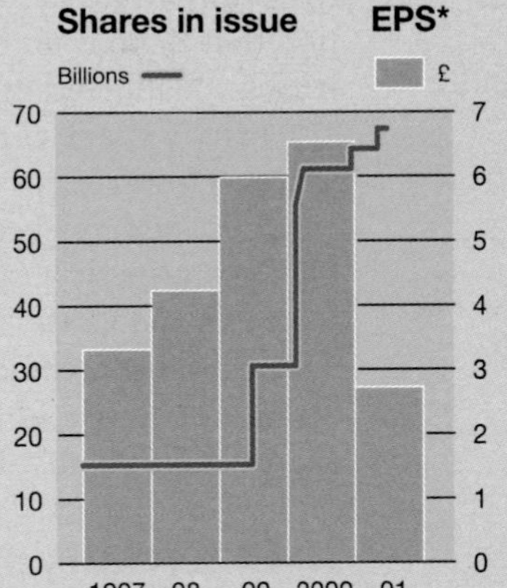

Vodafone shares have fallen 18 per cent since it produced its annual results on May 29, underperforming the sector as analysts have reduced forecasts. Its market capitalisation this week fell below £100bn – at the peak it was £270bn – with the shares at their lowest since October 1998.

Some of the pricing pressure reflects a share overhang, with recipients of Vodafone paper cashing in.

Source: Dan Roberts, *Financial Times*, 28 June 2001, p. 23. Reprinted with permission. Graphs: © Thomson Financial Datastream.

A second reason for using shares as the consideration is that the **price–earnings ratio (per) game** can be played. Through this companies can increase their earnings per share (eps) by acquiring firms with lower PERs than their own. The share price can rise (under certain conditions) despite there being no economic value created from the merger.

Imagine two firms, Crafty plc and Sloth plc. Both earned £1m last year and had the same number of shares. Earnings per share on an historic basis are therefore identical. The difference between the two companies is the stock market's perception of earnings growth. Because Crafty is judged to be a dynamic go-ahead sort of firm with management determined to improve earnings per share by large percentages in future years it is valued at a high PER of 20.

Sloth, on the other hand, is not seen by investors as a fast-moving firm. It is considered to be rather sleepy. The market multiplies last year's earnings per share by only a factor of 10 to determine the share price – *see* Exhibit 20.13.

Exhibit 20.13 Illustration of the price to earnings ratio game – Crafty and Sloth

	Crafty	*Sloth*
Current earnings	£1m	£1m
Number of shares	10m	10m
Earnings per share	10p	10p
Price to earnings ratio	20	10
Share price	£2	£1

Because Crafty's shares sell at a price exactly double that of Sloth it would be possible for Crafty to exchange one of its shares for two of Sloth's. (This is based on the assumption that there is no bid premium, but the argument that follows works just as well even if a reasonable bid premium is paid.)

Crafty's share capital rises by 50 per cent, from ten million shares to 15 million shares. However eps have doubled. If the stock market still puts a high PER on Crafty's earnings, perhaps because investors believe that Crafty will liven up Sloth and produce high eps growth because of their more dynamic management, then the value of Crafty increases and Crafty's shareholders are satisfied.

Each old shareholder in Crafty has experienced an increase in earnings per share and a share price rise of 33 per cent. Also, previously Sloth's shareholders owned £10m of shares in Sloth; now they own £13.33m of shares. (*see* Exhibit 20.14).

Exhibit 20.14 Crafty after an all-share merger with Sloth

	Crafty
Earnings	£2m
Number of shares	15m
Earnings per share	13.33p
Price to earnings ratio	20
Share price	267p

This all seems rational and good, but shareholders are basing their valuations on the assumption that managers will deliver on their promise of higher earnings growth through operational efficiencies, etc. Managers of companies with high PER may see an easier way of increasing eps and boosting share price. Imagine you are managing a company which enjoys a high PER. Investors in your firm are expecting you to produce high earnings growth. You could try to achieve this through real entrepreneurial and/or managerial excellence, for example by product improvement, achieving economies of scale, increased operating efficiency, etc. Alternatively you could buy firms with low PERs and not bother to change operational efficiency. In the long run you know that your company will produce lower earnings because you are not adding any value to the firms that you acquire, you are probably paying an excessive bid premium to buy the present earnings and you probably have little expertise in the new areas of activity.

However, in the short run, eps can increase dramatically. The problem with this strategy is that in order to keep the earnings on a rising trend you must continue to keep fooling investors. You have to keep expanding at the same rate to receive regular boosts. One day expansion will stop; it will be revealed that the underlying economics of the firms bought have not improved (they may even have worsened as a result of neglect), and the share price will fall rapidly. Here is another reason to avoid placing too much emphasis on short-term eps figures. The Americans call this the bootstrap game. It can be very lucrative for some managers who play it skilfully. However there can be many losers – society, shareholders, employees.

There are some significant dangers in paying shares for an aquisition, as Buffett makes clear in Exhibit 20.15.

Exhibit 20.15

Wealth for shareholders from mergers: the view of Warren Buffett

Our share issuances follow a simple basic rule: we will not issue shares unless we receive as much intrinsic business value as we give. Such a policy might seem axiomatic. Why, you might ask, would anyone issue dollar bills in exchange for fifty-cent pieces? Unfortunately, many corporate managers have been willing to do just that.

The first choice of these managers in making acquisitions may be to use cash or debt. But frequently the CEO's cravings outpace cash and credit resources (certainly mine always have). Frequently, also, these cravings occur when his own stock [shares] is selling far below intrinsic business value. This state of affairs produces a moment of truth. At that point, as Yogi Berra has said, 'You can observe a lot just by watching.' For shareholders then will find which objective the management truly prefers – expansion of domain or maintenance of owners' wealth.

The need to choose between these objectives occurs for some simple reasons. Companies often sell in the stock market below their intrinsic business value. But when a company wishes to sell out completely, in a negotiated transaction, it inevitably wants to – and usually can – receive full business value in whatever kind of currency the value is to be delivered. If cash is to be used in payment, the seller's calculation of value received couldn't be easier. If stock [shares] of the buyer is to be currency, the seller's calculation is still relatively easy: just figure the market value in cash of what is to be received in stock.

Meanwhile, the buyer wishing to use his own stock as currency for the purchase has no problems if the stock is selling in the market at full intrinsic value,

But suppose it is selling at only half intrinsic value. In that case, the buyer is faced with the unhappy prospect of using a substantially undervalued currency to make its purchase.

Ironically, were the buyer to instead be a seller of its entire business, it too could negotiate for, and probably get, full intrinsic business value. But when the buyer makes a partial sale of itself – *and that is what the issuance of shares to make an acquisition amounts to* – it can customarily get no higher value set

▶

Exhibit 20.15 continued

on its shares than the market chooses to grant it.

The acquirer who nevertheless barges ahead ends up using an undervalued (market value) currency to pay for a fully valued (negotiated value) property. In effect, the acquirer must give up $2 of value to receive $1 of value. Under such circumstances, a marvelous business purchased at a fair sales price becomes a terrible buy. For gold valued as gold cannot be purchased intelligently through the utilization of gold – or even silver – valued as lead.

If, however, the thirst for size and action is strong enough, the acquirer's manager will find ample rationalizations for such a value-destroying issuance of stock. Friendly investment bankers will reassure him as to the soundness of his actions. (Don't ask the barber whether you need a haircut.)

A few favorite rationalizations employed by stock-issuing managements follow:

(a) 'The company we're buying is going to be worth a lot more in the future.' (Presumably so is the interest in the old business that is being traded away; future prospects are implicit in the business valuation process. If 2X is issued for X, the imbalance still exists when both parts double in business value.)

(b) 'We have to grow.' (Who, it might be asked, is the 'We'? For present shareholders, the reality is that all existing businesses shrink when shares are issued. Were Berkshire to issue shares tomorrow for an acquisition, Berkshire would own everything that it now owns plus the new business, but *your* interest in such hard-to-match businesses as See's Candy Shops, National Indemnity, etc. would automatically be reduced. If (1) your family owns a 120-acre farm and (2) you invite a neighbor with 60 acres of comparable land to merge his farm into an equal partnership – with you to be managing partner, then (3) your managerial domain will have grown to 180 acres but you will have permanently shrunk by 25% your family's ownership interest in both acreage and crops. Managers who want to expand their domain at the expense of owners might better consider a career in government.) . . .

There are three ways to avoid destruction of value for old owners when shares are issued for acquisitions. One is to have a true business-value-for-business-value merger, . . . Such a merger attempts to be fair to shareholders of *both* parties, with each receiving just as much as it gives in terms of intrinsic business value . . . It's not that acquirers wish to avoid such deals, it's just that they are very hard to do . . .

The second route presents itself when the acquirer's stock sells at or above its intrinsic business value. In that situation, the use of stock as currency actually may enhance the wealth of the acquiring company's owners . . .

The third solution is for the acquirer to go ahead with the acquisition, but then subsequently repurchase a quantity of shares equal to the number issued in the merger. In this manner, what originally was a stock-for-stock merger can be converted, effectively, into a cash-for-stock acquisition. Repurchases of this kind are damage-repair moves. Regular readers will correctly guess that we much prefer repurchases that directly enhance the wealth of owners instead of repurchases that merely repair previous damage. Scoring touchdowns is more exhilarating than recovering one's fumbles.

The language utilized in mergers tends to confuse the issues and encourage irrational actions by managers. For example, 'dilution' is usually carefully calculated on a pro forma basis for both book value and current earnings per share. Particular emphasis is given to the latter item. When that calculation is negative (dilutive) from the acquiring company's standpoint, a justifying explanation will be made (internally, if not elsewhere) that the lines will cross favorably at some point in the future. (While deals often fail in practice, they never fail in projections – if the CEO is visibly panting over a prospective acquisition, subordinates and consultants will supply the requisite projections to rationalize any price.) Should the calculation produce numbers that are immediately positive – that is, anti-dilutive – for the acquirer, no comment is thought to be necessary.

The attention given this form of dilution is overdone: current earnings per share (or even earnings per share of the next few years) are an important variable in most business valuations, but far from all-powerful.

There have been plenty of mergers, non-dilutive in this limited sense, that were instantly value-destroying for the acquirer. And some mergers that have diluted current and near-term earnings per share have in fact been value-enhancing. What really counts is whether a merger is dilutive or anti-dilutive in terms of intrinsic business value (a judgment involving consideration of many variables). We believe calculation of dilution from this viewpoint to be all-important (and too seldom made).

A second language problem relates to the equation of exchange. If Company A announces that it will issue shares to merge with Company B, the process is customarily described as 'Company A to Acquire Company B', or 'B Sells to A'. Clearer thinking about the matter would result if a more, awkward but more accurate description were used: 'Part of A sold to

Exhibit 20.15 continued

acquire B' or 'Owners of B to receive part of A in exchange for their properties'. In a trade, what you are giving is just as important as what you are getting . . .

Managers and directors might sharpen their thinking by asking themselves if they would sell 100% of their business on the same basis they are being asked to sell part of it. And if it isn't smart to sell all on such a basis, they should ask themselves why it is smart to sell a portion. A cumulation of small managerial stupidities will produce a major stupidity – not a major triumph. (Las Vegas has been built upon the wealth transfers that occur when people engage in seemingly-small disadvantageous capital transactions.) . . .

Finally, a word should be said about the 'double whammy' effect upon owners of the acquiring company when value-diluting stock issuances occur. Under such circumstances, the first blow is the loss of intrinsic business value that occurs through the merger itself. The second is the downward revision in market valuation that, quite rationally, is given to that now-diluted business value. For current and prospective owners understandably will not pay as much for assets lodged in the hands of a management that has a record of wealth-destruction through unintelligent share issuances as they will pay for assets entrusted to a management with precisely equal operating talents, but a known distaste for anti-owner actions. Once management shows itself insensitive to the interests of owners, shareholders will suffer a long time from the price/value ratio afforded their stock (relative to other stocks), no matter what assurances management gives that the value-diluting action taken was a one-of-a-kind event.

Source: Warren Buffett's Letter to Shareholders in the *Berkshire Hathaway Annual Report 1982*. Reprinted with permission. © Warren Buffett.

Other types of finance

Alternative forms of consideration including debentures, loan stock, convertibles and preference shares are unpopular, largely because of the difficulty of establishing a rate of return on these securities which will be attractive to target shareholders. Also, these securities often lack marketability and voting rights over the newly merged company.

THE MERGER PROCESS

The regulatory bodies

The City Code on Takeovers and Mergers provides the main governing rules for companies engaged in merger activity. The actions and responsibilities of quoted and unlisted public companies have been laid down over a period of more than 30 years. The Code has been developed in a self-regulatory fashion by City institutions, notably the London Stock Exchange, the Bank of England, the investment institutions, companies, banks, self-regulatory organisations (SROs) and the accounting profession. It is administered on a day-to-day basis by the Takeover Panel Executive.

Statutory law is relatively unimportant in the regulation of mergers; its main contribution is to require that directors carry out their duty without prejudice in a fiduciary manner. That is, that they show trustworthy and faithful behaviour for the benefit of shareholders equally.

The self-regulatory non-statutory approach is considered superior because it can provide a quick response in merger situations and be capable of regular adaptation to changed circumstances. There are frequent occurrences where companies try to bend or circumvent the rules and it is useful to have a system of regulation which is continually reviewed and updated as new loopholes are discovered and exploited. Exhibit 20.16 gives some indication of the way in which the Takeover Panel responds to the changing

Exhibit 20.16

Flexibility is takeover body's key to escaping EU hangman

FT

A review of the 'creeper' rule may stave off a threat from Brussels, says Jane Martinson

Plans by the Takeover Panel, the UK's acquisitions watchdog, to review the 'creeping' provision of its rulebook come at the same time as the threat of encroachment from the European Commission.

Flexibility and speedy answers to members' concerns are key weapons in the panel's fight against further legislation and government intervention.

Action on the creeper provision – which allows shareholders slowly to gain control of a company without launching a bid would follow a relative flurry of activity from a body keen to demonstrate the adaptability of its system of voluntary agreement.

Few in the City support more legislation or much change to the 'regulation by club rules' that underpins the Takeover Panel, a self-regulatory organisation staffed largely by secondees from City firms.

But the panel's recent decision to modernise its rules follows criticism that it was not doing enough to ensure fair play.

'If the panel does not show itself to be flexible it's putting its head in the noose of European regulation,' said one institutional investor . . .

The decision of Alistair Defriez, the body's director-general, to raise the creeper provision at the next panel meeting comes less than a month after the High Court rejected an unprecedented legal action based on it. Minority shareholders in Astec, the electronic power supply group, went to the High Court after Emerson, the US group, increased steadily its stake in Astec to 51 per cent by using the creeper provision . . .

This decision, to be put to the 18-strong panel in July, has pleased several institutional investors . . .

Mr Defriez is adamant that extra legislation should be avoided. 'The great thing about the code is that it isn't legislation carved in stone which nobody can change for 20 years. If we believe it [the panel] isn't working to the highest standards we change it,' he said. He added that a simple statement is enough to signal a change in the code.

Action using legislation, in contrast, 'could keep a court case going for years'.

Source: Jane Martinson, *Financial Times*, 29 May 1998, p. 13. Reprinted with permission.

types of unfairness by changing the rules. Statutory law would not have the same degree of flexibility. (Note that 'creeping' means achieving control of a company by buying up to 1 per cent per year even though over 30 per cent of the shares are already held and a formal bid has not been made.)

The Code may not have the force of law but the Panel do have some powerful sanctions. These range from public reprimands to the shunning of Code defiers by the regulated City institutions – the Financial Services Authority requires that no regulated firm (such as a bank, a broker or an adviser) should act for client firms that seriously break the Panel's rules.

The fundamental objective of the Takeover Panel regulation is to ensure fair and equal treatment for all shareholders. The main areas of concern are:

- shareholders being treated differently, for example large shareholders getting a special deal;
- insider dealing (control over this is assisted by statutory rules);
- target management action which is contrary to its shareholders' best interests; for example, the advice to accept or reject a bid must be in the shareholders' best interest, not that of the management;
- lack of adequate and timely information released to shareholders;
- artificial manipulation of share prices; for example an acquirer offering shares cannot make the offer more attractive by getting friends to push up its share price;
- the bid process dragging on and thus distracting management from their proper tasks.

The Office of Fair Trading (OFT) also takes a keen interest in mergers to ensure that mergers do not operate against the public interest – this usually means the constraining of competition. An OFT initial screening may or may not be followed by a Competition Commission investigation. This may take several months to complete, during which time the merger bid is put on hold. More recently another hurdle has been put in the path of large mergers, with intra-European Union mergers being considered by the European Commission in Brussels. This is becoming increasingly influential: in 2000 it investigated 345 mergers.

Pre-bid

Exhibit 20.17 shows the main stages of a merger. The acquiring firm usually employs advisers to help make a takeover bid. Most firms carry out mergers infrequently and so have little expertise in-house. The identification of suitable targets may be one of the first tasks of the advisers. Once these are identified there would be a period of appraising the target. The strategic fit would be considered and there would be a detailed analysis of what would be purchased. The product markets and types of customers could be investigated and there would be a financial analysis showing sales, profit and rates of return history. The assets and liabilities would be assessed and non-balance sheet assets such as employees' abilities would be considered.

If the appraisal stage is satisfactory the firm may approach the target. Because it is often cheaper to acquire a firm with the agreement of the target management, and because the managers and employees have to work together after the merger, in the majority of cases discussions take place which are designed to produce a set of proposals acceptable to both groups of shareholders and managers.

During the negotiation phase the price and form of payment have to be decided upon. In most cases the acquirer has to offer a bid premium. This tends to be in the range of 20 per cent to 100 per cent of the pre-bid price. The average is about 30–50 per cent. The timing of payment is also considered. For example, some mergers involve 'earn-outs' in which the selling shareholders (usually the same individuals as the directors) receive payment over a period of time dependent on the level of post-merger profits. The issue of how the newly merged entity will be managed will also be discussed – who will be chief executive? Which managers will take particular positions? Also the pension rights of the target firm's employees and ex-employees have to be considered, as does the issue of redundancy, especially the removal of directors – what pay-offs are to be made available?

If agreement is reached then the acquirer formally communicates the offer to the target's board and shareholders. This will be followed by a recommendation from the target's board to its shareholders to accept the offer.

If, however, agreement cannot be reached and the acquirer still wishes to proceed the interesting situation of a hostile bid battle is created. One of the first stages might be a 'dawn raid'. This is where the acquirer acts with such speed in buying the shares of the target company that the raider achieves the objective of obtaining a substantial stake in the target before the target's management have time to react. The acquirer usually offers investors and marketmakers a price which is significantly higher than the closing price on the previous day. This high price is only offered to those close to the market and able to act quickly and is therefore contrary to the spirit of the Takeover Panel's rules, because not all shareholders can participate. It breaks the rules in another way: the sellers in a 'dawn raid' are not aware of all relevant information, in this case that a substantial stake is being accumulated. The Takeover Panel insists that the purchase of 10 per cent or more of the target shares in a period of seven days is not permitted if this

Exhibit 20.17 The merger process

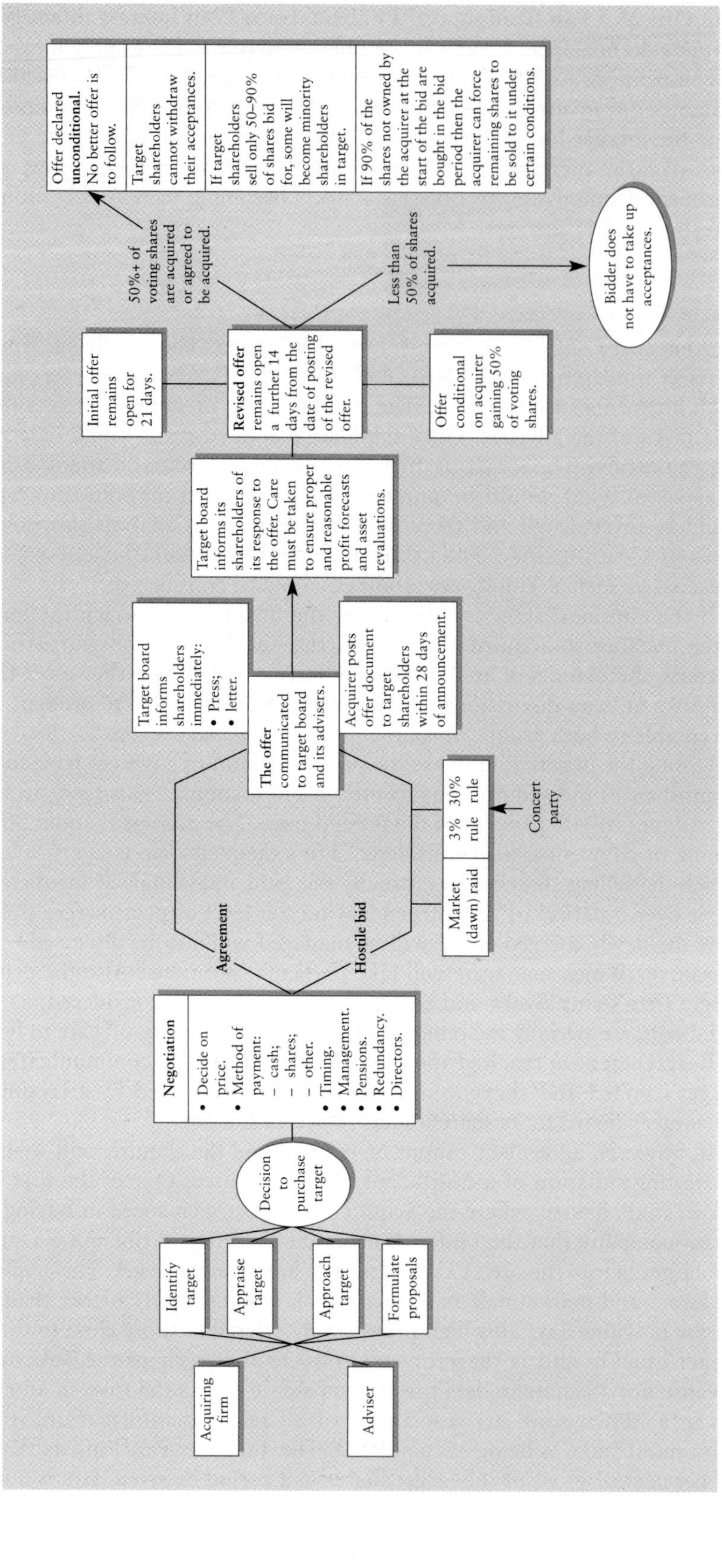

would take the holding to more than 15 per cent (except if the shares are purchased from a single seller).[11] Once 15 per cent has been accumulated any change in the holding greater than 1 per cent (up or down) must be notified to the market.

An important trigger point for disclosure of shareholdings in a company, whether the subject of a merger or not, is the 3 per cent holding level. If a 3 per cent stake is owned then this has to be declared to the company. This disclosure rule is designed to allow the target company to know who is buying its shares and to give it advance warning of a possible takeover raid. The management can then prepare a defence and present information to shareholders should the need arise.

If a company builds up a stake of more than 30 per cent the Takeover Panel rules usually oblige it to make a bid for all of the target company's shares. A 30 per cent stake often gives the owner a substantial amount of power. It is very difficult for anyone else to bid successfully for the firm when someone already has 30 per cent. It is surprising how often one reads in the financial press that a company or individual has bought a 29.9 per cent holding so that they have as large a stake as possible without triggering a mandatory bid.

Sometimes, in the past, if a company wanted to take over another it would, to avoid declaring at the 3 per cent level (or 5 per cent as it was then), or to avoid bidding at the 30 per cent level, sneak up on the target firm's management and shareholders. It would form a 'concert party' by persuading its friends, other firms and individuals to buy stakes in the target. Each of these holdings would be below the threshold levels. When the acquirer was ready to pounce it would already have under its control a significant, if not a majority, controlling interest. Today all concert party holdings are lumped together for the purposes of disclosure and trigger points.

The bid

In both a friendly and a hostile bid the acquirer is required to give notice to the target's board and its advisers that a bid is to be made. The Press and the Stock Exchange are usually also informed. The target management must immediately inform their shareholders (and the Takeover Panel). This is done through an announcement to the Stock Exchange and a press notice, which must be quickly followed by a letter explaining the situation. In a hostile bid the target management tend to use phrases like 'derisory offer' or 'wholly unacceptable'.

Within 28 days of the initial notice of an intention to make an offer the offer document has to be posted to each of the target's shareholders. Details of the offer, the acquirer and its plans will be explained. If the acquisition would increase the total value of the acquirer's assets by more than 15 per cent the acquirer's shareholders need to be informed about the bid. If the asset increase is more than 25 per cent then shareholders must vote in favour of the bid proceeding. They are also entitled to vote on any increase in authorised share capital.

The target management have 14 days in which to respond to the offer document. Assuming that they recommend rejection, they will attack the rationale of the merger and the price being offered. They may also highlight the virtues of the present management and reinforce this with revised profit forecasts and asset revaluations. There follows a period of attack and counter-attack through press releases and other means of communication. Public relations consultants may be brought in to provide advice and to plan strategies.

The offer remains open for target shareholders to accept for 21 days from the date of posting the offer document. If the offer is revised it must be kept open for a further

14 days from the posting date of the revision.[12] However to prevent bids from dragging on endlessly the Panel insists that the maximum period for a bid is 60 days from the offer document date (posting day). There are exceptions: if another bidder emerges, then it has 60 days, and its sixtieth day becomes the final date for both bidders; or if the Board of the target agrees to an extension. If the acquirer fails to gain control within 60 days then it is forbidden to make another offer for a year.

Exhibit 20.18, which reproduces an article on Westminster Health Care, shows that despite a 21-day rule, target shareholders have become accustomed to a 60-day period in which to make up their minds.

Exhibit 20.18

Westminster Health Care: quick bid fails

Institutions joined forces this week to stamp out sudden-death takeover bids by firmly rejecting Westminster Health Care's hostile offer for Goldsborough, a smaller nursing home group.

Confident of City support in the light of the target's share price weakness, Westminster quickly declared its £70m offer final, shortening the timetable for acceptance from the usual 60 days to 21 days. Three-week 'bullet' bids are permissible, but have proved unpopular with investors used to a 60-day timetable, in which the bidder normally raises its offer . . .

One leading Goldsborough investor called Westminster's offer 'unduly aggressive', forcing institutions to make snap decisions and preventing the target from mounting a proper defence. He added: 'Most fund managers are simple folk: stroke us and we roll over, but twist our arms and we bite back.'

Another Goldsborough shareholder, with some 6 per cent of its shares, said the 21-day issue was 'very relevant' to his rejection of the offer. 'This is a small company where there is little guidance from analysts. We need time to properly assess tricky points like asset values.'

Full-term takeovers offer more than just time to reflect. They give rival bidders the time to make a higher offer and advisers and underwriters more chances to earn fees . . .

'The 60-day bid process is a ritual,' sighed Westminster chief executive Pat Carter. 'We probably should have followed it.'

Source: Sameena Ahmad, *Investors Chronicle*, 19 July 1996. Reprinted with kind permission of the *Investors Chronicle*.

Post-bid

Usually an offer becomes unconditional when the acquirer has bought, or has agreed to buy, 50 per cent of the target's shares.[13] Prior to the declaration of the offer as unconditional the bidding firm would have said in the offer documents that the offer is conditional on the acquirer gaining (usually) 50 per cent of the voting shares. This allows the bidding firm to receive acceptances from the target shareholders without the obligation to buy. Once the bid is declared unconditional the acquirer is making a firm offer for the shares which it does not already have, and indicating that no better offer is to follow. Before the announcement of unconditionality those target shareholders who accepted the offer are entitled to withdraw their acceptance. After it, they are forbidden to do so.

Usually in the days following unconditionality the target shareholders who have not already accepted quickly do so. The alternative is to remain a minority shareholder – still receiving dividends but with power concentrated in the hands of a majority shareholder. There is a rule to avoid the frustration of having a small group of shareholders stubbornly refusing to sell. If the acquirer has bought nine-tenths of the shares it bid for, it can, within four months of the original offer, insist that the remaining shareholders sell at the final offer price.

If the bid has lapsed or not been declared unconditional the bidder cannot bid again for a 12-month period.

Exhibit 20.19 Defence tactics

Here are a few of the tactics employed by target managers to prevent a successful bid or to reduce the chances of a bid occurring.

Before bidding starts

- ***Eternal vigilance*** Be the most effective management team and educate shareholders about your abilities and the firm's potential.
- ***Strategic defence investments*** Your firm buys a substantial proportion of the shares in a friendly firm, and it has a substantial holding of your shares.
- ***Forewarned is forearmed*** Keep a watch on the share register for the accumulation of shares by a potential bidder.

After bidding has started

- ***Attack the logic of the bid*** Also attack the quality of the bidder's management.
- ***Improve the image of the firm*** Use revaluation, profit projections, dividend promises, public relations consultants.
- ***Try to get a Competition Commision inquiry.***
- ***Encourage unions, the local community, politicians, customers and suppliers to lobby on your behalf.***
- ***White Knight*** Invite a second bid from a friendly company.

  The following tactics are likely to be frowned upon by the Takeover Panel in the UK but are used in the USA and in a number of continental European countries.

- ***Poison pills*** Make yourself unpalatable to the bidder by ensuring additional costs should it win – for example, target shareholders are allowed to buy shares in target or acquirer at a large discount should a bid be successful.
- ***Crown jewels defence*** Sell off the most attractive parts of the business.
- ***PacMan defence*** Make a counter-bid for the bidder.
- ***Asset lock-up*** A friendly buyer purchases those parts of the business most attractive to the bidder.
- ***Golden parachutes*** Managers get massive pay-offs if the firm is taken over.
- ***Employee share ownership plans (ESOPs)*** These can be used to buy a substantial stake in the firm and may make it more difficult for a bidder to take it over.
- ***Share repurchase*** Reduces the number of shares available in the market for bidders.
- ***Give in to greenmail*** Key shareholders try to obtain a reward (for example, the repurchase of their shares at premium) from the company for not selling to a hostile bidder or for not becoming a bidder themselves. (Green refers to the colour of a US dollar.)

THE IMPACT OF MERGERS

There has been a significant amount of empirical research into mergers and their impact. Some of the questions asked and answered will be considered in this section.

Are target firms poor performers?

One of the proclaimed benefits of mergers is that they can be a spur to increased efficiency. Surely, it is argued, the most inefficient managers will be removed through a takeover by more efficient managers, won't they? Some evidence suggests that those firms which become targets are no less profitable than those which do not. Singh (1971) has provided some evidence on the best way to avoid becoming a takeover victim. It has little to do with performance and more to do with size. Singh concluded that once firms reach an average profitability there is no incentive to increase profits further in order to avoid being taken over. His rules to avoid being taken over are:

- *For small firms with low profitability* – increase profitability to just above average, (note: satisficing not maximising).
- *For medium and large firms* – increase size rather than the rate of profit.

Other researchers who have identified larger size as a factor that decreases the likelihood of being taken over include Hasbrouck (1985), Palepu (1986) and Ambrose and Megginson (1992), Levine and Aaronovitch (1981), Powell and Thomas (1994). This evidence sugests that the threat of takeovers, rather than inducing profit maximisation, encourages firms to grow bigger and faster.

Franks and Mayer (1996) found that hostile bids in the UK do not appear to be directed at poorly performing firms. Bhide's (1993) research, on the other hand, showed that US target firms generally had poor, or at best mediocre, performance records. Targets of friendly mergers were more likely to be well managed.

Does society benefit from mergers?

One way in which society could benefit from a merger is if the resulting combination could produce goods at a lower cost as a result of economies of scale or improved management. However set alongside this is the fact that mergers may also result in social costs in the form of monopoly power. Investigators have attempted to weigh up these two offsetting outcomes of mergers in general – *see* Exhibit 20.20.

The conclusions of researchers in this area generally are that at best mergers are neutral for society.[14] In some studies the cost is seen as greater than the benefit.[15] These analyses are based on the average outcome. They do not exclude the possibility that many mergers do produce social gains greater than the social cost.

The balance of social gains and losses was considered in the case of the bid by GEC (now Marconi) for the submarine maker VSEL. Two of the Monopolies and Merger (now the Competition) Commission commissioners said that the cost reductions resulting from the rationalisation of the shipyard industry would benefit the customer (the government) more than the disbenefit resulting from the loss of competition. The other four commissioners believed that the loss of competition was too great a price to pay. The President of the Board of Trade overruled the majority verdict of the MMC – *see* Exhibit 20.21.

Exhibit 20.20 Social benefits and costs of mergers

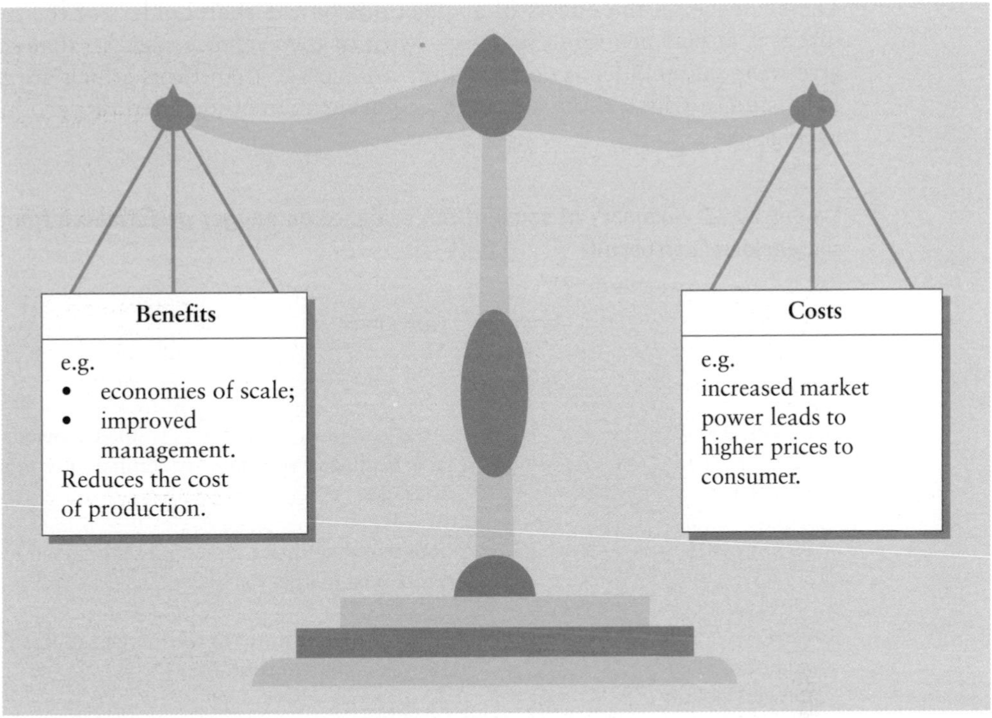

Benefits
e.g.
• economies of scale;
• improved management.
Reduces the cost of production.
Costs
e.g.
increased market power leads to higher prices to consumer.

Exhibit 20.21

GEC given go-ahead to bid for VSEL

FT

Heseltine overrules monopolies commission report after assurances on competition

Mr Michael Heseltine, trade and industry secretary, yesterday cleared General Electric Company to bid for VSEL, the submarine maker, overruling a recommendation by the Monopolies and Mergers Commission that GEC's pursuit should be blocked.

GEC, however, has had to agree – if successful in its bid – to maintain separate teams at VSEL's Barrow yard and its own Yarrow site on the Clyde to bid for future contracts in competition with each other.

British Aerospace, the other company pursuing VSEL, was cleared by the commission, and is also able to bid. A bidding war is now likely to resume in the stock market with BAe renewing its share offer for VSEL and GEC offering cash.

The commission was split over whether to block GEC, with two of the six members recommending that GEC should proceed if it could provide adequate safeguards. Mr Heseltine said that as GEC had offered assurances on competition and having taken into account the views of the Ministry of Defence, he would allow GEC's bid to proceed.

The commission's majority report said the proposed takeover of VSEL by GEC would reduce competition. As a result, the MoD would pay a higher price for ships and there would be a loss of potential design and production improvements. Assurances from GEC could not wholly replace the pressure of competition, they said.

In a minority report, however, two of the six members said they thought assurances from GEC would be enough to ensure the procurement system was not abused. They added that the reduction in costs that would flow from GEC's rationalisation of the shipyard industry would also benefit taxpayers.

Source: Bernard Gray, *Financial Times*, 24 May 1995. Reprinted with permission.

Do the shareholders of acquirers gain from mergers?

The evidence on the effects of acquisitions on the shareholders of the bidding firm is that it is at best neutral in its effect. Most of the evidence suggests that acquiring firms give their shareholders poorer returns on average than firms which are not acquirers. Even studies which show a gain to acquiring shareholders tend to produce very small average gains.

Exhibit 20.22 Summary of some of the evidence on merger performance from the acquiring shareholders' perspective

Study	*Country of evidence*	*Comment*
Meeks (1977)	UK	At least half of the mergers studied showed a considerable decline in profitability compared with industry averages.
Firth (1980)	UK	Relative share price losses are maintained for three years post merger.
(A review of monopolies and mergers policy) (1978)	UK	At least half or more of the mergers studied have proved to be unprofitable.
Ravenscraft and Scherer (1987)	USA	Small but significant decline in profitability on average.
Limmack (1991)	UK	Long-run under-performance by acquirers.
Higson and Elliot (1993)	UK	Poor relative performance on average (friendly bids produce much lower returns than hostile bids).
Gregory (1997)	UK	Share return performance is poor relative to the market for up to two years post merger, particularly for equity-financed bids and single (as opposed to regular) bidders.
Franks and Harris (1989)	UK and USA	Share returns are poor for acquirers on average for the first two years under one measurement technique, but better than the market as a whole when the CAPM is used as a benchmark.
Sudarsanam, Holl and Salami (1996)	UK	Poor return performance relative to the market for high-rated (PER) acquirers taking over low-rated targets. However some firms do well when there is a complementary fit in terms of liquidity, slack and investment opportunities.
Manson, Stark and Thomas (1994)	UK	Cash flow improves after merger, suggesting operating performance is given a boost.

KPMG sent a report to the Press in November 1999 showing the poor performance of cross-border mergers in terms of shareholder value. They then, embarrassed, tried to retrieve the report before it received publicity. Many commentators said that the evidence, that only 17 per cent of cross-border mergers increased shareholder value, would not help KPMG win business assisting firms conducting such mergers – *see* Exhibit 20.23.

Exhibit 20.23

KPMG withdraws merger study

FT

Report casts doubt on effectiveness of cross-border deals

By Norma Cohen, Property Correspondent

KPMG, the accountancy and consultancy firm increasingly involved in advising on mergers, this weekend sought to withdraw a study which concluded that 83 per cent of cross-border mergers have not delivered shareholder value.

The high proportion of mergers that fail to add value raises questions about the effectiveness of many cross-border deals – an area in which "Big Five" firms such as KMPG are increasingly seeking to expand their advisory role.

KMPG sent the report to journalists last week, noting that it was embargoed for publication today. However, late on Friday it asked that the report be withdrawn, saying it was postponing publication . . .

The study, commissioned by KPMG but carried out via confidential interviews by a third-party consultant, looked at a sample taken from the top 700 cross border deals by value between 1996 and 1998.

In all, 107 companies world-wide participated. Of these, the study found 53 per cent destroyed shareholder value, while another 30 per cent produced no discernible difference. The conclusions came after an analysis of share price movements relative to those of similar competitors in the first year following the merger.

Source: Norma Cohen, *Financial Times*, 29 November 1999, p. 23 Reprinted with permission

Do target shareholders gain from mergers?

Acquirers usually have to pay a substantial premium over the pre-bid share price to persuade target shareholders to sell. The empirical evidence in this area is overwhelming – target shareholders gain from mergers.

Do the employees gain?

In the aftermath of a merger it sometimes happens that large areas of the target firm's operations are closed down with a consequent loss of jobs. Often operating units of the two firms are fused and overlapping functions are eliminated, resulting in the shedding of staff. However, sometimes the increased competitive strength of the combined entity saves jobs and creates many more.

Do the directors of the acquirer gain?

The directors of the acquirers often gain increased status and power. They also generally receive increased remuneration packages – *see* Exhibit 20.24.

Do the directors of the target gain?

We do not have a definitive answer as to whether the directors of the target gain. In the Press they are often unfairly described as the failed managers and therefore out of a job.

Exhibit 20.24

Funds furious over RBS bonuses

FT

By Simon Targett, Investment Correspondent

The National Association of Pension Funds is to recommend that its members vote against the re-election of two Royal Bank of Scotland directors in protest against the pay-out to executives of "takeover" bonuses worth £2.5m . . .

But last night Sir George Mathewson, RBS executive deputy chairman, told the FT the size of the bonuses paid to him and three other executives – £2.5m in total – "wouldn't have given you bragging power in a Soho wine bar",

Sir George, who received a takeover bonus of £759,000 for his part in the acquisition of NatWest, said the special bonuses were not discussed with shareholders prior to their award in March 2000. "Frankly, [the award of the bonuses] was not worthwhile talking to shareholders about," he said . . .

The NAPF's opposition to RBS's takeover bonuses follows its protest against telecoms group Vodafone for last year paying a £10m bonus to Chris Gent, its chief executive, for winning the race to buy Mannesmann of Germany.

Institutional shareholders dislike takeover bonuses because they reward executives for completing acquisitions rather than building shareholder value.

Source: Simon Targett, *Financial Times*, 27 March 2001, p. 1. Reprinted with permission

They are the losers in the 'market for managerial control'. In reality they often receive large pay-offs on their lengthy employment contracts and then take on another highly paid directorship.

Do the financial institutions gain?

The financial institutions benefit greatly from merger activity. They usually receive fees, regardless of whether they are on the winning side in a bid battle.

Warren Buffett sums up the evidence on the winners from mergers:

> They are a bonanza for the shareholders of the acquiree; they increase the income and status of the acquirer's management; and they are a honey pot for the investment bankers and other professionals on both sides. But, alas, they usually reduce the wealth of the acquirer's shareholders, often to a substantial extent .[16]

MANAGING MERGERS

Many mergers fail to produce shareholder wealth and yet there are companies that pursue a highly successful strategy of expansion through mergers. This section highlights some of the reasons for failure and some of the requirements for success.

The three stages of mergers

There are three phases in merger management. It is surprising how often the first and third are neglected while the second is given great amounts of managerial attention. The three stages are:

- preparation;
- negotiation and transaction;
- integration.

In the preparation stage strategic planning predominates. A sub-set of the strategic thrust of the business might be mergers. Targets need to be searched for and selected with a clear purpose – shareholder wealth maximisation in the long term. There must be a thorough analysis of the potential value to flow from the combination and tremendous effort devoted to the plan of action which will lead to the successful integration of the target.

The negotiation and transaction stage has two crucial aspects to it.

1 ***Financial analysis and target evaluation*** This evaluation needs to go beyond mere quantitative analysis into fields such as human resources and competitive positioning.
2 ***Negotiating strategy and tactics*** It is in the area of negotiating strategy and tactics that the specialist advisers are particularly useful. However the acquiring firm's management must keep a tight rein and remain in charge.

The integration stage is where so many mergers come apart. It is in this stage that the management need to consider the organisational and cultural similarities and differences between the firms. They also need to create a plan of action to obtain the best post-merger integration.

The key elements of these stages are shown in Exhibit 20.25.

Exhibit 20.25 The progression of a merger

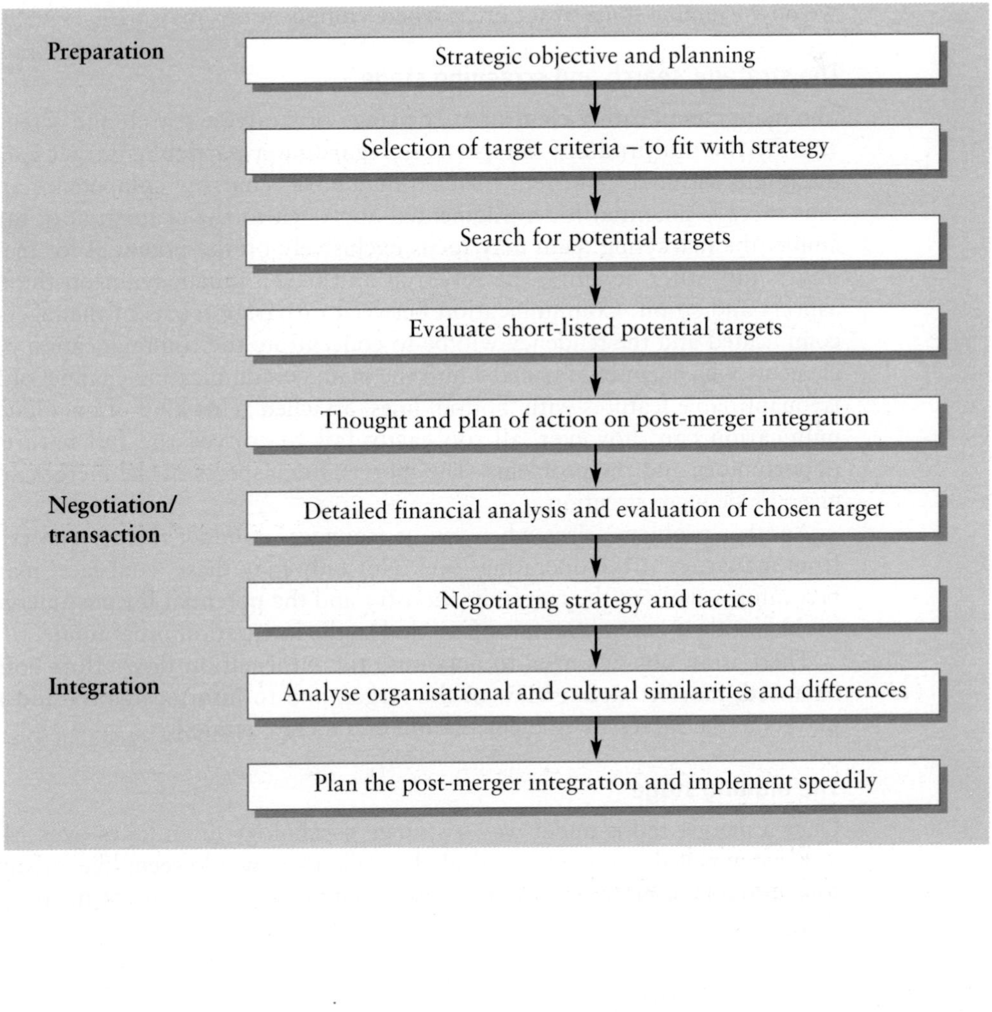

Too often the emphasis in managing mergers is firmly on the 'hard' world of identifiable and quantifiable data. Here economics, finance and accounting come to the fore. There is a worrying tendency to see the merger process as a series of logical and mechanical steps, each with an obvious rationale and a clear and describable set of costs and benefits. This approach all but ignores the potential for problems caused by non-quantifiable elements, for instance, human reactions and interrelationships. Matters such as potential conflict, discord, alienation and disloyalty are given little attention.[17] There is also a failure to make clear that the nature of decision making in this area relies as much on informed guesses, best estimates and hunches as on cold facts and figures.

The organisational process approach

The organisational process approach takes into account the 'soft' aspects of merger implementation and integration. Here the acquisition process, from initial strategic formulations to final complete integration, is perceived as a complex, multi-faceted programme with the potential for a range of problems arising from the interplay of many different hard and soft factors. Each merger stage requires imaginative and skilled management for the corporate objective to be maximised.

Problem areas in merger management

We now examine some of the areas where complications may arise.

The strategy, search and screening stage

The main complicating element at the stage of strategy, search and screening is generated by the multitude of perspectives regarding a particular target candidate. Each discipline within a management team may have a narrow competence and focus, and thus there is potential for a fragmented approach to the evaluation of targets. For example, the marketing team may focus exclusively on the potential for marketing economies and other benefits, the research and development team on the technological aspects and so on. Communication between disparate teams of managers can become complicated and the tendency will be to concentrate the communication effort on those elements which can be translated into the main communicating channel of business, that is, quantifiable features with 'bottom lines' attached. This kind of one-dimensional communication can, however, all too easily fail to convey the full nature of both the opportunities and the problems. The more subtle aspects of the merger are likely to be given inadequate attention.

Another problem arises when senior managers conduct merger analysis in isolation from managers at the operating level. Not only may these 'coal-face' managers be the best informed about the target, its industry and the potential for post-merger integration problems; their commitment is often vital to the integration programme.

There is an obvious need to maximise the information flow effort both to obtain a balanced, more complete view of the target, and to inform, involve and empower key players in the successful implementation of a merger strategy.

The bidding stage

Once a merger bid is under way a strange psychology often takes over. Managers seem to feel compelled to complete a deal. To walk away would seem like an anticlimax, with vast amounts of money spent on advisers and nothing to show for it. Also they may feel that the investment community will perceive this management as being one unable to implement its avowed strategic plans. It may be seen as 'unexciting' and 'going nowhere' if it has to retreat to concentrate on its original business after all the excitement and promises surrounding a takeover bid.

Managers also often enjoy the thrill of the chase and develop a determination to 'win'. Pay, status and career prospects may hinge on rapid growth. Additionally, acquirers may be impelled to close the deal quickly by the fear of a counter-bid by a competitor, which, if successful, would have an adverse impact on the competitive position of the firm.

Thus mergers can take on a momentum which is difficult to stop. This is often nurtured by financial advisers keen on completing a transaction.

These phenomena may help to explain the heavy emphasis given to the merger transaction to the detriment of the preparation and integration stages. They may also go some way to explaining merger failure – in particular, failure to enhance shareholder value as a result of the winner's curse.

Expectations of the acquiring firm's operational managers regarding the post-merger integration stage

Clarity and planning are needed to avoid conflict and disappointment among managers. For example, the integration strategy may outline a number of different tasks to be undertaken in the 12–24 months following an acquisition. These may range from disposal of assets and combining operating facilities to new product development and financial reconstruction. Each of these actions may be led by a different manager. Their expectations regarding the speed of implementation and the order in which each of these actions will be taken may be different. A clear and rational resource-planning and allocation mechanism will reduce ambiguity and improve the co-ordination of decision making.

Aiming for the wrong type of integration

There are different degrees of integration when two firms come together under one leadership. At the one extreme is the complete **absorption** of the target firm and the concomitant fusing of two cultures, two operational procedures and two corporate organisations. At the other extreme is the **holding company, preservation or portfolio approach** where the degree of change of the acquired subsidiary may amount merely to a change in some financial control procedures, but otherwise the target firm's management may continue with their own systems, unintegrated operations and culture.

The complete integration approach is usually appropriate in situations where production and other operational costs can be reduced through economies of scale and other synergies, or revenues can be enhanced through, say, combined marketing and distribution. The preservation approach is most suitable when it is recognised that the disbenefits of forcing organisations together outweigh the advantages, for example when the products and markets are completely different and the cultures are such that a fusion would cause an explosive clash. These arm's-length mergers are typical of the acquisitive conglomerates. In such mergers general management skills are transferred along with strict financial performance yardsticks and demanding incentive schemes, but little else is changed.

With **symbiosis-based** mergers there is a need to keep a large degree of difference, at least initially, in culture, organisation and operating style, but at the same time to permit communication and cross-fertilisation of ideas. There may also be a need to transfer skills from one part of the combined organisation to another, whether through training and teaching or by personnel reassignment. An example might be where a book publisher acquires an Internet service provider; each is engaged in a separate market but there is potential for profitable co-operation in some areas. As well as being aware of the need for mutual assistance each organisation may be jealous of its own way of doing things and does not want its *esprit de corps* disrupted by excessive integration.

Exhibit 20.26 expresses the failure of some acquirers to allow adequately for the complicating human factor.

Exhibit 20.26

Marrying in haste

FT

Mergers and acquisitions continue apace in spite of an alarming failure rate and evidence that they often fail to benefit shareholders, writes Michael Skapinker

A long list of studies have all reached the same conclusion: the majority of takeovers damage the interests of the shareholders of the acquiring company. They do, however, often reward the shareholders of the acquired company, who receive more for their shares than they were worth before the takeover was announced . . .

Why do so many mergers and acquisitions fail to benefit shareholders? Colin Price, a partner at McKinsey, the management consultants, who specialises in mergers and acquisitions, says the majority of failed mergers suffer from poor implementation. And in about half of those, senior management failed to take account of the different cultures of the companies involved.

Melding corporate cultures takes time, which senior management does not have after a merger, Mr Price says. 'Most mergers are based on the idea of 'let's increase revenues', but you have to have a functioning management team to manage that process. The nature of the problem is not so much that there's open warfare between the two sides. It's that the cultures don't meld quickly enough to take advantage of the opportunities. In the meantime, the marketplace has moved on.'

Many consultants refer to how little time companies spend before a merger thinking about whether their organisations are compatible. The benefits of mergers are usually couched in financial or commercial terms: cost-savings can be made or the two sides have complementary businesses that will allow them to increase revenues . . .

Mergers are about compatibility, which means agreeing whose values will prevail and who will be the dominant partner. So it is no accident that managers as well as journalists reach for marriage metaphors in describing them. Merging companies are said to 'tie the knot'. When mergers are called off, as with Deutsche Bank and Dresdner Bank, the two companies fail to 'make it up the aisle' or their relationship remains 'unconsummated'.

Yet the metaphor fails to convey the scale of risk companies run when they launch acquisitions or mergers. Even in countries with high divorce rates, marriages have a better success rate than mergers. And in an age of frequent premarital cohabitation, the bridal couple usually know one another better than the merging companies do.

A more appropriate comparison might be with second marriages, particularly where children are involved. This was the description used by John Reed, former chairman of Citicorp, which merged with Travelers Group in 1998 to create Citigroup. Mr Reed and Sandy Weill, head of Travelers, agreed to be joint chairmen of the merged company, a relationship that ended this year when Mr Reed retired.

Speaking to the US Academy of Management last year, before his departure, Mr Reed said: 'The literature on putting together two families speaks volumes to me. The problems of step-parents, the descriptions of some children rejecting other parents, and all of the children being generally ticked off, is all meaningful...Sandy and I both have the problem that our "children" look up to us as they never did before, and reject the other parent with equal vigour.'

But Prof Sirower, who has written a book on acquisitions called *The Synergy Trap*, rejects the view that the principal problem is post-merger implementation. 'Many large acquisitions are dead on arrival, no matter how well they are managed after the deal is done,' he says. Prof Sirower asks why managers should pay a premium to make an acquisition when their shareholders could invest in the target company themselves. How sure are managers that they can extract cost savings or revenue improvements from their acquisition that match the size of the takeover premium?

Prof Sirower denies he is saying companies should never make acquisitions. If 65 per cent of mergers fail to benefit shareholders, 35 per cent are successful.

Exhibit 20.26 continued

How can acquirers try to ensure they are among the successful minority? Ken Favaro, managing partner of Marakon, a consultancy the has worked for Coca-Cola, Lloyds TSB and Boeing, suggests two conditions for success. The first is to define what success means. 'The combined entities have to deliver better returns to the shareholders than they would separately. It's amazing how often that's not the pre-agreed measure of success,' Mr Favaro says.

Second merging companies need to decide in advance which partner's way of doing things will prevail. 'Mergers of equals can be so dangerous because it is not clear who is in charge,' says Mr Favaro.

Prof Sirower adds that managers need to ask what advantages they will bring to the acquired company that competitors will find difficult to replicate . . .

Given how heavily the odds are stacked against successful mergers, managers should consider whether their time and the shareholders' money would not be better employed elsewhere – improving customer service, for example. Above all, they need to ask whether they are launching a takeover because their acquisition will improve their performance or because they cannot think what else to do.

Source: Michael Skapinker, *Financial Times*, 12 April 2000. Reprinted with permission.

Why do mergers fail to generate value for acquiring shareholders?

A definitive answer as why mergers fail to generate value for acquiring shareholders cannot be provided, because mergers fail for a host of reasons. However there do appear to be some recurring themes.

The strategy is misguided

History is littered with strategic plans which turned out to be value destroying rather than value creating. Daimler-Benz in combining Mercedes with Fokker and Dasa tried to gain synergies from an integrated transport company then it tried to become a global car producer by merging with Chrysler. Marconi sold off its defence businesses to concentrate on telecommunication equipment. It spent a fortune buying companies at the forefront of technology only to slam into the hi-tech recession in 2001 – its shares lost 98 per cent of their value. Saatchi and Saatchi tried to create a global service industry through numerous takeovers and found themselves in dire straits in the early 1990s. Building societies, banks and insurance companies in the UK bought hundreds of estate agents in the 1980s in the belief that providing 'one-stop shopping' for the house-owner would be attractive. Many of these agency chains were sold off in the 1990s at knock-down prices. Fashion also seems to play its part, as with the conglomerate mergers of the 1960s, the cross-border European mergers of the early 1990s prompted by the development of the single market and the dot.com merger frenzy around the turn of the millennium.

Over-optimism

Acquiring managers have to cope with uncertainty about the future potential of their acquisition. It is possible for them to be over-optimistic about the market economics, the competitive position and the operating synergies available. They may underestimate the costs associated with the resistance to change they may encounter, or the reaction of competitors. Merger fever, the excitement of the battle, may lead to an openness to persuasion that the target is worth more than it really is. A common mistake is the underestimation of the investment required to make a merger work, particularly in terms of managerial time.

Exhibit 20.27

On masquerading skimmed milk, lame horses and sexy deals

We believe most deals do damage to the shareholders of the acquiring company. Too often, the words from HMS Pinafore apply: 'Things are seldom what they seem, skim milk masquerades as cream.' Specifically, sellers and their representatives invariably present financial projections having more entertainment value than educational value. In the production of rosy scenarios, Wall Street can hold its own against Washington.

In any case, why potential buyers even look at projections prepared by sellers baffles me. Charlie and I never give them a glance, but instead keep in mind the story of the man with an ailing horse. Visiting the vet, he said: 'Can you help me? Sometimes my horse walks just fine and sometimes he limps.' The Vet's reply was pointed: 'No problem – when he's walking fine, sell him.' . . .

Talking to *Time Magazine* a few years back, Peter Drucker got to the heart of things: 'I will tell you a secret: Dealmaking beats working. Dealmaking is exciting and fun, and working is grubby. Running anything is primarily an enormous amount of grubby detail work . . . dealmaking is romantic, sexy. That's why you have deals that make no sense.'

. . . I can't resist repeating a tale told me last year by a corporate executive. The business he grew up in was a fine one, with a long-time record of leadership in its industry. Its main product, however, was distressing glamorless. So several decades ago, the company hired a management consultant who – naturally – advised diversification, the then-current fad. ('Focus' was not yet in style.) Before long, the company acquired a number of businesses, each after the consulting firm had gone through a long – and expensive – acquisition study. And the outcome? Said the executive sadly 'When we started we were getting 100% of our earnings from the original business. After ten years, we were getting 150%.'

Source: Warren Buffett. Letter to shareholders, *Berkshire Hathaway Annual Report 1995*. Reprinted with permission. © Warren Buffett.

Failure of integration management

One problem is the over-rigid adherence to prepared integration plans. Usually plans require dynamic modification in the light of experience and altered circumstances. The integration programme may have been based on incomplete information and may need post-merger adaptation to the new perception of reality.

Common management goals and the engendering of commitment to those goals is essential. The morale of the workforce can be badly damaged at the time of a merger. The natural uncertainty and anxiety has to be handled with understanding, tact, integrity and sympathy. Communication and clarity of purpose are essential as well as rapid implementation of change. Cultural differences need to be tackled with sensitivity and trust established.

The absence of senior management commitment to the task of successful integration severely dents the confidence of target and acquired managers.

Coopers & Lybrand, the international business advisers, in 1992 conducted 'in-depth interviews with senior executives of the UK's top 100 companies covering 50 deals'. There emerged some factors which seem to contribute to failure, and others which are critical for raising the chances of success. These are shown in Exhibit 20.28.

Exhibit 20.29 discusses some of the personnel/cultural difficulties that occur after mergers.

The ten rules listed in Exhibit 20.30 are NOT recommended for shareholder-wealth-orientated managers.

Exhibit 20.28 Survey on the reasons for merger failure and success – Coopers & Lybrand

The most commonly cited causes of failure include:		*The most commonly cited reasons for success include:*	
Target management attitudes and cultural differences	85%	Detailed post-acquisition plans and speed of implementation	76%
Little or no post-acquisition planning	80%	A clear purpose for making acquisitions	76%
Lack of knowledge of industry or target	45%	Good cultural fit	59%
Poor management and poor management practices in the acquired company	45%	High degree of management co-operation	47%
Little or no experience of acquisitions	30%	In-depth knowledge of the acquiree and his industry	41%

Exhibit 20.29

The ills of dysfunctional deals: management takeovers

FT

New research turns conventional wisdom about successful company acquisitions on its head, writes **Alison Maitland**

One irony of takeovers is that shareholders in the target company often enjoy windfall gains, while employees suffer disruption, uncertainty and loss. Another irony that fascinates business economists is that shares in the predator company frequently underperform after the acquisition. Could the two be linked?

The question is of more than academic interest. Worldwide merger and acquisition activity reached an astonishing $2,242bn (£1,485bn) in the last quarter of 1999 and first quarter of this year, according to Thomson Financial Securities Data. Two years ago the figure for the comparable six-month period was $1,077bn. The deals are bigger too; those whose value has been disclosed are worth an average $295m, almost double what they were two years ago.

Although mergers have become more popular, they are as hard as ever to pull off. Cambridge University's Judge Institute looked at 77 large takeovers by UK companies from 1990 to 1996. It found that shares in the acquiring companies underperformed the FT All-Share index by an average of 18 per cent in the two years after their deals.

The secret of success, according to the conventional wisdom, is for predators to act fast. They should integrate the target company as completely as possible and make it absolutely clear who is boss and which corporate culture will dominate.

But a new study* turns this on its head. The research, by PA Consulting Group and the University of Edinburgh Management School, suggests that acquirers who avoid the slash-and-burn approach enjoy better shareholder returns. Deals should take a selective rather than an all-embracing approach to integration. Acquirers are more likely to be successful if they recognise the existence of cultural differences and, before the deal closes, form an 'integration team' that includes a substantial number of staff from the target company.

The PA study set out to establish objectively how acquirers could reduce the risks involved in post-merger integration. It surveyed 85 companies that made acquisitions worth at least £50m between the start of 1997 and mid-1999. The takeover targets were all UK-based, with buyers mainly from the UK, but also from North America, Australia, Belgium, Finland, Ireland and the Netherlands.

The researchers evaluated different approaches to post-merger integration according to short-term shareholder returns. They calculated these from the difference between share-price performance immediately before and after the merger announcement and its predicted value had the deal not taken place. (Previous research found a strong correlation between short-term share-price movements and long-term cash flows.)

The methods that appear to add shareholder value include early and detailed planning and communication, regular cash-based reports on progress, and explicit rewards for staff who achieve a successful integration.

Jeremy Stanyard, head of PA Consulting's M&A team, says speed is as important as ever. 'But people have mistaken this for doing everything very quickly. We're saying you should do certain things

►

Exhibit 20.29 continued

very quickly, but be selective about what you do.'

In one merger, two sales and marketing departments that had been deadly rivals were hastily integrated, leading to confusion over brand management and the loss of key people.

John McGrath, chief executive of Diageo, the food and drink group, is persuaded by the research findings. 'There are dangers in over-integration, or in moving too fast in an attempt to realise all your synergies at once,' says the man who presided over the 1997 merger of Guinness and Grand Metropolitan. 'It's a question of identifying where value is being created, and then making sure you protect it during the integration process.'

Few companies can be happy to see knowledgeable and talented staff walking out of the door. Why then, is it common to ride roughshod over people, even though that causes damaging culture clashes and can diminish employees' commitment?

Rob Yeung, a business psychologist at the London office of the Nicholson McBride consultancy, says acquisitions are often driven by ego. 'In many organisations that say they'll respect the target company's values, they're only paying lip service to it,' he says. 'They don't promote the best and brightest people, but the people who are best for their own purposes.'

Even sensitivity after the merger will not save deals that are done for the wrong reasons. The PA study also found that the motive for the merger appears to have a crucial effect. Acquisitions aimed primarily at cost savings are found to produce no shareholder benefits. By contrast, those aimed at increasing revenues, gaining access to new markets, or acquiring technology, do tend to deliver value.

Mr Stanyard believes that markets question the strategic value of cost reduction on its own. 'If the acquired company becomes leaner and fitter, is that doing anything to take the combined company forward strategically?'

In their book *After the Merger*,** three consultants with A.T. Kearney in Germany support this view. Synergies aimed at 'efficiency', rather than growth, can also have an unwelcome psychological impact on employees of the target company. Merged companies seek 'early wins', such as factory closures and job cuts, but the antipathy that is stirred up can cause them to backfire.

*Creating shareholder value from acquisition integration, available from Sheonagh Friend at PA Consulting, 020 7333 5260 or email: m-a@pa-consulting.com.

***After the Merger*, published by Financial Times Prentice Hall.

Source: Alison Maitland, *Financial Times*, 8 June 2000. Reprinted with permission.

Exhibit 20.30 Arnold's ten golden rules for alienating 'acquired' employees

1 Sack people in an apparently arbitrary fashion.

2 Insist (as crudely as possible) that your culture is superior. Attack long-held beliefs, attitudes, systems, norms, etc.

3 Don't bother to find out the strengths and weaknesses of the new employees.

4 Lie to people – some of the old favourites are:
- 'there will not be any redundancies';
- 'this is a true merger of equals'.

5 Fail to communicate your integration strategy:
- don't say why the pain and sacrifice is necessary, just impose it;
- don't provide a sense of purpose.

6 Encourage the best employees to leave by generating as much uncertainty as possible.

7 Create stress, loss of morale and commitment, and a general sense of hopelessness by being indifferent and insensitive to employees' needs for information.

8 Make sure you let everyone know that you are superior – after all, you won the merger battle.

9 Sack all the senior executives immediately – their knowledge and experience and the loyalty of their subordinates are cheap.

10 Insist that your senior management appear uninterested in the boring job of nuts-and-bolts integration management. After all knighthoods and peerages depend upon the next high-public-profile acquisition.

Exhibit 20.31 highlights some aspects not yet covered, including:

- a management and personnel audit;
- an alternative to merger is a strategic alliance;
- acquirers that fail to deliver value often become targets themselves.

Exhibit 20.31

A sometimes fatal attraction

FT

The problems with takeovers go beyond faulty strategic logic or paying too high a price. Even good deals founder if they are poorly managed after the merger . . .

The task of successfully implementing an acquisition or merger is formidable. If the acquiring company's shareholders are to make money from the deal, sales must be increased and costs reduced to a level that compensates for the premium over the share price paid for the company. This is rarely less than 20 per cent.

Unless there is a large overlap between the companies there are few easy savings. The targets of hostile bids are not necessarily poor performers, according to a study of takeovers in the mid-1980s by the London Business School . . .

[Most] companies delude themselves about the scale and nature of the task. They focus on revenue-enhancement opportunities rather than cost reduction, according to David Wightman, global head of strategy practice at PA Consulting Group. 'In fact revenue synergies are not often achieved in any great quantity, and frequently not at all.'

Companies also often delude themselves about the speed at which they should act. The desire to respect the culture of the acquired company and prevent the defection of important staff often slows the pace of integration . . .

The disadvantage with a slow approach to integration is that it tends to dissipate momentum and enthusiasm. Moreover, delays can dilute the financial benefits of a deal . . .

Nonetheless, the practical difficulty of integrating companies with different cultures cannot be underestimated. Recent research by London's Imperial College into European cross-border deals found that differences in management style – the formality of procedures, the adherence to job descriptions, the structure of communications – bore a strong correlation to deals' chances of failure . . .

[Consultants] urge managers to adopt different styles of management for different types of deal. Bill Pursche of McKinsey argues that different styles are appropriate depending on the degree of business overlap, the relative size of companies, the companies' skills, the urgency and source of the expected returns and the style of leadership.

For example, if cost savings are the main rationale of the merger, targets should be set at the top and passed through the organisation. If the goal is to achieve revenue synergies or longer-term skill transfers, then a more participatory approach, drawing recommendations from the 'grass roots', is appropriate. Pursche calls this 'empowering the troops' and says it can result in strong morale. But it is more common in merging companies to find poor morale, rising staff turnover and falling productivity.

There is probably no easy solution to poor morale. Reassuring staff about job security may not be possible – and may be counterproductive if proved false. Even so, companies are invariably advised to try to reduce uncertainty and explain the merger's rationale, through newsletters and meetings between senior executives and employees.

Unsurprisingly, pay is one of the most marked influences on morale. A London Business School study in 1987 found that in two-thirds of successful takeovers, the acquired management reported either improved performance incentives, better pension entitlements, better career prospects, or the introduction of share options.

The same study highlighted another important influence on the ultimate success of the acquisition: a thorough audit of the target company before the takeover.

Whereas all the buyers in the LBS study conducted financial audits of the acquired companies before they bought them, only 37 per cent carried out a management or personnel audit. Moreover, although buyers stressed the importance of the purchased company's middle management, 70 per cent did not meet these managers before the takeover.

The paucity of pre-merger planning causes frustration, particularly among managers concerned with human resources. A seminar of directors and financiers involved in takeovers sponsored by People in Business, a consultancy, uncovered a strongly held view that deals were too focused on financial measures . . .

However, institutional investors are imposing a tougher discipline on bidders than 10–15 years ago, according to Julian Franks of London Business School. 'People who acquire badly, frequently become targets themselves,' he says.

Another feature of the 1990s is the growth in strategic alliances as a cheaper, less risky route to a strategic goal than takeovers.

Source: Vanessa Houlder, *Financial Times*, 11 September 1995. Reprinted with permission.

CONCLUDING COMMENTS

At a minimum this chapter should have made it clear that following a successful merger strategy is much more than simply 'doing the deal'. Preparation and integration are usually of greater significance to the creation of value than the negotiation and transaction stage. And yet, too often, it is towards this middle stage that most attention is directed.

Doubts have been raised about the purity of the motives for mergers but we should restrain ourselves from being too cynical as many mergers do create wealth for shareholders and society. Industries with a shifting technological or market base may need fewer larger firms to supply goods at a lower cost. The savings from superior managerial talent are genuine and to be praised in many cases. Restructuring, the sharing of facilities, talent and ideas, and the savings from the internalisation of transactions are all positive outcomes and often outweigh the negative effects.

Like many tools in the armoury of management, growth through mergers can be used to create or destroy – often it ain't what you do, its the way that you do it.

KEY POINTS AND CONCEPTS

- **Mergers are a form of investment** and should, theoretically at least, be evaluated on essentially the same criteria as other investment decisions, for example, using NPV. However there are complicating factors:
  - the benefits from mergers are difficult to quantify;
  - acquiring companies often do not know what they are buying.

- **A merger is the combining of two business entities under common ownership.** It is difficult for many practical purposes to draw a distinction between merger, acquisition and takeover.

- A **horizontal** merger is when the two firms are engaged in similar lines of activity.

- A **vertical** merger is when the two firms are at different stages of the production chain.

- A **conglomerate** merger is when the two firms operate in unrelated business areas.

- **Merger** activity has occurred in waves, with peaks in the early 1970s the late 1980s and the late 1990s – times of good economic and stock market performance. **Cash** is the most common method of payment except at the peaks of the cycle when **shares** were a more popular form of consideration.

- **Synergistic merger motives**:
  - market power;
  - economies of scale;
  - internalisation of transactions;
  - entry to new markets and industries;
  - tax advantages;
  - risk diversification.

- **Bargain-buying merger motives:**
  - elimination of inefficient and misguided management;
  - undervalued shares.

- **Managerial merger motives:**
  - empire building;
  - status;
  - power;
  - remuneration;
  - hubris;
  - survival;
  - free cash flow.
- **Third-party merger motives:**
  - advisers;
  - at the insistence of customers or suppliers.
- **Value is created from a merger** when the gain is greater than the transaction cost.

  $$PV_{AB} = PV_A + PV_B + \text{gain}$$

  The gain may go to A's shareholders, or B's, or be shared between the two.
- The **winner's curse** is when the acquirer pays a price higher than the combined present value of the target and the potential gain.
- **Cash as a means of payment**

  For the acquirer

  Advantages
  - Acquirers' shareholders retain control of their firm.
  - Greater chance of early success.

  Disadvantages
  - Cash flow strain.

  For the target shareholders

  Advantages
  - Certain value.
  - Able to spread investments.

  Disadvantages
  - May produce capital gain tax liability.
- **Shares as a means of payment**

  For the acquirer

  Advantages
  - No cash outflow.
  - The PER game can be played.

  Disadvantages
  - Dilution of existing shareholders' control.
  - Greater risk of over-paying

  For the target shareholders

  Advantages
  - Postponement of capital gains tax liability.
  - Target shareholders maintain an interest in the combined entity.

  Disadvantages
  - Uncertain value.
  - Not able to spread investment without higher transaction costs.
- The **City Code on Takeovers and Mergers** provides the main governing rules. It applies to quoted and unlisted public companies. It is self-regulatory and non-statutory – but powerful. Its objective is to ensure fair and equal treatment for all shareholders.

- The **Office of Fair Trading (OFT)** and the **Competition Commission** investigate potential cases of competition constraints.
- **Pre-bid:**
  - advisers appointed;
  - targets identified;
  - appraisal;
  - approach target;
  - negotiate.
- A **'dawn raid'** is where a substantial stake is acquired with great rapidity.
- Shareholdings of **3 per cent** or more must be notified to the company.
- A stake of **30 per cent** usually triggers a bid.
- **Concert parties**, where a group of shareholders act as one, but each remains below the 3 per cent or 30 per cent trigger levels, are now treated as one large holding for the key trigger levels.
- **The bid**
  - notice to target's board;
  - offer document sent within 28 days;
  - target management respond to offer document;
  - offer open for 21 days, but can be frequently revised and thereby kept open for up to 60 days (or longer if another bidder enters the fray).
- **Post-bid**
  - When a bid becomes unconditional (usually at 50 per cent acceptances), the acquirer is making a firm offer and no better offer is to follow.
- **Target firms are not on average poor performers** relative to others in their industry.
- **Society sometimes benefits** from mergers **but most studies suggest a loss**, often through the exploitation of monopoly power.
- The **shareholders of acquirers tend to receive returns lower than the market** as a whole after the merger. However many acquirers do create value for shareholders.
- Target **shareholders, directors of acquirers and advisers gain significantly** from mergers. For the **directors of targets and other employees** the evidence is mixed.
- **There are three stages of mergers.** Most attention should be directed at the first and third, but this does not seem to happen. These stages are.
  - preparation;
  - negotiation and transaction;
  - integration.
- **Non-quantifiable**, 'soft', human elements often determine the success or otherwise of mergers.
- **Mergers fail for three principal reasons:**
  - the strategy is misguided;
  - over-optimism;
  - failure of integration management.

REFERENCES AND FURTHER READING

Ambrose, B.W. and Megginson, W.L. (1992) 'The role of asset structure, ownership structure, and takeover defences in determining acquisition likelihood', *Journal of Financial and Quantitative Analysis*, 27(4), pp. 575–89.

Bhide, A. (1993) 'The causes and consequences of hostile takeovers', in D.H. Chew, Jr (ed.), *The New Finance: Where Theory Meets Practice*. New York: McGraw-Hill. Target firms are poor performers.

Brett, M. (2000) *How to Read the Financial Pages*. 5th edn. London: Random House. Chapter 10 gives a clear, fluid and succinct account of the merger process.

Buffett, W. (1982) Letter to Shareholders accompanying the Berkshire Hathaway Annual Report. Omaha, Neb. www.berkshirehathaway.com. Words of wit and wisdom forged by business experience.

Buffett, W. (1995) Letter to Shareholders accompanying the Berkshire Hathaway Annual Report. Omaha, Neb. www.berkshirehathaway.com. Words of wit and wisdom forged by business experience.

Buono, A. and Bowditch, J. (1989) *The Human Side of Mergers and Acquisitions*. San Francisco: Jossey-Bass. Explains the importance of the management of people during and after merger.

Cartwright, S. and Cooper, C. (1992) *Mergers and Acquisitions: The Human Factor*. Oxford: Butterworth Heinemann. Cultural and other 'soft' issues of mergers are discussed.

Conyon, M.J. and Clegg, P. (1994) 'Pay at the top: a study of the sensitivity of top director remuneration to specific shocks', *National Institute of Economic and Social Research Review*, August. Growth of the firm (sales) is positively related to directors' pay.

Coopers & Lybrand and OC & C (1993) *A review of the acquisition experience of major UK companies*. London: Coopers & Lybrand. An interesting survey of the top 100 firms' reasons for difficulties and triumphs in post-merger management.

Copeland, T., Koller, T. and Murrin, J. (1996) *Valuation*. 2nd edn. New York: McKinsey & Co. and Wiley. Chapter 14 provides some useful and easy-to-follow guidance on merger management.

Cowling, K., Stoneman, P. and Cubbin, J. et al. (1980) *Mergers and Economic Performance*. Cambridge: Cambridge University Press. Discusses the societal costs and benefits of mergers.

The Economist (2000) 'Merger Briefs' (two-page post-merger analysis of successes and failures) in the following editions: DaimlerChrysler, 29 July 2000; HypoVereinsbank, 5 August 2000; Boeing, 12 August 2000; Compaq, 22 July 2000; AOL Time Warner, 19 August 2000; Citicorp, 26 August 2000;

Firth, M. (1980) 'Takeovers, shareholders' returns and the theory of the firm', *Quarterly Journal of Economics*, 94, March, pp. 235–60. UK study. Results: **a** The target shareholders benefit; **b** the acquiring shareholders lose; **c** the acquiring firm's management increases utility; **d** the economic gains to society are, at best, zero.

Firth, M. (1991) 'Corporate takeovers, stockholder returns and executive rewards', *Managerial and Decision Economics*, 12, pp. 421–8. Mergers leading to increased size of firm result in higher managerial remuneration.

Franks, J. and Harris, R. (1989) 'Shareholder wealth effects of corporate takeovers: the UK experience 1955–85', *Journal of Financial Economics*, 23, pp. 225–49. Study of 1,800 UK takeovers. Gains of 25–30% for targets. Zero or modest gains for acquirers. Overall there is value created for shareholders.

Franks, J. and Mayer, C. (1996) 'Hostile takeovers and correction of managerial failure', *Journal of Financial Economics*, 40, pp. 163–81.

Gregory, A. (1997) 'An examination of the long-run performance of UK acquiring firms', *Journal of Business Finance and Accounting*, 24(7–8), Sept., pp. 971–1002. More evidence on the poor performance of acquirers.

Hasbrouck, J. (1985) 'The characteristics of takeover targets: q and other measures', *Journal of Banking and Finance*, 9, pp. 351–62.

Haspeslagh, P. and Jemison, D. (1991) *Managing Acquisitions*. New York: Free Press. A thorough and well-written guide to the management of firms that engage in mergers.

Higson, C. and Elliot, J. (1993) 'The returns to takeovers – the UK evidence', IFA Working Paper. London: London Business School. More evidence on the poor performance of the shares of acquiring firms.

Hunt, J.W., Lees, S., Grumber, J. and Vivian, P. (1987) 'Acquisitions: The Human Factor'. London: London Business School and Egan Zehnder International. Forty UK companies investigated. Merger motives, success or failure rates and success factors (particularly people factors) are explored.

Jensen, M.C. (1986) 'Agency costs of free cashflow, corporate finance and takeovers', *American Economic Review*, May, p. 323. Dividend payouts reduce managers' resources and lead to greater monitoring if they go to the capital markets for funds. Internal funding is thus preferred and surplus cash flow leads to value-destroying mergers. Easy to read.

Jensen, M.C. and Meckling W.H. (1976) 'Theory of the firm: managerial behavior, agency cost and ownership structure', *Journal of Financial Economics*, October, pp. 305–60.

Kuehn, D. (1975) *Takeovers and the theory of the firm: An empirical analysis for the United Kingdom* 1957–1969. Basingstoke: Macmillan. Acquiring firms that engage in multiple acquisitions display profitability, growth rates, etc., that are no different from those of firms which engage in few takeovers.

Lev, B. (1992) 'Observations on the merger phenomenon and a review of the evidence'. Reprinted in J.M. Stern and D. Chew (eds), *The revolution in corporate finance*. 2nd edn. Oxford: Blackwell. Merger motives, and who wins from mergers, are discussed in an introductory style.

Levine, P. and Aaronovitch, S. (1981) 'The financial characteristics of firms and theories of merger activity', *Journal of Industrial Economics*, 30, pp. 149–72.

Limmack, R. (1991) 'Corporate mergers and shareholder wealth effect, 1977–86', *Accounting and Business Research*, 21(83), pp. 239–51. 'Although there is no net wealth decrease to shareholders in total as a result of takeover activity, shareholders of bidder firms do suffer wealth decreases.'

Lynch, P. (1990) *One Up on Wall Street*, New York: Penguin.

Manson, S., Stark, A. and Thomas, H.M. (1994) 'A cash flow analysis of the operational gains from takeovers', Research Report 35 of the Chartered Association of Certified Accountants, London. Post-merger and pre-merger consolidated operating performance measures are compared. Operational gains are produced on average. A study of 38 companies.

Meeks, G. (1977) *Disappointing Marriage: A Study of the Gains from Mergers*. Cambridge: Cambridge University Press. Evidence on merger failure from the acquiring shareholders' point of view.

Meeks, G. and Whittington, G. (1975) 'Director's pay, growth and profitability', *Journal of Industrial Economics*, 24(1), pp. 1–14. Empirical evidence that director's pay and firm sales (size of firm) are positively correlated.

'Mergers and acquisitions' (1995) *Bank of England Quarterly Bulletin*, August, pp. 278–9. A discussion of the close relationship between merger activity and share price levels.

Mitchell, M.L. and Lehn, K. (1990) 'Do bad bidders become good targets?', *Journal of Political Economy*, 98(2), pp. 372–98. 'Hostile bust-up takeovers often promote economic efficiency by reallocating the targets' assets to higher valued uses . . . In aggregate, we find that the returns to acquiring firms are approximately zero; the aggregate data obscure the fact that the market discriminates between "bad" bidders which are more likely to become takeover targets, and "good" bidders, which are less likely to become targets.'

Palepu, K.G. (1986) 'Predicting takeover targets: a methodological and empirical analysis', *Journal of Accounting and Finance*, 8, pp. 3–35.

The Panel on Takeovers and Mergers, *The City Code on Takeovers and Mergers and Rules Governing Substantial Acquisitions of Shares*. London. The complex set of rules are laid out in reasonably easy to follow fashion. Updated regularly.

Powell, R.G. and Thomas, H.M. (1994) 'Corporate control and takeover prediction', Working paper 94/07 (Department of Accounting and Financial Management, University of Essex).

Rappaport, A. (1998) *Creating Shareholder Value*. New York: Free Press. Revised and Updated. Chapter 8 provides a shareholder value perspective on mergers.

Ravenscraft, D. and Scherer, F. (1987) *Mergers, Sell-Offs and Economic Efficiency*. Washington, DC: Brookings Institution. An overview of mergers: rationale, activity, profitability, economics. US based.

A review of monopolies and mergers policy: a consultative document (1978). London: HMSO, Cmnd. 7198 (Green Paper).

Roll, R. (1986) 'The hubris hypothesis of corporate takeovers', *Journal of Business*, April, 59(2), pt. 1, pp. 197–216. 'Bidding firms infected by hubris simply pay too much for their targets.'

Singh, A. (1971) *Takeovers*. Cambridge: Cambridge University Press. Provides evidence on the type of firms which become targets.

Sirower, M.L. (1997) *The Synergy Trap: How Companies Lose the Acquisition Game*. New York: Free Press. A practical, easy-to-read guide to mergers and the reasons for the failure to create value.

Sudarsanam, S. (1995) *The Essence of Mergers and Acquisitions*. Hemel Hempstead: Prentice-Hall. An easy-to-read introduction to all aspects of mergers – more detailed than this chapter.

Sudarsanam, S., Holl, P. and Salami, A. (1996) 'Shareholder wealth gains in mergers: Effect of synergy and ownership structure', *Journal of Business Finance and Accounting*, July, pp. 673–98. A study of 429 UK mergers, 1980–90. Financial synergy dominates operational synergy. A marriage between companies with a complementary fit in terms of liquidity slack and surplus investment opportunities is value creating for both groups of shareholders. But high-rated acquirers taking over low-rated firms lose value.

Van de Vliet, A. (1997) 'When mergers misfire', *Management Today*, June. An excellent, easy-to-read, overview of merger problems with plenty of examples.

WEBSITES

www.berkshirehathaway.com

www.ft.com

www.kpmg.co.uk

www.londonstockexchange.com

www.thetakeoverpanel.org.uk

SELF-REVIEW QUESTIONS

1 List as many motives for mergers as you can.

2 Briefly describe the alternative methods of payment for target firms and comment on their advantages and disadvantages.

3 Explain the significance of the following for the merger process:
- a concert party;
- the 3% rule;
- the 30% rule;
- the Takeover Panel;
- the OFT;
- the Competition Commission;
- a dawn raid.

4 List the potential beneficiaries from mergers and briefly explain whether, on average, they do gain from mergers.

5 What are the three stages of a merger?

6 List some actions which might assist a successful post-merger integration.

7 Explain the following:
- synergy;
- the internalisation of transactions;
- bargain buying;
- hubris;
- the survival motive;
- the free cash flow merger motive.

8 How do mergers differ from other investment decisions?

9 Explain the terms horizontal mergers, vertical mergers and conglomerate mergers.

10 What is the winner's curse?

11 What does it mean when an offer goes 'unconditional'?

QUESTIONS AND PROBLEMS

1* Large plc is considering the takeover of Small plc. Large is currently valued at £60m on the stock market while Small is valued at £30m. The economies of scale and other benefits of the merger are expected to produce a market value for the combined firm of £110m. A bid premium of £20m is expected to be needed to secure Small. Transaction costs (advisers' fees, etc.) are estimated at £3m. Large has 30 million shares in issue and Small has 45 million. Assume the managers are shareholder-wealth maximisers.

Required

a Does this merger create value for Large plc?

b If the purchase is made with cash what will be the price offered for each of Small's shares?

c What would be the value of each of Large's shares after this merger?

2 Which of the following mergers is horizontal, vertical or conglomerate?
a Marks & Spencer and Next.
b Northern Foods and Sainsbury's.
c Philips and HMV.
d P&O and Electrolux.
e Ford and Microsoft.

3* Box plc is considering the acquisition of Circle plc. The former is valued at £100m and the latter at £50m by the market. Economies of scale will result in savings of £2.5m annually in perpetuity. The required rate of return on both firms and the combination is 11 per cent. The transaction costs will amount to £1m.

Required

a What is the present value of the gain from the merger?
b If a cash offer of £70m is accepted by Circle's shareholders what is the value created for Box's shareholders?
c If shares are offered in such a way that Circle's shareholders would possess one-third of the merged entity, what is the value created for Box's shareholders?

4* High plc has an historic PER of 22 and Low plc has an historic PER of 12. Both companies have 100 million shares in issue and produced earnings of £20m in the last financial year. High has offered three of its shares for every five held by Low's shareholders.

Required

a If you held 1,000 shares in Low and accepted the offer from High, by how much would your wealth increase assuming High's shares remain at the pre-bid price?
b What is the bid premium being offered?
c If High was able to increase the rate of growth of Low's earnings to the same as High's and therefore place them on the same PER as High, what would High's share price move to?
d If High makes no changes to Low's operations and so earnings growth continues at its present rate what will the intrinsic value of a share in High be?
e Explain the PER game and how High could continue to acquire firms, make no changes to underlying earnings and yet show a rising earnings per share trend.

5* Consider the following companies:

	A	*B*
Earnings per share (recent)	50p	10p
Dividends per share (recent)	25p	5p
Number of shares	5m	3m
Share price	£9.00	75p

The cost of equity capital for both firms is 12 per cent. B is expected to produce a growth in dividends of 5 per cent per annum to infinity with its current strategy and management. However if A acquired B and applied superior management and gained benefits from economies of scale the growth rate would rise to 8 per cent on the same capital base. The transaction costs of the merger would amount to £400,000.

Required

a What value could be created from a merger?

b If A paid £1.20 cash for each of B's shares what value would be available for each group of shareholders?

c If A gave one of its shares for seven of B's what value would be available for each group of shareholders?

d If none of the merger benefits is realised, because of problems of integration, what is the loss or gain in value to A and B shareholders under both the cash offer and the shares offer?

6 White plc and Black plc have made all-share bids for Blue plc.

	White	*Black*	*Blue*	*White + Blue*	*Black + Blue*
Pre-merger share price	£4	£3	£1		
Number of shares issued	1m	2m	1.5m		
Market capitalisation	£4m	£6m	£1.5m	£6.8m	£8.0m

Assume no transaction costs.

Required

a If you were the managing director of White what is the maximum number of White shares you would offer for every 10 Blue shares? (Fractions of shares may be used.)

b If you were the managing director of Black, what is the maximum number of Black shares you would offer for every 10 Blue shares? (Fractions of shares may be used.)

c Discuss possible reasons for the increase in value for the Black + Blue merger being less than that for the White + Blue merger.

7 (*Examination level*) Some of the reasons put forward for mergers are beneficial to society, some to shareholders, some to the management of the acquirer and others result in benefits to more than one group. Describe these in the form of an essay.

8 (*Examination level*) The directors of Trajectory plc have decided to expand rapidly through mergers. You have been asked to explain the process itself, from appointing an adviser to the offer going unconditional. Do this in the form of an essay.

9 (*Examination level*) Mergers fail to produce value for the shareholders of acquirers in many cases. Describe and explain some reasons for merger failure.

ASSIGNMENT

Obtain as much information as you can on a recent merger. Relate the elements discussed in this chapter (merger motives, process, planning and integration) to the merger under examination. Write a report and make recommendations for improvement should any future mergers be contemplated.

CHAPTER NOTES

1 Rappaport (1998), p. 138.

2 For example, *see* Cartwright, S. and Cooper, C. (1992); Buono, A. and Bowditch, J. (1989).

3 Tim Burt and Richard Lambert, 'The Schrempp Gambit . . .', *Financial Times*, 30 October 2000, p. 26.

4 Tim Burt, 'Steering with his foot to the floor', *Financial Times*, 26 February 2001, p. 12.

5 Charles Batchelor, 'Vertical integration sets building materials debate', *Financial Times*, 17 December 1999, p. 26.

6 For evidence on the monetary benefits to directors of expanding the firm, *see* Meeks and Whittington (1975), Firth (1991) and Conyon and Clegg (1994).

7 Warren Buffett, *Berkshire Hathaway Annual Report* 1994.

8 John Kay, 'Poor odds on the takeover lottery', *Financial Times*, 26 January 1996.

9 Lynch (1990), p. 204.

10 *The Economist*, 8 June 1996, pp. 92–3.

11 Or if the purchases are immediately before the buyer announces a firm intention to make an offer if the offer is agreed by the target Board.

12 If an offer is revised all shareholders who accepted an earlier offer are entitled to the increased payment.

13 If 90 per cent of the target shares are offered, the bidder must proceed (unless there has been a material adverse change of circumstances). At lower levels of acceptance, it has a choice of whether to declare unconditionality.

14 For example, *see* Singh (1971), Firth (1980) and Lev (1992).

15 For example, Cowling *et al.* (1980) concluded that in many cases efficiency was not improved but monopoly profits were made available to the acquirer.

16 Letter to shareholders in the Berkshire Hathaway Annual Report 1995.

17 For a more thorough consideration of the human side of mergers consult Haspeslagh and Jemison (1991), Cartwright and Cooper (1992) and Buono and Bowditch (1989).

Part VI

MANAGING RISK

21 Derivatives

22 Managing exchange-rate risk

Chapter 21

DERIVATIVES

INTRODUCTION

A derivative instrument is an asset whose performance is based on (derived from) the behaviour of the value of an underlying asset (usually referred to simply as the 'underlying'). The most common underlyings are commodities (for example tea or pork bellies), shares, bonds, share indices, currencies and interest rates. Derivatives are contracts which give the right, and sometimes the obligation, to buy or sell a quantity of the underlying, or benefit in another way from a rise or fall in the value of the underlying. It is the legal *right* that becomes an asset, with its own value, and it is the right that is purchased or sold. Derivatives instruments include the following: futures, options, swaps, forward rate agreements (FRAs), forwards.

The derivatives markets have received an enormous amount of attention from the Press in recent years. This is hardly surprising as spectacular losses have been made and a number of companies brought to the point of collapse through the employment of derivatives instruments. Some examples of the unfortunate use of derivatives include:

- Metallgesellschaft, the German metals and services group, which was nearly destroyed in 1994 after losing more than DM2.3bn on energy derivatives;
- Procter & Gamble, which lost $102m speculating on the movements of future interest rates in 1994;
- Orange County in California, which lost at least $1.7bn on leveraged interest rate products;
- Barings, Britain's oldest merchant bank, which lost over £800m on Nikkei Index (the Japanese share index) contracts on the Singapore and Osaka derivatives exchanges, leading to the bank's demise in 1995;
- Sumitomo, which lost £1.17bn on copper and copper derivatives over the ten years to 1996;
- Long-Term Capital Management, which attempted to exploit the 'mispricing' of financial instruments, by making use of option pricing theory. In 1998 the firm collapsed and the Federal Reserve Bank of New York cajoled 14 banks and brokerage houses to put up $3.6bn to save LTCM and thereby prevent a financial system breakdown.

In many of the financial scandals derivatives have been used (or misused) to speculate rather than to reduce risk. This chapter examines both of these applications of derivatives but places particular emphasis on the hedging (risk-mitigating) facility they provide. These are powerful tools and managers can abuse that power either through ignorance or through deliberate acceptance of greater risk in the anticipation of greater reward. However there is nothing inherently wrong with the tools themselves. If employed properly they can be remarkably effective at limiting risk.

Learning objectives

This chapter describes the main types of derivatives. Continued innovation means that the range of instruments broadens every year but the new developments are generally variations or combinations of the characteristics of derivatives discussed here. At the end of this chapter the reader will be able to:

- explain the nature of options and the distinction between different kinds of options, and demonstrate their application in a wide variety of areas;
- show the value of the forwards, futures, FRAs, swaps, caps and floors markets by demonstrating transactions which manage and transfer risk.

A LONG HISTORY

Derivatives instruments have been employed for more than two thousand years. Olive growers in ancient Greece unwilling to accept the risk of a low price for their crop when harvested months later would enter into forward agreements whereby a price was agreed for delivery at a specific time. This reduced uncertainty for both the grower and the purchaser of the olives. In the Middle Ages forward contracts were traded in a kind of secondary market, particularly for wheat in Europe. A futures market was established in Osaka's rice market in Japan in the seventeenth century. Tulip bulb options were traded in seventeenth-century Amsterdam.

Commodity futures trading really began to take off in the nineteenth century with the Chicago Board of Trade regulating the trading of grains and other futures and options, and the London Metal Exchange dominating metal trading.

So derivatives are not new. What is different today is the size and importance of the derivatives markets. The last quarter of the twentieth century witnessed an explosive growth of volumes of trade, variety of derivatives products, and the number and range of users and uses. In the ten years to 2000 the face value of outstanding derivatives contracts rose 60-fold to stand at about US$60 trillion (US$60,000,000,000,000). Compare that with a UK annual GDP of £950bn.

OPTIONS

An option is a contract giving one party the right, but not the obligation, to buy or sell a financial instrument, commodity or some other underlying asset at a given price, at or before a specified date. The purchaser of the option can either exercise the right or let it lapse – the choice is theirs.

A very simple option would be where a firm pays the owner of land a non-returnable premium (say £10,000) for an option to buy the land at an agreed price because the firm is considering the development of a retail park within the next five years. The property developer may pay a number of option premiums to owners of land in different parts of the country. If planning permission is eventually granted on a particular plot the option to purchase may be exercised. In other words the developer pays the price agreed at the time that the option contract was arranged, say £1,000,000, to purchase the land. Options on other plots will be allowed to lapse and will have no value. By using an option the property developer has 'kept the options open' with regard to which site to buy and develop and, indeed whether to enter the retail park business at all.

Options can also be traded. Perhaps the option to buy could be sold to another company keener to develop a particular site than the original option purchaser. It may be sold for much more than the original £10,000 option premium, even before planning permission has been granted.

Once planning permission has been granted the greenfield site may be worth £1,500,000. If there is an option to buy at £1,000,000 the option right has an intrinsic value of £500,000, representing a 4,900 per cent return on £10,000.

If the original developer had eschewed options and simply bought the site for £1,000,000, instead of purchasing the *right* to buy, then the return, should it decide to sell rather than develop, would be only 50 per cent. From this comparison we can see the gearing effect of options: very large sums can be gained in a short period of time for a small initial cash outlay.

Share options

Share options have been traded for centuries but their use expanded dramatically with the creation of traded option markets in Chicago, Amsterdam and, in 1978, the London Traded Options Market. In 1992 this became part of the London International Financial Futures and Options Exchange, LIFFE (pronounced 'life').

A share call option gives the purchaser a right, but not the obligation, to buy a fixed number of shares at a specified price at some time in the future. In the case of traded options on LIFFE, one option contract relates to a quantity of 1,000 shares. The seller of the option, who receives the premium, is referred to as the writer. The writer of a call option is obligated to sell the agreed quantity of shares at the agreed price some time in the future. American-style options can be exercised by the buyer at any time up to the expiry date, whereas European-style options can only be exercised on a predetermined future date. Just to confuse everybody, the distinction has nothing to do with geography: most options traded in Europe are American-style options.

Call option holder (call option buyers)

Now let us examine the call options available on an underlying share – Cadbury Schweppes, on 13 August 2001. There are a number of different options available for this share, many of which are not reported in the table presented in the *Financial Times* which is reproduced as Exhibit 21.1.

So, what do the figures mean? If you wished to obtain the right to buy 1,000 shares on or before late January 2002, at an exercise price of 500p, you would pay a premium of £300 (1,000 × 30p). If you wished to keep your option to purchase open for another three months you could select the April call. But this right to insist that the writer sells

Exhibit 21.1 Call options on Cadbury Schweppes shares, 13 August 2001 FT

	Call option prices (premiums) pence		
Exercise price	*October*	*January*	*April*
460p	36	51	59
500p	15	30	38½
Share price on 13.8.2001 = 482p			

Source: Financial Times, 14 August 2001. Reprinted with permission.

the shares at the fixed price of 500p on or before a date in late May will cost another £85 (the total premium payable on one option contract = £385). This extra £85 represents additional *time value*. Time value arises because of the potential for the market price of the underlying to change in a way that creates intrinsic value. The longer the time over which the option is exercisable the greater the chance that the price will move to give intrinsic value. Time value is the amount by which the option premium exceeds the intrinsic value.

The two exercise price (also called strike price) levels presented in Exhibit 21.1 illustrate an *in-the-money-option* (the 460 call option) and an *out-of-the-money-option* (the 500 call option). The underlying share price is above the strike price of 460 and so this call option has an intrinsic value of 22p and is therefore in-the-money.

The right to buy at 500p is out-of-the-money because the share price is below the option exercise price and therefore has no intrinsic value. The holder of a 500p option would not exercise this right to buy at 500p because the shares can be bought on the stock exchange for 482p.

(It is sometimes possible to buy an *at-the-money option*, which is one where the market share price is equal to the option exercise price.)

The option premiums vary in proportion to the length of time over which the option is exercisable (they are higher for an April option than for an October option). Also a call option with a lower exercise price will have a higher premium.

Suppose that you are confident that Cadbury Schweppes shares are going to rise significantly over the next five and half months to 700p and you purchase a January 460 call at 51 pence.[1] The cost of this right to purchase 1,000 shares is £510 (51p × 1,000 shares). If the share rises as expected then you could exercise the right to purchase the shares for a total of £4,600 and then sell these in the market for £7,000. A profit of £2,400 less £510 = £1,890 is made before transaction costs (the brokers' fees, etc. would be in the region of £40–£60). This represents a massive 371 per cent rise before costs (£1,890/£510).

However the future is uncertain and the share price may not rise as expected. Let us consider two other possibilities. First, the share price may remain at 482p throughout the life of the option. Second, the stock market may have a severe downturn and Cadbury Schweppes shares may fall to 400p. These possibilities are shown in Exhibit 21.2.

In the case of a standstill in the share price the option gradually loses its time value over the five and a half months until, at expiry, only the intrinsic value of 22 pence per share remains. The fall in the share price to 400p illustrates one of the advantages of purchasing options over some other derivatives: the holder has a right to abandon the option and is not forced to buy the underlying share at the option exercise price – this saves £600. It would have added insult to injury to have to buy at £4,600 and sell at £4,000 after having already lost £510 on the premium for the purchase of the option.

Exhibit 21.2 Profits and losses on the January 460 call option

	Assumptions on share price in January at expiry		
	700p	482p	400p
Cost of purchasing shares by exercising the option	£4,600	£4,600	£4,600
Value of shares bought	£7,000	£4,820	£4,000
Profit from exercise of option and sale of shares in the market	£2,400	£220	–*
Less option premium paid	£510	£510	£510
Profit (loss) before transaction costs	£1890	–£290	–£510
Percentage return over $5^1/_2$ months	371%	–57%	–100%

*Not exercised.

Exhibits 21.3 and 21.4 show the extent to which the option gears up the return from share price movements: a wider dispersion of returns is experienced. On 13 August 2001, 1,000 shares could be bought for £4,820. If the value rose to £7,000, a 45 per cent return would be made, compared with a 371 per cent return if options are bought. We would all like the higher positive return on the option than the lower one available on the underlying – but would we all accept the downside risk associated with this option? Consider the following possibilities.

- If share price remains at 482p:
  - Return if shares are bought: 0%
  - Return if option is bought: –57% ((£220 – £510)/£510)[2]
- If share price falls to 400p:
  - Return if shares are bought: –17% ((400 – 482)/482) × 100)
  - Return if option is bought: –100% (the option is worth nothing)

Exhibit 21.3 Profit if 1,000 shares are bought in Cadbury Schweppes in August 2001 at 482p

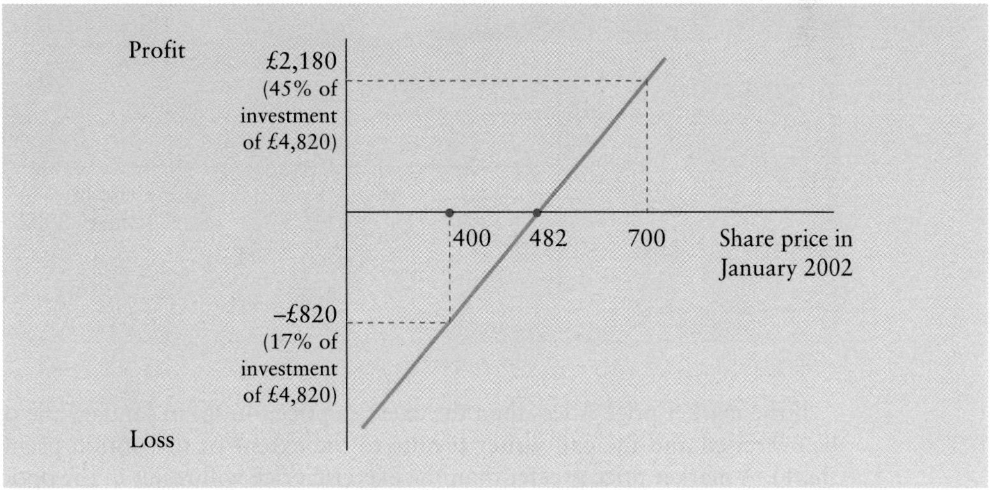

Exhibit 21.4 Profit if one 460 January call option contract (for 1,000 shares) in Cadbury Schweppes is purchased on 13 August 2001 and held to maturity

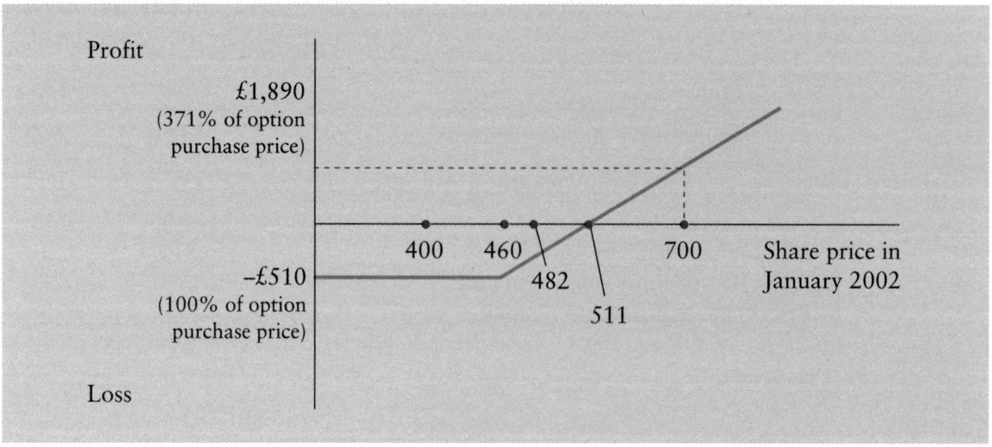

The holder of the call option will not exercise unless the share price is at least 460p: at a lower price it will be cheaper to buy shares on the stock market. Break-even does not occur until a price of 511p because of the need to cover the cost of the premium (460p + 51p). However at higher prices the option value increases, pence for pence, with the share price. Also the downside risk is limited to the size of the option premium.

Call option writers

The returns position for the writer of a call option in Cadbury Schweppes can also be presented in a diagram (*see* Exhibit 21.5). With all these examples note that there is an assumption that the position is held to expiry.

Exhibit 21.5 The profit to a call option writer on one 460 January call contract written on 13 August 2001

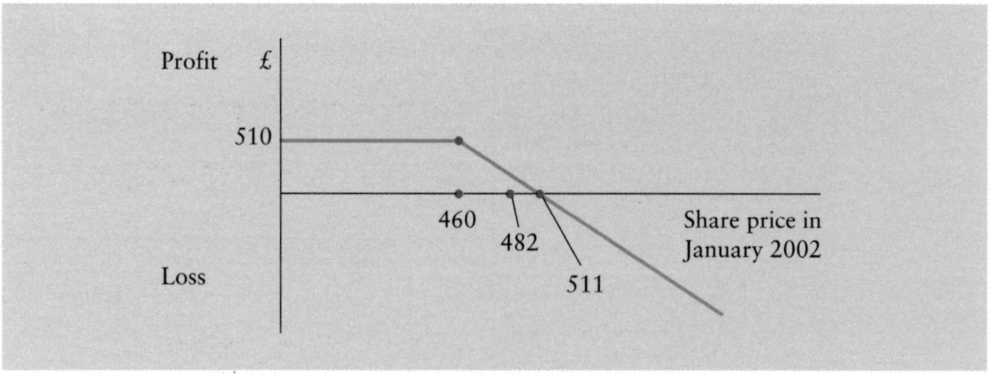

If the market price is less than the exercise price (460p) in January the option will not be exercised and the call writer profits to the extent of the option premium (51p per share). A market price greater than the exercise price will result in the option being exercised and the writer will be forced to deliver 1,000 shares for a price of 460p. This may mean buying shares on the stock market to supply to the option holder. As the share price rises this becomes an increasingly onerous task and losses mount.

Note that in the sophisticated traded option markets of today very few option positions are held to expiry. In most cases the option holder sells the option in the market to make a cash profit or loss. Option writers often cancel out their exposure before expiry – for example they could purchase an option to buy the same quantity of shares at the same price and expiry date.

LIFFE share options

The *Financial Times* lists over eighty companies' shares in which options are traded (*see* Exhibit 21.6).

Exhibit 21.6 LIFFE equity options

Share price of the end of the trading day

Premium payable per share for call options with a March 2002 exercise date

FT

Option		Calls Oct	Calls Jan	Calls Apr	Puts Oct	Puts Jan	Puts Apr
Abbey Natl	1150	64½	104½	126½	67½	95	118½
(*1155)	1200	44½	81½	104	97½	122½	148
Ald Domecq	390	36½	45	50	5½	13½	17
(*417½)	420	18	27½	33½	17	26½	30½
AstraZeneca	3300	158½	258	321	126	189½	242
(*3320)	3400	109	200½	268	178	231½	288
BAA	600	53½	63	77	7	15½	23
(*641)	650	20½	33½	47	24	36	43
BAT	550	38½	53	62	25	33½	48
(*559)	600	17½	31	39½	54	61	77½
Barclays	2100	164	227	269½	67½	115	155
(*2200)	2200	106½	177	216	107½	161½	199
Six Continents	700	34½	50½	62½	17	38½	50½
(*711½)	750	12½	27	40½	46	68½	80
Boots	650	37	50	65	16	29½	38½
(*665)	700	15	27	41½	44½	57	65
Br Airways	300	32½	40½	49	6	14½	20½
(*324)	330	14	24	33	17	28	34
BP	600	27½	42½	54	25	36½	45
(*601)	650	9½	22	32½	57½	66½	73
Cadbury Sch	460	36	51	59	10	19½	28
(*482)	500	15	30	38½	29	39	48
CGNU	1000	51½	81	104	48½	68½	97½
(*1005½)	1050	30	58	82	78½	96½	127
Corus	60	6½	9½	12	3½	6	7½
(*62½)	70	2½	5½	8	9½	12	13½
EMAP	700	52½	74	92½	28	47	59
(*718½)	750	29½	50½	68½	55	73½	84½
GlaxoSmKl	1900	111	163½	210½	59½	102	126
(*1935)	2000	60½	111	155	109½	148	171
HSBC 75p	800	47	73	90½	27½	45½	65
(*826)	850	23½	48	65½	54½	70½	91½
Halifax	800	56	78½	94	23	39½	59
(*833)	850	29½	53	69	48	64	84½
ICI	420	29½	44	55	18½	28	35½
(*434)	460	13	26	36½	42	50	57½
Intl Power	280	19	29½	37½	14	21½	26
(*282½)	300	10½	20½	28	25½	32½	37
Land Secur	850	55½	71½	90½	13	27	37½
(*885)	900	25½	43	64	33½	48½	61
Option		Oct	Jan	Mar	Oct	Jan	Mar
Lonmin	850	61	89½	98	31½	50½	70½
(*872)	900	37	64½	73½	57½	75½	97½

Option		Calls Oct	Calls Jan	Calls Apr	Puts Oct	Puts Jan	Puts Apr
Marks & S	240	21	28	34	7½	15	19
(*251)	260	10½	18	24½	17½	25½	29½
Natl Grid	460	42	53½	62	11	21½	27
(*487)	500	19½	32	41½	29	40	45½
Pearson	1000	98	145	178½	69	105½	135
(*1020)	1050	74	122½	155½	95½	132	161½
Psion	70	16½	23½	27	8½	14½	17½
(*78)	80	12½	19½	23	14	20½	23½
RTZ	1150	78½	116½	138	60½	86	111½
(*1174)	1200	54½	91½	113	86	110½	136½
Reuters	800	84	117½	140	57½	82	103½
(*820)	850	60½	94	116½	84	108½	129½
Royal Bk Scot	1700	107	166½	200½	87½	128½	156½
(*1718)	1800	63½	120½	154½	144	183	210½
Royal/Sun Al	460	33	48	57	17½	27	40
(*480½)	500	15	29½	39	40	48½	62½
Safeway	360	20	30	38½	14½	23	28
(*362½)	390	7½	17½	25½	32½	40½	45
Sainsbury	390	22	32	40	14½	23½	28½
(*394)	420	9½	19	26½	32½	41	45
Option		Oct	Jan	Mar	Oct	Jan	Mar
Shell Trans	550	25½	41	48	26	35½	38½
(*551)	600	8	20	27	59	65	68
Option		Oct	Jan	Apr	Oct	Jan	Apr
Std Chartd	800	64	93½	110½	33	52½	73
(*824)	850	39	67½	82	58	76	95
Vodafone	130	15	20½	25	9	13½	16½
(*135)	140	10	16	20	13½	18½	21½
Option		Aug	Nov	Feb	Aug	Nov	Feb
Allce & Leics	800	40½	64	86½	–	25	40
(*840)	850	4	37	61	13½	48½	64½
Anglo Amer	875	27½	81	–	4	57½	–
(*898)	900	11½	68½	59	13	69½	88
BAE Systems	330	21½	34½	44	–	12	18
(*351)	360	1	17½	27½	10	25½	32
Brit Telecom	449	14	49	–	4	34	–
(*458½)	494	1½	29½	–	35½	59	–
Capita	460	23	61½	81½	1½	35	50½
(*481)	500	2	43	60	21	55½	68½
Carlton Comm	330	8	33	45	2½	23½	32
(*335)	360	–	20	31½	25	41	48½
Diageo	700	39½	63	78	–	24	34½
(*739)	750	3	34½	52½	14	47½	59

Option		Calls Aug	Calls Nov	Calls Feb	Puts Aug	Puts Nov	Puts Feb
Gallaher	460	21½	37½	53	–	17½	28½
(*481)	500	½	19	34	19	39½	49½
Hanson	500	33	53½	67½	–	19	27½
(*532½)	550	½	28	42	22	43	52
Hilton	240	6½	16	22½	–	10	13½
(*246)	260	–	7½	13	14	21½	24½
Impl Tobacco	800	24	69	87	1½	37	58
(*822)	850	1	44½	62½	28½	62½	84½
Invensys	80	3½	11½	14	1	8	11½
(*82½)	90	–	7½	9½	7½	14	17
Kingfisher	360	14½	31	41	½	17	23½
(*373½)	390	½	17½	27	16½	33½	39½
Legal & Gen	160	7½	14	18½	–	6	8½
(*167½)	180	–	5	9½	12½	17	19½
Logica	650	30	112	148½	8½	84½	115
(*671)	700	6½	89	127½	35	111½	142½
Marconi	80	3½	14	18	2	12	16½
(*81)	90	½	10½	14	9½	18	22½
P & O	220	7½	16	22	½	11	15½
(*227)	240	–	7	13½	13	23	27
Prudential	850	17	57½	81½	3	42	56½
(*863)	900	½	35	57½	37	70½	82½
Rentokil Init	220	12½	21½	26½	–	7½	11
(*232½)	240	½	11	16	7½	17½	19½
Rolls-Royce	200	14	21½	26½	–	7½	11
(*213½)	220	½	11	16½	7	17½	21
Tesco	240	15	24	30½	–	7½	11
(*255)	260	1	13	20	5½	16½	20½
Option		Sep	Dec	Mar	Sep	Dec	Mar
ARM	280	37½	63	78	23½	46	58
(*292½)	300	28½	55	70½	34	57½	70
Autonomy	360	52	86	110	46	76	96½
(*364)	390	39	74	99	63	94	115
BG	260	23½	31½	38	3	9½	13
(*279)	280	10	18½	27	10	16½	22
Baltimore	20	5	7	8½	2	3½	5
(*23)	25	2½	5	7	4½	6½	8½
Bk Scotland	800	52½	73	91	17½	40	57
(*831)	850	26	47½	66½	40½	64½	82½
BSkyB	750	50	84½	108½	27	53	68½
(*769½)	800	27½	60½	85	54	79	94½
Brit Biotech	20	1½	3	4	1½	2½	3
(*20)	25	–	1½	2	5	6	6½

Option		Calls Sep	Calls Dec	Calls Mar	Puts Sep	Puts Dec	Puts Mar
CMG	220	35	55	66	16½	35	43½
(*237½)	240	25½	46½	58½	26½	46½	55½
Cable & Wire	330	25	44	55	21	36	47½
(*332½)	360	13	30½	41	38½	52½	63
Celltech	1000	58½	107	139½	48	85	107
(*1005)	1050	36½	82½	116	76½	111	133½
Centrica	200	21½	26½	31½	2	6	9
(*218)	220	8½	15	20½	9½	14	17½
Colt Tel	280	40½	67½	85	25½	48½	63
(*294)	300	32	59	77½	36½	60½	75½
Compass	550	25½	47	62½	18	33	47
(*557)	600	7½	26	41½	50	62	75½
Dixons	220	10½	21	27½	9½	17½	22½
(*224½)	240	3½	13	19½	22½	29½	34½
EMI	420	20	36	48½	21½	36	47½
(*425)	460	6	21½	33	49½	61	71½
Energis	90	11½	19	23½	7	14	17
(*94)	100	7	15	19½	12½	19½	23
Granada	152	10	–	–	5	–	–
(*156)	163	5	–	–	11	–	–
Gus	550	50½	72	79½	6	20	28
(*591½)	600	19½	44	53	25	42½	51
LloydsTSB	700	45	73	90½	18	37½	57½
(*725)	750	18½	47½	64½	42	62½	82
Misys	330	38	64	79	26½	48½	61½
(*340)	360	25	51½	67	43	65½	79
Amersham	600	41½	69½	89½	23½	47½	61
(*614½)	650	20	47	66½	52	75	88
Railtrack	300	30	44	51½	12½	28½	36½
(*316)	330	15	30	38	27½	45	53
Reed Intl	600	33	60	75	18	38½	47
(*615)	650	12	37½	52	47	66	73½
Sage	200	22	36½	45	12	24	31
(*209)	220	13	27½	36½	23	35	42
Scot Power	460	22½	36	47	11	23½	32
(*475)	500	5	18	28½	34	46	53½
Telewest	70	11	17	20½	6	11½	14
(*74½)	80	6½	13	16½	12	17½	20
Tomkins	180	15½	18	21½	3	7	11
(*195½)	200	2½	8½	12	14	17½	21½
Unilever	550	54½	68½	81½	3½	14½	22½
(*598)	600	19	37	52	18	33	42
Whitbread	609	46½	59½	–	4	16	–
(*648)	660	14½	30	–	23½	69	–

*Underlying security price. Premiums shown are based on settlement prices. Source: LIFFE

August 13 Total contracts. Equity & Index options: 59,059 Calls: 24,628 Puts: 28,616

Strike or exercise price for this line of options

Put option premium – in this case with a March exercise date

Source: *Financial Times*, 14 August 2001. Reprinted with permission.

Put options

A put option gives the holder the right, but not the obligation, to sell a specific quantity of shares on or before a specified date at a fixed exercise price.

Imagine you are pessimistic about the prospects for Cadbury Schweppes on 13 August 2001. You could purchase, for a premium of 19½p per share (£195 in total), the right to sell 1,000 shares in or before late January 2002 at 460p (*see* Exhibit 21.6). If a collapse in price subsequently takes place, to, say, 400p, you can insist on exercising the right to sell at 460p. The writer of the put option is obliged to purchase shares at 460p while being aware that the put holder is able to buy shares at 400p on the stock exchange. The option holder makes a profit of 460 – 400 – 19.5 = 40.5p per share, a 208 per cent return (before costs).

As with calls, in most cases the option holder would take profits by selling the option on to another investor via LIFFE rather than waiting to exercise at expiry (*see* Exhibits 21.7 and 21.8).

Exhibit 21.7 Put option holder profit profile (Cadbury Schweppes 460 January put, purchased 13 August 2001)

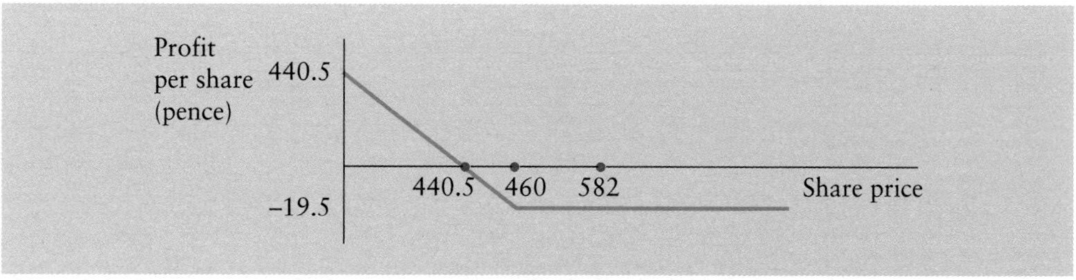

Exhibit 21.8 Put option writer profit profile (Cadbury Schweppes 460 January put, sold 13 August 2001)

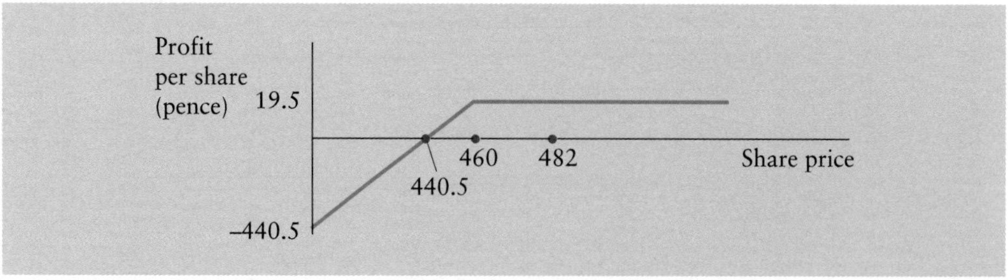

For the put option holder, if the market price exceeds the exercise price, it will not be wise to exercise as shares can be sold for a higher price on the stock exchange. Therefore the maximum loss, equal to the premium paid, is incurred. The option writer gains the premium if the share price remains above the exercise price, but may incur a large loss if the market price falls significantly.

Traditional options

The range of underlyings available on LIFFE and other exchanges is limited. Traditional options, on the other hand, are available on any security but there is no choice on the strike (exercise) price: this is set as the market price on the day the option is bought. Also all options expire within three months and the option cannot be sold on to another investor: it has to be either exercised by the original purchaser or left to lapse. The purchaser may close a position during the life of an option by doing the reverse (e.g. if he has bought a call option he could sell a call option at the same strike price).

Using share options to reduce risk: hedging

Hedging with options is especially attractive because they can give protection against unfavourable movements in the underlying while permitting the possibility of benefiting from favourable movements. Suppose you hold 1,000 shares in Cadbury Schweppes on 13 August 2001. Your shareholding is worth £4,820. There are rumours flying around the market that the company may become the target of a takeover bid. If this materialises the share price will rocket; if it does not the market will be disappointed and the price will fall dramatically. What are you to do? One way to avoid the downside risk is to sell the shares. The problem is that you may regret this action if the bid does subsequently occur and you have forgone the opportunity of a large profit. An alternative approach is to retain the shares and buy a put option. This will rise in value as the share price falls. If the share price rises you gain from your underlying share holding.

Assume a 460 April put is purchased for a premium of £280 (*see* Exhibit 21.6). If the share price falls to 380p in late April you lose on your underlying shares by £1,020 ((482p – 380p) × 1,000). However the put option will have an intrinsic value of £800 ((460p – 380p) × 1,000), thus reducing the loss and limiting the downside risk. Below 460p, for every 1p lost in a share price, 1p is gained on the put option, so the maximum loss is £500 (£220 intrinsic value + £280 option premium). The size of the gain should the share price rise is limitless, as is shown in Exhibit 21.9.

This hedging reduces the dispersion of possible outcomes. There is a floor below which losses cannot be increased, while on the upside the benefit from any rise in share price is reduced.

Exhibit 21.9 Profit profile for a put option and shares

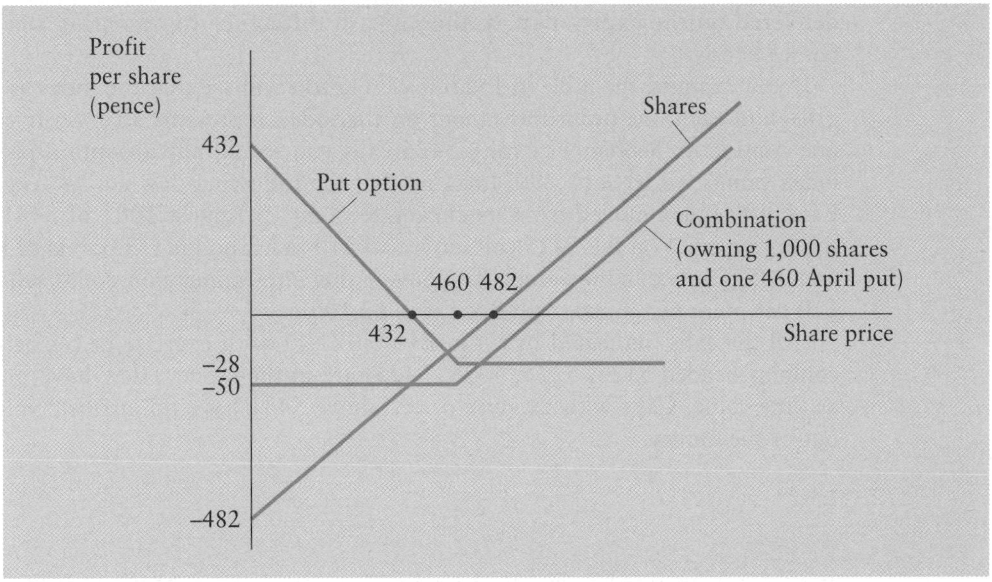

A simpler example of risk reduction occurs when an investor is fairly sure that a share will rise in price but is not so confident as to discount the possibility of a fall. Suppose that the investor wished to buy 10,000 shares in Diageo, currently priced at 739p (on 13 August 2001) – *see* Exhibit 21.6. This can be achieved either by a direct purchase of shares in the market or through the purchase of an option. If the share price does fall significantly, the size of the loss is greater with the share purchase – the option loss is limited to the premium paid.

Suppose that ten February 750 call options are purchased at a cost of £5,250 (52.5p × 1,000 × 10). Exhibit 21.10 shows that the option is less risky because of the ability to abandon the right to buy at 750p.

Exhibit 21.10 Losses on alternative buying strategies

Diageo share price falls to:	*Loss on 10,000 shares*	*Loss on 10 call options options*
700	£3,900	£5,250
650	£8,900	£5,250
600	£13,900	£5,250
550	£18,900	£5,250
500	£23,900	£5,250

Index options

Options on whole share indices can be purchased, for example, Standard and Poors 500 (USA), FTSE 100 (UK), CAC 40 (France), DAX (Germany) and so on. Large investors usually have a varied portfolio of shares so, rather than hedging individual shareholdings with options, they may hedge through options on the entire index of shares. Also speculators can take a position on the future movement of the market as a whole.

A major difference between index options and share options is that the former are 'cash settled' – so for the FTSE 100 option, one hundred different shares are not delivered on the expiry day. Rather, a cash difference representing the price change passes hands.

If you examine the table in Exhibit 21.11, you will see that the index is regarded as a price and each one-point movement on the index represents £10. So if you purchased one contract in September expiry 5425 calls you would pay an option premium of 139 index points × £10 = £1,390. Imagine that the following day, i.e. 14 August 2001, the FTSE 100 Index moved from its closing level on 13 August 2001 of 5431 to 5500 and the option price on the 5425 call moved to 210 index points (75 points of intrinsic value and 135 points of time value). To convert this into money you could sell the option at £10 per point per contract (210 × £10 = £2,100).

All the calls (indicated by C) in Exhibit 21.11 with exercise prices below 5431 (the columns headed 5125, 5225, 5325, 5425) are in-the-money; they have intrinsic as well as time value. Calls with exercise prices above 5431 have no intrinsic value and so are out-of-the-money.

Exhibit 21.11 **FTSE 100 Index option prices**

EURO STYLE FTSE 100 INDEX OPTION (LIFFE) £10 per full index point **13 Aug**

	5125		5225		5325		5425		5525		5625		5725		5825	
	C	P	**C**	P	**C**	P	**C**	P	**C**	P	**C**	P	**C**	P	**C**	P
Aug	**300½**	1	**203**	3½	**112½**	13	**42½**	43	**9**	109½	**1½**	202	**½**	300½	**¼**	400½
Sep	**349½**	40½	**270½**	61	**199½**	89½	**139**	128½	**90**	179	**54**	242½	**29½**	317½	**14**	401½
Oct	**396**	72½	**321½**	97½	**252**	127	**192**	165½	**140½**	213½	**99**	271	**66**	337	**41**	411½
Dec	**478½**	127	**408½**	155½	**343½**	189	**285½**	229	**233**	274½	**186**	326	**145**	383½	**110½**	447
Mar	**560½**	194	**494½**	225	**433**	260½	**375**	300	**321**	343	**272**	391	**227½**	443½	**188**	501

Calls 13,157: Puts 15,839. * Underlying index value. Premiums shown are based on settlement prices.

Source: *Financial Times*, 14 August 2001. Reprinted with permission.

By contrast, all puts (indicated by a P) with an exercise price lower than 5431 do not have intrinsic value and are out-of-the-money.

Hedging against a decline in the market

A fund manager controlling a £30m portfolio of shares on behalf of a group of pensioners is concerned that the market may fall over the next four months. One strategy to lower risk is to purchase put options on the share index. If the market does fall losses on the portfolio will be offset by gains on the value of the index put option.

First the manager has to calculate the number of option contracts needed to hedge the underlying. With the index at 5431 on 13 August 2001 and each point of that index settled at £10, one contract has a value of 5431 × £10 = £54,310. To cover a £30m portfolio:

$$\frac{\pounds 30\text{m}}{\pounds 54{,}310} = 552 \text{ contracts}$$

The manager opts to buy 552 December 5425 puts for 229 points per contract.[3] The premium payable is:

229 points × £10 × 552 = £1,264,080

This amounts to a 4.2 per cent 'insurance premium' (1.264m/30m) against a downturn in the market.

Consider what happens if the market does fall by a large amount, say, 15 per cent, between August and December. The index falls to 4616, and the loss on the portfolio is:

£30m × 0.15 = £4,500,000

If the portfolio was unhedged the pensioners suffer from a market fall. However in this case the put options gain in value as the index falls because they carry the right to sell at 5425. If the manager closed the option position by buying at a level of 4616, with the right to sell at 5425, an 809-point difference, a gain is made:

Gain on options (5425 – 4616) × 552 × £10 =	£4,465,680
Less option premium paid	– £1,264,080
	£3,201,600

A substantial proportion of the fall in portfolio value is compensated for through the use of the put derivative.

Exhibit 21.12 Aunt Agathas and derivatives

Millions of ordinary small investors (Aunt Agathas in the City jargon) have their money applied to the derivatives markets even though they may remain blissfully unaware that such 'exotic' transactions are being conducted on their behalf. Take the case of guaranteed equity bonds. Investors nervous of investing in the stock market for fear of downward swings are promised a guarantee that they will receive at least the return of their original capital, even if the stock market falls. If it rises they will receive a return linked to the rise (say the capital gain element – excluding dividends). The bulk of the capital invested may be placed in safe fixed-interest investments, with the stock market linked return created through the use of options and other derivatives. An alternative approach is to invest 85 to 95 per cent of the assets in shares and the rest in put options (these funds are designed to lose a maximum of 5 per cent per quarter). Following the Barings Bank fiasco there was some discussion over the wisdom of using such highly geared instruments. However the financial services industry easily defended itself by pointing out the risk-reducing possibilities of these products if properly managed.

Corporate uses of options

There are a number of corporate uses of options.

1 ***Share option schemes*** Many companies now grant (or sell to) employees share options (calls) as a means of achieving commitment and greater goal congruence between agents and principals. Employees are offered the right to buy shares at a fixed price some time in the future. They then have the incentive over the intervening years to perform well and push up the share price so as to realise a large gain when the options may be exercised. Continental has taken the use of options for employee incentive schemes one stage further through the use of put options – *see* Exhibit 21.13.

2 ***Warrants*** A share warrant is an option issued by a company which gives the owner the right, but not the obligation, to purchase a specified number of shares at a specified price over a given period of time. Note that it is the company that writes the option rather than speculators or hedgers.

3 ***Convertible bonds*** A convertible bond can be viewed as a bundle of two sets of rights. First, there are the usual rights associated with a bond, for example interest and principal payments, and second, there is the right, but not the obligation, to exercise a call option and purchase shares using the bond itself as the payment for those shares.

4 ***Rights issues*** In a rights issue shareholders are granted the right, but not the obligation, to purchase additional shares in the company. This right has value and can be sold to other investors.

5 ***Share underwriting*** Effectively when an underwriter agrees to purchase securities, if investors do not purchase the whole issue, a put option has been bought with the underwriting fee, and the company has the right to insist that the underwriter buys at the price agreed.

Exhibit 21.13

Options from Morgan and Dresdner

FT

Not every application of derivatives leads to losses for users such as Procter & Gamble, nor reputational damage for designers of tailor-made products such as Bankers Trust, nor catastrophic collapse for traders such as Barings. Options, a type of derivative financial instrument, also stand behind a novel and increasingly popular device to extend European employee share ownership.

J.P. Morgan and Dresdner Bank, the US and German banks, yesterday announced a partnership in Germany to market a sophisticated employee share ownership programme (esop). The venture's first client is Continental, the German tyre manufacturer, which wishes gradually to extend worker ownership from 0.5 per cent to 5 per cent.

Each employee in the 'Conti 100' scheme will be entitled to 100 shares which, at yesterday's share price of DM20.7, would be worth DM2,070. A participant in the programme provides 20 per cent of the investment and receives a two-year interest free loan for the remaining 80 per cent.

Employees are guaranteed against a fall in the company's share price. For a fee from Continental, J.P. Morgan and Dresdner write 'put' options on Continental shares. These give employees the right, but not the obligation, to sell their shares at the initial share price. If the market price falls below that level, they can exercise the option and avoid losses. If the market price rises, they can take a profit and let the option lapse.

The protection provided by J.P. Morgan allows employees to invest without jeopardising their savings; and it provides security for workers to borrow and thus leverage their investment. The company can introduce incentives without jeopardising employees' savings and morale.

Source: Nicholas Denton, *Financial Times*, 6 October 1995. Reprinted with permission.

6 *Commodities* Many firms are exposed to commodity risk. Firms selling commodities, or buying for production purposes, may be interested in hedging against price fluctuations in these markets. Examples of such firms are airlines, food processors, car manufacturers, chocolate manufacturers. Some of the commodity options available are:

- crude oil
- aluminium
- copper
- coffee
- cocoa

Operational and strategic decisions with options (real options)

Managers often encounter decisions with call or put options embedded within them. Examples of these are given below.

The expansion option

Firms sometimes undertake projects which apparently have negative NPVs. They do so because an option is thereby created to expand, should this be seen to be desirable. The value of the option outweighs the loss of value on the project. For example, many Western firms set up offices, marketing and production operations in China in the 1990s which ran up losses. This did not lead to a pull-out because of the long-term attraction to expand within the world's largest market. If they withdrew they would find it very difficult to re-enter, and would therefore sacrifice the option to expand. This option is considered to be so valuable that some firms are prepared to pay the price (premium) of many years of losses.

Another example would be where a firm has to decide whether to enter a new technological area. If it does it may make losses but at least it has opened up the choices available to the firm. To have refused to enter at all on the basis of a crude NPV calculation could close off important future avenues for expansion. The pharmaceutical giants run dozens of research programmes knowing that only a handful will be money spinners. They do this because they do not know at the outset which will be winners and which the losers – so they keep their options open.

The option to abandon

With some major investments, once the project is begun it has to be completed. For example, if a contract is signed with a government department to build a bridge the firm is legally committed to deliver a completed bridge. Other projects have options to abandon (put options) at various stages and these options can have considerable value. For example, if a property developer purchases a prime site near a town centre there is, in the time it takes to draw up plans and gain planning permission, the alternative option of selling the land. Flexibility could also be incorporated in the construction process itself – for example, perhaps alternative materials can be used if the price of the first choice increases. Also, the buildings could be designed in such a way that they could be quickly and cheaply switched from one use to another, for example from offices to flats, or from hotel to shops. At each stage there is an option to abandon plan A and switch to plan B. Having plan B available has value. To have plan A only leaves the firm vulnerable to changing circumstances.

Option on timing

Perhaps in the example of the property developer above it may be possible to create more options by creating conditions that do not compel the firm to undertake investment at particular points in time. If there was an option to wait a year, or two years, then the prospects for rapid rental growth for office space *vis-à-vis* hotels, flats and shops could be assessed. Thus a more informed, and in the long run more value-creating, decision can be made.

True NPV

True NPV takes into account the value of options.

True NPV = Crude NPV + NPV of expansion option + NPV of the option to abandon + NPV of timing option + NPV of other option possibilities

FORWARDS

Imagine you are responsible for purchasing potatoes to make crisps for your firm, a snack food producer. In the free market for potatoes the price rises or falls depending on the balance between buyers and sellers. These movements can be dramatic. Obviously you would like to acquire potatoes at a price which was as low as possible, while the potato producer wishes to sell for a price that is as high as possible. However both parties may have a similar interest in reducing the uncertainty of price. This will assist both to plan production and budget effectively. One way in which this could be done is to reach an agreement with the producer(s) to purchase a quantity of potatoes at a price agreed today to be delivered at a specified time in the future. Bensons, the UK crisp producer, buys 80 per cent of its potatoes up to 19 months forward. Once the forward agreements have been signed and sealed Bensons may later be somewhat regretful if the spot price (price for immediate delivery) subsequently falls below the price agreed months earlier. Unlike option contracts, forwards commit both parties to complete the deal. However Bensons is obviously content to live with this potential for regret in order to remove the risk associated with such an important raw material.

A forward contract is an agreement between two parties to undertake an exchange at an agreed future date at a price agreed now.

The party buying at the future date is said to be taking a *long position*. The counterparty which will deliver at the future date is said to be taking a *short position*.

There are forward markets in a wide range of commodities but the most important forward markets today are for foreign exchange, in which hundreds of billions of dollars worth of currency are traded every working day – this will be considered in Chapter 22.

Forward contracts are tailor-made to meet the requirements of the parties. This gives flexibility on the amounts and delivery dates. Forwards are not traded on an exchange but are over-the-counter instruments – private agreements outside the regulation of an exchange. Such an agreement exposes the counterparties to the risk of default – the failure by the other to deliver on the agreement. The risk grows in proportion to the extent to which the spot price diverges from the forward price as the incentive to renege increases.

Forward contracts are difficult to cancel, as agreement from each counterparty is needed. Also to close the contract early may result in a penalty being charged. Despite these drawbacks forward markets continue to flourish. Ashanti Goldfields of Ghana had reason to be grateful for the forward market in gold[4] (*see* Exhibit 21.14).

Exhibit 21.14

Hedging helps Ashanti mines break even

FT

Ashanti Goldfields annual 1998 results yesterday underlined the importance to gold miners of hedging profits. Hedging income amounted to $139m (£85m) – unchanged on 1997 – compared with operating profits after exceptional costs but before closure losses up 14 per cent at $90.3m. Turnover was 13 per cent ahead at $600m.

If Ashanti did not hedge its output by forward selling, its mines would not break even. Hedging allowed it to realise a gold price of $385 per once, $91 higher than the spot price.

Source: *Financial Times*, 25 February 1999, p. 33. Reprinted with permission.

FUTURES

Futures contracts are in many ways similar to forward contracts. They are agreements between two parties to undertake a transaction at an agreed price on a specified future date. However they differ from forwards in some important respects.

Futures contracts are exchange-based instruments traded on a regulated exchange. The buyer and the seller of a contract do not transact with each other directly. The clearing house becomes the formal counterparty to every transaction. This reduces the risk of non-compliance with the contract significantly for the buyer or seller of a future, as it is highly unlikely that the clearing house will be unable to fulfil its obligation.

The exchange provides standardised legal agreements traded in highly liquid markets. The contracts cannot be tailor-made. The fact that the agreements are standardised allows a wide market appeal because buyers and sellers know what is being traded: the contracts are for a specific quality of the underlying, in specific amounts with specific delivery dates. For example, for cocoa traded on LIFFE (*see* Exhibit 21.15) one contract is for a specified grade of cocoa and each contract is for a standard 10 tonnes with fixed delivery days in late September, December, March, May and July.

In examining the table in Exhibit 21.15, it is important to remember that it is the contracts themselves which are a form of security bought and sold in the market. Thus the December future priced at £761 per tonne is a derivative of cocoa and is not the same thing as cocoa. To buy this future is to enter into an agreement with rights. The rights are being bought and sold and not the commodity. When exercise takes place then cocoa is bought. However, as with most derivatives, usually futures positions are cancelled by an offsetting transaction before exercise.

Exhibit 21.15 Cocoa futures

COCOA LIFFE (10 tonnes; £/tonne) FT

	Sett price	Day's change	High	Low	Vol 000s	int 000s
Sep	742	+1	748	734	0.56	37.8
Dec	761	+1	766	753	0.66	33.6
Mar	778	+2	780	770	0.40	37.3
May	791	+1	792	785	0.09	25.9
Jul	803	+1	803	798	0.18	13.2
Sep	812	–	816	812	0.09	9.27
Total					**1.98**	**16.0**

Note: 'O int' means open interest and shows the number of outstanding contracts. Vol shows the volume of trading that day.

Source: *Financial Times*, 14 August 2001. Reprinted with permission.

Marking to market and margins

With the clearing house being the formal counterparty for every buyer or seller of a futures contract, an enormous potential for credit risk is imposed on the organisation – given the volume of futures traded and the size of the underlying they represent. (LIFFE has an average daily volume of £360bn.) If only a small fraction of market participants fail to deliver this could run into hundreds of millions of pounds. To protect itself the clearing house operates a margining system. The futures buyer or seller has to provide, usually in cash, an *initial margin*. The amount required depends on the futures market, the level of volatility of the underlying and the potential for default; however it is likely to be in the region of 0.1 per cent to 15 per cent of the value of the underlying. The initial margin is not a 'down-payment' for the underlying: the funds do not flow to a buyer or seller of the underlying but stay with the clearing house. It is merely a way of guaranteeing that the buyer or seller will pay up should the price of the underlying move against them. It is refunded when the futures position is closed.

The clearing house also operates a system of daily *marking to market*. At the end of every trading day the counterparty's profits or losses created as a result of that day's price change are calculated. The counterparty that made a loss has his/her *member's margin account* debited. The following morning the losing counterparty must inject more cash to cover the loss if the amount in the account has fallen below a threshold level, called the *maintenence margin*. An inability to pay a daily loss causes default and the contract is closed, thus protecting the clearing house from the possibility that the counterparty might accumulate further daily losses without providing cash to cover them. The margin account of the counterparty that makes a daily gain is credited. This may be withdrawn the next day. The daily credits and debits to members' margin accounts are known as the *variation margin*.

Worked example 21.1 Margins

Imagine a buyer and seller of a future on Monday with an underlying value of £50,000 are each required to provide an initial margin of 10 per cent, or £5,000. The buyer will make profits if the price rises while the seller will make profits if the price falls. In the following table (*see* Exhibit 21.16) it is assumed that counterparties have to keep all of the initial margin permanently as a buffer.[5] (In reality this may be relaxed by an exchange.)

Exhibit 21.16 Example of initial margin and marking to market

	Day				
£	*Monday*	*Tuesday*	*Wednesday*	*Thursday*	*Friday*
Value of future (based on daily closing price)	50,000	49,000	44,000	50,000	55,000
Buyers' position					
Initial margin	5,000				
Variation margin (+ credited) (– debited)	0	–1,000	–5,000	+6,000	+5,000
Accumulated profit (loss)	0	–1,000	–6,000	0	+5,000
Sellers' position					
Initial margin	5,000				
Variation margin (+ credited) (– debited)	0	+1,000	+5,000	–6,000	–5,000
Accumulated profit (loss)	0	+1,000	+6,000	0	–5,000

At the end of Tuesday the buyer of the contract has £1,000 debited from his/her member's account. This will have to be paid over the following day or the exchange will automatically close the member's position and crystallise the loss. If the buyer does provide the variation margin and the position is kept open until Friday the account will have an accumulated credit of £5,000. The buyer has the right to buy at £50,000 but can sell at £55,000. If the buyer and the seller closed their positions on Friday the buyer would be entitled to receive the initial margin plus the accumulated profit, £5,000 + £5,000 = £10,000, whereas the seller would receive nothing (£5,000 initial margin minus losses of £5,000).

The worked example illustrates the effect of leverage in futures contracts. The initial margin payments are small relative to the value of the underlying. When the underlying changes by a small percentage the effect is magnified for the future, and large percentage gains and losses are made on the amount committed to the transaction:

$$\text{Underlying change (Monday–Friday)} \quad \frac{55{,}000 - 50{,}000}{50{,}000} \times 100 = 10\%$$

$$\text{Percentage return to buyer of future} \quad \frac{5{,}000}{5{,}000} \times 100 = 100\%$$

$$\text{Percentage return to seller of future} \quad \frac{-5{,}000}{5{,}000} \times 100 = -100\%$$

To lose all the money committed to a financial transaction may seem disappointing but it is nothing compared with the losses that can be made on futures. It is possible to lose a multiple of the amount set down as an initial margin. For example, if the future rose to £70,000 the seller would have to provide a £20,000 variation margin – four times the amount committed in the first place. Clearly playing the futures market can seriously damage your wealth. This was proved with a vengeance by Nick Leeson of Barings Bank. He bought futures in the Nikkei 225 Index – the main Japanese share index – in both the Osaka and the Singapore derivative exchanges. He was betting that the market would rise as he committed the bank to buying the index at a particular price. When the index fell margin payments had to be made. Leeson took a double or quits attitude, 'I mean a lot of futures traders when the market is against them will double up'.[6] He continued to buy futures. To generate some cash, to make variation margin payments, he wrote combinations of call and put options ('straddles'). This compounded the problem when the Nikkei 225 Index continued to fall in 1994. The put options became an increasingly expensive commitment to bear – counterparties had the right to sell the index to Barings at a price much higher than the prevailing price. Over £800m was lost (*see* Exhibit 21.17).

Settlement

Historically the futures markets developed on the basis of the physical delivery of the underlying. So if you had contracted to buy 40,000 lbs of lean hogs you would receive the meat as settlement. However in most futures markets today (including that for lean hogs) only a small proportion of contracts result in physical delivery. The majority are closed out before the expiry of the contract and all that changes hands is cash, either as a profit or a loss. Speculators certainly do not want to end up with 5 tonnes of coffee or 15,000 lbs of orange juice and so will reverse their trade before the contract expires, for example, if they originally bought 50 tonnes of white sugar they later sell 50 tonnes of white sugar.

Hedgers, say a confectionery manufacturer, may sometimes take delivery from the exchange but in most cases will have established purchasing channels for sugar, cocoa, etc. In these cases they may use the futures markets not as a way of obtaining goods but as a way of offsetting the risk of the prices of goods moving adversely. So a manufacturer may still plan to buy, say, sugar, at the spot price from its longstanding supplier in six months and simultaneously, to hedge the risk of the price rising, will buy six-month futures in sugar. This position will then be closed before expiry. If the price of the underlying has risen the manufacturer pays more to the supplier but has a compensating gain on the future. If the price falls the supplier is paid less and so a gain is made here, but, under a perfect hedge, the future has lost an equal value.

Exhibit 21.17

Leeson hid trading from the outset

FT

Mr Nick Leeson opened 88888, the account in which he hid his unauthorised trading, just two days after Barings began trading on Simex at the start of July 1992.

The Singapore inspectors, who have had access to Simex data not made available to the Bank of England, show that Mr Leeson's secret futures and options positions grew slowly at first.

After losing S$10.7m (£4.8m) between July and October 1992, Mr Leeson brought the balance on the hidden 88888 account back close to zero in July 1993. This tallies with his own account, given in a television interview, of the relief he felt when he made back his losses in mid-1993.

But it appears that the main method by which Mr Leeson recovered his losses, initially made on futures positions, was by selling options in a way which stored up trouble. When the market moved against him and his futures lost money, he tended to write 'straddles', a combination of options.

These produced an immediate premium which reduced the deficit in the 88888 account. But the options, on the Nikkei index of Japanese stocks, exposed Mr Leeson to a movement in the market in either direction.

They produced an initial profit, with a counterbalancing risk of loss on expiry of the options contracts. It was a highly risky form of borrowing.

From the timing of Mr Leeson's trading, it appears that the sale of these 'straddles' was an attempt to plug the hole left by punts on the market which had gone awry.

Losses on account 88888

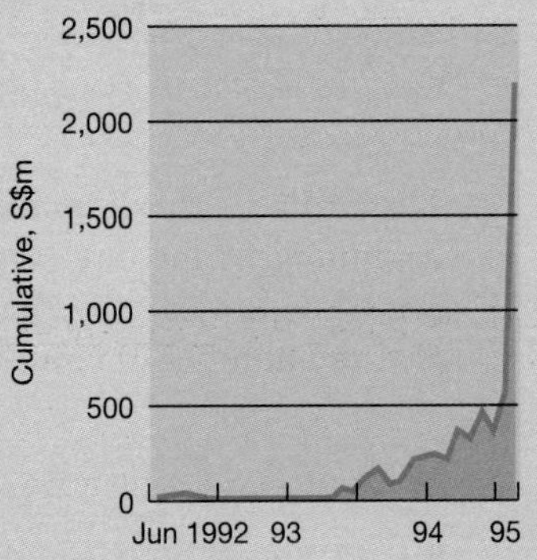

Source: Inspectors' report.

For example, in November 1993, Mr Leeson's futures losses had mounted to S$4.2bn from S$788m the previous month. This coincided with Mr Leeson's most intense bout of options trading, which lifted the value of the options portfolio to a surplus of S$478m the following month.

But their value collapsed after the Kobe earthquake, which triggered a sharp increase in the volatility of the Japanese stock market. In any case, Mr Leeson's profits on options in 1994 were not sufficient to offset his other losses.

Source: N.D., *Financial Times*, 18 October 1995, p. 8. Reprinted with permission.

As the futures markets developed it became clear that most participants did not want the complications of physical delivery and this led to the development of futures contracts where cash settlement takes place. This permitted a wider range of futures contracts to be created. Futures contracts based on intangible commodities such as a share index or a rate of interest are now extremely important financial instruments. With these, even if the contract is held to the maturity date one party will hand over cash to other (via the clearing house system).

For example, the FTSE 100 futures (*see* Exhibit 21.18) are notional futures and contracts. If not closed out before expiry they are settled in cash based on the average level of the FTSE 100 Index between stated times on the last trading day of the contract. Each index point is valued at £10.

Exhibit 21.18 FTSE 100 futures

FTSE 100 index futures (LIFFE) £10 per full index point FT

	Open	Sett price	Change	High	Low	Est. vol	Open int.
Sep	5450.0	5435.5	+5.5	5472.0	5410.0	25246	321935
Dec	5460.0	5482.5	+6.0	5510.0	5460.0	1750	19893
Mar	5509.5	5502.5	+6.0	5509.5	5509.5	50	10839

Source: *Financial Times*, 14 August 2001. Reprinted with permission.

The table in the *Financial Times* (Exhibit 21.18) shows the first price traded at the beginning of the day (Open), the settlement price used to mark to market (usually the last traded price), the change from the previous day, highest and lowest prices during the day, the number of contracts traded that day and the total number of open contracts.

Worked example 21.2 Hedging with a share Index future

It is 13 August 2001 and the FT 100 is at 5431. A fund manager wishes to hedge a £10m fund against a decline in the market. A December FTSE 100 future is available at 5482.50. The manager retains the shares in the portfolio and sells 184 index futures contracts (£10m/(£10 × 5431)).

Outcome in December

For the sake of argument assume that the index falls by 10 per cent to 4888, leaving the portfolio value at £9m. This £1m loss is offset by the closing of the future position by buying 184 futures at 4888, producing a profit of:[7]

Able to buy at	4888 × 184 × £10 =	8,993,920
Able to sell at	5482.50 × 184 × £10 =	10,087,800
		£1,093,880

Exhibit 21.19 discusses the increasing importance of derivatives to financial institutions.

Exhibit 21.19

Pension funds see less risk in derivatives

FT

UK fund managers have found derivatives are a safe investment alternative, writes Simon Targett, Investment Correspondent

Unilever Superannuation Fund, the $4bn pension fund of the Anglo-Dutch household product group, tried to minimise the risk on a £1bn portfolio by establishing 'an agreed downside tolerance' with Mercury Asset Management, its fund manager.

It is now embroiled in a costly legal case because, it claims, MAM disregarded their instructions by investing in stocks which were 'too risky'.

An increasingly popular alternative, and one gaining popularity among pension funds, is to use derivatives to minimise risk, says Sally Bridgeland, head of investment research at Bacon & Woodrow, the actuarial consultants.

But in continental Europe, derivatives remain an acquired taste. Vivienne Carnt, head of the continental Europe division in the investment practice of William M Mercer, the actuarial consultant, said: 'It is still patchy, and there tends to be a fear of derivatives. Some run a mile when you mention the word.'

In the UK, however, there is a greater readiness to allow fund managers to use derivatives.

Exhibit 21.19 continued

This dates back to 1990, when John Major's administration decided not to tax trades in derivatives, says John Rogers, head of investment at the National Association of Pension Funds.

Since then, the number of pension funds allowing their fund managers to use derivatives has climbed steadily.

Last year, according to a survey by the NAPF, 70 per cent of public schemes and 67 per cent of private schemes allowed investment managers to use derivatives.

Yet, not all fund managers 'felt comfortable' using them, according to Mr Rogers. This explains why only 26 per cent of private schemes and 44 per cent of public schemes actually used derivatives . . .

Actuarial consultants are now busily encouraging pension funds and their managers to turn to derivatives.

Ms Bridgeland says derivatives are being promoted as a means of protection...

The British Telecommunications pension fund, one of the UK's largest with assets of around £25bn, allows Hermes, its fund manager, to use derivatives for 'tactical asset allocation'.

Using equity futures, Hermes' fund managers can change the asset allocation on a short-term basis, moving faster and more cost-effectively than by buying or selling physical asset.

In the future, derivatives could be used to facilitate a long-term change to pension funds' allocation of assets, according to Ms Bridgeland . . .

In continental Europe, the potential for growth is huge, since countries are changing their asset allocation, shifting from bonds to equities. But actuarial consultants predict pension funds will not readily turn to derivatives.

UK pension fund investments

	Private schemes (%)	Public schemes (%)
Do you invest in derivatives?		
Yes	26	44
No, but they can	41	26
No, they can't	33	30
No. of respondents	417	50
Any limits?		
Yes	68	90
No	32	10
No. of respondents	188	31
What type of limit?		
Maximum percentage of fund value	40	25
Currency/other hedging only	33	38
With trustee approval	6	8
Other	21	29
No. of respondents	105	24

Source: National Association of Pension Funds, 1998

Source: Simon Targett, *Financial Times*, 14 October 1999, p. 33. Reprinted with permission.

Short-term interest rate futures

Trillions of pounds worth of trading takes place every year in the short-term interest rate futures markets. These are notional fixed-term deposits, usually for three-month periods starting at a specific time in the future. The buyer of one contract is buying the right to deposit money at a particular rate of interest for three months.

Short term interest rate futures will be illustrated using the three month sterling market.

The unit of trading for a three-month sterling time deposit is £500,000. Cash delivery by closing out the futures position is the means of settlement, so the buyer would not actually require the seller of the future to place the £500,000 on deposit for three months at the interest rate indicated by the futures price. Although the term 'delivery' no longer has significance for the underlying it does define the date and time of the expiry of the contract. This occurs in late September, December, March and June.

Short-term interest contracts are quoted on an index basis rather than on the basis of the interest rate itself. The price is defined as:

$$P = 100 - i$$

where:

P = price index;

i = the future interest rate in percentage terms.

Exhibit 21.20 Interest rate futures

Aug 13		Open	Sett	Change	High	Low	Est. vol	Open int.
Euribor 3m*	Sep	95.81	95.84	–0.02	95.86	95.83	57,495	464,515
Euribor 3m*	Dec	69.03	96.06	–0.02	96.08	96.05	37,173	388,027
Euribor 3m*	Mar	96.16	96.20	–0.01	96.22	96.18	42,802	335,124
Euribor 3m*	Jun	96.09	96.14	–	96.15	96.11	33,657	161,463
Euribor 3m*	Sep	95.95	96.00	–	96.01	95.96	16,081	144,472
Euroswiss 3m*	Sep	97.04	97.07	–	97.10	97.04	8,058	81,697
Euroswiss 3m*	Dec	97.21	97.26	+0.01	97.27	97.24	8,284	57,421
Sterling 3m*	Sep	95.09	95.11	+0.01	95.11	95.08	12,290	170,872
Sterling 3m*	Dec	95.20	95.23	+0.01	95.24	95.18	25,900	164,057
Sterling 3m*	Mar	95.10	95.16	+0.02	95.17	95.11	20,634	146,380
Sterling 3m*	Jun	94.83	94.91	+0.03	94.92	94.87	9,913	99,604
Sterling 3m*	Sep	94.58	94.67	+0.03	94.68	94.62	5,345	83,347
Eurodollar 3m†	Aug	96.42	96.43	–	96.44	96.42	2,222	24,699
Eurodollar 3m†	Sep	96.54	96.69	+0.16	96.56	96.50	91,607	680,305
Eurodollar 3m†	Dec	96.44	96.48	+0.04	96.45	96.44	108,116	687,650
Eurodollar 3m†	Mar	96.33	96.34	+0.01	96.35	96.28	119,231	503,911
Eurodollar 3m†	Jun	96.03	69.24	+0.23	96.19	95.97	96,517	559,242
Eurodollar 3m†	Sep	95.65	95.67	+0.04	95.66	95.59	64,549	418,399
Eurodollar 3m†	Dec	95.25	95.24	+0.01	95.26	95.19	50,145	383,548
Fed Fnds 30d‡	Aug	96.365	96.365	–	96.365	96.365	4,601	27,028
Fed Fnds 30d‡	Oct	69.545	96.550	+0.005	96.550	96.540	12,276	44,266
Fed Fnds 30d‡	Nov	96.675	96.680	+0.005	96.680	96.670	2,569	24,550
Euroyen 3m‡‡	Sep	99.905	99.905	+0.005	99.905	99.905	10	283,838
Euroyen 3m‡‡	Dec	99.870	99.875	+0.005	99.870	99.870	39	226,453
Euroyen 3m‡‡	Mar	99.865	99.865	+0.010	99.865	99.865	1,373	143,641

Notes: Euribor 3m: A benchmark interest rate in euros for three-month deposits.
Euroswiss 3m: Three-month interest rate in Euro-Swiss francs.
Sterling 3m: Sterling three-month interest rate.
Eurodollar 3m: Three-month notional deposit rate for Eurodollars.
Fed Fnds 30d: Federal funds 30-day interest – a US benchmark rate.
Euroyen 3m: Three-month interest rate for euroyen deposits.

Sources: * LIFFE. † CME. ‡ CBOT. ‡‡ TIFFE
Source: *Financial Times*, 14 August 2001. Reprinted with permission.

Thus, on 13 August 2001 the settlement price for a March three-month sterling future was 95.16, which implies an interest rate of 100 – 95.16 = 4.84 per cent. Similarly the June quote would imply 100 – 94.91 = 5.08 per cent. In both cases the implied interest rate refers to a rate applicable for a notional deposit of £500,000 for three months on expiry of the contract. Thus the 4.84 per cent is the rate for three-month money starting from March 2002. (The figure of 4.84 per cent is the annual rate of interest on a three-month deposit.)

The price of 95.16 is not a price in the usual sense – it does not mean £95.16. It is used to maintain the standard inverse relationship between prices and interest rates. For example, if the interest rates for three-month deposits starting in March 2002 rose to 6.8 per cent the price of the future would fall to 93.20. It is this inverse change in capital value when interest rates change which it is of crucial importance to grasp about short-term interest rate futures. This is more important than trying to envisage deposits of £500,000 being placed some time in the future.

Worked example 21.3 Hedging three-month deposits

An example of these derivatives in use may help you to understand their hedging qualities. Imagine the treasurer of a large company anticipates the receipt of £100m in March 2002, eight months hence. She expects that the money will be needed for production purposes in the summer of 2002 but for the three months following March it can be placed on deposit. There is a risk that interest rates will fall between now (August 2001) and March 2002 from their present level of 4.84 per cent per annum for three-month deposits starting in March. The treasurer does not want to take a passive approach and simply wait for the inflow of money and deposit it at whatever rate is then prevailing without taking some steps to ensure a good return.

To achieve certainty in March 2002 the treasurer buys, in August, March expiry three-month sterling interest rate futures at a price of 95.16. Each future has a notional value of £500,000 and therefore she has to buy 200 to hedge the £100m inflow.

In March suppose that three-month interest rates have fallen to 4 per cent. When the £100m is placed on deposit the return available is £100m × 0.04 × $^3/_{12}$ = £1m. This is significantly less than if interest rates had remained at 4.84 per cent.

Return at 4.84 per cent (£100m × 0.0484 × $^3/_{12}$)	= £1,210,000
Return at 4.0 per cent (£100m × 0.04 × $^3/_{12}$)	= £1,000,000
Loss	£210,000

However the cautiousness of the treasurer pays off because the futures have risen in value as the interest rates have fallen.

The 200 futures contracts were bought at 95.16. With interest rates at 4 per cent for three-month deposits starting in March the futures in March have a value of 100 – 4 = 96.00. The treasurer in March can close the future position by selling the futures for 96.00. The gain that is made amounts to 96.00 – 95.16 = 0.84.

This is where a *tick* needs to be introduced. A tick is the minimum price movement on a future. On a three-month sterling interest rate contract a tick is a movement of 0.01 per cent on a trading unit of £500,000.

One-hundredth of 1 per cent of £500,000 is equal to £50, but this is not the value of one tick. A further complication is that the price of a future is based on annual interest rates whereas the contract is for three months. Therefore £50/4 = £12.50 is the value of a tick movement in a three-month sterling interest rate futures contract. In this case we have a gain of 84 ticks with an overall value of 84 × £12.50 = £1,050 per contract, or £210,000 for 200 contracts. The profit on the futures exactly offsets the loss of anticipated interest when the £100m is put on deposit for three months in March.

Worked example 21.4 Hedging a loan

In August 2001 Holwell plc plans to borrow £5m for three months at a later date. This will begin in December 2001. Worried that short-term interest rates will rise Holwell hedges by selling ten three-month sterling interest rate futures contracts with December expiry. The price of each futures contract is 95.23 so Holwell has locked into an annual interest rate of 4.77 per cent or 1.1925 per cent for three months. The cost of borrowing is therefore:

£5m × 0.011925 = £59,625

Suppose that interest rates rise to annual rates of 6 per cent, or 1.5 per cent per quarter. The cost of borrowing for Holwell will be:

£5m × 0.015 = £75,000

However, Holwell is able to buy ten futures contracts to close the position on the exchange. Each contract has fallen in value from 95.23 to 94.00 (100 – 6); this is 123 ticks. The profit credited to Holwell's margin account of LIFFE will now stand at:

123 ticks × £12.50 × 10 contracts = £15,375

The derivative profit offsets the extra interest cost on the loan Holwell takes out in December (£75,000 – £15,375 = £59,625).

Note that if interest rates fall Holwell's gain, by being charged lower interest on the actual loan, will be offset by the loss of the futures. Holwell sacrifices the benefits of potential favourable movements in rates to reduce risk.

As Exhibit 21.21 shows, the price of short-term interest rate futures are followed closely as they give an indication of the market view on the level of short-term interest rates a few months hence.

Exhibit 21.21

Betting on interest rates

FT

The short sterling market has its own advice to offer

As the chancellor and the governor of the Bank of England sit down to ponder interest rate policy at their monthly monetary meeting today, a £40bn-a-day industry will be pronouncing its own judgment on where rates are going next.

The betting in the so-called 'short sterling' futures market is that policymakers will leave rates unchanged until well into next year. Banks and companies use this market to protect themselves against adverse changes in rates, while speculators use it to gamble on how rates might move.

Short sterling futures are traded on the London International Financial Futures and Options Exchange. Their current price implies a prediction that base rates will still be at 6¾ per cent by the end of this year, rising to 7 per cent by the end of next year. With more than £10,000bn each year backing these bets, this is a forecast that policymakers ignore at their peril.

'Short sterling takes in all the latest economic and political news to give an indication of where the money market thinks short-term interest rates will be going in the future,' said Mr Nigel Richardson, an economist at Yamaichi International, a Japanese bank.

The companies and banks buying short sterling futures are making a simple bet. The price of the short sterling contract is equal to 100 minus whatever interest rate is expected when the three month contract expires, so the price of the contract rises when interest rates fall.

If a company thought interest rates would be 6¾ per cent by December it would expect the price of the December contract to be 93.25. If the current price of the December contract was below 93.25 – in other words the market expected interest rates to be higher than 6¾ per cent at the end of the year – then the company could buy the contract and expect to profit when it expired in December.

This allows a short sterling trader to protect itself against a possible interest rate movement, effectively fixing the interest rate at which it borrows or lends. A more aggressive investor can use short sterling to gamble on an interest rate change.

Imagine a company has a sum of money to invest in a bank, but fears interest rates will fall. The company could buy a short sterling contract expiring in three months. If, by then, interest rates had not fallen, the company would have lost

Exhibit 21.21 continued

nothing. If rates did fall the company would get a lower return on its investment, but this would have been offset by a rise in the price of the futures contract.

Another company might want to borrow money, but fear that interest rates are set to rise. It could hedge against this risk by selling short sterling futures. If rates did rise the company's borrowing costs would be higher, but it would be able to buy the contract back at a lower price and use the profit to offset the cost.

This is useful for banks providing fixed-rate mortgages. They use the short sterling market to fix the interest rates at which they borrow, which they can then pass on to customers.

Economists in the City use the forecast provided by the short sterling market as a basis for their own projections. 'It is very useful. It tells you what the market is predicting and you then take the market into account when making your own forecast,' said Mr Stuart Thomson, economist at Nikko, a Japanese bank.

But there have been times when the forecasts have been very different – and short sterling has not always been right. This year the short sterling market was expecting interest rates to be close to 9 per cent by December. Economists were expecting a more modest increase, and in the event they were proved more accurate.

Similarly, after the pound's exit from the European exchange rate mechanism in 1992, short sterling predicted that interest rates would have to remain high. In event they were cut aggressively.

'If you just want an average of the views of everybody acting in the market, then short sterling is fine,' said Mr Ian Shepherdson, an economist at HSBC Markets. 'But if you want an opinion, you need an economist. Short sterling gives the consensus, but the consensus is not always right.'

Policymakers will no doubt draw solace from the fact that markets can be wrong sometimes too.

Source: Graham Bowley, *Financial Times*, 1 November 1995. Reprinted with permission.

FORWARD RATE AGREEMENTS (FRAs)

FRAs are useful devices for hedging future interest rate risk. They are agreements about the future level of interest rates. The rate of interest at some point in the future is compared with the level agreed when the FRA was established and compensation is paid by one party to the other based on the difference.

For example, a company needs to borrow £6m in six months' time for a period of a year. It arranges this with bank X at a variable rate of interest. The current rate of interest is 7 per cent. The company is concerned that by the time the loan is drawn down interest rates will be higher than 7 per cent, increasing the cost of borrowing.

The company enters into a separate agreement with another bank (Y) – an FRA. It 'purchases' an FRA at an interest rate of 7 per cent. This is to take effect six months from now and relate to a 12-month loan. Bank Y will never lend any money to the company but it has committed itself to paying compensation should interest rates (say on Libor) rise above 7 per cent.

Suppose that in six months spot one-year interest rates are 8.5 per cent. The company will be obliged to pay Bank X this rate: £6m × 0.085 = £510,000; this is £90,000 more than if the interest rates were 7 per cent.[8] However, the FRA with Bank Y entitles the company to claim compensation equal to the difference between the rate agreed in the FRA and the spot rate. This is (0.085 – 0.07) × £6m = £90,000. So any increase in interest cost above 7 per cent is exactly matched by a compensating payment provided by the counterparty to the FRA. However, if rates fall below 7 per cent the company makes payments to Bank Y. For example, if the spot rate in six months is 5 per cent the company benefits because of the lower rate charged by Bank X, but suffers an equal offsetting compensation payment to Bank Y of (0.07 – 0.05) × £6m = £120,000. The company has generated certainty over the effective interest cost of borrowing in the future. Whichever way the interest rates move it will pay £420,000.

The 'sale' of an FRA by a company protects against a fall in interest rates. For example, if £10m is expected to be available for putting into a one-year bank deposit in three months the company could lock into a rate now by selling an FRA to a bank. Suppose the agreed rate is 6.5 per cent and the spot rate in three months is 6 per cent, then the depositor will receive 6 per cent from the bank into which the money is placed plus $^1/_2$ per cent from the FRA counterparty bank.

The examples above are described as 6 against 18 (or 6 × 18) and 3 against 15 (or 3 × 15). The first is a 12-month contract starting in six months, the second is a 12-month contract starting in three months. More common FRA periods are 3 against 6 and 6 against 12. Typically sums of £5m–£100m are hedged in single deals in this market. Companies do not have to have an underlying lending or borrowing transaction – they could enter into an FRA in isolation and make or receive compensating payments only. The daily global turnover in FRAs in 2001 was US$129 billion.

Exhibit 21.22 A comparison of options, futures, forward rate agreements and forwards

Options	*Futures*	*FRAs and forwards*
Advantages		
Downside risk is limited but the buyer is able to participate in favourable movements.	Specific rates are locked in. No right to let the contract lapse, as with options.	No margins or premiums payable.
Available on or off exchanges. Exchange regulation and clearing house reduce counterparty default risk for those options traded on exchanges.	No premium is payable. (However margin payments are required.)	Tailor-made, not standardised as to size, duration and terms.
Usually highly liquid markets.	Very liquid markets. Able to reverse transactions quickly and cheaply.	Can create certainty. Locks in specific effective rates.
May be useful if no strong view is held on direction of underlying.	Exchange regulation and clearing house reduce counterparty default risk.	
Disadvantages		
Premium payable reduces returns.	If the underlying transaction does not materialise, potential loss is unlimited.	Benefits from favourable movements in rates are forgone.
Margin required when writing options.	Many exchange restrictions – on size, duration, trading times.	Greater risk of counterparty default – not exchange traded.
	Margin calls require daily work for 'back office'.	More difficult to liquidate.

CAPS

An interest rate cap is a contract that gives the purchaser the right to effectively set a maximum level for interest rates payable. Compensation is paid to the purchaser of a cap if interest rates rise above an agreed level. This is a hedging technique used to cover interest rate risk on longer-term borrowing (usually two to five years). Under these arrangements a company borrowing money can benefit from interest rate falls but can place a limit to the amount paid in interest should interest rates rise.

Worked example 21.5 Interest rate cap

For example, Oakham plc may wish to borrow £20m for five years. It arranges this with bank A at a variable rate based on Libor plus 1.5 per cent. The interest rate is reset every quarter based on three-month Libor. Currently this stands at an annual rate of 7 per cent. The firm is concerned that over a five-year period the interest rate could rise to a dangerous extent.

Oakham buys an interest rate cap set at Libor of 8.5 per cent. For the sake of argument we will assume that this costs 2.3 per cent of the principal amount, or £20m × 0.023 = £460,000 payable immediately to the cap seller. If over the subsequent five years Libor rises above 8.5 per cent in any three-month period Oakham will receive sufficient compensation from the cap seller to exactly offset any extra interest above 8.5 per cent. So if for the whole of the third year Libor rose to 9.5 per cent Oakham would pay interest at 9.5 per cent plus 1.5 per cent to bank A but would also receive 1 per cent compensation from the cap seller (a quarter every three months), thus capping the interest payable. If interest rates fall Oakham benefits by paying bank A less.

The premium (£460,000) payable up front covers the buyer for the entire five years with no further payment due.

The size of the cap premium depends on the difference between current interest rates and the level at which the cap becomes effective; the length of time covered; and the expected volatility of interest rates. The cap seller does not need to assess the creditworthiness of the purchaser because it receives payment of the premium in advance. Thus a cap is particularly suitable for highly geared firms, such as leveraged buyouts.

Floors and collars

Buyers of interest rate caps are sometimes keen to reduce the large cash payment at the outset. They can do this by simultaneously selling a floor, which results in a counterparty paying a premium. With a floor, if the interest rate falls below an agreed level, the seller (the floor writer) makes compensatory payments to the floor buyer. These payments are determined by the difference between the prevailing rates and the floor rate.

Returning to Oakham, the treasurer could buy a cap set at 8.5 per cent Libor for a premium of £460,000 and sell a floor at 6 per cent Libor receiving, say, £200,000. In any three-month period over the five-year life of the loan, if Libor rose above 8.5 per cent the cap seller would pay compensation to Oakham; if Libor fell below 6 per cent Oakham would save on the amount paid to bank A but will have to make payments to the floor buyer, thus restricting the benefits from falls in Libor. Oakham, for a net premium of £260,000, has ensured that its effective interest payments will not diverge from the range 6 per cent + 1.5 per cent = 7.5 per cent at the lower end, to 8.5 per cent + 1.5 per cent = 10 per cent at the upper end.

The combination of selling a floor at a low strike rate and buying a cap at a higher strike rate is called a collar.

SWAPS

A swap is an exchange of cash payment obligations. An interest-rate swap is where one company arranges with a counterparty to exchange interest-rate payments. For example, the first company may be paying fixed-rate interest but prefers to pay floating rates. The second company may be paying floating rates of interest, which go up and down with Libor, but would benefit from a switch to a fixed obligation. For example, imagine that firm S has a £200m ten-year loan paying a fixed rate of interest of 8 per cent, and firm T has a £200m ten-year loan on which interest is reset every six months with reference to Libor, at Libor plus 2 per cent. Under a swap arrangement S would agree to pay T's floating-rate interest on each due date over the next ten years, and T would be obligated to pay S's 8 per cent interest.

One motive for entering into a swap arrangement is to reduce or eliminate exposure to rises in interest rates. Over the short run, futures, options and FRAs could be used to hedge interest-rate exposure. However for longer-term loans (more than two years) swaps are usually more suitable because they can run the entire lifetime of the loan. So if a treasurer of a company with a large floating-rate loan forecasts that interest rates will rise over the next four years, he/she could arrange to swap interest payments with a fixed-rate interest payer for those four years.

Another reason for using swaps is to take advantage of market imperfections. Sometimes the interest-rate risk premium charged in the fixed-rate borrowing market differs from that in the floating-rate market for a particular borrower.

Worked example 21.6 SWAPS

Take the two companies, Cat plc and Dog plc, both of which want to borrow £150m for eight years. Cat would like to borrow on a fixed-rate basis because this would better match its asset position. Dog prefers to borrow at floating rates because of optimism about future interest-rate falls. The treasurers of each firm have obtained quotes from banks operating in the markets for both fixed- and floating-rate eight-year debt. Cat could obtain fixed-rate borrowing at 10 per cent and floating rate at Libor +2 per cent. Dog is able to borrow at 8 per cent fixed and Libor +1 per cent floating:

	Fixed	*Floating*
Cat can borrow at	10%	Libor +2%
Dog can borrow at	8%	Libor +1%

In the absence of a swap market Cat would probably borrow at 10 per cent and Dog would pay Libor +1 per cent. However with a swap arrangement both firms can achieve lower interest rates.

Notice that because of Dog's higher credit rating it can borrow at a lower rate than Cat in both the fixed and the floating-rate market – it has an absolute advantage in both. However the risk premium charged in the two markets is not consistent. Cat has to pay an extra 1 per cent in the floating-rate market, but an extra 2 per cent in the fixed-rate market. Cat has an absolute disadvantage for both, but has a comparative advantage in the floating-rate market.

To achieve lower interest rates each firm should borrow in the market where it has comparative advantage. So Cat borrows floating-rate funds, paying Libor +2 per cent, and Dog borrows fixed-rate debt, paying 8 per cent.

Then they agree to swap interest payments at rates which lead to benefits for both firms in terms of **a** achieving the most appropriate interest pattern (fixed or floating), and **b** the interest rate that is payable is lower than if Cat had borrowed at fixed and Dog had borrowed at floating rates. *One* way of achieving this is to arrange the swap on the following basis:

- Cat pays to Dog fixed interest of 9.5 per cent;
- Dog pays to Cat Libor +2 per cent.

This is illustrated in Exhibit 21.23.

Exhibit 21.23 An interest rate swap

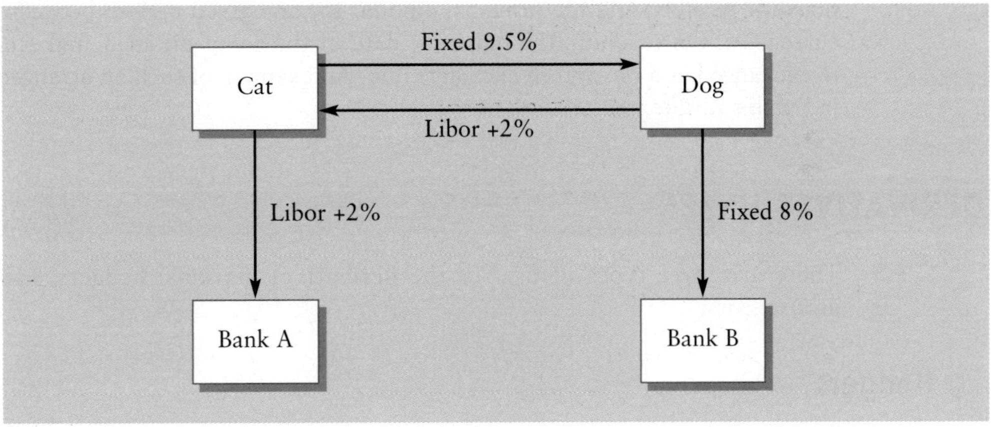

Now let us examine the position for each firm.

Cat pays Libor +2 per cent to a bank but also receives Libor +2 per cent from Dog and so these two cancel out. Cat also pays 9.5 per cent fixed to Dog. This is 50 basis points (0.5 per cent) lower than if Cat had borrowed at fixed rate directly from the bank. On £150m this is worth £750,000 per year.

Cat:

Pays	Libor +2%
Receives	Libor +2%
Pays	Fixed 9.5%
Net payment	Fixed 9.5%

Dog takes on the obligation of paying a bank fixed interest at 8 per cent while receiving 9.5 per cent fixed from Cat on the regular payment days. The net effect is 1.5 per cent receivable less the Libor +2 per cent payment to Cat – a floating-rate liability of Libor +0.5 per cent.

Dog:

Pays	Fixed 8%
Receives	Fixed 9.5%
Pays	Libor +2%
Net payment	Libor +0.5%

Again there is a saving of 50 basis points or £750,000 per year.[9] The net annual £1.5m saving is before transaction costs.

Prior to the widespread development of a highly liquid swap market each counterparty incurred considerable expense in making the contracts watertight. Even then, the risk of one of the counterparties failing to fulfil its obligations was a potential problem. Today intermediaries (for example banks) take counterparty positions in swaps and this reduces risk and avoids the necessity for one corporation to search for another with a corresponding swap preference. The intermediary generally finds an opposite counterparty for the swap at a later date. Furthermore, standardised contracts reduce the time and effort to arrange a swap and have permitted the development of a thriving secondary market, and this has assisted liquidity. The total value of outstanding swaps contracts rose to stand at $60,366bn in mid-2000 according to the International Swaps and Derivatives Association.

There are many variations on the swaps theme. For example, a 'swaption' is an option to have a swap at a later date. In a currency swap the two parties exchange interest obligations (or receipts) and the principal amount for an agreed period, between two different currencies. On reaching the maturity date of the swap the principal amounts will be re-exchanged at a pre-agreed exchange rate. An example of such an arrangement is shown in Exhibit 21.24.

DERIVATIVES USERS

There are three types of user of the derivatives markets: hedgers, speculators and arbitrageurs.

Hedgers

To hedge is to enter into transactions which protect a business or assets against changes in some underlying. The instruments bought as a hedge tend to have the opposite-value movements to the underlying. Financial and commodity markets are used to transfer risk from an individual or corporation to another more willing and/or able to bear that risk.

Consider a firm which discovers a rich deposit of platinum in Kenya. The management are afraid to develop the site because they are uncertain about the revenues that will actually be realised. Some of the sources of uncertainty are that: **a** the price of platinum could fall, **b** the floating-rate loan taken out to develop the site could become expensive if interest rates rise and **c** the value of the currencies could move adversely. The senior managers have more or less decided that they will apply the firm's funds to a less risky venture. A recent graduate steps forward and suggests that this would be a pity, saying: 'The company is passing up a great opportunity, and Kenya and the world economy will be poorer as a result. Besides, the company does not have to bear all of these risks given the sophistication of modern financial markets. The risks can be hedged, to limit the downside. For example, the platinum could be sold on the futures market, which will provide a firm price. The interest-rate liability can be capped or swapped into a fixed-rate loan. Other possibilities include using the FRA and the interest futures markets. The currency risk can be controlled by using currency forwards or options.' The Board decide to press ahead with development of the mine and thus show that derivatives can be used to promote economic well-being by transferring risk.

Exhibit 21.24

TVA, EIB find winning formula

FT

The back-to-back swap deal priced yesterday for the Tennessee Valley Authority and the European Investment Bank will give both cheaper funding than they could obtain through conventional bond issuance.

TVA, the US government-owned power utility, is issuing a 10-year DM1.5bn eurobond with a Frankfurt listing, while EIB is raising $1bn with a 10-year issue in the US market. The issuers will swap the proceeds.

Speaking in London yesterday, the treasurers of both organisations said the arrangement – now relatively unusual in the swaps market – had allowed them to reduce borrowing costs, although they did not specify by what amount.

Two elements of the deal were important in this respect. First, the EIB has a much stronger comparative advantage over TVA in funding in dollars than it does in D-Marks. Lehman Brothers, co-bookrunner on both deals, said the EIB priced its 10-year dollar paper at 17 basis points over Treasuries, about 6 to 7 points lower than TVA could have done.

In the German market EIB enjoys a smaller advantage; it could raise funds at about 4 basis points less than the 17 points over bonds achieved by TVA.

Second, by swapping the proceeds on a back-to-back basis rather than through counterparties, bid/offer spreads were eliminated and transaction costs reduced.

Resulting savings were pooled, providing benefits for both borrowers.

Both also diversified their funding sources. Lehman said some 65 per cent of the TVA bonds were placed in Europe, 20 per cent in Asia, and 15 per cent in the US. About half the EIB issue was placed in the US, 35 per cent in Europe, and 15 per cent in Asia.

Source: Richard Lapper, Capital Markets Editor, *Financial Times*, 12 September 1996. Reprinted with permission.

Speculators

Speculators take a position in financial instruments and other assets with a view to obtaining a profit on changes in value. Speculators accept high risk in anticipation of high reward. The gearing effect of derivatives makes speculations in these instruments particularly profitable, or particularly ruinous. Speculators are also attracted to derivatives markets because they are often more liquid than the underlying markets. In addition the speculator is able to sell before buying (to 'short' the market) in order to profit from a fall. More complex trading strategies are also possible.

The term speculator in popular parlance is often used in a somewhat critical fashion. This is generally unwarranted. Speculators are needed by financial markets to help create trading liquidity. Prices are more, not less, likely to be stable as a result of speculative activity. Usually speculators have dissimilar views regarding future market movements and this provides two-way liquidity which allows other market participants, such as hedgers, to carry out a transaction quickly without moving the price. Imagine if only hedgers with an underlying were permitted to buy or sell derivatives. Very few trades would take place each day. If a firm wished to make a large hedge this would be noticed in the market and the price of the derivative would be greatly affected. Speculators also provide a kind of insurance for hedgers – they accept risk in return for a premium.

Arbitrageurs

The act of arbitrage is to exploit price differences on the same instrument or similar assets. The arbitrageur buys at the lower price and immediately resells at the higher price. So, for example, Nick Leeson claimed that he was arbitraging Nikkei 225 Index futures. The same future is traded in both Osaka and Singapore. Theoretically the price should be identical on both markets, but in reality this is not always the case, and it is possible simultaneously to buy the future in one market and sell the future in the other and thereby make a risk-free profit. An arbitrageur waits for these opportunities to exploit a market inefficiency. The problem for Barings Bank was that Nick Leeson obtained funds to put down as margin payments on arbitrage trades but then bought futures in both markets – surreptitiously switching from an arbitrage activity to a highly risky, speculative activity. True arbitrageurs help to ensure pricing efficiency – their acts of buying or selling tend to reduce pricing anomalies.

Over-the-counter (OTC) and exchange-traded derivatives

An OTC derivative is a tailor-made, individual arrangement between counterparties, usually a company and its bank. Standardised contracts (exchange-traded derivatives) are available on dozens of derivatives around the world, for example the Chicago Board of Trade (CBOT), Chicago Board Options Exchange (CBOE) the Chicago Mercantile Exchange (CME), LIFFE, the MATIF in France and the Eurex in Germany and Switzerland. Roughly one-half of outstanding derivatives contracts are traded on exchanges.

Many derivatives markets are predominantly, if not exclusively, OTC: interest-rate FRAs, swaps, caps, collars, floors, currency forwards and currency swaps. Exhibit 21.25 compares OTC and exchange-traded derivatives.

Exhibit 21.25 OTC and exchange-traded derivatives

OTC derivative

Advantages

- Contracts can be tailor-made, which allows perfect hedging and permits hedges of more unusual underlyings.

Disadvantages

- There is a risk (credit risk) that the counterparty will fail to honour the transaction.
- Low level of market regulation with resultant loss of transparency and price dissemination.
- Often difficult to reverse a hedge once the agreement has been made.
- Higher transaction costs.

Exchange-traded derivative

Advantages

- Credit risk is reduced because the clearing house is counterparty.
- High regulation encourages transparency and openness on the price of recent trades.
- Liquidity is usually much higher than for OTC – large orders can be cleared quickly due to high daily volume of trade.
- Positions can be reversed by closing quickly – an equal and opposite transaction is completed in minutes.

Disadvantages

- Standardisation may be restrictive, e.g. standardised terms for quality of underlying, quantity, delivery dates.
- The limited trading hours and margin requirements may be inconvenient.

CONCLUDING COMMENTS

From a small base in the 1970s derivatives have grown to be of enormous importance. Almost all medium and large industrial and commercial firms use derivatives, usually to manage risk, but occasionally to speculate and arbitrage. Banks are usually at the centre of derivatives trading, dealing on behalf of clients, as marketmakers or trading on their own account. Other financial institutions are increasingly employing these instruments to lay off risk or to speculate. They can be used across the globe, and traded night and day.

The trend suggests that derivatives will continue their relentless rise in significance. They can no longer be dismissed as peripheral to the workings of the financial and economic systems. The implications for investors, corporate institutions, financial institutions, regulators and governments are going to be profound. These are incredibly powerful tools, and, like all powerful tools, they can be used for good or ill. Ignorance of the nature of the risks being transferred, combined with greed, has already led to some very unfortunate consequences. However, on a day-to-day basis, and away from the newspaper headlines, the ability of firms to quietly tap the markets and hedge risk encourages wealth creation and promotes general economic well-being.

APPENDIX 21.1 OPTION PRICING

This appendix describes the factors that influence the market value of a call option on a share. The principles apply to the pricing of other options. The complex mathematics associated with option pricing will be avoided because of their unsuitability for an introductory text. Interested readers are referred to the reading list at the end of the chapter.

Notation to be used:

C = value of call option
S = current market price of share
X = future exercise price
r_f = risk-free interest rate (per annum)
t = time to expiry (in years)
σ = standard deviation of the share price
e = mathematical fixed constant: 2.718 . . .

The factors affecting option value

1 *Options have a minimum value of zero*

$$C \geq 0$$

Even if the share price falls significantly below the exercise price of the option the worst that can happen to the option holder is that the option becomes worth nothing – no further loss is created.

2 ***The market value of an option will be greater than the intrinsic value at any time prior to expiry*** This is because there is a chance that if the option is not exercised immediately it will become more valuable due to the movement of the underlying – it will become (or will move deeper) in-the-money. *An option has time value* that increases, the longer the time to expiry.

Market value = intrinsic value + time value

3 ***Intrinsic value (S – X) rises as share price increases or exercise price falls*** However this simple relationship needs to be made a little more sophisticated because S – X is based on the assumption of immediate exercise when the option is about to expire. However if the option is not about to expire there is some value in not having to pay the exercise price until the future exercise date. (Instead of buying the share a call option could be purchased and the remainder invested in a risk-free asset until the exercise date.) So intrinsic value is given a boost by discounting the exercise price by the risk-free rate of return:

$$\text{Intrinsic value} = S - \frac{X}{(1 + r_f)^t}$$

4 ***The higher the risk-free rate of return the higher will be intrinsic value***, because the money saved by buying an option rather than the underlying security can be invested in a riskless rate of return until the option expires.

5 ***The maximum value of an option is the price of the share***

$$C \leq S$$

6 ***A major influence boosting the time value is the volatility of the underlying share price*** A share which has a stable, placid history is less likely to have a significant upward shift in value during the option's lifetime than one which has been highly variable. In option pricing models this factor is measured by the variance (σ^2) or standard deviation (σ) of the share price.

Black and Scholes' option pricing model

Black and Scholes' option pricing model (BSOPM) was published in 1973 and is still widely employed today despite the more recent modifications to the original model and the development of different option pricing models. The BSOPM is as follows:

$$C = SN(d_1) - \frac{X}{e^{r_f t}} N(d_2)$$

where:

N (.) = cumulative normal distribution function of d_1 and d_2

$$d_1 = \frac{\ln(S/X) + (r_f + \sigma^2 / 2)t}{\sigma\sqrt{t}}$$

ln = natural log

$$d_2 = d_1 - \sigma\sqrt{t}$$

In 1997 NatWest Markets, the investment banking arm of National Westminster Bank, was seriously damaged by the revelation of a longstanding failure of senior managers to recognise the mispricing of options – £77m was lost but the damage in terms of reputation was far greater than that (*see* Exhibit 21.26).

Exhibit 21.26

Options mispricing caused loss

FT

The role of Mr Kyriacos Papouis, the 30-year-old former trader at NatWest Markets, in apparently building up over-valuations of £90m in its option books, has not been examined directly during the initial stage of NatWest's inquiry.

However, an outline of what Mr Papouis appears to have done is emerging. Although it involved mis-valuations of options for two years, the bulk of the losses are accounted for by a relatively small number of large trades.

Mr Papouis appears to have amassed small losses as part of routine swaps and options market-making in 1995. However, the fact that option prices are derived from estimates of likely volatility in markets provided a loophole.

Mr Papouis could adjust his estimates of volatility in less liquid swaps and options so as to boost their values. He then managed to persuade risk managers in NatWest Markets to agree to his volatility estimates and valuations.

It is not clear why he was able to persuade other managers that he was right. NatWest says that there was no gap between computer models available to risk managers and to traders, so the mispricing came from volatility estimates.

As the potential losses that would emerge in future rose in size, Mr Papouis appears to have made a few large and complex trades in which volatility estimates were so awry that they offset a high proportion of potential losses.

Source: John Gapper, *Financial Times*, 14 March 1997, p. 6. Reprinted with permission.

KEY POINTS AND CONCEPTS

- **A derivative instrument** is an asset whose performance is based on the behaviour of an underlying asset (the underlying).
- **An option** is a contract giving one party the right, but not the obligation, to buy (call option) or sell (put option) a financial instrument, commodity or some other underlying asset, at a given price, at or before a specified date.
- The **writer of a call option** is obligated to sell the agreed quantity of the underlying some time in the future at the insistence of the option purchaser (holder). A **writer of a put** is obligated to sell.
- **American-style options** can be exercised at any time up to the expiry date whereas **European-style options** can only be exercised on a predetermined future date.
- **An out-of-the-money option** is one that has no intrinsic value.
- An **in-the-money option** has intrinsic value.
- **Time value** arises because of the potential for the market price of the underlying, over the time to expiry of the option, to change in a way that creates intrinsic value.
- **Traditional share options** are available on a wide range of securities whereas traded options are available on a restricted range. However traditional options' strike prices are limited to the underlying's market price, the expiry period is under three months and they cannot be sold.
- **Share options** can be used for hedging or speculating on shares. **Share index options** can be used to hedge and speculate on the market as a whole. Share index options are cash settled.

- **Corporate uses of derivatives include:**
  - share options schemes;
  - warrants;
  - convertible bonds;
  - rights issues;
  - share underwriting;
  - commodity options.

- **Operational and strategic decisions with options (real options):**
  - expansion options;
  - abandonment options;
  - option on timing.

$$\text{True NPV} = \text{Crude NPV} + \text{NPV of expansion option} + \text{NPV of abandonment option} + \text{NPV of timing option} + \text{NPV of other option possibilities}$$

- A **forward contract** is an agreement between two parties to undertake an exchange at an agreed future date at a price agreed now. Forwards are tailor-made, allowing flexibility.

- **Futures** are agreements between two parties to undertake a transaction at an agreed price on a specified future date. They are exchange-traded instruments with a clearing house acting as counterparty to every transaction standardised as to:
  - quality of underlying;
  - quantity of underlying;
  - legal agreement details;
  - delivery dates;
  - trading times;
  - margins.

- For futures, **initial margin** (0.1 per cent to 15 per cent) is required from each buyer or seller. Each day profit or losses are established through **marking to market** and **variation margin** is payable by the holder of the future who loses.

- The majority of futures contracts are **closed** (by undertaking an equal and opposite transaction) **before expiry** and so **cash losses or profits** are made rather than settlement by delivery of the underlying. Some futures are settled by cash only – there is no physical delivery.

- **Short-term interest-rate futures** can be used to hedge against rises and falls in interest rates at some point in the future. The price for a £500,000 notional three-month contract is expressed as an index:

  $$P = 100 - i$$

  As interest rates rise the value of the index falls.

- **Forward rate agreements** (FRAs) are arrangements whereby one party compensates the other should interest rates at some point in the future differ from an agreed rate.

- An interest rate **cap** is a contract that gives the purchaser the right effectively to set a maximum interest rate payable through the entitlement to receive compensation from the cap seller should market interest rates rise above an agreed level. The cap seller and the lender are not necessarily the same.

- A **floor** entitles the purchaser to payments from the floor seller should interest rates fall below an agreed level. A **collar** is a combination of a cap and a floor.
- A **swap** is an exchange of cash payment obligations. An interest-rate swap is where interest obligations are exchanged. In a currency swap the two sets of interest payments are in different currencies.
- Some **motives for swaps:**
  - to reduce or eliminate exposure to rising interest rates;
  - to match interest-rate liabilities with assets;
  - to exploit market imperfections and achieve lower interest rates.
- **Hedgers** enter into transactions to protect a business or assets against changes in some underlying.
- **Speculators** accept high risk by taking a position in financial instruments and other assets with a view to obtaining a profit on changes in value.
- **Arbitrageurs** exploit price differences on the same or similar assets.
- An **over-the-counter (OTC)** derivative is tailor-made and available on a wide range of underlyings. They allow perfect hedging. However they suffer from counterparty risk, low regulation and frequent inability to reverse a hedge.
- **Exchange-traded** derivatives have lower credit (counterparty) risk, greater regulation, higher liquidity and greater ability to reverse positions than OTC derivatives. However standardisation can be restrictive.

REFERENCES AND FURTHER READING

Arnold, G. (1996) 'Risk management using financial derivatives', in E. Gardener and P. Molyneux (eds), *Investment Banking: Theory and Practice*. 2nd edn. London: Euromoney. Some more applications of derivatives are illustrated.

Bank of England Quarterly Bulletins. An important and easily digestible source of up-to-date information.

Black, F. and Scholes, M. (1973) 'The pricing of options and corporate liabilities', *Journal of Political Economy*, May/June, pp. 637–59. The first useful option pricing model – complex mathematics.

Blake, D. (2000) *Financial Market Analysis*. 2nd edn. Chichester: Wiley. Some very useful material – but your maths has to be up to scratch!

Brett, M. (2000) *How to Read the Financial Pages*. 5th edn. London: Random House. A very simple introduction to these markets.

Brown, M. (1996) 'Derivative instruments', in E. Gardener and P. Molyneux (eds), *Investment Banking: Theory and Practice*. 2nd edn. London: Euromoney. A useful overview of the derivatives markets in one chapter.

Eales, B.A. (1995) *Financial Risk Management*. Maidenhead: McGraw-Hill. Introductory material on derivatives. Includes Lotus 1-2-3 spreadsheets as an aid to learning.

The Economist (1996) 'A survey of corporate risk management', 10 February. A survey of practice and thinking in the field – very accessible.

Financial Times. An important source for understanding the latest developments in this dynamic market.

Galitz, L. (1998) *Financial Engineering*. 2nd edn. London: FT Prentice Hall. A clearly written and sophisticated book on use of derivatives. Aimed at a professional readership but some sections are excellent for the novice.

Miller, M.H. (1997) *Merton Miller on Derivatives*. New York: Wiley. An accessible (no maths) account of the advantages and disadvantages of derivatives to companies, society and the financial system.

Taylor, F. (2000) *Mastering Derivatives Markets*. 2nd edn. London: FT Prentice Hall. A good introduction to derivatives instruments and markets.

Vaitilingam, R. (2001) *The Financial Times Guide to Using the Financial Pages*. 4th edn. London: FT Prentice Hall. Explains the tables displayed by the *Financial Times* and some background about the instruments – for the beginner.

Valdez, S. (2000) *An Introduction to Global Financial Markets*. 3rd edn. Basingstoke: Macmillan. Very good introductory description of instruments, with a description of markets around the world.

Winstone, D. (1995) *Financial Derivatives*. London: Chapman & Hall. An easy-to-follow introduction to derivative instruments and markets – great clarity.

WEBSITES

www.bloomberg.com	Bloomberg
www.reuters.com	Reuters
www.cnnfn.com	CNN Financial News
www.wsj.com	*Wall Street Journal*
www.ft.com	*Financial Times*
www.fow.com	*Futures and Options World*
www.cbot.com	Chicago Board of Trade
www.liffe.com	London International Financial Futures and Options Exchange
www.cboe.com	Chicago Board Options Exchange
www.amex.com	American Stock Exchange
www.nyse.com	New York Stock Exchange
www.eurexchange.com	Eurex, the European Derivative Exchange
www.isda.org	International Swaps and Derivatives Association

SELF-REVIEW QUESTIONS

1 What are derivatives and why do they have value?

2 Why can vast sums be made or lost in a short space of time speculating with derivatives?

3 Describe the following:

- traded option
- call option
- put option
- traditional option
- in-the-money option
- out-of-the-money option
- intrinsic value
- time value
- index option
- option writer

4 Compare the hedging characteristics of options and futures.

5 Distinguish between delivery of the underlying and cash settlement.

6 List and briefly describe the application of options to industrial and commercial organisations.

7 Explain the advantages of entering into a forward contract.

8 How do futures differ from forwards?

9 Describe the following:

- clearing house
- initial margin
- marking to market
- variation margin

10 Explain forward rate agreements, caps, floors and collars.

11 Describe what is meant by a swap agreement and explain why some of the arrangements are entered into.

12 Distinguish between a hedger, a speculator and an arbitrageur.

13 Why do the over-the-counter markets in derivatives and the exchange-based derivatives markets coexist?

QUESTIONS AND PROBLEMS

1 You hold 20,000 shares in ABC plc which are currently priced at 500p. ABC has developed a revolutionary flying machine. If trials prove successful the share price will rise significantly. If the government bans the use of the machine, following a trial failure, the share price will collapse.

Required

a Explain and illustrate how you could use the traded options market to hedge your position.
Further information:
Current time: 30 January.
Traded option quotes on ABC plc on 30 January:

		Calls			*Puts*		
	Option	*March*	*June*	*Sept.*	*March*	*June*	*Sept.*
ABC plc	450	62	88	99	11	19	27
	500	30	50	70	30	42	57
	550	9	20	33	70	85	93

b What is meant by intrinsic value, time value, in-the-money, at-the-money and out-of-the-money? Use the above table to illustrate.

2 Palm's share price stands at £4.80. You purchase one March 500p put on Palm's shares for 52p. What is your profit or loss if you hold the option to maturity under each of the following share prices?

a 550p

b 448p

c 420p

3 What is the intrinsic and time value on each of the following options given a share price of 732p?

Exercise price	*Calls Feb.*	*Puts Feb.*
700	55½	17½
750	28	40

Which options are in-the-money and which are out-of-the-money?

4 Adam, a speculator, is convinced that the stock market will fall significantly in the forthcoming months. The current market index (14 August) level is 4997 (FTSE 100). He is trying to decide between two strategies to exploit this market fall:

a Buy five 5025 December put options on the FTSE 100 Index at 191.

b Sell five FTSE 100 Index futures on LIFFE with a December expiry, current price 5086. Extracts from the *Financial Times:*

FTSE 100 Index option (LIFFE) (4997) £10 per full index point
5025 exercise price

	Calls	*Puts*
Aug.	31	34
Sept.	131	114
Oct.	182	148
Nov.	223	168
Dec.	268	191

FTSE 100 Index Futures (LIFFE) £10 per full index point

	Open	*Sett. price*
Sept.	5069	5020
Dec.	5128	5086

Assume: No transaction costs.

Required

i What would the profit (loss) be if the index rose to 5500 in December under each strategy?

ii What would the profit (loss) be if the index fell to 4500 in December under each strategy?

iii Discuss the relative merits of using traded options rather than futures for speculation.

5[†] On 14 August 1997 British Biotech traded options were quoted on LIFFE as follows:

		Calls			*Puts*		
	Option	*Sept.*	*Dec.*	*March*	*Sept.*	*Dec.*	*March*
British Biotech	160	30½	40	53	7½	16½	23½
(177½)	180	20½	31	45½	16½	27	34½

Assume: No transaction costs.

Required

a Imagine you write a December 180 put on 14 August 1997. Draw a graph showing your profit and loss at share prices ranging from 100p to 250p.

b Add to the graph the profit or loss on the purchase of 1,000 shares in British Biotech held until late December at share prices between 100p and 250p.

c Show the profit or loss of the combination of **a** and **b** on the graph.

6* A manager controlling a broadly based portfolio of UK large shares wishes to hedge against a possible fall in the market. It is October and the portfolio stands at £30m with the FTSE 100 Index at 5020. The March futures price is 5035 (£10 per Index point). A March 5000 put option on the FTSE 100 Index can be purchased for 210 at £10 per point.

Required

a Describe two ways in which the manager could hedge against a falling market. Show the number of derivatives and cash flows.

b What are the profits/losses under each strategy if the FTSE 100 Index moves to 4000 or 6000 in March?

c Draw a profit/loss diagram for each strategy. Show the value of the underlying portfolio at different index levels, the value of the derivative and the combined value of the underlying and the derivative.

d Briefly comment on the differences between the two hedging strategies.

7 (*Examination level*) A buyer of a futures contract in Imaginationum with an underlying value of £400,000 on 1 August is required to deliver an initial margin of 5 per cent to the clearing house. This margin must be maintained as each day the counterparties in the futures are marked to market.

Required

a Display a table showing the variation margin required to be paid by this buyer and the accumulated profit/loss balance on her margin account in the eight days following the purchase of the future. (Assume that the maintenance margin is the same as the initial margin.)

Day	*1*	*2*	*3*	*4*	*5*	*6*	*7*	*8*
Value of Imaginationum (£000s)	390	410	370	450	420	400	360	410

b Explain what is meant by 'gearing returns' with reference to this example.

c Compare forwards and futures markets and explain the mutual coexistence of these two.

8* A corporate treasurer expects to receive £20m in late September, six months hence. The money will be needed for expansion purposes the following December. However in the intervening three months it can be deposited to earn interest. The treasurer is concerned that interest rates will fall from the present level of 8 per cent over the next six months, resulting in a poorer return on the deposited money.

A forward rate agreement (FRA) is available for 'sale' at 8 per cent.

Three-month sterling interest futures starting in late September are available, priced at 92.00.

Assume: No transaction costs and that a perfect hedge is possible.

Required

a Describe two hedging transactions that the treasurer could employ.

b Show the profit/loss on the underlying and the derivative under each strategy if market interest rates fall to 7 per cent, and if they rise to 9 per cent.

9* a Black plc has a £50m ten-year floating-rate loan from bank A at Libor + 150 basis points. The treasurer is worried that interest rates will rise to a level that will put the firm in a dangerous position. White plc is willing to swap its fixed interest commitment for the next ten years. White currently pays 9 per cent to Bank B. Libor is currently 8 per cent. Show the interest rate payment flows in a diagram under a swap arrangement in which each firm pays the other's interest payments.

b What are the drawbacks of this swap arrangement for Black?

c Black can buy a ten-year interest-rate cap set at a Libor of 8.5 per cent. This will cost 4 per cent of the amount covered. Show the payment flows if in the fourth year Libor rises to 10 per cent.

d Describe a 'floor' and show how it can be used to alleviate the cost of a cap.

10 Three-month sterling interest-rate futures are quoted as follows on 30 August:

	£500,000 points of 100% *Settlement price*
Sept.	91.50
Dec.	91.70
Mar.	91.90

Red Wheel plc expects to need to borrow £15m at floating rate in late December for three months and is concerned that interest rates will rise between August and December.

Assume: No transaction costs.

Required

a Show a hedging strategy that Red Wheel could employ to reduce uncertainty.

b What is the effective rate of interest payable by Red Wheel after taking account of the derivative transaction if three-month spot rates are 10 per cent in December? Show the gain on the derivative.

c What is the effective rate of interest after taking account of the derivative transaction if three-month spot rates are 7 per cent in December? Show the loss on the derivative.

d Compare short-term interest-rate futures and FRAs as alternative hedging techniques for a situation such as Red Wheel's.

11 'The derivatives markets destroy wealth rather than help create it; they should be made illegal.' Explain your reasons for agreeing or disagreeing with this speaker.

12 Invent examples to demonstrate the different hedging qualities of options, futures and forwards.

13 Speculators, hedgers and arbitrageurs are all desirable participants in the derivatives markets. Explain the role of each.

ASSIGNMENTS

1 Describe as many uses of options as you can by a firm you know well. These can include exchange-traded options, currency options, other OTC options, corporate uses of options (for example underwriting) and operational and strategic decision options.

2 Investigate the extent of derivatives use by the treasury department of a firm you know well. Explain the purpose of derivatives use and consider alternative instruments to those used in the past.

CHAPTER NOTES

1 For this exercise we will assume that the option is held to expiry and not traded before then.

2 £220 is the instrinsic value at expiry: (482 – 460p) × 1,000 = £220.

3 This is not a perfect hedge as there is an element of the underlying risk without offsetting derivative cover.

4 Early in 1999, however, it was revealed that Ashanti was not simply using derivatives to reduce risk. It also lost a great deal of money as the gold price rose: Ashanti had switched from hedging to speculating – it was gambling on the price of gold.

5 Initial margin is the same as maintenance margin in this case.

6 Nick Leeson in an interview with David Frost reported in *Financial Times*, 11 September 1995.

7 Assuming that the futures price is equal to the spot price of the FTSE 100. This would occur close to expiry date of the future.

8 All figures are slightly simplified because we are ignoring the fact that the compensation is received in six months whereas interest to Bank X is payable in 18 months.

9 Under a swap arrangement the principal amount (in this case £150m) is never swapped and Cat retains the obligation to pay the principal to bank A. Neither of the banks is involved in the swap and may not be aware that it has taken place. The swap focuses entirely on the three-monthly or six-monthly interest payments.

Chapter 22

MANAGING EXCHANGE-RATE RISK

INTRODUCTION

This chapter discusses how changes in exchange rates can lead to an increase in uncertainty about income from operations in foreign countries or from trading with foreign firms. Shifts in foreign exchange rates have the potential to undermine the competitive position of the firm and destroy profits. This chapter describes some of the techniques used to reduce the risk associated with business dealings outside the home base.

CASE STUDY 22.1

What a difference a few percentage point moves on the exchange rate make

Until autumn 1992 sterling was a member of the European exchange rate mechanism (ERM), which meant the extent it could move in value *vis-à-vis* the other currencies in the ERM was severely limited. Then came 'Black Wednesday' when in order to prop up the value of sterling the UK government increased bank base rates to 15 per cent and instructed the Bank of England to buy billions of pounds to offset the selling pressure in the markets. It was all to no avail. The pound fell out of ERM, the government gave up the fight, and by the end of the year £1 could only buy you about DM2.35 compared with DM2.90 in the summer (a 19 per cent decline).

George Soros was one of the speculators who recognised economic gravity when he saw it, and bet the equivalent of $10bn against sterling by buying other currencies. After the fall the money held in other currencies could be converted back to make $1bn in just a few days. He was dubbed the man who 'broke the Bank of England'. While this was not exactly true, he and others did cause severe embarrassment. When sterling was highly valued against other currencies exporters found life very difficult because, to the foreign buyer, British goods appeared expensive – every DM, franc or guilder bought few pounds. However in the four years following 'Black Wednesday' UK exporters had a terrific boost and helped pull the economy out of recession as overseas customers bought more goods. Other European companies, on the other hand, complained bitterly. The French government was prompted by its hard-pressed importers to ask for compensation from the European Commission for the 'competitive devaluations by their neighbours'. Then things turned around. Between 1996 and 2001 the pound rose against most currencies. For example, whereas you could buy only DM2.2 at the beginning of 1996 by 2001 you could buy DM3.09 for every pound. Looked at from the German importers' viewpoint UK goods relative to domestic goods rose in price by something of the order of 30–40 per cent.

UK firms lined up to speak of the enormous impact the high pound was having on profits. British Steel (Corus) cut thousands of jobs in response to sterling's rise and started losing money at an alarming rate. It also passed on the pain by telling 700 of its UK suppliers to cut prices. In addition, it suffered because its UK customers which exported ordered less steel.

James Dyson, the vacuum cleaner entrepreneur, announced in 2000 that he was planning to build a factory in East Asia rather than Britain because of the strength of the pound. In the previous year Dyson had made a loss on its £60m of exports. The Japanese car makers, Toyota, Honda and Nissan, which had established plants in Britain, complained bitterly about the high level of the pound. Their factories were set up to export cars. They were hurt by having to reduce prices and also by their commitment to buy 70 per cent of components from UK suppliers (continental European suppliers benefited from a 30–40 per cent price advantage because of the high pound).

The message from the ups and downs of sterling and other currencies in the 1990s is that foreign exchange shifts and the management of the associated risk are not issues to be separated and put into a box marked 'for the attention of the finance specialists only'. The profound implications for jobs, competitiveness, national economic growth and firms' survival mean that all managers need to be aware of the consequences of foreign exchange rate movements and of how to prepare the firm to cope with them.

Learning objectives

By the end of this chapter the reader will be able to:

- explain the role and importance of the foreign exchange markets;
- describe hedging techniques to reduce the risk associated with transactions entered into in another currency;
- consider methods of dealing with the risk that assets, income and liabilities denominated in another currency, when translated into home-currency terms, are distorted;
- describe techniques for reducing the impact of foreign exchange changes on the competitive position of the firm;
- outline the theories designed to explain the reasons for currency changes.

THE EFFECTS OF EXCHANGE-RATE CHANGES

Shifts in the value of foreign exchange, from now on to be referred to as simply 'forex' (FOReign EXchange),[1] can impact on various aspects of a firm's activities:

- ***Income to be received from abroad*** For example, if a UK firm has exported goods to Canada on six months' credit terms, payable in Canadian dollars (C$), it is uncertain as to the number of pounds it will actually receive because the dollar could move against the pound in the intervening period.

- ***The amount actually paid for imports at some future date*** For example, a Japanese firm importing wood from the USA may have a liability to pay dollars a few months later. The quantity of yen (¥) it will have to use to exchange for the dollars at that point in the future is uncertain at the time the deal is struck.
- ***The valuation of foreign assets and liabilities*** In today's globalised market-place many firms own assets abroad and incur liabilities in foreign currencies. The value of these in home-currency terms can change simply because of forex movements.
- ***The long-term viability of foreign operations*** The long-term future returns of subsidiaries located in some countries can be enhanced by a favourable forex change. On the other hand firms can be destroyed if they are operating in the wrong currency at the wrong time.
- ***The acceptability, or otherwise, of an overseas investment project*** When evaluating the value-creating potential of major new investments a firm must be aware that the likely future currency changes can have a significant effect on estimated NPV.

In summary, fluctuating exchange rates create risk, and badly managed risk can lead to a loss of shareholder wealth.

VOLATILITY IN FOREIGN EXCHANGE

Exhibits 22.1 to 22.4 show the extent to which forex rates can move even over a period as short as a few weeks – 5 or 10 per cent point shifts are fairly common.

In the mid-1970s a regime of (generally) floating exchange rates replaced the fixed exchange-rate system which had been in place since the 1940s. Today most currencies fluctuate against each other, at least to some extent.

If a UK firm holds dollars or assets denominated in dollars and the value of the dollar rises against the pound a forex profit is made. Conversely, should the pound rise relative

Exhibit 22.1 Exchange-rate movements, US$ to UK£, August 1986 – August 2001 (monthly)

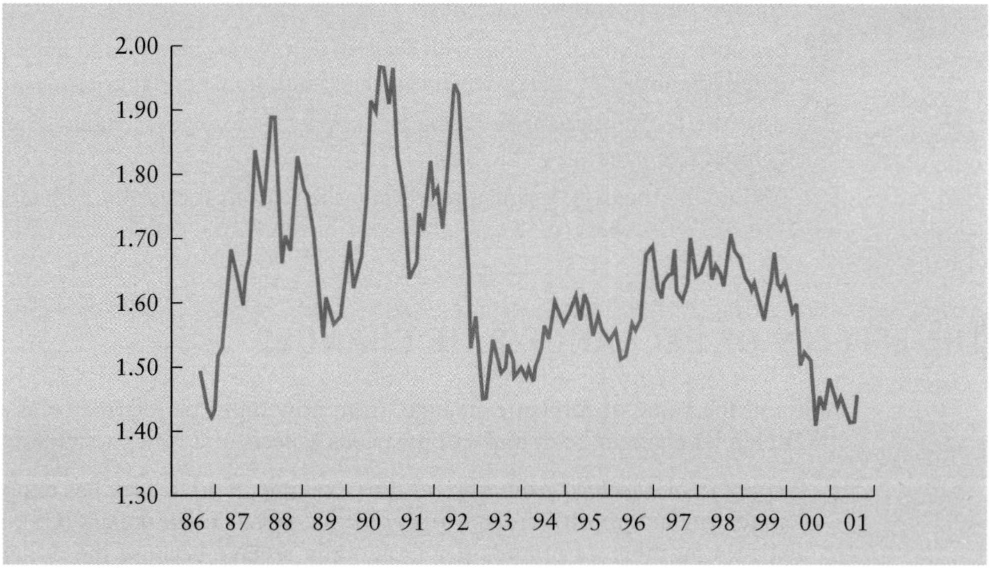

Source: Thomson Financial Datastream.

to the dollar, a forex loss will be incurred. These potential gains or losses can be very large. For example, between March 1992 and February 1993 the dollar appreciated by 17.8 per cent against the pound so you could have made a large gain by holding dollars even before the money was put to use, say, earning interest. In other periods fluctuating forex rates may wipe out profits from a project, an export deal or a portfolio investment (for example a pension fund buying foreign shares).

Exhibit 22.2 Exchange-rate movements, Japanese Yen to US$, August 1986 to August 2001 (monthly)

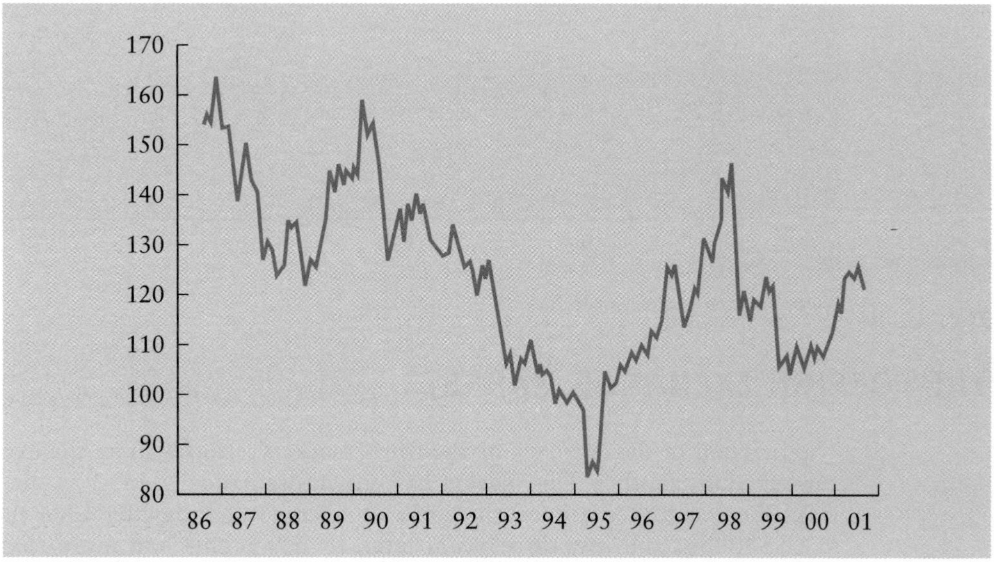

Source: Thomson Financial Datastream.

Exhibit 22.3 Exchange-rate movements, UK £ to euro, January 1999 to August 2001 (weekly)

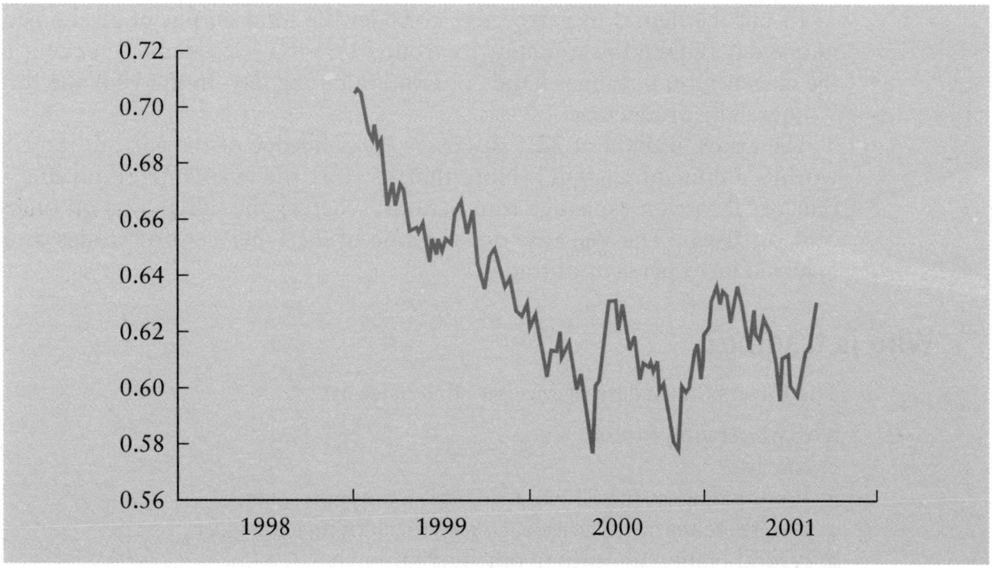

Source: Thomson Financial Datastream.

Exhibit 22.4 Exchange-rate movements, US$ to euro, January 1999 to August 2001 (weekly)

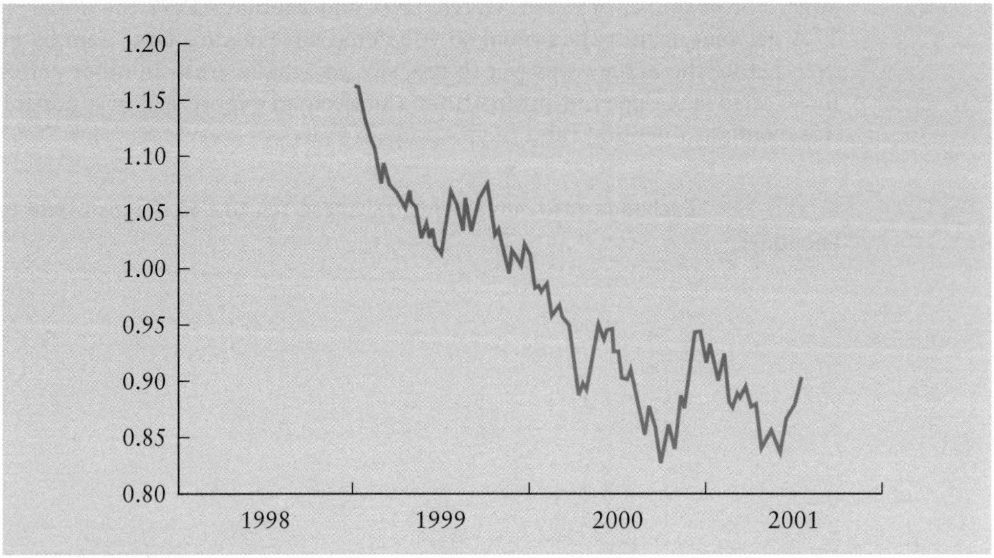

Source: Thomson Financial Datastream.

THE FOREIGN EXCHANGE MARKETS

The function of the currency or the forex markets is to facilitate the exchange of one currency into another. This market has grown dramatically. In 1973 the equivalent of US$10bn was traded around the globe on average each day. By 1986 this had grown to US$300bn, and just three years later, by 1989, this had more than doubled to US$590bn. In 1998 the daily turnover was over US$1,490bn. In 2001 it was estimated at $1,210bn. London is the biggest currency trading centre in the world, with US$504bn traded daily in 2001. There was US$254bn traded in the US. Japan had US$147bn and Singapore comes in fourth place with US$101bn per day.

To put the figures in perspective consider the total output of all the people in the UK in one day (GDP): this amounts to around US$4bn – less than 1 per cent of the value of the currency that changes hands in London in one day. In the USA the forex turnover is 9 times daily production.

The article in Exhibit 22.5 discusses the challenge of the euro to the US dollar as the world's dominant currency. Note that in 2001 the euro entered on one side of 38 per cent of all foreign exchange transactions, whereas the dollar was on one side in 90 per cent of cases. (The yen was on one side of 22.7 per cent of trades and sterling was involved in 13 per cent of trades.)

Who is trading?

The buyers and sellers of foreign currencies are:

- exporters/importers;
- tourists;
- fund managers (pensions, insurance companies, etc.);
- governments (for example, to pay for activities abroad);
- central banks (smoothing out fluctuations);
- speculators;
- banks.

Exhibit 22.5 Currency trading

Euro dawn promises challenge to mighty $

FT

By Richard Adams and Andrew Balls in London

The coming of the euro – the European single currency – means that the latest survey of the international foreign exchange market may soon look like a museum piece.

The survey – held every three years by the Bank for International Settlements and central banks around the world – revealed that the dollar is still far and away the dominant world currency.

In London, the world's leading centre for foreign exchange, buying or selling of the dollar accounts for 85 per cent of total turnover. That proportion is little changed from previous surveys.

But the latest survey, published yesterday, shows a rise in trading in the dollar against the currencies that will make up the euro when it is launched in January.

In 1995, the combined dollar-euro trades accounted for around 38 per cent of total turnover, with 22 per cent of the total market coming from dollar/D-Mark trading.

Three years later and the total has risen above 40 per cent, thanks to greater activity in lira and other member currencies.

Hal Herron, the global head of foreign exchange trading at Deutsche Bank in London, said: 'When the euro comes into being it will be as a major bloc. We will see it traded against a whole range of currencies. Things will look completely different, that's for sure.'

But it may take time for the euro to challenge the dollar as the international currency of choice, because of the deep reserves held in dollars worldwide.

A change in the dollar's status could hurt the position of the New York market, which remains the largest foreign exchange centre after London.

Source: Richard Adams and Andrew Balls, *Financial Times*, 30 September 1998, p. 4. Reprinted with permission.

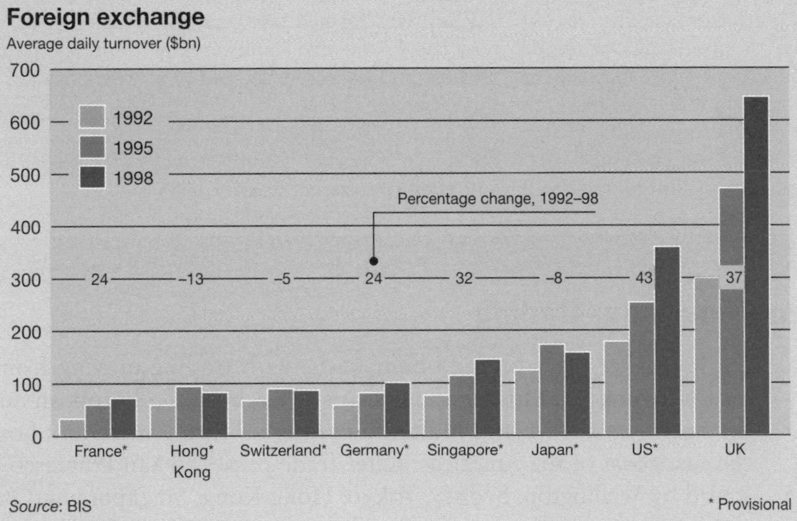

The first five groups account for only a small fraction of the transactions. The big players are the large commercial banks. In addition to dealing on behalf of customers, or acting as marketmakers, they carry out 'proprietary' transactions of their own in an attempt to make a profit by taking a position in the market – that is, speculating on future movements. Companies and individuals usually obtain their foreign currencies from the banks.

Foreign exchange interbank brokers often act as intermediaries between large buyers and sellers. They allow banks to trade anonymously, thus avoiding having the price move simply because of the revelation of the name of a bank in a transaction.

Most deals are still made over the telephone and later confirmed in writing. However the new electronic trading systems in which computers match deals automatically have taken a rapidly increasing share of deals – *see* Exhibit 22.6.

Exhibit 22.6

FXall set to intensify battle in online currency trading

FT

By Christopher Swann and Doug Cameron

FXall, the online currency trading system, is set to go live today, intensifying the battle among platforms to lure fund managers and treasurers away from traditional phone-based dealing.

FXall, owned by a consortium of seven banks, hopes to gain a lead over the Atriax platform backed by Citigroup, Deutsche Bank and JP Morgan Chase, which plans to open in June.

The launch of FXall is the largest to date among multi-bank online platforms seeking to cut the cost of providing wholesale banking services and meet client demands for quotes and research from a range of providers. 'There is only room for two survivors, and logically it should be FXall and Atriax,' said the head of e-commerce at one European bank. 'But there remain question marks over their high cost structure and [cash] burn rate.'

Banks have invested more than $5bn (£3.5bn) in internet platforms trading in equities, bonds, loans and derivatives.

However, limited client take-up and conflicting interests between backers of consortia portals could lead to a shake-out with many services folding or failing to launch.

FXall was formed last year and now has 47 member banks. Many of these also joined Atriax and two smaller online operators.

With daily turnover of $1,500bn, the currency market is competitive, and platforms are battling for bank members to maximise liquidity and minimise transaction costs for corporate clients.

The currency market has been slow to develop online trading, with about 5 per cent of deals conducted on the internet.

'Until now there has been no compelling offer for companies wishing to trade electronically and as a result they stuck to traditional means,' said Phil Weisberg, chief executive of FXall . . .

Atriax, which is backed by Reuters, has more than 60 members representing more than half of currency trading.

Source: Christopher Swann and Doug Cameron, *Financial Times*, 10 May 2001, p. 23. Reprinted with permission.

Twenty-four hour trading

Dealing takes place on a 24-hour basis, with trading moving from one major financial centre to another. Most trading occurs when both the European and New York markets are open – this is when it is afternoon in Frankfurt, Zurich and London and morning on the east coast of the Americas. Later trade passes to San Francisco and Los Angeles, followed by Wellington, Sydney, Tokyo, Hong Kong, Singapore and Bahrain.

Most banks are in the process of concentrating their dealers in three or four regional hubs. These typically include London as well as New York and two sites in Asia, where Tokyo, Hong Kong and Singapore are keen to establish their dominance.

The vast sums of money traded every working day across the world means that banks are exposed to the risk that they may irrevocably pay over currency to a counterparty before they receive another currency in return because settlement systems are operating in different time zones – this is called Herstatt risk. *See* Exhibit 22.7.[2]

Exhibit 22.7

IBM to build forex settlement bank

FT

By George Graham, Banking Editor, in London

IBM is to build and operate the new settlement bank which is being set up to handle the $3,500bn of foreign exchange trades settled each day.

CLS Services, the consortium set up by a group of leading international banks to handle the foreign exchange settlement problem, said it had chosen IBM to design and build the new settlement system and to operate it for at least five years after it starts up in mid-2000 . . .

Yesterday's announcement coincides with the deadline set two years ago by central bankers for the private sector to come up with a solution to the problem of settlement risk in foreign exchange trading. The deadline inspired creation of the settlement bank. It also spurred banks to tighten their internal procedures, and triggered the development of netting services.

Foreign exchange trades today are mostly settled by paying the two different currencies separately. Since banks settle in different time zones, there is a risk – known as Herstatt risk after the collapse of Bankhaus Herstatt in Germany in 1974 – that a bank could fail after receiving one leg of its foreign exchange trades but before paying the other leg.

When the CLS Bank starts up, it will allow both legs of the trade to paid simultaneously, eliminating the risk that one bank might fail in midstream . . .

Membership of CLS Services has already been broadened beyond the group of 20 banks which began the project and now has 40 shareholders. Other financial institutions will be given the chance to sign up over the next two months, as CLS finalises the funding for the settlement bank project . . .

The first stage of the banks' plan to tackle Herstatt risk was the merger of two competing multilateral netting services, Echo in the UK and Multinet in the US. The combined netting service allows banks to reduce their settlement risk by adding all the different gross amounts they owe each other and settling only the net difference . . .

After the CLS Banks starts up in 2000, some banks will use it as their main way of eliminating foreign exchange settlement risk, but others will still channel foreign exchange trades through the netting service, using the CLS Bank to settle the netted amounts.

Source: George Graham, Banking Editor, *Financial Times*, 28 April 1998, p. 4. Reprinted with permission.

EXCHANGE RATES

We now look more closely at exchange rates. We start with some terms used in forex markets. First, we provide a definition of an exchange rate:

An exchange rate is the price of one currency expressed in terms of another.

Therefore if the exchange rate between the US dollar and the pound is US$1.44 = £1.00 this means that £1.00 will cost US$1.44. Taking the reciprocal, US$1.00 will cost 69.44 pence. The standardised forms of expression are:

US$/£ : 1.44
or
US$1.44/£

Exchange rates are expressed in terms of the number of units of the first currency per single unit of the second currency. Also forex rates are normally given to five or six significant figures. So for the US$/£ exchange rate on 16 August 2001 the more accurate rate is:

US$1.4431/£

However this is still not accurate enough because currency exchange rates are not generally expressed in terms of a single 'middle rate' as above, but are given as a rate at which you can buy the first currency (bid rate) and a rate at which you can sell the first currency (offer rate). In the case of the US$/£ exchange rate the market rates on 16 August 2001 were:

US$1.4431/£ 'middle rate'

	bid rate	*offer rate*
	↓	↓
US$/£	1.4430	1.4432
	↑	↑
	You can buy dollars from a bank or broker at this rate.	You can sell dollars to a bank or a broker at this rate.

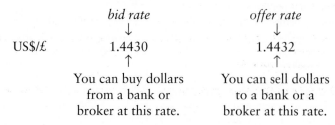

So if you wished to purchase US$1m the cost would be:

$$\frac{\$1{,}000{,}000}{1.4430} = £693{,}001$$

However if you wished to sell US$1m you would receive:

$$\frac{\$1{,}000{,}000}{1.4432} = £692{,}905$$

The foreign exchange dealers make profit in two ways. First, they may charge commission on a deal. Depending on the size of the transaction this can vary, but it is generally well below 1 per cent. Second, these institutions are dealing with numerous buyers and sellers every day and they make a profit on the difference between the bid price and offer price (the bid/offer spread). In the above example if a dealer sold US$1m and bought US$1m with a bid/offer spread of 0.02 of a cent a profit of £693,001 – £692,905 = £96 is made.

Worked example 22.1 Forex

The basic elements of forex are so important for the rest of the chapter that it is worth while to pause and consolidate understanding of the quoted rates through some exercises.

Answer the following questions on the basis that the euro/US$ exchange rate is 1.1168–1.1173.

1 What is the cost of buying €200,000?
2 How much would it cost to purchase US$4m?
3 How many dollars would be received from selling €800,000?
4 How many euros would be received from selling US$240,000?

Answers

1 $\frac{200{,}000}{1.1168} = \text{US}\$179{,}083$

2 $4{,}000{,}000 \times 1.1173 = €4{,}469{,}200$

3 $\frac{800{,}000}{1.1173} = \text{US}\$716{,}012$

4 $240{,}000 \times 1.1168 = €268{,}032$

The spot and forward exchange markets

There are two main forex markets.

1 *The 'spot' market* In the spot market transactions take place which are to be settled quickly. Officially this is described as immediate delivery, but this usually takes place two business days after the deal is struck.
2 *The 'forward' market* In the forward market a deal is arranged to exchange currencies at some future date at a price agreed now. The periods of time are generally one, three or six months, but it is possible to arrange an exchange of currencies at a predetermined rate many years from now.

Forward transactions represent about one-third to one-half of all forex deals. There are many currencies, however, for which forward quotes are difficult to obtain. The so-called exotic currencies generally do not have forward rates quoted by dealers. These are currencies for which there is little trading demand to support international business, etc. On the other hand, spot markets exist for most of the world's currencies.

The *Financial Times* reports the previous day's trading in the forex market. The figures shown in Exhibit 22.8 relate to dealing on 16 August 2001. Of course by the time a newspaper reader receives the information in this table the rates have changed as the 24-hour markets follow the sun around the world.

The second column in the table in Exhibit 22.8 gives the middle price of the foreign currency in terms of £1 in London the previous afternoon.[3] This is the spot price for 'immediate' delivery. The third column shows the change in prices over the day.

The next column entitled bid/offer spread shows the buying and selling prices, but rather confusingly leaves out the first few digits. So for the South African rand the bid and offer rates are 11.8831 and 11.8992.

The next two columns show the day's trading range for the mid prices. The first forward price (middle price) is given in the column entitled 'One month'. So you could commit yourself to the purchase of a quantity of dollars for delivery in one month at a rate which is fixed at about US$1.4415. In this case you will need fewer US dollars to buy £1 in one month's time compared with spot, therefore the dollar is at a *premium* on the one-month forward rate.

The forward rates for three months show a different relationship with the spot rate for the South African rand. Here more rands are required (R12.0299) to purchase £1 in three months' time compared with an 'immediate' spot purchase (R11.8912), therefore the rand on three-month forward delivery is at a *discount*. The rand is becoming less expensive to buy, or is depreciating against sterling.

The *Financial Times* table lists quotations up to one year, but, as this is an over-the-counter market (*see* Chapter 21), you are able to go as far forward in time as you wish – provided you can find a counterparty. For some currencies trading in three-month and one-year forwards is so thin as to not warrant a quotation in the table. However for the major currencies such as the US dollar, sterling, the euro, the Swiss franc and the Japanese yen, forward markets can stretch up to ten years. Airline companies expecting to purchase planes many years hence may use this distant forward market to purchase the foreign currency they need to pay the manufacturer so that they know with certainty the quantity of their home currency they are required to find when the planes are delivered.

The table in Exhibit 22.8 displays standard periods of time for forward rates. These are instantly available and are frequently traded. However forward rates are not confined to these particular days in the future. It is possible to obtain rates for any day in the future, say, 74 or 36 days hence. But this would require a specific quotation from a bank.

Exhibit 22.8

POUND SPOT FORWARD AGAINST THE POUND FT

Aug 16		Closing mid-point	Change on day	Bid/offer spread	Day's Mid		One month		Three months		One year		Bank of Eng. Index
					high	low	Rate	%PA	Rate	%PA	Rate	%PA	
Europe													
Austria*	(Sch)	21.7545	+0.0349	506 – 584	21.8035	21.6275	21.7462	0.5	21.7252	0.5	21.5486	0.9	100.5
Belgium*	(BFr)	63.7785	+0.1024	644 – 872	63.9200	63.4040	63.7518	0.5	63.6902	0.5	63.1723	0.9	99.3
Denmark	(DKr)	11.7700	+0.0216	673 – 727	11.7940	11.7199	11.769	0.1	11.7646	0.2	11.702	0.6	102.6
Finland*	(FM)	9.4000	+0.0151	983 – 016	9.4210	9.3450	9.3964	0.5	9.3874	0.5	9.311	0.9	78.6
France*	(FFr)	10.3705	=0.0167	686 – 723	10.3938	10.3100	10.3666	0.5	10.3566	0.5	10.2724	0.9	102.0
Germany*	(DM)	3.0921	+0.0049	915 – 926	3.0995	3.0724	3.0909	0.4	3.088	0.5	3.0628	0.9	99.0
Greece*	(Dr)	538.712	+0.8650	616 – 808	539.927	535.570	538.509	0.5	537.989	0.5	533.614	0.9	57.6
Ireland*	(I£)	1.2451	+0.0020	449 – 453	1.2479	1.2378	1.2446	0.5	1.2434	0.5	1.2333	0.9	88.1
Italy*	(L)	3061.16	+4.9100	062 – 171	3068.06	3043.31	3060	0.5	3057.05	0.5	3032.19	0.9	72.8
Luxembourg*	(LFr)	63.7758	+.01024	644 – 872	63.9200	63.4040	63.7518	0.5	63.6902	0.5	63.1723	0.9	99.3
Netherlands*	(Fl)	3.4840	+0.0056	834 – 846	3.4918	3.4636	3.4827	0.5	3.4792	0.5	3.451	0.9	98.3
Norway	(NKr)	12.8133	+0.0107	074 – 191	12.8548	12.7893	12.8369	–2.2	12.8875	–2.3	13.0731	–2.0	95.0
Portugal*	(Es)	316.954	+0.5090	897 – 011	317.671	315.112	316.835	0.5	316.528	0.5	313.955	0.9	89.7
Spain*	(Pta)	263.050	+0.4230	003 – 097	263.640	261.510	262.951	0.5	262.697	0.5	260.561	0.9	74.5
Sweden	(SKr)	14.6753	+0.0934	718 – 787	14.6965	14.5526	14.6673	0.7	14.6546	0.6	14.5871	0.6	75.7
Switzerland	(SFr)	2.4008	+0.0048	001 – 014	2.4059	2.3937	2.3975	1.6	2.3903	1.7	2.3508	2.1	109.0
Turkey	(Lira)	2099711	–21487	350 – 072	2151560	2092350	–	–	–	–	–	–	–
UK	(£)	–	–	–	–	–	–	–	–	–	–	–	104.4
Euro	(€)	1.5810	+0.0026	807 – 812	1.5850	1.5714	1.5804	0.5	1.5788	0.5	1.566	0.9	79.68
SDR	–	1.125200	–	–	–	–	–	–	–	–	–	–	–
Americas													
Argentina	(Peso)	1.4428	+0.0052	426 – 429	1.4515	1.4395	–	–	–	–	–	–	–
Brazil	(R$)	3.5926	–0.0034	916 – 936	3.6109	3.5704	–	–	–	–	–	–	–
Canada	(C$)	2.2087	+0.0072	081 – 093	2.2170	2.2010	2.2071	0.8	2.2042	0.8	2.1896	0.9	78.3
Mexico	(New Peso)	13.1063	+0.0239	981 – 144	13.1818	13.0691	13.1554	–4.5	13.2988	–5.9	14.049	–7.2	–
USA	($)	1.4431	+0.0050	430 – 432	1.4519	1.4398	1.4415	1.4	1.4382	1.4	1.4245	1.3	116.9
Pacific/Middle East/Africa													
Australia	(A$)	2.7355	+0.0053	350 – 359	2.7487	2.7192	2.7355	0.0	2.7357	0.0	2.7352	0.0	72.7
Hong Kong	(HK$)	11.2558	+0.0389	544 – 571	11.3241	11.2302	11.2415	1.5	11.2139	1.5	11.1051	1.3	–
India	(Rs)	67.9845	+0.2356	076 – 613	68.4020	67.9010	68.158	–3.1	68.5262	–3.2	70.3325	–3.5	–
Indonesia	(Rupiah)	12627.1	+7.80	902 – 641	12721.8	12288.9	12612.66	1.4	12583.96	1.4	12464.79	1.3	–
Israel	(Shk)	6.1058	+0.0068	981 – 134	6.1162	6.0981	–	–	–	–	–	–	–
Japan	(Y)	173.425	+0.9540	377 – 473	173.580	172.280	172.7	5.0	171.325	4.8	165.12	4.8	139.1
Malaysia†	(M$)	5.4838	+0.0190	834 – 842	5.5165	5.4720	–	–	–	–	–	–	–
New Zealand	(NZ$)	3.3148	–0.0065	134 – 162	3.3409	3.3060	3.3171	–0.8	3.322	–0.9	3.3452	–0.9	8.17
Philippines	(Peso)	73.5693	+0.2262	920 – 456	73.9049	73.4920	73.9213	–5.7	74.5699	–5.4	78.8555	–7.2	–
Saudi Arabia	(SR)	5.4122	+0.0187	117 – 127	5.4452	5.4000	5.4064	1.3	5.3948	1.3	5.3481	1.2	–
Singapore	(S$)	2.5205	+0.0091	198 – 211	2.5294	2.5142	2.5152	2.5	2.5043	2.6	2.4552	2.6	–
South Africa	(R)	11.8912	+0.0418	831 – 992	11.9600	11.8496	11.9413	–5.1	12.0299	–4.7	12.3623	–4.0	–
South Korea	(Won)	1845.73	–7.2600	838 – 307	1853.07	1838.38	–	–	–	–	–	–	–
Taiwan	(T$)	49.7870	+0.1006	114 – 626	50.0891	49.7114	49.7084	1.9	49.6026	1.5	49.3464	0.9	–
Thailand	(Bt)	64.4272	–0.1004	867 – 677	64.7160	64.2950	64.3752	1.0	64.3796	0.3	64.7387	–0.5	–

Bid/offer spreads in the Pound Spot table show only the last three decimal places. Sterling index calculated by the Bank of England. Base average 1990 = 100. Index rebased 1/2/95. EMU member. The exchange rates printed in this table are also available on the internet at **http://www.FT.com**.

Source: *Financial Times*, 17 August 2001, p. 26. Reprinted with permission.

The Special Drawing Rights or (SDRs) of the International Monetary Fund (IMF) are artificial currencies made up from baskets of other currencies. Finally the Bank of England index shows the extent to which the pound has strengthened (a number below 100), or weakened (a number above 100) against another currency since 1990. The figure in the UK row shows the trade weighted index – the extent to which sterling has moved against other currencies weighted according to the level of international trade. (A larger number means sterling has strengthened against a basket of currencies weighted accordingly to the proportion of trade in the currency.)

In 1999 the *Financial Times* introduced a new forex table for the euro – *see* Exhibit 22.9.

Exhibit 22.9

Real thing replaces the synthetic euro

FT

The FT will publish daily a table showing the spot (immediate delivery) and forward (settlement at a future date) values for the euro against more than 30 of the world's main traded currencies.

This takes the place of the FT Synthetic Euro table, which we began publishing last May and was designed to give readers a rough guide to the likely value of the euro.

The new table will appear from Mondays to Fridays on the Euro Prices page and on Saturdays on the Currencies and Money page.

It has a similar design to the tables already published for sterling and the US dollar . . .

The table does not include so-called 'legacy currencies' – the currencies of the 11 members of the euro-zone, which are now simply national sub-units of the euro, with fixed values against the currency. These fixed values will be shown daily in a footnote to the table.

For sterling, which is often quoted only on a 'certain for uncertain' basis against other currencies (so many \$ per £) we are following the European central bankers' suggestion in this table and showing the euro on a 'certain for uncertain' basis (so many £ per €).

Euro Spot forward against the euro

Dec 21		Closing mid-point	Change on day	Bid/offer spread	Day's Mid high	Day's Mid low	One month Rate	One month %PA	Three months Rate	Three months %PA	One year Rate
Europe											
Czech Rep.	(Koruna)	34.1809	+34.1809	376 – 242	34.1376	34.2242	35.9577	–62.4	36.5307	–27.5	38.9094
Denmark	(DKr)	7.4566	+7.4566	502 – 630	7.4502	7.4630	7.4848	–4.5	7.5054	–2.6	7.5883
Greece	(Dr)	330.382	+330.382	068 – 696	330.068	330.696	339.9966	–34.9	344.9414	–17.6	365.4205
Hungary	(Forint)	253.869	+253.8690	619 – 120	253.619	254.120	258.7088	–22.9	264.5668	–16.9	289.8696
Norway	(NKr)	8.7272	+8.7272	197 – 347	8.7197	8.7347	8.7834	–7.7	8.8369	–5.0	9.0354
Poland	(Zloty)	4.0429	+4.0429	375 – 482	4.0375	4.0482	–	–	–	–	–
Romania	(Lev)	11622.02	+11.0200	150 – 255	11591.50	11652.55	–	–	–	–	–
Russia	(Rouble)	18.8276	+18.8276	284 – 268	18.7284	18.9268	–	–	–	–	–
Slovakia	(Koruna)	41.5190	+41.5190	170 – 209	41.3170	41.7209	–	–	–	–	–
Sweden	(SKr)	9.2338	+9.2338	253 – 422	9.2253	9.2422	9.2020	4.1	9.2052	1.2	9.2634
Switzerland	(SFr)	1.6010	+1.6010	995 – 024	1.5995	1.6024	1.6171	–12.1	1.6103	–2.3	1.5885
UK	(£)	0.7136	+0.7136	130 – 142	0.7130	0.7142	0.6946	32.0	0.6981	8.7	0.7139
Americas											
Argentina	(Peso)	1.1822	+1.1822	814 – 829	1.1814	1.1829	–	–	–	–	–
Brazil	(R\$)	1.4091	+1.4091	081 – 100	1.4081	1.4100	–	–	–	–	–
Canada	(C\$)	1.8025	+1.8025	008 – 041	1.8008	1.8041	1.7848	11.8	1.7889	3.0	1.8095
Mexico	(New Peso)	11.8614	+11.8614	455 – 773	11.8455	11.8773	12.1079	–24.9	12.8244	–32.5	15.2878
USA	(\$)	0.8458	+0.8458	463 – 453	0.8463	0.8453	1.1676	–456.6	1.1701	–153.4	1.1828
Pacific/Middle East/Africa											
Australia	(A\$)	1.8885	+1.8885	863 – 907	1.8863	1.8907	2.0022	–72.2	2.0050	–24.7	2.0251
Hong Kong	(HK\$)	9.1557	+9.1557	497 – 617	9.1497	9.1617	9.0681	11.5	9.1543	0.1	9.6528
India	(Rs)	50.0320	+50.0320	965 – 675	49.9965	50.0675	49.9116	2.9	50.6275	–4.8	54.5182
Indonesia	(Rupiah)	10079.21	+10.2100	590 – 253	9895.90	10262.53	13695.91	–430.6	14948.19	–193.2	19930.42
Israel	(Shk)	5.0909	+5.0909	737 – 081	5.0737	5.1081	–	–	–	–	–
Japan	(Y)	136.302	+136.3020	179 – 424	136.179	136.424	157.1915	–183.9	156.1131	–58.1	152.1140
Malaysia	(M\$)	6.4199	+6.4199	161 – 237	6.4161	6.4237	4.4314	371.7	4.4314	123.9	4.4314
New Zealand	(NZ\$)	2.2243	+2.2243	215 – 270	2.2215	2.2270	2.3624	–74.5	2.3685	–25.9	2.4122
Philippines	(Peso)	46.8192	+46.8192	732 – 651	46.6732	46.9651	52.3986	–143.0	53.4190	–56.4	58.0581
Saudi Arabia	(SR)	4.4343	+4.4343	315 – 371	4.4315	4.4371	4.3828	13.9	4.3994	3.1	4.4784
Singapore	(S\$)	1.9154	+1.9154	136 – 171	1.9136	1.9171	2.0225	–67.1	2.0261	–23.1	2.0471
South Africa	(R)	6.6564	+6.6564	406 – 721	6.6406	6.6721	7.0155	–64.7	7.2134	–33.5	8.1081
South Korea	(Won)	1554.13	+15.1300	144 – 683	1551.44	1556.83	–	–	–	–	–
Taiwan	(T\$)	38.3781	+38.3781	476 – 085	38.3476	38.4085	40.4926	–66.1	40.8256	-25.5	42.2030

Source: *Financial Times*, 5 January 1999, p. 30. Reprinted with permission.

Covering in the forward market

Suppose that on 16 August 2001 a UK exporter sells goods to a customer in Singapore invoiced at S\$500,000. Payment is due three months later. With the spot rate of exchange at S\$2.5198–2.5211/£ (*see* Exhibit 22.8) the exporter, in deciding to sell the goods, has in mind a sales price of:

$$\frac{500{,}000}{2.5211} = £198{,}326$$

The UK firm bases its decision on the profitability of the deal on this amount expressed in pounds.

However the rate of exchange may vary between August and November: the size and direction of the move is uncertain. If sterling strengthens against the Singaporean dollar, the UK exporter makes a currency loss by waiting three months and exchanging the dollars received into sterling at spot rates in November. If, say, one pound is worth S\$2.7 the exporter will receive only £185,185:

$$\frac{500{,}000}{2.7} = £185{,}185$$

The loss due to currency movement is:

£198,326
£185,185
£13,141

If sterling weakens to, say, S$2.30/£ a currency gain is made. The pounds received in November if dollars are exchanged at the spot rate are:

$$\frac{500{,}000}{2.30} = £217{,}391.30$$

The currency gain is:

£217,391
£198,326
£ 19,065

Rather than run the risk of a possible loss on the currency side of the deal the exporter may decide to cover in the forward market. Under this arrangement the exporter promises to sell S$500,000 against sterling on 16 November. The forward rate available[4] on 16 August is S$2.5043/£ (*see* Exhibit 22.8). This forward contract means that the exporter will receive £199,657 in November:

$$\frac{500{,}000}{2.5043} = £199{,}657$$

In November the transactions shown in Exhibit 22.10 take place.

Exhibit 22.10 Forward market transactions

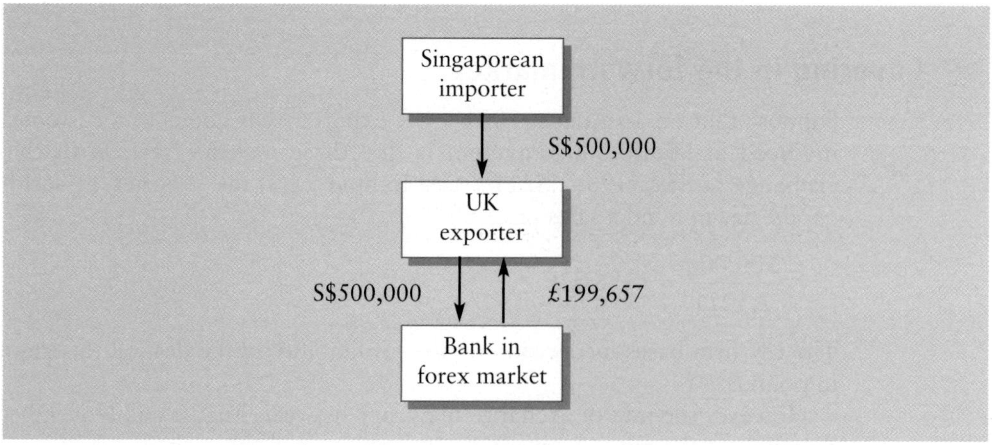

From the outset the exporter knew the amount to be received in November (assuming away credit risk). It might, with hindsight, have been better not to use the forward market but to exchange the dollars at a spot rate of, say, S$2.30/£. This would have resulted in a larger income for the firm. But there was uncertainty about the spot rate in November when the export took place in August. If the spot rate in November had turned out to be S$2.70/£ the exporter would have made much less. Covering in the forward market is a form of insurance which leads to greater certainty – and certainty has a value.

TYPES OF FOREIGN-EXCHANGE RISK

There are three types of risk for firms which operate in an international market place:

- transaction risk;
- translation risk;
- economic risk.

Transaction risk

Transaction risk is the risk that transactions already entered into, or for which the firm is likely to have a commitment in a foreign currency, will have a variable value in the home currency because of exchange-rate movements.

This type of risk is primarily associated with imports or exports. If a company exports goods on credit then it carries a figure for debtors in its accounts. The amount it will receive in home-currency terms is subject to uncertainty if the customer pays in a foreign currency.

Likewise a company that imports on credit will have a creditor figure in its accounts. The amount that is finally paid in terms of the home currency depends on forex movements, if the invoice is in a foreign currency. Transaction risk also arises when firms invest abroad, say, opening a new office or manufacturing plant. If the costs of

Exhibit 22.11

Indonesian group turns to Chase Manhattan for help FT

By Sander Thoenes and Peter Montagnon in Jakarta

Bakrie & Brothers, the diversified Indonesian conglomerate, has hired Chase Manhattan as its financial adviser to help the group meet looming off-shore debt obligation . . .

Bakrie & Brothers, the listed part of the Bakrie Group, is the first Indonesian company to publicise efforts to restructure and reduce exposure to short-term debt, which has tripled in rupiah terms over the past few months as the currency has collapsed . . .

Most Indonesian enterprises have been slow to respond to their debt exposure – and almost all have publicly denied it – expecting the currency to recover before debt payments start to hurt. But the rupiah fell from Rp2,600 to the dollar in July to Rp10,000 earlier this month, ending at Rp8,200 on central bank intervention on Friday.

Last week the government estimated foreign debt had reached $140bn (£85.8bn), including $20bn in short-term debt. At least $80bn was private debt and much of it was not hedged.

Bakrie and most other companies have in recent weeks negotiated rollovers for much of their debt, as they are technically bankrupt at the going exchange rate. Bankers fear any new fall of the rupiah could spark a debt moratorium, official or de facto. At least 40 companies have already defaulted, by market estimates, but lenders have rarely gone public on bad loans.

Source: Sander Thoenes and Peter Montagnon, *Financial Times*, 19 January 1998, p. 4. Reprinted with permission.

construction are paid for over a period the firm may be exchanging the home currency for the foreign currency to make the payments. The amounts of the home currency required are uncertain if the exchange rate is subject to rate shifts. Also the cash inflows back to the parent are subject to exchange-rate risk.

In addition, when companies borrow in a foreign currency, committing themselves to regular interest and principal payments in that currency, they are exposed to forex risk. This is a problem that beset a number of Far Eastern companies in the late 1990s. They had committed themselves to paying off borrowings in a hard currency (e.g. US dollars, sterling). This became a serious problem when the debt trebled or quadrupled simply because of the decline in their currency against the hard currency – *see* the example of Bakrie & Brothers in Exhibit 22.11.

Translation risk

Translation risk arises because financial data denominated in one currency are then expressed in terms of another currency. Between two accounting dates the figures can be affected by exchange-rate movements, greatly distorting comparability. The financial statements of overseas business units are usually translated into the home currency in order that they might be consolidated with the group's financial statements. Income, expenses, assets and liabilities have to be re-expressed in terms of the home currency. Note that this is purely a paper-based exercise; it is translation and not the conversion of real money from one currency to another. If exchange rates were stable, comparing subsidiary performance and asset position would be straightforward. However, if exchange rates move significantly the results can be severely distorted. For example, Reed Elsevier has a large proportion of its business in the USA and, despite a 10 per cent rise in profits in dollar terms, when profits were translated back into pounds the increase from one year to the next was only 1 per cent. This was because sterling rose against the dollar. *See* Exhibit 22.12.

Exhibit 22.12

Strong pound hits UK side of Reed Elsevier

FT

Operating profit growth at Reed Elsevier, the Anglo-Dutch media and information group, came virtually to a halt in the first half because of the strong pound.

There was a £36m negative effect on the company, which does a large part of its business in the US. Operating profits of continuing businesses rose only 1 per cent to £446m, but growth was 10 per cent at constant exchange rates.

Reed's shares dropped 40p or 6.3 per cent to close at 590p in a stock market that rose 1.2 per cent.

Mr Nigel Stapleton, co-chairman, emphasised yesterday that the currency impact was on the translation into sterling and did not affect the underlying performances of the businesses.

Source: Raymond Snoddy, *Financial Times*, 8 August 1997. Reprinted with permission.

There are two elements to translation risk.

1 ***The balance sheet effect*** Assets and liabilities denominated in a foreign currency can fluctuate in value in home-currency terms with forex-market changes. For example, if a UK company acquires A\$1,000,000 of assets in Australia when the rate of exchange is A\$2.2/£ this can go into the UK group's accounts at a value of £454,545. If, over the

course of the next year, the Australian dollar falls against sterling to A$2.7/£, when the consolidated accounts are drawn up and the asset is translated at the current exchange rate at the end of the year it is valued at only £370,370 (1,000,000/2.7) a 'loss' of £84,175. And yet the asset has not changed in value in A$ terms one jot. These 'losses' are normally dealt with through balance sheet reserves.

2 ***The profit and loss account effect*** Currency changes can have an adverse impact on the group's profits because of the translation of foreign subsidiaries' profits. This often occurs even though the subsidiaries' managers are performing well and increasing profit in terms of the currency in which they operate, as the case of Reed Elsevier (*see* Exhibit 22.12) indicates.

Economic risk

A company's economic value may decline as a result of forex movements causing a loss in competitive strength. The worth of a company is the discounted cash flows payable to the owners. It is possible that a shift in exchange rates can reduce the cash flows of foreign subsidiaries and home-based production far into the future (and not just affect the near future cash flows as in transaction exposure). There are two ways in which competitive position can be undermined by forex changes:

- ***Directly*** If your firm's home currency strengthens then foreign competitors are able to gain sales and profits at your expense because your products are more expensive (or you have reduced margins) in the eyes of customers both abroad and at home.
- ***Indirectly*** Even if your home currency does not move adversely *vis-à-vis* your customer's currency you can lose competitive position. For example suppose a South African firm is selling into Hong Kong and its main competitor is a New Zealand firm. If the New Zealand dollar weakens against the Hong Kong dollar the South African firm has lost some competitive position.

  Another indirect effect occurs even for firms which are entirely domestically orientated. For example, the cafés and shops surrounding a large export-orientated manufacturing plant may be severely affected by the closure of the factory due to an adverse forex movement.

TRANSACTION RISK HEDGING STRATEGIES

This section illustrates a number of strategies available to deal with transaction risk by focusing on the alternatives open to an exporter selling goods on credit.

Suppose a UK company exports £1m of goods to a Canadian firm when the spot rate of exchange is C$2.20/£. The Canadian firm is given three months to pay, and naturally the spot rate in three months is unknown at the time of the shipment of goods. What can the firm do?

Invoice the customer in the home currency

One easy way to bypass exchange-rate risk is to insist that all foreign customers pay in your currency and your firm pays for all imports in your home currency. In the case of this example the Canadian importer will be required to send £1m in three months.

However the exchange-rate risk has not gone away, it has just been passed on to the customer. This policy has an obvious drawback: your customer may dislike it, the marketability of your products is reduced and your customers look elsewhere for supplies. If you are a monopoly supplier you might get away with the policy but for most firms this is a non-starter.

Do nothing

Under this policy the UK firm invoices the Canadian firm for C$2.2m, waits three months and then exchanges into sterling at whatever spot rate is available then. Perhaps an exchange-rate gain will be made, perhaps a loss will be made. Many firms adopt this policy and take a 'win some, lose some' attitude. Given the fees and other transaction costs of some hedging strategies this can make sense.

There are two considerations for managers here. The first is their degree of risk aversion to higher cash flow variability, coupled with the sensitivity of shareholders to reported fluctuations of earnings due to foreign exchange gains and losses. The second, which is related to the first point, is the size of the transaction. If £1m is a large proportion of annual turnover, and greater than profit, then the managers may be more worried about forex risk. If, however, £1m is a small fraction of turnover and profit, and the firm has numerous forex transactions, it may choose to save on hedging costs. There is an argument that it would be acceptable to do nothing if it was anticipated that the Canadian dollar will appreciate over the three months. Be careful. Predicting exchange rates is a dangerous game and more than one 'expert' has made serious errors of judgement.

Netting

Multinational companies often have subsidiaries in different countries selling to other members of the group. Netting is where the subsidiaries settle intra-organisational currency debts for the *net* amount owed in a currency rather than the *gross* amount. For example, if a UK parent owned a subsidiary in Canada and sold C$2.2m of goods to the subsidiary on credit while the Canadian subsidiary is owed C$1.5m by the UK company, instead of transferring a total of C$3.7m the intra-group transfer is the net amount of C$700,000 (*see* Exhibit 22.13).

Ehibit 22.13 Netting

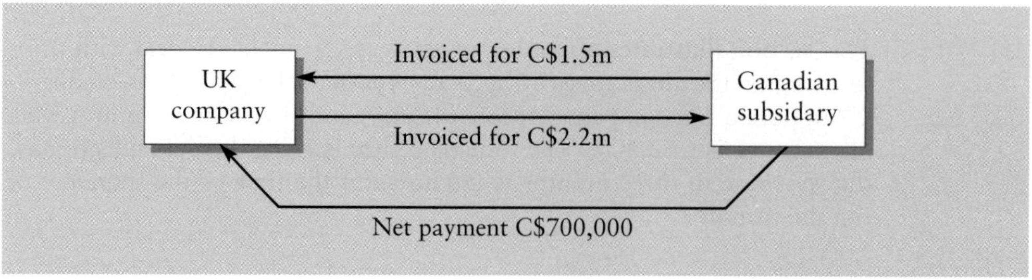

The reduction in the size of the currency flows by offsetting inflows and outflows in the same currency diminishes the net exposure which may have to be hedged. It also reduces the transaction costs of currency transfers in terms of fees and commissions.

This type of netting, involving two companies within a group, is referred to as bilateral netting, and is simple to operate without the intervention of a central treasury.

However for organisations with a matrix of currency liabilities between numerous subsidiaries in different parts of the world, multilateral netting is required. A central treasury is usually needed so that there is knowledge at any point in time of the overall exposure of the firm and its component parts. Subsidiaries will be required to inform the group treasury about their overseas dealings which can then co-ordinate payments after netting out intra-company debts. The savings on transfer costs levied by banks can be considerable.

Matching

Netting only applies to transfers within a group of companies. Matching can be used for both intra-group transactions and those involving third parties. The company matches the inflows and outflows in different currencies caused by trade, etc., so that it is only necessary to deal on the forex markets for the unmatched portion of the total transactions.

So if, say, the Canadian importer is not a group company and the UK firm also imported a raw material from another Canadian company to the value of C$2m it is necessary only to hedge the balance of C$200,000 (*see* Exhibit 22.14).

Exhibit 22.14 Matching

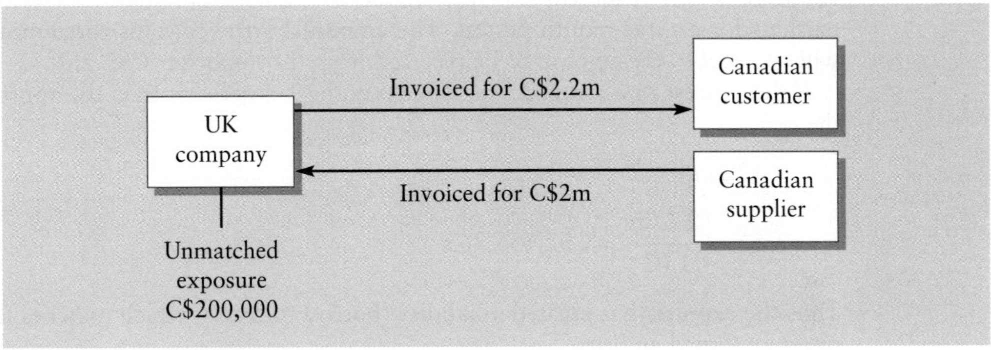

Naturally, to net and match properly, the timing of the expected receipts and payments would have to be the same.

Leading and lagging

Leading is the bringing forward from the original due date the payment of a debt. Lagging is the postponement of a payment beyond the due date. This speeding up or delaying of payments is particularly useful if you are convinced exchange rates will shift significantly between now and the due date.

So, if the UK exporter which has invoiced a Canadian company for C$2.2m on three months' credit expects that the Canadian dollar will fall over the forthcoming three months it may try to obtain payment immediately and then exchange for sterling at the spot rate. Naturally the Canadian firm will need an incentive to pay early and this may be achieved by offering a discount for immediate settlement.

An importer of goods in a currency which is anticipated to fall in value may attempt to delay payment as long as possible. This may be achieved either by agreement or by exceeding credit terms.

Forward market hedge

Although other forms of exchange-risk management are available, forward cover represents the most frequently employed method of hedging. A contract is agreed to exchange two currencies at a fixed time in the future at a predetermined rate. The risk of forex variation is removed.

So if the three-month forward rate is C$2.25/£ the UK exporter could lock in the receipt of £977,778 in three months by selling forward C$2.2m.

$$\frac{\text{C\$2.2m}}{2.25} = £977,778$$

No foreign exchange-rate risk now exists because the dollars to be received from the importer are matched by the funds to be exchanged for sterling. (There does remain the risk of the importer not paying, at all or on time, and the risk of the counterparty in the forex market not fulfilling its obligations.)

Money market hedge

Money market hedging involves borrowing in the money markets. For example, the exporter could, at the time of the export, borrow in Canadian dollars on the money markets for a three-month period. The amount borrowed, plus three months' interest, will be equal to the amount to be received from the importer (C$2.2m).

If the interest rate charged over three months is 2 per cent then the appropriate size of the loan is:

$$\text{C\$2.2m} = \text{C\$?}\ (1 + 0.02)$$

$$\text{C\$?} = \frac{\text{C\$2.2m}}{1.02} = \text{C\$2,156,863}$$

Thus the exporter has created a liability (borrowed funds) which matches the asset (debt owed by Canadian firm).

The borrowed dollars are then converted to sterling on the spot market for the exporter to receive £980,392 immediately:

$$\frac{\text{C\$2,156,863}}{2.2} = £980,392$$

The exporter has removed forex risk because it now holds cash in sterling.

Three months later C$2.2m is received from the importer and this exactly matches the outstanding debt:

Amount borrowed + interest = debt owed at end of period

$$\text{C\$2,156,863} + \text{C\$2,156,863} \times 0.02 = \text{C\$2.2m}$$

The receipt of £980,392 is £19,608 less than the £1m originally anticipated. However it is received three months earlier and can earn interest.

The steps in the money market hedge are as follows.

1 Invoice customer for C$2.2m.
2 Borrow C$2,156,863.
3 Sell C$2,156,863 at spot to receive pounds now.

4 In three months receive C$2.2m from customer.
5 Pay lender C$2.2m.

An importer could also use a money market hedge. So a Swiss company importing Japanese cars for payment in yen in three months could borrow in Swiss francs now and convert the funds at the spot rate into yen. This money is deposited to earn interest, with the result that after three months the principal plus interest equals the invoice amount.

Futures

A foreign currency futures contract is an agreement to exchange a specific amount of a currency for another at a fixed future date for a predetermined price. Futures are similar to forwards in many ways. They are, however, standardised contracts traded on regulated exchanges. Forwards can be tailor-made in a wide range of currencies as to quantity of currency and delivery date, whereas futures are only available in a limited range of currencies and for a few specific forward time periods.

The Chicago Mercantile Exchange (CME) operates a futures market in currencies including: US$/£, US$/¥, US$/ SFr (Swiss franc), US$/€. A single futures contract is for a fixed amount of currency. For example, a sterling contract is for £62,500. It is not possible to buy or sell a smaller amount than this, nor to transact in quantities other than whole-number multiples of this. To buy a sterling futures contract is to make a commitment to deliver a quantity of US dollars and receive in return £62,500. On 16 August 2001 the CME quoted contracts for delivery in late September and December (and for no months in between). For example, the December contract was priced at 1.4370 (shown in the *Financial Times*). This means that if you buy one contract you are committed to deliver US$1.4370 for every pound of the £62,500 you will receive in late December, that is US$89,812.50. If you *sold* one contract at 1.4370 you would deliver £62,500 and receive US$89,812.50.

Exhibit 22.15 Currency futures on the Chicago Mercantile Exchange FT

US $ CURRENCY FUTURES (CME)

Aug 16		Open	Latest	Change	High	Low	Est. vol.	Open int.
$-Euro €	Sep	0.9133	0.9106	−0.0012	0.9196	0.9106	35,151	107,739
$-Euro €	Dec	0.9130	0.9120	+0.0018	0.9162	0.9111	421	2,484
$-Sw Franc	Sep	0.6021	0.6022	+0.0011	0.6050	0.5990	11,121	61,508
$-Sw Franc	Dec	0.6027	0.6027	+0.0009	0.6032	0.6010	191	815
$-Yen	Sep	0.8400	0.8378	−0.0009	0.8412	0.8343	37,839	102,655
$-Yen	Dec	0.8441	0.8453	−0.0006	0.8453	0.8439	525	2,434
$–Sterling	Sep	1.4390	1.4418	+0.0030	1.4502	1.4386	13,520	39,110
$–Sterling	Dec	1.4390	1.4370	+0.0038	1.4400	1.4370	141	231

Source: CME. Euro: €125,000; Swiss Franc: SFr125,000; Yen: 12.5m ($ per ¥100); Sterling £62,500.

Source: *Financial Times*, 17 August 2001, p. 26. Reprinted with permission.

A firm hedging with currency futures will usually attempt to have a futures position which has an equal and opposite profit profile to the underlying transaction. Frequently the futures position will be closed before delivery is due, to give a cash profit or loss to offset the spot market profit or loss (for more details on futures *see* Chapter 21). For example, if a US firm exports £62,500 worth of goods to a UK firm on three months' credit for payment in late December and the current spot exchange rate is US$1.58/£ there is a foreign exchange risk. If we further assume, for the sake of simplicity, that the

December future is also trading at a price of US$1.58 per £ the exporter's position could be hedged by selling one sterling futures contract on CME.

If in December sterling falls against the dollar to US$1.40/£ the calculation is:

Value of £62,500 received from customer when converted to dollars at spot in December (£62,500 × 1.40)	US$87,500
Amount if exchange rate was constant at US$1.58/£	US$98,750
Forex loss	US$11,250

However an offsetting gain is made on the futures contract:

Sold at US$1.58/£ (£62,500 × 1.58)	US$98,750
Bought in December to close position at US$1.40/£ (£62,500 × 1.40)	US$87,500
Futures gain	US$11,250

(Alternatively the exporter could simply deliver the £62,500 received from the importer to CME in return for US$98,750.)

In the above example a perfect hedge is achieved. This is frequently unobtainable with futures because of their standardised nature. Perhaps the amount needed to be hedged is not equal to a whole number of contracts, for example £100,000, or the underlying transaction takes place in November (when no future is available).

Futures did not prove very popular in the UK when traded on LIFFE. This was largely due to the existence of more flexible and convenient forms of currency hedges such as forwards and currency options.

Currency options

The final possible course of action to reduce forex transaction risk to be discussed in this chapter is to make use of the currency option market.

A currency option is a contract giving the buyer (that is, the holder) the right, but not the obligation, to buy or sell a specific amount of currency at a specific exchange rate (the strike price), on or before a specified future date.

A call option gives the right to buy a particular currency.

A put option gives the right to sell a particular currency.

The option writer (usually a bank) guarantees, if the option buyer chooses to exercise the right, to exchange the currency at the predetermined rate. Because the writer is accepting risk the buyer must pay a premium to the writer – normally within two business days of the option purchase. (For more details on options *see* Chapter 21.)

Currency option trading was given a significant boost when the Philadelphia Stock Exchange began to trade currency options in 1982. The options on euro/$ and £/$ are shown daily in the *Financial Times* – see Exhibit 22.16. The crucial advantage an option has over a forward is the absence of an obligation to buy or sell. It is the option buyer's decision whether to exercise the option and insist on exchange at the strike rate or to let the option lapse.

With a forward there is a hedge against both a favourable and an unfavourable movement in forex rates. This means that if the exchange rate happens to move in your favour after you are committed to a forward contract you cannot take any advantage of that movement. We saw above that if the forward rate was C$2.25/£ the exporter will receive £977,778 in three months. If the spot exchange rate had moved to, say, C$1.9/£ over the three months the exporter would have liked to abandon the agreement to sell

Exhibit 22.16 Philadelphia currency options

FT

PHILADELPHIA SE EUROS/$ OPTIONS €62,500 (cents per €)

Strike	.... CALLS			.... PUTS		
Price	Sept	Nov	Dec	Sept	Nov	Dec
0.880	–	–	4.23	0.34	1.00	1.28
0.900	1.92	2.76	3.04	0.79	1.76	–
0.920	0.93	1.80	–	1.84	2.77	3.10

Previous day's vol, Calls n/a Puts n/a. Prev. day's open int, Calls n/a Puts n/a

PHILADELPHIA SE £/$ OPTIONS £31,250 (cents per pound)

Strike	.... CALLS			.... PUTS		
Price	Sept	Nov	Dec	Sept	Nov	Dec
1.420	2.39	3.18	3.48	0.52	1.67	2.10
1.430	1.19	2.62	–	1.33	2.11	–
1.440	0.45	2.16	2.51	2.56	2.57	3.02

Previous day's vol, Calls – Puts – Prev. day's open int, Calls – Puts –

Source: *Financial Times*, 17 August 2001, p. 26. Reprinted with permission.

the dollars at C$2.25/£, but is unable to do so because of the legal commitment. By abandoning the deal and exchanging at spot when the Canadian firm pays the exporter will receive an income of:

$$\frac{\text{C\$2.2m}}{1.9} = £1,157,895$$

This is an extra £180,117.

An option permits both:

- hedging against unfavourable currency movement; and
- profit from favourable currency movement.

Now, imagine that the treasurer of the UK firm hedges by buying a three-month, Canadian dollar put, sterling call option with a strike price of C$2.25/£ when the goods are delivered to the Canadian firm.

Worked example 22.2 Currency option contract

To induce a bank to make the commitment to exchange at the option holder's behest a premium will need to be paid up front. Assume this is 2 per cent of the amount covered, that is a non-refundable 0.02 × C$2,200,000 = C$44,000 is payable two business days after the option deal is struck.

Three months later

The dollars are delivered by the importer on the due date. The treasurer now has to decide whether or not to exercise the right to exchange those dollars for sterling at C$2.25/£. Let us consider two scenarios:

Scenario 1

The dollar has strengthened against the pound to C$1.9/£. If the treasurer exercises the right to exchange at C$2.25/£ the UK firm will receive:

$$\frac{\text{C\$2,200,000}}{2.25} = £977,778$$

If the treasurer takes the alternative and lets the option lapse – 'abandons it' – and exchanges the dollars in the spot market, the amount received will be:

$$\frac{C\$2{,}200{,}000}{1.9} = £1{,}157{,}895$$

Clearly in this case the best course of action would be not to exercise the option, but to exchange at spot rate. Note that the benefit of this action is somewhat reduced by the earlier payment of C$44,000 for the premium.

Scenario 2

Now assume that the dollar has weakened against sterling to C$2.5/£. If the treasurer contacts the bank (the option writer) to confirm that the exporter wishes to exercise the option the treasurer will arrange delivery of C$2,200,000 to the bank and will receive £977,778 in return:

$$\frac{C\$2{,}200{,}000}{2.25} = £977{,}778$$

The alternative, to abandon the option and sell the C$2.2m in the spot forex market, is unattractive:

$$\frac{C\$2{,}200{,}000}{2.5} = £880{,}000$$

Again, the option premium needs to be deducted to give a more complete picture.

With the option, the worst that could happen is that the exporter receives £977,778, less the premium. However the upside potential is unconstrained.

Option contracts are generally for sums greater than US$1,000,000 on the OTC (over-the-counter) market (direct deals with banks) whereas one contract on the Philadelphia exchange is, for example, for £31,250 or €62,500. The drawback with exchange-based derivatives is the smaller range of currencies available and the inability to tailor-make a hedging position.

Exhibit 22.17 discusses the attitude of some treasurers and analysts to hedging forex risk.

Exhibit 22.17

To hedge or not to hedge

FT

There is a range of futures, swaps and currency options from which to choose.

A company can expend blood, sweat and tears on achieving a 15 per cent rise in exports. But when it converts its foreign income into its home currency, it may be in for a nasty shock. If its domestic currency has risen by 15 per cent, all the extra profits will be wiped out.

The phenomenon is called currency risk. Corporate treasurers, the people who manage this risk for their companies, have a much more complicated life now than they did a decade ago, says Mr John Parry, director of Rostron Parry, a consultancy specialising in financial markets and derivatives.

Ten years ago there was little more a treasurer could do to hedge risk than buy a currency forward – that is, to set a price today for which he agreed to buy the currency at a certain time in the future. Now there is a range of futures, swaps and currency options from which to choose.

Perhaps the form of hedging that is growing fastest is the currency option. It gives a company the right to buy or sell a currency at a set price at a certain time in the future – for instance, the right to buy sterling at DM2.70 in 12 months. If sterling stays above that level, the user will exercise the option. This can be expensive: a 'plain vanilla' option

Exhibit 22.17 continued

can cost 4 per cent of the amount of pounds the user needs to buy.

But before treasurers even look into ways of hedging risk, they are faced with a big question: should they bother? Some companies never hedge, choosing instead to live with currency risk. They argue that while exchange rates sometimes move against them, they sometimes change in their favour. For instance, if the pound falls, a UK company will see the value of its foreign earnings rise when it converts them into sterling. To have hedged would have meant to lose these windfall gains.

UK and US companies would have mostly gained from leaving their currency exposure unhedged in recent years, as the pound and dollar have tended to fall. But there was a turnaround in recent months, when the pound's surge hit UK exporters. According to foreign exchange advisers, most have never hedged. Profits have been sliced at many companies.

Critics of hedging currency risk often cite companies which have come a cropper from dabbling in derivatives. Allied Lyons, the UK foods company, lost £150m after currency options positions went wrong in 1991. Orange County in California, the Belgian government, and the unlucky Nick Leeson of Barings Bank are no advertisements for buying "derivatives" either. 'Mention the word "derivatives" around a board table and everybody freezes,' says Mr Jeremy Wagener, director-general of the UK's Association of Corporate Treasurers.

The Allied Lyons affair has made UK companies more wary of derivatives than their rivals are in France, the US and Scandinavia, according to bankers. Even a company as large as British Steel proclaims proudly that it never uses currency options. 'We don't go in for anything fancy,' it says. 'We only buy straightforward forwards.'

Companies outside the UK often regard their currency management side as a profit centre, says Ms Lisa Danino, a saleswoman at Bank of America. She adds: 'In sophistication, the UK corporates are quite a way behind.'

Small businesses tend to be those most frightened of hedging. 'They often have no treasurer and no thoughts on the subject at all', says Mr Wagener. Mr Michele di Stefano, head of forex sales at BZW, says: 'In most cases, treasury operations are understaffed'. Even treasurers who themselves understand complex hedging products have to be able to explain them to their directors, often a tricky task.

Nor can customers always trust banks to give them impartial advice on derivatives. The banks, after all, are trying to sell products. Mr Bill McLuskie, treasurer of Canary Wharf Ltd in the UK, claims: 'I know bankers who say, "Given the quality of some treasurers, it's easy to con them".'

Mr McLuskie and Mr Wagener nonetheless preach the virtues of hedging currency risk. The main thing a company is buying is certainty, they say. No longer can its cash flow stall and start depending on which way the forex market moves. To hedge is to buy insurance, says Mr Wagener. A risk-averse company should hedge; a company with risk-appetite may well consider not doing so.

Many people regard buying currency derivatives as 'speculation', says Mr McLuskie. In fact, he argues, the opposite is true. *Not* to buy the products is to speculate on the foreign exchange market. And most companies have no special insight into which way a currency will move. Mr Parry says: 'Your job as a producer of goods and services is not to second-guess the foreign exchange markets'.

There are trends that may encourage more companies to buy hedging products. For a start, says Mr Howard Kurz, head of global forex at NatWest Markets, many corporates are becoming more sophisticated about derivatives. In the 1970s, Mr Wagener recalls, many had no treasurer at all. Now, a growing number of finance directors are former treasurers.

Second, as more banks pile into the options business, prices are falling. Most banks are now selling what they call 'zero-cost options' – although if the market moves more than the purchaser expects, the options can be far from zero-cost. Mr Parry says: 'The question in the end is what value you put on being able to sleep at night when the markets are moving all over the place.'

Source: Simon Kuper, *Financial Times*, 18 April 1997, p. 4. Reprinted with permission.

MANAGING TRANSLATION RISK

The effect of translation risk on the balance sheet can be lessened by matching the currency of assets and liabilities. For example, Graft plc has decided to go ahead with a US$150m project in the USA. One way of financing this is to borrow £100m and exchange this for dollars at the current exchange rate of US$1.5/£. Thus at the beginning of the year the additional entries into the consolidated accounts are as shown in Worked example 22.3.

Worked example 22.3 Translation risk

Opening balance sheet

Liabilities		*Assets*	
Loan	£100m	US assets	£100m

The US$150m of US assets are translated at US$1.5/£ so all figures are expressed in the parent company's currency.

Now imagine that over the course of the next year the dollar depreciates against sterling to US$2/£. In the consolidated group accounts there is still a £100m loan but the asset bought with that loan, while still worth US$150m,[5] is valued at only £75m when translated into sterling. In the parent company's currency terms, £25m needs to be written off:

Year-end balance sheet

Liabilities		*Assets*	
Loan	£100m	US assets	£75m
	£100m		£75m
Forex loss	–£25m		

Alternatively Graft plc could finance its dollar assets by obtaining a dollar loan. Thus, when the dollar depreciates, both the asset value and the liability value in translated sterling terms becomes less.

Opening balance sheet

Liabilities		*Assets*	
Loan	£100m	US assets	£100m

If forex rates move to US$2/£:

Year-end balance sheet

Liabilities		*Assets*	
Loan	£75m	US assets	£75m

There is no currency loss to deal with.

One constraint on the solution set out in Worked example 22.3 is that some governments insist that a proportion of assets acquired within their countries is financed by the parent firm. Another constraint is that the financial markets in some countries are insufficiently developed to permit large-scale borrowing.

Many economists and corporate managers believe that translation hedging is unnecessary because, on average over a period of time, gains and losses from forex movements will even out to be zero. Exhibit 22.18 considers the reasons for most companies taking no steps to hedge against profit translation risk.

Exhibit 22.18

When a hedge is not a gardener's problem

FT

As the half-yearly company reporting season has got under way, so too have the protests from UK companies that the strength of sterling is cutting profits.

BOC, the gas producer, estimated that sterling's rapid rise in the last 12 months would cut £46m off its annual profits because of the cost of translating foreign currency earnings into sterling.

But, as one letter writer to the Financial Times recently asked, surely UK companies could avoid these problems by hedging their currency exposure, using financial instruments to protect against exchange rate fluctuations?

In fact, exporters use a number of techniques to lower currency risks. An engineering firm exporting machinery to Germany, for example, could price its contracts in sterling and shift the exchange rate risk on to its customers. Exporters can also buy forward contracts for an exchange rate fixed at a future date.

An unpublished survey of corporate treasurers by Record Treasury Management, a London consultancy, found that 77 per cent of respondents used forward contracts and other currency derivatives.

But Les Halpin, chief executive of RTM, said while many companies were happy to use derivatives to hedge their cash positions, almost none was prepared to use similar instruments to protect profits earned overseas.

The result is companies with substantial overseas operations, such as BOC, Imperial Chemical Industries and Reuters, have reported translation losses in converting foreign profits. ICI said interim pre-tax profits were down £90m because of the rapid rise in sterling. It attributed £30m to the translation into sterling.

So why not use derivatives to hedge translation costs? UK companies rarely do, according to Mr Halpin, because they often don't understand them.

Treasurers' forecasts off the pace

Sterling against the DM

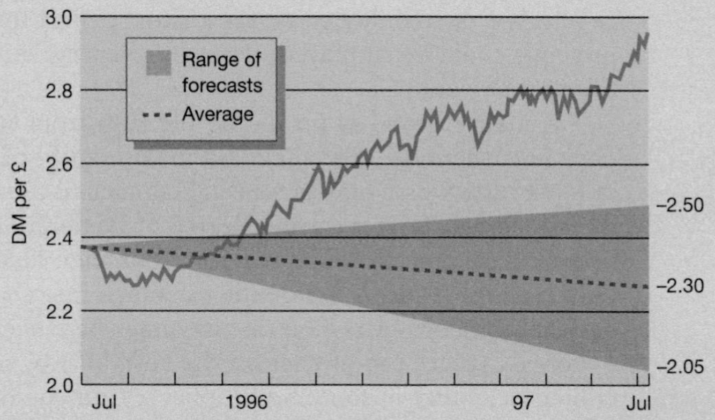

Source: Record Treasury Management.

The RTM survey found that 30 per cent said 'complexity' was the main risk in using derivatives. 'Most company executives think a hedge is something they get their gardener to trim,' grumbled one City equities analyst.

Another 35 per cent of treasurers said 'lack of control' was a significant risk – the fear that the spirit of Nick Leeson may live in a graduate trainee within the finance department. Since future profit levels are unknown, deciding how much to hedge is one barrier.

Sandvik, the Swedish industrial group, was recently caught out by currency hedging, as it reported an 18 per cent fall in first-half profits. In its case, the weakening of the krona meant its hedged positions made a loss.

UK finance directors are reluctant to hedge for several reasons. Profits lost in translation can often be 'paper losses' – it is only when the profits are converted into sterling that a loss is made. And there are complex accounting problems for representing derivatives on balance sheets, especially for instruments spanning several years.

But the most important reservation may be psychological.

If a corporate treasurer gets permission to hedge overseas earnings, and a currency shift makes the hedge unnecessary, then the cost and blame for the decision can be easily identified. But if the treasurer decides not to hedge, then the company is at the whim of the currency markets, an act of God for which no one is responsible.

Ironically, many corporate treasurers are happy to let their organisations dabble in currency speculation – even though treasurers are no better than anyone else in predicting rate movements.

In 1996, RTM asked them to predict sterling's rate against the D-Mark in a year's time. The highest reply was DM2.50. A year later, the pound rose above DM3.02 – 25 per cent more than the average forecast of DM2.40.

Hedging cannot protect a company from extended currency movements. John Rennocks, finance director of British Steel, said: 'Hedging is an important part of any exporter's business activity, but can only defer the impact of violent currency swings.'

But, Mr Halpin replied, well judged hedging can give a company 'breathing space', enabling it to take decisions on moving production or resources before the full impact of a currency swing is felt.

Source: Richard Adams, *Financial Times*, 18 August 1997. Reprinted with permission.

MANAGING ECONOMIC RISK

Economic exposure is concerned with the long-term effects of forex movements on the firm's ability to compete, and add value. These effects are very difficult to estimate in advance, given their long-term nature, and therefore the hedging techniques described for transaction risk are of limited use. The forwards markets may be used to a certain extent, but these only extend for a short period for most currencies. Also the matching principle could be employed, whereby overseas assets are matched as far as possible by overseas liabilities.

The main method of insulating the firm from economic risk is to position the company in such a way as to maintain maximum flexibility – to be able to react to changes in forex rates which may be causing damage to the firm. Firms which are internationally diversified may have a greater degree of flexibility than those based in one or two markets. For example, a company with production facilities in numerous countries can shift output to those plants where the exchange rate change has been favourable. The international car assemblers have an advantage here over the purely domestic producer.

Forex changes can impact on the costs of raw materials and other inputs. By maintaining flexibility in sourcing supplies a firm could achieve a competitive advantage by deliberately planning its affairs so that it can switch suppliers quickly and cheaply.

An aware multinational could allow for forex changes when deciding in which countries to launch an advertising campaign. For example, it may be pointless increasing marketing spend in a country whose currency has depreciated rapidly recently, making the domestically produced competing product relatively cheap. It might be sensible to plan in advance the company's response to a forex movement with regard to the pricing of goods so that action can be rapid. For example, a UK company exporting to Norway at a time when sterling is on a rising trend can either keep the product at the same price in sterling terms to maintain profits and face the consequential potential loss of market share, or reduce the sterling price to maintain a constant price in krona and thereby keep its market share. Being prepared may avert an erroneous knee-jerk decision.

The principle of contingency planning to permit quick reaction to forex changes applies to many areas of marketing and production strategies. This idea links with the notion of the real option described in Chapter 21. The option to switch sources of supply and output, or to change marketing focus, may have a high value. Despite the cost of creating an adaptable organisation, rather than a dedicated fixed one, the option to switch may be worth far more in an uncertain world.

Exhibit 22.19 describes the plight of UK exporters who suffered from the strength of sterling. Note that the pain is less for some than for others: 'Many larger exporters are substantial importers and so can offset their currency gains and losses. Some have production bases overseas.'

Exhibit 22.19

When the wheels come off

FT

The continued rise of the pound is putting unremitting pressure on some UK exporters

The workers at Alloy Wheels, a Kent-based maker of car wheels, need no reminder of the impact of the ascent of the pound on UK exports.

Fifty of the 430 staff are losing their jobs this month and most of the rest face pay cuts as the South African-owned company struggles to remain competitive overseas. 'We are in a very difficult position,' says Mr Lyn Evans, finance director at the factory, which exports about 40 per cent of its £35m annual sales.

Like many other British engineering companies, it capitalised on the pound's weakness in the early 1990s to get into exports for the first time. Now, following the 23 per cent appreciation in the pound's trade-weighted value since last summer, Mr Evans is having to reorganise the plant to stay in profit.

While Alloy Wheels may be an extreme example, its experiences are being repeated across swathes of UK manufacturing. The Engineering Employers' Federation reported this week that the industry had lost 18,000 jobs since the beginning of the year due – at least in part – to sterling. It warned there were more job cuts to come . . .

It is a far cry from the early 1990s, when Britain's exports soared after the pound's 16 per cent fall in the wake of its 1992 exit from the European exchange rate mechanism. With the global economy recovering from recession, UK export volumes jumped 10.8 per cent in 1994, followed by increases of 7.3 per cent and 6.7 per cent in 1995 and 1996. The government proudly declared an end to the long decline in Britain's share of world exports.

But many exporters are living on borrowed time: some are still benefiting from hedges taken out six or 12 months ago against adverse currency movements and others from the fact that customers have not yet found alternative suppliers . . .

British industry is so diverse that the impact of sterling's appreciation varies hugely. Many larger exporters are substantial importers and so can offset their currency gains and losses. Some have production bases overseas.

But the growing specialisation of companies means industry-wide generalisations are of limited value. Businesses differ in the degree to which they are exposed to short-term currency swings. Among the most seriously affected are those trading in price-sensitive commodities such as metals, chemicals and textiles.

In engineering, there is a contrast between leading companies such as GKN, IMI and TI, and some smaller businesses. The big groups have mostly established diversified operations across Europe and North America. Customers are often supplied from factories in their own countries. TI estimates that, even though it has customers in 45 countries, only 20 per cent of sales are exports and only half of that UK exports. These companies suffer when their foreign earnings are translated into sterling for accounting purposes, but this does not reflect any change in trading conditions.

However, smaller UK-based engineering companies have no such protection from sterling. For example, many machine tool makers, among the prime beneficiaries of sterling's weakness in the early 1990s, are now under pressure. Mr Keith Bailey, chief executive of BSA Tools in Birmingham, which saw sales double from £3m to £6m after 1992, this year expects sales to fall to £4m unless the pound drops back. 'It is an unprecedented situation. The City of London makes money whether sterling goes up or down. But we in manufacturing have got to have stability.

'In the last six months we have had to import machines that cannot be made here competitively,' he adds. 'We have also developed a joint venture in China where manufacturing costs are lower.'

Process Scientific Innovations, a maker of high-technology filters in County Durham, says it only broke even in the year to April after sterling's rise wiped £200,000 off profits. Ms Sue Hunter, managing director, says she is considering switching some purchasing to Germany and possibly locating any future expansions overseas.

Additional reporting by Chris Tighe and Richard Wolffe.

Source: Stefan Wagstyl, *Financial Times*, 11 July 1997. Reprinted with permission.

EXCHANGE-RATE DETERMINATION

There are a number of factors which influence the rate of exchange between currencies. This section briefly considers some of them.

Purchasing power parity

The theory of purchasing power parity (PPP) is based on the idea that a basket of goods should cost the same regardless of the currency in which it is sold. For example, if a basket of goods sold for £10,000 in the UK and an identical basket sold for US$15,000 in the USA then the rate of exchange should be US$1.50/£. Imagine what would happen if this were not the case; say, for example, the rate of exchange was US$3.00/£. Now British consumers can buy a basket of goods in the US market for half the price they would pay in the UK market (£5,000 can be exchanged for US$15,000). Naturally the demand for dollars would rise as UK consumers rushed out of sterling. This would cause the forex rates to change – the dollar would rise in value until the purchasing power of each currency was brought to an equilibrium, that is, where there is no incentive to exchange currencies to take advantage of lower prices abroad because of a misaligned exchange rate.

The definition of PPP is:

Exchange rates will be in equilibrium when their domestic purchasing powers at that rate of exchange are equivalent.

So, for example:

Price of a basket of goods in UK in sterling	×	US$/£ exchange rate	=	Price of a basket of goods in USA in dollars
£10,000	×	1.50	=	US$15,000

The PPP theory becomes more interesting if relationships over a period of time are examined. Inflation in each country will affect the price of a basket of goods in domestic currency terms. This in turn will influence the exchange rate between currencies with different domestic inflation rates.

Let us suppose that sterling and the US dollar are at PPP equilibrium at the start of the year with rates at US$1.50/£. Then over the year the inflation rate in the UK is 15 per cent so the same basket costs £11,500 at the end of the year. If during the same period US prices rose by 3 per cent the US domestic cost of a basket will be US$15,450. If the exchange rate remains at US$1.50/£ there will be a disequilibrium and PPP is not achieved. A UK consumer is faced with a choice of either buying £11,500 of UK-produced goods or exchanging £11,500 into dollars and buying US goods. The consumer's £11,500 will buy US$17,250 at US$1.50/£. This is more than one basket; therefore the best option is to buy goods in America. The buying pressure on the dollar will shift exchange rates to a new equilibrium in which a basket costs the same price in both countries. To find this new equilibrium we could use the following formula:

$$\frac{1 + I_{\text{US}}}{1 + I_{\text{UK}}} = \frac{\text{US\$/£}_1}{\text{US\$/£}_0}$$

where:

I_{US} = US inflation rate;
I_{UK} = UK inflation rate;
$US\$/£_1$ = the spot rate of exchange at the end of the period;
$US\$/£_0$ = the spot rate of exchange at the beginning of the period.

$$\frac{1 + 0.03}{1 + 0.15} = \frac{US\$/£_1}{1.50}$$

$$US\$/£_1 = \frac{1 + 0.03}{1 + 0.15} \times 1.50 = 1.3435$$

The US dollar appreciates against sterling by 10.43 per cent because inflation is lower in the USA over the period.

At this new exchange rate a basket of goods costing US$15,450 in the USA has a sterling cost of 15,450/1.3435 = £11,500 and thus PPP is maintained.

The pure PPP concludes that the country with the higher inflation rate will be subject to a depreciation of its currency, and the extent of that depreciation is proportional to the relative difference in the two countries' inflation rates. The PPP theory has some serious problems when applied in practice:

- ***It only applies to goods freely traded internationally at no cost of trade***
Many goods and services do not enter international trade and so their relative prices are not taken into account in the determination of currency rates. Medical services, haircuts, building and live entertainment, to name but a few, are rarely imported; therefore they are not subject to PPP. The theory also has limited applicability to goods with a high transportation cost relative to their value, for example, road stone or cement. The PPP disequilibrium would have to be very large to make it worthwhile importing products of this kind. There may also be barriers inhibiting trade, for example regulations, tariffs, quotas, cultural resistance.

- ***It works in the long run, but that may be years away***
Customers may be slow to recognise the incentive to purchase from another country when there is a PPP disequilibrium. There is usually some inertia due to buying habits that have become routine. Furthermore, governments may manage exchange rates for a considerable period, thus defying the forces pressing toward PPP. In addition, in the short term there are other elements at play such as balance of payments disequilibria, capital transactions (purchase of assets such as factories, businesses or shares by foreigners) and speculation.

The evidence is that relative inflation is one influence on exchange rates, but it is not the only factor. There have been large deviations from PPP for substantial periods.

Interest rate parity

PPP is concerned with differences in spot rates at different points in time and relating these to inflation rates. However, interest rate parity (IRP) concerns the relationship between spot rates and forward rates, and links differences between these to the nominal interest rates available in each of the two currencies.

The interest rate parity theory holds true when the difference between spot and forward exchange rates is equal to the differential between interest rates available in the two currencies.

The outcome of the IRP theory is that if you place your money in a currency with a high interest rate you will be no better off when you convert the sum back into your home currency via a prearranged forward transaction than you would have been if you had simply invested in an interest-bearing investment carrying a similar risk, at home. What you gain on the extra interest you lose on the difference between spot and forward exchange rates.

For example, suppose a UK investor is attracted by the 8 per cent interest rate being offered on one-year US government bonds. This compares well with the similarly very low risk one-year UK government bond offering 6 per cent interest. The IRP theory says that this investor will not achieve an extra return by investing abroad rather than at home because the one-year forward rate of exchange will cause the US$ to be at a discount relative to the present spot rate. Thus, when the investment matures and the dollars are converted to sterling the investor will have achieved the same as if the money had been invested in UK government bonds.

Consider these steps:

1 *Beginning of year*
   a Exchange £1m for US$1.5m at the spot rate of US$1.5/£.
   b Buy US$1.5m government bonds yielding 8 per cent.
   c Arrange a one-year forward transaction at US$/£1.5283 to sell dollars.
2 *End of year*
   Exchange US$1.62m (US$1.5m × 1.08) with the bank which agreed the forward exchange at the beginning of the year at the rate 1.5283 to produce 1.62 ÷ 1.5283 = £1.06m. This is equal to amount that would have been received by investing in UK government bonds, 6 per cent over the year. The differential between the spot and forward rates exactly offsets the difference in interest rates.

The formula which links together the spot, forward and interest rate differences is:

$$\frac{1 + r_{US}}{1 + r_{UK}} = \frac{US\$/£_F}{US\$/£_S}$$

where: r_{US} = interest rate available in the USA;
r_{UK} = interest rate available in the UK (for the same risk);
$US\$/£_F$ = the forward exchange rate;
$US\$/£_S$ = the spot exchange rate.

To test this relationship consider the case where both the spot rate and the forward rate are at US$1.50/£. Here the investor can prearrange to convert the dollar investment back into sterling through a forward agreement and obtain an extra 2 per cent by investing in the USA. However the investor will not be alone in recognising this remarkable opportunity. Companies, forex dealers and fund managers will turn to this type of trading. They would sell UK bonds, buy dollars spot, buy US bonds and sell dollars forward. However this would quickly lead us away from disequilibrium as the pressure of these transactions would lower UK bond prices and therefore raise interest rates, cause a rise in the value of the spot dollar against sterling, a rise in the price of US bonds and therefore a fall in interest rates being offered and a rise in the dollar forward rate. These adjustments will eliminate the investment return differences and re-establish IRP equilibrium.

The IRP insists that the relationship between exchange and interest rates is:

- ***High nominal interest rate currency*** Currency trades at a discount on the forward rate compared with spot rate (it depreciates).
- ***Low nominal interest rate currency*** Currency trades at a premium on the forward rate compared with spot rate (it appreciates).

The IRP theory generally holds true in practice. However there are deviations caused by factors such as taxation (which alters the rate of return earned on investments), or government controls on capital flows, controls on currency trading and intervention in foreign exchange markets interfering with the attainment of equilibrium through arbitrage.

Expectations theory

The expectations theory states that the current forward exchange rate is an unbiased predictor of the spot rate at that point in the future.

Note that the theory does not say that the forward rate predicts precisely what spot rates will be in the future; it is merely an unbiased predictor or provides the statistical expectation. The forward rate will frequently underestimate the actual future spot rate. However it will also frequently overestimate the actual future spot rate. On (a statistical) average, however, it predicts the future spot rate because it neither consistently under- nor consistently over-estimates.

Traders in foreign currency nudge the market towards the fulfilment of the expectations theory. If a trader takes a view that the forward rate is lower than the expected future spot price there is an incentive to buy forward. Then when the forward matures and the trader's view on the spot rate turns out to be correct the trader is able to buy at a low price and immediately sell at spot to make a profit. The buying pressure on the forward raises the price until equilibrium occurs, in which the forward price equals the market consensus view on the future spot price, which is an unbiased predictor.

The general conclusions from the empirical studies investigating the truthfulness of the expectations theory is that for the more widely traded currencies it generally works well. For the corporate manager and treasurer the forward rate is unbiased as a predictor of the future spot rate. That is, it has an equal chance of being below, or of being above, the actual spot rate. However it is a poor predictor – sometimes it is wide of the mark in one direction and sometimes wide of the mark in the other.

This knowledge may be useful to a corporate manager or treasurer when contemplating whether to hedge through using forward rates, with the attendant transaction costs, on a regular basis or whether to adopt a 'do nothing' policy, accepting that sometimes one loses on forex and sometimes one wins. For a firm with numerous transactions, the future spot rate will average the same as the forward rate, and so the 'do nothing' policy may be the cheaper and more attractive option.

The influence of a current-account deficit and capital flows

Another influence on exchange rate movements is the presence or otherwise of an unsustainable balance of payments. If an economy is importing more goods and services than it is exporting it is said to have a current-account deficit. The exchange rate will move (in theory) so as to achieve current-account balance. So, an overvalued exchange rate makes exporting difficult and encourages consumers to buy goods produced in other countries. If the exchange rate then declines exporters can sell more abroad and consumers are more likely to purchase the domestically produced version of a product as it becomes cheaper relative to imported goods. The trade deficit is eventually eliminated through this mechanism. The Fundamental Equilibrium Exchange Rate (FEER) is the exchange rate that results in a sustainable current-account balance. Any movement away from the FEER is a disequilibrium that sets in train forces that tend to bring the exchange rate back to equilibrium. That is the theory. In reality, there are many factors other than the trade balance causing forex rates to move.

Less than 1 per cent of all forex transactions are related to imports and exports of goods and services. Exchange rates can diverge from FEER for many years if foreign investors are willing to continue to finance a current-account deficit. They do this by buying assets (bonds, shares, companies, property, etc.) in the country with the negative balance of payments. The main influence on these capital transfers of money (and therefore demand for the deficit country's currency) is investors' expectations regarding the returns available on financial assets. If investors believe that the economy with a current-account deficit nevertheless offers good future returns on the bond market or the equity market, say, they will still bid up the value of its currency as they buy it to invest.

Around the turn of the millennium the USA ran a very large current-account deficit and yet the currency did not fall in value. Foreign investors thought that the returns offered on US financial assets, particularly shares, were attractive and so continued to support the dollar as they pumped money into the economy. While the American people went on a spending spree (with expenditure higher than take-home pay), in the process buying mountains of foreign produced goods, money flowed in as financial assets were bought, thus allowing the dollar to remain high. Of course, the dollar could plummet should overseas investors ever start to believe that the US economic miracle is over (or that it wasn't really a productivity miracle after all) as they sell US financial assets, sell the dollar and move funds to somewhere else in the world offering more exciting (or safer) returns.

The efficiency of the currency markets

Whether the forex markets are efficient at pricing spot and forward currency rates is hotly debated. If they are efficient then speculators on average should not be able to make abnormal returns by using information to take positions. In an efficient market the best prediction of tomorrow's price is the price today, because prices move in a random walk fashion, depending on the arrival of new information. Prices adjust quickly to new information, but it is impossible to state in advance the direction of future movements because, by its nature, news is unpredictable (it might be 'bad' or it might be 'good').

If the market is efficient, forecasting by corporate treasurers is a pointless exercise because any information the treasurer might use to predict the future will have already been processed by the market participants and be reflected in the price.

There are three levels of market efficiency:

- *Weak form* Historic prices and volume information is fully reflected in current prices, and therefore a trader cannot make abnormal profits by observing past price changes and trying to predict the future.
- *Semi-strong form* All publicly available information is fully reflected in prices, and therefore abnormal profits are not available by acting on information once it is made public.

- *Strong form* Public and private (that is, available to insiders, for example those working for a central bank) information is reflected in prices.

Much empirical research has been conducted into currency market efficiency and the overall conclusion is that the question remains open. Some strategies, on some occasions, have produced handsome profits. On the other hand, many studies show a high degree of efficiency with little opportunity for abnormal reward. Most of the studies examine the major trading currencies of the world – perhaps there is more potential for the discovery of inefficiency in the more exotic currencies. Central bank intervention in foreign exchange markets also seems to be a cause of inefficiency.

As far as ordinary humble corporate treasurers are concerned, trying to outwit the market can be exciting, but it can also be dangerous.

CONCLUDING COMMENTS

Managers need to be aware of, and to assess, the risk to which their firms are exposed. The risk that arises because exchange rates move over time is one of the most important for managers to consider. Once the extent of the exposure is known managers then need to judge what, if anything, is to be done about it. Sometimes the threat to the firm and the returns to shareholders are so great as to call for robust risk-reducing action. In other circumstances the cost of hedging outweighs the benefit. Analysing and appraising the extent of the problem and weighing up alternative responses are where managerial judgement comes to the fore. Knowledge of derivatives markets and money markets, and of the need for flexible manufacturing, marketing and financing structures, is useful background, but the key managerial skill required is discernment in positioning the company to cope with forex risk. The ability sometimes to stand back from the fray, objectively assess the cost of each risk-reducing option and say, 'No, this risk is to be taken on the chin because in my judgement the costs of managing the risk reduce shareholder wealth with little to show for it,' is sometimes required.

KEY POINTS AND CONCEPTS

- An **exchange rate** is the price of one currency expressed in terms of another.
- **Exchange rates are quoted** with a bid rate (the rate at which you can buy) and an offer rate (the rate at which you can sell).
- **Forex shifts can affect:**
  - income received from abroad;
  - amounts paid for imports;
  - the valuation of foreign assets and liabilities;
  - the long-term viability of foreign operations;
  - the acceptability of an overseas project.
- The **foreign exchange market** has grown dramatically over the last quarter of the twentieth century. Over US$1,210bn is traded each day. Most of this trading is between banks rather than for underlying (for example, import/export) reasons.

- **Spot market** transactions take place which are to be settled quickly (usually two days later). In the **forward market** a deal is arranged to exchange currencies at some future date at a price agreed now.
- **Transaction risk** is the risk that transactions already entered into, or for which the firm is likely to have a commitment, in a foreign currency will have a variable value.
- **Translation risk** arises because financial data denominated in one currency then expressed in terms of another are affected by exchange-rate movements.
- **Economic risk** Forex movements cause a decline in economic value because of a loss of competitive strength.
- **Transaction risk hedging strategies:**
  - invoice customer in home currency;
  - do nothing;
  - netting;
  - matching;
  - leading and lagging;
  - forward market hedge;
  - money market hedge;
  - futures hedge;
  - currency options.
- One way of **managing translation risk** is to try to match foreign assets and liabilities.
- The **management of economic exposure** requires the maintenance of flexibility with regard to manufacturing (for example, location of sources of supply), marketing (for example, advertising campaign, pricing) and finance (currency).
- The **purchasing power parity theory (PPP)** states that exchange rates will be in equilibrium when their domestic purchasing powers at that rate are equivalent. In an inflationary environment the relationship between two countries' inflation rates and the spot exchange rates between two points in time is (with the USA and the UK as examples):

$$\frac{1 + I_{US}}{1 + I_{UK}} = \frac{\text{US\$/£}_1}{\text{US\$£}_0}$$

- The **interest rate parity theory (IRP)** holds true when the difference between spot and forward exchange rates is equal to the differential between the interest rates available in the two currencies. Using the USA and the UK currencies as examples:

$$\frac{1 + r_{US}}{1 + r_{UK}} = \frac{\text{US\$/£}_F}{\text{US\$/£}_S}$$

- The **expectations theory** states that the current forward exchange rate is an unbiased predictor of the spot rate at that point in the future.
- The **Fundamental Equilibrium Exchange Rate** (FEER) is the exchange rate that results in a sustainable current-account balance.
- **Flows of money for investment** in financial assets across national borders can be an important influence on forex rates.
- The currency markets are generally **efficient.**

REFERENCES AND FURTHER READING

Brett, M. (2000) *How to Read the Financial Pages*. 5th edn. London: Random House Business Books. An easy introduction to this topic.

Demirag, I. and Goddard, S. (1994) *Financial Management for International Business*. Maidenhead: McGraw-Hill. More detailed and broader than this chapter. Introductory.

Eaker, M., Fabozzi, F. and Grant, D. (1996) *International Corporate Finance*. Orlando, Florida: Dryden. A wide-ranging international finance text. US perspective but with international examples. Easy to read.

Eales, B.A. (1995) *Financial Risk Management*. Maidenhead: McGraw-Hill. Contains some useful sections on currency risk management using derivatives.

Hallwood, C.P. and MacDonald, R. (2000) *International Money and Finance*. 3rd edn. Massachusetts and Oxford: Blackwell. Detailed discussion of economic aspects of forex.

Levi, M.D. (1996) Hallwood. *International Finance*. 3rd edn. New York: McGraw-Hill. Covers the international markets and the international aspects of finance decisions for corporations in an accessible style. US based.

McRae, T. (1996) *International Business Finance*. Chichester: Wiley. Deals with many international financial issues in a succinct fashion. UK-based writer with an accessible style.

Pilbeam, K. (1998) *International Finance*. 2nd edn. London: Macmillan. Detailed discussion of the models of exchange rate determination.

Roth, P. (1996) *Mastering Foreign Exchange and Money Markets*. London: Pitman Publishing. An introductory guide to practical forex and money market products, applications and risks.

Taylor, F. (2000) *Mastering Derivatives Markets*. 2nd edn. London: FT Prentice Hall. Contains some easy-to-read sections on currency derivatives.

Taylor, F. (1997) *Mastering Foreign Exchange and Currency Options*. London: Pitman Publishing. An excellent introduction to the technicalities of the forex markets and their derivatives. Plenty of practical examples.

Vaitilingam, R. (2000) *The Financial Times Guide to Using the Financial Pages*. 4th edn. London: FT Prentice Hall. A helpful guide to the way in which the *Financial Times* reports on the forex markets, among others.

Valdez, S. (2000) *An Introduction to Global Financial Markets*. 3rd edn. Basingstoke: Macmillan Business. A clear and concise introduction to the international financial scene.

Winstone, D. (1995) *Financial Derivatives*. London: Chapman and Hall. Clear introduction to the use of derivatives including currency derivatives.

WEBSITES

www.bis.org	Bank for International Settlements
www.bloomberg.co.uk	Bloomberg
www.reuters.co.uk	Reuters
www.ft.com	*Financial Times*
www.bankofengland.co.uk	Bank of England
www.ecb.int	European Central Bank

SELF-REVIEW QUESTIONS

1 Describe the difference between the spot and forward currency markets.

2 Explain through a simple example how the forward market can be used to hedge against a currency risk.

3 Define the following:

a transaction risk

b translation risk

c economic risk

4 What are the advantages and disadvantages of responding to foreign exchange risk by **a** invoicing in your currency; **b** doing nothing?

5 Draw out the difference between netting and matching by describing both.

6 What is a money market hedge, and what are leading and lagging?

7 How does a currency future differ from a currency forward?

8 Compare hedging using forwards with hedging using options.

9 Describe how you would manage translation and economic risk.

10 Explain the purchasing power parity (PPP) theory of exchange-rate determination.

11 Describe the relationship between spot rates and forward rates under the interest rate parity (IRP) theory.

12 What is the expectations theory?

QUESTIONS AND PROBLEMS

1 Answer the following given that the rate of exchange between the Japanese yen and sterling is quoted at ¥/£188.869 – 189.131:

a How many pounds will a company obtain if it sold ¥1m?

b What is the cost of £500,000?

c How many yen would be received from selling £1m?

d What is the cost of buying ¥100,000?

2 On 1 April an Australian exporter sells A$10m of coal to a New Zealand company. The importer is sent an invoice for NZ$11m payable in six months. The spot rates of exchange between the Australian and New Zealand dollars are NZ$1.1/A$.

Required

a If the spot rate of exchange in six months is NZ$1.2/A$ what exchange rate gain or loss will be made by the Australian exporter?

b If the spot rate of exchange in six months is NZ$1.05/A$ what exchange rate gain or loss will be made by the Australian exporter?

c A six-month forward is available at NZ$1.09/A$. Show how risk can be reduced using the forward.

d Discuss the relative merits of using forwards and options to hedge forex risk.

3 Describe the main types of risk facing an organisation which has dealings in a foreign currency. Can all these risks be hedged, and should all these risks be hedged at all times?

4* (*Examination level*)

a A UK company exports machine parts to South Africa on three months' credit. The invoice totals R150m and the current spot rate is R7.46/£. Exchange rates have been volatile in recent months and the directors are concerned that forex rates might move so as to make the export deal unprofitable. They are considering three hedge strategies:

i forward market hedge;

ii money market hedge;

iii option hedge.

Other information:

- three-month forward rate: R7.5/£;
- interest payable for three months' borrowing in rand: 2.5 per cent;
- a three-month American-style rand put, sterling call option is available for R150m with a strike price of R7.5/£ for a premium payable now of £400,000 on the over-the-counter market.

Required

Show how the hedging strategies might work. Use the following assumed spot rates at the end of three months in order to illustrate the nature of each of the hedges:

R7.00/£.

R8.00/£.

b Explain why it may not always make sense for a company to hedge forex risk.

5 British Steel (Corus) suffered greatly as a result of the high value of sterling because it is a major exporter (as are many of its customers). Consider the range of approaches British Steel could have taken to reduce both its transaction and economic exposure.

6 Describe how foreign exchange changes can undermine the competitive position of the firm. Suggest some measures to reduce this risk.

7 a A basket of goods sells for SFr2,000 in Switzerland when the same basket of goods sells for £1,000 in the UK. The current exchange rate is SFr2.0/£. Over the forthcoming year inflation in Switzerland is estimated to be 2 per cent and in the UK, 4 per cent. If the purchasing power parity theory holds true what will the exchange rate be at the end of the year?

b What factors prevent the PPP always holding true in the short run?

8 a The rate of interest available on a one-year government bond in Canada is 5 per cent. A similar-risk bond in Australia yields 7 per cent. The current spot rate of exchange is C$1.02/A$. What will be the one-year forward rate if the market obeys the interest rate parity theory?

b Describe the expectation theory of foreign exchange.

9* (*Examination level*) Lozenge plc has taken delivery of 50,000 electronic devices from a Malaysian company. The seller is in a strong bargaining position and has priced the devices in Malaysian dollars at M$12 each. It has granted Lozenge three months' credit.

Malaysian interest rates are 3 per cent per quarter.

Lozenge has all its money tied up in its operations but could borrow in sterling at 3 per cent per quarter (three months) if necessary.

Forex rates	*Malaysian dollar/£*
Spot	5.4165
Three-month forward	5.425

A three-month sterling put, Malaysian dollar call currency option with a strike price of M$5.425/£ for M$600,000 is available for a premium of M$15,000.

Required

Discuss and illustrate three hedging strategies available to Lozenge. Weigh up the advantages and disadvantages of each strategy. Show all calculations.

10† The spot rate between the euro and the US Dollar is €1.77/US$ and the expected annual rates of inflation are expected to be 2 per cent and 5 per cent respectively.

a If the purchasing power parity theory holds, what will the spot rate of exchange be in one year?

b If the interest rate available on government bonds is 6 per cent in the Eurozone and 9 per cent in the USA, and the interest rate parity theory holds, what is the current one-year forward rate?

11 The spot rate of exchange is Won1,507/£ between Korea and the UK. The one-month forward rate is Won1,450/£. A UK company has exported goods to Korea invoiced in Won to the value of Won1,507m on one month's credit.

To borrow in Won for one month will cost 0.5 per cent, whereas to borrow in sterling for one month will cost 0.6 per cent of the amount borrowed.

Required

a Show how the forward market can be used to hedge.

b Show how the money market can be used to hedge.

c What is the maximum that this company should offer as a discount to try and obtain payment immediately as an alternative to hedging in the markets, assuming all other factors remain constant?

ASSIGNMENTS

1 Examine a recent import or export deal at a company you know well. Write a report detailing the extent of exposure to transaction risk prior to any hedge activity. Describe the risk-reducing steps taken, if any, and critically compare alternative strategies.

2 Write a report for a company you know well, describing the extent to which it is exposed to transaction, translation and economic risk. Consider ways of coping with these risks and recommend a plan of action.

CHAPTER NOTES

1 It is also shortened to FX.

2 The CLS Bank launch is not expected to take place until 2002.

3 The *Financial Times* takes a representative sample of rates from major dealers in London at 4–5 p.m.

4 If we ignore the marketmakers' bid/offer spread and transaction costs.

5 Assuming, for the sake of simplicity, no diminution of asset value in dollar terms.

APPENDICES

I Future value of £1 at compound interest

II Present value of £1 at compound interest

III Present value of an annuity of £1 at compound interest

IV Future value of an annuity of £1 at compound interest

V Areas under the standardised normal distribution

VI Answers to the mathematical tools exercises in Chapter 2 Appendix 2.1

VII Solutions to selected questions and problems

Appendix I

FUTURE VALUE OF £1 AT COMPOUND INTEREST

Interest rate

Periods	1	2	3	4	5	6	7	8	9	10	11	12	13	14	15	
1	1.0100	1.0200	1.0300	1.0400	1.0500	1.0600	1.0700	1.0800	1.0900	1.1000	1.1100	1.1200	1.1300	1.1400	1.1500	1
2	1.0201	1.0404	1.0609	1.0816	1.1025	1.1236	1.1449	1.1664	1.1881	1.2100	1.2321	1.2544	1.2769	1.2996	1.3225	2
3	1.0303	1.0612	1.0927	1.1249	1.1576	1.1910	1.2250	1.2597	1.2950	1.3310	1.3676	1.4049	1.4429	1.4815	1.5209	3
4	1.0406	1.0824	1.1255	1.1699	1.2155	1.2625	1.3108	1.3605	1.4116	1.4641	1.5181	1.5735	1.6305	1.6890	1.7490	4
5	1.0510	1.1041	1.1593	1.2167	1.2763	1.3382	1.4026	1.4693	1.5386	1.6105	1.6851	1.7623	1.8424	1.9254	2.0114	5
6	1.0615	1.1262	1.1941	1.2653	1.3401	1.4185	1.5007	1.5869	1.6771	1.7716	1.8704	1.9738	2.0820	2.1950	2.3131	6
7	1.0721	1.1487	1.2299	1.3159	1.4071	1.5036	1.6058	1.7138	1.8280	1.9487	2.0762	2.2107	2.3526	2.5023	2.6600	7
8	1.0829	1.1717	1.2668	1.3686	1.4775	1.5938	1.7182	1.8509	1.9926	2.1436	2.3045	2.4760	2.6584	2.8526	3.0590	8
9	1.0937	1.1951	1.3048	1.4233	1.5513	1.6895	1.8385	1.9990	2.1719	2.3579	2.5580	2.7731	3.0040	3.2519	3.5179	9
10	1.1046	1.2190	1.3439	1.4802	1.6289	1.7908	1.9672	2.1589	2.3674	2.5937	2.8394	3.1058	3.3946	3.7072	4.0456	10
11	1.1157	1.2434	1.3842	1.5395	1.7103	1.8983	2.1049	2.3316	2.5804	2.8531	3.1518	3.4785	3.8359	4.2262	4.6524	11
12	1.1268	1.2682	1.4258	1.6010	1.7959	2.0122	2.2522	2.5182	2.8127	3.1384	3.4985	3.8906	4.3345	4.8179	5.3503	12
13	1.1381	1.2936	1.4685	1.6651	1.8856	2.1329	2.4098	2.7196	3.0658	3.4523	3.8833	4.3635	4.8980	5.4924	6.1528	13
14	1.1495	1.3195	1.5126	1.7317	1.9799	2.2609	2.5785	2.9372	3.3417	3.7975	4.3104	4.8871	5.5348	6.2613	7.0757	14
15	1.1610	1.3459	1.5580	1.8009	2.0789	2.3966	2.7590	3.1722	3.6425	4.1772	4.7846	5.4736	6.2543	7.1379	8.1371	15
16	1.1726	1.3728	1.6047	1.8730	2.1829	2.5404	2.9522	3.4259	3.9703	4.5950	5.3109	6.1304	7.0673	8.1372	9.3576	16
17	1.1843	1.4002	1.6528	1.9479	2.2920	2.6928	3.1588	3.7000	4.3276	5.0545	5.8951	6.8660	7.9861	9.2765	10.7613	17
18	1.1961	1.4282	1.7024	2.0258	2.4066	2.8543	3.3799	3.9960	4.7171	5.5599	6.5436	7.6900	9.0243	10.5752	12.3755	18
19	1.2081	1.4568	1.7535	2.1068	2.5270	3.0256	3.6165	4.3157	5.1417	6.1159	7.2633	8.6128	10.1974	12.0557	14.2318	19
20	1.2202	1.4859	1.8061	2.1911	2.6533	3.2071	3.8697	4.6610	5.6044	6.7275	8.0623	9.6463	11.5231	13.7435	16.3665	20
25	1.2824	1.6406	2.0938	2.6658	3.3864	4.2919	5.4274	6.8485	8.6231	10.8347	13.5855	17.0001	21.2305	26.4619	32.9190	25

Periods	16	17	18	19	20	21	22	23	24	25	26	27	28	29	30	
1	1.1600	1.1700	1.1800	1.1900	1.2000	1.2100	1.2200	1.2300	1.2400	1.2500	1.2600	1.2700	1.2800	1.2900	1.3000	1
2	1.3456	1.3689	1.3924	1.4161	1.4400	1.4641	1.4884	1.5129	1.5376	1.5625	1.5876	1.6129	1.6384	1.6641	1.6900	2
3	1.5609	1.6016	1.6430	1.6852	1.7280	1.7716	1.8158	1.8609	1.9066	1.9531	2.0004	2.0484	2.0972	2.1467	2.1970	3
4	1.8106	1.8739	1.9388	2.0053	2.0736	2.1436	2.2153	2.2889	2.3642	2.4414	2.5205	2.6014	2.6844	2.7692	2.8561	4
5	2.1003	2.1924	2.2878	2.3864	2.4883	2.5937	2.7027	2.8153	2.9316	3.0518	3.1758	3.3038	3.4360	3.5723	3.7129	5
6	2.4364	2.5652	2.6996	2.8398	2.9860	3.1384	3.2973	3.4628	3.6352	3.8147	4.0015	4.1959	4.3980	4.6083	4.8268	6
7	2.8262	3.0012	3.1855	3.3793	3.5832	3.7975	4.0227	4.2593	4.5077	4.7684	5.0419	5.3288	5.6295	5.9447	6.2749	7
8	3.2784	3.5115	3.7589	4.0214	4.2998	4.5950	4.9077	5.2389	5.5895	5.9605	6.3528	6.7675	7.2058	7.6686	8.1573	8
9	3.8030	4.1084	4.4355	4.7854	5.1598	5.5599	5.9874	6.4439	6.9310	7.4506	8.0045	8.5946	9.2234	9.8925	10.6045	9
10	4.4114	4.8068	5.2338	5.6947	6.1917	6.7275	7.3046	7.9259	8.5944	9.3132	10.0857	10.9153	11.8059	12.7614	13.7858	10
11	5.1173	5.6240	6.1759	6.7767	7.4301	8.1403	8.9117	9.7489	10.6571	11.6415	12.7080	13.8625	15.1116	16.4622	17.9216	11
12	5.9360	6.5801	7.2876	8.0642	8.9161	9.8497	10.8722	11.9912	13.2148	14.5519	16.0120	17.6053	19.3428	21.2362	23.2981	12
13	6.8858	7.6987	8.5994	9.5964	10.6993	11.9182	13.2641	14.7491	16.3863	18.1899	20.1752	22.3588	24.7588	27.3947	30.2875	13
14	7.9875	9.0075	10.1472	11.4198	12.8392	14.4210	16.1822	18.1414	20.3191	22.7374	25.4207	28.3957	31.6913	35.3391	39.3738	14
15	9.2655	10.5387	11.9737	13.5895	15.4070	17.4494	19.7423	22.3140	25.1956	28.4217	32.0301	36.0625	40.5648	45.5875	51.1859	15
16	10.7480	12.3303	14.1290	16.1715	18.4884	21.1138	24.0856	27.4462	31.2426	35.6271	40.3579	45.7994	51.9230	58.8079	66.5417	16
17	12.4677	14.4265	16.6722	19.2441	22.1861	25.5477	29.3844	33.7588	38.7408	44.4089	50.8510	58.1652	66.4614	75.8821	86.5042	17
18	14.4625	16.8790	19.6733	22.9005	26.6233	30.9127	35.8490	41.5233	48.0386	55.5112	64.0722	73.8698	85.0706	97.8822	112.4554	18
19	16.7765	19.7484	23.2144	27.2516	31.9480	37.4043	43.7358	51.0737	59.5679	69.3889	80.7310	93.8147	108.8904	126.2422	146.1920	19
20	19.4608	23.1056	27.3930	32.4294	38.3376	45.2593	53.3576	62.8206	73.8641	86.7362	101.7211	119.1446	139.3797	162.8524	190.0496	20
25	40.8742	50.6578	62.6686	77.3881	95.3962	117.3909	144.2101	176.8593	216.5420	264.6978	323.0454	393.6344	478.9049	581.7585	705.6410	25

Appendix II

PRESENT VALUE OF £1 AT COMPOUND INTEREST

Interest rate

Periods	1	2	3	4	5	6	7	8	9	10	11	12	13	14	15	
1	0.9901	0.9804	0.9709	0.9615	0.9524	0.9434	0.9346	0.9259	0.9174	0.9091	0.9009	0.8929	0.8850	0.8772	0.8696	1
2	0.9803	0.9612	0.9426	0.9246	0.9070	0.8900	0.8734	0.8573	0.8417	0.8264	0.8116	0.7972	0.7831	0.7695	0.7561	2
3	0.9706	0.9423	0.9151	0.8890	0.8638	0.8396	0.8163	0.7938	0.7722	0.7513	0.7312	0.7118	0.6931	0.6750	0.6575	3
4	0.9610	0.9238	0.8885	0.8548	0.8227	0.7921	0.7629	0.7350	0.7084	0.6830	0.6587	0.6355	0.6133	0.5921	0.5718	4
5	0.9515	0.9057	0.8626	0.8219	0.7835	0.7473	0.7130	0.6806	0.6499	0.6209	0.5935	0.5674	0.5428	0.5194	0.4972	5
6	0.9420	0.8880	0.8375	0.7903	0.7462	0.7050	0.6663	0.6302	0.5963	0.5645	0.5346	0.5066	0.4803	0.4556	0.4323	6
7	0.9327	0.8706	0.8131	0.7599	0.7107	0.6651	0.6227	0.5835	0.5470	0.5132	0.4817	0.4523	0.4251	0.3996	0.3759	7
8	0.9235	0.8535	0.7894	0.7307	0.6768	0.6274	0.5820	0.5403	0.5019	0.4665	0.4339	0.4039	0.3762	0.3506	0.3269	8
9	0.9143	0.8368	0.7664	0.7026	0.6446	0.5919	0.5439	0.5002	0 4604	0.4241	0.3909	0.3606	0.3329	0.3075	0.2843	9
10	0.9053	0.8203	0.7441	0.6756	0.6139	0.5584	0.5083	0.4632	0.4224	0.3855	0.3522	0.3220	0.2946	0.2697	0.2472	10
11	0.8963	0.8043	0.7224	0.6496	0.5847	0.5268	0.4751	0.4289	0.3875	0.3505	0.3173	0.2875	0 2607	0.2366	0.2149	11
12	0.8874	0.7885	0.7014	0.6246	0.5568	0.4970	0.4440	0.3971	0.3555	0.3186	0.2858	0.2567	0.2307	0.2076	0.1869	12
13	0.8787	0.7730	0.6810	0.6006	0.5303	0.4688	0.4150	0.3677	0.3262	0.2897	0.2575	0.2292	0.2042	0.1821	0.1625	13
14	0.8700	0.7579	0.6611	0.5775	0.5051	0.4423	0.3878	0.3405	0.2992	0.2633	0.2320	0.2046	0.1807	0.1597	0.1413	14
15	0.8613	0.7430	0.6419	0.5553	0.4810	0.4173	0.3624	0.3152	0.2745	0.2394	0.2090	0.1827	0.1599	0.1401	0.1229	15
16	0.8528	0.7284	0.6232	0.5339	0.4581	0.3936	0.3387	0.2919	0.2519	0.2176	0.1883	0.1631	0.1415	0.1229	0.1069	16
17	0.8444	0.7142	0.6050	0.5134	0.4363	0.3714	0.3166	0.2703	0.2311	0.1978	0.1696	0.1456	0.1252	0.1078	0.0929	17
18	0.8360	0.7002	0.5874	0.4936	0.4155	0.3503	0.2959	0.2502	0.2120	0.1799	0.1528	0.1300	0.1108	0.0946	0.0808	18
19	0.8277	0.6864	0.5703	0.4746	0.3957	0.3305	0.2765	0.2317	0.1945	0.1635	0.1377	0.1161	0.0981	0.0829	0.0703	19
20	0.8195	0.6730	0.5537	0.4564	0.3769	0.3118	0.2584	0.2145	0.1784	0.1486	0.1240	0.1037	0.0868	0.0728	0.0611	20
25	0.7795	0.6095	0.4776	0.3751	0.2953	0.2330	0.1842	0.1460	0.1160	0.0923	0.0736	0.0588	0.0471	0.0378	0.0304	25
30	0.7419	0.5521	0.4120	0.3083	0.2314	0.1741	0.1314	0.0994	0.0754	0.0573	0.0437	0.0334	0.0256	0.0196	0.0151	30
35	0.7059	0.5000	0.3554	0.2534	0.1813	0.1301	0.0937	0.0676	0.0490	0.0356	0.0259	0.0189	0.0139	0.0102	0.0075	35
40	0.6717	0.4529	0.3066	0.2083	0.1420	0.0972	0.0668	0.0460	0.0318	0.0221	0.0154	0.0107	0.0075	0.0053	0.0037	40
45	0.6391	0.4102	0.2644	0.1712	0.1113	0.0727	0.0476	0.0313	0.0207	0.0137	0.0091	0.0061	0.0041	0.0027	0.0019	45
50	0.6080	0.3715	0.2281	0.1407	0.0872	0.0543	0.0339	0.0213	0.0134	0.0085	0.0054	0.0035	0.0022	0.0014	0.0009	50

Periods	16	17	18	19	20	21	22	23	24	25	26	27	28	29	30	
1	0.8621	0.8547	0.8475	0.8403	0.8333	0.8264	0.8197	0.8130	0.8065	0.8000	0.7937	0.7874	0.7812	0.7752	0.7692	1
2	0.7432	0.7305	0.7182	0.7062	0.6944	0.6830	0.6719	0.6610	0.6504	0.6400	0.6299	0.6200	0.6104	0.6009	0.5917	2
3	0.6407	0.6244	0.6086	0.5934	0.5787	0.5645	0.5507	0.5374	0.5245	0.5120	0.4999	0.4882	0.4768	0.4658	0.4552	3
4	0.5523	0.5337	0.5158	0.4987	0.4823	0.4665	0.4514	0.4369	0.4230	0.4096	0.3968	0 3844	0.3725	0.3611	0.3501	4
5	0.4761	0.4561	0.4371	0.4190	0.4019	0.3855	0.3700	0.3552	0.3411	0.3277	0.3149	0.3027	0.2910	0.2799	0.2693	5
6	0.4104	0.3898	0.3704	0.3521	0.3349	0.3186	0.3033	0.2888	0.2751	0.2621	0.2499	0.2383	0.2274	0.2170	0.2072	6
7	0.3538	0.3332	0.3139	0.2959	0.2791	0.2633	0.2486	0.2348	0.2218	0.2097	0.1983	0.1877	0.1776	0.1682	0.1594	7
8	0.3050	0.2848	0.2660	0.2487	0.2326	0.2176	0.2038	0.1909	0.1789	0.1678	0.1574	0.1478	0.1388	0 1304	0.1226	8
9	0.2630	0.2434	0.2255	0.2090	0.1938	0.1799	0.1670	0.1552	0.1443	0.1342	0.1249	0.1164	0.1084	0.1011	0.0943	9
10	0.2267	0.2080	0.1911	0.1756	0.1615	0.1486	0.1369	0.1262	0.1164	0.1074	0.0992	0.0916	0.0847	0.0784	0.0725	10
11	0.1954	0.1778	0.1619	0.1476	0.1346	0.1228	0.1122	0.1026	0.0938	0.0859	0.0787	0.0721	0.0662	0.0607	0.0558	11
12	0.1685	0.1520	0.1372	0.1240	0.1122	0.1015	0.0920	0.0834	0.0757	0.0687	0.0625	0.0568	0.0517	0.0471	0.0429	12
13	0.1452	0.1299	0.1163	0.1042	0.0935	0.0839	0.0754	0.0678	0.0610	0.0550	0.0496	0.0447	0.0404	0.0365	0.0330	13
14	0.1252	0.1110	0.0985	0.0876	0.0779	0.0693	0.0618	0.0551	0.0492	0.0440	0.0393	0.0352	0.0316	0.0283	0.0254	14
15	0.1079	0.0949	0.0835	0.0736	0.0649	0.0573	0.0507	0.0448	0.0397	0.0352	0.0312	0.0277	0.0247	0.0219	0.0195	15
16	0.0930	0.0811	0.0708	0.0618	0.0541	0.0474	0.0415	0.0364	0.0320	0.0281	0.0248	0.0218	0.0193	0.0170	0.0150	16
17	0.0802	0.0693	0.0600	0.0520	0.0451	0.0391	0.0340	0.0296	0.0258	0.0225	0.0197	0.0172	0.0150	0.0132	0.0116	17
18	0.0691	0.0592	0.0508	0.0437	0.0376	0.0323	0.0279	0.0241	0.0208	0.0180	0.0156	0.0135	0.0118	0.0102	0.0089	18
19	0.0596	0.0506	0.0431	0.0367	0.0313	0.0267	0.0229	0.0196	0.0168	0.0144	0.0124	0.0107	0.0092	0.0079	0.0068	19
20	0.0514	0.0433	0.0365	0.0308	0.0261	0.0221	0.0187	0.0159	0.0135	0.0115	0.0098	0.0084	0.0072	0.0061	0.0053	20
25	0.0245	0.0197	0.0160	0.0129	0.0105	0.0085	0.0069	0.0057	0.0046	0.0038	0.0031	0.0025	0.0021	0.0017	0.0014	25
30	0.0116	0.0090	0.0070	0.0054	0.0042	0.0033	0.0026	0.0020	0.0016	0.0012	0.0010	0.0008	0.0005	0.0005	0.0004	30
35	0.0055	0.0041	0.0030	0.0023	0.0017	0.0013	0.0009	0.0007	0.0005	0.0004	0.0003	0.0002	0.0002	0.0001	0.0000	35
40	0.0026	0.0019	0.0013	0.0010	0.0007	0.0005	0.0004	0.0003	0.0002	0.0001	0.0001	0.0001	0.0001	0.0000	0.0000	40
45	0.0013	0.0009	0.0006	0.0004	0.0003	0.0002	0.0001	0.0001	0.0001	0.0000	0.0000	0.0000	0.0000	0.0000	0.0000	45
50	0.0006	0.0004	0.0003	0.0002	0.0001	0.0001	0.0000	0.0000	0.0000	0.0000	0.0000	0.0000	0.0000	0.0000	0.0000	50

PRESENT VALUE OF AN ANNUITY OF £1 AT COMPOUND INTEREST

Interest rate

Periods	1	2	3	4	5	6	7	8	9	10	11	12	13	14	15	
1	0.9901	0.9804	0.9709	0.9615	0.9524	0.9434	0.9346	0.9259	0.9174	0.9091	0.9009	0.8929	0.8850	0.8772	0.8696	1
2	1.9704	1.9416	1.9135	1.8861	1.8594	1.8334	1.8080	1.7833	1.7591	1.7355	1.7125	1.6901	1.6681	1.6467	1.6257	2
3	2.9410	2.8839	2.8286	2.7751	2.7232	2.6730	2.6243	2.5771	2.5313	2.4869	2.4437	2.4018	2.3612	2.3216	2.2832	3
4	3.9020	3.8077	3.7171	3.6299	3.5460	3.4651	3.3872	3.3121	3.2397	3.1699	3.1024	3.0373	2.9745	2.9137	2.8550	4
5	4.8534	4.7135	4.5797	4.4518	4.3295	4.2124	4.1002	3.9927	3.8897	3.7908	3.6959	3.6048	3.5172	3.4331	3.3522	5
6	5.7955	5.6014	5.4172	5.2421	5.0757	4.9173	4.7665	4.6229	4.4859	4.3553	4.2305	4.1114	3.9975	3.8887	3.7845	6
7	6.7282	6.4720	6.2303	6.0021	5.7864	5.5824	5.3893	5.2064	5.0330	4.8684	4.7122	4.5638	4.4226	4.2883	4.1604	7
8	7.6517	7.3255	7.0197	6.7327	6.4632	6 2098	5.9713	5.7466	5.5348	5.3349	5.1461	4.9676	4.7988	4.6389	4.4873	8
9	8.5660	8.1622	7.7861	7.4353	7.1078	6.8017	6.5152	6.2469	5.9952	5.7590	5.5370	5.3282	5.1317	4.9464	4.7716	9
10	9.4713	8.9826	8.5302	8.1109	7.7217	7.3601	7.0236	6.7101	6.4177	6.1446	5.8892	5.6502	5.4262	5.2161	5.0188	10
11	10.3676	9.7868	9.2526	8.7605	8.3064	7.8869	7.4987	7.1390	6.8052	6.4951	6.2065	5.9377	5.6869	5.4527	5.2337	11
12	11.2551	10.5753	9.9540	9.3851	8.8633	8.3838	7.9427	7.5361	7.1607	6.8137	6.4924	6.1944	5.9176	5.6603	5.4206	12
13	12.1337	11.3484	10.6350	9.9856	9.3936	8.8527	8.3577	7.9038	7.4869	7.1034	6.7499	6.4235	6.1218	5.8424	5.5831	13
14	13.0037	12.1062	11.2961	10.5631	9.8986	9.2950	8.7455	8.2442	7.7862	7.3667	6.9819	6.6282	6.3025	6.0021	5.7245	14
15	13.8651	12.8493	11.9379	11.1184	10.3797	9.7122	9.1079	8.5595	8.0607	7.6061	7.1909	6.8109	6.4624	6.1422	5.8474	15
16	14.7179	13.5777	12.5611	11.6523	10.8378	10.1059	9.4466	8.8514	8.3126	7.8237	7.3792	6.9740	6.6039	6.2651	5.9542	16
17	15.5623	14.2919	13.1661	12.1657	11.2741	10.4773	9.7632	9.1216	8.5436	8.0216	7.5488	7.1196	6.7291	6.3729	6.0472	17
18	16.3983	14.9920	13.7535	12.6593	11.6896	10.8276	10.0591	9.3719	8.7556	8.2014	7.7016	7.2497	6.8399	6.4674	6.1280	18
19	17.2260	15.6785	14.3238	13.1339	12.0853	11.1581	10.3356	9.6036	8.9501	8.3649	7.8393	7.3658	6.9380	6.5504	6.1982	19
20	18.0456	16.3514	14.8775	13.5903	12.4622	11.4699	10.5940	9.8181	9.1285	8.5136	7.9633	7.4694	7.0248	6.6231	6.2593	20
25	22.0232	19.5235	17.4131	15.6221	14.0939	12.7834	11.6536	10.6748	9.8226	9.0770	8.4217	7.8431	7.3300	6.8729	6.4641	25
30	25.8077	22.3965	19.6004	17.2920	15.3725	13.7648	12.4090	11.2578	10.2737	9.4269	8.6938	8.0552	7.4957	7.0027	6.5660	30
35	29.4086	24.9986	21.4872	18.6646	16.3742	14.4982	12.9477	11.6546	10.5668	9.6442	8.8552	8.1755	7.5856	7.0700	6.6166	35
40	32.8347	27.3555	23.1148	19.7928	17.1591	15.0463	13.3317	11.9246	10.7574	9.7791	8.9511	8.2438	7.6344	7.1050	6.6418	40
45	36.0945	29.4902	24.5187	20.7200	17.7741	15.4558	13.6055	12.1084	10.8812	9.8628	9.0079	8.2825	7.6609	7.1232	6.6543	45
50	39.1961	31.4236	25.7298	21.4822	18.2559	15.7619	13.8007	12.2335	10.9617	9.9148	9.0417	8.3045	7.6752	7.1327	6.6605	50

Periods	16	17	18	19	20	21	22	23	24	25	26	27	28	29	30	
1	0.8621	0.8547	0.8475	0.8403	0.8333	0.8264	0.8197	0.8130	0.8065	0.8000	0.7937	0.7874	0.7812	0.7752	0.7692	1
2	1.6052	1.5852	1.5656	1.5465	1.5278	1.5095	1.4915	1.4740	1.4568	1.4400	1.4235	1.4074	1.3916	1.3761	1.3609	2
3	2.2459	2.2096	2.1743	2.1399	2.1065	2.0739	2.0422	2.0114	1.9813	1.9520	1.9234	1.8956	1.8684	1.8420	1.8161	3
4	2.7982	2.7432	2.6901	2.6386	2.5887	2.5404	2.4936	2.4483	2.4043	2.3616	2.3202	2.2800	2.2410	2.2031	2.1662	4
5	3.2743	3.1993	3.1272	3.0576	2.9906	2.9260	2.8636	2.8035	2.7454	2.6893	2.6351	2.5827	2.5320	2.4830	2.4356	5
6	3.6847	3.5892	3.4976	3.4098	3.3255	3.2446	3.1669	3.0923	3.0205	2.9514	2.8850	2.8210	2.7594	2.7000	2.6427	6
7	4.0386	3.9224	3.8115	3.7057	3.6046	3.5079	3.4155	3.3270	3.2423	3.1611	3.0833	3.0087	2.9370	2.8682	2.8021	7
8	4.3436	4.2072	4.0776	3.9544	3.8372	3.7256	3.6193	3.5179	3.4212	3.3289	3.2407	3.1564	3.0758	2.9986	2.9247	8
9	4.6065	4.4506	4.3030	4.1633	4.0310	3.9054	3.7863	3.6731	3.5655	3.4631	3.3657	3.2728	3.1842	3.0997	3.0190	9
10	4.8332	4.6586	4.4941	4.3389	4.1925	4.0541	3.9232	3.7993	3.6819	3.5705	3.4648	3.3644	3.2689	3.1781	3.0915	10
11	5.0286	4.8364	4.6560	4.4865	4.3271	4.1769	4.0354	3.9018	3.7757	3.6564	3.5435	3.4365	3.3351	3.2388	3.1473	11
12	5.1971	4.9884	4.7932	4.6105	4.4392	4.2784	4.1274	3.9852	3.8514	3.7251	3.6059	3.4933	3.3868	3.2859	3.1903	12
13	5.3423	5.1183	4.9095	4.7147	4.5327	4.3624	4.2028	4.0530	3.9124	3.7801	3.6555	3.5381	3.4272	3.3224	3.2233	13
14	5.4675	5.2293	5.0081	4.8023	4.6106	4.4317	4.2646	4.1082	3.9616	3.8241	3.6949	3.5733	3.4587	3.3507	3.2487	14
15	5.5755	5.3242	5.0916	4.8759	4.6755	4.4890	4.3152	4.1530	4.0013	3.8593	3.7261	3.6010	3.4834	3.3726	3.2682	15
16	5.6685	5.4053	5.1624	4.9377	4.7296	4.5364	4.3567	4.1894	4.0333	3.8874	3.7509	3.6228	3.5026	3.3896	3.2832	16
17	5.7487	5.4746	5.2223	4.9897	4.7746	4.5755	4.3908	4.2190	4.0591	3.9099	3.7705	3.6400	3.5177	3.4028	3.2948	17
18	5.8178	5.5339	5.2732	5.0333	4.8122	4.6079	4.4187	4.2431	4.0799	3.9279	3.7861	3.6536	3.5294	3.4130	3.3037	18
19	5.8775	5.5845	5.3162	5.0700	4.8435	4.6346	4.4415	4.2627	4.0967	3.9424	3.7985	3.6642	3.5486	3.4210	3.3105	19
20	5.9288	5.6278	5.3527	5.1009	4.8696	4.6567	4.4603	4.2786	4.1103	3.9539	3.8083	3.6726	3.5458	3.4271	3.3158	20
25	6.0971	5.7662	5.4669	5.1951	4.9476	4.7213	4.5139	4.3232	4.1474	3.9849	3.8342	3.6943	3.5640	3.4423	3.3286	25
30	6.1772	5.8294	5.5168	5.2347	4.9789	4.7463	4.5338	4.3391	4.1601	3.9950	3.8424	3.7009	3.5693	3.4466	3.3321	30
35	6.2153	5.8582	5.5386	5.2512	4.9915	4.7559	4.5411	4.3447	4.1644	3.9984	3.8450	3.7028	3.5708	3.4478	3.3330	35
40	6.2335	5.8713	5.5482	5.2582	4.9966	4.7596	4.5439	4.3467	4.1659	3.9995	3.8458	3.7034	3.5712	3.4481	3.3332	40
45	6.2421	5.8773	5.5523	5.2611	4.9986	4.7610	4.5449	4.3474	4.1664	3.9998	3.8460	3.7036	3.5714	3.4482	3.3333	45
50	6.2463	5.8801	5.5541	5.2623	4.9995	4.7616	4.5452	4.3477	4.1666	3.9999	3.8461	3.7037	3.5714	3.4483	3.3333	50

Appendix IV

FUTURE VALUE OF AN ANNUITY OF £1 AT COMPOUND INTEREST

Interest rate

Periods	1	2	3	4	5	6	7	8	9	10	12	14	16	18	20	25	30	35	40	45	50
1	1.0000	1.0000	1.0000	1.0000	1.0000	1.0000	1.0000	1.0000	1.0000	1.0000	1.0000	1.0000	1.0000	1.0000	1.0000	1.0000	1.0000	1.0000	1.0000	1.0000	1.0000
2	2.0100	2.0200	2.0300	2.0400	2.0500	2.0600	2.0700	2.0800	2.0900	2.1000	2.1200	2.1400	2.1600	2.1800	2.2000	2.2500	2.3000	2.3500	2.400	2.4500	2.5000
3	3.0301	3.0604	3.0909	3.1216	3.1525	3.1836	3.2149	3.2464	3.2781	3.3100	3.3744	3.4396	3.5056	3.5724	3.6400	3.8125	3.9900	4.1725	4.3600	4.5525	4.7500
4	4.0604	4.1216	4.1836	4.2465	4.3101	4.3746	4.4399	4.5061	4.5731	4.6410	4.7793	4.9211	5.0665	5.2154	5.3680	5.7656	6.1870	6.6329	7.1040	7.6011	8.1250
5	5.1010	5.2040	5.3091	5.4163	5.5256	5.6371	5.7507	5.8666	5.9847	6.1051	6.3528	6.6101	6.8771	7.1542	7.4416	8.2070	9.0431	9.9544	10.9456	12.0216	13.1875
6	6.1520	6.3081	6.4684	6.6330	6.8019	6.9753	7.1533	7.3359	7.5233	7.7156	8.1152	8.5355	8.9775	9.4420	9.9299	11.2588	12.7560	14.4834	16.3238	18.4314	20.7813
7	7.2135	7.4343	7.6625	7.8983	8.1420	8.3938	8.6540	8.9228	9.2004	9.4872	10.0890	10.7305	11.4139	12.1415	12.9159	15.0735	17.5828	20.4919	23.8534	27.7255	32.1719
8	8.2857	8.5830	8.8923	9.2142	9.5491	9.8975	10.2598	10.6366	11.0285	11.4359	12.2997	13.2328	14.2401	15.3270	16.4991	19.8419	23.8577	28.6640	34.3947	41.2019	49.2578
9	9.3685	9.7546	10.1591	10.5828	11.0266	11.4913	11.9780	12.4876	13.0210	13.5795	14.7757	16.0853	17.5185	19.0859	20.7989	25.8023	32.0150	39.6964	49.1526	60.7428	74.8867
10	10.4622	10.9497	11.4639	12.0061	12.5779	13.1808	13.8164	14.4866	15.1929	15.9374	17.5487	19.3373	21.3215	23.5213	25.9587	33.2529	42.6195	54.5902	69.8137	89.0771	113.330
11	11.5668	12.1687	12.8078	13.4864	14.2068	14.9716	15.7836	16.6455	17.5603	18.5312	20.6546	23.0445	25.7329	28.7551	32.1504	42.5661	56.4053	74.6967	98.7391	130.162	170.995
12	12.6825	13.4121	14.1920	15.0258	15.9171	16.8699	17.8885	18.9771	20.1407	21.3843	24.1331	27.2707	30.8502	34.9311	39.5805	54.2077	74.3270	101.841	139.235	189.735	257.493
13	13.8093	14.6803	15.6178	16.6268	17.7130	18.8821	20.1406	21.4953	22.9534	24.5227	28.0291	32.0887	36.7862	42.2187	48.4966	68.7596	97.6250	138.485	195.929	276.115	387.239
14	14.9474	15.9739	17.0863	18.2919	19.5986	21.0151	22.5505	24.2149	26.0192	27.9750	32.3926	37.5811	43.6720	50.8180	59.1959	86.9495	127.913	187.954	275.300	401.367	581.859
15	16.0969	17.2934	18.5989	20.0236	21.5786	23.2760	25.1290	27.1521	29.3609	31.7725	37.2797	43.8424	51.6595	60.9653	72.0351	109.687	167.286	254.738	386.420	582.982	873.788
16	17.2579	18.6393	20.1569	21.8245	23.6575	25.6725	27.8881	30.3243	33.0034	35.9497	42.7533	50.9804	60.9250	72.9390	87.4421	138.109	218.472	344.897	541.988	846.324	1311.68
17	18.4304	20.0121	21.7616	23.6975	25.8404	28.2129	30.8402	33.7502	36.9737	40.5447	48.8837	59.1176	71.6730	87.0680	105.931	173.636	285.014	466.611	759.784	1228.17	1968.52
18	19.6147	21.4123	23.4144	25.6454	28.1324	30.9057	33.9990	37.4502	41.3013	45.5992	55.7497	68.3941	84.1407	103.740	128.117	218.045	371.518	630.925	1064.70	1781.85	2953.78
19	20.8109	22.8406	25.1169	27.6712	30.5390	33.7600	37.3790	41.4463	46.0185	51.1591	63.4397	78.9692	98.6032	123.414	154.740	273.556	483.973	852.748	1491.58	2584.68	4431.68
20	22.0190	24.2974	26.8704	29.7781	33.0660	36.7856	40.9955	45.7620	51.1601	57.2750	72.0524	91.0249	115.380	146.628	186.688	342.945	630.165	1152.21	2089.21	3748.78	6648.51
25	28.2432	32.0303	36.4593	41.6459	47.7271	54.8645	63.2490	73.1059	84.7009	98.3471	133.334	181.871	249.214	342.603	471.981	1054.79	2348.80	5176.50	11247.1990	24040.7	50500.3
30	34.7849	40.5681	47.5754	56.0849	66.4388	79.0582	94.4608	113.283	136.308	164.494	241.333	356.787	530.312	790.948	1181.88	3227.17	8729.99	23221.6	60501.1	154107	383500
35	41.6603	49.9945	60.4621	73.6522	90.3203	111.435	138.237	172.317	215.711	271.024	431.663	693.573	1120.71	1816.65	2948.34	9856.76	32422.9	104136	325400	987794	2912217
40	48.8864	60.4020	75.4013	95.0255	120.800	154.762	199.635	259.057	337.882	442.593	767.091	1342.03	2360.76	4163.21	7343.86	30088.7	120393	466960	1750092	6331512	22114663
45	56.4811	71.8927	92.7199	121.029	159.700	212.744	285.749	386.506	525.859	718.905	1358.23	2590.56	4965.27	9531.58	18281.3	91831.5	447019	2093876	9412424	40583319	167933233
50	64.4632	84.5794	112.797	152.667	209.348	290.336	406.529	573.770	815.084	1163.91	2400.02	4994.52	10435.6	21813.1	45497.2	280256	1659761	9389020	50622288	260128295	1275242998

Appendix V

AREAS UNDER THE STANDARDISED NORMAL DISTRIBUTION

z	0.00	0.01	0.02	0.03	0.04	0.05	0.06	0.07	0.08	0.09
0.0	0.0000	0.0040	0.0080	0.0120	0.0160	0.0199	0.0239	0.0279	0.0319	0.0359
0.1	0.0398	0.0438	0.0478	0.0517	0.0557	0.0596	0.0638	0.0675	0.0714	0.0753
0.2	0.0793	0.0832	0.0871	0.0910	0.0948	0.0987	0.1026	0.1064	0.1103	0.1141
0.3	0.1179	0.1217	0.1255	0.1293	0.1331	0.1368	0.1406	0.1443	0.1480	0.1517
0.4	0.1554	0.1591	0.1628	0.1664	0.1700	0.1736	0.1772	0.1808	0.1844	0.1879
0.5	0.1915	0.1950	0.1985	0.2019	0.2054	0.2088	0.2123	0.2157	0.2190	0.2224
0.6	0.2257	0.2291	0.2324	0.2357	0.2389	0.2422	0.2454	0.2486	0.2517	0.2549
0.7	0.2580	0.2611	0.2642	0.2673	0.2704	0.2734	0.2764	0.2794	0.2823	0.2852
0.8	0.2881	0.2910	0.2939	0.2967	0.2995	0.3023	0.3051	0.3078	0.3106	0.3133
0.9	0.3159	0.3186	0.3212	0.3238	0.3264	0.3289	0.3315	0.3340	0.3365	0.3389
1.0	0.3413	0.3438	0.3461	0.3485	0.3508	0.3531	0.3554	0.3577	0.3599	0.3621
1.1	0.3643	0.3665	0.3686	0.3708	0.3729	0.3749	0.3770	0.3790	0.3810	0.3830
1.2	0.3849	0.3869	0.3888	0.3907	0.3925	0.3944	0.3962	0.3980	0.3997	0.4015
1.3	0.4032	0.4049	0.4066	0.4082	0.4099	0.4115	0.4131	0.4147	0.4162	0.4177
1.4	0.4192	0.4207	0.4222	0.4236	0.4251	0.4265	0.4279	0.4292	0.4306	0.4319
1.5	0.4332	0.4345	0.4357	0.4370	0.4382	0.4394	0.4406	0.4418	0.4429	0.4441
1.6	0.4452	0.4463	0.4474	0.4484	0.4495	0.4505	0.4515	0.4525	0.4535	0.4545
1.7	0.4554	0.4564	0.4573	0.4582	0.4591	0.4599	0.4608	0.4616	0.4625	0.4633
1.8	0.4641	0.4649	0.4656	0.4664	0.4671	0.4678	0.4686	0.4693	0.4699	0.4706
1.9	0.4713	0.4719	0.4726	0.4732	0.4738	0.4744	0.4750	0.4756	0.4761	0.4767
2.0	0.4772	0.4778	0.4783	0.4788	0.4793	0.4798	0.4803	0.4808	0.4812	0.4817
2.1	0.4821	0.4826	0.4830	0.4834	0.4838	0.4842	0.4846	0.4850	0.4854	0.4857
2.2	0.4861	0.4864	0.4868	0.4871	0.4875	0.4878	0.4881	0.4884	0.4887	0.4890
2.3	0.4893	0.4896	0.4898	0.4901	0.4904	0.4906	0.4909	0.4911	0.4913	0.4916
2.4	0.4918	0.4920	0.4922	0.4925	0.4927	0.4929	0.4931	0.4932	0.4934	0.4936
2.5	0.4938	0.4940	0.4941	0.4943	0.4945	0.4946	0.4948	0.4949	0.4951	0.4952
2.6	0.4953	0.4955	0.4956	0.4957	0.4959	0.4960	0.4961	0.4962	0.4963	0.4964
2.7	0.4965	0.4966	0.4967	0.4968	0.4969	0.4970	0.4971	0.4972	0.4973	0.4974
2.8	0.4974	0.4975	0.4976	0.4977	0.4977	0.4978	0.4979	0.4979	0.4980	0.4981
2.9	0.4981	0.4982	0.4982	0.4983	0.4984	0.4984	0.4985	0.4985	0.4986	0.4986
3.0	0.4987	0.4987	0.4987	0.4988	0.4988	0.4989	0.4989	0.4989	0.4990	0.4990

Appendix VI

ANSWERS TO THE MATHEMATICAL TOOLS EXERCISES IN APPENDIX 2.1

1 a £124 b £125.97

2 a £26,533 b £163,665

3 a 14.2 years b 4.96 years

4 Present values of the four options:

a £1,000,000

b £1,104,883

c £1,500,000

d £1,283,540

Given the time value of money of 9 per cent per annum and certainty about the future (e.g. that you will live to enjoy the perpetuity) then the official answer is **c**. You may like to question whether this is what *you* would really go for. If you prefer another option, try to explain what that option says about your time value of money.

5 6%

6 £675

7 14.93%

8 a 32.20 b £31.18

9 £4,731

10 £6,217, 8.24%

11 Present value of a ten-year £800 annuity = £4,711. Therefore you could invest £4,711 @ 11% and receive £800 per year for ten years. Reject Supersalesman's offer.

12 £6,468

Appendix VII

SOLUTIONS TO SELECTED QUESTIONS AND PROBLEMS

This Appendix provides suggested solutions to those end-of-chapter numerical questions and problems not marked with an asterisk * or a dagger †.

Answers to questions and problems marked * are given in the *Lecturer's Guide*. Questions and problems marked † are left for the tutor or lecturer to discuss. Answers to discussion questions, essays and reports questions can be found by reading the text.

Chapter 1

No numerical questions; answers to all questions may be found by reading the text.

Chapter 2

1 Proast plc

a

Project A				*Project B*		
Point in time (yearly intervals)	*Cash flow*	*Discount factor*	*Discounted cash flow*	*Cash flow*	*Discount factor*	*Discounted cash flow*
0	–120	1.0	–120.00	–120	1.0	–120.00
1	60	0.8696	52.176	15	0.8696	13.044
2	45	0.7561	34.025	45	0.7561	34.025
3	42	0.6575	27.615	55	0.6575	36.163
4	18	0.5718	10.292	60	0.5718	34.308
		NPV	4.108		NPV	–2.460
			£4,108			–£2,460

Advice: Accept project A and reject project B, because A generates a return greater than that required by the firm on projects of this risk class, but B does not.

b The figure of £4,108 for the NPV of project A can be interpreted as the surplus (in present value terms) above and beyond the required 15 per cent return. Therefore, Proast would be prepared to put up to £120,000 + £4,108 into this project at time zero, because it could thereby obtain the required rate of return of 15 per cent. If Proast put in any more than this, it would generate less than the opportunity cost of the finance providers.

Likewise, the maximum cash outflow at time zero (0) for project B which permits the generation of a 15 per cent return is £120,000 – £2,460 = £117,540.

2 Highflyer plc

a First, recognise that annuities are present (to save a lot of time).

Project A: Try 15% $-420{,}000 + 150{,}000 \times 2.855 = +£8{,}250$.
Try 16% $-420{,}000 + 150{,}000 \times 2.7982 = -£270$.

$$\text{IRR} = 15 + \frac{8{,}250}{8{,}250 + 270} \times (16 - 15) = 15.97\%$$

Project B: Try 31% and 32%.

Point in time (yearly intervals)	*Cash flow*	*Discounted cash flow @ 31%*	*Discounted cash flow @ 32%*
0	–100,000	–100,000	–100,000
1	75,000	57,252	56,818
2	75,000	43,704	43,044
		+956	–138

$$\text{IRR} = 31 + \frac{956}{956 + 138} \times (32 - 31) = 31.87\%$$

b NPV: *Project A*
$-420{,}000 + 150{,}000 \times 3.0373 = +£35{,}595$

Project B
$-100{,}000 + 75{,}000 \times 1.6901 = +£26{,}758$

c Comparison:

	IRR	*NPV*
Project A	15.97%	+£35,595
Project B	31.87%	+£26,758

If the projects were not mutually exclusive, Highflyer would be advised to accept both. If the firm has to choose between them, on the basis of the IRR calculation it would select B, but, if NPV is used, project A is the preferred choice. In mutually exclusive situations with projects generating more than the required rate of return, NPV is the superior decision-making tool. It measures in absolute amounts of money rather than in percentages and does not have the theoretical doubts about the reinvestment rate of return on intra-project cash inflows.

4 *Point in time (yearly intervals)*	*0*	*1*	*2*	*3*
Cash flow	–300	+260	–200	+600
Discount factor	1.0	0.885	0.7831	0.6931
Discounted cash flow	–300	+230.1	–156.62	+415.86

NPV = +£189.31

Because the sign (+, –) changes three times, we may expect to find three possible IRRs.

Chapter 3

1 Tenby-Saundersfoot Dock Company

a London head office cost allocation is irrelevant as this is non-incremental.

Point in time (yearly intervals)	*0* *£000*	*1→∞* *£000*
Fees		255
Repairs	–250	
Employees		–70
Administration, etc.		–85
Electricity		–40
Other docks		–20
Cash flow	–250	+40

Additional overhead costs are included, but those which would have occurred, whether or not the dock project proceeded, are excluded. The loss of trade to other profit centres (docks) is included in the assessment of this project because this is an incidental effect which only occurs because of this new project.

b $\text{NPV} = -250 + \frac{40}{0.17} = -14.706$ or £14,706.

2 Railcam

Point in time (yearly intervals)	*20X2* *£m*	*20X3* *£m*	*20X4* *£m*
Sales	+22	+24	+21
Debtor adjustments			
Opening debtors	5.00	5.50	6.00
Closing debtors	5.50	6.00	5.25
	–0.50	–0.50	+0.75
Wages	–6.00	–6.00	–6.00
Materials	–11.00	–12.00	–10.50
Creditor adjustments			
Opening creditors	2.50	2.75	3.00
Closing creditors	2.75	3.00	2.625
	+0.25	+0.25	–0.375
Overhead	–5.00	–5.00	–5.00
	–0.25	+0.75	–0.125

3 Pine Ltd

a Recognition of sunk cost: £20,000 research.
Recognition of irrelevant data: depreciation.

£000s	*20X1 start*	*20X1 end*	*20X2*	*20X3*	*20X4*	*20X5*	*20X6*
Sales		+400	+400	+400	+320	+200	
Equipment	–240					+40	
Stock	–30					+30	
Working capital	–20					+20	
Overheads		–8	–8	–9.6	–9.6	–9.6	
Material		–240	–240	–240	–192	–120	
Variable costs		–40	–40	–40	–32	–20	
Debtors adjustment							
Opening debtors		0	400	400	400	320	200
Closing debtors		400	400	400	320	200	0
		–400	0	0	+80	+120	+200
Cash flow	–290	–288	+112	+110.4	+166.4	+260.4	+200
Discount factor	1.0	0.8929	0.7972	0.7118	0.6355	0.5674	0.5066
Discounted cash flow	–290	–257.2	+89.3	+78.6	+105.7	+147.8	+101.3

NPV = –£24,500

A negative NPV indicates that the project produces less than the opportunity cost of capital of the finance providers. This firm would serve its shareholders best by not proceeding with this project.

b The answer should explain, with a minimal use of technical language, the following:

- The time value of money.
- Discounting cash flows to a common point in time.
- Opportunity cost of investors' funds.
- Minimum rate of return required on a project.
- NPV = shareholder wealth increase.
- NPV decision rule
- The significance of being cash flow based rather than profit based.
- Only incremental cash flows are considered.

6 NPV = –5,000 + 2,000 × 0.885 + 2,200 × 0.7831 + 3,500 × 0.6931 = £919

$$\text{AEA} = \frac{\text{NPV}}{\text{annuity factor}} = \frac{919}{2.3612} = £389$$

9 Quite plc

Incremental cash flows for replacement:

Point in time (yearly intervals)	*0*	*1 → 15*	*15*
	+2,000 −7,000 −5,000	+500	+500

Incremental NPV = −5,000 + 500 × 8.0607 + 500 × 0.2745 = −£832.40

Incremental cash flows for overhaul:

Point in time (yearly intervals)	*0*	*1 → 15*
	−2,500	+300

−2,500 + 300 × 8.0607 = −£81.79

Recommendation: The best course of action is to continue with the old, unoverhauled machine.

13 Clipper plc

Point in time (yearly intervals)		*NPV*
0	10,000	= 10,000
1	12,000 × 0.909	= 10,908
2	14,000 × 0.826	= 11,564
3	15,500 × 0.751	= 11,641
4	16,500 × 0.683	= 11,270

The best time to cut the trees is in three years' time.

15 Hazel plc

a NPV of A: $-200 + \frac{220}{1.15} + \frac{242}{(1.15)^2} = +174$

b NPV of B: $-240 + \frac{220}{1.15} + \frac{242}{(1.15)^2} + \frac{266}{(1.15)^3} = +309$

c AEA for A: $\frac{174}{1.626} = +107$

AEA for B: $\frac{309}{2.283} = +135$

Preferred machine: Machine B.

d If C is used for a further five years:
£000s

$$(160 \times 3.3522) + (20 \times 0.497) + \frac{135/0.15}{(1.15)^5} = £993,751$$

If C is scrapped now:

£000s

$$87 + \frac{135}{0.15} = £987,000$$

Recommended option: do not scrap at time 0.

e Explanations in plain English are required, not passages of technical jargon.

Chapter 4

1 **Payback**
A: 6 years B: 3 years C: 4 years D: 4 years E: 5 years

Discounted payback

A	£	*Cumulative*
500 × 0.893	446.5	446.5
500 × 0.797	398.5	845
500 × 0.712	356	1,201
500 × 0.636	318	1,519
500 × 0.567	283.5	1,802.5
500 × 0.507	253.5	2,056
500 × 0.452	226	2,282

Discounted payback is not achieved (shareholder wealth-destroying project).

B	£	*Cumulative*
2,000 × 0.893	1,786	1,786
5,000 × 0.797	3,985	5,771
3,000 × 0.712	2,136	7,907
2,000 × 0.636	1,272	9,179

Discounted payback is not achieved (shareholder wealth-destroying project).

C	£	*Cumulative*
5,000 × 0.893	4,465	4,465
4,000 × 0.797	3,188	7,653
4,000 × 0.712	2,848	10,501
5,000 × 0.636	3,180	13,681
10,000 × 0.567	5,670	19,351

Discounted payback at year 5.

D	£	*Cumulative*
1,000 × 3.0373	3,037	3,037
7,000 × 0.5674	3,972	7,008

Discounted payback at year 5.

E	£	*Cumulative*
500 × 2.4018	1,201	1,201
2,000 × 0.6355	1,271	2,472
5,000 × 0.5674	2,837	5,309
10,000 × 0.5066	5,066	10,375

Discounted payback at year 6.

4 a Payback: 4 years

b

Point in time (yearly intervals)	*Cash flow*	*Discount factor*	*Discounted cash flow*	*Cumulative discounted cash flow*
0	(6,250)	1	(6,250)	(6,250)
1	1,000	0.9091	909.1	(5,340.9)
2	1,500	0.8264	1,239.6	(4,101.3)
3	2,000	0.7513	1,502.6	(2,598.7)
4	1,750	0.6830	1,195.3	(1,403.4)
5	1,500	0.6209	931.3	(472.1)
6	1,000	0.5645	564.5	92.4
7	500	0.5132	256.6	349.0
8	500	0.4665	233.3	582.3

Discounted payback = 6 years.

c NPV = £582.30.

Chapter 5

Self-review questions

2
$$(1 + m) = (1 + h)(1 + i)$$
$$(1 + 0.09) = (1 + h)(1 + 0.05)$$
$$(1 + h) = \frac{1.09}{1.05} - 1$$

$h = 3.81\%$

Questions and problems

1 Plumber plc

a *Project A:*

NPV = −1.5 + 0.5 × 0.8929 + 0.5 × 0.7972 + 1 × 0.7118 + 1 × 0.6355 = +0.69235

Accept.

Project B:

NPV = 2.0 + 4 × 0.6355 = +0.542.

Accept.

Project C:

NPV = −1.8 + 1.2 × 0.7118 + 1.2 × 0.6355 = −0.1832

Reject.

Project D:

NPV = −3.0 + 1.2 × 3.0373 = +0.64476

Accept.

Project E:

NPV = −0.5 + 0.3 × 3.0373 = +0.41119

Accept.

Project	*Investment £m*	*NPV £m*	*NPV/investment*	*Ranking*
A	1.5	0.69235	0.4616	2
B	2.0	0.542	0.271	3
D	3.0	0.64476	0.215	4
E	0.5	0.41119	0.822	1

Allocation of £5m:

Project	*Investment £m*	*NPV*
E	0.5	0.41119
A	1.5	0.69235
B	2.0	0.54200
D × $^1/_3$	1.0	0.21492
	5.0	1.86046

Maximum NPV available = £1.86046m.

b £2,290,300.

c

Project	*NPV*
A	0.69235
D	0.64476
E	0.41119
	1.74830

2 The Telescope Company

Project	*Investment*	*NPV*
C	10,000	6,000
E	7,000	2,100
A × 0.5	3,000	600
	20,000	8,700

3 Premiums: £25,194.
PV = 25,194/$(1.17)^3$ = £15,730

5 Hose plc

Point in time (yearly intervals)		*Money cash flow £000*		*Discounted money cash flow £000*
0		–800		–800
1	150 × 1.06	159	159 × 0.885	141
2	150 × 1.1236	169	169 × 0.7831	132
3	150 × 1.1910	179	179 × 0.6931	124
4	150 × 1.2625	189	189 × 0.6133	116
5	150 × 1.3382	201	201 × 0.5428	109
6	150 × 1.4185	213	213 × 0.4803	102
7	150 × 1.5036	226	226 × 0.4251	96
				20

This project produces a positive NPV and should therefore be accepted, all other things being equal.

6

Point in time (yearly intervals)	*Annual writing down allowance* £	*Written down value* £
0	0	10,000
1	2,500	7,500
2	1,875	5,625
3	1,406	4,219
4	1,055	3,164
5	791	2,373

Taxable profit can be reduced by £1,406 in the third year.
Present value of WDA in year 4 = £1,055 × 0.30 × 0.6830 = £216.17.

Balancing adjustment if the machine has a scrap value of £1,000 after 5 years:

Amount written off	10,000 – 2,373	= 7,627
Depreciation		9,000
		1,373

Chapter 6

1 +£348.7K a +£269.7K b +£198.8K

4 a *Annual cash flows:*

		£
Sales	22,000 × 21	462,000
Variable direct costs	22,000 × 16	–352,000
		110,000

$$-400{,}000 + 110{,}000 \times \text{af} = 0$$

$$\text{af} = \frac{400{,}000}{110{,}000} = 3.6364$$

From annuity tables: $24 + \dfrac{3.6819 - 3.6364}{3.6819 - 3.5705}(25 - 24) = 24.4\%$

IRR = 24.4%

b *Sales volume:*

		£
Sales	20,900 × 21	438,900
VDC	20,900 × 16	–334,400
		104,500

$$\text{af} = \frac{400{,}000}{104{,}500} = 3.8278$$

$$22 + \frac{3.9232 - 3.8278}{3.9232 - 3.7993}(23 - 22) = 22.8$$

IRR = 22.8%

Sales price:

		£
Sales	22,000 × 19.95	438,900
Variable direct costs		–352,000
		86,900

$$\text{af} = \frac{400{,}000}{86{,}900} = 4.6030$$

$$17 + \frac{4.6586 - 4.6030}{4.6586 - 4.4941}(18 - 17) = 17.3$$

IRR = 17.3%

Variable direct costs:		£
Sales	22,000 × 21	462,000
Variable direct costs	22,000 × 16.8	–369,600
		92,400

$$\text{af} = \frac{400{,}000}{92{,}400} = 4.3290$$

$$19 + \frac{4.3389 - 4.3290}{4.3389 - 4.1925}(19 - 18) = 19.1\%$$

IRR = 19.1%

c Consult the chapter for details.

5 **Project W**

Return	p_i	$R \times p_i$	*Expected return*	$(R_i - \bar{R})^2 p_i$
2	0.3	0.6	3.4	0.588
4	0.7	2.8	3.4	0.252
		3.4		0.840

Standard deviation £0.917m

Project X

Return	p_i	$R \times p_i$	*Expected return*	$(R_i - \bar{R})^2 p_i$
–2	0.3	–0.6	5.0	14.7
8	0.7	5.6	5.0	6.3
		5.0		21.0

Standard deviation £4.58m

Observation: W has a lower return and a much lower standard deviation than Y.
X has a higher return than Y, but also a higher risk.

6 $$\frac{-80{,}000 - 220{,}000}{160{,}000} = 1.875$$

Probability of insolvency = 50% – 46.96% = 3.04%

8	*Out-turn*	*Probability*	$R_i \times p_i$	$(R_i - \bar{R})p_i$
a	272,400	0.10	27,240	12,127,806,250
b	–46,500	0.10	–4,650	86,142,250
c	–75,200	0.56	–42,112	236,600
d	–234,700	0.24	–56,328	6,055,997,400
	Expected return		–75,850	18,270,182,500

Standard deviation £135,167

10 a *NPVs*
RJW's projections, +£138m
More optimistic scenario, +£1,077m
More pessimistic scenario, –£578m

NPV	p_i	$NPV \times p_i$	$(NPV - \overline{NPV})^2 p_i$
138	0.5	69	9,591
1,077	0.3	323.1	192,240
–578	0.2	–115.6	146,034
Expected return		276.5	347,865

Standard deviation 590

b $\frac{-550 - 276.5}{590} = -1.4$

Probability of avoiding liquidation = 50% + 41.92% = 91.92%

c $\frac{100 - 276.5}{590} = 0.3$

Probability of a rapidly moving share price = 50% + 11.79% = 61.79%

Chapter 7

1 32%

2 4.17%; 17.7% annualised return

3 84.9%; 22.74%

7 a 30%; 7.16%
b 32%, 16.7%

13 a Ihser: 18%; 18.33%
Resque: 16.5%; 2.29%

b (i) Expected return: 17.25
Variance: 64.3
Standard deviation: 8.0

(ii) Expected return 16.67
Variance: 0
Standard deviation: 0

15 a

Portfolio	Expected return %	Standard deviation %
All in A	20	7.1
1	26.6	20.3
2	22.2	7.3
3	20.9	6.1
All in B	28.75	27.7

b

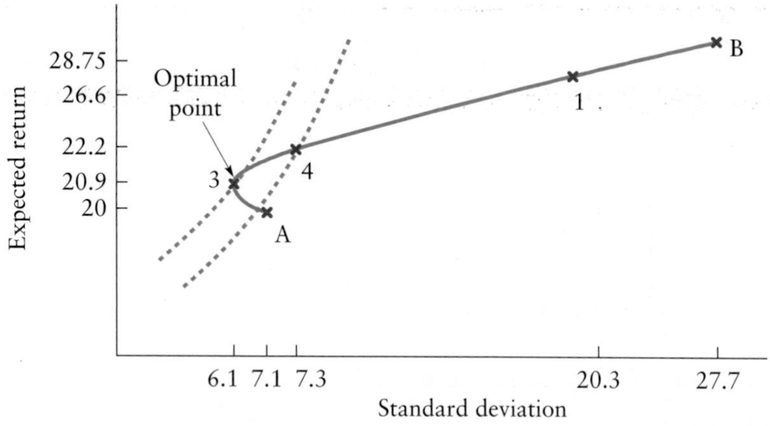

c The efficient region for the risk-return line drawn is between portfolio 3 and B. The inefficient region is between 3 and A.

d Indifference curves for a highly risk-averse individual are displayed, which result in portfolio 3 being optimal. Indifference curves with other slopes are acceptable, provided the optimal portfolio is shown to be where an indifference curve is tangential to the risk-return line – the highest achievable in the NW direction.

e See Chapter 7 for a description of the market portfolio; also consult Chapter 8.

Chapter 8

1 14.5%

3 A: 17% B: 9.5% C: 12%

4 7.33

5 a r_f = 10%; risk premium = 8%.

b P is above SML, offering a high return for risk level. The price will rise until the return offered is 23.6%.

c Q is below SML, offering a low return for its risk level. The price will fall until the return offered is 16.4%.

8 a Projects 1, 3 and 4.

Chapter 9

No numerical questions.

Chapter 10

12 £1.82; 8p.

Chapter 11

1 a £95.20 b 8.06%

2 a £100 b 10.15% c £103.62

3 a $9 \times 6.28115 + 100/(1.095)^{10} =$ £96.88

b $9 \times 6.56385 + 100/(1.085)^{10} =$ £103.30

c 8.255%

d 9%

5 a $\frac{100}{(1.05)^5} =$ £78.35

b $\frac{100}{(1.10)^5} =$ £62.09

6 Bond 1: £96.36 Bond 2: £101.82

10 16.08%

11 7.5%

13 a £78.71m

b

Year	*1*	*2*	*3*	*4*	*5*
Payments (£m)	4.75	4.75	4.75	4.75	54.75

c

Year	*1*	*2*	*3*	*4*	*5*
Payments (£m)	14.75	13.80	12.85	11.90	10.95
Outstanding at the beginning of the year		40.00	30.00	20.00	10.00

16 a 100/40 = £2.50

b (2.50 – 1.90)/1.90 = 31.6%

c $190 \times 40 =$ £76

Chapter 12

1

Interest on overdraft	£
$180{,}000 \times 3/12 \times 0.1$	4,500
$150{,}000 \times 3/12 \times 0.1$	3,750
$200{,}000 \times 3/12 \times 0.1$	5,000
	13,250
Arrangement fee	3,000
	16,250

Interest on loan	
200,000 × 0.1	20,000
Less Interest receivable	
200,000 × $^3/_{12}$ × 0.04	2,000
20,000 × $^3/_{12}$ × 0.04	200
50,000 × $^3/_{12}$ × 0.04	500
	£17,300

The loan is significantly more expensive. If cost is the only consideration, then the overdraft should be selected.

4 Overdraft interest over a 40-day period:

$(1 + d)^{365} = (1 + i)$

$\sqrt[365]{1 + 0.11} - 1 = 0.000285959$

$(1 + 0.000285959)^{40} - 1 = 0.011502$ or 1.15%
$10{,}000 \times 0.011502 = £115.02$

The value of the discount, £200, is greater than the cost of the additional overdraft and therefore Biscuit should pay on the 10th day.

10 $\sqrt[365]{1.09} - 1 = 0.000236131$

$(1.000236131)^{46} - 1 = 0.01092$ or 1.09%

It is more attractive to accept a discount of 1.5%.

11 a $\sqrt[365]{1.15} - 1 = 0.000382983$

Interest over 63 days:
$(1 + 0.000382983)^{63} - 1 = 0.02441$ or 2.441%

This is more than the discount and therefore Penguin should continue to pay on the 70th day.

Chapter 13

1 Cash flows: £10m/52 = £192,308 per week

Monday	*Tuesday*	*Wednesday*	*Thursday*	*Friday*
£82,418	£27,473	£27,473	£27,473	£27,473

$$Q = \sqrt{\frac{2 \times 35 \times 10{,}000{,}000}{0.11}} = £79{,}772$$

Interest cost:

Daily interest $\sqrt[365]{1.11} - 1$ = 0.0002859

4 days £82,481 × ((1.0002859)^4 – 1) = £94.29
3 days £27,473 × ((1.0002859)^3 – 1) = £23.57
2 days £27,473 × ((1.0002859)^2 – 1) = £15.71
1 day £27,473 × ((1.0002859) – 1) = £7.85

It would be best to pay cash into the bank account on Mondays and Fridays. The interest on Monday's cash inflow is greater than the cost of paying in. However, to pay in every day of the week would cost more in transaction cost than interest saved.

4 $\text{EOQ} = \sqrt{\frac{2 \times 300{,}000 \times 200}{10}} = 3{,}464$ units

Orders per year $= \frac{300{,}000}{3{,}464} = 86.6$

Total inventory cost $= \frac{AC}{Q} + \frac{HQ}{2}$

(300,000 × 200)/3,464 + (10 × 3,464)/2 = £34,641

5 a $\text{EOQ} = \sqrt{\frac{2 \times 10{,}000 \times 50}{7}} = 378$ units.

b Inventory cost: (10,000 × 50)/378 + (7 × 378)/2 = £2,646
Number of orders per year: 10,000/378 = 26.46

c Stock reorder level = 10,000/52 = 192 units

d Maximum inventory holding = 378 + 192 = 570 units

7 a

£000	*October*	*November*	*December*
Previous month's sales	165	180	45
Previous month's sales	55	315	385
This month's sales	90	110	140
Inflows	310	605	570
Materials	–270	–330	–420
Labour and other costs	–45	–55	–70
Total outflows	–315	–385	–490
Balances			
Opening balance	–70	–75	145
Net cash surplus (deficit)	–5	220	80
Closing balance	–75	145	225

Whitborrow will have sufficient cash to purchase the new equipment in December.

Chapter 14

2 Theory: 275p.
Practice: the scrip issue may be interpreted by the market as an optimistic signal from management that earnings and dividends will continue to grow in a satisfactory or better manner, and therefore the share price could settle above 275p. Fama *et al.* (1969) showed this phenomenon for US companies.

Chapter 15

8 a $\frac{10\text{m}}{0.13} = £76.92\text{m}$

b Cash flow: $-10\text{m} + \frac{2\text{m}}{0.13} = +£5.38\text{m}$

Earnings rise to £12m each year.
This is good investment, as the present value of the additional cash inflows is greater than the sacrifice. Here a rise in earnings coincides with a rise in value.

c Cash flow: $-5\text{m} + \frac{0.5\text{m}}{0.13} = -£1.154\text{m}$

Earnings rise to £10.5m each year.
This is bad investment, as the present value of the additional cash inflows is less than the sacrifice at time 0. Here a rise in earnings is achieved but value is lost.

9 Annual value creation: £300,000 × (0.19 – 0.13) = +£18,000
Performance spread = 0.19 – 0.13 = 0.06 or 6%
Value of the firm: 300,000 + 18,000 × 5.918 = £406,524

11 a $\frac{580 - 600}{600} \times 100 = -3.3\%$

b $\frac{580 - 450}{450} \times 100 = +28.9\%$

c $\frac{580 - 125}{125} \times 100 = 364\%$

To put additional meaning to TSR calculations, it is often useful to compare them with a benchmark:

Share index returns	3 years	24%
	5 years	68%
	10 years	210%

On the basis of these calculations, we observe that Tear has performed relatively well over a ten-year period but relatively poorly over three-year and five-year periods. This leads to a problem with TSR: it is highly dependent on the time period chosen.

Additional issues:
- It is important to relate relative returns to risk class.
- It measures in percentage terms rather than absolute terms.

Chapter 16

9 £5m – (£50m × 0.14) = –£2m

12 a $-80 + \frac{5}{1 + K_{DBT}} + \frac{5}{(1 + K_{DBT})^2} + \frac{5}{(1 + K_{DBT})^3} + \frac{5}{(1 + K_{DBT})^4} + \frac{105}{(1 + K_{DBT})^5} = 0$

Try 10%: +1.05
Try 11%: –2.178
$K_{DBT} = 10.33\%$
$K_{DAT} = 10.33\ (1 - 0.31) = 7.13\%$

b $K_E = r_f + \beta\ (r_m - r_f)$
$= 6 + 1.3(5) = 12.5\%$

c $K_{BANK} = (9 + 2)(1 - 0.31) = 7.59\%$

$$\begin{aligned} \text{WACC} &= K_E W_E + K_{DAT} W_D + K_{BANK} W_{BANK} \\ &= 12.5 \times 0.526 + 7.13 \times 0.211 + 7.59 \times 0.263 \\ &= 10.08\% \end{aligned}$$

Market values	*£*	*Weight*
Equity	2m	0.526
Loan	1m	0.263
Bond	0.8m	0.211
	3.8m	1.000

d *Corporate value*

£m	*1*	*2*	*3*	*4*	*5*	*6 → ∞*
Sales	1.1	1.21	1.331	1.464	1.6105	1.6105
Profit	0.11	0.121	0.1331	0.1464	0.16105	0.16105
Tax	–0.0341	–0.0375	–0.04126	–0.0454	–0.0499	–0.0499
IFCI	–0.017	–0.0187	–0.02057	–0.0226	–0.0249	0
IWCI	–0.006	–0.0066	–0.00726	–0.008	–0.0088	0
Operating free cash flow	0.0529	0.0582	0.06401	0.0704	0.07745	0.11115

Discounted cash flows (@10.08%)
= 0.0481 + 0.048 + 0.048 + 0.048 + 0.048 + 0.6822
= £0.9223m

Shareholder value = £0.9223m – £1.8m
= £0.8777m

Pre-interest cash flows are insufficient to cover the return to lenders and therefore shareholder value is negative.

e A possible element to the answer:
Operating profit margin = 15%
Planning horizon = 8 years

£m	*1*	*2*	*3*	*4*	*5*	*6*	*7*	*8*	*9*
Sales	1.1	1.21	1.331	1.464	1.6105	1.7716	1.949	2.1436	2.1436
Profit	0.165	0.1815	0.1997	0.2196	0.2416	0.2657	0.2924	0.3215	0.3215
Tax	−0.0512	−0.0563	−0.0619	−0.0681	−0.0749	−0.0824	−0.0906	−0.0997	−0.0997
IFCI	−0.017	−0.0187	−0.02057	−0.0226	−0.0249	−0.0274	−0.0302	−0.0331	0
IWCI	−0.006	−0.0066	−0.00726	−0.008	−0.0088	−0.0097	−0.0106	−0.0117	0
OFC	0.0908	0.0999	0.10997	0.1209	0.133	0.1462	0.161	0.1770	0.2218

$$\frac{0.0908}{1.1008}+\frac{0.0999}{(1.1008)^2}+\frac{0.10997}{(1.1008)^3}+\frac{0.1209}{(1.1008)^4}+\frac{0.133}{(1.1008)^5}+\frac{0.1462}{(1.1008)^6}+\frac{0.161}{(1.1008)^7}+\frac{0.177}{(1.1008)^8}+\frac{0.2218/0.1008}{(1.1008)^8}$$

Discounted cash flows:

0.0825 + 0.0824 + 0.0824 + 0.0823+ 0.0823 + 0.0822 + 0.0822 + 0.0821 + 1.0205 = £1.6789m

Shareholder value = £1.6789m − £1.8m
= −£0.1211m

Chapter 17

3 314p

4 240p

Chapter 18

6 a $6.1 \times 0.4 + 14.5 \times 0.6 = 11.14$
40% debt, 60% equity

9 WACC = $30 \times 0.4 + 9 \times 0.6$
= 17.4%

Chapter 19

8 a $g = 7.46$
$P_0 = 155\text{p}$

		Discounted
b	$d_1 = 4\text{p}$	3.54
	$d_2 = 4\text{p}$	3.13
	$d_3 = 10\text{p}$	6.93
	$P_3 = \frac{d_4}{K-g} = \frac{10(1.09)}{0.13-0.09} = 272.5$	188.86
		202.46

Answer 202p.
Therefore the sacrifice of short-term dividends is worth while.

c Issues to be discussed: signalling, information asymmetry, clientele effects and residual theory.

Chapter 20

6 a 4.667 shares

b 4.444 shares

Chapter 21

1 A possible hedging strategy:
Purchase 20 June 450 put options and hold to expiry.

If share price falls to 400p:

Loss on shares	£1 × 20,000	20,000
Gain on options	50p × 20,000	10,000
Less Option premium		3,800
		£6,200

Overall loss £13,800

If share price rises to 600p:

Gain on shares	£1 × 20,000	20,000
Less Option premium		3,800
Overall gain		£16,200

2 a £520 loss
b £520 – £520 = 0
c £800 – £520 = £280 profit

3

Option	*Intrinsic value*	*Time value*
700 call	32p	23.5p
750 call	0	28p
700 put	0	17.5p
750 put	18p	22p

In-the-money options: 700 call, 750 put.
Out-of-the-money options: 750 call, 700 put.

4 (i) Options loss £1,910 × 5 = £9,550

Futures:

Sold @ 5,086 × £10 × 5	= 254,300
Bought @ 5,500 × £10 × 5	= 275,000
Loss	£20,700

(ii) *Options*
Intrinsic value per option: 5,000 – 4,500 = 500

500 × £10 × 5	25,000
Less Option premium	9,550
Gain	£15,450

Futures	
Sold @ 5,086 × £10 × 5	254,300
Bought @ 4,500 × £10 × 5	225,000
Gain	£29,300

7 a

	£000s							
Day	*1*	*2*	*3*	*4*	*5*	*6*	*7*	*8*
Value of future	390	410	370	450	420	400	360	410
Initial margin	20	–	–	–	–	–	–	–
Variation margin	–10	20	–40	+80	–30	–20	–40	50
Accumulated profit (loss)	–10	+10	–30	+50	+20	0	–40	+10

10 a Red Wheel could sell 30 three-month sterling interest rate futures dated for December at 91.70.

b Rate of interest = 8.30%.
Gain on derivative: 91.70 – 90.00 = 170 ticks.
This exactly offsets the additional interest paid to the lender:
Gain on derivative: 170 × 12.50 × 30 = £63,750.
Loan interest above 8.3%:
£15m × 0.017 × $^{3}/_{12}$ = £63,750.

c Rate of interest = 8.30%.
Loss on derivative: 91.70 – 93.00 = 130 ticks.
130 × 12.50 × 30 = –£48,750.
Gain from interest rate being lower than 8.3%:
£15m × 0.013 × $^{3}/_{12}$ = £48,750.

Chapter 22

1 a £5,287.34

b ¥94,565,500

c ¥188,869,000

d £529.47

2 a

Expected income	A$10m
Actual income $^{11}/_{1.2}$	A$9.167m
Exchange rate loss	A$0.8333m

b

	A$10.0000m
A$10m $^{11}/_{1.05}$ =	A$10.4762m
Exchange rate gain	A$0.4762m

c Exporter agrees to deliver NZ$11m in six months to forward market counterparty. It will receive 11m/1.09 = A$10.09174m regardless of spot exchange rates in six months' time.

d See Chapter 22.

7 a $\frac{1 + 0.02}{1 + 0.04} \times 2 = \text{SFr}1.9615/£$

8 a $\frac{1 + 0.05}{1 + 0.07} \times 1.02 = \text{C\$}1.0009/\text{A\$}$

11 a Forward purchase of sterling

$$\frac{\text{Won } 1{,}507\text{m}}{1{,}450} = £1.03931\text{m}.$$

b Borrow in Won and exchange for sterling immediately.

Amount borrowed: $\frac{1{,}507\text{m}}{1.005}$ = Won 1,499.5m

Exchange: $\frac{1{,}499.5\text{m}}{1{,}507}$ = £995,023

In one month the lender is paid with the Won received from the customer.

c Won 7.5m.

GLOSSARY

'A' shares Usually shares which carry fewer or no votes are designated 'A' shares.

Abnormal return (residual) A return greater than the market return after adjusting for differences in systematic risk.

Absolute advantage A firm, body or country has an absolute advantage if it can obtain a benefit at a lower cost than other firms, bodies or countries.

Acceptance credit (bank bill) An institution (e.g. bank) commits itself to the payment of a sum of money in the future as stated in the acceptance credit document. The borrower is given this document in return for a promise to pay a sum on the maturity date to the institution. The acceptance credit can be sold in the discount market to obtain funds for the borrower.

Accounting rate of return A measure of project profitability. Profit divided by assets devoted to the project.

Additivity Able to add up.

Ageing schedule The total debtor figure is broken down to show how long invoices have been outstanding (remained unpaid).

Agency Acting for or in the place of another with his/her/their authority.

Agency costs Costs of preventing agents (e.g. managers) pursuing their own interests at the expense of their principals (e.g. shareholders). Examples include contracting costs and costs of monitoring. In addition there is the agency cost of the loss of wealth caused by the extent to which prevention measures have not worked and managers continue to pursue non-shareholder wealth goals.

Agent A person who acts for or in the place of another with that other person's authority.

Aggressive shares Shares having a beta value greater than 1.

Allocation of capital The mechanism for selecting a mixture of goods and services produced by a society.

Allocational efficiency of markets Efficiency in the process of allocating society's scarce resources between competing real investments.

Allotment In a new issue of shares, if more shares are demanded at the price than are available, they may be apportioned (allotted) between the applicants.

Alternative Investment Market (AIM) The lightly regulated market operated by the London Stock Exchange, focused particularly on smaller, less well-established companies.

American-style option An option which can be exercised by the purchaser at any time up to the expiry date.

Amortisation The repayment of a debt by a series of instalments.

Annual equivalent annuity (AEA) A regular annual amount which is equivalent, in present value terms, to another set of cash flows.

Annual percentage rate (APR) The true annual interest rate charged by a lender. It takes full account of the timing of payments of interest and principal.

Annuity An even stream of payments over a given period of time.

Arbitrage The act of exploiting price differences on the same instrument or similar securities by simultaneously selling the overpriced security and buying the underpriced security.

Arbitrage pricing theory (APT) A type of multi-factor model which relates return on securities to various non-diversifiable risk factors.The expected return on any risky security is a linear combination of these factors.

Arithmetic mean The average of a population equals the sum of the observations divided by the number of observation.

Asset-backed securities *See* Securitisation.

Asset liquidity The extent to which assets can be converted to cash quickly and at a low transaction cost.

Asset lock-up In a hostile takeover situation, the target sells to a friendly firm those parts of the business most attractive to the bidder.

Asset transformers Intermediaries who, by creating a completely new security – the intermediate security – mobilise savings and encourage investment. The primary security is issued by the ultimate borrower to the intermediary, who offers intermediate securities to the primary investors.

Asymmetric information One party in a negotiation or relationship is not in the same position as other parties, being ignorant of, or unable to observe, some information which is essential to the contracting and decision-making process.

At-the-money option The current underlying price is equal to the option exercise price.

Authorised share capital The maximum amount of share capital that a company can issue. The limit can be changed by a shareholder vote.

Average collection period (ACP) The average number of days it takes to collect debts from customers. The total debtors outstanding divided by the average daily sales.

Back office That part of a financial institution which deals with the settlement of contracts, accounting and management information processes.

Bad debts Debts that are unlikely to be paid.

Balance of payments A record of the payment for goods and services obtained by a country and other transfers of currency from abroad and the receipts for goods and services sold and other transfers of currency abroad. The balance on the current account (visible trade and invisible trade) is the difference between national income and national expenditure in the period. The capital account is made up of such items as the inward and outward flow of money for investment and international grants and loans.

Balloon repayment on a loan The majority of the repayment of a loan is made at or near the maturity date, with the final payment substantially larger than the earlier payments.

Bank for International Settlements (BIS) Controlled by central banks, the BIS was established to assist international financial co-ordination. It promotes international monetary co-ordination, provides research and statistical data, co-ordination and trusteeship for intergovernmental loans, and acts as a central bank for national central banks, accepting deposits and making loans.

Bank of England The central bank of the United Kingdom, responsible for monetary policy. It oversees the affairs of other financial institutions, issues banknotes and coins, manages the national debt and exchange rate, and is lender of last resort.

Bank of England index Shows the extent to which a currency has strengthened or weakened against sterling since 1990.

Barter To trade by exchanging one commodity for another, without the use of money.

Base case strategy A continuation of current strategy.

Base rate The reference rate of interest that forms the basis for interest rates on bank loans, overdrafts and deposit rates.

Basis point One-hundredth of 1 per cent, usually applied to interest rates.

Bearer bond The ownership of a bond is not recorded on a register. Possession of the bond is sufficient to receive interest, etc.

Benefit–cost ratio A measure of present value per £ invested. Benefit–cost ratio = Net present value divided by Initial outlay.

Beta This measures the systematic risk of a financial security. In the capital asset pricing model it is a measure of the sensitivity to market movements of a financial securities return, as measured by the covariance between returns on the asset and returns on the market portfolio divided by the variance of the market portfolio. In practice a proxy (e.g. FT-SE 100 index) is used for the market portfolio.

Bid premium The additional amount an acquirer has to offer above the pre-bid share price in order to succeed in a takeover offer.

Bid price The price at which a marketmaker will buy shares or a dealer in other markets will buy a security or commodity.

Bid-offer spread The difference between the marketmaker's buy and sell prices.

Bill of exchange A document which sets out a commitment to pay a sum of money at a specified point in time, e.g. an importer commits itself to paying a supplier. Bills of exchange may be discounted – sold before maturity for less than face value.

BIMBO A buy-in management buy-out. A combination of a management buy-out and a buy-in. Outside managers join forces with existing managers to take over a company, subsidiary or unit.

Black Monday 19 October 1987, the date of a large fall in stock market prices.

Black Wednesday 16 September 1992, a day of severe currency turbulence when sterling and the Italian lira devalued significantly and were forced to leave the exchange rate mechanism.

Bond A debt obligation with a long-term maturity, usually issued by firms and governments.

Bonus issue *See* Scrip issue.

Book-building A book runner invites major institutional investors to suggest how many shares they would be interested in purchasing and at what price in a new issue or secondary issue of shares. This helps to establish the price and allocate shares.

Book-to-market equity ratio The ratio of a firm's balance sheet value to the total market value of its shares.

Book value Balance sheet value.

Bootstrapping game *See* Price-earnings ratio game.

Borrowing capacity Limits to total borrowing levels imposed by lenders, often determined by available collateral.

Bought deal An investment bank buys an entire security issue (e.g. shares) from a client corporation raising finance. The investment bank usually intends to then sell it out to institutional clients within hours.

Break-even analysis Analysing the level of sales at which a project, division or business produced a zero profit (accounting emphasis).

Break-even NPV The extent to which a single variable can change before the NPV of a proposed project switches from positive to negative (or vice versa).

Broker Assists in the buying and selling of financial securities by acting as a 'go-between', helping to reduce search and information costs.

Bubble An explosive upward movement in financial security prices not based on fundamentally rational factors, followed by a crash.

Budget (national) Sets out government expenditure and revenue for the financial year. In the UK it is presented by the Chancellor of the Exchequer to the British Parliament.

Buffer stock Stock held to reduce the negative effects (stock-out costs) of an unusually large usage of stock.

Building society A UK financial institution, the primary role of which is the provision of mortgages. Building societies are non-profit-making mutual organisations. Funding is mostly through small deposits by individuals.

Bulldog A foreign bond issued in the UK.

Bullet bond A bond where all the principal on a loan is repaid at maturity.

Business angels Wealthy individuals prepared to invest between £10,000 and £100,000 in a start-up, early-stage or developing firm. They often have managerial and/or technical experience to offer the management team as well as equity and debt finance. Medium- to long-term investment in high-risk situation.

Business risk The risk associated with the underlying operations of a business. The variability of the firm's operating income, before interest income: this dispersion is caused purely by business-related factors and not by the debt burden.

Cadbury report The Committee on the Financial Aspects of Corporate Governance chaired by Sir Adrian Cadbury made recommendations on the role of directors and auditors, published in 1992.

Call option This gives the purchaser the right, but not the obligation, to buy a fixed quantity of a commodity, financial instrument or some other underlying asset at a given price, at or before a specified date.

Cap An interest rate cap is a contract that effectively gives the purchaser the right to set a maximum level for interest rates payable. Compensation is paid to the purchaser of a cap if interest rates rise above an agreed level.

Capital asset pricing model (CAPM) An asset pricing theory which assumes that financial assets, in equilibrium, will be priced to produce rates of return which compensate investors for systematic risk as measured by the covariance of the assets' return with the market portfolio return.

Capital budgeting The process of selecting long-term capital investments.

Capital gearing The extent to which the firm's total capital is in the form of debt.

Capital lease *See* Leasing.

Capital market line (CML) The set of risk-return combinations available by combining the market portfolio with risk-free borrowing or lending.

Capital rationing When funds are not available to finance all wealth-enhancing (positive NPV) projects.

Capitalisation An item of expenditure is taken on to the balance sheet and capitalised as an asset rather than written off against profits.

Capitalisation issue *See* Scrip issue.

Capitalisation rate Required rate of return for the class of risk.

Capped bonds The floating interest rate charged cannot rise above a specified level.

Cartel A group of firms entering into an agreement to set mutually acceptable prices for their products.

Cash-conversion cycle The stock-conversion period plus the debtor-conversion period minus the credit period granted by suppliers. It focuses on the length of time between the company's outlay on inputs and the receipt of money from the sale of goods.

Cash cow A company with low growth and stable market conditions with low investment needs. The company's competitive strength enables it to produce surplus cash.

Cash settlement Many derivatives are cash settled, meaning that the underlying is not delivered but a cash payment is made, calculated as the difference between the exercise price and the price of the underlying at expiry.

Central bank A banker's bank and lender of last resort, which controls the credit system of an economy, e.g. controls note issue, acts as the government's bank, controls interest rates and regulates the country's banking system.

Certificate of deposit (CD) A deposit is made at a bank and the certificate that a deposit has been made is given in return to the lender. This is normally a bearer security. The CD can then be sold in the secondary market whenever a firm needs cash.

CHAPS (Clearing House Automated Payment System) The UK same-day interbank clearing system for sterling payments.

Characteristic line The line that best relates the return on a share to the return on a broad market index.

Chartist Investment analysts that rely on historic price charts (and/or trading volumes) to predict future movements.

Chasing the trend Buying financial securities after a recent upward trend in prices and selling after a recent downward trend.

Chicago Board of Trade (CBOT) The futures and options exchange in Chicago, USA – the world's oldest (established 1848).

Chicago Board Options Exchange (CBOE) The largest options exchange in the world, trading options on shares, indices and interest rates.

Chicago Mercantile Exchange (CME) An exchange which trades a wide range of currency futures and options, interest rate futures and options, commodity futures and options, and share index futures and options.

CHIPS (Clearing House Interbank Payment System) The US system for US dollar payment between banks.

City Code on Takeovers and Mergers Provides the main governing rules for companies engaged in merger activity. Self-regulated and administered by the Takeover Panel.

City of London A collective term for the financial institutions located in the financial district to the east of St Paul's Cathedral in London (also called the Square Mile). However, the term is also used to refer to all financial institutions, wherever they are located.

Clawback Existing shareholders often have the right to reclaim shares sold under a placing as though they were entitled to them under a rights issue.

Clearing bank Member of the London Bankers' Clearing House, which clears cheques, settling indebtedness between two parties.

Clearing house An institution which settles mutual indebtedness between a number of individuals or organisations. The clearing house may also act as a counterparty.

Clientele effects In dividend theory the level of dividend may be influenced by shareholders preferring a dividend pattern which matches their consumption pattern or tax position.

Coefficient of determination, R-squared For single linear regression this is the proportion of variation in the dependant variable that is related to the variation in the independent variable.

Collateral Property pledged by a borrower to protect the interests of the lender.

Commercial bill (bank bill or trade bill) A document expressing the commitment of a borrowing firm to repay a short-term debt at a fixed date in the future.

Commercial paper (CP) An unsecured note promising the holder (lender) a sum of money to be paid in a few days – average maturity of 40 days. If they are denominated in foreign currency and placed outside of the jurisdiction of the authorities of that currency then the notes are euro-commercial paper.

Commitment fee A fee payable in return for a commitment by a bank to lend money.

Common stock The term used in the USA to describe ordinary shares in a company.

Companies Acts The series of laws enacted by Parliament governing the establishment and conduct of incorporated business enterprises. The Companies Act 1985 consolidated the Acts that preceded it.

Companies House The place where records are kept of every UK company. These accounts, etc. are then made available to the general public.

Comparative advantage A firm or a country has a comparative advantage in the production of good X if the opportunity cost of producing a unit of X, in terms of other goods forgone, is lower, in that country compared with another country, or in that firm compared with another firm.

Competition Commission The Commission may obtain any information needed to investigate possible monopoly anti-competitive situations referred to it.

Competitive position The competitive strength of the firm *vis-à-vis* rivals in a product market.

Compound interest Interest is paid on the sum which accumulates, whether or not that sum comes from principal or from interest received.

Concert party A group of investors, acting together or under the control of one person, which buys shares in a company.

Conflict of preferences There is a conflict of preferences between the primary investors wanting low-cost liquidity and low risk on invested funds, and the ultimate borrowers wanting long-term risk-bearing capital.

Conglomerate bank A bank with a wide range of activities, products and markets.

Conglomerate merger The combining of two firms which operate in unrelated business areas.

Consumer price index (CPI) The main US measure of general inflation.

Contractual theory Views the firm as a network of contracts, actual and implicit, which specify the roles to be played by various participants. Most participants bargain for low risk and a satisfactory return. Shareholders accept high risk in anticipation of any surplus returns after all other parties have been satisfied.

Controlling shareholder One with 30 per cent or more of the voting capital, or any shareholder able to control the composition of the board of directors.

Conventional cash flows Where an outflow is followed by a series of inflows, or a cash inflow is followed by a series of cash outflows.

Conversion premium The difference between the current share price and the conversion price, expressed as a percentage of the current share price for convertible bonds.

Conversion price The share price at which convertible bonds may be converted.

Conversion ratio The nominal (par) value of a convertible bond divided by the conversion price. The number of shares available per bond.

Conversion value The value of a convertible bond if it were converted into ordinary shares at the current share price.

Convertible bonds Bonds which carry a rate of interest and give the owner the right to exchange the bonds at some stage in the future into ordinary shares according to a prearranged formula.

Corporate broker Knowledgeable about the share and other financial markets. Advises companies on fund raising (e.g. new issues). Tries to generate interest amongst investors for the company's securities. Stands prepared to buy and sell companies' shares.

Corporate raider An organisation that makes hostile takeover approaches for quoted companies.

Corporate value The present value of cash flows within the planning horizon plus the present value of cash flows after the planning horizon.

Corporate venturing Large companies fostering the development of smaller enterprises through, say, joint capital development or equity capital provision.

Corporation tax A tax levied on the profits of companies.

Correlation coefficient A measure of the extent to which two variables show a relationship, expressed on a scale of -1 to $+1$.

Cost leadership strategy Standard no-frills product. Emphasis on scale economics and other cost advantages.

Cost of capital The rates of return that a company has to offer finance providers to induce them to buy and hold a financial security.

Counterparty The buyer for a seller or the seller for a buyer.

Counterparty risk The risk that a counterparty to a contract defaults and does not fulfil obligations.

Coupons An attachment to a bond or loan notes document which may be separated and serve as evidence of entitlement to interest. Nowadays it refers to the interest itself.

Covariance The extent to which two variables move together.

Covenant A solemn agreement.

Creative accounting The drawing up of accounts which obey the letter of the law and accounting body rules but which involve the manipulation of accounts to show the most favourable profit and balance sheet.

Credit period The average length of time between the purchase of inputs and the payment for them. Equal to the average level of creditors divided by the purchases on credit per day.

Credit rating An estimate of the quality of a debt from the lender viewpoint in terms of the likelihood of interest and capital not being paid and of the extent to which the lender is protected in the event of default. Credit rating agencies are paid fees by companies, governments, etc. wishing to attract lenders.

Credit risk The risk that a counterparty to a financial transaction will fail to fulfil their obligation.

Credit union A non-profit organisation accepting deposits and making loans, operated as a co-operative.

Creditor One to whom a debt is owed.

Crest An electronic means of settlement and registration of shares following a sale on the London Stock Exchange.

Crown jewels defence In a hostile merger situation, the target sells off the most attractive parts of the business.

Cum-rights Shares bought on the stock market prior to the ex-rights day are designated cum-rights and carry to the new owner the right to subscribe for the new shares in the rights issue (used as a substitute for the market portfolio).

Currency swop *See* Swop.

Current ratio The ratio of current liabilities to the current assets of a business.

Cyclical industries Those industries in which profits are particularly sensitive to the growth level in the economy, which may be cyclical.

Darling A stock market darling is one which receives a lot of attention and is regarded as very attractive.

Data-snooping Data-snooping occurs when a given set of data is used more than once for purposes of inference or model selection. This leads to the possibility that any results obtained in a statistical study may simply be due to chance rather than to any merit inherent in the method yielding the results.

Dawn raid An acquirer acts with such speed in buying the shares of the target company that the raider achieves the objective of a substantial stake in the target before its management has time to react.

Debentures Bonds issued with redemption dates a number of years into the future. Usually secured against specific assets (mortgage debentures) or through a floating charge on the firm's assets.

Debt capital Capital raised with (usually) a fixed obligation in terms of interest and principal payments.

Debtor conversion period The average number of days to convert customer debts into cash. Equal to the average value of debtors divided by the average value of sales per day.

Debtors Those who owe a debt.

Deep discounted rights issue A rights issue price is much less than the present market price of the old shares.

Default A failure to make agreed payments of interest or principal.

Defensive industries Those industries where profits are not particularly sensitive to the growth level in the economy.

Defensive shares Having a beta value of less than 1.

Deferred ordinary shares Rank below preferred ordinary shares for dividends.

Dematerialisation Traditionally the evidence of financial security ownership is by written statements on paper (e.g. share certificates). Increasingly such information is being placed on electronic records and paper evidence is being abandoned.

Demerger The separation of companies or business units that are currently under one corporate umbrella. It applies particularly to the unravelling of a merger.

Depository receipts Certificates, representing evidence of ownership of a company's shares held by a depository. They can be bought and sold.

Derivative A financial asset, the performance of which is based on (derived from) the behaviour of the value of an underlying asset. A financial instrument.

Deutsche Börse AG – DTB Deutsche Terminbörse (DTB) The German derivatives market, which merged with the central stock exchange in 1994.

Differentiation strategy The unique nature of the product/service offered allows for a premium price to be charged.

Diminishing marginal utility After some point, successive equal increments in the quantity of a good yield smaller and smaller increases in utility.

Direct foreign investment The purchase of commercial assets such as factories and industrial plant for productive purposes.

Disclosure of shareholdings If a stake of 3 per cent or more is held by one shareholder in a UK public company, then this has to be declared to the company.

Discount (a) The amount below face-value at which a financial claim sells, e.g. bill of exchange or zero coupon bond. (b) The extent to which an investment trust's shares sell below the net asset value. (c) The amount by which a future value of a currency is less than its spot value. (d) The action of purchasing financial instruments, e.g. bills, at a discount. (e) The degree to which a security sells below its issue price in the secondary market.

Discount house An institution that purchases promissory notes and resells them or holds them until maturity.

Discount market deposit Money deposited with a London discount house. Normally repayable at call or very short term. Clearing banks are the usual depositors.

Discounted cash flow Future cash flows are converted into the common denominator of time zero money by adjusting for the time value of money.

Discounted payback The period of time required to recover initial cash outflow when the cash inflows are discounted at the opportunity cost of capital.

Disintermediation Borrowing firms bypassing financial institutions and obtaining debt finance directly from the market.

Diversifiable risk *See* Unsystematic risk.

Diversification To invest in varied projects, enterprises, financial securities, etc.

Divestiture To remove assets from a company or individual.

Dividend The profit paid to ordinary shareholders, usually on a regular basis.

Dividend cover The number of times net profits available for distribution exceed the dividend actually paid or declared. Earnings per share *divided by* Gross dividend per share *or* Total post-tax profits *divided by* Total dividend payout.

Dividend policy The determination of the proportion of profits paid out to shareholders, usually periodically.

Dividend valuation models (DVM) These methods of share valuation are based on the premise that the market value of ordinary shares represents the sum of the expected future dividend flows, to infinity, discounted to present value.

Divisible projects It is possible to undertake a fraction of a project.

Divorce of ownership and control In large corporations shareholders own the firm but may not be able to exercise control. Managers often have control because of a diffuse and divided shareholder body, proxy votes and apathy.

Dominance When one (investment) possibility is clearly preferable to a risk-averse investor because it possesses a better expected return than another possibility for the same level of risk.

Dow theory A method of predicting share price trends by identifying primary trends from historic share price data.

Drawdown arrangement A loan facility is established and the borrower uses it (takes the money available) in stages as the funds are required.

Early-settlement discount The reduction of a debt owed if it is paid at an early date.

Early-stage capital Funds for initial manufacturing and sales for a newly formed company. High-risk capital available from entrepreneurs, business angels and venture capital funds.

Earn-out The purchase price of a company is linked to the future profits performance. Future instalments of the purchase price may be adjusted if the company performs better or worse than expected.

Earnings per share Profit after tax and interest divided by number of shares in issue.

EASDAQ (European Association of Securities Dealers Automated Quotation) A Europe-wide stock exchange aimed at innovative, young and fast-growing companies.

Economic book value A term used by Stern Stewart and Co. It is based on the balance sheet capital employed figure subject to a number of adjustments.

Economic order quantity (EOQ) The quantity of inventory items (e.g. raw material) to order on each occasion which minimises the combined costs of ordering and holding stock.

Economic profit (EP) For a period the economic profit is the amount earned by a business after deducting all operating expenses and a charge for the opportunity cost of the capital employed.

Economic risk The risk that a company's economic value may decline as a result of currency movements causing a loss in competitive strength.

Economic value added (EVA) Developed by Stern Stewart and Co. A value-based metric of corporate performance which multiplies the invested capital (after adjustments) by the spread between the (adjusted) actual return on capital and the weighted cost of capital. The adjustments are to the profit figures to obtain the actual return and to the balance sheet to obtain the invested capital figure.

Economies of scale Larger size of output often leads to lower cost per unit of output.

Ecu (European currency unit) A composite of European Union (EU) member states' currencies weighted by the member state's share of EU output.

Efficiency frontier (efficient set, efficient-boundary) The range of expected return and standard deviation combinations available from portfolios of assets, all of which are efficient portfolios.

Efficient portfolio A portfolio that offers the highest expected return for a given level of risk (standard deviation) and the lowest risk for its expected return.

Efficient stock market Prices rationally reflect available information. The efficient market hypothesis (EMH) implies that new information is incorporated into a share price (a) rapidly, and (b) rationally. In an efficient market no trader will be presented with an opportunity for making an abnormal return, except by chance.

Electronic funds transfer at a point of sale (EFTPOS) A computerised system allowing the automatic transfer of money from a buyer to a seller of goods or services at the time of sale.

Emerging markets Security markets in newly industrialising countries with capital markets at an early stage of development.

Employee share ownership plans (ESOP) Schemes designed to encourage employees to build up a shareholding in their company.

Endowment policies Insurance policies in which a lump sum is payable, either at the end of the term of the policy or on death during the term of the policy.

Endowment saving schemes Life assurance schemes with the additional feature of a huge lump sum payment at the end of a period, should the policyholder survive. One important use is for the repayment of house mortgages.

Enterprise investment scheme (EIS) Tax relief is available to investors in qualifying company shares (unquoted firms not involved in financial investment and property).

Enterprise value The sum of a company's total equity market capitalisation and borrowings.

Entrepreneur Defined by economists as the owner-manager of a firm. Usually supplies capital, organises production, decides on strategic direction and bears risk.

Equitisation An increasing emphasis placed on share (equity) finance and stock exchanges in economies around the world. A growing equity culture.

Equity kicker (sweetener) The attachment of some rights to participate in and benefit from a good performance (e.g. exercise option to purchase shares), to a bond or other debt finance. Used with mezzanine finance.

Equity-linked bonds *See* Convertible bonds.

Euro The name of the new single European currency.

Euro medium-term notes (EMTN) *See* Medium-term note.

Euro-commercial paper *See* Commercial paper.

Euro-security markets Informal (unregulated) markets in money held outside the jurisdiction of the country of origin.

Eurobond Bond sold outside the jurisdiction of the country in whose currency the bond was denominated.

Eurocurrency Currency held outside its country of origin.

Eurocurrency banking Transactions in a currency other than the host country's currency.

Eurodollar A deposit or credit dollars held outside of the regulation of the US authorities.

European exchange rate mechanism (ERM) A system set up by members of the European Union which restricts the movement of the currencies of those member states belonging to the system.

European Monetary Union (EMU) A single currency with a single central bank having control over interest rates being created for those EU member states which join. The process of moving towards a monetary union began in 1999.

European-style options Options which can only be exercised by the purchaser on a predetermined future date.

Eurozone Those countries that joined together in adopting the euro as their currency.

Event risk The risk that some future event may increase the risk on a financial investment, e.g. an earthquake event affects returns on Japanese bonds.

Ex-ante Intended, desired or expected before the event.

Ex-post The value of some variable after the event.

Ex-rights When a share goes 'ex-rights' any purchaser of a share after that date will not have a right to subscribe for new shares in the rights issue.

Ex-rights price of a share The theoretical market price following a rights issue.

Exchange controls The state controls the purchase and sale of currencies by its residents.

Exchange rate The price of one currency expressed in terms of another.

Execution-only brokers A stockbroker who will buy or sell shares cheaply but will not give advice or other services.

Exercise price (strike price) The price at which an underlying will be bought (call) or sold (put) under an option contract.

Exit The term used to describe the point at which a venture capitalist can recoup some or all of the investment made.

Exotic A term used to describe an unusual financial transaction, e.g. exotic option, exotic currency (i.e. one with few trades).

Expansion capital Companies at a fast-development phase needing capital to increase production capacity, working capital and capital for the further development of the product or market. Venture capital is often used.

Expectations hypothesis of the term structure of interest rates (yield curve) Long-term interest rates reflect the market consensus on the changes in short-term interest rates.

Expectations theory of foreign exchange The current forward exchange rate is an unbiased predictor of the spot rate at that point in the future.

Expected return The mean or average outcome calculated by weighting each of the possible outcomes by the probability of occurrence and then summing the result.

Expiry date of an option The time when the rights to buy or sell the option cease.

External finance Outside finance raised by a firm, i.e. finance that it did not generate internally, for example through profits retention.

External metrics Measures of corporate performance which are accessible to individuals outside the firm and concern the performance of the firm as a whole.

Factor model A model which relates the returns on a security to that security's sensitivity to the movements of various factors (e.g. GDP growth, inflation) common to all shares.

Factor risk/Non-factor risk A factor risk is a systematic risk in multi-factor models describing the relationship between risk and return for fully diversified investors. Non-factor risk is unsystematic risk in multi-factor models.

Factoring To borrow against the security of trade debtors. Factoring companies also provide additional services such as sales ledger administration and credit insurance.

Fair game In the context of a stock market it is where some investors and fund raisers are not able to benefit at the expense of other participants. The market is regulated to avoid abuse, negligence and fraud. It is cheap to carry out transactions and the market provides high liquidity.

Fallen angel Debt which used to rate as investment grade but which is now regarded as junk, mezzanine finance, or high-yield finance.

Filter approach to investment A technique for examining shares using historic price trends. The trader focuses on the long-term trends by filtering out short-term movements.

Final dividend A dividend payable after the year-end.

Finance house A financial institution offering to supply finance in the form of hire purchase, leasing and other forms of instalment credit.

Finance lease (also called **capital lease** or **full payout lease**) The lessor expects to recover the full cost (or almost the full cost) of the asset plus interest, over the period of the lease.

Financial assets (securities) Contracts that state agreement about the exchange of money in the future.

Financial distress Obligations to creditors are not met or are met with difficulty.

Financial gearing (leverage) *See* Gearing.

Financial risk The additional variability in a firm's returns to shareholders which arises because the financial structure contains debt.

Financial Services Authority (FSA) The chief financial services regulator in the UK, established in 1997.

Financial slack Having cash (or near-cash) and/or spare debt capacity available to take up opportunities as they appear.

Financing gap The gap in the provision of finance for medium-sized, fast-growing firms. Often these firms are too large or fast growing to ask the individual shareholders for more funds or to obtain sufficient bank finance. Also they are not ready to launch on the stock market.

Finished goods inventory period The number of days for which finished goods await delivery to customers. Equal to the average value of finished goods in stock divided by the average goods sold per day.

Fisher's equation The money rate of return m is related to the real rate of return h and the expected inflation rate i through the following equation: $(1 + m) = (1 + h)(1 + i)$.

Five-day rolling settlement The transfer and payment for most shares traded on the London Stock Exchange is now completed in five days through the Crest settlement system.

Fixed charge (e.g. **fixed charged debenture or loan**) A specific asset(s) is assigned as collateral security for a debt.

Fixed exchange rate The national authorities act to ensure that the rate of exchange between two currencies is constant.

Fixed-interest securities Securities such as bonds on which the holder receives a predetermined interest pattern on the par value (e.g. gilts, corporate bonds, eurobonds).

Fixed-rate borrowing (fixed interest) The interest rate charge is constant throughout the period of the loan.

Flat rate The rate of interest quoted by a hire purchase company (or other lender) to a hiree which fails to reflect properly the true interest rate being charged as measured by the annual percentage rate (APR).

Flat yield *See* Yield.

Float The difference between the cash balance shown on a firm's chequebook and the bank account. Caused by delays in the transfer of funds between bank accounts.

Floating charge The total assets of the company or an individual are used as collateral security for a debt.

Floating exchange rate A rate of exchange which is not fixed by national authorities but fluctuates depending on demand and supply for the currency.

Floating rate notes (FRNs) Notes issued in which the coupon fluctuates according to a benchmark interest rate charge (e.g. LIBOR). Issued in the Euromarkets generally with maturities of 7 to 15 years. Reverse floaters: the interest rate declines as LIBOR rises.

Floating-rate borrowing (floating interest) The rate of interest on a loan varies with a standard reference rate, e.g. LIBOR.

Floor An agreement whereby, if interest rates fall below an agreed level, the seller (floor writer) makes compensatory payments to the floor buyer.

Flotation The issue of shares in a company for the first time on a stock exchange.

Focus strategy The selection of a segment in the industry to serve to the exclusion of others.

Foreign banking Transactions in the home currency with non-residents.

Foreign bond A bond denominated in the currency of the country where it is issued when the issuer is a non-resident.

Foreign exchange control Limits are placed by a government on the purchase and sale of foreign currency.

Foreign exchange markets (Forex or **FX)** Markets that facilitate the exchange of one currency into another.

Forex A contraction of 'foreign exchange'.

Forfeiting A bank purchases a number of sales invoices or promissory notes from an exporting company; usually the importer's bank guarentees the invoices.

Forward A contract between two parties to undertake an exchange at an agreed future date at a price agreed now.

Forward-rate agreement (FRA) An agreement about the future level of interest rates. Compensation is paid by one party to the other to the extent that market interest rates deviate from the 'agreed' rate.

Founders' shares Dividends are paid only after all other categories of equity shares have received fixed rates of dividend.

Free float The proportion of a quoted company's shares not held by those closest (e.g. directors, founding families) to the company who may be unlikely to sell their shares.

Frequency function (probability or **frequency distribution)** The organisation of data to show the probabilities of certain values occurring.

Friendly mergers The two companies agree to the merger.

Friendly Society A mutual (co-operative) organisation involved in saving and lending.

FT-SE Actuaries All-Share Index (the 'All-Share') The most representative index of UK shares, reflecting over 900 companies' shares.

FTSE International (*Financial Times* and the London Stock Exchange) This organisation calculates a range of share indices published on a regular (usually daily) basis.

Full-payout lease *See* Leasing.

Fund management Investment of and administering a quantity of money, e.g. pension fund, insurance fund, on behalf of the fund's owners.

Fundamental analysts Individuals that try to estimate a share's true value, based on future returns to the company.

Fundamental beta An adjustment to the risk premium on the average share, developed by Barr Rosenburg and others, which amalgamates a number of operating and financial characteristics of the specific company being examined.

Future A contract between two parties to undertake a transaction at an agreed price on a specified future date.

Gearing (financial gearing) The proportion of debt capital in the overall capital strucutre. Also called leverage.

Gearing (operating) The extent to which the firm's total costs are fixed. This influences the break-even point and the sensitivity of profits to changes in sales level.

General inflation The process of steadily rising prices resulting in the diminishing purchasing power of a given nominal sum of money. Measured by an overall price index which follows the price changes of a 'basket' of goods and services through time.

General insurance Insurance against specific contingencies, e.g. fire, theft and accident.

Geometric mean The geometric mean of a set of *n* positive numbers is the *n*th root of their product. The compound rate of return.

Gilts (gilt-edged securities) Fixed-interest UK government securities (bonds) traded on the London Stock Exchange. A means for the UK government to raise finance from savers. They usually offer regular interest and a redemption amount paid years in the future.

Globalisation The increasing internationalisation of trade, particularly financial product transactions. The integration of economic and capital markets throughout the world.

Goal congruence The aligning of the actions of senior management with the interests of shareholders.

Golden handcuffs Financial inducements to remain working for a firm.

Golden parachutes In a hostile merger situation, managers will receive large pay-offs if the firm is acquired.

Golden shares Shares with extraordinary special powers over the company, e.g. power of veto over a merger.

Good growth When a firm grows by investment in positive performance-spread activities.

Grace period A lender grants the borrower a delay in the repayment of interest and/or principal at the outset of a lending agreement.

Greenbury report Recommendations on corporate governance.

Greenmail Key shareholders try to obtain a reward (e.g. the repurchase of their shares at a premium) from the company for not selling to a hostile bidder or becoming a bidder themselves.

Greenshoe An option that permits an issuing house, when assisting a corporation in a new issue, to sell more shares than originally planned. They may do this if demand is particularly strong.

Gross dividend yield

$$\frac{\text{Gross (before tax) dividend per share}}{\text{Share price}} \times 100$$

Gross domestic product A measure of the total flow of goods and services produced by an economy over a specified time period, normally a year.

Gross present value The total present value of all the cash flows, excluding the initial investment.

Growth industries Those industries which grow almost regardless of the state of the economy.

Guaranteed equity bonds Investment products which promise a stock market linked return if the market rises, and the return of the original capital if the stock market falls.

Guaranteed loan stock An organisation other than the borrower guarantees to the lender the repayment of the principal plus the interest payment.

Hampel report A follow-up to the Cadbury and Greenbury reports on corporate governance. Chaired by Sir Ronald Hampel and published in 1998.

Hard capital rationing Agencies external to the firm will not supply unlimited amounts of investment capital, even though positive NPV projects are identified.

Hard currency A currency traded in a foreign exchange market for which demand is persistently high.

Head and shoulders formation A chartists' (technical analysts) share price pattern in which the chart line forms the appearance of a shoulder followed by a head (a rise in price to a peak, followed by a fall) and then another shoulder.

Hedging Reducing or eliminating risk by undertaking a countervailing transaction.

Herstatt risk In 1974 the German bank Herstatt was closed by the Bundesbank. It had entered into forex transactions and received deutschmarks from counterparties in European time, but had not made the corresponding transfer of US dollars to its counterparties in New York time. It is the risk that arises when forex transactions are settled in different time zones.

High-yield share A share with high dividends relative to its price.

High-yield debt *See* Mezzanine finance *or* Junk bonds.

Hire-purchase (HP) The user (hiree) of goods pays regular instalments of interest and principal to the hire-purchase company over a period of months. Full ownership passes to the hiree at the end of the period (the hiree is able to use the goods from the outset).

Holding period returns Total holding period returns on a financial asset consist of (a) income, e.g. dividend paid, and (b) capital gain – a rise in the value of the asset.

Homemade dividends Shareholders creating an income from shareholdings by selling a portion of their shareholding.

Horizontal merger The two companies merging are engaged in similar lines of activity.

Hostile merger The target (acquired) firm's management is opposed to the merger.

Hubris Overweaning self-confidence.

Hurdle rate The required rate of return. The opportunity cost of the finance provider's money. The hurdle rate can be compared with the internal rate of return to make a decision on the shareholder value potential of a project.

Impact day The day during the launch of a new issue of shares when the price is announced, the prospectus published and offers to purchase solicited.

Income gearing The proportion of the annual income streams (i.e. pre-interest profits) devoted to the prior claims of debt holders. The reciprocal of income gearing is the interest cover.

Income yield *See* Yield.

Incorporation The forming of a company, including the necessary legal formalities.

Incremental fixed capital investment Investment in fixed assets which adds to the stock of assets and does not merely replace worn-out assets.

Independent variables The two variables are completely unrelated; there is no co-movement.

Index option An option on a share index, e.g. FTSE 100 or Standard and Poor's 500.

Index trackers Collective investment funds (e.g. unit trusts) which try to replicate a stock market index rather than to pick winners in an actively managed fund.

Indifference curve Alternative combinations of two goods, or one good and one bad (e.g. return on investment and risk of that investment) which are equally acceptable to the investor. That is, the alternatives provide the same level of utility.

Individual Savings Account (ISA) A special savings account with special tax privileges. The saver can invest savings in cash deposits, shares or insurance products.

Indivisible project With some projects it is impossible to take a fraction, e.g. shipbuilding. All or nothing options are presented.

Industry attractiveness The economics of the market for the product(s).

Inflation The process of prices rising.

Informed investors Those that are highly knowledgeable about financial securities and the fundamental evaluation of their worth.

Initial margin An amount that a derivative contractor has to provide to the clearing house when first entering upon a derivative contract.

Initial public offering (IPO) The offering of shares in the equity of a company to the public for the first time.

Inland Revenue The principal tax-collecting authority in the UK.

Insider trading (dealing) Trading shares, etc. on the basis of information not in the public domain.

Instalment credit A form of finance to pay for goods or services over a period through the payment of principal and interest in regular instalments.

Institutional neglect Share analysts, particularly at the major institutions, may fail to spend enough time studying small firms, preferring to concentrate on the larger 100 or so.

Institutionalisation The increasing tendency for organisational investing, as opposed to individuals investing money in securities (e.g. pension funds and investment trusts collect the savings of individuals to invest in shares).

Insurable risk Risk that can be transferred through the payment of premiums to insurance companies.

Interbank brokers Brokers in the forex markets who act as intermediaries between buyers and sellers. They provide anonymity to each side.

Interbank sterling The money market in which banks borrow and lend sterling among themselves.

Interest cover The number of times the income of a business exceeds the interest payments made to service its loan capital.

Interest rate parity (IRP) of exchange rate determination The interest rate parity theory holds true when the difference between spot and forward exchange rates is equal to the differential between interest rates available in the two currencies.

Interest rate risk The risk that changes in interest rates will have an adverse impact.

Interest rate swop *See* Swop.

Interest yield *See* Yield.

Interim dividend A dividend related to the first half-year's trading.

Interim profit reports A statement giving unaudited profit figures for the first half of the financial year, shortly after the end of the first half-year.

Intermediaries offer A method of selling shares in the new issue market. Shares are offered to financial institutions such as stockbrokers. Clients of these intermediaries can then apply to buy shares from them.

Intermediate debt *See* Mezzanine finance *or* Junk bonds.

Internal metrics Measures of corporate performance available to those inside the company. They can be used at the corporate, SBU or product line level.

Internalisation of transactions By bringing together two firms at different stages of the production chain in a vertical merger, an acquirer may achieve more efficient co-ordination of the different levels.

International Monetary Market (IMM) The part of the Chicago Mercantile Exchange which specialises in currency and eurodollar futures.

International Petroleum Exchange (IPE) The energy futures and options exchange in London.

International Securities Market Association (ISMA) A self-regulatory organisation designed to promote orderly trading and the general development of the Euromarkets.

In-the-money option An option with intrinsic value. The current underlying price is more than the option exercise price.

Intrinsic value (company) The discounted value of the cash that can be taken out of a business during its remaining life.

Intrinsic value (options) The payoff that would be received if the underlying is at its current level when the option expires.

Introduction A company with shares already quoted on another stock exchange, or where there is already a wide spread of shareholders, may be introduced to the market. This allows a secondary market in the shares.

Investment grade debt Debt with a sufficiently high credit rating to be regarded as safe enough for some institutional investors.

Investment Management Regulatory Organisation (IMRO) The self-regulatory organisation in the UK for managers of pooled investments, e.g. unit trusts, pension funds.

Investors in Industry (3i) The largest venture capital investor in unquoted companies in Europe.

Invoice An itemised list of goods shipped, usually specifying the terms of sale and price.

Invoice discounting Separate (or a select few of) invoices are pledged to a finance house in return for an immediate payment of up to 80 per cent of the face value.

IOU A colloquialism intended to mean 'I owe you'. The acknowledgement of a debt.

Irredeemable Financial securities with no fixed maturity date at which the principal is repaid.

Irrelevancy of the dividend proposition (by Modigliani and Miller) If a few assumptions can be made, dividend policy is irrelevant to share value.

Issued share capital That part of a company's share capital that has been subscribed by shareholders, either paid up or partially paid up.

Issuing house *See* Sponsor.

Joint stock enterprise The capital is divided into small units, permitting a number of investors to contribute varying amounts to the total. Profits are divided between stockholders in proportion to the number of shares they own.

Junior debt *See* Subordinated debt.

Junk bonds Low-quality, low credit-rated company bonds. Rated below investment grade. Risky and with a high yield.

Just-in-time stock holding Materials and work-in-progress are delivered just before they are needed and finished goods are produced just before being sent to customers.

Lagging The postponement of a payment beyond the due date.

Laissez-faire The principle of the non-intervention of government in economic affairs.

Lead manager In a new issue of securities (e.g. shares, bonds, syndicated loans) the lead manager controls and organises the issue. There may be joint lead managers, co-managers and regional lead managers.

Lead time The delay between placing an order with a supplier and the order being delivered.

Leading The bringing forward from the original due date of the payment of a debt.

Leasing The owner of an asset (lessor) grants the use of the asset to another party (lessee) for a specified period in return for regular rental payments. The asset does not become the property of the lessee at the end of the specified period. *See also* Finance lease; Operating lease.

Leveraged buyout (LBO) The acquisition of a company, subsidiary or unit by another, financed mainly by borrowings.

Leveraged recapitalisations The financial structure of the firm is altered in such a way that it becomes highly geared.

LIBOR (London Interbank Offered Rate) The rate of interest offered on loans to highly rated (low-risk) banks in the London interbank market for a specific period (e.g. three months). Used as a reference rate for other loans.

Life cycle stage of value creation The longevity of competitive advantage and favourable industry economies can be represented in terms of a life cycle with four stages: development, growth, maturity and decline. In the early stages superior long-term value performance is expected because of a sustainable competitive advantage and favourable long-term industry economics.

Life insurance Insurance against death. Beneficiaries receive payment upon death of the policyholder or other person named in the policy. Endowment policies offer a savings vehicle as well as cover against death.

LIFFE (London International Financial Futures and Options Exchange) The main derivatives exchange in London.

Limited companies (Ltd) 'Private' companies with no minimum amount of share capital, but with restrictions on the range of investors who can be offered shares. They cannot be quoted on the London Stock Exchange.

Limited liability The owners of shares in a business have a limit on their loss, set as the amount they have committed to invest in shares.

Liquidity The degree to which an asset can be sold quickly and easily without loss in value.

Liquidity risk The risk that an organisation may not have, or may not be able to raise, cash funds when needed.

Liquidity-preference hypothesis of the term structure of interest rates The yield curve is predominately upward sloping because investors require an extra return for lending on a long-term basis.

Listed companies Those on the Official List of the London Stock Exchange.

Loan stock A fixed-interest debt financial security. May be unsecured.

Local authority deposits Lending money to a UK local government authority.

London Metal Exchange (LME) Trades metals (e.g. lead, zinc, tin, aluminium and nickel) in forward and option markets.

London Stock Exchange (LSE) The London market in which securities are bought and sold.

London Traded Option Market (LTOM) Options exchange which merged with LIFFE in 1992.

Long form report A report by accountants for the sponsor of a company being prepared for flotation. The report is detailed and confidential. It helps to reassure the sponsors when putting their name to the issue and provides the basis for the short form report included in the prospectus.

Long position A positive exposure to a quantity. Owning a security or commodity; the opposite of a short position (selling).

Lowest common multiple (LCM) method Alternative regularly recurring projects are compared over a period of years, the period being equal to the lowest common multiple of the cycle length of the projects.

Low-grade debt *See* Mezzanine finance *or* Junk bonds.

Mainstream corporate tax (MCT) Tax paid by UK companies nine months after the end of the company's financial year.

Management buy-in (MBI) A new team of managers makes an offer to a company to buy the whole company, a subsidiary or a section of the company, with the intention of taking over the running of it themselves. Venture capital often provides the major part of the finance.

Management buyout (MBO) A team of managers makes an offer to its employers to buy a whole business, a subsidiary or a section so that the managers own and run it themselves. Venture capital is often used to finance the majority of the purchase price.

Managerialism Operating the firm for the benefit of managers, pursuing objectives attractive to the management team but which are not necessarily beneficial to the shareholders.

Marché à Terme d'Instruments Financiers (MATIF) The French futures and options exchange.

Market capitalisation The total value at market prices of the shares in issue for a company (or a stock market, or a sector of the stock market).

Market in managerial control Teams of managers compete for control of corporate assets, e.g. through merger activity.

Market index A sample of shares is used to represent a share (or other) market's level and movements.

Market portfolio A portfolio which contains all assets. Each asset is held in proportion to the asset's share of the total market value of all the assets. A proxy for this is often employed, e.g. the FTSE 100 index.

Market power The ability to exercise some control over the price of the product.

Market risk *See* Systematic risk.

Market segmentation hypothesis of the term structure of interest rates The yield curve is created (or at least influenced) by the supply and demand conditions in a number of sub-markets defined by maturity range.

Market to book ratio (MBR) The market value of a firm divided by capital invested.

Market value added The difference between the total amount of capital put into a business by finance providers (debt and equity) and the current market value of the company's shares and debts.

Marking to market The losses or gains on a derivative contract are assessed daily in reference to the value of the underlying price.

Matador A foreign bond issued in Spain.

Matching The company matches the inflows and outflows in different currencies covered by trade, etc., so that it is only necessary to deal on the currency markets for the unmatched portion of the total transactions.

Matching principle The maturity structure of debt matches the maturity of projects or assets held by the firm. Short-term assets are financed by short-term debt and long-term assets are financed by long-term debt.

Maturity date The time when a financial security (e.g. a bond) is redeemed and the par value is paid to the lender.

Maturity structure The profile of the length of time to the redemption and repayment of a company's various debts.

Maturity transformation Intermediaries offer securities with liquid characteristics to induce primary investors to purchase or deposit funds. The money raised is made available to the ultimate borrowers on a long-term, illiquid basis.

Maximisation of long-term shareholder wealth The assumed objective of the firm in finance. It takes into account the time value of money and risk.

Mean (a) arithmetic mean: a set of numbers are summed, and the answer is divided by the number of numbers; (b) geometric mean: calculated as the *n*th root of the product of *n* number, e.g. the geometric mean of 2 and 5 is $\sqrt{2 \times 5} = \sqrt{10} = 3.16$.

Mean-variance rule If the expected return on two projects is the same but the second has a higher variance (or standard deviation), then the first will be preferred. Also, if the variance on the two projects is the same but the second has a higher expected return, the second will be preferred.

Medium-term note (MTN) A document setting out a promise from a borrower to pay the holders a specified sum on the maturity date and, in many cases, a coupon interest in the meantime. Maturity can range from nine months to 30 years. If denominated in a foreign currency, they are called Euro medium-term notes.

Merchant banks Financial institutions that carry out a variety of financial services, usually excluding high street banking.

Merger The combining of two business entities under common ownership.

Metric Method of measurement.

Mezzanine finance Unsecured debt or preference shares offering a high return with a high risk. Ranked behind secured debt but ahead of equity. It may carry an equity kicker.

Mobilisation of savings The flow of savings primarily from the household sector to the ultimate borrowers to invest in real assets. This process is encouraged by financial intermediaries.

Model Code for Directors' Dealings London Stock Exchange rules for directors dealing in shares of their own company.

Modified internal rate of return (MIRR) The rate of return which equates the initial investment with a project's terminal value, where the terminal value is the future value of the cash inflows compounded at the required rate of return (the opportunity cost of capital).

Money cash flow All future cash flows are expressed in the prices expected to rule when the cash flow occurs.

Money market Wholesale (large amounts) financial markets in which lending and borrowing on a short-term basis takes place (< 1 year).

Money rate of return The rate of return which includes a return to compensate for inflation.

Moral hazard The presence of a safety net (e.g. insurance policy) encourages adverse behaviour (e.g. carelessness).

Multi-period capital rationing Capital constraints are imposed in more than one period to restrict the acceptance of positive NPV projects.

Mutual exclusivity If one is taken, the other cannot be.

Mutual funds A collective investment vehicle the shares of which are sold to investors – a very important method of investing in shares in the USA.

NASDAQ (National Association of Securities Dealers Automated Quotation System) A series of computer-based information services and an order execution system for the US over-the-counter securities (e.g. share) market.

National savings Lending to the UK government through the purchase of bonds, and placing money into savings accounts.

Near-cash (near-money) Highly liquid financial assets but which are generally not usable for transactions and therefore cannot be fully regarded as cash.

Negotiability (1) Transferable to another – free to be traded in financial markets. (2) Capable of being settled by agreement between the parties involved in a transaction.

Net asset value (NAV) Fixed assets, plus stocks, debtors, cash and other liquid assets, minus long- and short-term creditors.

Net operating cash flow Profit before depreciation, less periodic investment in net working capital.

Net present value The present value of the expected cash flows associated with a project after discounting at a rate which reflects the value of the alternative use of the funds.

Netting When subsidiaries in different countries settle intra-organisational currency debts for the net amount owed in a currency rather than the gross amount.

New issue The sale of securities, e.g. debentures or shares, to raise additional finance or to float existing securities of a company on a stock exchange for the first time.

Newstrack A small company news service and a place where J.P. Jenkins posts share prices for companies trading on Ofex.

Nikkei Stock Average A share index based on the prices of 225 shares quoted on the Tokyo Stock Exchange.

Noise trading Uniformed investors buying and selling financial securities at irrational prices, thus creating noise (strange movements) in the price of securities.

Nominated adviser (Nomad) Each company on the AIM has to retain a nomad. They act as quality controllers, confirming to the London Stock Exchange that the company has complied with the rules.

Nominated brokers Each company on the AIM has to retain a nominated broker, who helps to bring buyers and sellers together and comments on the firm's prospects.

Non-executive director A director without day-to-day operational responsibility for the firm.

Note (promissory note) A financial security with the promise to pay a specific sum of money by a given date, e.g. commercial paper, floating rate notes. Usually unsecured.

Objective probability A probability that can be established theoretically or from historical data.

Ofex An unregulated share market operated by broker J.P. Jenkins.

Off-balance-sheet finance Assets are acquired in such a way that liabilities do not appear on the balance sheet, e.g. some lease agreements permit the exclusion of the liability in the accounts.

Offer for sale A method of selling shares in a new issue. The company sponsor offers shares to the public by inviting subscriptions from investors. (a) Offer for sale by fixed price – the sponsor fixes the price prior to the offer. (b) Offer for sale by tender – investors state the price they are willing to pay. A strike price is established by the sponsors after receiving all the bids. All investors pay the strike price.

Offer for subscription A method of selling shares in a new issue. The issue is aborted if the offer does not raise sufficient interest from investors.

Offer price The price at which a marketmaker in shares will sell a share, or a dealer in other markets will sell a security or asset.

Office of Fair Trading The Director-General of Fair Trading has wide powers to monitor and investigate trading activities and to refer monopoly or anti-competitive situations to the Competition Commission (often via the President of the Board of Trade).

Official List (OL) The daily list of securities admitted for trading on the London Stock Exchange. It does not include securities traded on the Alternative Investment Market (AIM).

One-period capital rationing When limits are placed on the availability of finance for positive NPV projects for one year only.

Open interest The sum of outstanding long and short positions in a given futures or option contract.

Open offer New shares are sold to a wide range of external investors (not existing shareholders).

Open outcry Where trading is through oral calling of buy and sell offers by market members.

Open-ended investment companies (OEIC) Collective investment vehicles with one price for investors. OEICs are able to issue more shares if demand increases from investors, unlike investment trusts. OEICs invest the finance raised in securities, primarily shares.

Operating gearing *See* Gearing.

Operating lease The lease period is significantly less than the expected useful life of the asset.

Operational efficiency of a market The cost to buyers and sellers of transactions in securities on the exchange.

Opportunity cost The value forgone by opting for one course of action; the next best use of, say, financial resources.

Opportunity cost of capital The return that is sacrificed by investing finance in one way rather than investing in an alternative of the same risk class, e.g. financial security.

Opportunity set (feasibility set) All the possible expected return and standard deviation combinations available from the construction of portfolios from a given set of assets.

Optimal portfolio A portfolio which provides the highest possible utility, given the constraints imposed by the opportunity set and efficiency frontier.

Option A contract giving one party the right, but not the obligation, to buy or sell a financial instrument, commodity or some other underlying asset at a given price, at or before a specified date.

Option premium The amount paid by an option purchaser (holder) to obtain the rights under an option contract.

Order-driven trading system Buy and sell orders for securities are entered on a central computer system, and investors are automatically matched according to the price and volume they entered (also called matched bargain systems).

Ordinary shares The equity capital of the firm.The holders of ordinary shares are the owners and are therefore entitled to all distributed profits after the holders of debentures and preference shares have had their claims met.

Organic growth Growth from within the firm rather than through mergers.

Out-of-the-money option An option with no intrinsic value.

Overdraft A permit to overdraw on an account (e.g. a bank account) up to a stated limit; to take more out of a bank account than it contains.

Overhead The business expenses not chargeable to a particular part of the work or product.

Oversubscription In a new issue of securities investors offer to buy more securities (e.g. shares) than are made available.

Over-the-counter trade (OTC) Securities trading carried on outside regulated exchanges. Allows tailor-made transactions.

Overtrading When a business has insufficient finance to sustain its level of trading. A business is said to be overtrading when it tries to engage in more business than the investment in working capital will allow. This can happen even in profitable circumstances.

PacMan defence In a hostile merger situation the target makes a counter bid for the bidder.

Par value (nominal or face value) A stated nominal value of a share or bond. Not related to market value.

Partnership An unincorporated business formed by the association of two or more persons who share the risk and profits.

Pathfinder prospectus In a new issue of shares a detailed report on the company is prepared and made available to potential investors a few days before the issue price is announced.

Payback The period of time it takes to recover the initial cost of a project.

Pecking order theory of financial gearing Firms exhibit preferences in terms of sources of finance. The most acceptable source of finance is retained earnings, followed by borrowing and then by new equity issues.

Pension funds These manage money on behalf of members to provide a pension upon the member's retirement. Most funds invest heavily in shares.

Pension holiday When a pension fund does not need additional contributions for a time, it may grant the contributors, e.g. companies and/or members, a break from making payments.

Perfect hedge Eliminates risk.

Perfect market The following assumptions hold: (a) there is a large number of buyers; (b) there is a large number of sellers; (c) the quantity of goods bought by any individual transactor is so small relative to the total quantity traded that individual trades leave the market price unaffected; (d) the units of goods sold by different sellers are the same – the product is homogeneous; (e) there is perfect information – all buyers and all sellers have complete information on the prices being asked and offered in other parts of the market; and (f) there is perfect freedom of entry to and exit from the market.

Performance spread The percentage difference between the actual rate of return on an investment and the required rate given its risk class.

Perpetuity A regular sum of money received at intervals forever.

Personal equity plan (PEP) Personal investment vehicle with tax advantages. Directed mostly to encourage investment in quoted shares.

Personal investment authority (PIA) The UK self-regulatory body responsible for insurance brokers, independent investment advisers and the marketing of pooled investment products.

Philadelphia Stock Exchange (PHLX) The first stock exchange in the USA. Trades shares, index options, more than 290 equity options and currency options.

Physical delivery Settlement of a futures contract by delivery of the underlying.

Placing A method of selling shares and other financial securities in the primary market. Securities are offered to the sponsors' or brokers' private clients and/or a narrow group of institutions.

Planning horizon The point in the future after which an investment will earn only the minimum acceptable rate of return.

Poison pills Actions taken, or which will be taken, which make a firm unpalatable to a hostile acquirer.

Portfolio investment Investment made (usually in another country) in bonds and shares. An alternative form of foreign investment is direct investment, buying commercial assets such as factory premises and industrial plant.

Portfolio optimiser A computer program designed to select an optimal portfolio in terms of risk and return.

Portfolio planning Allocating resources to those SBUs and product/customer areas offering the greatest value creation, while withdrawing capital from those destroying value.

Post-completion audit The monitoring and evaluation of the progress of a capital investment project through a comparison of the actual cash flows and other benefits with those forecast at the time of authorisation.

Precautionary motive for holding cash This arises out of the possibility of unforeseen needs for cash for expenditure in an unpredictable environment.

Pre-emption rights The strong right of shareholders of UK companies to subscribe for further issues of shares. *See* Rights Issue.

Preference share These normally entitle the holder to a fixed rate of dividend but this is not guaranteed. Holders of preference shares precede the holders of ordinary shares, but follow bond holders and other lenders in payment of dividends and return of principal. **Participating preference share**: share in residual profits. **Cumulative preference share**: share carries forward the right to preferential dividends. **Redeemable preference share**: a preference share with a finite life. **Convertible preference share**: may be converted into ordinary shares.

Preferred ordinary shares Rank higher than deferred ordinary shares for an agreed rate of dividend.

Preliminary profit announcements (prelims) After the year-end and before the full reports and accounts are published, a statement on the profit for the year and other information is provided by companies quoted on the London Stock Exchange.

Present value Future cash flow is discounted to time zero.

Preservation approach to merger integration Little is changed in the acquired firm in terms of culture, systems or personnel. General management skills might be transferred from the parent along with strict financial performance yardsticks and demanding incentive schemes.

Press Collective name for newspapers and periodicals.

Price-earnings ratio (PER) Share price divided by earnings per share.

Price-earnings ratio game (bootstrapping) Companies increase earnings per share by acquiring other companies with lower price-earnings ratios than themselves. Share price can rise despite the absence of economic value gain.

Primary investors The household sector contains the savers in society who are the main providers of funds used for investment in the business sector.

Primary market A market in which securities are initially issued.

Principal (a) The capital amount of a debt, excluding any interest. (b) A person acting for their own purposes accepting risk in financial transactions, rather than someone acting as an agent for another.

Principal–agent problem In which an agent, e.g. a manager, does not act in the best interests of the principal, e.g. the shareholder.

Privatisation The sale to private investors of government-owned equity (shares) in nationalised industries or other commercial enterprises.

Profitability index A measure of present value per pound invested.

Project appraisal The assessment of the viability of proposed long-term investments in terms of shareholder wealth.

Project finance Finance assembled for a specific project. The loan and equity returns are tied to the cash flows and fortunes of the project rather than being dependent on the parent company/companies.

Proprietary transactions A financial institution, as well as acting as an agent for a client, may trade on the financial markets with a view to generating profits for itself, e.g. speculation on forex.

Prospectus A document containing information about a company, to assist with a new issue (initial public offering).

Provisions Sums set aside in accounts for anticipated loss or expenditure.

Proxy votes Shareholders unable to attend a shareholders' meeting may authorise another person, e.g. a director or the chairman, to vote on their behalf, either as instructed or as that person sees fit.

Public limited company (Plc) A company which may have an unlimited number of shareholders and offer its shares to the wider public (unlike a limited company). Must have a minimum share value of £50,000. Some Plcs are listed on the London Stock Exchange.

Purchasing power parity (PPP) theory of exchange rate determination Exchange rates will be in equilibrium when their domestic purchasing powers at that rate of exchange are equivalent.

Put option This gives the purchaser the right, but not the obligation, to sell a financial instrument, commodity or some other underlying asset at a given price, at or before a specified date.

Quick ratio (acid test) The ratio of current assets, less stock, to total current liabilities.

Quota Quantitative limits placed on the importation of specified goods.

Quote-driven trading system Marketmakers post bid and offer prices on a computerised system.

Random walk theory The movements in (share) prices are independent of one another; one day's price change cannot be predicted by looking at the previous day's price change.

Ranking (debt) Order of precedence for payment of obligations. Senior debt receives annual interest and redemption payments ahead of junior (or subordinated) debt. So, if the company has insufficient resources to pay its obligation the junior debt holders may receive little or nothing.

Rappaport's value drivers The seven key factors which determine value are: (1) Sales growth rate. (2) Operating profit margin. (3) Tax rate. (4) Incremental fixed capital investment. (5) Incremental working capital investment. (6) The planning horizon. (7) The required rate of return.

Raw materials stock period The average number of days raw materials remain unchanged and in stock. Equal to the average value of raw materials stock divided by the average purchase of raw materials per day.

Real assets Assets used to carry on a business. These assets can be tangible or intangible.

Real cash flows Future cash flows are expressed in terms of constant purchasing power.

Real option An option to undertake different courses of action in the real asset market (strategic and operational options), as opposed to an option on financial securities or commodities.

Real rate of return The rate that would be required in the absence of inflation.

Recapitalisation A change in the financial structure, e.g. in debt/equity ratio.

Receiver A receiver takes control of a business if a debtor successfully files a bankruptcy petition. The receiver may then sell the company's assets and distribute the proceeds among the creditors.

Recognised investment exchange (RIE) A body authorised to regulate securities trading in the UK, e.g. the London Stock Exchange.

Recourse If a financial asset is sold (such as a trade debt), the purchaser could return to the vendor for payment in the event of non-payment by the borrower.

Redemption The repayment of the principal amount, or par value, of a security (e.g. bond) at the maturity date.

Redemption yield *See* Yield.

Registrar An organisation that maintains a record of share ownership for a company. It also communicates with shareholders on behalf of the company.

Relationship banking A long-term, intimate and relatively open relationship is established between a corporation and its banks. Banks often supply a range of tailor-made services rather than one-off services.

Rembrandt A foreign bond issued in The Netherlands.

Repayment holiday *See* Grace period.

Residual theory of dividends Dividends should only be paid when the firm has financed all its positive NPV projects.

Resistance line A line drawn on a price (e.g. share) chart showing the market participants' reluctance to push the price below (or above) the line over a period of time.

Resolution of uncertainty theory of dividends The market places a greater value on shares offering higher near-term dividends because these are more certain than more distant dividends.

Retail banking Banking for individual customers or small firms, normally for small amounts. High-volume/low-value banking.

Retail service provider (RSP) Marketmakers were renamed RSPs in 1997 when the new order-driven trading system SETS was introduced.

Return on capital employed (ROCE); return on equity (ROE); return on investment (ROI) Traditional measures of profitability. Profit returns divided by the volume of resources devoted to the activity. *See also* Accounting rate of return.

Reverse floating rate notes *See* Floating rate notes.

Revolving credit An arrangement whereby a borrower can draw down short-term loans as the need arises, to a maximum over a period of years.

Revolving underwriting facility (RUF) A bank underwrites the borrower's access to funds at a specified rate in the short-term financial markets throughout an agreed period.

Rights issue An invitation to existing shareholders to purchase additional shares in the company in proportion to their existing holdings.

Risk A future return has a variety of possible values. Sometimes measured by standard deviation.

Risk averter Someone who prefers a more certain return to an alternative with an equal return but which is more risky.

Risk lover (seeker) Someone who prefers a more uncertain alternative to an alternative with an equal but less risky outcome.

Risk management The selection of those risks a business should take and those which should be avoided or mitigated, followed by action to avoid or reduce risk.

Risk transformation Intermediaries offer low-risk securities to primary investors to attract funds, which are then used to purchase higher-risk securities issued by the ultimate borrowers.

Risk-free rate of return (RFR) The rate earned on riskless investment, denoted $_{rf}$. A reasonable proxy is short-term lending to a reputable government.

Risk-return line A line on a two-dimensional graph showing all the possible expected returns, i.e. standard deviation combinations, available from the construction of portfolios from two assets. This can also be called the two-asset opportunity set or feasibility set.

Roadshow Companies and their advisers make a series of presentations to potential investors, usually to entice them into buying a new issue of securities.

Rolled-over overdraft Short-term loan facilities are perpetuated into the medium term and long term by the regular renewal of the facility.

RPI (retail price index) The main UK measure of general inflation.

R-squared, R^2 *See* Coefficient of determination.

Rule 4.2 Replaced rule 535.2 for a short period prior to the establishment of the Alternative Investment Market.

Rule 535.2 Under this rule stock exchange members were allowed to trade securities that were not on the Official List from the 1950s until 1994.

Running yield *See* Yield.

Sale and leaseback Assets (e.g. land and buildings) are sold to another firm (e.g. bank, insurance company) with a simultaneous agreement for the vendor to lease the asset back for a stated period under specific terms.

Sales ledger administration The management of trade debtors: recording credit sales, checking customer creditworthiness, sending invoices and chasing late payers.

Samurai bonds A foreign bond issued in Japan.

Satisficed When a contributor to an organisation is given just enough of a return to make their contribution, e.g. banks are given contracted interest and principal, and no more.

Scenario analysis An analysis of the change in NPV brought about by the simultaneous change in a number of key inputs to an NPV analysis. Typically a 'worst case scenario', when all the changes in variables are worsening, and a ' best case scenario', when all the variable changes are positive, are calculated.

Scrip dividends Shareholders are offered the alternative of additional shares rather than a cash dividend.

Scrip issue The issue of more shares to existing shareholders according to their current holdings.

SEAQ (Stock Exchange Automated Quotation System) A computer screen-based quotation system for securities where marketmakers on the London Stock Exchange report bid-offer prices and trading volumes, and brokers can observe prices and trades.

SEAQI (Stock Exchange Automated Quotation International) A computer screen-based quotation system for securities that allows marketmakers in international shares based on the London Stock Exchange to report prices, quotes and trading volumes.

SEATS plus (Stock Exchange Alternative Trading Service) A London Stock Exchange system for trading less liquid securities where there is either a single, or no, marketmaker. Displays marketmaker prices and/or current public orders.

Secondary market Securities already issued are traded between investors.

Securities and Exchange Commission (SEC) The US federal body responsible for the regulation of securities markets (exchanges, brokers, investment advisers, etc.).

Securities and Futures Authority (SFA) The UK regulatory body for dealing in securities (e.g. shares), financial futures, commodity futures and international bonds.

Securities and Investment Board (SIB) Until 1997 the chief regulator of financial services in the UK.

Securities house This may mean simply an issuing house. However, the term is sometimes used more broadly for an institute concerned with buying and selling securities or acting as agent in the buying and selling of securities.

Securitisation Financial payments (e.g. a claim to a number of mortgage payments) which are not tradable can be repackaged into other securities (e.g. a bond) and then sold. These are called asset-backed securities.

Security (1) A financial asset, e.g. a share or bond. (2) Asset pledged to be surrendered in the event of a loan default.

Security market line (SML) A linear (straight) line showing the relationship between systematic risk and expected rates of return for individual assets (securities). According to the capital asset pricing model the return above the risk-free rate of return or a risky asset is equal to the risk premium for the market portfolio multiplied by the beta coefficient.

Seedcorn capital The financing of the development of a business concept. High risk; usually provided by venture capitalists, entrepreneurs or business angels.

Self-regulation Much of the regulation of financial services in the UK is carried out by self-regulatory organisations (SROs), i.e. industry participants regulate themselves through organisations such as the Securities and Futures Authority.

Semi-annual Twice a year at regular intervals.

Semi-strong efficiency Share prices fully reflect all the relevant, publicly available information.

Senior debt *See* Subordinated debt.

Sensitivity analysis An analysis of the effect on project NPV of changes in the assumed values of key variables, e.g. sales level, labour costs. Variables are changed one at a time. It is a 'what-if' analysis, e.g. what if raw material costs rise by 20 per cent?

Separation theorem The choice of the optimal portfolio (the market portfolio) is made by all investors and is separate from the risk/return choice which is determined by the extent to which the investor lends or borrows at the risk-free rate. Applied to the capital asset pricing model.

Sequence A computerised share trading platform introduced by the London Stock Exchange in 1996.

SETS (Stock Exchange Electronic Trading Service) An electronic order book-based trading system for the London Stock Exchange. Brokers input buy and sell orders directly into the system. Buyers and sellers are matched and the trade executed automatically. In 1997 the system was used for the 100 largest UK shares and the Stock Exchange plans to increase the number of shares on SETS – eventually SEAQ might be completely replaced.

Settlement The completion of a transaction, e.g. upon expiry of a future, the underlying is delivered in return for a cash payment.

Settlement price The price calculated by a derivatives exchange at the end of each trading session as the closing price that will be used in determining profits and losses for the marking-to-market process for margin accounts.

Share market Institutions which facilitate the regulated sale and purchase of shares; includes the primary and secondary markets.

Share option scheme Employees are offered the right to buy shares in their company at a modest price some time in the future.

Share premium account A balance sheet entry represented by the difference between the price received by a company when it sells shares and the par value of those shares.

Share repurchase The company buys back its own shares.

Shareholder value analysis A technique developed by Rappaport for establishing value creation. It equals the present value of operating cash flows within the planning horizon *plus* the present value of operating cash flows after the planning horizon *plus* the current value of marketable securities and other non-operating investments *less* corporate debt.

Shareholder wealth maximisation The maximising of shareholders' purchasing power. In an efficient market, it is the maximisation of the current share price.

Short selling The selling of financial securities (e.g. shares) not yet owned, in the anticipation of being able to buy at a later date at a lower price.

Short-term interest rate future (colloquially known as **short sterling**) The three-month sterling interest rate future contract traded on LIFFE. Notional fixed-term deposits for three-month periods starting at a specified time in the future.

Short-termism A charge levelled at the financial institutions in their expectations of the companies to which they provide finance. It is argued that long-term benefits are lost because of pressure for short-term performance.

Sight bank account (current account) One where deposits can be withdrawn without notice.

Signalling Some financial decisions are taken as signals from the managers to the financial markets, e.g. an increase in gearing, or a change in dividend policy.

Simple interest Interest is paid on the original principal: no interest is paid on the accumulated interest payments.

Sinking fund Money is accumulated in a fund through regular payments in order eventually to repay a debt.

Small firm effect The tendency of small firms to give abnormally high returns.

Soft capital rationing Internal management-imposed limits on investment expenditure.

Solvency The ability to pay legal debts.

South Sea Bubble A financial bubble (*see* Bubble) in which the price of shares in the South Sea Company were pushed to ridiculously high levels on a surge of over-optimism in the early eighteenth century.

Special dividend An exceptionally large dividend paid on a one-off basis.

Special drawing rights (SDRs) A composite currency designed by the International Monetary Fund (IMF). Each IMF member country is allocated SDRs in proportion to its quota.

Specific inflation The price changes in an individual good or service.

Speculative motive for holding cash This means that unexpected opportunities can be taken immediately.

Speculators Those that take a position in financial instruments and other assets with a view to obtaining a profit on changes in their value.

Sponsor Lends its reputation to a new issue of securities, advises the client company (along with the issuing broker) and co-ordinates the new issue process. Sponsors are usually merchant banks or stockbrokers. Also called an issuing house.

Spot market A market for immediate transactions (e.g. spot forex market, spot interest market), as opposed to an agreement to make a transaction some time in the future (e.g. forward, option, future).

Stakeholder A party with an interest in an organisation, e.g. employees, customers, suppliers, the local community.

Standard deviation A statistical measure of the dispersion around an expected value. The standard deviation is the square root of the variance, σ^2.

Start-up capital Finance for young companies which have not yet sold their product commercially. High risk; usually provided by venture capitalists, entrepreneurs or business angels.

Statutory Established, regulated or imposed by or in conformity with laws passed by a legislative body, e.g. Parliament.

Stock exchange A market in which securities are bought and sold. In continental Europe the term bourse may be used.

Stock-out costs The cost associated with being unable to draw on a stock of raw material, work-in-progress or finished goods inventory (loss of sales, profits and goodwill, and also production dislocation).

Stocks and shares There is some lack of clarity on the distinction between stocks and shares. Shares are equities in companies. Stocks are financial instruments that pay interest, e.g. bonds. However, in the USA shares are also called 'common stocks' and the shareholders are sometimes referred to as the stockholders. So when some people use the term stocks they could be referring to either bonds or shares.

Straight bond One with a regular fixed rate of interest and without the right of conversion (to, say, shares).

Strategic business unit (SBU) A business unit within the overall corporate entity which is distinguishable from other business units because it serves a defined external market where management can conduct strategic planning in relation to products and markets.

Strategy Selecting which product or market areas to enter/exit and how to ensure a good competitive position in those markets/products.

Strategy planes chart Maps a firm's, SBU's or product line's position in terms of industry attractiveness, competitive advantage and life cycle stage of value potential.

Strike price (1) In the offer for sale by a tender it is the price which is chosen to sell the required quantity of shares given the offers made. (2) The price paid by the holder of an option when/if the option is exercised.

Strike price of an option *See* Exercise price.

Strong form efficiency All relevant information, including that which is privately held, is reflected in the share price.

Subjective probability Probabilities are devised based on personal judgement of the range of outcomes along with the likelihood of their occurrence.

Subordinated debt A debt which ranks below another liability in order of priority for payment of interest or principal. Senior debt ranks above junior debt for payment.

Sunk cost A cost the firm has incurred or to which it is committed that cannot be altered. This cost does not influence subsequent decisions and can be ignored in, for example, project appraisals.

Survivorship bias In empirical studies of share price performance the results may be distorted by focusing only on companies which survived through to the end of the period of study. Particularly poor performers (i.e. liquidated firms) are removed from the sample, thus biasing the results in a positive direction.

Swop An exchange of cash payment obligations. An interest rate swop is where one company arranges with a counterparty to exchange interest rate payments. In a currency swop the two parties exchange interest obligations (receipts) for an agreed period between two different currencies.

Swoption An option to have a swop at a later date.

Symbiosis type of post-merger integration Large differences between acquired and parent firms in culture, systems, etc., are maintained. However, collaboration in communications and the cross-fertilisation of ideas are encouraged.

Syndicated loan A loan made by one or more banks to one borrower.

Synergy A combined entity will have a value greater than the sum of the parts.

Systematic (Undiversifiable or **market) risk** That element of return variability from an asset which cannot be eliminated through diversification. Measured by beta. It comprises the risk factors common to all firms.

Takeover (acquisition) Many people use these terms interchangeably with merger. However, some differentiate takeover as meaning a purchase of one firm by another with the concomitant implication of financial and managerial domination.

Takeover Panel The committee responsible for supervising compliance with the City Code on Takeovers and Mergers.

Tariff Taxes imposed on imports.

Taxable profit That element of profit subject to taxation. This frequently differs from reported profit.

techMARK The London Stock Exchange launched techMARK in 1999. It is a subsection of the shares within the Official List. It is a grouping of technology companies. It imposes different rules on companies seeking a flotation from those which apply to the other companies on the Official List (e.g. only one year's accounts is required).

Technical analyst *See* Chartist.

Tender offer A public offer to purchase securities.

Term loan A loan of a fixed amount for an agreed time and on specified terms, usually with regular periodic payments. Most frequently provided by banks.

Term structure of interest rates The patterns of interest rates on bonds with differing lengths of time to maturity but with the same risk. Strictly it is the zero-coupon implied interest rate for different lengths of time. *See also* Yield curve.

Terminal value The forecast future value of sums of money compounded to the end of a common time horizon.

Third market A lightly regulated market in company shares introduced by the London Stock Exchange in 1987. Closed in 1989.

Tick The minimum price movement of a future or option contract.

Tier one ratio of core capital That part of a bank's capital defined as shareholders' equity plus irredeemable and non-cumulative preference shares.

Tiger economies The first four newly industrialised economies in Asia: Taiwan, South Korea, Singapore and Hong Kong (also referred to as dragon economies).

Time value That part of an option's value that represents the value of the option expiring in the future rather than now. The longer the period to expiry, the greater the chance that the option will become in-the-money before the expiry date.

Time value of money A pound received in the future is worth less than a pound received today – the value of a sum of money depends on the date of its receipt.

Total shareholder return (TSR) The total return earned on a share over a period of time: dividend per share plus capital gain divided by initial share price.

Trade credit Where goods and services are delivered to a firm for use in its production and are not paid for immediately.

Trade debtor A customer of a firm who has not yet paid for goods and services delivered.

Tradepoint A recognised investment exchange for shares established in the UK in 1995. A computer screen order-driven system of trading is used.

Traditional option An option available on any security but with an exercise price fixed as the market price on the day the option is bought. All such options expire after three months and cannot be sold to a secondary investor.

Transaction risk The risk that transactions already entered into, or for which the firm is likely to have a commitment in a foreign currency, will have a variable value in the home currency because of exchange rate movements.

Transactional banking Banks compete with each other to offer services at the lowest cost to corporations, on a service-by-service basis.

Transactional motive for holding cash Money is used as a means of exchange; receipts and payments are rarely perfectly synchronised and therefore an individual or business generally needs to hold a stock of money to meet expenditure.

Translation risk This risk arises because financial data denominated in one currency are then expressed in terms of another currency.

Treasury bill A short-term money market instrument issued (sold) by the central bank, mainly in the UK and USA, usually to supply the government's short-term financing needs.

Treasury management To plan, organise and control cash and borrowings so as to optimise interest and currency flows, and minimise the cost of funds. Also to plan and execute communications programmes to enhance investors' confidence in the firm.

Trust deed A document specifying the regulation of the management of assets on behalf of beneficiaries of the trust.

Trustees Those that are charged with the responsibility for ensuring compliance with the trust deed.

Tulipmania A seventeenth-century Dutch bubble. *See* Bubble.

Ultimate borrowers Firms investing in real assets need finance which ultimately comes from the primary investors.

Uncertainty Strictly (in economists' terms), uncertainty is when there is more than one possible outcome to a course of action; the form of each possible outcome is known, but the probability of getting any one outcome is not known. However, the distinction between risk (the ability to assign probabilities) and uncertainty has largely been ignored for the purposes of this text.

Unconditionality In a merger, once unconditionality is declared, the acquirer becomes obligated to buy. Target shareholders who accepted the offer are no longer able to withdraw their acceptance.

Unconventional cash flows A series of cash flows in which there is more than one change in sign.

Underlying The subject of a derivative contract.

Underwriters These (usually large financial institutions) guarantee to buy the proportion of a new issue of securities (e.g. shares) not taken up by the market, in return for a fee.

Undiversifiable risk *See* Systematic risk.

Uninformed investors Those that have no knowledge about financial securities and the fundamental evaluation of their worth.

Unit trust An investment organisation that attracts funds from individual investors by issuing units to invest in a range of securities, e.g. shares or bonds. It is open ended, the number of units expanding to meet demand.

Unlisted Securities Market (USM) A lower-tier (less stringently regulated) market for shares in London, which ceased in 1996.

Unsecured A financial claim with no collateral or any charge over assets of the borrower.

Unsystematic (unique or diversifiable) risk That element of an asset's variability in returns which can be eliminated by holding a well-diversified portfolio.

Utility The satisfaction, pleasure or fulfilment of needs derived from consuming some quantity of a good or service.

Valuation risk (price risk) The possibility that, when a financial instrument matures or is sold in the market, the amount received is less than anticipated by the lender.

Value action pentagon This displays the five actions for creating value: (1) Increase the return on existing capital. (2) Raise investment in positive spread units. (3) Divest assets from negative spread units to release capital for more productive use. (4) Extend the planning horizon. (5) Lower the required rate of return.

Value creation: four key elements The four key elements are: (1) Amount of capital invested. (2) Actual rate of return on capital. (3) Required rate of return. (4) Planning horizon (for performance-spread persistence).

Value creation profile An analysis of the sources of value creation within the firm from its products and market segments, which maps value creation against the proportion of capital invested.

Value creation quotient (VCQ) An external value metric developed by Rory Knight. The market value of equity and the balance sheet value of debt divided by the cumulative capital raised and retained (debt plus equity).

Value drivers Crucial organisational capabilities, giving the firm competitive advantage. Different from Rappaport value drivers.

Value investing The identification and holding of shares which are fundamentally undervalued by the market, given the prospects of the firm.

Value-based management A managerial approach in which the primary purpose is shareholder wealth maximisation. The objective of the firm, its systems, strategy, processes, analytical techniques, performance measurements and culture, have as their guiding objective shareholder wealth maximisation.

Vanilla bond *See* Straight bond.

Variable rate bond (loan) The interest rate payable varies with short-term rates (e.g. LIBOR six months).

Variation margin The amount of money paid after the payment of the initial margin required to secure an option or futures position, after it has been revalued by the exchange or clearing house.

Vendor placing Shares issued to a company to pay for assets, or issued to shareholders to pay for an entire company in a takeover are placed with investors keen on holding the shares in return for cash. The vendors can then receive the cash.

Venture capital (VC) Finance provided to unquoted firms by specialised financial institutions. This may be backing for an entrepreneur, financing a start-up or developing business, or assisting a management buyout or buy-in. Usually it is provided by a mixture of equity, loans and mezzanine finance. It is used for medium-term to long-term investment in high-risk situations.

Venture capital investment funds Standard investment trusts (without tax breaks) with a focus on more risky developing companies.

Venture capital trusts (VCTs) An investment vehicle introduced to the UK in 1995 to encourage investment in small and fast-growing companies. The VCT invests in a range of small businesses. The providers of finance to the VCT are given important tax breaks.

Vertical merger Where the two merging firms are from different stages of the production chain.

Volume transformation Intermediaries gather small quantities of money from numerous savers and repackage these sums into larger bundles for investment in the business sector or elsewhere.

Warrant A financial instrument which gives the holder the right to subscribe for a specified number of shares or bonds at a fixed price at some time in the future.

Weak form efficiency Share prices fully reflect all information contained in past price movements.

Weighted average cost of capital (WACC) The weighted average cost of capital (the discount rate) is calculated by weighting the cost of debt and equity in proportion to their contributions to the total capital of the firm.

White knight A friendly company which makes a bid for a company that is welcome to the directors of that target company, which is the subject of a hostile takeover bid.

Wholesale financial markets Markets available only to those dealing in large quantities. Dominated by interbank transactions.

Winner's curse In winning a merger battle, the acquirer suffers a loss in value because it overpays.

Withholding tax Taxation deducted from payments to non-residents.

Working capital The difference between current assets and current liabilities – net current assets or net current liabilities.

Working capital cycle Typically, investment in raw materials, work-in-progress and finished goods is followed by sales for cash or on credit. Credit sales funds are usually collected at a later date. Investment is needed at each stage to finance current assets. The cycle may be expressed in terms of the length of time between the acquisition of raw materials and other inputs and the flow of cash from the sale of goods.

Work-in-progress period The number of days to convert raw materials into finished goods. Equal to the average value of work-in-progress divided by the average cost of goods sold per day.

Writer of an option The seller of an option contract, granting the right but not the obligation to the purchaser.

Writing-down allowance (WDA) (capital allowance) Reductions in taxable profit related to a firm's capital expenditure (e.g. plant, machinery, vehicles).

Yankee A foreign bond issued in the USA.

Yield The income from a security as a proportion of its market price. The flat yield (interest yield, running yield and income yield) on a fixed interest security is the gross interest amount, divided by the current market price, expressed as a percentage. The redemption yield or yield to maturity of a bond is the discount rate such that the present value of all cash inflows from the bond (interest plus principal) is equal to the bonds current market price.

Yield curve A graph showing the relationship between the length of time to the maturity of a bond and the interest rate.

Z statistic A calculation of the number of standard deviations from the mean to the value of interest.

Zero cost option A combination of option purchase and option writing. The price of the written option (premium) is the same as the price (premium) paid for the option that is purchased, so the net cost is zero.

Zero coupon bond (preference share) A bond that does not pay regular interest (dividend) but instead is issued at a discount (i.e. below par value) and is redeemable at par, thus offering a capital gain.

BIBLIOGRAPHY

A review of monopolies and mergers policy: a consultative document (1978). London: HMSO, Cmnd. 7198 (Green Paper).

Abraham, A. and Ikenberry, D. (1994) 'The individual investor and the weekend effect', *Journal of Financial and Quantitative Analysis*, June.

Accounting Standards Committee (1984) *Accounting for leases and hire purchase contracts, SSAP 21*. London: Accounting Standards Committee.

Adedeji, A. (1997) 'A test of the CAPM and the three factor model on the London Stock Exchange', paper presented to the British Accounting Association Northern Accounting Group 1997 Annual Conference, 10 September 1997, Loughborough University.

Allen, D. (1991) 'The whiching hour has arrived', *Management Accounting*, November, pp. 48–53.

Altman, E.I. and Kao, D.L. (1992) 'Rating drift in high-yield bonds', *Journal of Fixed Income*, 1, March, pp. 15–20. Also reproduced in S. Lofthouse (ed.) (1994) *Readings in Investments*. New York: Wiley.

Ambrose, B.W. and Megginson, W.L. (1992) 'The role of asset structure, ownership structure, and takeover defences in determining acquisition likelihood', *Journal of Financial and Quantative Analysis*, 27 (4), pp. 575–89.

Anthony, R.N. (1960) 'The trouble with profit maximisation', *Harvard Business Review*, November–December, pp. 126–34.

Arnold, G. and Smith, M. (1999) *The European High Yield Bond Market: Drivers and Impediments*. London: *Financial Times* Finance Management Report.

Arnold, G.C. (1996) 'Equity and corporate valuation', in E. Gardener and P. Molyneux (eds) *Investment Banking: Theory and Practice*. 2nd edn. London: Euromoney.

Arnold, G.C. (1996) 'Risk management using financial derivatives', in E. Gardener and P. Molyneux (eds), *Investment Banking: Theory and Practice*. 2nd edn. London: Euromoney.

Arnold, G.C. (2000) 'Tracing the development of value-based management'. In Glen Arnold and Matt Davies, *Value-based Management: Context and Application*. London: Wiley.

Arnold, G.C. (2002) *Valuegrowth Investing*. London: FT Prentice Hall.

Arnold, G.C. and Davies, M. (eds) (2000), '*Value-Based Management*', London: Wiley.

Arnold, G.C. and Davis, P. (1995) *Profitability trends in West Midlands industries. A study for Lloyds Bowmaker*. Edinburgh: Lloyds Bowmaker.

Arnold, G.C. and Davis, P. (1996) *Profitability trends in East Midlands industries. A study for Lloyds Bowmaker.* Edinburgh: Lloyds Bowmaker.

Arnold, G.C. and Hatzopoulos, P.D. (2000) 'The theory-practice gap in capital budgeting: evidence from the United Kingdom', *Journal of Business Finance and Accounting*, 27(5) and (6), June/July, pp. 603–26.

Arya, A., Fellingham, J.C. and Glover, J.C. (1998) 'Capital budgeting: some exceptions to the net present value rule', *Issues in Accounting Education*, 13(3), August, pp. 499–508.

Association of Corporate Treasurers. *The Treasurer's Handbook*.

Atkins, A.B. and Dyl, E.A. (1993) 'Reports of the death of the efficient markets hypothesis are greatly exaggerated', *Applied Financial Economics*, 3, pp. 95–100.

Baba, N. and Kozaki, M. (1992) 'An intelligent forecasting system of stock prices using neural networks', *Proceedings of International Joint Conference on Neural Networks*. Baltimore, MD, vol. 1, pp. 371–7.

Ball, M., Brady, S. and Olivier, C. (1995) 'Getting the best from your banks', *Corporate Finance*, July, pp. 26–47.

Ball, R. (1995) 'The theory of stock market efficiency: accomplishments and limitations', *Journal of Applied Corporate Finance*, Winter and Spring, pp. 4–17.

Ball, R. and Brown, P. (1968) 'An empirical evaluation of accounting income numbers', *Journal of Accounting Research*, Autumn, pp. 159–78.

Ball, R. and Kothari, S.P. (1989) 'Nonstationary expected returns: Implications for tests of market efficiency and serial correlation in returns', *Journal of Financial Economics*, 25, pp. 51–94.

Ball, R., Kothari, S.P. and Shanken, J. (1995) 'Problems in measuring portfolio performance: an application to contrarian investment strategies', *Journal of Financial Economics*, 38, May, pp. 79–107.

Bank of England Quarterly Bulletin.

Bank for International Settlements Quarterly Review.

Banz, R. (1981) 'The relationship between return and market value of common stock', *Journal of Financial Economics*, 9, pp. 3–18.

Banz, R.W. and Breen, W.J. (1986) 'Sample-dependent results using accounting and market data: Some evidence', *Journal of Finance*, 41, pp. 779–93.

Barclays Capital (2001) *Equity-Gilt Study*. London: Barclays Capital.

Barry, C.B., Peavy, J.W. (III) and Rodriguez, M. (1998) 'Performance characteristics of emerging capital markets', *Financial Analysts Journal*, January/February, pp. 72–80.

Basu, S. (1975) 'The information content of price-earnings ratios', *Financial Management,* 4, Summer, pp. 53–64.

Basu, S. (1977) 'Investment performance of common stocks in relation to their price/earnings ratios: A test of the efficient market hypothesis', *Journal of Finance*, 32(3), June, pp. 663–82.

Basu, S. (1983) 'The relationship between earnings' yield, market value and return for NYSE stocks – Further evidence', *Journal of Financial Economics*, June, pp. 129–56.

Baumol, W.J. (1952) 'The transactions demand for cash: An inventory theoretic approach', *Quarterly Journal of Economics*, November, pp. 545–56.

Benartzi, S. and Thaler, R. (1995) 'Myopic loss aversion and the equity premium puzzle', *Quarterly Journal of Economics,* 110(1) pp. 73–92.

Bernard, V. (1993) 'Stock price reactions to earnings announcements', in Thaler, R. (ed.) *Advances in Behavioural Finance*. New York: Russell Sage Foundation.

Bernard, V.L. and Thomas, J.K. (1989) 'Post-earnings-announcement drift: delayed price response or risk premium?' *Journal of Accounting Research*, 27 (Supplement 1989), pp. 1–36.

Berry, A. *et al.* (1990) 'Leasing and the smaller firm', The Chartered Association of Certified Accountants, Occasional Research Paper No. 3.

Bhasker, K. (1979) 'A multiple objective approach to capital budgeting', *Accounting and Business Research*, Winter.

Bhide, A. (1993) 'The causes and consequences of hostile takeovers', in D.H. Chew, Jr (ed.), *The New Finance: Where Theory Meets Practice*. New York: McGraw-Hill.

Biddle, G. and Lindahl, F. (1982) 'Stock price reactions to LIFO adoptions: The association between excess returns and LIFO tax savings', *Journal of Accounting Research*, 20(2), Autumn, pp. 551–88.

Bierman, H. (1988) *Implementing Capital Budgeting Techniques*, Revised edn. Cambridge, Mass: Ballinger Publishing.

Bierman, H. and Smidt, S. (1992) *The Capital Budgeting Decision*, 8th edn. New York: Macmillan.

Black, F. (1972) 'Capital market equilibrium with restricted borrowing', *Journal of Business*, July, pp. 444–55.

Black, F. (1976) 'The dividend puzzle', *Journal of Portfolio Management*, 2, pp. 5–8.

Black, F. (1986) 'Noise', *Journal of Finance,* 41 (3), July, pp. 529–34.

Black, F. (1993) 'Beta and returns', *Journal of Portfolio Management*, 20, Fall, pp. 8–18.

Black, F. and Scholes, M. (1973) 'The pricing of options and corporate liabilities', *Journal of Political Economy*, May/June, pp. 637–59.

Black, F., Jensen, M.C. and Scholes, M. (1972) 'The capital asset pricing model: Some empirical tests', in M. Jensen (ed.), *Studies in the Theory of Capital Markets*. New York: Praeger.

Blair, A. (1997) 'EVA fever', *Management Today*, January, pp. 42–5.

Blair, A. (1997) 'Watching the new metrics', *Management Today*, April, pp. 48–50.

Blake, D. (1990) *Financial Market Analysis*. Maidenhead: McGraw-Hill.

Blake, D. (2000) *Financial Market Analysis*. 2nd edn. London: Wiley.

Blume, M.E. (1971) 'On the assessment of risk' *Journal of Finance*, 26(3), June, pp. 1–10.

Blume, M.E. (1975) 'Betas and their regression tendencies', *Journal of Finance*, 30 (3), June, pp. 785–95.

Blume, M. and Friend, I. (1973) 'A new look at the capital asset pricing model', *Journal of Finance*, 26(1), March, pp. 19–33.

Boardman, C.M., Reinhard, W.J. and Celec, S.G. (1982) 'The role of the payback period in the theory and application of duration to capital budgeting', *Journal of Business Finance and Accounting*, 9(4), Winter, pp. 511–22.

Boston Consulting Group (1996) *Shareholder value metrics*. Shareholder Value Management Series.

Bower, D.H., Bower, R.S. and Logue, D.E (1986) 'A primer on arbitrage pricing theory' in J.M. Stern and D.H. Chew (eds), *The Revolution in Corporate Finance*. Oxford: Basil Blackwell.

Bower, J.L. (1972) *Managing the Resource Allocation Process*. Illinois: Irwin.

Braxton Associates (1991) *The Fundamentals of Value Creation*. Insights: Braxton on Strategy. Boston, Mass: DRT International.

Braxton Associates (1993) *Managing for Value*. Insights: Braxton on Strategy. Boston, Mass: DRT International.

Brealey, R.A. and Myers, S.C. (2000) *Principles of Corporate Finance*. 6th edn. New York: McGraw-Hill.

Brealey, R.H. (1986) 'Does dividend policy matter?', in J.M. Stern and D.H. Chew (eds) *The Revolution in Corporate Finance*. Oxford: Basil Blackwell.

Breedon, F. and Twinn, I. (1996) 'The valuation of sub-underwriting agreements for UK rights issues', *Bank of England Quarterly Bulletin*, May, pp. 193–6.

Brennan, M. (1971) 'A note on dividend irrelevance and the Gordon valuation model', *Journal of Finance*, December, pp. 1115–21.

Brett, M. (2000) *How to Read the Financial Pages*. 5th edn. London: Random House.

Brigham, E.F. (1966) 'An analysis of convertible debentures: Theory and some empirical evidence', *Journal of Finance*, March, pp. 35–54.

Brigham, E.F., Gapenski, L.C. and Ehrhardt, M.C. (1998) *Financial Management: Theory and Practice*. 9th edn. Fort Worth: Dryden Press.

Brock, W., Lakonishok, J. and LeBaron, B. (1992) 'Simple technical trading rules and the stochastic properties of stock returns', *Journal of Finance*, 47, December, pp. 1731–64.

Bromwich, M. and Bhimani, A. (1991) 'Strategic investment appraisal', *Management Accounting*, March.

Brown, M. (1996) 'Derivative instruments', in E. Gardener and P. Molyneux (eds), *Investment Banking: Theory and Practice*. 2nd edn. London: Euromoney.

Bruce, R. (1995) 'Parting from your parent', *Accounting*, September, pp. 38–9.

Buckley, A. (2000) *Multinational Finance*. 4th edn. London: FT Prentice Hall.

Buckle, M. and Thompson, J. (1995) *The UK Financial System: Theory and Practice*. 2nd edn. Manchester: Manchester University Press.

Buffett, W. (1982) Letter to shareholders accompanying the Berkshire Hathaway Annual Report. Omaha, Nebraska: Berkshire Hathaway Inc.

Buffett, W. (1984) *Berkshire Hathaway Annual Report*. Omaha, Nebraska: Berkshire Hathaway Inc.

Buffett, W. (1995) Letter to shareholders accompanying the *Berkshire Hathaway Annual Report*. Omaha, Nebraska: Berkshire Hathaway Inc.

Buffett, W.E. (1984), 'The superinvestors of Graham-and-Doddsville', an edited transcript of a talk given at Columbia University in 1984. Reproduced in *Hermes* (Columbia Business School), Fall 1984 and in the 1997 reprint of Graham (1973).

Buffett, W.E. (2000) Letter to shareholders included with the 2000 Annual Report of Berkshire Hathaway Inc: www.berkshirehathaway.com.

Buono, A. and Bowditch, J. (1989) *The Human Side of Mergers and Acquisitions*. San Francisco: Jossey-Bass.

'The Cadbury Report' (1992) *Report of the Committee on the Financial Aspects of Corporate Governance*. London: Gee.

Cannon, T. (1994) *Social Responsibility*. London: Pitman Publishing.

Capaul, C., Rowley, I. and Sharpe, W.F. (1993) 'International value and growth stock returns', *Financial Analysts Journal*, 49, January–February, pp. 27–36.

Carsberg, B.V. (1975) *Economics of Business Decisions*. Harmondsworth: Penguin.

Carsberg, B.V. and Hope, A. (1976) *Business Investment Decisions Under Inflation: Theory and Practice*. London: Institute of Chartered Accountants in England and Wales.

Cartwright, S. and Cooper, C. (1992) *Mergers and Acquisitions: The Human Factor*. Oxford: Butterworth Heinemann.

Carty, P. (1994) 'The economics of expansion', *Accountancy*, March.

Carty, P. (1995) 'Marriages made in heaven?', *Accounting*, September, p. 42.

Chan, L.K.C., Jegadeesh, N. and Lakonishok, J. (1996) 'Momentum abnormal performance: do stocks overact?' The *Journal of Financial Economics*, 31, pp. 235–68.

Chan, L.K.C, Jegadeesh, N. and Lakonishok, J. (1996) 'Momentum strategies', *Journal of Finance*, 51, December, pp. 1681–713.

Chan, L.K.C. and Lakonishok, J. (1993) 'Are the reports of beta's death premature?', *Journal of Portfolio Management*, 19, Summer, pp. 51–62. Reproduced in S. Lofthouse (ed.) (1994) *Readings in Investment*. Chichester: Wiley.

Chan, L.K.C., Hamao, Y. and Lakonishok, J. (1991) 'Fundamentals and stock returns in Japan', *Journal of Finance*, 46, pp. 1739–64.

Chartered Institute of Public Finance and Accountancy (1983) 'Management of capital programmes' *Financial System Review*, 8.

Chew, D.H. (ed.) (1993) *The New Corporate Finance*. New York: McGraw-Hill.

Chopra, N., Lakonishok, J. and Ritter, J.R. (1992) 'Measuring abnormal performance: do stocks overact?', *The Journal of Financial Economics*, 31, pp. 235–68.

Christy, G.A. (1966) *Capital Budgeting – Current Practices and their Efficiency*, Bureau of Business and Economic Research, University of Oregon.

Clare, A. and Thomas, S. (1995) 'The overreaction hypothesis and the UK stock market', *Journal of Business Finance and Accounting*, 22(7) October, pp. 961–73.

Clark, T.M. (1978) *Leasing*. Maidenhead: McGraw-Hill.

Collier, P., Cooke, T. and Glynn, J. (1988) *Financial and Treasury Management*. Oxford: Heinemann.

Collis, D.J. and Montgomery, C.A. (1997) *Corporate Strategy: Resources and the Scope of the Firm*. New York: McGraw-Hill.

Conyon, M.J. and Clegg, P. (1994) 'Pay at the top: a study of the sensitivity of top director remuneration to specific shocks', *National Institute of Economic and Social Research Review*, August.

Cooper, D.J. (1975) 'Rationality and investment appraisal', *Accounting and Business Research*, Summer, pp. 198–202.

Cooper, I. and Kaplanis, E. (1994) 'Home bias in equity portfolios, inflation hedging and international capital market equilibrium', *The Review of Financial Studies*, 7(1), pp. 45–60.

Coopers & Lybrand and OC & C (1993) *A review of the acquisition experience of major UK companies*, London: Coopers & Lybrand.

Cope, N. (1995) 'Cashing in on household prestige', *Accounting*, September, pp. 44–6.

Copeland, T., Koller, T. and Murrin, J. (1996) *Valuation*. 2nd edn. New York: McKinsey and Co. Inc. and Wiley.

Corhay, A., Hawawini, G. and Michel, P. (1987) 'Seasonality in the risk-return relationship: some international evidence', *Journal of Finance*, 42, pp. 49–68.

Cornelius, I. and Davies, M. (1997) *Shareholder Value*. London: *Financial Times*: Financial Publishing.

Corporate Finance. London: Euromoney.

Coulthurst, N.J. (1986) 'Accounting for inflation in capital investment: state of the art and science', *Accounting and Business Research*, Winter, pp. 33–42.

Coulthurst, N.J. (1986) 'The application of the incremental principle in capital investment project evaluation', *Accounting and Business Research*, Autumn.

Cowling, K., Stoneman, P., Cubbin, J. *et al.* (1980) *Mergers and Economic Performance*. Cambridge: Cambridge University Press.

Crossland, M., Dempsey, M. and Moizer, P. (1991) 'The effect of cum- to ex-dividend changes on UK share prices', *Accounting and Business Research*, 22(85), pp. 47–50.

Cuthbertson, K. (1996) *Quantitative Financial Economics*. Chichester: Wiley.

Damodaran, A. (1999) *Applied Corporate Finance*. New York: Wiley.

Daniel, K., Hirshleifer, D. and Subrahmanyam, A. (1998) 'Investor psychology and security market under- and overreactions', *Journal of Finance*, 53(6), pp. 1839–85.

Davies, M. (2000) 'Lessons from practice: VDM at Lloyds TSB', in G.C. Arnold and M. Davies (eds) *Value-Based Management*, London: Wiley.

Davies, M., Arnold, G.C., Cornelius, I. and Walmsley, S. (2001) '*Managing For Shareholder Value*. London: Informa Publishing Group.

Davis, E.W. and Collier, P.A. (1982) 'Treasury management in the UK'. London: Association of Corporate Treasurers.

Dean, J. (1951) *Capital Budgeting*. New York: Columbia University Press.

De Bondt, W.F.M. and Thaler, R.H. (1985) 'Does the stock market overreact?', *Journal of Finance*, 40(3), July, pp. 793–805.

De Bondt, W.F.M. and Thaler, R.H. (1987) 'Further evidence on investor overreaction and stock market seasonality', *Journal of Finance*, 42(3), pp. 557–81.

De Long, J.B., Shleifer, A., Summers, L.H. and Waldemann, R.J. (1989) 'The size and incidence of the losses from noise trading', *Journal of Finance*, 44(3), July, pp. 681–96.

De Long, J.B., Shleifer, A., Summers, L.H. and Waldemann, R.J. (1990) 'Noise trader risk in financial markets', *Journal of Political Economy*, 98, pp. 703–38.

De Wit, B. and Meyer, R. (1998) *Strategy: Process, Content, Context*. 2nd edn. London: International Thomson Business Press.

Demirag, I. and Goddard, S. (1994) *Financial Management for International Business*. Maidenhead: McGraw-Hill.

Demski, J.S. (1994) *Managerial Uses of Accounting Information*. Boston: Kluwer.

Dhrymes, P.J., Friend, I. and Gultekim, N.B. (1984) 'A critical reexamination of the empirical evidence on the arbitrage pricing theory', *Journal of Finance*, 39, June, pp. 323–46.

Dimson, E. (ed.) (1988) *Stock Market Anomalies*, Cambridge: Cambridge University Press.

Dimson, E. and Marsh, P. (1986) 'Event study methodologies and the size effect: the case of UK press recommendations', *Journal of Financial Economics*, 17, pp. 113–42,

Dimson, E., Marsh, P. and Staunton, M. (2001) *The Millennium Book II: 101 Years of Investment Returns*. London: London Business School and ABN Amro.

Dissanaike, G. (1997) 'Do stock market investors overreact?', *Journal of Business, Finance and Accounting*, 24(1), January, pp. 27–49.

Divecha, A.B., Drach, J. and Stefek, D. (1992) 'Emerging markets: a quantitative perspective', *Journal of Portfolio Management*, Fall, pp. 41–50.

Dixit, A.K. and Pindyck, R.S. (1994) *Investment Under Uncertainty*. Princeton, NJ: Princeton University Press.

Donaldson, G. (1961) *Corporate debt policy and the determination of corporate debt capacity*. Boston: Harvard Graduate School of Business Administration.

Donaldson, G. (1963) 'Financial goals: management vs. stockholders', *Harvard Business Review*, May–June, pp. 116–29.

Doyle, P. (1994) 'Setting business objectives and measuring performance', *Journal of General Management*, Winter, pp. 1–19.

Dreman, D. (1998) *Contrarian Investment Strategies: The Next Generation*. New York: Wiley.

Dreman, D. and Berry, M. (1995) 'Overreaction, underreaction, and the low P/E effect', *Financial Analysts Journal*, 51, July/August, pp. 21–30.

Drury, J.C. and Braund, S. (1990) 'The leasing decision: a comparison of theory and practice', *Accounting and Business Research*, Summer, pp. 179–91.

Eales, B.A. (1995) *Financial Risk Management*. Maidenhead: McGraw-Hill.

Economist, The (1991) 'School brief: risk and return', 2 February.

Economist, The (1992) 'Beating the market: yes – it can be done', 5 December.

Economist, The (1996) 'A survey of corporate risk management', 10 February.

Economist, The (1996) 'Economic focus: stay-at-home shareholders', 17 February.

Economist, The (2000) 'Merger brief', 22 July, 29 July, 5 August, 12 August, 19 August, 26 August.

Eiteman, D.K., Stonehill, A.I. and Moffett, M.H. (2001) *Multinational Finance: International Edition*. 9th edn. Reading, Mass: Addison Wesley.

Elton, E.J. and Gruber, M.J. (1970) 'Marginal stockholder tax rates and the clientele effect', *Review of Economics and Statistics*, February, pp. 68–74.

Elton E.J. and Gruber, M.J. (1995) *Modern Portfolio Theory and Investment Analysis*. 5th edn. Chichester: Wiley.

Elton, E.J., Gruber, M.J. and Rentzler, J. (1983) 'A simple examination of the empirical relationship between dividend yields and deviations from the CAPM', *Journal of Banking and Finance*, 7, pp. 135–46.

Elton, E.J., Gruber, M.J. and Mei, J. (1994) 'Cost of capital using arbitrage pricing theory: a case study of nine New York utilities', *Financial Markets, Institutions and Instruments*, 3 August, pp. 46–73.

Emmanuel, C., Otley, D. and Merchant, K. (1990) *Accounting for Management Control*, 2nd edn. London: Chapman and Hall.

Fama, E.F. (1965) 'The behaviour of stock market prices', *Journal of Business*, January, pp. 34–106.

Fama, E.F. (1970) 'Efficient capital markets: a review of theory and empirical work', *Journal of Finance*, May, pp. 383–417.

Fama, E.F. (1978) 'The effects of a firm's investment and financing decisions', *American Economic Review*, 68(3), June, pp. 272–84.

Fama, E.F. (1980) 'Agency problems and the theory of the firm', *Journal of Political Economy*, Spring, pp. 288–307.

Fama, E.F. (1981) 'Stock returns, real activity, inflation and money', *American Economic Review*, 71, September, pp. 545–64.

Fama, E.F. (1991) 'Efficient capital markets II', *Journal of Finance*, 46(5), December, pp. 1575–617.

Fama, E.F. (1998) 'Market efficiency, long-term returns, and behavioural finance', *Journal of Financial Economics*, 49, September, pp. 283–306.

Fama, E.F. and French, K.R. (1988) 'Permanent and temporary components of stock prices', *Journal of Political Economy*, 96, pp. 246–73.

Fama, E.F. and French, K.R. (1992) 'The cross-section of expected stock returns', *Journal of Finance*, 47, pp. 427–65.

Fama, E.F. and French, K.R. (1993) 'Common risk factors in the returns on stocks and bonds', *Journal of Financial Economics*, 33, pp. 3–56.

Fama, E.F. and French, K.R. (1995) 'Size and book-to-market factors in earnings and returns', *Journal of Finance*, 50(1), March, pp. 131–55.

Fama, E.F. and French, K.R. (1996) 'Multifactor explanations of asset pricing anomalies', *Journal of Finance*, 50(1), March, pp. 55–84.

Fama, E.F. and French, K.R. (1998) 'Value versus growth: the international evidence', *Journal of Finance*, 53(6), December, pp. 1975–99.

Fama, E.F. and MacBeth, J. (1973) 'Risk, return and equilibrium: empirical test', *Journal of Political Economy*, May/June, pp. 607–36.

Fama, E.F. and Miller, M.H. (1972) *The Theory of Finance*. Orlando, Florida: Holt, Rinehart & Winston.

Fama, E.F., Fisher, L., Jensen, M.C. and Roll, R. (1969) 'The adjustment of stock prices to new information', *International Economic Review*, 10(1), February, pp. 1–21.

Finance and Leasing Association (FLA) Annual Report. London: FLA.

Financial Times (Lex Column) (1996) 'Return on investment', 7 May.

Finnie, J. (1988) 'The role of financial appraisal in decisions to acquire advanced manufacturing technology', *Accounting and Business Research*, 18(70), pp. 133–9.

Firth, M. (1980) 'Takeovers, shareholders' returns and the theory of the firm', *Quarterly Journal of Economics*, 94, March, pp. 235–60.

Firth, M. (1991) 'Corporate takeovers, stockholder returns and executive rewards', *Managerial and Decision Economics*, 12, pp. 421–8.

Firth, M.A. (1977a) 'An empirical investigation of the impact of the announcement of capitalisation issues on share prices', *Journal of Business, Finance and Accounting*, Spring, p. 47.

Firth, M.A. (1977b) *The Valuation of Shares and the Efficient Markets Theory*. Basingstoke: Macmillan.

Fisher, F.M. and McGowan, J.I. (1983) 'On the misuse of accounting rates of return to infer monopoly profits', *American Economic Review*, 73, March, pp. 82–97.

Fisher, I. (1930) *The Theory of Interest*. Reprinted in 1977 by Porcupine Press.

Foster, G. (1979) 'Briloff and the capital markets', *Journal of Accounting Research*, 17, pp. 262–74.

Foster, G., Olsen, C. and Shevlin, T. (1984) 'Earnings releases, anomalies, and the behavior of security returns', *Accounting Review*, 59(4), October, pp. 574–60.

Francis, G. and Minchington, C. (2000) 'Value-based metrics as divisional performance measures', in G.C. Arnold and M. Davies (eds) *Value-Based Management*. London: Wiley.

Franks, J. and Harris, R. (1989) 'Shareholder wealth effects of corporate takeovers: the UK experience 1955–85', *Journal of Financial Economics*, 23, pp. 225–49.

Franks, J. and Mayer, C. (1996) 'Hostile takeovers and correction of managerial failure', *Journal of Financial Economics*, 40, pp. 163–81.

Friedman, M. (1970) 'The Social Responsiblity of Business is to Increase its Profits', *New York Times Magazine*, 30 Sept.

Friend, I. and Blume, M. (1970) 'Measurement of portfolio performance under uncertainty', *American Economic Review*, September, pp. 561–75.

Friend, I., Westerfield, R. and Granito, M. (1978) 'New evidence on the capital asset pricing model', *Journal of Finance*, 33, June, pp. 903–20.

Froot, K.A. and Dabora, E. (1999) 'How are stock prices affected by the location of trade?', *Journal of Financial Economics*, 53, pp. 189–216.

Frost, P.A. and Savarino, J.E. (1986) 'Portfolio size and estimation risk', *Journal of Portfolio Management*, 12, Summer, pp. 60–4.

Fuller, R.J. and Wong, G.W. (1988) 'Traditional versus theoretical risk measures', *Financial Analysts Journal*, 44, March–April, pp. 52–7. Reproduced in S. Lofthouse (ed.) (1994) *Readings in Investment*, Chichester: Wiley.

Gadella, J.W. (1992), 'Post-project appraisal', *Management Accounting*, March, pp. 52 and 58.

Galbraith, J. (1967) 'The goals of an industrial system' (excerpt from *The new industrial state*). Reproduced in H.I. Ansoff (1969) *Business Strategy*. London: Penguin.

Galitz, L. (1998) *Financial Engineering*. 2nd edn. London: FT Prentice Hall.

Gardener, E. and Molyneux, P. (eds) (1996) *Investment banking: theory and practice*. London: Euromoney Books.

Gitman, L.J. and Forrester, J.R. (1977) 'A survey of capital budgeting techniques used by major US firms', *Financial Management*, Fall, pp. 66–76.

Gitman, L.J. and Maxwell, C.E. (1987) 'A longitudinal comparison of capital budgeting techniques used by major US firms: 1986 versus 1976', *The Journal of Applied Business Research*, Fall, pp. 41–50.

Gitman, L.J. and Mercurio, V.A. (1982) 'Cost of capital techniques used in major US firms', *Financial Management*, Winter, pp. 21–9.

Gordon, L.A. and Myers, M.D. (1991) 'Postauditing capital projects', *Management Accounting (US)*, January, pp. 39–42.

Gordon, L.A. and Stark, A.W. (1989) 'Accounting and economic rates of return: a note on depreciation and other accruals', *Journal of Business Finance and Accounting*, 16(3), pp. 425–32.

Gordon, M.J. (1959) 'Dividends, earnings and stock prices', *Review of Economics and Statistics*, 41, May, pp. 99–105.

Gordon, M.J. (1962) *The Investment, Financing and Valuation of the Corporation*. Homewood, IL: Irwin.

Gordon, M.J. (1963) 'Optimal investment and financing policy', *Journal of Finance*, May.

Gordon, M.J. and Shapiro, E. (1956) 'Capital equipment analysis: the required rate of profit', *Management Science*, III, pp. 102–10.

Graham, B. (1973) *The Intelligent Investor*. Revised 4th edn. New York: Harper Business (reprinted 1997).

Graham, B. and Dodd, D. (1934). *Security Analysis*. New York: McGraw-Hill.

Graham, G. (1999) 'HSBC's new guiding light aims to outshine peer group', *Financial Times*, 23 February, p. 25.

Grayson, C.J. (1966) 'The use of statistical techniques in capital budgeting', in A.A. Robichek, (ed.) *Financial Research and Management Decisions*. New York: Wiley, pp. 90–132.

'The Greenbury Report' (1995) *Director's remunerations: report of a Study Group chaired by Sir Richard Greenbury*. London: Gee.

Gregory, A. (1997) 'An examination of the long run performance of UK acquiring firms', *Journal of Business Finance and Accounting*, 24(7–8), September, pp. 971–1002.

Gregory, A. and Rutterford, J. (1999) 'The cost of capital in the UK: a comparison of industry and the city'. CIMA monograph, May.

Grinyer, J.R. (1986) 'An alternative to maximisation of shareholder wealth in capital budgeting decisions', *Accounting and Business Research*, Autumn, pp. 319–26.

Gurnani, C. (1984) 'Capital budgeting: theory and practice', *Engineering Economist*, Fall, pp. 19–46.

Hajdasinski, M.M. (1993) 'The payback period as a measure of profitability and liquidity', *The Engineering Economist*, 38(3), Spring, pp. 177–191.

Haka, S.F., Gordon, L.A. and Pinches, G.E. (1985) 'Sophisticated capital budgeting selection techniques and firm performance', *Accounting Review*, October, pp. 651–69.

Hallwood, C.P. and MacDonald, R. (2000) *International Money and Finance*. 3rd edn. Massachusetts and Oxford: Blackwell.

'The Hampel Report' (1998) *The Committee on Corporate Governance, Final report*. London: Gee.

Harris, A. (1996) ' Wanted: insiders', *Management Today*, July, pp. 40–1.

Harris, M. and Raviv, A. (1991) 'The theory of capital structure', *Journal of Finance*, 46, pp. 297–355.

Harris, M., Kriebel, C.H. and Raviv, A. (1982) 'Asymmetric information, incentives and intrafirm resource allocation', *Management Science*, 28(6), June, pp. 604–20.

Hart, O.D. (1995a) *Firms, Contracts and Financial Structure*. Oxford: Clarendon Press.

Hart, O.D. (1995b) 'Corporate governance: some theory and implications', *Economic Journal*, 105, pp. 678–9.

Hasbrouck, J. (1985) 'The characteristics of takeover targets: q and other measures', *Journal of Banking and Finance*, 9, pp. 351–62.

Haspeslagh, P. and Jemison, D. (1991) *Managing Acquisitions*. New York: Free Press.

Hawawini, G. and Klein, D.B. (1994) 'On the predictability of common stock returns: worldwide evidence', in R.A. Jarrow, V. Maksinovic, and W.T. Ziemba, (eds), *Finance*. Amsterdam: North-Holland.

Hawawini, G.A. and Michel, P.A. (eds.) (1984) *European Equity Markets, Risk, Return and Efficiency*, Garland Publishing.

Hayek, F.A. (1969) 'The corporation in a democratic society: in whose interests ought it and will it be run?' Reprinted in H.I. Ansoff (1969) *Business Strategy*. London: Penguin.

Hertz, D.B. (1964) 'Risk analysis in capital investment', *Harvard Business Review*, January/ February, pp. 95–106.

Hertz, D.B and Thomas, H. (1984) *Practical Risk Analysis: An Approach through Case Histories*. Chichester: Wiley.

Hickman, B.G. (1958) 'Corporate bond quality and investor experience', *National Bureau of Economic Research*, Princeton, 14.

Hicks, J.R. (1946) *Value and Capital: An Inquiry into some Fundamental Principles of Economic Theory*. 2nd edn. Oxford: Oxford University Press.

Higson, C. and Elliot, J. (1993) 'The returns to takeovers – the UK evidence', IFA Working Paper. London: London Business School.

Hillier, F.S. (1963) 'The derivation of probabilistic information for the evaluation of risky investments', *Management Science*, April, pp. 443–57.

Hirshleifer, J. (1958) 'On the theory of optimal investment decision', *Journal of Political Economy*, 66 (August), pp. 329–52.

Hirshleifer, J. (1961) 'Risk, the discount rate and investment decisions'. *American Economic Review*, May, pp. 112–20.

Ho, S. and Pike, R.H. (1991) 'Risk analysis in capital budgeting contexts: simple or sophisticated', *Accounting and Business Research*, Summer, pp. 227–38.

Ho, S.M. and Pike, R.H. (1991) 'Risk analysis techniques in capital budgeting contexts', *Accounting and Business Research*, 21(83).

Hodgkinson, L. (1987) 'The capital budgeting decision of corporate groups', Plymouth Business School Paper.

Hong, H., Kaplan, R. and Mandelker, G. (1978) 'Pooling vs. purchase: the effects of accounting for mergers on stock prices', *Accounting Review*, 53, January, pp. 31–47.

Hong, H. and Stein, J.C. (1999) 'A unified theory of underreaction, momentum trading and overreaction in asset markets', *Journal of Finance*, 54(6), pp. 2143–84.

Howells, P. and Bain, K. (2000) *Financial Markets and Institutions*. 3rd edn. Harlow: Financial Times Prentice Hall.

Hunt, J.W., Lees, S., Grumber, J. and Vivian, P. (1987) 'Acquisitions: the human factor'. London: London Business School and Egan Zehnder International.

Ikenberry, D., Lakonishok, J. and Vermaelen, T. (1995) 'Market underreaction to open market share repurchases', *Journal of Financial Economics*, October–November, pp. 181–208.

Ikenberry, D., Rankine, G. and Stice, E. (1996) 'What do stock splits really signal?', *Journal of Financial and Quantative Analyisis*, 31, pp. 357–75.

Investors Chronicle (1997) 'A week in the markets', 18 April, p. 10.

Jackson, T. (1997) 'A serving of added value', *Financial Times*, 13 January, p. 12.

Jaffe, J., Keim, D.B. and Westerfield, R. (1989) 'Earnings yields, market values and stock returns', *Journal of Finance*, 44, pp. 135–48.

James, A.N.G and Peterson, P.P. (1984) 'The leasing puzzle', *Journal of Finance*, September.

Jebb, F. (1997) 'Who's delivered the goods?', *Management Today*/William M. Mercer, March, pp. 48–52.

Jegadeesh, N. and Titman, S. (1993) 'Returns to buying winners and selling losers: implications for stock market efficiency', *Journal of Finance*, March, 48, pp. 65–91.

Jenkinson, T. and Ljungquist, A. (1996) *Going Public: The Theory and Evidence on How Companies Raise Equity Finance*. Oxford: Clarendon.

Jensen, M.C. (1968) 'The performance of mutual funds in the period 1945–64', *Journal of Finance*, 23, May, pp. 389–416.

Jensen, M.C. (1986) 'Agency costs of free cash flow, corporate finance and takeovers', *American Economic Review*, 76, pp. 323–9.

Jensen, M.C. (1989) 'Eclipse of the public corporation', *Harvard Business Review*, September–October, pp. 61–74.

Jensen, M.C. and Meckling, W.H. (1976) 'Theory of the Firm: Managerial Behavior, Agency Costs and Ownership Structure', *Journal of Financial Economics*, Oct., Vol. 3, pp. 305–60.

Johnson, G. and Scholes, K. (2002) *Exploring Corporate Strategy*. 6th edn. Harlow: FT Prentice Hall.

Jones, T.C. and Dugdale, D. (1994) 'Academic and practitioner rationality: the case of investment appraisal', *British Accounting Review*, 26, pp. 3–25.

Jorion, P. (1992) 'Portfolio optimisation in practice', *Financial Analysts Journal*, 48, January/February, pp. 68–74.

Journal of Economic Perspectives (1988) Fall.

Kahnemann, D. and Tversky, A. (2000) *Choices, Values and Frames*. Cambridge: Cambridge University Press.

Kamijo, K.-I and Tanigawa, T. (1990) 'Stock price recognition – approach', International Joint Conference on Neural Networks. San Diego, CA, Vol. 1, pp. 215–21.

Kaplan, R. and Roll, R. (1972) 'Investor evaluation of accounting information: some empirical evidence', *Journal of Business*, 45, pp. 225–57.

Kaplan, R.S. (1986) 'Must CIM be justified by faith alone?' *Harvard Business Review*, March/April, pp. 87–95.

Kaplan, R.S. and Atkinson, A.A. (1998) *Advanced Management Accounting*, International Edition, Englewood Cliffs, NJ: Prentice-Hall.

Kaplanis, E. (1996) 'Benefits and costs of international portfolio investments, *Financial Times Mastering Management*, January.

Kaplanis, E. and Schaefer, S. (1991) 'Exchange risk and international diversification in bond and equity portfolios', *Journal of Economics and Business*, 43, pp. 287–307.

Kay, H. (1994) 'Capital city', *Director*, October, pp. 34–40.

Kay, J. (1993) *Foundations of Corporate Success*. New York: Oxford University Press.

Kay, J.A. (1976) 'Accountants, too, could be happy in a golden age: the accountant's rate of profit and the internal rate of return', Oxford Economic Papers, 28, pp. 447–60.

Keane, S. (1974) 'Dividends and the resolution of uncertainty', *Journal of Business Finance and Accountancy*, Autumn.

Keasey, K., Thompson, S. and Wright, M. (1997) *Corporate Governance: Economic, Management and Financial Issues*. Oxford: Oxford University Press.

Kee, R. and Bublitz, B. (1988) 'The role of payback in the investment process', *Accounting and Business Research*, 18(70), pp. 149–55.

Keim, D. (1983) 'Size-related anomalies and stock return seasonality: further emprical evidence', *Journal of Financial Economics*, 12, pp. 13–32.

Keim, D.B. (1988) 'Stock market regularities: a synthesis of the evidence and explanations', in E. Dimson, (ed.) *Stock Market Anomalies*, Cambridge: Cambridge University Press and in S. Lofthouse, (ed.) (1994) *Readings in Investment*. Chichester: Wiley.

Kendall, M. (1953) 'The analysis of economic time-series prices', *Journal of the Royal Statistical Society*, 96, pp. 11–25.

Kennedy, A. and Mills, R. (1992) 'Post completion auditing: a source of strategic direction?', *Management Accounting (UK)*, May, pp. 26–8.

Kennedy, A. and Mills, R. (1993a) 'Post completion auditing in practice', *Management Accounting*, October, pp. 22–5.

Kennedy, A. and Mills, R. (1993b) 'Experiences in operating a post-audit system', *Management Accounting*, November.

Kennedy, J.A. and Mills, R. (1990), *Post Completion Audit of Capital Expenditure Projects*. London: CIMA. Management Accounting Guide 9.

Keynes, J.M. (1936) *The General Theory of Employment, Interest and Money*. London: Harcourt, Brace and World.

Kim, S.H. (1982) 'An empirical study of the relationship between capital budgeting practices and earning performance', *Engineering Economics*, 27(3), Spring, pp. 185–96.

Kim, S.H. and Farragher, E.J. (1981) 'Current capital budgeting practices', *Management Accounting (US)*, June, pp. 26–33.

Kim, S.H., Crick, T. and Kim, S.H. (1986) 'Do executives practice what academics preach?', *Management Accounting (US)*, November, pp. 49–52.

Kindleberger, C.P. (1996) *Manias, Panics and Crashes: A History of Financial Crises*, 3rd edn. New York: Macmillan.

King, P. (1975), 'Is the emphasis of capital budgeting theory misplaced?' *Journal of Business Finance and Accounting*, 2(1), p. 69.

Klammer, T., Koch, B. and Wilner, N. (1991) 'Capital budgeting practices – a survey of corporate use', *Journal of Management Accounting Research*, Fall, pp. 447–64.

Knight, R.F. (1996) *Value Creation among Britain's Top 500 Companies*. The Oxford Executive Research Briefings. Oxford: Templeton College.

Kothari, S.P., Shanken, J. and Sloan, R.G. (1995) 'Another look at the cross-section of expected stock returns', *Journal of Finance*, March, 50(1), pp. 185–224.

Kuehn, D. (1975) *Takeovers and the theory of the firm: An empirical analysis for the United Kingdom* 1957–1969.

Lakonishok, J. and Shapiro, A.C. (1984) 'Stock returns, beta, variance and size: an empirical analysis', *Financial Analysts Journal*, 40, July–August, pp. 36–41.

Lakonishok, J. and Shapiro, A.C. (1986) 'Systematic risk, total risk and size as determinants of stock market returns', *Journal of Banking and Finance*, 10, pp. 115–32.

Lakonishok, J., Shleifer, A. and Vishny, R. (1994) 'Contrarian investment, extrapolation and risk', *Journal of Finance*, 49, pp. 1541–78.

Lakonishok, J., Vishny, R.W. and Shleifer, A. (1993) 'Contrarian investment, extrapolation and risk', *National Bureau of Economic Research Working Paper*, May, No. 4360.

La Porta, R. (1996) 'Expectations and the cross-section of stock returns', *Journal of Finance*, 51(5), December, pp. 1715–42.

La Porta, R. Lakonishok, J. Shleifer, A. and Vishny, R. (1997) 'Good news for value stocks: further evidence on market efficiency', *Journal of Finance*, 52 (2), pp. 859–74.

Lawrence, A.G. and Myers, M.D. (1991) 'Post-auditing capital projects', *Management Accounting*, January, pp. 39–42.

Lee, D.R. and Verbrugge, J.A. (1996) 'The efficient market theory thrives on criticism', *Journal of Applied Corporate Finance*, 9(1), pp. 3–11.

Lefley, F. (1996) 'Strategic methodologies of investment appraisal of AMT projects: a review and synthesis', *The Engineering Economist*, 41(4), Summer, pp. 345–61.

Lev, B. (1992) 'Observations on the merger phenomenon and a review of the evidence'. Reprinted in J.M. Stern and D.H. Chew (eds) *The Revolution in Corporate Finance*. 2nd edn. Oxford: Blackwell.

Levi, M.D. (1996) *International Finance*. 3rd edn. New York: McGraw-Hill.

Levine, P. and Aaronovitch, S. (1981) 'The financial characteristics of firms and theories of merger activity', *Journal of Industrial Economics*, 30, pp. 149–72.

Levine, R. and Zervos, S. (1996) 'Capital control liberalisation and stock market development', *World Bank Policy Research Working Paper* No. 1622. World Bank.

Levine, R. and Zervos, S. (1996) 'Stock markets, banks and economic growth', *World Bank Policy Research Working Paper*, World Bank.

Levinson, M. (1999) *Guide to Financial Markets*. London: The Economist Books.

Levis, M. (1989) 'Stock market anomalies: a reassessment based on UK evidence', *Journal of Banking and Finance*, 13, pp. 675–96.

Levis, M. (1990) 'The winner's curse problem, interest costs and the underpricing of initial public offerings', *Economic Journal*, 100, March, pp. 76–89.

Levy, H. (1978) 'Equilibrium in an imperfect market: a constraint on the number of securities in the portfolio', *American Economic Review*, September, pp. 643–58.

Levy, R.A. (1971) 'On the short-term stationarity of beta coefficients', *Financial Analysts Journal*, November–December, pp. 55–62.

Lewellen, W.G., Stanley, K.L., Lease, R.C. and Schlarbaum, G.G. (1978) 'Some direct evidence of the dividend clientele phenomenon', *Journal of Finance*, December, pp. 1385–99.

Lewis, K. (1996) 'Consumption, stock returns and the gains from international risk-sharing', *NBER Working Paper*, No. 5410, January.

Limmack, R. (1991) 'Corporate mergers and shareholder wealth effect, 1977–86', *Accounting and Business Research*, 21(83), pp. 239–51.

Lintner, J. (1956) 'Distribution of income of corporations among dividends, retained earnings and taxes', *American Economic Review*, 46, May, pp. 97–113.

Lintner, J. (1965) 'The valuation of risky assets and the selection of risky investments in stock portfolios and capital budgets', *Review of Economics and Statistics*, 47, pp. 13–37.

Litzenberger, R.M. and Joy, O.M. (1975) 'Decentralized capital budgeting decisions and shareholder wealth maximisation', *Journal of Finance*, 30(4), pp. 993–1002.

Litzenberger, R.H. and Ramaswamy, K. (1979) 'The effect of personal taxes and dividends on capital asset prices: theory and empirical evidence', *Journal of Financial Economics*, 7, pp. 163–95.

Litzenberger, R.H. and Ramaswamy, K. (1982) 'The effects of dividends on common stock prices: tax effects or information effects?', *Journal of Finance*, May, pp. 429–43.

Lofthouse, S. (1994) *Equity Investment Management*. Chichester: Wiley.

Lofthouse, S. (ed.) (1994) *Readings in Investment*. Chichester: Wiley.

London Stock Exchange (2000) *A Practical Guide to Listing on the London Stock Exchange*. London: The Exchange.

London Stock Exchange Annual Report.

London Stock Exchange Fact File. (Annual.)

London Stock Exchange Publicity. (Quarterly.)

London Stock Exchange quarterly magazine.

Longmore, D.R. (1989) 'The persistence of the payback method: a time-adjusted decision rule perspective', *The Engineering Economist*, 43(3), Spring, pp. 185–94.

Lowe, J. (1997) *Warren Buffett Speaks*. New York: Wiley.

Lowe, J. (1999) *The Rediscovered Benjamin Graham*. New York: Wiley.

Lowenstein, L. (1991) *Sense and Nonsense in Corporate Finance*. Reading, MA: Addison-Wesley.

Luehrman, T.A. (1997) 'Using APV: a better tool for valuing operations', *Harvard Business Review*, 75 (May–June), pp. 145–54.

Lumijärvi, O.P. (1991) 'Selling of capital investments to top management'. *Management Accounting Research*, 2, pp. 171–88.

Lutz, F.A. and Lutz, V.C. (1951) *The Theory of Investment in the Firm*. Princeton NJ: Princeton University Press.

Lynch, P. (1990) *One Up on Wall Street* (with John Rothchild). New York: Penguin.

Lynch, P. (1994) *Beating the Street* (with John Rothchild). New York: Simon & Schuster.

Lynn, A. (1995) 'Creating wealth', *Sunday Times*, 10 December.

Lynn, M. (1998) 'Creating value: the best and the worst', *Sunday Times*, 27 September.

McConnell, J. and Muscarella, C. (1985) 'Corporate capital expenditure decisions and the market value of the firm', *Journal of Financial Economics*, March, pp. 399–422.

McDaniel, W.R., McCarty, D.E. and Jessell, KA. (1988) 'Discounted cash flow with explicit reinvestment rates: tutorial and extension', *The Financial Review*, August.

McIntyre, A.D. and Coulthurst, N.J. (1986) *Capital Budgeting Practices in Medium-Sized Businesses – A Survey*. London: Institute of Cost and Management Accountants.

McIntyre, A.D. and Coulthurst, N.J. (1987) 'Planning and control of capital investment in medium-sized UK companies', *Management Accounting*, March, pp. 39–40.

McRae, T. (1996) *International Business Finance*. Chichester: Wiley.

McTaggart, J.M., Kontes, P.W. and Mankins, M.C. (1994) *The Value Imperative*, New York: Free Press.

Macqueen, J. (1986) 'Beta is dead! Long live beta!' in J.M. Stern and D.H. Chew (eds), *The Revolution in Corporate Finance*. Oxford: Blackwell.

Magee, J.F (1964a) 'Decision trees for decision making', *Harvard Business Review*, July/August, pp. 126–38.

Magee, J.F. (1964b) 'How to use decision trees in capital investment', *Harvard Business Review*, September/October, pp. 79–96.

Malkiel, B.G. (1999) *A Random Walk Down Wall Street*, 7th edn. New York: Norton.

Maness, T.S. and Zietlow, J.T. (1993) *Short-Term Financial Management*. St Paul, MN: West Publishing.

Manson, S., Stark, A. and Thomas, H.M. (1994) 'A cash flow analysis of the operational gains from takeovers', Research Report 35 of the Chartered Association of Certified Accountants.

Markowitz, H.M. (1952) 'Portfolio selection', *Journal of Finance*, 7, pp. 77–91.

Markowitz, H.M. (1959) *Portfolio Selection: Efficient Diversification of Investments*. 2nd edn (1991): New York: Wiley and Cambridge MA: Basil Blackwell.

Markowitz, H.M. (1991) 'Foundations of portfolio theory', *Journal of Finance*, June.

Marsh, P. (1982) 'The choice between equity and debt: an empirical study', *Journal of Finance*, 37, March, pp. 121–44.

Marsh, P. (1994) 'Underwriting of rights issues: a study of the returns earned by sub-underwriters from UK rights issues', *Office of Fair Trading Research Paper No. 6*.

Martikainen, T. and Puttonen, V. (1996) 'Finnish days-of-the-week effects', *Journal of Business, Finance and Accounting*, 23(7), September, pp. 1019–32.

Martin, P. (1998) 'Goldman's goose', *Financial Times*, 11 August, p. 14.

Mason, C. and Harrison, R. (1997) 'Business angels – heaven-sent or the devil to deal with?', in S. Birley and D.F. Muzyka (eds), *Mastering Enterprise 3: Sources and Types of Finance*, London: Pitman Publishing.

Massey, D. (1995) *New Issues: Profit From Flotations and Initial Public Offerings*. London: Pitman Publishing.

Maude, D. (1996) 'Eurobond primary and secondary markets', in E. Gardener and P. Molyneux (eds), *Investment Banking: Theory and Practice*, London: Euromoney.

Meeks, G. (1977) *Disappointing Marriage: A Study of the Gains from Mergers*. Cambridge: Cambridge University Press.

Meeks, G. and Whittington, G. (1975) 'Director's pay, growth and profitability', *Journal of Industrial Economics*, 24(1), pp. 1–14.

'Mergers and acquisitions' (1995) *Bank of England Quarterly Bulletin*, August, pp. 278–9.

Michaely, R., Thaler, R. and Womack, K. (1995) 'Price reaction to dividend initiations and omissions: overreaction or drift?', *Journal of Finance*, 50, pp. 573–608.

Michaud, R.O. (1989) 'The Markowitz optimization enigma: is "optimized" optimal?', *Financial Analysts Journal*, 45, January–February, pp. 31–42.

Michaud, R.O., Bergstorm, G.L., Frashure, R.D. and Wolahan, B.K. (1996) 'Twenty years of international equity investment', *Journal of Portfolio Management*, Fall, pp. 9–22.

Miller, M. and Modigliani, F. (1961) 'Dividend policy, growth and the valuation of shares', *Journal of Business*, 34, October, pp. 411–33.

Miller, M.H. (1977) 'Debt and taxes', *Journal of Finance*, 32, May, pp. 261–75.

Miller, M.H. (1991) 'Leverage', *Journal of Finance*, 46, pp. 479–88.

Miller, M.H. (1997) *Merton Miller on Derivatives*. New York: Wiley.

Miller, M.N. and Orr, D. (1966) 'A model of the demand for money by firms', *Quarterly Journal of Economics*, August, pp. 413–35.

Mills, R. and Print, C. (1995) 'Strategic value analysis', *Management Accounting*, February, pp. 35–7.

Mills, R., Robertson, J. and Ward, T. (1992) 'Why financial economics is vital in measuring business value', *Management Accounting (UK)*, January, pp. 39–42.

Mills, R.W. (1988) 'Capital budgeting techniques used in the UK and USA', *Management Accounting*, January, pp. 26–7.

Mills, R.W. and Herbert, P.J.A. (1987) 'Corporate and divisional influence in capital budgeting', Chartered Institute of Management Accountants, Occasional Paper Series.

Mitchell, M.L. and Lehn, K. (1990) 'Do bad bidders become good targets?', *Journal of Political Economy*, 98(2), pp. 372–98.

Modigliani, F. and Miller, M.H. (1958) 'The cost of capital, corporation finance and the theory of investment', *American Economic Review*, 48, June, pp. 261–97.

Modigliani, F. and Miller, M.H. (1963) 'Corporate income taxes and the cost of capital: a correction', *American Economic Review*, 53, June, pp. 433–43.

Modigliani, F. and Miller, M.H. (1969) 'Reply to Heins and Sprenkle', *American Economic Review*, 59, September, pp. 592–5.

Mossin, J. (1966) 'Equilibrium in a capital asset market', *Econometrica*, 34, October, pp. 768–83.

Myers, R. (1996) 'Keeping score: metric wars', *CFO*, October, pp. 41–50.

Myers, S. and Majluf, N. (1984) 'Corporate financing and investment decisions when firms have information investors do not have', *Journal of Financial Economics*, June, pp. 187–221.

Myers, S.C. (1974) 'Interaction of corporate financing and investment decisions – implications for capital budgeting', *Journal of Finance*, 29 (March), pp. 1–25.

Myers, S.C. (1984). 'The capital structure puzzle', *Journal of Finance*, 39, July, pp. 575–82.

Myers, S.C. (1996) 'Fischer Black's contributions to corporate finance', *Financial Management*, 25(4), Winter, pp. 95–103.

Neale, C.W. and Holmes, D.E.A. (1988) 'Post-completion audits: the costs and benefits', *Management Accounting*, 66(3), pp. 27–30.

Neff, J. (1999) *John Neff on Investing* (with S.L. Mintz). New York: Wiley.

Nichols, N.A. (1993) 'Efficient? Chaotic? What's the new finance?', *Harvard Business Review*, March–April, pp. 50–58.

Northcott, D. (1991) 'Rationality and decision making in capital budgeting', *British Accounting Review*, September, pp. 219–34.

OFGEM (1999) 'Review of public electricity suppliers, 1998–2000. Distribution price control review: consultation paper', May. www.ofgem.gov.uk/public/pqarc.htm.

Osborne, A. (1996) 'Family firms place a price on a vote', *Investors Chronicle*, 22 November.

Outram, R. (1997) 'For what it's worth', *Management Today*, May, pp. 70–71.

Panel on Takeovers and Mergers, *The City Code on Takeovers and Mergers and Rules Governing Substantial Acquisitions of Shares*. London.

Palepu, K.G. (1986) 'Predicting takeover targets: a methodological and empirical analysis', *Journal of Accounting and Finance*, 8, pp. 3–35.

Patterson, C.S. (1989) 'Investment decision criteria used by listed New Zealand companies', *Accounting and Finance*, 29(2), November, pp. 73–89.

Peters, E.E. (1991) *Chaos and Order in the Capital Markets*. New York: Wiley.

Pettit, R.R. (1977) 'Taxes, transaction costs and clientele effects of dividends', *Journal of Financial Economics*, December.

Pike, R.H. (1982) *Capital Budgeting in the 1980s*. London: Chartered Institute of Management Accountants.

Pike, R.H. (1983a) 'The capital budgeting behaviour and corporate characteristics of capital-constrained firms', *Journal of Business Finance and Accounting*, 10(4), Winter, pp. 663–71.

Pike, R.H. (1983b) 'A review of recent trends in formal capital budgeting processes', *Accounting and Business Research*, Summer, pp. 201–8.

Pike, R.H. (1985) 'Owner-manager conflict and the role of payback', *Accounting and Business Research*, Winter, pp. 47–51.

Pike, R.H. (1988) 'An empirical study of the adoption of sophisticated capital budgeting practices and decision-making effectiveness'. *Accounting and Business Research*, 18(72), pp. 341–51.

Pike, R.H. (1996) 'A longitudinal survey of capital budgeting practices', *Journal of Business Finance and Accounting*, 23(1), January.

Pike, R.H. and Wolfe, M. (1988) *Capital Budgeting in the 1990s*. London: Chartered Institute of Management Accountants.

Pilbeam, K. (1998) *International Finance*. 2nd edn. London: Macmillan Business.

Pinches, G.E. (1982) 'Myopia, capital budgeting and decision-making', *Financial Management*, Autumn, pp. 6–19.

Pohlman, R.A., Santiago, E.S. and Markel, F.L. (1988) 'Cash flow estimation practices of larger firms', *Financial Management*, Summer.

Pontiff, J. and Schall, L.D. (1998) 'Book-to-market ratios', *Journal of Financial Economics*, 49, pp. 141–60.

Porter, M.E. (1985) *Competitive Advantage*. New York: Free Press.

Porterfield, J.T.S. (1965) *Investment Decisions and Capital Costs*. Upper Saddle River, NJ: Prentice-Hall.

Poterba, J.M. and Summers, L.H. (1988) 'Mean reversion in stock prices: evidence and implications', *Journal of Financial Economics*, 22, pp. 27–59.

Powell, R.G. and Thomas, H.M. (1994) 'Corporate control and takeover prediction', Working paper 94/07 (Department of Accounting and Financial Management, University of Essex).

Rappaport, A. (1998) *Creating Shareholder Value*. Revised and updated. New York: Free Press.

Ravenscraft, D. and Scherer, F. (1987) *Mergers, Sell-Offs and Economic Efficiency*. Washington, DC: Brookings Institution.

Reimann, B.C. (1989) *Managing for Value*. Oxford: Basil Blackwell.

Reinganum, M.R. (1981) 'Misspecification of capital asset pricing: empirical anomalies based on earnings' yields and market values', *Journal of Financial Economics*, 9, pp. 19–46.

Reinganum, M.R. (1982) 'A direct test of Roll's conjecture on the firm size effect', *Journal of Finance*, 37, pp. 27–35.

Reinganum, M.R. (1988) 'The anatomy of a stock market winner', *Financial Analysts Journal*, March–April, pp. 272–84.

Reinhardt, U.E. (1973) 'Break-even analysis for Lockheed's Tristar: an application of financial theory', *Journal of Finance*, 28, pp. 821–38, September.

Rendleman, R.J., Jones, C.P. and Latané, H.E. (1982) 'Empirical anomolies based on unexpected earnings and the importance of risk adjustment', *Journal of Financial Economics*, November, pp. 269–87.

Ridley, M. (1993) 'Survey of the frontiers in finance', *The Economist*, 9 October.

Ritter, J.R. and Chopra, N. (1989) 'Portfolio rebalancing and the turn-of-the-year effect', *Journal of Finance*, 44, pp. 149–66.

Roberts, H.V. (1959) 'Stock market "patterns" and financial analysis: methodological suggestions', *Journal of Finance*, March, pp. 1–10.

Rock, K. (1986) 'Why new issues are underpriced', *Journal of Financial Economics*, 15, January, pp. 187–212.

Roll, R. (1977) 'A critique of the asset pricing theory's tests: Part 1: on past and potential testability of the theory', *Journal of Financial Economics*, 4 March, pp. 129–76.

Roll, R. (1981) 'A possible explanation for the small firm effect', *Journal of Finance*, September.

Roll, R. (1986) 'The hubris hypothesis of corporate takeovers', *Journal of Business*, April, 59(2), pt. 1, pp. 197–216.

Roll, R. (1994) 'What every CFO should know about scientific progress in financial economics: what is known and what remains to be resolved', *Financial Management*, 23(2), Summer, pp. 69–75.

Roll, R. and Ross, S.A. (1980) 'An empirical investigation of the arbitrage pricing theory', *Journal of Finance*, 35, December, pp. 1073–103.

Roll, R.W. and Ross, S.A. (1983) 'Regulation, the capital asset pricing model and the arbitrage pricing theory', *Public Utilities Fortnightly*, 111, 26 May, pp. 22–8. Reproduced in S. Lofthouse (ed.) (1994) *Readings in Investment*, Chichester: Wiley.

Rosenberg, B., Reid, K. and Lanstein, R. (1985) 'Persuasive evidence of market inefficiency', *Journal of Portfolio Management*, 11, Spring, pp. 9–16.

Ross, S. (1977) 'The determination of financial structure: the incentive-signalling approach', *Bell Journal of Economics*, 8, pp. 23-40.

Ross, S.A. (1974) 'Return, risk and arbitrage', in I. Friend and J.L Bicksler (eds), *Risk and Return in Finance*. New York: Heath Lexington.

Ross, S.A. (1976) 'The arbitrage theory of capital asset pricing', *Journal of Economic Theory*, 13, December, pp. 341–60.

Ross, S.A. (1995), 'Uses, abuses, and alternatives to the net-present-value rule', *Financial Management*, 24(3), Autumn, pp. 96–102.

Ross, S.A., Westerfield, R.W. and Jaffe, J. (1999) *Corporate Finance*. 5th edn. New York: McGraw-Hill.

Roth, P. (1996) *Mastering Foreign Exchange and Money Markets*. London: Pitman Publishing.

Rozeff, M. (1986) 'How companies set their dividend payout ratios'. Reprinted in J.M. Stern and D.H. Chew (eds), *The Revolution in Corporate Finance*. Oxford: Basil Blackwell.

Rushe, D. (2000) 'Winners and losers in the drive to add value', *Sunday Times*, 24 September.

Rutterford, J. (1993) *Introduction to Stock Exchange Investments*. 2nd edn. Basingstoke: Macmillan.

Rutterford, J. (2000) 'The cost of capital and shareholder value', in G.C. Arnold and M. Davies (eds.) *Value-Based Management*. London: Wiley.

Samuels, J.M., Wilkes, F.M. and Brayshaw, R.E. (1996) *Management of Company Finance*, 6th edn. London: Chapman and Hall.

Sangster, A. (1993) 'Capital investment appraisal techniques: a survey of current usage', *Journal of Business Finance and Accounting*, 20(3), pp. 307–33.

Scapens, R.W. and Sale, J.T. (1981) 'Performance measurement and formal capital expenditure controls in divisionalised companies', *Journal of Business Finance and Accounting*, 8, pp. 389–420.

Scapens, R.W., Sale, J.T. and Tikkas, P.A. (1982) *Financial Control of Divisional Capital Investment*. London: Institute of Cost and Management Accountants.

Schoenburg, E. (1990) 'Stock price prediction using neural networks', *Neurocomputing*, 2, pp. 17–27.

Scholes, M. (1972) 'The market for securities: substitution versus price pressure effects of information on the share prices', *Journal of Business*, April, pp. 179ff.

Sharpe, W.F. (1963) 'A simplified model for portfolio analysis', *Management Science*, 9, pp. 277–93.

Sharpe, W.F. (1964) 'Capital asset prices: a theory of market equilibrium under conditions of risk', *Journal of Finance*, 19, September, pp. 425–42.

Sharpe, W.F., Alexander, G.J. and Bailey, J.V. (1999) *Investments*. 6th edn. Upper Saddle River, NJ: Prentice-Hall.

Shefrin, H. (2000) *Beyond Greed and Fear*. Boston, MA: Harvard Business School Press.

Sheridan, T. and Kendall, N. (1992) *Corporate Governance*. London: Pitman Publishing.

Shiller, R.J. (2000) *Irrational Exuberence*. Princeton, NJ: Princeton University Press.

Shleifer, A. (2000) *Inefficient Markets: An Introduction to Behavioural Finance*. Oxford: Oxford University Press.

Simon, H.A. (1959) 'Theories of decision making in economics and behavioural science', *American Economic Review*, June.

Simon, H.A. (1964) 'On the concept of organisational goals', *Administrative Science Quarterly*, 9(1), June, pp. 1–22.

Singh, A. (1971) *Takeovers*. Cambridge: Cambridge University Press.

Sirower, M.L. (1997) *The Synergy Trap: How Companies Lose the Acquisition Game*. New York: Free Press.

Smith, A. (1776) *The Wealth of Nations*. Reproduced in 1910 in two volumes. Londont: Dent.

Smith, C. (1986) 'Investment banking and the capital acquisition process', *Journal of Financial Economics*, 15, pp. 3–29.

Smith, T. (1992) *Accounting for Growth*, London: Century Business.

Smith, T. (1995) 'Many happy returns', *Management Today*, May, pp. 56–9.

Solnik, B. (2000) *International Investments*, 4th edn. Reading, Mass: Addison Wesley Longman.

Solnik, B.H. (1974) 'Why not diversify internationally rather than domestically?', *Financial Analysts Journal*, July–August, pp. 48–54.

Solomon, E. (1963) *The Theory of Financial Management*. New York: Columbia University Press.

Solomons, D. (1985) *Divisional Performance, Measurement and Control*. 2nd edn. Connecticut: Weiner Publishing.

Soros, G. (1987) *The Alchemy of Finance*. (Reprinted in 1994 with a new preface and a new foreword.) New York: Wiley.

Soros, G. (1995) *Soros on Soros*. New York: Wiley.

Soros, G. (1998) *The Crisis of Global Capitalism*. New York: Public Affairs.

Spiedell, L.S. and Sappenfield, R. (1992) 'Global diversification in a shrinking world', *Journal of Portfolio Management*, Fall, pp. 57–67.

Standard & Poor's (1999) *Ratings Performance 1998: Stability and Transition*, January.

Statman, M. (1982) 'The persistence of the payback method: a principle–agent perspective', *The Engineering Economist*, 11(1), Summer, pp. 95–100.

Statman, M. and Sepe, J.F. (1984) 'Managerial incentive plans and the use of the payback method', *Journal of Business Finance and Accounting*, 11(1) Spring, pp. 61–5.

Stephens, G. and Funnell, J. (1995) 'Take your partners', *Corporate Finance*, London: Euromoney, July.

Stern, J. (1998) 'The capital structure puzzle', *Journal of Applied Corporate Finance*, II(I), Spring, pp. 8–23.

Stern, J.M. and Chew, D.H. (eds) (1986) *The Revolution in Corporate Finance*, Oxford: Blackwell.

Stern Stewart and Co. (1995) 'Creating wealth', *Sunday Times*, 10 December.

Stewart, G.B. (1991) *The Quest for Value*. New York: Harper Business.

Strong, N. and Xu, X.G. (1997) 'Explaining the cross-section of UK expected stock returns', *British Accounting Review*, 29(1), pp. 1–23.

Sudarsanam, S. (1995) *The Essence of Mergers and Acquisitions*. Hemel Hempstead: Prentice Hall.

Sudarsanam, S., Holl, P. and Salami, A. (1996) 'Shareholder wealth gains in mergers: effect of synergy and ownership structure', *Journal of Business Finance and Accounting*, July, pp. 673–98.

Sullivan, R., Timmermann, A. and White, H. (1999) 'Data-snooping, technical trade rule performance, and the bootstrap', *Journal of Finance*, 54(5), pp. 1647ff.

Swalm, R.O. (1966) 'Utility theory – insights into risk taking', *Harvard Business Review*, November/December, pp. 123–36.

'Symposium on some anomalous evidence on capital market efficiency' (1977) A special issue of the *Journal of Financial Economics*, 6, June.

Tait, N. (1999) 'Ford aims to slash $1bn from cash base this year', *Financial Times*, 8 January, p. 17.

Taylor, F. (1997) *Mastering Foreign Exchange and Currency Options*. London: Pitman Publishing.

Taylor, F. (2000) *Mastering Derivatives Markets*. 2nd edn. London: FT Prentice Hall.

Thal Larsen, P. (1997) 'EVA: nice figures, but what do they mean?', *Investors Chronicle*, 17 January, pp. 18–19.

Thaler, R. (ed.) (1993) *Advances in Behavioural Finance*. New York: Russell Sage Foundation.

Tobin, J. (1958) 'Liquidity preference as behaviour toward risk', *Review of Economic Studies*, 26, February, pp. 65–86.

The Treasurers Handbook. London: Association of Corporate Treasurers.

3i (1993) 'Dividend policy, April'. Reported in *Bank of England Quarterly Review*. August, p. 367.

Train, J. (1980) *The Money Masters*. New York: Harper Business (reprinted 1994).

Train, J. (1987) *The Midas Touch*. New York: Harper & Row.

Treasurer. London: Euromoney.

Treynor, J. (1965) 'How to rate management of investment funds', *Harvard Business Review*, January–February.

Tully, S. (1993) 'The real key to creating wealth', *Fortune*, 20 September, pp. 38–50.

Tyrrall, D.E. (1998) 'Discounted cash flow: rational calculation or psychological crutch?', *Management Accounting* (UK), February, pp. 46–8.

Urry, M. (1996) 'The $45bn man makes his pitch', *Financial Times, Weekend Money*, 11/12 May, p. 1.

US Office of Business Economics (1966) *The National Income and Product Accounts of the United States 1929–1965*. Washington: Government Printing Office.

Vaitilingam, R. (2001) *The Financial Times Guide to Using the Financial Pages*. 4th edn. London: FT Prentice Hall.

Valdez, S. (2000) *An Introduction to Global Financial Markets*. 3rd edn. Basingstoke: Macmillan Business.

Van de Vliet, A. (1997) 'When mergers misfire', *Management Today*, June.

Wagner, W.H. and Lau, S. (1971) 'The effects of diversification on risk'. *Financial Analysts Journal*, November–December.

Wardlow, A. (1994), 'Investment appraisal criteria and the impact of low inflation', *Bank of England Quarterly Bulletin*, 34(3), August, pp. 250–54.

Watts, R. (1986) 'Does it pay to manipulate E.P.S.?' in J.M. Stern and D.H. Chew (eds), *Revolution in Corporate Finance*. Oxford: Blackwell.

Weingartner, H.M. (1969) 'Some new views on the payback period and capital budgeting', *Management Science*, 15, pp. 594–607.

Weingartner, H.M. (1977) 'Capital rationing: *n* authors in search of a plot', *Journal of Finance*, December, pp. 1403–31.

West, K.D. (1988) 'Bubbles, fads and stock price volatility tests: a partial evaluation', *Journal of Finance*, 43(3), pp. 639–56.

Westwick, C.A. and Shohet, P.S.D. (1976) 'Investment appraisal and information', ICAEW Research Committee, Occasional Paper, No. 7.

Wilkes, F.M. (1980) 'On multiple rates of return', *Journal of Business, Finance and Accounting*, 7(4).

Wilkes, F.M. (1983) *Capital Budgeting Techniques*. 2nd edn. Chichester: Wiley.

Williamson, O. (1963) 'Managerial discretion and business behaviour', *American Economic Review*, 53, pp. 1033–57.

Winstone, D. (1995) *Financial Derivatives*. London: Chapman and Hall.

Wright, M.G. (1973) *Discounted Cash Flow*. 2nd edn. Maidenhead: McGraw-Hill.

Wynne, G.L. (1988) 'Sources of UK short-term and medium-term debt', in J. Rutterford, and D. Carter (eds), *Handbook of Corporate Finance*. London: Butterworths.

Zimmerman, J.C. (1997) *Accounting for Decision Making and Control*, 2nd edn. Boston: Irwin/ McGraw-Hill.

INDEX

Aaronovitch, S. 896
Abbey National 372, 492, 538, 883
  as bank 32, 33, 34
ABN Amro bank 288
ABP 831
Abrahams, Paul 350
absorption, in mergers 903
acceptance credits 540–1, 543
Accor 488
accounting rate of return (ARR) 141–4
  drawbacks of 143
  in earnings-based management 667–9
  reasons for 144
  use of 138
accounting rules 14
acquisition for shares 421
actual rate of return 670
Adams, Richard 971, 991
Adedeji, A. 311
adjusted present value (APV) 835–7
Adler, Tamara 495
AEG 661
African lakes 349
Aga Foodservice Group plc 554
agency costs 825–6
agency theory 855–6
aggressive shares 305
Ahmad, Sameena 894
Airbus 96–7
airline profits 6
Airstream Finances 538
Airtours 425
Alchemy Partners 444–5
Alex Lawrie 526
Alliance & Leicester 33, 858
Allianz Capital Partners 472
Allied Lyons 989
allocational efficiency 606, 607
Alloy Wheels 993
Alternative Investment Market (AIM) 23, 41, 355–6, 358–60
  costs of joining 409
  growth of 359
  raising equity capital 408–10
AM Paper 441
Amazon 572, 756
Amber Day 394
ambiguity aversion 637
Ambrose, B.W. 896
Amec 831
American Allied Signal 883
American Express 626
Amstrad Group 385
Andarko 760
Anderson, Ed 629
Angel Trains 536
annual equivalent annuity method 115–18
  drawbacks 119
annuities 87–8
Apple Computers 431
Araki, Yuji 350
arbitrage 634–5
arbitrage pricing theory 314–15
arbitrageurs 954
Argentina 470
Arnold, G.C. 138, 151–2, 153, 519, 623, 655, 662, 671, 704, 735, 737, 739, 808, 908
Arnold, Harriet 434
Arsenal Football Club 363
Artoli, Romano 878
Ashanti Goldfields (Ghana) 348, 937
Ashley (London) 771
Ashworth, Peter 362
asset beta 834–5
asset divestment 675
asset securitisation 494
asset transformers 28–9
Associated Nursing Services 493
Association of British Insurers 417
Association of Corporate Treasurers 554
Association of Private Client Investment Managers and Stockbrokers 345
Astec 890
AstraZeneca 678, 681
asymmetric information
  on bonds 464
  and stock market efficiency 603–5
AT & T 721
Atriax 972
attitude as resource 703
Australia
  corporate governance in 17
  returns on equities, bonds, bills 289, 294
  share turnover 342
  small firm performance 618
  stock market correlation matrix 268
authorised shares 389
Autodis 473
availability heuristic 637–8

B Elliott 441
Baba, N. 615
Bacon & Woodrow 942
BAE Systems 828
Bailey, Anthony 639
Bailey, Keith 993
Baker, David 524–5
Bakrie & Brothers 979–80
Ball, R. 616
balloon payments on loans 516
Balls, Andrew 515, 971
Bamford, J.C. 386, 447, 451
Banham, Sir John 52

bank bills 540–1
Bank for International Settlements 365, 971
Bank of America 989
Bank of America International Finance Corporation 110
Bank of England 638, 889
Bank of Scotland 858, 883
banker's acceptance 540–1
Bankers Trust 935
Bankhaus Herstatt 973
Banking Act (1987) 373
banking sector 34–6
  debt finance by 463–6
    advantages 463
    costs 463–4
    repayments 465–6
    security 464–5
  retail 34–5
  short- and medium-term finance 511–16, 542
    overdraft 511–15
    term loans 516, 542
  and treasury management 563, 564
  and venture capital 430
  wholesale 35
Banz, R. 621
Barbour, Margaret 829
Barclays Bank 34, 740
  advisers, cost of 883
  bond issue 495
  economic profit 721
  returns on shares 302, 305, 678
  revenue sources 15
  and small businesses 515
Barclays Capital 288, 296, 302, 737
Barclays de Zoete Wedd (BZW) 219
Barings Bank, collapse of 923, 935, 940–1, 954, 989
Barker, Kate 764
Barker, Thorold 415, 513, 828
Barrell, Alan 448
barter system 20
Bass 263–4, 721
Basu, S. 620
BAT Industries 466, 721
Batchelor, Charles 536–7, 828, 831–2
Baumol's cash model 578–80
Baxter, Andrew 447
BDO Stoy Hayward 782
Beattie, Alan 32
Beattie, Vivien 536
behavioural finance 633–8
  cognitive errors 635–8
  and EMH 633–5
Belgium
  share turnover 342
  small firm performance 618
  stock markets in 343
Bell Atlantic 883
Benoit, Bertrand 412–13, 431–2
Bensons 937
Bentley Cars 136
Berkshire Hathaway 320, 625–6, 627–31, 698, 766, 850
Bernard, V.L. 619, 620
Benartzi, S. 637
beta 297–300
  asset 834–5
  calculating 303–4
  classifying shares by 304–5
  fundamental beta 741
  measuring 306–7
  reliability of 740–1
  and WACC 737
Bhide, A. 896
bills, rate of return on 287–95
bills of exchange 539–40, 543
Black, F. 308, 309, 310
Black and Scholes' option pricing model 956
'Black Wednesday' 966
Blackwell, David 15, 349, 363, 419, 442, 443, 444
Blair, Alistair 681
Blume, M.E. 307
Blyton, Enid 136
BMW 604–6
BOC 302, 740
Body Shop 8, 385, 446, 771
Boeing 97, 533
Boland, Vincent 368–9, 371
bond markets 39–40
bonds 35, 459–82
  convertible 475–8
  foreign 483
  high-yield (junk) 471–5
  interest yield 481–2
  rate of return on 287–95
  redeemable 479–80
  repayments 462
  valuing 478–82
  variations 462–3
  world prices 489
Bonfield, Sir Peter 803
Bonham, Derek 25, 759
book-building 406–7, 420
Boots plc 458, 757
Bosch 883
bought deal 422
Bovis Homes 660
Bowen, Sally 339
Bowie, David 495
Bowley, Graham 946–7
Boyle, John 424–5
BP Amoco 678, 681, 857, 870, 876
BPB Industries plc 477
Bradley, Nick 19
Branson, Richard 385, 446, 513, 533
Braveheart Ventures 424
break-even net present value 197–8
Bream, Rebecca 355, 469, 472, 473, 478
Breen, W.J. 621
Bridgeland, Sally 942–3
Bridgepoint 427
Brightreasons 403–4
Briloff, Abraham 617
British Aerospace 24, 828, 853, 897
British and Commonwealth 617
British Bankers' Association 515
British Gas 24, 372
British Petroleum (BP) 264
British Steel (*see also* Corus) 672, 883, 967, 989, 991
British Telecom (BT) 488, 492, 885
  asset value 758
  beta 740
  capital structure 803, 806, 828

credit rating 469
listing on stock exchanges 347–8
project appraisal 164–5
return on shares 302, 372
rights issue 415
value management in 678, 681
British Venture Capital Association (BVCA) 424, 429
Broadview 877
Brock, W. 614
brokers 25, 28
Brooke, Richard 24
Brooks Brothers 874
Brown, Gordon 434, 852
Brown, P. 616
Brown-Humes, Christopher 858
Brunault, Mark 473
BSA Tools 993
BSkyB 24, 621
BT Alex Brown 770
Buckley, Neil 446
Budge, Richard 219
Buffett, Warren 320–1, 625–31, 671, 698
on dividends 845, 850
on mergers 880, 881, 887–9, 906
building societies 36
bullet repayments on loans 516
Burns, Lord 821
Burt, Tim 759, 880
Burton 388
Burton, John 824
Busby, Colin 402
Bush, George W. 875, 876
business angels 424–5
business risk
in gearing 813
management of 565–6
Byers, Stephen 418–19
Byrne, Fergal 426–7
BZW 110, 272, 408, 776, 989

CAC-40 (France) 375, 932
Cadbury, Sir Dominic 4
Cadbury Schweppes 189
asset value 758
objectives 4
share options 925, 927, 930
call option holder (buyer) 925–8
call option writer 928–9
Camelot 189
Cameron, Doug 972
Campbell, Katharine 428–9, 434
Campeau Group 831
Canada
returns on equities, bonds, bills 289, 294
share turnover 342
small firm performance 618
stock market correlation matrix 268
stock markets in 337
Canary Wharf Ltd 989
Candover Investments 536
Canon 700
capabilities as resources 703
capital
cost of 725–42
and capital structure 814
CAPM in 728–9
debt capital 730–2
of equity capital 727–8
equity risk premium 738–9
retained earnings 730
risk-free premium 739–40
and share value 726–7
high cost of 391
management of, *see* working capital management
weighted average cost of 733–5
and capital structure 815–16
corporate practice on 735–8
in economic profit 720–1
information from 734–5
in SBUs 735
capital allowances 379
capital asset pricing model (CAPM) 285–323
applications 305–6
arbitrage pricing theory 314–15
beta 297–300
calculating 303–4
classifying shares by 304–5
capital market line 295–7
and cost of capital 728–9
expected returns
calculating 296–7
estimating 302
factor models 311–14
multi-factor 311, 314
one-factor 312–13
and risk-return relationship 316–17
three-factor 315–16
two-factor 313–14
practice of 308–11
reliability of 740–1
risk, perspectives on 319–21
security market line 300–2
shares, bonds, bills 287–95
and systematic risk 317–18
technical problems with 306–8
unrealistic assumptions of 308
capital flows, and exchange rates 997–9
capital gearing 804–5
capital market line 269–71
in CAPM 295–7
capital rationing 165–9
hard rationing 166–9
divisible projects 166–8
indivisible projects 166, 168–9
multi-purpose 169
soft rationing 165–6
capital structure 801–33
control of organisation 829
debt finance 802–4
efficiency 831
motivation 830
reinvestment risk 830–1
and financial distress 822–4
costs 825
financial slack 828
gearing, *see* gearing
Modigliani and Miller on 816–20
pecking order in 827–8
signalling 828
and taxation 820–2
and value of firm 814

and weighted average cost of capital 815–16
Caribiner 632
Carlton Communications 721
Carlyle 445
Carnt, Vivienne 942
Carter, Pat 894
cash-conversion cycle 569–73
cash float 100, 583–4
cash flows
and mergers 882
in project appraisal
annual equivalent annuity method 115–18
drawbacks 119
depreciation 99
discounting 178
incremental 102–10
information quality 97–8
make-or-buy decision 121–3
net operating 101–2
profit calculations 98–110
replacement cycles 113–19
replacement decision 110–12
timing 120
working capital 100–1
in value creation 710–12
valuing shares with 776–9
cash management 580–4
cash flow synchronization 583
cash trade-off 577
control cash flows 582–4
models 577
planning cash flows 580–2
policy framework 580
Cazenove 415
Celltech 24
central counter-party 371
Century Inns 403
certainty 191
chaebol 18
Chan, Louis 311, 619, 621
chaos in weak-form efficiency 614–15
Chase de Vere 616
Chase Manhattan Bank 979
Chernomyrdin, Victor 487
Chevron 876
Chicago Board of Trade 924, 954
Chicago Board Options Exchange 954
Chicago Mercantile Exchange 954, 985
China 337, 339, 349
China Petroleum and Chemical Corporation 355
Chirac, Jacques 85, 340
Chisholm, Sam 24
Chopra, N. 614
Chrysler 589
Citigroup 972
City Code on Takeovers and Mergers 889
Claas, August & Helmut 451
clawback 420, 421
Clearing House Automated Payments System (CHAPS) 584
Clearing House Interbank Payments System (CHIPS) 584
Clementi, David 32
clientele effects of dividends 851
Clifford-King, Martin 724
Close Brothers 413
Close Brothers Corporate Finance 831–2
Clover Corporation 359
CLS Services 973
CMGI 434
Co-operative Bank 8
Coca-Cola 626, 671, 701, 721, 905
Cochrane, John 294–5
cocoa futures 938
Coggan, Philip 446, 777
cognitive dissonance 637
Cohen, Norma 535–6, 899
Colder, Colin 426
Coleman, Mary 434
collars in interest rate caps 949–50
collateral for debt finance 464
Colle, Patrick 355
Collins, Simon 473
Coloroll 617
Combined Code 399
commodities 934–5
communism, collapse of 337
Companies Act (1981) 856
Compaq 431
Competition Commission (CC) 374, 739, 870, 896
competitive advantage in industry 704–5
competitive resource strength in value creation 699–704
compound interest 83–4
Computer Management Group 403
Confederation of British Industry 764, 855
conglomerate mergers 870
conservatism by investors 636
consumption in simple economies 19
Continental Tyre 935
continuous compounding 89–90
contractual theory of firm 8–9
conversion premium 475
conversion price 475
conversion ratio 475
convertible bonds 475–8, 485, 934
convertible preference shares 392, 542
Coopers & Lybrand 906
Copeland, T. 709
Corbett, Gerald 25
Coredeal 486
Cornelius, Ian 682
Cornerstone aggregates 759
corporate behaviour 353
corporate finance and stock markets 379
corporate governance
internationally 17–19
regulations 17
corporate investment in project appraisal 53–7
corporate value 671, 714
corporate venturing 433
corporation tax 379
Corus (*see also* British Steel) 672, 883, 967
Corzine, Robert 857
cost leadership strategy 705
cost reduction decisions 150
Costin, Alan 803
Court, David 659
covenants 460–2, 464
Cramb, Gordon 468
credit cards 495
Crèdit Lyonnais 412
Crèdit Lyonnais Laing 220

Credit Management Research Centre 524
credit policy in debtor management 520
credit rating in debt finance 467–70
Credit Suisse First Boston 404, 764
creditor management 589
creditors 101
CREST 367–8, 398
Criminal Justice Act (1993) 395
Crooks, Ed 764
cross-border mergers 899, 907
Cummings, Jo 403–4
cumulative abnormal returns (CARs) 619
cumulative preference shares 392
currency markets, efficiency of 998–9
currency risk 988
currency risk management 567
current-account deficit and exchange rates 997–9
current share price 11–12
cyclical industries, earnings of 769
Cytomyx 442

Dabora, E. 635
Daewoo 824, 878
Daimler-Benz 657, 661, 905
DaimlerChrysler 869, 905, 907
Dalglish, Kenny 10, 359
Daneshkhu, Scheherazade 494
Daniel, Caroline 14
Daniel, K, 614
Daniel Thwaites 363
Danino, Lisa 989
Darlaston, Lance 393
Datastream 302, 307
Davies, M. 682, 710
Davies, Simon 466
Davis, P. 519, 808
DAX (Germany) 375, 932
Day, Colin 404
Day, Timon 760
De Benedetti, Carlo 661
De Bondt, W.R.M. 614
De La Rue 189
De Long, J.B. 635
debentures and loan stocks 460, 542
debt capital
  cost of 730–2
  and share capital 803
debt finance 457–501
  bank borrowing 463–6
    costs 463–4
    repayments 465–6
    security 464–5
  bonds 459–82
    convertible 475–8
    high-yield (junk) 471–5
    interest yield 481–2
    repayments 462
    valuing 478–82
    variations 462–3
  in capital structure 802–4
    efficiency 831
    motivation 830
    reinvestment risk 830–1
  credit rating 467–70
  debentures and loan stocks 460
  features 458–9
  interest rates, term structure 495–501
    expectations hypothesis 497–8
    liquidity-preference hypothesis 498–9
    market-segmentation hypothesis 499
  international sources 482–90
    Eurobonds 484–8, 490
    foreign bonds 483
  for leveraged buyout 475–6
  mezzanine debt 471–5
  for project finance 490–2
  raising equity capital 388
  sale and leaseback 492–4
  securitisation 494–5
  syndicated loans 466
  trust deeds and covenants 460–2
  see also short- and medium-term finance
debtor management 589
debtors 100
decision making 135–54
  accounting rate of return 141–4
    drawbacks of 143
    reasons for 144
  internal rate of return 144–5
  investment process for, *see under* investment
  payback 137–41
    discounted 139
    drawbacks of 139
    reasons for 139–41
  'science' or 'art' 145–8
  sensitivity analysis in 198
  time, tyranny of 147–8
deep discounted bonds 462
defence tactics against mergers 895
defensive industries, earnings of 769
defensive shares 305
deferred tax payments 543
Denmark
  returns on equities, bonds, bills 289, 294
  share turnover 342
Denton, Nicholas 935
depositary receipts 354, 355
depreciation
  in project appraisal 99
  in shareholder value analysis 714
  and taxation 170
deregulation of stock markets 347
derivative markets 41
derivatives 923–57
  forward rate agreements 947–8
  forwards 936–7
  futures 937–47
    marking 938–40
    settlement 940–2
    short-term interest rate 943–6
  interest rate caps 949–50
  options 924–36
    call option holder (buyer) 925–8
    call option writer 928–9
    corporate uses of 934–5
    decisions with 935–6
    hedging 931–2
      against market decline 933
    index options 932–3
    LIFFE share options 929

derivatives (*continued*)
    mispricing 957
    pricing 955–6
    put options 930
    share options 925
    traditional options 930–1
  over-the-counter and exchange-traded 954
  swaps 950–2, 953
  users 952–4
    arbitrageurs 954
    hedgers 952
    speculators 953
Derwent Valley Foods 431
Deutsche Bank 495, 904, 971, 972
Deutsche Börse 343, 371
Deutsche Morgan Grenfell 441
Deutsche Telecom 164, 469, 488
developing countries
  HIV drugs for 9
  stock markets in 337
Diercks, Carsten 445
differentiation strategy 705
diminishing marginal utility 203
Dimson, Elroy 288, 289, 293, 294, 618
Diprose, Michael 359
Direct Holidays 425
discount rate, adjusting for risk 193–4
discounted cash flow (DCF) 55–7, 782
discounting 89
Discover 495
Disney 459, 671, 721, 809
Dissanaike, G. 614
diversification in portfolio theory 247–9
  benefits of 266–9
  boundaries 261–4
  international 266–9
  perfect negative correlations 261–2
  perfect positive correlations 262
  zero correlation 263
dividend growth model 762–3
dividend valuation methods 760–70
  dividend growth model 762–3
  dividends, non-payment of 766–7
  forecasting growth rates 767
  growth determinants 767–9
  to infinity 761–2
  non-constant growth 765–6
  normal growth rate 763–5
  problems with 767
dividends 845–61
  clientele effects 851
  information in 852–4
  Modigliani and Miller on 847–9
  non-payment of 766–7
  not tax deductible 391
  owner control 855–6
  as residual 849–50
  scrip 856
  share buy-backs 856–8
  and taxation 852
  uncertainty, resolution of 854–5
Dixons 771
Dixson, Maurice 880
Dodd, Dave 629
domestic commercial paper 490, 543
domestic medium-term notes 490
dominance in portfolio theory 254–7
Domino Printing Science 448
Done, Kevin 6, 12
Donner, Richard 362
Dorrell, Stephen 855
Dow, Charles 612
Dow Jones Industrial Average (DJIA) 375, 614, 627
Dow theory in weak-form efficiency 612–13
Dreman, David 319
Dresdner Bank 904, 935
Dresdner Kleinwort Wasserstein 366
Drew, Keith 449
Drew Scientific 449
Drexel Burnham Lambert 471
Drucker, Peter 906
Duckett, Stephen 434
Dumas, Angela 450
Dun and Bradstreet 521, 524
Duncan, Ian 25
Dunne, Nancy 539
Duyn, Aline van 469, 488, 821–2
Dwr Cymru 821
Dyson, James 450, 967

early-stage funds, venture capital as 425
earnings, manipulation of 616–17
earnings-based management 663–9
  accounting methods 664
  accounting rate of return 667–8
  and earnings-per-share 668–9
  investment 665
  risk 666–7
  time value 666
earnings-per-share
  in business strategy 706
  in earnings-based management 668–9
East Midlands Development Agency 434
EasyJet 385, 404, 407
economic profit 720–3
  drawbacks 722–3
  use of 721
  usefulness of 722
economic risk, managing 992–3
economic value added (EVA) 723–4, 725
economies, primitive and modern 19–22
  investment in 21–2
  money in 20
  simple economy 19–20
economies of scale
  in financial intermediation 29
  and mergers 875–6
The Economist 618
Edmonstone, Drew 362
Edwards, Geoff 452
Edwards, Keith 536
Edwards, Mark 10
efficiency frontier in portfolio theory 254–7
efficient market hypothesis (EMH) 604–7
  defence of 633–5
  implications of
    for companies 640–1
    for investors 639–40
  misconceptions about 638

Eidos 348
Electra Fleming 402
Electronic Communication Networks (ECN) 345
Elf 876
Elias, Michael 426–7
Elliot, J. 898
Elonex Computers 448
Elton, E.J. 852
EMI 758
The Energy Group 466
Enron 492
enterprise investment schemes 433
equipment replacement decisions 150
equities
  in primary market 355–8
  risk and return on 294–5
  risk premium on 302
equity capital
  acquisition for shares 421
  on AIM 408–10
  authorised shares 389
  bought deal 422
  cost of 727–8
  debt 388
  floating on official list 393–9
    conditions and responsibilities_395
    continuing obligations 398–9
    issuing process 396–8
    new issues, statistics 399
    prospectus 394
    suitability 395–6
  golden shares 393
  Gordon growth model on 729
  issuing methods 399–404
    failure to float 403
    intermediaries offer 402
    introduction 400
    offer for sale 400
    offer for subscription 400
    placing 400–2
  limited companies 390
  new issues, costs 410–12
  non-voting shares 392–3
  ordinary shares 387
    disadvantages of 388
  placings and open offers 420
  preference shares 390–2
  preferred ordinary shares 393
  quotation, dissatisfaction with 435
  raising 385–435, 541
  rights issues 412–19
    calculations 414–15
    ex-rights and cum-rights 416
    not taken up 415
    price discount decision 416
  script issues 422
  share issues 388–9
  timetable 404–8
    book-building 406–7
    Financial Times statistics 406
    Railtrack 404–6
  unquoted firms 423–34
    business angels 424–5
    corporate venturing 433
    enterprise investment scheme 433
    financing gap 423–4
    government sources 433
    incubators 433
    venture capital 425–34
    venture capital trusts 432–3
  vendor placing 421–2
  warrants 423
equity cost of capital 410
equity-linked bond 475
equity-related bonds 485
equity risk premium 738–9
  risk-free rate 739–40
Ernst & Young 776
Esser, Klaus 657, 883
Eurex 954
Euro
  exchange rate movements 969–70, 977
  medium-term notes 490
  trading volume in 971
Euro-securities market 482
Eurobonds 35, 354, 484, 543
  issuing 486–9
  market development 484–5
  types of 485–6
Eurocommercial paper 490
Eurocurrency 36
Eurodeposit account 482
Euronext 23, 343, 344
Europe
  merger activity 872
  stock markets in 343–5, 365
European Commission 875
European Investment Bank 953
European Private Equity 428
Eurotunnel 563
  debt finance 500–1
  inflation allowance 173
  present value of 85
  risk appraisal 189
Evans, Lyn 993
Eversholt 536
Exchange Rate Mechanism 966
exchange rates 966–99
  changes, effects 967–8
  determination of 994–9
    current-account deficit and capital flows 997–9
    expectations theory 997
    interest rate parity 995–7
    purchasing power parity 994–7
  forward markets 975–9
    covering 977–9
  spot markets 975–7
  see also foreign exchange
exchange-traded derivatives 954
expansion option 935–6
expectations hypothesis in debt finance 497–8
expectations theory 997
expected net present values 206–10
expected returns
  in CAPM
    calculating 296–7
    estimating 302
  in portfolio theory 239
    correlation coefficient 252–3
    covariance 250–2
    standard deviation for 250
    two-asset portfolio 249

export finance 543
extraordinary profits, and preference shares 391
ExxonMobil 857, 876

factor models in CAPM 311–14
  multi-factor 311, 314
  one-factor 312–13
  and risk-return relationship 316–17
  three-factor 315–16
  two-factor 313–14
factor risk 313
factoring 526–9, 542
  credit insurance 528
  invoice discounting 529
  recourse and non-recourse 529
  sales ledger administration 528
  stages in 527
Fairey 419
Fama, E.F. 308, 310, 610, 621, 729
Fama, G. 308, 315, 319
Fang Xinghai 349
Favaro, Ken 905
Federal Mogul 659
Federated and Allied department stores 831
Federation of Small Businesses 524
Fels, Gerhard 11
filters in weak-form tests 612
Fina 876
finance houses 36
finance lease 533–4
financial distress 822–4
  costs of 825
financial flows, globalisation of 346–50
financial gearing 804
  and preference shares 391
financial management 5
financial manager
  intermediation by 25–31
    asset transformers 28–9
    brokers 28
    conflict of preferences 26–8
    economies of scale 29
    primary investors 25
    ultimate borrowers 26
  role of 22–5
    in financial markets 23
    investment 23
    risk management 24
    strategy 24
    treasury management 23
financial markets
  financial manager in 23
  flow of funds in 31
  investment in 305–6
Financial Reporting Review Panel 493
financial risk in gearing 813
Financial Services Act (1986) 373
Financial Services and Markets Act (2000) 373
Financial Services Authority (FSA) 345, 364, 890
financial services sector 31–4
  changes 31–4
  reasons 31
financial slack 828
financial system 34–41
  banking sector 34–6
  long-term savings institutions 36–7
  markets 39–41
  risk spreaders 38
  unit trusts 38–9
Financial Times 663
  foreign exchange tables 977
  statistics on new issues 406
financing capital 556–68
  currency 561
  and financial community 563–4
  interest rates 561
  long or short borrowing 556–8
  matching principle 559–61
  retained earnings 561–2
Finelist 473
Finland
  share turnover 342
  small firm performance 618
  stock markets in 337
Firecrest 410
firms
  objectives of 4–15
    financial 7–10
    ownership and control 16–19
    profit maximisation 12–15
    shareholder wealth 11–12
  ownership and control of 16–19
    information flow in 17
    separation of ownership 16
  small, performance of 618
  see also unquoted firms
Firn, David 442
Firth, M. 898
Fisher, I. 174
Fitch IBCA 467, 468, 469
fixed capital, investment in 714
fixed-interest securities 354
floating-rate debt 732
floating rate note (FRN) market 462, 485, 542
floors in interest rate caps 949–50
focus strategy 705
Fokker 661, 905
Ford, Ken 409
Ford Motor Company 470, 532, 589, 883
foreign bonds 483
foreign exchange
  currency markets, efficiency of 998–9
  markets 970–3
  risk, types of 979–81
    economic 981
    hedging strategies 981–9
    transactions 979–80
    translation 980–1
  twenty-four hour trading in 972
  volatility 968–70
foreign exchange markets (Forex) 40, 973, 974
forfaiting 543
Forte, Charles 494
Forte Group 393
forward agreements 565
forward exchange markets 975–9
  covering 977–9
forward market hedging 983
forward rate agreements (FRAs) 947–8
Forward Trust 536–7
forwards 936–7, 948
Foster, G. 617, 619

founders' shares 541
France
  index options in 932
  returns on equities, bonds, bills 289, 294
  share turnover 342
  small firm performance 618
  stakeholders in 340
  stock market correlation matrix 268
  stock markets in 337, 343
    volatility of 428
France Telecom 164, 469, 478
Franks, J. 896, 898
Franks, Julian 909
free cash flow in value creation 713, 715
Freer, Penny 412
French, K. 308, 310, 315, 319, 621, 739
Friedman, Milton 5
Friends Provident 9
Froot, K.A. 635
Fry, Tony 412
Frye, Michael 441
FTSE *100* 375, 932, 942
FTSE *250* 377
FTSE *350* 377
FTSE *AIM* 377
FTSE *All-Share* 375–7
FTSE Eurotop 300 375
FTSE *Fledgling* 377
FTSE International 375
FTSE *SmallCap* 377
FTSE *techMARK* 377
FTSE *techMARK All-share* 377
Fuji Bank 430
Fuller, Russell 316–17
Funnell, Justin 782
futures 937–47, 948
  marking 938–40
  risks in foreign exchange 985–6
  settlement 940–2
  short-term interest rate 943–6
FXall 972

Gapper, John 15, 417–18, 957
Gardner, Roy 24
Gates, Bill 661
Gates Corporation 870
gearing 804–14
  agency costs 825–6
  and borrowing capacity 826–7
  business and financial risk 813
  capital gearing 804–5
  effect of 809–14
  and financial distress 822–4
    costs 825
  income gearing 806–8
  industry group 829
  relevance, lack of 809
Geberit 472
Gecas 875
General Cable Corporation 850
General Electric 875
General Electric Company 661, 896, 897
general inflation 173
General Motors Corporation 532, 589
Gent, Chris 420, 900
Georgo, Nicholas 443
Germany
  companies going private 445
  corporate governance in 17
  corporate restructuring 657
  index options in 932
  profit growth 764
  returns on equities, bonds, bills 289, 294
  share turnover 342
  small firm performance 618
  stock market correlation matrix 268
  stock markets in 340
    volatility of 428
  venture capital in 431–2
Gillette 626
gilts 354
Gimbel, Florian 461
GKN 993
Glas Cymru 821–2
Glasgow, Edwin 493
Glaxo SmithKline 8, 9, 150, 307, 564
  value management in 658, 674, 678, 679, 681
Glaxo Wellcome, *see also* Glaxo SmithKline 725, 870
globalisation 33
Glynwed International plc 554
GMAC 532
Goizueta, Roberto 721
golden shares 393
Goldman Sachs 420, 466, 472, 473, 702
Goldsborough 894
Goodacre, Alan 536
Gordon, M.J. 729
Gordon, Myron 854
Gordon growth model on equity capital 729
Gorman, Douglas 403
Goschalk, Stephen 409
Gott, Tony 136
Gourlay, Richard 403–4, 449
Graham, Benjamin 613, 624–5, 629
Graham, George 564, 973
Graham-Newman Corporation 625, 629
Grainger, Richard 413
Granada 263–4, 393
Grand Metropolitan 25
Gray, Bernard 897
Great Universal Stores 302, 305, 470
Greece 342
Green, Michael 721
Green, Philip 394
Greenbury, Sir Richard 25
Greenhills 476
Gregory, A. 737–8, 898
Griffiths, John 136, 443, 878
Gross, Bill 434
growth industries, earnings of 769
Gruber, M.J. 852
GTech 189
GTM Entrepose 110
Guerin, Rick 630
Guerrera, Francesco 513
GUS 740
Guthrie, Michael 403–4

Haji-Ioannou, Clelia 385
Haji-Ioannou, Polys 385
Haji-Ioannou, Stelios 385
Halcyon Finance Limited 555

Hale, David 351–2
Halifax plc 470, 883
Halifax Bank 33
Hall, Sir John 10
Halpin, Les 991
Hanbo Steel Group 18
Hang Seng (Hong Kong) 375
Hannah, John 403
Hanson, Lord 855
Hanson Trust 25, 402, 759
hard capital rationing 166–9
  divisible projects 167–8
  indivisible projects 168–9
Hargreaves, Deborah 875
Harney, Alexandra 593
Harnischfeger, Uta 445
Harris, Clay 418
Harris, R. 898
Hart, O. 830
Harverson, Patrick 10
Hasbrouck, J. 896
Hatzopoulos, P.D. 138, 151–2, 153, 685, 736–7, 739
Haverson, Patrick 393, 394
Hawawini, Gabriel 311
Hayek, Fredrich 5
Healthcall 441
hedgers 952
hedging 931–2
  in foreign exchange transactions 981–91
    currency options 986–8
    decisions to 988–9
    do nothing 982
    forward market 983
    futures 985–6
    invoice in home currency 981–2
    lagging 983
    leading 983
    matching 983
    money market 984–5
    netting 982–3
    and strength of sterling 991
  loans 945–6
  against market decline 933
  with share index future 942
  three-month deposits 945
Heidelberger Druckmaschinen 452
Henchey, Maurice 441
Hermes 943
Herron, Hal 971
Hertz 702
Heseltine, Michael 725–6, 897
Hickman, B.G. 470
high-tech industries 351–2
high-yield (junk) bonds 471–5
Higson, C. 898
Hill, Roy 412
Hill Samuel 402, 830
Hilton Group 493–4
hire purchase 515, 529–32
Hirshleifer, D. 614
Hocken, Barry 363
Hodge, Stephen 857
Hoechst 661
Hofman, Tracy 25
holding companies, in mergers 903
Holl, P. 898
Hollinger, Peggy 803
Holm, Gladys 294
Honda 700, 967
Honeywell 875
Hong, H. 614
Hong Kong
  share turnover 342
  stock market correlation matrix 268
Honsel, Hans-Dieter 445
Hoogovens 883
horizontal mergers 870
Houlder, Vanessa 909
Hovis Bread 870
Howson, John 359
HSBC 34, 264, 947
  debt financing 466, 537
  securities 760
  shareholder value 678, 681
HSBC Invoice Finance 526
Humber Power 538
Hunter, Sue 993
Hunter, Tom 394
Hunter Ground 476
Huntingdon Life Sciences 366
Hutchins, Greg 25
Hutchinson UK 491
Hutchinson Whampoa 478
hybrid securities 732

IBM 459, 973
Iceland 345
Iceland (food chain) 803
ICI 466
ICL 189
Idealab 434
Ikea 443
Ikenberry, D. 619
Illsley, Tony 404
IMI 993
Imperial Chemical Industries 991
Imprint Search & Selection 359
in-the-money-option 926
income flow methods of valuing shares 760
income gearing 806–8
incremental cash flows in project appraisal 102–10
incubators 433
index options 932–3
India 492
indifference curves in portfolio theory 257–9
  problems 260–1
Individual Savings Accounts (ISAs) 372
Indonesia 979
Industrial Development Leasing Company (Bangladesh) 539
industry attractiveness in value creation 699
Inner City Enterprises 409
inflation 54
  in project appraisal 172–9
    adjusting for 175–8
    and internal rate of return 178
    money cash flows 174–5
    money rates of return 173–4
    real cash flows 174–5
    real rates of return 173–4
    treatment of 178–9

information asymmetry and financial distress 826
Ingram, Rebecca Winnington 25
insider trading 631–2
insolvency 212–17
  probability distribution 215–17
Instinet 345
insurable risk management 566–7
insurance funds 37
Intel 150
interest
  and project appraisal 105–6
  semi-annual 481–2
  yield 481
interest rates
  converting to annual rates 90
  on derivatives, caps 949–50
  determining 86–7
  parity 995–7
  on sterling futures 946–7
  term structure in debt finance 495–501
    expectations hypothesis 497–8
    liquidity-preference hypothesis 498–9
    market-segmentation hypothesis 499
  in UK 591
  and working capital management 561, 567–8
    and risk 567–8
internal rate of return (IRR) 66–76
  characteristics of 76
  and inflation 178
  modified 77–81
  reasons for 144–5
  use of 138
International Air Transport Association (IATA)
international banks 36
international diversification in portfolio theory 266–9
International Finance Corporation 538
International Lease Finance Corporation 533
International Monetary Fund (IMF) 468, 976
International Securities Market Association (ISMA) 484, 486
International Swaps and Derivatives Association 952
Internet Capital Group 434
internet shares
  demand for 363
  valuation of 783
internet venture capital 434
Invensys 430
inventory 100
inventory management 584–8
  trade-offs 585
investment
  decision-making process for 148–54
    appraisal 151–2
    development and classification 150–1
    ideas, generation of 149–50
    implementation 153
    post-completion audit 153–4
    report and authorisation 152
    screening 151
  financial manager, role of 23
  in fixed capital 714
  in money economy 21
  in portfolio theory 241–9
    correlation scale 246
    diversification 247–9
    independent investments 244–5
    perfect negative correlations 243, 261–2
    perfect positive correlations 243–4, 262
  in positive spread 675
  in simple economies 19–20
  of surplus funds 589–92
    choice of investment 591
    objective 590
    policy 590–1
  and taxation 170–2
Investment Management Regulatory Organisation (IMRO) 373
investment period 87
investment trusts 38–9
  valuing shares in 760
Investors in industry (3i) 543, 782
invoice discounting 529, 543
Ireland 764
Iron Maiden 495
Iskandar, Samer 340
Island 345
Italy
  returns on equities, bonds, bills 289, 294
  share turnover 342
  stock market correlation matrix 268
  stock markets in 343
ITNet 14

J. Sainsbury 264, 302, 307, 740, 773
Jackson, Tim 572
Jaffe, J. 621
Jang Hasung 18
Japan
  profit growth 764
  returns on equities, bonds, bills 289, 294
  share turnover 342
  small firm performance 618
  stock market correlation matrix 268
  stock markets in 337, 343
Jarvis Hotels 493–4
Jazztel 470
J.C. Bamford Excavators (JCB) 386, 447, 451
Jeanniot, Pierre
Jeens, Robert 858
Jefferson Smurfit 774–5
Jegadeesh, N. 619
Jensen, M.C. 830, 882
Jiang Zemin 337, 339
Johnson, Richard 412–13
Jones, C.P. 619
Jones, Sheila 441
Josco Group 365
J.P. Jenkins 362, 363
J.P. Morgan 355, 487, 935
J.P. Morgan Chase 972
Jukes, Andrew 536
Jungheinrich 451
junk bonds 471–5
just-in-time stock holdings 588

Kamijo, K.-I. 615
Kamprad, Ingvar 443
Kaplan, R. 616
Kay, John 881
Kazmin, Amy 341
Keele University 495

Keim, D.B. 620
Kelly, Jim 493
Kendall, Maurice 608
Kennett Capital 426
Kenya 349
Kerins, Mike 442
Kernot, Charles 220
Kersley, Richard 770
Keynes, J.M. 623
Kier Group 402
Kingfisher 52, 758, 771, 853
  treasury policy 554, 555
Kingsman, Alan 335, 442
Kingsman, Sue 335
Kleinwort Benson 408
Knapp, Tom 629
Knight, Angela 345
knowledge as resource 703–4
Korea
  share turnover 342
  shareholder's rights in 18
Korea Development Leasing Corporation 539
Korea First Bank 18
Korniotis, Peter 632
Kottkamp, Eckart 451
Koutes, P.W. 662
Kozaki, M. 615
KPMG 473, 899
KPMG Corporate Finance 442
KPMG Transaction Services 412
KPN 469
KPN Qwest 472
Kuper, Simon 988–9
Kurz, Howard 989
Kynge, James 339, 349

Lac, Jean-Pierre 564
lagging in foreign exchange 983
Laing Construction 110
Lakonishok, Josef 311, 614, 619, 620, 621
Lapper, Richard 953
Lapthorne, Richard 24
LASMO 760
Latané, H.E. 619
Late Payment of Commercial Debts (Interest) Act (1998) 525
Latvia 345
Laura Ashley 771
Le Baron, B. 614
Le Carré, John 9
Le Méridien Hotels 494
Lea, Ruth 764
leading in foreign exchange 983
leaseback 492–4, 543
leasing 515, 532–9, 542
  advantages of 534–6
  and buying 537–8
  finance lease 533–4
  new rules for 535–6
  operating lease 532–3
  transaction 532
Leeson, Nick 940, 941, 954, 989, 991
Legal and General Ventures 430
Legge, Chris 469
Lehman Brothers 953
Leigh, Bernard 803
Lennard, Andrew 535
Lever, Ken 669
leveraged buyouts 831
  finance for 475–6
Levine, P. 896
Levis, M. 620, 621
Levy, R.A. 307
Lewis, Karen 268
Lewis, William 417–18
Liberfabrica 412
LibertySurf 52
Liedtke, Hugh 882
life assurance 37
life-cycle stage in value creation 704–5
LIFFE share options 929
limited companies 390
limited liability 336
Limmack, R. 898
Linaker, Paddy 855
LINC 425
Lintner, J. 310, 319, 853
liquidity-preference hypothesis in debt finance 498–9
Lithuania 345
Lloyd Webber, Andrew 385, 446
Lloyds TSB 34, 830, 905
  advisers' costs 883
  debt financing 513, 515, 526
  merger 905
  shareholder value 678, 681
Lloyds UDT Limited 519, 808
loan stocks 460, 542
London
  as financial centre 32
  Sony's move to 593
London Business School 404
London Business School Risk Measurement Service 302
London Clearing House 370
London Inter-Bank Offered Rate (LIBOR) 392, 463, 491
London International Financial Futures and Options Exchange (LIFFE) 33, 41
  derivatives 925, 946, 954
  equity options 929
London Market (Official List) 41
London Metal Exchange 924
London Stock Exchange 15, 32, 343, 353–8, 889
  Alternative Investment Market (AIM) 358–60
  on insider trading 632
  Ofex 362–3
  Official List 358
  primary market (equities) 355–8
  regulation of 373–5
  secondary market 358
  securities traded 354–5
  tasks for 364
  techMARK 360–1
  trading structure 371
  turnover 342
Long-Term Capital Management 923
long-term debt 542
Lotus 431, 878
low-risk portfolios 263–4

Lucas 883
Luesby, Jenny 829
Luke, Edward 495
Lycos 783
Lynch, Peter 321, 623–4, 882
Lyons Cakes 870

3M 150
M & G 855
MacBeth, J 308
Macfarlane, Sir Neil 493
Mackenzie, Craig 9
Mackintosh, James 363
Magee, John 611
Majluf, N. 827
Major, John 943
make-or-buy decision 121–3
Malkani, Gautam 366
Malkiel, B.G. 311, 621
management buy-in (MBI) 427, 430
management buyout (MBO) 35, 425, 430, 441
  in private companies 444
management evaluation in valuing shares 768
Management Today 678, 681
managerialism 16
Mankins, M.C. 662
Mannesmann 657, 883
  takeover of 11, 661, 885, 900
Manot, Virginia 533
Manson, S. 898
Mapp, Derek 434
Marconi 896, 905
margins 938–9
market portfolio
  in CAPM 295, 297
  unobtainable 307
market pricing costs of new issues 410–11
market-segmentation hypothesis in debt finance 499
market share, achieving 6
market to book ratio (MBR) 682–4
market value added (MVA) 679–82
Markowitz, Harry 235
Marks and Spencer plc 25, 33, 809
  asset value 758
  beta 307, 740
  leaseback 492
  PER 771
  returns on shares 302
  takeover by 874
Marsden, Philip 782
Marsh, P. 618
Marsh, Paul 288, 289, 293, 294, 417–18
Marsh, Peter 447, 451
Marshall, Alfred 721
Martin, Peter 147, 365
Martinson, Jane 890
matching
  in financing projects 559–61
  in foreign exchange 983
Mathewson, Sir George 900
MATIF 954
Matthes, Jürgen 11
Matthews, Bernard 385, 444
Maverick Entertainment 359
Maxwell, Conor 449
Maxwell Group 617
Mayer 452
Mayer, C. 896
MBNA 495
McCall, David 444
McDonnell Information Systems 403
McKinsey 904
McLuskie, Bill 989
McTaggart, J.M. 662, 709
McVicar, Mark 501
Médecins sans Frontières 9
medium-term notes 542
Meeks, G. 898
Megginson, W.L. 896
Mehdorn, Hartmut 452
mergers 353, 868–910
  advisers on 882–3
  decision to 869
  defence tactics 895
  definition 869–70
  failure of 904–5, 907, 909
  financing 884–9
    cash 884–5
    shares 885–7
  impact of 896–900
  managing 900–9
    failure to generate value 905–6
    organisational approach to 902
    problem areas 902–4
    stages of 900–2
  motives for 872–84
    bargin buying 879
    cash flow 882
    economies of scale 875–6
    entry to new markets 877–8
    hubris 881
    management inefficiency 879
    managerial motives 879–81
    market power 874–5
    risk diversification 878
    survival 881–2
    synergy 872–4
    taxation 878
    of third parties 882–4
    transactions, internalisation of 876
    undervalued shares 879
  process of 889–95
    bid 893–4
    post-bid 894–5
    pre-bid 891–3
    regulatory bodies 889–91
  statistics 870–2
Merrill Lynch 345, 404, 415
Messer Griesheim 472
Mestrallet, Gérard 340
Metallgesellschaft 923
mezzanine debt 471–5, 543
Mezzanine Management 473
MG Rover 443
Michaely, R. 619
Michel, Pierre 311

Michels, David 494
Microsoft 165, 320, 661, 809
  cash, generating 589
  competitive advantage of 704
  market capitalisation 352
Middelmann, Conner 407–8, 487
Midland Bank 515
Milken, Michael 471
Miller, M.
  on capital structure 801–2, 816–20, 827
  on dividends 847–9
MobilCom 557–8
Model Code for Directors' Dealings 395
Modigliani, F.
  on capital structure 801–2, 816–20, 827
  on dividends 847–9
Moffat, Simon 24
money
  in economies 20
  markets 39
  time value of 54–5
money cash flows 174–5
money rates of return 173–4
Monopolies and Mergers Commission 418, 739, 896, 897
Monsanto 563
Montagnon, Peter 979
Monument Oil & Gas 760
Moody-Stuart, Mark 857
Moody's 467, 468, 469
Morgan Stanley 25
Morris, Harvey 632
Morrison 773
Morton, Sir Alastair 500, 501
Mosenergo 784
Mossin, J. 319
Moulton, Jon 444–5
Munger, Charles 625–7, 630
Murray Motors Mowers 870
Myers, Stewart 822, 827
Myners, Paul 443

Nakamoto, Michiyo 350
narrow framing 636–7
NASDAQ 340, 344, 345, 348, 606
  equity turnover 342
  quota-driven 364
NASDAQ *100* 375
National Association of Pension Funds 417, 900, 943
National Grid 814
National Power 407–8
NatWest Bank 15, 34, 394, 443, 782
  leasing 538
  merger 870, 883
  and small businesses 512, 515
NatWest Markets 956, 957
NatWest Private Equity 441
NatWest Securities 776
Nedlloyd 660
Neff, John 624
negative operating cycle 572
Nestlé 877
net asset value (NAV) 757–60
  usefulness of 759–60
net operating cash flow
  in project appraisal 101–2
  in replacement decision 118–19
net present value (NPV) 57–76
  break-even 197–8
  and cash flow 710
  characteristics of 76
  expected 206–10
  of options 936
  in probability analysis 206–10
  use of 138
Netherlands, the
  returns on equities, bonds, bills 289, 294
  share turnover 342
  small firm performance 618
  stock market correlation matrix 268
  stock markets in 337, 343
  tax laws 857
Netscape 431
netting in foreign exchange 982–3
Network South East 538
Neuer Markt 604–6
neural networks 614–15
neutral shares 305
New Look 403
New York Stock Exchange 308, 340, 342, 606
Newcastle United 10, 495
News Corporation 470
Newstrack 362
Next 388, 771, 831
Nicholson, Mark 424–5
Nikkei 225 Index 940, 941, 954
Nikkei (Japan) 375
Nikko Bank 947
Nissan 967
noise trading 622
Nomura International 494, 495
non-factor risk 313
non-voting shares 392–3, 541
Noon Group 427
Norex Alliance 345
Northern Electric 814
Northern Foods 475
Norway 345
Nottingham Forest Football Club 393
NTL Communications 470
Nursing Home Properties 493

Oasis Stores 411
Oates, Keith 25
objective probabilities of risk 191–2
offer for sale by tender 400
Ofex 362–3, 402, 410
off-balance sheet schemes 493, 535
Office of Fair Trading (OFC) 374, 870, 891
Official List (LSE) 358
  raising equity capital on 393–9
    conditions and responsibilities 395
    continuing obligations 398–9
    issuing process 396–8
    new issues, statistics 399
    prospectus 394
    suitability 395–6

OFGEM 739
OFWAT 739
oil industry, economies of scale in 876
Olivetti 661
Olsen, C. 619
open-ended investment companies
operating gearing 804
operating lease 532–3
operating and strategic decisions with options 933
operational efficiency 605–6
opportunity costs 53
  in project appraisal 104
  of retained earnings 730
option on timing 936
option to abandon 936
options 924–36, 948
  call option holder (buyer) 925–8
  call option writer 928–9
  corporate uses of 934–5
  decisions with 935–6
  hedging 931–2
    against market decline 933
  index options 932–3
  LIFFE share options 929
  mispricing 957
  pricing 955–6
  put options 930
  share options 925
  traditional options 930–1
Orange 469, 478, 756
Orange County, California 923, 989
ordinary shares 387, 541
  disadvantages of 388
organisational structure as business strategy 707
Osaka rice market 924
Osborne, Alastair 501
Ostrovsky, Arkady 420–1
Otter Controls 451–2
out-of-the-money-option 926
over-the-counter derivatives 954
overdraft 511–15, 542
  conditions 513–15
overheads in project appraisal 105
overtrading 575–6
owner earnings, valuing shares with 780–1
ownership and control of firms 16–19
  information flow in 17
  separation of ownership 16
Oxfam 9
Oxford BioMedica 335, 758
Oxford Instruments 431
Oxley, Ann 452

P & O 659–60, 661, 717
Pacal 388
Page, Nigel 669
Palepu, K.G. 896
Panel on Takeovers and Mergers 374
Papouis, Kyriacos 957
Paragon Software 426–7
Parker, George 536–7
Parker, Iain 451–2
Parry, John 988
participating preference shares 392
payback 137–41
  discounted 139
  drawbacks of 139
  reasons for 139–41
  use of 138
Peabody 759
Pearson plc 238, 466, 593, 662–3, 765
Peel, Michael 14
Penguin 663
Pennzoil 882
pension funds 36–7
  in derivatives 942–3
performance spread 670
  in economic profit 720
Perimeter, Stan 630
perpetuities 88–9
personal equity plans 372
Personal Investment Authority (PIA) 373
Peru 339
Peston, Robert 855
Peters, Edgar 615
Phildrew Ventures 450
Philips 11, 564
Phoenix Consortium 443
Photobition 461
Pickard, Jim 512
Picken, Graham 537
Pierer, Heinrich von 657
Pike, Richard H. 138, 735
Pilkington 662, 679
Pilling, David 9
Pizzaland 404
placing 400–2
  and open offers 420
  vendor placing 421–2
planning horizon 670, 675
Plender, John 11, 18, 661
Polly Peck 617
Polygram 446
Poonawala, Akbar 355
Porter, Michael 705
Porterbrook 536
portfolio approach to mergers 903
portfolio performance, measuring 305–6
portfolio planning 707
portfolio selection in CAPM 305
portfolio standard deviation 249
portfolio theory 235–75
  application of 272–3
  capital market line 269–71
  diversification 247–9
    benefits of 266–9
    boundaries 261–4
    international 266–9
    perfect negative correlations 261–2
    perfect positive correlations 262
    zero correlation 263
  dominance 254–7
  efficient frontier 254–7
  expected returns 239
    correlation coefficient 252–3
    covariance 250–2

portfolio theory (*continued*)
standard deviation for 250
two-asset portfolio 249
holding period returns 236–8
indifference curves 257–9
problems 260–1
investment combinations 241–9
correlation scale 246
diversification 247–9
independent investments 244–5
perfect negative correlations 243, 261–2
perfect positive correlations 243–4, 262
low-risk portfolios 263–4
optimal portfolio, choosing 259–61
indifference curve analysis 260–1
problems with 273–4
securities in large numbers 264–5
shares
comparing 240–1
standard deviation for 240
two-asset portfolio
expected returns 249
Portugal 342
Powell, R.G. 896
PowerGen 407–8, 470, 491
preference shares 390–2, 541–2
as debt capital 732
preferred ordinary shares 393, 541
Prentice Hall 663
present values 84–5
adjusted 835–7
see also net present value
Pretzlik, Charles 444
Price, Christopher 409, 410
Price, Colin 904
Price, John 492
price charts in weak-form efficiency 611–12
price discount decision 416
price-earnings ratio (PER)
low, investing in 620–1
in mergers 886
in valuing shares 771–6
over time 772
prospective PERs 775–6
use of 773–5
Price Waterhouse 676
pricing efficiency 606
principal-agent problem 16
private companies 427
bought back 446
as family businesses 451
small companies as 442–3
staying private 447–52
privatisation 337, 346, 372, 407
Proactive Sports 359
probability analysis 200–11
expected net present values 206–10
expected return 201–2
independent probabilities 210–11
mean variance rule 205–6
risk and utility 203–5
standard deviation 202–3, 206–10
using, problems 217–18
Process Scientific Innovations 993
Proctor & Gamble 593, 923, 935
profit maximisation by firms 12–15
profits, airline 6
project appraisal 51–81
capital rationing, *see* capital rationing
cash flow for, *see* cash flows, in project appraisal
corporate investment 53–7
decision making for, *see* decision making
discounted cash flow 55–7
and inflation, *see under* inflation
internal rate of return, *see* internal rate of return
investment process for, *see under* investment
net present value, *see* net present value
risk, *see under* risk
and taxation 170–2
time value of money 54–5
value creation 53–7
project finance 490–2, 543
project finance, risk transfer in 491–2
property investment companies, valuing shares in 759–60
public limited companies (plc) 390
public-to-private company 427
Puplett, Peter 173
purchasing power parity 994–7
pure rate of interest 54
Pursche, Bill 909
Purser, Christopher 554
put options 930
PwC 428

Quaker Oats 721
Quelch, John 404
quoted shares, ownership of 372–3

Racal Electronics 189
Railtrack 404–6
random walks 608–10
Rangers Football Club 363
Rankine, G. 619
Rappaport, A. 709, 712–15, 720
rate of return
accounting 141–4
drawbacks of 143
in earnings-based management 667–9
reasons for 144
use of 138
and company growth 767–8
internal 66–76
characteristics of 76
and inflation 178
modified 77–81
reasons for 144–5
use of 138
required
calculating 306
lowering 676–7
in value creation 670
on shares, bonds, bills 287–95
Ravenscraft, D. 898
Rawsthorne, Alice 450
Read, Cedric 676
real cash flows 174–5
real options 933
real rates of return 173–4

Really Useful Theatre Group 385, 446
Reckitt Benckiser 404
Recognised Investment Exchanges (RIE) 373
Record Treasury Management 991
recourse finance 491
redeemable bonds 479–80
redeemable preference shares 392
Reed, John 904
Reed Elsevier 25, 980
regret by investors 637
Reimann, B.C. 709
Reinganum, M.R. 621
relationships as resources 701–2
Reliance of India 459
Rendleman, R.J. 619
Rennocks, John 991
Renwick, James 420–1
replacement, in project appraisal
  cycles of 113–19
  decision to 110–12
representativeness by investors 636
reputation as resource 702
required rate of return
  calculating 306
  lowering 676–7
  in value creation 670
residuals, dividends as 849–50
resource-based companies, valuing shares in 760
resources, and growth 767
retail banks 34–5
retained earnings
  and capital structure 827
  cost of 730
  as financing option 561–2
return on capital employed (ROCE) 52, 141, 668
  in business strategy 706
return on equity (ROE) 668
return on existing capital, increasing 674
return on investment (ROI) 141, 668
Reuters 24, 672, 972, 991
revolving underwriting facility 543
Rich, Motoko 411
Richardson, Nigel 946
rights issues 413–19, 934
  calculations 414–15
  costs of maintaining listing 413
  ex-rights and cum-rights 416
  not taken up 415
  price discount decision 416
Riley, Barry 302
Rio Pacific 427
risk
  assessing in trade debtor management 520–2
  in CAPM
    perspectives on 319–21
    risk-return relationship 316–17
    systematic 317–18
  defined 190–3
  diversification of in mergers 878
  in earnings-based management 666–7
  economic, managing 992–3
  in equities
    premium on 302, 738–9
    return on 294–5
  factor and non-factor 313
  gearing 813
  of insolvency 212–17
    probability distribution 215–17
  management of
    by financial managers 24
    and shareholder wealth 13
    and time value of money 54
  objective probabilities 191–2
  in portfolio theory 263–4
  and project appraisal 189–225
    adjusting through discount rate 193–4
    in practice 218–24
    probability analysis, *see* probability analysis
    scenario analysis 199–200
    sensitivity analysis 194–8
    and utility 203–5
  subjective probabilities 192–3
  transfer in project finance 491
  and working capital management 564–8
    business 565–6
    currency 567
    insurable 566–7
    interest rate 567–8
risk averter 205
risk lover 205
risk premium approach 193–4
risk spreaders 38
Ritter, J.R. 614
RJB mining 219–20
Robert Fleming 657
Roberts, Dan 885
Robertsons Jams 870
Roddick, Anita & Gordon 385, 446
Rogers, John 943
Rolf Benz 445
Roll, R. 616, 881
Roll, Richard 297, 307
Ross, S. 828
Ross, Sarah 359
Rostron Parry 988
Rowley, Rob 24
Rowntree 877
Royal Bank of Scotland 34
  advisers' costs 883
  debt financing 526
  executives' bonuses 900
  leaseback 494
  merger 870
  value creation 678
Royal Dutch Shell
  buyback 856, 857
  capital structure 803
  project appraisal 104
  share value 678, 681
RPG Group 363
RTM 991
Ruane, Bill 630
Russell, Neville 409
Russia
  bonds 487
  credit ratings in 19
  valuing shares in 783
Rutterford, J. 737–8

Saatchi and Saatchi 905
sacking of managers 16
Safeway 773
Sainsbury, J, *see* J Sainsbury
Salami, A. 898
sale and leaseback 492–4, 543
Sampdoria Football Club 460
Samsung Electronics 18
Sandvik 991
Saregama 363
Savoy Hotel Group 393
SBC Warburg 446, 487
Scardino, Marjorie 663
scenario analysis 198–200
Scherer, F. 898
Schlegel 430
Schloss, Walter 629
Schnabel, Claus 11
Schneider, Mark 468
Schoenburg, E. 615
Scholes, M. 640
Schrempp, Jürgen 657, 869–70
Schröder, Gerhard 11
Schroder Solomon Smith Barney 404
Schroders 418
Scott, Keith 427
Scottish Development Agency 433
scrip dividends 422, 856
script issues 422
Sealey, Steve 441
Securities and Exchange Commission 369
Securities and Futures Authority (SFA) 373
securitisation of debt finance 494–5, 543
security market line 300–2
seedcorn, venture capital as 425
Seeley, Alan 442
Self-Regulatory Organisations (SROs) 373
Selfridges 355
Semple, Bob 770
Send Group 359
sensitivity analysis 194–8
settlement cycle 368–9
Severn River Crossing 110
Severn Trent Water 803
Shapiro, E. 729
share buy-backs 856–8
share issues 388–9
share markets 41
share option schemes 934
share options 925
share premium account 389
share split 422
share underwriting 934
shareholder value analysis 712–20
  depreciation 714
  merits and problems 720
shareholder wealth maximisation 12–15
shareholders
  of Huntingdon Life Sciences 366
  and stock markets 352–3
  and treasury management 563
  wealth 7, 11–12
    rewards linked to 16
  wealth maximising goals 661–2
shares 35
  beta, classifying by 304–5
  in efficient markets 607
  mispriced 305
  in portfolio theory
    comparing 240–1
    standard deviation for 240
  quoted, ownership of 372–3
  rate of return on 287–95
  selling 16
  valuing, *see* valuing shares
Sharpe, W.F. 310, 319
Shefrin, Hersh 633
Shepherd Neame 363
Shepherdson, Ian 947
Shevlin, T. 619
Shiller, Robert 633
Shleifer, Andrei 633, 634, 635
Shohet, P.S.D. 735
short- and medium-term finance 510–43
  acceptance credits 540–1
  bank sources 511–16
    overdraft 511–15
    term loans 516
  bills of exchange 539–40
  factoring 526–9
    invoice discounting 529
    recourse and non-recourse 529
  hire purchase 529–32
  leasing 532–9
    advantages of 534–6
    and buying 537–8
    finance lease 533–4
    operating lease 532–3
  trade credit 515–19
    terms 519
  trade debtor management 520–6
    assessing risk 520–2
    credit policy 520
    payment 522–6
    terms 522
short-term interest rate futures 943–6
Siebe 449
Siegel, Jeremy 294
Siemens 657
signalling 828
Simes, Ivory 9
Simon & Schuster 466
Simon Engineering 880
Simonian, Haig 657
Singapore
  share turnover 342
  stock market correlation matrix 268
Singer & Friedlander 410
Singh, A. 896
sinple interest 83
Sirower, Prof. 904–5
SK Telecom 18
Skapinker, Michael 853, 904
small- and medium-size businesses
  flotation of 441, 442–3, 444
  late payment to 524–5
  as private companies 442–3, 444
Smith, Adam 9

Smith, Terry 617
Smith and Wesson 870
SmithKline Beecham 870
Snoddy, Raymond 980
soft capital rationing 165–6
Solnik, B. 266, 267, 268
Solomons, David 722
solvency and liquidity ratios 808
Sony 593, 702, 704
Soros, George 623, 637, 966
South Africa 342
South African Breweries 348, 702
South Sea Bubble 622
Spain
  credit rating, long-term 470
  share turnover 342
  stock market correlation matrix 268
Special Drawing Rights of IMF 976
specific inflation 173
speculators 953
Spirax-Sarco 452
Sports Division Group 394
spot exchange markets 975–7
stakeholder model 11
stakeholders 5, 340
Standard & Poor 19, 467, 468, 469, 932
Standard & Poor's 500 Index 375, 627
standardised unexpected earnings (SUE) 619
Stapleton, Nigel 25, 980
Stark, A. 898
start-up, venture capital as 425
Staunton, Mike 288, 289, 293, 294, 618
Stefano, Michele di 989
Stein, J.C. 614
Stena Sealink 660
Stephens, Gerry 782
sterling
  interest rates on futures 946–7
  rise of 993
Sterling, Lord 659
sterling corporate bonds 354
Stern Stewart & Co 679, 681, 682
Stevenson, Lord 662
Stewart, G.B. 709, 827, 830, 831
Stewart, John 858
Stewart, Rod 495
Stice, E. 619
stock 100
stock exchange, joining 435
Stock Exchange Alternative Trading Service (SEATS) 366, 369
Stock Exchange Automated Quotation (SEAQ) 364, 366, 369
Stock Exchange Automated Quotation International (SEAQI) 341
Stock Exchange Trading Service (SETS) 369, 370, 371, 372
stock market bubbles 622–3
stock market efficiency 603–41
  behavioural finance 633–8
    cognitive errors 635–8
    and EMH 633–5
  efficiency types 605–7
  levels of 610
  meaning of 604–7
  random walks 608–10
  semi-strong form 610, 615–31
    bubbles 622–3
    commentaries on 623–7
    cyclical effects 617–18
    earnings, manipulation of 616–17
    information 616
    in small firms 618
    underreaction 619
    value investing 619–22
  strong-form 610, 631–2
  value of 607
  weak-form 610–15
    chaos and neural networks 614–15
    Dow theory 612–13
    exceptions 614
    filters 612
    price charts 611–12
    trading rules 613
stock markets 335–80
  deregulation of 347
  in Europe 343–5
  financial flows, globalisation of 346–50
  financial pages 375–8
  importance of 350–3
  institution in 347
  multiple listings 347–9
  quoted shares, ownership of 372–3
  regulation of 373–5
  sharp decline in 636
  tasks for 364
  taxation and corporate finance 379
  trading systems 364–72
    order-driven 369–72
    quota-driven 364–9
  volatility of 428–9
  world survey 336–42
Straddling, Stuart 24
straight fixed-rate bonds 485
Strascherg, Falk 431
strategic business units (SBUs) 673
  management of 696–9
  strategy for 699–707
  value drivers in 707
  WACC in 735
strategy valuation 717–18
Strauss-Kahn, Dominique 340
Stretford, Paul 359
strike price of options 926, 931
Strong, N. 311
sub-underwriting 417
subjective probabilities of risk 192–3
Subrahmanyam, A. 614
Sudarsanam, S. 898
Suez Lyonnaise des Eaux 340
Sugar, Alan 385, 446
Sullivan, R. 614, 617
Sumitomo 923
Summers, Diane 676
Summers, Jeff 501
Sun Microsystems 431
sunk costs 105
surplus funds, investment of 589–92
  choice of investment 591
  objective 590
  policy 590–1

Swann, Christopher 362, 972
swaps 950–2, 953
Sweden
  returns on equities, bonds, bills 289, 294
  share turnover 342
  stock market correlation matrix 268
  stock markets in 337
Switzerland
  returns on equities, bonds, bills 289, 294
  share turnover 342
  stock market correlation matrix 268
  stock markets in 337, 345
symbiosis-based mergers 903
syndicated loans 466
synergy in mergers 872–4

T & N 659
Taiwan 342
takeovers
  share value in 759
  threat of 16
tangible resources 701
Tanigawa, T. 615
Targett, Simon 828, 900, 942–3
Tate & Lyle 831
taxation
  and capital structure 820–2
  of dividends 852
  and mergers 878
  in project appraisal 170–2
  and stock markets 379
Taylor, Andrew 402, 821–2
Taylor, Martin 15
Taylor, Paul 877
Taylor, Peter 441
Teather & Greenwood 409
techMARK 41, 360–2, 395
Technologieholding 431
Telecom Italia 478
Telewest Communications 404
Tennant, Christopher 450
Tennessee Valley Authority 953
term loans 516
Tesco 773
Texaco 876
Texas Utilities 466
Thailand 340–1
Thaler, R. 614, 619, 633, 637
Thames Water plc 556–7
Thoenes, Sander 979
Thomas, H.M. 896, 898
Thomas, J.K. 619, 620
Thommson, Geoffrey 424
Thomson, Stuart 947
Thorn EMI 446, 717
Thornhill, John 487
three-day rolling settlement 367
Tieman, Ross 776, 850
Tiger economies 337
time value
  of money in project appraisal 54–5
  of options 926
The Times 138
Timmermann, A. 614, 617
Titman, S. 619
Tomkins 25, 669, 870
Tomkins, Richard 874
Total Petroleum 876
total shareholder return (TSR) 677–9
Towers, John 443
Toyota 350, 967
trade credit 515–19, 542
  terms 519
trade debtor management 520–6
  assessing risk 520–2
  credit policy 520
  payment 522–6
  terms 522
traded debt, cost of 730–1
Tradepoint 345, 369, 606
traditional options 930–1
transactions
  hedging strategies 981–9
    currency options 986–8
    do nothing 982
    forward market 983
    futures 985–6
    invoice in home currency 981–2
    lagging 983
    leading 983
    matching 983
    money market 984–5
    netting 982–3
  internalisation of in mergers 876
  managing 989–90
  risks in foreign exchange 979–80
translation risks in foreign exchange 980–1
treasury management 23, 552
  corporate subjects 554
  main areas 553
  and relationship banking 564
  strategic level of 562–3
Trocadero 136
true NPV of options 936
trust deeds 460–2
TSB 34, 372, 830
Tube Investments 993
tulip bulb bubble 622, 924
Tully, S. 721
Turkey 342
Turner, Mark 349

UBS 394, 469
UBS Warburg 404, 420
uncertainty 192
underwriting
  rights issues 417–18
  secondary shares 418–17
Unilever 681
Unilever Superannuation Fund 942–3
UniPoly 430
unit trusts 38–9
United Kingdom
  capital expenditure by firms 152
  credit rating, long-term 470
  financial services sector growth 31–4

index options in 932
interest rates 591
merger activity 871
optimal weights for portfolio 272
profit growth 764
quoted shares, ownership of 372–3
returns on equities, bonds, bills 289
share turnover 342
small firm performance 618
stock market correlation matrix 268
stock markets in 337
United Kingdom Listing Authority (UKLA) 393, 395, 396, 398, 632
United States
corporate governance in 17
index options in 932
returns on equities, bonds, bills 289, 294
share turnover 342
small firm performance 618
stock market boom 351–2
stock market correlation matrix 268
stock markets in 337
volatility of 429
University Superannuation Scheme 36–7
unquoted firms, raising equity capital 423–34
business angels 424–5
corporate venturing 433
enterprise investment scheme 433
financing gap 423–4
government sources 433
incubators 433
venture capital 425–34
venture capital trusts 432–3
unquoted shares, valuing 781–2
untraded debt, cost of 732
UPC 467
Urquhart-Stewart, Justin 363
Urry, Maggie 427, 430, 770
utility and risk 203–5
Uzbek Leasing International 539

Vallance, Sir Iain 828
value-based management 655–85, 695–725
application of principles 696–710
corporate strategy 707–10
earnings-based, *see* earnings-based management
firm's objective 696
strategic assessment 699–705
competitive resource strength 699–704
industry attractiveness 699
life-cycle stage of value 704–5
strategic business units 696–9
strategic choice 705–7
strategy implementation 707
value creation 658–63, 669–77
asset divestment 675
external measurement 677–84
market to book ratio 682–4
market value added 679–82
total shareholder return 677–9
internal measurement 710–25
cash flow 710–12
economic profit 720–3
drawbacks 722–3
usefulness of 722
economic value added 723–4
free cash flow 713, 715
scenario analysis 718
sensitivity analysis 718
shareholder value analysis 712–20
strategy valuation 717–18
investment on positive spread, raising 675
mission statements 662–3
planning horizon, extending 675
in project appraisal 53–7
required rate of return, lowering 676–7
return on existing capital, increasing 674
strategic determinants 699–705
competitive resource strength 699–704
industry attractiveness 699
life-cycle stage of value 704–5
wealth maximising goals 661–2
value destruction 658–63
value drivers
in cash flow discounting 712–13, 715
in strategic business units (SBUs) 707
value investing 619–22
valuing shares 755–89
and cash flow 776–9
dividend valuation methods 760–70
dividend growth model 762–3
dividends, non-payment of 766–7
forecasting growth rates 767
growth determinants 767–9
to infinity 761–2
non-constant growth 765–6
normal growth rate 763–5
problems with 767
income flow methods 760
managerial control and 784–9
net asset value 757–60
usefulness of 759–60
and owner earnings 780–1
price-earnings ratio model 771–6
over time 772
prospective PERs 775–6
use of 773–5
unquoted 781–2
in unusual companies 782
variable-rate note market 462
variable rate preference shares 392
Varity 883
Vema 359
vendor placing 421–2
venture and development capital investment trusts 432
venture capital 425–34, 515, 543
and market volatility 428–9
providers 430
return on funds raised 429
Venture Capital Association 428
venture capital trusts 432–3
Vermaelen, T. 619
vertical mergers 870
Vietnam International Leasing Company 538–9
Virgin Direct 33, 639
Virgin Group 385, 446, 513, 533

Virt-x 345, 369–70, 606
Visual Action Holdings 632
Vivendi 340
Vodafone 11, 388, 420–1
  merger with Mannesmann 883, 885, 900
  value management in 660, 672, 678, 681
VSEL 896, 897

Wagener, Jeremy 989
Wagstyl, Stefan 993
Wainhomes 444
Wal-Mart 470
Walker-Duncalf, Paul 345
Wallis, Teresa 361–2
warrants 423, 541, 934
Washington Mutual 487–8
Washington Post 626
Wassall 850
Waterstones 431
wealth maximising goals 661–2
Weetabix 363
Weidner, Jan 445
weighted average cost of capital (WACC) 733–5
  and capital structure 815–16
  corporate practice on 735–8
  in economic profit 720–1
  information from 734–5
  in SBUs 735
Weill, Sandy 904
Weisberg, Phil 972
Welch, Jack 870
Wells Fargo 626
Welsh Development Agency 433
Wessendorff, Alexander 431
Westminster Health Care 894
Westwick, C.A. 735
Wetrin, Israel 448–9
White, H. 614, 617
White, Ian 658
Whitehead, Rod 446
Whitesmith, Howard 448
wholesale banks 35
Wickes 24
Wightman, David 909
Willett, Allan 447–9
Willett International 447
William M. Mercer 942
Williams, Christopher 632
Willmen, John 348
Wing Kong (Holdings) 363
Winterflood Securities 366
wireless communication licences 164–5
Womack, K. 619
Wong, Wenchi 316–17
Woodland, Phil 386
Woolwich 33, 858, 883
working capital in project appraisal 100–1
working capital management 551–93
  Baumol's cash model 578–80
  cash, importance of 576–7
  cash-conversion cycle 569–73
  cash management 580–4
    cash flow synchronization 583
    cash trade-off 577
    control cash flows 582–4
    models 577
    planning cash flows 580–2
    policy framework 580
  cycles 568–9
  dynamics of 573–4
  financing 556–68
    currency 561
    and financial community 563–4
    interest rates 561
    long or short borrowing 556–8
    matching principle 559–61
    retained earnings 561–2
  inventory management 584–8
    trade-off 585
  main areas 553
  overtrading 575–6
  policies 574–5
  risk management 564–8
    business 565–6
    currency 567
    insurable 566–7
    interest rate 567–8
  surplus funds, investment of 589–92
    choice of investment 591
    objective 590
    policy 590–1
  working cycle 568–9
World Wide Web 877
writing down allowance 170–1
WT Foods 427
Wyko 412–13

XTL Biopharmaceuticals 442
Xtreme Information 473
Xu, X.G. 311

Yahoo! 877
Yamaichi International 946
Yell 488
Yorkshire Electricity 814
Young, Steve 385–6

Z statistic 213
zero coupon bonds 460, 462